THE DIALECTS OF ANCIENT GAUL

THE DIALECTS
OF ANCIENT GAUL

by

JOSHUA WHATMOUGH

Late Professor of Comparative Philology
in Harvard University

PROLEGOMENA AND RECORDS
OF THE DIALECTS

HARVARD UNIVERSITY PRESS

Cambridge, Massachusetts

1970

70-9934

I wish to express my appreciation and sincere gratitude
to Harvard University Press for having undertaken and carried
to fruition this complicated and difficult publication.

V.Wh.

Winchester, Massachusetts
1969

CONTENTS

See page 4 of the *Dialects* for its contents. The original page numbering of both the Prolegomena and the *Dialects* has been retained.

From

Dialects of Ancient Gaul

Grammar: Part I

1963

INTRODUCTION

I begin with some additions to my Prolegomena (1944) and DAG (1949 - 1951).

Perhaps the most important, as well as the most interesting, is the treatise by Jean-Jacques Hatt, La Tombe gallo-romaine (Paris 1951), pp. 24 - 62 with its maps, showing the distribution of Keltic proper names and their proportion of occurrence in relation to non-Keltic names. Thus (p.26) Hatt gives a map of Gaul on which are marked sites showing respectively over 40% and over 25% indigenous names. These range (p. 27) from 75% at Briançon to 0% at Fréjus, Marseille, and Riez. The agreement with the collection of names in DAG, (by that time available in microfilm) is re-markable, and a welcome independent confirmation of the work of two in-dependent workers in the same field. Fuller details are given on the fol-lowing pages (29 ff.)

*   *   *

ADDENDA to PROLEGOMENA

Since 1944 I have accumulated two note books of addenda to the Prolegomena. These I now reduce to a minimum of important additions, not attempting, for example, to bring up-to-date mere bibliography - that fetish of the timid and incompetent compiler - but only matters of consequence. References are to pages of the Prolegomena.

p. 7 s. v. Spr FK, 1. 6 for LII read LI

    s. v. ILG, R. -G. K. Ber. after 107 add:, 198-214
            after 53-134 add: Indices to CIL XIII, 1943, viii + 234,
            with six plates.

p. 11   On Gallia (in Caesar's meaning) add: BG vi. 1-2.

p. 11, n. 9   Cf. gallus (?), gall (lime-gall i.e. Galloway pony?).
The clipped form gall (not in NED or EDD) is peculiar
to Lancashire, but there are hints of gallus "cock" in the
sense of pony or jack-ass in DuCange.

See also, in PID, Preface pp. viii - ix (on method); 166-202 (on
Gallic items in Italy); 65-165 (on Kelto-Liguric); and 202-206 (on Alpine
items).

Other references: Haberl in ZfCPh 8, 1910-12, 82-101; Jullian REA,
1911, 344-45 (cf. p. 95) a propos of Haberl. The bone of contention is
whether or not we must distinguish from one another three vocables lem- :
lim- viz. (1) lem- "cerf, " (2) lem- : lim- "ormeau, " and (3) lim-
"marais" (cf. Gr. λιμνη); and the argument is based on limeum :
ceruarium Pl. 27, 101; Lemouices as an animal-name (cf. Brannouices);
Limonum, Lemonum, Limonius, Limonia "source du cerf" (cf. Ep-, Bebr-,
Dam-, and Sir-ona); but Lemane, Limagne, Lemonnos contain lem-
"marais" (cf. Lemanae, now Lympne).

But Rudolf Haberl (Eger i Baden) Zur Kenntniss des Gallischen, loc.
cit., had argued: 1. Change of e to i in Fr. LNN of Gaulish origin. lem-[e̷]
thus Limoges from Lemouices; Limours from Lemausum; Limeil, Limeuil
Liméjouls from Lemoialum: Cf. Yverdun from Eburodunum; Ivry from
Eburiacu; Brionne from Breuiodurus, Briuodurum: Briare, Brières, Brieuilles;
Breuiodurus, Breuidorum - primary, but Briuodurum - secondary; Clichy
from Clippiacu : Cle̷ppius; Nimes from Nemausus, nemos

However, S. Fr. and Provençal have a̷ from e̷: Clapiers from Clep-
piacus; Averdon from Eburodunum; Alleyrat from Elariacu; Allier from
Elauer; Parignargue from Petroniacu; Amillac from Amiliacu (Ae-, E-).
And elsewhere: Avry from Eburiacu; Larrey from Elariacu(m); Alligny from
Eliniacu; Amilly from Amiliacu; Appoigny from Eponiacu; Craon from
Cregadunum

Manifestly the change affects open short e̷ under a secondary accent
(Nebenton), which therefore remained open, whereas otherwise in Romance
all open unaccented vowels became close (uenire becomes venir, but
uenit becomes vient); or with primary accent: eccu (ecce) illu becomes
OF icel, O Prov. aquel, aicel, Sp. aquel (It quello w. loss of a-), ebureu
[becomes ebur] becomes Fr. ivoire, It. avorio, O. Prov. avori; Germ.
Re̷ulf becomes OF. Rioul, Prov. Raoul. Theodónttus becomes O. Prov
Taudoret; A̷mílius whence A̷miliácu becomes Amillac.

Gallic LNN are compounds or derivatives; hence, with "Nebenton"
on first syllable, open e̷ and therefore short. But e̷ shifted to a in a syllable
next to "Nebenton, " Segisamon becomes Sp. Sasamon. PRESUMABLY THE
ACCENT IS GAULISH: Ve̷nedotio becomes Guined, De̷metia becomes Dy-
fed, cf. teg but tigern, Sigo-in cpds. beside Sego-, Virgilius beside Verg-;
but, Ve̷ragri beside Varagri; E̷rminius : Arminius, Erauisci : Arauisci
Petouio : Πατάυιον Cleppiacu : Clipiagum Lemouices : Λιμουικοι.

Therefore O Prov. Naiac must be *Na̷uius, and Nieuil-les-Saintes
*Neioialos (not ai), and Nueuil-sous Faye Neioialo; therefore i in Nieuil
is from e̷, not from a - hence Neuio-ialus "Newfield" (cf. Neuiodunum)

Naidunum (Thr.), N ἀιοδουνώ, Liburn. Nedinum (Nadin Dalm.),
N ηδινον ------ all from Neuiodunum. N ηδινον was pronounced
Nīd-. So Adnama (: nĕmos), but Adnamatos (: Nemetes) because Adnama
(-tos), not -nám-
Remarks.

1. On lĕm- and brĭg- in first syllable:

Lĕmouices (Limoges) from *lĕmos "elm, " cf. (-annos for -onnus
"water"? J. Wh.) Lemannos (Lemane, Limane, La Limagne), Lemanae
n. pl. (OE Limene, mod. Lympne) beside Germ. ĕlm-, Lat. ulmus i. e.
l (Gaulish li-, r Gaul ri, brĭg-), with ablaut: G. lem-, Germ. elm, Lat.
ŭlm-; cf. Ŧr. fĕr, Germ. wĕr, Latin uir. If so lem- would be for lim-
as in Limonum "Poitiers" Vendryès MSL 13. 380; Pedersen VKG I.175 and
lim- lem- are dialect variants, even though lem- appears in Ŧr. as Lim-,
unless Gaulish e was pronounced[i]. (And this, I hold, is the correct explanation, i written e before m, or i : e are allophonic; the phoneme is
/i/, often written e.)

2. Nimes, Blismes

Nimes, Prov. Nemze from Némausus; but also Nemours also from
Némausum, cf. Limours from Lémausu; i. e. e becomes i (no; [i] before m
has allophone e, so written: J. Wh.), Nemaus - cf.ναμαυσικαβο, Namausatis [Provençal dial.] ; cf. λεπας - ἀπος Prov. lapedo, Sp. lapa.
We should expect *Namze, but i : e occurs before m (Meyer-Lubke: ę before a nasal is ę in Provençal, hence Nemze).

Blisme from Belisama; Blesamius was a Galatian, Blesamus an Italian;
Fr. also has Bellême (Dep. Orne); hence no first syllable accent. If so beis a prefix, cf. Germ. bi-, be- Hence the stem is lĕs- becomes lis- (or[i],
allophone or written e?) unless e remained dialectally, and -āma has ā
(not superl. -ama, later -ima cf. Uxama, Oxima, Exmes or Axima Aime)
as in A-lĕs-ia Alise i. e. like ę becomes Fr. i before s, cf. Alisia i. e. phoneme [i]again (: allophonic e), in which a- is a prefix Germ. at-, Lat.
ad-. These prefixes are properly pre-verbs; hence lĕs verⱥbal, cf. lesan
"auflesen; glean, gather". Belisama is "Gatherer, " Alesia "place of assembly. "

3. Arras from Atrebates

-ăt- cf. Argentoráte becomes Argentré, Audrate becomes Orré,
Adesate becomes Axat, Cerate becomes Ceré or (accent forward) as in
Nemours but Nimes (Ném- but Nemaús-). Mimáte becomes Mimat but
Mímate becomes Mende, Condáte becomes Condé but Cóndate becomes
Condes

Thus Atrébates, whence a from e in Arras, so Medieval Atrábates; strictly
Atrèbátes (becomes Atrabátes, then Atrábates), like Varátes becomes Varas.
Hence ę becomes dialectal[cf. Eⱨuriacu becomes Avry beside Ivry.

Atrab^{e}/ₐₜes becomes Atrabtes, Arraz, Arras; so gabata *gabete *gabte, Fr. jatte.

Welsh tref from I. Eu. *trbo - like lim, lem, or *brig - i.e. *trib- with [i] allophonic e.

Compare, therefore, Latin turba, Goth þaúrp . The cognate of tref in Latin is turba, in Osc. trúbum But Haberl (p. 90) regards lĕm-, trĕb- as the normal grade, ļ (lim-), ṛ (trib-) as reduced grade, i.e. gradation not allophones or dialect variants.

4. Erlaf fl. (Lower Austria)
Erlaf from *Erlape or *Irlape , not Arelape (-te TP), confused with Arelate Arles (?). Yet cf. Arminius for Erminuis, Arcunia for Ercynia, Namausatis above, with ę becomes a. Analyze - ape, apa i.e. aqua aǀⱴa (or -apa J. Wh. , cf. Punj-ab); -e is gen. -ae, riuus Arelapae (why not loc. sg. ? J. Wh.) from *erel-, Corn. Bret. er, W. eryr, Goth ara Germ. Aar (Adler "eagle, " *er- plus Germanic -ila suffix).

5. On Gaulish u becomes e, i (or a).
Lug(u)dunum : Lyon, Lion, Laon, Laons, Laudun, Lauzun, Mont-La-hue, Loudon; Late L. Leudunum, Laudunum - g becomes 0, u becomes e, a, through Luuu- (cf. frigidus becomes freidus, freddo, froid).
-au- is specifically Provençal, not French; so in Gaulish tugurium becomes tegurium (Du Cange), tigurium. Gaulish *tegia becomes N. Ital. teggia, Are-tegias Fr. Arthies, Athies, Athée, cf. Τέγος , tĕgere, *tegernos "dominus, " W. tigern; Tigurini, Tejurini; Tuğurinis, Tugurinus, Tegernacu, Tigurnacu; Tugia becomes Span. Toia from tegia; nouio- from neuio-, Noyon (older Nouio-dunum), but Nyon (later Neuio-), i.e. e be-comes o before velar g or u. Then, with loss of velar ui or g, o becomes u: I. Eu. neuios, tegos, Gaul.nouios, tugurium, Late Gaul.*neios, *tejurium (j is [χ])
So Lugudunum becomes Leudunum (with ẹ, and tẹgurium), ĕ gives Fr. i, Prov. It. a.

Cf. Luxouii Lixouii Fr. Lezou, Lisieux; Uxellodunum becomes Yssoudun, Exoudun, Issolu. (Late Latin Ex-, Gaulish ĕ remains in Fr. , but becomes i Yssoudun, Lisieux : i.e. dialect variation)

6. ǫ before j ([χ]) becomes e
broialum : breuil, breil, Nouesium : Nivisium, Nieuil-les-Saintes, Nueil-sur-Faye; Nouiodunum becomes Neuio-, Thr. Ναϊοδουνῶ (Procop.); ę becomes a, Νὴ ϋιυου(η is [ī]) Ptol., mod. Nadin (Dalm.); Claudiomagus becomes Clǫd- becomes Fr. Clion, i.e. ǫ becomes ĕ or a.

7. Accent in Gaulish: p. 99ff. In Gaulish cpds. initial syll. accent as in Germ. (and Ital.). On Romanization the Latin accent prevailed (only in certain cases was equalization with Gaul. accent achieved, viz. not back beyond third last syllable, i.e. in long cpds. , only if second member rela-tively independent).

(Fr. Divonne is -ṓna, not Diuŏna i.e. -ŏna : -ṓna, cf. Bituriges becomes Bourges).

As usual, Jullian had the worst of the argument. Some qualification of Haberl's generally admirable thesis, closely knit and well argued, I have given above (2).

*   *   *

NOTE ON PROCEDURE:

Notwithstanding manifest difficulties, it is quite necessary to regard most solicitously the limits of dialect-areas. Exceptions may occur to this general principle in the narrower questions of strictly Keltic morphology, especially of the verb wherever attested Gaulish verb-forms are available in more than one such area; these do in fact show considerable agreement. In the verb, at least, it is possible to establish a pattern of Gaulish morphology, even in some small details of dialect, since such detail is a function of dialectal divergence; and also sometimes possible to observe chronological divergence. The verb system, as a functioning structure, was essentially the same all over Gaul so long as and wherever Gaulish was spoken. Major differences are lexical.

Methods of noun-formation may be approached in any I. Eu. language with ease by taking a given area and studying intensively, and statistically, all the items of a given word-category (here almost exclusively PNN) within that area. The only limitations to accuracy arise from the fact that the PNN represent a selective, not a random sampling of the material, from which a random sampling is to be made with the help of the coded cards. Moreover the selection is extensive enough to give quite trustworthy evidence, particularly, for example, when we have not only Gaulish but Aquitanian, Germanic, Greek, Latin, and even Semitic variants in evidence.

In principle we have to offer both descriptive and historical grammar, so far as the nature of the material permits. These will be given in sequence, first descriptive, then historical and comparative. Each area will be taken in turn, first Alpine, then Narbonensis, and so on; areas which have been done by former students, whether in print or not, are (with some necessary changes) given here, with appropriate credit to their authors.

Finally there is a unified grammar and index (particularly of lexical items); and a chapter of conclusions last of all.

Cultural and political background, archaeology and history, together with the reasons for considering a region as a dialect or language area, relatively uniform or not (as the case may be), have been given at the beginning of each regional section in DAG. Hence, at comparable dates, we reconstruct comparable dialects for comparable areas. The relative isolation of islands is a matter which, the case of Gaul (unlike Italy or Greece) is a problem which scarcely exists.

PNN of the same region and general provenance (economically and socially as well as geographically, e. g. terra sigillata) are in general a good indication of phonematic structure and tolerances, in some measure even of the language of the person who bore the name, particularly when, as is often the case, graphic variants (e. g. c : cc : g, or t : tt : d and ꝺ) indicate an attempt on the part of a Latin-speaking engraver (or author of a sepulchral insc.) to reproduce what he took to be the local pronunciation.

In Phonematics I have tried to give (a) an inventory of phonemes with their allophones if possible; (b) pattern, especially as regards distribution, clusters and the like; (c) some hint of frequency of distribution - but accurate statistics I have been obliged to leave to others, ars grammatica longa, uita breuis. In Morphomatics I have tried to give (a) the basic structure (largely I. -Eu.) in formation (substantival and verbal), composition and the like; (b) a list of formatives, and their distribution so far as significant; but (c) accurate statistics I have not yet been able to do, for the same reason as in Phonematics.

As to lexicon, the index of English words to the lexical items will suffice. All references are to the items in DAG 1-250, Notes i-lxi, rarely to pages (p.) of DAG.

A commentary to selected inscc. is interpolated, where appropriate, in the grammatical discussion of salient cruces (e. g. of the Coligny calendar), or of some particular epilegma (e. g. Καρνομου 78).

In historical grammar I work backwards from the description, avoiding unnecessary, but not irrelevant, I. -Eu. information. After that it is useful, and necessary, to add a brief sketch of the development from I. Eu. in phonematic or morphomatic terms (e. g. co-alescence, positional variants that became phonematic, infixation, suffixation), together with, for the sake of clarity, a formal but brief presentation of Keltic developments.

Syme (JRS 39, 1949, 14ff.), discussing Romano Hispone (Tac. A. 1, 74, 1) calls attention to the gentilicium (or cognomen) Romanus (Gaulish Εκυλιοσ ριουμανεοσ Venetic ka. n. ta ruman. n. a) in Cisalpine and transalpine Gaul by contrast with Italy. Over a dozen such items are recorded in Cisalpina, chiefly in Transpadana. Syme infers that anyone who took this name was highly unlikely to be a Roman at all (possibly, however, ciuis Romanus was meant - J. Wh.), but quite probably a Gaul, and probably with Quisling-like aspirations. With a different formation, but the same principle implied, note the attested PN Romatius.

Also in JRS 39, 1949, 1-5 Last explains the Roman prohibition of Druidism as perhaps not political in origin, but humanitarian, having arisen from repulsion at the practice of human sacrifice of a peculiarly cruel kind (burning alive).

1   hala Add; Die Sprache 2, 1950, 73-76.

25 bis   New insc. from Bouches-du-Rhône, see Gallia xi. 1, 1953, 112-113,
         Ogam VI. 6, no. 36, Dec. 1954, 258ff.

Ποϱειξου γαλλιανορ   δεδε   βελενο

43 bis   Cippus from Saint-Remy de Provence

Τ χ V κ   ολατ | ι σ κ ο σ

Gallia VIII, 1950, 124

83   Add Carpinarius ib. p. 148, Διένκαυνοι Kaibel 2379, Vuiltides(?)
      12. 2095 (577 or 597 A. D. , ? Vuitildes lapis).

90   Add new TS from La Graufesenque : RA 6, 37 (1951), 170-193; REA
      53, 1951, 71-81, Gallia 8, 1950, 8-9; REA 54, 1952, 93-101; from
      these sources I take the following - Cintusmus, Vebrullus, tesanares,
      Criciro Lecora, pannas, Louripa, pultario

137   For TS in the Orléans museum see Durand-LeFebre in Bull. de la Soc.
      arch. et hist. d'Orléans 24, 1940, 165-202.

Note xxv (c), cf. Note xxi Remark (iii): add, from EC vol. 5, 1950-51, pp.
237-247, the new inscc.

    monimentum | nertomari | namantobogi

and   moniminto | aθθedomari | orbiotali θ | fili

144 bis A new insc. from Bouy; see CRAI 1951, 131-134 after Union des
         Sociétés savantes de Bourges 2, 1951, pp. 10 sqq. (1949-50)

    etione Carantinae | Isosaegnato Hiduae | Mercurio M... ortiumi?

148   Add ad Canaunos Gallis 8, 1950, 34

178   (s. v. trade) add: tragula: J. Descroix, REA 50, 1948, pp. 309-312

    On tecco see Zaunick, Dornseiff Festschrift, 375-384 (APh 24, 1953,
    281)

181   Epona JRS 41, 1951, 166

182   Draccius Gallia 7, 1949, 235, Amceis (TS) AcS 3. 592

Add Gysseling, M. , and A. C. F. Koch Diplomata Belgica (Belgian Inter-University Centre for Dutch Studies, Brussels, 1950)

Clifford, Elsie M. Bagendon : A Belgic Oppidum, 1961.

For possible dialect divergence see Cobrunna, Cotira, Cricconia in the Glossary.

On Hieronymus and Lactantius at Trier see J. Heinhausen in TrZ 20, 1-2, 1951, 126-154; in Wainwright's book Problem of the Picts, 1955, the chapter on Pictish does not mention the link between the Picts and Aquitania, or deal adequately with *petia-; Ch. Verlinden, Frontier linguistique en Belgique 1955; C. F. Angus Diodorus' Primitive Britain, 1955; M.Deneckere, Histoire de la langue française dans les Flandres, 1770-1823, published 1954; M. Toussaint, La frontière linguistique en Lorraine.

189   An abecedarium (A to F only) TrZ., 18, 1949, 308

203   TS at Toule (Meurthe et Moselle), ib. 132-135 (Delort)

205   Tile-stamps at Trier, ib. 290-302

208D Add: a medallion found under the bridge at Trier (ib. pp. 44, 54, 320):
      Arecaippus   ⎰Conaldus

211, 213   (Mars) Lenus ib. p. 62; and see the treatise of E. Gose Der
                  Tempelbezirk des Lenus-Mars (Trierer Grabungen and For-
                  schungen) 1956

212   On laetus, litus add Bloomfield in Collitz Studies 1930, pp. 83-94.

On Bononia (-Gesoriacum) see Heurgon in Homages Bidez-Cumont pp. 127-133 (Cf. REA 51, 1949, 324-26; APh 20, 1949 [1951], 261).

Note xlv British Local Names, Amiens, a patera, JRS 41, 1951, 22

      (A) Mais Aballana Vxelodunum Camboglanis Banna Esica

xlv   (C) Other British names (inscc. 1950), PNN, ibid. pp. 142-145 C.
      Nipius Ascanius, Dulcius, Saufeius (-p-?), Axaunus, Matuacus,
      Bractus

Note xlv Add Richmond on Ravennas in Britain

Add Klingelhofer Germania Latina 1956; Scherer, Anton Die keltisch-germanischen Namengleichungen in Corolla Linguistica (Sommer Festschrift), 1955; Schwarz, Ernst Germanische Stammeskunde, Heidelberg 1956.

220 bis Couroos de la Seine

⌐are|Sequani|areos|iourus|Luceon Nertecomari

$\delta \alpha \gamma o \lambda \iota \tau o \upsilon \sigma \mid \alpha \upsilon o [\upsilon \omega] \Gamma$

See Lejeune and Martin REA 58, 1-2, 1956, pp. 71-82.

234 ca. 1185

Hardmannus, Heribertus

Note lvi On sub ascia Bober AJ Arch. 55, 1951, p. 40

On Pfyn-names Dickenmann, Beitr. z. NF, 2, 1950-1, pp. 68ff., 108ff.

Verodubna (insc.) Arch. Ertesitö 4, 1943, 89, Solia ib. 96, Aicca Cansalli(f.) Arch. Ertesitö 5/6, '44-5, 123, P. Atreuius (?) Cata Arch. Ertesitö 7/9, '46-8, 275

On Keltic names in Dacia - A. Alföldi, Zu den Schicksalen Sieben-bürgers im Altertum, Budapest 1944, 15-17

221 Niessen, Handatlas ... Rhein, 1950, TrZ 18, 1949, 253-58 (Stein-hausen).

240 hendinos see K. Malone Widsith pp. 15 f.

243 $B \epsilon \lambda \sigma o \upsilon \rho \delta o \varsigma$ cf. Cic. in Pis. 35.85 Iouis Velsuri

241 Marlis Franken Die Alamannen zwischen Iller u Lech RGK 1944 (ac-tually 1949) AJ Arch. 55, 1951, 217; Uslar TrZ 18, 1949, 264

Steinhausen, Kultrische Stammesnamen in Ostgermanien Die Sprache 2, 1950, 1-22

244 Add (from AcS): Ambudsuilius (-uis), Amilaius, Amludo, dabis Atico Luciano not Varisatico

H.-M. 320 (after Laur-Belart Schw. Urg. 34, 1943, 70; dabis at be-ginning of newly discovered writing tablets, H.-M. 326, Finke 115, Anz. Schw. Alt. 31, 1929, 182; Atticus (?) at Vindonissa, H.-M. 274.)

246 $\alpha \delta \alpha \hat{\iota} o \varsigma \cdot \alpha \lambda \epsilon \kappa \tau \rho \upsilon \omega \nu$ (Maced., see P-W, s.v.)

250   On Asse fl., Iura, Eno-s Ona "water" add Pokorny Beitr. z. NF, 2, 1950-1, 33-39

On names in -(a)nt(ia)- in E. Alps, Switzerland, France, Brit. Isles, Germ., Krahe ibid. 113-131

Add Fiebiger, O. Inschr .... Ostgermanen, ed. 2 (Denkschr. Akad. Wiss. Wien, Ph-H. Kl. 72, 2, 1947).

SIGNS AND ABBREVIATIONS

Ligatures are indicated by ‿ beneath the conjoint letters.

＿ beneath a letter indicates that it is damaged or otherwise imperfect in the original, or uncertain in other ways.

† indicates that the text given is probably corrupt, whether through injury to the original, or the engraver's (or copyist's) mistake.

* indicates an emendation.

*indicates a sign which, though clear, I cannot identify with certainty with any of the signs given in the table of $a\beta\beta$ but which is described (or reproduced) in the comment.

Square brackets are used for conjectural restorations.

. . . denote spaces in the inscription where letters once stood or may have stood. Each punct denotes room for one letter. Where a blank space is left between the last punct and | marking the end of the line, it is implied that the number of missing letters cannot be further defined. In other places than at the end a line, attention is called to the hiatus in the notes.

No marks of punctuation have been inserted in the text of the inscriptions in the body of the book.

] or [indicates places at the beginnings or ends of lines where, owing to the broken condition of the original, letters are or may be missing. Conjectural restorations at such places are printed (as already explained) within square brackets.

Interpuncts are reproduced in the form in which they appear in the originals (i.e. single, double, triple, or other forms).

| marks the end of a line in the original. The numbers at the left-hand side of the text of the inscriptions refer to these lines.

‖ marks the end of every fifth line.

r. = right, right-hand, or on the right-hand side.

l. = left, left-hand, or on the left-hand side.

insc. = inscription, inscc. = inscriptions.

$a\beta$ = alphabet, $a\beta\beta$ = alphabets.

In the gloss sections occasionally it seems desirable to include lemmata which are probably borrowed from some language or dialect (usually Latin or Greek) other than that to which ancient authority assigns them or than that with the records of which they are given; these are enclosed in [ ].

● below a letter indicates that while not uncertain, the letter is faint and worn.

KEΛTIKA

BEING PROLEGOMENA TO

A STUDY OF

THE DIALECTS OF ANCIENT GAUL

KEΛTIKA

BEING PROLEGOMENA TO
A STUDY OF
THE DIALECTS OF ANCIENT GAUL [1]

i. Prefatory

EVEN the late Sir John Rhys, although he was not a competent critic of such matters, came in time to understand that the pre-Latin dialects of Gaul and of northern Italy present related problems of classification, at least in Provence and the western part of Gallia Cisalpina: merely related, that is, not identical. Whoever tries to make up his mind about the one, must, sooner or later, make up his mind about the other. It was for this reason that at one time I intended to give some account of the inscriptions called "Celtican" by Rhys, "Ligurian" by d'Arbois de Jubainville, in the Appendix (A. Alien Inscriptions) of *The Prae-Italic Dialects of Italy* (Vol. II, 1933, see p. 612, no. 4). That plan proved impracticable. Hence I decided to expand what had begun simply as an account of the pre-Roman dialect of Provence into a survey of the linguistic remains, more or less contemporary, of Gaul as a whole — in the broadest interpretation of that variously defined geographical label.

NOTE: First published in *Harvard Studies in Classical Philology*, Volume LV (Cambridge, Mass.: Harvard University Press, 1944).

[1] There is no "medieval" or "modern" Gaul; but my concern is with geographical more than with chronological divisions, and "pre-Roman," "Roman," "Christian" would all be too trenchant for my purpose; "ancient" is intended to include them all, to the end of the Empire.

The decision was stimulated partly by the need, felt also by others,[2] of a critical edition of the pre-Latin inscriptions of Gaul (other than Greek or Phoenician); but even more by the statements, made by ancient writers, that differences in dialect (γλῶττη or *lingua*) existed between Aquitania and Gallia Lugdunensis and between Lugdunensis and Gallia Belgica; and by the desire which I felt either to substantiate, if I could, by as full a collection of evidence as possible, or else to disprove, those statements. For in the past it has been the inconclusive practice sometimes to dismiss the matter with an assertion that the differences are "not clear" to us, sometimes to accept the ancient authors at their face value, without making an attempt to assemble much, if any, of the extremely fragmentary yet abundant testimony that is now available, but, as a rule, not without conjecturing what the differences might have been. This dissipated evidence, which it was necessary to bring together into one place if its meaning was to be extracted from it, I have collected; and the conclusions that I shall offer are based upon its collection. With the three Gauls I have included the *prouincia* Narbonensis and the two Germanies, thereby affording as complete an account as possible of the dialects of ancient Gaul entire. Hence it is permitted to explain the differences that existed among them, and to do so by means of an ordered and unified documentation, instead of mere generalization resting on nothing more than vague memories of the scattered evidence or conjectures about its probable nature.

Inevitably evidence other than direct non-Latin epigraphic testimony had to be admitted. But I have neither repeated the task begun, if not quite completed, by Holder, of collecting the glosses and ancient proper names of Gaul, and all the ancient references to them — in fact every scrap of ancient writing that bears, however remotely, upon Gaul; nor copied his collections except by way of relevant citation. For the *testimonia*, not as a rule quoted by me, recourse must still be had to Holder's *Altceltischer Sprachschatz*. What I have done, in using Holder's work, has been to put into their proper geographical location, whenever that was possible, selected pertinent items — that is, items which give some clue to the local pre-Latin dialect — taken

---

[2] E.g., by Jacobsthal, see *Arch. Anz.* XLV 1930, 235–236.

from the medley which in Holder has no arrangement at all other than the conventional, and therefore readily consulted, but not illuminating, merely alphabetical order. (The few relevant items that have come to light since Holder was at work I have of course gathered in.) The selection of all this matter, however, has been made most rigorous, especially in those areas in which we can avail ourselves of at least two dialect inscriptions; elsewhere more liberal, for, without such inscriptions, glosses and nomenclature are now the only available evidence.

The testimony upon which any opinion about the classification of the dialects of ancient Gaul must rest is drawn, therefore, from material that is intractable chiefly because it is fragmentary. But some conclusions emerge which, while not startling, are both positive and clear; and which, while they confirm (or are confirmed by) ancient tradition about the linguistic situation in Roman Gaul, are drawn primarily from extant documents, not from such tradition.

(1) It is certain, then, that a Keltic dialect of the Brythonic group was spoken in pre-Roman, and, for some centuries longer, in Roman Gaul. (2) It is probable that there was at least one enclave there in which a Keltic dialect of the Goidelic group was spoken. (3) It is certain that Iberian was, or had been, spoken in Aquitania and in parts of Narbonensis. (4) It is certain that a Western Germanic dialect was spoken in Belgica in regions adjoining the river Rhine (the later Germania inferior) from which it tended to spread westward; and less extensively in Germania superior, where Keltic was spoken on both sides of the river but was less subjected to Germanic influence or mastery than in Germania inferior or in Belgica. (5) It is presumable that other dialectal differences within Keltic itself had arisen in the course of time in the several parts of Gaul, of the kinds that normally occur when communication between speakers of the same or of a related language is long interrupted or completely severed. (6) It is probable that Ligurian was or had been spoken in Narbonensis. (7) It is probable that the inscriptions commonly called "Gaulish" actually are, with few exceptions, in Keltic. (8) It is, however, certain that Greek and Latin influences are manifest in word-order, and possibly also in a few instances of (a) sound-substitution and (b) word-forms. (9) Lexicographical differences, so far as they can be traced, are, as

would be expected, most clearly marked; less clearly, differences in the development of speech-sounds; differences of accidence and syntax, if they existed, as is probable enough, escape us well-nigh entirely.

These conclusions are an adequate answer to the question what the ancients meant by their statements about differences of language in Roman or pre-Roman Gaul. It has been disappointing to spend many hours, in total far out of proportion to the results obtained, going through the vast amount of printed material that undiscriminating editors and publishers year after year thrust upon scholars, on the chance (I will not say in the hope) that some item of real importance might have come to light since the industrious Holder laboriously compiled his thesaurus. But the very paucity of the scant and meagre scraps of new evidence that remained to be gleaned in this way, despite the prodigious activity of the archaeologists, professional and amateur, in France and in the Rhineland, is itself a sufficient indication that the conclusions set forth above are not likely to be overturned, or the general statement of them that I have given to become much more precise, by way of addition or even illustration, in detail.

I do not refer, save most exceptionally, to sources of information which I have not myself seen, nor to items which proved inaccessible in first-hand sources of information. Most of the texts of the dialect inscriptions I had copied in 1929 or later years, and some I had expected to see again in 1939 and 1940. The outbreak of war in Europe prevented that; it has also made unobtainable some new books, and recent issues of periodicals. But although I have examined for myself all that I cite or quote, I do not cite or quote a great deal that I have seen. I have read everything pertinent that I could find. Much of it was not worth reading, much less worth mentioning, either intrinsically or for my immediate purpose. But if critics conclude that because some bibliographical item is not mentioned, therefore I am unaware of its existence, they are more likely to be wrong than right; if a thing is not mentioned, it is probably because I have read it, but do not quote or cite it because I found it unacceptable or actually worthless.

CHIEF WORKS OF REFERENCE

CA   *Carte archéologique de la Gaule romaine* (dressée sous la direction de Adrien Blanchet). Institut de France, Académie des Inscriptions et Belles-Lettres, viz. *Forma Orbis Romani* (Union Académique Internationale). Paris, 1931– .

Fasc. i: Partie orientale (carte) et texte complet du département des Alpes Maritimes, par Paul Couissin; Partie orientale (carte) du département des Basses-Alpes, par Henry de Gérin-Ricard, 1931.

Fasc. ii: Carte (partie orientale) et texte complet du département du Var . . . par P. Couissin . . . A. Donnadieu . . . Paul Goby . . . A. Blanchet . . . H. de Gérin-Ricard, 1932.

Fasc. iii: Carte et texte du département de la Corse . . . par Ambroise Ambrosi, 1933.

Fasc. iv: Carte de la partie occidentale du département du Var et de la partie orientale du département des Bouches-du-Rhône . . . P. Couissin, H. de Gérin-Ricard, Fernand Benoît (sic), 1934 [*no text*].

Fasc. v: Carte (partie occidentale) et texte complet du département des Bouches-du-Rhône, par F. Benoit, 1936.

Fasc. vi: Carte et texte complet du département des Basses-Alpes . . . par H. de Gérin-Ricard . . . A. Blanchet, 1937.

Fasc. vii: Carte et texte complet du département de Vaucluse, par Joseph Sautel, 1939.

K.   Henrici Kiepert *Formae Orbis Antiqui* (Berlin, 1894–1914), viz. maps no. xxiv (1913) *Galliae partes quae erant Caesaris tempore* with *Civitates trium Galliarum et provinciae tempore Augusti* and *Germania altero p. Chr. n. saeculo*; xxv (1912), *Gallia secundo et tertio p. Chr. n. saeculo*; xxiii (1902) *Italia superior cum regionibus Alpinis*.

Compare the maps in *CIL* III, V, XII. But observe the strictures of C. Jullian in *REA*, XVI, 1914, 63–70.

Bibl.   Robert de Lasteyrie, Eugène Lefèvre-Pontalis, Alexandre Vidier, *Bibliographie générale des Travaux historiques et archéologiques publiés par les Sociétés savantes de la France*, Paris, I–VI, 1888–1918, I–III, 1906–1914.

Useful in tracing the place of publication of many papers (within these years) which later writers (*more suo*) are apt to cite with inadequate bibliographical detail.

Mont. Raoul Montandon, *Bibliographie générale des travaux pal-ethnologiques et archéologiques* (Époques préhistorique, proto-historique et gallo-romaine), I–VI, 1917–1938, and Supplé-ments I–III, 1921–1929, France; and (separately, 1917) Canton de Genève et régions voisines; Paris, Geneva, Lyons.

IJ *Indogermanisches Jahrbuch* (since 1914), Strassburg, Berlin, and Leipzig.

AcS Alfred Holder, *Altceltischer Sprachschatz*, Leipzig, 1891–1913. Cf. Johann Sofer, "Das keltische Wortgut in den klassischen Sprachen" in *Commentationes Vindobonenses*, II, 1936, 70–92.

Cf. the criticisms of Ludwig Christian Stern in *Kritischer Jahresbericht über die Fortschritte der romanischen Philologie . . . herausgegeben von Karl Vollmöller*, IV, 1898–1900, i, 48, with the reviews cited there; to which add Dottin in *Revue critique d'histoire et de littérature*, nouvelle série, LXXVII 1914, 147–148, and W. Meyer-Lübke in *Berliner Philologische Wochenschrift*, XXXV, 1915, 1509–1511.

VKG Holger Pedersen, *Vergleichende Grammatik der keltischen Sprachen*, 2 volumes, Göttingen, 1909–1913.

There is an abridgement in English (by Henry Lewis), *A Concise Comparative Celtic Grammar*, Göttingen, 1937, containing later views on a few matters.

Do. Georges Dottin, *La langue gauloise*, Paris, 1920.

Cf. the reviews by Vendryes in *Revue celtique*, XXXVIII, 1920–21, 179–185; by Loth in *Revue archéologique*, 5e série, XIII, 1921, avril–juin, 108–119 (cf. *RC* XXXIX, 1922, 387–388); by Jud in *Archivum Romanicum* VI, 1922, 188–211; and by Terracini in *Rivista di filologia e d' istruzione classica*, XLIX, 1921, 401–430.

Rh. John Rhys, "The Celtic Inscriptions of France and Italy," *Proceedings of the British Academy*, II, 1905–06, 273–373; [Sir John Rhŷs] additions and corrections, V, 1911–12, 261–360.

Cf. the criticisms by d'Arbois de Jubainville in *Revue celtique*, XXVIII, 1907, 209; and by Thurneysen in *Zeitschrift für celtische Philologie*, VI, 1908, 557–558.[3]

---

[3] See also the criticisms passed upon another paper of Rhys ("Celtic Inscriptions of Cisalpine Gaul," *Proc. Brit. Acad.*, VI 1913–14, 23–112) by Loth in *RC* XXXV

SprFK | Leo Weisgerber, "Die Sprache der Festlandkelten," *Deutsches Archäologisches Institut, Römisch-germanische Kommission*, XXter Bericht, 1930, Frankfurt-am-Main, 1931, 147–226.
Cf. the reviews by G. B[onfante] in *Emerita*, III, Madrid, 1935, 184–185; J. Vendryes in *RC*, LII, 1934, 120–22.

KR | Rudolf Thurneysen, *Keltoromanisches*, Halle, 1885.

MHC | W. Dinan [Liam Ó Doighnéain], *Monumenta Historica Celtica*, I, London, 1911.

FHRC | Johannes Zwicker, "Fontes Historiae Religionis Celticae," in *Fontes historiae religionum ex auctoribus graecis et latinis collectos* edidit Carolus Clemen, Fasc. V i, Berlin, 1934, ii–iii, Bonn, 1935–36.
Cf. the review by R. Th[urneysen] in *Zeitschrift für celtische Philologie*, XX, 1936, 524.

RL | Max Ebert, *Reallexikon der Vorgeschichte*, Berlin, 1924–1932.

CIL | *Corpus Inscriptionum Latinarum* XII (Gallia Narbonensis), 1888, supplemented by E. Espérandieu, *Inscriptions latines de Gaule* (Narbonnaise), Paris, 1929.
ILG |
 | XIII (Tres Galliae et duae Germaniae), since 1899, supplemented in part by H. Finke, "Neue Inschriften" (Belgica, Germania superior et inferior) in XVIIter Bericht, 1927, of
R.-G. K. Ber. | *Röm.-Germ. Kommission, Deutsches Archäologisches Institut*, Frankfurt-am-Main, 1929, 1*–107 (Register, 215–233); and by Herbert Nesselhauf, "Neue Inschriften aus dem römischen Germanien und den angrenzenden Gebieten," XXVIIter Bericht, 1937, *R.-G. Komm.*, 1939, 51–134.

AE | Where these fail, recourse must be had to *L'année épigraphique* (published in *Rev. arch.*), or to the *Rassegna di epigrafia Romana* of Aldo Neppi Modona (i–viii in *Historia* IV–IX 1930–35, ix in *Aevum* XI 1937), and to the "Chronique gallo-romaine" (published in *Revue des études anciennes*).

TopF | Auguste Vincent, *Toponymie de la France*, Brussels, 1937.

NLB | *Les noms de lieux de la Belgique*, Brussels, 1927.

1914, 370–375, and by Dottin in *Rev. crit. d'hist. et de litt.*, nouv. sér., LXXVIII, 1914, 114.

I cite *Rh.* by pages as numbered in *Proc. Brit. Acad.*; the numbering, but not the pagination, differs in the separate issues. It can readily be found by a simple calculation. The writing $\hat{y}$ affected by Rhys, about the time he was knighted, may well yield to y except when quoted directly from his own title-pages.

FrON   Hermann Gröhler, *Über Ursprung und Bedeutung der franzö-
          sischen Ortsnamen*, 2 volumes, Heidelberg, 1913–1933.

NLF   Auguste Longnon, *Les noms de lieu de la France* (edited by P.
          Marichal and L. Mirot), Paris, 1920–29.
          Cf. Albert Dauzat, *La Toponymie française*, Paris, 1939.

          Henri Hubert, *Les Celtes*, 2 volumes, Paris, 1932. Cf. the
          criticisms of J. Toutain in *Revue de l'histoire des religions*,
          CXIV, 1936, 222–235.

Mnl.   Albert Grenier, *Manuel d'archéologie gallo-romaine*, Paris, I,
          1931, II i–ii, 1934; continues Déchelette's *Manuel d'arch.
          préhistorique, celtique et gallo-rom.*

DA   *Dictionnaire archéologique de la Gaule*, 2 volumes, Paris, 1875–
          1919.

M.-C.   Ernest Muret and Anatole Chabouillet, *Catalogue des mon-
          naies gauloises de la Bibliothèque Nationale* (Département des
          médailles et antiques), Paris, 1889.

Atl.   Henri de la Tour, *Atlas de monnaies gauloises*, Paris, 1892.

Tr.   Adrien Blanchet, *Traité des monnaies gauloises*, 2 volumes,
          Paris, 1905, supplemented by the same author's "Chronique
          de numismatique celtique," *Rev. celt.* XXVIII, 1907, 73–78;
          XXIX, 1908, 72–79; XXX, 1909, 189–197; XXXI, 1910,
          49–59; XXXII, 1911, 396–406; XXXIV, 1913, 397–405;
          XXXIX, 1922, 338–347; XLVIII, 1931, 149–162.

HG   Camille Jullian, *Histoire de la Gaule*, I–VIII Paris, 1908–26.
          There is a bibliography of the prodigious and in part mis-
          directed output of C. Jullian (see Arnold J. Toynbee's witty
          criticisms in *A Study of History* I [Oxford and London,
          1934], 11–12), compiled by Maurice Toussaint and pub-
          lished in *Revue des questions historiques*, CXXII 2, mars
          1935, 179–214; CXXIII–CXXIV 3, mai 1935, 35–62.

REA   *Revue des Études Anciennes*, Bordeaux and Paris, since 1899;
          contains valuable "chroniques gallo-romaines, notes gallo-
          romaines, d'archéologie gallo-romaine, d'archéologie rhé-
          nane," and "chroniques de toponymie."
          Tables analytiques des Tomes I à XV (1899–1913), 1933.

RC   *Revue Celtique* I–LI, Paris, 1870–1934.
          Tables des volumes I–VI (1886), VII–XII (1891), XIII–
          XVIII (1898), XIX–XXIV (1906), XXV–XXX (1911),
          XXXI–XLV (1928).

ZfCPh   *Zeitschrift für celtische Philologie*, Halle, since 1896.
         Register, Bände I–V in V (1904–05); VI–X in X (1915),
         XI–XV in XVI (1927).

ZNF   *Zeitschrift für Ortsnamenforschung*, Munich and Berlin,
         1925–1937, I–XII, XIII i, continued as *Zeitschrift für
         Namenforschung*, Berlin, XIII ii ff., since 1937.
         Register, Bände I–XIII (1925–1938), Berlin, 1939.

II. INTRODUCTORY

As the language of official use in the Roman empire, Latin came to be extended, more or less completely, to many peoples of many different nationalities and civilizations, and, above all, of different speech-habits. What Augustus saw with his own eyes, Vergil pictures Aeneas as seeing, as it were prophetically, upon the shield made for him by Vulcan. The peoples of the empire had not only their peculiar appearance and garb, like the Gauls who had scaled the Capitoline hill long before empire was dreamt of,[4] but also diversity of language —

> *incedunt uictae longo ordine gentes,*
> *quam uariae linguis, habitu tam uestis et armis.*[5]

This is commonplace enough; so too is a more explicit assertion about differences of speech in Gaul. What Caesar wrote about the differences to be observed there *lingua institutis legibus*,[6] may be found also in Strabo;[7] it appears further that this information was to be had in the older writer Posidonius, from whom, it is maintained, Caesar and Strabo in fact drew it independently.[8]

---

[4] *Aen.*, VIII 659–662.

[5] *Op. cit.*, 722–723.

[6] *B.G.* I 1.2.

[7] IV 1.1, C 176.

[8] It is clear that *B.G.* I 1 goes back to Posidonius, and therefore describes a state of affairs that obtained at a time somewhat earlier than Caesar's own, say c. 80 B.C. On the sources of *B.G.* I 1 and of Strabo IV 1.1, see Karl Barwick, "Caesars Commentarium und das Corpus Caesarianum," *Philologus*, Supplementband XXI 2, 1938; Franz Beckmann, *Geographie und Ethnographie in Caesars Bellum Gallicum*, Dortmund, 1930 (cf. E. Löfstedt, *Syntactica*, II 1933, 175 n. 2); A. Klotz, "Geographie und Ethnographie in Caesars Bellum Gallicum," *Rheinisches Museum*, LXXXIII 1934, 66–96, especially 74–87; Matilde Truscelli,"I Κελτικά di Posidonio e loro influsso sulla posteriore etnografia," *Rend. d. r. Acc. naz. dei Lincei*, Cl. di

Know'edge of the western provinces of the empire has grown greatly through archaeological discoveries, even within recent decades. Excavation has been active especially in the Rhineland, and also in France and Holland, and in Belgium. It is not claimed, indeed, that there is a neat agreement of dialectal and cultural areas of a kind that is so striking in the map of pre-Roman Italy. But it would be mere folly to deny the existence of dialectal areas in pre-Roman Gaul just because a detailed map, like that of Italy, with its dozen or so ancient dialects, is more a vision than a reality. The fact is that the dialects of Gaul are ill documented merely because the art of writing hardly was diffused in Gaul (except in Provence) in advance of the spread of the Latin language. This lack of direct evidence, however, may be in some measure countered by indirect evidence. The systematic study of Latin inscriptions and of notices in ancient writers encourages the hope that a more precise meaning can be given to the remark, recorded by some early but acute or well-informed observer,

---

sc. mor., stor. e filol., serie sesta, XI 1935, 609–730, where (697) a reconstruction of Posidonius on tripartite Gaul is attempted. See also, more generally, Giorgio Pasquali, "Cesare, Platone e Posidonio," *Studi ital. di filologia classica*, nuova serie, VIII 1930–31, 297–301 (also on *B.G.* VI 13–14).

The same tradition is echoed by Ammianus Marcellinus XV 11. 1–3.

On all this see Ernst Kalinka, "Cäsar und die Fortsetzer seiner Werke: Bericht über das Schrifttum der Jahre 1929–36," *Bursians Jahresbericht über die Fortschritte der klassischen Altertumswissenschaft*, CCLXIV (1939), 169–256, especially 190, 201–202 (with the references to Eduard Norden, *Die germanische Urgeschichte in Tacitus Germania*, ed. 3, 1923, 365); Friedrich Frahm, "Cäsar und Tacitus als Quelle für die altgermanische Verfassung," *Historische Vierteljahrschrift* XXIV 1928, 152; W. Capelle, "Poseidonius der Entdecker der 'nordischen' Völker," *Geistige Arbeit*, IV 1937, xi, 7–9, gives a "popular" account.

On an allied topic see F. Frahm, "Die Entwicklung des Suebenbegriffs in der antiken Literatur," *Klio*, XXIII 1929, 181–210.

The relevant place in Strabo may be quoted:

οἱ μὲν δὴ τριχῇ διῄρουν, ᾿Ακυιτανοὺς καὶ Βέλγας καλοῦντες καὶ Κέλτας· τοὺς μὲν ᾿Ακυιτανοὺς τελέως ἐξηλλαγμένους οὐ τῇ γλώττῃ μόνον, ἀλλὰ καὶ τοῖς σώμασιν . . . τοὺς δὲ λοιποὺς Γαλατικοὺς μὲν τὴν ὄψιν, ὁμογλώττους δ' οὐ πάντας, ἀλλ' ἐνίους μικρὸν παραλλάττοντας ταῖς γλώτταις, κτλ.

On this see Robert Munz, "Über γλῶττα und διάλεκτος und über ein posidonianisches Fragment bei Strabo: ein sprachwissenschaftlich-philologischer Excurs zu Posidonius bei Strabo C 176 über dialektische Verschiedenheiten bei den Galliern," *Glotta* XI 1921, 85–94.

about varieties of language and customs among the tribes of north-western Europe.

Let us begin, then, with Caesar's opening statement, which, as every schoolboy knows, was not intended to include Narbonensis, despite the fact that it begins with the words *Gallia . . . omnis*: "Gaul, taken as a whole, is divided into three parts, one of which is inhabited by Belgae, another by Aquitani, and the third by people who are called in their own language 'Kelts' and in Latin 'Gauls.' All these differ from one another in language, institutions, and laws. The 'Gauls' are separated from the Aquitani by the river Garonne, from the Belgae by the Marne and the Seine." These first words of Caesar's *de bello Gallico* [9] are so well known as hardly to need quotation, so

[9] Gallia est omnis diuisa in partes tres, quarum unam incolunt Belgae, aliam Aquitani, tertiam qui ipsorum lingua Celtae, nostra Galli appellantur. hi omnes lingua institutis legibus inter se differunt. Gallos ab Aquitanis Garunna flumen, a Belgis Matrona et Sequana diuidit (*B.G.* I, I. 1–2).

Gallus, Galli was the Latin name for the invaders who sacked Rome in 390 B.C. Any country which they occupied could be called, by the same name, *Gallia*. Why they were so called we do not know. The etymology of their name and its source are likewise unknown. It may have been an appellative, and, if so, it may have meant "warrior," or "foreign, strange." Or it may have been a tribal or local name, the name that is of the tribe where, or of the locality, in which, the Romans first learned to know "Gauls." But in no sense was it, or could it be, a national or political designation. Only after the conquest by Caesar was *Gallia* accepted, in the administrative language of Rome, with the more exact geographical meaning, common to the historians of imperial and all later times, which will be stated presently (p. 20).

On the names *Celtae, Galli,* Κελτοί, Γαλάται in Latin and Greek writers generally, see H. d'Arbois de Jubainville, "Les Celtes et les langues celtiques," *Revue archéologique*, nouv. sér., I 1882, 87–95, 141–154 (add to his references Diod. Sic. V 32.1). For another suggestion (*gallus, cf. Becco*) see *REA* XII 1910, 295.

The sham hare "Celtae and Galli" started by Rhys, *Transactions of the Philological Society*, London, 1891–94, 104–131, was shown to be what it was by E. Zupitza, "Kelten und Gallier," *ZfCPh* IV 1902–03, 1–22. Rhys still pretended that it was a live hare, *Proc. Br. Acad.* II 1905–06, 71–134, warily avoiding the mention of Zupitza's name. But Zupitza had the better of the argument. Cf. R. Thurneysen in *ZfCPh* VI 1907–08, 244–245.

The modern name *Gaule, Gaul* is another story, yet to be told. Albert Sjögren, *Studia Neophilologica*, XI 1938–39, 210–214, has the suggestion that it comes from Wace who adopted in his *Roman de Brut* the local name [*La*] *Gaule* (several hamlets near Caen and Bayeux), which he knew had in scholastic Latin traditionally been

forthright in what they affirm as hardly to need interpretation. Yet they have become the text of many a laborious dissertation. For example, the long discussion, in many chapters, which the late T. E. Rice Holmes, who had no taste for nonsense or humbug, felt himself obliged to write [10] about the peoples of pre-Roman and Roman Gaul, shows clearly how the words of Caesar have been obscured by a superimposed mass of modern, and silly, interpretation and argument.

In part the dispute is perverse. No one reading without preconception the simple statement *ipsorum lingua Celtae, nostra Galli, appellantur* could take it to mean other or more than what it says, namely that a certain people whom Caesar had encountered in a large stretch of territory between the Garonne and the Marne called themselves by a different name from that by which Caesar himself and other speakers of Latin were wont to designate them. That is all. Caesar says nothing, it ought to be unnecessary to point out, about "Kelts" as distinguished from Gauls. He merely mentions two different names, a native one and a foreign one, of one and the same people. Who in his senses would maintain that the Welsh are a different people from the Cymry, the Allemands (or Germans) from the Deutsche, the Graeci from the Hellenes? Yet this is precisely what Rhys did.

But in part the dispute springs from the desire to know more about the differences which Caesar declared existed "in language" and in other matters between the Belgae, Celtae (or Galli), and Aquitani. It springs also from carelessness or absence of definition, and as we proceed it will be necessary to make clear the meanings in which we use *Gallia* or Gaul (a purely geographical term) and *Keltic* (a purely linguistic term) as well as *Galli* or Gauls, which we shall use consistently in the meaning "inhabitants of Gaul, *Gallia*" (as defined). That part of the dispute which is perverse may be left to the fate which awaits all perverse disputes, a fate which in fact already has overtaken it. But the desire to discover just how those three peoples differed in language from one another and from their neighbors is legitimate

---

Gallia, as an equivalent also of the name of the classical Latin *Gallia*. But I am reluctant to believe that the extremely common and well established *Gaule* is a mere literary accident; besides, the manuscripts of Wace actually have *Gaulle* as well as *Gaule*. *Gallia* would, of course, normally become **Jaille* in French.

[10] *Caesar's Conquest of Gaul*, ed. 2, Oxford, 1911, 257–338.

enough. It is an enquiry easily trapped in the pitfalls of excess of zeal and misplaced ingenuity. In the effort to shun them it is not necessary, however, to go to the other extreme of inhibiting common sense, and of doubting whether any of the inscriptions known as Gaulish are in a Keltic language.[11] And in all that has been written on this subject, one thing at least has been done neither by Rhys nor by Dottin, nor by any one else who has written about the Keltic dialects of Gaul, and that is: so to arrange the linguistic evidence as to show clearly what truth, if any, there is in Caesar's assertion, on the basis of the materials now extant. Caesar, or his authority, is not indeed made a liar, merely if the assertion cannot be justified on that basis, for the basis itself may now be inadequate. No one was so learned or so unlearned, or at least no one so interested, in Caesar's own day, as to have disputed the statement. Its truth was as self-evident as a comparable statement made to-day about India or South America.

We must be content, therefore, with what evidence we have, and not attempt to go beyond it. But the required arrangement of the evidence demands two simple rules of procedure: first, an orderly geographical classification of it, the broadest outlines of which Caesar himself has given us; and, second, a rigid separation of what is certain from what is merely probable. To these I have added a third rule, which needs no justification, that is to reject the irrelevant. The materials which will be offered have been severely selected from a mass of records, on the principle of admitting only those which throw light on the dialectal conditions of pre-Roman Gaul.

It is necessary, however, to extend somewhat the geographical limits with which Caesar begins. Taking into consideration only the Galli, we know that other peoples called by this name lived in ancient times in other parts of Europe, as well as in Gaul. On the other hand, at *B.G.* I 1, 1 Caesar, in his threefold partition of Gaul, uses the term *Gallia* in a narrower sense than that in which the imperial provincial administration used it, or in which it is commonly understood. Any enquiry, therefore, into the linguistic situation in ancient Gaul, must take into account any other ancient dialects that may have existed

---

[11] See the *Transactions of the Philological Society* (London), 1933, 102. The opposite view is strongly stated by C. Jullian, *HG* II 1908, 360–375, especially 371 n. 6, 366 n. 3 ad fin.

there in addition to the three which Caesar specifies ("Belgic, Celtic, Aquitanian"); and also, granted that one (or more than one) of such dialects (taken all together) belonged to that subdivision of the Indo-European languages which modern philologists, using the ancient name, call Keltic, must take some account, by way of comparison, of related dialects spoken outside of the boundaries of Gaul, as for example in the adjacent territories of Germany, Switzerland, and Italy — not to mention the ancient Keltic dialect of Galatia.[12]

It was, in fact, the study of the problems presented by the Lepontic inscriptions and by the remains of Ligurian as well as of Keltic in Gallia Cisalpina, that led naturally to the present study. At first the intention was simply to deal with the texts of those non-Latin and non-Greek inscriptions of ancient Gaul which are commonly regarded as Keltic. Then the plan gradually took shape of presenting a linguistic survey of Gaul as a whole, *Gallia omnis*.

Even from the little that has been said about "Keltic" dialects and about "Gaul," it will be evident that both of these terms require definition. Definitions, it need hardly be said, properly come at the end, not at the beginning, of an investigation. If, therefore, it is possible to define the terms *Keltic* and *Gallia* here, without further delay, that is because their meanings have been made sufficiently clear by previous investigations.

It is a little over one hundred years since Franz Bopp, in 1838,[13] demonstrated, what had been doubted or denied, namely, that the Keltic languages are Indo-European, though that essential fact had been stated by Sir William Jones in 1786 and recognized by Rasmus Rask in 1818;[14] and, since 1853, the year in which the *Grammatica Cel-*

---

[12] On this see now L. Weisgerber, "Galatische Sprachreste," in *Natalicium Johannes Geffcken*, Heidelberg, 1931, 151–175, reviewed by J. Vendryes, *RC* XLIX 1932, 299–300.

[13] *Die celtischen Sprachen in ihrem Verhältnisse zum Sanskrit usw.*, Berlin, 1839 (Gelesen in der Akademie der Wissenschaften am 13. Dec. 1838).

[14] In a letter dated 11 June 1818, see Rask's *Samlede . . . Afhandlinger* II 1836, 281: Denne (vor) Rase inddeler jeg således: *den indiske* (den dekanske, hindostanske), *irâniske* (pers. armen. osset.), *trakiske* (graeske og latinske), *sarmatiske* (lettiske og slaviske), *gotiske* (gjerman. og skandinav.) og *keltiske* (brittaniske og gæliske) Stamme eller Folke og *Sprogklasse*. Sir William Jones' famous statement of 1786 is quoted in every text-book and need not be repeated here. It will be seen that by

tica appeared, their chief characteristics have been made well known.[15] By Keltic, then, we understand that variety of western Indo-European speech [16] which is recognizable both by those features that it possesses in common with other Indo-European languages, and also, more particularly, by those peculiar features of its own that distinguish it among them; and which we find to be spoken in modern times in Brittany, Cornwall, Wales, the Isle of Man, Ireland, and Scotland (not to mention the Welsh-speaking colony of Patagonia), and to have been spoken in ancient times in Great Britain and Ireland, in Gaul (except in the corner between the river Garonne and the Pyrenees mountains), and at least temporarily in many parts of the central European, Alpine, and Danubian regions, in some parts of the Spanish, Italian, and Balkan peninsulas; and in Asia Minor. The term Keltic, therefore, applies properly to language and to language only. The extension of it so as to designate people ("Kelts") is justified when and only when it is restricted to the meaning "Keltic-speaking" at that period at which it is known the people who are designated Keltic were actually Keltic-speaking. In any other usage the term is misleading if not meaningless. Thus we can say that Keltic speech was in use in certain parts of Gaul in the last century before Christ, and we may designate the communities, who used such a speech, as Keltic or Keltic-speaking, so long and only so long as they used it, but not, for example, after they had discarded that speech and learned Latin in its place.

1818 Rask had revised his earlier opinion, set forth in his prize-essay "Undersøgelse om det gamle Nordiske eller Islandske Sprogs Oprindelse" (1814, first published in 1818, now reprinted in *Udvalgte Afhandlinger* [*Ausgewählte Abhandlungen*] of Rask, edited by L. Hjelmslev, 1932), that Keltic is not Indo-European, but owes its Indo-European elements to borrowing.

[15] For readers of this monograph the most useful summaries are those of Ernst Windisch, "Keltische Sprache," in Gröber, *Grundriss der romanischen Philologie* I, ed. 2, 1904–06, 371–404, or of Julius Pokorny, "Kelten: B. Sprache," in Ebert, *Reallexikon der Vorgeschichte*, VI 1926, 296–300. Cf. H. d'Arbois de Jubainville, *Éléments de la Grammaire celtique*, Paris, 1903. Those who desire detail may be referred to Pedersen, *VKG*.

On the progress of Keltic studies see R. Thurneysen, "Die keltischen Sprachen," in Streitberg, *Geschichte der Indogermanischen Sprachwissenschaft* II 1 1916, 281–305.

[16] Cf. Hubert, *Les Celtes* I 23–40, where the fact is emphasized more than once, that the "Kelts" are not a race or people, but a group of communities or societies, one of the most clearly marked characteristics of which is their language.

As for ancient Gaul, we appeal not only to the large group of people living there called, according to Latin and Greek testimony, Celtae or Κελτοί by themselves and often also by ancient writers, so that their communities are called by the adjective *celticus* or κελτικός, terms which are also used by ancient glossographers and other writers to describe their speech and certain words quoted by them from it, both as it was then current in Roman Gaul and in other regions where that speech and its dialects were or had been current; but we appeal also to the long history of certain dialects spoken in the British Isles and in Brittany, reaching down to modern times, dialects which linguistic comparison proves beyond all doubt to be kindred to the ancient Keltic dialect or dialects of Gaul as recorded in those mere isolated fragments, so that the name is justifiably extended to cover all of these; and further we appeal to other linguistic remnants, to which allusion has already been made, found in Gaul itself, and proved by the same method, to belong to the same subdivision of the entire group of dialects as Welsh and Cornish and Breton. There would seem, then, to be no possibility of misunderstanding what is meant by the term "Keltic," whether generally or (more particularly) with reference to ancient Gaul.

The relation of Keltic, as we have defined Keltic, to other Indo-European languages has often been discussed,[17] and again recently by J. Vendryes.[18] It is necessary here to narrow the discussion to the ancient Keltic idioms of Gaul. The fact is familiar, that recorded forms such as *petuar[, pinpetos, epocal(l)ium, petrudecameto* (Gélignieux, Ain), with *p*, do not pass unchallenged, but are confronted by other forms such as *equos* (Coligny, Ain), *Sequana*, with *qu*; and hence a most telling shibboleth would seem to have lost its usefulness.[19] Two, in part

---

[17] By none better than by Holger Pedersen "Le groupement des dialectes indo-européens," *Det Kgl. Danske Videnskabernes Selskab, Historisk-filologiske Meddelelser,* XI 3, 1925.

[18] "La position linguistique du Celtique," *Proc. Br. Acad.,* XXIII 1937, 333–371. Vendryes is wrong, by the way, in claiming *asia* as Keltic (336).

[19] But not in the way in which Iowerth C. Peate "The Kelts in Britain," *Antiquity,* VI 1932, 156–160, and "The Kelts: a Linguistic Contribution," *Archaeologia Cambrensis,* LXXXVII 1932, 260–264, argues. His "contribution" (!) is *nihil ad rem*. That of R. G. Collingwood in R. G. Collingwood and J. N. L. Myres, *Roman Britain and the English Settlements,* Oxford, 1936, 19 is worse. For it is pure non-

contradictory, admissions are made: (1) that in Gaul, the language so far as it was Keltic, agreed in general with Brythonic, despite the treatment of *u̯r-*, which gave *br-* (at least in some areas), but in Welsh *gwr-*, later *gr-*; and (2) that there was no unity of Keltic language in Gaul, that historical and political conditions as well as explicit testimony and archaeological evidence are all against the assumption of such a unity. We know that, before the Romans, the Kelts were the last people to arrive in Gaul, but also that they came in several waves of migration, at different times, and that their predecessors were not Keltic. Usually it is supposed that documentary evidence is completely lacking from which differences of dialect might be deduced, though it is admitted that not all the peoples of Gaul spoke Keltic even at the time of the Roman conquests, and that traces of language anterior to Keltic itself may be observed.

Nevertheless it is contended that proper names, particularly local names, which are something apart within the norm of a spoken language, show great uniformity from one end of Gaul to the other. Attention is called, however, to differences of distribution of certain types of proper names, local names in *-briga* "mount" being especially numerous in Celtiberia, names in *-ialum* "clearing" in certain parts of Gaul. Moreover, in addition to, or side by side with, Keltic proper names there are names, particularly of rivers and mountains, which do not show Keltic formations or Keltic words, or agree with the phonematic or other usage of Keltic, and these are thought to be anterior to Keltic. As examples are quoted the names of mountains *Alpes, Morvan, Cévennes* (to quote the modern forms), and of rivers *Arar, Elauer, Garunna, Icauna, Liger, Rodanus, Samara, Tarnis*, and of towns *Agedincum, Durocortorum*. Despite, therefore, the Keltic alternation, as it would appear, of *p*: *qu*, or the alleged, but extremely doubtful, loss of initial *s* (as in Brythonic), it is conjectured that traces

---

sense to write "It is now held . . . that the Q-variety" [of Keltic] "arose in Ireland, perhaps in the third century before Christ, by a change of *p* into *q*." If Professor J. R. R. Tolkien, who helped Mr Collingwood "untiringly with problems of Celtic philology" (vii), is the author of this extraordinary gaff, he must stand alone in it. Irish preserves Kelt. *q̯ʷ* (from I. Eu. *q̯ʷ*) as late as the Ogam period, later it has *k‘* and the normal subsequent development *k‘*. True, Latin *p*, in the oldest borrowings, is identified with *q̯ʷ* in Irish; later it is *p*.

of Iberian speech in south-west Gaul, and of Ligurian in south-east Gaul, are to be found; or so it was conjectured, for one authority, completely carried away by the now fashionable Illyriomania, would substitute "Illyrian" for Ligurian in the latter area. Finally, King Charles' head, or the atavistic "substratum," reappears from time to time, when traces of Keltic or of Keltic influence, are proclaimed to exist, not merely in the vulgar Latin of Gaul, but also in the French language, and not merely in its vocabulary but also in other features, at various times in its history.

Thus we have a certain number of Keltic words surviving into modern French, e.g., *alouette, vergne, lieue, arpent, marne, ouche, marchais, breuil.*[20] The fact is not surprising; and the ascription of *ixi* "ipsi" at Suetonius *Aug.* 88 to a Gaul is plausible, since the change from *ps* to χ*s* in Keltic is universal. But it is more doubtful whether there is justification for the comparison of French with Irish constructions and prepositions which Vendryes[21] suggests. Far less remote and far more convincing is the comparison between Keltic multipersonal passive forms in Welsh and Irish, and the Gaulish *marcosior,* if that is correctly interpreted as a passive verbal form. Doubts too are awaked by Vendryes' appeal to "substratum" in Keltic, Etruscan, and Italic, the "substratum" in this case being supposed to be ancient, Mediterranean, and pre-Indo-European.

Within Indo-European itself, however, it is a commonplace observation that Keltic has many items of vocabulary and grammar shared in common with Germanic[22] and Italic, or with both, e.g. Gaulish

---

[20] Cf. Dottin *REA* VII 1905, 42–44.

[21] 369.

[22] The subject demands more accurate study than that given to it by C. S. Elston, *The Earliest Relations between Celts and Germans,* London, 1934 (see the reviews by M. L. Sjœstedt, *RC* LI 1934, 305–309, H. Krahe, *Idg. Forsch.,* LII 1934, 258–259, and by G. Neckel in *Deutsche Lit.-ztg.,* LV 1934, 1797–98), or by Sigmund Feist, *Indogermanen und Germanen* ed. 3, Halle, 1924, 71–77, and *Germanen und Kelten in der antiken Überlieferung,* Halle, 1927 (see the review by W. Steinhauser in *ZfCPh,* XVII 1928, 423–426). Among older discussions note J. Mansion, "Kelten en Germanen," *Verslagen en Mededeelingen der koninklijke vlaamische Academie voor Taal en Letterkunde,* Gent, 1912, 1293–1308 (cf. 1285–1286, and the summary in French, *REA* XV 1913, 198–199), H. d'Arbois de Jubainville, *Celtes et Germains,* Paris, 1886 (from *Comptes Rendus de l'Académie des Inscriptions et Belles-Lettres,* 4e série, XIII 1885 [published 1886], 316–325, where it appeared under a different

celicnon, which appears to mean some kind of building or structure, cf. Gothic *kēlikn* "upper-room, tower;" but this agreement, like many others (e.g. Ir. *marc* "horse") in Vendryes' list of words dealing with warfare, is due to borrowing.[23] On the other hand, Keltic and Italic have a great many features in common, not by borrowing, but, so to speak, by inheritance, notably a large number of words connected with religion.[24]

title, "Unité primitive des Italo-celtes, relations de l'empire celtique avec les Germains antérieurement au second siècle avant notre ère"), and most recently J. Pokorny in *ZfCPh* XX 1936, 500–508; cf. H. Hirt, *Indogermanische Grammatik* I 1927, 57–59, id., *Handbuch des Urgermanischen*, I 1931, 11–13. It is well to recall the distinctions implied by Caesar *B.G.* I, 47 (cf. VI 21–24) and by Tacitus *Germ.* 2.5 (on the text see the conjectures of R. Meissner and E. B[ickel], *Rh. Mus.*, LXXXVIII 1939, 379–384).

The first attempt to grapple seriously with this problem was perhaps that of Adolf Holtzmann, *Kelten und Germanen*, Stuttgart, 1855, quickly followed by the more painstaking H. B. Christian Brandes, *Das ethnographische Verhältniss der Kelten und Germanen*, Leipzig, 1857. Some recent judgements must be read with caution (Gustav Neckel, "Germanen und Kelten," *Zeitschrift für Deutschkunde*, XLVII 1933, 497–574; Rudolf Much, "Kelten und Germanen," *Volk und Rasse*, III 1928, 143–154 and 193–201). A. Schulten, "Germanen und Gallier," *Forschungen und Fortschritte*, VIII 1932, 121–122, argues that "Germanen" reached Spain in the sixth century B.C.!

Some further bibliographical items will be given in connexion with Germania inferior in the main body of the work. Add M. Mauss, *Rev. de Synthèse*, XVII 1939, 22–23; M. Dillon, *JEGP* XLII 1943, 492–498.

[23] Cf. Vendryes, *RC*, XLIX 1932, 300 (citing Weisgerber) on the possibility that both *kelikn* and *siponeis* came into Gothic from Galatian rather than from Gaulish. On *siponeis* see, in addition to R. Much in *Beiträge zur Gesch. der deutschen Spr. u. Lit.*, XVII 1892, 33 and W. Luft in *Zts. f. deutsches Altertum*, XLI 1897, 239 (both cited by S. Feist, *Etym. Wtb. der gotischen Sprache* ed. 2, 1933, s.v.), A. Cuny *REA* XII, 1910, 15. Add also Carl J. S. Marstrander, "A Celto-Germanic Correspondence of Vocabulary," *Norsk Tidsskrift for Sprogvidenskap*, VII 1934, 347–349; id., "Une correspondance germano-celtique," *Skrifter utgit av Videnskapsselskapet i Kristiania* 1924, II Historisk-filosofisk Klasse, 8. But Collitz, *AJP* XLVI 1925, was quite wrong in his guess (σύμπονος).

[24] See, in general, Richard von Kienle, "Italiker und Kelten," *Wörter und Sachen*, XVII 1936, 98–153; J. Vendryes, "Italique et Celtique," *RC* XLII 1925, 379–390; A. Walde, "Über älteste sprachliche Beziehungen zwischen Kelten und Italikern," Rektoratsschrift, Innsbruck, 1917; on Rhys *loc. cit.* n. 9 supra ("The Celts and other Aryans of the P and Q groups," *Trans. Phil.Soc.*, 1891), see the criticisms of J. Loth in Vollmöller's *Kritischer Jahresbericht*, IV 1895–96: i 44–46. Recent

The Roman or greater Gaul of which we have spoken extended beyond the frontiers of modern France, for it stretched as far east as the Rhine so as to include, besides Alsace and Lorraine (which at present are no longer French), the western and north-western lowlands of Switzerland from Geneva to the western end of lake Constance; the Rhenish provinces of Germany; Luxembourg, Belgium, and the southern part of the Netherlands. Thus, for the ancients, Gallia in the broad sense of the term meant the north-western land-mass of continental Europe, enclosed by the Mediterranean and the Pyrenees on the south, by the Atlantic and the English channel on the west and north, by the Rhine and the Alps on the east.[25] Galli are inhabitants of Gallia. This is greater than Caesar's Gallia too, for he excluded the Roman province into which, after the Civil War, the territory of Massilia was to be incorporated. But then there are also certain frontier-districts, lying between Germany, Raetia, and Italy, which were more or less Keltic in character, and of which, therefore, it is convenient and, for the purposes of a linguistic enquiry, proper to take account. The peculiar organization of some of these regions sufficiently indicates the difficulties which the Roman imperial administrators themselves felt, on territorial and other administrative grounds, in including them in the adjacent provinces. In addition to the three military districts between Italy and the province of southern Gaul, there was the *uallis Poenina*, corresponding roughly to the modern canton Wallis of Switzerland; that part of the country of the Keltic Vindelici in the

scepticism on the agreements between Italic and Keltic (see, e.g., C[arl] M[arstrander] "De l'unité italo-celtique," *Norsk Tidsskrift for Sprogvidenskap*, III 1929, 241–259, and "A West-Indoeuropean Correspondence of Vocabulary," VII 1934, 335–343) has gone too far. But the views of C. Jullian "L'Époque italo-celtique," *REA*, XVIII 1916, 263–276; XIX 1917, 125–133; XX 1918, 43–46, were just as extreme. Something may be gleaned from J. Vendryes, "Mélanges italo-celtiques," in *Mémoires de la Société de Linguistique de Paris*, XIII 1905–06, 384–408 (cf. *ZfCPh*, VI 1907–08, 251), *id.*, "Les correspondances de vocabulaire entre l'indo-iranien et l'italo-celtique," XX 1918, 265–285 (summary in *Rev. arch.* 5e sér., VIII 1918, 347), and from G. Devoto "Italo-greco e Italo-celtico," in *Silloge linguistica dedicata alla memoria di Graziadeo Isaia Ascoli*, Turin, 1929, 200–240 (*Arch. Glott. Ital.*, XXII–XXIII). Cf. Vendryes, *EC* II 1937, 405; Bonfante, *Emerita* II 1934, 263–306; *Riv. IGI* XIX 1935, 49–69; M. Dillon, *AJP* LXV 1944, 124–134.

[25] The evidence is assembled by Holder *AcS* I, s.v. Gallia (1896); cf. J. Toutain in E. de Ruggiero, *Dizionario epigrafico di antichità romane*, s.v. Gallia (1905).

map I

GAUL AT THE TIME OF CAESAR

northern province of Raetia (later Raetia secunda), which, on their western confines, adjoined Gaul proper; and the *agri decumates*, which lay between Gaul and Germany — in all, therefore:

I. ALPINE REGIONS
    1. Alpes Maritimae
    2. Regnum Cottii
    3. Alpes Graiae
    4. Vallis Poenina

II. GAUL PROPER
    1. Narbonensis
    2. Aquitania
    3. Lugdunensis
    4. Belgica
    5. Germania inferior
    6. Germania superior

III. MIDDLE RHINE AND UPPER DANUBE
    1. Agri decumates
    2. Vindelici

The maps set forth the republican and imperial subdivisions of Gaul. I have used the latter for the purposes of a geographical classification of the dialectal evidence, (1) because most of it is actually of imperial date; (2) because the dialects were not, or at least Keltic was not, extinct before the third century of our era; and (3) because the imperial subdivision provides areas more instructive and also more manageable than Caesar's or Strabo's do.[26] (Caesar's tripartite division, let us recall, is not his own, but that of Posidonius.) It must be understood that the precise boundaries of the imperial subdivisions cannot be accurately indicated, for they are not accurately known. Still

---

[26] It is not worth while to give a sketch of Strabo's Gaul (with the Pyrenees running north and south). Those who want it may find a map of sorts in the Loeb Strabo, II.

The two Germanies (*inferior* and *superior*) were "im officiellen Sprachgebrauch keine Provinzen, sondern regiones oder dioeceses der Provinz Belgica im weitern Sinn;" this truth (Mommsen, *Gesammelte Schriften* VIII, 1913, 153–154) cannot be too much emphasized.

Map II

GAUL AT THE TIME OF AUGUSTUS

later divisions, whereby there was set up a varying number of provinces, are of no interest here.[27]

In its main features the history of the latinization, this term being
used in its strictest (i.e. linguistic) sense, is very similar in Gaul to
what it had been in Italy. In both lands there are records of languages
spoken before the spread of Latin, and some hints, but no actual records, of still others. Moreover we do not suppose that the ancestors
of the people whose linguistic remains are the oldest known to us in
either Gaul or Italy were dumb. What we have to ask is the question
what languages, so far as we can now tell, were spoken in the several
regions of Gaul and its frontier-districts before the spread of Romance
(that is Latin) or Germanic speech. The ultimate fate of the pre-Latin
dialects in Gaul, as in Italy, was that at last they were abandoned,
almost everywhere, in favor of other forms of speech, usually Latin.
And if, as some hold, modern Greek is in Italy nowhere descended
from the ancient Greek of Magna Graecia, a view mentioned here only
for the sake of comparison and not because it is thought to be truer
than the opposite theory, no more is Breton in France descended from
the ancient Keltic dialect of Brittany, but (like Albanian in Italy) was
introduced there from outside. But Basque, spoken in the arrondisse-
ments of Bayonne and Mauléon, is usually maintained to be descended
from Iberian, spoken in the ancient Aquitania and presumably anterior to Keltic.

To repeat, then, we must ask, not what was the Iberian or the
Ligurian language respectively of Aquitania or eastern Narbonensis,
for in that form the question implies a denial of the sure fact that a
more or less racially stable people on occasion does change its language
as easily as its culture; but, rather, what languages were spoken, at
successive periods, in Aquitania or in Gaulish (and in Italian) Liguria;
and likewise with respect to the other regions of Gaul proper and to
the frontier-districts. We are entitled, moreover, once these questions have been answered, also to assign geographical names, for example Iberian or Ligurian, to certain of their dialects, if only as a

[27] A recent discussion may be had of Herbert Nesselhauf, "Die spätrömische
Verwaltung der gallisch-germanischen Länder" (*Abhandlungen der preussischen
Akademie der Wissenschaften*, 1938, Phil.-hist. Klasse, 2), pp. 8–21; cf. Grenier,
Mnl. I 138–141.

Map III

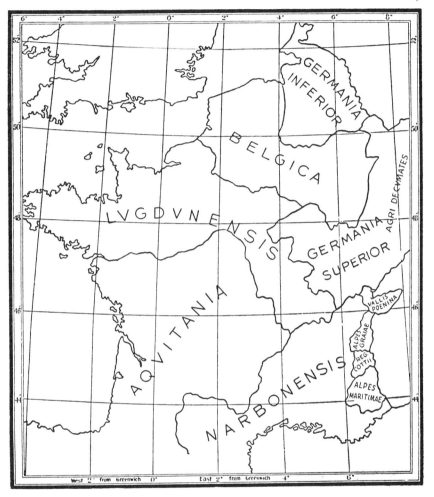

GAUL IN THE SECOND AND THIRD CENTURIES AFTER CHRIST

means of identification, and then to ask what were the affiliations of the dialects so designated. And these geographical names, it ought not to be necessary to point out, must not be assigned to fit some preconceived theory.

The very fact that Ligurians are known to have lived in Gaul as well as in Italy, if not the theory of d'Arbois de Jubainville and others that these Gaulish Ligurians at one time spoke a non-Keltic but nevertheless Indo-European speech, raises the question what had been the language or languages of this wider Liguria that straddled the Alpes Maritimae from Italy to Gaul, before Latin became its language. Again the fact that a Keltic language was brought into Italy from across the Alps about the beginning of the fourth century before Christ or the end of the preceding century, raises important questions of the relations between that Keltic dialect of north Italy and the Keltic dialects of Gaul, and also of the nature of the latinization in north Italy and Gaul respectively.

It is all the more necessary to consider these preliminary questions, since erroneous views concerning the answers to them are still bandied about by the reckless or prejudiced. First, then, the Ligurian question.[28] For the moment, the problem of the Narbonese inscriptions may be left in abeyance. What it is important to emphasise here is the incontestable fact that there was spoken in the ancient Liguria, before the use of Latin, an Indo-European language that cannot be classified as a dialect of any other Indo-European speech, but must be put in an independent place within that family of languages. The evidence even for this guarded form of statement has been given elsewhere, and I do not intend to repeat it. It is necessary, therefore, only to point out, first, that no argument has yet been advanced to alter that fact in the slightest degree; and hence, second, that the sole ques-

---

[28] I cannot enter into the problems raised by Eduard Mauritz Meijers, "Le droit ligurien de succession," *Revue d'histoire du droit,* V 1923–24, 1–32, elaborated in his larger work with the same title, published as *Rechtshistorisch Instituut,* Leiden, Ser. II. 2, vol. I 1928 ("Les Pays Alpins"), eagerly as Jullian welcomed any excuse for identifying Ligurian with "l'italo-celtique" (cf. Julien Havet, "Les institutions et le droit spéciaux aux italo-celtes," *RC* XXVIII, 1907, 113–116). Jullian's own attempts to separate Ligurian names of cities and rivers in France (*REA* III, 1901, 317; V, 1903, 28–29, cf. 36 n. 2; VIII, 1906, 250–252; 343; cf. XV, 1913, 453 n. 1) cannot be called successful.

tion that remains is whether or not the conclusion to which the evidence leads should be formulated in the general undefined shape in which it has just been stated above, and only so — and a more definite form of statement may indeed be modified to that extent, without making any essential change in my view; in other words, whether or not it is justifiable to give the conclusion a less vague shape by saying that the pre-Latin Indo-European speech of Liguria is appropriately to be described as Ligurian. The answer is that there are good and sufficient reasons for taking this further step.[29]

Next the Keltic dialect of north Italy. The gradual, but almost uninterrupted, process of supplanting the Keltic dialects has been at work in Europe for over two thousand years, until to-day Keltic is not commonly spoken anywhere except in restricted parts of the British Isles and Brittany. When and how did Keltic cease to be spoken in north Italy? That a Keltic dialect was spoken there before Latin is certain, and the general character of that Keltic dialect is also well known; that is to say, it belonged to that branch of Keltic known as *p*-Keltic, because it substituted, in part, labial plosives for the older Indo-European labio-velar plosives and also for the combination $\hat{k}\underset{\sim}{u}$. Thus, like Welsh and Cornish *ebol* (*b* for older *p*), we have Keltic *epo-* in north Italy (*Eporedia*, *Epona*) in contrast with Irish *ech*, Venetic *e·kupeθari·s·*, *ecupetaris*, or even Umbrian *ekvine*. The interpretation "charioteer" of the Venetic word just cited was first proposed by Torp, and nothing that has been said against it since then either by Danielsson or by others is convincing; still less are the other interpretations suggested in its place. In general I often find myself in agreement with Pedersen's conclusions, but not in his criticism of Torp's brilliant explanation of that Venetic word.[30]

But comparisons of Keltic words with words in other Indo-European languages in Italy, apart from the well-known agreements on which the Italo-Keltic hypothesis was based, are not notably closer than with words in Indo-European languages outside Italy.[31] Nothing is gained, for example, by insisting on a comparison of Welsh *iach* "healthy" with Venetic *akeo*, even though Greek ἀκέομαι also regularly has the smooth breathing, for the absence of initial $\underset{\sim}{i}$- would be quite as irregu-

---

[29] See note A, pp. 77–80 below.
[30] See note B, pp. 80–82 below.
[31] See *Do.*, 126–132.

lar in Venetic as are the few forms with rough breathing (e.g. Delph. ἐφακέομαι) in Greek.[32] It is, moreover, certain that linguistically the Gauls had no lasting influence in Italy, apart from the well-known borrowings of single words into Latin; and, in fact, it is only in the western part of the country about the Po that "we can assume from the testimony of the inscriptions the existence of a compact Gaulish-speaking population."[33] This inscriptional evidence is of two kinds: first, the three isolated but actual Keltic inscriptions of Briona (No-vara), Todi, and Zignago; and, second, the manifestly Keltic names which appear in "good measure, pressed down and running over" in the Latin inscriptions of Cisalpine Gaul. Mr D. O. Robson, of the University of Western Ontario, London, Ontario, writes in opposition to my view (namely, that these Keltic names prove the survival of a rapidly latinized but previously Keltic-speaking population of the Po valley) that they "may equally well point to a much later influx." As to that, it need only be pointed out that the moon may be made of green cheese. The objections of a critic who confuses Hittite hiero-glyphic and Hittite cuneiform need not, indeed, be taken very seri-ously, but the interpretation of an often-quoted place in Polybius[34] dealing with the latinization — or, from Polybius' point of view, the romanization — of Cisalpine Gaul, calls for more careful consideration.

Elsewhere[35] I have, like others before me,[36] interpreted that place in Polybius as being greatly exaggerated if taken in its literal meaning. From this view, which is at least no "mis-interpretation" of the facts, I see no reason to depart. In the first place, it has constantly to be remembered that even Greek writers about Italian affairs invariably tell their stories from the Roman point of view, and in the matter of the conquest of Cisalpine Gaul Polybius is no exception to the rule. Next, the very fact that the Romans had by no means done with the turbulent Alpine and Cisalpine tribes, even after the days of Polybius, proves that he exaggerated. Then the considerable evidence of Keltic

---

[32] See *Classical Philology*, XXXVI 1941, 409.

[33] H. Pedersen, *Linguistic Science in the Nineteenth Century*, 1931, 54.

[34] II 35.4; see note C, pp. 82–85 below.

[35] *Prae-Italic Dialects*, II 170; cf. *Foundations of Roman Italy*, 1937, 106, 153.

[36] E.g., H. Nissen, *Italische Landeskunde*, I 1883, 482; cf. von Duhn quoted, and Chilver cited, in nn. 176, 178 below.

cults, which, in Cisalpine Gaul, survived even the romanization,[37] above all that of the *matronae*, is perhaps the most convincing proof that the Gauls were not "expelled" or removed root and branch, so much as absorbed into the older population and, with the plantation of colonies, the spread of agriculture and commerce, and above all the adoption of Latin, became "extinct" in the sense that with the loss of their Gallic characteristics, and especially of their ancestral language, the descendants of the Gauls of Gallia Cisalpina ceased to be Kelts and became rather Italians in the course of the last two centuries B.C.

The process of romanization in Transalpine Gaul, then, was not essentially different from what it had been in Cisalpine Gaul;[38] it took place at later dates, and it operated on different tribes, that is all. Indeed it clearly must be regarded as substantially an extension, beyond the Alps, of that same process which in the end not merely justified but actually had compelled, when at last it could no longer be denied, the extension, as far as the Alps, of the Roman franchise even to the most Keltic part of Cisalpine Gaul, the Transpadana (49 B.C.).

There is, however, a great contrast between Narbonensis and the three Gauls, where the latinization was affected much more slowly and was not in fact completed before the sixth century of our era. The spread of Christianity had much to do with the introduction of Latin into the remoter parts of Gaul, and, outside of the towns and permanent camps, Christian preachers must have played at least as large a part as Roman soldiers, traders, and officials in spreading the Latin at the same time that they spread the faith of the Church. It is, therefore, all the more remarkable that a large proportion out of the total number of dialect inscriptions preserved to us in Gaul have been discovered in southern Gaul, which was earlier and more rapidly latinized, and not from the Tres Galliae, which maintained their Keltic speech longer and more tenaciously, thoroughly latinized as the whole of Gaul was in the long run.

[37] See *Foundations of Roman Italy*, 157–160; G. E. F. Chilver, *Cisalpine Gaul*, Oxford, 1941, 183–192.

[38] This was also Mommsen's view, *History of Rome*, Eng. tr. by W. P. Dickson, New York, 1872, IV 645–647.

But manifestly it would be absurd to conclude that in the Tres Galliae the Keltic-speaking people were exterminated, and not in Narbonensis. The true explanation is that the absence of written documents is part and parcel of their more persistent Kelticism. The druids refused to commit their traditional lore to writing, and all but the nobles, who were educated by the druids, remained illiterate. Thus there was no common practice of writing before the Latin language was introduced, and with it the free use of the art. Hence, when the people began to write at all, they did so, with hardly an exception, in Latin and in the Latin alphabet. The statement is sometimes made, especially in popular works, that just as Latin, the common language of the empire, was taken over by the Gauls, so the Latin alphabet was taken over by the Keltic languages. But this statement needs some modification. In general it may be said that in the Tres Galliae we find (except at Mont-Auxois) only the Latin alphabet in use for writing dialect inscriptions, in Narbonensis only the Greek alphabet; in Italy the North-Etruscan alphabet appears in all three extant Keltic inscriptions.

What is true of the three Gauls, is true at first also of Britain. The native Irish or *ogam* script was not only proper to Ireland, whence it spread to Wales, Cornwall, Scotland, and the Isle of Man; it is itself of uncertain origin.[39] It was never threatened by competition with Greek writing; on the other hand the Latin alphabet first began its triumphal progress, not yet stayed, beyond the borders of Italy, when it was adopted for writing the Keltic languages, not only of Gaul, but also of the British Isles. There can be no doubt that the people of Roman Britain generally spoke not Latin but British.[40] They did not

[39] Helmut Arntz maintains a Runic origin (see Müller's *Handbuch der Altertumswissenschaft*, ed. W. Otto, VI *Handbuch der Archäologie*, 1939, 353–356, with the references to his earlier and fuller discussions, and to the criticisms of Thurneysen and Keller). Neither this view nor the commonly accepted derivation from the Latin alphabet is satisfactory; but at all events there is no question of a Gaulish origin, or of a native script peculiar to the Keltic peoples as a whole, even if *ogam* should be of independent Irish origin. In his article, "L'Écriture chez les Celtes," *RC* XLIV 1927, 1–13, unfortunately Loth takes Glozel seriously.

[40] See, for example, the conclusions of K. H. Jackson (in *Proceedings of the British Association for the Advancement of Science*, 1935, 425), whose statement is to be preferred to that of R. G. Collingwood ap. T. Frank, *Economic Survey of Ancient Rome,*

write it down, however. In Britain the speaking of Latin, among the officials and perhaps as a second language — a polite tongue of the upper classes — coincided roughly with the ability to read and write. Certainly we have in the end a very different situation from what obtained even in the three Gauls, where eventually Latin was established firmly and developed into a Romance language. Yet Latin was not without influence on the British tongue, as modern Welsh proves. Hence the Keltic epigraphic evidence from Britain, where the speakers of Keltic were by no means exterminated by the Romans, or for that matter by their Anglo-Saxon conquerors either, is insignificant and negligible, if not actually zero, as in fact more than once, erroneously, it has been declared to be.[41] But even if we have no British inscriptions, it was in Britain that Keltic survived, to be re-introduced, in the fifth and sixth centuries of our era, from Cornwall into the northwestern corner of Gaul; and the Keltic dialects of Britain were never so much in danger of being supplanted by Latin as was Albanian, which almost became a Romance language, or as the Keltic dialects of Gaul, which actually were supplanted. Educated natives in Britain, who must have understood Latin in imperial times, were therefore bilingual, and some of the western dialects of the native speech of the

III 1937, 67–68. I find the statement of E. Zachrisson, "Romans, Kelts, and Saxons in Ancient Britain," *Skrifter utgivna av Kungl. Humanistiska Vetenskaps-Samfundet i Uppsala*, XXIV 1927 (Festskrift tillägnad Uppsala Universitet) 25, far too sweeping.

[41] Writers who declare that no Keltic inscriptions have been found in Britain would do well to say what they mean by Britain (which for me includes Wales) and by Keltic (they seem to mean Brythonic). A declaration so incautiously worded is manifestly so false as not to need refutation. Granted that the inscriptions listed by Rhys in the Appendix to his *Lectures on Welsh Philology*, ed. 2, 1879, 357–407, are at most debased Latin, as well as late, and that the *ogam* inscriptions of Britain (*op. cit.*, 272–285; add the Silchester *ogam* discovered in 1893, see *Archaeologia*, second series, IV 1894, 233) are Goidelic and presumably the work of Irish immigrants, it is true only to say that Britain has no early Keltic inscriptions comparable to those of Gaul, and none at all that are Brythonic. At least the announcement made in the London *Times* 4 August 1930, p. 6, middle of column 7, of a "Brythonic" *graffito* discovered at Colchester in 1930 was, so far as I can find, premature. We are left, therefore, only with such indirect evidence as proper names in Latin inscriptions and the early history of the Welsh language and of Cornish and Breton furnish.

people, though much modified in form both during and just after the period of the Roman domination of Britain, so far from becoming extinct, still survive to this day as Welsh — but Welsh, in all its periods, has been written in the Latin alphabet.

The explanation is the same as in Gaul, that the great mass of the people could not write. Civilisation was backward, the population meagre and scattered, and illiteracy general and inevitable. The so-called Welsh "alphabet of Nemnivus," which probably never was in use, is said to have been invented in answer to a Saxon's taunt that the Britons had no letters, and it in fact is actually based on the Latin alphabet.[42] So the Saxon's taunt was well founded.

Outside of Narbonensis, then, what Keltic inscriptions we have from Gaul are written in the Latin alphabet, and inside of it in the Greek alphabet, taken over from the Massiliots before the conquest of that province by the Romans and long before their conquest of the Tres Galliae. Three texts from Narbonensis which have been claimed as Keltic and not written in the Greek alphabet, from Marseilles, Vaison, and Annecy, are of doubtful kelticity. But even in Narbonensis the Greek alphabet which had thus been freely used for the writing of the native speech eventually gave way to the Latin script, especially after the Roman conquest, just as the language gave way to Latin speech, and finally Latin writing must have been used for all except inscriptions in the Greek language. This way of putting it admits the three dubious inscriptions; if they are excluded as being Latin in language as well as in alphabet, then we may say that Narbonensis has no Keltic inscriptions in anything but the Greek alphabet, and that this alphabet survived only for writing Greek: but Latin quickly won the mastery both in writing and in language after the conquest of Narbonensis by Rome.

The druids are said [43] to have used Greek writing for purposes other than their sacred lore, but if Caesar was able to use merely Greek letters (even, as is probable enough, also in cipher), and not the Greek language, as a means of disguising his communications with Quintus Cicero,[44] then it is evident that knowledge of them had not penetrated

---

[42] See J. Morris Jones, *Welsh Grammar*, 1913, 9.

[43] Caesar, *B.G.* VI 14.3; cf. Strabo IV 1.5, C 181, on the spread of Greek among the Gauls as the language of commerce (τὰ συμβόλαια Ἑλληνιστὶ γράφειν).

[44] *B.G.* V 48.4.

so far north as the country of the Nervii, whereas we have the direct testimony of Caesar himself that the Helvetii were familiar with the Greek alphabet.[45] It may be recalled, however, that Tacitus[46] reports the use of "Greek" writing by the Germans who lived on the Raetic frontier. This statement on the part of Tacitus is most plausibly interpreted to mean that some form of "Sub-Alpine" or "North Etruscan" alphabet had crossed the Alps (later to become the source of runic[47] letters), and it is possible that Caesar, or his informants, may have made the same mistake, in this matter of writing, about the Helvetii, as the informants of Tacitus did about the Germani. That explanation cannot be applied to Caesar's account of his own practice; nor is it likely to be right as regards the practice of the druids, for we actually have preserved Keltic inscriptions of Narbonensis written in the Greek alphabet, but it is by no means excluded in the case of the Helvetii. It has been held, for example by Rice Holmes,[48] that knowledge of writing was more general in Gaul in the middle of the last century B.C. than the evidence indicates. He calls attention to the remark of Diodorus[49] that the Gauls used to throw letters, addressed to the dead, on the funeral pile. But since such letters must have had a ritual value, it may be considered certain that they were written by the druids, and it by no means follows, as Rice Holmes assumed, on the ground of Diodorus' statement, that the knowledge of writing "was not confined to the priests." The main contention, however, that the art of writing was far from being general among the Keltic-speaking tribes prior to the Roman conquest is not seriously affected by these doubts, and the druids of Gaul, by countenancing writing at all,[50] were perhaps departing from the stricter druidical tradition of Britain. One

[45] *B.G.* I 29.1.

[46] *Germ.* 3.3; Solinus XX 1, 100.3 M. asserts that Greek letters were used in a votive inscription in honor of Ulysses set up by the Caledones.

[47] See *PID* II 505 n. 1; *Foundations of Roman Italy* 188 n. 1; but the suggestion seems to have been made first by G. Hempl as long ago as 1899; see *Journal of English and Germanic Philology* II 370–374.

[48] *Caesar's Conquest of Gaul* ed. 2, 1911, 17; *The Roman Republic and the Founder of the Empire* II 1923, 6.

[49] V 28.6.

[50] We are not here concerned with druidical oral poetry, on which see C. Jullian, "De la littérature poétique des Gaulois," *RA*, 3e sér., XL 1902, 304–327; H. M. and N. K. Chadwick, *Growth of Literature*, I, Cambridge, 1932, 607–611.

of the chief contributions, then, of the process of romanization in the Tres Galliae, when at last it did come, was, as in Narbonensis, the Latin alphabet itself. It is unfortunate for us that this form of writing, once acquired, was so little used as it was for inscriptions in the Keltic dialects of Gaul.

III. GAUL BEFORE THE ROMANS [51]

The infamous Glozel fraud [52] having gone the way of all frauds, the fantastic posers that were debated for some years after the "discovery" was first announced have vanished into limbo, whence there is no need to resurrect them. We start, therefore, with the coming of the Gauls, for Gaul was not the cradle of the Keltic peoples. Hecataeus of Miletus [53] was right when he counted the Phocaean colony of Massilia "a city in the land of the Ligurians" (πόλις τῆς Λιγυστικῆς) "below" or "adjoining the land of the Kelts" (κατὰ τὴν Κελτικήν). For in the sixth and fifth centuries B.C. the Kelts had not conquered, they

[51] See, inter alia, the articles *Frankreich, Französische Urbevölkerung,* and *Kelten,* in Ebert's *Reallexikon der Vorgeschichte* (O. Reche, H. Obermaier, P. Bosch Gimpera, J. de C. Serra Ràfols, E. Rademacher); and, above all, Déchelette and Grenier's *Mnl.* To these add L. Mirot, *Manuel de Géographie historique de la France,* Paris, 1929, chap. i, ii; C. Jullian, *De la Gaule à la France,* Paris, 1922, chap. iii, iv; A. Grenier, *Les Gaulois,* Paris, 1923; J. Loth, "La première apparition des Celtes dans l'île de Bretagne et en Gaule," *RC* XXXVIII, 1920–21, 259–288 (cf. *id.*, *REA* XXIII, 1921, 327–328; C. Jullian, *REA* XXIV, 1922, 160); O. Hirschfeld, "Timagenes und die gallische Wandersage," *Kleine Schriften,* Berlin, 1913, 1–18 (*SB der Berl. Akad.*, 12 April 1894, 331–347); H. d'Arbois de Jubainville, *Les Celtes,* Paris, 1904; J. Vendryes and H. Hubert, "Notes d'archéologie et de philologie celtiques," *RC* XXXIV, 1913, 1–13, 418–447; H. Hubert, "Bulletin des études archéologiques," *RC* XLII, 1925, 244–272; XLIV, 1927, 382–439; L. Joulin, "La protohistoire de la France du sud," *C. R. Acad. Insc. et Belles-Lettres,* 1922, 88–93, and *RA*, 5e sér., XVI 1922, 1–43; *id.*, "Les Celtes d'après les découvertes archéologiques recentes dans le sud de la France," *RA*, 5e sér., VIII, 1918, 74–109; Carl Schuchhardt, *Alteuropa,* ed. 3, Berlin and Leipzig, 1935.

[52] The articles of C. Jullian in *REA* make amusing reading: XXVIII 1926, 23, 361–362; XXIX 1927, 59; 157–186; 210; 259–299; 376–392; XXX 1928, 63–67; 107–114; 205–210; 211–214; 302–306; XXXI 1929, 37–41; 151–160; 230–235; 327–333. His attempts at interpretation are even more ridiculous (e.g. XXXI 40–41). A bibliography of "l'affaire Glozel" would fill pages, see *Mont.* IV Index, s.v. Glozel.

[53] Ap. Steph. Byz., s.v. Μασσαλία (F. Jacoby, *F. Gr. Hist.* 1, 1923, 1 fr. 55).

did not in fact conquer until about 300 B.C., south-eastern Gaul. So much is proved by archaeological evidence.[54] The region of the Pyrenees, however, they had reached much earlier, sometime in the fifth century; and it was about 400 B.C. that they crossed the Alps and burst into upper Italy.

In south-western Gaul, in the regions of Béarn, Gascony and western Languedoc, regions north of the Pyrenees from which Iberian coin legends are recorded, they found Iberians in occupation of the soil, and in south-eastern Gaul Ligurians, among whom, on the coast, Greek settlers had preceded them. North-eastern Gaul was subsequently occupied by Germans or mixed Kelts and Germans. Germanic tribes who are named on the west side of the Rhine are the Condrusi, Eburones, Caerosi, Paemani, Segni, Tungri, Sunuci, Baetasii, Vangiones, Nemetes, Triboci, and there were Germanic settlers among the Treueri. Even in imperial times there was at first a high proportion of Gauls enrolled in what were reckoned German legions, though as romanization advanced the Gauls showed less and less taste for military service. The ancients in fact found Kelts and Germans alike μορφαῖς καὶ ἤθεσι καὶ βίοις,[55] and to the inexpert they both sounded equally foreign in language, just as a man who knows only English will

[54] In addition to the results of modern archaeological research we have the testimony of ancient writers, especially Strabo IV; and Caesar B.G. passim. The attack made by Klotz on the authenticity of the geographical excursus in B.G. is generally discounted since the disproof of his contentions made by R. Koller. A popular account of the Kelts may be read in Edward Eyre, *European Civilisation*, I 1934, 220–225, 237 (on Keltic origins); II 1935, 163 (on the Kelts generally).

The work of W. H. Bullock Hall *The Romans on the Riviera and on the Rhone*, London 1898, besides being eminently readable, makes some points that are worth recalling here. He rightly stresses the importance of the *Ora Maritima* of Festus Avienus (fourth century of our era), since it was based upon the *periplus* which the Carthaginian navigator Himilco had compiled eight centuries before; hence the importance of the statement of Festus that the Rhone divided the Iberi and Ligyes (cf. Strabo III 4.19, C 166), and of assertions concerning incursions of Kelts into Gaul (Hall, 9, 10). Hall interprets (86) *Gallus* as meaning "living in Gaul" (not necessarily Keltic-speaking), pointing out that Provence was thus never occupied by Gauls, for it was not part of Gallia (53); with *Libica*, the name of the western mouth of the Rhone (Pl. III 5) he compares (48) the name of the *Libui*, a Ligurian tribe who lived near Verona (Livy V 35). The Belgae themselves, he reminds us (5, n. 1), had come from across the Rhine and expelled "Galli" (Caesar, B.G. II 3).

[55] Strabo VII 1.2, C 290. Cf. A. Helbok, *Grundlagen der Volksgeschichte Deutsch-*

hear Italian and Spanish as foreign and yet somehow alike. Not only
fundamental agreements,[56] but borrowings, back and forth, made for
some superficial points of agreement between Germanic and Keltic
especially in frontier regions, and even modern criticism, which usually
can distinguish, no matter which of the two ascriptions ancient writers may give, is occasionally at a loss and unable to determine definitely
between them. A typical situation that may have given rise to such a
linguistic confusion is, for example, created by a migration such as that
of the Germanic Sugambri to the left bank of the Rhine, which took
place in 8 B.C.; [57] for confusion of the same order does actually extend
itself also to material remains. Thus a fortress at Allenbach [58] shows
defenses which, it is claimed, may be interpreted either as early
"Keltic" defenses against the Germans, or as late "Keltic" against
the Romans!

There are, therefore, at least all these five linguistic elements (Ligurian, Iberian, Greek, Germanic, Keltic) to be distinguished in pre-
Roman Gaul, the Keltic being by far the most conspicuous and most
important, and the territorial limits of the other four being in general
well known, even if their precise boundaries are not. Thus it was in
the Rhineland that the population was German or strongly germanized,
but in close contact with "Keltic" influences and "Keltic" civilization; and Keltic peoples had preceded the Germans there. After the
conquest by Caesar, however, even on the Rhine there was no further
"Keltic" expansion, but rather a fusion of Kelts and Germans, with
romanizing tendencies, and in imperial times articles of trade in that
region are definitely provincial Roman in character. The Ligurians
stretched as far north as the Isère, and the boundary between the
Iberians, or rather the Aquitani, and the Gauls is stated by Caesar
himself to have been the river Garonne. So we have the Aquitani of

---

lands und Frankreichs, Berlin, 1937, 74–237; with Atlas of maps (1938), especially
nos. 80, 117–119.

[56] Cf. p. 19 above.   Matteo Bartoli has called attention to some agreements
between Keltic and Germanic that are not merely lexical in *Neophilologus*, XXIV
1939, 140 nn. 5, 6 (where he gives references to some relevant, and some quite
irrelevant, discussion in *Festschrift für Herman Hirt*, q.v.).

[57] Fortifications belonging to this period were reported in *Germania*, XX 1936,
173–183.

[58] *Loc. cit.* 93–100. I do not defend this use of "Keltic."

Caesar's grouping between the Garonne and the Pyrenees, largely Iberian in their make-up, and therefore akin to the people of Spain; the Belgae, mixed Keltic and Germanic, to the north-east of the Seine and the Marne, in the plains of Picardy, Artois, and Champagne, along the Scheldt, lower Rhine, and in the Ardennes; and the Celtae proper occupying the lowlands of Switzerland, Alsace, Lorraine, part of the Rhenish provinces, and the great plains and uplands of central France as far as the Atlantic seaboard; while a large part of Provence, from the Alps and the Isère, at least as far west as the river Rhone, was occupied by Ligurians, who also stretched east and south into Italy, and who, whatever view be taken of their ethnic and linguistic connexions, were certainly on the soil long before the Kelts.

The current view held by competent archaeologists [59] is that the early home of the Kelts was to the east of the Rhine, perhaps stretching as far as Bohemia. The Bavarian barrow-builders have been claimed by one authority [60] as "proto-Kelts." Attention is called to the frequent occurrence of old Keltic names of mountains, rivers, and forests between the basins of the upper Danube and Rhine, and this area is accordingly claimed as the "Keltic" cradle, appeal being made for confirmation to a druidic tradition preserved in a fragment of Timagenes as recorded by Ammianus Marcellinus; [61] in contrast the ancient name of a settlement *Liguria*, in modern form Livière, near Narbonne according to Gregory of Tours,[62] is thought to chime with the assertion of Hecataeus [63] that the Ἐλίσυκοι were Ligurians.[64] At-

[59] See, for example, C. F. C. Hawkes, *Prehistoric Foundations of Europe*, 1940, 370: the home of the Kelts was in S. W. Germany, with the Swiss plateau and eastern France, extending to the east more than to the west of the Rhine, and including N. W. Germany. He, however, also appeals to linguistic evidence — namely, river-names.

[60] V. G. Childe, *Proceedings of the British Association for the Advancement of Science*, 1926, Section H, 392. Cf. G. Sergi, *Italia: le origini* (Turin, 1919) 154, 322, 409; J. Pokorny, *ZfCPh*, XX 1933–36, 518. But see my criticism, *Foundations of Roman Italy*, 1937, 107.

[61] XV 9.2–4 (F. Jacoby, *F. Gr. Hist.* 2 A, 1926, 88 fr. 2).

[62] *Miraculorum Lib. I de gloria martyrum*, 92 (Migne, *Patrol. Lat.*LXXI col. 786), cf. *REA* VII, 1905, 389 n. 1; VIII, 1906, 250–251.

[63] Ap. Steph. Byz., s.v. Ἐλίσυκοι (F. Jacoby, *F. Gr. Hist.* 1, 1923, 1 fr. 53).

[64] J. M. de Navarro, *Proceedings of the First International Congress of Prehistoric and Protohistoric Sciences*, 1932 [1934], Oxford and London, 277–278.

tempts to apply linguistic evidence to the problem of "Keltic" origins
and relationships are confusing. A. Meillet, for example, would cut
the Gordian knot of agreements not merely between Keltic, Italic,
Slavonic, and Germanic [65] but also of Keltic etc. with Greek and Hittite by ascribing them all quite simply to conservatism, and made no
attempt to approach the question where Keltic or any other of these
languages evolved. Similarly, S. Feist,[66] dealing with identical evidence, left open the question precisely where on the right bank of the
Rhine was the original home of the Kelts — possibly, he granted,
while admitting no proof, in the Danube valley. Julius Pokorny has
now worked out his theories [67] in much greater detail, since he stated
them in 1928 and 1933.[68] He thinks of a western group of Indo-
European-speaking people as splitting into Germanic and Italo-Keltic
groups. To the north of a line running from Bremen through Magde-
burg and Eberswalde to Stettin were the "Nordic" tribes; between
this line and the Alps is a territory bisected by a line Saale-Chemnitz-
Enns to the east of which the archaeologists find the Lausitz-culture
characterised by urnfields, and to the west the people who from their
type of graves are called the tumulus-builders. Now according to
Pokorny the Lausitz-people spoke Illyrian, and from the tumulus-
builders sprang both the Italici and the Kelts. After the Italici had
moved off into Italy, there were left behind "Kelto-Italici" whom he
regards as proto-Kelts, whence arose (c. 1200 B.C.) the true Kelts of
history in the course of a great expansion which upset all the peoples
of central Europe. These true Kelts were evolved from the admixture

[65] *Actes du deuxième Congrès international de Linguistes*, 1931 [1933], 203.

[66] *Op. cit.* 186.

[67] "Zur Urgeschichte der Kelten und Illyrier (mit einem Beitrage von R. Pit-
tioni)," Halle, 1939, reprinted from *ZfCPh* XX 2 (1935), 315–352; XX 3 (1936),
489–522; XXI 1 (1938), 55–204. But see the reviews, mostly unfavorable: KHM
in *Rocznik Slawistyczny*, XIII 1937, 134; M.-L. Sjœstedt-Jonval, *Bull. de la Société
de Linguistique de Paris*, XL 1939, 105–111; K. H. Jackson, *Antiquity*, XV 1941,
96–100, V. G. Childe, *ibid.*, 100–102; M. Lejeune, *REA* XLI, 1939, 93–95.
Cf. Hawkes *op. cit.* (n. 59 above), 363–364.

[68] *Actes du premier Congrès international de Linguistes*, 1928, 175–176; *A. du
troisième Congr. internat. de Linguistes*, 1933 [1935], 82–86 (cf. J. Vendryes in
Études celtiques, II 1937, 185–186); *Nature*, CXXXII 1933, 648 (cf. *Proceedings of
the British Association for the Advancement of Science*, 1933, 517–518).

of Lausitz-people, some of whom had moved westwards to conquer and settle among the tumulus-builders, pushing as far aş Belgium and central France, while others went southwards to Hungary and over the eastern Alps into Italy to become respectively the Illyrians and Veneti of history. This reconstruction of the prehistoric situation is supported by strong archaeological evidence, and from the linguistic side Pokorny attempts to bring the testimony of ancient local names into accord with it. His efforts are not completely successful, however, for they require us to see Illyrian names extended over an area so wide that for Pokorny Illyrian would seem to cover a multitude of Indo-European dialects; and they overlook completely the strong Italic flavor of Venetic. He has performed a valuable service by selecting and re-arranging some of the evidence to be had from nomenclature, and he has called attention to a number of linguistic features which appear to link Keltic and Illyrian closely together. But the interpretation of ancient names is usually a matter of questionable etymology, and their evidence often open to more than one seemingly defensible reading. As for agreements between Illyrian and Keltic, they are not notably more marked than such coincidences between any two Indo-European dialects; where they are not due to conservatism they may be as much the result of independent development as of a common origin. In particular, as Kuryłowicz pointed out in 1933 during the discussion of Pokorny's paper read to the Third Congress of Linguists, the development of r to ri and of l to li in Keltic is comparatively late, and therefore to be dissociated from the same development in Illyrian. And in general, the theory [69] which Pokorny

---

[69] Cf. Max Vasmer "Beiträge zur alten Geographie der Gebiete zwischen Elbe und Weichsel," *Zeitschrift für slavische Philologie*, V 1928–29, 360–370; *id.*, "Beiträge zur slavischen Altertumskunde: i. Nochmals die Nordillyrier," *ibid.*, VI 1929–30, 145–151; *id.*, "Beiträge etc.: vi. Neues und Nachträgliches," *ibid.*, VIII 1931, 113–119. Without returning to the explanation of Al. Schachmatov, "Zu den ältesten slavisch-keltischen Beziehungen," *Archiv für slavische Philologie*, XXXIII 1912, 51–99, which tended to see the Slavs as Kelts, we may readily admit an I. Eu. linguistic stratum as a common source of much that Keltic, Germanic, Slavic, Italic, and Illyrian hold in common, and that is doubtless the best view to take of agreements in toponymy between Keltic and west Slavonic areas; see Lubor Niederle, *Manuel de l'antiquité slave* I, 1923, 25–26 (cf. *REA*, XXVI 1924, 145). At all events Pokorny's use of historical labels to designate prehistoric cultures is completely unjustified.

has followed and elaborated deprives Illyrian of all geographical, and of almost the whole of its linguistic, meaning — everything from Poland to Spain and from the Baltic to the Mediterranean becomes grist to his Illyrian mill.

The facts, then, do not warrant a more precise statement than the one given above (p. 37) that the early home of the Kelts was to the east of the Rhine. This view has some positive support from scattered notices in ancient writers, as we have seen, and also the negative support of language, in so far as the fact that the river-names of Gaul, which in general may be supposed to be older than the names of towns, are not as a rule Keltic, whereas the latter are, may be taken to show that in the local names of Gaul there is a stratum which was laid down, so to speak, by a people or peoples who preceded the Keltic-speaking tribes there.[70] Thus, even so Keltic-seeming a mountain-name and river-name as *Ceuenna, Cebenna* (the Cévennes) is probably pre-Keltic; for it appears to show a Gaulish sound-change (lenited *m*)[71] as compared with Ligurian *Cemenelon* (Cimiez), and in fact, in Greek sources it is written Κέμμενον. Ultimately the centre of distribution of the Keltic languages must be the same as that of all the other Indo-European languages, which in no event can be placed in Gaul.

Since there is independent testimony that the Belgae arose from the fusion of the remnants of a Keltic population settled to the west of the lower Rhine with Germanic invaders, it would be an obvious assumption that their speech, so far as it remained Keltic, must have shown marked dialectal differences as compared with that of the Celtae or Gauls, precisely as Caesar avers to have been the fact. Moreover, since Iberian is admittedly not an Indo-European language at all, it is evident that, so far as Iberian still survived at that time, or its influence, Caesar or his source must have been rightly informed that the language of the Aquitani was also different from that of the Celtae. Again, those who hold that Ligurian was not Indo-European, must

---

[70] On the "pre-Keltic" and "pre-Italic" substratum see the papers of Bertoldi summarized in *REA*, XXXII 1930, 305–308; cf. *id.*, "Problèmes du substrat: Essai de méthodologie dans le domaine préhistorique de la toponymie et du vocabulaire," *Bulletin de la Société de Linguistique de Paris*, XXXII, 1931, 93–184.

[71] Pedersen, *VKG*, 165; the ancient sources for the forms quoted are given in *AcS*, s.v.

take the same view of the language of the greater part of Narbonensis, if not in Caesar's day, then a century earlier or more; and those who regard Ligurian as having been Indo-European still are agreed in distinguishing it from Keltic. Whether or not the non-Latin and non-Greek inscriptions of Narbonensis, however, are Ligurian is another question; even if they are counted Keltic, it still remains to ask how far, if at all, they differ from the other Keltic inscriptions of Gaul. If they are Ligurian, then, first, Ligurian certainly was Indo-European but not Illyrian; and, second, a question of the relation between Ligurian and Lepontic in Cisalpine Gaul is raised, since Lepontic is not Keltic but Ligurian or rather Kelto-Ligurian.

The diffusion of the Keltic languages is plausibly associated with a series of migrations that took place in the first half of the last millennium B.C. from a region that corresponds roughly with what is now north-western Germany. The causes of these migrations are supposed to have been the pressure of alien peoples, the stress of climate that produced it, and perhaps the growth of population and love of plunder. However that may be, there were movements into Britain; and also, more important for us, a large-scale migration, thought to have taken place in the latter part of the sixth century, in a south-westerly direction across France towards the Pyrenees. Some detachments of the people who thus migrated even reached Spain, but the great mass of them seem to have settled in new homes in central and western Gaul.[72]

---

[72] Cf. A. Grenier, *La Gaule romaine* (pp. 379–644 of T. Frank, *An Economic Survey of Ancient Rome* III 1937), 396–417; Eoin MacNeill, *Phases of Irish History*, 1919, 11–30; Hans Philipp, *Vor- und Frühgeschichte des Mittelmeerraumes*, 1937, 94–98 and 248–255; Auguste Vincent, *Toponymie de la France*, 1939, §§ 173–202; P. Bosch Gimpera, "Two Celtic Waves in Spain," *Proceedings of the British Academy*, XXVI 1940, 25–148 (really an archaeologist's survey of the "Keltic" problem, according to modern theory).

A summary statement may be useful:

c. 1000 B.C.: Formation and expansion of the Kelts.

Between c. 950 and 500: Hallstatt; Kelts move as far as central France.

c. 450: A second expansion (La Tène).

c. 450–300: Kelts dominant in Gaul.

c. 300: Kelts from the right bank of the Rhine move west (Belgica) and also much later into Britain from Belgica; last of all the Treueri, followed by the Germanic tribes (Nemetes, Vangiones etc.) across the Rhine.

113–102 B.C.: Cimbri and Teutones.

In Gaul the beginning of the Iron Age, that revolution in civilization which is supposed to have had its centre at Hallstatt, is placed about 800 B.C. The expansion of the Kelts falls within the following two centuries, marked by the movement of warlike migratory bands, builders of tumuli, from southern Bavaria along the Rhine and Moselle, and thence via river-valleys into the heart of Gaul. The form of burial of the chieftain with his warriors around him, all of them equipped with weapons and accoutrements, is held to prove a feudal organization; just as in the fifth century B.C. in Champagne tombs containing chariots and harness mark another stage in the development of this conquering aristocracy who settled on the soil of France, subjecting and uniting with the previous population, imposing its language, its ethnic names, and its social organisation upon them. It has been conjectured, not very convincingly however, that the ancient territorial divisions corresponding to more than sixty peoples, which we find in Gaul in Roman times, may go back even to the pre-Keltic period. But the names of the huge terrains into which Gaul came to be divided are usually derivatives of personal names, and mainly Keltic. By the fifth century the country had become rich and overpopulated, and the Bituriges, with their centralised political organisation aimed under their chieftain Ambigatus to secure a hegemony over the other Gauls.[73] This was about 400 B.C. The policies of Ambigatus, as described by Livy, are perhaps to be associated with the diffusion of the La Tène civilisation, which followed closely the direction of the Rhine and the Danube. But *Celtica* properly so called was the territory between the rivers Seine and Garonne, and by the fourth century its frontiers and tribal boundaries, under the regime of an aristocratic oligarchy that was replacing the older system of royalty, were probably established very much as we find them in Roman times. Not later than the beginning of the third century a new Keltic expansion occurred in several parts of Europe, bringing the La Tène period I to its close. This was the period of the Belgic invasions, and by the end of the century the Belgae had occupied the territory north of the Seine and Marne, where Caesar found them. From what is conjectured of their historical evolution it would be natural for them to have a dialect different from the Celtae, much as the details of the differences may escape us. During

[73] Livy, V 34.1.

this La Tène period II hegemony over the Celtae passed into the hands of the Arverni, the last two leaders of whom were Luerius (or Luernius), a contemporary of Aemilius Paulus, and his son and successor Bituitus, whom the Romans captured in 121 B.C.

La Tène I and II were periods of considerable luxury and magnificence. The following period, La Tène III, is much poorer and marked a regression, at least on the continent. It was, in fact, opened by a catastrophe, such as more recent events can parallel, the invasion of Gaul by the Cimbri and Teutones. The hegemony of the Arverni was broken by the Romans, and among the Gauls themselves were division and dissension. It was, nevertheless, old memories of the Arverni that, about a century later, inspired the exploits of Vercingetorix.[74] Romans and Gauls alike in Provence were overwhelmed by the Cimbri and Teutones, and Gaul had scarcely had time to repair its ruins after their onslaught before Caesar appeared on the scene in 58 B.C. But the rivalries of the Aedui and Sequani, together with the threat to Gaul from the Suebi and others led by Ariovistus, the overflowing of the Kelts of the Danube valley and from the right bank of the Rhine, particularly in the southern part of its upper course, between the Alps and the Jura mountains — the country of the Helvetii —, compelled rather than invited the intervention of Caesar in the affairs of Gaul proper that, in the end, led to the subjugation of the entire land to the Romans. The final period, therefore, La Tène III, preceding the Gallo-Roman period, was by comparison with those that had gone before, one of poverty and collapse.

That a people entered Gaul, coming from the lower Rhine, is held to be proved by the similarities which have been observed, for example, in the structure of their graves and in much of the pottery which they made. The migration into north-eastern France (the Belgae) took place, as we have seen, somewhat later, in the course, perhaps, of the fourth century B.C.,[75] and, as is well known, there were other movements further south, into Italy, and also to the south-east, into the Danubian regions, the Balkan peninsula, and even Asia Minor. The Germanic tribes, whose expansion is thought to have been one of the

---

[74] *B.G.* VII 4.1.

[75] Opinion on the date varies; some archaeologists say c. 500, others not later than the beginning of the third century B.C.

causes of these migrations, bordered the Keltic peoples on the east, and there must have been some intermixture of the two groups, notably along the valley of the Rhine, where, as we have seen, the Belgae of history may be supposed to have been descended from the older Keltic and later Germanic invaders. Finally, Belgae themselves moved to Britain in large numbers between about 100 and 60 B.C. Meanwhile, not only did the Kelts advance towards developing something like an urban life of their own, and so prepare the way themselves for a more rapid romanization, but, in the course of the second century B.C., Roman interests had actually begun to be established in southern Gaul, at least in Narbonensis, on what was destined to be an enduring basis.

Evidently, then, the native material civilization of the Gauls was entering upon its final stages of the La Tène culture in the second century B.C., and had reached its end by the end of the last century B.C. What with the Roman conquest and annexation of Provence, and the advance of Germanic tribes from beyond the Rhine, the Gauls were already being placed on the defensive by the middle of this period.

It is probably the mere lack of evidence that gives us the impression that pre-Roman and Keltic Gaul endured the period of romanization in religion and in political organization far more successfully than in language, at least superficially. Though the worship of Roman deities was introduced, under Latin names, still the native names survived in many localities, either alone, or, by the easy process of syncretism, identified with the Latin names. Or where we have actually only Latin names, the underlying concept was usually native, even where it is a concept that is found also in Roman or Greek religion — in fact the "interpretatio Graeca" often preceded the "interpretatio Romana" so far as Keltic religion and its native survivals are affected. Thus we have, for example, Teutates, Esus, and Taranis (identified respectively with Mercury, Mars, and Jupiter), Maponus, Grannus, and Belenus (all three identified with Apollo), Taruos Trigaranus "the bull with the three cranes," Boruo or Bormo[76] (the god of warm springs), Mercurius Dumias (a local god, at Puy de Dôme), Magusanus and Deusoniensis (Hercules), Ogmius (the god alleged to have presided over eloquence and the power of speech), Cernunnus (thought

---

[76] The relation between these two forms seems to be the same as that between *Ceuenna* and *Cemenelon*, cf. p. 40, n. 71 above.

to have been a chthonic deity), Epona (the goddess of horses and horsemen, whose name was left undisturbed), Iouantucarus (Mercury), Cobledulitanus (Apollo), Sucellus, Segomo (Mars), Camulus (Mars), Clauariates (Mercury),[77] the deae Matres (Matrae, Matronae — spirits of the springs, rivers, forests, or mountains, guardians of the land and its inhabitants) who are often further found designated and localized by the addition of a local epithet. Again we find Mercury associated with Rosmerta (*f.*), and Apollo with Sirona (*f.*). To the druids, a sacerdotal caste, passing reference will suffice. As for the Jupiter-columns, as they are called, these are partly non-Keltic as well as non-Roman. But the Campestres, Suleuiae or Triuiae, or Fatae (to give them their Roman name), a trinity of goddesses, were as native as the "genius cucullatus." Of the Roman gods, Hercules perhaps enjoyed the greatest popularity.

Although, therefore, as a matter of policy, the cult of the emperor was introduced quite early (Drusus established an altar to "Rome and Augustus" in 12 B.C. at Lyons,[78] where the cult was administered by the *concilium Galliarum*) and druidism repeatedly suppressed (first by Tiberius in A.D. 16),[79] still, so long as paganism lasted, the spirit of druidism in Gaul evidently remained Keltic at least as much as it became Roman or Italian. In that sense, therefore, the advent of Christianity, as it brought about the gradual disappearance of paganism, marched with the advance of the Latin language; for example, ancient secret charms and remedies which the old faith had prescribed appear couched in what passed for the old language, even if sadly corrupt in form. But there can be no doubt that the diffusion of Latin was completed by Christian preaching; at the end of the empire, it was the only language of Gaul. And the situation is in some ways analogous to what we find in nomenclature. "The reproduction of the Gallic proper names in Latin, not seldom with the retention of non-Latin forms in sound," was natural enough, for Latin names were not

[77] For some of these see, e.g., Dessau, *Insc. Lat. Sel.*, 4538, 4500, 4599, 4601, 4638; but full references to *CIL* will be given in the appropriate places in the main body of the work.

[78] Dio Cassius, LIV 32.1; cf. Dessau 112 (Narbo, *numini Augusti*), *CIL* XIII ii 2, p. 505 (ara Vbiorum, at Cologne, 9 B.C.–A.D. 4).

[79] Cf. *Cambridge Ancient History*, X 645, n. 1.

adopted wholesale, especially for names of places, any more than English or other European names have totally displaced Indian names in North America; nor were the Roman or Italian personal names which veterans, settlers, and merchants brought with them universally acceptable to Gauls. But we are not entitled to conclude on this ground, as Mommsen did, that "the vigorous survival of the national language is most distinctly shown" [80] by the survival of Keltic proper names, or that Keltic religion "vanished even more rapidly" than the language.[81]

As with religion, language, and nomenclature, so it was in matters of political organization. Yet there is a difference. The framework of the native cantonal organization was respected by the Roman imperial administration, but for all official purposes Latin was required almost from the beginning. Gallic coins under Roman rule follow Latin types, and we have virtually no public document in any Keltic dialect of Gaul. The one notable exception, the famous calendar of Coligny, is more apparent than real; for it is at least as much a religious as a political document, and it was deliberately smashed into fragments in ancient times. The large three-fold subdivision of the three Gauls, then, the Belgae, Celtae, and Aquitani, rested on a corresponding grouping of tribes (*ciuitates*); and each tribe was made up of an aggregate of communities, called *pagi* in Latin, whose relationship to one another might be based on nothing more than that of neighborhood, though usually it implied blood-kinship, real or assumed. A very small tribe might, indeed, consist of a single *pagus*, with its own presiding magistrate, and even among the united *pagi*, each community, before the coming of the Romans, had retained some degree of independence. The larger unions were characteristic especially of central Gaul, but among the Aquitani the smaller units persisted. Again, smaller unions sometimes appear as bound by *clientela* to a larger or central *ciuitas*. Thus the Segusiani, Ambiuareti, Aulerci Brannouices ("raven-warriors"), and Brannouii are named by Caesar[82]

---

[80] *Provinces of the Roman Empire*, I 100.

[81] *Op. cit.* 106. Contrast Mommsen's own statements elsewhere about the suppression of Keltic (82, 99, 100), or the survival of non-Roman worship (103), where he seems to contradict himself.

[82] *B.G.* VII 75. For names of the type of *Brannouices* cf. *Eburones* "people of the yew." But *Brannouii* is probably mere dittography.

as client-unions of the Aedui, smaller, that is, than appear among the cantons as re-organized by Augustus.[83] The native title of the chief magistrate, at least among the Aedui, has been preserved to us, namely *uergobretus*,[84] and neither title nor office appears to have become extinct in early imperial times. We have some hints, too, of social organization in the native words for "servant" and "serf," viz. **uassalus* and *ambactus*; large numbers of these, and clients also, were bound to each member of the nobility, whom Caesar designated as *equites*. And the much later survival of native road-measurements is implied in the official recognition by Severus, early in the third century after Christ, of the Keltic unit of length, the league (French *lieue*), *leuga*, which was about one and a half Roman miles.

From the historical evidence, then, taken alone, it would appear that the Belgic Kelts were the latest comers into pre-Roman Gaul, and, if Caesar was rightly informed, that the languages of the Belgae and of the Celtae were, or had been, distinct. Both, however, were presumably Keltic, and therefore the differences may not have been very great. Again, the conquering Kelts, as the evidence of nomenclature shows, had advanced, probably in not very large numbers, beyond the Garonne: it is not astonishing that *Gallus* acquired the meanings of "stranger" and "enemy." But without careful analysis the evidence of nomenclature may easily be deceptive. Recent studies of personal names among the Treueri, for example, reveal a smaller proportion of Keltic and Germanic names than might have been expected from a cursory survey of the evidence. And even when accurately determined, percentages of relative frequency of occurrence of names of given origin are not to be taken merely at their face value. Nevertheless, it seems improbable that the Keltic language ever was generally spoken in Aquitania, but Iberian instead; and altogether probable that, both among the Belgae and among the Celtae, the conquerors had imposed their own language upon the conquered peoples. Further, if, in Caesar's day, some knowledge of Latin had penetrated even to the Belgae, as Caesar's own precautions against knowledge of his plans reaching the enemy, in case his communications to his legates should fall into their hands, imply,[85] yet it is also true that at the be-

---

[83] Mommsen, *op. cit.*, I 95, n. 2.

[84] *B.G.*, I 16.5; see *AcS* III 213–214 for some variant forms or spellings.

[85] *B.G.*, V 48.4, cf. p. 32 above.

ginning of his campaigns he had to converse through an interpreter with Diviciacus, who either could not or would not talk Latin (or Greek).[86] For in Provence the language of Rome had begun to take root even before Caesar's arrival.

Most attempts to give substance to Caesar's assertion about differences in language between the Belgae, the Aquitani, and the Celtae, apart from the obvious explanation that covers the Iberian Aquitani and the partly Germanic Belgae, can hardly be regarded as more than mere conjecture. This conclusion is true notably of well-nigh everything that Sir John Rhys wrote on the subject.[87] But Caesar, as we have seen, was not alone in what he said, for Strabo had made the remark that the inhabitants of Gaul, though the appearance and material civilization of all were identical or similar, did not all speak the same language. Unfortunately Strabo, like Caesar, gives us no detailed information, and his remark, which stems from the same source as Caesar's, may refer to nothing more than the obvious distinctions between Provence and Aquitania and the rest of Gaul.[88] In that case, nothing more recondite is meant than Keltic as contrasted with Iberian and Ligurian and Germanic — or various degrees of intermixture of some of these (as Iberian and Keltic, Germanic and Keltic, or Ligurian and Keltic or Iberian and Ligurian), at least in frontier-districts.

Linguists have usually ignored the problem, not altogether without reason. Those of them who have discussed it at all have, without exception, committed themselves to some particular theory, however wild, and have supported that theory through thick and thin, on the slenderest evidence, or no evidence at all. One of the least prejudiced accounts that I have read, and one in which the author tried to give a survey of conflicting opinions, without trying to reconcile contradictions, was not written by a linguist at all, but by a schoolmaster-

---

[86] *B.G.*, I 19.3.

[87] Compare also the note by Rice Holmes in his edition of Caesar's *de Bello Gallico* I, 1914, 37, where, after pointing out that "Most of the Celtae spoke Gaulish or Gallo-Brythonic," and that the language of the Belgae presumably must have been, in the main, the same tongue, he continues "Perhaps . . . some spoke a different Celtic dialect; . . . for at a later period inscriptions were erected in Gaul in a language which was different from Gaulish," and then adds that this other language may already have been a dead language!

[88] So *Do.* 26–27.

historian. In 1911 the late T. E. Rice Holmes, in the second edition of his *Caesar's Conquest of Gaul*, gave a résumé [89] of the theories then current on the subject of the dialects of Gaul which showed all his usual shrewdness and common sense. After calling attention to the possibility that traces of *q*-Keltic may lurk hidden in the magico-medical formularies of Marcellus of Bordeaux (which some scholars "do not take seriously") or in local names like *Sequana, Sequani* (which some hold are "not Keltic" — and to which he might have added the divine name *Sinquatis*), Rice Holmes, following Rhys and Nicholson in their studies of the calendar of Coligny, accepted them as tending to show that Goidelic as well as Brythonic Keltic was at some time spoken in Gaul. The view of d'Arbois de Jubainville that the Coligny calendar is written in Ligurian he dismisses. And he concludes that the Belgae and Celtae spoke one and the "same [Keltic] language or dialects of it." This language, moreover, was not a language that could have been spoken in Gaul before the arrival, in the first half of the last millennium B.C., of the invading peoples from the east of the Rhine, but was one which they had brought with them; for, where even some of the local names, as well as most of the personal names are Keltic, including those of the nobility, "is it credible that the chiefs of the conquering race should have been called by names that were not their own but those of their subjects?"

But for the student of language the best and, I think, the most recent, account of the problem and of the present state of knowledge is unquestionably that by L. Weisgerber, *Die Sprache der Festlandkelten*, published in 1931.[90] Weisgerber rightly maintains that many of the variations which we find in our written records must reflect actual differences within the dialects of continental Keltic: "dass das weite Keltengebiet eine völlig einheitliche Sprache aufgewiesen habe, ist trotz der auffälligen — nur der Gleichförmigkeit auch in der materiellen Hinterlassenschaft der Latènezeit vergleichbaren — Gleichheit der Ortsnamen nicht anzunehmen." But he will have none of Nicholson's conjectures concerning the preservation of initial *p* in "Sequanian," "Continental Pictish," and in the Keltic of north Italy, nor of Feist's theories about "Kelto-Germans" (which boil down "in gewöhnlichen

[89] 318–321, 329.
[90] Cf. p. 7 above; see especially *SprFK* 183–188.

Wörten" to the simple statement "sie sind sprachlich zweifellos Germanen"). And he is highly sceptical, and rightly, of any assumption of dialectal differences which rests upon, or is made to bolster up, some isolated etymology. As for the statement in Caesar, echoed in Strabo, "gerade hier ist es nicht möglich, auf Grund unserer Kenntnis des Gallischen einen Dialektgegensatz festzustellen." But, in this connexion, it must be pointed out that Weisgerber's own discussion of the problems raised by certain forms presented in the calendar of Coligny (*equos, prin(n)i, petiux*), and of numerous other alleged instances of dialectal variations (e.g. *-cenna*: *pennos,* ειωρου: *ieuru*), is quite inconclusive, although, by its very admission of such variations, it is also inconsistent with his own opinion as just quoted.

Weisgerber stresses "Substratforschung." This emphasis upon substratum is important enough, if it is limited to the time when the new language (namely Latin) was being learnt, but not if it is extended to show Gallic influence in later Romance developments. The atavistic interpretation of the substratum-theory is pure fancy; [91] and it is most actively plied where the substratum is well-nigh unknown. Then too Weisgerber stresses the modern method of dialect-geography, which also has its dangers if interpreted, as it were, once (and even more than once) removed: "namentlich die Romanistik arbeitet in weitem Umfang mit der Annahme mundartlicher Entwicklungen im Gallischen." The danger here is the obvious one that what is merely hypothesis for Romance linguistics is apt to be taken as fact for Keltic. However, it is possible to show that some fairly trustworthy conclusions have been reached: "danach ist man berechtigt, eine gallische dialektische Entwicklung anzunehmen, wenn bei unzweifelhaft gallischen Namen oder Wörtern in den romanischen Deszendenten Lautwandel eingetreten ist, der den romanischen Mundarten in der Verbreitungszone des gallischen Wortes fremd ist." Thus the change of *st* to *þ*, or of *nn* to *nd*, or a variation in writing (and pronunciation) such as *rc*: *rg* (*arcanto-*: *arganto-, uerco-*: *uergo-*) can be shown to be essentially dialectal. Another example of some interest is the change of *u̯*- to *f*- (regular in Goidelic, cf. Eng. *flannel* but W. *gwlan*), which

[91] Cf. *Cinquième Congrès International de Linguistes: Réponses au Questionnaire,* Bruges, 1939, 48.

is attested by French *flanelle*,[92] or Fr. *faner* (cf. Gael. *fann*), Fr. *félon* (Gael. *feall*), so that apparently the Irish change ("seit dem 6. Jahrhundert bezeugt") "mundartlich auch im Gallischen gelebt hat," though there is no clear, undisputed case of initial *f-* to be found in extant Gaulish records. But, as Weisgerber himself points out, much still remains to be done in the work of collecting relevant evidence, especially from the development of local names, before definite boundaries can be drawn; and his final remarks are worth quoting:

> Von Seiten der Keltologie selbst wäre besonders eine Vorarbeitung der altkeltischen Sprachreste nach einzelnen Landschaften bzw. Stammesgebieten nötig, um überhaupt Anhaltspunkte für die Feststellung der Besonderheiten einzelner Gebiete zu liefern. Aber selbst die Zusammenstellungen der inschriftlichen Funde aus bestimmten Bezirken . . . widmen diesen Fragen wenig Beachtung . . . ; so kommen Versuche in dieser Richtung . . . noch nicht über erste Ansätze hinaus.

The cantonal organization of the Gauls would naturally lead to the development of dialectal variations among them. Much has been made by all writers on this subject of the form *equos* in the Coligny calendar. But we should remember that Umbrian has *ekvine* (cf. Sabine *tescua*), despite its treatment of I. Eu. $q\underset{.}{u}$ as *p*. The best solution of this problem would seem to be that $q\underset{.}{u}$ and $\hat{k}\underset{.}{u}$ were distinguished; [93] possibly the same solution is to be applied also to the local names that derive from **Aequoranda*.[94] But if *Sequana* does contain not $\hat{k}\underset{.}{u}$ but $q\underset{.}{u}$, then there is clearly a difference of sound-change in Gaulish *petru-* "four," though the Germanic *f-* (Goth. *fidwor*) is worth consideration in this connexion. Again, the pronunciation *i*, as contrasted with Latin *e*, attested by Consentius,[95] would appear to be Keltic and perhaps dialectal. Dottin [96] calls attention to **bruca*, implied by Fr. *bruyère*, as contrasted with *matres Vroicae* (**u̯roica* cf. Ir.

---

[92] Some hold that the French is borrowed from the English word; but if so, whence came English *flannel*?

[93] Cf. *SprFK* 184–185.

[94] *AcS* I 1485.26–1486.17. I conjecture that this is related to Umb. *eikvasese, eikvasatis.*

[95] *Gram. Lat.* V 394. 11 K.

[96] 360 (addendum to 306). Cf. *SprFK* 185, where doubt is expressed, and the observation made that **brucus* lies behind *bruyère*.

froech), and suggested that **bruca*: **uroica* (*br*: u̯r, *u*: *oi*) point to different Gaulish developments in different dialects. Attempts have been made to distinguish, within Gaul, between two different developments of m̥, n̥ (*em*, *en* and *am*, *an*) that would correspond to the Goidelic and Brythonic treatment respectively of those sounds,[97] but the "evidence" is itself hypothetical. Dottin [98] has collected a large number of variants most of which appear to be graphic; and of those which are phonetic very few (e.g. *cantlos* beside *cantalon*) are comparisons of different forms within Gaul; the vast majority are pairs of words, one from Gaul, the other outside of Gaul. Mention was made above of the recent revival of an old scepticism concerning the inscriptions of Narbonensis. Many years ago d'Arbois de Jubainville expressed the opinion, afterwards accepted by Bréal, that the inscriptions containing the words δεδε and βρατουδε are Italic rather than Keltic; they have been regarded as Ligurian or (by Rhys) as "Celtican." But as Dottin remarked,[99] "on peut, au moins provisoirement, ne pas séparer ces inscriptions des autres inscriptions gauloises." In that case, however, they would seem to belong to a different dialect from the others. From this summary account alone it is evident that no real advance whatever has yet been made towards an interpretation of ancient doctrine concerning the dialects of Gaul.

IV. THE ROMANIZATION OF GAUL [100]

Narbonensis, particularly the hinterland of Marseilles, was hellenized first, and then romanized. To speak of a *Gallia Graeca* there is no mere title or phrase. The romanization of Gaul is essentially the fusing of a Graeco-Roman culture with a native Gallic civilization, the Greek

[97] *SprFK* 185–186.
[98] 54–56, 101.   [99] 36–37.
[100] Ernest Desjardins, *Géographie historique et administrative de la Gaule romaine*, 4 vols., 1876–1893; *id.*, *Géographie de la Gaule d'après la Table de Peutinger*, Paris, 1869; Fustel de Coulanges, *Histoire des Institutions politiques de l'ancienne France*, I, La Gaule romaine, revue par . . . C. Jullian, 1908; H. d'Arbois de Jubainville, *Recherches sur l'origine de la Propriété foncière et des noms de lieux habités en France* (période celtique et période romaine), avec la collaboration de G. Dottin, 1890; C. Pallu de Lessert, "L'Oeuvre géographique d'Agrippa et d'Auguste," *Mémoires de la Société nationale des antiquaires de France*, 7e sér., VIII 1909, 215–298; Héron de

element becoming the less pronounced and the less independent the further one moves from the Mediterranean coast. Roman penetration, as usual, begins as a military intervention; again, as often, it ended with the imposition of the Latin language upon the inhabitants of Gaul, and that is the feature in which we are here most interested.

In the course of the second century B.C. Roman armies had appeared in southern Gaul more than once. Assistance was given by Rome to the Greeks of Massilia against Gauls and Ligurians combined in 154 B.C.,[101] but Gallic pressure upon the Greek city was renewed

Villefosse, "Les Agents de recensement dans les trois Gaules," *ibid.*, 8e sér., III 1914, 249–300; A. Blanchet, *Les enceintes romaines de la Gaule*, 1907 (cf. *RC* XXVIII, 1907, 87); Julius Beloch, "Die Bevölkerung Galliens zur Zeit Caesars," *Rh. Mus.*, LIV 1899, 414–445 (but see the criticisms of A. Grenier ap. Frank, *Economic Survey*, III 452–454); Hermann Dessau, *Geschichte der römischen Kaiserzeit*, II 2, 1930, 480–534; Otto Hirschfeld, *Kleine Schriften*, 1913, ii–xi, 19–238; *Notitia Galliarum* (Monumenta Germaniae historica, auctorum antiquissimorum Tomus IX, ed. Th. Mommsen, 1892), with the observations of Duchesne in *Bulletin de la Soc. nat. des antiquaires de France*, 1892, 247–252 (administrative not ecclesiastical basis); J. Markowski, "De Galliis, Hispaniis, Germania in indice rerum gestarum diui Augusti laudatis," *Eos*, XXXIV 1932–33, 427–459; R. Syme, "The Origin of Cornelius Gallus," *CQ*, XXXII 1938, 39–44; Martroye, in *BSAF*, 1926, 285–288 (cf. Collinet, *ibid.* 278), discussing *B.G.*, VI 19.1–2, explains *pecuniae* as "wealth," not "coined money;" Meriwether Stuart, "The Date of the Inscription of Claudius on the Arch of Ticinum [*CIL*, V 6416 [10]]," *AJA*, XL 1936, 314–322; A. Grenier, "La Gaule indépendente et la Gaule romaine," *Revue des Cours et Conférences*, XXXVIII i, 1936–1937, 98–108; L.-A. Constans, *Guide illustré des campagnes de César en Gaule*, 1929; N. J. DeWitt, *Urbanization and the Franchise in Roman Gaul*, 1940; P. Jacobsthal and E. Neuffer, "Gallia Graeca: Recherches sur l'hellénisation de la Provence," *Préhistoire*, II 1933, 1–64; A. Grenier, *Mnl.* (cf. the review by I. A. Richmond, *Antiquity*, X 1936, 498–501); *id.*, *La Gaule romaine* (see n. 72 above); L. C. West, *Roman Gaul: Objects of Trade*, 1935 (in general, unfavorably reviewed); C. Benedict, *History of Narbo*, 1941 (cf. *CW*, XXXV 1942, 163); Philippe Héléna, *Les origines de Narbonne*, 1937 (cf. the review in *RA* 6e sér., XIII 1937, 181); H. Leclerc, "*Pagi* de la Gaule," in *Dict. d'archéologie chrétienne*, XIII i, 1937, 380–436 (ecclesiastical divisions correspond to the old *pagi*?); Charlotte E. Goodfellow, *Roman Citizenship*, 1935; A. N. Sherwin-White, *The Roman Citizenship*, 1939; on the economic reconstruction of Gaul, see A. Grenier, *Revue des Cours et Conférences*, XXXVIII, 1936–1937, 209–218, 430–441; *Revue des études latines*, XIV 1936, 373–388; on the *concilium* see E. G. Hardy, *Studies in Roman History: First Series*, ed. 2, 1910, 235; D. Vaglieri in *Diz. Epigr.* s.v.; J. S. Reid, *Municipalities of the Roman Empire*, 1913; see also the relevant chapters in *CAH*, which I have found helpful.

[101] Polybius XXXIII 8–10; Livy, *per.* xlvii.

within thirty years, and culminated (125–118 B.C.) in the establishment of the *prouincia Narbonensis*, and, in the long run, in the permanent occupation of Gaul by Rome. This began with Roman intervention (125–123 B.C.) against the Salluuii,[102] and a temporary fortification (*castellum*) at Aquae Sextiae, established in order to keep open communication between Italy and Spain,[103] was converted into a fixed or permanent camp (*castra statiua*); it was but a day's march north of Massilia, to which it afforded good protection. In 121 B.C., therefore, steps were taken to reduce the warring tribes and to pacify the territory of Massilia;[104] the Allobroges were defeated on the Rhone between Orange and Avignon, and a road (the via Domitia) constructed from Tarascon to the Col du Perthus. These operations, together with the defeat of the Aruerni not far from Valence, sealed the fate of southern Gaul. The Narbonese province was established, then, at the end of the second century B.C., and secured by the foundation of the military colony of Narbo Martius (118 B.C.),[105] but the greater part of the coastal strip of territory from Montpellier to Nice still belonged to Massilia, though the Ligurian and Keltic cantons of the interior were no more subject to the Greek city than before.

Gaul was thrown into confusion afresh by the wandering hordes of Cimbri and Teutones (with some accompanying Kelts) in 111 and 110 B.C.; and the defeat inflicted by them upon the Romans in 109 B.C. left both Provincia and Italy open to attack for some years after 105 B.C. Meanwhile the Cimbri moved into Spain and the Teutones roved through Gaul. It was only their defeats at Aquae Sextiae (102 B.C.) and Campi Raudii (Vercellae) a year later that removed the peril from the gates of Italy. A year before, in the course of his campaigns against these invaders, Marius had caused a canal to be cut at the mouth of the Rhone,[106] the *fossa Mariana*, that ensured the development of Arles. About the same time (103 B.C.) the Cimbri and Teutones were contending with the Belgae, and six thousand of their

[102] Livy, *per.* lx.

[103] Livy, *per.* lxi; cf. *Act. Triumph.* 123, 122.

[104] *Act. Triumph.* 120.

[105] Cicero, *Brut.* 43; Vell. Paterc. I 15; cf. II 7.8; Eutrop. IV 23.

[106] R. D. Oldham, "The Age and Origin of the Lower Rhone," has an interesting account of the Rhone delta, with identifications of some ancient sites, in *Quarterly Journal of the Geological Society of London*, XC 1934, 445–461.

number are said to have been left behind in the Meuse valley, where later they were known as the Atuatuci. Thus the prestige of Rome in Gaul was temporarily restored, but plans for colonies to be planted there, apart from some allotments in 100 B.C., came to nothing.

First, then, their interest in the overland route to Spain through southern Gaul,[107] and then the necessity for holding the northern invaders back, brought about active military intervention of the Romans. But once these needs had been filled, latinization and exploitation of Provence began and continued apace and uninterruptedly, until, as Cicero remarked in 69 B.C.,[108] no business transaction in Narbonensis could be completed without the intervention of a Roman citizen as middleman. These *negotiatores* played an important part in the romanization; Narbonensis, already in part hellenized, now received an Italian stamp and long retained it; it was more completely romanized than any other part of Gaul, and to this day its Roman ruins bear witness to the truth of Pliny's assertion that Narbonensis was one with north Italy.[109]

Before Caesar's wars in Gaul (58–51 B.C.) the Roman domain extended as far as Toulouse, Vienne, and Geneva; after them, it had expanded to the Atlantic Ocean on the west and north, and along the whole course of the Rhine easterly. Many tribes had indeed been bound to Rome by treaty (*foedus*),[110] but the conquest of Gallia Comata, whence later were formed three imperial provinces of Aquitania, Lugdunensis, and Belgica, destined to be united by the imperial cult also, was Caesar's achievement. Although, therefore, Roman authority had been restored in Transalpine Gaul after the battles of Aquae Sextiae and Campi Raudii, outside its borders the Keltic tribes continued to struggle among themselves for the supremacy, and even Transalpina revolted in 77 B.C., only to be defeated by Pompey on his march to Spain. But the ruthless exactions of the Romans that followed the defeat provoked a desperate situation, and in 63 B.C. the

[107] Cic., *pro Font.*, V 13: *specula populi Romani.*

[108] *Op. cit.*, V 11.

[109] *NH*, III 31: *Narbonensis Italia uerius quam prouincia.*

[110] Cicero, *pro Balbo* 32; Tac. *Hist.*, IV 67; Amm. Marc., XV 12.5; Pliny, *NH*, IV 106–107.

Allobroges appealed for relief directly to Rome. Receiving no satis-
faction, in 61 they revolted and again were "pacified" after a fashion.
These troubles, and what was perhaps more dangerous for undisturbed Roman control in southern Gaul, namely the contest for
hegemony that kept central Gaul in a turmoil, and the intrigues that
went on constantly among the Gauls themselves both inside and outside of Narbonensis, brought about a series of events that led first to
the intervention of Caesar, as governor of Provincia (58 B.C.), where
he had tried to meet the needs of the Gauls as far as possible, and then
to a military occupation by him that ended, in 51 B.C., in the final
subjugation of the whole of Gaul. Thanks to Caesar's conciliatory
policy, there was little trouble for many years thereafter, so that the
pax Romana started to extend Roman civilization and the Latin
language throughout the length and breadth of the vast provinces that
Caesar had added to the Roman empire with a frontier on the Rhine.

The generous allotments made to Caesar's veterans, as, for example,
of the sixth legion at *Arelate* (Arles) and of the tenth at *Narbo Martius*
(Narbonne), both in the old province of Transalpine Gaul, that part
of the ancient Mediterranean world outside Italy which was already
most Italian in character and most italianized in tradition, hastened
the process of romanization. But although the enfranchisement of the
Transpadana in 49 B.C. had prepared the way for further enfranchisement in romanized regions, the assassination of Caesar himself in 44 B.C.
prevented the fulfilment of whatever plans he may have had for en-
franchising romanized urban communities beyond the Alps, and
Caesar was so far in advance of his contemporaries in his liberal attitude toward provincials that, despite the advance of Roman civilization and of the Latin language in and beyond the Alpine regions, anything more than the gift of citizenship to certain individuals was long
delayed.

Narbonensis remained separate from Gallia Comata, however.
Caesar had tied it administratively with Spain,[111] while the rest of
Gaul was subdivided into two divisions. Lepidus also had adminis-
tered Narbonensis together with Spain, but Antonius reunited all
Gaul, and after Philippi the *Prouincia* was joined with the rest of Gaul.
The provincial command of Transalpine Gaul had been assigned to

[111] Dio Cass., XLIII 51.8.

Antonius in 44 B.C. for a period of five years; Decimus Brutus he dislodged. After 40 B.C., however, it was Augustus who had control of Gaul (except Narbonensis), and in due course it was he who organized the four Gallic provinces (including Narbonensis). The Civil wars had annihilated Massilia politically; in theory it continued free of the empire, a Greek city, but as a small provincial town, that played the same rôle in Gaul that Naples had done in Italy. Some four years later, Octavian, following the example of Caesar, established a colony for veterans of the seventh legion at Baeterrae in Narbonese Gaul, and about 32 B.C. he received the submission of the three Gauls and of Germany, whose chieftains swore an oath of allegiance to him, as he himself records in his *Res Gestae*.[112]

It is true that Augustus "pacified" Gaul and that his "pacification" was not disrupted, despite sundry localized conflicts during the decade 38 to 28 B.C. But notwithstanding these outward marks of conquest, the people of Gaul were almost as far from being completely settled, especially in the north and west, as they had been after the campaign of Agrippa seven years before. Hence again in 29 and 28 B.C. we find the Romans obliged to suppress rebellions among certain tribes, the Suebi, Morini, and Treueri; Messalla defeated the Aquitanians in 28–27 B.C. not far from Narbonne, and it was perhaps about this time that fourteen Keltic tribes living between the Loire and the Garonne were transferred, in a general re-organization of the Gauls under Augustus, to Aquitania and joined to the many but small Iberian communities who lived between the Garonne and the Pyrenees.[113] This transfer was in accord with the geographical conditions, but it was none the less temporary: within three centuries at the most the Aquitani were separated from the Gauls north of the Garonne (the "*Nouempopuli*") once more.[114]

Augustus visited Gaul four times in all between 27 and 8 B.C.; first, after the principate was established (28 B.C.), on his journey to and

---

[112] V 4–5, 10–12, 17, 36.

[113] See J. P. Postgate, *CR*, XVII 1903, 112 (the chief ancient authorities are Strabo IV, C 189–190; Pliny *NH*, IV 108).

[114] See the insc. of Hasparren, CIL XIII 412 (*CLE* 260), the date of which is disputed (third century after Christ according to Grenier, *La Gaule rom.*, 435; second century, Jullian, *REA*, IV 1902, 46); Salvianus, *de gub. dei*, VII 8.

from Spain (27–26 B.C.), when the administrative rearrangements were being made that broke even Narbonensis away from the senate and made it an imperial province (though in 22 B.C. it was returned to the senate,[115] so that its distinctive position in Gaul, among other causes, contributed to its separate development); a second time in 16 B.C., in the course of an absence from Rome that lasted three years, at the end of which period (13 B.C.) Tiberius was made *legatus* of the three Gauls, i.e. the three praetorian provinces (Lugdunensis, Belgica, and Aquitania), an arrangement which renewed the territorial division that Caesar had found in 58 B.C. (together these provinces numbered sixty-four *ciuitates*); third, in 10 B.C., when he was at Lyons; and last of all in 8 B.C., when he returned to Gaul after the death of Drusus. Each of these visits was occupied in dealing with administrative and other questions, which included the organization of the two Germanies — military areas, which only later became provinces. In 19 B.C. Agrippa was in Gaul as governor; and the campaigns of 17–14 B.C., when the Alpine passes were secured, and the political arrangements made which placed the three small but important frontier military districts of the Maritime Alps, the Cottian Alps, and Graian Alps, together with the territory of the Raeti and Vindelici, and four tribes of the Vallis Poenina, under equestrian governors, prefects, equestrian prefects or procurators, as well as the census conducted in 27 B.C., again in 12 B.C.,[116] and yet again after the death of Augustus (this was conducted by Germanicus in A.D. 15), were all part of the general policy of the pacification and settlement of Gaul.

As we have seen, the old three-fold division of the country was found not quite practicable by Augustus — the purely Keltic tribes between the Garonne and the Loire were assigned to Aquitania which would otherwise have been disproportionately small; and the left bank of the Rhine, from lake Geneva as far north as the Moselle, was joined with Belgica, though most of these cantons included tribes counted Celtae by Caesar. In general, the Keltic division (Celtica, or "Gallica") preponderated, however, so that together the expression the "three Gauls" is justified.

Sporadic risings occurred from time to time, as for example when

---

[115] As far as the territory of the Aedui, Tac. *Ann.* XI 25.
[116] Livy, *per.* cxxxix.

the people of Nemausus overthrew the statues of Tiberius.[117] These were not unnaturally provoked by census-taking and the levying of taxes, but they sprang also from internal feuds and from the discord that was rife among the Keltic tribes. Even after the days of Augustus difficulties often arose in imposing tribute on the tribes of Gaul. More serious were the revolts of Keltic nobility on a larger scale led by Julius Florus and Julius Sacrovir (A.D. 21), after which there was a determined attempt to disarm the natives at the same time that the druids were suppressed; and again, the rebellion led by Vindex that preceded the downfall of Nero (A.D. 68),[118] which for a time seemed as if it might succeed in its declared object of establishing an independent *imperium Galliarum*. The Keltic cantons were raised and a Gallic empire of Julius Classicus proclaimed among the Treueri, of Julius Sabinus among the Lingones. But all this ended in farcical tragedy. In the long run the insurrection could not succeed, and the turn of the tide came early; a year later (A.D. 70), the power of Rome was restored, and thereafter the process of romanization went on undisturbed.

As for the rôle played by the druids,[119] the united druids, as Caesar described them, belonged actually to the monarchical period in Gaul, before 112 B.C. Their unity, in fact, was dependent upon a measure of political unity, and declined with it. It was the social and political revolutions that took place during the last century of Gallic independence and the early years of the Roman period that brought about the weakening of the druidical power and organization.

Nevertheless, in some ways there was a survival of Gallic sentiment. The *ara ad confluentes*, for example, fostered a feeling of Gallic individuality in the Tres Galliae, such as found open expression in the revolt of A.D. 70; and such as still lasted on in the time of Gallienus to launch the Gauls on a line of action of their own. But such influences were rare. And there were many and more powerful influences that worked in the opposite direction.

Rome being traditionally jealous of her privileges,[120] even the Trans-

[117] Suetonius, *Tib.* 13. This seems to have occurred towards the end of Tiberius' retirement in Rhodes, perhaps c. 1 B.C.

[118] Tac., *Hist.*, I 65; IV 17; Dio Cass., *frag.* LXIII 22.

[119] Cf. N. J. DeWitt, *TAPA* LXIX 1938, 319–322.

[120] Note especially Suetonius *Iul.* 80.

padanes had not received the franchise until 49 B.C. But the stage
of *attributio* was attained in the Transpadana in 89 B.C. under the Lex
Pompeia, and this was an important step towards romanization, by
which less advanced communities were placed under the protection
of a neighboring city, and through it they paid *tributum*. The *attributi*
were practically on an equal footing with the people of the place to
which they were attached, and gradually the distinction disappeared,[121]
and hence the process of romanization was hastened, even though the
grant of franchise was delayed. Julius Caesar probably intended to
apply the same liberal policy to the Transalpines that he had to the
Cisalpines, but his successors were more cautious. Those cities of
Narbonensis which were not *coloniae ciuitatis Romanae*, by virtue of
being settlements of veterans, seem in fact to have received Latin
rights, so that the province, at Caesar's death, was very much in the
same position as Cisalpine Gaul during the years 89 to 49 B.C. The
extension of the franchise beyond the Alps was therefore merely part of
a larger policy of Caesar, who had sympathies that went far outside
the frontiers of Italy. But it is clear that in Gaul the people in general
were not ripe for Roman citizenship. There were still extensive areas
in which there were no regular cities, the unit being the tribe and not
the city. Augustus, so far from being ready to enfranchise all the
Gauls, is recorded as having on occasion refused the grant of the
franchise even for a particular Gaul who had been recommended for
it, lest it should be too easily won, and thereby cheapened. But despite occasional disturbances, and despite the difficulties of maintain-
ing security along the frontier of the Rhine, which the Germans were
astride and which was still but lightly held, Gaul began to move
towards a new prosperity, almost without interruption, once the entire
country had succumbed to Caesar and peace had been declared.

To natural communications along waterways — helped out by
portages — were added good roads, for example, the one constructed
in 27 B.C. by Agrippa, from Lugdunum to open up new country; agriculture was supplemented by commerce and town-life fostered. For-
tunes were made in rapidly growing cities not only at Narbonne or
Arles, but at Bordeaux or Lyons, or even Trèves. Currency in circu-

---

[121] On Brixia (the canton Brescia) cf. Note C below.

lation increased enormously, and instead of the crude imitation of
Greek types (with Keltic inscriptions in some cases) or original types,
we find Roman types copied and the Latin alphabet in use for the
inscriptions. About the same date (27 B.C.) Aquitania was pacified
and in the main the Gauls were loyal to their new governors. The
visits of Augustus, and his complete reorganization of the country
contributed not only to the growing trade and prosperity, but also to
the increasing diffusion of Roman civilization. Narbonensis [122] already
had abandoned war for agriculture and urban life; stock-farming was
extensively practiced, and by Augustan times the manufacture of
terra sigillata had begun on a large scale, for example at La Graufesenque, to be carried on later at other centres, for example Lezoux
(after A.D. 50).[123] There was an active trade north and south in these
"Samian" wares (as they used to be called), which became fashionable
all over western Europe, but Gaul was predominant in output, though
Germany had native manufactories. Industrial relations sprang up
between Gaul and Spain, Italy, the Danubian lands, Africa, Britain
and elsewhere, as this one merchandise alone testifies. Some measure
of the prosperity of a land traditionally rich is afforded by the gift of
four million sesterces sent from Lyons to Rome to help in the restoration of the city after the fire of A.D. 64. Handicrafts of every kind are
named in the Latin inscriptions of Gaul. From having been merely a
new master to Gaul, therefore, Rome rapidly became a leader. Tiberius had new roads laid out in Narbonensis, and the old ones repaired.
And if the visit of Gaius in A.D. 40 contributed little or nothing to the
development of the provinces, Claudius not only fostered their material progress by planting colonies at Lugdunum Conuenarum in
Aquitania, and among the Vbii, but also bestowed the highly valued
privileges of the *ius Latii* or in many cases the whole franchise. It was
under his principate that Gauls began to be admitted to magistracies
and to the senate, despite vigorous opposition in Rome, admirably expressed by Seneca in the *Apocolocyntosis*, [124] — as it appears, Gallic
nobles might be enrolled in the senate, and any Roman citizen of Gaul

---

[122] Strabo IV, C 190.

[123] Estimates of date vary; compare *CAH* X 405 with *CAH* XI 503.

[124] vi (cf. iii), a reference which I owe to Dr H. Bloch; Tac., *Ann.* XI 23–25;
Dessau 112.

was eligible for election to office. From the famous inscription *CIL* XIII 1668 we know that Claudius proposed the *ius honorum* for certain Gauls: a rich noble might thus become a Roman senator when Claudius threw open the senate to provincial citizens of Gallia Comata — a strange contrast to earlier days when a wealthy Gaul would eagerly barter a slave in exchange for a jar of wine.[125] In republican times extension of the franchise would have been unthought of. It was only under the principate that there was gradually achieved the inclusive imperial citizenship. In this the policy of Claudius was far more generous than anything that Augustus or Tiberius had considered wise. Besides special grants made freely to individuals or entire communities, the enfranchisement of non-Italian troops on their discharge became the rule; and, at last, in A.D. 212, Caracalla made all but the most backward tribes citizens of Rome. Thus Gaul partook of what was the general imperial policy. Reorganization was from time to time necessary, as under Diocletian, but this did not interrupt the steady development of the provinces.

As for the Germanic tribes on the left bank of the Rhine, they were allowed to retain their native institutions. Even in Gaul proper the tribal system had been left intact. Representatives of the three Gauls were brought together in the annual assembly of the *concilium Galliarum* at Lyons,[126] which thus inspired a growing sense of unity in the native population. Even Caesar had held these conventions of the nobles during his campaigns,[127] and in imperial times they served to convince local opinion that it was not utterly disregarded. Many Gauls were entrusted with the command of military units, and a few, like Vindex, were raised to the position of governor of a province. If in his case this trust was misplaced, on the whole the Gauls were beginning to acquire a firm sense of loyalty to Rome. On the frontier of the Rhine, the activity of Trajan in building roads and fortifications before his return to Rome in A.D. 99 added a new sense of security.

Several factors played a part in the process of romanization. (1) Once any territory was annexed to Rome, there always followed an emigration of numbers of Italian-born speakers of Latin for the pur-

---

[125] Diod. Sic., V 26.3-4.
[126] *CIL* XIII pp. 227 ff.
[127] *B.G.* IV 6.5; V 2.4; VI 3.4; cf. I 30.

poses of private trade and the collection of public and private revenue, and of these the traders frequently settled in the new territories and took root there. They were followed, especially in Narbonensis, by peasant-settlers who actually farmed the land. There was, then, a marked drift of population from Italy towards the west that had set in by the second century B.C. Polybius noted the existence of Roman milestones in Transalpine Gaul even in his own day, as well as the important sea-going traffic of the Rhone. The existence of commercial relations between the Hellenistic east and the Italo-Keltic west is attested also by the fact that Keltic coinage begins about the first half of the third century B.C. It must by no means be supposed, therefore, that Gaul lived in a state of complete barbarism before the Roman conquest. There was a fairly stable political and social life, especially in Narbonensis, not without comforts or knowledge of the arts. But everywhere the political horizon was a limited one; there was no great state, and commerce was narrow. There was little urban life, save in a few places, to which foreign influence had permeated. Rome expanded both the political and the commercial horizon. This expansion was accomplished through a small minority of immigrant settlers who diverted the activities of the mass into a new channel. Although, therefore, the Gauls gradually conformed to a Roman way of life, received the grant of citizenship and might thus rise to the governing class, yet Gaul continued to be inhabited by Gauls. The great mass of the people were now becoming farmers and artisans; there was a certain survival not only of the native language but of native culture, with which the process of romanization came less into conflict than with language, and the three Gauls at least remained for some time related by language. But the civilization of Roman Gaul is a mixture of Gallic and Roman elements. Old habits of dress and housing died hard; something of old Keltic customs and unruliness survived. The foundations of this Romano-Gallic culture were laid by Caesar and Augustus, just as were the foundations of the modern Romance language that we call French. And even it was affected by the old native language so long as that was spoken.

(2) Next there is to be noted the effect of military settlements. The late W. Meyer-Lübke was one of the first to recognize the importance of permanent encampments (*castra statiua*) of the Roman standing

army in spreading Latin and developing the several Romance dialects. The military colonies of Caesar and Augustus in Narbonensis as elsewhere quickly passed beyond the stage of being merely military colonies; Arles (*Arelate*), which in those days could be reached by sea-going vessels up the Rhone, became a commercial center in the first century of our era, and a century later had surpassed and displaced the old Greek foundation of Massilia. Nor was it merely the units of the camp for the time being that counted. There was also the continuous process of recruitment and discharge. During the Julio-Claudian period, when the legions were chiefly of Italian blood, and again later, when more provincials were enrolled, time-expired soldiers tended to settle where they had been stationed.[128] Still later, under Hadrian, this became the normal practice; and, at the same time, it was also regular for the garrisons to obtain recruits from the districts in which they were stationed. Besides, Roman citizenship followed as a rule on discharge; the auxiliary troops associated with an army that spoke Latin, and were commanded by officers who were Roman in outlook and Italian in tone. No wonder if the permanent camps brought the provincials rapidly into contact with Roman civilization. So long as recruits were raised in Italy, the legions took many thousands of Italians permanently to Gaul, and at the same time spread the language and ideals of Rome and Italy among the native population through troops afterwards locally enrolled.[129] And in most cases, at least in Gaul, the camps led to the formation of nearby civilian settlements, through which they were even more effective as centres of Roman influence: first came the demand for agricultural produce from military lands, then the growth of markets (*canabae*), with their swarms of traders, and finally a permanent town. Examples of this course of development often named, even outside of Gaul, are Vetera in lower Germany, or the *canabae* at Carnuntum which became a *municipium* in the time of Hadrian, or Moguntiacum which was progressing to that stage by the end of the third century; [130] there are exceptions of course — thus Argentorate always remained a market associated with the camp. But whatever stage of development was

---

[128] Tac., *Ann.* XIV 27.
[129] Cf. Aristides XXVI 75 ff., K.
[130] *CIL* XIII 6727.

reached, everything tended to bring Rome and Italy to the provinces. For there were always groups of Italians who settled in the provinces without military reasons, and except in the most remote districts there could usually be found a *conuentus ciuium Romanorum* acting under the protection of a *curator*. The institution of this latter was due probably to Trajan.

(3) Last of all, and most important, was the attitude of the Romans, especially in imperial times, to the provincials whom they governed. They were not "superior," but on the contrary "receptive in their turn," so that they "escaped the failure of the cultural crusade." Rome's prestige grew inevitably in proportion to the growing gratitude of the provincials to the authors of the *pax Romana*. For if the world was at peace, that peace, which Gaul enjoyed in common with the other provinces, depended for its preservation on Rome. Naturally, devotion to the imperial power grew in strength and found expression in the wide-spread imitation of its buildings, institutions, and language. A prosperous town always was eager to become a colony, with the suggestion of closer connexion with Rome which the status of *colonia* implied, and citizenship came to be an object of justifiable ambition and pride. It can hardly be supposed that the Roman citizenship did not imply some acquaintance with and knowledge of the civilization and language that lay behind it.

The contrast, however, between Narbonensis and the Tres Galliae is deeply marked, and cannot be too much emphasized. In the former romanization went deep. Narbonensis was already Mediterranean in character and had been affected by long standing Greek influences, so that it was part of the early nucleus of the empire. But the Tres Galliae served rather to support the two Germanies and so to protect the empire. In Narbonensis there was a large number of towns and cities, many of which ancient testimony and modern research agree in showing to have been centers in which Roman civilization had planted its roots firmly: Tacitus [131] remarked on the progress of letters at Massilia; from Arles we have an unusually large number of inscriptions testifying to the popularity of that Roman institution the *collegium* or trade-guild; *Nemausus* (Nimes) had its famous buildings in the Roman style, still partly extant, from the time of Augustus; [132] *Tolosa*

[131] *Agr.* 1. Cf. *CAH* XI 445.   [132] Mela 2.75; cf. *CIL* XII 3151.

(Toulouse) was known for its learning and oratory;[133] Vienne (*Vienna*), Aix-en-Provence (*Aquae Sextiae*), *Baeterrae, Cularo, Forum Iulii* (Fréjus), *Narbo, Valentia* (Valence), all were sharing in the same rapid progress; at *Vasio* (Vaison) excavations conducted within the last decade have revealed an unsuspected city altogether Mediterranean in character, quite as much Hellenistic as Roman.[134] The younger Pliny[135] tells us of the *eques*, who after having fulfilled his term of military service and administrative work as procurator in Narbonese Gaul, took up agriculture and literature, turning his farm into a miniature "Athens;" and the contribution of *Prouincia* to Roman letters is well known from names such as those of Cornelius Gallus, Pompeius Trogus, Voteienus Montanus, Domitius Afer and Rutilius Namatianus. No wonder, then, if, with its important Italian leaven, this old province was latinized at once and completely; its distinctive form of Romance language, the Langue d'oc, in fact still survives as something different from French, perhaps from a different substratum. It has often been remarked that there is a certain difference in the names of the modern cities in Provence (e.g. Nimes from *Nemausus* — not from Volcae) and in France, where they are tribal (e.g. Paris from Parisiis, not from *Lutecia*). Arles and Fréjus, with the larger centres such as *Auennio, Aquae Sextae, Apta Iulia*, organized on the basis of Latin rights, were virtually Italian communities within the Gallic cantons, and Arles the true heir of that great emporium of Gallo-Italic commerce, the Greek city of Massilia. Something of Hellenistic culture survived in the south, just as romanization was always stronger in the east of Gaul than in the west and north. But, generally speaking, we may say that the lower Rhone was romanized on both banks, both in language and in manners, by the end of the Augustan age; even the remnants of the cantonal organization were but slight. Architecture too tells the same story; in the cities of Narbonese Gaul, beside the hellenizing or Hellenistic features, we have the magnificent structures of the early empire and succeeding years in the grand Roman style. Perhaps it is chiefly in the minor arts that there remains something of an independ-

---

[133] Martial IX 99; Hieron., *Chron.* an. 2072; cf. *AcS* II 1878.
[134] See the works of J. Sautel, *CA* fasc. vii, pp. xxiv–xxv.
[135] *Ep.* VII 25.

ent Keltic spirit, as in the picture of an artisan and his tools on a Gallic *cippus*. But, after all, the flourishing of the arts was dependent in a large degree upon the *pax Romana*, with its economic prosperity and rise in population.

The Tres Galliae present the greatest contrast with all this. The process of romanization was slower and less intensive. Gallic speech survived later; for there were no colonies, since the old cantons were preserved. In the Rhine districts in particular Roman influences permeated slowly. In Aquitania we hear only of Burdigala (Bordeaux) as a centre of Latin learning and literature; in Lugdunensis there was an important centre for the training of Gallic youth, after the Roman manner instead of the displaced native one, namely *Augustodunum* (now Aûtun), Lugdunum being the political centre. In fact this Gallic capital was the only city in the three Gauls organized on a basis that so many towns enjoyed in *Prouincia*; the Keltic diet of the three provinces met there, but later even it fell behind Trèves. The three Gauls, we must remember, extended properly as far as the Rhine, though the Vbii were not part of the sixty-four cantons; but the Heluetii and Triboci were included among them, the Heluetii and Sequani being counted by Caesar [136] among the Celtae. Caesar, of course, excluded or ignored the old Roman *Prouincia*; and for him the Treueri seem to have been reckoned with the Celtae, though it is not absolutely certain in what group he placed them. At a later date the Sequani were counted in Upper Germany (to the end of the third century of our era), and even the Lingones also in Upper Germany (to the end of the second century). In Belgica the only important towns were Durocortorum and, definitely so reckoned, the Treueri. The three Gallic provinces, then, maintained the old organization into cantons, *pagi* or *ciuitates*, and being more or less denuded of native troops, were left with a civilian population among whom was slowly disseminated the Helleno-Roman culture of the Mediterranean. The nearer the frontier was approached on the Roman side, the more pronounced this became, on the German side, the less pronounced. The two Germaniès were originally military commands established on the Rhine — Upper Germany to take in the Heluetii, Sequani, Lingones, Rauraci, Triboci, Nemetes, and Vangiones, and Lower Germany the

[136] I 1.2–4.

Vbii, Tungri, Menapii, Bataui — these last named being originally
Keltic; so Metz and Trèves both fell in the three Gauls. Clearly if
they left it undisturbed in Gaul, the Romans must have left the old
cantonal system undisturbed, as in fact they did, in the Germanies
and in Raetia. Trajan did something to forward a sort of romanization by his building of roads in the Germanic provinces, before he returned to Rome in A.D. 99. Although, therefore, we find the Roman
form of expression in the Germanies as in the Gauls, this romanization
was by comparison, quite superficial. Native Germanic names of
deities (e.g. Nerthus, *fem.*) survived as did Keltic in Gaul — sometimes
along the Rhine Keltic and Germanic names are not so easily distinguished one from another — but where romanization was effective,
in religion or in other spheres, its subjects were mostly of the Gallo-
Roman immigrant class. Keltic name-material, it is true, survives,
but its bulk is often less than would be expected, and its very occurrence, therefore, proportionately deceptive. Thus, an examination
of the names of the Treueri [137] reveals only 16.5% Keltic names against
63.5% Italo-Roman and 20.0 % non-Keltic. But even these figures
may be misleading, for there were many valid reasons why Italian or
Roman names might be favored to the point of adoption. In Raetia
the advance of Roman civilization was also long delayed, and the
same delay obtained both among the Vindelici and in the neighboring
lands — the *agri decumates*, all of them territories in which Keltic
peoples had at one time lived.

v. The End of Keltic in Gaul [138]

How long did any Keltic dialect continue to be spoken in Gaul?
This question has often been asked, and there is a certain amount of
direct evidence from which to answer it. Again, to what extent may

[137] L. Weisgerber, *Rh. Mus.*, LXXXIV 1935, 289.

[138] See *Do.* 69–79; *SprFK* 176–179; Nyrop, *Grammaire historique de la langue
française*, I ed. 2, 1904, 5–7; Brunot, *Histoire de la langue française* I, 1905, 17–37;
M. K. Pope, *From Latin to Modern French*, 1934, 1–6, 16–18, 70, 89, 136–137 (with
the authorities cited, viz. Meyer-Lübke, *Gr. Fr.*, §§ 48, 50; *Einführung* § 221 and
pp. 207–216 in ed. 2; *Zts. f. frz. Spr. u. Lit.* XLI 1–7; XLIV 75–84; XLV 350–351);
Vendryes, "Celtique et Roman," in *Revue de linguistique romane* I, 1925, 262–277;
W. von Wartburg, *Évolution et structure de la langue française*, ed. 2, 1934, 11–21;

the influence of Keltic upon the Latin spoken in Gaul, and its modern descendants, the dialects of France, be traced? To what date do such influences go back? For clearly Keltic was not altogether extinct so long as it could affect the popular Latin of Gaul. These questions may well be considered together.

That a certain number of Keltic words, e.g. *leuga*, taken over into Gallo-Latin, survived long enough to appear in modern French (*lieue*, Eng. *league*, a measure of length), is well known. Others are: *arpent* (*arepennis*), *brueil* (*brogilos*), *bruyère* (**u̯roikos*, dial. **urūkos*, **brukos* and **u̯raukos*, **braukos*), *charue* (*carruca*), *chouan* (*cauannus*), *changer* (*cambiare*), *encombrer* (*combri*), *vassal* (*uassallus*), *veltre* (*uertrăgus*). A longer list may be found in R. Thurneysen's *Kelto-romanisches* (1884), and to his collections later gleanings have added not a few items.[139]

---

id., *Die Entstehung der romanischen Völker*, Halle, 1939; B. A. Terracini, "Sostrato," in *Scritti in onore di Alfredo Trombetti*, Milan 1938, 321–364.

On the problems of Vulgar Latin in general, see also H. F. Muller, *A Chronology of Vulgar Latin*, Halle, 1929 (Heft LXXVIII of the *Beihefte zur Zeitschrift für romanische Philologie*); F. George Mohl, *Introduction à la Chronologie du Latin vulgaire*, 1899; W. Meyer-Lübke, "Die vorromanischen Volkssprachen," in Gröber's *Grundriss der romanischen Philologie* ed. 2, I 1904–06, 451–497; K. von Ettmayer, "Vulgärlatein," in Streitberg's *Geschichte der indogermanischen Sprachwissenschaft*, II i, 1916, 231–280.

[139] See, for example, Vendryes, *loc. cit.* 274 (*baume, ouche*), and, above all, the great etymological dictionary of W. Meyer-Lübke, *Romanisches etymologisches Wörterbuch*, ed. 3, 1935, in which many words are traced back to recorded or restored Keltic forms; cf. the still incomplete *Französisches etymologisches Wörterbuch* (since 1922) of W. von Wartburg (with the reviews by H. Pedersen in *Litteris* II 77–94; VII 17–25); much the same ground is covered in E. Gamillscheg's *Etymologisches Wörterbuch der französischen Sprache*, 1928; a masterly handling of the whole question of Keltic words in Romance is the review of *Do.* by J. Jud in *Archivum Romanicum*, VI 1922, 188–211, with the series of articles by the same scholar in *Romania*, XLVI 1920, 465–477; XLVII 1921, 481–510 (cf. *RC* XLII, 1925, 241); XLIX 1923, 389–416; LII 1926, 328–344; *Bündner Monatsblatt* 1924, 205–226; *Bull. de dialectologie rom.*, III 1911, 74 (on *nantu-*); (with Aebischer) *Archivum Romanicum*, V 1921, 29–52; single items often appear in the journals (e.g. L. H. Gray, *Romanic Review*, April 1942), but these are usually words for which a Keltic origin is alleged, the Keltic original being unattested. The important articles by Meyer-Lübke in *Zeitschrift für rom. Philologie*, XIX 1895, 94–99, 273–281; XX 1896, 529–535, should not be overlooked. A few Keltic items that survived not only Latin but also the barbarian invasions of the late Empire, chiefly local names, may be gathered from Th. Frings, "Germania Romana," *Teuthonista*: Beiheft 4,

There are, it is true, a number of words, appearing in writers such as Fortunatus (sixth century after Christ), which are not Latin, and which may have been acquired in Gaul.[140] But, apart from the few scraps of direct testimony, the significance of which is not always beyond dispute, the evidence consists entirely in the survival, into medieval and modern times, of Keltic words and names in regions in which Keltic was spoken before the spread of Romance or Germanic idioms. Within recent years, the discussion of Keltic survivals in modern proper names has been actively resumed.

Unfortunately, however, the very important question of date remains without a definite answer. But these recent discussions have revealed clearly the certainty that Keltic must have survived much later, in remote districts, than had generally been admitted, or than the explicit evidence would suggest. Nomenclature is notoriously tenacious, especially toponomy, and it is possible to overestimate its significance. But J. U. Hubschmied has made a strong case for the late survival of Keltic among the Heluetii and their neighbors to the south.[141] All over France Keltic elements are disguised in modern local names, e.g. -*dunum* (Verdun, Laon, Lyon), -*dŭrum* (Auxerre), -*brĭga* (Deneuvres), -*măgos* (Caen, Rouen), -*ācum* (Cambrai), -*ĭălum* (Bailleul), to mention only a few. The marked weakening of medial syllables (e.g. Nimes from *Némausus*) has suggested to some the influence of an ancient Keltic accentuation.

Commonly, then, as Latin must have been adopted after the conquest by Caesar, Keltic doubtless lingered on in rural districts, perhaps as a second language; a reasonable estimate puts the date of its complete disappearance, even from remote country districts, not earlier

---

1932, and from E. Gamillscheg, *Romania Germanica*, 3 vols., 1934–36. Werner Kaufmann in his Zurich dissertation "Die gallo-romanischen Bezeichnungen für den Begriff 'Wald,'" 1913, has called attention to pre-Roman terms, some of which are not even Keltic (e.g. *barto* in Gascony).

[140] See D. Tardi, *Fortunat*, Paris, 1927, p. 224, for words of "origine barbare." But *leudus* "song," *ganta* "wild goose," *r[h]una* "letter of the alphabet," are Germanic, and *flado* "a kind of cake," *stapio* "a head-dress (?)" not Keltic; . . *cidar* "tiara," *manzer* "bastard" are Semitic; this leaves, of Tardi's list, only the familiar *raeda*.

[141] "Sprachliche Zeugen für das späte Aussterben des Gallischen," *Vox Romanica*, III 1938, 48–155.

than the fifth century after Christ.[142] From the *Digests* [143] of Ulpian (222–228 A.D.) it is clear that Gaulish must still have been current in many places in the third century, for its use in pledges and trusts (*fideicommissa*) was expressly permitted, and the well-known passage in St Jerome,[144] comparing the language of the Treueri and that of the Galatians, which was Keltic, has been cited frequently to show that Keltic was still spoken in the Rhineland in his day (late in the fourth century). It has been both maintained, however, and also denied that this famous citation actually derives from forbears of the first century B.C., in whom it would be appropriate and from whom it was directly or indirectly copied.[145] Yet, as Loth has pointed out,[146] the inscriptions of Le Morvan which clearly show that Keltic had not become everywhere completely unintelligible, though it was no longer everywhere in common use, date from the third or fourth century of our era, and might, therefore, be claimed as confirming Jerome's assertion. What does weaken that assertion, is the possibility that in Trèves we should expect any non-Latin speech at the end of the fourth or early in the fifth century as likely to have been Germanic as Keltic. Much earlier Irenaeus Bishop of Lugdunum is said to have studied Keltic,[147] perhaps with the intention of preaching in that language. Again, in the middle of the third century, his impending death is said to have been predicted in Keltic to Severus Alexander,[148] who, as is clear from the evidence of papyri,[149] did actually allow the validation of wills in

---

[142] See, in addition to the works cited in n. 139, Fustel de Coulanges, *La Gaule romaine*, ed. 3, 1908, 125–134.

[143] XXXII 1.11: *fideicommissa quocumque sermone relinqui possunt, non solum latina et graeca, sed etiam punica uel gallicana uel alterius gentis.* Fustel de Coulanges, *op. cit.* 127 n. 1 compares the more dubious κελτιστί of Lucian, *Pseudomantis* 51.

[144] *Ep. ad Gal.*, Migne *Patrol. Lat.* XXVI [Hieron. VII] col. 357 *a* 26.

[145] A. H. Krappe, *RC* XLVI 1929, 126–129. Johann Sofer, "Das Hieronymuszeugnis über die Sprachen der Galater und Treverer," in *Wiener Studien*, LV 1937 (*Festgabe für L. Radermacher*), 148–158, accepts and defends Jerome's statement as an independent observation. Cf. on the general question of the "death" of languages, Vendryes, *Bulletin de la Société de Linguistique de Paris*, XXXVI 1935, 4.

[146] *Comptes rendus de l'Académie des Inscriptions et Belles-Lettres*, 1916, 168.

[147] *Contra haeres.*, proem. (Migne VIII 3.4.1), 177 A.D.

[148] Lampr., *Alex.*, 59–60.

[149] See *CAH* XI 447, and the source there cited.

languages other than Latin. Both Vendryes and Brunot [150] hold that the *defensor*-pun in Sulpicius Severus implies a general knowledge of Latin, and that, therefore, the phrase *celtice aut . . . gallice loqui*,[151] also in Sulpicius Severus, proves nothing, for it may not have meant literally "in Keltic," in fact Wilmotte interprets it to mean "talk in Gallo-Latin." The reference to an *incultum transalpini sermonis horrorem* in Pacatus' panegyric on Theodosius (389 A.D.) is likewise unconvincing.[152]

The conclusion to which we come is that Latin was undoubtedly the common language of Gaul, as of the western Empire as a whole, by the third or fourth centuries, especially wherever Christianity was introduced. If, here and there, a fragmentary knowledge of Gaulish survived, the Latin alphabet was used to write it. The language of Rome early took firm root in Narbonensis, and was understood well enough elsewhere in Gaul, even if the mass of the people often must have clung to the native tongue, so that the final disappearance of Keltic was a long-delayed process, the work of generations. After all, native words are quoted not only in Ausonius and Claudian, but also in Venantius Fortunatus and even in Gregory of Tours. Some of these may well have been learned through written sources, but some could have survived from the vernacular to creep into spoken Latin. If, then, Keltic was not favored by the educated classes in Gaul, the people of the country, in contrast with those of the towns, probably remained largely Keltic in speech as well as Gallic in spirit, until the

---

[150] Vendryes 269; Brunot 17 (see n. 138 above); Sulp. Sev., *vit. Mart.* 9 (363–425 A.D.).

[151] Sulp. Sev., *dial.* I 27; Wilmotte, *Mélanges Tille* [*Sborník Praci venovaných prof. dru Václavu Tillovi*] Prague, 1928, 223. Wilmotte's view seems improbable. In *tu uero uel celtice, aut, si mauis, gallice loquere, dummodo Martinum loquaris* there can be no opposition between *celtice* and *gallice* other than "or if you prefer so to call it," which is what *aut, si mauis* must mean here. The words seem to have been literally intended. Compare the story told by Aulus Gellius IX 7.4 of the lawyer, *quasi nescio quid tusce aut gallice dixisset*, which proves the survival of outlandish talk, exactly like the story of Pollio's attack upon Livy's "patauinitas." Moreover, since it was "homo Gallus" who hesitated to talk Latin "apud Aquitanos," he may have been more at home in Gaulish than in Latin, not to mention Iberian. In fact the whole chapter distinctly suggests a variety of speech in fourth-century Gaul. Cf. Gloss. Lat. V 1931, p. 378 (AA, v. 154), *CGL* V 488. 45; 518, 15; Gellius II 25. 8.

[152] *Pacati paneg. Theodos.* I (Baehrens 271.20).

spread of Christianity, bringing Latin with it, completed what the conquest by arms had begun.[153]

Discounting as much as possible the evidence of local names, which proves little or nothing about the date at which Keltic ceased generally to be spoken, especially in the north-west, where the reintroduction of a Keltic dialect (Breton) in the fifth century of our era makes the problem even more complex, we may confidently accept the judgements of Nyrop (p. 5, § 3) and of Brunot (p. 34) that Keltic was not yet completely extinct in the fourth century, but was far advanced along the road to extinction, and that Latin must have won complete mastery soon after the time of St Jerome, certainly in the fifth, or, at the very latest, in the sixth century of our era. Even so, of words which survived into French, most are, significantly enough, nouns, and all, or nearly all, pertain, again significantly, to rural life.

But Keltic had survived long enough to produce some effect, before it completely disappeared, upon the Latin of Gaul.[154] The change of

[153] On Gaul in the late Empire, see Courtenay Edward Stevens, *Sidonius Apollinaris and his Age*, 1933 (reviewed by O. G. S. Crawford, "Sidonius and his Times," *Antiquity*, VIII 1934, 81–84), Raymond Thouvenot, "Salvian[us] and the Ruin of the Roman Empire," English translation by O. G. S. Crawford, *ibid.*, 315–327; Jacob Peter Jacobsen, *Les Manes* (French translation from the Danish, by E. Philipot), vol. III 1924, "Le sentiment religieux populaire en France" (pp. 13–182 "Le christianisme gallo-roman"); cf. *REA* XXVII 1925, 331; and on the spread of Latin by the church into the Rhineland, Wilhelm Neuss, *Die Anfänge des Christentums im Rheinlande*, ed. 2, Bonn a. Rhein, 1933 (Rheinische Neujahrsblätter, 2). But both language and religion travelled along the imperial roads; on these we now have the important work *Le grandi Strade del Mondo romano*, Rome: Istituto di Studi romani, by Grenier and others (cf. *Classical Review* LII 1938, 159; and LIII 1939, 28–30, a review by R. Syme).

[154] The problem is vexed. I have indicated only a few certain items. Those who wish to pursue the problem further should consult: Vendryes, *op. cit.* n. 138 above; A. Brun, "Linguistique et peuplement," *Revue de Linguistique romane*, XII 1936, 165–231 (cf. the critique by C. Bruneau, *ibid.* XIII 1937, 26–32); Jan de Vries, "De hypothese van het keltische Substraat," *Tijdschrift voor Nederl. Taal- en Letterkunde*, L 1931, 181–221; V. Bertoldi, "Sopravivenze galliche," *RC* XLVI 1929, 16–28 (Alpine regions), L 1933, 327–338, A. Graur, "*Ab, ad, apud* et *cum* en Latin de Gaule," *Bull. Soc. Ling.*, XXXIII 1932, 225–298 (G. claims to see Keltic influence in the confusion of these prepositions in the popular Latin of Gaul); as well as the older studies of V. Brøndal, *Substrater og Laan i Romansk og Germansk*, 1917 (condemned by O. Jespersen, *Language*, 200–201) and P. G. Goidànich, *Zeitschrift für romanische Philologie, Beihefte*: Heft 5 (1907), 131–141.

[*u*] to [*y*] or of *ct* to *χt* and *it* in French are, what has often been observed, also Keltic, and are therefore commonly ascribed to the influence of the Keltic substratum upon Vulgar Latin as spoken in Gaul; so also is the appearance of the vigesimal system of reckoning (quatrevingts), the shift of intervocalic -*g*- to -*h*-, which was then lost (e.g. -*bria* for an older -*briga* in local names, or the *uertraha* of Grattius Faliscus, for older *uertraga*), and, in inflexions, the nom. pl. fem. in -*as* (as at La Graufesenque). In Gaulish itself there are isolated instances of variation in writing of intervocalic consonants, analogous to the change -*g*-: -*h*-, as *d*: *d̃* or *d*: *dz*, *t*: *θ* and *b*: *v* (Cebenna: Cevenna), which likewise are ascribed to Keltic. The argument against the assumption of Keltic influence has been stated by Meyer-Lübke,[155] but it is not convincing, and in the particulars listed above Keltic utterance is generally admitted, and by some scholars, also in the isolative forward pronunciation of vowels.

Divergence between southern and northern Gaul in the spoken language, it has been assumed, in late Latin was due to the divergent organic basis of an Iberian and Ligurian substratum in the south as distinguished from Keltic to the north; and north of the Loire there is also Germanic influence to be reckoned with. Nevertheless, in the north itself there is no trace of a difference that can be clearly drawn between Belgae and Celtae (Galli) in early times other than the presumed Germanic admixture in the former. The commonly made assumption that the influence of the substratum was slighter or slower wherever Latin was superimposed upon Keltic than elsewhere, because of the close relationship between Italic and Keltic, really has little to commend it beyond mere conjecture. We are on much firmer ground in comparing the voicing and opening of single breathed and plosive consonants (intervocalic *b* to *b̃*, *p* to *b* to *b̃*), a process which in Gaul gained ground rapidly, with similar changes in Keltic; the opening began as early as the second century, and voicing in the fifth century after Christ.

It has been held, for example by Brunot,[156] that Cicero was exaggerating in his opinion of the extent of romanization, but Cicero's testimony is confirmed by that of Strabo (born 63 B.C.), who speaks

---

[155] Cf. n. 138 above.

[156] I 23.

of the people of Narbonensis as being Roman in language and custom, if not by that of the later Pliny, who, as we have seen, describes it as Italian rather than as a province. Greek, however, was not dead at Marseilles even in the time of Varro,[157] and was used there and in the vicinity, by the Christian church, a usage which has left its mark even on Provençal. But there is no question of the usage of Greek in daily life except in a very limited area and that not for long after the decline of the Massiliot power. The Belgae, as we have seen, must have spoken Keltic, with some Germanic traits, and were in fact themselves sometimes confused with purely Germanic-speaking tribes. And in Aquitania were Iberians, who were spreading further into Gaul in the early empire. Yet this language also gave way to Latin and to Romance in its Gascon form.

Vexed as is the question of Latin orthography in Gaul, which prevents us from taking at its face value the epigraphic evidence, rare as are the Keltic inscriptions in the Latin alphabet, and granted that there are Latin inscriptions from Gaul even in Republican times, yet it is possible to put the date of the disappearance of Keltic too early. The facts that Latin literature was not merely read, but in due time also written in Gaul (Ausonius c. 310–395 A.D.), that Latin became the medium of education, and in the north the main vehicle for the diffusion of the Christian faith, that it was the language of the soldiers and of slaves as well as of administration and of all but purely local trade, do not seriously weaken the force of evidence which points to a situation comparable with that of Scotland or Wales or Ireland some centuries after the English conquest — in all of which Keltic persisted in remote or forested or highland districts and now even shows signs of new vigor. In that there is a difference. In Gaul Keltic did finally and permanently disappear (apart from its re-introduction in Brittany in the course of the fifth to seventh centuries after Christ); and evidently, when the Franks and other Germanic tribes came in, Latin was strong enough to absorb the invading speech — there was at that date no sign of the survival of Gaulish, or the least possibility of its revival.

The diffusion of Latin was completed, then, by Christian preaching, so that at the collapse of the empire it was the only language of Gaul. But in the second century Christianity itself had not advanced

[157] Ap. Hieron., Migne XXVI col. 354c.

beyond the romanized south. And, so long as Keltic sentiment and religion survived (even in an *interpretatio Romana*), it found expression in the use of the Keltic names at least of deities, whether or not joined with Latin names. But through the Church, Latin in Gaul seems to have gone deeper still, so as to become the universal vernacular. For a time many people, especially in the country-side, must have been bilingual (compare again Wales or Ireland), and in the towns there would be a constantly increasing proportion of those who knew only Latin. Already in the first and second centuries after Christ the schools — for example of Toulouse, Trèves, and Marseilles — aided in the diffusion of Latin, and we see from inscriptions that greetings and salutations were commonly made in that language. At Marseilles Latin eventually effaced Greek, and some Gaulish cities produced famous Latin authors.

Romanization in the Germanies is difficult to estimate. Doubtless it went far in the cities and larger communities. Latin must have been widely known, and it was of course the rule in the army. But inscriptions often show a defective Latinity that tells its own story. This state of affairs presents a certain contrast as compared with latinized Gaul. But even there, besides the direct evidence quoted above, we have the abundant evidence of personal and local nomenclature to show a specialized survival of the Keltic vocabulary, and also the adoption of occasional words as in the names of army manoeuvres,[158] technical expressions relating to cavalry, or to local products (e.g. beer, *ceruesia* Fr. *cervoise*), and a multitude of glosses preserved in ancient writers at a time when Latin was universal for spoken intercourse, and finally the influence of Keltic upon the development fo Romance in Gaul. Everything points to a gradual cessation of Keltic that must be reckoned in terms of centuries, and the commonly accepted estimate (fifth to sixth centuries after Christ) cannot be far from the mark.

[158] Arrian, *Tact.*, 43, 2.

NOTE A (p. 27)

On the name "Ligurian"

To assert that "Ligurian was a non-Indo-European language" is simply to echo, nay even to re-echo,[159] a preconceived prejudice, as well as to misconceive the nature of the whole problem of linguistic classification. Again, to suggest that the Ligurians were Indo-Europeanized by "proto-Kelts"[160] is to become involved in still more serious error. What Krahe, for example, wrote in the *Hirt Festschrift* I had, of course, read between the publication of *PID* and the writing of my *Foundations of Roman Italy*, and if I passed it over in silence in the latter book, that was because I was then, as I am still, completely unconvinced, not because I had not read it. Here, as heretofore, it is conceded at once, that any Indo-European language or languages of which records are preserved to us in Liguria, that is in the land of the Ligures, whether in Italy or in Gaul, may be presumed to have been introduced there in succession to some pre-Indo-European and non-Indo-European speech, since we know that region to have been inhabited by man from a time far too remote to have been peopled for the first time by speakers of any Indo-European tongue. Thus the dispute is partly nothing more than a dispute about names; it is, however, partly a dispute about linguistic evidence and its classification, partly also a dispute about chronology. Fundamentally there are four questions to be put: (1) What evidence is there, if any, to prove, what is a perfectly valid assumption, namely the existence, in Liguria, of a non-Indo-European language spoken there before the adoption of Indo-European? (2) What is the correct classification of the Indo-European but pre-Latin speech that we find spoken there, Keltic, Italic, or neither? (3) By what names should those pre-Indo-European and Indo-European languages be designated? (4) By whom, and at what date, was that Indo-European language introduced? It is nothing short of astonishing that so many comparative philologists do not see that these are the questions, and that they are fundamental, not only to their own discussions but also to mine. It ought to be unnecessary to say so, but they so far repeat their prejudices or misconceive the problem that it has become necessary for me to state it in this elementary way. Fortunately, since the evidence is already collected and classified, the answers can be stated briefly.

[159] *Year's Work in Classical Studies* 1937, 93. Contrast Pokorny's judgement, *ZfCPh* XXI 1938, 74. But Pokorny's own theory, that what is I. Eu. in Ligurian must have been Illyrian is devoid of foundation, and inconsistent with his "proto-Keltic" theory.

[160] *ZfCPh* XX 1936, 518 (Pokorny).

(1) There is no evidence of the use in Italian (and Gaulish) Liguria, prior to Indo-European, of any non-Indo-European speech other than that contained in proper names of the region, local, personal, and divine. Here the evidence is mixed. Some of the names, and of their constituent elements, are unquestionably non-Indo-European, but the greater part by far are just as unquestionably Indo-European. It was Niedermann, if I mistake not, who first observed, in 1918, that in view of the proper name *Caeptiema* (Tab. Gen.), Kretschmer's analysis of *Berigiema* (*ib.*) is by no means assured, and I alluded to Niedermann's observations by my reference to Bertoldi's article in *PID* III 22 s.v. *giem-*, then the latest discussion of that point. If my readers cannot read, that is their misfortune. But if we no longer accept the analysis *Beri-giema*, and the forms *Blustiemelus, Lebriemelus* perhaps tell against it in the same direction as *Caeptiema*, though *Quiamelius* does not, for it cannot be analysed as *Qu-iam-el-ius* (and if it could -*iam*- is not -*iem*-), neither does *Intimilium*, yet it still stands true that an overwhelmingly large number of proper names from the Ligurian area can be nothing but Indo-European. In fact the total number of these will be diminished now exactly by one, or at the most by three. Nevertheless, it is doubtless true that at one time there was spoken in that area a non-Indo-European language; for, as I said before, we do not suppose that the ancestors of the pre-Latin Indo-European speaking people of Liguria were dumb. But the traces of that non-Indo-European speech are extremely scanty and some of the elements which have been ascribed to it, for example -*a* or -*asca*, are at least just as easily explained, as I have shown elsewhere, as Indo-European.

(2) Since some of the Indo-European proper names from the Ligurian area show features which distinguish them both from Keltic and from Italic, they cannot be correctly classified as belonging to either of those branches of Indo-European. As for the material of the Lepontic inscriptions, the same conclusion holds good, with the qualification that their dialect appears to be more closely related to Keltic than that of the Ligurian proper names does.

(3) Hence it follows that neither Italic nor Keltic can be justified as a linguistic designation either of the Indo-European proper names of Liguria or of the dialect of the Lepontic inscriptions. "Proto-Keltic," which is Pokorny's label, at least for the onomastic material, is no better, for it only means "earliest Keltic," and their dialect is not Keltic, either early or late, but only closely related to Keltic, just as it is related, and as closely, to Italic. The term proto-Keltic is fantastic as applied to the Ligurian names; it might conceivably be applied to the oldest known remains of Keltic, say the Keltic inscriptions of Gaul and Italy, but to nothing else. Of course, if by "proto-Keltic" something is meant so far different from Keltic as not to be recognizable as Keltic, then the entire argument is a dispute about names, and the name "proto-Keltic" is doubly unjustifiable and had better be dropped at once, and another name put in its place. Again the "proto-Kelts" of

Sergi or Childe,[161] who are concerned with archaeology, are just as much a phantasy, even on archaeological evidence, which has no place for them. Even if it had, their use of the term is fantastic, for "Keltic," we have already seen, has no meaning except as a linguistic term. Now granted that the Indo-European speech of Liguria, like that of Greece or of Italy, was preceded by a non-Indo-European form of speech, what name shall we give to it? The remains of non-Indo-European are just about as impressive in Liguria as in Greece. But the name Greek is usually reserved for the infinitely more impressive Indo-European remains, and, in Italy, the name Italic for the infinitely more impressive Osco-Umbrian and Latin-Faliscan; in like manner I maintain that the name Ligurian should be reserved for the infinitely more impressive Indo-European remains of Liguria — especially since linguistically they can be classified as intermediate between Italic and Keltic, but neither the one nor the other. If anyone wants a name for the non-Indo-European remains of Liguria, I advise him to call them precisely that — non-Indo-European, just as he does in Italy or in Greece, or if he prefers it, pre-Indo-European, since linguistically they can no more be further classified in Liguria than in Greece and Italy; and not to distort the linguistic situation and put it all out of proportion by taking the only geographical name that we have from the more important in order to attach it to the less important and almost negligible pre-Indo-European fragments of speech in Liguria. "Lepontic" as a geographical label remains unaffected by this discussion; so does the view (it is Pedersen's and Kretschmer's more than mine) that it is essentially Ligurian or Kelto-Ligurian in character.

(4) Ligurian, the term being used as determined above, must have been introduced by Indo-European speaking folks who linguistically were a link between the Keltic-speaking and the Italic-speaking people of the Italo-Keltic group of Indo-European. Italo-Keltic, as Pedersen has seen, thus receives a tripartite (not bipartite) subdivision. But we have no other name for them, any more than we have for the other tribes who introduced Indo-European speech into Italy or the tribes who introduced Indo-European speech into Turkestan. Their history is too remote for that. The name "proto-Kelts" as we have seen is ruled out. It would be ruled out, if there were no other reasons, solely by its implication that the people of Liguria spoke four different languages in succession within a thousand years, an implication that is patently absurd. But those who wish to use the name Ligurian for the non-Indo-European speech of Liguria (or, to use their misleading phraseology, who say that Ligurian was a non-Indo-European language) are the ones who must face and, if they can, answer at least two further questions squarely and honestly. They admit that an Indo-European language came to be spoken in Liguria. Who then, I ask them, introduced

[161] G. Sergi, *Italia: le origini*, 1919, 154, 322, 409; V. G. Childe, *Proc. Brit. Association*, 1926, 392.

it? Not "proto-Kelts," for there is no such thing; nor Keltic-speaking people, for it is not Keltic; nor Italic-speaking, for it is not Italic. Pokorny's "Illyrian" I have dealt with above. Who then? There is no answer other than the one I have given. Neither archaeology, nor history, nor language has any acceptable name to give to that Indo-European dialect better than, indeed other than, Ligurian. But when was it introduced? At a remote date, far more remote than any that can be assigned to the imaginary "proto-Kelts" of the archaeologists. For, as Pedersen has seen,[162] the period of Italo-Keltic unity probably reaches back well into the second millennium B.C., before which it can no longer be perceived. But it was only at the time when Italic and Keltic were developing independently that the intermediate Ligurian came into existence, for there is no indication of linguistic mixture, such as is found in Lepontic. Hence Pedersen's chronology seems to me to be sound.

NOTE B (p. 27)

On Venetic ECUPETARIS

It may have been, as Pedersen declares,[163] "beschämend" (so I thought it at the time), that Conway kept Pauli's old transcription of the Venetic symbol ı|ı, as everywhere to be written *h*. Loyalty to Conway's memory forbids me say more here about the several appeals which I made to him between 1924 and 1929, asking him to reconsider his theories of the value both of the symbol ı|ı and of the Venetic medial puncts; and likewise loyalty to my collaborator forbade me depart then from his system of transcription, little as I approved of it.[164] But if the adjective used by Pedersen is applicable to any interpretation of *e·kupeθari·s·* that I have yet read, then it is to Pedersen's own:[165] "der erste Bestandteil gehört zu gr. νέκυς, der zweite zu πέτρᾱ," for that requires us to believe that an initial *n*- had been lost in Venetic, or else added in νέκυς (and, therefore, presumably in Latin *nex* and its congeners), and also to regard the vowel *a* as due to anaptyxis. His appeal to Hittite *aki* "dies" is not conclusive.

It would have been easier to swallow an appeal to Irish *ēc* "death" and to assume *eku-* beside *enku-* from *ņku-* with a loss of *n* before *k* such as took place also in later Venetic before *t*, e.g. *vh[ou]χotna·i·* (*PID* no. 134) beside *vho·u·χo·n·tna* (*ib.* no. 16), cf. *vho·u·χota* (*ib.* no. 136 bis v),[166] and *kuito* if

---

162 H. Pedersen, *Linguistic Science in the Nineteenth Century*, 1931, 313, 319.

163 Cf. n. 159 above.

164 *PID* II 79, 511, 547; III 39 (s.v. *ritiei*); cf. *Classical Philology*, XXIX 1934, 283.

165 Characterized as "poco persuasivo" even by the writer of an article in *Enc. Ital.* XXXV 1937, 47.

166 Suppl. I, *Classical Philology*, XXIX 1934, 286.

rightly so read and interpreted as "Quintus." In this the development would be the same as in Old Irish, for *n* is regularly preserved before *k* and before *t* in Venetic, as in the oldest Keltic; but the assumption is unjustified without the occurrence of the older spelling *enk-*, especially in a document as old as the Venetic inscriptions *PID* nos. 141, 142, not to mention the fatal *p-* in -*petari·s·*, for the etymology of πέτρᾱ which connected it with -*quetro-* in Latin *triquetrus* is no longer accepted, and even Rhys stopped short of claiming Venetic for Keltic, just as Fraser has stopped short of claiming it (with Pauli's predecessors) for Etruscan.

As for the ending, it would be better to compare Ven. *kluθiiari·s·*, which must have had an original *r*, since intervocalic -*s*- was preserved in Venetic. No one will deny that Latin -*arius* stands for an older -*asios* (both Oscan and Umbrian testify to -*s*-); and Latin *Clutorius*, *Clutorianus* contain -*tor-io-*, not -*aris*. Besides, Venetic shows no evidence that would lead us to suppose that it has nominatives in -*is* beside -*ios*, like Oscan (*Pakis*) and, in a few forms, dialectal Latin too (*Clodis*). Accordingly, in ·*e·kupeθari·s·* it is necessary to see an I. Eu. -*ri*- form. Such forms do exist, even if they are not numerous. But we have not only the comparatively isolated formations such as Lat. *imber* (*imbris*), Osc. *anafriss*: Skt. *abhrá-m*, Lat. *uter* (*utris*): Gr. ἄνυδρος, ὑδρία, or Skt. *asri-*, Gr. ἄκρις: ἄκρος, Lat. *ācer*, *ocris*, Osc. *akrid*, Lat. *sacer* (O.L. *sacres*, pl.), Osc. *sakrim*, Umb. *sacre*, with -*ri*- beside -*ro*-;[167] Lat. *puter*, *putris* (: *puteo*), Gr. ἴδρις (ἰδεῖν). Italic has also a widely spread -*aris* ending which is commonly supposed everywhere to stand for an older -*alis*, -*l*- being dissimilated to -*r*- when another -*l*- already stands in the word (e.g. *popularis*). If, however, Italic properly has only -*alis* and not -*aris* (Vestinian *flusare* but Latin *floralis*), then in some words at least -*aris* is secondary, for there is no cause for dissimilation in Osc. *dekkviarím*, Umb. *sehmeniar*; and, dissimilated or not, -*aris* appears in Osc. *luisarifs*, which has the same phonetic complex as *flusare*. But if Osco-Umbrian has a secondary -*aris*, why should not Venetic also show it? And derivatives with -*r*-, from various sources, do make their appearance in more than one Indo-European language in forms that cannot contain an older -*s*- like Latin -*arius*, for example Greek -*αριον* in diminutives, Germanic -(*u*)*ario*- in ethnic names, or (obviously from *bher-*) O.H.G. adjectives in -*bári*.

There is, however, at hand a very simple way of accounting for Venetic -*petari·s·*, without appealing to Greek πέτρᾱ, πετρι- (cf. πέτρινος), an appeal that has involved Pedersen in the assumption of a Venetic anaptyxis (why not metathesis?) otherwise entirely unknown. For, side by side with the verbal derivatives ἴδρις and *putris* cited above, we have *r*-derivatives from the root of Latin *peto* (*pet-*, *petā-*, *pet-*, with an old *r/n* stem *pétr̥*, *petnés*)[168]

---

[167] Brugmann, *Grundriss* ed. 2, II 1 (1906), 381–384. Cf. M. Leumann and J. B. Hofmann, *Lat. Gram.*, 1926 (1928), 233, 238. On Lat. -*alis* (∾ Etr. -*al*) G. Herbig, *Glotta* IV 1912–13, 186. Cf. O.L. *sacris*, *pac(a)ri*.

[168] Walde-Pokorny, *Wtb.* II 1927, 19–21; cf. I 1930, 172.

in Skt. *patará-*, *patáru-* and perhaps in Greek πτέρις (-εως, acc. πτέριν, pl. πτέρεις, beside gen. πτέριδος); the alternation *-ro-*: *-ru-*: *-ri-* is normal, and the assumption of anaptyxis totally unnecessary (cf. Skt. *patará- patáru-*),[169] even if we take the final step of comparing the compound *acci-piter*, older **acu-petri-s* [170] (cf. Gr. ὠκύπτερος, ὠκυπέτης, Skt. *ašupátvan-*, *ašupátvā*). For this very word gives us not only an old Latin genitive *accipiteris* [171] "apud uetustissimos," but also a by-form *acceptor* (with its derivative in *-arius*), said to have been used by Lucilius (fr. 1130); [172] and, last of all, if we may trust the testimony of Placidus [173] *accipitres: equos celeres*, a shadow of the literal meaning of *accipiter* "swift-flying" still lurked in the Latin *Accipiter*, even if "Hawk" was merely the name of a swift race-horse (like *Aquila*, *Tigris*).

But "swift-flying" would be a good nick-name for a jockey or charioteer as well as a good name for a race-horse. A possible ablaut-variant of **ōk̑ú-* "swift" is **ēk̑ú-*, and it is preferable to see even that in Venetic *e·kupeθari·s·* rather than Pedersen's (*n*)*eku-* "corpse," if, despite the Pannonian name *Ecco* and Latin *eculus*, *eculeus*, *ecus* (*equŏs*), we may not assume a Venetic *eku-* for an older **ek̑uo-*; for one of the three inscriptions which bear the word *e·kupeθari·s·*, *ecupetaris* shows us a horseman driving his two-horse chariot (*PID* no. 142), and if Pedersen objects that another (no. 141) does not, then I must insist that a bronze urn, the object on which the third was engraved (no. 157*a*), can not conceivably be described as a "grave-stone," which is Pedersen's interpretation of the word! Finally, the Keltic compound *eporedias* "bonos equorum domitores" makes a satisfactory parallel to the formation of *e·ku-peθari·s·*.[174]

NOTE C (p. 28)

On Polybius II 35.4

If it were worth while, which it is not, either on his account or on mine, to confute one by one the several mis-statements in which Mr Robson has indulged himself,[175] it would be an easy matter to do so. Two examples must

[169] Brugmann, *Grundriss* ed. 2, II i (1906), 355–356.

[170] Cf. Walde-Hofmann, *Lat. etym. Wtb.*, ed. 3, 1930, 6.

[171] Priscian, *Gr. Lat.* II 229.7 (Keil).

[172] Charisius, *Gr. Lat.* I 98.9 (Keil).

[173] *Glossaria Latina* IV (1930), 13 no. 42 (= *CGL* V 516).

[174] It should be recalled that Conway's interpretation was actually not his, but Torp's in the first place; *e kupeθari·s·* is conceivably a proper name; if so, compare *Assedomarus*, *Aθθedomarus* beside *assidarius*, *essedarius*.

[175] *CW* XXXI 1938, 85–86.

suffice, for his merely subjective judgements are of no importance either way, any more than his complaint that I have not included in my *Foundations of Roman Italy* whatever I judged to be irrelevant to its subject, as the rape of the Sabine women and such like old wives' tales; but it is of some importance not to let pass unchallenged the extraordinary and false assertion that of the Indo-European-speaking tribes who migrated into Italy "no others are mentioned" than the Samnites.

Mr Robson exaggerates. I do not profess to mention by name so many even as *one* people in "the migration of Indo-European speaking tribes into Italy;" but if he can count, Mr Robson will find half-a-dozen and more names of tribes, the Samnites among them, who lived in Italy in historical times and spoke Indo-European languages, which is a very different thing. Mr Robson's real grievance, as a glance at his reference told me, is that I decline to accept his ill-founded theory of a migration from Samnium to the valley of the Po, which he supposes to have taken place at the end of the Second Punic War, but which neither Polybius nor any other historian has perjured himself into witnessing. I profess to mention such names, just as I profess to set forth the precise manner of the establishment of the Indo-European languages in Italy, *not at all*, inasmuch as I confess myself ignorant, like everybody else except Mr Robson, of those things. Had I been writing a work of fiction, of the kind of Mr Robson's thesis, nothing would have been easier than to make precise, but imaginary, what is now left vague in order that it may also be both accurate and honest.

However, if you must have an imaginary migration of Samnites into the Po valley, you must first extirpate the previous inhabitants in order to make room for the new-comers. What Mr Robson calls a mistaken assumption is neither mistaken nor an assumption. I observe with pleasure Mr Robson's epigraphic leanings. Well, there are literally hundreds of inscribed gravestones of men, women, and children, who were born, lived, died, and were buried, in Cisalpine Gaul, in the centuries after Polybius, and who bore names that can be nothing else but Keltic [176] — and that was knowledge even before Holder had collected them. It is a choice, therefore, between the strait literalism of an only too "precise statement" of an ancient author and an overwhelming combination of interpretative and yet historical though not literary testimony. Of course, you can have the *uox* of Polybius, *et praeterea nihil*, and conveniently empty the Po if you like, but then you will have an ancient error, which Nissen saw through long before the archaeological and linguistic research of this present century gave us the only interpretation of Polybius' exaggerated assertion that can save it from outright rejection as being either a blunder or a fabrication, and reconcile it with the evidence of later writers, for example of Strabo (V 1.6) that Insubres still survived in his day in the vicinity of Milan, which Strabo, almost in the

[176] Cf. G. E. F. Chilver, *Cisalpine Gaul*, 1941, 81–83, who makes the same point against Robson, and who also interprets Polybius as I do.

words of Polybius, describes as being near the Alps! As Mommsen rightly saw, "Mediolanum and Brixia were indebted for their wide bounds and their lasting power essentially to the fact that they were, properly speaking, nothing but the cantons of the Insubres and the Cenomani." [177]

Polybius meant that the Kelts "were expelled" from Cisalpine Gaul in the sense in which Strabo (V 4.8) meant that the Samnites "were ejected" (ἐξέπεσον) from Pompeii, namely from any political control or autonomy — for their language also and their family names endured in Campania for centuries after the "ejection." Similarly von Duhn, speaking on archaeological grounds, has insisted: [178] "Die Bemerkung des Polybius (II 35.4), schon zu seiner Zeit, um 150, seien die Gallier bis an den Fuss des Gebirges hinaufgedrängt darf nicht mit Niese im Sinne gänzlicher Ausmerzung im übrigen Po-Land, sondern nur als Aufhören ihrer politischen Beherrschung der Po-Ebene verstanden werden"; and again a recent writer in the *Cambridge Ancient History*,[179] declares, quite rightly, that "even in Italy we can perceive beneath the crust of romanization something of the Keltic tradition in the North." If the Etruscans and Gauls lived side by side (Polyb. II 17), why not the Gauls and the Romans?

The argument based on the paucity of Keltic inscriptions, if it were valid, would prove that the Keltic-speaking people of Gaul itself were almost exterminated by the Romans. In fact, it only shows that they learned to talk Latin almost everywhere in Gaul, as in Italy, before they learnt to write. Long after the days of Polybius, Cisalpina was still Gallia; are we then to be told that the people of England are no longer English?

Much recent study, for example the paper of Vittorio Bertoldi in *Vox Romanica*,[180] goes to show that much more of Keltic survived in North Italy than we have hitherto supposed. And the language of the Lepontic inscriptions likewise can only be explained by the assumption of profound Keltic influence upon the Ligurian substratum. As for names in *Sab-* Pokorny also has observed that in Cisalpine Gaul they by no means imply a migration from central Italy.[181]

So my second is a much more serious objection altogether. The familiar method of omission is easily the most deadly way of practising the art of mis-representation. Twice Mr Robson deliberately suppresses some words in the sentences which he quotes from me. The suppression of the words

---

[177] *Provinces of the Roman Empire*, Eng. tr. by W. P. Dickson, new edition, 1909, I 55.

[178] Ebert, *Reallexikon* VI 1925, 287.

[179] XI 1936, 803.

[180] III 1938, 229–236; cf. G. Alessio, "Il nome del fiume Savuto ed una nuova base mediterranea *Sap-*, *Sab-*," in *L'Italia Antichissima*, N. S. fasc. XI, 1937, 53–59.

[181] *ZfCPh* XXI 1938, 79–80.

"or extinct" (p. 153) is tantamount to a *suppressio ueri* calculated to deceive; and by omitting the words "the point is not pressed" (p. 182), he contrives to throw into the eyes of his readers the very dustiest dust of the whole silly dispute about Vergil's birthplace and ancestry, and at the same time to mis-represent my position.

THE DIALECTS OF ANCIENT GAUL

PREFACE

Notwithstanding warnings such as those uttered from
time to time by the eminent Romance scholar J. Jud, the
assumption is commonly made that the Latin of any one of
the provinces of the Roman Empire was a uniform Latin, free
from dialectal differences; and the assertion is at least as
commonly made that the Latin of the entire Empire was likewise uniform. This cannot have been so, much as the details
of the differences, that must have existed, escape us. It
certainly was not true of Gaul[1] in the days of Caesar or in
the next three or four centuries. To make clear, so far as
the evidence can make clear, the differences that existed in
the non-Latin dialects of different parts of ancient Gaul, is
the purpose of the present work, as explained in my Prolegomena

1   Jud, Romania, 52, 1926, 331: l'unité lexicologique
de la Gaule n'est qu'une hypothèse sans valeur; 49,
1923, 397-98: nous sommes encore trop enclin à
admettre l'existence d'un gaulois uniform et nivelé;
c'est une conception que la linguistique romane est
la première à ébranler à mesure que nous pénétrons
mieux dans la structure des survivances celtiques.

1

(published in HSCP 55 1944), to which reference should be
made for all other matters of a prefatory or preliminary
nature, including the list of works of reference.

In the map I have indicated not only the provenances
of inscriptions but also the chief sites in Gaul at which
terra sigillata is known to have been manufactured. The key
to the map and the index of sites, like the table of contents,
are given complete now. The grammar, which will appear with
the commentary, glossary, and other indexes, in the last part,
will be made available in printed form only if there is demand
enough to justify the cost of printing and publication. The
index to CIL 13 (part 5, 1943, cf. AE 1945, p. 178), still
inaccessible to me in 1949, appeared after I had made my collections of names from that volume -- actually seven volumes,
the supplements in RGK Ber. and elsewhere (Prolegomena p. 7)
not counted -- by working through its many thousands of inscriptions. I did use the index to CIL 12, but (as a pre-

Preface

caution) I also read the volume and thereby gleaned a few

noteworthy items. The maps in Stroux's index to volume

13 I should expect to be valuable, and therefore mention

their reported existence. Instead of repeating it, I

refer to the system of signs and abbreviations given in

PID volume 2, pp. xxix-xxx, which I have used (with a few

insignificant changes) in the present work.

J. Wh.

Cambridge, Massachusetts
5. x. 1949

CONTENTS

PART I   THE RECORDS OF THE DIALECTS

Contents

Contents

Contents

Contents

Contents

Contents

Contents

INTRODUCTORY NOTE (on Boundaries). When Caesar began his campaigns in Gaul, only the "prouincia" Narbonensis can be said to have had boundaries at all clearly defined in the mind of its Roman governor and his contemporaries. The rest was Gaul taken as whole, from the Pyrenees and Ocean, to the Rhine; but the lines between the Belgae and Lugdunensis, and between Lugdunensis and Aquitania, were only vaguely drawn. Portions were carved out of Belgica in the formation of the two Germanies only at a later date, and the frontiers of Belgic Gaul were in due time strictly determined;[1] for Caesar, everything on his side of the Rhine, from its mouth to the point at which it left lake Constance (lacus Venetus), and west of a line running thence to the north-eastern angle of Prouincia near the head waters of the Rhône was counted within Gallia (i.e., the land of the Galli), the Heluetii included.

The boundaries of the prouincia Narbonensis were, on the other hand, quite clearly distinguished. From the source of the Rhône the line ran south-westwards and southwards along the summits of the Alps (Alpes Penninae, Graiae and Cottiae) to strike the Mediterranean just west of Nicaea; and westwards along lake Geneva to the junction of the Saône (Arar) and the Rhône, which it crossed to follow the range

1 Cf. A. Grenier, La Notitia Dignitatum et les front-
   ières de l'est et du nord de la Gaule, in Mélanges
   Paul Thomas, Bruges 1930, 378-393.

Note on Boundaries

of the Cévennes and thence to the Garonne and the Pyrenees, excluding the Ruteni to the north but including Tolosa and the Volcae Tectosages. We shall count the records within this boundary as belonging to Narbonensis.[1] The Alpine regions were not included in Narbonensis strictly defined.

See, further, Prolegomena, pp. 20-22, 24-26, 51; PID 2, Preface p. viii and pp. 166-169.

1 Cf. Grenier Mnl., vol. 1, 1931, 129.

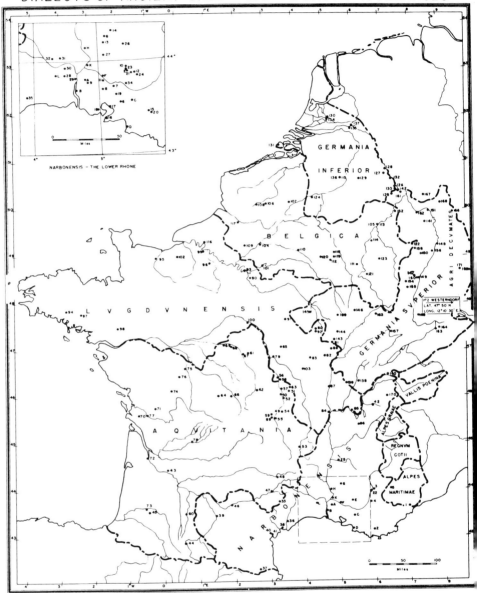

NARBONENSIS — THE LOWER RHONE

KEY TO MAP

16

Map

23

PART I

THE RECORDS OF THE DIALECTS

Alpine   Regions

Gallia   Narbonensis

1949

Of all the tasks which Augustus had to face during
his principate none was more urgent or more momentous than
that of creating an efficient administration of the empire
that Roman arms had conquered. The Alpine regions, between Narbonensis and Italy, were seen to have peculiar
problems that made it necessary to give them a separate
organization. Hence, in 14 B.C., these districts, perhaps
more Ligurian than either Liguria itself or Narbonensis,
were constituted imperial provinces. The southernmost
province, that of the Alpes Maritimae, which was placed
under an imperial prefect, seems not to have reached the
coast, where Narbonensis marched with Liguria, at the mouth
of the Var (save that Antipolis, now Antibes, belonged to
Italy). But the frontiers of the Alpine provinces are uncertain, see CIL 12 pp. xii-xiii, and the meagre linguistic
records that we have are confined to such as have been preserved indirectly through Greek and Latin channels, chiefly
in Latin inscriptions, and consist almost entirely of
proper names. Some of these were given in PID, vol. 1,
385-369, and are not repeated here.

COINS Coin-legends of the Alpine regions are to be
found in PID vol. 2, 129-128 (nos. 324, 326-328, 330 bis).

A. GLOSSES

A Note on Glosses.

By "gloss" I understand an item in an ancient author,
or glossary; not a word claimed by a modern etymologist as
Keltic or Germanic or Alpine or what not. Few items of
the latter category are admitted; the former are not excluded even if the ascription of dialect or language is
erroneous. But such ancient mistakes are corrected, either
tacitly by the use of square brackets, or explicitly. My
concern is to collect the ancient testimonia, not to com-
pile an etymological dictionary. But any reader, who will
take the trouble, can see for himself that I frequently
criticize the ancients, and the moderns.

I have referred to a few items in PID 2, without repeating them, where the territorial limits are not to be
clearly distinguished, e.g. an item belonging to Cisalpine
Gaul is sometimes attested also for the Maritime regions,
or even for Transalpine Gaul. But Keltic items put into
PID 2, on the ground that they were current in Cisalpine
Gaul, are not as a rule mentioned here, unless ancient
testimony explicitly refers them also to Transalpine Gaul,
probable, or even certain, as it may be, in many a case,
that the word in question was current in Gaul proper.

Cf. items 178, 207, 220, 233 below.

30

Glosses

1 Glosses of the Alpine Regions

Testimonia are reduced to the necessary minimum. More is, as a rule, available in Holder or in the places cited in the discussions of the several items.

I have been obliged to omit a bellicum "prunelle" ascribed merely "des gloses," without reference, in BSL 32, 1931, 139n. (cf. belloce "fruit du prunellier," Savoy), as if *belluca beside bulluca, Holder I 631, see 158 below; Baluci (pers. name) 6 Remark. For a summary of Bertoldi's work see REA 32, 1930, 307-308.

alpes "Gallorum lingua alti montes," Serv. G 3.474

But the word is probably pre-Keltic; see Bertoldi ZfRPh 56, 1936, 181-184; cf. BSL 32, 1931, 148 and Berl. Beitr. z. R. Ph., 1, 1929, 278-284. There is also a variant with -b-, in Ἄλβια ὄρη (Strabo 202 C.), and perhaps also in Albici "homines...montani" Caes. BC 1.57.3, cf. 34.4; Ἀλβίοκοι Strabo 203 C. See also PID 2.180. This alp-: alb- must be distinguished from albo- "white," which may have been Keltic as well as Latin, and may appear in the following word.

ἄλβολον "pennyroyal," Diosc. 3.31: γλήχων ... Γάλλοι ἄλβολον, οἱ δὲ γαλίοψις

Cf. Plin. NH 27.81, who gives also galion, i.e. Gr. γάλιον, probably from γάλα. If *albūca "white, marly earth" (Prov. aubugo, Meyer-Lübke, Wtb., 325) and albucium are to be counted Ligurian (Bertoldi, Berl. Beitr., loc. cit.), ἄλβολον may provisionally be classified here; but albo- is probably to be analyzed *al-bho-, and this al- to be recognized in alutiae (Aquitania), albucrarensis (Callaecia), Albocola (Vaccaei). Latin according to Do.32.

asinusca (uitis), rabuscula (uitis) "vines of inferior

quality," Plin. NH 14.42

See Marstrander, Skrifter utg. av. Videnskapsselskapet i Kristiania, 1924 (2), Hist.-Fil. Kl. 8, 18, who counts both

Glosses

words Ligurian on the ground of -sc-; the context in Pliny
(41-43) suggests an Alpine origin, but the etymology commonly accepted (asinus), if it were proven, would favor a Latin
origin for asinusca. The etymology of rabuscula is unknown;
the word is quoted only from Pliny; perhaps we should read
rauuscula and compare rauus "grayish," OHG. grāo, with the
alpine change of gr- to r- (Raecus, Raet-i, from Gr-, cf.
Alpes Grai-ae, PID 2.473; dial. rauistellus beside urban
grauastellus; *Ico-randa: Aquae-granni?).

atrusca also a kind of vine, Macrob., Sat. 3.20.7

   The formation is the same as in asinusca above (cf.
Marstrander, loc. cit.); moreover Hubschmied has demonstrated
the existence of an Alpine *atro- 'black' (RC 50, 1933, 266-
267). A word so ill known can hardly have been native Latin,
all appearances to the contrary.

bala (-anis) "having a white blaze" (of a horse)

   Only in Ennodius episc. Ticinensis, carm. 2.136 tit.
Cf. Procop., Goth. 1.18, τοῦτον (sc. ἵππον) Ἕλληνές μέν
φαλιὸν, βάρβαροι δὲ βάλα καλοῦσιν, whence it has been
inferred that bala is Germanic, Goth. bala, Eng. dial. ball.
To Ennodius, however, the word may have become known from
inhabitants of his see, and Livy (see Holder, AcS I 337)
speaks of a mountain-peak (cf. Belchen Walde-Hofmann 1.559-
560) in Liguria, Balista (i.e. "white-peaked"). It is certain
that Keltic had a form bal(i)o- "white" independently of the
cognate Germanic bala. Cf. Bertoldi RC 48, 1931, 291 n. 2;
BSL 32, 1931, 167 (with 138-141). The meaning "peak, crag"
appears also in the following. On Βαλίος , the horse of
Achilles (Il. 16.148) see P.W. s.v.

balma (1) "pointed rock, peak," (2) "grotto"

   Holder 1.337 cites, besides many local names, Acta
Sanctorum 28 Feb., III 746 A: quam in cingulo illo uel
balma, Gallico, ut reor, sermone, sic uocatam.

   The distribution of modern derivatives and of local
names proves beyond doubt that the word is of Alpine origin;
comparison with Corn. bal "mine" has been suggested, and
also a Keltic variant *balba (b from m, after l), as represented (Balba) in local names: see J. Loth, RC 38, 1920,
47-58; Battisti, Arch. Glottolog. Ital. 22-23, 1929, 419

32

(citing Bertoldi Rev. Ling. Rom., 3, 263-281; cf. BSL, 32, 1931, 167).

In Riese Anth. Lat., 1.204, 11 for ualmam read balmam; I take the obscure words vv. 10-12 to be a list of punishments for which Seruandus medicus is destined (cf. v. 2: Tartareo missum de carcere).

Cf. perhaps φάλα below.
Walde-Hofmann 1.864, 865 (s. vv. fala, feruo).

basium: see 240.

[? boiae "shackles for the neck." Plautus, Paul. ex Fest.,

Gl., Hieron., etc.; Holder, AcS 3.897

If from Boii (Thurneysen in Thes. Ling., after Solmsen, KZ 37.24), then, since it appears in Plautus, Cisalpine rather than Transalpine; boia the name of a fish, Diosc. Lat., Gl., see Thes. Ling. 2.2063. 29-32, is even more a riddle. Perhaps cf. baiulare (Plt.)?]

bronda "twig, shrub, leaf" (14th c., Du Cange)

As Jud has shown (Bull. dial. rom., 3, 1911, 68 n.), this word has been current chiefly in Alpine areas, and is probably the Keltic equivalent of Latin frons.

[bruscum "maple knot," Plin. NH 16.68

The context in Pliny (66-69) may imply an Alpine or Transalpine source; Bruscus is a Keltic name, and a Keltic etymology would easily be supplied, Walde-Hofmann 1.117.]

[bulga (not-ia): see PID 2.183; Keltic, pace Brüch Einfl.10]

camox "chamois" Polem. Silv., see Holder, AcS 3.1064

Probably an Alpine and pre-Keltic (Ligurian?) word, possibly pre-I.Eu. See Walde-Hofmann 1.148, 854, with Bertoldi ZfRPh 57, 1937, 147, 158 n. 1; Jud in Howald and Mayer Röm. Schweiz 1940, 367.

Glosses

?capanna "casula," Isid., Orig. 15.12.2 (rustici);

"tugurium" id., Gl., later cabanna and -ae, especially

in local names; also written cau-; Holder, AcS 1.757,

cf. 871; 3, 1020, cf. 1171

Neither modern derivatives nor the distribution of the
local names help to fix the geographical source of this interesting word. The etymology is also uncertain. The Alpine
variant camanna, from cabanna (see J. Sofer, Lat. u. Rom. aus
den Etym. des Isidorus von Sevilla, 1930, 125) is some justification for including it here, whether or not the now commonly
accepted explanation (metathesis for canaba) be followed;
more probable to me seems a connexion with cappa (capanna for
*cappanna), capella— hood and hut have a very similar shape,
—(cf. Isid. Et. 19.24.17; Glotta 18.147). Pokorny (Urg.,
69) reckons the word Illyrian; his etymology, as well as
this ascription, strikes me as highly hypothetical. If Illyr.,
it may well stand here with the Alpine words; as strong a case
for putting it with words of the upper Rhine and Danube
(Section VIII below) might be made.

carpenta (-um) "charpente," cf. carpentarius

See Jud, Arch. Rom. 6, 1922, 195 (cf. Romania, 52, 1926,
347); Weisgerber SprFK 183. For carpentum "waggon" see PID
II 187 (and, on the later history of the word, W. Ensslin,
Klio 32, 1939, 89-105). Cf. Carbantorate.

carpinus "hornbeam." Transpadane, Plin. NH 18.201

On the survival in French dial. (south of a line from
Grenoble to the Gironde), see G. Walter Giessener Beitr.z.
Rom.Ph. 10, 1922, 66-68.

Cognate with Illyr. $\gamma\rho\acute{\alpha}\beta\iota o\nu$, PID 2.69, 429; cf. Walde-
Hofmann 1.171.

daculum "gladium, ensem, telum, mucronem, sicat (leg. sicam)"

Syn. Cic., CGL 1.84.91

Niedermann's conjecture of a Ligurian *ďalklā (cf. O.Fr.
dail, Catalan dalla "sickle") is confirmed by this gloss.

Glosses

Related to Sicel δάγκλον(PID 2.450), Latin falx (cf. perhaps fancua, CIL I ed. 2, 1614, on which see now Vendryes
Rev. de Philol. 70, 1946, 93-95, *ghankū: *kankū W. cainc).

damma: see PID 2.162

gaesum Alpinum, Verg. A 8.661; of the Veragri and Sinduni,

Caes. BG 3.4; on the Rhine, Prop. 5.10.39. Cf. CGL

4.595.37 (lingua Gallica)

See PID 2.184, and for the (quite uncertain) etymology, Walde-Hofmann s.v. (with Add.). The constant v.l. cesa,
caesa seems too frequent to be insignificant. On CGFr 214,
no. 183 see Kaibel ad loc., cf. Dechelette, REA 13, 1911,
455, and note the S. Ital. ethnicon Ἀγγαισοι (Cuny RC 28,
1907, 413-415), AcS 3.623; pers. name Gaeso (Greg. Tur.)
ib. I 1517.

gandadia (v.l. gang-) "gold-bearing earth," Plin. NH 33.72.

That this word is of Alpine origin was proved by Bertoldi, BSL 32, 1931, 93-128; cf. ZfRPh 57, 1937, 142. But
it appears also in Iberian territory, and is probably neither
Keltic (despite Gandanium, Ghent) nor I.Eu. even.

[(?)*garra (carra) "rock"

Dial. French (S.W.) garric "chêne," cf. garrigues (in
the Cévennes), Basque (h)arri "stone," (h)ariz "chêne."
Dauzat, REA 42, 1940, 610. But all this (after Alessio) is
hypothetical in the highest degree.]

genista "broom"

Balboni Stud. Etr. 16, 1942, 403-408 compares W. banadl,
and sees genista as an Alpine cognate (I.Eu.gu̯).

[? giluus "pale yellow," Verg. G 3.83

Cisalpine according to Walde-Hofmann. But see now Die
Sprache 1, 1949, 127.]

35

Glosses

[? gladius "sword." In Plaut., Lucil.; therefore an early

borrowing, and like gaesum, perhaps Alpine

On the relationship of gladius to Keltic cognates, see
Vendryes Mél. de Saussure, 1908, 309-310, Walde-Hofmann,
s.v.]

ibex "chamois." First in Pliny NH 8.214; now considered to

be of Alpine origin (cf. camox)

Etym. unknown. Jud (in Howald and Mayer, Röm. Schweiz
367) derives mod. Alpine vesina from *ibicina.

[? ibiscum "marsh-mallow," Verg. E 10.71. Keltic or Ligurian

(-sc-); Cisalpine rather than Alpine]

ἴορκος "mountain goat" (ἴορκες, ἰυρκες Hesych.) Oppian.

cyneg. 2.296, 3.3 (Holder, AcS 2.65)

Cf. Iurca f. CIL 12.152; Welsh iwrch, caer-iwrch Walde-
Hofmann s.v. caper; and perhaps the Keltic *iuris "mountain"
which underlies the Iura mons of Caesar BG 1.2.3; Iures Plin.
NH 3.31, cf. mod. dial. joux, older jour "forêt (de sapins),"
"chiefly in the Rhône valley, above lake Geneva"(Atl. ling.
Fr. 594); see de Saussure ap. Loth, RC 28, 1907, 340; Werner
Kaufmann, Die gallo-rom. Bezeichnungen für den Begriff "Wald"
(diss. Zürich, 1913), 18-20; J. H. Hubschmied, Z.f. deutschen
Mundarten, 19, 1924, 189-193; Vox Rom. 3, 1938, 142 n. 3;
E Muret, Romania 15, 1924, 446-449. There appear to be no
Keltic cognates, and the word may be Ligurian, as Holder AcS
2.94 (after d'Arbois de Jubainville) and Muret maintain. Greek
δόρκας i.e. ζ- (Boisacq s.v.), but cf. Ed. Diocl. 4.15 (d-).

? ligurium: see PID 2.164, cf. langurus ib. 2.203

? orombouii (lectio inc.) "uitam in montibus degentes" (near

Bergomum), Plin. NH 3.124. Hybrid (Greek and Keltic?),

but clearly corruptin our texts of Pliny

Glosses

φάλα· ὅροι, σκοπίαι. φάλα· ἡ μικρὰ κάρα. βάλον ·οὐρανον,

all in Hesych.

The Alpine origin of this word, and its wider extent (Iber.? Ligur.?) is now clearly recognized, see Walde-Hofmann, s.v. fala, with Add., (to his references add Devoto, Stud. Etr. 13, 1939, 311-316, who stresses, unconvincingly, the meaning "rotondità.")

Cf. perhaps balma above, Lep. pala "grave-stone." But Walde connects Lat. pala with pastinum rather than with sepelio, Umb. pelsa. It is doubtless irrelevant that pastinaca is Gallica to Plin. NH 19.89 (the same paragraph as ibiscum, q.v. above).

pennum "acutum," Gloss. Lat. 1 BI.112-115; 4.15, B11 (*CGL

5.9.8, 50.23; cf. 608.31; 4.212.20), Isid. 19.19.11,

but pinnum in Quint. 1.4.12, Isid. 11, 1.46; cf. pen(n)is

"caput," CGL 4.139.43

If bipennis (Varro, Verg.) is actually connected, not with penna or pinna, but rather with this word, it must be a dialectal (O.-U., or Kelt.) form; but this assumption, likely as it is, is not necessary in order to make acceptable a Keltic pennum, pinnum (for e, i cf. Consentius, Gr. Lat. 5. 394.12 K) represented in Penninus (Alpes Penninae), cf. Appenninus mons, Pennelocus (i.e. "Summo-lacu," PID 1.451), summus Penninus (a hybrid, like Lingua-glossa, cf. Cuno-pennus at Brescia, CIL 5.4216, Penno-crucion Staffs., Cuno-cenni(s) Brecon), and possibly the Roman (dial.?) cognomen Pennus (dict. de Galleis, act. tr. capit., a.u. 393). Cf. are-pennis; Greg. Tur. h. Fr. 10 (cf. 17) bipennis quod est francisca. Said to survive in Fr. dial. (Comminges) pène (Lizop I 59).

The meaning "tip, point, headland" beside "sharp, pointed" is obvious. Jud, Romania 47, 1921, 489 would see penno-also in a Keltic talo-penno- "pignon," cf. M.-L. 8544 b; Dauph. talapent, talapet, Lyon. talapen, Sav. talapon.

Ir. cenn (Belg. Nemeto-cenna; Sumelo-cenna in Agr. Decum.), W. penn, Pedersen 1.157; cennum "acutum," CGL 5.177. 8; possibly Lat. cuneus is cognate (*q^{u}e/o-).

Glosses

<u>rabuscula</u> (uitis): see asinusca above

<u>saliunca</u>: see PID 2.160; Weisgerber, SprFK. 208

?(<u>s)asia</u>: see PID 2.158

<u>uatusicus</u> (caseus): Plin. NH 11.240 (Ceutrones)

<u>uerbascum</u> (-<u>u</u>-) "mullein"

    Plin. NH 25.120, with Isid. 17.9.94; CGL 3.539.2,
630.46, 563.53 etc. (cf. Thes. Gloss. Emend. s. vv. phlomus,
lupicuda)

    Pre-I.Eu. and Ligurian according to Alessio, Stud. Etr.
13.1939, 317-330 (cf. uerpa?); but see also the discussion
by Bertoldi, RC 50, 1933, 330-335.

<u>uiburnum</u> "the way-faring tree"

    Verg. E 1.26. For the form compare the Alpine laburnum
(see PID 2.203). Meyer-Lübke, W.u.S. 11,1928, 143-144; G.
Walter, Giessener Beiträge 10.66.

LOCAL NAMES - ALPINE

B. Ethnic, Local, Divine, and Personal Names

1. Alpes Maritimae

This province extended westwards as far as the head-
waters of the Durance. Of the names which follow but few
must be Keltic; some are Ligurian, one or two Greek or Latin.
Of the glosses above, there is probably a greater proportion
that can be counted pre-Roman.

(i) Ethnic and Local Names

From CIL 12.1-164, 5702-5720; Espérandieu, Inscriptions
Latines de Gaule, Paris, 1929, nos. 1-11, 15-19. Once more
(cf. Prolegomena p. 3), the names are selected for their linguistic interest. Complete lists are not given; those who
want them may refer to CIL 12 (with Espérandieu), or to Holder,
AcS. And names given in PID 1 358-360, 363-369 must be sought
there. Testimonia easily accessible in Holder are not as a
rule repeated. In particular, references are given in the
lists of personal names only to sources not used by CIL,
Espérandieu, Holder, or PID.
See further (for all sections containing local names)
E. Desjardins Géographie de la Gaule d'après la Table de
Peutinger, Paris 1869; and L. Duchesne Fastes épiscopaux de
l'ancienne Gaule, Paris 1894-1915, three volumes.
At PID 1.358 Cemenelum (cf. Cebenna infr.) add kem[in
an Etruscan insc., Fabretti Atti d. R. Acc. d. Sc. di Torino
7, 1871-72, 854-859 with 894-896. If the insc. is genuine,
and if correctly interpreted, kem[must be the oldest record
of this name. Cenabon 179 (Orléans) is commonly compared
with Genua; at all events it can hardly stand (by metathesis)
for Ceb-(Cem-), the meaning of which would be inappropriate
there.
On CIL 12 see Sautel BA 1925, cxxv; and for recent excavations at Cimiez, Gallia 4, 1946, 77-136.

39

2

?Adunicates Pl.

Agodano Rav.

Alma IA

Alpes (Maritimae) cl.,
e.g. CIL 13.1802, ILG
3 Ἄλπεις (παράλιοι,
παραθαλάσσιοι IG 14.
2429, 2433), Alpicus
(carm.) Esp.- de Rugg.
523 (otherwise Alpi-
nus); Ἀλβία Str.,
Ὄλβια ....νῦν δὲ Ἄπλια
Posid. ap. Athen.,
Σάλπια Lycophr., cf. 1
above, AcS 1.107

Anaone portus IA

Ἄρπων Polyb.

Auisione portus IA

Beriti[ni] pag[ani] insc.,
mod. Beritins (?)

Brig[insc., num., prob-
ably Brig[omagus or
-omagensis (Brigianni
BSAF 1898, 263-4) mod.
Briançonnet

?Buriates Flor., Iordan.,
AcS 1.640

Caenia mons., Pl., Cae-
[n]in[ensis] CIL 12.
671?

Contubr(ici) and Contrubii
act. tr. cap. (see AcS
1.1111, and REA 29,
1927, 302,whence AE
1926, 121)

?Epanterii montani Liv.

Glannatina (or -ua?)
ciuitas NG, mod.
Glandève

Lumone IA

?Nemesii insc.; perhaps a
common noun (collegium
lignariorum iuuenum
nemesiorum) cf. Νεμητον
57, and gl. 79; AE
1945, pp. 171 Nemesis
and 175

[Oliuula portus. IA, AcS
1.844; Latin; cf. Pl.
15.1. Like Gallitae,
PID 1.364, this name
has a Sicel analogue]

Σαλῖναι Ptol, Salin-
[iensis] insc., cl.;
CIL 12, p. 9; 5.7817,
7900; CA 7, p. 13, no.
35

Σάλπια see Alpes above

Σανίτιον Ptol., Sanit-
[iensis] insc., NG.
Cf. Σάὐνιον 246 below,
mod. Senez

Σουήτριοι Ptol. 3.1.38
(AcS 2.1308), cf. PID
1.364. Compare the
numerous names in Su-
or Sue- (Suebi, Sues-
siones, Sudeta, to
name no others)

?Ta...rnei act. tr. cap.
a.588 (CIL I ed. 2, p.
48)

Turamina (Et-?) AcS 1.
1482; 2.1993, mod.
Thorame

Local, Divine, Personal Names

Οὐίντιον Ptol., Vint-
    (iensis) insc. BSAF
    1923, 199; mod. Vence

Vulpis fl. TP. Cf.
    nimphae Volpinae 236
    infr. (Coblenz)

3   Further Modern Local Names

Balur, Blausasc, La Boissa (cf. Buxea, Longnon no.
656), Cassiannes, Castellar, La Fuye (cf. Fagea, Longnon
657) Lantosque, Malvans, Roure (cf. Robur, Longnon 626),
Thorenc, Vaquairie, Vignols (*Vinoialum): CA 1.53.

4   (ii) Divine Names

(Mars) Ieudrinus CIL 12.2
    (Puget-Théniers, La
    Penne), S. d. Ricci RA
    1,1900, 430 (cf. 438);
    Ieusdrinus or Leus-
    drinus in CIL l.c. and
    add. p. 803; Leusdrtno
    Pais; cf. Ludrianus
    (Feltria) PID 1.254?

Lauaratus insc. (La Broc),
    see CIL 12.5702

(Mars) Vintius insc., mod.
    Vence (local, see above)

[Mars Veracinius (?):
    insc., forged, see CA
    1.44, no. 226]

(iii) Personal Names

a.   Nomina

Note.   The Roman system of personal nomenclature is
by no means invariably followed in the Latin inscc. of
Gaul.   Nomina are listed separately only if clearly used
as such (i.e. as gentilicia), otherwise as cognomina.
The latter, therefore, include many individual, distinctive names, which may or may not be accompanied by
a nomen gentilicium.   Some doubtful cases, names of the
types that in Latin would be definitely nomina, are also
included; and occasionally, when it is uncertain how the
name was used, a mark of interrogation calls attention
to the doubt.   But this mark is, of course, used to indicate other doubts or uncertainties (e.g. of reading or
language).

Personal Names

5

Braebius	Pescennius CA 1.48, no. 253
Cenouilius	?Setosius
Certia ILG 7	??Sextorius CIL 5.7982
Cimbrius	Vectinia ILG 2
Cremonius (cf. Cremonis iugum 10)	Velabel[l]ius
	Veludius (cf. ueleda 220)
?Cupitius	?Vialius CIL 12.68
Matuconius	

Vlattius (see cogn. below)

b. Cognomina

6

Ἀλεβίων	Iucius (and Iusius?) REA 21, 1919, 149
Brectenus	Mantus AE 1912, 135
Catullinus	?Matuconus
Cimogio	Meducinus
Cragus (cf. Adamn. vit. Columb. 1.12, p. 19: qui Scottice uocita-batur Columb Crag), but cf. Ven. Glagus	Niger, CA 1.48, no. 253
	Πυθώνακτος IG 14.2425
	Σειλός IG 14.2428
Cremonius (cf. nomina above)	Sura REA l.c.
Δέρκυνος	Tauriscus Amm. Marc. 15.10.9
Enig(e)nus	
?Flauimius	

Corsica, Sardinia

6 ctd.   (Alp. Marit.)

Tutus   ?Vlattius 1b.

Velagenus RA l.c., cf.   Vlatuna
   Klio 21, 1927, 84.3;
   uela 178

Remark:

   CIL 12.15 Pannunia, with u for ʊ.

Note 1

  CIL 12.41 (Vence):

  ... Baluci │ Lanc │ Ciuotegetis │ oup

  i is ├ , (i or e, cf. Gram.)

Note 11

  <u>Corsica</u> Of the little that is known concerning pre-
Roman Corsica, still less is relevant here. Perhaps
attention may be called to the following ancient local
names viz.:

    Aliso, Caesiae litus, Cersunna

and modern names viz.:

    Populasca, Venzolasca

see CA 3.1, 17, 24; cf. BSAF 1893, 85 (local); see also
Berthelot, on Ptolemy's account of Corsica, RA 11, 1938,
28-29, 133; cf. my Foundations of Roman Italy, pp. 375,
380.

Corsica, Sardinia

Personal names:

Baslel (or -iel) ILG 12

Caninius ib. 14

Turbellus ib. 12

SARDINIA   The Iberian evidence is collected by A. Garćia
y Bellido in Emerita 3, 1935, 225-256.

Ethnic and Local Names

2. Regnum Cottii

(or Prouincia Alpium Cottiarum, the boundary of which

ran just west of Chorges)

(i) Ethnic and Local Names

7

Aquisiana fl. Pardessus
  Dipl., La Guisane

Aquisleuae (in pago Bri-
  gantino) ib., Eygliers

Βριγάντιον cl. -io insc.,
  Briançon

Caesao (G-), Goesao,
  Gaesaeone itin., Rav.,
  insc., also called
  Tyrio; see CIL 11,
  3281-84, cf. 5, p. 811
  n. 3, Césanne

(Musticae) Calmes Greg.
  Tur., cf. calmes 207

?Cammuntii insc., RA 14,
  1939, 253 no. 60 (cf.
  p. 257, col. 1 ad fin.)

Caturiges cl., insc.,
  -ensis, Caturigomago
  TP, insc., -ensis,
  Chorges

Cinisius mons Fredeg.,
  Mt-Cenis

Cottiae cl., Cottianae
  insc., Alpes, previous-
  ly called Iuliae (Livy
  5.34.8), on which see
  my Foundations of
  Roman Italy, 177 n. 1;
  Nissen 2 i, 151

Druantio (Gr-) CIL 11.
  3281-84

Ebrodunum (Eburo-) cl.,
  itin., TP, ILG 15
  -ensis, Embrun

Ἐξκιγγόμαγος , Scingomagus
  cl., Exilles (?)

Iuliae see Cottiae above

Matrona mons itin., Am.
  Marc., Ennod. carm. I
  1.23

Ocelo CIL 11.3281-84,
  La Chiusa

[Quariates PID 1.365, now
  Queyras. See H. Fer-
  rand in Bull. Géogr.
  36, 1922 (1923), 67-69]

Rama CIL 11.3281-84

Rigomagus NG (at Barcelon-
  nette?)

Scingomagus see Ἐξκιγγο-
  above

Segusio CIL 11.3281-84
  Suse

Stabatio TP

Tyrio see Caesao above

Divine and Personal Names

There is ample evidence here, not to mention the name of Cottius, regis Donni filius, to show Keltic-speaking settlements. Presumably rex translates donnus.

7 bis   (ii) Divine Name

Albiorix AE 1945. 105, 106
(cf. CIL 12.1300, 1062)

(iii) Personal Names

8   a. Nomina

?Albiorigius AE 1945.106   Leuconius
  (or Albiorigi u.s.?)
                                Macrima AE 1945.105
Allius
                                Parridius
Blaesia
                                Tittonius
Cominia
                                Vennonius
Corsius
                                Vesomnius (or Vessonius?)
Egeius
                                Vestonius
Escigius AE 1945.105
                                Vlattia

46

Personal Names

9   b.   Cognomina

Albanus CIL 12.80, REA
    39, 1937, 366

Adnema

Adretilis (?)

Alpina

?Anais CIL 12.86 (see
    Fitreso below)

Atiliana

Baro

Bituuo

Bonucius CIL 12.76
    (Corsius)

Bussullus, -a

Butuna

Cottius

Δόννος, Donnus

Eamon (?)

Excingus

?Fitreso Anais CA 6.29,
    no. 98 (CIL 12.86
    Fitresomais,cf. AcS 1.
    1495), read Titreso-
    mais (?) or Feltre(n)-
    sis Mai(en)s(is)?   See
    Anais above

?Gobannicn(o)

?Lu[tatia] CIL 12.80 (REA
    39, 1937, 366)

?Namicus

Nemateuus

Nertoualus

Parrio

Salonina

Smertullus

Solicia

Solicil(l)us

Solita

Sueta AE 1945.105

?Titresomais, see Fitreso
    and Anais above

Titto

Velagenus; cf. uela 178

Venna

V[ennus]

Ves[AE 1945.105

Remark:

> CIL 12.86 pereggre, with -gg- before -r-.

3. Alpes Graiae

The westernmost point of the boundary is a little west of that of the Regnum Cottii (2 above), but runs thence in a north-easterly direction, the prouincia Alpium Graiarum becoming narrow at its northern end, until it opens out into the Vallis Poenina (15 below).

10   (i) Ethnic and Local Names

?Alsede AcS 3.576

Arebrigium itin., TP, Rav. Derby

Ariolica TP

Atrect(i)ani (Atract-), Alpes Atrectianae insc., see CIL 12 p. 20, 5 p. 757; CIL 12.80, cf. REA 14, 1912, 55-59 and 39, 1937, 366 (a different reading, Adanates, Keune in PW s.v. Sauincates), AcS 1.271, 3. 730

Axima (Ceutronum) cl., TP, Rav., num., also a divine name; later called Forum Claudii; apparently the form contains the usual superlative ending -sima. Aime

Bergintrum TP, IA, Rav. Bourg (Saint Maurice)

Cana (Venusta) NG, AcS 3. 1070

Ceutrones (or -ae) cl., inscc. (CIL 12.113, cf. REA 14, 1912, 188); Ceutronicae (Alpes) Pl.

Cremonis iugum cl., cf. pers. Cremonius 5 above, Monte Cramont (cf. Grimsel: AcS 1. 1164?)

Local and Divine Names

Darantasia (Tar-) TP, IA, NG, num., Ennod.; mutatio Darentiaca (REA 20, 1918, 198, mod. Daraize, after H. Ferrand in Bull. de l'Acad. Delphinale 9, 1914-1917, Grenoble 1917, p. 340) It. Burd. 554.6 (Cuntz, p. 87), but if this identification is correct the item is mis-placed in It. Burd.; Tarentaise

Druentia fl., cl.; Druenticus (nauta) inscc.; Durontia, Durentia in ASS (see AcS 1.1321), Durance (Pokorny Urg. 37)

Graiae (Alpes) cl., ?Graioceli cl. BG 1.10.4 (v.l. Grai Oceli), Graius mons. cl., saltus (Zwicker, FHRC 38. 23)

Isara fl. cl., Isère

Medulli cl., insc.

?Sauatio Rav. (an Stabatio, cf. 7 above?)

?Sebagini Cic. pro Quinctio 25. 80 (Cebennas cl. Hirschfeld)

11   Further Modern Local Names

Arc fl., Chamonix, Forclez-du-Prarion, Lans le Bourg, Modane, Saillans, Saint Sorlin d'Arve, Salins, Verney

12   (ii) Divine Names

Aximus CIL 12.100 (Aime)

Graius (Hercules), numen Graium, arae Herculeae FHRC 38.23; 47.15-17

Matronae CIL 12.100

Saluennae Matronae ILG 17

Vallis Poenina   Introduction

13   (iii) Personal Names

a. Nomina

Laudius   Vireius

14   b. Cognomina

?Carianus   Mallianus

Cladaeus lib.   Montanius

Exomnus   ?Nigria

4. Vallis Poenina

The valley of the Rhône -- from its head-waters to
its entrance into lake Geneva. Cf. CIL 12, p. 20. See
further Riv. di Stud. Lig. 9, 1943, 171-174; Zts. f.
schweiz. Arch. u. Kunstgesch. 3, 1941, 1-24, 63-76;
RELat. 19, 1941, 37-39 (AE 1945, p. 169).

mango "gallodromus" CGL 5.620.8, NdSc 1892, 68, cf.
CIL 13.8348, whatever its origin (cf. CP 42, 1947, 203),
was, it would appear, known locally in the sense of
"travelling salesman."

15   (i) Ethnic and Local Names

Acaunum (-g-), Acaunensis (-g-) in ASS and other late documents and insc. (AcS 1.13-14), cf. agaunum 178 below

Auriates (v.l. Or-) Rav.

?Bellenica Rav.

Daliterni Avien.

Drusomagus (Sedunorum) Ptol.

Ebrudunum Sapaudiae, with its classis barcariorum (cf. 158) ND, apparently (see CIL 12, p. 27) the place also called Pennolucos (-elocos, -us) TP, IA, Rav. (cf. 1 above), a Keltic equivalent of Latin Summolaco (for -u), see PID 1.451; for penn- cf. pennum (1) and Penninus below. Distinguish four places of this name, items 7, 15, 241, viz. Alpes Cottiae (Embrun), Vallis (nr. Villeneuve, Geneva), Yverdun, and Brünn

Lemannus lacus, Λημέννα Λίμνη, cl., inscc. H.-M. 92, 152

Minnodunum, -dunensis inscc. TP, IA, Moudon (Milden); on the meaning "Burg des Ziegenflusses" (?) cf. H.-M. p. 249 (Aebischer RC 44, 1927, 324)

Nantuates cl., cf. nanto 178 below; in Latin Vallenses q.v. infr.

Octodurum (-us) cl., cf. PID 1.453, Octon

Oriates: see Auriates above

(summus) Poeninus (Penn-) cl., perhaps a hybrid like Linguaglossa etc. (penninus meaning almost the same as summus), or cf. (for the formation) Pennolucos and Summolaco

Pennolucos: see Ebrudunum above

(Alpes) Poeninae (Penn-) inscc., cl.

(Vallis) Poenina (Penn-): see Vallis below. On the spelling Poen- see my Foundations of Roman Italy 158

Rhodanus fl., cl., Rhône and Rodden

Sapaudia: see Ebrudunum above; and sappinus (79), uidubium (178). Cf. REA 22, 1920, 273-82. Now Savoie

Seduni, Sedunensis cl.

Tarnaiae (v.l. -adae) TP, IA, Rav.

16

Local and Divine Names

Tauredunum Greg. Tur.,
 Tauredunensis mons
 (-tun-) Mar. Avent.
 chron. (563 A.D.)

[Vallis] Poenina CIL 12.
 118, 147; 9.3044;
 [Vallenses] ILG 20,
 NG, CIL 13.5006, 5520,
 5522, 5523, 6361;
 P.-W. 16.1684; cf.
 Poeninus, Nantuates
 above; Wallis, Valais

Varagri, Veragri cl.,
 insc.

Vberi cl., insc.

Verusager NG (i.q. Octo-
 durum)

Viromagus, TP, IA

Viuiscus (-um), Viuisci
 (Bib- CIL 13.11, 1 p.7)
 cl., inscc. (also in
 Aquitania), Vevey; cf.
 ibiscum (1)?

16   Further Modern Local Names

Clarens, Drance, Joux (cf. Iurca 19, below), Martigny,
Massonger, Promasens, Saint Saphorin, Saint Triphon, Siders
(Sierre), Sion (Sitten)

17   (ii) Divine Names

Alpes RA 26, 1927, 349 no.
 6, cf. 14, 1939, 324.
 This, the first re-
 corded dedication Al-
 pibus (cf. other names
 of mountains used also
 as divine names, e.g.
 Abnoba, Penninus, Vose-
 gus), comes from All-
 mendingen near Thun,
 but may be included

here (cf. 1, 2, 6?, 8,
 9, 15 above)

Cantismerta CIL 12.131

?Iolla "deus Montanorum"
 (v.l. Mantuanorum)
 Schol. Verg. E 3.76
 (Thilo 3.2, p. 62,
 13 ff.); on terra sig.of
 Vertault ('Ιολλο) as pers.
 name (see 282)

Personal Names

Poenina dea, Poeninus
   (deus) FHRC 30.14;
   34.31; Ioui Pynino

(Great St Bernard)
BSAF 1904, 181

Sedatus H.-M. 62

18   (iii) Personal Names

a. Nomina

Acaunensis H.-M. 55, AE
   1945.123

Cassius AE 1945.122

Coelius AE 1945.124

Caurius

Massonius (v.l. V-, S-)
   H.-M. 69

Nitonia, -ius H.-M. 66, 68

Pansius

Sassonia (V-?) H.-M. 69

Sentius

Seppius H.-M. 425

Tincius (cf. tinca 207)

Varenius

Vassonius H.-M. 66, 69?

Vinelius H.-M. 62-63

Vinia

Vintelius (for -nd-?)

19   b. Cognomina

Adnamu f.

Ambitoutos H.-M. 461

Ἀνηροέστης (-ος) cl.
   (the same is also
   called, erroneously,
   Ariouistus)

Auitiana H.-M. 66

Cantorix

Carantinus H.-M. 58, AE
   1945.122

C..enianus H.-M. 44

Personal Names

Κογκολίτανος Polyb. 2.22.2

Decumina

Deppus

Diuicianus

Iurca (cf. Ἴορκος 1, Iura?)

Matuio

Montanus H.-M. 54, AE 1945.123

Nitiogenna

Scaurus H.-M. 461

Successianus

Tefeuo CIL 12.134 (an Teđ- ?)

Turconos

Varenus

Vegetinus

Vrsulus

Remark:

Modern Switzerland represents much more than the Vallis Poenina (in which Latin uallis renders the Gaulish nantos, Latin uallenses and Germanic daliterni the Gaulish Nantuates, cf. Pauly-Wissowa 16.2, 1935, col. 1684). The territory of the Heluetii (here reckoned with Germania Superior) fell within what is now the Swiss frontier. In these two well defined territories (Poenina and the Heluetii) Keltic was doubtless the predominant language in pre-Roman times; but other idioms are not excluded from them, at least not from Vallis; and the evidence of nomenclature, both ancient and modern, shows that Keltic was or had been at some time spoken in areas of Switzerland other than these two. See Section VIII below.

54

Vallis Poenina

In remote and isolated districts Keltic seems not
to have died out before the incursions of the Alemanni
in the fifth century of our era. (See the important
article by J. H. Hubschmied in Vox Romanica 3, 1938,
pp. 48-155, with the review, by M. L. Sjoestedt-Jonval,
BSL 39, fasc. 117, 1938, pp. 113-15.) It is not astonishing, therefore, that some traces of Keltic are to be
found to this day in modern Switzerland, and it is worth
while to call attention to a few of the more striking of
them here, despite the fact that not all of them belong
specifically to the Vallis Poenina, but to the country
of the Heluetii or to other parts of Switzerland. A
large part of the evidence made available by Hubschmied
(l.c.) comes of course from the German-speaking part of
Switzerland; most of it also pursues extant items of
vocabulary or toponomy to their Keltic prototypes.
Hubschmied's argument is nearly always convincing. He
has added to our knowledge of the extent and persistence
of Keltic speech in Roman and pre-Roman Switzerland. The
examples cited below are but a few selected from his collections, for preference those in which the ancient Keltic
form is actually attested.

Translations, such as Eschental of Ὀσκέλα (Domo
d'Ossola), Hauptsee of Caput loci or Pennelocus (Summo

Vallis Poenina

lacu? cf. Sumeloc-enna?), Daliterni of Vallenses or of
Nantuates, if not its counterpart Tulingi, demonstrate
the validity of Hubschmied's contention that Keltic survived long enough to produce, with the invading Germanic,
a temporary bilingualism, unless (in the latter instance
and in others of its kind) we are to suppose that Keltic
was first supressed by Latin, not by Germanic. Hubschmied
has endeavoured also to unveil some of the phonematic and
other features of late Gaulish, parallel in part to those
found in the development of the insular Keltic dialects,
especially in the treatment of the diphthongs, of the
spirant s, and of some consonant-clusters.

In Pennelocus we have -locus gen. sg. *lokous of
the u-stem *locu- "lake," cf. Segelocus near Lincoln.
The familiar superlative formants emerge in Huemoz (in
Canton Waadt above the Rhône-valley, *ouksamo-, cf.
Clutamus, Rixsamae, Axima, Auxuma). If the modern
Alpine local name Palpuogna contains *pelpa- from *quel-
"turn" (see Vendryes' summary RC 51, 1934, 149), that at
least still points to Brythonic Keltic.

It seems clear, too, that -etum (tuccetum, rumpotinetum, uernetus, νεμητον, combretum) must be reckoned
Keltic in the Vallis Poenina (cf. Bertoldi, Vox Rom.

56

Vallis Poenina

3, 1938, 229-236) as well as in Cisalpine Gaul and in
Narbonensis. But Hubschmied's account of the Swiss
local names <u>Seewis</u> and <u>Valzifens</u> in the Bündener Ober-
land (Über Ortsnamen des Silvretta- und Samnaun-gebietes,
see Clubführer durch die Bündener Alpen 8, 1934, 421-460;
known to me only at second hand, but see RC 51, 1934,
338-339; Vox Rom. 3, 1938, 64, 114; Pokorny, Urg. 153-154,
cf. 133 n.1), <u>See-</u> in the former as standing for *sequ<u>ā</u>,
and <u>-zifens</u> in the latter for *sequiēnos (cf. Sequana,
Sequani, and redupl.*si-sk-uo, W. hysp; cf. Siscia,
Siscii 241 and perhaps Lat. siccus, Sicel σᾱυκός?), if
right, presents the highly improbable coincidence of q<u>u</u>
preserved in two different localities but in one and the
same word, and in that word only. This is incredible if
that word really contained q<u>u</u> and was also Keltic, save
on assumptions which neither comparative nor Keltic grammar is prepared to make. On the other hand, if we are
postulate I.Eu. k<u>u</u> (cf. Sabine tesqua) and not I.Eu. q<u>u</u>,
Hubschmied's explanation is confirmed by other examples
of a distinction between k<u>u</u> and q<u>u</u> (cf. Prolegomena 51,
with n. 94). For -k<u>u</u>(o)- not -q<u>u</u>(o)- see Brugmann Grds.
ed. 2, II i, 474.

For further attempts of Hubschmied to disentangle
Keltic words in the modern dialects of Switzerland see

Vallis Poenina

RC 50, 1933, 254-271 (on *bag$\overline{o}$n(o-) "forêt de hêtres,"
cf. Bagacum now Bavay), add Vox Rom. 1, 1936, 186; ib.
88-105 (on terms used in the dairy -- Ausdrücke der
Milchwirtschaft gallischer Ursprungs, see the summary
in Etudes Celtiques 2, 1937, 362-363). His article
Verkehrswege in den Alpen zur Gallierzeit nach der
Zeugnissen der Ortsnamen, Schweizerischer Lehrerzeitung
1933, 27 Jan., I know only from ZfRPh Suppl. Bd. 47-55,
1927-35, item. 1068. See also 240 Remark.

II GALLIA NARBONENSIS

Narbonensis was bounded, as we have seen (Introductory Note), on the east by the Alpine regions, almost
from the sea to lake Geneva; its northern frontier (Pl.3.
31-37; cf. PW 7.653-660; Grenier, Mnl. 1.130) ran along
the southern side of the lake, then followed the Rhône,
from Geneva almost as far as Vienne, just north of which
it crossed the Rhône and followed the line of the Cévennes
to a point south of the upper waters of the Tarn; thence
the frontier turned north-west (thus excluding the Ruteni,
who belonged to Aquitania), and west as far as the junction
of the Tarn and the Garonne, whence it ran due south almost in a direct line, until it reached the Pyrenees.

Within this area we may further distinguish that
part of it which, between 76 and 49 B.C., was subject to
the Greek city of Massilia, namely the coastal region as
far west as Agáthe and northwards, between the Rhône and
the western boundary, as far as Vienne. This is a veri-
table "Gallia graeca," (i.e. a Hellenistic rather than
Hellenic Gaul; distinguish Gallograeci, -ia of Asia Minor);
and Varro (ap. Hieron. epist. ad Gal. 2, praef., quoted
AcS 1.1924, 41-43) reported that Greek, Latin, and Keltic
were all spoken in Massilia, a statement confirmed (and

broadened) by the presence not only of Latin and Keltic
inscriptions (CIL 12 and the present work), but also of
Greek inscriptions (IG 14.2424-2537; CIL 12.3406, 3672,
5690.138 sqq., 5691.3, 5696.22), of Greek and Latin bilingual inscriptions (CIL 12.174, 306, 1038, 1277, 1686,
4015), of what looks like a Keltic and Latin bilingual
(ib. 3044; see Note xiv b below), of one with a Greek
word written in the Latin alphabet (ib. 5687.38), and
of one with a Gaulish divine name written in Greek letters
(ib. 5693.12), exactly like the majority of the Gaulish
inscriptions of Narbonensis. Livy's remark (21.32.10) on
the uniformity of language in Narbonensis and the Alpine
regions (he clearly means Gaulish) is not inconsistent
with the comment of Polybius (2.16), who refers merely
to different tribes, not to different dialects on opposite
sides of the Alps. It is noteworthy also that Sicilian
influences have been traced there (see Centenaire SAF,
Recueil de Mémoires 1904, 61 ff.), the more so since I
have noted some six or seven glosses common to Sicel and
Gaulish, some of them clearly Keltic words that had somehow got into Sicily (perhaps, however, through the mercenaries employed by Dionysius of Syracuse, see PID 2.168
n.2), others items which may have gone from Sicily to
Gaul, one or two possibly a common inheritance. It is
not to be hastily assumed, however, that Greek products

or imitations of thom found in the interior of Gaul, at
least along the middle Rhine, had spread from Massilia
rather than from the Danube route (Grenier ap. Frank,
Economic Survey 3, 1937, 423, criticizing de Navarro,
Antiquity 2, 1928, 423-442; cf. Jacobsthal and Neuffer,
Préhistoire 2, 1933, 49 on de Navarro's later paper,
Antiquity 4, 1930, 130). But it is from this part of
Narbonensis, and chiefly from the southern half of it,
that a large number of our dialect inscriptions have
come, so that less stress is to be put upon the testimony of glosses and of proper names.

Moreover, with hardly an exception, these dialect
inscriptions are written in the Greek alphabet; and it
is clear from this peculiarity to what we must attribute
the unequal geographical distribution of our texts, namely
the limited knowledge of writing before the advent of
Roman power, and with it, of the Latin language as well
as of the Latin alphabet. It hardly needed Christianity,
save in the less accessible parts of Narbonensis (see G.
de Manteyer's papers cited in REA 28, 1926, 28), to
bring knowledge of these (on the Roman roads of the
Dauphiné see H. Ferrand, BA 1914, 3-37). How far this
Latin was affected by a pre-Roman, and even pre-Keltic,
substratum is a question that has often been discussed;

and if the peculiarities of the langue d'oc are in any degree due to such a substratum, then we must recognize that its extent exceeded the boundaries of Narbonensis and included a good deal of Aquitania also (see A. Brun Rev. de Ling. Rom. 12, 1936, 165-251, especially 192-246). The paper of Funel (L'article celtique dans les parlers provençaux, Nice Historique 1913, 5-54; Mont., Suppl. 1, 44.9214) I have not seen.

Massilia itself was ringed by a number of fortified oppida which have been ascribed to a mixed Kelto-Ligurian population (see H. de Gérin-Ricard, RA 3, 1934, 226 ff.; 4, 191-194); further inland was another series of settlements, some of which are the sites of a number of dialect inscriptions. M. de Gérin-Ricard (Prouincia 14, 1934, 38-88; cf. REA 37, 1935, 48) has described one such oppidum (Vieux-Port) cf. 400-100 B.C., that was encircled by Gauls c. 125 B.C. If this is correct, the question of dialect in older inscriptions (I mean as between Ligurian and Gaulish) will have been re-opened. With these we begin; for in Narbonensis the unit of political organization was the municipality, elsewhere in Gaul the canton (cf. Nesselhauf, Verwaltung, Abh. d. Preuss. Akad. der Wiss., 1938. 2, 5; Mommsen Provinces 1.80).

Gallia Narbonensis

The old collection of texts, both literary and epigraphic, by Ernestus von Herzog (Galliae Narbonensis prouinciae Romanae historia, Leipzig 1864) is still valuable.

Note iii

On a silver cup found at Belgentier (Var), 22 km. from Toulon.

ουενικοιμεδου

(or ουενιχ -).

Published by Blanchet CRAcInscBL 1933, 365, who sees the Greek name Νικομήδης, which, in itself, would be likely enough in view of Greek influence in Narbonensis (to the references already given, add, for example V. Bertoldi Antichi correnti di cultura greca nel mediterraneo occidentale, La Parola del Passato 1, 1946, 33-68; or, on the archaeological side, the Repertoire archéologique announced in REA 39, 1937, 363, cf. 257). But a Keltic Venic(h?)oi Medou (i.e. -ū) or medu would be easily defended, and would not leave an unexplained ουε .

20   1. Basses-Alpes

Keltic or Kelto-Latin insc. from Volonne (on the Durance, west of Digne); on the fragment of an altar, 0.29 by 0.25m.

63

Basses-Alpes

20 ctd.

<u>ma</u>]trabo |]tabo

CA 6, 1937, 24 no. 79. For a clearly Keltic name at
Volonne see 25 below (Venimara).

Remark:

    I see no reason to suppose that the quasi-inscc. on
a bas-relief of Montsalier (divine figures?), apparently

(a)   ]τουδ[|]παπ[|]πυσ|

(b)   ?]πυ.[??

must be Keltic. But they are not, in their present form,
if they ever were, articulate; REA 5, 1903, 298 (cf. CA
6, 20, no. 62); (b) is written serpentine boustrophedon
as compared with (a). See now P. Jacobsthal Early Celtic
Art, Oxford 1944, 1 p. 7, and 2 Plate 6 (Catalogue 1, p.
165), who thinks the inscc. ancient, but "not contemporary"
with the sculpture. The letters have finials, and υ is V,
σ is ⟩ . See also Espérandieu, Recueil des Bas-reliefs de
la Gaule no. 36; Jahreshefte des Öst. Arch. Inst. 26, 1930,
37, fig. 25.

      (c) But it may be worth-while to call atten-
tion to a fragment of pottery from Valensole (CA 6.2, no
7), which begins

piales| |

since this is evidently the Greek φιάλη, like the manifestly Greek names of earthenware at La Graufesenque,

Basses-Alpes

(90-131 below), less likely a personal name.

      (d) Not much more significant is the insc.,
also from Valensole, first published CA l.c., after a
copy by H. de Gérin-Ricard, apparently

    ]pis .... ucicurai | caugpriioi | dp. qrsiimi

(for carisimi at the end?); Cicarus, Criciro, Crucuro
are common on terra-sigillata (see Oswald's Index, East
Bridgford, 1931), and compare the gloss gigarus (158),
and the divine names Cicollus (181, 236), Cicinus (23).
But in the first line the division may come at curai.

      (e) Definitely interesting, as showing the
same style of document as the pottery-lists from La
Graufesenque (90 sqq. below) is an inscribed tegula
found at Thorame-Haute (Colmars) ca. A.D. 200, see CA
6.11, no. 20, which reads

        supposuit furno III Idus Iulias | die

        solis | abuit (sic) tegulas   imbrices

      (f) CIL 12.372 (Riez)

        ceruesia

See 178 below.

Basse-Alpes

21   Local Names

(References are to CA 6, 1937, by page and number, unless otherwise indicated).

Alabonte(m) 31, cf. CIL 12, p. 104; AcS 1.73, 3.545; Allemont

Alaunium CIL 11.3281-84 TP, IA

Alebece v. Reii infr.

Banonum 20.58

Bodiontici Pl.

Catuiacia 18.54; IA

Δίνια, Dinia 9.16; Ptol., Pl.; Dinia Lub. [CIL 12.6037a; Digne

[Aquae] Griselicae (Griseli AcS) 2.5; Gréoulx

Reii [Apollinares] 3.8, cf. CIL 13.6913, AE 1935.15; Alebece

(Alaebaece), Reiorum (cf. Albici, Ἀλβίοικοι 80 below, and the gloss alpes 1 above?) cl.; in late documents R(h)eg(i)enses and Regium (Galliae) v. AcS 2.1114; c(olonia) u(etus) R(eiorum) CIL 12.360 and H. de Gérin-Ricard, Bull. Soc. Sc. Litt. des Basses-Alpes 22, 1928-29, 237; BSAF 1899, 307; now Riez (cf. Ries, Switzerland)

Σέντιοι Ptol.

Stablo uilla, now Estoublon; REA 44, 1942, 87

22   Further Modern Names
                (cf. CA 6.33)

In medieval sources: Archanthioscus, Catalioscus, Marzoscu; modern Albiosc, Aubignosc, Briasc, Le Brusc, Curiusque, Demandolsc, Manosque, Peyresq, Velhosc, Venascle all show the familiar -sc-.

Others: Castellar(d), Soleilhas, Tabourne, Tavernoulas, Villard (or -ars).

Divine and Personal Names

23   Divine Names

Alaunius CIL 12.1517; cf.
21 above; 179, 211, 243,
244 below

(Mars) Beladon(n)is CIL
12.503; ILG 219, 220

(Mars) Bruatus ib. 221;
cf. 80 ad fin., 82
below

(Mars) Carrus Cicinus CIL
12.356, cf. Cicinenses
6.9103a, Cicollus (181,
236); and the divine
names Garre (C-) 86
and Crarus 82, modern
local names Le Caire,
Gar (AcS 1.815); gloss
*carra (ga-) 1 above

Cicinus v. Carrus

(Nymphae) Griselicae CIL
12.361, cf. 21 above

(Mars) Nabelcus ILG 22 (cf.
CIL 12.1169-1171`;
commonly counted Keltic,
and as related to Lat.
nebula, Greek νέφος
(CA 7.19, 40), but
Semitic forms would be
as easily compared

Osdiauae CIL 12.362

?Reia (mater), cf. local
names; doubtfully so read
by H. de Gérin-Ricard,
see REA 34, 1932, 291;
but Reii.... in CA 6.
5,10 (cf. AE 1931.50)

Personal Names

24   a. Nomina

Cael(i)us CA 6.23, 74

Kareius 12.983

Connius ILG 219

Linaria CA 6.18, 53

Oltini[us] CIL 12.369

Siccius CA 6.18, 56;
ILG 221

Vectimarius ib. 6 (BA
1911, ccxxi)

?Ven(ticius) ILG 220

?Venni... CIL 12.370

Viriatius ib. 1514

Vitrasius CA 6.2, 5

Personal Names

25   b. Cognomina

Avitus CIL 3.7397

Birro ILG 227

Catus CA 6.23, 74

?Cintugnatus ILG 40

Cursus ib. 228

?Esaludi (Tesallydi?) CA
    6.8, 9; CIL 12.5754

†Gisberga ib. 16.44

?Grae... |ipo ib. 8.13
    (or divine?)

Λίγυς IG 14.2427 (cf.
    Ligur CIL 13.2197,
    -ius 1921)

Mociantus ILG 228

Mogetiuarus CIL 12 add.
    378 (p.810). But cf.
    Mogitumarus 83 below

Pandus ib. 2926 (cf.
    Pandusa: AcS 2.925)

Pedullo CIL 12.349

?Pefirus ILG 224

Premicca CA 6.18, 53; cf.
    Praemiaca 153 below?

Seranus 12.5753

Suramus ib. 362

]somni CA 6.25, 81

?Tesallydi v. Es- above

Titullus ILG 229

Venimara ib. 228

]ugenonis g.sg., CA 6.25,
    81

Veronus ib. 5.13

Vettius CIL 13.6193

?Viriatus CA 6.15, 41 (but
    see cogn.)

Vitio 12.350

Vrsus ILG 219

    CA 6,20.63 reports a number of names from lamps,
said to be common in other parts of Provence, but some
of them not reported by Holder or by Oswald (Index),
e.g. Hoscri, Pulli, Strobil[. Cf. CA 7.126,271; 91,3;
126, 268.

Inscription of Ventabren

2. Bouches-du-Rhône

Paul Masson ed. Bouches-du-Rhône: Enc. Départementale
(numerous contributors) 1, 1932 (Les Origines), 4 i, 1932
(Archéologie) gives useful information of a general character; cf. 2, 1924 (L'Antiquité); RA 3, 1934, 140-141.

26

A pyramid-shaped block of red stone, discovered in
1902, at Ventabren, seen by me in the Musée d'Archéologie
at Marseille (Château Borély), inventory no. 239 of 10
Aug. 1904; first published by H. de Gérin-Ricard and
Arnaud d'Agnel, CRAcInscBL 1903, 58-61 (with discussion
by H d'Arbois de Jubainville, 108-111, facsimile); CA
5, 1936, 91.278; Arch. Anz. 19, 143.

32.75 in. high; 15.75 in. wide at the bottom of the
inscribed face, 18.5 in. at the top; 12.75 in. thick at
the top, 10.75 in. at the bottom on the left; 12.5 in.
(bottom), 13.75 (top) on the right. Edges bevelled,
corners now broken.

The insc. is complete, letters 1.5 to 1.25 in. high
(except ο), with finials; ε is Ϝ. Date: ca. 150 B.C. or
a little earlier. Do. 149, 6 bis.

ΟΥΕΝΙΤΟΥΤΑ | ΚΟΥΑΔΡΟΝΙΑ

Note iv

A fragmentary insc., also in the Château Borély, inventory no. 240, discovered at the same time and place as
26; 18.625 in. high, 15.5 in. wide (bottom) to 18 in. (top)
— owing to a break; 13 in. thick; letters 1.5 to 1.75 in.
tall.

uectit[us | birac[i

ILG 97

Inscription of Alleins

27
    An almost square block of white limestone (14 in.
by 13.375 in.), now built into the wall of the baptistry
in the parish church at Alleins, said to have been discovered not far away; first published by G. Lafaye, Bull.
épigr. de la Gaule 2, 1882, 127, when it was "encastrée
à l'angle d'une maison." The corners are indented after
the modern style of a mural tablet, and the stone was
originally much larger, perhaps a pyramid, like those of
Saint-Remy. But the text is complete (blank spaces 2 in.
at r. in lines 1, 2; space for five or six letters line 4
at end, and room for two more rows of writing beneath it);
seen by me.

    Letters 1 to 1.25 in. tall, not deeply cut. Puncts
inside each ο (except the first in line 2), an apparent
interpunct in line 3 (unless it belongs to (σ); the punct
in line 1 after γ, if original, must be accidental.
Characteristic letter forms Α, Κ and κ, ε . No finials.

κογ·γενν | ολιταvo | σ· καρθιλιτα | vιοσ

    Reading everywhere certain except in line 3, where
the cross-bar of θ is very faint and may not be ancient
(Καροι- ?).

        Cf. Κογκολίτανος 19 above (Polyb. 2.22.2).
        CA 5.114, 373; Do. 149, 6

Graffiti of Eyguières

Note iv bis

A defixio (?), engraved on a silver plate, discovered before 1870, at LaRocque d'Anthéron (c. 10 miles east
of Alleins), see Rev. Epigr. 5, 1903-1908, 7; the reading
is quite uncertain.

]tialniarduinn[?

ILG 75

28

A patera discovered in the necropolis of Mont-Menu,
near Saint-Pierre de Vence (Commune d'Eyguières), associated with the oppidum of Costefère (cf. CA 5.115);
graffito:

μα

P. de Brun, Note sur la nécropole gallo-grecque du
Mont-Menu, (in Mem. de l'Institut Historique de Provence,
Marseilles, 1931), a reference which I take from Rolland,
Cahiers d'hist. et d'arch., Nimes 6, 1933, 285 n. 31.

29

Another graffito "sur pot. italique," now in the
museum at Arles; from Servane (Eyguières), CA 5.119, 393
(not "Mouries," Cahiers l.c., n. 30).

Κρ

Inscription of Eyguières

Note v

A small plaque of lead, engraved on both sides in
cursive Greek script, discovered at Eyguières in 1899
(BA 1899, cxii cf. cxxiiii) on the plateau of Costefère;
in the possession of its discoverer M. Auguste Perret
at Eyguières, by whose courtesy I was allowed to examine
it. CA 5.116, 381.

3.2 by 2.75 in., not more than .03 in. thick; letters
from .25 to .375 in. in height. First published by
Camille Jullian REA 2, 1900, 47-55, but the writing is
too carelessly engraved and too confused for confidence
in any transcription. I compared Jullian's text with
the original, and offer the following copy with all re-
serve:

In (a) line 5 is actually written at the end, on top
of the last four letters of line 4. In (b) line 1 the
strokes added to μ (and taken as ς′ by Jullian) are

Inscription of Les Baux

probably accidental; I can make nothing of the three
symbols in line 5 (after α), which Jullian optimistically
read $\varsigma'\varsigma'\beta$ (or $\epsilon\alpha\beta$).

$\sigma\mu\epsilon\rho$- and $-\rho\iota\xi$ (b) lines 1, 4 are familiar in
Keltic names. Otherwise the text is so uncertain so to
render all guesses about its meaning totally misplaced.
In (a) $\epsilon\sigma\sigma o$ line 2 as a demonstrative pronoun, and (line 1)
$\sigma\iota\gamma\lambda\alpha o$ "sigillum" are remotely possible. In (b) line 2
for $\gamma\lambda\lambda\iota\alpha$ read perhaps $\gamma\alpha\lambda\iota\alpha$, and in lines 6 and 7 $\sigma\int\tau o\chi\iota$
(i.e. $\sigma\tau o$-?) appears to be repeated; 7 $\alpha\kappa\tau o\rho\gamma\iota\varrho$ "actor
Ger["(?).

Audollent 113; cf. Do., p. 43

30
"Prope ecclesiam uici dicti <u>les Baux</u> ... in cippo
rotundo fracto," Lenormant, after a copy made in 1856 by
H. Revoil, Rh. Mus. 21, 1866, 223; repeated by Héron de
Villefosse, Bull. Mon. 45, 1879, 52-53. Unlike the next
item, this seems not to have been repeated in IG 14, or
elsewhere.

$]\iota\cdot\sigma\mu\epsilon\rho[$ | $]\mu\alpha\tau[$

There is nothing to show the language of the insc.,
but it might well be a fragment of a text similar to those
of Saint-Remy and elsewhere in the Bouches-du-Rhône. Les
Baux is a few miles south of Saint-Remy-de-Provence; traces
of an ancient oppidum (older than the end of the third

Inscriptions of Les Baux

century B.C., see RA 4, 1934, 193) have been found there.

31
    "Inter rudera eiusdem loci in cippo rotundo prope
uiam quae ducit ad uicum dictum Paradou," Lenormont and
de Villefosse loc. cit.

αχιτοσ

CA 5.202, 521, IG 14.2478 (if genuine, not Greek). This
may be incomplete, like 30 above.

32
    An amphora found c. 1888 at Les Baux ("cimetière
de la Catalane"), now in the Musée des Alpilles (Saint-
Remy); first published BSAF 1890, 77-79, whence AcS 2.
1448. Often repeated since then, cf. CA 5.203, 521;
seen by me. Graffito:

σε|γομαρ[

in which σ and γ are scarcely distinguishable. F. Benoit,
"Les Bringasses," Préhistoire 5, 1936, 120-139.

Saint-Remy-de-Provence

About a mile south of the modern Saint-Remy-de-
Provence, in the rising ground of the foot-hills of the
Alpilles (or Alpines), stood the ancient city of Glanum
(Pl., Γλανόν Ptol., Glanici 12.1005, γλανικων num.; and,
Actes du Congrès de Nîmes Paris, 1932, Association
Guillaume Budé, p. 137, γλανιχου, later, in TP and IA,
also Clanum; cf. AcS 1.2025), belonging to the tribe of
the Salluuii. A colony of Marseille, it shared in a high
degree the Gallo-Greek civilization of the third and second
centuries B.C., to the latter of which presumably the
inscriptions given below are to be assigned. Various
objects, among them Massiliot coins, have been unearthed
there sporadically; and more systematic excavations conducted during the second and third decades of this century
have revealed many others in the ruins of a Gallo-Greek
temple, of baths, houses, tombs, aqueducts, and other
structures.

See CA 5, 1936, 204-212. 529, with the map B (p. 192)
and plan C (208), and ample bibliographical notes to which
reader must refer. These notes are gratefully mentioned
here, since they make it unnecessary to repeat a mass of
references which I had gathered myself. Only occasionally
do I give references to sources cited in CA l.c.; but a
few additional items are of course added.

Glanum was destroyed by Caesar in 49 B.C., and none
of the dialect inscriptions from that site can be of

later date, if indeed they are later than c. 125-75 B.C.
The smashing of Keltic monuments is usually assigned to
Caesar's times; but can it be shown that similar destruction was not carried out sporadically, and at some
sites at least, by the Cimbri and Teutones? Subsequently
the city was rebuilt by the Sixth Legion stationed at
Arles (founded in 46 B.C.), some 15 miles to the south-
east. The inhabitants moved to the modern site on the
plain under the late empire.

Among the stones of Saint-Remy-de-Provence bearing
Keltic inscriptions, now mostly gathered into the Musée
des Alpilles at Saint-Remy, a number share certain
characteristics. These great monoliths, tall square
columns, surmounted by a pyramid, are usually ornamented
on one or more faces near the top, and on the pyramid
itself, with linear triangular designs (see for example
the Plate in Bull. Monumental 7, 1879, at p. 38; most
recently, H. Rolland, Bull. de la Soc. préhist. française
32, 1935, 647). The insc. is sometimes cut over this
design, or the design may take the place of the insc.
The stelae are clearly funerary, and usually the inscc.
give nothing more than the names of the dead with whose
tomb or remains the stone is associated.

Cf. H. Hubert, Stèles funeraires gauloises en Ligurie,
Paris (Leroux, 1909) 3 pp. (Mont. I 1917, 311.5510);
H. Rolland, La Maison hellénistique de Glanon, Bergerac

(J. Castenet, 1932), reviewed in RA 1, 1933, 277. An
uninscribed stele from St. Remy, BSAF 1933, 171-173.

In addition to the inscribed specimens listed
below, there are those of Cavaillon (50-55), and a number
of others discovered at various times at Les Baux, said
to have been destroyed (cf. 27 above). In north Italy
we have similar monuments from Levo (PID 2.107-108), and
some of the pyramid-shaped Venetic inscribed stones are
essentially of the same type, though much smaller in size.
It is believed that the pyramid has been developed from
the house-urn with sloping roof, and Jacobsthal (Schumacher
Festschrift 1930, 189-194, Pl. 20-21) derives the specimens
of Provence from an Etruscan source. There is evidence
in fibulae of the Certosa type discovered near Saint-Remy
and in ruins of hut-dwellings to show that Provence was
in contact with northern Italy by the sixth century B.C.
(cf. REA 37, 1935, 347). A somewhat different view would
connect the stelae of Provence more nearly with those of
Cisalpine Gaul (ib. 38, 1936, 343), but they in their
turn are ultimately Etruscan in inspiration.

The stelae both of Les Baux and of Saint-Remy are
dated by Rolland (Cahiers d'Histoire et d'Archéologie 6,
1933, 288) c. 150 B.C., on the basis of associated objects
from the graves to which they presumably belonged (late

Inscriptions of St-Remy

La Tène III). Similarly at Cavaillon, the pre-Roman

sepultures, with which the inscribed stelae found there

belong, are assigned to La Tène III (Déchelette Mnl. 4,

ed. 2, 1927, 560 n. 2 [on p. 561]). This date may be

accepted as an upper limit; the late Hellenistic lamps

give us a lower limit 100-50 B.C., so that c. 125-75 B.C.

would be a reasonable dating of the inscc., with which

the epigraphic evidence, especially the forms of the

letters α, β, ϵ, σ, well accords.

33
    A lime-stone stele nearly 9 ft. high in all, 16 in.
by 18 in. at the base, 14 by 11 in. at the top, where it
terminates in a pyramid 14 in. high. Found in 1836 "au
Nord du quartier de la Galline" (or Galine) near Saint-
Remy-de-Provence "le long de l'ancienne voie Aurelienne"
(Rolland), formerly "in the old collection of the Marquis
de Lagoy" (P. de Brun), now in the public collections in
the Musée des Alpilles at Saint-Remy, seen by me.

The front face of the pyramid has an incised

triangular pattern; both front and back faces of the

stele have a St Andrew's cross similarly incised a few

inches from the top. Then, just beneath this, the insc.,

letters 3 in. tall, except o (1.5 in.)

ουριττα | κοσηλο | υσκονι | οσ

78

Inscriptions of St-Remy

The text is certain and complete. Slight finials.
A (α) and C (σ) are characteristic letter forms.

First published by Lenormont Rh. Mus. 21, 1866, 223
and frequently since then; Do. 148.4; CA 5.204, 527;
Jacobsthal op. cit. 191 (A), Pl. 20.1.

34
Another lime-stone stele, originally like the last
item, but now broken at the top, and only 5 ft. 3 in. in
height. Discovered in 1836 at "Le Mas de Bigot, au
quartier de la Galline," and also at one time in the
collection of de Lagoy, now in the Musée des Alpilles
(Saint-Remy); seen by me.

17 in. by 7.13 in. at the bottom, 12.5 in. by 6 in.

at the top. A stele so far from square, i.e. wider than

it is thick, is held to be the more ancient, since it is

closer to the pattern of the hut-urns. First published

by Lenormant l.c. An incised line runs across the front,

at the top; just beneath it, the insc.

βιμμοσ | λιτουμ | αρεοσ.

Letters 3 in. tall (except o 2 in.); μ is $\mathcal{M}$ (third

letter) and M(elsewhere); but the fifth stroke of that μ

may be accidental, or (less likely) the remains of the

St Andrew's cross deliberately cut deeper in modern times.

Not N γγα (Dottin), or μυ or νυ (CIL 12, p. 127),

or μι (Rolland). ρ is P, ϵ is Є, α is A, punct at end; and in the preceding letter ο (Θ, not O).

Do. 148.5; Jacobsthal l.c. (E), Pl. 21.1; CA, l.c.

35

Lime-stone stele, discovered in 1925 near the Pont de la Pistole, west of Saint-Remy, not far from the uia Aurelia (cf. 33), and presented to the Musée des Alpilles (seen there by me) by M. Bremond "agent-voyer, à qui l'on en doit la découverte."

6 feet 2.5 in. by 17 in. wide by 19 in. thick at the bottom, 13 in. by 13.75 in. at the top, just before it narrows into the surmounting pyramid (each face an equilateral triangle, 13 in. along each edge) 10.5 in. in height. There is an incised triangular panel within the front face of the pyramid and a bisecting vertical line within it. Near the top of the front face of the stele, the insc., very faintly incised, the reading of which is uncertain. In the darkened room of the museum, in which I was obliged to observe it, I did not observe the final ξ of line 2, which photographs reveal (‡).

σιγο...[| τιορειξ | εσκεγγορ | .ουι[(?)

Inscriptions of St-Remy

Letters from .625 in. (γ, line 3) to 1.5 in. (o, line 2, circular; lozenge-shaped lines 3, 4) to 2 in. (τ line 2) high, and even a little taller (σ C in line 3); the insc. is engraved once more over the double-axe or St Andrew's cross pattern.

Before ου in line 4, probably ι or o is to be read. But is -ουι a dative ending (-ui)? I formerly so took it, with -ει (read now -ειξ) in line 2 (cf. Thurneysen Gram., 1946, 193; Pisani Riv. IGI 17, 1933, 189 n. 1; Arch. Glott. Ital. 27, 1935, 168). Both would be welcome, but unusual, forms; for these stones usually give a nom. sg., not a dat. sg. in memoriam. It is hardly possible to take -ι as a genitive sg., for o-stems in -ūo- are unknown. If ου is u, then -uos is a possible nom., gen. -uī. Moreover a dative -ui (from -ōi), common in Lepontic, is not definitely attested for Gaulish (perhaps Cicollui?). But Lepontic has the dative construction (rarely the nominative), pala being written or understood. Most probably line 4 is incomplete, everything after ι being illegible (restore δεδε or βρατουδε , cf. 39?).

HSCP 44, 1933, 227-229; Jacobsthal l.c. (D), Pl. 20.2-3; CA 5.214, 534(4). I have not seen the supplementary notes of Rolland in Courrier Numismatique 1933, nos. 33-34, the only file in this country (of the American Numismatic Society) lacking those parts.

Inscriptions of St-Remy

36

Another funerary stele from the Mas du Cloud in the district called La Galline, Saint-Remy. Now in the Musée des Alpilles; 2.77m. high by 0.32m. by 0.31m. (top) and 0.40m. by 0.40m. (base). Pyramid and incised lines, diagonal on the front.

Previously considered uninscribed (like two others at Saint-Remy); a weathered, all but illegible, text was detected by H. Rolland, see Cahiers d'histoire et d'Archéologie, Nimes, 6, 1933, 279

$$]\alpha[\qquad]\upsilon[\qquad]\rho\epsilon\iota\xi \quad ?$$

CA 5.214, 534 (1)

37

The fragment (moulded upper part) of an altar, 0.16m. by 0.24m. by 0.15m., with a fragmentary text. Discovered during the official excavations (Beaux-Arts) of 1930 at the site of Glanum. Apparently broken in ancient times and used "comme moellon, dans le mur est, ou mieux, peut-être les étuves -- du Balneum romain de Glanum" (Rolland), the date of which is put shortly after 45 B.C. by a coin of L. Plautius Plancus found embedded in the mortar of the east wall. But the altar must be much older than that, as the alphabet shows (А not A, Υ not Υ, Ϟ not Ϲ line 3 [?]), so in 38 below Γ not Γ . Doubtless it was

Inscriptions of St-Remy

broken during the destruction of Glanum by Caesar in 49
B.C., if not earlier by the Teutones. Now in the Musée
des Alpilles at Saint-Remy, seen by me.

$$\kappa \underset{\cdot}{\alpha} \mu o \upsilon \lambda \alpha \tau \iota \vert \alpha \underset{\cdot}{o} \upsilon \tau \rho o \upsilon \iota. \vert. \upsilon \iota \upsilon \underset{\cdot\cdot}{o} \sigma$$

I take the second letter of line 2, like the fifth
(and first?) of line 3, apparently mere puncts, as o ,
which in line 1 and line 2 (sixth letter) is much smaller
than the other letters. In line 3 what looks like a
double punct stands before the first ∨.

CA 5.209,529 (8); Rolland l.c. 273-302, Pl. 6(a);
Congrès de Nîmes, 1932, 147; Saint-Remy de Provence,
Bergerac 1934, 53 and 57; P. de Brun Prouincia (Revue
trimestrielle d'histoire et d'archéologie provençales
publiée par la Société de statistique et d'archéologie
de Marseille et de Provence) 15, 1935, 251; BSAF 1931,
192 (Καμοφλατι|ασυτρονι|νινα).

38

Another altar, lime-stone, also re-used for secular
purposes in ancient times, apparently in the rebuilding
of a house on the north side of the Roman baths at Glanum,
in the wall of which it was discovered still embedded in
1931.

0.26m. by 0.13m. by 0.03m. On the top, a small

Inscriptions of St-Remy

quadrangular depression. Now at Saint-Remy, Musée des Alpilles, seen there by me.

$$\epsilon \pi o \nu \alpha [$$

CA l.c. (9); Rolland l.c., Pl. 6(b); Congrès de Nimes, p. 148; id., Saint-Remy de Provence, 53; cf. REA 35, 1933, 310.

39
Presumably also an altar, from Saint-Remy, discovered in the sixteenth century, now lost.

$$]o\nu \quad oo\upsilon o\pi \delta \iota o\upsilon \iota \cdot \beta \rho \alpha \tau o\upsilon [$$

The third letter is given as $\odot$.

Do. 148.3; CIL 12, p. 127 (reading $\iota \iota$ instead of π); CA 5.209, 529(27).

40
A small piece of lime-stone, c. 5 in. square, said to have been found near Saint-Remy, seen by me in the Musée des Alpilles. Too fragmentary to make the dialect certain, a text possibly containing the form $\alpha \upsilon o \tau$ is worth reporting:

$$? \ ]\alpha \upsilon o\tau . [\qquad \qquad | \ \nu \iota [$$

Inscriptions of St-Remy

ひ O   both damaged at the top, but ○ is certain and ひ

probable; ⊤ (?) is more doubtful, the cross-bar being

missing

HSCP 44, 1933, 230-231

Note vi

Four blocks of soft lime-stone from the aqueduct
that served the Hellenistic buildings of Glanum; discovered in 1928 along the highway between the Jewish
cemetery and the Vallon de Gros.   The inscc. are too
brief to be of linguistic significance, and may be no
more than mason's marks.

Each block is c. 2.35m. by 0.32m. by 0.32m.   The
upper surface was excavated to form a channel c. 0.18m.
deep and the same width.   Only three are inscribed, and
of these two (a) and (c) have been removed to the Musée
des Alpilles at Saint-Remy.

(a) ठ८   (b) K   (c) ριK

Deeply cut in letters 0.16m. tall.

Rolland l.c., 272-275 and 297-299 (where an interpretation as numerals is suggested); Congrès de Nîmes,
147; CA 5.213, 532; Rolland, Saint-Remy-de-Provence 52,
where rik is interpreted as Keltic for "canal" (sic);
BSAF 1930, 92 the text is given as ठ८ ρικ .

41
 A patera of red-ware, discovered in 1929 in a grave
near the uia Aureliana; covered with a black varnish and
restored from the many fragments into which it had been
broken. Now in the Musée des Alpilles, seen by me.

 9.75 in. in diameter; at the edge, on the rim itself, two letters 1 in. and .50 in. high respectively,
apparently the Latin alphabet,

 (a) su

Rolland takes this as λF (i.e. λ is my u, F my s) and
interprets it as a numeral.

 Then, 3.5 in. to the right, much smaller letters
(.20 in. high), the graffito

 (b) $\sigma \mu \epsilon \rho [$

 CA 5.212, 529 (D iii); Rolland, Cahiers d'histoire
et d'archéologie 6.1933, 283.25, Pl. V b; Jacobsthal et
Neuffer Gallia Graeca (in Préhistoire 2, 1933) 57, fig. 63.

 CA l.c. (D ii) reports a potter's mark Smertalitanus,

assigned to "at. de Germanie (?)," but it does not appear

in Oswald's Index. And many of the "names" given by P. de

Brun in Rhodania (Association des Préhistoriens et Arché-

ologues classiques et des Numismatistes du Bassin du Rhône)

1925 and 1928 are badly misread. Out of his lists I

select only Angius and Tasco on potsherds found at Saint-

Remy, both potters attributed by Oswald to South Gaul.

Graffiti of St-Remy

Remark:

From the same tomb is reported (Rolland l.c.)
a funerary urn, bearing the single letter, graffito: ʋ

42

A flat patera of red earthenware, black varnish,
10 in. in diameter, a graffito of one word, near the rim,
in letters of varying height. From a trench tomb discovered in March 1928 at le Mas du Cloud (quartier de la
Galline), Saint-Remy, lined with flat stones and covered
by two others. Now in the Musée des Alpilles, seen by me.

$$ \epsilon\beta o\upsilon\rho o\sigma $$

(σ, ᛒ β , small ○ .

CA 5.214, 534; Jacobsthal Schumacher Festschrift
189, fig. 1 a (p. 190); HSCP 44, 1933, 229-230.

43

Another (complete) patera, with a small foot; found
in the same grave; 10.5 in. in diameter. Just inside the
rim, a graffito, which I read doubtfully as

uis (?)

P. de Brun Prouincia 10, 1930, 36; Rolland Cahiers
l.c., 300 (interpreted as numerals, but seemingly confused
with 41a above).

Inscriptions of St-Remy

Note vii

(a) On a "plat, rouge brun sombre," published by
H. Rolland Prouincia 18, 1938, 201-210, fig. 8 (p. 208),
beneath the foot:

σ

(b) Two graffiti, Rolland Cahiers l.c., 285 nos.
32, 33:

(i) on an amphora   (ii) on the fragment of a vase

    lae   ]κου

(c) On an altar

        Siluano | ∧ ∧ ∧ | u s l m

CA 5.209, 12 (CIL XII 1000)

(d) On two fragments of stone, reported by Formigé,
Bull. Mon. 1931, 192:

(i)   (ii)

        συ   πρ

(e) Jacobsthal o.c. 191.6 reports an "illegible"
graffito on the base of a lamp, possibly

                    υι (?)
Cf. Préhistoire 2, 34 n. 5(i)

88

Inscriptions of St-Remy

Remark:

(i) CIL 12, p. 127 n. 4, cf. CA 5.204, 528, an insc. copied in 1856 by Lenormont (Rh. Mus. 21, 1866, 224, cf. Bull. Mon. 45, 1879, 40 n. 27): "prope Glanum in cippo quadrato iuxta uillam quae dicitur le mas de Durand,"

$$]..\upsilon\rho \,|\, \alpha\kappa\lambda \,|\, \eta o\sigma \,|\, \upsilon\epsilon\alpha $$

(A α, C σ) is usually considered Greek. But Héron de Villefosse's Ἡρακλειος (sic) Bull. Mon. l.c. is not satisfying.

(ii) RA 10, 1937, 375 reports a dedication di (sic) <u>Budeno</u> from Glanum (dibus deab[usque Espérandieu ILG 149), but di for deo casts doubt on the reading.

Addendum. H. Rolland Fouilles de Glanum, Suppl. to Gallia, Paris 1946 (AJA 52, 1948, 411) I have not seen.

An interesting confirmation of the memory of the old ties between the Gauls of the Rhône valley and the Galatians of Asia Minor is furnished by a decree of Lampsacus (195 B.C.), see Michel, Recueil d'inscriptions grecques, Paris 1900, no. 529 (B 48).

Inscription of Orgon

44

   A small piece of smooth, white limestone, discovered in Oct. 1886 at Orgon (on the south side of
Durance, opposite Cavaillon), "dans un monceau de
décombres provenant des demolitions d'une chapelle dite
de Notre-Dame;" but the ultimate source was doubtless
a Gallo-Roman temple, the existence of which is indicated by dedications to Apollo and other deities found
at the same site (CA 5.197, 492 n. 3). Since 1887 in
the Musée Calvet at Avignon (no. 1 in the catalogue by
E. Espérandieu, Inscriptions antiques du Musée Calvet
d'Avignon, Avignon Seguin, 1900, p. 7), seen there by me.
Published simultaneously in Bull. Épigr. de la Gaule 6,
1886, 296-7 and in Rev. Épigr. du Midi 2, 1884-1889, 259
no. 643; Photograph in A. Sagnier, Mémoires de l'Académie
de Vaucluse, 6, 1887, 61-69.

   18.75 in. high, 8.5 in. wide (base) narrowing to
6.5 in. (top, originally rounded, now broken), 6.5 in.
from front to back (bottom) 5.5 in. (top). Doubtless a
small altar, as the remains of the top at the front
clearly show. The text is complete (5.75 in. blank
beneath line 3).

ουνβρουμαρος|δεδεταρανοου|βρατουδε καντεμ

Fragmentary and Doubtful Inscriptions

Letters at the beginning nearly 1 in. high, but mainly .5 to .375 in., except o (.25 in. or a little larger); β is open, ρ has a small hook; A α, E ε, K κ.

At the end of line 1 o is almost closed; at the end of line 3, μ is certain (not vα Espérandieu), but the engraver may have intended to cut Ʌ (i.e. vα), and have forgotten the cross-bar.

Do. 146.1; CIL 12, p. 820; L. H. Gray Revue des Études Indo-Européennes (Bucharest) 1, 1938, 298-300. The items Mont. Suppl. 1. 9437, 9852 I have not been able to obtain.

Remark:

(1) Arles (Arelate, previously Theline, Avienus Or. mar. 690) has not yet yielded the dialect inscc. that might have been expected there. At all events the fragmentary

αΠι   (BSAF 1930, 92)

]ierodu (CA 5.191, 463);   and

? Πρει φγατης (ib. 148. 448-9, 9.7)

tell us nothing. The gloss peironus ... in camino

91

Fragmentary and Doubtful Inscriptions

arelat(ensi) ib. 219. 562, CIL 12.5558 (from Du Cange,
an. 1234) is of course Latin (*petronius i.e. milliarum,
cf. Prov. peiro "stone" from petro, so the local name
Peyruis i.e. Petrosium).

      (ii) The same remark is true of Aix (Aquae
Sextiae); at least I can make nothing of the alphabetic
tablet published by Clerc in REA 11, 1909, 50-52, on
which single letters, viz.

$$\delta\ \epsilon\ \theta\ \circ\ \sigma\ \tau\ \upsilon$$

and the group

$$\sigma\ \upsilon\ \vee\ \ \ (?)$$

are said to occur.

    But there are a number of curious, if doubtful,
other epigraphic fragments from various sites in the
Bouches-du-Rhône, which may be noted here for the sake
of completing the record.

      (iii) Marseille
(a) From I.G. 14.2453, apparently

     ? τι ƒ ο ρ ƒ ι δ υ

     ? ρ ο ƒ ο ν ο σ   (i.e. Rufōnus?)

ib. 2465, perhaps not Greek (Mommsen)

  ... σ... | ... ου |... τρου y

Fragmentary and Doubtful Inscriptions

ib. 2466 (cf. Note lxi)

σταδισ

(b) From CIL 12.5686, 1179

ενισισ   (?)

ib. 5679.49, r. to l.

γλαουι   (?)

On Marseille see R. Pernoud Essai sur l'histoire du Port de Marseille, 1935.

(iv) Trets (cf. the divine name Trittia below), ib. 5686.1115.

ιʃεπο

CA 5.53, 174 (on a lamp)

]eurdus

(v) Les Martigues (Maritima Auaticorum, on the étang de Berre, the stagnum Mastramela, see CA 5.50-51, cf. RA 31, 1930, 182 and 9, 1937, 120), on a lamp (CA l.c. no. 163), cf. 158 below

barga

Graffiti from Fos (Canton d'Istres), c. 5 miles from Les Martigues, l.c. 94.288

Fragmentary and Doubtful Inscriptions

(v) ctd.

coemo

cinnatu

(the latter no doubt the same as Cennatus, South Gaul, in Oswald's Index).

(vi) Saint-Blaise (also on the étang de Berre) (a) An inscription "encastrée dans le mur d'une chapelle situe a Castel-Veire," "non dechiffrée," see Bull. Arch. 1930-31, 274.

(b) Graffiti on pot-sherds from the oppidum excavated between 1935 and 1938 at Saint-Blaise, see H. Rolland in Monuments hist. de la France (Paris) 3, 1938, 104:

Τουιο[

Χαροβυ[

διο[

The third is most probably Greek.

(vii) Rognac (on the opposite side of the étang de Berre), described as an "autel magique" (genuine?), with the groups of letters

ΟΕα   ιαο   Εοαι

or other combinations of them (gnostic?), see REA 34,

Inscription of Saignon

1932, 291 (cf. 29, 1927, 163-165; 31, 1929, 363). But
Espérandieu 658 renders this as gen[io] Accon (sic).

(viii) From Bouc (across the entrance of the
étang de Berre from Les Martigues), a fragment of orange-
colored pottery, with

]ουο[

See H. de Gérin-Ricard and G. Arnaud d'Agnel, Antiquités
de la Vallée de l'Arc, Aix 1907, 43, better H. de Gérin-
Ricard, Mém. Acad. Vaucluse (Avignon) 16, 1916, 89.

3. Vaucluse

45
A much broken and worn piece of lime-stone dis-
covered c. 1867 in the garden of the presbytery at
Saignon (near Apt), now secured to the west wall of the
church there, near the entrance, on the south side.
Seen there by me.

19 by 6.5 in.; letters 1.5 or 1.625 in. high
(except o 1.25 in.); υ is apparently $\bar{Y}$, but the
cross-bar may be modern.

]δβο..τοο[|]ουειματικαν[? |]αι
ουει καρνιτου[

Line 1 τ or ς ? Line 3 α or λ ? Not much can be
missing (perhaps two letters in line 1 on left, one or

Inscription of Saignon

two on right; line 2 only one on l., none on r.; line 3

complete?), if the present size of the stone is any

indication of the extent of the originally engraved part

of it.

First published in Rev. épigr. du midi de la France
1, 1878-1883, 366-67.409; Do. 153.16; CIL 12, p. 822.

46
A single line of text cut near the top of a huge
block of stone discovered in 1880 at Gargas (c. 3 miles
north-west of Apt), taken in 1881 to Avignon (Musée
Calvet, Espérandieu 12.5); seen there by me.

17.75 in. by 3 ft. 9.75 in. (length) by 2 ft. 7 in.

(front to back). The text is complete; the traces of

letters above it have nothing to do with this insc.

Fine letters 2 to 2.25 in. high, with finials; the insc.

is the best, in style of lettering, of all those now at

Avignon, where it is left exposed to the weather in the

open courtyard of the museum. The letters marked .

are chipped, but the reading is everywhere certain.

ΕΣΚΕγγαι βλανδοουικ ο υ νι αι

First published Rev. épigr. 1, 176.209 (with the
misreading βλοουι , cf. BSAF 1880, 245-246 βλαοουι);
Do. 151.10; CIL 12, p. 137; CA 7, 14.24.

Inscription of St-Martin-de-Castillon

47

The fragment of a lime-stone drum of a column, discovered Nov. 1882, at Saint-Martin-de-Castillon, a little over 1 km. from Apt, removed in 1886 to the Musée Calvet at Avignon (Inv. 23A; Esp. 14.7); seen there by me.

First published Rev. épigr. 1, 333.370 (cf. 384, facsim.); cf. CIL 12, p. 822.

Height 17.5 in., diameter 17.25 in. Letters 1.5 and 1.625 in. tall, except ο (.625 in.). The text is both uncertain and incomplete, and line 1 is so different in style from the rest that it is either a distinct text or has been worked over in modern times.

?]σουι̣λ̣λιϙυ̣ιτουσ[|]να κ̣νοσ[|]αδ̣ε

σ is ⊏ and Ϲ, likewise ε is E, ϙ is Ϙ (not Ρρ), λ is Λ.

In line 2 κ has been "emended" into R. I saw no trace of ι before α in line 3. If, as is likely enough, the inscription has been tampered with, in line 1 emend]σουι καρνιτουσ[

Do. 153.17

48

A curious monument, not an altar as hitherto described, but funerary. It is a square pillar, 2 ft. 5.5 in. high, terminating in a pyramid; 14 in. by 10 in. at the base, 8.5 in. by 7 in. at the top moulding; above it the pyramid. The curious feature is the incised

outline of a pair of feet, toes downwards, beneath the
insc., which perhaps was added after the feet were drawn
in, for line 3 is tilted upwards, in smaller letters, to
right, so as to avoid the heel of the left foot. The
same feature appears at Cadenet, see 58 below, and elsewhere (see CIL 13 vi 1, 1933, p. 19: "pedes duo in
laterculis;" St Just Pequart and Le Rouzic Signes gravés
du Morbihan, Paris 1927, Pl. 136, the dolmen of Roch Pol.
The symbolism is familiar in India, where the imprints
are believed to be those of the Buddha's feet and to
imply security and sanctity in a place visited by him;
see W. Crooke Things Indian, New York 1906, 231-237).

This block of calcareous stone was discovered in
1870 at Saint-Saturnin d'Apt, some 25 miles north-east
of Apt, in the valley of the Coulon, a tributary of the
Durance. It was placed in the Musée Calvet at Avignon
(Inv. 65; Esp. 12.4); seen there by me.

ουαλικιο | ονερεστ. | αιουνιαι

Letters 1.25 in. high (lines 1,2), 1 in (line 3);
(σ and Єє .

The stone is broken on right edge; hence the last
letter of line 1 (after which nothing is missing) may
have been ο , as generally taken, or σ ; line 2 lacks
one letter at end, in line 3 there is space for one
letter at the end.

Do. 150.8; CIL 12, p. 137; CA 7.15

Inscription of L'Isle-sur-la-Sorgue

49

    From L'Isle-sur-la-Sorgue. The Sorgue and the
Ouvèze unite at Bédarrides, a few miles from Sorgues
on the main line between Orange and Avignon.   But
L'Isle-sur-la-Sorgue is reached most quickly from
Avignon itself, 15 miles to the east, and 4.5 miles
short of the famous Fontaine de Vaucluse, immortalized
by Petrarch. The spring, "chiare, fresche, e dolci
acque," was doubtless known in antiquity; it is the
source of the Sorgue, springing from rocks 650 ft.
high to pass through a cave 25 feet wide.

    The mutilated insc. that we now have, on the semi-
circular drum of a great engaged column of calcareous
stone, probably recorded some structure or dedication
connected with the cult of the spring. Only two lines
survive out of originally at least four; there may have
been writing also above what is now line 1.

    4 ft. 5 in. high, diameter 17.5 in. at the top
(19 in. bottom). The letters, much broken and difficult
to decipher, vary in height: ϵ 1.625 in., δ .875 in.,
α 1.5 in., o .875 in.

    Discovered in 1884, now in the Musée Calvet (Inv.
23B, Esp. 13.6), seen by me.

]ασγεννοριγ. | ουρετε. μα[τ]ρε[βο]

υι[   ]...   ...[   ]...   ...[

    In line 2 there is space for letters as indicated,
but the stone is damaged and the writing all but illegible.

99

Cavaillon

At the end of line 1, possibly ι (now apparently a
double interpunct), in line 2 the seventh letter appears
as ε superimposed upon an erroneously repeated τ .

Published simultaneously Rev. épigr. 2, 1884–1889,
39.483 and Bull. Épigr. de la Gaule 4, 1884, 189; Do.
150.9; CIL 12, p. 822 add. 137, 6; CA 7.25, 54 (where
it is given twice, as if two identical inscc.). Photograph in Mém. de l'Acad. de Vaucluse 4, 1885, 105–111
(no sign of the repeated τ).

Cavaillon

The Cabellio of classical writers (Pl. 3. 36, καβε
and cabe on coins antedating the Roman conquest, see 78
below; ciuitas Cauellicorum in NG 11. 13), modern
Cavaillon, stood upon the lower ground to the east of
the slight rise, now known as the Colline Saint-Jacques,
lying between it and the Durance (see the sketch-map,
REA 11, 1909, 54). This hilly ground was the site, in
more or less continuous human occupation from neolithic
times, of a pre-Roman oppidum assigned by Déchelette
(Mnl. 3, 1054 n.; cf. Mazauric, REA 13, 1911, 82; Grenier
in Frank 3, 425 n.29 with the references given there)
to the period La Tène III, i.e. it lasted not later than
the opening decades of the last century B.C.

Inscriptions of Cavaillon

The six following inscriptions, written in the Greek alphabet, may, therefore, be dated confidently c. 125-100 B.C. (cf. p. 77 above). One of them, engraved in the sloping face of the rock above the bed of the Durance, is still in situ (55 below); the other five were removed to the disused Hôpital at Cavaillon, where I examined them in 1929. There is a cast of the rock-inscription in the museum at Nimes. Of the five inscc. at (but not in) the Hôpital, one is said to be on "a fragment of a column" (50), the other four are stelae, or parts of stelae, similar to those of Saint-Remy and Les Baux. We are indebted to the Jouve family of Cavaillon for the preservation of these five inscc., all discovered in 1909, first published by F. Mazauric in the Revue du Midi (Nimes, 63, 1910, 45-51 with Pl.; see REA 12, 1910, 199); the rock insc. was first observed and described in 1903.

CA 7, 26-29 strangely omits all mention of these inscc.; from P. de Brun and A. Dumoulin La Colline Saint-Jacques de Cavaillon avant l'occupation romaine, Cahiers d'histoire et d'archéologie 12, 1937, 449-487, it would appear that all except 55 have now been deposited in the Musée lapidaire de Cavaillon. On Cavaillon itself see REA 20, 1918, 242-243.

Inscriptions of Cavaillon

50

    Generally described as "a fragment of a column," but the stone may well be part of a stele of the usual type. Present dimensions: 2 feet high on the unin-scribed side, 17.5 in. to 19.5 in. on the inscribed face, a step 6.5 in. to 4.5 in. deep having been cut out about half the entire thickness (10 in.) of the slab, just beneath the insc. Thus the inscribed face now measures 17.5 in. on left, 19.5 in. on right, 14 in. across; 9 in. blank above the insc., which is no doubt complete. Fine, well cut letters 2 in. in height (ο) to 2.5 in. (υ) or 3 in. (β), with slight finials.

βαλαυδο|υι μακκαριο|υι

    The reading is certain, the damage in line 3 at the bottom being insignificant. Υυ , κκ, ββ, Αα, Ρρ Observe the consistent division before -υι in both lines.

    Rh. Add., Pl. 1 (facsimile); Do. 151.12

51

    A lime-stone stele 5 feet 8 in. high, 13.5 in. thick and 13 in. wide, surmounted by a pyramid 18 in. high, base 12 in. square.

Inscriptions of Cavaillon

Letters 1.25 in. to 1.5 in. high, not so well cut
as in 50, but in a good, later style, thus Υυ , Αα , Εε ,
Cσ . Recent damage on left, but the text is not in doubt.

ελουισσα|μαγουρει|γιαουα

Photographs in Rh. l.c.; Do. 151.11.   The text
given by de Brun-Dumoulin Cahiers l.c. 479.1 (ελουσσα
in line 1, with ξ(, τι in line 3) is untrustworthy.

52
Part of a similar stele, now 4 feet 6 in. high,
12 in. thick, and 13 in. across the front face.   No
pyramid now; the stone appears to have been rudely cut
down just above an incised line that runs across the
face above line 1.

καβιροσουι|νδιλικοσ

Letters unevenly cut and somewhat worn; α is Α ,
Ββ , small ο , Cσ , Υυ .
In line 1 ι is chipped at top.   In line 2 Rhys
read -διακοσ .   But the stone has ΙΔ .   This cannot be
read ια, for α is Α not Δ .   Accordingly I take the

symbol as ligatured for ιλι or assume the accidental
omission of ι (thus ιλ⟨ι⟩), perhaps added beneath as
an afterthought.

Rh. Add., Pl. 2 (photograph); Do. 152.13

53   Another part of a similar stele, now 4 feet 9 in.
high, 17.5 in. wide, 13.5 in. thick. Large letters 3 in.
(o) to 3.5 in. and 4 in. high, evenly engraved, a central
punct in o and σ (Ϲ); υ is Υ and κ Κ.

Rh. Add., Pl. 3; Do. 152.15

54   Another stele, present dimensions 4 feet 2 in. by
16 in. by 15 in. Letters deeply incised, but the face
of the stone is worn, the whole of line 1 damaged at the
top, and all four lines on left; 1.5 in. high (except o
1.125 in. or 1.25 in., and υΥ or Υ 2.25 in.), α is Α ,

Inscriptions of Cavaillon

y ⌐ and ⊤⊤ .

] ἀιτεσ·ατ|ε μαγουτι · ovvα|κουι

A whole line or more may be wanting at the top.
In line 1 there is considerable doubt about the reading.
Rh. gives μιτιεσι·μιτ , in which the ι after μιτ- , and
the ι after σ are certainly wrong; they are not in the
original at all. De Brun gives ... τεο ..τ| ... The
⋏ in line 1 is the lower half of Λ in both cases (not
μ), and the stroke, apparently joined to the limb of α
far from certain (hardly conjoint ꭤυ ?). Then, after
the interpunct, the stone has Λ⊤ (broken at the top),
which must be for ατ , for there is no trace of ι
between the two letters. In line 2 at the beginning ε
or σ (damaged), not ισ .

Rh. Add., Pl. 2; Do. 152.14

55
Known to me only from the plaster cast at Nîmes
(Inventory no. 141), the original being on the banks of
the Durance at Cavaillon (Colline Saint-Jacques) and
frequently covered with mud or water or both. The

Inscriptions of Cavaillon

letters, to judge from the cast, are 3.25 to 3.5 in. in
height, and occupied (what is left of them, or has been
observed of them) a space c. 2.5 feet by 1.5 feet. I
read

$$]o\nu\epsilon\lambda\rho o\upsilon[\quad | \quad]\upsilon\iota\kappa\iota\kappa[$$

Almost certainly incomplete, both right and left;
the ου of line 1, ν of line 2, are both very faint in
the cast, and it appears that the original is worn to
the point of illegibility "à cause de l'usure de la
pierre par les eaux," L.-H. Labande, by whom the insc.
was first published, Mémoires de l'Academie de Vaucluse
(Avignon) 3, 1903, 164, where the reading φηκικος is
given in line 2. But of all the inscc. in Greek alphabet
two only (44,57) have η , and the φ is given here as Φ.
The cast suggests rather |ˋ|| , which I have taken
doubtfully as νι . In line 1 Labande's Λ for Λλ is
not supported by the cast, nor his ος at the end of
line 1. An alleged φ in 37 is altogether erroneous.

Do. 152.15 bis

Note viii

(a) Cahiers d'histoire et d'archéologie 12, 1937,
474 (Plate 7, fig. 13), a fragment of lead plate, 72 by

Inscription of Grozeau

29 mm., found at the Colline Saint-Jacques, with a
doubtful text:

?]ι Ϝολεϭαϭιτ. εξ[|].τ

I have taken Χ as ξ , on the ground that Ϝ appears;
but if in line 1 for Ϝ we read ϵ , Χ may be χ . The
alphabet is a curiously mixed affair, with Λ , Ϲ and
Ε , Α , Ϲ . There is a scratch beneath Ϝ (Ϝ?) which
might justify the reading ϵ .

(b) Ib., 469, a fragment of pottery:

]ου[

Cf. p. 95.

56
This insc. is now to be seen in the church-yard
of the Chapelle Pontificalle de Notre-Dame-du-Grozeau
(or Groseau, or Grosel), about .5 mile from Malaucène
(see Note ix). It is all very much weathered, and the
reading frequently quite uncertain.

Originally on the front face of an altar, 3 feet
5.5 in. high, 14 in. thick, 10 in. wide, except where
it widened at the top in volutes to 12 in., 16 in. and

Inscription of Grozeau

then 20 in. This original width has been much diminished
by cutting down on one side, and by the building of the
altar into the church-yard wall. The altar is now surmounted by a cross, and has been repaired with cement
in quite recent times, much to the detriment of the
insc. which is in places all but illegible. Seen there
by me.

Said to have been found c. 1805, and put to its
present use as early as 1810. First published by A.
Deloye, Bibliothèque de l'École des Chartes 4, 1847-48,
329. At one time it was actually inside the church, as
a support to the altar (BA 1889, 204; cf. BSAF 5, 1884,
187-189, and 297-300). Letters 1 in. to 1.25 in. and
1.5 in. high, except smaller o .

$$...\iota\tau\lambda o\upsilon\sigma|..\nu\alpha\lambda\iota\alpha\kappa o\sigma|.\rho\alpha\sigma\epsilon\lambda o\upsilon.|$$

5 $.\rho\alpha\tau o\upsilon\delta\epsilon.|\kappa\alpha\nu\tau\epsilon[\nu\alpha$

Line 1: ι is merely a half hasta, a trace of the
cross-bar of τ is visible, then λ (clear), next o quite
uncertain. 2: before a worn α (Λ?), an upright,
possibly ι , more likely ν , not λ . There are faint
traces of the slanting stroke before it. The second α
was left incomplete, Λ (for Λ); oσ are crowded in at
the end of the line, o (worn) is certain, σ altogether
doubtful. 3: ρ doubtful, only the hasta being visible.
The rest, except ε (worn) is clear. 4: scarcely room

Inscription of Vaison

for β before ρ , but it could not, I think, have stood
at the end of 3. Of υ only the upper part remains.
5: after $\top$ a worn ϵ , then a big patch of cement covers
everything; but in 1884 (BSAF l.c.) $\nu\alpha$ was still to be
seen.

Do. 147.2; CA 7, 48, 84; CIL 12, p. 824, add p.
162; Espérandieu Musée Calvet 8.2

57
A small slab of calcareous stone, 2.25 in. to
2.75 in. thick, now in the Musée Calvet at Avignon, seen
there by me; Inv. no. 23, Espérandieu 10.3. Discovered
at Vaison in 1840, deposited in the museum in 1841.

Present dimensions: 12 in. wide, 10.25 in. top
to bottom on right, 9.875 in. on left. The letters
come to the very edges, and the stone is probably not
in its original condition or size. There is no clue to
the nature of the object with which the insc. was in the
first place associated. But the text is complete,
certainly on right, at top, and at bottom, and probably
also on left. Lightly cut in a quasi-cursive style Λ ,
Λ λ , ω ω , ϵ ϵ , $(\sigma$, letters from .75 in. (o) to
1.375 in. high. Date: not before 50 B.C. First pub-
lished in 1842 by Louis de la Saussaye, Numismatique

109

Inscription of Vaison

de la Gaule Narbonnaise 163.

σεγομαροσ|ουιλλονεοσ|τοου

τιουσ|ναμκυσατισ|ειωρουβη

5   λη‖σαμισοσιν|νεμητον

Do. 150.7; CIL 12, p. 162; CA 7.58, 88 (39); cf.
I. Becker Rh. Mus. 13, 1858, 295; id. Kuhn und Schleichers
Beiträge zur vergleichende Sprachforschung 3, 1863, 162-
163

L. H. Gray AJPh 63, 1942, 442-443 takes this (as
well as 68, 63, 160, 161, 162, 169 below) as a metrical
text (in trochaic dimeters). I am not convinced.

The divine name Belisama, and connected local names,
are discussed by F. Lot RC 45, 1928, 315-317; the former
is known from other inscc., cf. Rev. épigr. du Midi 3,
1890-1898, 375-376 (no. 1134), BSAF 1883, 171-174; deo
Belisamaro (Chalon-sur-Saône), Revue épigraphique 1,
1913, 95.

The discussion of this insc. in the Maruéjol
memorial volume (see REA 26, 1924, 132) I have not been
able to see.

Inscription of Beaumont

Note ix

A sand-stone cippus, discovered c. 1847 at Beaumont, near Vaison, first published by A. Deloye,
Bibliothèque de l'École des Chartes, 4, 1847-48, 326;
now at Malaucène (some three miles east of Vaison), in
the private collections of M. A. Chastel, seen there
by me.

21 in. high by 13 in. wide; corners broken, and

also right side. But the last line is complete, and not

more than one letter has been damaged on right in lines

1-3. Latin alphabet, letters 1.875 in. to 2.125 in.

high, painted red in modern times (the remains of the

last letter in line 1, and of the punct in line 2

having been overlooked). Style of early empire, wide-

spread M, O the full height of the line, R (open in

line 4, not elsewhere) and E narrow, S very slightly

curved (especially in line 1), slight finials, lozenge-

shaped interpunct (lines 2,4).

subroni | sumeli· | uoreto(u) | uirius·f

1. iubron the early editors, wrongly; subron Do.,

Rh. 3. The engraver started to put in u at the end, then

left it incomplete, and put the entire letter into line

4; there is an apparent (accidental?) thorn to the 4th

letter in line 4.

In line 4 f presumably stands for fecit. But if

Inscription of Carpentras

the insc. is in Latin, it is not easily construed.

Do. 147.2 bis; CIL 12.1351; CA 7.48, 85B

Note x

A lead plaque, 0.57m. x 0.50m., 0.009 thick, discovered at Carpentras, sometime in or before 1845, when
it was deposited in the Musée Calvet at Avignon (Espérandieu 146.197), letters 0.020 to 0.025m. high, clearly
and deeply engraved; but the alphabet and (if articulate,
at all) the dialect are uncertain; Jullian REA 2, 1900,
136-141 argued for Iberian, but presumably we have a
mere jumble of alphabetic or quasi-alphabetic symbols
intended to serve some magical purpose:

$$? \, \delta\epsilon h \, \upsilon\mu \, o\chi[\quad |\upsilon \, \lambda\alpha\gamma\upsilon\kappa\upsilon \, \epsilon\delta\tau\rho\int. \, : \theta o|\varsigma. \, \lambda$$

Note xi

Although I am familiar with Thurneysen's explanation (I.F. 42, 1924, 143 n. 1) of the form auot in the
sense seruus or libertus a uotis (cf. a marmoribus, a
statuis), I am constrained to include here two formulae
that occur on the Triumphal Arch of Orange (L. Chatelain,
Les monuments romains d'Orange, Paris 1908, 50-55; CIL
12.1231, not later than the time of Tiberius, and
possibly older, see P. Coussin RA 24, 1926, 210-211, cf.
CA 7.104, 98), of which one contains auot.

This word is best known on terracotta figurines

and pottery, but it appears also on andirons, fibulae,

a ring, coins and in inscriptions of some length, cf.

Notes xii, xix, 136 Remark, 175, Notes xxxiv, xxxix,

On AVOT at Orange

xlix, liv, lv, lx below; thus Thurneysen's view (accepted
by Weisgerber SprFK 193, cf. Walde-Pokorny 2.12) must be
declared quite unconvincing for that and the following
reasons, viz.

(1) The names on the Arch of Orange are not those
of slaves, but of Gaulish chieftains; auot has, moreover,
a counterpart in]uaune (see below).

(2) The alleged expression "a uotis" is nowhere
else known.

(3) If auot actually occurs on coins of the Lexouii
(AcS 1.317), it cannot stand for "a uotis." Moreover,
andirons are unlikely, terra sigillata impossible votive
objects.

(4) The writing auotis occurs only once, a uotis
never, auotti, auote, auoti, auot, auuot, auo, au being
the usual writings, clearly abbreviations, but certainly
not of "a uotis," unless proof can be adduced from a
certain text. The abbreviated Latin is totally different
(namely V S L M), and of a totally different expression.
On terra sigillata such an expression as "a uotis,"
parallel to "ab epistulus, a pedilus" in literary texts,
would make nonsense.

(5) Two inscc. of Alise-Sainte-Reine (165,166),
in Greek alphabet, have αϝουωτ; a third, of St Remy,

On AVOT at Orange

has αυoτ (40, above); and yet another, of Mont Ventoux (Note xii, below) also has αυoτ .

(6) The formula appears not to occur outside Gaul, where

(7) it is restricted, except for the inscriptions just mentioned and (?) the coins of the Lexouii, to pottery and figurines, or other small objects.

(8) The accompanying names on pottery are usually Keltic, and not servile e.g. Reχtugenos, Aucirix.

(9) Beside Rutenus au (CIL 13.10010, 1670 b 1) we have Ruten(us) fecit (ib. 1670 b 2), and beside Boudillus auot (infr.) we have Ioui (?) Boudillus pos(uit) BSAF 1885, 190; Auctus auote and Auctu fecit (La Grauf., Oswald p. 31); As auo and Asiaticus fecit in CIL 13.10010, 178. Similarly (cf. CIL 13 iii, fasc. 1, p. 121) we have such pairs as Bollo auot and Bollus fecit, Acutios auot and Acutios fecit, Flauus auot and Flauus fecit, Buccus auot and Buccus fecit.

(10) Thurneysen's "form(auit), bisher fälschlich zu form(am) ergänzt" (Sacrillos Carati auot form) is put out of court by a formula such as Seuerianus fecit formas (see Oswald, Index of Potters' Stamps 1931, p. vii).

(11) Finally, and this clinches the matter,

On AVOT at Orange

terra sigillata was not produced by slave-labor at all,
so competent authority assures me. See further my paper
in The Journal of Celtic Studies 1, 1950. The unique
cruciform arrangement of _auot_ in CIL 13.10010, 248 is
no proof of a magical or religious implication (notwithstanding arepo 79 below), for it appears also even
in personal names on terra sigillata (10010, 1333 and
1653). And if auot stands alone in 10010, 248, so does
fecit in 885.

      CIL 12.1231, on shields
          (a) 1   Bo]udillus _auot_
          (b) 8   Boduacus]uaune (?)

The restoration of (a) 1 is certain (despite Budillus
in CIL 12, Index); the figure given by Déchelette in
BSAF 1910, 386 shows that two letters are wanting before
u, which would give the usual spelling (AcS 1.498, Bu-
being otherwise unattested ib. 628). Déchelette has
the interesting suggestion that the inscc. are "simples
marques de fabrique indiquant l'origine gauloise des
trophees;" but if _auot_ (not to mention]uaune) means
"posuit" rather than (or as well as) "fecit," this
assumption is unnecessary.

On AVOT at Orange

The auot figurines and pottery are widely distributed all over Gaul. But they seem to have been diffused from a few centers such as Lezoux (Aquitania), a site in western Gaul (Lugdunensis?), Rheinzabern (Germania Superior), and the original types perhaps from but one or two such centers, probably located in southern Gaul (Lezoux?). Accordingly the form auot, though attested for all parts of Gaul, must be regarded as proper only to the south.

Perhaps attention should be called to the fact that one of the shields on the Arch of Orange (CIL loc. cit. 2) has the reading ...e (or Is)... fe..., in which it is conceivable that fe stands for "fe[cit]." It would not be easy to find a personal name, to fit the few remaining letters, on the assumption that only one word is required; on the other hand, we should expect fe[cit in a second line, and beneath the personal name. In any case f is rare in Gaul except in pure Latin forms.

As for the arms represented on the arch of Orange, some of them at least are definitely Iberian in character, according to H. Breuil RA 16, 1922, 188-190.

Remark:

The reading given in CA 7.125, 221

iennioriulior

from the handle of an amphora found at Orange (cf. CIL 12.5683, 89), if correct, is striking enough to be noted here, since it appears to contain more than mere names. But cf. Iii En, CA 7.125, 220, and Inniii ib. 124, 206.

116

Inscription of Cadenet

58

     Almost certainly a funerary (not votive) monument,
like 48 above. Discovered at Cadenet (Vaucluse, about
midway between Apt and Aix); it is in fact described
as "sur un tombeau de marbre" by the informant of
Christophe, comte de Villeneuve [-Bargemon], by whom it
was first published, Statistique du Département des
Bouches-du-Rhône, Marseilles, vol. 2 1824, 235; then
given by Ch. Alex. Roland, Cadenet historique 1, 1837,
261, after whom it was repeated by Rabiet in MSAF 8,
1887, 337, with Roland's sketch: "encastrée autrefois
dans les murs d'enceinte du Castelar," destroyed or
lost sight of long ago.

$$\mu \epsilon \tau \epsilon \lambda \mid \alpha \iota \, o \, \sigma \, \lambda \alpha \mid \delta o \, \sigma$$

Instead of λ , de Villeneuve gave δ , and in

Roland and Rabiet τ is a possible reading for ι ($\bar{\mathsf{I}}$).

Beneath the last line of text, two feet (just as in the

insc. of the nearby Saint-Saturnin-d'Apt, 40 above), on

which see Rabiet l.c. 338.

     CIL 12, p. 137.3; CA 7.3, 8

59

     "Une pierre de molasse" found near the Castellar
de Cade at Cadenet, and reported by H. de Gérin-Ricard
in Mém. de l'Acad. de Vaucluse (Avignon) 16, 1916, 88-89;
0.65 by 0.40 by 0.25m., bearing four letters (0.10 to
0.15m. high); said to have been associated with a tomb
(incineration).

$$] \, o \upsilon \underset{.}{\epsilon} \rho \, [$$

The last extant letter is R , which can hardly

be anything but ρ (not v); the ^{o} is lozenge-shaped, and

Inscriptions of Cadenet and Mt-Ventoux

59 ctd.
ϵ (η ?) apparently ⊢ (for Ɛ ?). CA l.c.

Remark:

        The Latin insc. CIL 12.1148, found at Buoux
(4 km. south of Apt) is certainly genuine (pace CA 7.17,
31). It was beyond the power of a forger to fabricate
such genuine Keltic names in 1827; but the insc. was no
doubt mis-copied. Read

                uebromara Atepomari   f

Verbronara Apete- lapis. Cf. AcS 1.258, 22; 3.130, 22

(Vebru-).

Note xii

        On a female statuette (cf. 175, Note xxxvi), found
at Mont Ventoux, CIL 12.5689, 3 (cf. CA 7.20, 45). I
read this as

            ἀυοτ αλπ ρου[

For ἀυοτ see Note xi above; αλπρου is probably not a
Greek gen. sg., but an incomplete Keltic name.

Remark:

        Mommsen regarded (perhaps wrongly) the name
Ουαλος, Vaalus in the bilingual insc., Gr. and Lat.,

118

Inscriptions of Avignon and Redessan

IG 14.2480 (CIL 12.1038), from Avignon, as identical
with Vacalus. It is in any event worth noting here.

Less significant, if correctly read, is the text,
certainly Greek, Εὐφραινου ἐφωπαρει , on a goblet of
blue glass, also found at Avignon; but, as Blanchet
observes (CA 7.37, 64; 8 with n. 1), "la lecture du nom
du fabricant...devrait etre revisée."

In BSAF 1886, 134-135 H. Gaidoz published (after
Rochetin) a bronze tablet with an insc. "en caractères
grecs" from Montdragon (Vaucluse), implying that it was
"suspendue...par un devot gaulois" in a shrine sacred
to the goddess of a spring. But the text, if articulate
at all, is not Gaulish, but Greek.

4. Gard

(Repertoire archéologique, see REA 39, 1937,
310; 37, 1935, 452-453.)

60

A tall square column, with a recessed area at the

top about .75 in. deep, to support a bust or statuette.

Not an altar, but a funerary stele. Discovered at

Redessan (8 km. east of Nimes) in 1891, first published

by Maruéjol, BA 1891, pp. xxv, 280-282. Given by

119

Inscriptions of Beaucaire

Dr. J. Reboul to the museum at Nîmes, seen there by me.

11 in. wide by 4 ft. 8.5 in. tall, of which height 18 in. (unworked) was set into the earth. Letters 2.25 in. high, beautifully cut, with finials, 3 in. from the top of the stone:

ΚρΕΙΤΕ

Do. 159.31. Cf. ecritusiri (239)?

61, 62
Two inscc. on capitals discovered with other architectural fragments in July 1809, during the diggings conducted to draw water from the Rhône for the canal at Beaucaire, the site of the ancient Vgernum; the texts were copied by the civil engineer in charge of the works, a M. Méjean, for the Académie du Gard, where his notes are said to have been preserved at Nîmes, see CIL 12, pp. 356, 832, and all subsequent copies appear to derive from them, the originals being lost.

61   ΚρΑΥΣΙΚΥΟ|ΣΕΚΣΙΥΥΟΣ ?

62   ΣΙΜΙΑΣ[

The text of 62 is not disputed, pace Holder I 1017.3, who gives cimiao. In 61 I have given what I think was possibly the original reading; but line 2 was carelessly and incompetently copied; the last letter of line 1 appears to have been carried over (by the copyist?) into line 2. I suspect that line 1 might be

120

Inscription of Collias

further emended to read κραϭϭικνοϭ, cf. craxantus (178)

and krasanikna (PID 321), line 2 έϭκ- .

First published by César Blaud, Antiquités de la
ville de Beaucaire 1819, Tab. 7.2 (cf. p. 26), thence
by A. Eyssette Histoire de Beaucaire depuis la 13ᵉ siècle
jusqu'à la révolution de 1789, 2, 1867, 317 (both works
inaccessible to me), and in the following places, which
I have seen: Ph. Eyssette in Congrès Scientifique de
France: 35ᵉ session, Montpellier 1868, vol. 2 (published
at Montpellier, 1872), 383-388; E. Germer-Durand in Mém.
de l'Acad. du Gard (Nîmes) Nov. 1866-Août 1867 [1868],
249-263; id. Procès-Verbaux de l'Acad. du Gard 1866-67,
Nîmes 1867, 125-128.

63

An almost square pillar of limestone (8 in. by 9

in.), 4 ft. 4 in. high, discovered at Collias. In 1869

it was still built into the exterior south wall of the

"petite chapelle romane de Notre-Dame-de-Laval" there

(see Bull. Épigr. de la Gaule 4, 1884, 253), but was

probably discovered much earlier. The insc. clearly

deals with a dedication (-αβο dat. pl., line 6), probably

to goddesses of a spring, for there is at Laval, "ermitage

N.-D., fondé au Xᵉ s., au bord d'une source ferrugineuse,"

and the altar of the "chapelle romane" there ("des XIIᵉ

et XVᵉ s.") is "formé des pierres tumulaires romaines"

(Joanne, Dict. Géogr., 2, 1892, 1024). No doubt this

stone came from the immediate vicinity. It was removed

Inscription of Collias

c. 1889 ("récemment," Rev. épigr. du Midi de la France 2, 1884-89, 404 no. 754, in a fascicle dated Jan.-Mar. 1889) to the Museum at Nîmes (no. 125), seen there by me. First published Bull. Épigr. l.c. (cf. 5, 1885, 188-206) and BSAF 1884, 267.

The insc. is complete, in letters 1.5 in. to 1.75 in. tall, very faint and almost illegible, of the usual style: $C \sigma$, $\mathcal{E} \epsilon$, A (and A ?) α . There is also a plaster cast at Nîmes, made c. 1888, which is of some slight help in deciphering the weathered original; cf. the plate published by M. F. Germer-Durand in Mémoires de l'Academie de Nîmes 11, 1888 [1889], 55-59.

$$\epsilon \kappa \upsilon \lambda \iota o | \sigma \rho \iota o \upsilon | \mu \alpha \nu \epsilon | o \sigma \alpha \nu . | \delta o o \upsilon$$

5 $$\nu \| \nu \alpha \beta o \delta | \epsilon \delta \epsilon \beta \rho \alpha \tau o | \upsilon . . \kappa \alpha \nu | \tau \epsilon \nu \alpha$$

In line 1 K ($\epsilon \kappa$); then I read $\curlyvee / \backslash$, the υ not uncertain, but faint and worn, as are all the letters marked with . in my transcript. But the text is easily restored in line 8 ($\delta \epsilon$), and perfectly intelligible.

Do. 159.32; CIL 12.5887

Inscription of Uzès

64

A fragment of an abacus from a large lime-stone capital, now 3 ft. 1 in. long, about 8 in. thick. The insc. stands on a face 5 in. deep, beneath two rows of moulding.

Discovered in 1869 at Uzès, the ancient Vcetia. Reported by A. Aures, Procés-verbaux le l'Académie du Gard 1868-69, 42, cf. Mém. de l'Acad. du Gard 1868-69 [1870], 90-92, and given by M. Alphonse Abauzit, in whose vineyard it had been discovered, to the Musée Archéologique et Épigraphique de Nîmes, seen there by me.

Clear, well-incised letters, 2.75 in. to 3 in. high.

]σενικιο σ·αβρω[

Incomplete on right, possibly on left. Presumably Keltic (cf. the names Senec-, Senic- etc., AcS 2.1467-1476). From what happened at Glanum (see p. 76), it is clear that native monuments, even in Provence, were destroyed by the Romans at the time of Caesar, and this fragment is no doubt to be ascribed to the period ending c. 50 B.C.

Do. 157.26; cf. BA 1887, 206; in Ed. Barry, E. Germer-Durand, A. Lebègue, F. Germer-Durand, A. Allmer, Recueil des Inscr. Antiques de la Provence de Languedoc 1893 (Vol. 15 of Dom A. Devic and Dom J. Vaissette's Histoire Générale de Languedoc), it is p. 572, no. 105 (Nîmes).

Inscription of Collorgues

65

Discovered by accident in the course of agricultural operations, c. 1869, at Collorgues near Uzès;
part of a large oil or wine jar, smashed at or before
discovery, and only a fragment of the inscribed part
was recovered and eventually placed in the Museum at
Nimes, seen there by me. First published by Allmer in
1885, Rev. épigr. 2, 1884-1889, 82.519.

What survives is a piece of the upper rim; 11 in.

long, 6 in. wide, 3 in. at the edge, much thicker below.

As restored in the museum, the jar stands 2 ft. 6 in.

high, 2 ft. 6 in. in diameter.

Sprawling letters, .5 in. to .625 in. high (o),

and (the rest) 1 in. or a little more. Broken, and not

easy to read:

$$].\alpha\tau\alpha\beta[\qquad]\kappa o\nu\nu o\upsilon\beta\rho[$$

All the letters in line 1 broken at top, and also

β in line 2 at the bottom. The latter is certain; but

in line 1 β is much more doubtful, and τ far from certain.

It appears as Υ (commonly read τι), perhaps not π ,

though Υ would be an unusual form of τ . The first

letter in line 1 may have been μ, or α, or λ . In

line 2 ν is N .

Heichelheim in PW 16, 1933, 953.60a manifestly

would read $\mu\alpha\tau\rho\alpha\beta[$ for Dottin's $\mu\alpha\tau\iota\alpha\beta$, though $\mu\alpha\tau\rho\iota\beta o$,

not even $\mu\alpha\tau\rho\epsilon\beta o$, would be better Keltic. If the insc.

is indeed votive, then in line 2 $\beta\epsilon$ may be expanded $\beta\rho\alpha\tau o\upsilon\delta\epsilon$

Do. 158.29; CIL 12, p. 832. Cf. 74 bis below?

124

Inscription of Montmirat

66

Observed in Nov. 1907 at the Castellar de Montmirat, the hill towering above the plain of Montmirat itself, and evidently the site of an ancient oppidum, whence this and other ancient stones had been taken for modern buildings, see F. Mazauric, Mém. de l'Acad. de Nimes 30, 1907, 364-365, who first reported this insc. Given by M. Hippolyte Martin to the Musée arch. et épigr. de Nimes, seen there by me.

12 in. by 12.5 in. by 5 in. thick, apparently a fragment of the top of an altar; lime-stone. At the right corner, beneath the moulding, in letters 2 in. high (except o , 1.125 in.), broken on right.

$$\beta\rho\alpha\tau{ou\tau[}$$

τ has lost its cross-bar; otherwise the writing is perfect, and τ at the end, instead of the usual - δ (ε), is remarkable.

Do. 157.24

Human occupation of the site of Nimes (Nemausus,
also the name of the local god of springs) and its
neighborhood goes back to prehistoric times. But the
Keltic oppidum does not antedate c. 300 B.C., when the
Kelts reached Languedoc, viz at Nimes ancestors of the
tribe known to the Romans as the Volcae Arecomici. It
shared the development both of the late La Tène period,
and of the Greek civilization spread by Marseille. The
element nem- of the name is doubtless I.Eu. (Lat. nemus)
and may be Keltic (cf. Nemesii 2 above), but -ausus is
not so clearly defined (cf. Gröhler FO 1, 1913, 160).
The insc. 67 has γαμκυσικαβο, and native coins have
Ναμασατ (ισ) as well as νεμαυ(σατισ?), cf. 78 below.
It is striking that the similar name of another place
(Νέμωσσος, capital of the Aruerni, Str. 4.2.3, 191C)
shows the -ss- suffix associated with pre-I.Eu. settlements (cf. perhaps Tartessus; and note the Ispana [regio?]
at Nimes, CIL 12.3363); and that yet a third place, modern
Nemours (Seine-et-Marne), assumed to come from *Nemau(s)sos
(or -ōssos), shows a characteristically Keltic substitution of -rs- for an older -(s)s- (see Weisgerber,
SprFK 187; Geffcken Festschr. 171), not shown in the
development of the modern name Nimes. Iberian names
have -sx- as well as -ss-. But I now think that the

Nimes

supposed connexion of these with Νέμωσσος and *Nemaus(s)os
(-ossos) is merely superficial, and that we have to do
with a change from -aus- to -a(s)s- or -o(s)s-, see
further the Grammar.

Roman influence began with the conquest of
Narbonensis in the last quarter of the second century
B.C., and a Roman colony was planted at Nimes itself in
46-45 B.C. Gaulish inscriptions in the Greek alphabet
cannot be later than the latter date; more probably they
belong to the earlier period, say c. 125-120 B.C., before
the influence of Marseille was undermined. The epigraphic testimony is in accord with this date.

The magnificent ruins of the Roman period no less
than the network of roads which diverged from the city,
testify to the importance which Nimes held for the
imperial administration. See E. Linkenheld in PW, s.v.
Nemausus (16 ii, 1935, 2286-2310); E. Espérandieu, Le
Musée lapidaire de Nimes 1924 has proved inaccessible
to me; CA 8, 1941; R. Naumann, Der Quellbezirk von Nimes
(Arch. Inst. des deutchen Reiches, Denkmäler antiker
Architektur, Bd. 4), Berlin and Leipzig, 1937; F. Benoit,
Nimes Arles et La Camargue, Paris 1946.

Inscriptions of Nimes

67
    Since its discovery "dans les travaux de la
Fontaine" at Nimes (cf. 73 below) in 1742, this important
votive insc., in honor of the "Mother-Goddesses of
Namausus," has been damaged in several places. But there
is an early account of it by the architect Dardailhon,
preserved in the archives of the public library of Nimes
(Séguier, ms. 13802 I 10), ca. 1745.

    The abacus of a capital of white marble on which

the insc. stands came to light during excavations con-

ducted that year at the spring in association with which,

as with so many springs in Gaul and elsewhere, a cult

existed in ancient times. Almost 3 feet long, 21.75 in.

from front to back; the vertical face, 3 in. deep, in

front of the abacus, is filled by the two lines of text,

in neat letters of 1 in. to 1.25 in. high (except o ,

.75 in.), with A , M , open β , Y , E , Σ .

    Now in the Musée archéologique et épigraphique at
Nimes (Ancien Lycée, 17 Grand' Rue), seen there by me
(no. 168.43). First published by Colson, Mém. de l'Acad.
du Gard 1850-51 [1851] 75-96 (cf. Procès-Verbaux, 254-
272)

κ]αρταρ[οσι]λλανουιακοσδεδε|

ματρεβοναμαυσικαβοβρατουδε

    The restorations in line 1 are based upon the old

ms. copy and the older editions; the letters marked with

a dot beneath are now all more or less damaged, [οσι]

had vanished before 1850, and κ] was so imperfect then

as to be misread as ι , and ρ as β . Colson gives a

Inscriptions of Nimes

clear ιτ for ι in line 1.

Do. 155.19; CIL 12, p. 383 n. 1, p. 833; Hubert,
RC 11, 1890, 249-252

Remark:

On the "Culte des Sources dans la cité gallo-
romaine de Nimes," see the article by Marrou in Congrès
de Nimes (Association Guillaume Budé) 1932, 186-195.
Cf. AcS 2.463-473 (dedications to the Matres, Matrae,
Matronae); Heichelheim in PW 14, 1930, s.v. Matres;
R. Meissner ibid. 2219 f., 2245 (where Aufaniae is held
to be cognate with Ubii), E. Bickel Rh. Mus. 87, 1938,
193-141 (some additional evidence; summary in Ph. Woch.
1939, 425); 88, 1939, 348 (not altogether convincing);
BJ 143-144, 1939, 209-220. Other references, 223 Remark
below, where I shall return to the question. My view
is that the cult of matres or Iunones in the Rhineland
is a cult adopted by Germanic-speaking tribes, who took
it over from the older Keltic-speaking tribes who preceded them. Ihm in BJ 83, 1887, 9 (cf. 122) assigned
the insc. 67 above to the (frankly impossible) date of
the first century of the present era.

129

Inscriptions of Nimes

68

On two adjoining faces of a rectangular block of
hard, reddish-colored stone, discovered at Nimes in the
rue de la Lampèze in 1876 (see Germer-Durand, Procès-
Verbaux de l'Académie du Gard 1876, 40-42; id. Revue
des Sociétés Savantes 4, 1876 [1877], 266-270, with
interpretation by d'Arbois de Jubainville; cf. BSAF 1876,
95-97). Now in the museum at Nimes (no. 128, together
with a plaster cast of the insc.), seen there by me.

15.75 in. by 8.75 in. by 8.75 in. The insc. is

on the upper part of two adjacent faces, somewhat

roughly cut, with a few peculiar letter-forms, e.g. $'O o$

(if the "apex" is original) in line 3, B β , $\lceil$ and $\lceil \sigma$,

$\wedge$ as well as A , M and $\mathsf{N} v$. The puncts, which have

been questioned (I think, without good reason) are clear

enough, but may not be original. No finials; the alpha-

bet (note σ, $\lfloor$) is probably later than that of no. 67.

The inclined line in my transcription indicates the edge

of the stone, the two faces adjoining which bear the

insc.

$$\kappa\alpha\sigma\sigma\iota/\tau\alpha\lambda o\sigma|o u\epsilon\rho\sigma\iota/\kappa v o\sigma\,\delta|\epsilon\delta\epsilon$$

5    $$\beta\rho/\alpha\cdot\tau\cdot o u\,\delta|\epsilon\kappa\alpha v\tau/\epsilon v\alpha\cdot\lambda\alpha|\mu\iota\cdot\epsilon\iota v o/u\iota\iota$$

μ in line 4 is doubtful ($v\iota$?); at the end of that

line v is V (elsewhere Y), taken (with $\iota\iota$) as a

numeral (VII) in BSAF l.c., but $v\iota\iota$ ib. 1881, 284.

Do. 155.20; CIL 12, pp. 383, 833

Inscriptions of Nimes

69

A well preserved insc., very clear and everywhere certain. On a piece of brown stone, over 3 feet high, 10 in. wide, ca. 12 in. wide at the bottom, and ca. 5 in. thick at the top, perhaps 6 in. at the bottom (it was impossible to take more precise measurements). Said to have been discovered in the eighteenth century, at "les Garrigues" (quartier Calinier or Gallinié) at Nimes, recorded in the Séguier mss. (1703-1784) nos. 13801 and 13802 (at Nimes) and 16930 (Bibl. Nat., Paris). The stone itself was long lost sight of; shortly after its rediscovery "au quartier des Tours-Seguin" ca. 1890 (see Hippolyte Bazin, Nimes Gallo-Romaine, Paris 1892, 128 n. 1), it was given to the Museum at Nimes (no. 138), where it still is; seen there by me.

Rounded at the top, insc. 4.5 in. below the highest point; letters 1.5 in. to 1.625 in. (except о, 1.25 in. to 1.375 in.): Є , (σ , Ξ ξ , Ν ν .

ЄσΚιγγο | ρ ЄΙ ξ Κ0 | νδιλλЄ0σ

The misreading κονδειλλεος appears to go back to Séguier (cf. CRAcInscBL 8, 1881, 259).

Do. 156.21; CIL 12, p. 383

Inscriptions of Nimes

70
    Discovered in April 1906, in excavations at Saint-
Baudile-le-Vieux, Nimes, built into a medieval wall,
but clearly sepulchral in character, doubtless having
been taken from the nearby ancient cemetery, see F.
Mazauric, Mém. de l'Acad. de Nimes 30, 1907, 308. Now
in the museum at Nimes, seen and copied by me.

    A block of reddish stone, 2 feet 8 in. high, 7.5

in. square at the top, unworked at the bottom, where

some two-thirds of the whole is left in the rough and

probably was set into the earth above a grave. The

writing is now very faint, and almost illegible in

places, letters ca. 1.25 in. or 1.5 in. high. The text

stands on two opposite faces, and I thought I detected

traces of writing on a third face, as well as traces of

other letters in addition to those now barely visible

on faces A and C.

(a)   α δ γ ε . ν ο υ ι | [

(b)   ] . . .   . . . [

(c)   α δ γ ε ν | ο ο υ

Cf. no. 49 above.

Rhys's δ | ε δ ε β in lines 2-3 of (a) is pure
imagination. Nor did I see any final ν in (a) 1
(Mazauric). Both Rhys and Mazauric have οουδ in line
2 of (c), with ν at the beginning of that line in M.'s
copy; neither is there. If this is a sepulchral insc.,

132

Inscriptions of Nimes

why look for ϳεδε or βρϥτοοδε? Why, indeed!

Do. 156.23

Note xiii (Do. 157.25)

After Mazauric, l.c. 365: "Au cours d'une promenade à Saint-Césaire" [two miles S.W. of Nimes, in the direction of Montpellier] "je remarquai dans un fossé, coté droit de la route, en face le Café de Font Jaïsse, une pierre très fruste sur laquelle apparaissaient quelques charactères qui me parurent antiques."

Now in the museum at Nimes, seen by me.

2 ft. 4 in. by 14 in.(left) and 7 in. (right) by 15 in. thick. Great sprawling letters, ρ 9 in. high, τ 7.5 in., ο 3.75 in., υ (what is left of it) 6 in., all somewhat suspicious in character, cf. 66 above.

βριτου[

The insc. breaks off on right, where υ is damaged at the top; ο has a central punct, and before ρ , on left, I detected part of what was intended for β , viz the lower part, ℔ .

Authentic? It looks to me like a misguided attempt to reproduce the familiar βρϥτουδε .

133

Inscriptions of Nimes

71
    This fragment of an abacus of white marble, very
similar to, and with writing of a style identical with
that of, the insc. no. 67 above, was found in 1886 at
Saint-Cosme in the vicinity of Nimes (see Bulletin de
l'Acad. de Nimes 1886, 133). Despite that fact, it may
belong originally to the same structure. Deposited in
the museum at Nimes, seen and copied there by me.

    The letters are exactly the same size, 1 to 1.25
in. high, as in 67, and are engraved upon the front face
of an abacus of exactly the same width, viz. 3 in.   The
other dimensions are: at the front 15 in. long, at the
back 22 in., from front to back 19 in.   Fine alphabet,
with finials, broken only on left.

]αδρεσσικνοσ|]υιβρατουδεκα

which must have continued]ντενα on another piece (cf.
Note xiv bis, unless κα is an abbreviation.

        Do. 157.27; CIL 12, p. 833.   Cf. Guillemaud RA 8,
1886, 362; Bull Épigr. de la Gaule 5, 1886, 294-296;
BSAF 1886, 254; 1887, 67

72
    Said to have been visible at one time in the vine-
yard of the Guirand family at Nimes, presumably discovered there.   The first record of it is in the Guiran
(sic, Do.) ms. dated 1652, now preserved in the Bibl.

impériale at Vienne (2, p. 391), see CIL 12, p. 383.
Enquiries addressed to a member of the family still
resident at Nimes have been unfruitful, and the stone
may now be considered lost. Apparently in two lines,

$$\text{καTO} | \text{υαλοσ}$$

with ⱷ recorded as A , σ as C , and υ as V (not Υ).

Do. 158.30

73
     This insc., discovered in 1739 at the Fontaine of
Nimes (cf. 67), was too imperfectly reported in the
first place (Histoire de l'Académie des Inscriptions
et Belles-Lettres 14, 1743, pp. 106-7, Plate I c) to
make restoration certain. The original is long since
lost. Cf. BSAF 1881, 284.

$$]\text{υιιρυρεουεο}[\quad | \quad]\text{ουαβ}[\text{ο}]\text{δεδε}$$
$$\text{λε}[\qquad |\text{βραT}]\text{ουδεκαντεν}[$$

The mixture of Greek and Latin alphabetic forms
(e.g. L in lines 1 and 2, read by me as ε ; D as well
as △ in line 2, read as δ and δ respectively; F in
line 3, read here as κ) is mere blundering; so for A
(line 3, third extant letter) I have given δ . In line 1

135

Inscriptions of Nimes

the fourth letter appears as $)$ (for φ?), and the sixth
as b (for P_ρ, or for $\mathsf{B}\beta$?). If -υι in line 1 ends a
word, ιουρεου will make sense, and εο[is a possible
beginning of a word. In line 4 βρατ] is an obvious and
certain restoration.

Do. 158.28; CIL 12, p. 383 no. 4

74

This inscription, if not Greek, may be Keltic. It
has often been regarded with suspicion, but to fabricate
a Keltic insc. was beyond the powers of any forger in
1742.

μεθθιλλος καστ|ιμοτουλου σε

γο|μανικοσ· κεκονιακε

On a mosaic fragment, discovered in 1742, at the
Fontaine at Nimes. From the ms. of Séguier, see Barry,
Lebègue, Germer-Durand, Insc. antiques de Languedoc
1893, p. 779 no. 560, the reading of which is certain.
My conjectures (Hermann Festschrift) may, therefore, be
misplaced, viz. that καντενα may be concealed in κε-
κονιακε.

136

Inscriptions of Nimes

74 bis

Inscription of uncertain provenance. I was unable, even after a long search, to find this insc., said to be preserved in the museum at Nimes, and presumably found somewhere in the neighborhood. But it was seen there by Rhys in 1905, and may have been temporarily "lost" or misplaced when I sought it in 1929. Rh. describes it as being "on a small piece of brick-like substance," Do. "tablette de grès rouge." It turned up in 1879 in the Bibliothèque, but there is no record of its actual provenance.

First published BSAF 1879, 293, cf. CIL 12, pp. 383, 838. It is read

$$]\mu\beta\alpha\tau\iota[\quad | \quad]\tau o o \upsilon[\quad | \quad]\tau\iota\nu[$$

Do. 156.22. Cf. no. 65 above?

Note xiv (IG 14.2510)

Discovered in 1734, near the Fontaine at Nimes. "Cubus lapideus in Dianae templum ablatus" Dardailhon ap. Séguier cod. Nem. 13802, p. 10, whence Durand, Inscr. de Nimes, ms. no. 408. "Dubito num Graeca sint uocabula" Kaibel. But $\epsilon\phi o\rho o\sigma$, which is given as the first word, can hardly be anything else; as for the second, zminbr (sic), if this is in the Latin alphabet, is presumably not Keltic. But if the original shows the Greek alphabet, then perhaps read

$$?] \sigma\mu\iota\nu \beta\rho[\alpha\tau o\upsilon\delta\epsilon\ ?$$

In this at least $\beta\rho$ would be familiar. Z may be mis-copied for Σ , or Γ , or Ξ , or even Λ .

137

Inscription of Substantion

Note xiv bis (CIL 12.3044)

Just as in 68, 70 and 71 above, the text was inscribed on two adjoining faces, so an insc. discovered
in 1739 at the Fountain of Nimes seems to have had a
Keltic inscription similarly engraved. But in ancient
times it was recut, so as to make a new surface for a
Latin text. The remains of the Keltic text appear now
only on the adjacent face, and read

$$] \sigma \ldots \quad | \quad \ldots \quad]\varkappa \nu \tau \epsilon \nu.$$

with $\Sigma\, \sigma$, and then obviously $\kappa]\alpha\nu\tau\epsilon\nu\alpha$.

It is not to be confused with 73 above. According
to Hist. de l'Académie 14 (Paris, 1743) p. 107, Pl. 3 (r),
it comes from the ms. of Séguier, and served as the
capital of a column. The restoration of the Latin text
given in CIL is doubtful, for it is then made a dedication to Apollo; we should assume rather some Keltic
divine name.

5. Hérault

75

On the abacus of a lime-stone column, with a rude
capital, broken at the corners, 28 in. by 27 in. by 7 in.
The insc. is incised on two edges, and these are now
fragmentary; letters 2.5 in. high (except $\circ$, 1.75 in.).

Discovered in 1840, see Inscriptions de Languedoc
(cf. 64, 74 above) 1893, p. 573 no. 107; CIL 12, p. 383.
Given by its discoverer, M. l'abbé Bourgade, to the

Inscription of Substantion

collections (Musée lapidaire) preserved in the first
court of the Palais de l'Université at Montpellier, the
property of the Société d'Archéologie de Montpellier,
it is reported to have come from Substantion, the ancient
Sextantio (CIL 12.3362, 6), now Castelnau-le-Lez, which
stands 2 miles north-east of Montpellier, across the
river Lez. Seen there by me.

 The provenance was given erroneously as Murviel
by Héron de Villefosse (BA 1887, 206), or as Pignon
(by Hirschfeld, CIL 12, p. 508); see, for the correct
account, the Procès-verbaux de la Soc. Archéologique
de Montpellier, 8 fév. 1840, and E. Bonnet in Mém. de
la Soc. arch. de Montpellier, 9, 1924, 93-120; id.,
Monspeliensia 1, 1930, 79-85, cf. Congrès de Nîmes
(Assoc. Guillaume Budé), 1932, 123.

 (a) μ̣ . στιλλ[

 (b) .ιvουσιδ[

 Bonnet (Mém., l.c.) reads]ιγλλ[and]ιvουειδ[,
in the latter of which he interprets δ as δ[εδε], and
takes -ουει as dat. sg.

 The stone appears to have been cleaned, and some
of its cement removed since Rhys saw it in 1910 (Add.
and Corr., 27-28), so that much more is now legible on
face (a), where, near the left, we have a doubtful letter
(broken at the top), either μ or α, then a break followed
by σ, next two upright strokes (either ιι, or ιτ, or τι),

139

Inscriptions of Substantion and Montagnac

λ (almost complete), another λ , or rather the bottom
of the left limb, with space for four or five letters
thereafter.

In (b) only one letter is wanting on left, five
or six on right; between them everything is certain.
σ has a middle punct, as occasionally elsewhere (e.g.
35,53); not an interpunct between words.

Do. 154.18

76
Engraved around the lower part of the circular
lime-stone capital of a column (not the base of a
column), discovered at Montagnac in 1898, now in the
cloisters of the cathedral of Saint-Nazaire at Béziers;
seen there by me. First published by Noguier and Héron
de Villefosse, BSAF 1899, 274-275; cf. Noguier, Bulletin
de la Société archéologique, scientifique et littéraire
de Béziers, 3, 1899, 190-192.

2 feet 1 in. in diameter at the top, 19 in. high.

There is a round hole at the top, into which a key was

fitted to hold the capital in place (an old "messendes

Dübellock" 12 c. deep, 5.5 cm. square, Jacobsthal);

around this are incised concentric rings, and around the

edge itself, linear looped and angular patterns. The

insc. is near the lower edge, 2 in. or 3 in. from the

bottom, lightly cut, in letters .5 in. high (o) to .75

in. (Κ,Τ), up to 1.5 in. high (ρ,υ); σ is Σ , Α.

Inscription of Montagnac

I read the text as follows:

$$\alpha\lambda\lambda\epsilon\tau\epsilon\nu o\sigma\kappa\alpha\rho\nu o\mu o\upsilon\alpha\lambda\iota\sigma o..\epsilon\alpha\sigma$$

in one continuous line, no interpuncts. The third letter is probably λ, not α, but damage to the stone makes it uncertain. Then, after τ, either ϵ or η, not ι, for the cross-bars are clear (E or H). Before $o\upsilon$, almost certainly μ, not ν; there are three strokes surviving, thus N (not N, as elsewhere in this insc.), followed by a broken surface of stone, where the final stroke of μ must have come. In $\lambda\iota$ the iota is broken at the top, but τ could not have stood here. Space for two letters before $-\epsilon\alpha\sigma$ at the end.

Cf. Jacobsthal, Arch. Anz. 45, 1930, 235-236; I agree with him that this text is one of the oldest, if not the oldest, of our extant Keltic inscc., written in a Greek alphabet of the third, rather than the second, century B.C., and certainly not of the Roman period (Dottin).

Do. 159.32 bis; Rev. Épigr. du Midi de la France IV 1899-1902, 83.1326; J. Dardé [et J. Sournies], Histoire de Béziers racontée par ses pierres (Musée lapidaire), Béziers 1912, 11-12, Pl. II; BSAF 1899, 274-75 offers a v.l.-νισκ.

Defixio of Amélie-les-Bains

Note xv

    I see no reason to doubt the authenticity of a
defixio found in 1845 "dans la principale source
thermale" at Amélie-les-Bains (in the Pyrénés-Orientales,
ca. 35 km. south-west of Perpignan), CIL 12.5367 (cf.
A. Audollent, Defixionum Tabellae 1904, 173-5, 114-120),
facsimile in Inscr. de Languedoc (see 64, 74 above) 387-
388, 1306. The text is uncertainly read; but it appears
to contain at least some names, and possibly other words,
of a dialectal character (Iberian or Gaulish?), cf.
R. Wünsch, Rh. Mus., N.F. 55, 1900, 270, as well as
familiar Latin items; Do. p. 43.

       (a) kantasnis kat | rogamos et de | petamukiosot |

5   sa uate non | lerano et de ‖ ux nesoapeteia |]et

    eleta nesoa..la |]nuki[|]   [

       (b) nisqie | kilitiusi | metat | ulaten |

5   ]ruet[‖]p[

       (c) nikasquite | rogamus ..s | ssyatis numena |

5   s.. niueldela | res..nuquai ‖ autete   cuma[

       (d) kenumene maximie flaucre | illiussiroes...

    quae ant quid..ruid | asetiuat laaokrios | ucapos-

5   ima atxexiaia | os niam cat.. on   ... ‖ s   non

    euostrim|m..t.atinum | ul(l.)xki..ki | ohir

       (e) demeti[

       (f)]αμικιου[

       (g) axx ... |]eaub[| axsonis

       (h) domxsaa| niskasrog[| mos et de[|

    ]tamus |]dinno[|]nn[

       (i)]colos[

Defixio of Amélie-les-Bains

Noteworthy are at least kantas niskas, in (a)
line 1, (h) line 2, cf. nisqie in (b) line 1(?), and
ucaposima in (d) 4, the former of which recalls not
only Ven. ka·n·ta (see PID 3.11), but also certain
Keltic forms, e.g. Candai, Cantismerta, cantalon,
cantlon, ϗɑντενɑ́ , cantuna, cantus, Cantium (cf. AcS
1.737-757, 3.1071-1083 cf. Canta insula [Illyr.], Thes.
Ling. Lat., Onom., s.v.; see also the Glossary; Pokorny,
Urg. 149, 153, cf. 46, 155), just as Ven. lau·s·ko·s·
and Vpsedia have Gaulish equivalents (Lascus 132,
uχsedia at La Graufesenque); the latter recalls Vιϭκɑ(?)
in 74 above, Nescato in 87. The k- of kanta, and -sk-
of niska(s), lau·s·ko·s·(cf. p. 57, 19 Remark; and 82
below) should be considered in connexion with the whole
problem of the treatment of $\hat{k}$, q, $\hat{k}\underset{\sim}{u}$, q$\underset{\sim}{u}$. The form
ucaposima wears the appearance of a quasi-Keltic superl-
ative; but cf. paramus (158). The repeated nesoa
(a 6, 8) is probably a complete word; with ulaten (?)
in (b) 4 cf. the coins in -en (77) and the names in
Vlat(t)- in AcS 3.20-22. But (d) 2 is obvious Latin
(illustres or illius sorores?), as are certain other
words; numenas and (?) kenumene (c) 3-4 and (d) 1 might
well be Greek, but cf. Leherenni (86); so perhaps l[aa]o-
krios in (d) 3; there are no doubt also several nonsense-

Defixio of Amélie-les-Bains

words, e.g. (d) 4 atxexiaiaos of the type familiar
enough in curses; as well as, finally, the usual mixture
of languages and dialects.

I have given the reading of CIL l.c., with one
correction, k for c in (c) 1 third letter; but it is
admittedly dubious, and other readings may be found in
Inscr. de Languedoc l.c.; note especially (c) 1: niskas
aquis (?), and (ib.) the suggestion that the kantai
niskai were goddesses of healing springs, a suggestion
which the provenance of the entire defixio makes highly
probable.

deux at (a) 4-5 and, if rightly divided, atxesc
in (d) 4, ull.xki (ib. 7) definitely suggest Iberian
(-qš, -qs is a frequent ending, e.g., bulaqš, libaqš,
uaraqš, aratqš, eoalaqš, ilacapqš; cf. the glosses
camox, ibex [Alpine, item 1 above] and balux 158); and
in fact a strong case has been made for considering
much in the Roussillon that used to be considered
Ligurian (e.g. Elisykes n.sg. Elisux or -yx, cf. Βέβρυξ)
as Iberian, see P. Fouché "Les Ligures en Espagne et
en Roussillon," in Revue Hispanique 81 i, 1933, 319-346.

Remark:

On Le Roussillon in general, see the useful
summary by R. Lantier REA 21, 1919, 271-289; Répertoire
archéologique (since 1930) of the Féderation historique
de Langedoc méditerranéen et du Roussillon (RA 10, 1937,
397; cf. REA 39, 1937, 363). To this day the Roussillon,

Graffiti of Ensérune

which was politically part of Spain until 1659, preserves in language, architecture, the arts, and in the physical appearance of its people, a great deal that reminds the visitor more of Spain than of France.

Chronique de toponymie by Fouché in REA 38, 1936, 431-438; the same author has a useful Chronique philologique des parlers provinçaux anciens et modernes [1913-24] in Rev. de ling. rom. 2, 1926, 113-136; cf. Revue hispanique 81, 1933, 319-346; J. Jannoray Gallia 4, 1946, 357-360. H. Breuil sees Iberian influence in arms on the ancient monuments of Provence, RA 6, 1917, 68-74.

Note xvi

Excavations at Ensérune (cf. 77b below) have brought to light large quantities of pottery of various styles and date, among it a quantity of Iberian ware, some specimens with inscriptions, see Corpus Vasorum Antiquorum, France Fasc. 6 (Collection Mouret, Fouiles d'Ensérune) 1927 [?], Texte p. 28. The reading is dubious, chiefly because of the uncertainty that surrounds the phonetic values of the Iberian symbols. I have followed, in the main, Manuel Gómez-Moreno's La escritura ibérica in Boletín de la real Academia de la Historia 112, Madrid 1943, 251-278 (cf. Word 3, 1947, 228-29).

nos. (1), (2) aveṭirišanmi

(3) boboalcarteabiṛli

(4) ulisanmi

(5) iabobᵓe

(7) oa ?   (8) ucece ?

(9) κιν   (10) βαλ

(11) ars   (12) ošann n n ?

Ib.,p.38,no.(1) v   (2) cotina

p. 39, no.(9) e

    Since certain symbols denote either a voiced or
a breathed consonant followed by a vowel, it is possible
to read di instead of ti in 28 (1), and go and di instead
of co and ti in 38 (2); 28 (6) appears to be in Greek
script (βε), and also (10). But some or all of the
vases with Iberian inscc. found at Ensérune, no less than
of the other kinds of pottery, may well have been imported
and, therefore, be no indication of the local dialect.
It is difficult, however, to believe that both Iberian
ware and Iberian coin-legends would have been found so
plentifully at Ensérune unless an Iberian settlement
existed there, speaking some variety of Iberian.

    Additional references (cf. 77; 79, Remark ii;
Aquitania Introduction; 157 Remark viii); BA volumes for
1910-13, 1918 (cf. REA 13, 1911, 204; 14, 1912, 415; 16,
1914, 96-97; 19, 1917, 215; 21, 1919, 288 n. 10; 22, 1920,
128; 23, 1921, 59); CRAcInscBL 1910, 517 and 1916, 397;
Assoc. Budé, Congrès de Nice 1935, 131-135; Hubert RC 11,
1890, 488-490 (on local names); Formigé Gallia 1, 1943,

refs. ctd.]
1-14; RA 7, 1936, 95-109; 8, 1936, 211-212; 26, 1946, 5-41.

From Formigé loc. cit., p. 14 fig. 12 I take an
Iberian pottery stamp found at Ensérune, viz.

tiri (or d-)

As for IG 14.2573.3 (Toulouse, on a seal)

ασσι

may be Iberian; but

Vαματιoν

ib. 2573.10 (Arles, on a cachet d'oculiste) is presumably
Greek.

77
Coins of Narbonensis with Iberian Inscriptions.
See, in general, Hübner Mon. Lang. Iber. 1893, pp. 13-28,
nos. 1, 2, 10-12, 14, 15(a)-(c) with (e) and (g); G. F.
Hill in Numismatic Notes and Monographs 44, 1930 (cf.
Blanchet RC 48, 1931, 151-153); G. Amardel in Bulletin
de la Commission archéologique de Narbonne, N.S., 2,
1892-3, 153-158, 328-354; 3, 1894-5, 13-16; 4, 1896-7,
463-478; 9, 1906-7, 317-339, 341-362, 482-490; 10, 1908-9,
xxxvii and 593-628.

These are coins, imitations of Massiliot types,
struck by a number of tribes, more Iberian in character

147

than Gaulish or Ligurian, who lived west and south of
the Volcae Arecomici, in the neighborhood of Baeterrae
and Narbo Martius. Presumably the legends are local or
personal names; as such they are given here, as part of
the linguistic record of this portion of Narbonensis,
since they testify clearly to the existence there, in
pre-Roman times, of a language quite different from the
language or languages of the rest of the province. Its
Iberian affiliations are also clearly shown by other
issues, with the same and related types, of Emporiae
and adjoining sites south of the Pyrenees.

(1) Bronze Coins

(a) Montlaurès (a few kilometers north-west of
Narbonne; on Montlaurès see the, for the nonce, illum-
inating note of Jullian, REA 9, 1907, 271; id. ib. 7,
1905, 389; 12, 1910, 195), a site that preceded that of
Narbo (Hill 2-13; Hübner nos. 1, 2, 14; Blanchet Traité
des monnaies gauloises 1905, 276; Muret-Chabouillet,
Catalogue des monnaies gauloises de la Bibliothèque
Nationale 1889, 2444-2498).

neronc

neroncn

neroncen

neroncen šo

neronen

Iberian Coin-legends

The sign H , formerly read h, has been shown to
have the value rather of the o-vowel (Gómez-Moreno in
Homenaje a Menéndez-Pidal III 1925, 484; so far as I
can see J. Cejador Alphabet et inscriptions ibériques
Paris 1929, Arch. Bibl. 1932 no. 2688, is worthless;
for other references to discussions of the Iberian alphabet see Note xvi). The termination -cn or -cen is
believed to be equivalent to a gen. pl. by Schuchardt
Iberische Deklination (SB. ph.-hist. Kl. Akad. Wien
157.2, 1907-08, 37, cf. Rev. internat. des études
Basques 4, 1910, 323). It is possible that šo is an
abbreviation of the name seloncen below.

With neron-, Narbo cf. Naro in Avienus Or. Mar.
587, Νύραξ· πόλις Κελτική Hecetaeus ap. Steph. Byz.;
AcS 2.814; RC 38, 1920-21, 259; but Grenier Les Gaulois,
1945, 121 thinks of Noricum.

On the obverse of these coins:

tuiš

eba (or eva ?)

ecc

The second is also read ei (Hübner).

149

Iberian Coin-legends

There is a rare variety with the legend

neronc   pu[

(Berlin 368, 1877, Pl. I 6), a specimen of which at
Béziers is said to read pu[r]pcn, cf. purp on the coins
of the Longostaletes below (connected by some with the
name Pyrene, Pyrenaeus; by others with the modern local
name Perpignan): AcS s.v. Longostaletes; F. Mouret in
Congrès de Nimes (Association Guillaume Budé) 1932, 128-
134). According to Hill (p. 9), Paris 2496 (neroncencen)
"is a freak."

    Date: ca. 175-71 B.C.

    (b) "Selo" (from coins only; no literary record),
found at Ensérune (9 km. south-east of Béziers) and
elsewhere (Hill 13, Hübner no. 12; M-C 2468-2469)

šeloncen │ eva (?)

Cf. eva above, and also šo (a). On the recent excavations at Ensérune see Mouret l.c. (cf. ib., 119-120);
REA 36, 1934, 483-485; Philippe Héléna, Les Origines de
Narbonne 1937, 208-210 (where the Iberian invasion of
southern Gaul is dated ca. 475 B.C.) and Note xvi.

    (c) Of uncertain attribution, but from the same
district as the above (Hill 15-16; Hübner no. 15b) ĭerhĭ
(Hü., i.e. everovo ?), stigmatized by Hill as a barbarous
attempt to write neron.

Iberian Coin-legends

(d) Hübner no. 10 (public and private collections, Paris, Nimes, Béziers)

1 · šu | eva (?)

"in Hispania nunquam reperta est" (Hü., who [p. 13] assigns the coins in question to this region on the grounds of similarity of type, and of the legend eva). But the name 1 · šu is not identified.

(e) From Montlaurès and other sites.

pricatio

pricantio

(or, at the end -tin?). On the obverse

eva (?)

From Hill 16-18, Hü. no. 11; M-C 2499-2506

This name (Brigantio) is undoubtedly Keltic, and presumably the Iberians here succeeded a Gaulish tribe to the site. But Hill (18) calls attention to CIL 12. 3362 (Nimes, cf. p. 346) Brugetia. More likely, perhaps, is comparison with the personal name, known from coins of the region of Narbonne and Béziers βριγαντικοσ (AcS 3.937-938; cf. Mouret l.c. 132; Bonnet ib. 135), cf. (f) below.

Date: 2 - 1c. B.C.

151

(f) Coins of the Longostaletae (or -es; known only from coins, with the Greek legend λογγοϲταλητων, and on the obverse βωκιοϲ, λουκοτικνοϲ and apparently also λουκορικνο ϲ) and the Iberian legend

purp

Cf. (a) above, Πυρήνη Hdt. 2.33, Pyrene Avienus Or. Marit. 568 (south of the Pyrenees).

Hill 18-22; Hü. 2(b)-(c); M-C 2350-2399; Tr. 272-278

Date: ca. 250 B.C. Hill (23-26 cf. 33) observes that the coins of Narbo, with the same types as those of Béziers (βητ αρρατιϲ) and the names (in Greek alphabet) Amytos, [B]rigantikos, Bitoukos (or Bitouios), Kaintolos (Kaiant-) are contemporary, or even earlier; there was, therefore, an Iberian "risorgimento" in which the Iberian replaced, at least partially, the Greek alphabet.

(ii) Silver Coins

(g) Of uncertain ascription; a barbaric imitation of an Iberian legend of Narbonensis (Hü. 13) from "much nearer the Spanish border than any of the places of provenance mentioned," but some of them so far afield as Saint-Étienne (Landes), Hill 37 (writing of "unblun-

Iberian Coin-legends

dered [sic] examples").

acoequntin

Hü. 15(a), M-C 3548-3549; Tr. 284

Perhaps an attempt at writing Aquitani(a), or its Iberian equivalent.

(h) Unknown provenance. From Hill 38, Hü. 15(g), M-C 3558, Tr. 283:

untga

(i) A unique coin in the British Museum; Hill 38, Hü. 15(c):

d | iece

(k) See PID 2.616, 6* bis (c), M-C 2177-78; belonging to a town "under the supremacy of Marseilles," M-C, (Sextantio ?); Tr. 149. If the alphabet is Iberian, read perhaps:

ṣetetuce (?)

Remark:

For Hill's pirako (39 n. 1), Hü. 15 e (cf. pp. 27-28) see PID 2.131, no. 323.

78   Other Coins of Narbonensis

For primary sources see the references in AcS vols. 1-3, unless given here.

ade[

amacos

ambilli, ambilo[s]

an[

anduarto (RC 28, 1907, 276)

?anteios, antinos (but cf. Tr. 595)

ᾱοσσ[

ᾱουενιοᾱ

ᾱππε, ᾱππ

arec[omici] Tr. 435

arelat[e]

ᾱρητοιᾱμοσ (but cf. Tr. 101, 436)

ᾱνθεν (or ᾱθευ ?)

auscrocos and -us (cf. RC 48, 1931, 155)

βητᾱρρᾱτισ

βιτουκοσ (or -ουιοσ)

?βιτουιοτουο [σ], but cf. Tr. 105

βριγᾱντικοσ

βοκιοσ (cf. p. 152)

? ca[

cabe, κᾱβε

Καιᾱντολου, cf. ΚΑΙΙΙΤΟϹ (i.e. Καιᾱⁿτ ?)

κᾱινικητων

caitio[

calitix

cand[

carisius

cau[ares?]

?κιμενουλο Cf. p.39 above; but see Tr. 125

coma[nus?], coman[

?coou (for coue?)

cosii

coue[

?couepus (Tr. 262-3)

?cous[

?κρισσο Cf. Tr. 240; de Brun Cahiers 12, 1937, 484 has apparently ΚΦΞΞΟ

donnus (cf. Tr. 262)

durnacos (cf. auscrocos)

eburo[Tr. 262

Coins of Narbonensis

ηλικιοτ(αγ) Ascribed to the Elesykes (PID 1. 376) by G. Amardel, Bull. Comm. Arch. de Narbonne, 9. 1906-7, 482-490

esianni (Tr. 121)

γλανικων

λακυδων Tr. 230

λογ

λομ and λομβο

λογγοσταλητων

λοσσ[or λοσσ Tr. 240

λουκοτικνοσ (or -ρικνοσ)

μα Tr. 128

μασσα

να[

ναμασατ[

ναμανσατ[Tr. 130

?νεμαυ[Tr. 101

oltuba

?oma

ϖαρ Cf. Tr. 133

perrucori (Tr. 264; but cf. AcS 2.980 and items 153, 158 below)

πν

πο

πυδ AcS 1.683

ra[

ricant[

roueca, ροουικα (arc-antodan-type)

σαμναγητων

σεγοβι (? or ρ̇ -)

σεμερ (for ιεμερ ?)

setu, setubo

turoca (cf. Tr. 88)

ued[

?uirodu[Cf. Tr. 263

?uolk (AcS 3.424, Tr. 147 read uock)

uol(cae)

Items in Latin Inscriptions

Remark:

(i) CIL 12.1657 (Die, Drôme)

arep[ennis

cf. 158 below

(ii) ib. 372 (Riez)

ceruisia (?)

cf. 178 below

(iii) IG 14.2578, 2 (Nimes)

qu   X

on weights.

(iv) CIL 12.2404 (a Christian insc., 523 A.D.)

aliberga

usually considered a personal name, has been interpreted
as the Frankish *(h)aliberga, heriberga "auberge" by
Pirson p. 236; cf. REW 4045.

79   Glosses

Only the minimum of testimonia is cited or quoted;
for the rest see Holder or the ll. cc. Cf. items 1; 200.

<u>acerabulus</u>: mapuldur (O.E.) CGL 5.340.1

adarabulum 149 Rem., Prov. ardzerable, izrable,
Fr. érable (cf. Meyer-Lübke, REW 93), and also Prov.
azedur (on this see Bertoldi BSL 32, 1931, 130); Vendryès,
RC 32, 1911, 128 deduces a Gaulish *abulos "tree;" cf.
opulus PID 2.204, but not Lat. ebulus (Gaul. odocos).
Probably, therefore, a hybrid of acer Lat., *abulos Kelt.,
both meaning "maple."

That a genuine Narbonese (Massiliot?) form is
preserved in Hesych. ἄκαστος· ἡ σφένδαμνος, Prov. agast,
agas, is at least possible.

<u>allo-</u> "other, second," <u>allobrogae</u> (-<u>es</u>) "exiles"

Sch. Iuv. 8.234 brogae Galli agrum dicunt, alla
autem aliud. Cf. PID 3.4 (alios); at La Graufesenque
(92-3 below) allos; cf. SprFK 192. Hence allobrogae
"ex alio loco translati." (Sch. Iuv. l.c.; Do. 225),
cf. W. allfro "exile," Terracini in Scritti Trombetti
339. On broga see below, with Housman CR 37, 1923, 60
(nom. sg. Allobrox).

<u>ambannus</u> "auvent"

Du Cange quotes a text of 1327 from Solignac
(Haute-Loire). See Jud, <u>Romania</u>, 49, 1923, 39; Jud
derives the word from <u>ande</u> and <u>banno-</u> "horn," in the
sense of "le grand jet an avant du toit." Cf. Meyer-
Lübke, <u>Einf</u>. 39.

Apparently related to Benacus with an:en (both
from ṇ), cf. Proleg. 52 (with n. 97), K. Meyer ZfCPh 7,
1909-10, 270 and 509; Cantobennicus mons (148) i.q.
Candidensis (AcS 3.1080, 54) so that canto- is rendered
"candidus," cf. Candidus (DN, 181) perhaps i.q. "Loucetius."
It is not likely that either Cebenna or penno- belong here,
despite a certain similarity of meaning.

157

Glosses of Narbonensis

ambrox: Gallus CGL 5.491.5

Probably the ethnicon Ambro(n), like Allobrox ib.

?andosa: invictus CIL 12.4316 (Narbonne)

So Holder 1.149-150. But it would seem rather
that Ilunno Andose together correspond to the Inuictus
of his second text. Presumably Iberian, not Keltic.
Cf. 82, 86-7.

[?arepo

This "form" in the well-known word-square (CIL
12.202* cet.) is translated ἄροτρον in a Greek version,
see Holder AcS 1.206 (cf. 3.677). Hence, compared with
the genuine arepennis (e.g. CIL 12.1657), it was accepted
as Keltic. But discovery of the square, in varying
arrangements, both at Pompeii and at Doura-Europos, makes
this explanation very unlikely. Moreover the entire
square, it has been supposed, is a concealed "pater noster"
combined with ᾱ and ω. But was there a Latin version of
the Lord's prayer in existence before the destruction of
Pompeii, and a Latin version written in Greek letters at
that — at least the first two words? An earlier attempt
to solve the problem by a cruciform arrangement may be
found in MSAF 5, 1904-05, 160-186; the most recent appears
to be Déonna's (after Jerphanion) Genava 22, 1944, 135.
(In passing, we may note that the arrangement of auot,
mentioned p. 115 above, appears in some of Déonna's
examples, see for instance his p. 134 with footnotes.)
The explanation "a rerum extremarum principio omni" (AE
1945, p. 174) is wide of the mark; on Sundwall's in Act.
Acad. Aboensis Hum. XV 1945, no. 5, see AE 1946, p. 240.
From A. Bezzenberger's Litauische Forschungen (1882)
p. 72, it appears that a corrupt form of the "square"
has been current in Lithuania in modern times. Hence,
the attempt to extract articulate sense from arepo, even
in the ancient version, seems a forlorn endeavor. C.
Wendel Z. f. neutest. Wissenschaft 40, 1941 [1942], 138-
151, 255, gives a summary of recent theories. The possibility that arepo should be read as a personal name is
not to be overlooked; it may even be, as has been suggested, a Vulgar Latin arripo "robber," otherwise unrecorded. [Add now Mus. Helueticum 5, 1948, 16-59]

Glosses of Narbonensis

It is evident, however, (1) that arepo may not be a real word; and (2) if it is, that it is hardly a genuine Keltic word. A very large number of discussions of the problem has appeared during the last two decades. With a few earlier ones, dated during the present century alone, I have noted some fifty references, which it would be useless to repeat here. The conclusion to which I come is, that, whatever the meaning of arepo, its resemblance to arepennis, although perceived early enough to account for ἄροτρον in the Greek version, is merely accidental; on arepennis see 158 below.]

bacuceus "possessed of evil spirits"

Cassianus Massiliensis, conlat. 7.32, 2 (AcS 1. 324–5), cf. CGL 4.599.12, the Narbonese form corresponding to Gaulish dusius, q.v. 178(?): alios ita eorum corda quos ceperant inani quodam tumore uidemus infecisse, quos etiam bacuceos uulgus appellat...

banno- v. ambannus

boscus (medieval Lat.) "wood"

This word appears in a number of medieval Latin texts (9th to 11th centuries), see Werner Kaufmann, Die gallo-rom. Bezeichnungen für den Begriff "Wald" (Diss. Zurich, 1913), 45–49. Its source and etymology are disputed; neither Latin buxus nor Greek βόσκη, both of which are proposed, satisfy semantic requirements, and Kaufmann's conjecture of a pre-Roman (Ligurian?) word seems as likely as any.

Modern derivatives are widely diffused (Prov. bosc, Ital. bosco, Fr. bois), but, as Kaufmann suggests, the word appears to have spread from Narbonensis (where βόσκη in Massiliot Greek may have been confused with it). See now my paper in Havers Festschrift (Die Sprache 1, 1948, 123); Boxsani (80 below).

brīsare "exprimere" Schol. Pers. 1.76; cf. brīsilis

    "fragilis" Schol. Hor. C. 3.23, 16

    Ancient authority naturally regarded brisare as a denominative formed from brisa; modern authority regards brisa as Illyrian in origin (βρύτεα), the Latin cognate being defrutum, and compares brisare (from which Fr. briser is supposed to come) with Ir. brissim "break," the Latin cognate being frango. But brisare does not mean "break," nor briser "express." Unless, therefore, the shift of meaning, from "express" to "break," is considered acceptable, the source of briser, brissim must be sought elsewhere, appearances notwithstanding.

    Otherwise we must accept the ancient association of brisare with brisa. The latter word (the Illyrian origin of which there is nothing to prove), being known to Columella, may have come from Narbonensis rather than Lugdunensis; that Keltic had a stem bris- Thurneysen (KR 93) recognized, but its relation to the Germanic group of words (including brittle as well as break) is far from clear.

brisconis "hulsi minuti" CGL 3.587.41, cf. 608.36

    Modern representatives locate this word (apparently confused with bruscum, item 1 above, at CGL 3. 628.43) in the south of France, see Jud Romania 49, 1923, 398; whereas the by-form frisgone (CGL, loc. cit.) appears in OFr fresgon, fregon, Fr. fragon, cf. 178.

    On another name for the "holly" in parts of the Ouest, ku and cognates, evidently the modern representative of a Keltic (Gaulish) cognate of holly, Frankish hulis, see Jud Romania 52, 1926, 328-330.

broga "ager, country"

    See allo- above. But the meaning is (1) "boundary," (2) "territory" (like Latin fines), and the word is cognate with Lat. margo, Germ. marca, see Jud Arch. Rom. 6, 1922, 193; Walde-Hofmann (ed. 3) 2, 39, s.v. margo;

Glosses of Narbonensis

SprFK 183: Norden Altgermanien 1934, 100; Hubschmied
Vox Rom. 3, 1938, 141 n. 3; A. Thomas RC 15, 1894, 216;
Ernout and Meillet (ed. 2), s.v. margo (p. 593); Jud
Romania 47, 1921, 482 n. (cf. 52, 1926, 347); Ir. bruig,
W. bro (Do. 238).

Cf. breialo 178 (s.v. caio); brogilus (whence Fr.
brueil) certainly acquired the meaning of "grove, clearing, lucus," and "park, estate, fundus" (see AcS 1.619-
20, 3.984); broialos (A.D. 572, ib. 3.986), see W. Kaufmann Begriff "Wald" (boscus, above), 64-65. Distinguish
bria (246) and brio (178); Messapic broge (PID 546e) may
be this word.

bucca "buck"

This word in Petronius 64.13 is manifestly a
different word from Latin bucca "mouth," see Sedgwick's
note ad loc. (Oxford, 1925), and the article by B. L.
Ullman, CP 38, 1943, 94-102, where the Plautine buccones
also is connected with bucca "buck;" but this bucca can
hardly be a native Latin word, for the Germanic and
Keltic forms are identical both with it and with one
another (Walde-Pokorny 1.189), the Keltic being most
likely borrowed from the Germanic. The Keltic names
Bucca, Buccus, Bucco, Buccio, especially Bucca at Nimes,
CIL 12.3095, suggest that Narbonensis was the source of
the Latin borrowing, though bucco in Plautus (unless
connected with bucca "mouth," Walde-Hofmann I 120) would
point rather to Cisalpine Gaul.

It is interesting to observe that both the game
and the name have reached South Africa (CJ 39, 1943-44,
293).

buttis "crater" CGL 4.325.53 (Fr. bouteille from the

    diminutives butticula, butticella)

Commonly supposed "to have been borrowed from
Greek;" but (1)βυτίνη , πυτίνη are Tarentine, not Greek;
(2) what Latin has is not buttis but patena, patella;
(3)πατάνα , πατέλλιον etc. are not Greek, but Sicel (PID
2.456-457); (4) the Greek for buttis is κρατήρ , according

161

to the glossographers, though buttis doubtless had other meanings; (5) Etr. has puti as well as parla (cf. Lat. patera).

It appears clear, therefore, that buttis is a word of Mediterranean origin, probably connected with the Mediterranean wine-trade, cf. Medieval Lat. boterius "doliarius" (Du Cange), and above all the striking fact that boteria, bouteria came to mean not simply "wine-route," but "route" in general in the Rhone valley, see REA 38, 1936, 426 (Fr. boutière), citing the monograph of L. Bodey, Les premières routes des vins de France, commentaire géographique sur le sens du toponyme "Boutière" au long de la Saône et du Rhône (Annales de Bourgogne, 1935, 3), reviewed RA 11, 1938, 368. (J. Germain, Routes du Rhône Paris 1936, is inaccessible to me.)

I conclude that buttis is of pre-Roman (and non-Greek) origin. It is not Keltic either, probably not even I. Eu., but "Mediterranean."

calo v. gallica below

?cartamera, cartalamon ἡ ὅλη κατασκευὴ (or παρασκευὴ)
τοῦ περιζώματος

Gaulish according to Lydus de mag. 2.13, quoting Varro; cartamera may have arisen from catalamon by metathesis and dissimilation. If so, cartalamon is the older form, and despite the difference of meaning may be cognate with the κάρταλλος (246) of the LXX and of the Glossaries (Holder 1.816, 3.1125), the root meaning being "wind," cf. the cognates suggested in Walde-Hofmann 1.286. The source from which Varro learnt the word is not apparent; possibly Narbonensis, but quite conceivably Galatia.

[The local name Cartima (Holder 3.1126) in Andalusia, if the name of the article of clothing came from it, a common enough derivation, would make cartamera the older form; but this seems on all counts much less likely.]

162

Glosses of Narbonensis

Mid. Ir. ceirtle "Knäuel," Pedersen VKG 1.160,
2.54. Hardly cf. κυεϱιά (158), carti (Note xxvi).

catanus "juniper (?)." Cf. "cytisum: genus arboris

quasi catanum, ⟨h⟩erba odoribera (sic)" CGL 5.179.6,

Lib. Gloss. CI 427 (where a totally different

solution of the problem presented by this gloss is

proposed; but at CI 411 I should now read catanus

for citaxus, or else accept the ceu taxus of Thes.

Gloss. Emend.).

The word appears to be located in Narbonensis in
view of Prov. cade, and of the local name Cadenet
(Vaucluse and Bouches-du-Rhône), i.e. *Catanetum AcS
3.1146; cf. calocatanus 158 below; Walde-Hofmann 1.181,
Ernout-Meillet (ed. 2) 162 ("sans doute mot gaulois"),
Meyer-Lübke 1760.

It would be going too far to attach much significance to the spelling odoribera, but cf. Porcobera:
Porcifera.

cimenice "mons dorsa celsus," Avienus or. marit. 622, 625

Cf. the local names Cemenelum (Lig., PID 1.385),
Κέμμενον and Cebenna 148, AcS 1.880-882; on Lucan's
cana...rupe 1.435 cf. Jullian, REA 12,1910, 164-65.

On m:b see Pedersen 1.117, 165; cf. Loth, R.C. 39,
1922, 51; Vendryes BSL 34, 1933, p. xxi (cf. 36, 1935,
130) appeals to Basque for an explanation, but that
seems unconvincing as well as unnecessary.

Does Comacinas rupes (leg. cimenicas?) AcS 3.1257
belong here? Cf. Cimiacinus 243; hardly comanus (below).

Glosses of Narbonensis

circius, cercius

See PID 2.188, AcS 1.1025-28 (in Narbonensi
prouincia, Plin. NH 2.121); to which add now Walde-
Hofmann 1.220, Weisgerber SprFK 197.

comanus "paganus"

Auson. cl. urb. 115 usque in Tectosages (v.l.
Teutosagos) paganaque nomina Volcas (Belcos, -as codd.).
No doubt Auson. was thinking of Greek κώμη rather than
of Comum, Comani, Are-comici. Cf. AcS 1.189, 30; 369.
30. Whence Holder ib. 1.1088, 49 got his Coms "plebs"
I do not know. Cf. 78 above. Ligurian according to
Brunel Rev. de Philol. 10, 1936, 333-344.

darpus "mole" Polem. Silv. 1.543.11

The word (*darbo) is best represented by modern
derivatives (Meyer-Lübke 2473, cf. Bertoldi BSL 32,
1931, 149-150) in southern France; it appears to be
proper to that area, but is probably pre-Keltic (Lig.,
Iber.?).

What is its relation (if any) to talpa (Aquit.)?

durnus "a fist-full, hand's breadth"

At Toulouse; cf. AcS 1.1382, 54; Du Cange s.v.;
Jud. Arch. Rom. 6, 1922, 194.

gallica, gallicola "galosh," properly "Gaulish shoe"

First in Cicero, Phil. 2.30.76 (cf. Gellius 13.22.6),
of Antony (qui uero Narbone reditus?); I believe that in
the Rhineland this had become *caliχa, *caliʒa, with a
somewhat different meaning, and was borrowed into Latin
(temp. Cic.) as caliga, cf. Caligula the association of
whom with Germania is well known (Tac. Ann. 1.41; Sen.
dial. 2.18.4).

164

Glosses of Narbonensis

This suggestion was anticipated by Oxé, Germania
15, 1931, 17, and it seems to me to be right, though
rejected by some, and not very clearly stated by Oxé.
At AcS 1.704, 11 (s.v. calo) read gallicae? Even though
caliga and gallica were in the end distinguished from
one another (e.g. in price, Ed. Diocl. 9.5), the names
may be of common origin. On calo see Ernout-Meillet
ed. 2, 136.

[garum: see lupus below]

[laena

Borrowed from Greek through Etruscan, despite
ancient authority, which seems to have confused laena
with linna. See PID 2.197-198.]

lupus

The name of a fish, so called at Fréjus, and used
in the manufacture of garum: Pl. 31.95, cf. REA 34,
1932, 291 (with Grenier ap. Frank 3.586 n. 84).   The
word garum is usually counted Greek (Walde-Hofmann 1.583;
Ernout and Meillet ed. 2, 411), but see 158 below. There
is no reason, however, why lupus could not be Keltic (as
well as dialect-Latin, lupus "pike,"); Dottin, Mélanges
Loth 1927, 92-98; cf. AcS 2.347-350, Loewenthal W.u.S.
10, 1927, 168; perhaps called lucius in Belgica (see 207),
unless that contains *leuk- "white;" note Leuponus Boruonicus (Port-sur-Saône, CIL 13.10025, 146)?

martensis, martisia: see muria below

μεντασῶνϵ "wild mint" (Ϝάλλοί) Diosc. 3.36; mentadione

Ps.-Apul. herbarius 91 (Galli...uocant); CML 4,

1927, 165.10 add.

165

Glosses of Narbonensis

Apparently a word of "Mediterranean" origin, borrowed, in various forms into Greek, Latin, Gaulish and
other languages. For the ending compare δουκωνέ (:odocos
158); ſ may come from di.

muria "brine, pickle"

Evidently cognate with mare, but not necessarily
itself Latin; cf. Ir. muri, muir, Lugd. more (v.l. mure)
Endl. gl., Mori- (and Mari-)-dunum, see AcS 2.628-630;
Benveniste Origines de la formation des noms en Indo-
Européen 1935, 81.

The corresponding word in Aquitania is garum q.v.
below (158). Plin. 34.94 expressly mentions the muria
of Antipolis, though both it and garum are also associated with Spain (Grenier Mnl. 2 ii, 1934, 616-617). A
similar product is martensis or martisia Isid. 20.2.29,
now explained by Heraeus (cf. Walde-Hofmann 2.46) as
named from Narbo Martius; cf. Sofer Lat. u. Rom. 41, 171;
Grenier ap. Frank 3.585-586.

[murmillo "gladiator;" murmillonicum genus armaturae

Gallicum est Fest. 358.8

But cf. Gr. μόρμυλος, μορμύρος, for which, however,
there is no I.Eu. etymology, and this word is ascribed
(by Boisacq) to a "Mediterranean" source, like μεντ*δῶνε.
But there is nothing to distinguish a Keltic or Gaulish
from the Latin form; first in Cic. Ph. 3.12.31.]

nimida (i.e. nemeta), nemet "woodland or mountain shrine."

Late documents only give these forms (Indiculus
superstitionum, 6.223: de sacris siluarum quae nimidas
uocant; Cartulaire de Quimperlé [1031], 1.368: silua
quae uocatur nemet), but it is unquestionably the well
attested νεμητον of the insc. of Vaison (57 above), and
may occur in montibus nimidis (86 below; cf. 157, Remark
v), and in other texts quoted in AcS 1.712. Cf. Caes.
BG 6.13.10 (Carnutes) certo anni tempore...considunt in
loco consecrato.

166

Glosses of Narbonensis

Cf. CIL 2.5607 (Citania) nimidi ? Less likely Numidae (223).

The word has well-known cognates (nemus, νέμος), and exists in OIr nemed gl. "sacellum;" it appears in the divine name Nemetona and in a large number of widely-distributed personal and local names. It cannot, there-fore, be considered peculiar to Narbonensis but is Keltic as a whole, cf. δρυνέμετον (δρυναίμετον) Strabo 12.567 C (Galatae, 278 B.C.).

The formant -etom is also very frequent in Keltic words or words with Keltic associations (candetum, com-bretum, tuccetum, rumpotinetum, to mention no others), cf. W. -edic (*-etiko-), d'Arbois de Jubainville, RC 28, 1907, 144.

Cf. J. Loth, RA 20, 1924, 57.

panicum, panicium "panic grass, wild millet"

Not before Caesar, who speaks of it at Massilia (BC 2.22.1, cf. Strabo 4.190 C, Aquitania), see also AcS 2.926-27.

I see no reason to connect the word with Latin panus "bobbin, tumour, ear (of millet)," but rather (modifying a suggestion of E. Gwynn accepted by Vendryes, RC 47, 1930, 200; the criticisms of H. Lewis, EC 1, 1936, 320, are idle) with Latin canicae, Ir. canach, W. pan, panog, and to mean any tufted growth, or fluffy material, tuft, plait, down, cotton, or the like; hence caneco-sedlon (Autun) either "rush-bottom chair," or "stuffed chair," will be a relic of q-Keltic in Lugdunensis (hardly a borrowing from Goidelic).

panicum (-ium) is, then, borrowed into Latin from Narbonensis, canicae pure Latin.

paraueredus: a hybrid compound (cf. orombouii, ἰμαξο-

κάριον Hesych., and others), Greek παρά and Keltic

(Isid.) ueredus (PID 2.200), "palfrey"

167

Glosses of Narbonensis

Both ueredus and paraueredus are attested only in
imperial times; the hybrid cpd. might (theoretically)
have arisen either in Galatia or in Gaul, but its association with the western empire is manifest (Holder,
s.vv.), no less than its modern representatives (in
Ital., Catalan, Sp. and Ptg., all borrowed from Provençal
— it is French independently, M-L 6231). Cf. rēda,
raeda.

passernix "whetstone;" repertae sunt (sc. cotes) trans

    Alpes, quas passernices uocant, Plin. NH 36.165

There is nothing to show precisely what "trans
Alpes" means here, whether Narbonensis or Raetia, or
some other locality. Dottin REA 7, 1905, 44 took it
to mean "dans la Gaule transalpine," which is the most
obvious interpretation. But the word, if rightly trans-
mitted by Pliny, appears to have no modern derivative.

[peculium

This word must be borrowed from some non-Keltic
language, doubtless Latin, since it preserves I.Eu. p-,
other objections to the assumption of a genuine Keltic
word apart. But it appears to have acquired the peculiar meaning of "a wife's personal property" in Gaul,
Ulpian, ad Sab. lib. 31, Dig. 23.3.9 (3), see AcS 2.961:

    ea quae Graeci παράφερνα dicunt, quaeque
Galli peculium appellant; cf. CIL 12.1005 curator
peculi r(ei) p(ublicae) Glanico(rum), cf. Espérandieu ILG 227, Caluentius et Birro patri et matri
de suo peculio etc.; and an insc. from the neighborhood of Angora (CR 37, 1923, 8 cf. 60-61),
Διογνητα Τεκτομαρου ... ανεθηϲεν βωμον Πεκο(υ)λιου ,
cf. RA 19, 1924, 389 no. 63.

M-L 6337; CIL 3.287 (6776), 8.20223; Thes. Ling.
Lat., s.v.]

Glosses of Narbonensis

?perta

(1) the letter p, see Marstrander in Norsk
Tidsskrift for Sprogvidenskap 1, 1928, 139-141 (French
summary, 182-183), whence the name of the Rune perÞa
beside kwerÞa, querta (Ir. cert), i.e. q; (2) a divine
name, fem., in an insc. of Uchaud, see Espérandieu ILG
519. Marstrander explains the divine name as that of
"en gallisk gudinde for den indhegnede jord," and it is
certainly recorded also as a local name, AcS 2.970-971,
but, unfortunately for Marstrander's hypothesis, it is
the name of a spring Peiroou (du Chaudron) at the site
of the insc. Esp. 519, and therefore Perta is more
likely to have been one of the many divinities of springs
and fountains worshipped in Narbonensis; the letter-
name may or may not be related -- I should be prepared
to believe it, if a satisfactory etymology could be
found: cf. perhaps Latin cortina, *qrto- (: q_o^u- ?),
for which Walde-Pokorny 2.368 postulate a root (s)quer-,
Lat. curuus. As for Peiroou cf. Prov. pairol "kettle"
(Ir. coir, W. pwr).EC 4, 1948,193

[rufius, "a kind of lynx (?)," rufus "a fish"

See AcS 2.1242-3, who gives the former from Pliny
NH 8.70 and 84: Italic, not Keltic.]

[sagarius in inscc. of Narbonensis, AcS 2.1287

Clearly a Latin derivative of sagus, for which
see PID 2.189; Pokorny Urg. 66 would count sagus Illyr.
— without, so far as I can see, any reason. Ed. Diocl.
19.60, σάγος Γαλλικός ,τοῦτ' ἐστιν Ἀνβιανησιος (sc.
Ambianensis, 212 Belgica) ἤτοι Βιτουρητικός (Bituregicus,
153 Aquit.) On the sagum itself cf. W.u.S. 11, 1928, 56-
57.]

sappinus "pine-tree" (Varro, Vitruv., Col., Pl.)

Possibly Keltic (SprFK 208), at least sapo- cf.
AcS 2.1362 (for *sapopinus Ernout and Meillet ed. 2,
895), cf. Sapaudus (-ia, Sapa-uidus; modern Savoie);

Glosses of Narbonensis

G. Walter in Giess. Beitr. vol. 2, no. 10, 66; H-M p. 371; Walde ed. 2, 678; M-L REW 7592; Terracini Riv. di Filol. 49, 1921, 429. W. Meyer KZ 28, 1887, 172 (sapipinus): sapo- for *saqu̯o- (OChSl. sokъ "saft der Pflanzen und Früchte"), Pokorny Urg. 66; F. Lot Rev. Savoisienne, 1935, 146-156 (REA 38, 1936, 430).

Pokorny ZfCPh 20, 1933, 158 (in reviewing Weisgerber), points out that W. sybwydd (with -y-, cf. OE saeppe) cannot correspond exactly to sapaudia.

[scarpa "footwear"

From uita S. Honorati, cf. Löfstedt Festschrift, 1945, 73. Germanic]

sil (Gallicum) Plin. NH 26.42, a plant (saxifrage?)

A curtailed form (cf. sili, M-L 7918) of sesilium or σέσιλι (Μασσαλιωτικόν cet., Diosc. 3.53), a word of Mediterranean origin (Ernout-Meillet ed. 2, 940, no doubt rightly, for Diosc. and other ancient authorities place it in many other lands as well as in Gaul), cf. AcS 2.1526-27, 1545-6 (to be distinguished from Plin. NH 33.159, sil, -is "ochre").

Yet another variant appears to be siser, σίσαρον (also a plant-name); and Dottin (pp. 286, 261) goes so far as to suggest that halus is a genuine Keltic (Brythonic) equivalent; but see 158 below. σέσιλι was Egyptian according to Nencioni AGI 33, 1941, 125. For siser at Gellep see Plin. NH 19.90.

tatula "(grand-)daddy"

Apparently appellative "father, grandfather," in CIL 12.3518 (Nimes), cf. W. tad. But it is a word of universal baby-talk, sometimes becoming a proper name (e.g. Tata, CIL 12.4830 (Narbonne); cf. Sab.-Lat. Tatius, Illyr. Tat(t)a, Gr. Τατᾶς, PID 3.45, s.v. θαοταras).

Glosses of Narbonensis

[t(h)au "the letter t" (?)

In Greg. Tur. hist. Franc. 4.5 (at Arles):
parietes uel domorum uel ecclesiarum signari uidebantur,
unde a rusticis hic scriptos tau uocabatur, tau is either
a letter of the alphabet, T or Γ, cf. PID 2.190, or else
the Keltic *tauos "silence" (cf. Dottin 291; Loth in
MSNAF, 7, 1924-7 [1928], 17-24.

Since the publication of PID, I have noted these
discussions of tau Gallicum: T. Frank, AJPh 56, 1935,
254-6, cf. REA 38, 1936, 200 (cf. 31, 1929, 235: sil
perhaps abbrev. for silēre?); Miller CP 37, 1942, 319-
321 (emends tau out of existence in Petronius 62.9);
Wickersheimer Strasbourg Medical Nov. 1928 (cited in
REA 31, 1929, 176) I have not been able to see. Whether
any light is to be had from Lucian Ind. Vocal. 10 (the
contest of τ and δ), discussed by Dornseiff, Das Alphabet
in Magie und Mystik, ed. 2, 1925, I should doubt.

If a letter of the alphabet is intended by tau
Gallicum, then Þ or Ჰ does occur in Narbonensis, CIL 12.
686, 2882, 5682, 5686. For tau in the arepo-square see
RA 6, 1935, 101; and for local names in Tau- AcS 2.1774.]

taurus "carduelis"

At Arles, Plin. NH 10.116; but if Pliny's account
of the name is right, the word is Latin. Yet we have a
Gaulish plant-name Τωρούκ , as well as the personal,
local, and divine names in taur- or taru- (in not all
of which is it clear that cognates of Latin taurus are
involved), AcS 2.1757-1772. Cf. thauori "camomile" (?)
SprFK 211.

*trebo "dwelling place, habitation"

Cf. Prov. treva, Lat. trabs, and the local name
Trebur (241); Jud Romania 47, 1921, 493 and 52, 1926, 347.

Glosses of Narbonensis

*trincare "cut"

    Prov. trincar, trencar "cut, cut short," from a
Gaulish (?) trincus, trinquos "gladiator, swordsman,"
attested by two Latin inscc., from Seville and Sardes
(Dessau 5163, 9340), see Piganiol REA 22, 1920, 283-290.

    Cf. perhaps W. trin "fight," Walde-Pokorny 2.628,
Lat. stringo, strictus id., ib. 650?

turia: nomina fluminum CGL 5.487.56

    Cf. Thyrius (80 below),Turia in Spain; Duria (PID
3.63), Durontia 10 above; Tor, Thor 81 below.

ueredus: see paraueredus above

    Remark:

    (i) On the graffito (Keltic ?) found at Les
Fins d'Annecy see Note xxi (a) below.

    (ii) Among the languages that must have been
heard occasionally in the coastal cities of Narbonensis,
and at times even inland, were the Semitic Phoenician
and Punic of traders; and for a short time, after 218
B.C., of Hannibal's soldiers. But no certain linguistic
record of them has ever been found. One long Phoenician
inscription has been found at Marseilles (CIS Pars 1
tom. 1, 1881-1887, 217-238 no. 165), and one short one

Narbonensis

at Avignon (Répertoire d'Épigraphie sémitique 1, 1900-1905, no. 360), but it is not clear that either was actually cut at those places, or even in Gaul at all. (There are, of course, Jewish funerary inscriptions of later date, irrelevant to the scope of this book.) It is possible that other evidence has escaped my search; but it cannot be far from the truth to say that there is no clear trace of any Semitic influence in the pre-Roman speech of Narbonensis, or of the rest of Gaul. The local name Roscynus, ῾Ρόσκυνος (Avien., Or. mar. 567, Polyb. 34.10.1, cf. Str. 4.1.6) mod. Roussillon, has indeed been claimed as such, on uncertain grounds (Ruscinona at Carthage, see P-W s.v.); cf. P. Fouché, Rev. hisp. 81, 1933, 339-340, and Note xv above.

(iii) CIL 12.4378 (Narbonne) dictator in iuniliciis (if correctly read); the last word is supposed to refer to a festival in June, and to follow the pattern of aedilicius. But we may have haplology for iunoni-licia, cf. Iunones (AcS 2.89-91), Osc. iuvil(l)a-?

(iv) In CIL 12.3345 (Nîmes) patillus (copo) seems to mean "qui patinam, i.e. cibum in patina coctum, uenalem proponit" (so ed.), rather than to be an additional cognomen (Patillus) as Mommsen took it. For

173

patina cf. 178 (s.v. anax), panna at La Graufesenque
(90 ff. below), canna 220 (Germ. Inf.)

Names of Narbonensis

Note on Names (Local, Divine, and Personal). In
all the lists of names that follow, to the end of this
book, observe: (1) that the names are not "collected,"
as would-be "complete" lists, but selected for their
linguistic interest; (2) that the primary sources are
given in Holder's AcS; such references are given here,
so far as possible, only for those names not to be found
in AcS; (3) that names given in PID are not, as a rule,
repeated.

In REA 14, 1912, plates 1-8 will be found a reproduction of that part of TP which deals with Gaul; ib.
15, 1913, pp. 181-184 Gaulish names in Not. Tir. For
Gaul as a whole the two works of E. Desjardins, Geogr.
de la Gaule d'après le Table de Peutinger 1869, and
Geogr. hist. et administrative de la Gaule romaine ed. 2,

174

Local and Ethnic Names

4, 1893, are still valuable.

For Narbonensis the chief sources are CIL 12 (1888), occasionally other volumes of CIL, and Espérandieu's ILG (1929). Hübner's MLI, Index pp. 244-247 is also useful. Cf. Jacob Rev. de Philol. 36, 1912, 151 ff. (on Strabo lib. 4); Blanchet EC 2, 1937, 246-253 (on Gaulish names in modern France).

80   Local and Ethnic Names

Abate

Accion palus Avien. 683;
   cf. 241, 243 infra

Acunon, -um

?Ἀκουϲιῶν

Adgentii (Argence?)

Aegitna ins. Polyb. 30,
   9, cf. RA 33, 1931,
   69-101.

Aemines portus (v.l.
   Minus, -es; mod. Miou?);
   cf. RA 34, 1931, 134-135

Aerardiarenses

Aerarium (pons)

Ἀεϼίᾳ , Aeria

Agathon (-ensis) now Agay

Agrizama

Agunna (cf. Agunia, Trans-
   pad. AE 1913, p. 470)
   Agonès

Alabon, now Allemont (?)

Alaudes

?Alanus CIL 12.1122

Alba Heluorum, ciuitas
   Albensium, modern Aps

Albiga, Albigenses

Albienses, mod. Albi

Albic(c)i, Ἀλβίοικοι

Albenno, Albinnum,
   Albinnenses (Albens)

Alconis portus IM, Ἀλωνίς
   (-ίτης) Steph. Byz.

175

Local and Ethnic Names

Aletanus pagus (cf. REA
26, 1924, 79)

'Αλγοι[κώμη IG 14.2490

? 'Αλιβωκοι (-οικοι?),
but cf. Albic(c)i

Allobrox, -ges (on-a, -ae
see CR 37, 1923, 60)
-gicus and (late)
-gicinus, 'Αλλόβριγες
(-βρύγες)

Almanticensis cf. AE 1945.
171; BSAF 1901, 72
(Mantega)

Ambrusium (-s[s]um),
-osium Pont-Ambruis.
Cf. Vmbranicia infr.?

Anarias ILG 257

?Anatilia, -lii (cf. CA
5.120, 399)

Anconiana uilla (Kiepert)

Andusia, now Anduze

Anteae (-eiae), now
Lantier

Apristia

Apta, Aptenses, mod. Apt
CIL 12, p. 931; insc.
AE 1910.62

Aquenses CIL ib., AE 1934.
165; cf. REA 36, 1934,
199-205 (with 201 n.
8); Aix

Aquotis fl., now Agout

Arandunici (Hournèze?)

Araura, also called
Cessero

Arauris fl., Arauricus
(Hérault), (?)Oranis
fl., Avien. 612. Cf.
179, 234 below; Cuny,
REA 29, 1927, 47-51

Arausio, Araus(i)ensis,
Arausicus, -ionensis
(Orange). Thurneysen
KZ 59, 1931-32, 13
(Mid. Ir. ara "cheek,
brow," Gr. παρειά,
Lesb. παραύα); CA 7.
112, 2

Arceuoturum

Arearum municipium (vita
Hororati) Yères; but
see RA 22, 1925, 95-
104

Arec[

Arecomici

Arelate, -ensis, -essis
(Arles); cf. ILG 111,
and see Theline below

Argenteus fl. Argens

Arisitum (-d-), Arisi-
tensis (-d-) Arese-
tensis

Arnemetici cf. REA 13,
1911, 348

Atau[(AcS 1.251, 51)

Atax fl., Attagus (Aude);
cf. RC 38, 1920-21,
88-89; RLRom. 2,1926,
130; REA 20, 1918, 195;
RA 6, 1917, 427; CRAc
InscBL 1917, 314

Local and Ethnic Names

Atacini

?Atius pagus ILG 340

[Atlantici Cambolectri]

Atrapensis ins. (vita Honorati)

Auantici (Avançon?)

Auatici: see Maritima

Aueii (not Aulii) ILG 344; REA 29, 1927, 286-94; 30, 1928, 121

Auennio, Ἀ(ο)υεννιῶν, Auenni-ensis, Auenionensis, Auennicus, Auenniocus (Avignon) CA 7.30, 64, cf. 34 n. 1; Duprat, Annales de Provence 23, 1926, 81-102

Auria uallis (11th cent.)

?Baciana (Vac-, Bat-)

Badera Bazîège

Baeterrae, Βαίτερͷ , Betar-ratis, Besara Avien. 591 Béziers

Bag(inensis?) pagus

Bautae (Bou-), Bouz, Bos (13-15th cent.)

Βέββρυκες Scymn., Steph. Byz. Cf. BA 1932-33, 351

?Belcae (for Vol-?)

?Beleno castro Beaune (Drôme)

Bellintum

Berconum oppidum

Bergine ciuitas; cf. 158 (barga)? Barca Hü. 225

Bergusium (-ia), Birg-, Berg- usitanus? (cf. 169) Bourgoin

Besingus

Blasco ins., Βλάσκων, Blasci Brescou

Bo[ ]tiorum pagus

?Bocconi Rav., for Voconi (Forum) IA, TP

Bolbro, Borbro (?)

?Bonomagus

Borman(n)i oppidum

Borodates

Bosedo Bezaudun

Boutae see Bau-; cf. 83

Boxs[ani] uicani (Buis, Drôme), cf. Boxsum 179, and gl. boscus 79 supr.; this is evidently the clue to Fr. bois; cf. Buxea silua (153), uilla Buxarias (212), Buxuil-lare (234), Buxenus (82); and my paper in Havers Festschrift (1948). But Boiscus (83), while con-ceivably from *Boscius, *Bok-s-ius, is more like-ly to be a derivative of Boius

Local and Ethnic Names

Brandobrici

Briginn[, B[riginnenses]
   Aquae (Brignon or
   Brienne?)

Brugetia (Bruzet). Cf.
   gl. brucarius (178),
   DN Vroicae (82)

Budencicenses (Bezouce
   or Bézuc?)

Burrea; cf. Buriates 2
   above, gl. burrus 158
   infr.

Cabellio, Cabellienses,
   ?Kablies[es], Cabel-
   licus, Cabellonensis
   (Cavaillon)

Caccabaria (?) v. Grenier
   ap. Frank 3.418

Cadienses

Caenicenses cf. Καινικητων
   78, Cainonensis 179,
   Καινός fl., perhaps
   read Καινην (sc. δι-
   ωρυχα, the fossa
   Mariana), or Σηκοανός
   (the Arc) AcS 3.1040,
   17; Sicel Καινός

?Calera (Hübner s.v.
   Narbo)

Camactulici

Cambolectri (Atlantici)

Candidum prom. Avien. 602

Capannae (at Gap) A.D. 739

Carbantorate Meminorum,
   Carpentorate, Carpen-
   tora(c)tensis (Carpen-
   tras)

Carcarium (v.l. Carn-)

Carcas(s)o, -ona, Car-
   casum; cf. TLL Onom.;
   and add CIL 13.7234
   Carc[(Phoen.?)
   (Carcassonne)

Carpentorate see Carbant-

Carsici, ?Charsitanus
   (Cassis). CIL 12.37*
   has been rediscovered
   and is now considered
   genuine, cf. CA 5.2,
   6; RA 34, 1931, 364 no.
   100 (cf. Mouquet ib.
   pp. 123-135; 33, 1931,
   174; 12, 1938, 330,
   citing Labande CRAc
   InscBL 1938, 294-297),
   REA 36, 1934, 395. Cf.
   possibly di Casses
   (211), but hardly carra
   (1)

Casiriaci agri

Cassauda AcS 1.824

Castellana uicinia ILG 44

Casuaria (Chaise?)

Catorissium, Cantourissa(?)

Catuiacia

?Caucoliberi AcS 3.1166,
   45; but see 84

Caudellenses

Local and Ethnic Names

Cauares, Cauari; cf.
  Glotta 28, 1940, 241
  n.1

Cecylistrium prom. Avien.
  703

Cedrus, Caedros

Κελτογαλατία 'Gallia'

? Κελτόριοι

Cessero, -aro see Araura

Ceuenna see 148

?Cinga see Sulga below

?Cipr[CIL 12.308
  (Cypres)

Citharista portus La Cio-
  tat (not Ceyreste),
  see REA 36, 1934, 395;
  cf. 22, 1920, 298

Clahilci (Clachili, Cha-
  bilci?) Avien. 675 (see
  the editions of Schul-
  ten, and of Berthelot)

Clanum (dép. Aude)

Classius amnis

?Cobiomagus uicus (cf.
  Grenier ap. Frank 3,
  432 note b)

?Comacinas (-tinas) rupes;
  cf. 79

Comani (?Comoni); cf. 79

Combusta

Condate (AcS 1.1093, 2)

Conuerantia Aquae (CIL 13
  1, p. 6)

?Copia

Coriossedens[es (Collias?)
  Cf. assidarius, essedum?
  Or names such as Tarues-
  sedum, Manduessedum,
  Metlosedum

[Cotini, Gothini]

?Cottion

Crindaui[nus] portus
  (Chamone?)

?Crodunum (cf. Grenier
  l.c.)

Cularo (Gratianopolis,
  now Grenoble), Cularo-
  nenses, Calarone,
  Curarore; cf. Boisacq
  s.v. Κάρυον

Cyneticum litus Avien. 566

Cypresseta It. Burd. 553.6
  (cf. Cipr[above?)

Darentiaca (Daraize, v.
  REA 20, 1918, 198 after
  Bull. de l'Acad. Del-
  phinale, 9, 1914-17,
  340)

Dea (Vocontiorum), Δία ,
  Deenses; mod. Die; cf.
  REA l.c.

Deobensis pagus

Dexiuates, Dexuates
  (Dezeaumes?)

Local and Ethnic Names

Dia[pagus

Diarenses

?Dibialimon

Dilis (portus?)

Druna fl. (Drôme)

?Duluscantum

Durentia see 10 above

Durotincum (-ng-)

Eburomagus, Ebro- (dép. Drôme)

Elesiodunum Cic. pro Font. 9.19 (cf. Grenier ap. Frank 3, 432 note b) Elusio It. Burd. 551.5

Elesyces Avien. 586

?Ellincum v. Eluicus

?Ἐλούκωκοι

Elusa, Elusates, Elusanus; Elusensis, Elosates; Elusio (Eauze). Cf. Elesyces above? Cf. 84

Eluii (H-), Eluicus, ?(H)- eluencus; for [h]eluen- nacus see 178

Epaona, Epaunon (6th cent.); Evienne (Valois) or (?) Yenne (Savoie) REA 11, 1909, 331

Ἐπίκιον κώμη IG 14.2476 (unless for ἐπιοίκιον ?)

Epotius pagus (Upaix?)

Etanna (Étain, Savoie), cf. gl. 158, divine names 181; but Yenne (between Vienna and Genaua) ac- cording to Gallia 1, 1943, 138-151

Gargarius (Garguier), Cf. REA 23, 1921, 120-4; CIL 12.71* Gargaricis is perhaps genuine, CA 5.5, 20

[Garunna, v. 148]

Genua, Genaua, Genuensis, Genauensis, Geneuentes, Geneuensis (Genève, Genf); cf. BSL 40, 1939, 119; Genava 19, 1941, 80; ILG 363

Glanum, Glanicus

Grinincenses, Gren- cf. gl. 220, Grinnes 221

?Heledus fl. Avien. 592, cf. Ledus

Helice palus id. 590

Helenae castrum Eutrop. brev. 9 (Elne); v. Iliberris

(H)eluina (Ceres) see 82

Iconii

180

Local and Ethnic Names

Iliberri, Ἰλέβεϼϼις, cf.
84; Hübner MLI, p.
245. Identified not
with Elne but with St
Cyprien Ann. du Midi
1938, 157-9 (RA 15,
1940, 293)

Incaro (Phoen.?)

Isarnus (Marseille) Merov.
num.

Ispana CIL 12.3363, cf.
AcS 1.1470, 41; Sieglin
ZONF 10, 1934, 253-275
(cf. PhW 1935, 1271-80).
On Hispania cf. PhW
1936, 623; 1937, 63;
1938, 142-44

?Iturium ins.; v.l. Sturium

Iuenalis pagus (La Jouine,
see CA 5.63, 232) CIL
12.512; cf. Lucretius

(Foro)iulienses, cf.
Iuliae above

Iunius pagus CIL 12.1307

Latara (-era) uicus, now
Lattes

Lauisco; cf. Lauscus 82
below

Ledus (Heledus?) fl., cf.
ledo gl. 158; now Liron
or Lez? On the inter-
pretation of Ledus,
Lidius, Lecius, mod.
Lez, as "eau courante"
cf. REA 28, 1926, 263
(after Bull. Geogr.,
1925). But v. AcS s.vv.

Lemannus lacus ILG 361

Lemincum (Lémenc)

Leris portus (A. D. 916,
CA 7.135) now Lers;
cf. 221?

Lero, Lerinus (-a) ins.,
Lirinensis (Lérins);
cf. 221

Lesura pagus, Laesara
(Lozère); cf. Λέσυϼος
ποταμός AcS 2.191?

?Letoce (Adl- AcS 1.42)
Per. Eg. (CA 7.130,
108)

Letus mons (Hübner 245)

Libica Proleg. 35 n.54;
for Libui: Ligyes see
PID 2.148 n., and cf.
Sebusiani: Segusiaui
Do. 55

Licirrus pagus

[Ligauni PID 1.368]

Liguria (Livière) Proleg.
37

Liria fl. Pl. 3.32

Λώβητον, Λωβητανοί (Iber.?)

Lub[(colonia Dinia Lub[ )
Cf. 21 above

Lucretius pagus; cf. 221

Lucus Augusti CIL 13.5207,
cf. 6.22981 (Luc en
Diois, Drôme); cf. per-
haps uernemetis, Ver-
nemeton 158, Augusto-

nemetum 148, so that
Lucus Augusti may be
for lucus augustus as
a Latinization of
uernemeton

Lugdunus mons 13th cent.
(Montlahue[?], Drôme)

Luteua fl., Luteuani,
Luteuensis (Lodève)

Macho uilla, now Magues?
See REA 19, 1917, 46

Macra uallis REA 17, 1915,
271-274 (for Marca
"fines"?)

Mantala

[Marbacum CRAcInscBL 1943,
476]

Maritima Auaticorum (Mar-
tigues) CA 5.50, 163.
See also below, Mastro-
mela

?Martinenc[Marsens(?),
REA 19, 1917, 136

Massilia, Μασσαλία, Mas-
silienses (also the
name of a river in
Crete, Ptol. 3.15.3),
Marseille

Mastromela, Μαστραμέλη,
Mastrabala
    The identifica-
tion of this site, of
Maritima Auaticorum,
and of Ratis, as well
as correct readings in
the text of Avienus are
perhaps beyond us: here
are some references to
the confused discus-
sion, REA 3, 1901, 333
n.2, 342-3; 5, 1903,
137; 13, 1911, 467-8;
16, 1914, 434; 28,
1926, 102-3; 31, 1929,
53; 36, 1934, 380-386;
42, 1940, 567-572; RA
31, 1930, 182; 9, 1937,
120; CA 5 51 163. Be-
sides Martigues, Aigues
Mortes, Saintes-Maries-
de-la-Mer, the étang de
Berre have all been
brought into the ques-
tion

Note:

    An important article, that makes use of the testi-
mony of Avienus and identifies a number of the ancient
names of Narbonese coast between Setius (Cette) and
Mastromela (v.l. -bala, note m:b) now Miramas(?) or
Malestron(?), Étang de Berre, appeared in Quart. Journal
of the Geolog. Soc. of London 90, 1934 (cf. Ph. Woch.
1935, 1210) 445-461 (Richard Dixon Oldham, The Age and
Origin of the Lower Rhône); the Accion palus of Avienus

Local and Ethnic Names

(682), it is argued, so far from being Lake Geneva
(Holder), was a marsh long since dried up as a result
of changes, natural or artificial, in the Rhône delta.
On the excursus of Ammianus on the Rhône valley cf.
Bickel in Oxé Festschrift (1938) 164-169. Cf. Berthelot,
A., ed. Avienus, Paris 1934; and the edition of A. Schul-
ten (in Schulten and Bosch Fontes Hisp. Ant. part 1
Avienus, Barcelona 1922).

A somewhat similar problem, namely that of the
coastal route, in Augustan times, from Italy to Spain
through Arles, has been attacked by F. Benoit in REA 40,
1938, 132-148, in which the local names Ernaginum,
Mastromela, Tericias (TP?), Vallis Sobrana (1429) and
others are examined; Pisauis (TP) is identified with
Saint Jean de Brenasse; and older maps (e.g. Kiepert)
corrected in some details.

An attempt, not altogether satisfactory, to con-
struct a map of Gaul after Ptolemy, was made by A.
Berthelot in REA 35, 1933, pp. 430 f.

Matauo, Matauonium, pagus
   Matauonicus

?Medianae insulae

?Melaconditia (cf. Micalo?)

?Mellosedum, Metroselon,
   Metiosedum? Distin-
   guish Metlosedum (-dunum)
   179; for the ending cf.
   Coriossedenses above

Memini, Μήμινοι see Car-
   bantorate

Mesua collis, now Mesve

Metapinum fl. (an outlet
   of the Rhône)

Metina ins.

?Micalo colonia Diceorum

(?Melaconditia; cf.
   Deciates PID 1.359)

Morginnum (Maurogena)

Narbo, Νάρβων , Narbonen-
   sis, Ναρβωνίτης , λιμνὴ
   Ναρβωνῖτις , Ναρβώνησ-
   ιος , Νάρβα , Ναρβαῖος ,
   ?Narbo]niensis RA 14,
   1936, 31; cf. CIL 12.
   6038, 13.1808

Naustalo oppidum

?Nearchi, see Ernaginum
   (Jullian HG 1.180 n.5;
   CA 5.222)

Nemausus (-m), Νέμαυσος
   (-ον), Νεμαύσιοι IG 14.
   2503, Namausatis, Ναμ-

183

Local and Ethnic Names

ꟼΟΥϹΙΚΟ - see 67, 78 above; cf. 83; Nemausensis (-iensis); Nemuso TP, cf. Νὲμ ωϭϭόϛ 148; Nimes (Prov. Némze)

Nouencrares(-ae) mutatio (Nouem Craris? Cf. 82)

Νοιόμαγος , Noiomagenses (Drôme), apparently miswritten Bonomago Rav., Senomago TP, mod. Nyons

?Obilonna (-innum, v.l. Billunum), Obelonon

Oct[pagus (Vienne)

?Oeusona (?for Leus-, Lous-)

Olbia, Olbienses ILG 44

Oliui mons (Montolieu, AcS 2.844, 1)

Olonna ib. 849, 7

Oranus fl. (for Arauris?)

Orbis fl., Orobus,"Ορoβιϛ , now Orb

Orga fons

Ouidis fl. (Ouvèze)

Pacatianus fundus CIL 12. 6032a

Περγάντιον, ethn. -ιοϛ Fort Bregançon?

Phila ins.

Piplae insulae, Avien. 585 (cf. Iber. Bilbilis, plplis num., Hü. 85)

Pisauae

Pomp[CIL 12.410

Prusianus fundus (Brésis)

Pyrene prom. Avien. 533

Ra[tis], Ratis, Radis; see above Mastromela, and add CA 5.120, 399. Cf. ratin 152 below; distinguish ratis 158 (REA 23, 1921, 335 "fougère," Basque iratze); AcS 2. 1077-78

?Rauelae uicus (Revel)

Renis fl.

Rep[uicani CIL 12.1844

Ritona fl.? (recorded only as a divine name) Rieu

R[h]odanus, -anicus, -anitis, -aniticus (Rhône)
     Cf. the gloss roth 178, and see the discussions by Kretschmer WPZ 19, 1932, 279, Glotta 24, 1935-6, 3; Mélanges van Ginneken 1937, 207-210; Mélanges Pedersen 76-87; Pokorny Urg. 97, 162; Mélanges Boisacq vol. 2 (Annuaire de l'Inst. de Philol. et d'Hist. orientales et slaves 6, 1938)

184

Local and Ethnic Names

193-197; F. Lot RC 45,
1928, 312-317; W. Stokes,
Academy 30, 1886, 43

Ῥοδανουσία, Rodanusia
(also called Theline)

Rubrensis, -aesus lacus

Ruscino, Ῥοσκυνον, Ῥου-
σκίνων fl., opp., Ro-
schinus, Rusino (Ca-
stell-Rossillo, Rou-
sillon; Phoen.?)

Salsulae fons (Salées)

?Sambracitanus sinus

Samnagenses Σαμναγητων
(78 above) cf. MSAF 2,
1903, 241-292 (Nages)

?Sarralis

?Saxar v. Sulga

Scarpiana

?Se[   ]carum uicus

Σηκοανός v. Caenicenses

Segobrigii, -es CA 5.5, 20

Segouellauni

Segusio (Suzon)

Segustero(n), Segesterii,
Segestericus, Sistar-
icensis (Sisteron)

Seleucus mons (Montsaléon)

?Senomagus, v. Bono-
(Noio-?)

Serta (Serres?)

Setius mons Avien. 608
(Cette)

Sextantio, Sostantio,
Sestatiensis (Substan-
tio)

Siccae Aquae; cf. 19 Re-
mark; 241

Sordus amnis, Sordicen
palus Avien. 570, 574;
Sordones Mela 2.84,
Plin. 3.32

Solon, Solonion (Salagnon)

Sotanum

Statumae

Stablonem, Stu-? Estoublon

Sturium(?) Pl. 3.79, v.
Itur-

Suebri; v. l. Suetri, Pl.
3.35, but cf. 3.137;
the Suelteri, Selteri
(mod. Esterel?) of
Holder and Hübner ap-
pear to be imaginary.

Sulga, Σούλγας Sorgue(s)
(Vaucluse); cf. REA 12,
1910, 165; 13, 1911,
459-464; but the Med.
Ms of Livy has Sarar;
read perhaps Saxar,
see RA 6, 1917, 427

Taburnus Pl. 14.18

Tarusco, Ταρούσκων, Taru-
sconiensis (Tarascon)

Tanconisi[colon(ia)
  BSAF 1914, 142 (Vénas-
  que, Vaucluse; Esp.
  175 is inadequate);
  also a divine name?

[Ταουσῶν κωμὴ IG 12.2517?]

Tasgoduno, now Tescou(?)
  or (REA 37, 1935, 214)
  Texon?

Tauroentum, Ταυρόεις , Ταυ-
  ροέγτιον , mod.
  Tarente, cf. AcS 3.
  1125, 25; REA 38, 1936,
  416-420; RA 9, 1937, 120

Taurus palus (Étang de
  Thau)

Tectosages, -i

Tecus fl., Tetum, Tetis,
  Ticis (Tech, or Têt?)

Tedusia (Tésiès, Thé-
  ziers); for the ending
  cf. Bergusia 169, 181

Tegna (Tain)

Telo, Telonno, Telonensis
  (Toulon)

Te[r]iciae cf. CA 5.197;
  209

Theline, also called Ro-
  danusia; identified
  with Arelate, Gallia
  2, 1943, 246

Thyrius fl., cf. 7, gl.
  turia 79

Ticinus fl. (dép. Ardèche)

Tolos(s)a, Tolosanus
  (Britannus natione AE
  1939. 53, Arles),
  Tolosates (Toulouse);
  cf. REA 17, 1915, 139;
  23, 1921, 63

Tononia rupes Avien.

Treuidon (Trèves), i.e.
  "three trees," cf.
  Sexarbor(86), Sapaudia
  (15); uidubion(178)

Tricastini, Tricassini,
  -stiniensis, Trica-
  strina (Tricastin, St
  Paul-Trois-Châteaux?)

Tricorii, Τρίκουροι Appian
  Kelt. 1

Tritolli

Τροίζην (leg. Τριττίη ?)
  Steph. Byz. (Trets?)
  cf. divine name Trittia?

?Tulingi, Tylangii

Turedonnum Tourdan

Tur[no?] Tournon

Valentia, Valentinus
  (Valence)

Valer[pagus

Vapincum, Vappincensis,
  now Gap, see Remark
  below

Vardo fl., (le Gard, lou
  Gardoun), cf. Vardacate
  PID 1.357, Iber. num.

Local and Ethnic Names

uardus Hübner MLI no.
34; Gardo AcS 1.1982;
cf. ZONF 4, 1928, 271

Vasio, Vasionensis, Va-
sensis, Vasiensis
(Vaison); also div.
name

Vatrute (Vie?)

Vatusicum

Vcetia, Vcetiensis, Vzen-
censes, cf. 169 and
the following item

Vseticus pagus AcS 3.50?
(Uzès)

[Οὐελλάυγιοι IG 14.2432]

Vendasca ciuitas CA 7.22,
49 (Vénasque)

Venusca

Vernodubrum fl. (Verdouble)

Vernosole

Verucini

Vgernum, Οὔγερνον, Vierni,
Vgernensis (Beaucaire)

?Vgium CIL 11.3281-84,
usually put in Spain,
but v. REA 42, 1940,
653-59; Gallia 2, 1943,
246 (Lavalduc)

Vienna, Vian(n)a, Βίεννος,
Βιεννήσιος, Vianensis,
Οὐίεννα, Viennensis
(Vienne)

Vindalon, Vindalium, Vin-
delicus amnis (Védène),
cf. 52

Vindausca, Vindasca,
Vindesca AcS 3.330,
i.q. Vendasca above.
Cf. Venax- 241?

Vindomagus pagus, Οὐ-
ινδόμαγος

Virinn[Védrines

Visoroncia, Vesaroncia,
Visurontia Vézerance

Viuarium, Viuarensis,
Viuariensis Viviers

?Vl[riuus

Vmbranici, -icia, cf.
Umbranates(?) now Città
d'Umbra in Cisalp. (Pl.
3 116 G, Vrbinates May-
hoff) with Serv. A. 12.
753 (= Solin. 2.11), E.
Bondurand Revue du Midi
23, Nîmes, 1898, 456-463,
Déjardins Geogr. 4, 1893,
97.

It may be hoped
that no one will be so
misguided as to argue
that the Umbrians mi-
grated to Narbonensis.

Vocontii (i.e. "Twenty"
REA 9, 1907, 172-4,
13, 1911, 351 (OW.
uceint), cf. tricontii
Note xxix (b), below.

Vocronesses (for -enses,
cf. Arelatesses; and
in Brit. Bindolandesses
AE 1917-18.131)

Volcae (Volqua REA 13, 1911,
70 n. 4); cf. W.u.S. 12,
1929, 304

187

Local and Ethnic Names

Volocates mutatio

Voludnienses Velieude?

Vordenses Gordes

?Vorocingus (-nc-)

Vra fons Eure (Gard); cf.
Varus and the other
names in ur-, uar-
(e.g. Ambi-uareti)

"river, water," Berthoud
Bull. Géogr. 1927 (REA
31, 1929, 60)

Vrsoli IA

Vulchalo (cf. Grenier in
Frank 3.432 n. b)

Vulgientes, cf. Vogientes
(div. name)?

Remark:

On the complex subject of modern toponymy, see
for Narbonensis (in addition to the works cited Proleg.
pp. 7-8; and the important "Chroniques de Toponymie" in
REA e.g. 35, 1933, 51-56 and 39, 1937, 263-266 on Provence,
ib. 133-138 on the Dauphiné; 34, 1932, 411-416 on Savoy;
for the Aude, Bull. de la Commission arch. de Narbonne
9, 1906-7, 288-316; cf. REA 28, 1926, 359; and the new
journal Onomastica):

(1) On -acum, -anum, -ascum, -uscum the dissertation
of P. Skok (Die mit den Suffixen -acum etc. gebildeten
sudfranzösischen Ortsnamen, 1906); (2) on -sc- also CA
5.229, 7.135-6; (3) on -ennus, -ennacus see Bull. de la
Comm. arch. de Narbonne 1925, 159; (4) -inco- is generally conceded to be Ligurian; (5) on -anus, -inus,
-ensis see the dissertation of I. Collijn Les Suffixes
toponymiques dans les langues françaises et provençales,
Upsala 1912.

Note also:

A. Magnan, Les noms de montagne niçoise, Nice
1938; Ch. Marteau, Répertoire de noms de lieu de l'arrondissement d'Annecy (Acad. florimontane: Mémoires et
Documents 1, 1935; 2, 1937; 3 not yet published); A. Gros,
Dict. étymologique des noms de lieu de la Savoie, Belley
1935 (cf. REA 38, 1936, 53-54); E. von Ettmayer in
Kretschmer Festschrift 1926, 23-34; A. Dauzat "Glossaire
onomastique" (in his Glossaire du patios de Vinzelles,

Local and Ethnic Names

Montpellier 1915); the treatises of Nicollet and E.
Melbois (on modern local names in Provence) cited REA
12,1910, 297; 33, 1931, 261-262; Jullian commented
briefly ib. 13, 1911, 344 and 348 on the translation of
local names into new languages, a subject that (with
consideration of hybrids e.g. Linguaglossa) would repay
study.

Modern names which continue an ancient name are
usually attested throughout the middle ages; but I have
not given medieval forms unless they are especially significant (e.g. Bouz above, s.v. Bautae). There are,
however, a few important modern local names, without any
ancient record at all, to which it may be worth while
to call attention. The list could easily be greatly
extended.

Biturrita 898 A.D., Bédarrides (not Béziers)

Graselum 698, cf. CIL 12.56 Griselicae (if genuine), Groseau, Gréoulx?

Vindasca, Vend- (Vénasque) but Vindauscia (as a
personal name) CIL 12.1751; cf. REA 17, 1915,
71; CA 7.135; BSL 32, 158 n. 2.

Rotmanis (Romans), see REA 34, 1932, 418

Tritis (Trets) ib. 41, 1939, 141

Camargue, cf. the pers. name Camars, ib. 24, 1922,
379-380

Local and Ethnic Names

Names in -sc- are especially numerous in the Var
(CA 2.75-76), where the Keltic element is less abundant.
Note, however:

Les Brignoles (brig-), Nans (nanto- ?), Brue-
Auriac (*brugaria, CA 2.76, but cf. Bruatus 23 above or
bruco- 178, div. name Vroicae 82).

Porquerolles (*porcaria) may translate Stoichades
insulae, the Iles d'Hyères (RA 22, 1925, 95-104), but
cf. Arearum (80 above)

Thor, Tor has been held to represent *torus "bord
de rivière;" cf. rather the gloss turia (79 above).

A name of peculiar interest is the modern Gap for
ancient Vap(p)incum, with the Germanic substitution of
g or gu for u-. At least there is no evidence to suggest, what might be tempting, a Brythonic pronunciation
of u- (gw-). But where Germanic g(w-) appears for u̯-
there is usually conflation of Germanic and Romance forms
(e.g. gâter, gué Prov. gua); so here, cf. Germanic gap,
geographically appropriate, which will also account for
the total loss of -incum. But does this orthodox explanation cover also Gascon: Vascones, Gard: Vardo, Gordes:
Vordenses? On u̯- becoming g(u)- see in general Hubschmied
Vox Rom. 3, 1938, 103-105, Jud ib. 1, 1936, 201; Arch.

190

Local and Divine Names

80 ctd.

Rom. 6, 1922, 339. Aebischer Zts. f. Schw. Gesch. 14, 1934, 309 interprets Marquisanes (Pyr.-Orient.) as Matres *Caxanae, i.e. Cassanae (cf. Deruonnae) "chênes."

81   Further Modern Local Names

Allan, Alleins, Ampus, Barbaïra, Baron, Le Barroux, Boulbon, Chusclan, Clarensac, Cruas, Cruples, Cuech, Curnier, Duin, Gajan, Gréasque, Lambesc, Moussac, Roujan, Texon, Thor (Tor), Tornac.

82   Divine Names

Abianius REA 16, 1914, 334

Abianus CA 5.209; ILG 666

?Aciannus

?Acilu deo CA 5.54, 179, cf. 2.66, 271; or Aciludeus?

Ac(c)orus

?Aethucolis

Alambrima

[?Albarinus ILG 173, cf. REA 24, 1922, 254; 25, 1923, 174; REA 41, 1939, 345. But it is also a personal name, 83 below; and CA 7.47, 83]

Albiorice (dat.)

Albiorigi (dat.)

Ald[e]me[hen]ses ILG 87

?[Al]isanus CIL 12.665

Allobrox

Almahae (matres)
Cf. Alma fl. AcS 1.106;
if strictly a local
name, then perhaps for
*Albae (*Alp-, mod.
Aups?), with m:b? Cf.
CA 5.11, 40, REA 22,
1920, 53

Andarta v. Dea

Andose dat. sg. m. "inu-
icto;" cf. 79, 86, 87,
and v. Illunnus inf.;
Becker Rh. Mus. 17,
1862, 14-28

?Anoniredi dat. CIL 12.
1285

Aramo Cf. BSL 32, 1931,
164 n. 2; and Aramici
(241 below)

Arausio ILG 184

Artaius Cf. Ardeia (now
Ardiège) Cart. (Lizop,
Comminges 113)

?Athubodua v. Cath-

?Attae (nymphae), ?Aptae.
Or, rather, personal
name Att(h)is?

Auicantus Cf. BSL l.c. 158
n. 3, REA 24, 1922, 164,
260; Liricantus (179)

Baginas CIL 12.2383 (m.)

Baginus ILG 251

Baginatiae ib.; cf. pagus
Bag[80 above. In

RE 2.437, 777 given as
Baginahae

Bel(1)enus (-inus, -innus)
Add ILG 34; cf. gl.
belinuntia 178

[Βῆλος IG 14.2482]

Bergonia

Borbanus ILG 58, RA 14,
1921, 409; Bormanus,
Bormana, Bormo, Boruo
These deities are
found where there are
warm springs; cf. For-
miae, Θερμαί, Phryg.
Γέρμη, Dac. Germisara,
Lig. Bormiae (PID 2.
156, AcS 1.492), Bor-
betomagus (Worms, ib.
489); forms with -e-
(Beru-, Berm-, Berb-)
are lacking. Therefore
the connexion with for-
mus "warm" (u or b aris-
ing by lenition, cf.
Loth RC 39, 1922, 50;
Pedersen-Lewis p. 55;
Jud. Arch. Rom. 6, 1922,
204; Hubschmied Vox.
Rom. 3, 1938, 119) is
preferable (pace Ernout-
Meillet, Walde-Hofmann,
et huius generis omnis)
to connexion with feruo,
but conflation with it
is probable (cf. AcS
3.913, 40)
See further Oehl ZONF
11, 1935, 103-111; 12,
1936, 53 - 64; (Gavia)
Burmina BSL l.c. 141;
mod. bourme "fumier dé-
layé" (Alpine), borme
"pus" (Lyon.) Vox. Rom.
l.c. 120 (cf. W. gor "pus").

Divine Names

But what clinches the
matter is calentes
aquae (AcS 1.493), cf.
Aquae Calidae 148;
Boruonicus 237

Br[Aquae; cf. 23, and
Vroicis below

Br[   ]us Hübner 253

Britouius (Mars)

Budenicus (Mars)

[?Budenus CA 5.208, cf.
APh 14, 1939 [1941],
p. 264; but ILG 149
reads dibu(s) de(a)bus,
cf. Note vii, Remark
(ii) above]

Buxenus (Mars) Cf. Buxea
silua 153, Boxsani 80,
boscus 79; Buxenus is
"deus robur," like Fagus
and Sexarbor 86, Silua-
nus infr., Alisanus 178,
181; i.e. as divine
names. See BSAF 1935,
175-178; 1936, 147-148;
CIL 9.3375, 12.103; gl. 79

Caiiarus

Candua Congrès de Nimes
191; cf. BSL l.c. 112
n. 1, kanta Note xv,
Auicantus above? La
Candoule

Carpantus

Carinnae (nymphae) REA 41,
1939, 345; AE 1940.158;
CA 7.46, 82

?Cathubodua (Ath-?) Pic-
tet, Rev. Sav. 1867,
112-113

Cautes

Caudellenses? But cf.
80 above

(?Cell[v. Bellenus)

Comedouae (or -i) augustae
(-i?)

?Crarus v. Diocrarus, and
cf. Nouencrares 80
above, AcS 1.1155

Cur]reti (i.e. -iti?) RA
14, 1936, 26 (Orange);
or Reti[?

?Dalla conseruatrix CIL
12.1719

Dea Andarta (add ILG 230)
cf. Artaius above.
For the comparison with
Ἀνδράστη or Ἀνδάτη
(read Ἀνδάετη) in Bri-
tain cf. Zwicker FHRC
84-85 (n. 14). Much
clearer is Artio 211,
243 below, and Arta-
(e, -he, -ehe) 86,
hardly Harsi 87

Deuiatis (dat.)

Dex(s)ius, i.e. -χ(s)- cf.
θέξιμον (δέξιƒον ?) 178

Digenibus (dat.), cf.
Diginibus at Cologne
(223)

193

Divine Names

Diiona (for Diuona?)

Dinomogetimarus; -moge-
    may be Illyr. But cf.
    Mogiancus, Mogiancius
    83

Diocraro (dat.); or Dio
    Craro? Me]diocraro?
    See Crarus above

Diuanno (add ILG 159),
    W.u.S. 11, 1928, 56.
    On this and Dinomo-
    getimarus cf. E. Krüger
    TrZ 15, 1940, 8-27, but
    cf. RA 23, 1945, 160

Dul(l)ouius cf. dolua,
    πεμπέδουλα 178

Dunatis

Elitiuae (matres)

(H)eluina (Ceres) cf. AcS
    1.1432; FHRC 68 (also
    a local name), cf. 247
    (Irish Cera)

Erditse (dat.?)

Ferontis templum FHRC 300.
    11

Fines REA 16, 1914, 233

Genaua ILG 357; RA 2,
    1933, 399.108; Genava
    10, 1932, 168-69 (cf.
    2, 1924, 99-106; BSAF
    1924, 243)

Gerudiatiae (matres)

Giarinus

Helioucmoun (-g-)

Hercules inuictus, v.
    Andose; Herculeius
    Graius CIL 12.5710

?Hos[v. Clerc Aquae
    Sextiae no. 86; but
    cf. REA 12, 1910, 197

Ialonus

Iboite (dat.) cf. REA 14,
    1912, 80; ILG p. 26

?Icotiis (dat.)

Idennica

]idonius (Mars)

Ignes aeterni (add RA 14,
    1939, 259; cf. Chevalier,
    Bull. Acad. Delphinale
    18, 1927 [1929], 1-5)

Ilunnus (Hercules) Andosa
    (-ss-us)

Iunones aug[ustae] Cf. REA
    16, 1914, 435; with
    Mastromela 80 (above)

Iunones montanae

Lacauus

?Lanoualus CIL 12, 1065

Divine Names

Larraso Cf. Λαρρασῶνι IG
14.2520; CIL 12.5369-
70; and 86 infr.

Lauaratus

Lauscus ILG 45; cf. CA 2.
224-5; 5.32; CIL 12.616
(and p. 816). Cf. Ven.
lav·s·ko·s· (Note xv
above)

Letinnoni (dat.), mod.
Ledenon

Lucus (pl.)

Macniaco Vellauno (corr.
for ueil-) CIL 12.2373;
Byvanck 1417, cf. 1416

M]agius (Mars) ILG 394

Maiurrus

Matrae (-abus dat.) Cf.
REA 9, 1907, 370

?Matruiles (-ae?) RA 14,
1939, 28; AE 1940.137
(gen. sg.?) Hardly a
corruption of Nemetiales?

?Me]diocrarus v. Crarus

Menmandutis (dat.?) Cf.
Skt. manma, Ir. menme,
and (for the ending)
Germanic -duÞs; Guten-
brunner 110 compares
Manmanhia CIL 6.31158

di Mitid[CA 5.209, 25;
cf. BSAF 1934, 124

Nabelcus v. 23

Nemausus

Nemetiales (matrae)

Nimpae BSAF 1927, 248-49,
nenfis (dat.) BΛ 1900
xxxii (Clerc, Aquae Sex-
tiae no. 81) ILG 64, 82.
In the former apparently
piain[or piam[as an
epithet? Or Priam(us)?

Obeleses (matrae)

Obioni (dat.)

Ocellu (dat.) AE 1940.159

]olatonae (matres?)

Olloudius (Mars) Cf. Loth
CRAcInscBL 1923, 345
("maître de la des-
tinée")

Osdiauae

Parcabus (dat.) Cf. ILG 83

Percernes (nymphae; cf.
Nimpae *piain above?);
cf. CA 7.49, 86. Pokorny
Urg. 174 interprets
this as *querc-

Perta cf. 79

Pipius Cf. REA 24, 1922,
260

195

Divine Names

Prox(s)umae (add ILG 174
  cet.) ? Proxam[REA
  37, 1935, 458. Cf. RA
  10, 1937, 334.26; 14,
  1939, 28-29. With
  Matruiles(?) RA l.c.,
  s.v.; cf. AE 1940.137
  (-as gen. sg.?). The
  plural of divine names
  is, of course, common-
  place: Siluanae AcS
  2.1556, 2, Nymphae,
  Martes CIL 5.3262,
  Mercurii IA 24.4,
  Iunones, Eponae 3.7904,
  Mineruae 13.4475

Reti v. Curreti; AE 1940.
  136

?Ricoria (Tr.?)

Ritona

Roqu[ILG 36

Rudianus (Mars) mod. Royans?
  Cf. Rudiobus (181); Loth
  RA 22, 1925, 210-227.
  Presumably not connected
  with Rodanus

?Sabelcus (for Nab-?) CIL
  12.1171

Segomanna ILG 393

Siluana

Siluanus (with mallet and
  bipennis, CIL 12, p.
  927)

Soioni (dat., fem.)

Sol[mo[CIL 12.1185

Sucellus

Suleuae m(ontanae?)

Suleuia (Minerva)

?Tangonae ILG 175; but cf.
  Tanconisi[above (80);
  P-W s.v. Tangonis; CIL
  12.1805

Thucolis

Tricoria v. Ric-

Trittia (from Pierrefeu,
  not Trets, Tritis:
  REA 41, 1939, 141-142)

?Vaeosus

Vasio, mod. Vaison

Vbelkabus (matribus), mod.
  Huvaeune? For the end-
  ing cf. Nabelcus; but
  CA 2.65, 261 reads
  Vbellabus or Vbelnabus

?V]gius (Mars?) RE 1902,
  p.277; cf. AcS 3.19
  (Serviers, Gard)

Veator (i.e. Vi- Mercurius)

Vellaunus v. Magniacus (-c-)

Venti (with Volcanus)

Viama BSAF 1937, 198 (Grenoble), RA 12, 1938, 325.
  88

196

Divine Names

Vienna (dea?), mod. Vienne
    BSAF 1899, 382, cf.
    Cent. Vol. SAF 1904,
    196; CIL 12.5864

Vintius (Pollux), cf. 80
    above

Vintur, mod. Ventoux; cf.
    CA 5.61, 222 (Ventur?),
    REA 1, 1899, 56-58:
    Vinturius (AcS 3.356)?

Virotuti (dat.) Apoll[ini],
    cf. Pictet Rev. Sav. 15
    Dec. 1867, 112-113 (-tut-
    as in Toutiorix) "chef
    (magistrat) des hommes"
    (RA 18, 1868, 1-17) But
    see Menmandutis above

Vogientis (dat.) CIL 12.
    1082 (cf. Vocontii,
    or Vulgientes)

Volcanus Cf. Volcae,
    Vulchalo 80 above

Vra fons Cf. 80 above;
    Vaillat Culte des
    Sources dans Gaule an-

tique 1932; cf. Congrès
de Nîmes 186-195 (RA 2,
1933, 425)

Vran[CIL 12.1111

Vrnia l'Ourne

Vrobrocis dat.

Vroicis dat. ILG 87. Cf.
    Proleg. 51, 69; among
    etymological discus-
    sions see also RC 48,
    1931, 312-324; Romania
    52, 1926, 338; 58, 1933,
    599-601; SprFK 214, Do.
    238; W-P 1.273, 319
    (Grds. 2 ed. 2, 151).
    Compare perhaps Vindo-
    (u)roicus (?) CIL 3.
    4604, AcS 3.350, 7

?Vssia

Vxellus (-lio lapis)

Vxouinus

Vxsacanus

Remark:

On the Keltic Iuppiter see now van Hoorn in
Med. v. Ned. Hist. Inst. te Rom 5, 1935, 23-30; RA 7,
1936, 156. On Apollo, Aebischer RC 51, 1934, 34-45.

Personal Names

83

Observe that from this point on, nomina and cognomina are given in a single alphabetically arranged
list; and that, as hitherto, the lists contain only
names selected for their linguistic interest; that names
which appear on terra sigillata are usually dealt with
according to the rules laid down at 88 (Remark). As to
sources, see 80; add Ch. Marteaux and M. Le Roux, Boutae
(Annecy, 1913). Some incomplete attempts to assemble
Keltic names may be found in RE 2, 1888, 382-384 (Nîmes,
cf. H. Bazin Nîmes Gallo-Romain, 1892, 132-133); and, by
Thédenat, RC volumes 8 (1887) to 14 (1893)

Abascantus CA 5.230

Abau[CA 7.120

Abel[ib.

Abicelia

Abillius

Abucatus

Abudius

Akanius

Accauus

Acedillus (Boutae)

Acica, -us

Ἀκίλις IG 14.2468

Acilius

Aco (Boutae)

Aconius

Ἀκόντιος IG 14.2483 (but

cf. Thes. Ling. Lat.
1.420)

Actalus

Actulus

Acutus, Aqutus

Acus (Pro Alesia 11, 1925,
62; Geneva)

Adbitus

Adbucillus

Adcennus

Adgennia, -us

Adgennus

Adgonna

Adgubillus

Adgubiounus

Adiatus

Adius (cf. BA 1932-3, 483;
AE 1934.32)

Personal Names

Admatius

Adreticia, -us

Adretonius

Adrettio

Adroarius ILG 609

Adulus

Adesi[

Aduentus

Aduetisso ILG 34

Aebutius

Aecus BC 3.79.6

Aegle ILG 590, 545 (Eclae)

?Aegus (Eg-, Ec-)

Aemicis

Aesilus

Aetoria, -us

Aetronius BA 1932-3 [1936]
  119

Aetus

Aeuillia, -us

Agidius ILG 187

Agileius CA 7.57, 20

Agio ILG 510

Agrecius

Aicorus, Aicor

?Aimie CA 7.119, 40

?Ainlioχ[

Aisugius (E-)

Alacca

Alaucus

Albanus

Albarinus

Albisia

Alboinus

Alcius

Aleasiumara

Alfia, -us

Algo

Alleticia ILG 445

Alliola

Alletroris (-ey- lapis)

Allurius

†Alonius (?) CIL 12.5344
  (A.D. 568)

Alpina ILG 168, 213; cf.
  REA 28, 1926, 43 -us
  CA 7.96, 5

Ambidauus

Ambillus

Ambridius

Amiteius ILG 232

199

Personal Names

Ammatiacus

Ammia, -us

Ammilla

Ammo

?Amneraix

Amon[CA 7.117, 23

Ananthailda ILG 297

Andebrocirix f. (Cf.
   Ascafotorix f. RA 35,
   1932, 145)

?Anderus

?Anderourus

Andius

Ando

Andolatius

Andorourus

Anicia CA 7.109, 13

Anilla

Ἀγισσεν

Annianus ILG 503

Annicco

Anniccus

Annius

Annonius

Anteremius (Afer) RA 14,
   1939, 25; AE 1940.135

Antessius

Anthillus ILG 85

Antillus

Antodon

Antulla -us

Anullinus

?Anutus

?Aombo

Apa m.

Aper

Apetemarus CIL 12.1148;
   read Atepomarus?

?Apho[BA 1916, lxii

Apilius

?Apo[

Aponius ILG 441, 558, 573

Appeus (Boutae)

Apronius ILG 213

Apronianus

Aprulla (add ILG 468)

?Aquius Esp. Syll 333

Arabus

?Aranto (Car-?)

Arbonius

Arbacia

Personal Names

?Arcanus

Arcessus

Arcusa

Arecorus

Aretullus

Argentilla -us

Arguria ILG 29

Arlenus

Arruntius

Arsius

Articilla

Aruenius

Aruntio RA 14, 1921, 278

?Arus (Boutae)

?Ascitus

Ascius

Asicius

]asirigia

Asisa ILG 583

ασσι IG 14.2573, 3

Assorenus

Assuia, -ius

Asucius

Ateieuo CA 7.120, 58

Ateioucus

Ateblinus (Boutae)

Atellius

Atepatus

Atepilla

Atepiot[CA 7.60, 75

Atepo

Atepomarus

Ateros CA 5.116, 381

Atessas, -atis

Atettia, -ius

Atgite

Athamallus

?Ati[ILG 128

Atilia, -ius

Atiamoenus ILG 377

Atimetes

Atimetio (-mit-)

Atimetus (-mit-)

Atisia, -ius

Atislius

Atismaria

Atiso RA 14, 1921, 260

Atita

Personal Names

Atleas REA 22, 1920, 172;
    ILG 114

Ato, Atu (Boutae)

Atolisus

Attalio

Attillus

Attius, -ia

Atto

Atucia

]atuedus (Gérin-Ricard
    et d'Agnel: Arc,
    1907, 188)

Atullus ILG 404

Aturenus

Aturia, -ios

Atusa

Aucalo

Aucasus

Aucia, -ius

Audax (cf. Audagus?)

Audemaces

Aueius (add ILG 344)

Auentus

Aufustia, -ius

Auitiana, -us

Auitus, -a

Aura

Auscus

Autestius

Auiul(l)a, -us

Axia, -ius

Axiounus

?Babbus CIL 12.767

Bacculus ILG 62

Βαίβιος Dessau 8814

Balonia

Bandinus

Banona

Bara

Bargates

Barnaeus (cf. CIL 13.7011)

Bassus

Becco

Beccus

?Beilona CA 7.37, 3

Belatulla, -us (add ILG
    162)

Belia

Bellatur

Bellica, -us H-M 430

Personal Names

Belli[

Bellicco

Bellicia -ius

Bellic(c)us (add ILG 229)

Bellinus

Bella, -us

Bellir[

Bello

Belue (-ne?)

Belurs

Belus

†Benenata BA 1934-35, 587

Bepo (Boutae)

Betutia, -ius

Bicatius

Bicirius

]bimmius Espérandieu Syll.
362. Cf. CIL 12.1082;
or βιμμοσ (34 above)

Bilcaisio

Billo

Biracus ILG 97

Birria -ius (add ILG 194,
201)

Birro ILG 227

]bito (?Bito)

Bittius

Bituka

Bitucius

Bitugia

Bitulla

Bituna (add ILG 77)

Bitunia

Bitutio

Bl]aesia ILG 562, -ius
CA 7.64, 8

Blanda, -us

Blandinus

Blandius

Blandola

Blastus

Blattius

Blatu

Bocurus

Boduacius

Boiscus

†[B]o[n]osa ILG 313

?Borustus

Botta, -us

Bottia

Boturo

Personal Names

Bouda (add ILG 535), -us
  (add ib. 416)

Boudia, -ius

Boudilla ILG 151

Boutius (perhaps an ethnicon?) Cf. Oswald, Index
  s.v.

Braetius

Brancus (v.l.-es Livy 21.
  31.6); cf. gl. branca
  220(?)

Bredo

†Bricciofrida

Briccius

Brico

Brin[

Brittius CIL 12.3353

Brocchus cf. gl. broccus
  158, num. βροκχοι AcS
  1.618.13

B]roius (Hispanus) ILG 366

?Brouaccus (Ebro-?)

Bru[

Bubata, -us

?Bucamia

Bucanus

Bucca cf. gl. bucca 79

Buccio

Bucconia

Buccula

Bucculius

Buddarus

Bulicus

Bulla

Bullia, -ius

Bullo

Bullonius

Burdo cf. gl. burdo 158

Buricus cf. gl. buricus
  158

Burranus

Burrus

Byrria

?Caamus (leg. Cadmus?)

Cab[

Cabellio

Cabirius

Caburus (cf. CQ 32, 1938,
  43)

Cacusius

Caesius

Caesta

Personal Names

Caetronius

[Cafatius]

Caiaucus

Caiena

Cala

Kalauia, Calauius

?Calendio

Calemerus BSAF 1893, 240;
   ILG 273)

?Calissus

Calitius

Callo

Callonius

Calomallus

Calosus, Kallosus ILG 402

Calpitanus CA 5.39.87

Caluo, -uus (ILG 144, 570)

Cam[

[Camars]

Camasius

Cambaria, -ius

Cambia

Kamenus

Camomilus

Campil(i)us

Camula[

Camulata, -us

Camulatia

Camul(l)ia, -ius

Camurrus

Canacia

]candua[

Canicus ILG 81

Canius, Canus

Cantia, -ius

Capauso

?Capeiil (Cape[g]ilsa?
   CIL 12.5686, 172)

Capeius

Capella

Capiatus

Kapinius

Cappia

Canestin(us) Esp. Syll.
   55 (CIL 12.2821)

Capit[

Capitoius

Capnus

Caprarius

Capreolus Dessau 9090,
   Riese 1683

Personal Names

Caprilia, -ius (ILG 350)

Capronia

Capus

Car[

Carantia, -ius

Carantiana, -us

Caranticconus (sic; an
    -icco?) ILG 151

Caranto

Carassounius

Carata

Caratius

Carauso

Careius (K-)

Caresus

Caretenus

Carilla

Carintianus

Carisia, -ius

Caritus

Carosenus

Carpus

Carsia, -ius

[Carsiaudia(?) Cf. Cassauda
    80]

Karus

Casaria

Casata

Cascelliu(s) ILG 436

?Casponius

Cassibr[a]tius

Cassicia, -ius

Cassicus

Cassilius

Cassillus

Cassiolus

Cassi[g]netus(?)

Castina

Castius

Casuna

Casunia

Casuria, -ius

Catalia

Catcatus (i.e. Cadgatus)

Catia, -ius

Catianus

Catilo ILG 461

Catinia

Catisius

Personal Names

Cattaius

Cattia, -ius

Catto

Cattu[

Cattura

Κατούγνατοσ

Catumandus (cf. REA 35,
   1934, 474)

Catullia

Κατούλλοσ IG 14.250

Catullus

?Catuper (-pris gen.)

Catus

Catuso

?Cauca

Caupicus

Cauia (G-)

Celaedo

Kel[CA 7.88, 27

Celatus

Ceionius

Celinus

?Celisus

Celtiliu(s) ILG 156

Celtilla

Celto

Celtus

Cemellus (G-); add REA
   22, 1920, 185

Cenetus

Ceniter

Censa (add ILG 368)

Censilla

Ceragius

Cerealis

[Cermanus i.e. Ger-]

Cermo

Certulus

Cerudius

Cerue[(cf. EC 2, 1937,
   30)

Cestia, -ius

?Cesuro

Cialb[CA 7.125, 216

?Cicelb[

Cicorelliu(s) AE 1921.95

Cil[

Cila

Cilon

Ciltius

207

Personal Names

Cimarius

?Cincnus CA 7.85, 4

Cinge

Cingetius

Cingius

Cinnamis

Cinnamus

Cintia

Cintugnata, -us (ILG 40)

Cinr[

Cintullus

Cippacus

Ciratus

Ciria, -ius

Cirratius ILG 453, cf.
  CIL 12.5388 (47 B.C.)

Cirrilus

Ci(s)sus

Citronius AE 1921.95

Cladaeus

?Clarianus

Classius

Cletus

Clinta

Cludia ILG 592

Cluuius ib. 409, 547

Cloustria

Cnisa ILG 66

Coblanuo f.

Cobnertus

Cogrouillus

Cocca

Cocusia

Codelo

Codonius (?Codo)

Coilanus CA 7.69, 21

Coinus

Coionius

Coius (add ILG 364, 585)

Colia, -ius

Comagius

Comanus

Combarillius

Combarillus

Comianus ILG 50

Cominia, -ius (cf. REA
  22, 1920, 183)

Comio f.

?Comtullus (cf. Tullus)

?Concennus (Congennius?)

Personal Names

Condercus

Condianus

Condita

Condo

Condolus

Condus

Congenncia

Congenniccus

Congenno

Connia, -ius

Conniola

Connius add ILG 219, 377, 455

Connil[

Consuadullia

Contessia, -ius

Κόπιλλοσ

Corasia

Cordius ILG 154

Cornaiius

Corradius

Cosconius ILG 401

Cosp[

Corsius

Cossutius

Cotillus

Cottilus

Cottulla(?) ILG 544

?Co]uertina ILG 239 Cf. REA 17, 1915, 75

Couxollius

Crac[

Cracco

Crappaus

Crasia, -ius

Crax[

Craxa

Craxanius

Crax(s)ius (-xx-)

Craxo BSAF 1937, 198 (Grenoble); or -us? (AE 1938.58)

Cremius

Creperius

Crinas

Cul(l)i(us)

Cummius

Cupita, -us

Cupitia

Cupus (Oswald Index, 200)

Curmilla (cf. EC 2, 1937, 30)

209

Personal Names

Curmisso (AE 1940.159)

?Curuardigia

Cusanus CA 7.122, 121

Dacminus

Dacurdo

Dagidius

Damanaus REA 12, 1911,
   70, n. 4

Damas

?Damus

Dancu CA 7.122, 123

Dannia, -ius

Dannomarus

Danomarus

Danotala

Dapsilis ILG 563

Darrantus

?Dasuius

Datiua

Dattouir

Dauarius

Dauerus

Dauerius

?Dauilus

Dauus

?Decnus

Δεκριζ IG 14.2441 (for
   Δερκ-?)

Decumo (add ILG 532)

Decumilla ILG 119

?Demogeta

Derceia

Derco

Δερκύλος IG 14. 2438

Des(s)ius

Deuillia, -ius

Diallus CIL 12.5388 (47
   B.C.)

Dimarius

Diorus

Disenius

Diselo

Diu[ILG 159

Diuc(c)ius

Diuicia, -ius

Diuilia

Diuius

Dius CA 5.148,4

Dognia

Personal Names

?Doliens

Δολου CIL 12.5686, 1177;
  cf. πεμπέδουλᾳ gl. (178)
  and Dula below

Domitus ILG 559

Donax CA 7.122, 125

Donnia, -ius

Donnotaurus

Donnus

?Doufus

?Dous[

D]ouiccorix CIL 12.1147

Dousarnus

Draccius

Drau[ILG 484

?Draucus

Drippinus (Oswald Index)

Drippius

Drippus

Drusius

Drutalus

?Druta

Duac[

Dubia, -ius

Dubnacus

Ducenius

Duccia

Dudio

Dudistia, -ius

Duel(l)us

?Duφius

Duill[CA 7.88, 22

Dula AE 1940.134 (not
  Duia CA 7.108, 10 f);
  cf. Δολου above

Dumerius

Dumnia ILG 396

Dunatius

Duronia, -ius

Duuius (Riese 351)

Ebideos CA 7.69, 21

?Ebrouaccus (Brou-)

Eburia, -ius

]eccarius RE 2, 1888, 383

Eccia, -ius

Ecimaria, -ius

Ecrito, Aegritomarus

Eϒ[

Edia

211

Personal Names

Egus

Ἐ?βύκοσ IG 14.2485

]eitri?

Eliponia, -ius

(H)eluia, -ius

(H)eluianus

Empiuius CA 5.224, 584

Enimanuus ILG 2

[Eorticus]

Epato f.

Epatus m. (ILG 128?)

Epia ILG 386

Epicifius AE 1936.112

Epidia, -ius (add ILG 308)

Epit[BA 1932-33 [1936],
   483

Epo[

Epotius

Eppius

Eprius

Ep(t)acus

?Equatia CA 7.30, 63

Erasus

Eripius

Ermetio (H-)

Ernus

Erucia, -ius

Escengolatis

Esciggorix

?Escornb[(for Escobnus?)

Esdius CA 5.186, 34

Esmerius ILG 211

Essius

]essol[?

Essuuius CA 5.224, 584

Esunertus (add ILG 303?
   Or Cobn-?)

?Etrilia

Ettamecia

Etuuius (Riese 1683)

Euenus ILG 363

Euis (Oswald, Index), cf.
   Idmeuis?

Exapila

Excingillius

Excingilla, -us

Excingomarus

Excingus

Exomn[us]

Expentanius ILG 92

212

Personal Names

[Faltonia ILG 559]

?Fasuri

?Finanus CIL 12.888

Ferreo ib. 5683, 272a, b

Filo ILG 243

Fromene ib. 964 (for
    Phronime?)

Gaberia, -ius

Gainia

Galeonus (gen. sg.?)

Galla, -us

Gallicus

Gal(l)icanus

Gallicia, -ius

?Galligenia RE 2.383

Gallius

Gallonia, -ius (C-)

Gamicus

Ganapo cf. Gamapia 179
    below

Gappius

?Garkol[

Gatiena CA 7.157, 13

Gauia, -ius (cf. gloss
    158)

Gauiatia

Geli[CA 7.88, 19

Geme ib. 122.34

Gemito

Gena[ca] ILG 553

Genesia, -ius ILG 22, 259,
    606

Germo (C-) f.

Gerus

Gessius

Gettius

Giamillius; cf. AE 1945.72?

Giaria

Gillius

Gimia

Gingetius

Glaidis f. BA 1918, xlix

Glo[CA 7.91, 1

Gnatia, -ius

Goas

Graeipo[CIL 12.355

Grania, -ius

Granianus

Greicus

Greius

Personal Names

Gresia ILG 559

Gudomarus

Heca ILG 113

Hiberus

Hirpidia, -ius

Hispanus ILG 366

Homonea ib. 524

Hosela

[Hotarzaradus]

Ὑρία IG 14.2433

Iacaena CIL 12.790 (Lac-?)

Iallius

Ia[ ]nns ILG 180

Ianinus CA 7.28, 4

Iapis

Iapys

Iaracio

Iarilla

Iaronius

?Iausus (Lausus)

Iaxsucus (i.e. Laχs-?)

Icarus

?Icca(u)us (Boutae)

Iccianus

Iccinus (Boutae)

Iccius

Icelus (Boutae)

Idmeuis

?Ieguiuo

]ilia (Suadurigii f.)

Iliomarus

Ilidius

Illiomarus

Ilo

Inacus ILG 239

?Inaumona

Indamia, -ius

Indedius

Indeles

Indutiomarus

Indutus

Ingerosa ILG 316

Inulus

Inus

Inuentus

Iop[

Personal Names

Ior[(or Ioru, Boutae)

Υ’]ωσή IG 14.2476

Iouenales ILG 317

Iouincatus

Isidus (Boutae)

?Isilus

Ismar[CA 7.88, 23

Isugius

Itauus

Itero

Iti[CA 7.110, 32

Iuantus

Iuencus (for Iuu-?)

Iuinaui CA 7.120, 66, cf.
110, 33

Iuito

Iunicilla

Iuo (or Iuon[us?] Boutae)

Iuuentia, -ius

Labricius

Lais ILG 408

Lalia

Lalianus

Lal(l)us

Lagge (i.e. -ng-?)

Lamponicus

Lardarius AE 1912.25

?Larienus CA 7.11, 49
(L. Arlenus?)

Lasciuus

Laticcus ILG 490

Latinius

Latinus

Lattius

Lat(t)o

Laurens

Laurinus

Lausus

Lauenus

Laχtucus

Leda

Leiturro

Lemiso

Ληναίσ IG 14.2447

Lenc[

Lentius

Lerissus

Letius

Leuanius

Personal Names

Leuconia, -ius

Lexius (Oswald Index)

Λιβάσ IG 14.2448

Licinilla

Licnus

Licorix (-ux?)

Lictauius CIL 13.6868

Lidauilla

Ligus

Lionus CA 7.69, 11

Litogene(s)

Lituccia, -ius

Lituccus

Litugena, -us

Litugius (-c-?)

Liuanius

†Liubani A.D. 568; gen.
  sg.?

Liuianus

Liuia, -ius

Logius

Λομβο CA 5.11, 39

Loreia

Lorinus

Lottus

Lotusius

Lucceius (add ILG 26)

Lucconius

Luccunius

?Lucenia

Lucilla

Lucinula, -us

Lucius

Luconianus

Lucritianus ILG 92

Lugius

Luliu[s]

Lullus

Lupa, -us

Lurius

]lurus CIL 12.1344

Lussor

Lutatia ILG 477

Luteua, -us

Lutonia

Luttacus

Luttius

Lutto (Iu-?)

Mab[BA 1941-42, 353

Personal Names

Macareus

Macaria

Maccianus

Macciril(l)a

Maccia, -ius

Maccis CIL 12.5699.2

Macco

Macellio

Μάκελλος IG 14.2451

Macio REA 17, 1915, 71;
  cf. ILG 175; gl. macio
  220

Macor[

Macrinus

Madi[

Maelinus

Maelo (add ILG 131)

Maeta m. (add CA 7.122,
  144)

†Mafortio

†Mafusio

Maganus

Magiacus

Magia, -ius

Magunia, -ius

Magunt[

Magusius

Mahaia

Mahes

Maina

Mainatis

Mainuilo RA 14, 1921, 277

Maionus

Maiorix

Maiuddilo

Malia, -ius

Malicco ILG 150

Malisius (serv.) CA 7.119,
  24

Mallo

Mallonius

?Maltrebrius CIL 12.1209

Mamidia

Mancius

Mandatus

Mangius

Mangonius ILG 584

Manigidia BA 1918, xcviii

Mantius

Mantro

Mapilla

Personal Names

Mara ILG 131

Marcio

Marcula, -us

Marcus

Maria, -ius

Maricus

Marila

Μαρίσκη IG 14.2450

Marra

Martiola (Boutae)

Marullianus 13.6863

Marullus

Maskarus

?Mascarpus (Boutae)

Mascelinus ILG 584

Mascellio

Masclus (add ILG 514)

Mascuricus

Masidia

?Maso (add ILG 347)

Maspetia, -ius

Massa

Masso

Massonia

Mastria

Masucia

Masuetus ILG 279

Masuinnia, -ius

Maternius 13.7007

Maticius

Matislius

Mato

Matrona (add ILG 596)

Matronilla

Matrus[CA 7.124, 208

Mattia, -ius

Matto

Matucenia, -ius (-g-)

Matugenus

Matuilo

Matullo

Matura, -us

Matuso

Meculonia, -ius

?Medɣcatus

?Mefinitus CA 5.103, 317

Melaenus

Melissaeus

Personal Names

Melissa, -us

Mel(l)ius

Mellinius

Menatus

Menio

Meno[ILG 484

Menos

Mentonus ILG 143

Mercatia

Mercatilla

Mereus (Boutae)

?Mesima

Messianus

Messina, -us

Messius

Messulus

Messurius

Messus ILG 521

Meuius ib. 229

Miccio

Mich[ILG 8

Micia

Micli[CA 7.28, 26

Minia (Esp. Syll. 326)

Minnius

Minuso

Minuta

?Miogmius

?Mirmius

Moccia

?Mociacus

Mocia

Μόκιμοσ IG 14.2490

?Moclii CA 7.82, 41 (cf.
    90, 5)

Moconia RE 2, 1888, 383

?Mocus

Mogetius

Mogiancus AcS 1.609

Mogia[n]cius BA 1932-3
    [1936], 484

Mogillo

Mogitumarus

Mogonia

Mogouius

Moltelius (cf. Mult-)

Moneius CIL 2.4161

Moniccia

Μοψεᾱτησ IG 14.2516

219

Personal Names

Mopsinus CIL 12.1110

??Mordmux RA 16, 1921, 280

Multelius, -il- (cf. Molt-)

Mulus ILG 150

Mummius

Muncu(?) CA 7.88, 32

Muninielia

Munnius

?Musa

?Musicus

Mutius

?Mutr[

Nagelius

Namantius

Namatius

Namerius

?Namidia RE 2, 1888, 383

Namilius

Nammia, -ius (cf. REA 19, 1917, 46)

Namuta

Nάνοσ

Nasonius

Nasso (add CA 5.14, 55;

cf. Prouincia 11, 1931, 8.161)

Nattia

?Naturius (add CIL 12. 5701, 10)

Nauica

Nauus

]ndoerdus?

Nebrigiad[

Necteria, -ius

Nem[

Nemausina (cf. local names)

Nemonia, -ius

Neria, -ius

?Nertus (Boutae)

Neuienorius CA 5.169, 34

?Neustomi

Neuatus

Neuia (Galla)

Neχt[

Nicaris

Nicasius ILG 255

]niccus

Nigella, -us

Nigrina, -us

220

Personal Names

Nisa ILG 66

Niua ILG 368

Niuatus

Nonius

Nonnius ILG 362

Nonnus

Noricus

Nouanus

Nouia, -ius

Nundina, -us

Obauus

Obellius

Obienia

Occia, -ius (add ILG 238)

Ocellus REA 41, 1939, 345

Oconia

Ocumisa

Oeizisd[CA 7.120, 43
  (Of Iz-?)

Oη πλ CA 7.124, 205 (Of
  Pl-?)

Oicanus (-auus?)

?Oida CA 7.120, 78

]olato

Oldrauus

Olidius ILG 596

Olia, -ius

Olitia, -ius (Cf. MSAF
  1914, 165)

Olluna (add ILG 87)

Olondia ILG 480

Olosto

Ombania, -ius

?Ombecco CIL 12.5381 (cf.
  87 infr.); but perhaps
  read Becco

Omiuius

Omos (Boutae)

]ompous

Omulla, -us

Onalisus

?Oncanio

]oniissio RA 17, 1941, 271

Oniu[CA 7.110, 33

Onsuadulia

Oppianus (cf. 160 and Note
  xlv C)

Orbia

]orgen[

Orgesa Germ. 22, 1938, 55;
  ZfdAlt. 75, 116

Orimundus ib.

Ortelius

Ortrus

?Osirinus

Otacilia, -ius

Oteia

Otinus (cf. CA 7.42, 71)

]ouicorix

Ouidia, -ius

P.aar[

Paconius (add ILG 597)

Pacullius

Pap(p)itus CA 7.70, 6-7

Papus ILG 599

Paquius

Parassius

Pardus

Partegoria

Parucia, -ius

Patruuius

Peccio

Pedo

Pedullius

Pedul(l)us

Pedusia

Pefirus ILG 222

Pel(l)ius

Pennius

Pentodia ILG 669

Pequ(ius) CIL 12.4225

Perus

Pert[CA 7.11, 49; 26.
     57. Cf. 82 above

Pescennius (add ILG 32)

Petita ILG 83

Petrusonia

Pixtilos

Pila (Boutae)

Pillo

Pillus (Oswald, Index)

Pinite ILG 406

Pipia ILG 447

Pipo

Pisinus ILG 88, 89

Planta m.

Plinius

Plutia ILG 478

Pocius

Personal Names

?Pollus (Boutae)

Pompulla

Pompullina

Poppo

Pontias

Porcia, -ius

Porro

Pottia

Precilia, -ius

Pretenius ILG 215

Pric[ILG 126

Pt..nni REA 41, 1939, 345

Pupa

Pupasius (Boutae)

Puster (-rus)

Qaris, Quaris CA 7.125, 225

Qial CA 7.125, 237

Quelia, -ius ILG 641

Quiamelius

?Rabano

Raielia

Ranilo ILG 542

Rarious

Rauricia

Rebrullus ILG 171

Reburrius

Reburrus (cf. REA 22, 1920, 183)

Reiconius

Rematia

Remulla

Reniccius

Rennius

R(h)enus (Rienus REA 36, 1934, 204)

Reppauus

?Resius (cf. CA 7.122, 141)

?Restus

Reticius

Retillus

Reuconius

Reuscina

Riccius (add ILG 368)

]riccus

Rigius

Rigom[ILG 440

Rinnia, -ius

Personal Names

Riouercus

?Rissam[

?Ritminia

Rituca

Riue[

]rmano?

Roccius

Rodanicus

Rodanius

Rhodinus ILG 202

R(h)odismianus

Rhodochus

Romogillia

Romogillus

Rotania

Rotanus

Roucillus

Roucius

Roudius (add ILG 234)

?Rouicus (Roucillus
  BC 3.79.6)

?Ruerius

Rufio

Rug[

Ruittacus

Rulina?

?Rulus Genava 18, 1940,
  60 (for Aulus CIL 12.
  2591)

Ruma

Runnius

Rusius

Ruso

Rusonius

Rutaius (Boutae)

S[   ]cnus

Sabina, -us

Sabineius ILG 276

Sabinius

Sabinula ILG 369

Sacco

Sacconia, -ius

Sacratus

Sacrinus

Sacrouir

Safinius CA 7.125, 225

Saedius ILG 530

?Sagitti

?Saiaonn[

Personal Names

Saiius (Esp. Syll. 236)

Salauerus

?Salitus

Saiius

Salonia, -ius

Saluentius BA 1938-40, 73

Samicius

Samicus

Samih[?

Samis?

Sammia, -ius

Sammo

Σάμμιοσ IG 14.2497-8

Samoniccius

Σάγγα, Sanga m.

Sandyceus ILG 469

Sanuillus

Sapalo

Sapaudus

Sapauidus

Sappius

Sapricia, -ius

Saprinius (CIL 12.1561)

Sarro

Satia

Satrius (add CIL 13.6945; ILG 257, 489)

Sattianus

Sattia

Satto BA 1932-33 [1936], 119

Satulla, -us

Sauria m.

Sauricus

Sauinis (Esp. Syll. 153)

Sauus (add Oswald, Index)

Saxo CIL 12.5683, 272

?Scaeuaeus

Scarpius

Scarpus

Scatnilla

?Scoilias CA 7.124, 186

?Scorobres

Scotaus

Scotia(n)us ILG 204

Scoto

Scotta, -us

Scottius

Scum[

Personal Names

?S△ RA 11, 1920, 120

Seccarus

Seccia, -ius

Secia

Secolasia

Secunius

Sedata, -us

Sedulus

Sega

Segeia, -us

Segellius

Segla

[Sego]marus ILG 461

Segolatia, -ius

Segorix

Segudia

Selia (for -d-?)

Seleucus, -ou-

Sencio

Seneca

Senecio

Senenia

?Seneucus

Senex

Senguesn[

Senicatus

Senilius

Senilus

Senissius

Sennius (add ILG 174)

Senno

Senocondius (Senu-)

Senonus (Boutae)

Senorix

?Senourus

Senouir

Senquri CA 7.123, 180
  (Senouir?)

Senter

Sentrius

Sentro m. f.

Senucia, -ius

?Sepullas Genava 4, 1926,
  121-22

Sepullius

Sequanus

Ser[   ]o

Serana, -us

Serania ILG 493

Personal Names

Serenua ILG 53

Sergianus ILG 474

Serra

Sertor ILG 26

Sertullius

Sescius

Set[

Setulcia (-eia?)

Seuua ILG 371

Seu...ois...

Sextilla

Sextus

Siccius ILG 221

Sico

Σίδη IG 14.2440

Sigal[AE 1939.47

?Sige

Sigerus

Silanus (add ILG 147)

Silo

Silonius

Silu[

Similis

Sina ILG 547

Singenia

Sinicus

Sintacius (-g- ILG 177)

Sion[(Oswald Index; cf.
    Pro Alesia 11, 1925, 67)

Siora

Sirico

Sirinus

Syronia (-y- for -i-?)

Sme[

Smeria, -ius

Smertullus

Zmertuccius REA 36, 1934,
    201

Smerus ILG 251

Soillius

Solibitis (Solibis?)

Solicana

Solicius

Solico

Solimario

Solimarius

Solimarus (add CIL 12.1157)

Solimutus

Solirigus

Personal Names

Solirix

Solisetia

Sollario (Esp. Syll. 499)

Sollauius

Sollia, -ius

Sollo

Sontoseia

Sores[ia] Prouincia 11,
    1931, 8; 172

Soricio

Soricina

Sornius

?Sorolia CIL 12.2488

Sorumbo

Spanilia

Sparacus

Spartius

Sparus (add ILG 350)

Speccius

Spinus

Stabilio

Stabulo

Staius AE 1945.72

Stardius

Statuta, -us

Strato (Boutae)

Su[

Suaducco f.

Suaduilla

Suadulius

Suadurigius

Suagria, -ius (Sy-)

Sualeius

Sual(l)ia, -ius

Subrius

Sucaria, -ius

Sucesa

Sueua

Suillius

Suria

Suril(l)io

Surus

Tabius

Tacitius

Taetania

Tagassus

Tagidius

Taietius

Personal Names

Taia, Taius

Tallius

Tallutius

Talusius

Tamecia

Taminia, -ius

Tancius

Tannonius

Tappius (Boutae)

Tarcia, -ius

?Tascus (Boutae)

Tasgius

Tatinus

Taua CA 7.124, 188

Taucius

Tauganius

Tauillia, -ius

Taurina REA 38, 1936, 195

Taurinus

Taurus (add ILG 214; CIL 13.6874)

?Tenconisius CA 7.17, 33

Terialia ILG 189

Tertiolus (add ILG 174)

Tese[

Tessia, -ius cf. Teθθ-

Tessilla, cf. Tettḍ-

Teθθicnius

Teto

Tetricus

Tettius

Teucidia ILG 498

Teun[

Teutomalius

Texatius

Tigorninus ILG 94
    (Tigornnus?)

Tillia, -ius

Tincia, -ius

Tincianus

Tincorix ILG 393

Tingandus

Tingolonaia (or -onnia)

Tinius

Tioccia

Tirro (Esp. Syll. 315)

Tissius

Titia ILG 546

Titinia CIL 12.1412

Titiola

Personal Names

Titius

Tittilus (Boutae)

Titucius

Titul(l)a, -us (add ILG
     479)

Tleisa

Tocidia

Togiacia, -ius

Togiacus

Togius

?Tomeracus (Clerc, Aquae
     Sextiae no. 40)

Tonna

Tonneius

Tossius

Toutilla, -us

Toutius

Touto (add ILG 150)

?Toutodiuix

Toutodiuicus

Tradic[

Tramuleius

Trasia

Trebonia ILG 368

Treptenius CIL 12.1210

Trexius

Triccos

Troccius

?Trocinoia

Trogius

Trogom[ILG 38

Trogus

Trouces

Trouceteius

Troucillus (add BG 1.19.
     47, 53; 7.65; CQ 32,
     1938, 43)

Tu[

Tuccius

Tulla, -us (cf. REA 22,
     1920, 183)

]turco

Turpio

Turrania, -ius

?]tusogit

Tuta

Vaalus, Ουαλοσ

Vacusus (Boutae)

Vadullus

Vaetius

Personal Names

?Valcius

Valicinia

?Valirmus

†Valho f., AE 1945.73

Vallo

Val(l)ia, -ius

Vanus

Vardigia

Varena, -us

Varenia, -ius

Varius CIL 3.107

Varus (add ILG 45)

Vassatus

Vassia RA 24, 1926, 364

Vassedo (cf. AE 1941.30)

Vassetius

Vassilia, -ius

Vassilus

V(a)sso

Vasso (Boutae)

Vateria

Vatia

Vatticinus

Vatto (-us RE 2, 1888, 383)

Vaturus

?Vaua

Vbila]tro

Vbilatronia

Vcceius (Esp. Syll. 492)

Vccius

Vcco (-u)

Vco (Boutae)

Vcusso

Vdalcai

Vdia (read as Vrsia CA 5.208, 5)

Vebruius

Vebrullus ILG 95, 171

Vebruou[

Vecco ILG 280

Vecticia, -ius

Vectirix

Vectitus

Vegeta ILG 659

Vegiso

Vel[

Velabellius

Veladus

Velagenus

Personal Names

Vellaco

Velloudius (Velud-)

Vena

Venaesia, -ius

Vencius

Venecrius

Veniclutius

Venicotenius

Venilatus

Venimara ILG 228

Venimarus

Veninia (cf. Gérin-Ricard et d'Agnel, Arc 1907, p. 191)

Veniuallia RE 2, 1888, 384 (for Vin- ?)

Venius

Venn(onius) ILG 179

Vennus ib. 494

Venticius

Venucia

Venulus

Venus CIL 12.234 (cf. RA 6, 1935, 222)

Vep[

Vepus

Verberi gen. sg.

Verbronara CIL 12.1148 (read Vebromara)

Verc[

Vercatus

Vercellius

Verci[

Vercilla, -us

Vercius

Verconnia, -ius

Verg[

Verilla

Verina, -us (add ILG 483)

Veriucus (-g-)

Vero or]uero ILG 98

Verno

?Vernonius (Ven-)

Vernus

Veronia

Verpa[n]tus F. 123

Verria, -ius (add ILG 79)

Verter

Vertico

Verto RE 2, 1888, 383

Verucius

Personal Names

Verulia

Verullia

Veruinius

Vesidia, -ius

Vesmerius

Vessonius

Vestinus

Vesuccia

Vesus (Esp. Syll. 297)

Vethonianus ILG 475; cf.
 Ven.vo.θ.o

Vettonianus ib. 474

Vetul(l)ia (cf. ILG 504)

?Viamelius (or Qu- ?)

Vianena CA 5.186, 34

Viasus (Boutae)

Viattius (for Vi- ?)

Vibius cogn.

Vibullius ILG 198

?Vicorlius

Viccia BA 1932-33 [1936],
 119

Vigellia ILG 33

?Vilaysio (Vn-?)

Vimpa (Boutae)

Vinatius

Vindauscia

Vindicatus

Vindius (cf. BSL 32, 1931,
 158 n. 2)

Vindo ILG 151

Vindulo

Vinicia, -ius (add ILG
 99)

Vinitor ILG 540

Vinius (cf. BSL l.c.)

Viniuallia

Vinnucia

Vinoualeios

Vinuleius

Vipillus

Vipius

Vipongius

Viredius

Vireia, -ius (add ILG 276)

Virga..tus

?Virosbicrius (Esp. Syll.
 1279)

Viricia

Viril(l)io

Virillia, -ius

Personal Names

Virilla

Virius

Virrius ILG 364, 412

Vorotouta

?Virus CIL 12.1124

Vintio (Boutae; but cf. 2, 4 above)

Vitia RA 11, 1920, 118

Vitousurix

Vittia

Vitto (Boutae)

Vitus

Viχtu[

Vlattius

]ulau[

Vleius

Vli[

Vlina

Vmbrus (Oswald, Index)

?Vnasus

?Vnaχsio

Vnseinius (cf. REA 24, 1922, 161-162?)

Voccius

Vocontius (B-), cf. 80

Vola, -us CIL 12.1120

Vosegus (Boutae; but see 236, 237 below)

Vossaticcius; -iccus (?) AE 1946.16

Vossilla, -us (-lia, -lius?)

Votienus

Voto (cf. Ven. vo.θ·o)

Votonna

Voturia, -ius

Vpeius

Vppiritio ILG 388

Vrassia

Vritea

Vrit(t)ia, -ius (RE 1, 23)

Vritto (cf. ILG 364)

Vrsa ILG 49, -us 219, Vrssa

Vrsia (but see Vdia)

Vrsio ILG 436

Vrso (Boutae)

Οὐρσόλη IG 14.2455

Vruimus CIL 13.6884

Vspirniolus (or Spir-? or Pir?) AE 1945.70; CIL 12.2440

Personal Names

Vtul(1)ia, -ius   ?Ximaii[(CA 7.124,
                                              202)

?Xari[?Xihii[(ib. 124, 203)

Addenda and Corrigenda

Page

35   On the later history of gaesum (Fr. guise)

         see J. Decroix in REA 47, 1945, 153-55.

40   s.v. Alpes for Ἀπλια read Ἀλπια

77   H. Rolland has dealt with the inscriptions

         of St Remy in volume 2 of Gallia 1944, 167 ff.

         From it, add now (82, Divine Names) Ippona (sc.

         Epona), Meldius, and (?) Tellura; and (83, Per-

         sonal Names) Γοργονι(ος) IG 14.2479, Smertalit[anus.

         But (p.89) the same author's Fouilles de Glanum

         (which I have now procured) adds nothing.

136   For κασσ|ι read καοβι

138   Read κ]αντενα

170   sentis: According to P. Grosjean (ALMA 17,

         1943, 73-77) not Gaulish in origin, but Latin.

235

Aquitania

1950

III   AQVITANIA

The elder Pliny's remark (14.149) on lexical differences between Spain and Gaul, in the terminology of
alcoholic beverages, was probably pertinent to other
terms too; and also to the smaller original Aquitania
(south of the Garonne) and the rest of Gaul. The name
Aquitania was extended, in the imperial division of
Gaul, to a territory that stretched as far north as the
Loire and as far east as the head-waters of that river;
an area, that is, comparable in size with the other
geographical subdivisions used in this book for the
purpose of classifying the linguistic remains of ancient
Gaul. But direct non-Latin evidence is less in bulk
even than in Narbonensis, and we are forced to make what
shift we can with the indirect testimony of ancient
authors and of Latin inscriptions (CIL 13.i 1, 1899, 1-
1622; iv, 1916, 11001-11170). This testimony, however,
makes it certain that a language quite different from
Keltic had been spoken in Aquitania, particularly in the
districts adjoining the Pyrenees; that this language was
Iberian, or akin to Iberian, can hardly be doubted; and
it is highly probable both that Basque is its modern
representative and also that in the modern Romance dialects of south-western France (e.g. in Gascon), the influence of the same or of a related language is observable.

237

Bibliography:

See, in general, Strabo 4.1.1 (176 C), quoted
Prolegomena n.8, and id. 4.2.1 (190 C) on the resemblance
of the Aquitanians (excepting only the Bituriges) to the
Iberians; Pliny 4.105-9; Grenier Mnl. 1.131-3; A. Blanchet
Les Ibères en Gaule, Revue de Synthèse 17, 1939, 33-6 (cf.
Rev. Belge 18, 1939, 737); G. Fabre Contribution à l'étude
du Protohistorique du Sud-Ouest de la France (Départements
des Hautes-Pyrénées, du Gers, et du Lot-et-Garonne), Gallia
4, 1946, 1-75; H. Kühn Kelten nach Spanien, IPEK 1935
[1936], 133; P. Bosch Gimpera, see Prolegomena p.41 n.72;
Pauly-Wissowa 7.652; H. Nesselhauf Spätrom. Verwaltung
(Abh. d. Preuss. Akad., Ph.-Hist. Kl., 1938), 15-6.

On Iberian and its relation to Basque there is a
readable account by W. J. Entwistle (The Spanish Language, London, 1936, 14-37); to the references which he
gives, add: H. Gavel, Éléments de la phonétique basque,
Paris, 1920; id., Rev. de ling. rom. 12, 1936, 36-43 (on
the substratum of Gascon), cf. J. Orr ibid. 10-35 (against
ascribing to Iberian the change Lat. f to Sp. h); C. Jullian REA 5, 1903, 383-4; G. Lacombe and R. Lafon, Basque,
aquitain, ibère, in Festschrift für Hermann Hirt 2.1936,
116-20 (on the writing, in Latin inscc. of Aquitania,
-ehe-, -oho-); A. Luchaire, Les origines linguistiques
de l'Aquitaine, Bulletin de la Société des Sciences,
Lettres et Arts de Pau 6, 1876-7 [1877], 349-423 (still
valuable); id. Études sur les idiomes Pyrénéens de la
region francaise, Paris 1879; on the work of E. Philipon,
Les Ibères, Paris, 1909, see the (unfavorable) review by
A. S[chulten] in Lit. ZtBl. 1910, 432-3; J. Pokorny
Iberer (B. Sprache) in Ebert's RLV 6, 1926, 5-8; G. Rohlfs,
Le Gascon, Halle 1935 (Beiheft 85 zu ZfRPh); H. Schuchardt
in Mitteilungen d. anthropol. Gesellschaft in Wien 45,
1915, 109-24 (Basque descended from Iberian, not from
Ligurian); id., Nubisch und Baskisch, Rev. internat. des
Études basques 6, 1912, 267-84 (REA 15, 1913, 197).

Although this book is not directly concerned with
the Iberian language or alphabet, references to a few
additional discussions may be useful, viz. those of
Schulten, Meinhof, Schoeller and Zylharz in Zts. d.
deutschen Morgenländischen Gesellschaft 78, 1924, 1-18;
84, 1930, 239; 85, 1931, 351; 87, 1934, 50-67. See also
M. Gómez-Moreno 77a above with Note xvi; and 157 Remark
viii below (S. Miguel de Liria). Since Corp. Vas. Ant.
(Hispania) takes cognizance of such Iberian inscc. as
may appear on vases, pertinent material and comment is

occasionally to be found there, cf. AJA 51, 1947, p.206.

L. H. Gray, BSL 36, 1935, 163-6 sees in -ez in modern Spanish personal names a suffix -iqo- based on a Keltic model. For a recent critique of Lafitte's Grammaire basque and Schuchardt's Primitiae Linguae Vasconum, see Gernika in Études Basques, vols. 3 and 4, 1947. Some characteristics of Iberian, Meyer-Lübke, Einführung, 242 (especially the paucity of labials); -sk- in local names, note the new insc. published in Jahrb. des deutschen arch. Instituts 48, 1933, 518-9.

But in the rest of Aquitania, north of the Garonne, the few non-Latin inscriptions that we have presumably are written in the language spoken, before the introduction of Latin, by people whose own names are Keltic, who lived in settlements the names of which are Keltic, and who worshipped deities the names of which are Keltic. The contrast between the Petrucorii, for example, and the Consoranni (with the Conuenae) or the Ausci, in this matter of nomenclature is striking. It is somewhat less obvious in local names, which are often to be compared with those of Spain, but this only means, and it is a generally recognized fact, that local names are relatively persistent. We may conclude that in Aquitania, south of the river Garonne, we have an Iberian substratum of language, over which was imposed, except in the extreme south-west, first Keltic and then Latin itself.

239

Cf. V. Bertoldi Rev. de ling. rom. 4, 1928, 222-50
(Antichi filoni nella toponomastica mediterranea); id.
ZfRPh 57, 1937, 137-69 (Contatti e conflitti di lingua
nell' antico Mediterraneo, esp. 141-58); G. Rohlfs
ZfRPh 47, 1927, 398-408 (Baskischen Reliktwörtern in
Pyrenäengebiet).

Of comparisons that are advanced in support of
this conclusion, the following seem instructive:

deo Artahe (-ehe): Basque arte "oak." But we
may as justly compare Gaul. Artaius(?) divine
name 82; Andarta ib.; Artacus pers. name 237;
and these are cognate with L. ursus, Ir. art,
Ernout-Meillet ed. 2, 1138; Walde 861; Walde-
Pokorny 1.322.

Sutugio (deo): B. su "hearth, fire," cf. deo
Suttunio CIL 2.746, infixed or prefixed -t-
being Iberian (e.g. Ilurgis): Iliturgis), B.
sutargi "fire-light;" see further Ebert
Reallex, 6, p.7, Bertoldi ll. cc. (Zts. 145,
Rev. 235), cf. the glosses alutiae: talutium
(158; Bertoldi Rev. 248 with n.1)

camox: B. gama (Bertoldi, Zts. 147, 158 n.1)

Ausci (mod. Auch): euskara "Basque" (Jullian in
REA 3, 1901, 330-2)

Leherenno, Leren- (deo): B. leher, ler "crever,
aplatir, épuiser" (?), see Lacombe-Lafon Hirt.
Festschr., 2, 117. Cf. dat. sg. both -ehe
and -e for the variation in spelling.

A number of technical terms connected with mining
(Pl. 33.69-75), so far as they can be assigned definitely to the Pyrenees' region, may well be Iberian;
but such identification is not always certain (e.g.,

gl. gangadia 1 above), or a corresponding Basque form
always available (? andyelo Hautes-Pyr., Bertoldi Zts.
142). Moreover there are Keltic forms that are comparable in some instances, e.g. urium (158 below) cf. the
Baetic local name Vrium fl. (Pl. 3.7), B. ur "water"
(H. Schuchardt ZfRPh 32, 1908, 77), but observe also
Vra fons, Vrnia (82).

The absence of initial f-, often noted as characteristic of Iberian and Basque, is of course also
characteristic of Gaulish, independent as the phenomena
are; more significant is the fact that Iberian, like
Basque, has no words beginning with r-. The similarity,
however, between an ancient local name such as Gabarus
fl. (AcS 1, 1509) and B. gabi, gao "river" (Bertoldi
Rev. 224); or between the ancient personal names Cison
(G-), Harsus (Harspus), Andere, Nescato (cf. niskas
Note xv above) and the Basque words gison "man," hartz
"bear," andere "girl, young woman," neskato "maid, young
girl" is possibly superficial or accidental, or at most
due to borrowing. Indeed hartz may well come from Keltic
as we have seen (W. arth, Ir. art "bear"); on the other
hand, Basque andere and izoki(n) may be the source not
only of Ir. ainder (cf. RC 48, 468) but also even of
Gaulish esox (see Tovar's Notas sobre el vasco y el

celto, Publ. de la Real Soc. Vascongada 1, 1945, 31-9,
reviewed in Word 3, 1947, 140; cf. id. ib. 1946, 1948;
cf. Eranos 45, 1947, 81-87; Piel in Humanitas 1, 1947,
122-129 on hysex, esox, Ptg. irze I have not seen). In
Spain too Keltic has left clear traces of influence
upon Iberian, as Tovar has shown (Las inscripciones
ibericas y la lengua de los Celtiberos, Boletín de la
Real Academia Española 25, 1946, 7-42; cf. Gray, Foundations 1939, 377-8). But there is probably a historical
connexion between B. (h)iri berri "new town" and the
local names Elimberris (84), Illiberris (80). That
Latin developed between the Garonne and the Pyrenees
in a manner analogous, in general, to that in which it
did south of the Pyrenees is clear (see, e.g., A. Kuhn,
ZfRPh 57, 1937, 326-65, cf. BSL 39, 1938, 79; on the
Berlin dissertation Zur Sprachgeographie Südwestgalliens
of M. Henschel, cf. Philipp in Idg. Iahrb. 6.23, 20).

Speakers of Keltic of later date entrenched themselves more securely at Bordeaux (the Biturges Viuisci,
see 153 and cf. 156 Remark) than elsewhere south of the
Garonne. Accordingly their names are given with those
of Aquitania north of that river, in order to avoid this
additional complication, which obscures the linguistic
contrast between the two regions.

1. Aquitania between the Pyrenees and the Garonne
(except Bordeaux)

Arabic numerals, without other indication of source, are references to CIL 13.i 1 (1899) 1-565; ii 2 (1907) 8888-93 (cf. REA 13, 1911, 80-81; 14, 1912, 174-88); iv (1916) 11001-31. On the Ora Maritima of Avienus see now PW, s.v. Periplus.

References to ancient sources which appear in AcS are not given at all; save that I have included many references to inscc. for which Holder furnishes, in his first volume, only citations dated earlier than 1899, even though the CIL number is added, in some instances, in AcS vol. 3. The peculiarities of the Latin inscc. of this district are such as to stimulate the ambitions of forgers; and spurious inscc. are more numerous than usual (cf. Sacaze, l.c. 86 infr., p.1091 n.1); it is probable, however, that caution, as usual, has been extreme, and that the authenticity of some alleged forgeries can be demonstrated (see e.g., MSAMidi 19, 1939, 217-30).

Cf. R. Lizop Les Conuenae et les Consoranni, Toulouse, 1931; id. Le Comminges et le Couserans avant la domination romaine, Toulouse, 1931 (cited as Lizop 1 and Lizop 2 respectively; both works reviewed by Vendryes RC 51, 1934, 127-9). For more recent discoveries see the reports of the Commission des fouilles de Saint Bertrand de Comminges published in the Mémoires de la Société archéologique du Midi de la France since 1931 (cf. REA

Nouempopulana and Inscription of Aubagnan

35, 1933, 44; 43, 1941, 216; 45, 1943, 276; Historia 8, 1934, 701.1046; RA 18, 1941, 164-7; 26, 1946, 103-4; CP 43, 1948, 139; APh 14, 1939, 287 and 15, 1940-1, 295, 322 gives two further works: B. Sapène Au Forum de Lugdunum Conuenarum 1924-38, Paris, 1940; and J. Zeiller, Fouilles de S. Bertrand de Comminges, 1933-38, in CRAc-InscBL 1941, 278-85). On Aymard's Toponymie pré-indo-européenne dans le Sud-Ouest in Rev. géogr. de Pyrénées et du Sud-Ouest 12, 1941, 360-72, see CP 43, 1948, 139.

Hübner MLI 1893, 244-7, 253-4, 261-4.

The misplaced ingenuity of S. Ferri (Atti d. R. Acc. dei Lincei, Cl. Sc. Mor., Ser. 6, Rendiconti 8, 1932, 760-4) discovered a mare's nest of Germanic tribal names (e.g. Chat]ti Tu[bantes, Hi]laeui[ones) in a few epigraphic fragments discovered at Saint Bertrand de Comminges. But the subsequent discovery of other scraps (see MSAMidi 19, 1939, 174-88; reported also in AE 1938, 169-71) has made Signor Ferri's hypothesis ridiculous (e.g. re]stitu[it, praef]ec[t]us alae VI[I Phry]gu[m) and the Siduni, Suebi, and Vsipii have gone the way of the Chatti, Tubantes, and Hilaeuiones.

Note xvii

This fragmentary Iberian insc. was discovered about 1914 at Aubagnan (Landes), in the district known as Tursan (perhaps *Atursanus for Aturensis, see 84) near Saint Sever, to the south of Mont-de-Marsan; first pub-

Inscription of Aubagnan

lished by P. Dubalen in REA 16, 1914, 217-18 and 339, cf. BA 1914, lxxi; afterwards by A. de Paniagua Les Celtes...dans le Sud-Ouest de la Gaule, Paris 1926, p.55.

On two fragments of a silver band, repoussé, which came to light with other metal objects and cinerary urns in the excavation of a number of tumuli in the Tursan region, presumably Iberian.

The text, in Iberian alphabet, reads, l. to r.

(a)]an. iduo[

(b)]tur[

(c)]to[

There is nothing to show whether these are parts of a continuous text or not. In (a) I have left un-transcribed a sign | (?) which can hardly be i, if the next symbol ⋈ , the normal i, has that value. If Gomez-Moreno's transcription is accepted, | is ba; otherwise it must be a misreading of ↑ (v) or ⊤ (according to Hübner, z); du is the familiar △ .

Local and Ethnic Names

84

Ages(s)innates

Alingo -onensis mod.
  Longon

Aquae: see Tarbellicae

Aquenses uicani 389, NG
  14.3, now Acqs, Dax

Aquitani, Ἀκουιτανοί,
  Ἀκυι- Aquitania cl.
  insc. (17)

Arnespe (or -um) 6th cent.,
  R. de Comminges 1930,
  94 (Lizop 1, 147), now
  Arnesp

Aspalluga (-c-) ?Aspe

Atur fl., Ἀτούρι-(o)ς,
  Atur(r)us, Atur(r)icus,
  Atures (pl.). Cf. REA
  12, 1910, 167

Atura, Aturensis (Adour)

Ausci, Αὔσκιοι, Auscius,
  Ausc(i)ensis modern
  Auch. Cf. euskara;
  and perhaps Osci-dates,
  -neum?

?Basaboiates (or -boc-)

Basates v. Vasates

Belendi (cf. BSL 32, 1931,
  134) Bal-. Cf. Bosch-
  Gimpera BA 1932-33
  [1936], 351. Iber.
  Belennes (Meyer-Lübke,
  Einf. 245); perhaps
  -nd- from -nn-

Belsinum

Bene(h)arnum, Benarni,
  Benarnenses, cf. Venami?
  now Béarn

Bercorates

Bigorra ciuitas (Cieutat)
  or castrum (Be- , Bo-);
  Biger(r)itanus (Be- ,
  -gor-), Beorritana (-et-);
  Bigerriones; Bigerricus;
  Begerri (Bi-). Cf. gl.
  bigerricus, clefabo 158.
  Modern Bigorre

Boiates, Boates, Boias
  ciuis 570, 615 (insc.
  Bordeaux); Boii REA 7,
  1905, 74; [but Bogiensis
  ib. 25, 1923, 268 is
  more likely Bayeux]; 13,
  1911, 128; 24, 1922, 128;
  28, 1926, 241-6; insc.
  CIL 13.11036. I have
  not seen Bertrand Peyneau,
  Découvertes archéolo-
  giques dans le pays de
  Buch, Bordeaux, 1926.
  Now Buch. Cf. Basa-
  boiates

Borodates (consacrani) 397
  (CIL 12.5379), cf. 147.
  Cf. Δάτιοι

Bucconis mutatio (Itin.),
  cf. divine name Bocco

Caauus mons 320 (Cclapis),
  cf. REA 13, 1911, 497

Cambolectri (Agesinnates);
  CIL 13.3087, cf. 80

246

Camponi (v.1. Campoi),
cf. Campsi (Hisp.)?
Cf. pers. names

Calagorris IA 457.9, cf.
Hieron. contr. Vig.,
Patr. Lat. Migne, 23.
353; Calagurritanus
ib. Cf. REA 27, 1925,
307

Carasa (Garris)

Casinomago TP

?Caucoliberi cf. AcS 3.
1166, 45-7; Lizop 2.
70, n.52, 82; REA 5,
1903, 384; Ann. du
Midi 50, 1938, 157-98
(RA 15, 1940, 293).
But the identification
of the site is uncer-
tain (? Collioure, see
80). The formation
recalls Illi-, Eli(m)-
berris. Cf. also Cauca
MLI 229; AcS 1.865-6;
and]cauce num. Lugd.
(177)

Cebenna, Ceuenna, Κέμμενον ,
now Cévennes

Cocosa, Cocosates (Sex-
Signani), Coequosa

Consoranni, Consuarani,
Consoranicus, Consoran-
nensis, Censerannis
(Rav.), Coserannus
(-amnis) conc. Burd.
? Cous[and Con[num.
(cf. CIL 13, p.3),
now Couserans

Conuenae, Κονουένοί (Κομ-)
num. Coue[? (CIL 13,

p.6, with n.5, cf. p.
57), Κωνουέναι Str.;
inscc. 254, 255, 257
The forms Commenae,
Commenicus, Κομουέναι
are for Comb-, Comu-;
Combinias Rav.; ciuis
Conuena, Conuenicus,
Conueniensis; Cobenin-
sis, Communica (i.e.
Conuen-).
Comminges, Capvern
(see Lizop 1.18-9),
Campan (CIL 13, p.6).
Lot RC 45, 1928, 312-7;
cf. REA 42, 1940, 628-
35 (Latin!)

Κόσσιον , Cossio Vasatum

Κουρίαν (ν)ὸν ἄκρον

Crebennus (cf. pers. names)

Δάτιοι (cf. Osci-, Boro-
dates

Egericius (-ir-) fl., Auson.
Gers

Eliumberrum (Mela chor.
3.2), Eliberre TP, Elim-
berrum IA. Cf. Iliberris
80, and see REA 3, 1901,
330-2, (Basque iri-berri
"new town"), Lizop 2.82-
3. Now Lombers, Lombez

Elusa, -ates, Elosates cl.
insc., also assigned to
Narb. (H)elusanus, Elo-
sanus. Eauze (Ciotat
"ciuitatem")

Local and Ethnic Names

Ferrarienses pagani 384

Florentinus uicus 258
　　Fleurance

Forum Ligneum IA 452.10

Garites BG 3.27 (v.l.
　　Gates)

Garunna (-umna) fl.,
　　Γαρούνᾱς , Garunni,
　　mod. Garonne

?Hebromagus (Narb.?)

Hungunuerro Itin. (cf.
　　pers. Orgo-uarra?)

Ilixonensis pagus Cf.
　　Rev. Com. 4, 1888, 275
　　(Lizop 1.67); Luchon.
　　Cf. divine names

Iluro, Elluronenses (Il-),
　　Olorone insc. (8894),
　　NG, Itin. Now Oloron

Lactora(-ura), -ates cl.
　　inscc., Lactorensis,
　　Lectoure

Landini Rav.

Lapurdum -ensis. Modern
　　Lampourdan, Labourd
　　(Bayonne)

Lassunni

Latusates

Losa uicus, mod. Losse

Lugdunum, Λούγδουνον
　　(Conuenarum, Consor-
　　annorum), insc. 255,
　　REA 46, 1944, 164-5,
　　AE 1945.15

Medulla fl., Rav., now
　　Midouze

[Monesi Pl. 4.108, leg.
　　Onesii?]

Mosconum

Narbona CIL 2.3876, v. REA
　　1, 1899, 232-7; Arbonne

Nouempopuli, -ana 412 CIL
　　6.32981 (REA 4, 1902,
　　46; 17, 1915, 143;
　　Haverfield, Athenaeum
　　13 Mar. 1915)

Onesi, Ὀνήσιοι , Aquae
　　Onesiae; Oneil, Oonne?

Onobrisates (v.l. -briuates,
　　-busates)

Oppidum Nouum IA, cf. Oppi-
　　dana f. (506)

Ophiussa (O[i]asso?) Avien.,
　　?Oyarzun (Lizop 2.173)

Oscidates (campestri, mon-
　　tani) Pl, 4.108, cf.
　　Ausci, Δατιοι

Local and Ethnic Names

Oscineum It. Burd.

Pinpedunni Pl. 4.108 (v.
1. Pinde-). Cf. Oxé,
BJ 130, 1925, 71

Ptianii (corrupt) BG 3.
27.1 (Preciani?)

Pyrene, Πυρήνη , Pyrenaeus
saltus (Pl. 4.108),
Pyrenaeo summo, imo
(Itin.)

Quattuorsignani (Tarbelli),
cf. Sex-, Pinpe-,
Petru- corii, Tri-,
Vocontii, Decumates

Sacer, Sacerons Rav.

?Sal(l)ates Not. Tir.
(Lizop 2.44), Salat

?Sarnali (-rralis) TP

?Sedibouiates AcS 1.462,
48; cf. Sibuzates (ib.
2.1538) Sybillates

Segosa IA, cf. Suc(c)asses?

Sennates

Serio fl., Sirio; Serones,
Seronensis pagus; Ci-
ron or Cerons (Lizop
2.44)

Sexsignani (Cocosates)
Pl. 4.108; cf. Quat-
tuor- Pinpe-

Sibuzates v. Sedi-

Siccae Aquae IA (an Cisiae
?); Saint Cizy (Lizop
1.118, cf. 132-4, 361)

Sigmatis fl.

Sotiates (-otes), Σωτιάτες
Sotiota (num.); Sos

Spariani uicini insc. AE
1928.13, REA 30, 1928,
121-2, Lizop 1.293,
Plate 7. Cf. gl. 240;
and perh. modern local
names Lesparre and
Hasparren (on the dis-
puted insc. of the
latter see Mnl.1, 133
n.1)

Subola uallis Fredegar;
Soule

Suc(c)asses, cf. Seg-?

Sybillates v. Sibuz- (pays
de Soule, CIL 13, p.53)

Tarba, Tarua (-lua), ?Tur-
ba, now Tarbes; Tarbelli
(Tere-), Tarbellicae
Aquae, v. Aquenses (Dax)
Quattuorsignani (cf. REA
11, 1909, 362). Cf. 158

Tarusates, modern Tursan,
Teursan

Τάστα (leg. Τάσγα ?)πόλις
(cf. gl. 158, 220)

Telonnum

Toruates (-n-?) Cf. REA
8, 1911, 97

Local and Ethnic Names

Tres Arbores IA 550; cf.
    Sexarbor div. name,
    and (for the meaning)
    Treuidon (80)

?Turba v. Tarba

Vanesia fl. (Cf. Besinum?
    Bels-?) AcS 1.396, 409;
    3.99

Vasates, -ensis, -icus
    (cf. Bas-), Vasatae
    Amm. Marc. (Cf. Va-
    scones, Gascony?),
    perh. mod. Bazás,
    Bazadais. I.q. Vassei
    Pl. 4.108?

Οὐασσάριοι CIL 13, p.75

Vassei v. Vasates

Vellates Pl. 4.108

Venami ib., v. Beneharni

Vernosole IA (Narb.? But
    Lavernose according to
    Lizop 1.118)

Vestianum? Rav.

?Vocates (cf. Boiates,
    Vassates)

Vesubium IA, Vesubio TP,
    Οὔσβιον Ptol., but cf.
    Vssubius 919, and gl.
    usubiom (178)?

85   Further Modern Names

    See the two works of Lizop given above, and add:
Chroniques de Toponymie (REA 39, 1937, 370-4, H. Gavel,
Le ʻToulousain' méridional; 36, 1934, 489-96, id., Pays
Basque, with Bibliography by G. Lacombe; 37, 1935, 205-
10, P. Barrière, Gascogne); H. Gavel, Sur quelques noms
de lieux aquitains ou espagnols (Calagurris, Illiberris,
Baiona; mod. Lukugaine), in REA 32, 1930, 342-54 (cf.
Jullian, ib. 27, 1925, 307-11); J. Laserre, L'origine de
la Nouempopulaine, Bayonne, 1928 (see REA 31, 1929, 61);
B. Sarrieu, Persistance de radicaux celtibériens dans
quelques noms de lieux de Gascogne, 1910 (ib. 13, 1911,
97). On the three works of Meillon treating of toponymie pyrénéenne, see REA 20, 1918, 253-4.

    Aymard (Rev. géogr. l.c., p.244 above) seeks to
identify the following lexical elements:

cara- "stone" (p.363): Ptg. carvalho, Basque
    harri, hariz "stone" and garric, garrigue
    "chêne" (roche from *hrocca, *harrocca,
    carrocca, but v. rocca 178; so that car(a)-
    rocca will be a binominal intensive [hybrid?]
    cpd.); Garunna, -umna (Gar, Garonne, Gironde),
    cf. the divine name Garri (-e), Carre (366)

cala- "rock" (363)

mala, mel "mountain" (365)

tala- "clay" (ib.), cf. talutium 158 below

gorri- "red" (366): Calagurris, now Calahorra (cf.
    Gavel, Études régionales pour l'enseignement
    1, 1941, 49)

ar- "water," aran "valley" (369): Araris, Arauris,
    modern Aar.

aven "water" (Gascon; 369 n.12): abon- (Keltic)

dur(ia) "water" (ib.): Dordogne, Ptg. Douro

gave (id., ib.): Gabarus; *atur: Adour

vara "water" (370): Vaberos, Voberos

But some of his deductions, and some of the sound changes
alleged (c- becoming g, ch, j; r geminated) are dubious.

Andorre (or -ra), Anos, Aran (pagus Aranensis, A.D.
1387, see Lizop 1.67-8), Ardiège (Ardeia, ib.; cf. 82
above), Arrie (Arria), Aussonne fl. (cf. divine name
Axoniebus?), Bachos (Vaxsosium), Bagnères, Baïgorry
(uallis Bigur, later Beyguer), Baretgie, Bavarthès,
Bayonne (Baiona, cf. gl. 158), Benque (Bencus, Vinca,
Vincum), Binos, Boussenac, Campan (pagus Campanus),

251

Divine Names

Capeurtoun or Capbreton (see REA 21, 1919, 296), Cieutat
or Cieutadès (pagus Ciuitatensis, Ciuitas), Ferrère
(Ferraria, pagus Ferrariensis 85 above), Gascogne (cf.
Vascones, Vasates above, and see 80 ad fin.), Lavedan
(Leuitani, -ie), Lescar (Lascurris), Lourdes (Lorda,
Lurda), Loures-Barousse (Lora, Lura), Luys, Nébouzan,
Neste fl., Nestier (Nestarium), Ourse fl., Sarrancolin
(Salangolinum), Sérou (pagus Seronensis?), Vénasque
(Lizop 2.60), Viella (Vetula), Vic (Vicus, Vico Iuli,
Vicoiulienses NG).

86 Divine Names

Abel(l)ion(n)i deo 30, 39,
40, 77, 148, 166, 171,
333, 337, 338; Gallia
1, 1943, 200.
  Sacaze (Nos anciens
dieux: Épigr. Pyr.,
Toulouse: Assoc. fr.
pour l'avanc. des Sc.,
16ᵉ Session à Toulouse
en 1887, pp.1077-1103)
identified this with
the modern "génie
familier" Hillon

Aberri deo 1101la

?Act[a]c[o] deo 379 Add.

Aχtouri m. (?) 371; or
  Aχto Vri (?)

Aereda deo 312

?Ageio deo 386; Ageioni
deo 180, 221 (-c-), 251,
379 Add. (?), 383, 385,
386; REA 13, 1911, 80
(-c-)

Ageioni Bassiario deo 221
Add. (Ac- REA 14, 1922,
88, i.q. 221 and 221
Add.)

Aherbelste deo 174

Divine Names

Alar[47; Alardossi 48,
222; A]lardos[tis 432;
Alardosto deo 313. See
also 11013b

?Algassi (Alc- , Arg-)
72; but the correct
reading is probably
H]alossi

Andei (or Ander[ ) deae
15

Andosso v. Bascei, Toli;
and cf. pers. names

Arardo daeo 41

Arixo deo 365, Arixoni
(-rr-) Marti 366, cf.
63. Aymard compares
the mod. local names
Carixo, Carice

Arpenino deo 167

]arsoni deo 168

?Artae 71; deo Artahe 70,
-ehe 64, 71 (deo)? Cf.
mod. local name Ardet
(Aymard)?

?Auerano deo (if genuine,
see MSAMidi 19, 1939,
223), cf. mod. local
name Aoueran

Asto Ilunno 31, cf. 371

Axoniebus dibus BSAF 1933,
81; AE 1935.61. Cf. mod.
local name Ausonne
(*Axona?)

?Baconis (gen.?) 557

Baeserte deo 85

Baicoriso deo 162, Bai-
co[r]ixo 323, -g- 92,
Buaigorixi (-e) 124
Add. Modern "génie"
Baian, Bigos (Sacaze
l.c.)

Baiosi deo 86, Baiase AE
1939.49; cf. mod. local
name Bazus (Gallia 1,
1943, 200)

?]bahaloisso 14; better
read as two words]ba
Haloisso 14 Add.

?Barcae deae (if genuine,
see MSAMidi 19, 1939,
230)

Bascei Andosso 26 (or one
word?). Cf. Vasates,
Vascones?

Bassiario (Ageioni) 221
Add.

Beisirisse 370

Belco 354 Add.

Belgoni dat. 11014

Belisama (Minerua) 8

?Benzozia (14th cent.,
see Lizop 1.360)

Bocco Harausoni 78, 79.
Cf. local name Bucco,
modern Boucou (Sacaze),
Bucco num. (Celsa)

Borienno deo 301; cf. Bori-
nas Fort. vit. Mart. 1.
290?

Divine Names

Buai- v. Bai-

?Carrenio 93 Add. (G-?),
  v.l. Carrnio, Carpnto

?]cuii REA 14, 1912, 79

Daho Marti 87

?Dunsioni (-z-) deo, if
  genuine AcS 1.1378,
  MSAMidi 19, 1939, 224

Edelati deo 146

Ele deo 58; ?Elh[59

]eni AcS 1.1438

Erdae 307

Erditse 397 (also ascribed
  to Narb.)

Erge deo (-c-) 181, 182,
  184, 186, 187-96, 198-
  204, 206-7; Erga Ano(?)
  197. Cf. mod. Mon[t]s-
  érié

Exprcennio deo 329. Cf.
  num. purpcn (77 i a)?

Fago deo 33, 223-5

Fontibus 343

Garre (-i) deo (C-?), cf.

Garumna, mod. Garros?

?[H]aloassi 72 (v. Algassi)

Haloisso 14, cf. pers.
  Lohissus

Harausoni v. Bocco; cf.
  mod. local name Arousec
  fl. (Sacaze)

Herauscorritsehe fano 409
  (with Add.). Perhaps
  to be divided Her[ ]
  Auscor[um] Ritsehe. Cf.
  REA 19, 1917, 261-8;
  Pisani RIGI 17, 1933,
  189; AGlItal. 27, 1936,
  168-9

Horolati. Cf. mod. local
  name Ore (Aymard)?

]ibus 68

Idiatte deo

Ilixoni deo 345-8; AE 1939.
  50; cf. ZfRPh, Beiheft
  78, 1929, 111. See also
  local names (Luchon)

Ilumber(o) 42 (with Add.)

Ilun(n)i deo 27 (with Add.),
  cf. 371, 374; Iluno BA
  1932-3 [1936], 120; cf.
  RA 36, 1932, 198; 11013a
  (AE 1913.181, REA 13,
  1911, 81; 14, 1912, 420;
  AE 1927.152). Cf. also
  Asto above, Lelhunno be-
  low]s Iluno (or Siluno?)
  MSAMidi 19, 1939, 218;

254

Divine Names

Ilun[Gallia 1, 1943, 200. Cf. perhaps the local name Ilunon (Spain), Lizop 2.83, 87

Iluberrixo 33, -oni 231

Iluroni 154

?Isornausi deo MSAMidi 1939, 229

Iscitto deo 334, 335 Sacaze compared the modern "génie" Ischit

Lahe deae On Lahe cf. Sacaze, Bull. Épigr. 5, 1885, 185-8

Larasso, Λ α ρ ρ α σ ωνι v. 82 above

?Lauictus

Leheren(n)i and -o deo (Marti), Lerenno. Cf. Mém. Acad. Toulouse 3, 1857-62, 353-439

Lelhunno (Marti) deo, Lelno(?)

?Lurgorr[BSAMidi 40, 1909-11, 140

Mitr deo 379

montes 349, 382

nimidi (Numidi?) montes 38 (with Add.) Cf. gl. nimida 79

Nymphae, Nimpae, Nympae 21, 50, 350-60, 390, 391, 437, 438; BSAMidi 47, 1921-5, 309

?]oism[11013

Oson[i BSAMidi 47, 1921-5, 304

?Ostia 11013 Add.

Πυρηναία (Ἀφροδίτη) Str. 4.1.3, 178 C, cf. Ptol. 2.10.1

?]resumailii..[74

Sex arbor, Sexs arbori, Sex arboribus 129, 132, 175; cf. BSAF 1935, 175-8; 1936, 147-8; Pro Alesia 4, 1918, 130-4; Rev. des eaux et forêts 74, 1936, 432; cf. Buxenus 82 above, Robur 155 below. Sacaze compared modern local name Arbas

?Siluno v. Iluno

?Stoico deo

Sutugio

T[411 Add.

Toliandosso (or Toli An-dosso?)

Personal Names

Tutelae 57, 159, 246, 328,
   411, 439, 440, 11015,
   11031; cf. REA 14,
   1912, 71, 412, with
   181 and 154 below

Vaxas (Gallia 1, 1943,
   200)

Ventis 441

Vax[o] deo (Lizop 2.223)

Xuban 130

To the "génies familiers" mentioned above Sacaze
(l.c., s.v. Abellis) adds Hades, Incantades, Tantugou
(cf. Lizop 1.360).

87   Personal Names

Abarcerius MLI (Index)

Acan (not -g-) 130

Accaten[555

Aconius 11007

?Ac[   ]stor 66

Act[37

Actiliona 165

Adaugus 412 (cf. REA 4,
   1902, 46)

Adehio(s) 11031 (Adeius?)

Adeiharbelesteg(is) 11031
   (But probably two words;
   divide at Adei? Or at
   Adeihar?). REA 12, 1901,
   71 suggests -g(enses),
   i.e. a local name

?Adeilus (not Adeituus)
   268 Add. (11011)

Adiatunnus, Ἀδιάτουνος
   cf. num. Adietuanus
   (The v.l. at BG 3.22.2
   is doubtless wrong)

Aedun(n)ia 552

Aeuadia 363

256

Personal Names

Ahoissus 406, 477

Albina 288 -us 176, 288,
449, 553; Albula 176

Alcimus 63, 146

Aldeni (dat.f.) 5

Alelpis MSAMidi 19, 1939,
218

Aleouos 10010.2817

Alfia (Bulluca) 261

Alpina, -us 11, 209

Amandinus REA 16, 1914,
83

Amelaius 407

Ampl[240

?An[   ]a 371 Add.

And[56, Ande[460

Andere f. 138, Andereni
dat. f. 169, cf. Ann-;
Andereseni (Lizop 2.
118)

Anderes 187, Anderexo 23,
Anderexso f. 324 (or
Anderex?), Ande]resse
46. Cf. BSL 32, 1931,
133, 166

Anderitia 344 (cf. 351)

Andos 226 (with Add.),
247; Andossic[gen.
(?) 263; Andossus 124,
188, 192(?), 202 (?),
264, 268 (with Add.
11011), Cf. Ann-.

Andosinus BSAF 1880, 157;
cf. REA 4, 1902, 214;
14, 1912, 78

Andost[321; Andosten m.
84, -stenni dat. 268
(with Add. 11011),
-stenno dat. 321

Andoston (v.l. -sion) 188,
-stonis gen. m. 89

Andoxponni dat., m. 80

Andoxus 26

Andrecconi dat. f. 280

Andus 53 (cf. 156 infr.)

Anerdesini dat. f. 343

Anesorinus 276

Anetus (AcS 3.622)

Annereni 11044; cf. And-

A.nnic[189

Annius 138

A]nnoss[us 199; cf. And-

Annous m. 60, 315

Anta 10010.2816a

Anteros 136

?Ant[i]nous 60

Antistius 73 Add., 177,
445; -ia 447; -ius
11023

Antullus 368

257

Personal Names

Anu[10010.2816b

Aptus 235

]arbelsis 54

Argesis

?Arhonsus 188 (leg. Nar-?)

]arris 11009.4

Arrulianus 451

Arserris gen. m. 95

Asspericus 314

Atilia 76

Attaconis gen. m.; -i
    dat. 265

Attaiorix m. 463

Attius 420, 426, 435; -ia
    454

Attixsis 76

?Aufius (leg. aueto) 480

Auitus 11001

Aucasius (Luc-?) 553

]aurias[m.172

Axionnis 323

Ausonius

B[56 Ba[557

Baesella 90

Baiexe 455

Baisothar[? 46 (i.e.
    -harris gen. f.)

Balluca MLI Index

Bambix 96, 109

Barba Lizop 1.53

Barhosis gen. m. 39,
    Barosis 247

Bassinus 372

]bele[151

Belesteg(is) v. Adeihar

Belex 167, -ix (or Belix[
    ?) 307

Belexconis gen. m. 167,
    214

Belexeia 456

Belexennis gen. m. 190

Belheiorix m. 90

?Bellaisis gen. m. 53
    (vv. 11. Biil- , Bil- ,
    Bill-aisis, Beilasis)

Berhaxsis gen. m. 343

Bersegi 456

Berulius 422

?Bexonis gen. m. 4 (but
    see Sem-)

Bihoscinnis gen. m. 59

Bihotus (v.l. -xus) 230

Personal Names

[?Bihotar (given only by
   Lizop 2.116)]

Bihoxus 321 (cf. Bihotus)

Bilossi (for Bihossi?)
   393

Binmandenus REA 16, 1914,
   83

Blandus 415

Bo[326

Bocontia (i.e. Voc-) 160

Bonbelex m. 338

Bonexsi f. 178, Bonixsus
   (Ion- lapis) 173,
   Bonnexsi(s) 72

Bonici (case?) 328; v.l.
   Bonio-seuria or -seuri;
   Bonici Spuria Hirsch-
   feld; Bonio Lizop 2.116

Boni AE 1927.152

Bonna f. 179

Bonnoris m. 267

Bonsilexsi dat. f. 62
   (Cf. Silex?)

Bontar 342

Bonten[? 191

Bonxorius 241

Bonxsoni m. (case?) 326

Bonxsus 260; Bonxus 223,
   Bo[nxus?] 326, Bonxi
   11016

Boriennus 301

Borei[gen. 309

Borroconis gen. m. 30

Borsei gen. m. 55; Borso
   268 Add. (11011)

Bortossi 443

Britexanossi (or Britex
   An[d]ossi?) 192

†Brittula 497, cf. gl. 220
   (s.v. brittia)

Bulluca 261, cf. gl. 158

Cahenna AE 1914.198, REA
   15, 1913, 430

Caelius 211

Calixsonis gen. m. 54

Calua 138

Caluesia MSAMidi 19, 1939,
   218

Cambuxae dat. 449

Campanus 120, 175

Camulus 537

Candida 210

Canio 10010.2814

Canpanus (Hisp.) 259

Karina 170

Cartulla 29 Add.

Personal Names

Cassia 352

Cassillus 138

Ceniuria 86

Censoin[454

Cerdo 554

Cesellius 11021

Cintugnatus 11005

Cison (G- ?) 125

Cisonten[? 337

Cissonbonis gen. m. 337

Clamosa (Treuera) 233

Clocoi 10010.2817

Cloepius, -ia 141

Coelia 193

Coeran[478; Coerana
  11008

Comba[, Comba[rillus
  458

?Comenua 533

Cominia 11001

Condannossus 324; but
  see also Socon-

Conditus 311

Condai gen. 555

Congus 311

?Conis[557 (or Baconis
  div. name?)

Crepen[BSAF 1870, 146-7;
  cf. local names

Cugur (i.e. Cucurus?) 312

Cuduesenus 125

Cupitius 547

Damcixa 557

Dannadinnis gen. m. 260

Dannonia 118

Dannonus 17

Dannorix m.5

Dantio 10010.2817

Derro 30

Derus 485

?Dinomagius (AcS, after
  Sacaze)

Donnia 530

Donnus 5

Dunaius 456, 459

Duniosus MLI Index

Dunnis gen. m. 260

Dunohorix m. 267

Dunohoxsis gen. m. 138

Dunomagius 17

Dun[s]iosi[nn]is gen. m.
  270; cf. divine names

Personal Names

?Dus 11019

Ebelc (i.e. -lo?) 354

Edunn[is f. 326 (or
    Edunn[se?)

Edunx[f. AE 1906.130;
    BSAMidi 35, 1905,
    326 (Edunxe); BSAF
    1906, 149; Edunx mater
    11005

?Eizia 419

[?Eliamarus 29*]

Elonus 342

Ennebox 194

Eppamaigus 268 Add.
    (11011)

Eranus 11008

Erdenius 33

Erdescus 33

]erennate[m. (gen.?)
    305

Ereseni dat. f. 341

Erhexoni dat. f. 267

Erianosserionis 366 (two
    words: Eria? Erianos?)

Estenconis gen. m. 271

Eunus 48

?Eutazia 460

Fafierus 173

?Fannac AcS 1.1492,20

Festa 345

Fitulius AcS 1.1495,53

Fortis 335

?Fressus 266

Fronto 10, 56(?), 257,
    264, 280, 552

Frontaccus 280; Froni.ac[
    450

Gallus 235

Galus 156, AE 1922.51;
    Gal[272

Gelais 55

Gerex(s)o 164, 369

Germanus 163

?Gison v. Cison

Gisondoni(?) dat. 278

[?Gruminiti 564]

Hahanni f. (case?) 273

Hahentenn f. 32 (not -tenu),
    173 (for Nah- ?)

H]aloassi 72 Add.

Halsconis gen. m. 341; cf.
    BSL 32, 1931, 101. (Cf.
    also Talsconis?)

Personal Names

Halscottarris gen. m. 277;
  cf.]arris 11009.4 (cf.
  289, 306)

Han[n]abus (or Hambus?)
  288

Hanaconis gen. m. 344

Hanarrus 5

Hanna 174, 195 (?);
  Hannac[87, cf. 195,
  Hannas(?) 195, 201

Hannaxsus 323

Harbelex m. 85, 173, 316;
  Harbelexsis and -exsi(s)
  gen. 327, 324. Cf. Belex

H]arbelsis 54

Harbelesteg(is) AE 1912.
  275; REA 14, 1912,
  70-1; 11031 (cf. Adei)

Harontarris gen. m. 289

Harsori (case?) 270; nom.
  m. 369 (for -is?),
  gen. 369

Harspus 118

Harsus 85

?Hauni MLI Index

Hauteten B.S. Ariégeoise
  1919, 139-40 (Lizop
  2.118)

Hautense f. 369, Hauten-
  soni dat. f. 277

Herr[, Herri 479 Add.

?Herossis MLI Index

?Holox[465, ?h]olox[
  11027a

Hontharri[s] gen. m. 306;
  cf. 11009.4

?Hortus MLI Index

Hotarris gen. m. 267, 342
  -i dat. 342, Hotarri[?
  46

]hosxi[s] gen. m. 282

Hunnu 334

Iacessis gen. m. 289

Ianuaria 387

Iarbonis gen. m.

Igillus

]iin[11010

Illai gen. m. 477

]illanis 183

Illixo CIL 12.5686, 426
  (from MLI Index)

Ilunnosi gen. m. (Cf.
  divine names)

]inoss[199

Inua AE 1935.61

Iricconis gen. m.

Ittixonis gen. m. 17

Personal Names

]iuet[229

Iullus (Espérandieu,
    Lectoure 31)

Labusius 386

Laetus 15, 341

Laetinus 15

Laeuina 553

Lana 266

?Lanipendia 447 (if a
    name)

Lasciuus 31, -ius 131;
    cf. 150

Laurco 472

Laureia 11021

?L]aurias 172

Laurina

Lentina 141

Lexeia

Lexanik·i·s gen. m. (an
    Lex... rigis? v.l.
    Lextinikis) 105; cf.
    -niska Note xv (?)

Liannassis gen. m. 280

Licinus 84, -ia 197, -ius
    277, 421

Ligurius 462

Litano[127

Litouir AcS 2.249

Lohisus 261

Lohitton (dat.?) 268 with
    Add. (11011)

Lohixsus 173

Luc[165

Lucanus 355, 367; -a 367

Lucid[242

†Luminatius 531

?Luxsa 471; but v. Titi-

Macrio 473

Mandatus 98-100, 335

Manutia 356

Marin[us 374

Marullus 169

Martus 236

Mati[454

Matico

Maurus 169; -a 54, also
    the mother of Ausonius,
    par. 17.7

Minicia 171

Minius AcS 2.596

Moau... AcS 2.602

Monsus 301

Montanus 34, 117, 119,
134, 158, 170, 222,
357, 471; -a 274, -ia
34, 158, 277

Montin[336

Muia (a pet dog) 488

Mundus 286

Mutanus AE 1928.13

N[ ]nis 59

Nacu[476

Naes[11027

?Namroni 351 (but v.
Hannaconis 344?)

Nescato f. 314 (Inesc-
sic Bladé); cf. niska
Note xv; Nixae, Nixi-
bus 243; Nisincii 179

?Netelia (Metellina?) 383

Neu[198

Neureseni dat. f.2

Neurus 304

?Nexius 439 (cf. Nesc-)

]nibo[305

Nic[or Nio[93

]nica 215

Nonia 11

†Nonnita 563

?Nosserionis gen. m. 366;
but v. Eria

Noualis 196

Nymfius 128

Ocar[MLI p.263

Occasus

Ocello 475

?Ocianus 551 Add.

Odannus

Odossus 400

Odoxus 268 with Add.
(11011)

Ofil[279

Ohasseris (Ona- ?) gen.
m. 74

Oiso oll[478

Oltaca 10010.2813

Ombex (F- ?) 11019

Ombexonis gen. m.; cf.
Ombecco (if correctly
read) CIL 12.5381

Ona- v. Oha-

Onesicrate 468, Onesima
468, Onestus 11017
(REA 14, 1912, 412)
cf. local name Onesii
(84 above)

]oniu[11011

Personal Names

]onna 29

]ontolion[280 Add.
  (cf. 6*?)

Oppidana 506; cf. Oppidum
  nouum (84 above)

Orcot[i] gen. m. 288

Orcotarris gen. m. 342

Orcuarus

Orgoannus

Orguarra; cf. Hungunuerro
  (84)

]origis MLI Index (Bladé)

Oro

Osaherr(us) 479

?Oscitaris REA 15.1913,
  430; but v. Sci-

]ose 54

Osson

]ouadius 161

Oxson 369

Pacius 299, †Pac[

Pal[469

Paulinus (Nolanus) b.
  A.D. 353 (cf. CIL 13,
  p.76)

Pelester (for -d-?) BSAF
  1870, 146-7

Pelopsis gen. m. 136

Petronia 37

Piandossonnius (-sp-, or
  -s P- ?) 124 Add.

Ponn[124 Add.

Pomptinius 14

Porc[ius 394

Priamus 101

Putus | erspa 380 (v.l.
  Ruiu. |. rra)

Rem[o   521

]resse 46

Rhe[a] 199

Rhexoni 267

]rica REA 16, 1914, 83

]ritsehe 409, v. Heraus-
  (86)

Rocius 534

Rufina 306, 447

Rufino (-us) 283

Rufio 277

Rufonius 358

Rufus REA 28, 1926, 255

Rurinus (-f-) 283

Rutundus 306

Sabina, -us, -ula, -ianus:
  twenty-four times in
  inscc. (22, 39, 75, 81,
  83, 104, 119, 249, 258,
  264, 267, 327, 335, 368,
  373, 374, 420, 422, 435,
  456, 487, AE 1939.50).
  Cf. Lizop 2.116 n.39

Saherossis gen. m. 287

Saleduna

Salinis[? gen. m. 381

Salisius 263

?Salus 156

Sambus

Sambilius (or -tus) AE
  1914.198; cf. REA 15,
  1913, 430

Sapalonis gen. m.

Sarmisibia 11030a

?]scinni | fonney (sic)
  11009

Scitaris AE 1914.197;
  cf. Oscitaris?

Segusiaua 352; cf. local
  names (84)

]selexse 11009

Sem[b... 238

?Sembecconi dat. (Cf.
  Becco) Or Sembecconisa?
  Cf. Om-

Sembedonnis gen. m.

Sembetel[? gen. m. 46

Sembetar (Lizop 1.113,
  n.102)

Sembetten, -ennis gen.

Sembexonis 4, -xsonis 62,
  both gen. m.

Sembus

Semperrus 141; BSAMidi
  1901-3, 227

Sendus

Senicco m.

Seniponnis gen. m. 267

Senitennis (Senhennis?
  Senilennis?) gen. m.
  125

Senius 174, 288, 311

Senixsonis gen. m.

Sennacius (-g-?)

Sennagi gen. or dat.?

Sentarri (-harri?) Senar-
  ri?) f. 342. Cf.]arris
  11009

Serana 13, 175; -us 42,
  92, 112, 142, 273, 330,
  369, 375, 391, 471

Serenus 473

Serio 366; cf. local names

Serranconi dat. m.

Sextillus 112

?Silabina 443

Silex 173, 329, 381; f.
268 with Add. (11011).
Cf. Bonsilexsi,]se-
lexsi 11009 (v.l.
]belexsi)

Silexconis gen. m. 283

Silana 507

Silania 330

Siluana 368; -us 137,
259, 271, 289, 325,
416; -ius 410

Siluina, -us 169, 343,
410, 449; AE 1939.49

Siradus

Siricconis gen. m. 111;
-i gen. m. 265

Sirico 173 (also as-
cribed to Narb.)

Sixsio AE 1928.13

?Socondanossi, but v.
also Con-

Soemuti (Soli-?) gen.
m. 471

Somenaris gen. m.

Sonbrabonis gen. m.

Sori[

Sorinianus MLI p.263

Sorinus 276

Sorus 96, ASS

Sosonnis gen. m.

Sotericus 424

Staphylius (Auscius) CIL
13, p.57 (from Ausonius);
cf. 36*

Sunducca

Surus

Surusis gen. m. 29

Talsconis gen. 555; cf.
BSL 32, 1931, 101 n.

Talseia 452

Tarc[(Taro[?   Tarc[o
?) or Tar[   ]osa 479
with Add.

Tariebissus (for Tarle- ?)

Tarlebissus (cf. 152 infr.)

Tarros 555 (cf. Tarusates?)

Taure 246

Tauricus 10, 485

Taurinus 212, 222, 301,
313, 338, 385, 485, 486

Taurus 30, 179, 313, 485,
11007, AE 1939.50

Tautinnus 483

Teixsossix f.; CRAcInscBL
1921, 156; AE 1922, 51;
REA 24, 1922, 54, cf.
Tasg- ? Cf. 36*

Personal Names

Tertullus 105

Tici 422

?Titiluxsa 471

Titulinus 440 (cf. Espér-
andieu, Lectoure 9)

Titullius, -a

Titullus, -a; and add
11005

Torsteginnus

Tottonis gen. m.

Touta 352

Toutannorix m.

Toutaronia

]trillion 362

Troccus

Tucc[538

Turranius 539

Vcoetixix BSAMidi 1921,
301.25; Lizop 1.509;
cf. RC 51, 1934, 129:
cf. Vcetia (80),
Vcuetis (169)

Vennonius 122

Vera 393

Verana 339

Verina 393

Verinia Espérandieu, Lec-
toure 50

Vernus 92

Veruic[542 (Treuer)

Vindemialis 180, 308

Viohossius, Vinussius REA
15, 1913, 430; AE 1914.
198

Vip|ɔ oi 561

]uir 46

Vitel(l)ia 34

Vlohoxo dat. m.

Vlohoxis gen.

Vlucirris gen. m.

?]ulux[MSAMidi 19,
1939, 217

?Vnagilla MLI Index

Vochio BSAMidi 1931, 301.
25

Vocontia v. Boc-

]uni 371, cf. 11010

?Vria 52 (v.l. Furia), 327

Vriassus

Vriaxe

Vrus 371

†Vrsicinus 500

Vrupatis gen. m.

Personal Names

?Vyc[ri 11004   Zan[11027

Remark:

(i) I see nothing in the alphabetic symbols
(Ariège), engraved on rock, published in Gallia 5,
1947, 29, that can be construed as Iberian. They are
more likely Latin graffiti.

(ii) Ausonius (epicedion in patrem 9) implies
that his father was not at home in Latin; but whether
he spoke Keltic or Iberian, and among the Vasates
(Bazas), near Bordeaux, either is possible, is not made
clear. Cf. Sofer ZfCPh 22, 1941, 113.

A.   Aquitania Prima

88   Graffito of Montans

It might be held that this sherd properly belongs
to La Graufesenque, with the graffiti of which (90-131)
it is identical in all the characteristic features.
But, if so, did the Blickweiler fragment (229) also
come from La Graufesenque? It, however, shows internal differences of text; the geographical distance is
greater; and, far as the products of La Graufesenque
were carried, it does not appear that the graffiti,
which are potters' accounts, written on broken and discarded plates, not bills of lading, were exported,
unless that has happened by accident in these two instances.

```
       ]dcc pannas [∞∞∞∞dcc │ c]atilli dc │  ]us
    pannas s⇄d cruminis[   │     ]li dcc acitabli cccl
5   p·m │ ∞∞∞∞dcclxxu ‖  ]ius et dercillus │ xxxx
    pannas s⇄[
```

CIL 13.10017, 46; Hermet Pl. 145; Oxé BJ 130, 1926, 51

On Terra Sigillata

1. caracsui Bohn, paracse[di] Oxé: pannas ego
3. crumina (sc. "crumenae") Oxé, gluannis (?) Bohn
4. p(lus) m(inus) Bohn, pl(us) Oxé; an ∞ ? The numeral
in line 1 is crowded beneath pannas.

On Montans terra sigillata see now Durand-Lefebvre in
Gallia 4, 1946, 137-94.

Remark:

Names from terra sigillata present peculiar
problems: (a) they are often badly written, or difficult to read for other reasons, or both; (b) it is
necessary, so far as possible, to determine the place
at which a potter worked, in order to classify his name
strictly on a geographical basis. But it happens commonly that we do not know where a potter worked, only
where a piece bearing his name has been found, and then
we have to be content with this less satisfactory ascription. For my purpose, of geographical classification, I have used Oswald's Index of Potters' Stamps on
Terra Sigillata, 1931. But I have no confidence that
all, or many of the names said to be recorded, shall
we say, at Orange (see, for example CA 5, 120-6), are
even accurately copied. I have done what I could,
little enough, to identify some of these strangers;
but there must remain a certain residue of names that
are mere ghosts. It is for the students of terra
sigillata to put their house in order. The rest of us
are helpless until they do.

The known sites at which potters worked in Aqui-

tania are Montans, La Graufesenque, Banassac, Lezoux,

Saint-Rémy-en-Rollat, Lubié-la-Palisse, and Vichy (Aquae

Calidae). In addition a number of potters are said,

more broadly, to have worked in South Gaul, which in

practice means Aquitania, not Narbonensis. The industry

On Terra Sigillata

flourished in Aquitania, at the sites named, and in
Eastern Gaul (Belgica, the two Germanies, and at a
number of sites in the Upper Rhine and Danubian districts), but not in Lugdunensis or Narbonensis, both
of which depended on imported fabrics. The interest
of terra sigillata for us lies in the fact that something has been gleaned from it wherewith to increase
our knowledge of Keltic, notably from the graffiti of
La Graufesenque; and also from the shorter inscriptions,
most of which consist of no more than proper names.
Thus we have (1) a large number of personal names that
are clearly Gaulish, such as Cintusmus, Dagobitus,
Ritomarus, Atepomarus, and present familiar elements
such as -rix, -dubnos, -maros, -genos, -rantos, Cintu-,
Matu-, Illio-, Biraco-, and many others; (2) Gaulish
affective names in -o, from Latin as well as native
names, e.g. Satto, Sacco, Seuuo, Peppo, Patto and
others; (3) a few local and ethnic names, e.g. Aquitanus,
Aruernicus, Biturix, Tribocus, occasionally from outside
of Gaul, e.g. Britannus; (4) the Gaulish word auot or
auoti(s), see Note xi; (5) n. sg. -os (for -us) is
probably a mark of Gaulish, rather than of vulgar Latin,
and so too -as n. pl., f., -i neut. pl., e.g. tri; but
it is easy to exaggerate the importance of writings

272

Potters of Montans

such as -ai for -ae; or c (before u) for q, e.g. Cuarti,
Anticui. The omission of -n- before -s- is due perhaps
to a V.L. change, and the confusion (in the writing) of
e, i is not peculiar to Gaul; in the symbol đ (or θ),
on the other hand, we have evidence of a dental contin-
uant (fricative or affricate) that is characteristic of
Gaulish.

89   Potters of Montans (A.D. 15 to 90)

Acutus (Aruernus)	Cacus	Felix
Aimo(n)	Caius (for G-)	Firmanus
Ainicicus	Celer	Firmo
Aluinus	C(h)resimus	Fronto
Ampio	Contouca	Helius
Andoca	Corius	Iullus
Apronius	Criatus	Lepta
Attillus	Crispinus	Macio
Aucius	Cunasus	Matugenus
?Aurelios (or Nigelios? see AA 29, 1914, 64-75)	Donicatus	Mitus
	Draucus	Nomus
	Eppia	Reburrus
?Bilicatus (Aruernus), Oswald p.4	Eppius	Repentinus
	Famius	Reus

273

La Graufesenque

Saluetus? (REA 24, 1922, 254)	Surdinus	Verces
Saluius?	Surius, Surus	Veretonus
Scipiu(s)	Tarus	Vicarus
		Vlatus

LA GRAUFESENQUE

A discovery which in interest almost matched that of the Calendar of Coligny was unpretentiously announced in 1923 by the publication, under the auspices of the Société des Lettres, Sciences et Arts de L'Aveyron (Carrère, Rodex 1923), of a modest work: Les Graffites de la Graufesenque. This was brought out by the unassuming Curé de l'Hospitalet-du-Larzac, the late Abbé Frédéric Hermet, Honorary Canon of Rodez.

La Graufesenque is the name of a small plain, about one kilometer square, on the left bank of the river Tarn opposite Millau in the Cévennes and just below the confluence of that river and the Dourbie (see the map in Hermet, La Graufesenque, Paris, 1934, vol. 1 Plate 1). The name (Gaufresenca in 1309) means "propriété de Gaufre," the latter being a family-name (Hermet op. cit. 1.356; A. Thomas ap. Loth, R.C. 41, 1924, 58 n.2; L. Constans REA 5, 1903, 191-2 has a different explanation).

274

La Graufesenque

Here there stood a great manufactory of terra sigillata
in the first century of our era, part of the Gallo-Roman
settlement, the Condatomago(s) of the Peutinger Table,
thirty leagues from Rodez (Segodunum) and twenty-three
from Lodève (Luteua).

The chief interest of La Graufesenque, for us, lies
in the two score fragmentary "plats" and "assiettes" of
terra cotta, covered with a red varnish. These were
used by the potters, whose native speech was evidently
Gaulish, though they had acquired some Latin, for the
purpose of keeping records of their output, which they
scratched on discarded pieces, large and small plates
or saucers, sometimes on mere fragments or broken pieces,
in the cursive Latin script of the time. The records
had only a temporary value, and were themselves cast
aside. It is from such broken pieces that, upwards of
forty, more or less incomplete, records or tallies have
been reassembled and restored by the patient industry
of Hermet, who published his final results in 1934 (La
Graufesenque 2 vols., Paris). The excavations that
brought them to light began in 1901 and ended in 1906;
Hermet published five texts in 1904 (RA 3, 1904, 74-91),
to be reproduced by Déchelette the same year (Vases ornés
1, 1904, 87-92, Pl. 13, 14). In fact two graffiti had

275

been discovered by l'abbé Cérès in his desultory and
incompletely recorded excavations of 1882-3, and were
published by Héron de Villefosse between 1882 and 1886
(BSAF 1882, 297-9; 1884, 83-5; cf. 1904, 307; Mém. Soc.
Lettres, Sc., et Arts de l'Aveyron 13, 1886, 200-1) and
again by Déchelette in 1904 (op. cit. 1.86, fig. 61-2).
But these (110, 115, 117, 119, 122, 129 below) created
no stir at the time. They are brief and incomplete;
even the largest of them (110) was not enough to give
warning of the surprise in store.

However, after the publication of Hermet's monograph of 1923, interest was aroused and the bibliography,
on the linguistic side alone (see below), is now extensive. To Hermet, who permitted me to study his collection at L'Hospitalet in 1929, I am very grateful. He
died in 1939 (RA 13, 1939, 256); his collection had
already been given to the Société des Lettres, Sciences
et Arts de l'Aveyron, and was deposited in its museum
at Rodez (see Hermet La Graufesenque 1.356, and Blanchet's
preface). Two of the graffiti discovered in 1882-3 (119,
122) have long been lost, and those I have not seen; 118
was temporarily lost when I was at L'Hospitalet, and for
it also I depend upon older copies. No. 129 I tried,
without success, to see in 1929. It had been given to

La Graufesenque

M. Antoine de Carlshausen of Millau. All the rest,
thirty-nine items in all, I saw for myself, 91, 109
included (the property respectively of M. Jules Artières
and M. Dieudonné Rey, both of Millau).

Déchelette in 1902 (see REA 5, 1903, 38-78) recognized certain vases discovered at Pompeii as having come
from La Graufesenque, where the moulds from which the
products of Mommo, Secundus, and Vitalis, and also their
stamps, had come to light. And in 1914, D. Atkinson
(JRS 4, 1914, 27-64) called attention to cases of "Samian"
ware found still unpacked at Pompeii, where they must
have arrived shortly before the eruption of Vesuvius in
79 A.D., also from La Graufesenque. These two observations prove (1) that La Graufesenque was a center of
mass-production (the graffiti, 90-131 below, record a
total of more than 750,000 vases, the work of some
seventy potters) and distribution of wares found all
over the western Empire; and (2) that its productivity
had reached a high peak in the middle of the first century of the Christian era. It is noteworthy that products of La Graufesenque have been found also in the
Roman camp at Hofheim (Taunus), which was occupied only
between 40 and 60 A.D. Of the total number, viz. forty-
three, of the graffiti of La Graufesenque, twenty-nine

were found all together and the rest not very far away; twenty of them have the stamp of Castus, and other potters who are named are known to have been his contemporaries. Moreover, the manufactory cannot have been established long before the time of Tiberius; evidence of an earlier date is completely wanting both at La Graufesenque itself and at the sites where its exports have been found (cf. Grenier apud Frank 3.545). But it had fallen into decadence by the time of Trajan, when it was supplanted by Lezoux and other centers of production (Heiligenberg 85-160 A.D., according to Forrer; or 100-130, Oswald; Rheinzabern c. 130 to 200 or 250 A.D.; Blickweiler; and Faulquemont-Chémery).

Details of the decoration of terra sigillata ("Romano-Gaulish" or "Gaulish-Arretine" ware, cf. Antiquity, 12, 1928, 103) need not detain us, except perhaps to note in passing the presence of the hound (cf. leporem laesum gallici canis dente Mart. 3.47.11; gl. uertragus 178), and of the ammentum (Blanchet, Pref. to Hermet's "La Graufesenque," viii-ix, cf. P. Couissin, "Les armes romaines," 1926, 121-9); nor need we stay over the distinctions of style made by Hermet. What we must notice, as a matter of capital importance, is the use of Gaulish mixed with Latin (like the mixed Etrusco-Latin of vase-inscc. at Commachio and in Campania) in the middle of the first century of the Empire at Condatomagus (condato- i.e. "confluence") in the country of the Ruteni, i.e. on the frontier between Narbonensis and Aquitania (cf. Pl. N.H. 3.37 with 4, 109; cf. PW s.v.). The potters of La Graufesenque at that date counted in Keltic, and talked a mixture of Keltic and Latin, as possibly workers in their other industries also, which are said to have been linen (Pl. 19.8) and (with the Gabali) silver (Strabo 4.2.2, 191 C.).

The graffiti, the linguistic contents of which are, therefore, of great interest, are almost without exception, potters' reckonings of production; two apparently are of a different type (130, 131 below). In addition to the graffito, most pieces also bear a potter's stamp, but it is not certain that the workmen named in a given reckoning had anything to do with the manufacturer whose name is stamped on the same piece. The drawings of a bird or a cross, whatever their real significance, have no apparent interest for us.

The graffiti evidently were written on sherds, not on whole pieces, for the writing is made to fit the shape of the sherd (e.g. 102). Usually a graffito fills only one side of the fragment with its rows (not columns) of items; but two specimens (120, 123) have two sets (or columns) of such rows of entries and two others (124, 115) have entries on both sides. Oxé first propounded the view, now generally accepted, that the records are simply the totals of the number of pieces deposited by different potters for a single firing in a common kiln (see, e.g., RA 6, 1935, 102-4), averaging thirty thousand pieces more or less (in four graffiti the total is approximately double the normal total, and perhaps implies the simultaneous firing of two kilns). Similar records are known not only from Montans (88), Blickweiler, and Rheinzabern (229, 230), but also from

279

Colmars in the Basses-Alpes (20, Remark e, cf. AE 1935.
144), from Bavay (AE 1928.138), from Montenach (REA 19,
1927, 205-7; AE 1927.155) and from Chémery in the Moselle
(see E. Delort, Annuaire de la Société d'Histoire et
d'Archéologie de la Lorraine 44, 1935, 355-67, pl. 19).

The readings of these are:

(1) Bavay (cf. Pro Nervia 3, 1927, 356, 369-373, 391)
     ]acit̞ | catilli ii | san[

(2) Montenach
      cum Anaillo dies. | cum Tertio dies i |
  inbricis dies iii | inbricem baiolandam mortari
  ui dies iii | tegule in campo Rassure dies i |
  .aterdi dies i

(3) Chémery
      ]tata |]lxx uasa x̄x̄x̄x̄uiii cclxxx |]luii
  uas mmd̄ccxxxxiiii |]uas mc |]lla cclxxii uas
  mmd̄ccxxx[|]ccliiii

Note also, in Italy, CIL 11.6702, 1 (Arezzo), which is
similar; 6702, 5 (also from Arezzo), which mentions
acet[abula] and pul[taria]; 6702, 23a (Horta), with

cat]illi[(?). One might also compare the ostraka from Carthage (AE 1912.61-70) the style of which is strikingly similar. They are apparently "quittances donnés par le mensor olei... pour des livraisons d'huile," and they are regularly dated at the top.

To these may be added:

(4) from Holdoorn (CIR 114, Byvanck Excerpta Romana, 2.102)

    kal iuni Quartus laterclos

    n ccxiiii

    Much more remarkable, for its bearing on the interpretation of tuθos, is the tile-inscription given by Byvanck (ibid., p.104), after Jensen, and also by Riese 4612 (CIR 1397), from Hummetroth (Hesse), cf. Walters History of Ancient Pottery 2.358, viz

    stratura tertia latercli capitlares

    n ccclxxu

Comparison of export-tax marks on vases (cf. Tenney Frank AJPh 57, 1936, 87-90) is less apt. There are possibly similar tallies CIL 11, 6709.30 and 35.

    Four different elements are to be distinguished in the potters' records of La Graufesenque, though no single extant graffito shows them all, and the second, a sort of post-script as Hermet called it, appears in only a few. They are:

(1) A heading, that is a brief formula regularly consisting of the Gaulish word tuθos or tuθθos followed by an ordinal numeral, either written out in full in Gaulish, or indicated simply by the Roman numeral, but never higher than tenth; instead of the numeral, or in addition to it, there occasionally stands the word luχtos, once luχtodos; and in perhaps four specimens a Gaulish official title, in full or abbreviated, cas(s)idan(n)o(s), and accompanied by a proper name (90, 92, 94, 102).

(2) Moreover, in four specimens (90, 93, 103, 109) the post-script, which in three of these is simply the word legitum, in the other, what must be its Gaulish equivalent, viz. autagis (whatever its etymology, see the Glossary), has become, as it were, incorporated into the heading. But the explanation of this peculiarity would seem to be that the post-script was inserted in any available space, at the top (before or immediately after the tuθos-formula); or (as in 114) in the margin. In this last, the post-script differs also in meaning, since it notes a correction of the reckoning, presumably an addition or supplement to rectify an oversight, as

the term extratuθ(o)- would seem to imply, instead of recording the approval (legitum, autagis) of the cassidannos, if indeed that is the significance of those terms. The alleged reading legitumum is a guess, and the final -m uncertain in legitu[m(?). Irish lige is from *leghiom, Latin has lectus (dim. lectulus), and we may, I think, infer a possible *leghitom "layer." A tuθos, therefore, will be a subdivision of an autagis or legitom (stratura). See now my paper in the F. N. Robinson volume (Journal of Celtic Studies 1, 1949).

(3) The body of each text is of considerable length, being the actual enumeration of manufactures, entered, row by row, under four heads. These give, in the normal but not invariable arrangement, the following details. First the name of a potter; second the name of the type or pattern of vase made by him; third the size of the vase (its capacity or diameter); and last of all, in Roman numerals, the number of vases turned out. The potters of La Graufesenque often worked in association; hence we sometimes find two or more names, up to as many as five, listed together, connected by the particles duci or toni (e.g. 99, lines 10, 16; 104, line 12). If the names thus fill the entire line, the rest of the information is carried into the next line. There appears to

be nothing corresponding to Gr. ἐποίει or ἐποίησε , to
Latin fecit or manu, or to Gaulish auot. Occasionally
the name of the potter stands last, after the numeral
(98, line 2; 110, line 17); or, if a potter had manufactured a variety of vases for a given firing, the
totals are accounted for in two or more successive lines,
and the potter's name may then be omitted after one
mention (111, line 6; contrast line 4), or the particle
eti, et may be used instead of the repeated name (103,
lines 4, 6). In some cases (93, 95, 98, 100, 101, 104,
106, 108), after the heading, there follows no potter's
name for several lines; it is suggested that the kiln-
master himself was the owner or manufacturer in such
instances.

The second item (the name of the type of vase) is
sometimes omitted (e.g. 99, lines 2-3). But precisely
as in the case of the names of potters, so the name of
a type-vase may be understood from a preceding line
(e.g. 99, line 8; 105, line 4); not infrequently the
name of the potter precedes, instead of following, the
name of the vase (e.g. 111, line 9; 98, line 8).

Third comes an indication of the size of the vases,
designated by the words pedalis (i.e. 1 foot), triatalis

(one third of a foot, i.e. 4 inches), or by the symbols
S ═ and ═ ═ (S standing for .5 in.). In these last,
the symbol ═ commonly degenerates into ═ or a z-like
mark. Formerly interpreted as marks of capacity, these
symbols are now believed to indicate the diameter of the
vases in question, thus, the duodecimal division of the
as (cf. Roby, Latin Grammar, vol. 1, Appendix D) being
applied to the foot, S ═ means bes (i.e. 8 inches),
═ ═ means triens (4 inches), pedalis means 1 foot,
and tria(n)talis means one third of a foot (4 inches),
i.e. there would be two means of marking a bessalis.
In fact, in three graffiti (90, line 4; 96, line 6; 114,
line 6) both ways are used together; but in 99, line 9
triatalis is followed by S ═, which is either an error
for ═ ═ , or else implies that the total number of
vases included some of the one, some of the other, size.
Only once (92, line 5) is the designation pedalis followed by the symbol S ═ or ═ ═, the explanation
of which must be the same. Another suggestion, that
both width and height are given, seems less likely.

The largest size of vase (pedalis) was made, as
would be expected, in smaller quantity, and the only
vases made in it were the canastri, catinos, catili(-ll-),
mortaria and uinaria. If no name of vase appears im-

mediately before the mark of dimension, then the type
of vase last mentioned is presumably to be understood
(e.g. 109, line 4; 105, line 6; 111, line 2; 113, line
4). Occasionally S == or the like is omitted altogether,
and sometimes the symbol stands before, instead of after,
the name of the vase; but the written designations
pedalis and triatalis invariably stand before it, though
usually in the case of triatalis the symbol == ==   also
stands after it (e.g. 114, line 6). The terms sext and
bisexti in 119, Hermet holds, also indicate size of diameter, i.e. respectively 2 inches (sext being abbreviated
for sextans, or rather sextantalis) and 4 inches (bisexti for bisextialis, synonymous with triatalis). Thus
the variety of dimensions named is one foot, eight
inches, four inches, and two inches.

The precise meaning of the term uχsedia or uxedia
(abbreviated uχs, ux, us, uxedi) is not determined; it
seems to imply something like "roughly, approximately,"
or perhaps "at most, not more than," and to apply to the
total number of a firing (as when it qualifies summa),
and also (as when it stands after the name of a type of
vase) either to the number of vases of that type, or its
dimension, or perhaps to its quality. The interpretation of us as usuales or usitati seems wrong, since us

corresponds to ux or uᵪs in other graffiti; moreover
catilli described as us are contrasted with catilli
described as bol. Both terms might be regarded as
standing in the place of the more precise indications
of diameter or size which we have already noted. The
corresponding idioms at Blickweiler appear to be uass
at (also rendered as aequat at), and gol or gollat respectively. In like manner luᵪtos at La Graufesenque
may be represented by carnuat at Blickweiler. On all
these terms, which are thus supposed to qualify, in a
general way, the dimensions or capacity or quantity,
or even the quality of the vases, see further the Glossary. It is perhaps worth noting that not all types of
vases have dimensions stated (unless by implication).
Smaller sized products, e.g. acitabli, atramentari, are
not so described. Of the rest, some invariably have
the dimension specified, e.g. canastri, others sometimes
have, sometimes not, e.g. catil(l)i, or, if not precisely, then only in general terms, by means of us, ux,
uᵪs or the like.

After the dimension stands simply a Roman numeral
indicating the number of vases of the type and size
specified that was produced by the potter named in the
same line. These numerals are used in precisely the

Roman way: i.e. a lower digit or integer set to the
left of a higher indicates subtraction; and thousands
are denoted by means of a stroke drawn above the nu-
merical symbol.

   Only six graffiti (95, 97, 100, 106, 121, 124)
actually have a summation; of the rest, some now lack
it merely by accident, from others it was perhaps deliberately omitted. It consists merely of the word
summa, with or without uχs(edia) added, and then the
Roman numeral giving the addition (not free from error)
of all the vases enumerated in the graffito.

   The mixed character of the language of the graffiti will be clear already from these descriptive notes.
It is shown also by the names of the potters themselves,
if not from the names of their products. But both of
these are Greek as well as Latin or Keltic, the Greek
names having clearly entered by way of Latin (e.g.
Mirtilos, Sum[m]acos; Castus, Felix, Verecundus; Mommo -u,
Vindulus; duprosopi, paraxidi, acitabli, atramentari;
pannas, broci). Evidently the influence of Gallia
Graeca extended beyond Narbonensis. In counting, however, the Italian entrepreneur, like his modern representative in non-European lands, seems to have had to

accept the native names of numbers, and presumably the
workmen interpreted the Roman numerals in their own
tongue, for when they spelled them out they used the
Gaulish forms, the ordinals of which from first to
tenth, only one of them in severely abbreviated form,
La Graufesenque has given us. In addition to the numerals and the words tuθ(θ)os, autagis, luχtos (-todos),
cas(s)i-dan(n)os, duci, toni, eti, uχsedia (ux-), we
have also luritus, prinas, ris, ariciani, tecuanbo-ebo,
sioχti which presumably are Keltic. Moreover, if not
the n. sg. -os (for -us, except in the constant -oius),
certainly the neut. pl. -i; -as, n. pl.; -us acc. pl.
of o-stems (used as nom); -os gen. sg. in u-stems are
clearly Keltic.

Among names of potters which Hermet (1.313-5, 317)
claimed as Keltic are Agedil(l)os, Ceruesa, (?)Depro-
sagi(los), Martalos, Mommu, Moretoclatos, Scota, Stamulos,
Vacaca (of which some are known nowhere else). But he
was wrong in reading Vinoulus (Lat.) for Vindulos (Keltic); some names which must be Keltic he did not identify
as such, e.g. Cosoius, Dario(s), Lousios, Meddilos,
Regenos, Sennilo, Tecci (?), to mention no others. And
he claimed as names some words which certainly are not
such, viz. autagis, bipros[, cassidannos, duci, toni,

and a few which probably are not, (deprosogi, moreto-
clatos, sioχti), or may not be such (ceruesa, circos?).
Names peculiar to La Graufesenque are, according to
Hermet (1.313-6), in addition to any given above, Agios,
Cotutos, Lucanus; other noteworthy names are Alibanus,
Carilo(s), Coros, Froncu (for -tu, -to?), Illios, Malcio
Montanus, Qutos, Siluinus. Beside Alibanus we have not
only Albanus (cf. Corntus: Cornutus, Masclos: Masculus,
though the former is perhaps a merely graphic variant)
but also Albinus (cf. Siluinus). Primus, Secundus,
Terti(us) may be Latin renderings of the Keltic Cintuxos,
Allos, Tritos.

In general I have ignored slight variations of
letter forms, notwithstanding Oxé's attempt at classification, based upon the style of the letter a, except
when there is a question of reading. But I have sought
to distinguish, in my transcription, between đ ($\ominus$ and
$\mathcal{P}$) and θ (Θ), even though the distinction be merely
graphic, as it appears to be. Interpuncts are reproduced exactly as they appear in the originals, and also
the symbols $=$ (or $\rightleftharpoons$) and $=$ $=$ ($\rightleftharpoons$ $\rightleftharpoons$); e is
regularly $\parallel$, and f is $\mathsf{I}^{\shortmid}$ but c and g are not always to
be distinguished with confidence, nor χ and x, nor $\cap$
and m, $\oplus$ and m. There is perhaps a conjoint us in 99,

lines 15, 16; cf. 98.7, 103.1, 104.9, 104.12, 106.11, 108, 111, 114, 119, 123.

Bibliography

A. Albenque Inventaire de l'archéologie gallo-romaine du département de l'Aveyron, Rodez (Carrère), 1947, reviewed in CR 1949, 37; id., Les Ruthènes, Paris 1949; D. Atkinson JRS 4, 1914, 27-64; A. Aymard Études régionales fasc. 3, 1942, 150-60 (see CP 43, 1948, 139); O. Bohn Germania 8, 1924, 19-27 (cf. RC 42, 1924, 493-94); E. Bonnet Carte archéologique du département de l'Aveyron, Paris 1944; G. Chenet Germania 14, 1930, 64-73 (cf. REA 34, 1932, 58); G. Dottin REA 26, 1924, 73-77 (cf. Glotta 15, 1927, 248); H. Drexel Germania 1927, 51-53 (cf. Röm. Mitth. 1921-1922, 34-35); J. Fraser RC 42, 1925, 93-96 (cf. Glotta 16, 1928, 223); A. Ernout (on acetabulum) Rand Studies, 1938, 101-03.

Grenier in Frank, vol. 3, 1937, 540-62; and in Oxé Festschrift (Darmstadt, 1938) 84-89 (Sur la coutume ouvrière des poitiers gallo-romains) discusses (after Gummerus) the title cassidannus, comparing magister figulorum (CIL 13.8729; Riese 2421); he argues, like Gummerus, that the workmen were independent, freely associated with one another for mass-production administered by "fondés de pouvoir qui étaient eux-mêmes des ouvriers." That is, there is no question of slave labor. Gummerus Soc. Sc. Fenn., Comm. hum. litt. 3 iii, 1930, 1-21; F. Hermet, La Graufesenque, 2 vols., Paris 1934 (reviewed by Davies Pryce JRS 24, 1934, 231-34; de Weerd Ant. Cl. 3, 1934, 543-47; Oxé BJ 140-41, 1936, 325-94; R. Lantier RA 9, 1937, 121); H. Hubert RC 44, 1927, 410; Jud RC 42, 1925, 196, (RA 24, 1926, 344); Jullian REA 24, 1922, 250-51 (on aricani luritus); R. Knorr Germania 21, 1937, 240-47 (cf. REA 41, 1939, 35); Loeschke Trierer Zeitschrift 3, 1928, 69-81.

J. Loth CRAcInscBL, 1924, 49; 67-75; and in RC 41, 1924, 1-64, 493; 42, 1925, 221-22 (cf. Glotta 15, 1927, 248); A. Meillet BSL 29, 1929, 29-33; A. Oxé BJ 130, 1926, 38-99 (cf. RC 43, 1926, 441-44), id. ib. 140-41, 1936, 325-94 (cf. REA 32, 1930, 261); S. Reinach RA 18, 1923, 180-81 (on Jullian above); R. Thurneysen ZfCPh 15, 1925, 379-83; 16, 1927, 285-304 (cf. RC 43, 1926, 262; 44, 1927, 249-50; 45, 1928, 415); id. ib. 20, 1936, 368; J. Vendryes BSL 25, 1924, 34-43 (cf. RC 41, 1924, 493-94; 43, 1926, 441-44; Glotta 16, 1928, 222); J. Whatmough in Robinson Studies (Journal of Celtic Studies, vol. 1, 1949).

La Graufesenque

90 (H.12)

    (a) casti

    (b) tuꝺos · cintuxo[| luꭓto†dos · casidana-

lone · le̦[gi]tum̦[| cornuto · cana · s = cc·|

eti · triatali · = = cc · | eti · pedalis ·

5   lx · ‖ albanus · panna · ∞ l | scota · felix ·

sumaco · catili · x̄ccc · | priuatos · tritos ·

licuias · ī̄xd̄ccc · | paraxidi · cccc · | acitabli·

10   ī̄x ‖

     (b) 1. cintu [30000?] Oxé   2. Read luꭓtos
tuꝺos?   cass- Loth (wrongly)   le[ ]tu[m Hermet
ed. 2, le[ ]tus Hermet ed. 1, Loth   After le[space
for one or two (not three) letters (e doubtful)   7.
icola Loth (wrongly), but scota is quite certain   10.
-bli There is a punct over the second i

91 (H.24)

    (a) casti

    (b) tuꝺos · c[|]ucanus · [|]dalis ·

uerecundo̦ș[| m]ortari s ==ccxxc · |]ecundo ·

5   = = mor · ccc · ‖]erecundos · = = canas ·

ccx · |]ari · peda · cxxu · |]anos · panias · s

= ∾ |]ciu · licuas · = = cc · |]ix ·

10   scota · catili · īīic ∾ · ‖].agos · catili ·

292

La Graufesenque

~ ~ d̤1̣[|].etos · paraxidi · mmc · |]xidi ·

~ cc |].tos · acitabli · ūiii p]riuatos ·

15   īx d̶1 ‖

2. ucanus Hermet ego, ucanos Loth   ]u- at
the beginning I did not find; but it is in Hermet's
plate   Similarly in line 4, m] is wanting (also from
Hermet's plate)   9. Not licuias (Hermet, Loth)   This
is certain; so Hermet's plate offers licuas   15. At
end d̶1, not di

92 (H.17)

(a) casti

(b)] allos : casidano[|]ontano · agedili-

os |]s · canastri · s ═ ccc · |]os · pedali ·

5   lu |]pedalis · xx · ‖]rtari · pe · 1 |]so ·

10   to.... : cc |] · cl |]cl |]uinar.. c̣ ‖]atra-

mit.. cccxxu · |]to · licuia · ūid̶cccc · |] ~

15   ~d̶ |]osagi | catili · ūi cc · |]xidi · exan·[‖

]īi·d̶

2. m]   3.]us Hermet, but his plate has]s
5. pedalis Oxé ego, pedali s ═ Hermet   7. tr.....
Oxé   8. mor·cl Hermet; mor must have been on a fragment since lost   14. Sc. depr]osagi[los   15. exan[-
decotti Loth (p.18)

La Graufesenque

93 (H. 16)

    (a) casti

    (b)]ẹ · alos · lu[.tos |].ṣ · legit[um. |

5   ]ạ s $=$ cclxx |]ạli · lu | mo]rta · s $=$ ccxx ·

   || morta $==$ cl | uinari · cl | canastri · $=$

   $=$ cc · |].us · panni · [$\sim$ |].atos · licuias ·

10 $\overline{\text{ui}}$[$\overline{\text{ii}}$ ||]tos · paraxiḍi · $\overline{\text{u}}$ cl |]bli · $\overline{\text{x}}$ |]mạ...

   felix · catili[| ....

       A small piece of (b), namely the ends of lines
1, 2, was missing when I saw this graffito   Before leg
(line 2),]s (or]si), not in Hermet's or Loth's text,
but clear in the original   10.]rus Hermet, Loth
13.]macos Hermet   Numerals at end of 9, 10 (broken
when I saw it) are restored from Hermet   11. Space
between u and cl

94 (H.11)

    tuθo · tṛ[| casidani · tri · moṛ[| agedilio ·

    mater · c[| masuetos · canas s $=$ ccc · | eti ·

5   canast · $==$ ccc · || regenos · pe xxxu | eti ·

    morta†bi · pe · xiix · | atramitari · ccclxx · |

10 mortari s $=$ cl | eti · mort · $==$ cl || masue-

    tos · panias s $=$ $\overline{\text{d}}$cclxx · | tritos · priuatos ·

    licuias · $\overline{\text{uiii}}$ | masuetos · paraxidi · $\sim$ $\sim$ |

    trito · priua·paṛax $\sim$ cđ | deprosagi · felix ·

La Graufesenque

15   paraxi ·   N cc̦c̦[‖ c̦atili · feli · depra ·

ī̄īīic N | terti · catili · m · | acitabli · ū̄īīi

        The stamp is illegible   1. tr[itos or tr[-
itios Loth; cf. trit[131 infr.   2. mon[tanos] Oxé
3. For mortar[i ?   7. For mortari   14. trito· not
tritos (Hermet, Loth)   18. Not ī̄īīi (Hermet ed. 1,
Loth), nor ū̄īīid̄ (Hermet ed. 2), but ū̄īīi ego, Oxé
18. acetabli Loth

95 (H.9)

        (a) casti

        (b) tud̄d̄os · petu[a]r̦[| can · s ══ ccl

5   can· | ped · xc | mor s ══ ccc | pan s ══ N · ‖

    mor ══ ══ ccc | can̦a ══ ══ | c uin [p]e̦d · cc |

10   felix cat N D) dccc | summacus c̦at N dc̦l ‖

    tri̦tus li̦c̦[ua]ș   D) N . . . . . | m]ansuetus par

    N N N | tri̦tus par   N Nccc | atramentari cc |

15   acet   D) N N N N d̄ ‖

        (c) summa̦ | x̄x̄xc

        (b) 1. Clearly d̄d̄, not θθ   ar doubtful
11. licvias Hermet, lequas(?) or lecuos(?) Oxé   After
D) N   the rest has been erased   15. Apparently
D) N N d̄(N d̄ but N for d̄ is a certain correction
        (c) stands opposite lines 8-9 to the right

295

La Graufesenque

96 (H.20)

(a) of casti

(b) tuθos · petuar.[|]erecun : canas · s
== ccxxxx |]rtari · uere · s == ccl · |]lis ·
5   uere · cu |]ano · panis · s == ᴎcl ‖ t]rian-
talis · uere · == == ccxxx | mortari · == == cc
· | asati · mortari · martalos · **xc** | tritos ·
10   liculas · == == cc | masuetos · pultari · đcc ‖
duprosopi · ᴎ l | felix · catili [   ]ᴎᴎᴎ
ccc · | tritos · catili · [   ]ᴎccl | mortari ·
ux · [   ]ccc · | tritos · liculas · [u]x · ᴎᴎ
15   cđl ‖ primos · liculas · ux · ᴎᴎ đl | macer ·
liculas · ux · ccc · | masuetos · licui · ux ·
ᴎᴎcc | lousios · paraxidi · ᴎᴎ đc | primo ·
20   paraxidi · ccc ‖ masuetos · paraxidi · ᴎ çđ |
masuetos · $\overline{\mathrm{ix}}$ |]a uerecun · liculạ == [

2.]erecus Loth (wrongly)   5. sc. mont]ano
Read pani⟨a⟩s   14. at end, perhaps cc not çcc   15.
At end apparently gđl for cđl   18. Not liculas pace
Hermet (ed.1 and ed.2), Loth, Oxé   23. The]a (omit-
ted by Hermet, Loth, Oxé) is clear

97 (H.19)

(a) casti of

La Graufesenque

97 (H.19) ctd.

     (b)].os · p[|]ṣ · catilus s ⹀ c.xx |

]irtilos · ⹀ ⹀ cccxxx | ue]recundos · mor · s

5 ⹀ ccclxxxu | ue]recundos mor · ⹀ ⹀cccc ‖

m]aṣuetos · uinareus · cccxxu | uẹ]recundos · pe-

dalis · clxu |]lciu · licuas · ⹀ ⹀ cxxx |

]lciu · licuas · s ⹀cc | ma]ṣuetos · pannas

10 s ⹀ d̄ccclxu ‖ fel]ix catili · uīd̄c̣ |]lciu ·

catili ᴎdc | mạsu]etos · catili c | mas]uetos ·

15 parasidi · ūīdccc | de]prosagilos parasidi d̄cc[‖

m]aṣuetos · mor · uχs · ccc[| masuetos · acitabli

ū[| summa · uχs · x̄x̄xcc.

     1. For p[Oxé reads i[2.]ṣ omitted by
Hermet   3. Apparently]irtilos or]atilos (or -teos)
Read c]atilos (not m]irtilos)?   6. -eus has ╿ for e
8, 9. Perhaps ma]   18. Perhaps l at end

98 (H.8)

     (a) casti of

     (b) tuθoṣ pịnpetos | canastri · s ⹀ ccc ·

cot.[| masuetos · s ⹀ cxl | cotutos · ⹀ ⹀

5 cccl | ẹti · morta · ⹀ ⹀ i̇cccxl ‖ mortari ·

s ⹀ · cccxxu | albano · moretoc̣latos · secu ·

La Graufesenque

```
      pan · s[    |  pedali · xxc|uinari cxx  |  catili ·
10    summac[o]  mmd̄cc ‖ felix catili · mmmccl  |  masueta ·
      paraxidi · mm  | tritos · paraxidi · mmmcm  | aci-
15    tabli · īx  |  masclos · paraxidi đ ‖ catil[i · ] çc
```

(b) 2. Perhaps cotụ at end   5. i before
cccxl is presumably an error   There is a clear initial stroke (omitted by Hermet, Oxé), and at the end l
is ⌊ with the hasta prolonged into the line above   10.
[o] is lost in the stamp   11. Omitted altogether by
Hermet (ed.1, ed.2), Loth, Oxé

99 (H.21)

    (a) martị

    (b) tuθos · suexos : | polos · s ══ ccc: |

```
 5   castos · ══ ══ cc ·  |  broci · xxx· | uinari · l
     ... ‖ albanos panna · s ══ m  | masuetos · pann
     s ══ đl  |  secundos · s ══ cl  |  .ario · triatalis
     ══ ══ cc ·  |  tritos · duci    deprosagi · toni ·
10   felixx· ‖ catili · īīīī · đ  |  cotutos · catili ·
     mmccl  |  ceruesa · catili · đ : cc ·  |  priuatos ·
     paraxidi · mmmd̄cccl  |  uindulụs · paraxidi · m :
15   cṃl ‖ uindulụs · duci · cosọị : paraxid · md̄cl |
     masuetos ·· acitabli · ūīīī
```

298

La Graufesenque

99 (H.21) ctd.

(a) is stamped in center; cross on reverse
(b) 1 ϑ or ā̃ ? (℮)   4. an croci??   5. after 1
apparently xx in rasura   7. an dann?   9. M]ario[s
Gummerus, Oxé, D]ario Hermet, arig Bohn triatali s =
Hermet   10. an ouci?   The following punct is doubtful   felix is followed by X' i.e. felixx· (not felix
xi?) or felixxi (hardly -xi from -ti "-que"?)   15, 16
uindulus (not -oulus Hermet, Bohn) has ⅄ (ụs) both times
conjoint, Oxé, Grenier, ego   Not uindulos or -is
16. an ouci?   cosoi[us Oxé, coscios Gummerus; not
cosoa

100 (H.21)

(a) casti of

(b) tuϑϑos ui · [| catinos s = c.[|

catinos = = cc[| cotutos · morta = = [|

5   masuetos pedalis lu ‖ masuetos mor pedalis · lxxx |

alibanos : pannas · s = cccc | ma]suetos : pannas

· s = ccl · | masuetos inbrataria · s = ccl |

10   priuatos · licuas = = ccc ‖ cotutos · mor ·

s = cc · | fe]lix catili $\overline{iii}$dcl | s]ummacos

catilus Ⱶdccccl | masuetos · cati [   ]cc |

15   tritos · parasidi · $\overline{uiid}$ ‖ masuetos · par.. idi ·

iiid | ma..etos acitabli · $\overline{ix}$ |]uxs $\overline{xxuiiid}$

4. mortari = = ab ipso scriba deletum;
thus mor is faintly, ta barely legible, rest illegible
10. pr seen on separate piece   licuas Hermet ed.2,

La Graufesenque

liculas ed.1 (wrongly)   13. an catil · us (?), not
catili Hermet ed.1, punct faint   Perhaps catili us ??

101 (H.13)

   (a) of casti

   (b) tuϑϑos · ui·| catinos · s ═ cccclx |

catinos · ═ ═ ⁚cc | catinos · pedalis · c|

5 uinaria c ‖ pannas · s ═ ∾c∾xxx |]stos ·

catili · ∾đcl |]s · c[a]tili ⁚ ∾ᴂdcc|

10]li ∾cc.l |]tili cl ‖]s · parasidi iiidccc.|

]tos parasidi ∾cccc |]parasidi ∾ᴂ∾cc|

]s · acitabli · x̄d

   1. ϑ in tuϑϑos, but (?) đ ϑ clearly distinguished After ui · (line 1) nothing is wanting
8. ∾∾∾cc Hermet, ∾∾∾cclx Oxé 12. Or]ios ?

102 (H.15)

   (a) casti

   (b) tuϑos · sextametos | cassidanno montanos |

a]gedilli canastri s ═ cccxx | canastri ═ ═

5 ccl | pannas s ═ đc ‖ uinari xxc | pedalis lx|

300

La Graufesenque

    liculas = lxx │ mortari s ⇌ cl │ mortari = =

10   cc ‖ u]inari xxc │ f]elix catilli liii │ masuetos

    ç[a]ṭ[i]lli · ꝺcl │]eṭos lxxxi. licu[│]gios

15   par[‖]s acita[

       1. punct faint   8. An licula s = ?   11.
Entire line deleted by original writer himself (cf. line
6)   14. '\ (i.e. ‖ e) before tos, i.e.]etos not
]itos   16. acila testa, lege acita[

103 (H.10)

    (a) casti of

    (b) legitum[

    (c) tuos · oxtumeto · │ uitali · canast ·

s = ccxc │ eti · canastri · = = ccxx · │

cotutos morta · s = ccxx │ eti · morta · = =

5   cxc · ‖ pedalo · mos · lx │ uinari · [│ atram[│

10   inbrat[│ panas · s = ∾ ꝺcccl ‖ trito · priuato ·

licula · cccxx│mortari · uxedi cccxx │ tritos ·

priuato. · licui ulīc │ masueto · par[a]xi ·

15   īīīīdc │ summaco · feli · s[cot]a cati ulcc ‖

sumaco. [c]ạtili · ex ccxl │ acita[b]li - uīīīd

    Badly shattered   1. at end umeto Loth, ego;

301

La Graufesenque

unnito Hermet (or uanito)   5. For pedale · mor
12. mortari Hermet, not mortaria (Loth); an uxed· ?
15. masueto· is certain pace Hermet, Loth (masuetos)

104 (H.2)

(a) of casti

(b) tuθos namet[os │ canastri s ══ cxxx │

mortari · s ══ ccc │ mortari ══ ══ ccc │ canastr·

5   ══ ══ ccl ‖ albanos · panna s ══ mccl │ masue-

tos · pann.. s ══ ccl │ felix · catili · md │

10 cotutos · mccc · catili │ masuetos · catili·dcc ‖

deprosagi · paraxidi · mmd̃l │ tritos · duci ·

uindulus · licuias - x̄.mcm │ masueto·acitabli ·

ūii d̃

1. namet[not naumet[(Loth), with ⋏ a
(not au)   7. panna Hermet; an pannas ?   But cf.
line 6   8. d̃ is ꝋ   12. duci, not ouci (Ꝺ)   13.
masueto (not masuetos Loth)

105 (H.3)

(a) casti of

302

La Graufesenque

        (b) t]uθos · ··init[| masuetos · can[|

    et · canas = = c[| mortari · == == cc |

5   masuetoṣ · morta s = · cl · ‖ pedalis · lu |

    pannas · s = m | uinari · c · | inbratari ·

10 s = cxu | t]riti · priuati · licuias · u͡ic · ‖

    f]elix · scota · c̣atili · u͞cc | sumacos · catili ·

    mcm | masuetos · paraxidi · u͞i | masueto · acita ·

    i͞i͞xd̄

        A mere fragment, 4 by 4.5 inches, engraved
after stamping and baking; two long strokes (accidental?) at beginning   1. After t]uθos the reading is
quite uncertain   Apparently anli   Perhaps namet[?
Or pinpe[?   Hardly trinis (?), cf. 122]nis; or
ince (cf. 119 incepit); or prinit ? cintux ?   But
this is all conjectural   6. d or d̄ ?   lu Hermet
ed.1, ego; not [(Hermet ed.2)   10. u͡ic Oxé, Hermet
ed.2, ego (u͞c Hermet ed.1)   13. u͞i ego, u͞ Hermet ed.
1, ed.2, Oxé

106 (H.6)

        (a) casti

        (b) ṭuθθos uiiii | pannas · s = mcc | c]a-

    tilus s = c̣x̣x̣x̣ | pedalis · .lu | catilus · == ==

5   cccxxx ‖ mor · s = cc | mor · == == c : |

    uinaria lxxx | tecci · catili i͞i͞d̄ | felix · catili

10 i͞i͞i͞i͞cl ‖ deprosagilos · parasidi i͞i͞i͞cccl | masuetos·

La Graufesenque

. parasidi ū · d̄ccc | priuatos · licuas ūiiccccl |

15   masuetos acitabli ūiiid̄ | summa · u⋌s·x̄xxiiid̄ ‖

(c) to

      Four pieces, re-united by Hermet   Text un-
usually clear   5. catilus, not catil us   11. gi
conjoint   At the bottom a single line (c) faint, and
upside down; perhaps not part of original graffito
But the same two letters (to) appear also on reverse
Perhaps both are merely an error or false start for
tuḷos ?

107 (H.30)

(a)   ]bus fe

(b) tuθθos · ix · |]ṭili · s == ccc |

5   ]ḷis cl |]s == ccxxxx |] == == ccclxxu ‖

10   ] == == cccc |]ṣ == d̄cl |]ccl |]cccc |]lɔo ‖

      5. ccclxxu Hermet, Oxé, ego; not ccclxxx Loth
On reverse non-alphabetic scratches

108 (H.7)

(a) casti

304

Potters' Names of La Graufesenque

Cantiorus?	Coelius	Dassi (B-?)
Cantus	Collo (or Cotto?)	Decumus?
Canus?	Copiro	
Capito	Cornutus	Eluinus
Cara[	Cosius	Epponus
Caratus (-nt-)	Cospalus?	
Carbo	Cotto	Firmo
Caril(l)us	Cotulo (-us)?	Fronicus?
		(Ronicus)
Carotalus?	Crassus	
Carus	Crestio (-is?)	Gagabio
Casillus?	Crestus	(Cacabus)
Cass(i)us	Cretus	Gallicanus
Castus	Crispus	Gallicus?
Catus	Crucia	Gallus
Celadus	Crucuro (cf.	Gelicus?
Celer	Criciru on coins	Gemma
Celeros	of Suessones;)	Generus?
	Criciro TS at	
	Trier	
Celsus	?Cunasus	Germanus
Cennatus	Cus[	
Cera		Homobonus
Cinus?	Damonus	
Citur?	Daribitus	Illus
Cnonc?	Dario	
Cocus	Darra	Labio

321

La Graufesenque

         (b) tuθos · decametos · | canas · s ═══

    cccxxx | canastri · ═══ ═══ cclx | morta · ═══ ═══

5   xxx · | canas · pedali · cxx · ‖ mortari · s ═══

    cxxx · | uinari · cx · | pannis · s ═══ m | in-

10 bratari · s ═══ l | atramitari · cl ‖ licu[i]as ·

    ═══ ═══ ccc | felix · scota · [c]atili · īud̄ |

    summacos catili · mmd̄l | catili · cxx | mosueta ·

15 paraxi · ūd̄ ‖ priuatos · trito · licu · ūcm · |

    acitab · īx | m]ortari · uxedi ccc

         Broken into two pieces   The stroke extend-
ing from line 1 to line 4 on left is apparently the
lower part of t in tuθos   8. pannis sic   15. mosueta
Hermet, ego; not masueta Loth

109 (H.23)

         (a) casti

         (b) autagis · cintux xxx

         (c) tuθos · decametos · luχtos · | uerecunda ·

    canastri · | s ═══ d̄ | eti · pedalis · cx | eti ·

5   canastri · ═══ ═══ d̄ ‖ alibanos · panias · ∾ xxx·

    · | a†.lbinos · uinari · d̄ | summacos · catili ·

    ∾∾ cd̄lx | felix · scota [cat]ili · ūcc | tritos ·

10 priuatos · paraxi · ūdl ‖ deprosagi · paraxidi ·

    ∾ ∾ d̄c · | masuetos · acitabli · īxd̄

                        305

La Graufesenque

Formerly the property of M. D. Rey of Millau. A complete plate, 6 inches in diameter, presumably discarded as somehow imperfect. Underneath, beneath the foot, a rooster in outline.

(b) cintux xxx an cintu xxxx ?   Impossible to say.   cintu $\overline{\text{xxx}}$c Oxé is an error   Not cint ux etc.

(c) 1. decametos Hermet, ego   decometos Oxé, Thurneysen   Unquestionably λ not $\lrcorner$ or $\lrcorner$ 3 is in a line by itself, but belongs with line 2   6. After the numeral x Hermet, but I saw nothing that could be so read; not ux   6. A clear i, short as usual, after al; possibly to be read al·banos   albanos Hermet, Loth   7. Apparently a·lbinos, possibly ailbinos (?) 10. An parasi- ?

Oxé takes luxtos (c) line 1 with (b), after the numeral

The varnish in lines 6 (over the numeral) and 9 (between]ili and $\bar{\text{u}}$cc impairs the reading slightly, but not enough to make it doubtful

110 (H.40)

I. (a) of g[

(b)]x[

(c)]xiiii |]s $=$ ccccl |] $=$ $=$

đ..cxxx |]os · pannas s $=$ ∾ |]s pannas

5   s $=$ ccl ‖]nutos pannas s $=$ ccc |]pannas

s $=$ cccc |]cos mortarus · s $=$ l $=$ $=$ cc |

306

La Graufesenque

10   ]ra catilli · us cc | g]enialis · catilli · us .d̄l ‖

    ]panos catilli · us · ccl · |]us catilli · us ·

    ccc |]ṣcus catilli bol · ⎯iīd |] · ca[ ]bol ·

15   cl |]bol cl ‖]ī d̄l · catilli |] · bol · ccc ·

20   moes · a[|]bol d̄l · |]bol · d̄cccccli |] dc ‖

    /// |] d |] l

II. prinas · silu[| ⎯iīu   tuddus[

    I. (b) possibly χ

        (c) 6.]eutos Hermet, Loth, Oxé   ]utos
Déchelette,]nutos ego   8.]gos Oxé   Read perhaps
mortar[i (not [ia) us (not uχ or uχs), mortar us Loth
9-13. catili (sic) Hermet, Loth, Déchelette   9-12. ui
Hermet ed.1, us Hermet ed.2, Loth   The second symbol
is virtually | (not ⸦ or ⸦), so that epigraphically
there is nothing decisive   13-19. dol Déchelette (Vases
ornés 1.88), bol Hermet, Loth, ego (cf. Martial 14.101)
In the original (e.g. line 13)⸦   19. At end li or l· ?
22.]r Hermet ed.1, Loth   ]d Hermet ed.2

        II. On reverse of I; plate in Hermet ed.2
only   1. brinas Oxé   sibu Hermet, alii alia (pri-
nassit or prinassitu?)   Analogy of other texts suggests rather s followed by a numeral   2. tu Hermet,
Oxé, Loth; sibutu Vendryes (apud Loth, p.29)   This
is hardly possible

307

La Graufesenque

111 (H.4)

      (a) c̣[

      (b)]ra[|]mortar · [| de]prosagi ·

pedali · lịị[| deprosagi · catili · = = c[|

5   deprosagi · mortari · = = cc[‖ masuetos ·

rostrati · s = ccx | rostrati = = cxxc |

masuetos · uinari · c. | pannas : s = ṃḍc |

10 inbratari · priuatọs c̣c̣ ‖ priuatos · ḷic̣uị.ş ·

]...[cc | tritos · catili]....[ccml | catili

· duprosopi d̃c | .erti · catili · d̃cl | scota ·

15 catili · mdc ‖ priuatos · licuias : u͞i͞icd | masu-

etos · paraxidi · i͞ud | lousios · paraxidi · m̃l |

20 mortari · ux · ccc | duprosopi · m ‖ acitabli ·

i͞ixd̃

      Spoiled before engraving   Fragmentary, and broken across   1.]ra[or]ba[?   7. cxxc or cxxl, not cxxi   8. After c, a chipped piece of surface, not clearly l or x   10. Not imbratari (Loth)   An c ?
11. licui[a]s Hermet ed.2, Oxé, ego; licuas Hermet ed.1
14. sc. t]   17. Omitted by Hermet ed.1, Loth

112 (H.14)

      (a) c̣aṣti

      (b)]mạ..[| albanos · | pann[| masuetos ·

La Graufesenque

```
      panna[  |  et · masueto · uinar[  |  statilos · mor-
  5   tari · s ══ ccx ‖ masuetos mortari · s ══ lx[x  |
      stamulos mortari ══ ══ cc.  |  ]mulo · iulianas ·
      c  |  ]x duci scota · catili · ūcc[ccl  |  ]si ·
 10   par[  ] ∾ ccdl ‖ ...eto · ]  parax[  ] ∾∾         |
      tritos · licuia. ūic ∾  |  eti·trito · par..idi · ∾ |
      masueto · acitabli · ūiii  |  masueta mortar · uxed
 15    · cc ‖
```

It appears from this item (cf. 109) that not
all the tallies were actually written on broken discarded pieces, but on whole (perhaps imperfect) plates,
afterwards shattered, like this.

4. eti Hermet, Oxé; et· ego   6. [x now lost;
so [ccl in line 9, and in line 11 cotutos (not seen by
me) Hermet, but in his plate (both editions) it is
rather -eta (i.e. masueta), not -utos; there is no trace
of -s   8. iulianas Hermet (perhaps intended to represent the clear i longa here)   9-10. There is a gap
(of about three lines' space) between these lines; but,
I think, only one tally   13. tritos Hermet, but the
original has trito·   15. an mortari uxedi (?) Hermet;
mortari uxedi Oxé, mortar· uxed· ego

In line 10 ∾ccdl "Schreibfehler für ∾∾ dl"
Oxé

113 (H.5)

(a) casti

(b) tuθ[| cornutos · br[| canastri · ══ ══

309

La Graufesenque

5 cc.[| pedalis · xc | uinari cc ‖ mortari s ＝

cxxu · | morta ＝ ＝ c | pannịas · s ＝ d̄cccl |

atramita · cclx· | scota · duci felix· catili·

10 ūd̄. · ‖ trito · duci · priuatos · licuias · ūīī·cc |

deprosagi · parax... · mmd̄ | masuetos · paraxidi

mmmd̄cc | acitabli · īx

Broken into two pieces.

2. br[ego, da[nnos (?) or at[(?) Oxé 3.
ccl[or ccc[(?) 8. i in rasura (or corrected from
o?) 10. duci (not ouci) with d certain 11. Not
liciuas Hermet (ed.1, ed.2) 12. deprosagi or -aci ?
idi lost (in stamp)

114 (H.22)

(a) marti

(b) .tu[ ]...os · | malso · [ ]... |

cornutos[| albanos · pa[ ]· s ＝ | ᴎccc · |

5 masuetos·p[ ]a s ＝ cccc· ‖ triatalis · can[as]-

tri · ＝ ＝ ccc · | deprosaga · licu[i]as · cl |

secundas · mortari · s ＝ ccl · | eti · triatalis

10 · mortari · ccxl | albinus · uiniri · c ‖ ceruesa ·

catili · ᴎcc· | cotuto · catili · ᴎ lxxx· |

castos · catili · ᴎ cl | tritos · duci · felix·

310

La Graufesenque

15 catili · ∾ ∾c∾ | deprosagi · paraxịdi · ∾∾ đl ‖

uindulos · ducị · priuato · paraxi ∾∾∾ ccc · |

eti · liculas · ∾ đl | cotu · liculas · đc | aci-

tabli· u̅i̅i̅i̅

(c) sio⤬ti·albanos · | panna · extratuθ · ccc

1. Apparently oc (or co?) before tu   2. post
malso·(Hermet, Bohn, ego : mario(s) Oxé) rasura   5.
p[ann]as =   or p[ann]a s =   ?   7. deprosagi Hermet
ed.1, Oxé, Loth; -aga Hermet ed.2, ego; an -aca?
8. secundas (?) : -us Hermet, Loth; secundụs Oxé, fortasse recte   10. uinari Hermet; uiniri Oxé, ego   16.
uindulos certain, not uinoulus (Hermet, Loth) or uindulus Oxé   duci ego, Oxé not duca Hermet, Loth (there
is a short scratch over the i)   19. cotu Hermet, ego;
cotutos (sic) Oxé

(c) is entered at the side, opposite lines 3-13

115 (H.38,39)

I. (a)] augustas · |]s · cxx |]usus ccc |

5]ạ·· · s = cc |]. ..̣ccl ‖]asidi · i̅i̅i̅ccl |

] parasidi · u̅c |] parasidi · đc , |] catili ·

10 ∾cccc |] catlli : i̅i̅i̅i̅ ‖]tios · catili cccc |

]lios catili ∾ cc |] magiu · catịḷị ... | qutos

15 cat[| ///////// ‖ primigen[   ]u̅i̅i̅i̅i̅ mommu · paɾ

(b) su⤬sed[

311

La Graufesenque

II. atticos · ca[| agio · cat[| cornutos cati[|

illios catili[

A flat plate, much damaged; II is on the reverse.

3.]reus (?) Oxé; an ..risus (?) id.; ...ausus
Hermet   4.]o.. Loth; om. Hermet   7.]p barely visi-
ble   10. sic; catili Hermet, Oxé   14. Note q   15.
The entire line has been erased   16. mommu ego, Oxé,
Thurneysen, Hermet ed.2; mommo Hermet ed.1, Loth

In (b) no space after s- ; should we read
s(umma) uχsed, like luχtodos (for luχtos tudos, 90)? Or
one word suχsed (cf. suexos, 99)?

II. 3. corn(u)tos Hermet, Oxé, Loth; corntos
or cornutos ego, cf. 99, 103, 104 for conjoint letters
(and pp. 290-91 above)

116 (H.18)

(a) of casti

(b) ?] catinos · s ꞊ cccc | pedales : lx |

catinos · ꞊ ꞊ clxxu | pannas · s ꞊ cc. |

5   mortaria : s ꞊ l ‖ pannas : s ꞊ c ⪕ · | uinaria

lxxu | m.rtaria · ꞊ ꞊   c | catilus iii̅. | [c]a-

10   tilus · [‖ [ca]tilu · [

5. s ꞊ c Hermet   6. ccu Hermet ed.1, Loth;
c ⪕ ego, Oxé   9, 10, 11. No space before us (or u[s);
not ux Loth; and it is not likely that we should read
catil us

La Graufesenque

117 (H.41)

      (a) of modesti

      (b)]arasidi · [|].· duca parasidi · [|

].θθilos parasidi ...mccc[|].lbus mor · uχs cl

     1. Too damaged for certainty; Hermet, Oxé, Loth made no attempt to read it   3. meddilos Hermet, Loth 4. morr Loth (wrongly)

118 (H.26)

      ]. = = luχto[| ... |] · s[|].= =

5   c[|]ri s = lu[||] · s c[|]t[| c]ela-

10   dos · [|] panias ccl[|] . = = [||]

    albanos · [|] panias [

     "Lost" in 1929; Hermet had found it again before 1934.   1. buxe Hermet, Loth, Thurneysen; buxe (?) Oxé; but cf. 121 An puxi? auxi? ruxi? luχtos?   A line appears to be missing between 1 and 2, and (my]t[ ) after 6   8. đ (not d Hermet) is quite clear

119 (H.43; CIL 13.10017,47)

      (a) .iuiici

313

La Graufesenque

119 ctd.

       (b)]ṇus incepit naṇius i..[|]os s ⚌

    ccl ⚌ ⚌ đcc]pannas s ⚌ $\overline{\text{iii}}$] $\overline{\text{iiii}}$ cc |

5   ]es ccc ‖] ..ū đ |] . ī đ |]s · cccc sext

    ccl bisexti l[|]tem acetabli[

        Long since lost, see note to 122; Déchelette,
Vases ornés I p.86, fig.62. The reading of (a) is altogether conjectural   1. an]rus ?   an naṇeus (or
naṇitus?)? ibo[?   Or pan[?   2. đ (not d Hermet,
Loth)   5. pedal]es Hermet ed.2   6. u or u? or s?
7. i or i?   8. Not bissexti Hermet, Loth (but see
Hermet p.306, and his plate)   Not ccc Hermet, Loth;
but cccc   9. accitabli Hermet ed.1, accetabli ed.2,
acetabula Loth

120 (H.27)

      (a) of germaṇ

      (b) 1.   ċ[| aċ[| circos · a[

          ii.   ]tos |]iii · ∿ ∿ ccl

         iii.   ṣ[| uinari · ccc | acitabli ·

  strogia · đ | panias · đxl

         iv.   coros · paroxe · ∿ ∿ dccl·

         v.   malciu catili cđxlu ·

      (c) 1.   ca[|

         ii.   alba[| panias · [

         iii.   siluinoṣ[| pan.[| mor[|

5 licu | pan[‖ .[

La Graufesenque

(121 ctd.)

Fragment of a large flat plate; arranged in
two columns (b and c respectively)   iii 2. lenari
Hermet ed.1, uinari ed.2; either is possible   The s
in line 1 is simply a straight upright   (c) i stands
opposite (b) ii 2; ii opposite (b) iv; iii 2 opposite
(b) v 2 iii;5. par[Oxé

121 (H.28)

    catilos · | paroxed · prina · puxi[|

   iuliani · đcxl | ciupalini · cđx[| catilos ·

5   prin[‖ paroxe · đcl[| paroxe · [|]aroxe[

A mere fragment   1. s a straight upright;
catilos ego; carilos Hermet, Loth, Oxé; r (for t)
appears to be an error   2. brina Oxé and buxi id.
If prina, then puxi (not buxi or auxi) must be read
The first letter is not l, unless miswritten; uxi is
very clear in the original   5. an carilos ? brin Oxé;
an prini (or arini)?   Here (and in line 2) b or p
very much like a   So (line 4) "on peut lire cuiba-
lini" Hermet, as Oxé does   Cf. 118 and 110 II above

122 (H.42; CIL 13.10016,7)

    ]nis tuθ[|]s catinos |]s rostrat[|]s

5   tisenar[|].enius r[‖]seno[

Now lost; sketch in Hermet ed.2, CIL l.c.;

La Graufesenque

Déchelette, Vases ornés I 86, fig. 61; Mém. Soc. Aveyron
13, 1881-86, 200; BSAF 1882, 298; RA 3, 1904, 75.   4.
]sti senar Hermet ed.1, Loth;   ]s tisenar Hermet ed.2

123 (H.29)

    I. (i)]catili[

        (ii) froncu | mortari · s = c[| mortari ≡≡≡

           ccc[| pedali · l

  II.(iii)]ntu · |]abli · ∿∿ dc

      (iv) catilo · [| paroxe[|]arox[

      (i) broken at top   (ii) 1. sic (not frontu,
or eroncu); but frontu (Thurneysen) is a likely emendation, notwithstanding the potter's name Fronicus (?)
Hermet, La Graufesenque 1.203   (iii) 1.]ciu (sc.
Malcius?) Hermet, Loth, Oxé; an Fro]ntu ?   2. sc.
acit]abli   (iv) 1. Not carilo Hermet, Loth, Oxé

124 (H.25)

    I. summa uxedia $\overline{\text{xxxiiiidxxu}}$[

    II. $\overline{\text{xxxiiiidcxxu}}$[

    A small fragment; I and II on different sides.
uxedia is below summa, but must be read with it.   In II
(not shown in Hermet's plate) Ð đ, in I d.   At end
of II possibly cxxx[, more likely cxxu[

La Graufesenque

125 (H.31)

      ]sidanus[|]lli bipros ◠[|]..ni

= = cccl

      A mere fragment.   1.]donus[Hermet ed.1,
]donus[or]danus[ed.2 (after Loth]danvs[ ), but I
saw]sidanus very clearly   2. dupros[or bipros[,
but not bitros[(Hermet ed.2), possibly dipros[(dep-
ros[?), most likely bipros

126 (H.32)

5   tu[| com[| et[| eti[| ma[‖ ma[

ma[| ma[| .[

      A mere fragment.   2. cor(nutus) Oxé, com[
Hermet, ego

127 (H.33)

      ] = = īu[? |]rtari · ccc |]īīidclxx

      A mere fragment. 1. Hermet, Loth have ū[,
but I saw iu[(presumably īu[ )

317

La Graufesenque

128 (H.34)

    I.   (i)]aci̠[? |] ∾ cc ca[|] ∾ [

          (ii)]t̠inos[|]nari ccc

    II. fr̠[ ]pa[

        An irregular fragment. (i) 1. an acc ?
Not occ (Loth), or go (Hermet)   2. ca[or ac[or
m[??   Column II: fr in same line as]nari (not as
]tinos Loth, Hermet), but I think it was part of a
separate column

129 (H.37)

          fuscus[| malcio · | eti can̠[| felix · ca̠[|

  5   momo · ca[‖ eti uinar[| eti · acet[| cosoius

 10   par c[| lousius par đ[| cornutus · par đc̠[‖

        uacaca par[

        Belongs to A. Carlshausen (Millau), not seen
by me. 2. cat[Oxé   8. ∾ [Oxé   c[Hermet,
ego

La Graufesenque

130 (H.36)

    (a) Germani of

    (b) aricani luritus | ris tecuan · boebo |

tidrus trianis

    Cf. REA 24, 1922, 250. The text was engraved before firing; this is exceptional, and may have some bearing on the interpretation.

    R. Thurneysen in ZfCPh 15, 1925, 379-83 reads tecuanboebo, though he interprets this as tecuanbo ebo (two words), something like "die Lehmarbeiter haben vor diesen (eben vergangenen) tecuan's geliefert (und zwar alle) drei Drittelschaften (etwa Knappschaften)." The reading is clear and certain, except in (b) 3 tidres (Thurneysen); not tudus, for this is no potter's account

131 (H.35)

    trit | sennilo | tuei

    On the base (underside) of the foot of the vase. All but illegible in line 3 (not tuθ, for this is no potter's account).

Note xviii

    Two bowls from La Graufesenque, apparently with the graffito φυρ on the outside, are recorded by A. W. Frothingham, Sigillate Pottery of the Roman Empire, New York, 1937, p.29 no.42.

Potters' Names of La Graufesenque

132

Potters of La Graufesenque, A.D. 20-90
(cf. 88 Remark, above)

Of the names of potters who worked at La Graufesenque (including some who are named in the graffiti above)
the following are selected for their linguistic interest
from the lists assembled by Hermet 1, 201-288, Oxé B.J.
140-141, 1936, 380-94. A complete catalogue of materials
from La Graufesenque is announced as in preparation by
Doranlo.

Abitus?	Aruernicus	Bit[illus?]
Acuitanus (for -qu-)	Attianus	Bollus
Aetus (L-?)	Attillus	Butiro (-uro)
Afer (-p-)	Attius	Bitrio, -iu (P-)
Agedillus	Auiaricus	See JRS 20,
Ainus?	Auitus	1930, 71-77
Albanus	Aullus (P-)	Cabiatus
Albinus	Auus	Cabuca?
Allus (G-)		Cacabus
Alrus (-bus)	Baccinus	Cailu(u)s
Andecarus?	Bacilus	Caldonus
Andillus	Bassenus (P-?)	Caldus?
Aper	Bassilus	Caluinus
Aquileus?	Bassus	Calus, -uus
Aquitanus	Bilicatus	Camius?
Ardacus	Bio	Canrucatus
Ardanus	Biracillus	Cantianus?

Potters' Names of La Graufesenque

Laetus

Lascus?
  (Masclus?)

Lasimappidus

?Legitumus (-c-)

Libertus

Libnus

Liciniana

Licinus

Licnus (-g-)

Logirnus

Lucanus

Lucceius

Lucianus

Lupus

Mabio (L-?)

Maccarus

Mac(c)ius?

Macer

Macrinus

Macus

Maesa

Malcio

Mammaca?

Manduilus

Manertus

Maponius

Marinus

Marosus?

Marsus

Martio, -ius

Masclus

Masculus

Maso

Masuetus

Matugenus

Mercator

Meddil(l)us (-θ-)

Melain

Melatio (Hermet
  1.275 "honey,"
  cf. Ceruesa
  "beer")

Melo, -us

Milo(n)

Mommo (-u)

Mont[

Muranus

Murus (-rr-)

Namus

Ne(c)qures?

Nicia, -ius?

Osbimanus

Patr[

Pass(i)enus

Paullus

Perrus

Picus?

Pol(l)io, -ius

Ponteius

Pontinus

Pontus

Potitus

Priamus

Pricenus

Primicus

Primulus

Primus

Priscinus

Pudens, Pudinis
  (RA 16,1940,
  146)

Pugnus

Potters' Names of La Graufesenque

Quintus

Qutus?

Regenus

Riomarus

Ritomarus?

Rogatus

Ronicus

Roppus

Ruf(f)us

Rufinus

Rusticus

Rutaenus

Sabinus

Saciro

Salarius Aptus?

Saluetus?

Saluianus

Samo (D-?)

Santonus

Saricus? -nus?

Sarra (D-); cf.
  Note xxvii

Sarrut(us)

Sasmonos

Satto (cf. RA 7,
  1936,126-28)

Scotnus?

Scot(t)ius

Senecio

Senicio

Senilis

Senis

Seno

Sentrus

Serro, -us

Seχ[tus]

Silanus?

Siluanus

Siluinus

Silius

Stabilio

Strobili

Suarad[

Suerius

Sulpicius

Sulma?

Sumi?

Surrius

Tetius

Tet(t)us?

Tertius

Tfse? (CA 5,
  211-12)

Tusso?

Vanderio

Vapus?

Vapuso

Varra?

Vassilus

Vebrus

Vegenus (-c-)

Vegetus

Viranus?

Virt(h)us

Voluso?

Votornus

Vrap(p)us

Vrsus

Vruoed?

323

La Graufesenque

Note xix

(a) A text reported by Cérès (cf. p.276 above), long since lost, is said to have had (CIL 13.10010, 2893n; AcS 3.780)

ss diu | auote

For auot see Note xi.

(b) The "names" commonly read as Vrituarus and Vriu(s) Aruernicus respectively may actually contain

uritu 'fecit'

(sc. Arus, Aruernicus), for which see the Glossary. See also RA 26, 1927, 165.249 (a cachet d'oculiste with urit[?) from Beaumont (Puy-de-Dôme).

(c) "Chaton de bague en fer, surmonté d'une agathe onyx. Trouvé tout récemment sur le plateau de Gergovia;" Mioche, Ann. scientif. de l'Auvergne 28, 1855, 482 (CIL 13.10024, 301), appears to read

uiriou

But cf. perhaps ieuru, ειωρου (e.g. 57, 161)?

Banassac

133

Graffito (cursive) "sur un petit pot" discovered
about 1872 at Banassac (Lozère, Bannaciaco num. Merov.,
AcS s.v.; on the Lozère see the Répertoire archéologique
du dép. de la Lozère by M. Balmelle, Montpellier, 1937,
cf. REA 39, 1937, 257); said to be preserved at Saint-
Germain-en-Laye, it could not be found when I sought it
there in 1929. Banassac stands at the confluence of the
Lot and the Urugne, c. 35 m. north of Millau. First
published by H. de Villefosse, BSAF 1872, 141-44; e̱ is ‖ ,
as usual.

neddamon | delgu linot

But linot is otherwise unknown; the correct reading, I suspect, is auot (see Note xi).

Do. 44; CIL 13.10016, 13

134   Potters of Banassac, A.D. 30-100
(cf. 88 Remark, above)

Biragillus (-c-)	Criciro (Cre-, for Crucuro?)	Iabus (Ta-?)
Coccillus		Maesus
	Dometos, Domitus	
Cocus		Manus?
	Eruipinus	
Comicato		Perrus (cf. gl.158)
	Geamil(l)us (for Gia-)	Suarad[

Miscellaneous Graffiti

Remark:

    (i) On the title

gutuater

which appears in the Latin inscc.   CIL 13.1577 (Le Puy
en Velay) cf. 2585, 11225-26, see the gloss 178.

Attention may be called also to these texts:

    (ii) Lezoux (CIL 13.10016,14)

magio nonumanu | uutlobilicedoni

which appears to show Keltic features (dat. sg. -u;
uutlo?)

    (iii) Banassac (10012, 7 a-b)

ceruesar[ius

Cf. gloss 178

    (iv) Montans (10012,18)

        (a)   ]louolles · aenea(e) som II alloboesio[rum

326

Miscellaneous Graffiti

(iv) ctd.

 (b)]que nouissimus heres ui[

 (c)]agrandisom[

Cf. AcS 3.570; RC 3, 1876-78, 315: Déchelette Vases ornés 1, 133-35 takes it as a writing exercise.

(v) On a statuette (10015, 89)

 is por(r)on istillu

(vi) From Lezoux (10017, 65)

 ]t sole · se solsoliasebso[

(vii) From Molles, Allier (10017, 66)

 op · letedosts · o

In both of these last (vi, vii) I have taken ⤫ as the interpunct (cf. 147 below); the o is merely ⌒ .

Miscellaneous Graffiti

(viii) Abecedaria, more or less incomplete, from Martres-de-Veyres (A-Q), Vichy (A-F, then M repeated eight times), Moulins (A-S), Varenne-sur-Allier (A-D) see CIL 13.10016, 2; 10017, 67; Déchelette Vases ornés 1, 134-35. Peculiar is CIL 13.10017, 68 (of unknown provenance)

$$\wedge\, \wedge\ B\ D\ \Phi\ D\ ||\ ||\ X\ Q\ Q\ S\ X$$

with variant forms of certain letters. The alphabet of Martres-de-Veyres (10016, 2) is preceded by the text:

draucus fecit et[   ]Mageni (sc. filio)

Note xx

H. de Villefosse reported in BA 1917, 81-84 (cf. REA 20, 1918, 126), a sherd with an insc. in Greek alphabet, discovered in 1891 at Chaysieu (Loire), which he claimed as "un graffite gaulois." It appears to read

$$\eta\, \upsilon\, \sigma\, \upsilon\, \iota\, [$$

the first letter being taken as η rather than h. The last is too imperfect to be certainly transcribed; de Villefosse suggested a possible Χ, which his photograph does not support at all, and would compare ἥσυχος , - ιος which is not Gaulish, and would also imply a blundering

Lezoux

transposition in the original. For the Greek alphabet
elsewhere in Aquitania, cf. 145 below.

ᵤ   If we read ἡυσουᴸ [, compare perhaps the gloss
υσσος (158 below, s.v. coccolobis) and the curious
graffito CIL 13.10016, 44 (Note xxxvi, Remark).

135   Inscription of Lezoux

Engraved on the back of a stone statue of Mercury

(with the regulation winged hat and money-bag), c. 2.5

feet across the shoulders and tall in proportion, cf.

Pliny 34.45; letters c. 4 inches high (except o 3.5 in.);

discovered at Lezoux (Puy-de-Dôme) in 1891, see BSAF

1891, 393 (cf. 1901, 102), now in the Musée des Antiqui-

tés nationales (Saint-Germain-en-Laye, no. 46273; see

Reinach Catalogue illustré 1, 213-15; cf. Espérandieu

Receuil de Têtes antiques 83, pl. 105), seen by me in

August 1929. Faint, and hard to read:

apr[onios │ ieu[ru · s]o[sin │ esum[aro

Of the letters enclosed in square brackets there

are only the merest traces; the letters not so enclosed

can with difficulty be made out; the rest, pace Rhys

Lezoux

and Jullian, is pure conjecture. In line 3, hardly
esiom[(?)

    Do. 42; CIL 13.1514 add.; Grenier ap. Frank 3.528-
28 (with n.63), 548

Note xxi

    There is nothing in this (fragmentary?) stamp of
Lezoux, two specimens of which are known, to demonstrate
its supposed Keltic character. The uncertainty of the
reading of line 3 (probably cob[n]erte, for -ti?) leaves
in complete doubt the one word (toberte?) which was supposed to prove the point, and the alleged mouno (rather
m[anu ouno?), if dat. sg. masc., would be Latin (-o),
not Gaulish (-u), while no one has yet claimed of(f)icina
as Keltic.

    calia · ue | biusiuniti | cob[n]erte · m |
    ouno ∴ caleni   oficina

    CIL 13.10012,19

330

Lezoux

(Note xxi ctd.)

The texts are, then:

(a) A fragment of a red-varnished vase (terra sigillata), acquired for the Musée d'Annecy (inventory no.
10057) with other materials excavated between 1879 and
1882 at Les Fins d'Annecy, see C. Marteau and M. Le Roux
"Boutae" (Annecy, 1913), 91 (cf. 84–90), and Catalogue
descriptive 1896, 14–15 (cf. 116, fig.5), viz. a bronze
of Nîmes (Augustus, Agrippa) and other coins (Augustus,
Vespasian, Hadrian) which afford useful indications of
date.   The Annecy fragment had actually only part of the
text, thus 2-6]iti |]e · m |]uno |]alen. ‖ oficina,
apparently with the leaf-shaped punct at the end of line
5 (not line 4, unless it is out of line); seen by me
July 1929.

(b) Found at Lezoux in or shortly before 1880 (see
Plicque, Congrès Archéologique de France 47, Arras 1880,
224–25), now at Saint-Germain-en-Laye (no. 1228/51880),
seen by me in August 1929.   In both (a) and (b) the writing, being imprinted from a left-to-right original, is
reversed; Rhys' "facsimile" (Additions Plate 9.18) is
from a plaster cast, in which the left-to-right arrangement is restored.   Letters about .375 in. high.

        e| is ‖ , and hence some read uii at the end of line
1 (ue | bius); in line 2 the reading is iuniti, not
nniti or a(n)niti.   In line 3 the first letter is ⅄
which I think must be a badly-formed c, not x or i or
(Thurneysen) t; elsewhere t is ⊤ .   Perhaps a punct is
lost after s in line 2, or it may have been so carelessly made as to appear as i.   The punct at the end of
line 4 (here given as ∴) is actually the familiar leaf.
In line 5 all that now remains is o[at the beginning.

        Do. 43, 43 bis.   Cf. Déchelette Vases Ornés 1,
1904, 217-18, figures 128, 129; Thurneysen ZfCPh 14,
1923, 10.

331

Lezoux

Note xxi bis

    (a) Déchelette op. cit., 218 (fig. 130) gives yet
another fragment of a vase found at Lezoux, an incomplete graffito, which might be either Gaulish or Latin:

]i[|]toca[|]uoga[

    (b) To these I add, from BA 1932-33 [1936], 167
(Lezoux)

Dontio   feci

for comparison with the personal and divine names Dunzio
or Dunsio (see 86, 87); and

    (c) From RA 5, 1935, 107 (Lezoux), said to be a
dedication, reading

rufius   uangroni   (?)

for comparison with uang-a (see 220).

Lezoux

Potters of Lezoux, A.D. 40-170
                  (see 88 Remark, above)

        The manufactory was at its height ca. 75-120 (cf.
Grenier in Frank 3.549; Doranlo REA 42, 1940, 6.6-20.

?Abalanis	Alexanus	Asiaticus
?Abalus	Aliatus	Ateclos
?Acapus	Al(l)ius	Ateius
Acaunus	Alpinius	Atepomarus
Acer	Amato	Atilianus
Acurio	Am(m)ius	Atrucianus
Acutinus	Anaillus	Attianus
Acutus	Andegenus	Attillus
Adiectus	Anicius	At(t)inus
Aduocisus	Annius	Attius
Aelius, Ailus	Antistii (pl.)	Aucella
Aestiuus	Anunus	Aucurinus
Aetaxus	Aper	Aufus
Agedillus	Apolauster	Auitus
Alaucus	Arcanus	Aunatus
Albinus	Ardacus	Aunus
Albucianus	Aricus	Aurelus
Albucius	Arncus	Austrus
Albus	Ar(r)o	

Lezoux

Baccatus (Bucc-)	Buccula	Capellio, -ius
Balbinus	Bucura	Capitu
Banoluccus	Burdo	Carantinus
Banuillus	Butrio	Cara(n)tedo
Banuus	Buturo	Caratillus
Bassus	Butturrus	Caratus
Belenicus		Carbo (?)
Belinus	Cabusa	Carrucalus
Bel(l)iniccus	Cacasus	Carus 10014.2
Belsa Aruernicus	Cadgatus	Carussa
Bigatus	Caillus	Casittus
Billicedo	Calaua	Cassignetus
Birrantus	Calendio	Cataseχtus
Birrus	Calenus	Catello
Bisrus	Caletinus	Catianus
Biturix	Caletus	Catillus
Boduocus	Caluus	Cato
Bonox(s)us	Cambus	Cattio
Borillus (cf. Βορίλος AcS 3.911, 52)	Campanus	Catto
	Camulinus	Catullinus
Borio	Camulixus	Catullus
Briccus	Cantomallus	Catussa
Buccius	Cantoseno	Caupirra
Bucco	Capellianus	Cautus

Lezoux

Cedoni	Cocurus (-o)	Dagomarus
?Ceflicio	Comicato	Daminus
Celticus	Comprinnos	Dano
Celtus	Condollus	Dauius
Celsianus	Congius	Dec(i)mus
Cenillo	Coppuro	Dec(u)manus
Censorinus	Cosaχtis	Decuminus
Cerialis	Cosminus	Dester
Ceroticus	Cotius	Diogensis
Certus	Cottius	Diuicatus
Cestus	Cracissa	Diuicus
Cettus	Cracuna (-i)	Diuiχtus
Cetus	Criciro	Doccalus
Cigetoutus	Crispinus	Docilis
Cina	Cristinus	Domitus, -etus
Cinnamus	Crobiso	Donatus
Cintio	Cucalus	Donnaucus
Cintussa	Cuccillus	Dontio, Donti
Cirro, -us	Cudus	Doueccus, Doeccus
?Cnaius (Gnatius?)	Cunissa	Drusus
Cobnertus	Cunus	?Duratus, Dura (-u)
Cocatusus	Curmillus	Duppius
Cocillus		
Cocisus	Dagodubnus	Ecusius

335

Lezoux

Eluillus (for H-)	Granio, -ius (C-)	Lollius
Eppillus		Lottius
Ericus	Ic[	Lotto
Esuateros	Illiomarus	Lucinus
	Illixo	Luppa
Fabus	Immunus	Lusa
Ferronius	Indercillus	
Fortis	Iouis	Maccalus
	Irnus	Maccirra
Gabrinus	Isteino	Maccus, -ius
Gemenus (C-)	Iuliccus	Maceratus
Geminus	Iullicus	Macerianus
Genetius	Iullinus	Macrianus
Genetlus	Iu(u)enis	Macrinus
Genitor		Macro
Genius	Laytucissa (Last-)	Magio
Gess(i)us	Lalianus	Maior
Giamillus	Lal(l)us	Malledo
Gio	Lamatutus (-toutus?)	Malliacus
Gippus		Malluro
Giro	Lartius	Mallurus
Gluppius (G. Luppius?)	Liltanus	Mallus
	?Littera	Mammius
Graecus	Litugenus (-cenus 10006.44)	Ma(n)suetus
Granianus		

336

Lezoux

Mapillus	Mettus (?)	Opillus
Marcellinus	Miricanus	Oppulo
Marcellus	Momilus	Ortus
Marianus	Montanus	Osbimanus
Maritumus	Morinus	Ouidius
Martianus	Mossius	
Mascellio	Moxillus	Pacatus
?Masclus	Moxius	Pallio
Mascuillus	Moχsius	Pateratus
Maternianus	Mulinus	Paterclinus
Materninus	Muχtullus	Paterclos (-us)
Maternus		Paternulus
Matrinus	Namilianus	Paternus
Mattius	Nattus	Patna
Maturus	(Aruernicus)	Patto
Maximinus	Nobilianus	Pauitus
Maximus	Nonu	Paullinus
Meddirius	Norus	Peculiaris
Melledo	Nudinus	Pentilius
Mentus	Numidus	Petrecus
Mercianus	Nundinus	Pinna
Mercussa	Nunnus	Pistillus
Mesillus		Piturix (B-)
Mettius	Ocarus (-o)	Potitianus
	Ollognus (-cn-)	

Lezoux

Pottacus

Primanus

Primulus

Priscianus

Priscillus

Pugn[

Putriu

Ramus

Ranto?

Redillus

Renatus

Regalis

Reginus

Regulinus

Regulus

Rentus

Reus (or Rhus?)

Ripanus

Rippinus

Ritogenus

Roppus

Roselus?

Rottalus

Rullinus

Rutenus

Sabinianus

Sacer

Sacilantro

Sacirapo

Saciro, -us

Saco (for Sacco)

Sacrantius

Sacrapus (-o)

Sacremius

Sacrillus

Sacro

Sacroticus

Sacrotus

Sacrouirus

Saluinus

Samillus

Samogenus

Sanctianus

Saniluus

Santianus

Sanuillus

Saturninus

Saxamus

Sciuli (?) 10010.
  1351, but see
  BA 1941-2 [1944]
  100

Scoplus

Scottus

Scotus

Secundinus

Securus

Sedatianus

Sedatus

Senex

Senila

Senilis

Seniserus

Sennius

Seruilis

Seruilio

Sernus

Sestus

Seuerianus

Seuerinus

Seu(u)o

Sileus

338

Lezoux

Siluinus	Tauricus	Vasilius
Siluius	Taurinus	Vatus?
Sinturo	Taurus	Vegetus
Sissus	Teddillus	Velox
Siticula	Tetturo	Verecundus
Solinus	Tintirio	Venermidus (sic, read Vernemidus?)
Sorinus	Titticus	
Sosimus	Tittius	Ver(i)anus
Suobnedo	Tituro	Veriugus
Suobnillus	Titurus	Verticissa
Suobnus	Titus	Vespo
Surburo	Titusius	Viamos
Surdillus	Toca? (10010.20)	Virtecissa (Ve-)
Surdus	Togosa	Viuus
Surillus	Toutos	Vllinus
Susus	Toutus	Voga[(10012.20)
	Tritus	Vogenus
		Vrbilus
Talussa		Vridaus
Tasgillus	Vagiro	Vxopillus
Taurianus	Vagirus	Vxsellus

339

Inscriptions with auot

Remark 1

The form

auot

or its variants (see Note xi) appears frequently at various sites in Aquitania, on vases, terracottas, and andirons, viz.:

(a) Toulon-sur-Allier, near Moulins, where the names of the potters concerned (assigned by some authorities to Lezoux) are

Anailos

Ateano (not Atilano)

Sacrillos (Carati, gen. sg.)

CIL 13.10015,1 and 38 a-d. The text of 38(a) has auot form Sacrillos Carati, usually read form(as) or form(am).

(b) Lezoux itself (in addition to the four names above):

Durati(s)	Rutenus
Ericu	Tocos (-g-)
Flauus	Valenc

cf. CIL 13 iii (1), 1901, p.121.

Here note Dura auote (CIL 13.10010,831) beside

Inscriptions with auot

Dura f(ecit) ib. 830, and Dura iu (for ieuru?) ib. 833,
unless this is to be read Durucu (sc. auot).

(c) La Graufesenque (cf. Note xix, a)

Auctus

Rutenus

(d) Southern Gaul (see 139)

Cotoio

and perhaps also

C Anton[

assigned by some to Bourbon-Lancy (Lugdunensis), see
CIL 13.10010,136; 10015,10; together with (10010,870;
2864)

Euini

]ucoto

both assigned to Vichy. Also from Vichy comes an andiron with

Iulos auot

AcS 3.781, and from Clermont-Ferrand another, reading

Gauidus auot

BSAF 1910, 387.1 (cf. CIL 13, 10020.14 ?]ouidu auot).

Inscriptions with auot

Note, finally, the personal name (?) at Bourges

(e)   auoto

CIL 13.10010,2855c

See, in general, CIL 13 iii (1), 1901, p.121; iii
(2), 1906, p.465; Audollent REA 42, 1940, 553-59 (on
the andirons). For auot see Journal of Celtic Studies
1, 1949, 9-10.

Remark 2

Names on tile-stamps from Aquitania (cf. 205 below):

Anchi	Lenturius
Catulus	Lugra (La-?)
Euintac (?)	Mapilli (?)
Gem[	Merula (Cubus)
Hano (?)	Sisso
Iaeiui (?)	Tal(uppa?)
Iuli	Toutissa (m.)
Licinus (Licus?)	Tiaurle (?)

342

Potters of South Gaul

Remark 3

Five vases from Lezoux (CIL 13.10016,15) offer a
number of women's names, apparently compounded with
amica or ama, thus:

Amdamica	Tlota
Medlotama	Tlotamica
Medilotamica	Vertamaca
Mucta[	Vertamica
Simcera (Sinic-?)	

137

Potters of Lubié-La Palisse, A.D. 120-160
(see 88 Remark)

Aduocisus	Casurius	Martinus
Al(l)billus	Cintugenus	Miccio
Aricus	Corisillus	Sacero
Banuus	Lupinus	Viducos, -us
Caletus	Mainacnus (-g-)	

Potters of South Gaul

138

Potters of Vichy, the Roman Aquae Calidae
A.D. 80-130

Acaunissa	Cocceius	Marillus?
Atimetus	Docnius	Marinianus
Cadilo	Euinus (Euini auotti)	Medetus
Cambus		Ociuus
Canaus	Gemellinus	Opiucnus (for Op[p]ianicnus?)
Canauus	Iateus	
Carassounus	Ioenalis	Priscinus
Cartus	Luciolus	Rutaius
	Macirus	Varucius

139
Other names of Potters known to have
worked in "South Gaul" (i.e. Aquitania),
sites not identified (cf. 88 Remark)

Abianus	Adinus	Alatus
Abus	?Adnadgenus	Albanus
Acanthus	Agedus	Albinianus
Acastus	Agrillus	Albinus
Acodillus	Aidacus	Al(l)ius
Acutillus	Ainibinus (E-)	Anextia

344

Potters of South Gaul

Angius	Biga	Cernus
Anteros	Billicuro	Chrestus
Apias	Billicus	Clarus
Aricus	Bissunus	Clemens
Arinus	Blaesus	Coius
Armandus	Buccillus	Comos
Arnus		Conatus
Aro	Cabitanus	Constic[
Artius	Cabuca	Cotto
Aruernicus	Cadmus	Crescens
Aruus	Cadurcus	Curius
Attis	Caleda	
Atuius	Callo	Daccus
Atxixus	Ca(n)rucatus (-g-)	Diocarus
Aucius	Cantirrus	Dodo
Audo	Capito (-us)	Donatus
Auetus	Capius	
Aufinus (R-?)	Carbo	Ebenus
Auilius	Carinus	Emia (or Emid[ )
Auitanus	Castrus	Enibinus
	Catenus	Epidius
Baccinus	Catillus	Errimus
Baccos	Catlus	Ertius
Bassinus	Cennatus	Esuac[

345

Potters of South Gaul

Esumus	Louius	Ocellus
Esu[	Lucillus	Oclatus
Euanus	Lucius	
Eust[		Paestor
	Mabio	Paternus
Fabio, -ius	Maio	Pilemus
Felicissa	Mars(s)us	Piper
Fontus (Foi[?)	Mario, -ius	Pleueus
	Masclinus	Pompeius
Garutius	Maximus, -umus	Pupus
Gemma	Maxmos (RA 5, 1935, 227)	
Gracchus	Meuus	Qaris (for Carissimus?)
Habius	Miccio	Quadus
	Mimo	Quaris (Isae? or L. Saf.?)
	Mirus	
Ianus	Motus	
Idmeius	Murus	Rasinus
Iluus		Rigenus
Iothur		Rispus
[?Isae (v.Saf)]	Naeuius	Ronicus
	Nalis	
Iuratus	Natomus	Roppus
	Nerus	Rosus
Labiatus	Nigrinus	Rutus
Laurus	Nitor	

Potters of South Gaul

Sabianus	Tasco	Verus
Sacirius	Triarius	Vicio
Saf v. Qaris	Tulus	Villio, Villo
Samia		Vimmus
Samilus	Vaisenus	Vin(n)ius
Satos?	Valis	Virecus
Sauus	Valuco	Virtus
Scottus (Cotus?)	Vanus	Vitlus
Semper	Varius	Vitulus
Seno	Varus	Vlatugnus
?Senome	Vassalus	Vlicus
Suarus	Vassenus	Volus
	Vassilius	Vrappus
Tabus	Vaxtius	Vruoed
Talis	Venus	Vtilis
Tanda	Verius	
Tanisius	Vertougus	Xantus

140
Names of Potters, not known to have
worked, but found, in Aquitania (cf. 88 Remark);
some of the following items are from BA 1941-42
[1944] 477-491.

Abreχta	Axus	Cunetus
Adgenus?		
Aegitus	Baciro	Demioncus
Agilis	Baquili?	Diauχsus
Ainicesi	Bollucus	Dimiono (?)
Aius	Burus	Dioratus
?Alanus		Dittanus
Alex[	Cabiatus	Don(i)us
?Alfo	Camulirilis (-gis)	Drutalus
Amonus	Carix (-ss-?)	Duciauus
Amuta	Cenicus?	Ducius
?Anor	Ceno	Ducri
Anullus	Cintusmus	Duocis?
Anutalis	Cintutus	
Ascla (?)	Cocasus	Egenus (-i-)
?Asdesmios	Combara?	Egualarus?
Asus	Com(m)o	Elussiu
Ateinus	Comornus	Ertius (for
Ateius?	Conetodus	T]er-?)
Atepus	Coticorix	
		Frontu
Atersus	Crixus	

348

Names of Potters found in Aquitania

Ibertus	Nicret[	Talussanus
Iccalus		Tanratus
Idmeuis	Ogarius	Tetio
Iperus?	Olognato?	Togidus
Itius	Olecsissus?	Tongus
Iurus		Toutissa (m.)
	Panic[	Tretios
Lasiuca (-st-)	Pottinus	Triccos
Lemo	Protis	Turrino
Lita		
Littus	Ritminus	Vatus
Losorus	Rumus?	Varucius
Luscilia		Vaulianus
	Sana	Vcatus
Macellus	Scabus	Vicanus
Maccirilla	Sceus?	Vindus
Mammillius	Senonius	Vssomarus
Massillus	Solanus	
Meda		

Remark

    At Saint Bonnet we have (CIL 13.10010,566)

               Cintu ieru

usually read as one word; perhaps for ie(u)ru "fecit"?

Néris-les-Bains

141
    Inscription of Néris-les-Bains (Allier)

Discovered in 1836, but not published until 1877,
see R. Mowat CRAcInscBL 5, 1877, 267 (cf. 256); id. RA
35, 1878, 94-108 (cf. 188-89) and BSAF 1887, 265-66;
placed in the Musée de Cluny in 1860, seen there by me
in 1929, inventory no.19262.

A block of stone 12.5 in. by 11.5 in. by 6.5 in.;

the insc., engraved in a panel 9.75 in. by 9.5 in., is

much weathered, letters 1 in. high (except o, .5 in.);

open r and b.

        braᵗronos | nantonicn | epaḍate͡xto | rigi ·
5   leucullo | suiorebe · logi ‖ toṵ

The t and e of lines 1, 3 are faint, but certain;

in line 6, however, the reading is very doubtful (ioe

is possible, and the last letter has also been read k);

the punct in line 5 may be accidental.

    Do. 48; CIL 13.1388 (with addendum); Catalogue
général, Musée des Thermes et de l'Hotel de Cluny, vol.
1, Paris 1922, p.95, no.520

Inscription of Néris-les-Bains

Remark

CIL 13, 1378 (cf. 1376-77, 1132, 11151; and see
also BSAF 1915, 107-14) gives us diribitoria (n. plu.),
on which see now my paper in Die Sprache vol.1, 1949
(Havers Festschrift), 124.   See also Note xxvii Remark
(below).

Note xxii

The letters engraved on "le nodule en schiste noir"
discovered at Sorbier near Montcombroux (Allier), repeated by Jullian REA 30, 1928, 66 (cf. 31, 1929, 236)
from Bull. Soc. préhistorique fr. 14, 1917, 512 fig. 2,
may be, as Jullian suggests, merely magical; but their
resemblance to Iberian alphabetic symbols (read ustigi?)
is striking.   The object itself appears to me to be an
unfinished spindle-whorl (cf. 147 below).

Inscriptions now at Guéret

The three following inscc., partly Keltic in some
of their features, are now at Guéret (Creuse) in the
museum of the Soc. des Sciences naturelles et archéologiques de la Creuse, where I saw them in 1929.

142

Roughly engraved on a block of granite discovered
in 1864 at Sazeirat near Marsac (Creuse), inventory no.
C 2 in the Museum at Guéret; 26.5 in. by .5 in. by 12
(at left) to 10 (at right) in.; broken at the corners,
but complete, only one letter being badly damaged;
letters lightly incised, 2 in. (u in line 2) to 2.5 or
3 in. (m in line 3) high. No puncts except in line 3,
where u s l m may have been added later, thus giving a
mixed appearance to a text which otherwise would pass
as Gaulish.

sacer peroco̧ | ieuru | duori|co · u·s·l·m

Do. 41; CIL 13.1452 (with older references) and
Addendum; cf. RA 13, 1866, 214-16 (anonymous, but evidently by A. Pictet); Pictet RA 15, 1867, 397

Inscriptions at Guéret

143

A long slab of granite, perhaps part of the lid of
a sarcophagus, now 51.25 in. by 14 in. by 2.5 in.,
broken all round, and the insc. cut short on right;
letters 2 in. (o) to 3.5 in. (b, l) in height.

bodocenus file · brot[

c has the form [(not l)

CIL 13.11163a (after Rhys, Proc. Brit. Acad., vol.
2, 1905-06, p.316).   Provenance not recorded.

Note xxiii

Another block of granite, now broken into two
pieces, 31 in. by 15.5 in. by 16 in.; letters 3 in. (m)
or 2.5 in. (o, d) in height. Presumably discovered in
or near Guéret, but I have been unable to find any other
record of it. The single line of text, broken in the
middle, may be the last line of a larger insc.

]modenac[

a is simply ∧ ; beneath the writing, on left, is an
upright cross (+ 4 by 5 in.).

HSCP 44, 1933, 231

Graffito of Séraucourt

144

Graffito of Séraucourt (Bourges)

Written in a spiral arrangement around the neck of
an urn of black ware, discovered in 1848 at Séraucourt,
Bourges (Cher), see A. de Longpérier, RA 6, 1849, 554-
56; reported by Buhot de Kersers, Mém. de la Soc. des
Ant. du Centre 4, 1870-72 [1873], p.175.72 as being in
a private collection at Nantes, it is said subsequently
to have passed to the museum at Saint-Germain-en-Laye,
but it could not be found there when I enquired for it
in 1929. Facsimile, Lenormant Rev. des Soc. Savantes
4, 1858, 565.

buscillasosiolegasitinalixiemagalu

The usual reading, sosio legasit...magalu, is not
borne out by the facsimile of Lenormant, which reads
licasit and macalu.

Do. 47; CIL 13.10017,70

Inscriptions of Genouilly

There are two Gaulish inscc. of Genouilly (Cher),
both engraved on large monoliths (menhirs), one of them
tri-lingual. It is likely that they were engraved only
long after they had been set up as standing stones, for
writing was itself of far later date than the period in
which menhirs are supposed to have been erected in Gaul.
The stone is striated, and not easily engraved; in fact,
in the tri-lingual a fault runs through the block, along
which it has split into two pieces. Both were discovered
in 1894, and both are now in the museum of the Société
des Antiquaires at Bourges (inventory nos. 268, 269 respectively), seen by me in 1929; see Ch. de Laugardière
in its Mémoires 20, 1893-94 [1895], 1-16; BA 1894, pp.
xxiii, xli, 127-37, Pl.9.

145

62 in. by 21.5 in. by 6.5 in. The inscc. are (a)
and (b) merely two proper names, the first incomplete,
in Latin and Greek alphabet respectively; then (c) a
brief Greek inscription; and next, below the fracture,
(d) a Keltic insc. in Latin alphabet. The inscc. need
not have been added at the same date, for they are not
identical in meaning, but they seem to refer to members
of one and the same family, and I take (b) and (c) together as making one continuous text.

Inscriptions of Genouilly

(a)   ]os · uirillios

(b)   ]τος· ουιρίλλιο [(c)]ἀνέϙυνοσ|
        ἐπόει

(d)   eluontiu | íeuru · aneuno | oclicno ·
        luguri | aneunicno

(a) Letters 1.25 in. (o) to 1.75 in. tall, (b) 1 in.
(o) to 1.375 in., (c) 1 in. (o) to 1.75 in.   These
appear all three to have been engraved by the same cutter,
at the same time, but (c) is separated from (b) by a
wider space than (b) from (a).   On the other hand (d)
is almost certainly by a different mason; the letters
are 2.25 in. high in line 1, 2 in. in lines 2-4, except
o which is everywhere smaller (in line 1 it is 2 in., in
lines 2-4 it is 1.75 in. high).   Finials in the Latin
alphabet, i.e. (a) and (d).   Iota longa in íeuru.

In (b) the final σ may be wanting by accident;
(c) is faint, and ἀν and o (fourth letter) are all but
illegible; ε is Є.

The ll of (a) is apparently Ь ; in (c) the lines
of the letters appeared to me to have been cleaned or

356

Inscriptions of Genouilly

recut slightly in modern times, especially the finials.
Perhaps the joining together of l and i in oclicno is
recent, crowded as line 3 is.

Do. 45; CIL 13.1326 (with add.); CR Cong. Arch.
Bourges 1898 [1900], 160-64

146

50 in. by 19 in. (greatest width) by 5 in., broken
into two fragments, on the upper of which stands the
single line of text, letters 1.5 (o) to 1.75 in. high,

]ruoni:u[

Very faint letters, each formed by a series of
points—not continuous strokes. Before u a faint double
interpunct, and before it i (not t); but cf. CIL 13.
11131 (Bourges) d. rontu (or rontiu?) · m, with † (read
as t or ti)?

Do. 46, CIL 13.1325 (with add.).

Inscriptions of Genouilly
and vicinity

Note xxiv

(a) I can make little or nothing of the insc. CIL 13.1311, discovered at Bourges in 1873, "fortasse recens," and said to read

arad · m · | rasiam sit | omnia ue̦|situas | tansna

(Is nsna at the end a garbled u·s·l·m ?)

(b) The same remark applies to CIL 13.1327 (Lury, Cher), "haud dubie male lecta."

b   d   puy | me̦stroc

(c) As for CIL 13.11161, these four lines of doubtful letters, if not masons' marks, may conceal something articulate:

saλλ | ιλι.αν | ιϭει | κυο(?)

From Drévant (Cher).

(d) Puy-en-Velay, CIL 13.1577

gutuater

See Note xxix and gloss 178 below.

Inscription of Gièvres

147

Two lines of text on the bevelled edges of a thick circular piece of serpentine, with a hole through the middle, clearly a spindle-whorl. Discovered at Gièvres (Loir-et-Cher), first published by Bourgoin in Mém. de la Soc. des Sc. et Lettres de Loir-et-Cher 7, 1867, 175; cf. Bull. de la Soc. arch., scient., et litt. du Vendômais 11, 1872, 165, fig. no.1.

tionouimpiχ | morucin χ

This is commonly read pixtionouim/xmorucin (cf. AcS 2.1011), the symbol χ being transcribed as x (better χ?); but it is obviously intended to show where the beginning and end come in a continuous sequence of letters, and gives us at least one intelligible word if so interpreted, viz. uimpi.

Ever since its discovery this object, with which Note xxii above may be compared, has been described as an "amulet;" it is, nevertheless, identical in shape with the spindle-whorls of Lugdunensis (Note xxxi, 164) as a glance at the illustrations in Bulletin de la Société arch., sc., et littéraire du Vendômois 11, 1872, Pl.2 fig.2 (at p.102) and in BA 1914, p.214, will show. I conjecture that the correct reading may be moru cintiono uimpi. Cf. Language 25, 1949, pp. 388-391.

CIL 13.1324

Names of Aquitania Prima

As before, sources given in AcS are not, as a rule, repeated here; arabic numerals, without other indication of source, refer to CIL 13, viz. i (1899) 1189-1622 (pp. 158-220) with iv (1916) 11082-11170 (pp.12-21), with ii 2 (1907) 8861-8887 and 8903-8923. Corrections (de Ricci) REA 4, 1902, 213-16.

148   Ethnic and Local Names

?Abrianeco num. AcS 3.474 is dubious (cf. AcS 1.9, 167; and 212 infr.) Note also Abrincatui (179), Obrincas (221), Obrege (148), but hardly Brancus (83) or branca (220)

Acitodunum modern Ahun

?Adedunum (cf. divine names)

Albeta fl. (ASS) Aubois

Albigi Rav. -ensis Not. Gal., Greg. Tur.; Albi[(?) 1121-23 add.; now Albi

Alerta

?Alyssontes RA 16, 1940, 136 (Alièzes)

Alsone uicaria

?Ambiuareti AcS 3.590

Andecamulenses 1449

Anderitum, Ἀνδερηδόν,

Andereton (-um), cf. pers. name Anderedus (AcS 1.145) and (234) local name Anderetiani (ib.); Antérieux.   Cf. gl. AcS 2.1195, 30

]riti ciu[1392 (?)

Anger, Angeris fl. Rav., Greg. Tur. Indre (Cf. Icara)

Angulis fl. Rav., Angolin

Anicium

Antros ins. (Mela)

Aquae Calentes CIL 13, p.200 (Baiae) Chaudo-saigues

Aquae Calidae (Vichy) TP

Argantomagus Argenton

Ariolica Avrilly-sur-Loire?

Artona (-th- Greg. Tur.) Artonne

Aruerni, Ἀρούερνοι, cl.

inscc. Aruernus, -as
(-atis); Aruernicus
(ter. sig.), Aruernen-
sis, Aluernis -nicus,
often Al- in late
documents; cf. divine
names. Auvergne

Arula fl. Aigre

Auara (-era) fl. Èvre

Auaricum, -ensis (cf.
BSAF 1919, 128; REA
23, 134)

Auario fl. Aveyron

Augustonemetum, -on,
-nimidum, Ag- Cf. gl.
79, 158; Jullian REA
15, 1913, 421-26. Now
Clermont-Ferrand (on
Clermont see Pasquali
Rend. Ist. Lomb. 72,
29-61; Ernout BSL 41,
1940, 45 [APh 15, 1940
-41, 206]). Cf. 136
above, and gl. verneme-
ton (158 below), which
evidently is translated
Augusto-nemeton, just
as Augustodunum (179)
is also rendered Au-
gusti montem (178 be-
low); Augusto- may
also correspond to
Vxello(-dunum inf.) as
well as to uer- (cf.
Virodunum, Verdunum
212?)

Augustoritum, -on, Au-
gustoredo; cf. insc.
1392 (or read eme-
]riti?)

Auitacus (-um) Aydat

Baiae v. Aquae

Belenatensis mons Greg.
Tur. (in gl. conf. 5;
FHRC 179.38)

Berbera (or -is) fl.,
Berberensis Greg.
Tur., Bèbre

Bicera fl. Rav. Vezère

Bituriges Cubi 1197,
Biturix Cubus 1337,
Biturix 1393; 1667,
1693, 1707, 2025a,
2835, 2929; 1376-77
addenda; CIL 13, vi
(1933), p.107; 6812,
6821 (cf. 8, 21024);
Vollmer 142; Bituri-
cus, -igicus, Bituri-
genses; modern Bourges
(Biturigas), Berry,
Berrichons

Blezis, Blesco castro,
Blesensis Rav., Greg.
Tur., Merov. num. now
Blois (Loir-et-Cher)

Borma (Vormes?) AcS
3.912-13

Briua Curretia Ruric.
Epist., Greg. Tur.
(Corrèze), Briuensis
(Brive)

Briua uico (Indre) now
Brives

Briuates Sid. Apol.,
Briuatenses Greg.
Tur. now Brioude
(Haute-Loire)?

Cadurci cl., cf. 1541,
   1547, 1551, 2001, 2011;
   -inus, -ensis, Caturca,
   Caturcensis, Caturnius,
   Caturcina, pagus Ca-
   thorcinus; cf. gl. 158;
   num.; now Cahors, Le
   Quercy

[Caesarodunum, Cas-
   (Turonum, Tours)]

Cambiouicenses TP, Cam[
   num. Chambon

Canauilium monasterium
   AcS 1.731,5

Cantilia, -llensis
   Chantelle

Cantobennicus mons Greg.
   Tur.

?Cantus blandus Fort.

Carantomagus TP Cranton(?)
   REA 19, 1917, 284

Caratiaco loco Fredeg.
   Charcé

Cariacus Fort. Chirat-
   l'Église

Caris (-us) fl. Cher

Caro uicus Chervix

Carobriae Chabris

Cas(s)inomagus

Claudiomagus (Clion;
   BSAOuest 9, 1931, 121
   -39; REA 35, 1933, 415)

Clausetia Sid. Apol.

Ceuenna (-b-) mons

Condate TP

Condatomagus TP (Rodez)

Consacrani 1561, cf. 147,
   397

Cosa (Cos), cf. Cocosates
   84

Cottion Sid. Apol.

Crosa fl., Rav. ASS,
   Creuse

Cubi v. Bituriges; Cuba
   1353 (but see BSAF 1915,
   230-238), Cubi 1333,
   Κοῦβοι Str., Cubii
   Frontin.; Cubis, -iio
   and (?)Οὐι[Τουριγεσ]
   κυ[βοι] num.

Curretia v. Briua

?Diolindum TP

Diuon(n)a, Deuona; cf.
   gl. 158

*Dumia (-ius) mons Dôme

Duno AcS 1.1376,20; Merov.
   num., Dun-le-Poelier

Duranius fl., Doranonia,
   Doron- , Dornonia,
   Dronona Dordogne

Eborolacensis praedii
   Sid. Apol.

Local Names

Elauer, Elauaris, Alere
  fl. Allier; cf. gl.158

?Eleuteti

Ernodorum (-ur-) Arnon

Euaun[1334? Cf. 1368
  and divine name Iuauus;
  Euauensis (Greg. Tur.),
  for Euauensis? Euaux
  cf. Epaona (80)?

?Exold]unesses 1351
  Issoudun

Gabali (-es), -iensis
  -itanus cl.; Gabali-
  bus 10012.3 (CIL 13
  vi, p.21), cf. gl.
  PID 340 D; Javols
  (CIL 13 ii 2 [1907]
  p.646), Gévaudan

Gabrae TP Gièvres

Gaudiacus (-g-) for
  *Gauid-(?) ASS Jouet-
  sur-l'Aubois

Garumna fl. (cf. RC 45,
  1928, 312-317) Garonne

Gergouia Gergovie Cf. Ét.
  Cl. 2, 1933, 306-11,
  529; REA 39, 1937, 44.
  The treatise of Hatt
  (see APh 18, 143) I
  have not seen

Gredonense castrum
  Grèzes-le-Château

Gurdonis castrum, cf.
  Gurdonicus (159)

Helarius mons FHRC 179.9

Icara Rav. (AcS 2.16),
  for Incara (Anger)?

Icidmago TP, Icutmageon
  Rav., for Ic(c)iomagus?
  Usson?

Iciodorensis uicus Issoire

Ἰόντωρα (?)

Iuauo- , v. Euaun[

Ledoso Merov. num. Lezoux;
  Lusianum REA 42, 1940,
  614

Lemane, Li- Limagne

Lemouices, Λεμοουίκες,
  Λιμουϊοι , Lemo-uicus
  622, -uicinus, -uicen-
  sis 1700, 1803 (cf.
  AcS 2.180-181),†Limoui-
  censis (?) 1487; cf.
  AcS 2.227,38 (Limoue-
  cas, -gas or Limouicas),
  Limoges, Limousin On
  lem- , lim- REA 13,
  1911, 345; 20, 1918, 126

Lentinum insc. Chr., BSAF
  1872, 74 Lempty (Puy-
  de-Dome), AcS 2.184

Leucus mons C.13 p.702 n.1

Liger fl., Loire Licania-
  censes Greg. Tur.

Linicassium REA 35, 1933,
  416 (Lenquais)

Local Names

?Lusianum v. Ledoso

Mantalomagensis uicus,
  Mantalomaus Manthelan

Mediocantus Greg. Tur.
  BSL 32, 1931, 158

Mediolanum (Biturigum)
  TP, Greg. Tur.
  Châteaumeillant

Milmandra fl. ASS.,
  Marmande; cf. gl.158

Νεμωσσός Str., cf. gl.
  79, 158; -nemetum
  (Augusto- etc.)

Neriomagus -ensis, Aquae
  Neri (TP), Nereensis
  uicus, cf. divine
  name Nerius; Néris-
  les-Bains

Noioialus (Nojals) REA
  35, 1933, 416

Nouiodunum Nouan-le-
  Fuselier? REA 26, 1924,
  322-26; 27, 1925, 133-
  34

Obrege (AcS 2.823), cf.
  personal name Obricus
  1195 (for Obrinc-[?]
  Or read Cob. ?) Cf.
  Abria- above?

Oltis (-us) fl., Lot. Cf.
  153 (Vl-)

Pocrinium Pringues or
  Périgny? (Cf. Prumiaco
  153?)

Pretoria TP (C.p.656)

Rigomagus -ensis, Greg.
  Tur., Merov. num. Riom

Ro(i)dumna Roanne

Ruessium, Ρουέσσιον,
  Reuessio, Ribision

Rutaini, -aeni, -eni,
  inscc., e.g. 13.629,
  Vollmer 350; Ρουταιν-
  οι, Ρουτανοί, Ruteni-
  cus, Rotenus, Rodin-
  gis; Rodez, le Rouerge

Segodunum TP, Not. Tir.
  Ptol.

Silanum TP

]spana 1547 addendum (iv
  p.20). Cf. mod. Is-
  pagnac, and v. 80, 83
  above; (?) Spaniacus
  AcS 2.1623

Stomatas Stontas

Tarnis fl., Tarnisca
  uallis Tarn

Tantalius (at Albi) MG

Tasciaca (C-?), Taseiae
  Thésée

Tigernense (Thigernum)

364

castrum, now Thiers,
Greg. Tur. Cf. AcS
2.1842; RA 28, 1923,
180 and cf. the gl.
tigernos (207), i.e.
teg- , tog- (moritex
207, su-teg- 178, tolu-
tegon 178, attegia
Note lii item k (bis);
[?] tugurium 240,
Tigurini 241)

Tincontium (C-), Tincollo
Sancoins

Tolnacum (Tounac) RA 16,
1940, 137

Transalium Greg. Tur.,
Tresalium, Transalien-
sis, -saliacensis
Trezelle

Triobris fl., Sid. Apol.,
Truyère

Varatedo (for -dum), or
Varadetum TP, (?)
Varaire

Vb... uum TP (Desjardins

Geogr. 295-96, REA 16,
1914, 339)

Vellaui, Ὀυελλάϊοι cl.,
inscc. (3240, cf. C.
13 ii 2, p.646), -crum
ciuitas, Vellauensis,
Vellauus, mod. Velay

Vialoscensis pagus AcS
3.273, but for Narbo-
(na) see 84 above

Vincenna fl., Vig- mod.
Vienne

?Virisionenses FHRC 195
Vierzon

Volouicus, Vuluicus ASS,
modern Volvic

Vorocium, Vorogio, Voro-
cius (also divine name,
1497 with add.); Voro-
cio uico Merov. num.;
mod. Vouroux; Desjar-
dins 286 (-glo?)

Vosagensis pagus Greg.
Tur.

Vxellodunum Puy-d'Issolu

The name Vxellodunum (cf. the hybrids Augustodunum,
Aûtun and Castello-dunum, Châteaudun) is of frequent
occurrence (AcS 3.62-67), and has given rise to many
problems of identification. This instance, among the
Cadurci, is simple; but others are disputed, see the

Local Names

discussions listed in REA 15, 1913, 452 (cf. 305); 16,
1914, 95 (cf. 99), 234, 338, 345, 432 (most of which is
comic enough), Bibliogr. in Bull. Soc. préhist. de la
France 1915 (ib. 17, 1915, 141); REA 28, 1926, 359; RA
11, 1938, 361-62. Dauzat discusses local names of the
Auvergne REA 32, 1930, 139-148 (cf. RC 48, 1931, 468-69);
on frontier terms such as fines, terminus, uxellum,
icoranda, randa see REA 49, 1947, 160 ff.; J. E. Dufour's
Dictionnaire topographique de Forez (Mâcon, Protat 1946,
1184 pages quarto, cf. EC 4, 1948, 426) I have not seen;
Viré (Les voies romaines du Quercy RA 16, 1940, 138-143)
is insignificant.

Chronique de Toponomie (Bourbonnais) REA 38, 1936,
345-348; on names in -ac- and -at- in the Limousin ib.
37, 1935, 213.

Remark:

I have given here (148) Claudiomagus and one or two
other names the precise ascription of which is uncertain;
for the Turoni or Turones belong properly to Lugdunensis,
not to Aquitania, and Claudiomagus is said to have been
on the frontier between the Biturges and the Turones
(modern Tours). It is advantageous, however, to take
the river Loire as a dividing line, at least for our

Local Names

present purpose, even though it was not always the precise political dividing line; for a wide river frequently
is an effective linguistic barrier, except occasionally
along its own course.

149   Further Modern Local Names

Allenc, Alléan, Arnaise, Aurillac; Bas-en-Basset,
Bonnet, Borde-Rouge, Breith, Brugès, La Celle-Bruyère,
Bugeac; Ceyssac, Chanac, Chezelles, Condat, Couchezotte,
Coudes; Déols (Dolus uicus), Le Dorat, Dore l'Eglise,
Dovie, Driaude; Escourolles, Espalion, Espaly, Espris;
Felletin; La Ganne (BSL 32.108), St Geneys, Gouzougnat;
Herry; Imbèque; Lanuéjols, Lavoûte, Levroux, Lury;
Magnac-Laval, La Marche (Marchia, CIL 13, p.181), Mari-
joulet, Mauvières, St Médard, Mende (Mimate), Menetou-
Salon, Molles, Montluçon, Moulet, Moutier; Neuilly-le-
Real, Neuvic, Neuvy-sur-Baranjon; Parsac, Perpezac-le-
Noir, Pern, Polignac, Ponsat (Potincaco castro num.
Merov.), Puy (Podium); Quintignac; Rancon, Reillac;
Salagnac (num. Merov. have Selaniaco), Sauzelles, Solig-
nac, Souvigny (Siluiniacum; cf. REA 38, 1936, 348);
Tarognat, Tintignac, Tulle; Ussel (Oxxello num. Merov.);
Vendoeuvres-en-Brenne, Vignarnaud.

Local Names

On Place-de-Jaude (Clermont-Ferrand) see REA 13,
1911, 94 (platea *Galata?); Chaulgnes has been derived
from *Cauannia (Vollmöllers Jahresber. 11, 1907-8, i
p.109).

Remark:

The Cartular A of S. Sulpicius of Bourges, edited
by L. de Kersers Mém. Soc. Ant. du Centre 35, 1912, [1913]
gives a large number of names, local and personal (151,
Remark infr.), some few of which may be noted here (cf.
REA 16, 1914, 337), viz.

Adarabulum Azerables
   (cf. 79)

Adenai Lazenay

Agenaico

Algiacum Augy

Alloniacum Allogny

Armilliacum Milly?

Belloiouis (-ioco)
   Beaujeu (cf. 1)

Boiago Bouy?

Boronus fl. Bouzon

Carontomago Charenton

Dadomna fl., Daona Dame

Duno, Dunensis Dun-le-Roi

Exsoliduno, Isolduni,
   Isodunensis Issoudon
   (148 above)

Glenessa Liénesse

Graciaco uilla Crécy

Iacerigas Sassièrges

Ioiacum Jouy (cf. 1)

Isora Yseure

Iuetum Ivoy

Local Names

Lauatensis uicaria Lavet

Linerensis Linière

Lupperii (?)

Maciacensis Massay

Madriacum, Meriacum
  Méry-ès-Bois

Magdunum, Maidunum Mehun

Marciliago uilla

Marmannia Marmagne

Marralupum

Molendinis, Mollinis
  Moulins?

Nantua uilla

Naonis fl. Nahon?

Narsena, Nersena

Negromentinsis, Nerunden-
  sis uicaria Nérondes

Orciacum Orçay?

Oriensis uicaria Ouzy?

Pancerius mons

Pariniaco Parigny

Poliniacum Pouligny

Quintiaco Quincy?

Sagonna fl., le Sagonnin

Sagonna, -onium Sagonne

Salebriuae Salbris

Sariaco Séry

Sigalonia Sologne

Siuriacum Civray

Solumniago Soulangy

Stagno (molendinum de),
  Stanno; cf. 150, 155,
  158

Suboculi

Teleidum, Tel(l)iacum
  Theillay

Telus, -is fl. Théols

Tresgolio uilla

Treuinum Entrevin

Varenae Varennes de
  Fougerolles

Vassalaicum, -etum
  Vasselay

Vauera, Veura, Vivra,
  Vauerensis Vèvre

Venesminsis, Venesininsis
  uiuaria Venesmes

Local and Divine Names

Vernoica Verneuil

Vernonensis aqua le Ver-
non

Vernucia Vernuce

Vidiliacum

Vinogilum, -oilum Vignoux

Viriacus

Vnbralia Ambrault

Volunniago, -iacensis
uicaria Volangis

Voseto Vouzay?

150   Divine Names

Adido 1575

Aruernus (Mercurius) 1522,
Aruernus (Genius) 1462
(Ad-), cf. Dumias and
(243 below) Aruernorix

Atepomarus (Apollo) 1318;
RC 17, 1896, 34-40.
Cf. 151

Bassoledulitanus (or
Bassus Led-?) Apollo
AE 1914, 246; BSAF
1914, 240; 1913, 368;
cf. REA 17, 1915, 216;
and 155 infr. (Coble-
du-), 237 (smertu- ,
Argiota-), 83 (Smerta-
litanus), PID 2.185

?Bellino deo 1461 (if
genuine); cf. FHRC
105.13, 179.38

Cososus deus 1353; but
cf. BSAF 1915, 230-
238, REA 18, 1916, 213

Dumias, -iatis (Mercuri-
us), 1523 (Puy de)
Dôme, cf. Aruernus;
and on dumias see also
Vendryes RC 33, 1912,
463-466; REA 8, 1906,
341. Cf. perhaps
dum(ani etc.) in the
Coligny calendar

Dunisia(?) BSAF 1879,
160-164

Etnosus(?) ib. 1882, 204;
1885, 96

Divine Names

?Flamoni 1376-1377 Add.
   (or flamini?)

Ibosus deus 1370

Iuauus deus 1368, cf.
   10008.22, 10027.42;
   local names and
   Lacauus? (82 above)

Iunones 1373, 1374

Mauida 11082

Mogetius (Mars) [Add BSAF
   1902, pp.198, 205,
   214] Illyr.?

Naga 11153

?Nennerius 1372

Nerius (also local name)
   1371, 1372, 1376,
   1377, 1379

Randosas (-ati Marti)

Rigisamus (Mars), cf.
   (AcS 2.1199) Rixama

?Romogill[ius 1524 (or
   pers. name? Cf. 1467)

?Secuelos 11135 (for
   Sucellus?)

Siann[us 1536 (for Stan-
   nus?) cf. Stanna 149
   Remark above, 155 be-
   low (with 158)

Solimara 1195

dea Soucon(n)a 11162 cf.
   modern local name
   (149 Remark) Sagonne;
   cf. P-W s.v., and
   also Saucon(n)a (179,
   181 Remark)

?Subremis 11160, cf.
   10027.246 and Subre-
   mus (151 below)

Tritullus (Mars)

V(asso) K(aleti) genio
   10017.958; cf. iv
   (1916) p.19, and 158
   below

?Vindon[(Mercurius)
   1518, 1518a, 1519,
   cf. 1520 (most likely
   personal name)

Vorocius (Mars), also
   local name

371

Acirgus 10002.5-6

?Acaionu 1527

?Acutibilus 1538 (add.
10010.33; not Acuus
1538) But read Acut-
(us) Bili(catus)
Ar(uerni)

Adcenus

Adnama 1398

Adnametus 11086; AE 1916.
66; REA 17, 1915, 275

Aduentus 1196

Adue(n)tinius 1196

?Aednimosta 1574

?Aeneaesus 10012.18; but
see 134 Remark iv
above

Afinius (Albenque Rutênes
1949, 290)

Agileius 1194

?Agrandisom 10012.18; but
see 134 Remark iv above

Aiseus AE 1928.141; RA 27,
1928, 209; cf. 10010.
72?

Alanus 10010.2859

Alcouindus 1551

Allia 1461

Alloboesius 10012.18; but
see 134 Remark iv
above

†Allouira 1323

Allus(a) 10015.77

Alogiosus 1331

Alpina 1447, -us 1620

?Amatio 1584

Ambigatus cl.

Amuc[10010.2861

Anauus 1189

Andecarius 1328

Apinossa 1398; -us 1439

Apius 10027.134

Apronius 10023.3

?Arad[1311

Ardossus 1336 Add.

Arecumbu 10016.19

Aribo 10015.1 (cf. arepo
79?)

Arisella 1203

Arrigario 11085 (an trig-?)

?Asdesmios Esp. Lem. 144;
AcS 1.246

[?Ascouindus AcS 1.243-49
(cf. 246.4), source
not stated]

?Ataaχti 10029.326

Ategnutis gen. 1193

Atepomarus (Lezoux); cf.
  150

Ateponus 1204

Ateratos 11090

Atespatus 1366; VKG 1.77
  (-sku-); Gutenbrunner
  12.4^

Atimetus 1430

Atisius 10006.9

Atrectus 1318

Atrianus 1328

Atticinus 10006.14

Attinus 1620

Attiolus 1437

Atuanus 1328

Atuirus 1206

Auienus 11152

Aucilo 1411

Aueta 1207

Auita 1437, 11101; -us
  1300

Aunia 1211

Aunilla 1210

Aurinus 1209

Auspenus 10006.16

Baluui gen. 11092

Bantius

†Bardtario 1530

Bassinus 1516

Bassulus 1516, 1567

†Baudulfus (6th cent.)
  1352

Bellinicus 10015.16

Bellouesus cl.

Benus 1330

]biba 1467

Biborigis gen. 11127
  (Bituo-?)

Biga AE 1928.31 (v.
  Carissa)

Biliap[1538; but see
  Acutibilus above

Biroi galli 11114b (two
  words?)

Birtiolos 10010.2875

?]bitu[10027.202

Bituitos (Bet-) cl.,
  insc.; ΒιΤΰιΤοϛ Str.,
  Betulto (sic) Act. Tr.

Bladamus 1316; cf. gl.
  blada 220

Blaesianus 1393

Bollaco 10010.2895

Bolus 10010.2889

Brigio(s) num.

Budaracus 1454

Burdecato 10010.2886

Burdonus 10015.22

Cacculla 11082

Cadgatus 1466

Cadonus 1551

?Caenidianus 1214

?Caetaurus 1399

Calenus 1453; BSocHist
    Corrèze 37, 1915, 241-
    253

Calepa 1347

Caleticcus 11094

Camelius 1215

Camerianus 1569

Camuledu 11095

Camulo[1465

Canidus 1216

Cantus 1332

Cantusius 1501

Cappellianus 1217

Caran[11096

Carantius 10015.18

Carassonius 1355

Carassounus 1496

Caratilla 11097

Carigus 1438

Carinnius 1218

Carisius 1385

Carissa m. AE 1928.31;
    BA 1928-29, 74; REA
    31, 1929, 59

Carix 10010.2859

Cartullus 1355

Catius 1364, 11154 (AE
    1911.21, REA 15, 1939,
    197)

Catus 1364

?Catuoppus 1219

Cedonius 1551, -us (Al-
    benque 301)

Celtillus cl.

†Cenos(?) f. 1443
    (Caroling.)

Ceruesarius (as pers.
    name?) 10012.7

Ceruius 1500

Cesord[1220

Cessorinus 1330

Cestia 1319

Personal Names

Cicedu num.

Cictouanus AcS 1.1012

Ciltica 1606

Cimber 1356

Cinamus 1222

Cintusmo(s) 11085, -us
    11099

[Cliternius 1383; but
    hardly cf. gl. 158]

Cnaiu (-tu?) 1318 Add.

Cobl[11114a, AcS
    3.1245

Cobricius 1195

?Cobrunnistitii 1474 (an
    statui?)

Combricus 1456

Comistri gen. 1460

Comprinnus 1468, 10027.
    245

Congonetiacus (Biturix)
    CIL 8.21024

Conted(d)ios AcS 3.1276,
    39

Contiioius Germ. 7, 1923,
    16

Conus 1474

Cossus 1223

Cotis 10002.170

Craecus 11113

Craxantus 1318

?Craxaucus 10008.16-17

Critognatus cl.

Crixus 1366

Cunuanos num.

Damonus 1364 bis (p.177)
    and Add.

?Daunilla AcS 1.1244

Daχsantinos 10015.25

Demioncia 11105 -ca BA
    1941-2 [1944] 217

Diauxis AcS 1.1281

Dicaeus 1364 Add.

?Diceata 11106

Dicus 1356

Dimiono (Demionc-) 10010.
    2858

Dioc[10027.23

Dioce|ni 11107 (-geni?)

Diopantus 1402

Diuiχtus 1400, 10025.59,
    11162; -iχχtus 1226
    (or -χx-?)

?Dodica 1416

Dommus 1255

375

Personal Names

Donnus 1576

]dubno 1579

Dusius 10008.40

[Duuius Pl. 34.47]

Eburila 1228

Ennius 10002.200

?Epaphrod[1368, 10027.
   42 Stepaprod[insc.

Epasnactos cl., cf. 141,
   157

Epos num.

?Eriaunus 1334 (an Euaun-,
   cf. Iuauus 1368? an
   Eridubnus?). Cf. 148

Ermeroti 11151

Esiub[10015.7

[Esuuius num.]

[Etruscilla 1519]

Etuosus 1189

?Eumfiyus REA 34, 1932,
   59

Eunus 1190

Euoccus 10002.203

Faltonia BSAF 1912, 273

Gabr[10024.200

?Gatpas BSAF 1884, p.84

Gaudilla 11110

Gauia 1197 (cf. gl. 158)

Genillus 10002.245

Germaniccus (sic) 1111

Gnatus 1318

Gobannitio cl.

Gresius BSAF 1912, 273

Iaberti 10010.2855 (Lib-?)

Idallus 1322

?Idorina (an Idomina?)
   11153

?Ierha f. (Albenque 283),
   or -ia (ib. 296)

Ietta 10010.2888

Igocatus 10010.2886

Illo 1335

Illumarus 1606

?Imoards[1336

?Inia[Esp. Lem.139

[Insidiator 1404]

[Insidiola 1404]

376

Personal Names

?Ioblicus 1409 (Po- , Pu-
 BA 1941-42 [1944] 216,
 AE 1945 [1946] 18)

Ioppillo 10015.22, 76

Ioppios 10015.75

?Iua(u)os 10008.22; but
 see 150 above

Iulitta 1413

Iunimus 1241

Ladanus (Lau-?) 1407

Lalianus 1198

Lallino (-us) 1337 with
 Add.

?Leaiussi[BSAF 1915, 113

Lemo Esp. Lem.149

Lera 1245

Liberina 1246

Liccaeus AE 1921, 95

Licentiossa 1608 (cf.
 1583)

?Lienus Esp. Lem.137

Lino[1617 Add.

Lita 10010.2858

Littiossa 1254

??Lomaxannas 10010.2893

Luccia 10010.2886

Lucterius 1541 with Add.;
 num.

Λουέργιος Strabo (v.l.
 - ριος, father of Bi-
 tuitos), Luerius CIL
 13 p.193. Cf. AcS 2.
 293 ("fox," i.e. for
 *lupo-) Rhys, cf.
 Dottin Mél. Loth, 1927,
 92-98. But *lupo- has
 p from qu, and ought
 to survive at this
 date; is the name an
 erroneous reading of
 'Α(ρ)ούεργος ?

Lupa 1458, †Lupa 1481;
 (-ula 1338), Lupus
 1201, 1213

Luttius 1428

Macuso MSA Centre 4,
 1870-72, 173.70

[Maeuia 1395]

Magninus (cogn.) 1517

Malucnus 1248

[Mamercus 1201]

[Mamrti 11097]

Manirius 1348

Mansuiola 1471

Manutia Lizop 2.318 n.67

[Marcellus 1192]

Marcilla 1249

Personal Names

Marco 1250

[Martialis 1325]

Martidia (-iia?) 11118

Marulla 1258

?Masces 1440 (cf. gl. 246)

Maspius 1259

Masueto(s), -a 11122,
    Mang- 11156

Matidia 11124

Matridia 1257

Matta 11116

Matuiia 1408

Matullina 1408

Medianus, Medius AcS
    2.497,24

?Megentira Auson.

Meliddus 1243

Merula (Cubus) CIL 13,
    p.158

?Metullus 1414

Mias[1339

?Moigetus 1472 (Molgenus
    AcS)

Motuidiacos num.

Moxius 1400; ?Moxme
    10010.2886

Mutenia

Naga 11153

Namatius Greg. Tur.

Namia Auson.

Nammius 1332

?Nano 1261 (Nanto? Nanio?)

Nannenus (Vernemetensis)
    AcS 2.682

Nariti 10010.2858

Nattos (Aruernus) 10015.
    32, 82

?Nemetus 1389

?Nem[(if pers.) 1371

?Nennerius, Nerius 1372
    (unless divine name)

Nertacus

Nertinus (-ius) AcS 2.722

?Nertius ib. (Nertus?)

Neruci 10011.238

?Nerundus 1262

Nimo 10010.2858

Nironius (or Niro)

?Noliccin AcS 2.757

?Noma

Nonnius 1577

Norbanus 1265

?Noto (auot) 10010.2855

378

Personal Names

Nutrobie AE 1926.127

Obricus 1195 (but cf.
    Obrege local name
    AcS 2.823)

Octa 1454

Oppius 10001.234-5, 378

Oppo 10015.62

Orbia 1266

Orgius (-c-)

Origanio 1412

Orin[10027.140

]osseni 10010.2858

[?Patauinia 1196]

Pătēra Auson.

Potitus 11128

Pupila 1272

?Puy|mestroc 1327

Rasia(m) 1311

Recca 1274

Regenus, Regina 1413

†Remesto 1485

?Rippo[(or]rippo[)
    10015.63

Ritminia 10006.138

Romo]gillus 1524

Rontu (or -iu?) 11131,
    for Fr-? Cf.]ruontu[
    (?) 1325

Rorilus

Roupia

Rutatus 10010.2863

Sabinius 1364 Add.

Sace[11132

Sacrila 1596

Saempritu 1319 Add.

Salluc[11114b

Sammius

San[1279

Sasouna

Scorpianus (Bourges; ego
    uidi)

?Secuelos 11135 (Suc-?);
    cf. 150

Sedatus

Sedulius CIL 13 p.181; or
    Sedullus cl., num.;
    AcS 2.1434

Segouesus cl.

Sen[num. Arvern.

Personal Names

Senecianus

Senillus 10015.39

Seposa 11138

[Sergius 1589]

Seros 1410

Sidonius CE 1516

Sigin[1270

†Siggecondis 1367

?Silo 10025.105

Siluectius Finke 342

Siluinus (Biturex) ib.

Simomarus (-ius) 1582

Sinotarii 10010.2883

Sinturo

S /// |ixitus 1401

Sog[1475

Soiana

Solie(-a) 11140

Solimara

Solimuto 11141

Sorus (Aruernus) ASS

]spana 1547 Add. (or
   local name?)

?Stepaprod[, v. Epa-

Suadulla 1319 Add., 11142

Suadutio 1137 Add.

Suauis (-us?) 11143

Subremus AcS 2.1651; but
   see 150 above

Succamo 10010.2862

Suloleno 10010.2884

?Suloriganio 1412

Sumenu

Smeratus 10015.46

Suoliccenc[(or Suolic-
   cin[?)

Surcici 10010.2858

Tacccus (Accu?) 10027.133

Talonius

?Tansna 1311 (cf. gl.
   tanda 220)

Taurilla 11144

Taurus 10015.47

Tecessi 10006.91

?Tegen[(an Tergenius,
   Tigern- ?)

Teθθ.. (Aruerni) 12.5686,
   1211; Teddilos (Tu-?)
   10016.34

Tergenius Esp. Lem.

Togimarus

Personal Names

Tota

Toutilla

Trebonianus (Albenque 290)

Tritogeno 10015.49

Tuddilos (?) 10016.34

[Tullia 1454]

Tura, Turaenia 1451

Vadutio

Valicius 1572

Vasueual 10010.2858

Vasueus ib.

Vebrumna 1298

Veldumnianus (Albenque 290)

Venilla

Veni✕samus

Ventianus 11145

Venuleius 10002.525

Vercassiuellaunus cl.

Vercingetorix cl., cf. C.2, p.65

?Verelobi 10008.39

Vergasillaunos(?) num. cl.? (-c-), for Vercassiuellaunus?

Vericus 1446; cl., num.

?Vernanis (Ar]uern-?) 1527

[?Vesituas 1311]

]uexora

Vibius (Albenque 290)

Vid[1617 Add.

Viduco

Vigeus 10008.6

Vimpuro 1368, 10027.42

?Vindonius 1518-1520 (or divine?)

Viniola 1349

?]ulerunde 1441

Viridomarus (Biturix)

Vlatcani 11103

Vlattius 10010.2072

Vocconianus Mél. d'Arch. et d'hist. 55, 1938, 89

?Vommi 10010.2886

Names of Potters

Remark:

(A) Several of the personal names in the Cartular A of
Sulpicius of Bourges (149, Remark) seem worthy of note,
viz.:

Ardicco	Pincerna (cf. 82; and, for -erna, 178 s.v. maderna)
Billo (coquus)	
Deuaus	Remigius
Gim(m)o, Gimonus?	Sado (puer)
Iuuo Carnotensis	Sebbaudus
Melantius (miles)	Vrso (miles)
Morinus	Villemarus (ledarius)
Nutridus (cf. Nutrobie 151)	

(B) Doubtful Names of Potters from Aquitania Prima

Abudinos	Adgenus	Ain[, Aen[
Acurio	Aeilos	Ainaicesus
?Acussi (-ri)	Aetus	Ainsa
Agapa (Ac-)	Aiamia	Airamn
?Acrinus (Ma-)	Aiato	Aisa
?Actanus	Aicea	Aisius
?Adfe (Ad[fe[cit)	Ailo	Aitinacus

382

Names of Potters

Aldunus	Ardacus	Aui, Auus
Aleouas	Ardasina	]axquius
?Alimiti	Aril(l)us (Car-)	
Alinus	Aroi	Bacil
Amai	Arecumbu (Lezoux)	Baquili
An[	Arucca, -us	Barnaeus
?Amdamica 10016.15	Asa	Bel[
?Amen[us	Ata	Bi[
?Amicus, -a	Atci	Biracadus
Ananditos	?Atdanus	Biracillus
Ananus	Atilus	Birarcus
Anarius	]atini	Bollaco
Anasa (Au-?)	Atita	Boril(l)os
Anexia	Atoos	Borius
Anianus	Atricus	Broc[
Anius	Attilianus	Broi[
Anoxus	Attius	Bualia (-t-)
Aoa	Atur	Bugatus
Apanin[	Aubion	Buccus, -a
]apanus	Auctus	Burdecato
Apicle	(avotti)	Burt[
Apillus, -a	Aurat[	Bus[
Ar[	Austrus	
?Aranteo	Aussinus	
	Autarix	Ca..us[

383

Names of Potters

Cabellio

Cabeo

Cacer

Cadmus (for
  Catumagos?)

Cadurcus

?Caeueituus

Caletius, -a

Casius

Cadilon

Caetaurus

Cailuus

Calemisus

Cal(l)us

Can[

Candinus

Canio

Cantus

Cantussius

Capani

Car...ua

Carantianus

Carasounos

Cara

Carix

Catidia (K-)

Catuganis

Catusa

Cau.erti

]ccei

Cel[

Census, -a

Ceres

Cesianus

Cesor[d]

Cesura

Chastus

Cheti

Chir[

Cho[

Ci[

Cialco[

Cic[

Cice[

Cidiui

Cint[

Cipario

Cippus (G-)

Cirmarcus

Cituros, -a

Ciu[

Ci.ueci

Cobnertus

Cleus (Clii-)

Clilui

Cl.mi

Clocoi

Cmamiri

Cniari

Co[

Cobino (-do?)

Coc[

Cocis

?Coilusyb.ie

Collus

Comosus

Condollus

Congus

Conteđ(đ)ios

Cop

Cor[

Dimiono

Ducri

384

Names of Potters

Elius	Gedillus	Mahes
Elussius	Genetlus	Mainacnos
Emia	Gio (Bio?)	Maisto
Estius	Gondius (Congius)	Mando
?Estrus (Festus?)	Grecus (-ae-)	Mario (for
Esumus	Gubrus (Ga-)	Solimario?)
Euinus		Matto
		Meddi
	Habitus (Ab-)	Meθillos
Febriscus	H·m·s	Meius
Felicente		Melissus
Felite	Ilatis	Melus
Flauinus	Illio	Miono
?Floridus	Iothur	Monus
Fontus		
?Fuca	Lastuca	Nattus
	Lauratus	Nerucus
?Gabalar	Liomarus	Niualis
Galbinus (C.Alb-)	Lituccus	Nonnit(t)us, -a
Galenus (Cal-)	Lobasio	
Galus (C-)	Losorus (-ius?)	Odel[
Gamus (C-)	Lou[	Odma
Garutius		Oico
Gastus (C-)	Maginnus	Oimn
Gato (C-)	Magiononus	Olosinus

385

Names of Potters

Olosinus

Oncus

Onnio

Onon

Opiso

Orius

Orumus

Parrhia

πιιμλι | νυμ
(IG 14.2577, 10)

Pistil(l)us

Pleuei

Riocenus

Riomarus (for Rigo-)

Rita

Saciro, -u, -us

Sacrilus

Salu

Saria

Sarinus

Sarrinus

Scap[

Scoplus

Sec[

Sella

Sextati[

Seuuo

Silo

Sottillus

Suces(s)us, -a

Surcicus

Tabur

Taesius (Lezoux) (Apotasgiu?)

Tausius, -a

Tauis

Ticinus

Titos

Tlota

Tlotamica

Toca

Toutissa

Tr[

Trasia

Tulo

Vacus

Vercinus

Vertamaca

Vertamica

Vertecillus

Vertecissa

Via

Viamius

Viasus

Viatoc?

?Viattius (Vlat[t]-)

Viciχtillus

Vid.i

Vindos, -a

Vintio

Viriou (iuriou?)

Viuex[

Viuos

Vixus

Vlatucnos

Vli[

Vltius

Voga

Voni

Vrappus

Vrida

Xeno

386

Miscellaneous Inscriptions

B.   Aquitania Secunda

Note xxv   Inscriptions of the Santones

(a) REA 5, 1903, 129-135, Pl.4. Jullian gives
here an "inscription" discovered in 1902 at Toulon-en-
Saintonges (Charente-Inférieure). It consists, if
ancient, most probably of mason's marks; but the letters
bear a remote resemblance to those of Iberian inscriptions (read, possibly n p i l k z ??).

(b) In Bull. Soc. arch. et hist. Charente 1926,
xlix, J. Marveau gives from a piece of terra sigillata,
as a continuous line of text, what is probably to be read

dometio m crumin

and therefore to be compared with the graffiti of La
Graufesenque.

(c) CIL 13 iv 1916, 11069-11070; Audollent, Defixionum Tabellae 1904, 111-112 (pp.167-171); Diehl
856; Dessau 8752. This is a curse, of the familiar
type, engraved on two lead plates measuring 0.10 by
0.085 m., that came to light in 1897, at Chagnon (also
in the Charente-Inférieure), noteworthy less for the
ἐφήσια grammata with which both tablets end, but which
have not been shown to be based on Gaulish,

atracatetra catigal│lara (v.l. ctigallara) precata

egdarata│hehes celata mentis ablata

387

Marcellus of Bordeaux

than for the forms

potesti

and

monimont

in 11070, lines 3 and 6 respectively, unless the former
is a mere slip for potest, or the result of Greek influence (which is most unlikely); for the latter compare
moniminto Note lii (a) below. The victims of the curse
are Lentinus and Tasgillus, of which at least the latter
name is to be noted as Keltic. Cf. Do. p.71; Deonna
has an interesting article on magic words in Genava 22,
1944, 116-137.

Remark: On the formularies in Marcellus of Bordeaux

Marcellus Burdigalensis himself tells us that some

of his remedies were obtained "ab agrestibus et plebeis"

(Praef. 2). It is not straining matters to apply this

statement to his magical formulae, or incantations, as

well as to his prescriptions. That the formulae which

are not intelligible to us contain some nonsense words

or syllables is probable enough; but it is certain that

he offers many incantations in perfectly good Latin (e.g.

12.46, 14.67-68) or Greek (e.g. 15.89), to take examples

at random, that in two places he gives what is virtually a

rendering of apparently inarticulate charms (8.193 φεῦγε,

Marcellus of Bordeaux

φεῦγε κριθή, κριθή σε διώκει and 31.33 tollo te hinc totam, haemorrhoida), that some of the formulae have received interpretations of scholars of repute (e.g. Vollmer, Wölfflin, see Niedermann's notes at 8.64, 12.24), and that one or two words seem not to defy interpretation (e.g. dercomarcos, σουρωρβι, see 190 below and the Glossary). It is not improbable, therefore, that some genuine fragments of the pre-Latin speech of Bordeaux and its vicinity, Keltic or Iberian, are preserved in these formulae. Each should, of course, be considered in its context (e.g. no.9 below was to be chanted with a remedium hordiolis).

1. 8.56 ουβдικ
2. 57 φυρφαρдη
3. 58 ✗ ουβρσρ ποπαιρασρ (ρ "scruple")
4. 59 ορυω ουρωδη
5. 64 excicum acriosos (v.l. crisos)
6. 170 tetunc resonco bregan gresso
7. 171 inmon dercomarcos axatison
8. 191 rica rica soro
9. 192 κυρια κυρια κασσαρια σουρωρβι
10. 193 uigaria gasaria

389

Marcellus of Bordeaux

11. 10.34 sicycuma cucuma ucuma cuma uma ma a

12. 55 socnon socnon

13. 56 sirmio sirmio

14. 69 ϭοκϭοκαμ ϭυκυμα (cf. 34)

15. 70 ψα ψε ψη ψε ψη ψα ψε

16. 12.24 argidam margidam sturgidam

17. 14.24 crissi crasi cancrasi

18. 15.105 heilen prosaggeri uome si polla nabuliet
    onodieni iden eliton

19. 106 xi exucricone xu criglionaisus scrisumioue-
    lor exucricone xu grilau

20. 21.8 Καρυανκω Καρυανκων Καρυανκων

21. 26.43 καραββραωθ

22. 18.72 adam bedam alam betur alam botum

23. 73 alabanda alabandi alambo

24. 19.26 1 ψ m θ k i a

25. 45 trebio potnia telapaho

26. 31.33 absi absa phereos

27. absis paphar

28. 32.25 κυϭτος

See, in general, the edition of M. Niedermann (CML
5, 1916); Dottin La langue gauloise 28 n.4, 214, 355;
O. Haas Die Sprache 1, 1949, 50-55; P. Marchot ZfRPh 50,
1930, 348-350; Weisgerber, SprFK 156, 160-161, cf. 209
(s.v. soro); R. Heim in Fleckeisen Jahrbücher Suppl. Bd.

Inscription of Rom

NF 19, 1893, 463-575; Zeuss in ZfCPh 3, 1900, 372-3;
J. Grimm and A. Pictet in Abh. Berl. Akad. Ph.-Hist.
Kl., 1855, 51-68 (cf. J. Grimm Kl. Schr. 2, 1865, 114-
172); and the other authors cited in Schanz-Hosius-
Krüger, Gesch. d. röm. Lit. 4.2, 1920, 278-282. The
dissertations of Chapot (1897) and Liechtenhan (1917)
throw no light on the formulae. For trebio cf. perhaps
*trebo (79 above) and the divine name Trebarunna (-onna)
AcS 2.1906 and AE 1934.20. Is 15 (10.70) to be compared
with the combinations of letters on the Venetic alphabetic tablets?

Note xxvi

Hints of excavations conducted in 1887 by a M.
Blumereau at Rom (Deux-Sèvres), the ancient Rauranum,
and eventually of an inscribed lead tablet, leaked out
through BSAF 1887, 122; 1888, 126-127; 1895, 122; cf.
MSAF 8, 1897 [1899], 118-148; but the great news of a
stupendous "discovery" was reserved for RC 19, 1898,
168-176 (Jullian).

A thin lead plate, about 2.75 in. by 4.50 in.,

lightly engraved on both sides in a mixture of uncial

and cursive styles, so worn as to be partly illegible

in most lines on Face A; seen by me in August 1929 at

the country-house of M. Guy Blumerau of Loudon (Vienne),

the son of the discoverer. I do not believe that the

"dialect" of this defixio is Keltic, save in the sense

that a few Keltic words may be interlarded in the vulgar

Latin of Roman Gaul, itself half-unintelligible in the

Inscription of Rom

mumbo-jumbo verbiage of incantations, cf. Thurneysen
ZfCPh 14, 1923, 11. The Colonel of Spahis, M. Saint-
Hillier, who aroused the wrath of Jullian by a somewhat
similar, if more extreme, assertion (CRAcInscBL 1921,
345-6) showed far more good sense than either Jullian
himself (l.c.) or Rhys, or the late Mr E. W. B. Nicholson
(ZfCPh 3, 1900, 310-321).

Letters 0.25 in. tall; noteworthy letter-forms are

$\wedge \wedge \lambda$ a, λ b, $\partial \partial \partial$ d, $\in$ e, σ g, $\dagger$ h (?),
$\llcorner$ l, M and $\hbar$ m, $\mathcal{N}$ and $\hbar$ n, open $\cup$ o, Γ p,
R r, $\curlyvee \vdash \Upsilon$ s, τ t, $\cup$ u, $\zeta \zeta$ z, and
the conjoint N nt; the rest will give no difficulty.

Where the lead is now too much worn by constant
handling to be legible, I have given, in square brackets,
the reading of Jullian; but I have no great confidence
in it. It is not astonishing that no official photograph of this lead plate was published until 1925; for
then it was seen to be largely blank on one side.

      A.   areciallicarti | etiheiontcaticat. |
na[de]mti[ssi]eclotu | epasedemttionti | b.car-
5   taoontdibo.. ‖ niasio[deeipia | sosiu[pu]raso[si]o |
10   gou[isasue]iotet | sosopour.ta... | s[u]ad.e.m.... ‖
duntna..e...

392

Inscription of Rom

        B.   te.[u]oraim.o │ eh.aatatθte... │ zoatan-
5   tatecom │ priatososioderti │ noipomnaioateho ‖ tis-
       sepogiatepri │ auim·oatan̯te │ o̯ntes·ati·meto │
10   a̯tate̯uraiimo │ are̯[sos]i[o]dert[i.. ‖ i[mo]n̯t̯[a]-
      demtisse. │ upe]... [a]......

   A. Line 1: r̯, not p; l̯ broken.   2: h is † (for ⱦ
or ꬱ ?); or is this a non-alphabetic symbol? No trace
of o after -cat. 4: At the beginning ep, not lil- .
There is no i between m̯t (m faint) and ti- ; following
the conjoint n̯t is a clear i. 5: Possibly a faint i (?)
after b; aoon not aon. 6: After io the line is completely smooth; for Jullian's eipia Rhys gives uapia.
They must have worn the spectacles of Joseph Smith.
7: Likewise pu and si, and isasue (8) must be taken,
if at all, on trust. 9: No i after sos; ta is certain,
followed by space for three letters. 11: First letter
may be a, not d.

   B. Line 1: u comes from Jullian; the original has
space for two letters after te, and for one between m
and o at the end. 2: Here h is Ⱨ ; there is a clear
cross-bar in θ . In lines 7 and 8 the puncts are unmis-

Inscription of Vieux-Poitiers

takable. At the end of line 7 there is a blank space
(four or five letters) which never was engraved. 9:
ziateuorauiimo Jullian. 10: After the final i, space
for two letters. 12: Nothing whatsoever is visible in
the original.

Do. 52 (cf. p.43); to his references (p.170 n.3)
add CIL 13.4 (1916) p.12; Chapeau BSAOuest 6, 1922-24
[1925], 686-698 (facsimile), cf. REA 38, 1926, pp.29,
261; O. Haas ZfCPh 23, 1943, 285-297; Terracini in Trombetti Studi, 1938, 356

152   Inscription of Vieux-Poitiers

An enormous monolith of irregular shape, project-
ing 9 ft. or more above the ground-level, 5 ft. wide,
and 2 ft. or more thick where it is set into the earth,
with the insc., some 4 ft. above the ground-level, three
lines of large letters, much weathered and moss-grown,
so as to be almost illegible, on the north face. The
field in which the stone stands is at Les Barres or
Vieux-Poitiers in the valley of the Clain, not far from
Cenon (Vienne) and about 15 miles north-east of the
modern Poitiers. Presumably the stone was set up long

Inscription of Vieux-Poitiers

before it was engraved, for the date of menhirs is far
earlier than that of writing (cf. 145, 146 above and
PID 338; perhaps also 50-55 above). Seen by me in
August 1929, when it appeared to me that the last word
(line 3) must originally have stood not by itself at
the extreme right, but was preceded by ten or twelve
letters now completely weathered away, with but a few
vague traces observable in a slanting light from the
west. First reported in 1786 by Bourgignon de Saintes,
Dissertation sur le Vieux-Poitiers 25 (published at
Poitiers), having been observed three years earlier;
and often reproduced since then.

rati̯n | briu̯ati̯omu̯ | fronty̯|tarbelionios |]i̯euru

Line 1: After Ν (interpreted as i̯n), space for
two letters (no punct); u̯a is Ѧ , and m̯u is Ѡ (hitherto read as m̯ł   2: Ν n̯t; after e (?), the lower part of
1 and i, then a doubtful o, followed by an inclined Ν
n, with i set over o and a small s.   3: the punct after
fronty̯ is no longer visible. In both line 2 and line 3
we have Ѳ , usually read e, rather than ei̯; this unusual form, for Ε , may be due to modern tampering.

395

Inscription of Vieux-Poitiers

r is Ꝛ and b open (ꞵ or ꞛ , ꞵ). The cross-bar in o (line 1) must be due to mischief, unless we have a genuine variant (⊖ for o).

    Do. 51 (cf. p.43), to whose references add de Longuemar BSAOuest 7, 1853-55 [1855], 303-306 (facsimile); Becker Rh.Mus. 13, 1858, 291; Flouest BSAF, 1889, 281; Lièvre BA 1889, 155-156; Stokes Academy 37, 1890, 392; Ernault BSAOuest 10, 1904-06 [1907], 368-373; Jullian REA 23, 1921, 335 (on ratis); cf. Menard in BSAOuest 1865-67 [1868], 543-44.

    CIL 13.1171, with Add; ZfCPh 8, 1910-12, 380

Remark:

    On Poitiers see Ginot in BSAOuest 5, 1919-21 [1921], 515-545; Tourneur-Aumont ib. 7, 1925-27 [1927], 40-60 (REA 27, 1925, 334-35); F. Eygun MSAOuest 11, 1934 (excavations of 1878-79, cf. RC 51, 1934, 340; REA 36, 1934, 482); and on the subject of menhirs, see the monograph of Octobon Rev. Anthrop. 1931, 299-577 (but note the review in Antiquity 9, 1935, 120).

Inscription of Vieux-Poitiers

Note xxvii

A thin silver plate (lamina argentea Marc. Burd.,
saepe), 5.25 in. by 1.50 in., discovered in 1858 at
Poitiers (Vienne), in a meadow at the intersection of
the rues Riffault and St Denis, in which were remains
of human burials; it is, however, a prescription, not
a defixio. The script is Latin cursive (fifth century),
neatly engraved, legible enough except where the plate
is broken; the last line occupies only about half of
the available space. Letters 0.19 in. high. The language is a mixture of Latin and Greek, with perhaps a
word or two of Gaulish thrown in; its formulae can
easily be matched in Marcellus of Bordeaux (Note xxv
Remark), as was observed both by d'Arbois de Jubainville
RC 1, 1872, 499 (cf. CRAcInscBL 1872, 131), and by Rico-
chon, La Tablette de Poitiers et une formule Byzantine,
Paris and Vienne, 1901 (cf. REA 3, 1901, 182 and ZfCPh
3, 1901, 619).

Now in the museum at Saint-Germain-en-Laye (inventory 16589), seen there by me in August 1929.

     bisgontaurionanalabisbisgontauriosu|ceanal-

     abisbisgontaurioscatalages|uimcanimauims-

     paternamasta|madarssetutateiustinaquempepe-

5   ritsarra

Line 1 at end, perhaps n instead of su. 4: a is
slightly oxydized; tinaqu broken, but otherwise certain.
Space for two letters at the end of line 3; and in line
5 the writing becomes wide, in a vain attempt to fill
all the available space. Wünsch BJ 119, 1910, 11 reads

Miscellaneous Words

at the end tuta(m) f(ac) Iustina(m), quem [sic] peperit
Sorra; CIL (l.c. infr.) has essentially the same reading.
Not, I think, F(a)ustina; as for Sarra (not Sorra) it
is a well attested name, e.g. at La Graufesenque (132),
as well as a common noun *sarra (implied in sarralia,
beside serralia, serra, see the gloss 158 below). It
is possible that sorra is a variant of sarra.

Do. 60 (pp.43, 210); facsimile ap. J. Becker, Kuhn
u. Schleichers Beitr. zur vergl. Sprachforschung 3, 1863,
170; to Dottin's references add: de Longuemar, Procès-
verbaux, Congr. sc. de France (Limoges) 1, 1859 [1860],
244-46; E. Ernault and L. Fayolle, BSAOuest 10, 1934-
35 [1936], 213; Terracini in Trombetti Studi, 1938, 359;
CIL 13.10026,86

Remark:

Attention may be called here to the following
items in Latin inscriptions of Aquitania Secunda:

> bur[rarius] 1056, cf. burra 158 below
>
> diribitorium 1132 (see 141 Remark)
>
> ?r]edia 1157
>
> ueredus 927
>
> uergobreto 1048 (cf. REA 49, 1947, 130)

Local and Ethnic Names

To which add CIL 13.10017,45

acitapulus canua Virilis fecit

Of CIL 13.890 (cf. AcS 2.1628)

ssari aucano (?)

I can make nothing.

For leuga (abbreviated L in inscc.) see CI. 13 ii.2
(1907) pp.645-646 (and 8898-8945) saepe; REA 37, 1935,
213.

Names of Aquitania Secunda

Arabic numerals, without other indication of source,
refer to CIL 13, viz. i (1899) 566-1188 (pp.75-158),
with ii.2 (1907) 8861-8886, 8898-8916, 8924-8950 and iv
(1916) 11032-11081 (pp.6-12); sources given in AcS are
not, as a rule, repeated here.

153   Ethnic and Local Names

Aginnum 916; Agennensis
    now Agen

?Ampennum portus, now
    Empan, AcS 1.133

Anagnutes Pl. 4.108, cf.
    Steph.Byz. s.v. ʾΑγν-
    ῶτες (AcS 3.602-603)?

Aquitanus 691

Aunedonnacum IA; Auedon-
nacus TP; cf. W.u.S.
11, 1928, 149; mod.
Aulnay

Beleno castro Merov. num.,
Châteaubelin, cf. ciuis
Belinas 1113? (Cf. 148
above; Esp. Sant. 144)

Bituriges Viuisci cl.
inscc. (CIL 13.613, 614,
1697), Bituricus, -ri-
gensis, -rigicus,
Biturex f. F.342; for
Viuiscus see 241

?Blaccicum Plassac

Blauia itin. Greg. Tur.
Blaye

Bracedone Merov. num.;
cf. BSAF 1913, 83;
Bresdon

Brigiosum, Briosum Brioux

Burdigala -enses (cf. REA
6, 1908, 271; 12, 1910,
301; 15, 1913, 294)
mod. Bordeaux. The
etymology (cf. Portu-
cale, Cala-gurris) is
much disputed (REA 22,
1920, 300; 26, 1924,
395-6; 27, 1925, 307-
11; 29, 1927, 310; AcS
2.1038; the Italian
modern name Porto-gallo,
near Pavia can hardly
be in question). Since
both burdus and cala
are Aquitanian glosses
(158 below) I believe

they furnish the best
clue. Castaignet (RL
Rom. 2, 1926, 130) I
have not seen

Buxea silua vit. S
Amantii (AB 8, 1889,
347), quoted in FHRC
3.255; now Boixe,
Boisse. Cf. Boxsani
(80), boscus (79)

Ca...nao TP 268 (CIL 13
ii.2, p.661)

?C[alambri]o TP or
C[alendri]o?

Carantonis (-us) fl.
Charente

Κανέντἀλος fl. Ptol.

?Cassanomum uicaria
(?*Cassanomagos Cf.
REA 39, 1937, 241-
255; ZfSchwGesch. 14,
1934, 284; RC 50,
1933, 263; EC 1, 1936,
179; W.u.S. 11, 1928,
148), Cassinomago TP,
now Chassenon

Clennus, Clinnus fl.
Greg. Tur., now Clain

Condate TP (Desjardins
274)

Condatis portus Auson.

Corterate Coutras

Cunnacus TP, Connezac?

Local and Ethnic Names

Dumnotonus (-ni- , -a)
    uilla Auson.

Ecolisnenses, Iculisna,
    Aquil- AcS 2.24,47
    Angoulême (BA 1932-3,
    345, 605-19)

Edobola silua (in pago
    Petrocoreco) Double
    (see AcS 1.1407)

Espaniacus (Isp-) Merov.
    num., Espagnac; cf.
    148 above,]spana

Excisum Eysses

[Fines La Croix d'Hins]

Gabris Chabris?

Garronenses (C-?) ND

Gauiriacum Gauriac cf.
    CIL 13 (i) p.76

Germanicomagus TP (see
    REA 3, 1901, 324 n.13;
    12, 1910, 196; 20,
    1918, 231-25)

Iculisna v. Ecol-

Ircauium 1041

Liger fl., Loire

Limonum, Lem- cl. inscc.
    (cf. 8928), now Poi-
    tiers; REA 13, 1911,
    345

Locodiacensis Fortun.,
    -teiaco num. Merov.,
    Logotigiacenses Greg.
    Tur. (for *Luco-teia-
    cus) Ligu. (Vienne)

Lucaniacus Loigny

Marciacinsis uilla Marsas

Mediolanum (Santonum) cl.,
    num.

Meduli cl., -llinus Auson.,
    Médoc. Cf. Metellum
    uicum (Castelneau de
    Médoc or Melle en Poi-
    tou?) CIL 13, p.75

[?Nateiaci 11032 (REA 12,
    1910, 68), but see 241
    below]

Nitiobroges (-ig-) 916,
    cl.; Nisiobrox not Tir.,
    Nisiobroges Sid. Apoll.

Nouarus pagus Auson.,
    Nouliers; cf. Nouiore-
    gum inf.?

Νουιόμκγος Ptol. For the
    various places with
    this name, see P-W s.v.

Nouioregum IA (now Royan)

Local and Ethnic Names

Ogia, Oga ins. Rav.(?),
ASS; Île d'Yeu?

Ol(l)ario ins., Vliaros
(P.4.109), Olario-
nenses, Oléron (AcS
3.24)

(?Pel[pagus AE 1939.
133; but if correctly
restored Pel[ecianus,
then v. CIL 14.4012)

Petrucorii now Périgueux
(cf. Tricorii Tréguier)
i.e. "the four armies
or clans" (cf. Quat-
tuorsignani 84 above,
Tetrapolis, Nouem-
populi, Δεκαμέρη, Sex-
signani, decumates and
the like). On the Pe-
trucorii see the mono-
graph of P. Barrière
"Vesunna Petrucori-
orum" Périgueux 1930
[1932], Société d'-
Histoire et d'arché-
ologie du Périgord,
reviewed by Grenier
REA 34, 1932, 333; cf.
id., Congrès de Nîmes
1932, 154-7; Gosseler
in P-W.
   Inscc., CIL 13.972,
1038, 1704, 7031,
11040, cf. 8895; AE
1910.123; 1911.238;
1939.165; CIL 12.275.
In cl. authors BG 7.
75.3; Str. 4.2.2, 190-
191C.; Pl. 4.109; Ptol.
2.7.9; 2.7.11; NG,
Rav., Sulp. Sev.; num.?

Pictones cl. insc., 1129,

8928; Pictaui 1697,
10017.23, -auicus,
-onicus, now Poitiers,
Poitou

[Portunamneto TP]

?Prumiaco....Pict[cf.
mod. Prigny? (CRAc
InscBL 1921, 424; 1926,
67-76; REA 28, 1926,
247-251; 29, 1927, 58;
RA 26, 1927, 386.) There
is a Praemiaco....uilla
in Ven. Fortun., now
Preignac (AcS 2.1040,
cf. 1043), and Prumia-
cum in cart. Redon.
(11th cent.); Prigny
presumably stands for
*Prinniacum. Other
references RA 24, 1926,
241; REA 23, 1921, 245-
6, 333; 24, 1922, 128
n.1; 25, 1923, 261; 26,
1924, 146; JRS 14, 1924,
123-136

Raraunum (Rauran-) Rom
(but see REA 34, 1932,
57; 35, 1933, 415-16;
BSAOuest 1931, 92-111)

Ratiaton (-ate), Ratia-
tensis Rézé-les-Nantes

Ratis ins. Ré or Retz
(Charente-Inférieure)

Reontium Greg. Tur. Riom

?Riuisum AcS 2.1197 (but
cf. Ruessium 148 above)

Salomaco IA, Salles

?Σαμνῖται at the mouth
   of the Loire, Str.;
   perhaps read Ναμνῖται?
   In Dion. Hal. appar-
   ently Ἀμνῖται , Anni-
   tae Prisc., but Σαμν -
   ῖται Ptol., Σαπινῖται
   Marcian. Heracl. Cf.
   2 above; not for sq.?

Santones or Santoni (-us
   1041, 1136, 1716; -es
   1070), Santonicus,
   Saintes, Saintonge;
   Portus Santonum BA
   1932-33 [1936], 421;
   REA 37, 1935, 212;
   num.; Oceani Santon-
   ici (cf. CIL 13, p.133)

Sarrum TP

Segolmettius (or -ttsus?)
   10008.3 (at Saintes)

Segora TP

?Senonno (San-) num.
   Merov., AcS 2.1355;
   Cenon (CIL 13, p.154;
   cf. 212 below)

Σῖκος λιμήν MLI 246, Ptol.
   2.7

Tamnum (L-) IA, TP

Teodeberciaco, Teoderi-
   ciaco num. Merov.

Tincillacensis Ven. Fort.

Vallebana Auson.

Varatedo TP, Vayres

Vereginis Ven. Fort.,
   Baurech?

Vesunna Petrucorionum
   (also divine name),
   Vesunnensis 943, cf.
   949, 955, 956, 11040;
   TP, IA, Ptol., CIL 1,
   ed.2, 2654; Vesunni-
   cus Sid. Apoll., La
   Visone (CIL 13, p.
   122); see also Petru-
   corii above

?Vibriacensis Greg. Tur.
   (AcS 3.275)

Vincenna fl., Vig- ,
   Vienne

?Vincentiana CIL 13, p.
   76

Vliaros Pl. 4.109, see
   Ol(l)ario above

Viuisci v. Bituriges
   above; cf. Viuisci
   (Vevey), Hirschfeld
   SB Preuss. Akad. Wiss.,
   Ph.-H. Kl., 20, 1926,
   452-56 (24-28) "Aqui-
   tania in d. Römerzeit,"
   cf. REA 15, 1913, 47-
   52, 186

Vlta fl. Rav., ASS, Lot
   (cf. Oltis above)

Vssubium IA Ves- TP,
   Ptol., cf. 154 below

Modern Local Names

Remark:

I have not been able to procure C. Dangibaud's
work Mediolanum Santonum 2 vols. 1933 (see RA 3, 1934,
115); or Busset on Gergovia, also 1933 (ib. 139); or
Janicaud on La Creuse 1932 (REA 37, 1935, 212), or his
later work Evaux Gallo-Romain (1934). For the Petrucorii see especially Goessler in P-W s.v.

154   Further Modern Local Names

(Le Mas d') Agenais, Ambernac, Antigny, St Apré,
l'Aunis; Badefols-de-Cadouin, Bérouges, Bessac, Bour-
bonne, Bourg (de-Visa); Chadenac, Charroux, Chauvigny,
Civaux, Civray, Les Cléons, Consac, Le Cormier, (St
Vincent de) Cosse, Cubzac, St Cybardeaux; Exoudun (cf.
148); Le Fleix; Gaillardon, La Gaubretière, Goulaine;
Hautefage; Ingrande-sur-Anglin; La Langon, Loupiac; St
Maixent, Magnelles, Marcay, Monségur, Nanteuil, Neuvicq-
sous-Montguyon; Pareds, Persac; St Romain, Roudoulous,
Rouillé; Sanxay, Sauvagnas, Savigné (-y), St Savin;
(St-Cyr-en-) Talmondois, Teuillac, Tonneins, Le Touron;
Le Veillon, Verrines.

As to La Vendée, the name most likely represents
a *Veneto- (cf. RA 33, 1931, 162) to be distinguished
from Veneti (Vannes, 179)

404

Modern Local Names

Some modern discussions: Barrière RA 1, 1933, 13-
23; M. Besnier REA 28, 1926, 337-351; M. Clouet in Rev.
d'Aunis et de Saintonge 1937 (see REA 40, 1938, 298);
A. Dauzat in La Toponymie française, Paris 1939, 175-
322 (Auvergne and Velay, cf. REA 32, 1930, 139-148; 33,
1931, 357-388; 36, 1934, 80-84); L. Fayolle REA 37,
1935, 58-62 (Poitou; Charentes); id. BSAOuest 1929 (see
REA 34, 1932, 419), ibid. 1928; id. BS hist. et arch.
du Périgord 1935, 163-169 (on bodica, broga, toia; Bergerac, Riberac); id. BSAOuest 1934-35, 347-350; M. Du-
portet Topobibliographie de la France (Creuse, Allier,
Indre); P. F. Fournier in BS hist. et sc. de l'Auvergne
52, 1932, 113 (on Ygrande: *Equo-randa, cf. REA 38,
1936, 54 and 348); A. Nicolaï, Noms de lieux de la
Gironde, Bordeaux, 1938 (known to me only from Ann. Ph.
1938 [1939], 212). On the older work of Delzon (1845)
see Rev. Ling. Rom. 4, 1928, 108. On Badet (both in
Aquitania and Lugdunensis) see Badey REA 39, 1937, 44.
The Dictionnaire des noms de lieux... de l'Allier by
G. Grassoreille, Moulins 1881 (REA 38, 1936, 346) I have
not seen.

Remark:

Arcachon (if for *Arcaisso) may be Iberian (REA
31, 1929, 55); for local names of the Charente see the
works of E. Béquet listed ib. 32, 1930, 23; 35, 1933,
414-415; Chronique de Toponymie, Gironde ib. 40, 1938,
404-410 (A. Nicolaï); names of the Bordeaux region, ib.
26, 1924, 255; names in -ac of Centre and Ouest REA 29,
1927, 305-306 (cf. 28, 1926, 26 [Jarnac]; 30, 1928,
122); names of Limousin, ib. 14, 1912, 405, cf. 20,
1918, 181-184; Saintonge ib. 231-36; Tulle [the divine
name Tutela, cf. above 86; 155, 181 below?) 14, 1912,
406; cf. 15, 1913, 451-52; 16, 1914, 345; 18, 1916, 210;
19, 1917, 47; 22, 1920, 54; 25, 1923, 385, local name
Tudela A.D. 1227, at Orléans); La Ligoure (Limousin) ib.
14, 1912, 201; river-names in Limousin, ib. 19, 1917,
282; Indre-et-Loire (so far as it is part of Aquitania)
ib. 23, 1921, 243; Dordogne, F. Lot RC 45, 1928, 312-
317; Ptolemy's account of the west coast of Gaul RA 31,
1930, 74-92 (C. Denancourt); Chronique de Toponymie:
Agenais by A. Nicolaï, REA 41, 1939, 252-258; ancient
routes, REA 39, 1937, 37-38; Chronique de Toponymie:
Limousin and Marche, Périgord by G. Lavergne in REA 36,

Local and Divine Names

1934, 397-400 (cf. 402); see also the papers by Dauzat
in ZONF 4, 1928, 257-269 (Berry); 6, 1930, 234-239
(miscell.); 8, 1932, 206-237 and 9, 1933, 10-45 and
108-132 (Auvergne and Vellay); Rev. Ling. Rom. 4, 1928,
62-117.

155   Divine Names

Adsmerius (Mercurius)
  1125

Aritmatho Marc. Burd. 20.
  60, cf. FHRC 115.10-
  14 (after Grimm)
  ardhmhath "summum
  bonum" or τὸ ἀγαθὸν
  δαιμόνιον (?)

Belenus FHRC 105.13,
  106.4

Boruo Albius CRAcInscBL
  1918, 479-484; cf. RC
  38, 1920-21, 89-90

Cobledulitauus 939 (cf.
  Bassoledulitanus 15
  above; Specht KZ 64,
  1937, 8)

Damona Matuberginnis
  See the references at

Boruo Albius above,
and add REA 22, 1920,
55; Mél. d'Arch. et
d'Hist. 50, 1913, 10;
RA 10, 1919, 417 (from
Rivières, Charente);
the epithet appears
to be a local name,
but for the ending cf.
Ilunnis (86)

Iunones 567

Maglo|matonio (dat.; or
  two words?) 915

Matuberginnis v. Damona

Minmantiae(?) 940; cf.156 infr.

?Merc[BSAOuest 1931,
  92-99 (REA 34, 1932,
  57), or personal name
  (?), but see also REA
  2, 1900, 363

Divine Names

Onuaua 580(?), 581

Robur deus 1112, cf. EC
1, 1936, 179; cf. 86

Stanna dea 950, 953(?).
But cf. Siannus 1536
(150 above), 1669
(181 below)? See also
149 Remark, 157 Re-
mark, and gl. 158 be-
low; possibly Siannus
(?) 10010.1813 qq (un-
less that is an error
for Siluanus); Etanna
(Narb. 80)

Sirona 582 (cf. perhaps
]ona 586, though that
might be for Epona,
or Diuona); Đirona,
Dir- cf. AcS 1.1286

Telo deus 948, 950(?),
952

Tutela dea 583-585, 939,
955, 956; cf. C.p.77;
154 Remark (above)

Tutela Vesunna 949

[Tutela Boudiga insc. of
Bordeaux (AE 1922.116,
cf. REA 24, 1922, 236-
246; 26, 1924, 256;
JRS 11, 1921, 102-107;

Macdonald, Roman Bri-
tain 1914-1928, p.110)
was worshipped by Bri-
tish soldiers from York,
and is herself no doubt
British]

Vesunna 949, 11040 (or
local?); cf. CIL 1,
ed.2, 2654; Germania
7, 1923, 15; 8, 1924,
80; and cf. Vesunia-
henae (223) Roscher
Lex. s.vv. Cf. Umb.
etc. Vesune, Osc.
Vesulliaís (ID 2.668),
Lig. Vesulus (PID 3.
50); REA 3, 1901, 212
n.1

Verpantus 1180, if divine
(i.q. Priapus), but
possibly personal;
-nt- a reverse writing
for -t- , since -nt-
may become -t-

Viducus (đ?), Visucius
(Mercurius) 576-577

Vssubius (genius loci)
919, cf. 84, 153 above;
Vsso-marus 156 Remark
B, gl. usubim (178);
useilo[(171)?; but
not ussibus 3202 or
usibus 1351, 11151
unless this Latin form
somehow suggested the
divine name Vssubius

Personal Names

Remark:

It is likely that other divine names were current in Aquitania, though not actually attested; thus Barrière p.86 reports a bronze figurine of a youth with a bear's head, compare Artio (CIL 13.5160), Artaius (12. 2199). Note also BSAF 1904, 319 (a head with three horns), CRAcInscBL 1939, 366 (Morlet on solar cults among the Aruerni); JCS 1, 1949, 35-46 (Pettazzoni on the three-faced god).

156   Personal Names

Abascantus 723

Abase? 937 add.

Ac[ed]omopas 1042-45, num.; cf. -patus 1366; Ag- Esp.; for the ending cf. Gatpas (151), Esumopas (182), but perhaps not Auopate AcS 3.779

Acau[1157

?Acaunus 685 v. Caunus

Acialico 10010.2851

Adbogius 7031 (cf. C. p.122)

Adbucietus 582

Adbugius 11877

†Adelfi 912

Adluc[us 1177 (or -[ctus Esp.)

Adnamatinia 11044, Riese 1313a

Adnametus 708, 979

Adnamita AE 1911.239

Personal Names

Adruppos (-us?) 994

Adtusta 819

Aduorix 750

?Aepurita 837 (Ate-?)

Aetunessus 1066

Agedillus 1041

Albilla 767

[Alcimus C.p.76]

Alpuni 10024.310

Ambiorix 1120

[Aman(da) 1063]

Ande 10010.2851

Andel(i)pa 750

?Andra 10010.2851

Andus 608

Aneχtlus 1165

Anna 768

Annibertus 960

Annius 11063

?Anodisim (-bim) 650

Aper 653

Aplonius 751

Aquitanus 750

Aqutus 7297, 10002.79

Argenus Esp. Sant. 134

Artelia Barrière p.75

A]ruereiho MLI 262

Arula 569

Atectorigiana 1041, cf.
157 below

Ateχtorix num.

Aterta 764

Ateula m. 800

Ateuritus 656, 837(?);
Esp. Sant. 168;
10016.35

Atioχta 658, -us 659

Atreba 807

Atrinius Esp. Sant. 152,
cf. Atrinu 10010.2838

Attaius 575

Attillius 11037

Atto 915, 922

Atunessus Esp. Sant. 111

Aturios 1089

Atturita MLI 262

Attusiola 662

Atusius 982

Aucauo 890

Aueta 664-666, 772

Personal Names

Aueticcus 1090

Auetius 667

Auita 602; -o, -us
10017.207

Auitianus 1090

Aulicus 857

A]uor AcS 1.317

Auro 822

Ausonius (cf. C.p.76;
REA 12, 1910, 196)

Autuis 1121

Axula 672

?Balorix (Bai-) *118, v.
REA 23, 1921, 128-29

Bassiania 11052

Batrusco 675

Belestus 781

Belgius 1165 (if personal)

Beliccus 949

?Belinas 1113 (-ate|pus?)

Belinia 658(?), 676,
1076

Bello Esp. Pér. 22

??Berinus BSAF 1914, 173

Betudaca 73 (cf. Bit-)

Bitudaga 774 (cf. Bet-)

[Bituna REA 13, 1911, 208]

Bitugnata 10017.225

Blandus 11059

Blastus 679

Bloxus 843

Boias 570, 615 (properly
ethn. cf. 84)

Brennos 677

Brig[10017.230, Brigia
231

?Cabilius Esp. Sant. 90

?Cabtiue 1138

Cahedo 11010.2838

Caisiccus 755

Caletia 986

Camulatucus 1120

Camulia 679

?Camulinus 680, 681;
Camul[10017.246

Camulus 682

Canius 587

Cantosenus 752 (Cauto-
AcS 1.870)

Cantus 583, cf. 1013

?Cantusa 797

Caprius 1061; cf. BSAF
   1914, 173

Carantilla 1092

Carasoua 820

Carina 1181

?Carneolus *119, REA 23,
   1921, 128-29 (cf.
   Corn-)

Castricia 613

Catilia 1130

Catius 1031

Cattius 11070a, AE 1912.
   279

Catullus 1140

Catus 1062

Cauaria 1139, -ius Esp.
   Sant. p.247

Cauarianus Esp. Sant. 81

Caunus 685 (Acaunus?)

Celta 800

Cessorinus 11044

?Cetrus Esp. Sant. 70

Chaudos 10010.2954

[Chlodouus (A.D. 643) 905]

Cicelauus 1140, cf. gl.
   cic- , gig- (158)

Cictouanus AcS 1.1012

Cinnamus 1096

Cinto 653, 688, 702

Cintua 690

Cintucnatus 844

Cintugena 664, 691-693,
   -us 672, 694, 1031,
   1163

Cintuginatus 708

Cintugnatus 695, 6969,
   cf. 10010.2847

Cintus 653, 689; 10010.
   2848

Cintusma 697, -us 698, 699

Classu[11054

Cobea 675

?Cobnertis 1097 (an
   collibertus?)

Cocceianus 729

Cocumbus 10025.178

Cogidubnus 1040

Coinagius 7031 (cf. C.
   p.122); not for
   Comagius?

Coinitus 1163

Columbus 10025.178

?Comagius 699; cf. Coin-

Comartiorix 720

Personal Names

Comeliddus 959 (read
  -ssus by some)

Comerta 710 (for Cobn-)

Comnertus 1061

Comnitsia 800

Conculcanus 927

Conetodu[bnus] 10010.
  634

Congonnetiacus 800

Congonnetodubnus 1040,
  1042-1045

Conmolnico (dat.?) 712

Conisouinus 711

Corentius 1066

Corin[713

Corneola 647 (cf. Carn-)

Cornicus Jullian Bord.
  247

Corobilla 1139

?Corr...is Jullian Bord.
  232

Corritia 1066

Cosconius 715

Cossa, -ius Esp. Sant.
  149

Coχt[829

Cratin[sin?] 669

Crax[754

Craxxillus 659

Crepio 1107

Crito 858

Crodoleno 10024.313

?Cronopiles 10017.35

Cru[636, 637

Cumpirtius? 848 (for
  Compertus?)

Dagobius 720 (-itus?)

Dapsilis 1006

?Decumo Esp. Sant. 78

[Diceratus 1055]

Diratus 721

Dioran(n)us Esp. Sant. 98

Diorata 721

Diuica Jullian Bord. 113

Diuiciaco 1048 add.

Diuiχta 666(?), 722, 1067,
  1068

?Diuiχtianus 666

Diuiχtus 579, apparently
  -uir- i.e. R for ⋏
  or Χ (?); 811, 817,
  854, 1068, 11079

Diχtus linarius 639 (for
  Diui -?)

Personal Names

Diuogen[ia] 571

Docius 1116

Donnus 1120

Doroicu 909 add.

Doromenus 10008.43

Draucus 724

Drutedo 1092, *118 (REA
    23, 1921, 128-29)

]dubita 725

Dubna 10017.333

Ducani 10010.2840

?Duetil Jullian 84

Dumnomotus 1069, 11045;
    cf. BA 1910 cxlvi, AE
    1910.123 and 158 (p.
    448); REA 12, 1910,
    295

Duratius BG 8.26.1

Durnacus 726

?Duruinnu 1157

Eb[11053

Ebelias (Ep-) 10017.338

Ebucia 727

Ebures BSAF 1899,163

?Eburius 617

Ecritus 1173

Egidius 11036

(H)eluinia 1115

Epotsorouidus (-tsio- ,
    -ster- vv.ll.; cf.
    Esp. Sant. 30) 1036 ii

Eppimus Jullian 84

Eppo 10017.345

Escingus 568

Esenocarus Barrière p.75

?Etucari 1069 (cf. Loset-)

[†Foegadius Sulp. Sev.
    Chr. 2.44.1]

Forconi[ ]us 909 add.

?Forens[11074

Fronto 1068

Gaii f?, Gauf? REA 42,
    1940, 600-608

Galactorius Fortun.

[Galeo CIL 1 ed.2, 2654;
    Cic. Att. 11.12.4 (47
    B.C.), cf. Germania
    7, 1923, 15; 8, 1924,
    80]

?Galulircli 645 (with
    other faked names:
    Duetil, Tiblik,
    Eppimus, Soris)

Gealus (Gea?) 821

413

Gedomo(n) and Gedemo(n) 1036 ii

Gemellus 579

Gnatusius 982

Harcola 740

Iabba 10010.2847

?Iardarius 851 (L-?)

Ibinuus 10010.2849

Ica m. 800

[Icco 922 (Alpin.)]

?]ictipo[909 add.

?Iedurui 1157

Ignius 631

Illius, -ia AcS 2.33

?Incianueruaus 746

Inderca 747

Indrcillus 747

Intercillus 608 (-ius lapis)

Inucenus (-g-) 748

[?Iounm (A.D. 466) AE 1927.154 (Ionah?)]

Irutnii 10010.2848

Iscanius Esp. Sant. 151

?Iuarus 1143 (cf. 150)

Iuorix 679

Lae[756

Laenas Esp. Sant. 73

Laftus 787 (Lae-)

Lagisse 646

Laguaudus 788

[Lampridius C.p.76]

Lasciuus 583

Leduccus 855

Λείψανα IG 14.2521

Lendu 10010.2847

Lenti[11075

[Lentulius C.p.149]

Ligurius 965

Lima, Limaretus 10017.524

Littus 10010.2854

Lituci 10017.525

Liuius 571, 804

?Losetucari 1069 (or Etucari?)

?Lubius 1080

Lucere 712

Lucterius 1024

Personal Names

Lugaunus 804

Luguselua 996

?Luppa (Taluppa?) 732

Lupus 614

Maccha 10010.2854

Macer 1041

Macuso 10017.549

Magirra 1032

Magnilla 1083

Maio (Mato?) 816

Malla CRAcInscBL 1918,
    479; RA 10, 1919, 417

Malluro ib.

Mamma 999

Mantusa 667

Map[10017.562

Marcus 1061

Marcen[1187

Maricca 1084, -us Tac.h.,
    2.61

Marinco? 1048, but
    Marino[1048 add.

Marina 1048

Maritalus 740

?Marmo 915

Marulla 1000

Marullius 966, 977

Mascellio 11057, -ius
    1058

Masclus 1058

Masma AcS 2.170?

Mato see Maio

Matrona 758, 1041

Matua (Natua?) 844, 866;
    -us 773

Matugenus 570

Matutio 570

?Mauetus (Masu-?) 799

Maurusius 912

Medi[1136

Meddillus BSAF 1891,83

Meduas 1170; cf. REA 22,
    1920, 211

Melausus 801

Meliddus 959

Melissus 1085

Memantusa 667 (Mim-?)

Mercantillus 1120

Mesniu 10010.2837

Micurita 802

Mimantusa v. Mem- and cf.
    Memmatinsis AcS 2.586
    (Greg. Tur.) and 155 above

Personal Names

Minicia Esp. Sant. 118

Molnicus 712

†Mommolenus (A.D. 643) 905

Mona/cur, see Brunet Rec. Commiss. Arts et Mon., Charente Inf. 20, 1927, 130

Monda 10010.2847

Moneta 1001

Moria 712

Mucc[10010.2854

Mutacus 631

Natua (Ma-?) 844

Namatius cf. AcS 2.675

Nemmia 804

Nammiola 1007

Nantius 666, 805; 10017. 618

?Nasbinus 635

?N|conisouini 711, but v. Con-

Nemetocena 806; -gena 603

Neptacus 857

Nepusa 638 (Greek?)

?Nertinius Jullian 182

Nertus 860, -a 752

?Nicenis 1094 (if genuine)

Noniconius 738

Nonna 1003

Nonnita 536

Nunu 10017.646

[Ocellio (a bird) 612 [Bilbilis]]

Odma 10010.2834

Ogilolus 806

Ollouico cl., BG 7.31.5

[Onatedo (Bellouacus) 611]

[Otacilia (Lugd.) REA 31, 1929, 259]

Otuaneunus 1036 ii

?Ouetil (Du-?) 645

Paedocaeus 642

Pari[AcS 2.932

Pascu[817

[Paulinus Nolanus]

[Pellaeus C.p.76]

Petrahes 10025.178; so Esp. Sant. 169, but Petraites or Tetraites (-des) in CIL

Personal Names

Petronius 1090

?Pilinis 658

?Pi⨯ticenus 870

Ponis f. 763

Potitianus 11056

Prito[1157

Pupius 821

Quadratus 925

[Rasinius Esp. Sant. 174]

Regrin[723

Remo 628 (unless ethn.)

Rennini 10010.2837

Reueta 988

Ricoueriugus 1048 (-g-)

Rosicia 863

?Ruso 7031

[Sabinianus Esp. Sant.
    79]

[Sabinus ib. 93, 103]

Sacrapo 829

Sacrina 830, 996

Sacuro 586; Auson.

†Saffarius (episcopus)
    1028

Saius 831

Sal[756

Sam[10017.756

Samocenus 806 (-g-)

Samius 10006.81

Samo 834 (for Sammo)

Sam[m]onicus 832 (-mm-),
    833 (-m-)

Santia 1148

Sau[676

Sanuacus 764

Scottus Barrière p.56

?Seasciatonos 1157, v.l.
    Seassiaturias

Secol[11074 (or Secol
    ...cera)

Sedatus 846

Segolmettus C.p.134,
    Segolmettsus BSAF
    1891, 83

Seius 8.2103

Sena 10017.784

Senecianus 738, 763

Senecio BSAF 1914, 173

Senilis 1090

417

Seniulus 848 (cf. 58
  Remark)

Seno 837

Senocarus 1000

Senodona 697, -donna 844,
  1146

Senon[da?] 849

Senonia 921

Senoruccus 685

Sentilla 686

Senus 847

[Serclus (Sendrus?)
  Parisius 629]

?Seuorus 853

Silanus(?) BSAF 1928,
  155-156

Silann[Esp. Pér. 64

Sintaugus 855

Siora 856

Soillius 767

Solda Esp. Sant. 170

[Solimarius Treuerus
  634]

Solinus 857

Soll[610

Soriolito 740

Soris 645

Sottus 956 (Sc-?)

Spartola 799

Sparsiolus 703

Suadugena 11050, AE 1911.
  238

Sulla 804

Sumer[774

Summina 864

Sunutua, -ius 865

?Sura 866

?Taluppa (Luppa?) 732

Tascus 11073

Tasgillus 687, 11069

Tate[891

Tatinus 868

?Tatmaluius 10002.495

Tauratis 1097 (Tauras)

Taurianus 769

Taurica 1098, -us 11081

?Tercetrus Esp. Sant. 70

Teretina Esp. Pér. 64

Tesco m. 694

?Tetraites (-des) v.
  Petrahes

Personal Names

[Tetricus (Imp.) REA 37,
    1935, 213; C.pp.76,
    77]

Teutomatus C.p.117; cf.
    Vendryes CRAcInscBL
    1939, 465-480; P-W
    s.v.

Tharto C.p.159

?Thelegusa 575 (Greek?)

Thorybius 11033

Tigota 10010.2847

?Tilblik[645

Titilius BSAF 1914, 173

Tocetus 582

Toci(us) 11059; Tocus
    Barrière pp.78, 124

Toglus 10017.848

Tolonio 10010.2839

Toutissa Jullian 976; cf.
    10017.849

Trilicus 870

Tro[CIL 1 ed.2, 2654

?Tuboglirila[1012, cf.
    645?

?Tucci CIL 1 ed.2, 2654

?Turias 1157

Tutus 924

[Varenilla 1129, cf.
    C.p.149]

[Varenus 1129]

[Ven]antia 884

Venixsama Bull. Mon.
    1881, 120-121

Venixxamus 1125, cf.
    Bull. Mon. 1880,
    297-299

Venopis 1087

Verpantus 1180 (unless
    divine)

Verrio 10010.2833

Vertamica 10017.889; cf.
    136 Remark 3 above

Verter 1059

Veruicia 878

Vestinus 611

Viblina 11052

Viduco 576

[Vilatessa 960]

Vilius BSAF 1914, 173

Vimp(us) 1031

Vindi 10017.915

Vindicianus 804

Vinícius 969

Vipodualis 1095

Personal Names

Virdomarus C.p.159;
  3.2065

Vlat(tia) 884 -ius 993;
  AcS 3.21

]ulpuro 759

?Vnagus 570

[Vocconianus, Bocc- ,
  Bucc- AE 1939.133]

Vodeluteiaci (gen.) 1081

Vol[1048

Volt[1040, 1042-5

Voltinus 1041

Vrittius 784; cf. RE 1,
  1913, 23; AE 1913.233

Vrsa 885, 912

?Vrus 784 (Vritior? uritu?)

?Xiduis 10010.2837

Note xxvii bis

    Names of Potters found at Bordeaux (BSAOuest 1934-
35, 214-232) and at Périgueux (Barrière pp.126, 129),
cf. 88 Remark above, include the following:

Adamatus

Anteius

Ateihus (-tus)

Lucius?

Mucus?

Ocella

Sertorius

Titullus, and

the noteworthy
  Sphanir (or
  Spanair)

420

Names of Potters

Remark:

(A) There is reason to believe that the Bordeaux and
Saintes districts were colonized by settlers from the
Rhineland, as well as by occasional migrants from Belgica or Lugdunensis; this may help to explain some rather
striking coincidences in the lists of Glosses of Aquitania and Belgica (including some items from Britain),
see 158 and 207 below. Thus in the inscc. we have

Aulercus 610

Belgus 1165, cf. 1042-5

Bellouacus 611

Britan[nicus] 636

Coriosoles 616

Mattiaci 11032

Mediomatricus 623

Menap[624

Neruius 1056

Parisius 629

Remus 628, 1055, 1091;
  -o 628

Sequanus 631

Senones 929

Treuerus 633, 634, 635

Viennensis 636, 637

Vosagensis pagus, see
  148 above

    Cf. Zangemeister on CIL 13.6607 (AcS 2.1351);
Jullian REA 4, 1902, 302, also called attention to the
fact that S. Seuerinus of Bordeaux (uita, Mélanges
Couture, Toulouse 1902, pp.23-63) hailed from Trier;
moreover, the name Senodonnus (above) is also found on
coins of the Caletes (Belg.)

Names of Potters

(B) Doubtful Potters' Names from Aquitania Secunda

Abal(1)an(o)

Abbo

Abitus

Abreχta

Acadillus

Acapus |Cos

Acapusos

Accauus

Accu, Acco

Acedilu (-g-)

Aco, Acu

Adlucus

Adn[

Aiasa 10010.2819

Ainaicesus

Ainicesus

Airamnus

Aitula

Albilla

Alus(s)a

Ambaris

Amilus

Amunius

Anb[

Ande[

Andoca

Andra

Aneχtolatius

Anunus

Aolid[
10010.2837

Apa[

Apamos

Apasa

Apaua[

Apronius

Apu[r..

Ar[

Arabus

Ardacus

Artelia

Aseros

Asiticus (-iat-)

Astucis (gen.)

?Ata|aχtus

Ate[

Ateixanti

?Aten[

Atepsi

Atilus

Atios

Atrinu 10010.2838

Atusos

Auaui 10010.2837

Aumom

Aχto?

?Bauliusi

B(b)ixi?

Belenios, -inios

Belli[

Belsus, -a

Bitugnata

]bius

Bollucius
10010.336

Bre[

Bulini

422

Names of Potters

Bus[

Ca..u

Cadu

Caiaciac[us]
  10010.2851

Caicu

Callis[

Cal(l)us

Camelus

Caminus

Canini 10010.2851

Cantomallus

Capito, -us

Caratuc(c)us

Caserus

Casurus

CD

CDP

Cenalus

Cenian[us 10010.
  2851

Cermuru 10010.
  2836

Ceus

Chaudos

Ciali

Cicer[

Cicr

Cictouanus

Cidiui 10010.
  2835

Cinia

Cinticatus

Cintu

Cintucra

Cipario 10010.
  2835

[Ontu]ciso (V-)

Cisus

Clam

Clulusau 10010.
  2838

Cna

Cni

Co[

Cobi 10010.2851

Cobsi 10010.
  2847

Coca

Cociru

Comos, -us

Condo

Conetodu[bnus]
  10010.634

Coppus 10010.
  2851

Coro

Cracines

Crasisa

Criuib[
  10010.2837

Crocu 10010.2851

Cuc[

Cucab (Cucar)

Cucesa 10010.
  2851

?Cure

?Curita

Cusa 10010.2833

Daluisius

Dassen[

Dauno

Dioranus

Diorix

Doni[cus

Doeccus, i.e.
  Doueccus

423

Names of Potters

Dourcus 10010.
  2851

?Drecinus (Derc-)

Duc[

Duratios, -us

Ebredus

Elussius

Emocus

Epi(us)

Epr.in[

Epron

Euutinic 10010.
  2848

Fatm

Iccnus

Illius

In[

Inoci

Inulus

Lupus

Macar(i)us

Malcio

Mascius

Meccessus

Meddillus

Melissus

Micra

Milia

Minirata
  10010.2848

Niramus 10010.
  2838

Nonnit(t)us, -a

Oeco

Oepia
  10010.2849

Ogarius

Oico

Olognatus

Omp[

Orusius

Ouo

Pairus

Pistil(l)os

Piᵪtaucus
  10002.399

Ratiatus

Reen

Regalis

Rinnin[
  10010.2838
  (cf. Renn-)

Rioge[nus
  10002.428

Rosculi 10010.
  2851

Salu

Sannin[

Sanuacus, -a

Sanus, -a

Saria

Scorobres

Sena

Soiata

Solimarius

Sollitus AcS
  2.1608,38

Succus[
  10010.2847

Coin-legends

Succusius 10010.2849	Tiseno[	Vic[
	To[	Vicanus
Surburo	Toglus	Vigeus
Sutticus 10010.2851		Viniu 10010.2847
	Verelob[	Virius
Tabilio	Verna 10010. 2854	Vlatucnos
Tatmaluius		Vssomarus
	Viatinus	
Tau[		Vsucius
	]uiatu	
Tecessus		Vtrianus

3. Coin-legends and Glosses

157   Coin-legends of Aquitania
        (from Blanchet Traité, and AcS)

ab	aχitos
abucatos (-g)	adcanaunos (cf. Concan-aunae PID 1, p.321)
abudo(s), abuds	adietuanus(?), cf. 87 above
aka	
acincouepus Bl.-Dieudonné 4	anadgouoni (not andugouo-nius ?)

Coin-legends

andu

anniccoios

[αρ (?) see Tr. 86, 211-
  16; not αρ(ουϵρνοι)
  AcS 3.700]

ariuos

atau (cf. Tau[156 Re-
  mark?)

?atc

atectorix

??ateuloib Bl.-Dieudonné
  289 (as a correction
  of παυλοιβ)

audos (for abud-)

belinos (or bienos?)

biotau[? AcS 3.866

bri[cos?], v. cicedu

brigios Tr. 106, 421

bucios (-g-) AcS 3.997,
  cf. SprFK 195; cf.
  βωκιος (78)

caledu, καλϵδυ

caliages(?), not g- (Tr.
  107)

?caloduanus AcS 1.704

cam[

cambil[

cambotre

camulo[genus]

Καπιτος (?)

cas

celecorix

cicedu (or cicedubri, or
  -u bri-)

?comolones AcS 3.1263

conno, κοννο

contoutos

cosius

κυ(βα?) | ουι, see 148
  above; cubio(s),
  cubiio

?cunuanus (AcS 1.1196;
  for adcanaunos?)

dara

diarilos

donnadu

durat(ios)

earos

eiqitiaco

embau?

426

Coin-legends

eoe

epad (i.e. -ā)

epil(l)os

epomeduos

epos

esu(u)ios

]iliouico(s)

isunis

iulios | aged]omopatis

iurca Bl.-Dieudonné 197

lemiso

luc(c)ios

luχterios, cf. lu tos(?)
  at La Grauf. (90 sqq.);
  RC 4, 1879-80, 317-323
  and 156 above

?luernes cf. 151 above

motuidiacos

nercod[

nes (or sen?)

oeo? (cf. eoe)

omondon

osne[

ουι·κυ (v. κυ)

pen(n)obrias (Merov.), a
  local name

perrucori

piχtilos (Lugd.?)

?pom[Gallia 5, 1947,
  288-289; Tr. 135 (T.
  Pom)

που (or απου, υπου ?), πθυ
  (for πoυ?)

]raob

re[(cf. urdo-)

sactnos, sacto

santonos

se[

sedul(l)os, sedulix AcS
  2.1434, cf. BG 7.78.4

sen (or nes?)

σμερ

solima(ros), but v. AcS
  3.866,39 (-ra)

sotiata

Iberian Words in Inscriptions

tatinos

[triccos, -us (Turones)]

uandetios (cf. mod. Ven-
   dée), -elos, -enos,
   -nenos, uadnelos
   (-elios)

uepotalus (not uero-)

uercingetorixs Cf. BA
   1932-3 [1936], 265-66

uerga or -ca (for Verca-
   [ssiuellaunus])

ουυ (i.e. Bituriges?)

uirc[

uiredios, -etios, -edisos

uirota(los?); but cf.
   uepo-

uirt, uirtu, uirtuas;
   hardly cf. uritu,
   ieuru?

urdo|ri(x) ?

υvo (AcS 3.463)

urippanos

Remark:

   It is well to call attention here to certain Latin
inscriptions of Iberia (Spain and Portugal) for the sake
of comparison of particular words or forms with glosses
or epigraphic items of Gaul proper, viz.

   (i) CIL 2.2660 (cf. p.912), Dessau 3259, CE 1526,
line 12:
                     in parami aequore
Cf. AcS 2.928, paramus "tableland" (Sp. páramo), 158 below.

Iberian Words in Inscriptions

(ii) ib. 3361.3-4, Dessau 5688:

agnuar(um) | trecentarum

A measure of area, see 158 below; cf. CIL 2.430, 3-4
(an | cnunarum?).

(iii) ib. 738.5, 739.2-3:

arimo(m) · sintamo

AcS 3.684, MLI p.181 nos. xlvi-xlvii.

(iv) ib. 430, MLI p.184 no. lvi, v. 3:

ueamuaearum tarboum

(v) ib. 5607, MLI p.183 no. liii a:

nimidi

Cf. 79 above.

(vi) And especially the famous lex metalli Vipascen-
sis, see EE 3. pp.165-189, CIL 2 Suppl. 5181, a further
table of which was discovered subsequently, see AE 1906.
151 (after Journal des Savants 1906, 442), cf. SB Preuss.
Akad. Wiss., Ph-H Kl. 1931, 2 p.836 and Cahiers d'histoire et d'archéologie 11, 1936, 527-547 (Les mines romaines d'Aljustrel, by P. Finiels and M. Louis); Dessau
6891:

Iberian Words in Inscriptions

(vi) ctd.

v. 28 recisamina

47 rutramina

50 ubertumbis

54 lausiae

58 pittaciarium

Cf. Buecheler ALL 2, 1885, 606 (lausiae: Sp. losa);

from AE 1906.151,7-8:

cuniculus

ternagus

Cf. 158 below.

On the tin mines of the Lemouices see REA 13, 1911, 350; compare the gloss (158) stannum and the divine name (155) Stanna. Further: Frank Economic Survey 3, 167 ff.; Sutherland Romans in Spain, 196; Oliver Davies Roman Mines in Europe (reviewed in JRS 26, 1936, 107; Ulf Täckholm Römischer Bergbau 1937 (cf. PhW 58, 1938, 1418; Klio 32, 1939, 119).

(vii) To these may be added the following:

umtrubos (CIL 2.2848), cf. μdτρεβο(?), unless we have to deal with the suffix -oba, -uba (Iberian?) e.g. Maenoba, Lenuba, Lenubar, Maenuba, see Schulten F.u.F. 14, 1939, 18; or the suffix -ibas of Iberian ethnica (see PID 2, p.474).

lugouibus (div. name) CIL 2.2812, cf. lucouebus at Sinoza, RA 19, 1912, 457 (no.12) and 33, 1931, 364 (cf. 102-106), Ir. Lugh, Gaul. Lugu-dunum.

nimmedo (pers. name?) ib. 6, 1935, 210.

Iberian Words in Inscriptions

On personal names the work of A. Carnoy (Éléments celtiques Louvain, 1907) is in need of revision; and many Keltic elements are to be recognized also in local and divine names of the Iberian peninsula, the collection of which cannot be undertaken here.

The name Hispania, cf.]spana (148), Ispana [regio] (80), Espaniacus or Isp- (153), Spanilia (83), but perhaps not Ssipan AE 1921.95, is doubtless Iberian (not Basque, Ph.W. 56, 1936, 632; cf. 57, 1937, 63; 58, 1938, 142-144).

(viii) The insc. on the vase of San Miguel de Liria that reads

gudua deitzdea

is interpreted both from the scene that it depicts and from Basque as a battle cry; see RA 7, 1936, 95-100; 8, 1936, 211-212; P. Dixon, The Iberians of Spain, 1940, p.8; some other references on Iberian and Basque: REA 23, 1921, 59; E. S. Bouchier, Spain under the Roman Empire; C.H.V. Sutherland, The Romans in Spain, 1939; G. Bonfante, Emerita 4, 1936, 326 (Basque gudu "war," deitzea "llamada, grito"), but against this interpretation A. Garcia y Bellido (quoting D. Julio de Urquijo) in Archivo Español de Arqueologia 15, 1942, 170; cf. Arch. Anz. 48, 1935, 519.

See also *247 ii-iv below. On Toncius (-g-), Toncetamus (-g-) see J. Leite de Vasconcellos Arch. português 1, 1895, 228-232 (cf. Vollmöllers Jahresbericht 4, 1895.96, 1 p.49; RC 17, 1896, 110-111). Iberian inscc. at Ensérune and coins of Narbonensis with Iberian legends were given above (Note xvi; 77)

Glosses

158   (cf. 1 above, Note on Glosses;
             79 above, 220 below)

acatus "skiff" Auson. ep. 22.2.31

        Cf. picatus (pe-) 207 below, of which this may
be a variant form; AcS 2.986 (s.v. picatus), Do. 223.

[?adarca: see PID 2.190

        But the word is now claimed as Iberian, cf.
Basque adar, with a Keltic suffix, see Pokorny ZfCPh 16,
1926-7, 112; for Iber. -ar, -ara cf. Bertoldi, ZfRPh 57,
1937, 165-6, and cf. Arar (179), Arauris (80).]

[agnua, acnua "a piece of ground 120 ft. square"

        Apparently the Iberian equivalent of arepennis;
cf. perhaps also V.L. acina (?).

        First in Varro; Baetic according to Columella,
see Holder AcS 1.60, 3.523; but (cf. Walde-Hofmann,
s.v.) the formation of the word hardly appears to be
Latin. The Italic acun- , akno- , means "year," and
CIL 2.430 ancnunarum, 3361 agnu(arum) help to associate
the word with Iberia, cf. Hübner MLI p.lxxx, who rightly
expunges the latine foisted upon Varro by Vittorio and
Keil.

        Etymology unknown; the alleged connexion with
Lat. actus is altogether doubtful. The term may be the
Iberian equivalent of either candetum (cf. P-W 3.1464-
65) or arepennis, but I have not found any Basque words
that would establish the former hypothesis.]

agoga "a channel in a mine" Pliny NH 33.76

        At first sight, none other than Greek; but, as
Bertoldi has observed (ZfRPh 57, 1937, 142), this, like

432

Glosses

other technical terms ascribed to the miners of the
Pyrenees, appears in Basque (agogai, ahogai "bocca,
apertura, entrata," and may, therefore, be Iberian.

ala "elecampane" Isid. 17.11.9 (rustici alam uocant)

Sofer, Lat. u. Rom. aus den Etym. des Isidorus,
1930, 96-99, defends the mss. reading alam (usually
emended to alum), but accepts the word as Keltic (cf.
PID 2.202); Kluge Arch. Rom. 6, 1922, 300 would have
it Germanic (OHG alant; but this is probably borrowed
from ala, with the addition of the Germ. suffix -nt);
Catalan and Sp. (whence Ptg.) ala points rather to
Iberia, where it is most likely Keltic in origin (cf.
[h]alus), not pace Holder ('span.') Iberian.

[albucrarense (metallum) apud Callaecos, see Plin. NH

33.80, cf. CIL 2.2598 metalla Albocol[ensia]?

In the latter (also Callaeci) clearly a local
name, cf. Albocola (Vaccaei). I cite the form here
only for comparison with albucium (s.v. ἄλβολον 1,
above), with alutia infr., and with Nouencrares (80)
Crarus, ?Me]diocrarus (82); but of these the former
comparison, if right, discredits the proposed I.Eu.
etymology; Iberian?]

[?alibrum, v.l. alabrum "reel, staple" Isid. 19.29.2;

cf. Sofer 116-117

Nothing is known concerning the origin of this
word; since it appears only in Isid., Gloss., and medieval Latin (uertitur hoc alabro quidquid net femina
fuso quoted in Du Cange), it is probably not Latin,
despite the ending -brum; in Isid. it may have come
from almost anywhere, but there is the possibility that
it is Iberian or Keltic, and I have ventured to put it
into Aquitania since he is the first to vouch for it.]

433

Glosses

[alutia "metallum aurarium" (Callaecia) Plin., NH 34.157

     Cf. al-bucrarense above? But Pliny also has
talutium ("si [aurum] inventum est in summo caespite
...si et aurosa tellus subest," in Spain, 33.67), and
Bertoldi explains the relation between alutia and talutium by an appeal (from Iberian) to Berber, ZfRPh. 57,
1937, 145. On aluta, alumen see also CGL 2.565,44 and
566.14, quoted AcS 2.1719-20 s.v. tanna (cf. 220 infr.).
The shift of meaning may have been runnels (1) for gold
washing; (2) for tanning. But I see no other connexion
between tannare and talutium (in which t- is an article
or other prefix).]

[amentum "alumen scissum" Theod. Prisc. eup. faen. 47

     Perhaps for *al-mentum? Cf. al- "white" (see 1
above)? Or Lat. alumen, which is supposed to contain
an I.Eu. alu- "bitter"? Or read a⟨lu⟩mentum?]

[amma "strix" Isid. 12.7.42; Sofer, Lat. u. Rom., 65,

172]

andera (1) "young woman;" (2) "andiron"

     Postulated by M-L REW 449, and by Dottin 227,
as the source of Romance or Basque forms as well as
Welsh and Irish, the word appears to have existed also
as a proper name in Aquitania, CIL 13.15, 138, 187, cf.
169 (AcS 3.615). But Pedersen JCS 1, 1949, 4-6 now
takes the word as Keltic and compares Gr. παρθένος .
Haberl ZfCPh 8.1910-12, 233-235 attempted unsuccess-
fully to demonstrate an ándēra (beside andéra).

anderitum "urbem sublimem" Sid. Apoll., apparently

    glosses the local name (148)

     Cf. Jullian REA 18, 1916, 205; Reinach RA 3,
1916, 127-134

Glosses

[ἀπαρία "a kind of grass," attributed to the Σπάνοι by

    Dioscarides 4.29.]

apitascudem "farinam [auri]" Pliny NH 33.69 appears to

    be corrupt. Cf. tasconium below?

apoperes, apopores "a kind of gourd or pumpkin" Isid.

    17.10.16

      Apparently a native word, see Sofer 118; but
Alessio Riv. di Filol. 56, 1938, 377 would find a Greek
origin (quasi * ἀποπεπειρα).

arpennis, arepennis, and arapennis: "actus quadratus;

    half an acre (semiiugerum); also a measure of

    length (one-fifth of a stade)"

      This Keltic word, the proper meaning of which
appears to have been "the end of a furrow, at which the
plough is turned round," more literally "forehead" or
"headland," is one of two partial synonyms of the Iberian (?) agnua discussed above, the other being candetum
(178).

      Its use among the Gauls (Galli) is attested by
Columella (RR 5.1.6), in the form are-pennis, in Spain
(Baetici) by Isid. (Etym. 15.15.4), in the form ara-
pennis. arepennis is also attested, e.g. for Narbonensis and Lugdunensis, in insc. CIL 12.1657 and 13.2465;
cf. CIL 3.3294 (i.q. 10275) arp[(from Baan, Danube),
and AcS 3.677 also adds CIL 5.6587 (Sizzano), but the
correct reading may be aream(?). In Aquitania the
proper form seems to have been arpennis (cf. the divine
name derived from it, Arpeninus CIL 13.167), with syn-
cope of e, as in the Liber Hist. Franc. 299.23 (Mon.
Germ. Hist., Scr. rer. Merov. vol. 2), as in French
arpent, Prov. arpen, cf. Aruerni for older are-uerno-

Glosses

(the writing Areuernus is late, but that fact does not
invalidate this explanation of Aruernus), and Armorius
beside Aremoricus; whereas ara-pennis is Ibero-Keltic,
cf. the spellings Ara-tispi, Araceli(um), Arabriga
(Sofer 120), Sp. arapende.

The t, d of Romance is problematical; the best
account is that -nn- became -nd- (cf. arependia in CGL
2.19.6) and later -nt- (arpentum Lex. Baiuv., A. Thomas,
Romania 39, 1910, 393); this is a regular Gaulish change,
see SprFK 186.

As for the etymology (see Walde-Hofmann 1.66,
848 s.v., with the authorities there cited), we have
the preposition are- and penn- "head, top" (cf. above),
Mid. Ir. airchenn.

arrugia "gallery in gold-mine" (a technical term) Plin.

NH 33.70

Romance forms point also to a by-form *rugia
(M-L REW 678), and the prefix a- is explained by Bertoldi BSL 32, 1931, 121-123, as Iberian, cf. Basque
arroil "rigole, fosse, cavité, creux," Gascon arrouio
"rigole, ruisseau;" RC 49, 1932, 308. Cf. perhaps
cor-rugus inf.

[baca, bacca "uinum in Hispania" Varro L.L. 7.87

With this belong a number of related or derivative forms: baccea (bachia), bacar, bacarium, bacrio
(but not bacausa AcS 1.322,18 which is an error for
bascauda), probably all of "Mediterranean" pre-I.Eu.
origin: Walde-Hofmann 1.91, Ernout-Meillet 98. Fr.
baie, Prov. baga]

baditis "nymphaea" (quae Gallice baditis appellatur,

Marcell. de medic. 33.63)

Since Marcellus (Burdigalensis) himself reports

436

Glosses

that he gathered information from rustic and popular
sources, it is possible that he learnt this word in
Aquitania. His actual words are ab agrestibus et plebeis (praef. 4). On Isidore see the work of Sofer
cited above (especially pp.162-165); on fish names in
Polemius Silvius see Schuchardt ZfRPh 30, 1906, 712-
732; and on the names of animals (ib.) see E. Zavattari
in Arch. Rom. 6, 1922, 462-493. The late Sir d'Arcy W.
Thompson called my attention to the works of Eugène
Rolland Faune and Flore populaire (1877-1915, 1896-1913)
and of Oken (Isis 1817-48). The latter is now in part
of historical interest only.

But baditis has a satisfactory Keltic etymology
(Ir. baidim "immerse," Lat. imbuo, Walde-Hofmann 1.92),
and may well have been known in other parts of Gaul.

The b- represents an I.Eu. $\mathcal{G}^u$, and need not
therefore testify to p-Keltic rather than to q-Keltic.

?badius "chestnut" (of horses) Varro, ap. Non. 80.2

Cf. O.Ir. buide "yellow," in Gaul Bodiocasses,
in Baetica Badia. [Whatever the origin of Sp. bazo
"dark brown" may be (M-L REW 6069), the *basus with
which it and badius have been connected (Ernout-Meillet
and others) does not exist; the reading of the mss. LP
at Lib. Gloss. BA 173 is, as I gave it in Gloss. Lat.
vol. 1, and as the alphabetic order shows, barus (not
basus, as CGL 5.170,28), which is further a corruption
of burrus (Lib. Gloss. BU 58).]

baia "harbor"

It seems to me highly probable that Isid. 14.8.
40 has preserved a genuine Iberian word (the source of
Sp. Pt. bahía, whence Fr. baie, Ital. baia), despite
the fact that he has confused it with the name Baiae
and interlarded his account with misunderstood glosses
on Aen. 9.707 (cf. 3.441, 6.107) and a fantastic etymology. Cf. Sofer 32-35.

Cf. baiolus "laborer," Tert. ad ux. 1.4.10 (Riese
Lit. 446, German?); baiolare (p.280 above). In Hispanic

Review 12, 1944, 11-28 a Germanic etymology (O. Frisian
*baga "curve, bend") is proposed; cf. Nykl Cronaca 1942,
48-49. Is the modern local name Bayonne related? Baiae
Calentes Sid. Apoll. 5.14.1.

From "harbor" the derived meaning is "long-shore-
man, laborer" (baiolus), and hence baiolare "load;" but
this can have nothing to do with boiae "shackles" (gl.1).

balisca (uitis) apud Bituriges, Columella RR 3.2.19 al.,

see AcS 3.796

Now commonly emended to read basilica; but it is
remarkable that Plin. NH 14.29, which clearly stems from
Columella l.c., as the phrase Hispaniae coccolobin uocant Pl., coccolobin uocant Hispani Col. proves, testifies to balisca (so Mayhoff) but oddly ascribes that to
the Dyrrachini (for which the correct reading may be
duracinam). Cf. Isid. 17.5.22, and for the ending cf.
(gl.1) asinusca, atrusca, rabuscula.

balisca is most likely the famous wine of Bordeaux, i.e. presumably the Bituriges Vivisci, not Cubi,
are meant; cf. Grenier (in Frank Economic Survey vol.3)
583, n.67, uitis Biturica (AcS 1.439).

[?balsa "paludibus...cinctum" Pl. NH 4.116

Cf. Basque balsa, ballsa. See Bertoldi BSL 32,
1931, 161 (cf. 126); ZfRPh. 57, 1937, 141.] belsa inf.

balux, baluca "gold-bearing sand"

See Plin. NH 33.77, where the names, doubtless
related, palaga and palacurna (cf. santerna, maderna,
pincerna) are also used, and other sources given by AcS
1.338-339; and, above all, Strabo 3.146 C., where πάλα
is evidently the same word. The alternation p:b and c:g
Bertoldi BSL 32, 1931, 99 (cf. 134) finds to be Iberian;
cf. Sp. baluz (M.L., REW 920). On gold-mining in Aquitania cf. Grenier in Frank 3, 456. But J. Bloch claims
an Iranian cognate, Mélanges Ernout 1940, 19.

438

Glosses

<u>barca</u> "barque," of late occurrence, e.g. Isid. 19.1.19

    This is one of several non-Latin terms for "ship, boat" (ascus, calo, curucus, nausum) current in various parts of Gaul; like ascus it seems also to have had the meaning of "vase" (i.e. a low, boat-like vase), see Blanchet, REA 25, 1923, 164-168₃ (his etymological guesses may be dismissed) cf. barisa: εἶδος ποτηρίου , CGL 2.28. 26; and like calo also to have had the meaning of "shoe" at least in N. Ital. barka (M.L. REW 952). So in English "shoes," especially if large and clumsy are "barges," not only in Dickens (American Notes ch. 1), but still in popular usage.

    Not necessarily borrowed from βᾶρις (Propertius has baris, cf. barisa above); rather barca, βᾶρις , and the Coptic bari "barque" are all representative of the same Mediterranean source.

    Derivatives are barcula, barcella, and barcarius e.g. 207 below (on this see BSAF 1896, 239, cf. 246).

    The divine name Barca or Barsa (Comminges, 86 above) can hardly be connected; and barga (M.L. REW 957, 958) is a different word. Hardly Punic? Otherwise c:g (cf. arcanto- , uerco- beside forms with-g-) would be significant, especially in view of Jud's claim (Rom. 46, 1920, 468-475) that barga is Keltic, cf. BSL 32, 1931, 144 and 161 (Bertoldi); but see PID 2.63.

    With barga "hut" Bottiglioni (Il Mondo Classico 2, 1932, 83) would connect both bargus: ἀφυής , sine ingenio (Gl.) and bargena: homo uitiosae gentis, νεκροφόρος (Gl.), both commonly supposed to be Etruscan (Walde-Hofmann 1, 97); but cf. K. Kerényi's discussion, summarised in Historia, 8, 1934, 557.

    Kluge AR 6, 1922, 231 claimed the word as Germanic. P. Katz I.F. 57, 1940, 264 (cf. APh 15, 1940-41, 204) observes that borrowed words which take -(1)ca (e.g. tunica) regularly become feminine. For barcarii see for example, ND Occ. 40; 35.12 (cf. Grenier in Frank 3, 637; Bregenz, Ebrudunum [Sapaudia]). The local name (Spain) Barca, also called Vxama, can hardly have any connexion.

Glosses

[bardocucullus

　　Santonicus (Mart. 14.128.1), cf. sellam sintoni-
acis... CIL 9.2125 (A.D. 236), read perhaps sant- (but
note the personal name Sinto AcS 2.1575)?　But also
Lingonicus (id. 1.53.5).　See bardus 178 below, and
cucullus ibid.; Neruicus Ed. Diocl. p.2209]

*barta "wood"

　　In Gascony and Narbonensis, claimed as pre-Roman
by Werner Kaufmann, Die gallo-rom. Bezeichnungen für
den Begrift "Wald" (Diss. Zurich, 1913), 62; cf. M.L.
REW 9643.

[?basterna "uehiculum itineris," Isid. 20.12.5

　　Conjectures on the etymology (bastum) in Walde-
Hofmann; but bastum is itself of doubtful origin and
burdabasta (Petron.) shows probably two foreign elements (Keltic, Ernout-Meillet ed.2, 122), not one
merely (burdo), though the meaning of that one suggests
Spain or Aquitania very strongly.

　　There is nothing to be deduced from the fact
that Lampridius is the first to use the word; but the
contexts in which it is used point rather to the Eastern empire.

　　For the ending cf. mad- , pinc- , sant-erna.
Apparently the meaning is comparable to that of pilentum
or carpentum.]

beccus "beak"

　　Antonio..., cui Tolosae nato cognomen in puer-
itia Becco fuerat; id ualet gallinacei rostrum (Suet.
Vitell. 18).

　　Cf. Beccus in CIL 12.2514 (Ain); Becco 5381 (Toulouse); and in Greg. Tur., mirac. lib. 2 (de uirt. Iul.)
16 (where Becco appears to be Aruernus).

440

belsa "campus...ob hoc dicitur, quia belsa plurima

quae sunt gramina profert" Virg. gram. (Tolo-

sanus) epit. 4.20.21

Cf. the local names Belsa (Beauce, Orléannais), Belsinum (Gers; Spain); REA 30, 1928, 69. Hence belsa is probably pre-Keltic; at all events, Bertoldi's conjectures (BSL 30, 1930, 170-2) are unconvincing; cf. rather balsa above, since marshy ground often has an abundant growth of grass. Iberian? Not Iranian or I.Eu. (Mélanges Ernout, 1940,17).

What is the connexion, if any, with belsauia (or belsa uia?), also known only from Virg. gram. Tolos. (epit. 15.90.12), who gives its meaning as "peruersa," apparently "irregular" in grammatical terminology? [Hardly bessa uia, cf. bessus (u-stem) below, for -ls-does not give -ss-].

Pedersen VKG 1,85 (cf. 537) derives belsa from *belisa.

berula (older *berura) "cress"

Marcellus de medic. 36.51, where it is called Latin, which may be right to the extent that the pure Keltic seems to have been *berura (Walde-Hofmann 1.101, M.L. REW 1054); in the glossaries we have a syncopated berla. Cf. Meyer-Lübke Einf. 42.

Cf. Bertoldi Arch. Glottolog. Ital. 22-23, 1929, 486; if Bertoldi is right, and indeed even if he is not, the word cannot be limited merely to Aquitanian on the ground that it is known from Marcellus Burdigalensis.

bessus "mos feritatis"

Virg. gram. epit. 14.85.18; hence possibly a term in use in Aquitania or Tolosa; cf. belsa above? Commonly equated with Ir. bés "custom." The Thracian name Bessus is no doubt unrelated.

Glosses

bettonica (u-)

Keltic according to Pl. 25.84; Cantabrica Cels. med. 5.27.10; commonly supposed to contain the name of the tribe Vettones (Lusitania), but the modern derivatives (M.L. 9290) point rather to b- ; Do. 234.

bicerra, bicerres "a kind of coarsely woven garment"

only in the Glossaries

Probably the same as bigerrica uestis (Sulp. Sev.), palla (Fortunatus, cf. Aquitanica palla in Greg. M.), -us turbo Sidon. Apoll., bigerrus (-icus?) sermo (Virg. gram. Tolos.), AcS 1.417-18, cf. Terracini in Scritti in onore di Alfredo Trombetti, 1938, 345; if so, and if the forms bicerra, bicerres are sound (cf. the Sp. becerro, bicerra, Ptg. bezevro discussed by Schuchardt ZfRPh 40, 1919-20, 103), these must be curtailed from bigerricus, the transmission of which is better supported, and which is presumably an ethnicon (cf. gallica, lesbium, cadurcum, English port, damson, sherry, and many others of the same sort in every language; so ϲάγος .... Βιτου ντικόϲ [-ηγ-?] Ed. Diocl. 19.61).

Metathesis (for birrica) has been suggested, but bigerricus puts that out of court, as much as Thurneysen's bi- and cirrus (!); as for -c-: -g-, see the Grammar.

birrus "a hooded cape" Gallicus...apud Santonas, Schol.

Iuv. 8.145

For other citations see AcS 1.425-426; deriv. birretum (described as auriculare) Pard. dipl. 1.105 (no.139, the testament of Caes. Arelatensis), and surely this (not birrus M.L., REW 1117a) is the source of O. Prov. beret (Fr. béret, Ital. berretto), O.Fr. barrete.

birrica "uestis ex lana caprarum ualde delicata" CGL 5.347,41, probably also is derived from birrus (not, pace Weisgerber and others, from burra).

Glosses

birrus (ctd.)

birrus would therefore appear to be the Iberian equivalent of Keltic sagum, as basterna of pilentum or carpentum (above). In the corrupt (?) bribetham "cloaked" (Vit. Sams., ASS 28 Jul. 6.580) may lurk a form birrata (i.e. clothed in a birrus). For the meaning cf. bardo-cucullus above.

blutthagio: Gallic, according to Marcell. de medic.

9.132

Etymology entirely unknown. As a remedy for earache, perhaps the poppy. Not a corruption of bul-gago (cf. bugillo)?

bricumus: see briginus

brigantes "uermiculi in oculis" Marcell. 8.127

For *urig- (W. gwraint, Ir. frigh), like *broica for uroica; see Loth REA 22, 1920, 121-122, where Prov. bregûent (from Mistral) is cited.

The Corpus Glossary (BR 179 Lindsay) has briensis: hondwyrm; cf. Jud Rom. 46, 1920, 475-477 (O.Prov. brian, Gasc. braguen). See also Journal des Savants 1920, 20 (bibliogr.); Riv. di Filol. 49, 1921, 430. According to Bertoldi Arch. Glott. Ital. 22-23, 1929, 495-496 *brigantios "absinthe" (Val Tell. briánz), cf. RC 46, 1929, 16-28, quasi "herba uermicularis," is derived from the same source as brigantes. But compare rather the next item.

briginus "artemisia, wormwood" CGL 3.631,22 (Gallice...

appellant), bricumus Marcell. 26.41

If this is actually connected with the preceding, then Eng. wormwood (O.E. wermod, Vermouth) has, through

443

sheer confusion, introduced the same idea (uermicularis) that the derivative *brigantios had etymologically. English "worm-wort" (O.E. wyrmwyrt) is entirely different.

Is not briginus a corruption of bricumus, and this a mis-writing of britumus, cf. Brito-martis, Artemis (hence "artemisia")?

broccus "pointed" specifically of the teeth dentes

brocc[h]i in Varro R.R. 2.7,3; cf. Mulomed. Chiron.

241.14 Oder (who reads brocchi for brumatici of

the ms., but as to that see Sofer, Lat. u. Rom.

aus den Etym. des Isidorus, 36 n.1); in Lucil.

and Plaut. apparently "having protruding teeth,"

Non. 25.22, Fest. 514.15 (L.).

Probably Keltic (Walde-Hofmann 1.116), cf. Broc-(c)o- in local and personal names, O.Ir. brocch, W. broch, Br. broc'h "badger" (hence in Latin perhaps brocchus is better than broccus); Dottin Mélanges Loth, 1927, 92-98; Pokorny Urg. 10.

With this has been compared broci n. pl. at La Graufesenque (90 sqq. above), the name of a vase, see Loth RC 41, 1924, 49; hence I include the Latin broccus here, cf. Prov. broc "can." Vendryes, however, BSL 25, 1925, 40, assumes broc[c]i[s] to have been borrowed from Gr. βροχίς. Since that means (1) a small noose, (2) a spider's web, (3) a measurement of land; and occurs only once (Anth. Pal.) in the sense of "ink-horn," the shape of which suggests a tusk or protruding tooth, I prefer (with Loth) to connect broci with broccus, taking it as a native Keltic word, and regarding βροχίς as borrowed (through Latin) into Greek. This gives a better etymology of βροχίς in the sense "ink-horn" than the conjectured relation with βρέχω. In the other meanings βροχίς is a different word, of different origins, just as much as mod. Germ. netzen and Netz (Kluge). Cf. βρούκος (PID 2. 429; 3.11 s.v. broge)?

Glosses

broccus (ctd.)

The existence of a V.Lat. brocc- in the required
sense is proved also by the Romance forms (cf. Weisgerber
SprFK 195); brocci were in mass-production, hence the
wide diffusion of the word (cf. Eng. borrowings such as
flask, tass, epergne), and may have reached Greek through
southern Italy (Tarentum). For the meaning cf. Germ.
Schnabelkanne.

bugillo -onis Marcell. 8.115, 25.14

Commonly supposed to be the same as bulgago in
the Glossaries, also the name of a plant, and this to
be connected with bulga (PID 2.183); but see Bertoldi
RC 50, 1933, 329 n.1, Arch. Glott. Ital. 22-23, 1929,
494.

bulluca (v.l. bulloga) "pomum paruulum" Vit. Columb. 16

(AcS 1.631)

Bertoldi BSL 32, 1931, 138 n.3 makes a case of
sorts against counting this word as Keltic, chiefly on
the ground of the alternation of c:g and p:b (see also
ZfCPh 17, 1927-8, 189). But actually there are hundreds
such (see the Grammar) in Gaul.

Note also the personal name Bulluca (87 above and
207 below with 1, note at alpes); Balluci 6 Remark. So
in English Johnny Appleseed, Plumstone as by-names; on
the ending -uca see Bertoldi, Berl. Beitr. 1, 1929, 280.
Zamor. (W. Spain) bollaca M.L. REW 1390. See in general
A. Cronenberg Die Bezeichung des Schlehdorns in Gallo-
romanischen, Berl. Beitr. 7 (2), 1937, 13-30.

burdus -i and burdo -onis "mule;" burdunculus, burdon-

arius, burdonicus, and burdatio are derivatives,

and perhaps burdabasta in Petron. shows in the

first element the same word (on basta cf. basterna

above)

445

Glosses

burdus (ctd.)

The Romance derivatives (cf. M.L. REW 1403, 1405)
suggest that burdus belongs to southern France, burdo
being more widely represented. Ancient local names, in
less degree personal names, suggest Aquitania as the
possible source of this certainly non-Latin term, for
which there appear to be no Keltic cognates. Grégoire
Études Horatiennes 1937,84 would count the word Germanic;
Kluge Urgerm. ed.3,13 takes it as borrowed into Germanic
(OHG burdihhîn), which is the wiser judgement. It must
be related somehow with the bur(r)ic(c)us.

?burina AcS 3.1007 from Not. Tir. 128,51

But Not. Tir. is far from clear; and I can see
nothing apposite except the hypothetical *Buriniacum
(Belg. local name) AcS 1.641, modern Burigny.

bur(r)ic(c)us (1) "small horse" (2) "mule" (Sp. burro

etc. "donkey," retroformate according to M.L. REW

1413)

This appears to be the Iberian equivalent of
Illyr. (Kelt.?) mannus. The v.l. brunicus in Isid. and
Lib. Gloss. (cf. Sofer 67) is probably due to confusion
with the Germanic *brun- "brown," but burriccus (*burrus) may have arisen from an older burdus through association with Lat. burrus "red, reddish." The relation
to burdus, burdo, however, is complicated by the existence of yet another word burrae, glossed as "stupidae,"
which would suit either donkeys or mules well enough.
As with burdus, this classification among Aquitanian
glosses rests on presumptive rather than conclusive
grounds.

burra "coarse garment"

Eucheria, Anth. Lat. 390.5 (composed in Gaul,
perhaps in Aquitania; cf. Skutsch in Pauly-Wissowa,
s.v.); cf. burrarius in CIL 13.1056 (Saintes), if not
birrus, birretum, and burina above.

446

cadurcum "bed-spread" Iuv. 6.537, 7.221

From the ethnicon Cadurci, cf. Plin., NH 19.8-13.

*cala "shelter; ravine" (?)

Cf. perhaps the local name Cala-gurris, in which
cala- is pre-Keltic according to Dauzat "Cala dans la
toponymie gauloise" (ZONF 2, 1926, 216-221; cf. P.S.
Pasquali, Ph. Woch. 1939, 814-816; REA 27, 1925, 307-
311; 33, 1931, 373; Revue des Langues romanes 67, 1934,
5). The element -cala or -gala occurs in Burdi-gala
above 153 (q.v.), and in many other names (AcS 1.685).
It has been the subject of much discussion. In addition to the references given I note (inter alia) BSL
32, 1931, 116 n. (cf. 161, 167 n.), Pokorny Urg. 86,
Benoit REA 40, 1938, 138 (calanca). Presumably not the
same word as cala "uallum" Serv. A. 6.1 (cf. Ernout-
Meillet ed.2, 132). Leite de Vasconcellos Revista
Lusitana 28, 1931, 50-60; P-W s.v. Cale (Iberian); Gr.
Encicl. Portuguesa e Brasil. 5 (no date), 488 s.v.
Cale (cf. Galécia?), but Mendes Corrêa cited there adds
nothing.

[celia, caelia "a fermented drink" in Spain Pl. NH 22.164

But Pliny has caelia et cerea in Hispania, the
mss. of Isid. 20.3.18 celia (also assigned to Spain),
and it would appear that celia is nothing more than a
variant of *ceria, cerea, cf. the Keltic ceruesia, κοῦρμι. For cilicia: ζῦθος (AcS 3.1033,54-1034,2) read
cilia, a variant of celia (?).]

[caetra "shield;" cf. κυρτία PID 2.195

In Spain, see Holder, AcS 1.679; but also amongst
the Britanni, Tac. A. 36. Probably an Iberian word,
not Keltic.]

The resemblance to cartallus (-ell-) CGL 5.349,
41 (240 below), Sic. karteddu (M.L. 1722), and to cartamera (79 above), cartaont (Note xxvi) is perhaps

superficial, unless there is a common element of meaning "to wind, weave."]

<u>calliomarcus</u> "colt's foot" Marcell. 16.101

But the Keltic name (Gallice Marcell.), is
actually better rendered into Latin not by equi ungula
(Marcell.), even though that may have been its name in
Latin, but by the emendation equi inguina (*callio-
"testiculus"), cf. 178 below epocalium, ebulcalium,
see Loth RC 37, 1919, 25; Pedersen, VKG 1.69. The
local names Calimarcensis and Callemarcium AcS 1.700,5;
3.1049,17 may be related.

[?<u>calmes</u> "waste land" AcS 1.703; 3.1050]

<u>calocatanus</u> "papauer siluestre" Marcell. 20.68

The formation is far from certain; comparisons
have been made both with catanus (79 above) and with
calox Ps.-Apul. 25 (AcS 1.705). Hardly a corruption
of καλυκάνθεμον?

<u>cama</u> "bed," <u>camisia</u> and <u>camisa</u> "shirt," <u>camisile</u> "fine

linen"

Isid. 19.22.29; 20.11.3; cf. Hieron. Epist. 64
ad. Fab. 11 (sermone uolgato); and (for camisile) AHD
Gl. 3.619,37. AcS 1.707, 719; 3.1064. Probably Ibero-
Keltic, Sofer 121-122; cf. Walde-Hofmann 1.145 and 854;
M.L., 1537, 1550.

But it is not clear that camisia, camisile are
connected with cama; if camisia stands for *kamitia
then Germanic (OHG hemidi "shirt") has forms most closely
related, and the Keltic (if not actually borrowed from
Germanic, but at an unusually early date) is to be
added to the few items which Keltic and Germanic have
in common without borrowing. Cumont Comment la Belgique

Glosses

fut romanisée p.35 took it as possibly Keltic; cf. E.
van Overloop in Annales Acad. royale d'archéologie de
Belgique 76 (7e Sér., 6) 1929, pp.49-59.

[campagus "a soldier's boot" (ed. Diocl. 9.11)

     Cf. possibly Campagones (cam-?) Hispani in
inscc. of Dacia, Holder 1.721. Written κομβάων Ed.
Diocl. 19.11]

cantabrum "standard" Tertull., Minuc. Fel.

     Generally supposed to come from the ethnicon
Cantabri (Vascones, Spain); if so, cf. campagus: Cam-
pagones above. But G. Heuten, Mélanges Boisacq (Ann.
de l'Inst. de Philol. et d'Hist. orientales et slaves
5, 1937) 478-484, arguing from an insc. of Aquincum,
takes the word as Keltic.

     Jud, Arch. Rom., 6, 1922, 211 postulated a
*cantosrin to account for Fr. chanfrein "partie antéri-
eure de la tête du cheval du front au naseau," i.e., I
suppose, srin- cf. Gr. ῥίς (denied by M.L. 1688); rather
we may suppose a by-form *cantafri- (cf. Porcobera beside Porcifera?), canta- being the prefix canta- , I.Eu.
*kmta, Gr. κατά (Walde-Pokorny 1.459); for the meaning,
the blaze on horse's head may be compared with a pennant
or standard (canta-brum lit. "going with, carried with"?);
or, less likely, cant(h)o- , see cantus below and *bhro- .

     To be distinguished from cantabrum "spelt," which
is Oscan according to G. Alessio in Annali della R.
Università degli Studi Economici e commerciali di Trieste
8, 1936, fasc. i-ii, 174-178 (Salentine kámfara, kanfre
from Osc. *cantafrum = Lat. cantabrum "crusca d'orzo").

     Since the word is known also from the inscrip-
tion of Aquincum AE 1935.164, cf. 1939.297, it may be
Illyrian. But the history of -br- , which is doubtless
of multiple origin (uergobreto, alibrum, Cobruna, artabri, combri, combretum), needs further study. It
has been suggested that cant(o)- appears also in candosoccus (178).

Glosses

[cantherius "gal (i.e. "pony," Lancs. dial.)," gallicus

Plaut. Aul. 495

But probably pre-Keltic, and somehow related, not necessarily by direct borrowing, to Gr. κανθήλιος, κάνθων, cf. G. Alessio Riv. di Filol. 66, 1939, 151 (from Magna Graecia, where it persists), PID 2.194, perhaps alien to Greek, Latin, and Keltic alike (cf. caballus), Cocco St. Etr. 16, 1942, 387-401; Grégoire Byzantion 13, 1938, 289 n.1.

The canterma "maleficium" of Greg. M., quoted AcS 1.748, cf. cantennus "maleficus" CGL 5.444,25 is perhaps to be corrected to canterina (in CGL read canterinus), see the contexts (worship of Epona) in Apul. met. 3.27, Tertull. apol. 16; and the meaning of canterius "frame" might suggest "rack, torture." The suggested incantatio (Zwicker FHRC 191.21) will not do; for maleficium is not maledictum. If we read canterna, the termination is presumably the same as in santerna, maderna, pincerna.]

cantus, "felloe"

Despite Quint. 1.5.7-8 (who would make it Spanish or African), the word is now usually compared with Gaulish κάντένα or κάντεν (68,73), cantalon (160), and therefore claimed as Keltic, see, e.g. Walde-Hofmann and Ernout-Meillet, s.v.; Weisgerber SprFK 196, Bertoldi BSL 32, 1931, 154 n.3.

The etymology proposed would make "bend, turn, circuit" the literal meaning, and I see no reason why canterius may not be a derivative of this; from time immemorial gals and ponies have been used at circular tasks, wells, mills and the like. Cf. Sicel κάνθος (PID 2.465; Ed. Diocl. 15.36).

κασσίτερος "tin"

Possibly the Iberian (?), or at all events pre-Keltic and pre-I.Eu. word (cf. Walde-Hofmann s.v.) corresponding to the Keltic stannum (below).

Glosses

Κασσίτερος (ctd.)

Cf., Diod. 5.38.4 (γίνεται δὲ κασσίτερος ἐν πολλοῖς τόποις τῆς Ἰβηρίας κτλ.), Plin. 4.119 ex aduerso Celtiberiae complures sunt insulae Cassiterides dictae Graecis a fertilitate plumbi. Not, I think, connected with the numerous names in Cassi- . But the original Cassiterides have now floated through the Indian ocean and into the Persian Gulf, and the name of the metal is explained as "from the land of the Kassi" (d.i. Kossäer), see Walde-Hofmann 1.178. Elamite according to Liddell and Scott.

[?celdo (-onis), v.l. tieldo: Plin. 8.166 equini generis

quos celdones uocamus; in Spain (Gallaica...et

Asturica gentes).

Holder 3.1179 compared Basque zaldi, zaldia, dim. zaldinca "horse, pony;" evidently one of a number of words for "pony, nag, hack, mule" with which Iberian enriched Latin and Romance (burdo, burricus, cantherius), not unnaturally, the mule being well adapted to the difficulties of travel in the Pyrenees and in Spain. Perhaps, however, for *calido, cf. Calidonia (like English gal, if "gallus"); W. cel(i)do, see Mod. Philology 43, 1945, 48.]

cerea "a fermented drink" (in Spain, Plin. NH 17.164)

Cf. ceruesia, κοῦρμι , and celia, caelia above.

[?cerrus "a kind of oak," Plin. 16.16 al.

Claimed as Iberian, cf. Basque harri "stone," Sp. Ptg. carrasca (from *carrasca "stone-oak, oak" M.L. 1718a); cf. Bertoldi, Stud. Etr. 7, 1933, 287, harriaga "saxetum," id. BSL 32, 1931, 172 (pays Basque). See 85 above; W.-P. 1.31; but harriaga has no connexion with arrugia above.]

Glosses

cicolus, v.l. ciculus "cuckoo"

     Isid. 12.7.67: tucos quos Hispani ciculos uocant. But 12.8.10 cicades ex ciculorum nascuntur sputo shows that the cuckoo was meant. Folklore still preserves in England the legend of cuckoo spit. Perhaps read cuculos, quos Hispani tucos (cf. Lib. Gloss. TU 26) uocant. Not connected with the divine name Cicollus (181) but simply onomatopoetic, cf. Sofer, 12-13.

clarnus "dish;" Gl. Prud. Cathem. 3.16 (p.22, Burnam,

    1905) ferculos (-a): discos uel clarnos, cf.

    satira genus est clarni uel lancis...clarnus

    potest appellari discus uel mensa, Schol. Pers.

    p.241 ed. Jahn (1843).

     The word probably comes from Spain or Gaul, as a marginal adscript in Prud. l.c., afterwards interlarded into the prefatory notes in Pers. ed. pr. post uitam, whence Jahn took them.

     Cf. Ir. clār, W. clawr "board, plank, table;" O.W. gl. claur (pl. clouriou) "tabellis;" and note procellunt sese in mensam Plaut. Mil.Gl. 762, procellunt: procumbunt Paul. ex Fest. 251 L. Ernout's "étrusque" is a mere guess.

clefabo (?)

     Meaning unknown, and perhaps corrupt. Given simply as sermone bigerr⟨ic⟩o (cf. bigerra above) by Virg. Tolos. Gr. 2, p.8.13 H. (AcS 1.417-18)

clintinna "uestis orbiculata" Gl. Prud. Ham. 289 (p.49,

    Burnam, 1905) scutulis: scutulatam uestem appel-

    lat orbiculatam quam rustici clintinnam (v.l.

452

clintinna (ctd.)

clintint) uocant.

Scaliger rightly interpreted scutulis in Prud.
l.c. as uestes in scutularum i.e. quadrarum (retium)
formam textas. But clintinna, though a genuine word,
is probably corrupt; unless it is cognate with clarnus
above, which seems unlikely (despite orbiculata in the
gloss, which might be associated with orbis or mensa),
it seems most reasonably connected with the Keltic linna
(sagum quadrum, Isid. 19.23.1 and 3), caracalla (if for
*caracpalla), Lat. palla (?), i.e. older *pl- . Since
I.Eu. p passed through f and h before it was completely
lost, the writing clin- may contain a vestige of p
(*χlin- , or rather *hlin-), note especially the reading litina of D¹ E¹ at Isid. 19.23.3: for the rest,
the word may have become confused with Latin linteum
or its derivatives (cf. linum, said to be non-I.Eu.),
or even with Gr. χλαῖνα , hence clintinna by conflation.
Quiggin RC 33, 1912, 100 reading glitinne thinks the
word "may very well be Welsh," but does not explain why.
Cf. linna below.

[clocca "bell"

Dottin REA 22, 1920, 39-40 would supply this word
in a text said to belong to the "sacramentaire de l'église
d'Angoulême," ad signum ecclesiae benedicendum quod Galli
lingua celtica cloccam uocant.

There is nothing to show that the word is proper
to Gaul or to Aquitania; but it may well have existed
there, quite independently of insular Keltic. In gender
it agrees with W. cloch (Ir., Gasc., Bret., Corn. masc.).
Cf. AcS 1.1045; 3.1238,36.]

[coccolobis "a kind of vine"

Iberian or Spanish according to Columella and
Pliny (see balisca above); but it is probably Greek
(κοκκός and λοβός) as Thurneysen (AcS 1.1056) claimed;
however, κοκκός itself was borrowed into Greek W.H. 1.
240-41; REA 7, 1905, 47.]

453

<u>corroco</u> (v.l. -ch-) "sturgeon (?)," Ausonius ep. 4.59

  Cf. Galic. corrujo "turbot," creac "sturgeon"
at Bordeaux, Toulouse (AcS 1.1135).

<u>corrugus</u> "water course"

  A technical term in gold-mining (cf. arrugia
above), Plin. NH 33.74; Bertoldi, BSL 32, 1931, 99 cf.
123 n.1.

<u>crāma</u> n. pl. "cream"

  Only in Ven. Fort. (carm. 11.14.2) and Gl., and
Romance M.L. 2294. Probably the same as κοῦρμι (also
neut.), both having a frothy appearance; in England
cream stout used to be advertised i.e. a rich frothy
stout or beer. So Irish Cream Ale, and Bristol Cream
(Whitewash) Sherry. κοῦρμι seems to have no survivals
in the Romance languages (except possibly Ptg., Fr.
corme), whereas crama has. (In O.Ch.Sl. krŭma means
"nourishment," cf. (?) κεράννυμι.) See now JCS 1, 1949,
52. There can be no connexion with χρῖμα, χρῖσμα.

[κρόβουλα, <u>creobula</u>

  Given as the word for "mint" used by the Σπάνοι,
Spani by Diosc. 3.35, Ps.-Apul. 91. Cf. perhaps Κρόβα-
λος· τρίχες αἰδοίων Hesych., and Lat. mentula?]

[<u>culcita</u> "pillow"

  Ascribed to the Cadurci, Plin. NH 19.13, cf.
Martial 11.56.9 al. (AcS 2.196); but the word itself is
actually Latin and as old as Plautus.]

Glosses

<u>cuniculus</u> (1) "coney-rabbit," (2) "tunnel (in a mine)"

Plin. NH 8.217, cf. Aelian h. anim. 13.15

See the discussion by Bertoldi Romania 54, 1928, 453,464; cf. ZfRPh 57, 1937, 146 (Basque unchi "rabbit").

<u>cumba</u> "valley" Isid. 19.2.1

AcS 1.1189, REA 7.50, local name Cumba (Pardessus 2.10, cf. Lizop 1.59) in pago Lemouicino. Cf. gamba, camba (207)? W.H. 1.305.

<u>curmi</u> "beer," κόρμα Poseid. ap. Ath. 4.36 (152c),

Diosc. 2.88, curmi (gen. sg.) Marcell. de medic.

16.33, curmen Gl. ... ὡς ἐν τῇ πρὸς Ἑσπέραν Ἰβηρ-

ίᾳ καὶ Βρεττανίᾳ , Diosc. l.c.

Presumably a neuter n-stem (Ir. cuirm, pl. cuir-menn); cognate is ceruesia (178 below), a possible case of lenition (cf. Bormo, Boruo), if not celia, cerea; cf. also crama above. Hubschmied Vox Rom. 3, 1938, 142 n.2.

For wider relationships of this undoubtedly Kel-tic word see Walde-Hofmann s.v. cremor (with addendum). In Marc. curmus (see SprFK 198), the name of a tree is, I suppose, unrelated.

<u>Dīuŏna</u>: Celtarum lingua, fons addite diuis, Auson. ord.

urb. nob. 160

This, in its context, is clearly imitated from Verg. A. 8.301 (decus addite diuis, addressed to Her-cules). It is possible, however, with Reinach (RA 20, 1924, 248) to suppose that Ausonius had in mind -ona as meaning "fons," cf. onna (178 below); but the suffix -ona reappears in Epona and other divine names (AcS 2. 858), its first syllable being short, and should there-

Glosses

fore be distinguished from -onna (ib.) in local names
(especially springs and the like, sometimes deified),
as well as from -ona in local names. Cf. FHRC 106.14;
RC 51, 1934, 314-16; REA 24, 1922, 158-159; "fons addite
diuis" is no more than "a spring to the glory of heaven"
(like decus addite diuis).

Dēuona (later dį-) appears as a local name
(Cadurci) TP., and Δηοὐονα Ptol.; Ausonius' line puts
another Diuona near Bordeaux, cf. possibly CIL 13.586
]onae, but the restoration is not certain to be Diu]onae.

Cognate with Latin diuus (deiuos), deus, Ir. dia
etc.; ei giving ē:i is possibly dialectal.

draucus "athlete" (Housman CR 44, 1930, 114-116)

Martial saepe, and as a personal name, Draucus
in Spain, Britain, Narbonensis; Etym. unknown. Cf.
drau-sus, Drauus, Druentia (PID 2.192)? Die Sprache 1,
1949, 127.

dureta "solium ligneum" Suet. Aug. 82, where it is des-

cribed as "uerbum Hispanicum."

Schwyzer KZ 62, 1934, 199-203, makes it the Greek
δροίτη "bath-tub," δρύτη . But if Augustus believed the
word to come from the Iberian peninsula (or from Aquitania), it is at least as likely that we have the familiar -etum, -eta ending and the Keltic duro- . Cf.
dur-atia (246), duratios (157); AcS 1.1379; Ernout-
Meillet 291.

elauer "alacris" AcS 1.1412,40

This is the local name (148 above) explained by
Greg. Tur. as meaning "swift."

Glosses

ἐμβρεκτόν "gravy, sauce," embractum and imbractum (Apic.)

Hesych. (s.v. ἐντριτον) assigns the word to the Γαλάται , but inbrataria at La Graufesenque testifies to the existence of the derivative if not of the simple form in Aquitania. Cf. bracis Pl. 18.62 (see 178 below); and see Stokes Academy 28, 1885, 226. On this etymology we have br- from older mr- . But was there not some confusion with ἐμβρέχω ?

[gabitariu

A nonsense-word in Virg. Tolos. gram., Epit. 15.6, according to the editors (Ernault, Tardi); but possibly for gabatario- , cf. gabata "dish" AcS 1.1509,28 cf. W.H. 575; Καβάθα in Ed. Diocl. 15.5,1. Less likely cf. the local name Gabatum AcS 1.1509,31. Not Keltic in any event (despite M.L. Einf. 243, cf. 40); Bertoldi's *gaba "torrent" (BSL 32, 1931, 141) adds nothing. If simply a nonsense-word cf. perhaps gabbarus "insulsus, barbarus" (Egyptian according to Aug. serm. 361.12.12, cf. E.M. 407; but gabbarus is formed like barbarus it-self).]

gaitanum (linum) "a kind of bandage for the eyes,"

Marcell. de medic. 8.27

Keltic according to Helmreich Philologus 69, 1910, 569, citing Galen who refers the remedy (and there-fore presumably the word) to Gaul.

galleta "a large wine-bowl," CGL 5.564,48; and perhaps

in Isid. 20.5.5 (calati codd.)

The word is certain, for it survives in Romance (M.L. REW 3656, where the origin is said to be unknown; if we read galleta in Isid., as the glossary-item strongly suggests, perhaps Iber. or Aquitanian). Cf. the ethnic name Caleti (Galeti, Plin. 19.8 puts them with the Cadurci and Ruteni), and note such names of

vases as Calena (obba), Lesbium (uas). That ethnica
often are used of products is a commonplace (cadurcum,
sherry, port, damson, campana "bell," brundisium "bronze,"
to mention no others.) Hardly to be compared with gollat at Blickweiler (229); annapus (178) is given as a
synonym in the Glossaries.

gammus "deer" Virg. Tolos., Gl. (CGL 3.431)

        Possibly Iberian, cf. Ernout-Meillet ed.2, 410;
Sp. Ptg. gamo "deer, buck" (M.L., REW 3668). Loewenthal
WuS 10, 1927, 185; 11, 1928, 73 offers a conjectural
(Keltic) etymology, and compares camox (1 above). For
Gammus personal name see 237, 244.

garum "fish-sauce," garus (-a) a fish

        Usually counted Greek (as by Pliny 31.93). But
Meyer-Lübke in Thes. Ling. Lat. 6.1695,33 calls attention to Prov. garle, garlesco; note also the names
Garos (Iber.?), Garra f. (at Nimes), the divine-name
Garra (Pyrenees, CIL 13.49), and the river-name Garumna
-unna Aquit., Gary-eunos Brit. (AcS 1.1988). Garunna,
then, would stand for -onno "river" (178 below) and
gar(o)- "fish." Cf. g(arum) Hispa(num), with the discussion by Grenier Mnl. vol.2, 1934, 616 (inter alia:
"Le garum était une spécialité espagnole"). Hor. S.
2.8.46; I do not think ui-garia (Note xxv Remark) can
be connected.

gauia "mew" (Plin., Apul.)

        Cf. Span. gavia, Basque gabi; possibly cognate
with cauannus, cauua (178 below); but both may be merely
onomatopoetic. A number of items found in Aquitania are
not limited to that province (e.g. κασσίτερος , cicollus,
clocca, curmi).

Glosses

gaulus "merops" Isid. 12.7.34

    For galbus, *galuus, according to Walde-Hofmann
1.585; but gallus itself may have come into Latin from
Keltic in the first place (ib. 578). The form with
metathesis, since it appears only in Isid., with the
Glossaries (and in Romance), may have become known to
him in Gaul or Spain. Cf. Sofer 134-36. I now think
that -ll- in gallus arose from -ul- in gaulus, see Die
Sprache 1, 1949, 127.

gigarus "dragon's wort"

    Keltic according to Marcell. de medic. 10.58;
Dottin (259) saw the word in Ital. gicaro "pied de veau,"
and Bertoldi Études celtiques 3, 1937, 28-32 (cf. Stud.
Etr. 10, 1936, 6 ff.) has a long discussion of the etymology of gigarus (W. cig "flesh"). One important point
in it is the comparison (of the ending) in gilarum,
uelarum. In TLL 6.1975 gigeria "intestina gallinarum"
may be cognate.

gilarum "wild thyme"

    Keltic according to Marcell. de medic. 11.10.

gurdus "stolidus," deriv. gurdonicus (Sulp. Sev.)

    ...ex Hispania dixisse originem audiui, Quint.
1.5.57; probably Iberian (Walde-Hofmann 1.627).

[?guursebalt "eseforium, parua tunica"

    Gl. Prud. p.69 Burnam; cf. Quiggin in RC 33, 1912,
100]

[?habia (auia) the name of a plant, Col. 4.14.3, 6

    Cf. Béarn. auyou, Basque abi. M.L. REW 842.]

459

Glosses

halus "samphire" (also written alus, alum n.)

Marcell. de medic. 31.29 (cf. 10.68) labels it
Keltic, but the word is found in Pliny (who gives sil
[79 above] as the Keltic form); cf. ala above? Jud,
Arch. Rom. 6, 1922, 208-209, does not accept halus as
Keltic, but anagallicum is probably a vulgar dissimilation (for alu-); it would appear that sil and halus
(alum, alus, ala) are somehow related, with a loss of
s- in Keltic utterance, cf. PID 2.202. Only the authority of Marcellus, and the presence of ala, suggest
ascription to Aquitania (sil being left in Narbonensis).

A suggested Keltic etymology may be found in
Walde-Hofmann 1.33; Ernout-Meillet incline to regard
this word as non-I.Eu. Cf. SprFK s.v.; Hoppe in Philologus 91, 1937, 449-52; hardly Alus (Venetic divine
name); HSCP 42, 1931, 145; Ernout-Meillet s.v. alium.

?hoclamsanus the name of a plant

Marcell. de medic. 20.115 (corrupt, see the ap.
cr. in Niedermann's edition).

iberis, ἰβηρίς "a kind of cress"

Pl., Galen; perhaps the ethnicon Ἴβηρες , Hibēri;
but cf. berula above.

[īda said to mean "place"

CE 479.5, Eph. Epigr. 5.999 El Kantara (omitted
from CIL 8 Suppl.), read eidais in Thes. Ling. Lat.,
s.v.; claimed as Iberian in the etymological dictionaries, but more likely to be N. African, cf. idurio,
CIL 8.23422, which may have a comparable meaning.]

[iouetanum "plumbum nigrum" Plin. 34.164

Perhaps simply the Spanish local name Iouetum,
AcS 2.68.]

460

Glosses

[lancea   See PID 2.197, Walde-Hofmann 1.757-8.]

[?laurio "wild thyme"

Either this or gilarum (above) is a figment.
Plin. Val. 1.33 has serpyllum quae Gallice laurio dicitur (but serpullum quam Galli gilarum dicunt Marcell.,
both continue ieiunus diu commanduces Pl., -et Marcell.).
I do not accept the Etym. Dictionaries (: Latin laurus),
whose authors clearly never have read the text. Cf.
the local (in Spain) and personal names AcS 2.162-63.]

laurex "coney-rabbit"

Iberian (Balearic Islands and Spain), see Plin.,
NH 8.217-218, probably cognate with the Ligurian λεβηρις
(PID 2.160), cf. Sicel λέπορις (ib., 454). For the
ending cf. βέδοξ , calox, camox, esox, hysex, ibex.

lausiae "flag-stones"

Only in the Lex metalli Vipascenis (Eph. Epigr.
3.165, Aljustrel in Portugal), and in Romance (M.L.
REW 4946), preserved as a common noun in South and South-
eastern France, in Spain and Portugal, perhaps in local
names further east (Lousonna, Hubschmied Vox Rom. 3,
1938, 102-103). The etym. is uncertain (Walde-Hofmann
1.776-777 offers some conjectures).

ledo: see liduna below

lellus: a pet appellation?

I take this from M.G.H. Script. rer. Merov. 4.547
ff., vit. S. Desiderius (Bishop of Cahors) cap. 33, as
addressed to Leodelenus. If it is merely a pet-name,
it is not peculiarly Aquitanian (or Germanic; Gutenbrunner Teuthonista N.F. 9, 1937, 74).

461

Glosses

lemiga: see limeum below

leuga "league"

See 178 below; the word appears everywhere in Gaul. For Aquitania, see (for example) CIL 13.8895, AE 1939.165; REA 25, 1923, 383.

liduna, ledo (-onis) "neap-tide" Marcell. de medic. 15.9

et al. (AcS 2.213), Baeda de temp. rat. 19, CGL

5.571,37 (ib. 2.168).

liduna (with u from ō) appears more definitely the Keltic form than ledo; the former is from Marcellus, the latter from Bede. It is another of the words common to Aquitania and (through the Belgae of Britain) to Belgica (or Britain).

Perhaps cognate with Goth. flōdus, O.E. flod (*plē(u): *plō(u)- , Walde-Pokorny 2.94-95), with ī from ē in liduna. But if the latter is genuinely Keltic the suffix must have contained -d- or -dh- , not -t- . Note also Basso-ledu-litanus (150), Cob-ledu-litanus (155) Camuledu (151), Ledus fl. (80), Adledus (CIL 13.5278 cf. Adletace fl. AcS 1.42, 2.168), and possibly Lindum, Dio-lindum (ib. 228-29, W.P. 2.438). In Finnish luode "north-west" is literally "open-water" and is, perhaps, flodus (with loss of f-) rather than a Keltic form without p- . So too Φροῦδις (212) is possibly flodus (with -r- for -1-), rather than fr- (Brythonic) from sr- (ῥέω, Skt. sr-). Hermathena 65, 1945, 2-3 (d'Arcy W. Thompson) takes us no further. Zwicker FHRC 165.24-26 gives from Palchus astrologus λιδοῦναι and μαλῖναι cf. 166.7-15, and again from Rhetorius astrologus 182.2. But Zwicker's dies idoneae for liduna and maligna for malina are out of the question.

limeum: a plant from which a poison (uenenum ceruarium)

for arrows was obtained; lemiga "mushroom" (and

462

Glosses

limeum (ctd.)

also poisonous fungi?) Hardly cf. limus?

Pliny NH 27.101 vouches for the former and for its Keltic usage; the latter, in which g is probably ȝ or i comes from the Vita Pardulphi (Lemouicensis) 2.10 (ASŜ 6 Oct. 3.435 E).

Now considered to be connected with the local name Lemouices (Limoges), cf. Lemannus, Lemausum (Limours), Limici (Spain), Lemuris -inus (Lig.), see Bertoldi W.u.S. 11, 1928, 153, Walde-Hofmann 1.804, Weisgerber SprFK 203, Pokorny Urg. 137-139; possibly Raetic leima (C.P. 35, 1940, 187); PID 2.164, but see also 3.27 (the connexion with ulmus must now be given up); Jullian's interpretation ("stag"), REA 13, 1911, 344-45 cf. 29, 1927, 166-168, is unlikely. But for a botanical term that also means "poison" cf. eburo- (207), Dottin in Mélanges Loth 1927, 92-98.

[linna: see PID 2.198

Cf. λινουργίαι ap. Cadurcos Str. 4.2.2, linificium (Vienne) N.D. Occ. 2.62; 10; Grenier in Frank 3.586, 638; lenteamenta FHRC 179.11. There is little doubt that linna, linum (246), linteum and even laena came to be confused in popular usage, though linna has been derived from pḷn- . Cf. clintinna above.]

mantum and -us (-ūs) "breue amictum"

Iberian (Hispani) according to Isid. 19.24.15 (not, pace M.L. REW 5328, "nach Probus iberisch"), and it does actually survive in Basque, Sp., Cat., Ptg., as well as in Italian (l.c.); supposed to be a retroformate from mantellum, but ultimately of Keltic origin; if so, why should not mantellum be the diminutive of mantum? mantum actually occurs in testam. Caes. Arelat. (Pardessus Dipl. 1.107), 542 A.D.; Ed. Diocl. 19.59; cf. T.L.L.

marathum "fennel" Marcell. de medic. 20.64, cf. Diosc.

   3.44 maratru (CML 4.213,11, cf. Thes. Ling. Lat.

   8.372,4, μαραθ[ρ]ον

     μάραθρον (dissim. to -θον) is not I.Eu. (Boisacq, s.v.), but there is nothing to show that the word existed independently in the western Mediterranean. In Anth. Lat. 209.5 R. (de Abcare) maratros (v.l. -dros) may be this same word; and Abcar is not surely a Semitic name (T.L.L. 1.74,36). The alternation -t(h)r- : -dr- represents a change of pronunciation.

[?mecia "anagallis"

    Marcell. de medic. 1.35; but Diosc.(2.178 RU, 1.247.15 W.) has μάκια , which he ascribes to the Romans, i.e. Latin.]

[mespilus, -um "medlar"

    Cf. FHRC 180.8 (Greg. Tur., Pyrenees). Commonly taken to be μεσπίλη . But what is that? Note the local name (?)Mispiliacus AcS 2.600 (Ain), and Misquillenses PID 1.241. For the rest refer to the usual sources T.L.L., E.M., W.H. As for duratia "mespila" see 246 and cf. dureta above. Plin. NH 15.84 (Gallicum).]

milimindrum "hen bane" (ὑοσκύαμος , calicarca AcS 1.699)

    Given as a popular term by Isid. 17.9.41; it evidently corresponds in Isid. to βελενούντιαμ in Diosc. 4.68 RV, and it may be that the two words are closely connected, despite popular corruption in one or both of them, and that in b:m (cf. bellocandium: μυλλόφυλον?) we should recognize a possible example of lenition, and in -(n)d- : -(n)t- a similar alternation. Not I.Eu. -dro- : -dhlo- (-tlo-)? For survivals into Sp. Ptg. see M.L. 5571 (with 1022); cf. Sofer, Lat. u. Rom....Isid., 146-148, Walde-Hofmann 1.99-100. Note also the river-name Milinandra, *Milmandra, now the Marmande (Cher), Holder AcS 2.585; or compare perhaps melinus "gelblich" SprFK

204, cf. Terracini Riv. Fil. 49, 1921, 428 (unless, as
I suspect, that is merely "quince-yellow, luteus," i.e.
μηλινοειδής), cf. AcS 2.536; local name Beliandrum (?)
AcS 1.385. If mil- : bel- go together, then presumably
the former is the southern form (Loth, RC 39, 1922, 50).
[Possibly confused with millefolium which appears to
stand for μηλόφυλλον, Ernout-Meillet 615; cf. REA 15,
1913, 304.]

[minium "cinnabar"

    Iberian according to Prop. 2.2.21 [3.11], cf.
Isid. 13, 21.32 (mod. Minho).]

[mus "terra"

    Isid. 12.3.1 and 20.3.4, cf. Diff. 1.552, gen-
erally considered a ghost-word for humus, cf. Sofer 15.
But although defended by Tietze Glotta 18, 1940, 279
who takes it as Iberian, Friedrich has identified it as
Lydian from Hesych. μωύς· ἡ γῆ Λυδιοί , see Glotta 19,
1941-42, 61 (cf. Idg. Jahrb. 26, p.368; A.Ph. 14, 1939
[1941], 197; 15, 1940-41, 189). But what is μωύς? Is
it a genuine Lydian form? Or a misreading of some corruption of humus misinterpreted as Lydian?]

odocos "dwarf elder"

    Marcell. de medic. 7.13, where it is said to be
Keltic; the δουκωνέ of Diosc. (read perhaps *ὀδουκωνεμ?)
and ps-Apul.(CML 4.167,23) appears to be a corruption
of this, the uaria lectio ebucone a mixture of odocos
or ducone and the pure Latin ebulus (OHG. attuh) for *%dho-
lo-(-ko-), W.H. 1.388-9. Cf. Bertoldi Arch. Glott. Ital.
22-23, 1929, 489; Sofer in Comm. Vindob. 2, 1936, 82;
SprFK 199; AcS 1.1363; 2.834. For ebulus cf. CIL 13.10008,
43 (Saintes) eb(uli) re(centis) sucus, but not (I think)
suc[in Note xxvii; and notes in CIL ad loc. (Pl. 25.164;
26.119); acerabulus (79 above). CLM l.c. gives olma as
the Dacian form, but this is not likely, if possibly, to
be connected.

Glosses

olca "plough land"

> Greg. Tur. in glor. conf. 78, cf. Octauiolca
(Galicia) M.L. REW 6050 (Prov. olca, Fr. ouche), local
names dép. Indre and Aisne (Greg. l.c. ascribes the
word also to the Remi, cf. 207 below). Jud, Romania,
52, 1926, 347 and 48, 1922, 451; Spitzer Zts. neufr.
Spr. u. Lit. 44, 1916-17, 251; Marstrander NTS 7, 1934,
349 (:OHG falga); Sofer ZfCPh 22, 1941, 115 n.1.

ontax "genus marmoris" CGL 5.377a,3

> Cf. ontes insc. Rom. (Note xxvi B 8), and perhaps
the Iberian coin-legend, Hübner MLI 15g, p.28: untga
(regio Emporitana), Ir. ond (Stokes B.B. 29, 1905, 170;
but it is unnecessary to alter the gloss to ondax). The
alternation -nt- : -nd- is not unusual; note also the
ending -ax (Iberian?).

orca (1) a sea-monster, (2) a large jar, dolium

> The association with Spain depends upon Varro RR
1.13.6, Plin. NH 9.12, cf. Isid. 20.6.5, but the etymological hand-books usually appeal to ὄρυξ and urceus.

> The meaning (2) may well come from (1), and it
may be compared with Orcades, which Stokes connected
with Latin porcus. I see no reason for not counting
the word Keltic. Cf. orcibeta Isid. 17.9.84?

pala, palaga, palacurna

> See balux above (palux in Iustin. 44.1.7)

paramus "plateau" (157 Remark)

> Cf. Sp., Ptg. páramo. Iberian or Keltiberian.
Iul. Hon. cosmogr. 36B, CIL 2.2660 (CE 1526) in parami
aequore; AcS 2.928-929. But as Meyer-Lübke Einf. 237
(cf. 242) pointed out p- is suspect in Iberian.

466

Glosses

perrus "Merry Andrew, clown," properly "quadruped" (i.e.

    *per-ros for *petr-pods), Sp. perro, Fr. pierrot

    In personal names (AcS 2.970); see the discussion
by C. Hernando Balmori, Rev. de Filologia Hispánica 3,
1942, 43-50, and EC 4, 1948, 48-54; M-L REW 6449; Perri-
cori for Petrucorii (e.g. Do. 64), perrucori 157 above,
and insc. peroco 142 (?); Perrus (Banassac) 134 above.

[pulluga (-ca)

    See bulluca above; the forms with p- are said to

    survive chiefly in the Graubünden.]

ratis "fern"

    Marcell. de medic. 25.37 (Keltic), Ir. raith.
On the etymology see Walde-Pokorny 2.21, Ernout-Meillet
852 (*pratis). Cf. Basque iratze REA 23, 1921, 335; and
distinguish Gaulish ratis "rampart" (152).

reburrus "with upstanding hair"

    Ammianus 28.4.7, cf. Aug. c. Faust. Manich. 6.1,
Gl.; and abundantly as a personal name in CIL vols. 2,
7, 12; AcS 2.1089-1092, M.L. 7105, but perhaps not Keltic (SprFK 207); yet cf. burra above. The modern Fr.
rebours etc. cannot in any event represent reburrus
directly.

salmo "salmon"

    In Aquitania, Plin. NH 9.68; cf. Ven. Fort. c.
7.4,6; but also Aus. Mos. 97-100, 129; and note Salmona,
a tributary of the Moselle (now Salm), salar 207 below.
L. H. Gray AJPh 49, 1929, 346; Kluge Urgerm. 12; apparently common to Aquitania and Belgica, cf. gauia above.

Glosses

[salpuga, solipuga "a poisonous insect" living in Spain

and Sardinia

Lucan 9.837 (and schol. ad loc.), Plin. NH 8.104; 22.163; Sol. 4.2; Isid. 12.3.4. Cf. Sofer Lat. u. Rom... Isid., 58-59. A variant with -f- (?) is dubious, but cf. rufius : rucca, lupus : lucius.

Santonica herba, santonicum "absinthe"

Marcell. de medic. 28.2, cf. AcS 2.1354-1353. It is, of course, from the ethnicon Santones; but it survives in Fr. santoline, Ptg. santonina "vermouth" (M.L. 7583b).

sarna (zerna) "impetigo" Isid. 4.8.6., who describes it

as the vulgar usage, Gl., Diosc., see Sofer Lat.

u. Rom. 154, 177.

Sp., Cat., Ptg. sarna, Basque zarra; also in proper names (AcS 2.1369). The deriv adj. was serniosus "petiginosus" (Theod. Prisc. 1.12).

Unless this is Iberian, corresponding in meaning to the Keltic derbita, derbiosus (see 178 below), cf. possibly O.E. sār "sore," for the etymology of which see Walde-Pokorny 2.445. Cf. ϲουρωρβι above (Note xxv, Remark).

?sarralia (serr-) "lactuca agrestis"

Isid. 17.10.11 and the Glossaries. The explanation of Isidore, who describes the term as current (quam s. nominamus), would imply a variant serralia, cf. serracum beside sarracum.

If a native word, evidently confused with serra "saw," though Isidore does not shrink from popular ety-

mology, and the alternation e:a (before r), is not difficult to account for; if a Latin word, then the a vowel
may have been induced by confusion with scariola (cf.
CGL 3.540,36; 567,16?). The Romance forms (Cat. serralha,
Sp. cerraja and sarraja, Ptg. serralha, M.L. 7865) point
to serr- as having prevailed, but not necessarily as
original. Cf. perhaps Sarra (132, Note xxvii).

scandala (-e) "spelt"

According to Pliny NH 18.62 the Latin for Gallic
bracis; but M.L. 7650 gives Cat. escandia, Sp. escanda,
Ptg. escandea, Astur. eskana, from the source of which
Pliny's scandala and Parm. skandzla, would appear to be
derivatives. Probably Iberian. Cf. Terracini Riv. di
Filol. 49, 1929, 430; secale (240). Distinguish scandala: σκανδούλη Ed. Diocl. 1.8. Cf. BB 23, 1897, 59;
in Festus scandalaca appears to be yet another word.

[scotica "whip" Isid. 5.27.15 (uulgo)

Survives only in N. Italy and Switzerland. Hor.,
Iuv., Mart. have scutica; and Walde regards the word as
merely the Greek σκυθική (scyt- Paul. ex Fest. 449.9 L.),
but the first author to use scutica is Hor., and we expect either O.L. scutica (Fest. 448.30 L., from σκῦτος,
which will not do, with ū); or, if a later borrowing
scythica. Despite the difference in meaning, there may
have been a popular confusion with the next item.]

scotta "ferrum anceps"

Acta Austregisili 1.2.15, ASS 26 May 5.231* F
(again: quod uulgus sc. uocat). Austregisilus (†624)
is described as Bituricensis, which locates the word in
Aquitania. Cf. Scot(t)ius (personal name) at La Graufesenque (132)?

Glosses

segullum (v.l. segutilum) "a kind of earth that indicates

the presence of gold"

A Spanish mining term, Pliny NH 33.67, cf. Sp.
segullo; see also Bertoldi, ZfRPh 57, 1937, 142. For
other such terms cf. alutia (talutium), apitascus (tasconium) above.

serniosus: see sarna above

soldurius, solidurius "deuotus"

Caes. BG 3.22.1 (apud Sotiates, in Aquitania).
In Athenaeus 6.54, 249 A-B (Nicol. Damasc.) the MSS have
φιλοδούρους or φιλοδούνους, for which Kaibel reads σολι-
δούρους, and Holder calls attention to British coins
with Cuno[belinos solidu[.

The most obvious guess would be to compare Latin
solidus, soldus, but a mercenary is not what the context in Caes. or Athenaeus demands, nor is a mercenary
usually "deuotus," the self-sacrificing Gallic warrior
of whom there is independent evidence (see AcS 2.1600-
1601). Walde thinks of *sollo- "whole" and *durios
"enduring" or *drurios "true." Latin has solliferreum
(of weapons), of which at least the first element is
comparable. I see no way of relating -durios and -fer-
reus, though ferreus is commonly applied to men. Stokes
(ap. Fick 2 ed.4, 304) suggested *sol(i)do-uirio- . But
solliferreum translates ὁλοσίδηρος (cf. gaesum 1 above,
σαύνιον 246; REA 13, 1911, 455) and there may be some
reference to the weapon in a garbled tradition.

stagnum, stannum "tin"

Pliny, and later writers; since tinning is said
to have been a Keltic invention (Pliny, NH 34.162), the
word may also be Keltic (Ir. stan, W. ystaen, Bret. sten).

In Gaul, as both local names and remains of mining operations show (see A. Grenier Mnl 2 11, 1934, 966-

Glosses

970), the départements of Haute-Vienne and the Creuse
are important, as well as Brittany; Grenier cites the
local names Etignières, A.D. 1247 Estaignères, 1392
Estanereis.   There is also the divine name Stanna 155
above.   Cf. REA 13, 1911, 94.

[stringes (v.l. striges): the name of a garment in

Spain, Isid. 19,23.1; Sofer, Lat. u. Rom. 45]

[strigilis "auri paruola massa"

In Spain, Plin. NH 33.62; on this, and the last
item, see Ernout-Meillet 987-988. For other mining
terms see segullum above.]

suapte "fittingly"

Virg. Tolos. gram. 116.10; thence into Irish
Latin, see K. Meyer Zur keltischen Wortkunde 2 (in SB.
K.Pr.Akad.d.Wiss., 1912, vol.2) p.1144, no.25.

Evidently a hybrid (see the Grammar), Kelt. su-
"well," and Latin apte. Cf. sua in the insc. of Rom.
(Note xxvi)?

?talamasca "larua de cortice arboris facta"

Gloss, cod. Bern. 386 f. 9ᵃ ad Comm. Einsidlense
in Donati artem minorem; Mon. Hist. Germ., Poet. 1.554
de talamasca (Theodulphi carm. 57 tit.). These references I take from AcS 2.1707.

The function of the talamasca was doubtless magical and apotropaic; cf. then Poitev., Saint. talbó "Holz-
stück das man den Tieren um den Hals hängt, um sie am
Weglaufen zu hindern," in which a practical use has been
developed; M.L. REW 8535 c-d.

Or compare *talamun (Ir. talam, gen. talman "earth"),

471

Glosses

talamasca (ctd.)

Dottin 290, if the meaning "ghost, revenant" comes from
"earthly, buried." Cf. Bertoldi, BSL 32, 1931, 151.
Weisgerber SprFK 210 refers to the Keltic or Iberian
talo- , tala- (in local names) "forehead." For masca
see 246 below; the -sc- need occasion no difficulty.

talutium (vv. ll. talutatium, alutatium) "gold-bearing

earth" Pliny NH 33.67

Pliny would suggest an Iberian source; but Keltic
is advanced by modern critics, e.g. Jud, Romania 47,
1921, 487-488 (cf. 52, 1926, 347); Bertoldi, however,
ZfRPh 57, 1937, 145 compares alutia (see this word above),
and would analyse ta-lutium, a-lutia (cf. Basque doub-
lets tarte beside arte, talde or alde, which, Bertoldi
claims, is a "traccia dell'articolo berbero femminile.");
P. S. Pasquali, Ph. Woch. 59, 1939, 813-816. See also
tannare 220 below (with aluta, alumen quoted there).

[?tamarix

See Ernout-Meillet, ed.2, 1016, for a suggested
Iberian origin, and note once more the ending -(i)x.]

?Ταρβηλοθάδιον From Diosc. 2.126 RV (1.198, 12 W.), who

makes the word Gallic, for ἀρνόγλωσσον (plantago

minor)

v.l. Ταρβηλοδάθιον , and in ps-Apul. (CML 4.25,70)
tarbidolotius (v.l. -slotius, -lopius, -lopium). The
reading Ταρβοταβάτιον in Diosc. was a conjecture of Zeuss.

The most recent suggestion is (Weisgerber, SprFK
210) to accept the reading tarbidol- (dol- "leaf").
Compare, in any event, taruo- "bull," and the Aquitanian
local names Tarbelli, Aquae Tarbellicae (84), and (152,
Vieux-Poitiers) the personal name tarbelionius, which,
or like forms, may have affected tarbidol- , if that is

472

Glosses

Ταρβηλοθάδιον (ctd.)

the correct form; otherwise they rather cast doubt on
Weisgerber's suggestion.

tasconium "terra alba similis argillae" Pliny, NH 33.69

(cf. apitascudem above)

Bertoldi BSL 32, 1931, 100-102, cf. ZfRPh 57,
1937, 142 calls attention to Basque tosca, said to mean
"white clay used in the manufacture of porcelain" (which
is exactly Pliny's definition).

Presumably distinct from tasco- "peg" (Galatian),
on which see Weisgerber, Natalicium Geffcken 1931, 163;
and (s.v. drungus) 220 below. And from Germanic tasca
"pocket" (Brüch p.6). But there may be some connexion
with Sabine-Latin tesca, tescua (which, like W. hysb
*si-s-k̂-u̯o- , contains k̥u̯ not q̯u̯), AcS 2.1588,1748.

tautanus "cateia, claua"

Said by Isid. 18.7.7 to be both Gallic and Iberian; what he describes is apparently a sort of boomerang.
The etymology is unknown; Sofer 46-47, 171 fancies an
Iberian au from Keltic ou or eu. See now Rh.Mus. 86,
1937, 97-126.

What is to be made of tautones "palpebrae" (AcS
2.1774, from cod. Sangall. 238, p.149)?

? θισάρικαμ (v.l. θησάρικάμ) Diosc., thetarion (vv. ll.

thicarica, thearica) ps-Apul., loc. cit. s.v.

Ταρβηλοθάδιον above, the Iberian for ἀρνόγλωσσον

[? titio "torris, lignum adustum"

Isid. 17.6.27 (cf. Sofer, pp.89, 174), but at

473

least as old as Varro; Isidore's source seems to have
been Lactantius, and Romance derivatives are abundant,
M.L. REW 8758. I cite the form here for comparison
with titiont in the insc. of Rom. Hardly cf. tuθos?]

[?titumen ps-Apul. 10.5 (CLM 4.43,18), artemisia mono-

clonos; cf. πόνεμ 178?]

[tomentum (Leuconicum)

　　　　See AcS 2.196-196, 1884. Like culcita above;
the object described is Gaulish, but the word Latin.]

tripetia "three legged seat"

　　　　Sulp. Sev. Dial. 2.1.4 (p.181 Halm) in sellula
rusticana...quas nos rustici Galli tripeccias (vv. ll.
tripecias, tripetias), uos scholastici tripodas...nuncu-
patis. Terracini Scritti...Trombetti p.345 and n.2
calls attention to this as "a mere vulgarism." But perhaps it is not to be so readily dismissed. If it really
contains ped- "foot," then we should read tripedia. But
if that were Keltic, -p- would disappear (cf. candetum?),
though treide (178) is a totally different word. Another
suggestion would be to read tripautia cf. pauta (220;
see also Die Sprache 1, 1949, 126), and tripautia would
almost certainly be corrupted in the course of the ms.
tradition. Again we have pet- in petisia (246; perhaps
distinguish piccis 240, but cf. Die Sprache l.c., 127-
28), which is, I think, most unlikely to be involved
here. On the other hand petia (178), pecia in Du Cange
s.v., which Thurneysen took as the source of Br. pez, W.
peth, Ir. cuit (i.e. *qᵘe/ot(t)i- , see KR pp.70-71),
Fr. pièce (denied by Fraser Scottish Gaelic Studies 5,
1 April 1938, 71 cf. 2 ii Feb. 1928, 192), is perhaps
to be recognized here, compounded with tri- "three."
There is also the Coligny peti ux (227; Die Sprache,
l.c.); the local name Trepitia (221), if not Triputenses
(241). Names in Pec(c)- , Pet(t)- AcS 2.960-61, 972;
finally loss of -r- by dissimilation from *tri-qᵘetria
(?) is not impossible.

Glosses

[tritanus, -ianus a variety of cabbage, Pliny NH 19.139,

    141. Cf. the local name Tritium?]

[?trixago or trissago " χαμαίδρυς "

    Latin, Pliny NH 24.130. From AcS 2.1961]

tucus "ciculus" Isid. 12.7.67; see cicolus above

uassallos "vassal, servant"

    Dim. of uassus 220 below (but note also Germanic
baro ib.); cited AcS 3.119 from Vita Menelei (Menatansis,
i.e. near Puy-de-Dôme) 4.35, ASS Iul. 5, 314 D, but also
from Pardessus Dipl. 2.284 (A.D. 710) near Liège, and
there can be no question but that the term, like uassus
itself, was in use, wherever Keltic was spoken. The institution is described by Caes. BG 6.15.2 (where he uses
the Latin cliens), in reference to Gaul and the Gauls
generally. However, note also the following item.

    uassos stands for I.Eu. *uposto-s (Pedersen 35,
Pedersen-Lewis 2; Pokorny, Urg. 43); Welsh gwas, Ir. foss.

uasso-galete "templum, delubrum" Greg. Tur. Hist. Fr.

    1.32: ueniens uero Aruernus, delubrum illud quod

    Gallica lingua uassogalate uocant...

    Stokes interpreted this as "uassorum...templum"
but it is apparently also a divine epithet, CIL 13.10017,
958 (Puy-de-Dôme) g[enio] u[asso] k[aleti], if correctly
expanded (which I doubt); this is found several times in
the Rhineland, to which the cult of Mercurius Aruernus
was successfully transplanted. Hence Mercurius Dumias
(i.e. Aruernus) is supposed to be the same as Vassocaletis, and G. Poisson derives modern Jaude (Clermont-
Ferrand) from (uasso)caletis, see Revue d'Auvergne 27,

Glosses

1910, 233-240 (cf. Rev. d. Ling. rom. 4, 1928, 95), but
cf. 149 above. On the temple of Mercurius Dumias see
A. Audollent in Le Puy-de-Dôme (published by L'Auvergne
littéraire artistique et félibriénne 4, no.32, June-
July 1927), 48-64. Unluckily the excavations of the
temple have yielded no positive evidence for the identification of Dumias and Vassocaletis (cf. A. Grenier,
La Gaule romaine in Frank 3, 1937, 529 n.63).

     There is the further difficulty of reconciling
Gregory's definition of uassogalate with the use of
the term as a divine epithet; that Mercury should be
the defender of uassi is not hard to understand. Perhaps uassocaletis is then, as an adjective, "at the
shrine of the uassi," as a neut. noun -e "the shrine
of the uassi." AcS 1.238,6; 697-698; 1942, 20-23; 3.
122-123; FHRC 175.22; 281.10; 306.27; CIL 13 iv (1916)
add. p.194. Greg. Tur. l.c. 33 suggests that the correct interpretation of uasso caletis is "seruo templi"
or "delubri," so that Stokes may have been on the right
track after all (*kel- : Germ. Halle, see AcS 1.697,12-
15; 3.122,30). As for delubrum cf. CA 2.35 (item 76)
and 5.229 (items 206, 223) modern délubre, but hardly
Le Brus, Narb. Isid. Etym. 15.4.9: delubra...templa
fontes habentia).

uergobretus: see 178 (e.g. CIL 13.1048, Santones)

uerna and uernus "alder"

     In glosses and local names (AcS 3.223-224, 227-8),
cf. areuernus 178 below, where the impv. uernus "obsta"
in the Endlicher glossary is discussed.

     Holder identifies uerna (-us) with the deus Sex-
arbor 86 above, cf. Fagus deus ibid., which is indeed
possible (cf. BSAF 1936, 148), but quite unproven; if
it were proven, it would help to locate uerna in Aquitania, cf. uerno-dubrum Pliny NH 3.32 (dép. Aude 80
above, and Pyrenées-Orientales), and, in fact, many of
the local and personal names containing this element do
belong to southern and western France. The Vernapia of
Bertoldi BSL 32, 1931, 159 I cannot locate, and he gives
no reference.

476

Glosses

uernus (ctd.)

Cf. Lat. uernilago ps-Apul. 110 (CML 4, 1927, 195.13, i.q. Diosc. 2.14, οὐρνιλάγω), and uernetus Marcell. de medic. 9.131 (herbam, quae Gallice uernetus dicitur), which perhaps should be read uernus. The word is Keltic (Ir. fearn, W. gwern), well represented in Romance (Bertoldi, Arch. Glott. Ital. 32-33, 1929, 490), especially in S. W. France (M.L. REW 9232; cf. Walter in Giessener Beiträge zur Rom. Philologie 2, no. 10, 1922, p.67 n.2). Among local names we have uerno- in 80, 84, and 149 Remark above, e.g. Vernosole. Cf. REA 42, 1940, 612.

uernemetis (abl. pl.)

"quod quasi fanum ingens Gallica lingua refert" Venantius Fortunatus carm. 1.9, 5-10 (with reference to a site in the Agenais), cf. the local names (AcS 3.218-219) Vernem(e)tas -on in the Gironde and in Maine-et-Loire; from nemeton (see 79 above) and the intensive prefix uer- (cognate with Greek ὑπέρ etc.); Loth RA 20, 1924, 52-53. The Endlicher glossary (cf. 178) is made up of items that started evidently as Latin explanations of Gaulish local names, such as this in Venantius Fort.

It is clear that uer-nemeton neut. sg. is trans-lated Augustonemeton (148 above) i.e. uer- "augustum" (or as Ven. Fort. has it "ingens") and nemeton "fanum," like anderitum "urbem sublimem" (above) cf. Anderitum (148) and Augustoritum (148), even though the Vernematis of Ven. Fort. is not Clermont-Ferrand, but apparently between Bordeaux and Toulouse. The termination -is is probably abl. pl. (in apposition with nomine), though a neut. pl. *Vernemeta is not, I think, attested beyond doubt, and still less a nom.-acc. fem. plu. *Vernemetas (AcS 3.218,35). For other places of the same name, in-cluding one in Britain see AcS 3.218-219; cf. BSAF 1913, 83; REA 13, 1911, 95. A compound with ar- (instead of uer-) is Arnemeza (AcS 3.688,18), Arnemeti (80 above) cf. REA 13, 1911, 348. For uer-nemeto- as a personal name (assumed AcS 3.219,11) cf. 136 above (uenermidus, read Vernemidus?); "eximio loco" (Ven. Fort. l.c., line 8) as well as "fanum ingens" (line 10) may also be per-tinent. The recognition of Gallica uerba is attested in a passage of Claudian often overlooked, but cited by AcS 1.1939,25; and canis Gallicus (Ov. Met. 1.533, cf. Mart. 3.47.11) is perhaps Gallic in name (uertragus 178

477

Glosses

uernemetis (ctd.)

below; or segusius 207 [ǯγ-] and PID 2.193?) as well as
in breed; for uer- , then, cf. AcS 3.179.

uettonica "betony" properly a local name (Spain)

     Pliny NH 25.84: Vettones in Hispania eam (sc.
herbam inuenere) quae uettonica dicitur in Gallia...
But see bettonica above.

[uipio "a small crane" (Balearic) Pliny NH 10.135. Cf.

     perhaps uibo (220), and (for the meaning) geranium.]

uiriae (Celtiberice), uiriolae (Celtice) "bracelets"

     Pliny NH 33, 39-40, cf. Weisgerber SprFK 213.
It is doubtful, however, whether uiriatus (AcS 3.365-
378) belongs here. Nor is it clear whether Germanic
(e.g. OE wír) has this word by inheritance or by borrowing (Kluge Urgerm. ed.3, p.6).

uisumarus "trifolium" Marcell. de medic. 3.9

     Cf. perhaps μερι-σει-μόριον (178).

uitrum "woad"

     In Britain (Caes. BG 5.14.2) and in Aquitania,
Marcell. de medic. 23.10 (herba quam nos uitrum...
[uocamus]), cf. 207. Compare OHG weit, OE. wād? But
the etymology is unknown. Presumably a different word
from Latin uitrum "glass," though Ernout-Meillet ed.2,
1117 think differently, and glastum (207) means both
"woad" and "amber;" glaesum (220) "amber" and (?) "glass."

478

Additional Personal Names of Aquitania

urium "sludge, the muddy water of a stream, water-course"

Pliny NH 33.75 (à propos of gold-mining). Cf.
the Baetic river-name Vrium (Pliny 3.7), Basque ur "water"
(Bertoldi BSL 32, 1931, 100 and 105; id. ZfRPh 57, 1937,
142), Vria (personal name, CIL 13.327), Vra fons (CIL
12.3076 Nimes).

Skt. var "water," Latin urina; and perhaps a
Gaulish uara- "water-course" (Weisgerber, SprFK 212),
Lig. Varus fl. But uara (Auson. Technopaegn. 4) is
presumably a different word (though the meaning "error"
could be got from the winding course of a stream); and
different also from ura "orchis" (ps-Apul., CLM 4.50,
15). Not urinum (178) unless the correct reading is
urium.

159   Additional Personal Names of Aquitania
                (from authors)

Auolus Fortunat.

?Baccara Martial

Baudillius Greg. Tur.

Βριτόρης Appian (for
   Vercingetorix?)

Britta Greg. Tur.

Cantianus Fortunat.

Dracco id.

Edobeccus Greg. Tur.

Gergissus Virg. Tol.

Gurdonicus Sulp. Sev.
   cf. gurdus (158)

Iumerus Fortunat.

Liger Sil. Ital.(4.120)

Ligerios Fortunat.; Merov.
   num.

Marturius Fortunat.

Metiscus Auson.

Namatius see AcS 2.675

Nunnichius Fortunat.,
   Greg. Tur.

Corrigenda and Addenda

Nunninus Greg. Tur.	Saruco Auson.
Nunnio id.	Suagrius Sidon. Apoll., Greg. Tur.
Ruricius Fortunat.; see also AcS 2.1248-49	Talas(s)us (Burdigal.) Auson.

To these may be added, from CIL 3.2065, Viridomarus (Biturix)

Corrigenda and Addenda

Page

241 On andere see JCS 1, 1949, 4-6 (παρθένος.)

242 Add Tovar JCS 1, 1949, 11-23

246 s.v. Caauus read Cc- lapis

295 At 95(b) line 7, for |c read c|

328 Remark (viii) for $\int$ read ζ

361 At Augustonemetum for "178 below" read "178 below s.v. dunum"

In the first part:

  Item 6

Iucius REA 21, 1919, 149	Velagenus AE l.c.; Klio 21, 1927, 82-86
Mantus AE 1913.135	?Vlattius AE l.c.
Sura REA l.c.	

  Item 79

  brisare: add JCS 1, 1949, 50

Lugdunensis

1950

"La province Lyonnaise de l'époque impériale ne
répresente plus qu'un reste bien réduit de l'ancienne
Celtique" (Grenier, Mnl. 1.133; cf. P-W 7.652-53).
Caesar's celtica (see Prolegomena, Map 1) had stretched
from the Garonne to the Seine and the Marne, from the
Rhine to the Atlantic, with its core centered in the
Bituriges Cubi, almost in the center of Gaul itself,
and a number of sea-faring tribes (aremorici) settled
on the west coast chiefly at and north of the mouth of
the Loire. But the establishment of the Belgic power
north of the Marne, the loss of their hegemony by the
Bituriges to the Aruerni, the succession of defeats at
the hands of the Romans as well as of the Cimbri and
Teutones, and finally the Roman conquest of Gaul, followed by the political re-organization under Augustus,
left of the ancient Celtica only a narrow strip of territory, stretching from the Saône to Brittany, and lying
between the Loire and the Belgic frontier, which at that
time was set not on the Seine but a few miles north of
it and almost parallel to it, a location doubtless intended to keep the Belgae under restraint. In the same
way some of the old ciuitates that had straddled the
Loire, as the Carnutes and Turones, preserved their old

boundaries more or less intact, so that between Iuliomagus and Briua the frontier of Aquitania is actually
south of the Loire.

Not a few of the tribal names of the restricted
Gallia Lugdunensis (cf. Pliny NH 4.107) survive in the
modern names of French cities (Sens, Meaux, Paris,
Tours: Senones, Meldi, Parisii, Turones); the territory
itself took its name from that of the city of Lugdunum,
which, unlike the ancient capital of the Bituriges Cubi
(Auaricum, Bourges), instead of being centrally placed,
was set near the frontier of Narbonensis, perhaps for
protection, but at a point at which it also served as a
meeting place for Gaulish gatherings, giving a sense or
shadow of unity, rather than the reality or substance
of it.

The paucity of pre-Latin inscriptions in Lugdunensis makes the ancient proper names of this territory
more important. Selection is necessary, as hitherto,
but does not exclude modern local names whenever they
represent, as they may even in Brittany, Keltic names
anterior to the Roman conquest, ambiguous as their interpretation often is. Thus Lugdunum itself (see 178
below), has been the subject of repeated conjecture,
ancient and modern:

(1) the derivation from λοῦγος· κό ρᾰξ (ps-Plut., de fluuiis 6.4) may have been accepted by its own inhabitants, cf. Bidez, Mélanges Navarre, Toulouse 1935, 29; P. Wuilleumier RA 8, 1936, 50; AJA 41, 1937, 132.

(2) "mons lucidus" is the interpretation offered in the uita S. Germani of Heiricus (Héric, ob. 880) 4.295-298, and this, it has been suggested (cf. Blanchet and Chabot in CRAcInscBL 1940, 54-58), is thought by some to be supported by the name Photinus of the first bishop of Lyons; cf. REA 24, 1922, 162-163.

(3) The Endlicher glossary gives "mons desideratus," on which see S. Reinach in REA 18, 1916, 277-279.

(4) Modern etymologists have appealed to the divine name *Lugus (u-stem), pl. Lugoues at Avenches (CIL 13. 5078), Bonn (13.8026), Osma (2.2818) and Sinoza (AE 1912. 12); cf. deo Bemilucioui (-g-) ap. Mandubios CIL 12.2885, and Ir. Lug(h), gen. Loga, -o, Luga; see Loth RA 24, 1914, 205-230; REA 18, 1916, 63-64; 20, 1918, 127; RA 23, 1931, 102-106. But

(5) some other recent suggestions (e.g. Philipp in Ph.W. 1913, 1146, cf. REA 15, 1913, 451; or Gröhler Fr-ON 1, 99) may be ignored. And

(6), so far as I know, no one has yet suggested comparison either with the ethnicon Lugii of eastern Germany, an idea that ought to commend itself to Pokorny (Urg. 4-5), or with λούγεον "marsh, swamp" Str. 7.5.2, 314 C (see 170 and 240 below). Vendryes (CRAcInscBL 1940, 55) maintains the traditional explanation: "cité du dieu Lug." The name is widely distributed (80, 84, 212, 221, 241) and appears even in Germania Magna.

Even more confused (and confusing) is the argument that has raged around modern French names that represent a prototype *equoranda or *icoranna, see the lengthy discussion by P. Lebel Romania 63, 1937, 145-203 (with the criticism of L. Roger Zts.nfr.Spr.u.Lit. 63, 1939, 169-175; J. Vannérus in Handelingen van de Koninklijke

Commissie vor Toponymie en Dialectologie 12, 1938, 321-

344; and Jeanton REA 39, 1937, 43-44).

This name is found not only in Lugdunensis, but
all over Gaul. It is believed to be Keltic and -ranna,
-randa is usually explained by comparison with Ir. rann,
Bret. ran "part, portion," since it is evident that the
term designates a frontier-site (like Lat. fines); but
what is ico- , equo- ? No explanation hitherto proposed
is acceptable; and I hesitate to offer yet another conjecture. Since, however, Coligny shows equo- like Umb.
ekvine, it is at least possible that Umb. eikvasese (for
*eikua(n)si-fs with the postposition -e(n), cf. castren-
sis, canabensis), eitipes (if that contains eik(u)- in
the first syllable, cf. Germ. eigen, Eng. own), and eikvasatis furnishes a clue to ico- , equo- in this puzzling
Gaulish local name. The former is "(in) pagis, collegiis"
or the like, the latter perhaps "paganicis," cf. possibly Osc. eikviaris(?) in ID 114, and (with Buecheler,
Umbrica 29) local names such as Aequi, Aequicoli, Illyr.
(Krahe, PN 132) Aecicus lacus (which gives a water-
boundary). The meaning required in equoranda is that
of "common boundary," and this etymology (cf. Lat. ae-
quos with ku, not qu ?), see von Planta, Gram. 1, 346-
348 (Devoto Tab. Iguv. 317 n.2) fits all the requirements better than any yet proposed. The spelling ei-
in Umb. eikva- is probably archaic (for e from older ae,
ai). Finally, note the coin-legend eiqitiako (or -aico,
possibly -uico?) from Graçay (Cher), Blanchet Tr. 119,
219.

For iron and bronze work in Lugdunensis cf. CIL
13.10029 and 10027; A. N. Newell has a brief account of
Gallo-Roman religious sculpture in Greece and Rome 3,
1913, 74-84; Florance Répertoire des antiquités celtiques
(Loir et Cher), cf. REA 29, 1927, 59; Mémoires de la
Commission des Antiquités du département de la Côte-
d'Or (1927-37), see RA 18, 1941, 169-172.

Words in Latin Inscriptions

Note xxviii

A few items of linguistic interest in the Latin inscc. of Lugdunum, other than proper names, are worth noting here, not all of them Keltic, viz. CIL 13:

1751   occabo (abl. sg.) "armlet, bracelet"

Cf. ὄκκαβος Et. M., Hesych. The formation is apparently similar to that of kanabae, Entarabus (In-) see 211 and 213 below; Iotacabo 182.

1954,206   in kanabis, in canabis

See 178 below; cf. Notes xlvi (17), lii (h), lvi; and CIL 13.1788 c[anabenses], but not Cenabum (179 below).

1954, 1960, 1966   loc. sg. Arare

2003   ?laudicarii (?lod-)

But the reading is doubtful; on lodix (Keltic?) cf. Walde-Hofmann 1.819; not laudicenari!

2008, 2010   sagarius

Cf. sagum PID 2.189.

2023   ars prossaria

Rostovtzeff CRAcInscBL 1930, 250-260 reads brossaria; but p- is right, cf, pro(s)a 178, 220 below. This must be the source of French brosse, English brush. Meyer-

Words in Latin Inscriptions

2023 (ctd.)

Lübke's *bruscia and *burstia (Germ.) REW 1340a, 1417
take no account of this insc. or of the gloss, and the
relationship of the words is not clear (p- the Keltic
pronunciation as heard by a speaker of Latin, and -ss-
for -st-). W.P. 2.132 throws no light either. Gaulish
brushed wool was, of course, famous.

2309   ]uxassoni

Probably a name; but the form is noteworthy, cf. words
in ux- AcS 3.67-68 (Vxuma, Vxono, Vxisama etc.)

†2374   saraga[

Apparently a name, but cf. sarracum, σάραγον (240).

     The insc. published in REA 15, 1913, 187 (AE 1913.
124) contains a reference to a

                    schola polionum

which seems to have baffled the editors. It has been
considered a miswriting of pellionum, cf. pellionarius;
polliones is "dealers in skins" (cf. JRS 26, 1936, 221),
but polliones (Dig. 50.6.7) is accepted by Byvanck Excerpta Romana 2.649.

     2448 (from Genay, in the country of the Ambarri)
is a bilingual (Greek and Latin) that testifies to Greek-
speaking traders under the Empire at Lyons and in Aquitania (negotiatori Lugduni et prou[incia] Aquita[ni]ca).

                        487

Words in Latin Inscriptions

Note xxix

(a) From Briord (Br]ioratenses, see CIL 13.2464, in the territory of the Ambarri) 2465 (cf. 12.1657, and 158 above)

arepe[nnis]

(b) From Géligneux (or -ieux) ib. 2494, in part:

...aediclam cum uinea et muris ad opus consumman-

dum et tutelam eius et ad cenam omnibus tricontis

ponendam XII in perpet[uum] sic ut petrudecameto

consumatur...

Cf. Loth, CRAcInscBL 1909, 16-28.

(c) From Macon (Matisco, in the territory of the Aedui), ib. 2583

?combucouati

Usually taken as a name, gen. sg. (Cambudouatus?), with the following f, but the reading is uncertain (not two words, combuco uati).

(d) 2585 (CIL 13.p.406, q.v.)

p. ogen (dei Moltini)

A priestly title, cf. pogdedorton (-onin) at Coligny (227)? And pogia at Rom (Note xxvi B 6 above)? Cf. AcS 2.901. In the same insc. (2585):

gutuatri Mart

Cf. Note xxiv(d) above; and the gloss 178 below (BG 8. 38.3); gutuater appears in two inscc. of Aûtun pub-lished in Mém. Soc. Éduenne, N.S. 28, 1900, 353-356 (Dessau 9308-09), CIL 13.11225-26. In the latter Appa[

Inscription of Auxey-le-Grand

(line 4) is more likely to be a cognomen than a common
noun (apparator?), and therefore does not bear on the
meaning of gutuater.

   (e) 2494   This insc., cf. (b) above, ends

        haec o s l h n s

which must stand for heredem non sequ(uentur, or the
like?) preceded by a phrase the precise expansion of
which is uncertain. In no event, however, is a Keltic
word likely to be concealed, like triconti "thirty"
and petrudecameto "fourteenth (day?)" (AcS 2.980; 1949;
cf. REA 7, 1905, 55; 9, 1907, 173; 13, 1911, 351). For
the later cf. decumates (see Section viii.1 Introduction;
BSL 29, 1929, 34) and see 179 below (mantalo- not "ae-
qualitas" Do. 74 n.4, but "uiacum" cf. Mantalo-magus
AcS 2.411 and [?] Aequo- , Equo- randa, as well as
Quadruuiae ib. 1058; REA 18, 1916, 282-283).

160

     From Auxey-le-Grand, near Volnay (Côte-d'Or), four
miles north-west of Beaune; discovered at the end of the
eighteenth century by a M. Boillot of Auxey, it remained
at Volnay until 1885, when it passed into the collection
of Gallo-Roman remains preserved in the small Museum of
the Société d'Archéologie at Beaune (Hotel de Ville),
no.17, seen there by me in July 1929.

Apparently the lid of a small sarcophagus; the

insc. is cut on a surface 18.5 in. by 11.5 in. sunk

into the face of a broken block of the local igneous

stone, now 23 by 14 by 5 in., probably never much larger.

The damage is at the top left corner, along the right

Inscription of Auxey-le-Grand

side, and along the bottom; but the word ieuru, being
divided between lines 2-3, shows that not much is wanting (room for one letter at left in line 3, probably
complete in line 4). A plaster cast at Saint-Germain-
en-Laye (22294) shows the insc. unbroken, and is said
to have been made when the stone was entire.

iccauos · op|pianicnos · ieu|ru·
brigindoni[. | cantalon[

The interpunct now appears clearly only in line 1,
but there can be no doubt that the older copies show its
position correctly. Letters 2.5 in. high (line 1), 2.125
in. (line 2), 1.625 in. (line 3), 2 in. (line 4), except
p in line 1 (3.375 in. high), with which o is conjoint.
In line 2 the letters are now no longer clear. In line
4, only the hasta of l remains; de Ricci, who first
pointed out traces of the horizontal, proposed cantalon,
Hirschfeld has cantaion, de Belloguet cantabon (-lon in
ed.2), cantaron alii. The plaster cast, for what its
evidence is worth, appears to favor cantalon; but de
Ricci's statement (ap. Hirschfeld) is based only on it.
In the original, the end of line 4, like the beginning
of line 2, is worn and broken, and now quite indistinct.

Cut in fine style, letters with finials; probably
of Augustan date. Rhys treated this text, and some
others, as metrical (cf. Gray AJPh 63, 1942, 443); I
mention his conjecture only to dismiss it. He also
supposed (Insc. p.11) the meaning of cantalon to be
"song," a fancy unlikely in itself, and refuted by the

Inscription of Auxey-le-Grand

fact that the insc. belongs to "un petit sarcophage."
De Belloguet, who did not lack common sense, saw that
the word must refer to some (larger?) structure of which
the inscribed stone was merely a part, if connected at
all; perhaps "mound, cairn" cf. cant(h)os (158) or
possibly "urn." On brigindoni see BSL 32, 1931, 158
n.2; on oppianicnos cf. 83 and 138 above, Note xlv C
below, Cic. pro Cluent. 4.10 (Oppianicus, Apulian) AcS
2.862; the likeness of the modern Le Cantal to cantalon
is fortuitous, and modern names in Cantal- , Cantel-
(Gröhler FrON 2.204) are commonly derived from Lat.
cantare.

Do. 38; CIL 13.2638 (where metre is condemned);
first published by Dominique Francois Louis Baron Roget
de Belloguet, Ethnogénie gauloise vol.1 (Glossaire
gaulois), Paris 1858 (ed.2, Paris 1872), 204 (ed.2, 289-
290), after a copy supplied by L. Renier.

Note xxx

On a stele discovered "en Bolard" near Nuits-Saint-
Georges (Côte-d'Or, 20 km. southwest of Dijon): "jeune
homme portant de la main droite un pot à anse et, de la
gauche, une bouteille; au fronton est inscrit le mot"

uinaris

BA 1932-33 [1936], 627.

161

Couchey (Côte-d'Or, canton Georey, Chambertin, seven miles south-west of Dijon) lies virtually on the frontier of Lugdunensis and Germania Superior; the insc. which follows (CIL 13.5468 with Add.) seems to me to belong more closely to the former than the latter area. Geographically it might be claimed with some reason by either; but (1) alisanu definitely recalls the insc. CIL 13.2843, deo Alisano Paullinus | pro Contedio (Contesoio BSAF 1881, fig. at p.281) fil suo u s l m, (2) it also associates the object with Alesia (Alise-Sainte-Reine) rather than with Diuio (Dijon), (3) actually from Alesia comes also a comparable object (Note xxxii below), probably, like the present one, manufactured at Alesia. Another (presumably imported: it has the Latin inscc. Q. Lussi Terti and Q. Lussi[ ) is recorded from Bremen by G. Schwantes in Schumacher Festschrift, 1930, 316-318, Pl.37. For tin-working in general cf. 158 s.v. stannum.

Inscribed "au pointillé" on the handle of a bronze pan, rather like a modern sauce-pan; discovered at Couchey in 1853, and presented that same year to the museum at Dijon (see Mém. de la Commission des Antiqui-tés du Département de la Côte-d'Or, 4, 1853-56 [Dijon, 1856], pp.x-xi, xxvi; cf. Rossignol, ibid. 281; Rép. arch. col.91), seen there by me in July 1929. Cf. Cata-logue de Musée de la Commission etc., Dijon, 1894, 89 no.445; first published (apart from an announcement in the journals in 1853) by Abbé Auber, Bull. Soc. Ant. Ouest 7, 1855, 327-330, Plate 2, frequently repeated since then.

Exterior circumference of the pan, 28.5 in. at the top, 19.75 in. at the base. Four concentric rings are

Inscriptions of Couchey and Aûtun

attached to the bottom of the pan, the object of which
is believed to have been to keep the contents of the
pan warm longer; a decorative "saw-tooth" motif runs
round the top rim. Handle 8.75 in. long, ending in a
broad flat ring (3.25 in. diameter) with a hole in the
center (1 in. diameter).

The insc., perfectly preserved, two lines of text,

along the handle:

doiros · segomari | ieuru · alisanu

in fine Latin alphabet (R , L , M , A) with slight

finials, letters .25 in. to .375 in. (1) tall, single

interpunct, and (at the very end) the "leaf" punctuation.

Do. 37. Cf. (on deus Alisanus) J. Toutain Pro
Alesia N.S. 3, 1917, 129-140; id., BSAF 1917, 214-216,
cf. 1919, 103; M. Besnier REA 21, 1919, 149; 22, 1920,
204-206; RA 14, 1939, 137; Gray AJPh 63, 1942, 443. On
the earlier periods see F. Henry Les Tumulus du dép. de
la Côte d'Or, 1932.

162

Although assured that this insc. should be in the
Musée lapidaire Saint-Nicolas at Aûtun (Saône-et-Loire),
in which city it was discovered in 1844, prolonged
search for it in July 1929, failed to disclose it. It
is described as being on a fragmentary sculpture, 1 m.
in height, "quatre femmes adossées" (RA 1, 1844, 698),
and is said to have come to light in the "avenue de la

Inscription of Aûtun

Gare, chemin de la Grange-Vertu." I am, therefore, dependent upon the text given by Devoucoux in his introduction, p.lxviii (facsimile), to the work of Edmonde Thomas (ob. 1660), Histoire de l'antique cité d'Autun, 1846. The stone was already broken into three pieces, vertically from top to bottom through o in licnos, and horizontally from that letter through line 1 to right. These fractures are responsible for the letters marked in the text as damaged. Otherwise the reading is not questioned. It is not, however, clear whether the text is complete. So far as the facsimile indicates, more might have followed line 4.

The whole is described as "une pierre méplate avec cadre" (the bottom of which is wanting) "et champ refouillé pour l'inscription."

licnos · con|teχtos · ieuru |
anualonnacu | canecosedlon

Latin alphabet, large letters in line 1. I have not given the interpunct shown by Devoucoux at the ends of lines 3, 4; it does not appear in other reproductions. The symbol transcribed χ (before t) is, of course, X .

Do. 39. For older references see CIL 13.2733 with Addendum (add Becker, Rh. Mus. 13, 1858, 293). On the deus Anual(l)us see J. G. Bulliot Mém. Soc. Éduenne, N.S. 28, 1900, 349-357. Pictet BSAF 1867, 114-119 interpreted canecosedlon as "siège de loi, ou de justice, tribunal," comparing CIL 13.3487 Apollini et Veriugodumno tribunalia duo Setubogius Esuggi f̂ d s d and others; compare also the local name Metlo-sedon (179 below), and perhaps CIL 13.2706 (Aûtun) ussedati (?) Note xxxi Remark below (ii), uχsedia (La Graufesenque above, 124),

Inscribed Spindle-Whorls

Taruessedum PID 1.451, monomalesedlin (?) CIL 6.2844
(AcS 2.625). In Metlosedum there is a v.l. Metio- (cf.
AcS 2.579,12), as perhaps in Anextio- : Anextlo- (ib.
1.153 and 3.622-23). In Mém. Soc. Éduenne 46, 1928-31,
388—389 (cf. 37, 1909, 393) it is re-affirmed that the
insc. is preserved "sous le préau du musée lapidaire de
la rue Saint-Nicolas" and further added that "la rue
de la Grange-Vertu" is now known as the "rue Bernard-
Renault;" but the comparison of caneco- with Doric κνᾶκός
"tawny" seems more than doubtful, cf. rather κνῆκος ,η-
"thistle-down," cognate with Skt. kañcanam "gold," OPr.
cucan "brown," OE hunig "honey," panicum 79 above. For
"metre" in this text cf. (besides Rhys) L. H. Gray AJPh
63, 1942, 443.

Note xxxi

Eight inscc. analogous to that of Saint-Révérien
(164 below) are reported from Aûtun and Sens, which
show Gaulish words or formulae. All on "pesons de
fuseau" (spindle-whorls, cf. 147 above). From Aûtun:

(a) nata uimpi | curmida◊

(b) geneta · | uiscara·

(c) taurina · | uimpi ///

(d) matta dagomata · | baline enata·

(e) marcosior · | maternia

(f) ueadia tua | + enet(u?)

Inscribed Spindle-Whorls

From Sens (discovered in 1913):

    (g) geneta imi · | dagauimpi[x]

The interpunct (×) of (g) confirms my transcription of 147 above. I have given this, and other interpuncts, as well as the word-division, as they stand in
the originals. Again in (g) the readings daga and uimpi
are confirmed by the inscc. (a), (c) and (d) above; de
Villefosse had geneta, mihi da gaudium, which seems
impossible from his own copy. So in (f) the original
has in line 2 [+] at the beginning, \ / at the end, of
which the former is a punct (not t), the second either
u (?) or a punct.

To these may be added, from Auxerre:

    (h) nata uimpi | pota · ui..m

See Héron de Villefosse BA 1914, 213-230 (repeated
in Bull. Soc. arch. de Sens 29, 1915 [1918], 19-41);
J. Loth, CRAcInscBL 1916, 168-182; cf. RC 38, 1920-21,
86-87. Loth dates the inscc. "vers le IIIe-IVe siècle
de notre ère," but he gives no reasons for this assign-
ment. Cf. Do. p.70. In (h) read no doubt uinum. The
text (g) comes not from Reims (AE 1914.232), but (as I
said) from Sens; on the interpretation of gomota (com-
moda?) see also Terracini in Scritti... Trombetti p.359;
on uimpi see now my paper in Language 25, 1949, 388-391
[for taurina cf. δάμαλις , also used as a term of endear-
ment; and for nata note also especially the variant enetu
in (g)].

Miscellaneous Inscriptions

Remark:

(i) A gaming die discovered in 1839 at Aûtun, now lost, and reading on its six sides (apparently in the order 1-6)

i   ua   est   orti   caius   uolo te

(evidently equivalent to numerals) is discussed by P. Wuilleumier in Istros 1, 1934, 14-18 (see Ph.W. 56, 1936, 55); CIL 13.10035,24.

(ii) In the Latin inscriptions of Aûtun, the following forms seem worthy of note, CIL 13.2706

ussedati (?)

(cf. Note xxviii and 162 above; uxsedia at La Graufesenque, which corresponds to Ven. Vpsedia).

ib. 2711, note the ending -u in

crigiru

(cf. danu 2712, drienu 2715, epiu 2716); in 2812 (between Aûtun and Nevers) we have

augu(sto) sacru deo | Brixantu propitiu

in which Brixantu is apparently abl. sg. (not dat.).

(iii) But in 2646 (Beaune) the form monimentu (i.e. monumentum) pace Dottin p.70 (cf. AcS 2.624) is probably but V.L., rather than Keltic or even mixed Kelto-Latin, despite monimenton at Til-Châtel, Côte-d'Or, CIL 13. 5628, cf. moniminto 5502, monimet 5495, monem ib. 5635 (see Note iii.a below), and mentobeto (178 below, life of Saint Symphorien d'Aûtun, Do. p.71). Cf. Note xxv(c) above.

Miscellaneous Inscriptions

(iv) In CIL 13.2863 (Fontes Sequanae) the spelling
doa (i.e. deae) is a mere blunder; but in 2864 (ib.)

dia(e)   Siqu[a]nn(ae)

shows two noteworthy variants (dia and -nn-). For dia,
dea dat. sg. cf. Word 5, 1949, 111.

(v) On the scrap of Keltic supposed to exist in
the Fragmenta Burana (vit. S. Symphorianus of Aûtun,
ob. ca 180), see 178 below.

(vi) CIL 13.10017,71-93 Graffiti on vases (chiefly
black ware) discovered at Mt Beuvray (Bibracte), now in
the museum (Hôtel Rolin) at Aûtun. Since the site was
abandoned under Augustus, the inscc. are all of older
date. The interesting feature, apart from Keltic names,
and perhaps a dat. sg. $-\omega\upsilon$ (i.e. $-\bar{u}$?) is the use of the
Greek alphabet (cf. κοσ/τεγος at Trier, see Intro. Note
to 208A below, beside Cossicus 194?). I select the
following items:

72	αμ[ουτ]ων	84	ουρκκ
74	γαιια	85	οχιροκ[(?)
76	δοννιαс	86	σεν
77	λουγουρ [	87	οτυχ
79,80	νεππτ and νηππτο	88	]βιιο
81	ουακα	89	]υτερ (?)
82	ουγοππα	90	] δουν
83	ουγιτιωυ	91	]υνουκιας
		94	καβο [κοια [

498

Inscription of St Révérien

163

Said to have been discovered in 1492 at Nevers
(Nièvre), the following text is now known only from
old manuscript copies. It is described as a stone
measuring 1.5 feet by 1 foot, with five lines of text:

ande|camu|los touti|ssicnos | ieuru

Do. 40; CIL 13.2821 (older references; add Becker,
Rh. Mus. 13, 1858, 292); repeated recently by Marius
Gerin, Mém. de la Soc. académique du Nivernais 26, 1924,
123-131 (but see the review by S. Reinach RA 19, 1924,
271).

164

Another spindle-whorl (cf. 147 and Note xxxi above),
with two lines of text arranged in the same way. Discovered at Saint-Révérien (Nièvre) in 1845, "lost" according to RC 38, 1920-21, pp.87-88 (cf. CIL 13.2827),
"conservée au musée de Nevers" BA 1924 p.cxii, but I
sought it there without success in 1929, despite written
and personal enquiry both before and during my visit to
Nevers in that year.

monignathagabi · | budduttonimon

in which d is the familiar Ð .

Inscriptions of Alise-Sainte-Reine

164 ctd.

Do. 59, CIL and RC ll. cc.; H. de Villefosse BA
1914, 489-490 (Bull. Soc. arch. de Sens 29, 1915, 42-
43); Loth CRAcInscBL 1916, 182-186; Gerin, Mém. Soc.
acad. du Nivernais 26, 1924, 133-141.

165-169   Inscriptions of Alise-Sainte-Reine

The famous Gaulish stronghold of Alesia, stubbornly
defended by Vercingetorix against Caesar in 52 B.C., is
now positively identified with Mont-Auxois, the flat-
topped hill that rises above the village of Alise-Sainte-
Reine, about two miles east of Les Laumes (Côte-d'Or).
The part which it played in the final desperate struggles
of the Gauls to escape the power of Rome, no less than
the successful excavations conducted there, have made
Mont-Auxois both a site of surpassing interest in itself, well worth more than a passing visit, and also the
subject of a vast amount of description and discussion.
For us interest centers around the five (or six?) Keltic
inscriptions discovered there, especially since four of
them stand alone, among all the Keltic inscriptions
found outside Narbonensis (except graffiti on vases, see
Note xxxi, Remark vi above and coin-legends), in being

500

Inscriptions of Alise-Sainte-Reine

written in the Greek alphabet. It is highly probable
that the insc. of Couchey (161) properly belongs here
also, for the evidence of excavation sustains that of
Pliny (NH 34.162) in proving that Alesia was closely
associated with the Gaulish art of silver and tin plat-
ing. The word for tin itself (stannum, cf. 158) seems
to re-appear in the epithet Stannus (?) of Apollo (CIL
13.1669, cf. 1536), as well as in several modern local
names (cf. Grenier Mnl. 2.970) and perhaps in the divine name (properly local) Stanna (CIL 13.950-954);
moreover, among the numerous non-Latin divine and personal names of Alesia, those of the deities Vcuetis and
Bergusia in particular have been associated with the
industry in metal for which Alesia was renowned (see
Mnl. 2.705).

Of the vast amount of literature on Alesia it will
be enough to refer here to A. Grenier, Mnl. 1.206-225,
2.702-712 (cf. Grenier ap. Frank 3.528); J. Toutain, La
Gaule antique vue dans Alésia, La Charités-sur-Loire
1932; Alésia gallo-romaine et chrétienne, same place
1933; Alésia son histoire, sa résurrection, Paris 1913
(cf. RC 32, 1911, 119-120; REA 15, 1913, 445). The
periodical Pro Alesia (1906-1932) and a large number of
reports in the archeological journals, and of monographs,
have contributed to these more comprehensive accounts;
in later years reports, more or less extensive, have
been made elsewhere (e.g. BSAF 1935, 185; CRAcInscBL
1937, 305-310). For a popular account see G. H. Allen
CW 28, 1935, 169-176.

Inscriptions of Alise-Sainte-Reine

S. Reinach RA 21, 1925, 26-100 (cf. 352) gives a bibliography of Alesia (down to 1924); see also H. de Villefosse MSAF 5, 1904-05, 207-272.

165

A block of sandstone, discovered in 1906, in fragments, at Lapipe-Séné on Mont-Auxois, and deposited in the museum there (Musée Alesia) of the Société des Sciences historiques et naturelles de Semur, seen by me in July 1929.

The assembled fragments, some thirteen of them, of which fewer than half can be fitted closely together, give some notion of the size and general character of the unbroken stone, 33.5 in. long by 11.5 in. high, c. 11 in. thick, and perhaps of the same type as the inscc. of Narbonensis. Doubtless the stone was smashed deliberately, either in ancient "times of trouble," or, long after its purport was lost, to be used as "filling."

Letters 1.5 in. high (o and Ϭ) to 2.25 in. (e.g. κ, ρ, β); characteristic forms are β , Ε , Ϗ (κ), Μ , Ν , Ρ (ρ), Ϲ (σ), Υ (υ), Ѡ and Ѱ (ω). Double interpunct.

Date c. 100-50 B.C. (cf. 169 below).

Inscriptions of Alise-Sainte-Reine

First published by Espérandieu Pro Alesia 1, 1906,
43-45, Pl. xi (cf. id. Les Fouilles d'Alesia de 1906,
Semur-en-Auxois 1907, 134-36, Pl.29); drawings and
photographs in Rhys Additions, Pl.4-6.

(a) σαμ..ταλ[οσ]αυουωτ.κνω|δω|σεσρ..λα
μα: γαρμα.σ|βιρακοτωυτι[α]ννο|κο
βριτουλωυ[ρα].β:ατο

(b) L   (c) ο|ρ

The fragments (b) and (c) may not belong to (a);
hitherto no one has succeeded in placing them in it.
The same doubt applies, in less degree, to the groups
of letters enclosed in square brackets in (a) lines 1,
3, 4; and in the last instance [ρα], the reading ρ (or
β ?) and α (or λ ?) is doubtful also, if not in the first,
in which so little is preserved of each letter as to
make identification uncertain (ο or ρ , σ or ο ?). Those
in lines 3, 4, placed here tentatively by Rhys, are on
one piece of stone, [.α] above [ρα].

503

Inscriptions of Alise-Sainte-Reine

Further, it is far from certain that line 1 was
the beginning of the insc. in its original state. The
two letters δω are on the side of the stone adjacent to
line 1 on the front, and may have belonged to part of
the insc. (or to a different insc.) written on the side,
rather than to line 1 of this, or (as Rhys took them)
to line 4. Cf. 68, Note xiv bis above.

Line 1. There is space for two or three letters
after the restored μ.   2. All that remains of ρ
(fourth letter) is a trace of the hook at the top; before σ at the end, perhaps κ (?).   3. Read perhaps
α]⟨λισ⟩αννο ? At the end, after ο, a break (space for
one letter), and then, to the end of the line, a blank
space, without any trace of engraving.   4. Cf. Βρίγουλος
AcS 1.544, 38-50? If [ρα] belongs here, space for only
one letter before β . After ατ the pieces fit well
enough together to leave no space for anything between
τ and ο, so that ν (Rh., Do.) is illusory; on the original there is nothing but the fractured face of the
stone, not Ν or ν . Do.'s printed text gives an erroneous impression of the extent of the lacunae.

Do. 35; CIL 13.11258

Inscriptions of Alise-Sainte-Reine

166

A fragment of sandstone, 7 in. wide (at the top), 7 in. tall. The two brief lines of text are near the top, with a number of mouldings beneath, i.e. probably we have part of the face of a square capital or pedestal. Broken on both sides, but no letter followed the final T in line 2.

Discovered in 1907 at La Fanderolle on Mont-Auxois (see the "plan parcellaire," in Pro Alesia 1, 1906, Pl.i; or Espérandieu Fouilles...de 1906, Pl.ii), now in the Musée Municipal there, seen by me July 1929

$$\text{ιτοσ αυου} \mid \text{ωτ}$$

Faint letters, .875 in. high (except smaller o); it is possible that the text is incomplete both right and left in line 1, right in line 2, but the existing text is intelligible (cf. auuot, auot in the Glossary; cf. Note xi above; and observe that if δυουωτ here and in 165 is the same word, Thurneysen's interpretation is impossible, for a Latin phrase can hardly have occurred in a pure Keltic insc.). Letter forms: Α α , Ϲ σ , Υ υ , Ω ω, which point to a date not earlier than c. 100 B.C., for the cursive ω does not make its appearance even in the Greek alphabet of Magna Graecia before the end of the second century B.C., in Attica c. 160 B.C. (see the Table in Larfeld, Hdb. d. gr. Epigr., Leipzig 1902), and can hardly have reached central Gaul before c. 100-50 B.C.

Do. 34; CIL 13.11259

Inscriptions of Alise-Sainte-Reine

167-168

Like Dottin (36; cf. CIL 13.11260-61), I depend
upon Rhys (Additions 311-312, Pl.vi nos.10-11) for two
brief inscc. (or fragments of a single insc.) on two
pieces of leaden plate (defixiones?) found at Mont-
Auxois in 1909; according to Do. "in the museum" (which?)
at Alise-Sainte-Reine, according to a letter from M. J.
Toutain they should be at the Musée des Antiquités
nationales de Saint-Germain-en-Laye, but no record of
them is available there, nor did I find them at Alise-
Sainte-Reine in 1929. Rhys' own account is based only
on a photograph; apparently the writing was in a cursive Greek alphabet (Rh., Do.). The larger (167) is
said to be c. 4 cm. by 1 cm., the size of the other is
not recorded. For its γ an alternative reading β or ρ
is suggested.

167   ]καρο μαρο [

168   ]ουιγρα [

Presumably neither text is complete.

169

A block of sandstone, discovered in 1839, at Le
Cimetière Saint-Père on the plateau of Mont-Auxois,
first published in Echo du Monde savant 5, 1839, 534,
and frequently since then (see the references below,
and in Do. 33, CIL 13.2880). At one time transferred
to Dijon, it was restored to the Musée Municipal founded at Alise-Sainte-Reine after the excavations (1861-
1869) inspired by Napoleon III; seen there by me in
1929 (inventory no.82). Measurements 29 in. by 19.5 in.
by 5.5 to 6 in.; broken along the bottom edge and at the
bottom left corner; otherwise the text is complete. It

Inscriptions of Alise-Sainte-Reine

was cut on a surface (19.5 by 13.25 in.) sunk into the stone for it, enclosed by mouldings with the conventional key-stone ornament right and left. A leaf serves as the interpunct between the two clauses of the text (i.e. before etic), and as ornament to fill the blank spaces at both ends of the last two lines. Otherwise the interpunct is triangular. Photograph in Rh., Additions, Pl.iv.

Doubtless this insc. was cut after the conquest of Gaul, the Latin alphabet having been adopted, though sparingly, for writing Gaulish which was hitherto totally unwritten (with a few exceptions in the Greek alphabet) in Lugdunensis. So far as the general style of the insc. is any indication of date, it may lie anywhere in the latter half of the last century B.C., hardly much later, though the long i in dugiiontiio (with the value i, fifth and tenth letters) and in alisiia (sixth letter) suggests the end of that period.

martialis · dannotali | ieuru · ucuete ·
sosin | celicnon ᵛ etic | gobedbi ·
5 dugiiontiio | ucuetin · ‖ in...alisiia

Letters 1.75 in. high in line 1, elsewhere 1.5 in.; except that at the end of line 1, in order to get in the word dannotali unbroken, t is superimposed on a small o (0.5 in. high) and a (0.75 in.) written above

507

Inscriptions of Alise-Sainte-Reine

li (both 0.5 in.); o is 0.5 in. also in dugiiontiio.
The i of ieuru is rather widely separated from e, but
the reading is of course certain; the letters in in
line 2 are conjoint. The red paint in all the letters
is modern. Well marked finials as in good Latin style,
but in the last i of line 4 so large as to make the
letter resemble the preceding t (read dugiont · to?).

There is space for one letter in the break before
uc (line 5), but there is no trace of such a letter,
and it is improbable that a letter ever stood there.
But in line 6 there is a great break before al, where
something must have been lost (brie "city," cf. penobrias
177 below, and gloss 246 below; or the like?). For an
attempt to read this inscription as verse see L. H. Gray
in AJPh 63, 1942, 442.

The discovery of a Latin insc. (CIL 13.11247)
reading

deo Vcueti et Bergusiae Remus Primi f donauit u s l m

settled once for all the meaning of ucuete(-in); and a
sanctuary, near which the insc. 169 had been found, was
excavated on Mont-Auxois in 1908 and 1911; bergusiae is
perhaps not a divine, but a local, name (cf. 80; and on
-usia, -isia cf. Kretschmer Glotta 22, 1934, 162) i.e.
"(mountain-) citadel, city," which would strengthen the
proposal to read [brie] i.e. *brige(?) in line 6. With
dugiiontiio cf. perhaps Raetic dugiaua (see PID 3.18).

508

Inscriptions of Alise-Sainte-Reine

Together the two inscc. have given rise to many discussions; see, with those listed in Do. 33 and CIL 13.2880,
the following:

Stokes Academy 30, 1886, 210; Eretta Origine et
traduction de l'insc. celtique d'Alise-Sainte-Reine,
Georg, Lyon 1904, 410 (from Montandon 1.8753); Pro
Alesia 1, 1906, 71-72 (after Allmer); 3, 1907-9, 338
(Espérandieu); ib. 385-390, 412-417 (L. Berthoud), 447-
48; 4, 1909-10, 569-575 (Besnier); 583-596 (L. Berthoud),
see RA 16, 1910, 364; REA 10, 1908, 353 and 11, 1909,
258 (Jullian, after Poisson); Thurneysen ZfCPh 6, 1907-
8, 558 (cf. REA 13, 1911, 467); H. de Villefosse CRAc
InscBL 1908, 498-500; G. Poisson Bull. Soc. géogr. de
Rochefort 30, 1908, 259; Vendryes RC 33, 1912, 101-103
and 119; Pro Alesia N.S. 5, 1919, 59-67, photograph ib.
1, 1906-07, at p.77 (Hirschfeld); cf. REA 23, 1921, 61;
31, 1927, 179 and 254; Lantier BSAF 1928, 244-45; J.
Toutain Pro Alesia N.S. 4, 1918, 191-192 (on alisa- in
river-names, cf. M. Besnier REA 22, 1920, 204-206; G.
Alessio Annales de Burgogne 1938, 130-133; summary in
REA 41, 1939, 347-48; G. Poisson Pro Alesia N.S. 11,
1925, 114-123 (condemned as "wertlos," Idg. Iahrb. 15,
244, "hypothetical" RC 46, 1929, 425); Pisani RIGI 17,
1933, 189, cf. AGI 27, 1936, 168-169 and Herauscoritsehe
fano 86 above); for Vcuetis cf. perhaps Vcoetixix 87
above; Vendryes RC 51, 1934, 129 n.1 and 337 n.1; G. H.
Allen CW 38, 1935, 169 n.2; id. AJA 39, 1935, 113-114;
Newell RA 14, 1939, 137; cf. J. Toutain Gaule antique
vue dans Alesia, 1932, 88; O. Haas ZfCPh 23, 1943, 285-
297

Note xxxii

The following items from Alise-Sainte-Reine may
be noted here:

(a) In the municipal Museum (no.339), on the broken

handle of an earthenware pan or ladle

$$]deo \cdot un[\quad | \quad]rro \cdot do[$$

(do[i.e. donauit?); on the reverse side, the single
letter u[. Seen by me, July 1929. In CIL 13.2875 line
1 reads um[at the end (so Pro Alesia 1, 1906, 24),
but Espérandieu Fouilles de 1906, 37 (no.173) has un[.
Cf. Rev. Epigr. 5, 1903, 8; MSAF 5, 1904-05, 245-47.

        (b) On the base of a silver cantharos, Greek cur-
sive

μεδ [| αραγε [

CIL 13.10026,24; MSAF 5, 1904-05, 256-262.   Cf. Arragenus
224, Ἀρηγενουα 179 below.

        (c) CIL 13.11240 (cf. 5408); see also J. Toutain
Alesia gallo-romaine et chrétienne 157, and (for Moritasgus CIL 13.2873) AE 1910.121-122, CRAcInscBL 1910,
555, with 1912, 47; RA 17, 1911, 215 and 20, 1912, 457;
BSAF 1910, 133; REA 12, 1910, 285-286; RA 14, 1939, 133-
158; Rhys Additions 312:

        aug sac | deo apollin[i | moritasgo |

        catianus | oχtai

For Oχtaius cf. AE 1925.98.

        (d) On a block of stone (Pro Alesia 1, 1906-07, p.13)

ψυ

Masons' marks? Or does this go with 165 above?

Inscriptions of Paris

(e) In view of the writing Alexia (twice in ASS,
cf. AcS 1.91), in alixie (144 above), but alisiens(is)
in Pro Alesia 3, 1908-9, 409, CIL 13.10029,216 a-b, the
reading Alixia at Pl. NH 34.162 and in the mss. of Caesar
may be correct (x with the value -ss- or -s- from -χs-).

(f) A dedication to Epona, discovered in 1931, is
recorded in AE 1939.235. On Epona in general at Alesia,
see G. Chenet Pro Alesia NS 11, 1925, 198-203 (cf. S.
Reinach RA 26, 1895, 163-195; REA 35, 1933, 411).

(g) A lead pig published in AE 1941.28, like CIL
13.2612 a-b bears (in part) the enigmatic

d l′ p | luicuc

(perhaps D libras pondo and Leg. VI Cuc[ ), but there
is no reason to suppose anything but Latin involved here.

170-173   Inscriptions of Paris

There are four inscriptions on four altars of lime-
stone which came to light in March 1710 at Paris, in the
Île de la Cité, beneath the choir of the cathedral of
Notre-Dame-de-Paris, first published by Charles César
Baudelot de Dairval, Description des bas-reliefs anciens
trouvés depuis peu dans l'église cathédrale de Paris

(1711), and frequently since then. At least part (a) in the second (171) is frankly Latin, and it is difficult to say, except where proper names are concerned, how much (if any) of the rest, whether on this or on the other three altars, must be regarded as Keltic. The altars, commonly agreed to be of the Gallo-roman period, have become, with their reliefs and inscriptions, the subject of a vast literature, some of which is cited below.

The ancient name of Paris itself, Lutecia or Lutetia has been the subject of much etymological speculation (see, e.g. R. Mowat, RA 35, 1878, 94-108; H. Gröhler, FrON 1.85, 159; H. Philipp, Woch. f. kl. Philol. 30, 1913, 1146, with Jullian's comment, REA 15, 1913, 451, cf. 22, 1920, 129; one guess is to regard it as standing for Lucotecia or (as in Strabo) Λουκοτοκία, i.e. the abode of Lucotios "the mouse-god (?)," cf. the gloss quoted by Holder AcS 2.303 from the Vita Comgalli, ASS 10 May 2.584F, luch ... quod sonat Latine mus, cf. Ir. luch, lochad, i.e. a t-stem, lucot-). But since the site of Paris is described as marshy (e.g. Caesar BG 7.57.1) perhaps we have *luco- (-g-) "marsh" (see p.484 above), and the gloss in the Vita Comgalli may somehow be confused with mus "humus" in Isid. (158 above); the form Λουκετία is yet another variant (178 below) for the citadel (πολίχνη) of Paris. Another suggestion REA 15, 1913, 451. No less dispute centers around the names of the deities that appear on these famous altars. The altars passed in due course into the Musée de l'Hôtel de Cluny, where I saw them in 1929 (inventory nos. 18602-605); see E. Haraucourt and F. de Montremy, Catalogue général 1, 1922, 19-21, where references to older catalogues are given, Plate 1; Do. 50; CIL 13.3026 with addendum; Stokes Academy 30, 1886, 210; Jullian REA 7, 1905, 373-374; 9, 1907, 263-264 and Plates 11-14; id. ib. 14, 1912, 88-89; F.-G. de Pachtère Paris à l'époque gallo-romaine 1912, 22; see also BSAF 1880, 260-261.

Inscriptions of Paris

Some further references: Toutain RA 23, 1934, 159-
160.   On taruo- cf. Taruisium, Taruessedum, PID 1 pp.
239, 451; Tarua 84 above, tarbelionius 152 above; for
the formation of Taru-essedum cf. Mandu-essedum (Britain)
AcS 2.405 (mandu- , mannu-s 240 below and PID 2, p.198).
On tri-garanos Heichelheim PW 2te Reihe s.v. Tierdämonen
(Keltisch) 6, 924-25; τρυγέρανος Philem. 47, CP 37, 1942,
97; Dottin Mélanges Loth 1927, 97 compared the local names
Garaninga quae et Romerteria (AcS 1.1982,18); but of
course not τρικάρανος (- ηνος) Anaximenes Lamps.   (L. and
Sc. s.v.) cf. Varro (Appian BC 2.9); J. Guiart Biologie
médicale 27, 1937, 91 compared the Indian triad (Brahma -
Visnu - Siva); P. Jacobsthal Early Celtic Art 1, 1944,
pp.10 n.4, 16, 23; cf. REA 10, 1908, 172-74; Drexel Jahrb.
d. Arch. Inst. 1915, pp.1, 96; RC 42, 1925, 268; REA 10,
1908, 70-75 Pl.5.   Note also Tribanti (dat. sg.?) 236
below (CIL 13.6061), with the figure of a three-horned
deity; MZ 27, 1932, 89 (horned head on vase).   A different (magical?) use of three in the "three fold death"
MacNeill Festschrift 1940, 535-550.

Monument of four deities Behn F.u.F. 5, 1929, 282
cf. MZ 24-25, 1929-30, 94; Klumbach ib. 26, 1931, 141-
144 (Grannus [Apollo] appears here, cf. 211, 223, 236
below).   On Cernunnus Ihm PW 3.1948; AcS 1.993,52; TLL
Onom. 3.348; REA 7, 1905, 373-74.   In the Val Camonica
(?) Altheim Welt als Gesch. 3, 1937, 5; Jacobsthal JRS
l.c. and Plate 11.4; Early Celtic Art 1, 1944, p.3 with
n.1, Plate 217a; and p.208 (addendum to pp.2-3); Altheim
RM 54, 1939, 1; Howald u. Meyer Röm. Schweiz 1941, 364.
Mosaic of a horned god, Wheeler Verulamium Pl.41 (at p.
144 of Rep. Research Com. Soc. Antiqu. London 11, 1936.
Note also κάρνυξ (-ον) gloss 178 below, and κάρνονον
(-μου?) at Béziers (76 above); less likely †Cernuus (pers.
name, eighth century, Arles) Bull. Monum. 1935, p.143
(which refers to cernuus "abiectus, humilis" Du Cange);
Cernus 176 below; κέρνα·ἀξίνη (Hesych.); Κάρνειος Apollo;
but not κόρνα (178).

Inscriptions of Paris

Catalogue no.2. The so-called "altar of Jupiter,"
showing on its four faces respectively (a) a bearded
Jupiter, with sceptre and thunderbolt, at his feet an
eagle; (b) a bull, caparisoned, with three cranes sit-
ting on his head and back, against a background of
foliage; (c) Vulcan, wearing a cap, and holding hammer
and tongs; (d) a male divine figure, cutting down a
tree (willow?) with an axe. Dimensions: 31.5 in. by
31.625 in., 43 in. high

(a)   iouis

(b)   taruos · trigaranus

(c)   uolcanus

(d)   esus

Each of these is complete as it stands; (b) fills

the whole side, being 29 in. long; in the others there

is ample space left blank, on right and left, to show

that nothing is wanting. But some modern jester has

added i before e in (d), and converted the first letter

of (a) into l! The letters are 1.5 in. tall in (a), 2

in., or a little less, in (b)-(d). Interpunct triangular.

On taruos trigaranus and esus see d'Arbois de Ju-
bainville RC 19, 1898, 245-251 cf. 28, 1907, 41-42 and
RA 11, 1908, 4-8, cf. ZfCPh. 7, 1910, 294; S. Reinach
RC 18, 1897, 137-149, 253-266 and Cultes, Mythes, et
Religions 1, 1905, 233-246; S. Czarnowski RC 42, 1925,

Inscriptions of Paris

1-57; J. Vendryes CRAcInscBL 1935, 324-341; A. N. Newell
RA 14, 1939, 133-158. And on the more general question
of "trinités gauloises," in addition to the references
given above, REA 28, 1926, 270, with H. Usener, Rh.Mus.
58, 1903, 1-47; 161-208; 321-362. It is noteworthy that
we also encounter elsewhere the "taureau à trois cornes,"
see BSAF 1890, 232-234; 1894, 68; 1898, 199-202; 1900,
111; 1911, 220-222, cf. Drioux BA 1926, 81-83; the figure
corresponding to cernunnus below, on whom see P. Wuilleumier RA 8, 1936, 51, and especially F. Altheim Welt
als Geschichte 2, 1936, 83-86; id. (with E. Trautmann)
ib. 3, 1937, 83-113 (but note the objections of P. Jacobsthal JRS 28, 1938, 66), is that of a bearded god
with two horns. According to F. R. Schroeder Germ.-
rom. Monatschrift 22, 1934, 180-212, the bull-god is
"pre-Indo-European."

171

Catalogue no.1. Dimensions: 28.75 in. by 29 in.
by 18.25 in., inscribed on three sides, good Latin alphabet with finials, open b and p, letters 2.75 in. high.
The reliefs are (b) three bearded figures, with flat
round caps on their heads, each armed with a spear and
a hexagonal shield; on (c) three male unarmed figures,
seen in profile; (d), uninscribed, two beardless figures
with the same kind of cap as in (b), and armed with
oval shields and with spears; (a) has no reliefs.

(a) Enclosed in a panel, 18.75 in. by 14.75 in.;
triangular interpunct.

tib · caesare · | aug · ioui · optum[| maxsumo ·
5 ... | nautae · parisiac | publice · posier. ‖ n.

The letters marked are damaged, but not illegible;

in line 3, however, it is no longer possible to read anything after the interpunct (suo Dottin, u... Catalogue). The mark ⌃ beneath s in line 4, is not an interpunct (Dottin), but probably accidental, hardly u reversed, or, indeed, articulate at all.

    (b) On the face opposite to (a); letters originally c. 2.5 in. high, but now broken at the top. Complete on right and left:

eurises

    (c) A similarly mutilated insc., on the border; possibly incomplete to right, if not also left:

senani · u.eilo[

Older editions (cf. CIL 13.3026 add.) give useilo, but no letter is now visible after u. Only a portion of face (d) remains, without insc. to right, all the rest being broken away.

According to the catalogue the scenes on this altar "de la Dédicace," a votive monument set up by the nautae Parisiaci, represent a ceremony of homage rendered by Gauls to Tiberius, who, wearing a laurel

crown and assisted by two Roman officials, receives them
seated.

172

     Catalogue no.3. The so-called "autel des quatre
dieux," (a) a bearded deity, with stag's antlers, each
of which bears a torques; on (b) and (c) the heavenly
twins, beardless; (d) a bearded god, holding in his
right hand a weapon (a club or pike?), with which he
is attacking a snake. Dimensions: 29.25 in. by 29.25
in., 19 in. high; inscc. at top, letters 1.625 to 2 in.
high, now very faint and much mutilated.

(a)   ].ern.nno.

Only nn is certain. Nothing is wanting to right,
perhaps five letters to left. The commonly accepted
reading Cernunnos, therefore, not being otherwise attested, must be regarded with scepticism; it has been
compared, however, with $\kappa\acute{\alpha}\rho\nu\upsilon\xi$ (AcS), with Ir. cern
"victory" (Do.), with the river-name Cernone, Cernune,
the modern Sanon (Jullian); and the same figure, of a
horned god wearing the torques on his antlers, has been
recognized in the Val Camonica (Altheim, but cf. Jacobsthal). Much safer, it seems to me, is Vendryes' iden-

tification (after Ihm) with Cernenus (243 below) in
Dacia (MacNeill Festschrift, 1940, 162).

(b)   ]smert...os[

Broken at top; 7.5 in. blank to left, then possibly
two letters before s; broken on right also, but perhaps
os (still visible in the eighteenth century, lost before 1880, cf. BSAF 1880, 260-261) was the end of a
single word, read (?) smertrios (not smertullos), cf.
CIL 13.4119, 11975-76; RA 16, 1922, 380; also at Trier
Mars Smertrius, see Germania 5, 1921, 104-105 (cf. REA
25, 1923, 63), CIL 13.11975-76 (Liesenich, Moselle);
REA 22, 1920, 211.

(c)   castor

Complete, but all except s appear to have been recut. The insc. of (d), if any, is now completely lost.

Inscriptions of Paris

173

Catalogue no.4. Dimensions: 35.5 in. by 36 in. by 18.75 in. high, much broken, "autel des huit dieux," viz. two clothed goddesses on face (a), a god (Mars?) and goddess on (b), a naked god and goddess on (c), and on (d) a god (Mercury?) and a goddess. Letters 1 in. high, at top:

(a)   ]for[

Perhaps complete on left, where there is a large space (19 in.) blank. On the opposite face:

(b)   ]eu · s[

Everything else is lost. The catalogue reads]eru[, cf. BSAF l.c., for Minerua according to Mowat, but the r (?) seemed to me impossible, unless an accidental scratch is to be taken seriously.

Note xxxiii

A small leaden plate, obviously a defixio, discovered rolled-up in 1847 at Paris, Quartier Saint-Marcel, on the breast of a skeleton; size not stated.

Inscriptions of Paris, Provenchères

Note xxxiii ctd.

First published by Th. Vacquer RA 37, 1879, 111-114
(facsimile), who reads the graffito:

χirisinallisoliciom |

socsinconoiosuoilsoci |

asunna aulu

The original was retained by its discoverer (cf.
Bull. Soc. de l'hist. de Paris et de l'Île de France
5, 1878, 100) and is now "lost;" there is a copy at
Saint-Germain-en-Laye which throws doubt upon Vacquer's
transcript, e.g. -noi instead of -iom at the end of
line 1, see CIL 13.3051 and 10029,328 where the reading
is given as xirimi iai soll o | socciuc oso oosa cisoc |
iu | ias .i(u) na; Audollent Defix. Tab., 108; cf. Loth
CRAcInscBL 1909, 19.

Note xxxiv

(1) CIL 13.3097 (o) from Provenchères, near Craon,
dép. Mayenne; on a tubulus ("conduit en chaux et sable"),

Inscriptions of Provenchères and Vieux

apparently uierui, for which read perhaps,

cint]u ie[u]ru(i) ?

or the like. Cf. 140 Remark above; CIL 13.10010,566;
AcS 3.1224. Otherwise (Mowat) a name (Vierui?).

(2) ib. 3162 (a long insc. on the base of a statue
discovered at the village of Vieux, the ancient Aregenua
of the Viducasses, now at Thorigny) face (ii) lines 11-
12

rachanas duas, tossiam Brit(annicam)

See the notes ad loc., and cf. 207, 220 below; rachana

"sagum," tossia (for *toxa?) "sagum, uel uestis." Cf.

AcS 2.1069 and 1893 (late authors, OE gloss, dim. ra-

chanella); Mommsen Ges. Schr. 8, 1913, 155-159 (Anal.

Epigr. 22); Besnier BA 1913, 21-50; ib. 1920, 287-297;

A. R[einach] RE 2, 1914, 159-160; MSAF 1910, 225-335;

Ernout-Meillet ed.2, 848 (raganus, racana); M-L 6983.

Ed. Diocl. 7.60 (Frank 5, 1940, 345).

Inscriptions of Vieil-Évreux

174

Inscription of Vieil-Évreux (Eure), the site of
the ancient Mediolanum of the Aulerci Eburouices; cf.
J. Mathière La Ciuitas des Aulerci Eburouices à l'
époque gallo-romaine, Evreux 1925 (reviewed by Jullian
Journal des Savants 1926, 231-32), and, for a more recent, but idle, argument concerning the location of
Mediolanum (CIL 13.3202), see REA 38, 1936, 39 and 39,
1937, 128-29; cf. L. Berthoud Pro Alesia 10, 1924, 234-
247 (on the distribution of the local name Mediolanum);
REA 8, 1906, 347; cf. 27, 1925, 333; 28, 1926, 24; and
29, 1927, 306.

This is a remarkable, but fragmentary and puzzling,

insc. engraved on bronze in a good Latin alphabet of

the early empire. Discovered at Vieil-Évreux in 1836,

seen by me in the public Museum at Évreux in 1929 (in-

ventory no.618).

Complete top and bottom, where there are remains
of a border, but broken right and left. Originally 24
in. high, but the original width can only be estimated.
The remaining border at the bottom is 28.5 in. long,
but the remaining inscribed part is considerably narrower (15 in.); within this inscribed part, c. 15 in.
high, are seven incomplete lines of text in letters of
varying sizes (1.5 in. in line 1, 1.375 in. line 2,
1.25 in. line 3, 0.875 in. and 1 in. in lines 4-7),
regular finials; a small ◡ placed high in the line serves
as interpunct. Perhaps less than half of the original
has survived. Lines 6-7 are Latin, but the rest can
hardly be anything but some form of Keltic.

```
     ]s · crisposboui[  |  ]ramedon[  |  ]iaχtac biti
5    eu · [  |  ]. o caradiionu[  |  ]n ia selaniseboddu·‖
     ]remi filia[  |  ]drutagisaciciuissue[
```

Inscriptions of Vieil-Évreux

174 ctd.

Line 1: first letter s or o. No punct after crispos. At right, i not t.   2: n is followed by a blank space, no punct.   3: before a$\wedge$ a certain, but broken, i.   4: before o, either s or d(?); u breaks at the broken edge of the bronze.   5: a wide space before ia, less after it. No space before seboddu, which is followed by the interpunct.   6: space after remi, but no spaces in line 7.

Do. 49; CIL 13.3204 with addendum (iaselani one word in line 5).

Note xxxv

Also from Vieil-Évreux comes the following Latin insc. (CIL 13.3197), seen at Évreux by me in 1929. A small piece of marble, broken into three pieces; 8 in. by 5.5 in. by 1 in. thick; neat letters, 0.5 in. high.

au]g · deogisaco | eb]urigiusagri |]lade

suopo|suit

It is quoted here for the purposes of comparison of line 1 with 174 line 7 above. On the Eure in general see L. Coutil Archéologie Gauloise vols 1-5, 1895-1925 (cf. RA 22, 1925, 367).

175

Specimens of a curious earthenware figurine,
covered with a white slip, with a text believed to be
Keltic, in letters moulded with the figure itself, not
inscribed, are known from a number of sites within or
near the borders of Lugdunensis, viz. Angers, Fégréac
(Loire-Inférieure), Corseuil (Côtes-du-Nord), Saint-
Jean-Trolimon (Somme), Caudebec-lès-Elbeuf (Seine-
Inférieure), Breteuil (Somme); the source or sources
from which they were distributed is thought to be somewhere between the Loire and the Seine, possibly Sully-
sur-Loire (uicus Sauliacus, Solliacus, Sulliacus on
Merovingian coins), cf. CIL 13 iii fasc. 2, 1906, pp.
464-466, AcS 3.780.

The only example which I have myself actually seen
is that found in the Roman cemetery at Uggate near
Caudebec-lès-Elbeuf; it was then (1929) in the possession of Mme Jules Leblond of Caudebec. 7.75 in. long,
0.75 in. thick, 2.5 in. across the shoulders; apparently a figure of Venus, much ornamented with rosettes, or
perhaps solar disks, or stylized representations of the
eye (cf. Walters Hist. of Anc. Pottery 2, 1905, 383-4),
and wearing a necklace. The insc. stands on the reverse,
running from the shoulder (r) to the feet (t) in letters
from .375 in. (r) to .19 in. (o) high, Latin alphabet
(with ‖ e, open ʁ , n reversed Ⱅ , g quasi-cursive ʂ
and hence hardly distinguished from s ʂ or ʅ , so that
erroneous readings have been published, e.g. rex tusenos
or rextusimos).

reᛪtugenossulliasauuot

One specimen has only the personal name reᛪtugenos.

Inscriptions with auot

175 ctd.

Do. 58; CIL 13.10015,85; BA 1887, 323-25; to their references add J. Drouet Bull. Comm. Ant. de la Seine-Inf. 7, 1885-87 [1889], 308; Blanchet MSAF 1890, 65-224; 1901, 189-272; id. Mélanges d'Archéologie gallo-romaine 2, 1902, 93. Blanchet (ib., 91) calls atten-tion to the discovery of ovens at Treguennec (Finistère), and, beside them, eighty statuettes of Venus; that would seem to indicate at least one certain place of manufac-ture.

Note xxxvi

The chief interest in the following items, as in

the last, is the presence of the word a(u)uot "fecit"

(cf. Note xi above). CIL 13, viz:

(a) 10015.90 (figurine), from Les Moines (Morbihan)

]s auuot

("figure vetue d'un sarreau gaulois"); v.l.]i

Ib. 10015.7 Anaogeno (for Anauo-)   34 Pistillus fecit

     10   Anto au(o)t   84 Pistillos

     69   Bot[Pixtillos

on which cf. Blanchet Mélanges 2 p.90. The name Pis-tillus appears also on a vase from the vicinity of Chagny (near Aûtun) ib. 10016.44, accompanied by three crosses

Inscriptions with auot

and the inscriptions

zuy   yyssuuii   ysys

presumably of a magical or gnostic character, or perhaps Christian (Iesus?). But cf. Note xx above; possibly only a writing exercise (e.g. 176 Remark, below).

(b) 10010.249 (on a vase), from Jublains

auota | max(i)mu[s

(c) 10027.116 (a fibula), Chalon-sur-Saône

iulios | auo[t]

(d) AE 1924.62 (from Bull. Soc. des Antiquaires de
Normandie 35, 1921-23, 604-05), a glass vase found at
Lisieux has on the rim front $\frac{2}{c}$ii, i.e.

front(u?) s ii

and in the center

auot

Cf. CIL 13.10025,50; SprFK 150; REA 26, 1924, 345. This
is read BSAF 1934-35 [1940] as front ~~sii~~ auotn+ (p.550).

Remark:

The mould which came to light at Meaux, reported

Dubious Inscriptions

by Gassies REA 2, 1900, 142-44, and reading

ateano sacrillos auot anailos

is believed to belong to Aquitania, since the names,
all three of them, belong to Moulins, see 136 Remark
above, with CIL 13.10015,1.

Note xxxvii

(1) There is (or was) a curious object in the
Museum at Nantes, a piece of schist .09 m. by .06 m.,
with rounded corners, discovered in a neighboring salt
marsh, probably an amulet and possibly an imported object. It was published by René Kerviler Armorique et
Bretagne 1, 1892, 186; see Bull. de la Société poly-
mathique du Morbihan (Vannes) 1907, 141-151 (H. Ramin);
and compared by C. Jullian (REA 17, 1915, 68) with a
somewhat similar object discovered at Münsingen (Switzerland), Déchelette Mnl. 2.1321. But the Nantes object, if genuine, and if correctly reported by Ramin,
appears to show, in Greek alphabet:

$$\alpha y \iota \alpha \rho \tau o \iota o \sigma \pi h o \sigma \quad (?)$$

(ʁ ρ, ⊂ and ⋜ σ, ⋀ π, Ⱶ h), or, reading ⋀ as λ (?),
and Ⱶ as η (?), - λησσ. But all this, if articulate,
appears more Greek than Keltic.

(2) The famous megaliths of the Morbihan are supposed by some to show alphabetic symbols. As to that,
see M. de Saint-Just Péquart and Z. le Rouzic Corpus
des Signes gravés des monuments mégalithiques du Morbihan, Paris 1927, 84-88; cf. REA 26, 1924, 143. So far
as I can see, not one of them is alphabetic, much less
articulate.

176

Names on terra sigillata found in Lugdunensis (cf. 88 Remark above), and on other portable objects.

From CIL 13.10010; AcS; Oswald's Index; Blanchet's Mélanges 2, 1902. Other sources are BA 1932-33 [1936], 634-35 (Nuits-Saint-Georges); Espérandieu BA 1908, 167-68 (Alesia), cf. Fouilles...de 1906, 150-154; R. Doranlo Vases sigillés gallo-romains inédits trouvés en Normandie in Bull. Soc. normande d'études préhistoriques 25, 1922-24 (Rouen 1926), pp.57-81; BA 1934-35 [1940] pp.540-559 (cf. 133); together with a few items on tile-stamps (cf. 205 below) from CIL 13 vi (1933), 141-176. I have no doubt that many readings are inaccurate, or the original corrupt or debased.

?Acensem	Adgenus	Almacin[
Abal(l)us	Aegit[	Amai[
Abasc[antus	Aelo[	Amallos
Abascus	Aenir[	Amarantus
Abrelus	Agricola	?Ambacius (-tus)
Abreχta	Ailo	Amceis
Abudinus	Ain(us), Aen[	Amioco
Abuso	Airocus	Amo
Acapus, -os (-g-)	Airu	Amuto
	?Aixixus (-ius)	Anaogeno
Acco	Alb[	Ancrini (Van-?)
Aco (with Catullinus)	Aleucus	And[
Acus	Alic[	Andeen[
Adgatus	Alocus	Andegenus

528

Names on Terra Sigillata

Anminos	Ascius	Aupianus
Annus	Assin[	Aupmir[
Anonius	Assutalus (not	Aurius, -a
Ant[	Talass- , Taluss- ?)	Auscus
Antenus	Astuus	Austerinus
Anullu	Asus (with	Axi, Axo, Axd
Aoa?	Cigetoutos)	
Ap(p)a	Ateanus	Baccos
Apiauus	Atecnudis (-tis)	Banillus
Apilo	Ath[	Barmasus
Apius	Atiad[	Barnaeus
Apro	Atinus	Be[, Becnic[
Apu[	Atis	Becuro (Đe-), -q-
Ar[	Atit[	Bemaius
Arasius	Atpi[	Biaucu[
Arat[	Atraicu	Bis[
Arbanus	Atusa (Atiusa?)	Biseaesi
Arcellus	Aucissa	Bisen
Ariba	Audio	Bitus
Arius	Auetus	Bocco
Aron	Auirio	Boccorus
Artas?	Auiua[	Boduos
Arusius	Auonus	Brennos
Ascen[	Auota (?)	Brigino

529

Names on Terra Sigillata

Brim[	Can[	Ceiite
Broc[	Candinasi	Celau[
Buc[	Cantiori	Celiandus
Bucura	Cantinorus	Celius
Budacius	Capinna	Cella
Bue[, Buf[	Capus	Cellirius
Burdiuus	Car[, Cara[	Celtianus
	Caranenus	Cenicus
Cab[	Caratan[	?Centor
Cabellio (?)	Caratuc(c)us	Centus
Cabil(l)o	Carah[	Cemianus
Cabiatus	Carbes[	Cer[
Cabillus	Carsaro	Cerdo
Caburus (with Comma)	Cart[ius?]	Cereius
	Casiu	Cermanus (G—)
Cacabus	Catulus	Cern[us
Caem[	Caturcus	Cerulus
Caes[	Caχtos	Cetsi
Caicesisis	Caueatus	Cexal[
Calixa	Cauouie	Ceχtis
Camilus	Cauus	Cfu uini
Campilius	cciprma	Chendo
Canauos, Canaus	Ccoi	Ciab[
?Canisma	Ced[	C.i.a.c

Names on Terra Sigillata

Ciamic[	Comma	Darrantus
[Cigetoutos]	Commio	Darsa
Cilu	Commo	Decanni?
Cimil	Commuos	Dessus
Cintuieru (but see 140 Remark and Note xxxiv above; 13.10010, 566)	Comnius	Diacus
	Como	Diauχsus
	Condatus	Dioratus
Cintutus	Conetodu	Docca
Cir[	Conetodubnus	Docnibo, -us
Circus	Conimarc[?	Dogirix
Ciril[	Copius	Dola[
Cirimns[	Coronca	Dolin[
Cirimnus?	Cosoiuia	Dometullus
Cla[	Counus	Dommia
Cliuaila	Coxxus (-χs- , -χx-?) χ	Donius
Clouius		Dous[
Cnc[	Crasisa (-si- for -χsi-?)	Dracc(i)us
Cniama	?Crui	Dripenni
cnssap?	Csamia	Drusa
Cocasus	?Cuaseturna	Drutalus
Cocinus	Curruro?	Dudenis?
Cocuda?		Δουγουρ[
Columilius	Daccius	Duii
??Comforfron (for ... of Front?)	Darius	

Names on Terra Sigillata

Eba	Fabracus	Ient[
Ebelus	?Facullia RA 11, 1938, 295; BSAF 1938, 123	Iera
Ebredus		Iger
Ecto	Faⅹtucis (La-?)	Ilenu
Egenus (-i-)	Febriscus	Illa
Egit[	Fouri	Imprito
Egular	Frontiniana	Inulus
Elissi(?)	Front | Proti	Ioppus
Eluilus	Froti	Irmo
Emta	Fuca?	Itius
Epacus		Iuatus (Iuu-)
Equirus	Gaenus (-ai-)	Iuinus
Eranus	Gagua	Iuio
Ercus	Galaunus	
Erecaius	Gecaud	Laguaudus
Ericus	Gemialo (Genialis?)	Licinus
Eridubnus, -os		Likui
Esieb?	Gemilius	Limetius
Esto	Gri	Lingonis(?)
]ettus(]ertus)		Liofita
Eu.ed[	Hoscri	?Lirinus RA 11, 1938, 293; but more likely lirini i.e. lil- , BSAF 1938, 123; AE 1945.74
Euis		
Exsobno	Icuco	
	?Icusisi	
	Icurisi	

Names on Terra Sigillata

Liunim?

Lou[

Lud[

Luscilia (-ll-)

Maccira

Macciril(l)a

Macinia

Macor

Mado

Maiuddilo

Malu

Mamb[

Marillus (-p-?)

Martiola

Marullus

Mascioi

Mascitus

Massa

Masuri (Chalon-
   sur-Saône)

Matiticius
   (Chalon-sur-
   Saône)

Mato

Matuci

Melil[

Melissus

Meltus

Mena

Menilus

Militus

Milus

Minurio

Mol[

Mucus

]murn[(AcS
   3.43,53)

Musa

Nasucus

Nep[

Nerius

Nertus

Nerucus

Nigelli

Nilus

Nitioceni

?Noiobito

Nonus

Nor[

Obelius

Obuius

Oc(c)oc[

Occitani

[Occocnus]

Ociocnus (for
   Ollognus, -cnus)

Octocni

Ocituis

Octa

Oicituis

Olicios

Olillus

Ollocnus (-g-)

Olliadu

Omouir

Onaiu[(Chalon-
   sur-Saône)

Ononi

Onuerh[

Onuphrus

Oppo?

Orius, Orinus

Oruita (-b-)

Osaria

Names on Terra Sigillata

Osc[ ]o[

Osinit

Otrimus

Paimn[

Petius

Petrahes

Petreci

Pilistrio

?Piroc[

Poppo?

Pricianus

Proti

Rannius

Rictus

Rimitanus

(Rimunatus?)

Ritminus

Rituarus

Rocus (-χ-, -os)

Romogillus

Roppus?

Rubellinus

Rucius

Ruscatu

Saeniani

Sagiro

Sallus

Samitus

Samtis?

Saoafa?

Sar[

Saridius (Cha-
 lon-sur-Saône)

Sarmus

Sarsicus

Satti[

Sc]oppus

Scorobres

Secco

Seclatu(s)

Seco[

Secos

Sedni?

Segolatius

Sel[

Sen[

Senecianus

Senex

Sentius

Serutus

Set[

Seχturi

Sicaop[

Sil[

Sintuciso

Silo, -u

Soillus

Sol[

Solano

Solit(us)

Soricio

Sottail(?)

Suobnedo

Suobnillinus

Susci

Tabius

Tabur

Talussanus

Tanconus

534

Names on Terra Sigillata

Tappu(s)	Turo	?Viato
Tarinus (-an-?)	Turonis (?)	Vibruiu
Tauatillus?	Turrilio	Vicanus
Tauic[?	]ttusco	Vigius
Taxapo?	Tu(o)ticius	Vilu[
Taurri		?Vindilicus
Tecessus	Vallo	Vinduro
Tic[	Vam[	Vira
Tiotag[	Vancrin[(or Ancrin[ )	Virlus
Titos		Viriodacus
Titulcanius	Varus	Virioru (?)
Titullus	Vaua	Vironus
Tit(t)us	Vauliani	Vosecun(n)us
Tituro (?)	]ubelino[(-cn-)	Vret[
Titusius	Vbertus	Vritti[
Togidu	Vbua	]urnusi
Togidius	Vcemus	?Vrtricus
Tourorix (-tiorix?)	Vcumu	Vssomarius (-ur- , with Cerealis)
Toutillus	Vegiso	Vtilus
Toutissa	Venesi[	Vtrianus (Vet-?)
Tricci, -os	Venirus	Vxsasus
Troxo, Troχso	Vererius	
Tullus	Vernacellus	Xex
Turilio, -llo	Vertia	
	Vertros	

535

Coin-legends of Lugdunensis

Remark:

The writing in CIL 13.10017,68 (see 134 Remark viii above), however it is to be read and whether it belongs to Lugdunensis or to Aquitania, is merely a "probatio pennae" or crude and incomplete alphabet, perhaps:

a   a   b   d   đ(?)   e   f(?)   χ (=h?)   g(?)   q   s (ƶ)   x

177

Coin-legends of Lugdunensis (from Blanchet, Tr., and AcS; with a few items from Blanchet and Dieudonné vol. 1)

aka (or ακα)

aco AcS 1.31, but v. 3.496; Tr. 96

acussros

acutios

αγηδ

αλακοσ (υλ-?)

alaucos

ama[

andecombo(gius)

anorbus

απαμοσ

arcantodan (see the Re-mark below)

aremagios (-c-)

αττι

arim

arus (cf. 181 below)

atepilos

ateula (Caletes? Or, according to some, Remi?); with ulatos

ateuloib (?)

atpilos

atranou (-nol)?

aulircos

aur, aurc?

536

Coin-legends of Lugdunensis

βελινος, βιλινος, βιεν-
ος(?) Cf. AcS 1.373,
386; Bl. 81, 101; gl.
(178 below) and div.
names (181). These
coins are ascribed by
some to the Aruerni

bouibitouios, -uix,
βουιβιιον(?)

caballos, καβαλλ

καλ, καλεδου, καλετεδου,
caledu (the last also
Aquit.)

calitix? (cf. 78 above)

cantorix

καριθα (i.e. -issa)

cassis|uratos

catal(os)

cattos

(κατωτ AcS 1.848 ??)

]cauce (Jersey; British?)

cecisu; cf. ces-

cel?

cesicou; cf. cec- ; read
σεγισου?

cicutanos (Jersey)

cinciunu?

cisiambos

ciu

cnce|ra (see]cauce)

κοιακα

κοιιος (κωιος ??)

coios

conat, κοναт

cone, conte

cone[   ]d i.e. coneto-
dubnos?)

conteciod

[copia (Lugdunum) 43 B.C.]

cosii (Narb.?)

cucinacios (cup-?), with
ulatos

d]eiuiciacos? (AcS 1.1262,
35-44)

diasulos

?doci[rix (q doci); but
see 232 below

drucca

dubnocou, dumno- , -cou-
eros, -couiru

dubnor(e)ix, dub]norex
BA 1941-42, 117

δουβνο, δουνο, δοβνο,
δονο, dubno(s)

Coin-legends of Lugdunensis

eburo

eburouicum

eburouix, ibruix (?)

eccaios

eduis

ελκεϭοουιξ (-ʃ)

επηνοϭ, epenos (eplenos, elp-?)

η ϭουαγεγι

esuios (Jersey)

essui

euornos

giamilos

]giantos (Jersey), v. tog- below

ibruix (?), v. ebur-

?imioci MSAF 5, 1904, 45-90; for doci|sam?

?ιγκι (said to be a debased καριθα)

licutanos (?), v. cic-

lita, litau, litauicos

lixouio, lixouiatis

magurix

mandubenos (cf. Mandubii, Epo- Vero-mandui)

maufennos, -eno- (?)

med, medlu, mediol[?

naca?

ndn

ned

]oa[

]obnos

οχδκνο ?

oiiuko?

[oino (or οιλιο ?), also read dino]

orcetirix, org- , orget[Cf. Orgetorix 182 below

orcopril (Jersey)

org- v. orcetorix

pennille

(penobrias | modericu or d]acomeris] Merov. num.) Both this and the next item are also assigned to Aquitania by some authorities

538

Coin-legends of Lugdunensis

piχtil(l)os

]ra (Jersey)

ratumacos (Rouen)

ri[

roueca, ρoουικα

rupil (Jersey)

sam (Tr. 115); for sam-
   [otalos (doci)? But
   see 232 below

segisu? (cf. AcS 2.1443;
   Tr. 426); v. ces-
   above

semissos, simissos [Latin?
   But cf. semi- , simi-
   uisonn- at Coligny
   (also Lat.?)]

senodon(nos)

senu, senui, senus (?),
   senua (?); cf. seno
   (British)

ϭϵπ, ϭϵππ

sesedi (Jersey)

slamb[

snia?

ϭολιμϰ, solima; but cf.
   157

stratos or siratos (?)

sula (Tr. 125, 401.1)

sutic(c)os

tasgetios

togiantos

togirix; but v. 232 below

toutobocio(s)

toua (Tr. 321; not auot?)

triccos

turonos

[ual]etiac(os)?

ulakos (cf. ϫλ-)

ulatos (or Belgic?), with
   ateula, cucinacios
   (cup-)

ulattu

ulucci (cf. ulakos?)

ueliocaθi

ueneχtos (cf. REA 3, 1901,
   85)

uercobreto (see below)

uericio, uericiu

uirici, uiriciu

uocunilios

χe (?)

Uνo (?)

Coin-legends of Lugdunensis

Remark:

The most interesting of the above coin-legends (auot being removed, see toua?), by all odds, are

(a) arcantodan

(Lexouii, also Meldi and Mediomatrici), on which see SprFK 198 (s.v. danno-), Thurneysen IF 42, 1924, 144 and 192; Walde-Hofmann Wtb. s.v. argentum; Loth REA 21, 1919, 263-270; Stokes Academy 30, 1886, 43; Blanchet Tr. 85-87; ZfCPh 8, 1912, 373; W-P 1.763 and 853. For other occurrences of dannos, alone or in compounds, see items 90, 92, 94, 102 above and 178, Notes xli, xlvi, lii, and lvi below.

The seals dredged from the Saône at Lyon (CIL 13. 10029,43) with ἀναβολικ and anabolici (sc. uectigalis) testify to the influence of Greek in fiscal and commercial usage at Lyon under the Empire.

(b) ulatos

(Caletes? Remi?), apparently "chief" (Ir. flaith i.e. an i-stem); cf. CIL 13.10027,127 (ulati), 10010.2073 (ula-tucni, -gni); and

(c) uercobreto

(Lexouii), perhaps a dual (cf. SprFK 211), also found in insc. (CIL 13.1048) and in Caesar (BG 1.65.6).

Note xxxvii bis

I can make nothing of an insc. reported from Thisy (Rhône) by Kaibel IG 14.2581,5, on a "petasus Mercurii," viz:

αδεα γ ρ υπευεσ

Glosses

(Cf. 1 above, Note on Glosses; 79 above, 220 below)

Again, I cite only the minima of testimonia. I have put into Lugdunensis a number of glosses, the Keltic nature of which is unequivocal, but which are not clearly assigned to a particular area, on the ground that Lugdunensis is more specifically "Celtica;" but many other unassigned glosses, less clearly Keltic in character, are put into the category of Unassigned Glosses (246 below).

Since some of the more interesting dialectal differences in Gaul are lexical variants, it is worth while calling attention to Dauzat Tableau de la Langue française (Paris 1939; cf. ZfCPh 23, 1943, 394) and in particular to such pairs as

lotta, soccus (Northern) : bana (Southern)

epo- (religious term) : caballus (popular)

deruo- : cassanos "oak"

garric- , harri- (i.e. carra : garra "stone,"
    cf. Hamitic akerrus, axerrus "oak," according to Dauzat pp.395-96, cf. 399) : alisia
    (older *palis- "rock" according to Dauzat,
    but see below).

What purports to be an incantatio druidum is quoted by Zwicker FHRC 1,100 (11-15) from Med. Plin. Sec. iun. (ca. A.D. 300-350) 3.16 p.268. But there is nothing in it that can be considered Gaulish; or, for that matter in the sixth century anecdotum Latinum printed by Zwicker 2,182.25 : irrifa epona nupsit illegy (except, of course, the familiar epona).

For Polemius Siluius cf. 158 above s.v. baditis; the supposition that he was Bishop of Martigny seems illfounded (Romania 35, 1906, 162); for the latter see Smith and Wace Dict. Chr. Biogr. 4, 1887, 581-82.

541

ἀβάνας (m., acc. pl.) "ape"

Hesych. has ἀβάνας (so Holder; ἀβράνας codd., ἀβάννας Reinesius)· Κελτοὶ τοὺς κερκοπιθήκους . From this the Germanic forms (with p from b) must have been borrowed, not (pace Dottin REA 7, 1905, 46) vice versa; cf. Walde-Pokorny 1.51-52. Skt. kapí-? But cf. Arabic al aftas "ape, pug-faced" (Schiaparelli Vocab. 581).

acaunumarga "stone marl" Pliny NH 17.44

The second element is marga (ib. 42), in Gaul and Britain "clay, marl" (cf. Breton marg), whence the di-minutive *margila (OFr marle, Fr marne, Br mercl, Basque merla), cf. the cpd. glisomarga (Pliny NH 17.46). As a synonym *albuca is postulated by M-L Einf. 243; the first element is:

acaunum (or -us) "stone"

Written agaunum (-s) in ASS 28 Feb. 3.741A and 22 Sept. 6.345D where it is defined as "petra" and "saxum" respectively (Gallico sermone .... accolae). Cf. Pliny's intermixto lapide (17.44). Common in local names, and occasional also in personal names, once even a divine name (CIL 3.14359,27), the word has not survived into modern times. Cf. acnua 158 above (?); acona below; Acunum TP, Rav. (dép. Drôme, Holder 1.34); and also glisomarga below.

TLL 1.250.33ff., 8.390,80; Holder AcS 1.12-14, 2.424-425; 477-479, 518; M-L REW 5351, 5354; Bertoldi BSL 32, 1931, 171 n.; Jud, Arch. Rom. 6, 1922, 209; Walde-Hofmann 1.5; 2.39, with G. Bonfante Emerita 2, 1934, 281, and (on the relation to Lat. acus), E. Ben-veniste, Origines de la formations des noms en Indo-Européen, Paris 1935, 6; acaun- : acamn- (lenition?).

?acona "whet-stone"

Pliny NH 27.10, Serv. G. 2.152, CGL 5.260,53. Thurneysen ap. Holder (3.497) is reported as connecting

Glosses

this word with the preceding; it is now usually believed
to be simply the Greek ἀκόνη.

ἄδες· πόδες (Hesych.)

alauda "lark"

Pliny NH 11.121, Suetonius Caes. 24; insc. e.g.
leg. V Alauda CIL 11.5211; Marcell. de Medic 28.50, cet.;
gl. Deriv. alodarium "a bird-net" Schol. Bern. Georg.
1.140. Perhaps alausa (207 below) is a variant; REA 34,
1932, 451.

[alica "spelt, spelt-grits;" or a "drink prepared from

spelt"

Starting from Pliny NH 18.113-116, where stress is
laid upon the whiteness of alica, Bertoldi Stud. Ital.
di Filol. Class., N.S. 7, 1930, 254 argues that al- ,
supposed to mean "white" (cf. 1 and 158 above), is the
source of this word. Accordingly he connects *alisa
"populus alba" also.

Be that right or not, there remains a curious
Gloss, CGL 3.597, 14a azyma: id est alisum (i.e. un-
leavened bread), which has never been satisfactorily
explained, though it is the source of Fr. alis (M-L REW
346a; on the etymology cf. A. Thomas CRAcInscBL 1909,
448-449, and Romania 38, 1909, 358-359, from which it
appears that the name of Alesia was popularly connected
in the middle ages with alisum, and it can hardly be
doubted that alisa and Alisia, Alesia are connected.
For another explanation cf. alis- (*palis-) see Dauzat
EC 4, 1948, 202; REA 42, 1940, 111 (and hence "falaise").

A. J. Reinach Pro Alesia 2, 1907-8, 209-223 has an
interesting theory that Alesia had a monopoly in the
preparation and sale of "panis praepinguis," i.e. gras-
cuit.]

543

Glosses

ἄλιζα "white poplar" (*alisa)

Hesychius gives ἄλιζα as Macedonian. On -ζα see
Hatzidakis Glotta 23, 1935, 268-270 (for -δια, as in
ἔνδα, cf. κόνυζα and plant-names generally). The Macedonian ἄλιζα is discussed also by E. Sapir I.Eu. prevo-
calic s- in Macedonian, a paper printed twice in 1939,
viz. in Language 15, 178-80 and AJPh 60, 463-464. He
accepts a "Visigothic" *alisa, cf. Schwyzer Gr. Gram.
1.69 n.3, Walde-Pokorny 1.151. But it may have been of
Keltic origin there, even if it is not actually a word
of wider range (Mediterranean?) al- "white" (cf. alica
above), as Bertoldi argues Rev. Ling. Rom. 3, 1927, 263-
282, and is generally admitted by the comparison of the
Gaulish local name Alisia, Alesia (cf. the divine name
Alisanus) as well as Aliso, Alisontia, Alisincum, see
P. Kretschmer Glotta 15, 1926-27, 305-306; Walde-Hofmann
1.31 (s.v. alnus), 845; Bertoldi ZfCPh 17, 1927-28, 184-
192; Pokorny Urg. pp.46, 81, 85, 93, 102, would make
alisa Illyrian (or Ligurian), like everything else.
Other modern theories of the etymology of Alesia: REA
3, 1901, 140, cf. Weisgerber SprFK 191-192, hardly any
better than an ancient one (Diod. 4.19,1 ἀπὸ ... τῆς ἄλης).
Hardly to be compared with *arg- "white," i.e. r:l
(*alig-).

[?aloxinum "absinth" Anthimus 15; Gl.

    Supposed by Kluge and others to be Greek, viz.
ἄλοη ὀξίνης (as if anyone would mistake aloe for vermouth); but the context in Anthimus (ceruisa bibendo
uel medus uel aloxinum) suggests not only a western
European origin but also a drink more palatable than
aloes. In ὀξύφυλλος, unless the reference is to the
shape of the leaves, -ks- stands for -sk- (W-P 1.185).
Cf. perhaps λάψανον below? O.H.G. alahsan is borrowed.

    There are no Keltic cognates, and the origin re-
mains obscure. Elsewhere bricumus was used, see 158
above.]

ambactus "seruus" Caes. BG 6.15.2

    Cf. Paul. ex Fest. p.4 L. (PID 2.181) who gives

Glosses

am "circum," cf. ambe below. Hence the amactum quoted
by Holder AcS 1.111 from cart. Senon., where it appears
five times in connexion with argentum, so that Holder
translates it "geprägtes geld," is probably the same
word "money (argentum) or serf (amactum)." At one time
I thought of comparing the coins of the Mediomatrici
with ARG | AMB or ARC | AMBA i.e. arcantodan[Ambacti
(or -u[s), but that seems a less likely explanation.
Spelled ambacthius in CIL 13.8788 (Doomburg), i.e. probably *ambaᵧtius; see 206 and Notes xlvi, lvi.

    Cf. abantonia and ambascia (-actia) 220 below,
the latter of which, according to Jud Romania 47, 1921,
305-308, has become confused with a Keltic *ambi-bascia
"charge," (cf. Lat. fascis), though the Romance derivatives which Jud cites in the Lyonais and adjoining dialects, are clearly enough distinguished by their meanings. Ambactus appears also a personal name (e.g. CIL
13.3686, Treveri).

ambe: rivo, [inter]ambes: [inter]riuos; de nom. Gall.

    6 (Endlicher Glossary), MGH auct. ant. 11,613.

    Cognate with Latin imber; cf. the river-names
Amber, Ambris, Ambra (Stokes Phil. Soc. Trans., 1868-69,
253; PID 3.58); Jullian REA 3.1901, 342 finds a survival
in the modern local name Ambès, and Thurneysen IF 42,
1924, 145 sees both Interambes and Trinanto (below s.vv.
nanto, tri-) as local names; cf. Intrambensis mod. En-
traigues M-L Einf. 272, Lognon 735 and perhaps Intaranum
179 below; see Zimmer KZ 32, 1893, 230-240 on Endl. Glossary as a whole.

    ambicus, given as the name of a fish by Polem.
Siluius, MGH auct. ant. 9.544,6, is probably no more than
a derivative of ambi- , like amulus (for *ambulus, cf.
am- above, s.v. ambactus), also in Polem. Siluius, l.c.
544,18 (for other suggestions, e.g. ambiguus, hamulus
cf. Schuchardt ZfRPh 30, 1906, 717); Romance derivatives,
Jud Arch. Rom. 6, 1922, 201; M-L REW 432; i.e. both mean
"belonging to, creature of the river."

    A possible derivative is ambiosas "circulos" CGL
5.345,25, if the winding of a river is implied; but far
more likely this belongs with ambi- as in ambactus, if

Glosses

it is accepted as Gallic at all (Stokes BB 29, 1905, 169; but see Heraeus in Walde-Hofmann 1.845). At Coligny (227 below) amb- is no doubt the same word (*m̥bhí, but -e in are- , ate- from -i)

[?ameia "alder" medieval Lat.

Cf. Meyer-Lübke W.u.S. 11, 1928, 64.]

anam "paludem" Endlicher gl. (613.9)

Dottin (after Stokes) compares Goth. fani "dirt, mud" (cf. Walde Lat.Et.Wtb. ed.2, 557 s.v. palus), Vasmer (see Boisacq in RA 19, 1924, 402) compares Pannona, Pannonia; and Hubschmied (Vox. Rom. 3, 1938, 125 n.1) a number of modern Swiss local names (e.g. Ins).

anax "pan, pitcher" Greg. Tur., mir. (de uirt. Iul.)

2.8 patenam et urceum, qui anax dicitur.

Holder AcS 3.606 cites Stokes, who compares OE ponne, E. pan, Germ. *panna (itself borrowed?), cf. 90 ff. above (La Graufesenque) panna (i.e. V.L. for patina?); but note also 240 below panaca Martial 14.100 (cf. E.W.B. Nicholson ZfCPh 3, 1901, 333), which suggests a form independent both of Latin (panna) and of Keltic (W. pann), viz. Illyr. (perhaps Raetic, see the context in Martial) or, less likely, Iberian. Dottin quotes an Ir. an "vase à boire," and Jud (Arch. Rom. 6, 1922, 201) calls attention to the medieval uses of anax (Du Cange); distinguish panacem (PID 2.164). But if anax is for an(n)ax the next word may be related. There remains, however, the even more complicated question of what relationship exists (if any) between panna (: anax?) and canna (220 below).

annapum (-us): "bowl, cup" CGL 5.564,48 cratera, uas

uinarium quod et galleta, annapum, scalam

546

Glosses

annapum ctd.

     Ernout-Meillet ed.2 p.54, count annapus Germanic; and, since it is well represented in the Germanic dialects (O.E. hnæp, Germ. Napf, cf. Kluge Et.Wtb. s.v., id., Urgerm. ed.3 p.17) it seems at first sight reasonable to count V.L. (h)annapus such; but did it not enter Germanic from Keltic? We seem to have an(n)a- as in anax above, and either a -po- (-qⁱⁱo-) suffix or (less likely) apa "water." The borrowing into Germanic, in that case, was subsequent to the first sound shift.

are "ante" Endlicher Gl., see sq.

Aremorici: antemarini, quia _are_ "ante," _more_ "mare,"

    morici _morini_ "marini" (Endlicher Gl., 613.2)

     Cf. Aruerni, Arecomici etc. (Holder AcS 1.188; 3.675,19-20; Weisgerber SprFK 192; are- "to the east of," after K. Meyer), the former of which the Glossary itself (613.3) gives as areuernus: ante obsta (obsita, Thurneysen IF 42, 1924, 145), are-pennis (158 above).

     There is a hint of a similar explanation in Hirt. BG 8.31.4 as well as in Caes. BG 7.75.4 (see Holder AcS 1.202,37-47): *p₂ri- (cf. περι) W-P 2.30-33.

areuernus "ante obsita" (Endlicher Gl., 613.3) i.e.

    (loca) consita

     I give Thurneysen's emendation (see above) for the meaningless obsta of the ms. All attempts to explain uernus as an impv. (cf. cecos 246 below) have failed; Thurneysen connects it with the tree-name (158 above).

arinca: a kind of grain

     Pl. 18.81 (Galliarum propria), cf. 61, 92; 22.121. Pokorny Urg. 86 sees the suffix -nc- as Ligurian; cf.

Glosses

Walde-Hofmann s.v. for the etymology (so Stokes compared
Greek ἄρδκος). Hardly cf. aricani 130 above?

?artuosus

　　　This adj., applied to callis in vit. Sequani
(Segestrensis, i.e. near Dijon) 1.6, ASS 19 Sept. 6.38A,
unless it is merely corrupt for arduosus (Lat. arduus,
cf. Arduenna) may be genuinely Keltic, cf. artuas (PID
339b.9) Ir. art "stone"(?), and (Du Cange) artauus
"knife" (EC 4, 1948, 203); W-P 1.148.

[?atinia "ulmus Gallica" see PID 2.194

　　　The connexion of this word with Atinius is now
generally denied, and a Keltic origin assumed (OIr aitten
"juniper"), cf. Walde-Hofmann 1.76,850.]

[?auca "goose," occa in CGL 5.615,40

　　　Attested in Avianus; usually counted a derivative
of auis, but Ernout-Meillet cast reasonable doubts on
that.]

avallo (i.e. ab-) "poma" Endlicher glossary 613.14

　　　Cf. Br. aval, Ir. aball; and perhaps the local
name Aballo (Holder AcS 1.5).

?ausaca　 the name of a fish Polem. Silu., MGH auct. ant.

　　　9.544,19

?bacc(h)inum (-on) "wooden bowl, basin" Greg. Tur. h.Fr.

　　　9.28, W-H 1.91

548

Glosses

bagaudae "latrones"

Aurel. Vict. de Caes., 39.17. Also written
bacaudae; bagaudica (rebellio), Eumen. or. pro restaur.
sch. 4; cf. REA 22, 1920, 107; Riese Lit. 9.2-3; Lizop
2,46. Used also as a personal name, and perhaps a tribal name to begin with (cf. PID 2.159); but cf. Ir. bag,
bagaim "fight." For the ending cf. bascauda, alauda(?).

[?ballatio FHRC 196.24; 198.1; 222.4]

bardus "bard" cf. PID 2.191

Apparently first in Poseidonius (ap.. Athen.), see
Holder AcS 1.347-348, 3.806, and the places quoted by
Zwicker FHRC (Index, e.g. 138.21; 224.1; 224.10; 228.6;
275.26); cf. bardocucullus 158 above, bardala and perhaps
barditus 246, 220 below. Deriv.: bardaicus, bardigiosus.
Also as a personal name, but not in Gaul; and in Bardo-
magus (near Milan). Not found outside Keltic; distinguish Latin bardus (even if the poet often has a "straw
in his hair.")

beber (-ri) "beaver" Schol. Iuu. 12.34: castorem bebrum

dicunt; Polem. Silu. (biber), Priscian

In local names Bibrax, Bibracte, Bebronna, Bebrini-
um, Bibroci, Bebriacum? (REA 7, 1905, 50 n.1), Βέβρυκες
(80 above)? Cf. Weisgerber SprFK 194. The literal meaning is "brown;" cf. Lat. fiber etc. (W-H 1.490). bebra
"beaver" Veget. de re mil. 1.20, is probably but the fem.,
this attachment to a helmet perhaps being made of beaver-
hide (sc. pellis, cutis, cf. parthica). Deriv. bebrinus;
cf. Vendryes W.u.S. 12, 1929, 241-244 on names of skin in
Keltic; Ernout-Meillet ed.2, 355 (s.v. fiber); Dottin
Mélanges Loth 1927, 92-98.

549

βελένιον the name of a plant, ps-Aristot. 7.821.32; cf.

the following item.

belinuntia, bilinuntia (-ll-) "herba Apollinaris"

Keltic according to Diosc. 4.68, ps-Apul. 4.
(CML 4.33,26 adn.) and generally derived from the divine
name Belenus (Apollo), cf. Bellenica (15 above). Much
has been made of the -nt- element in order to claim an
Illyrian origin (Kretschmer Glotta 14, 1925, 97; Bertoldi Rev. Ling. Rom. 3, 1927, 277; Pokorny Urg., 83),
but it should be observed that ps-Apul. vouches for
bellinoton or -tem, (cf. Weisgerber SprFK 194), and that
ps-Arist. has βελένιον (above), while beneola in Isid.
17.9.84 is probably an error (pace Sofer, Lat.u.Rom. 5),
if not for belenea (-ia), then for betilolen (q.v., below). Bertoldi AGI 22-23, 1929, 501-502. Cf. milimindrum 158 above (b:m). It is unlikely (cf. W-H 560) that
Latin fullo (on which cf. REA 28, 1926, 264) is related.

belion (AcS 3.833), foisted upon ps-Apul. 57 is a
figment (see CLM 4.110,6 adn.); but note the following
item.

βελιοκάνδος(?), mulicandos "herba millefolium"

Dios. 4.113, ps-Apul. 89 (CML 4.160,13), both of
whom vouch for the term as Gallic. Etymological guesses
are reported in Walde-Hofmann 1.151 (s.v. candeo), 523-24
(s.v. folium); cf. Weisgerber SprFK 194, 205. Is b:m
another example of lenition?

?betilolen "herba personacia" ps-Apul. 36 (CLM 4.82,24

(v.l. -rem), also called bardana (246 below)

Zeuss proposed to read -dolen (i.e. Keltic -dol-
"leaf"); and beneola also at Isid. 17.9.84 may be a corruption of this word. Cf. beta (itself perhaps Keltic,
W-H 1.102)? Or betula below?

Glosses

[↑beto (Holder AcS 3.856)

On this vox nihili, see mentobeto below.]

betul(l)a "birch," Gallica arbor Plin. NH 16.75, from

which bitumen was extracted by the Gauls, id. ib.,

cf. 176.

Cf. beta (leg. -tua?): berc (i.e. birch) CGL 5.
347,15; bitulus 402,69; the former at least may have
been confused with the name of the second letter of the
alphabet (Marstrander NTS 1, 1928, 132); Fr. bouleau
(cf. M-L Einf. 42).

On Pliny's testimony, taken together with the W.
and Br. forms bedw-en, bézo the Latin betul(l)a is supposed to be of Keltic origin; bitumen will show i for e
(see the Grammar). See, for example, Ernout-Meillet
ed.2, pp.108, 111 (where Keltic names in Bit- , more
usually connected with Ir. bith, betho are brought in);
Kuryłowicz Etudes 6, Skt. játu- (I.Eu. *gʷetu-); W-H 103,
107 (where bitumen is separated entirely from betulla,
and compared with OE cwidu "mastic"), 852; Sofer in
Comm. Vindob. 2, 1936, 83. Names in use in lands where
bitumen and bituminous products were known in ancient
times suggest any other than a Keltic origin for this
latter word (cf. R. J. Forbes, Bitumen and Petroleum in
Antiquity, Leiden, 1936; and also his article in Mnemosyne N.S. 4, 1936, 67-77).

bidubium (uid-) "pruning hook" Vita Leutfredi abbas

(Évreux) 3.24, ASS 21 June 4.110C, and in Glosses

(AcS 3.290-291), e.g. Schol. Iuv. 3.311

Holder gives a number of possible Keltic cognates;
note, in addition, Messap. β(σ)βη (i.e. ϝισϝη ?) "pruning
knife" (PID 2.424). On the ending -bio- see NTS 1, 1928,
227; SprFK 195; cf. K. Meyer in SBPrAkadWiss 1912, 2.800,
no.23 (Ir. -be "hew"), who neatly interprets Betuuius as
"Birkenschläger."

bidubium ctd.

But there is also to be considered a uidu- "tree"
(AcS 3.290), in Viducus (BSAF 1898, 296) Treuidon (80
above), and in Sapaudia (15 above; cf. SprFK 208), which
seems to favor the variant uidubium (-uium). Cf. 180.

[bigardio: see caio below]

?bitriscus (ui-) a small bird

Vita Auiti abb. (Micacensis, Aquitania), and Cari-
leffi abb. (Anisolensis, Lugdunensis), see AcS 3.413;
M-L REW 1137b.

?bodina (medieval Lat.)

See Thurneysen KR 91; Jud Arch. Rom. 6, 1922, 204.

bolusseron (v.l. bolbo-) "ivy" ps-Apul. 99.27 (Gallic);

elsewhere called ϛου βίτης, q.v. below

On the etymology see Bertoldi AGI 22-23, 1929, 498-
499 *uxello- (reading bol-usellon).

brāces: see PID 2.182 (add Lucan 1.430)

Cf. bracilis Isid. 19.33.5 (Sofer, Lat.u.Rom. 80)
and tubruci (220 below); beside the deriv. bracatus note
also bracarius (Ed. Diocl. 7.42 and 46). Borrowed from
Germanic into Keltic (cf. Vendryes RC 48, 1931, 429; W-H
1.113-114; Pisani JCS 1, 1949, 47; Kluge Urg. 33; d'Arbois de Jubainville RA 1, 1903, 337-342).

552

Glosses

__bracis__ "malt" for the manufacture of beer (ceruesia),

 Pl. NH 18,62; CGL 5.616,26

  On the etymology see now W-H 2.36 (s.v. marceo). Cf. not only imbractum (see the Glossary), ἐμβρεκτόν 158 above, but also Mars Braciaca CIL 7.176 (a dedication by an Aquitanian; Lentier Monum. Piot 34, 1934, 58: "à propos le dieu celtique de Bouray," Seine-et-Oise), and perhaps bractari, bractamentum (Ernout-Meillet ed.2, 117).

__bracus__ "uallis" Gesta abb. Font. (Script. rer. Germ. II)

 279 (p.24 ed. Loewenfeld 1886)

  At the mouth of the Seine; cf. OFr braie, Eng. braye. But the etymology is unknown. Cf. perhaps broccus "sharp" i.e. "steep (?)" (158 above), with a:o as in Bodio- , Badio-casses and many other words.

__breialo__: see caio below

__brio__ "ponte" (Endlicher Glossary, 613.5)

  Cf. bria; -briua and Briua in local names (AcS 1. 529,23; 610), briuatiom (152 above). Cognate with Skt. bhrū-š, Gr. ὀφρῦς , OHG brawa; Stokes Trans. Phil. Soc. 1868-69, 253; Zimmer KZ 32, 1892, 237; Dottin REA 9, 1907, 174-180.

__brucos__ "herba saxifraga" ps-Apul. 98 (CLM 4.177,8)

  Cf. Jud Romania 52, 1926, 338; Bertoldi AGI 22-23, 1929, 487. To be distinguished from bruco- in brucarius (Mul. Med. 532) and from *brugaria (80 Remark, above), uroicae (82 above).

Glosses

caballus and caballa (with numerous derivatives, e.g.

    caballinus, cabellaris and -ius, caballicare,

    caballatio, strutho-caballus, caballicatio, cabal-

    lista) and also a shortened form cabo, cauo "equus"

    (Gl., cf. AcS 1.655,11-17), as well as in proper

    names, ib. 1.651-658; 3.1016-1020

       It is now agreed that this is a pre-Indo-European
word that entered Greek and Latin and Keltic, perhaps
independently, and is not in any event of Keltic origin.
Cf. H. Grégoire Byzantion 11, 1936, 615-627 (Études
Horatiennes 1937, 81-93) and 13, 1938, 287-290, who
argues for a "Balkan" origin; cf. J. Loth Les noms du
cheval chez les Celtes in Mém. de l'Inst. nat. de France,
43.1, 1933, 113-148. Cf. W-H 125-26 and 853; V. Cocco
Caballos (Studio lessografico ed etimologico, Coimbra
1945), reviewed in Word 2, 1946, 95-97; Nehring Die
Sprache 1, 1949, 164-170. The caballus is the heavy
European draught-horse.

caio "enclosure, fortification" (Endlicher gl. 613.10)

       The actual gloss reads caio: breialo siue bigardio.
Here not only the lemma but also breialo in the gloss is
Keltic, cf. brogo- (-a) brogilo- 79 above (on brogilo-
cf. BSAF 1937, 159); and bigardio in the gloss is also
not Latin, but perhaps Germanic (cf. 220 below, and see
a suggestion of H. Zimmer in KZ 32, 1891, 237-238 with
238 n.1; Kluge AR 6, 1922, 236 [misprinted 232].

       The meaning of caio and bigardio must agree with
that of breialo, brogilo- , which is known (see 79 above);
besides we also have glosses caii: cancelli in CLG, and
Keltic cognates, e.g. OW cae "sepimentum," OBr cai-ou
"munimenta," and the etymology is clear, *kagh- Skt.
kakṣa (Kuryłowicz, Études I.Eu. 1, p.9), Gr. κοίτη ,κώμη,
OE hāg, hege ("hedge"), mediev. L. cayum "house" (Zimmer
l.c.; cf. Stokes Trans. Phil. Soc. 1868-69, 259), cohum
(-us) Isid. nat. 12.3, cf. W-H 1.244; M-L REW 1480; Cai-
ocum (Cayeux-sur-Mer) Gröhler FrON 1.316; cf. 207 below.

Glosses

?cala "uilla"

    See AcS 1.686,28; cf. below 179, the local name
Cala-rona

cambiare "rem pro re dari" (Endlicher glossary 613.13)

    For the word in actual use, see the extracts from
Lex.Sal., ASS etc. in AcS 1.711-712, 3.1057-58. Romance
forms (Fr. changer etc.) are from the Latin borrowing,
not directly from the Keltic.

candetum (older *cantedum?)

    A Gaulish land measure (100 or 150 feet) Columella
RR 5.1.6, Isid. 15.15.6, called in Aquitania acnua (158
above). Cf. P-W 3.1464-65; W. cant- "hundred," Ir. ed
"foot." The personal name Cantedus (214 below) can
hardly be connected.

candosoccus "sucker" (viniculture)

    Gaulish according to Columella RR 5.5.16; the ety-
mology is uncertain. Recent conjecture (Jud Arch. Rom.
6, 1922, 211, cf. 202) favors canto- "rim, edge" and
socco- "cep de vigne," rather than socco- , succo-
"plough-share, lit. snout;" Hubschmied RC 50, 1933, 258-
259, cf. Fr. souche (*tsukko-); SprFK 209; ZfCPh 23,
1943, 217.

[cannabis "hemp"

    Mistakenly listed in AcS as "germanisch, trotz
Athen. 5.206F κάνναβιν ... ἐκ τοῦ Ῥοδανοῦ ποταμοῦ."
Perhaps Holder (1.735) wrote germanisch, by mistake for
griechisch; and it is now generally agreed that Greek
(whence the Latin cannabis) borrowed κάνναβις from some
eastern language, not identified. However, the word
was widely current in Gallic lands, cf. cannabetum CIL
5.3072; and just as in English "canvas" means also "tent,"

so the frequent <u>canaba,</u> <u>kanaba</u> of Lugdunensis (CIL 13.
1911, 1921, 1954, 2033, 2016, 11179), Belgica (Note xli
below), Germania Inferior (Note xlvi) and Superior (Note
xlii), and of the Upper Rhine (Note lvi below) means (1)
"tent" or "barracks," and then (2) "wine-shop, cabaret."
I see no reason for assuming can(n)aba to be borrowed
from Gr. κάν(ν)αβος "wooden frame or model;" but there
seems also to have existed a form *canafa (M-L REW 1566),
cf. perhaps Canafates CIL 5.5006, usually read Cannanefates (see 221 below); in CIL 3.4850 we have canapa and
von Blumenthal, Glotta 18, 1930, 147 takes as Illyrian
the Greek κάλυβη "cover, screen; hut, cabin," which
(with l:n) may well be related. It is striking that
Cenabum (179 below) is called ἐμπόριον by Strabo (4.2.3),
negotiandi causa by Caesar (BG 7.3.1), and that the bilingual insc. (CIL 13.2448, Greek and Latin) in honor of
a negotiator brings him from the Syrian city Canath,
Canotha. In Gaulish both this and Canafa (with -f- for
-th-) or canapa would be unpronounceable; hence perhaps
canaba.

Further references AcS 3.1071 (local name *Cana-
pus?), ib. 1076 (-cannae "city"?); Ed. Diocl. 1.29 al.;
P-W 3.1451f., 1484f.; ZfCPh 20, 1936, 519 (on capanna);
but there is no connexion with Canauus (138 above) or
Cannaban (Kluge Urg. 10).

Deriv. canabarius, canabensis; in CGL 5.595,69 the
meaning "camera post cenaculum" is given for canaba.

If the connexion with cannabis is rejected, then
<u>canaba</u> is probably pre-Keltic and pre-I.Eu., a word
associated with the viniculture and wine-trade of the
Mediterranean basin.]

<u>cappa</u> "caracalla" Isid., Gl., Greg. Tur., ASS; AcS 1.759-

780; 3.1086

Deriv. capellus, cappula; and perhaps (?) capanna
(gloss, item 1 above), unless this is for canapa, can-
(n)aba (above), by metathesis, as some conjecture. Etym.
unknown. For the meaning cf. Isid. 19.24.17 (cucullata
"casula," cuculla "minor casa;" so chapel from capella,
capanna : cappa?

Glosses

caracalla "cape, cloak (with a hood)"

From Gaul, according to Aurelius Vict., de Caes.
21.2; hence the proper name. Cf. W-P 2,58; W-H 1, 164-
165; Ed. Diocl. 7.44-45.

caragus, caragius "fortune teller"

The authors who use this word (Caes. Arelat., uit.
Sancti Eligii, Conc. Autissodor., Conc. Narb.), for
which see the texts in Zwicker FHRC Index, point strongly to a Gaulish (not necessarily Keltic) origin.

κάρνυξ "trumpet" Eustath. Hom. Il. 18.219 (p.1139.57)

ὑπὸ τῶν Κελτῶν (after Poseidonius?), but cf. κάρνον
Hesych. (Γαλάται), Diod. 5.30. Cf. carnuat (below, 229),
cernunnus (172 above), ? Καρνονον(76), ?Cornuti Amm. 16.
12.43. Cognate with Latin cornu. For an ancient repre-
sentation of the κάρνυξ see REA 9, 1907, 58 with Plate 6.
A river-name Carnun is quoted from the Cartulaire of
Redon in REA 9, 1907, 273; for more obviously related
local names see AcS 1.794-801. Finally, the name of a
bird carnotina (Polem. Silu., MGH auct. ant. 9.543,22)
may be related.

caddos (i.e. caddos, casso-?) "sanctus" CGL 5.493,30

In BB 19, 1905, 169 Stokes compares Ir. cad; Hebrew according to Thes. Gloss. Emend., just as the Endl.
Gl. makes dan Hebrew too.

Cf. Riv. di Filol. 49, 1921, 430. Doubtless the
explanation of di Casses (211, 236, 243), Velio- Vidu-
Bodio-casses (179, Vidu-cassis), cassi-dannos (90, 92,
94, 102), and perhaps even of the apparently Greek Ca-
tharus (Iuppiter) in FHRC 296.27 lies here. But the
etymology is far from clear. The roots kad- W-P 1.340
are not helpful; words for water often imply sanctity
(Isara : ἱερός), and so κάδοας (246 below) may also be
concerned, but hardly *cassano- "chêne" (RC 50, 1933,
263; M-L Einf. 242).

557

Glosses

cauannus (-a) "ulula" Eucherius (Lugd.) Instr. 2.9;

Schol. Bern. Ecl 8.55

There is no lack of either Keltic (Brythonic) or
I.Eu. cognates, cf. W-H 1.184, M-L REW 1785-87. The
form cauua (glossed as γλαῦξ), cited by Terracini Riv.
di Filol. 49, 1921, 427, is probably a curtailed form,
unless cauanna is a derivative (cf. cappa : capanna),
which is less likely; but cf. also gauia "sea-gull,
mew" (158)?

Ultimately onomatopoetic. On the history of the
word in glossaries cf. Lindsay CP 13, 1918, 4; Holder
AcS 1.872, 3.1171 (cab- ib. 1020, cabalos and cebena
ib. 1172); Zwicker FHRC 224.15-18, 249.33 adds testimonia from OE glossaries and from Saloman (episc. Constant., i.e. of Konstanz), and also (77.27) calls attention to a canana which I think must be a corruption for
cauanna.

?cectoria "boundary" Grom. Lat. 333.19 al.

Cf. Vendryes EC 2, 1937, 131-3 and CRAcInscBL
1933, 376-377, where a Keltic origin is claimed; Ir.
cécht "plough." The meaning is against the suggestion
of a corruption of tectoria.

[?celtis a fish, CGL 2.99.14

Claimed as Keltic by Skutsch BB 22, 1896, 126; but
cf. W-H and E-M ed.2, s.v. The word celtis, celta
"chisel" is best disregarded, A. E. Housman CQ 20, 1926,
26, Proc. Camb. Phil. Soc. 1916, 12.]

ceruesia, ceruisa "beer" Pl. NH 22.164, and other au-

thorities, AcS 1.995-997, including glosses (ib.

3.1027)

Cf. κοῦρμι, crama, caelia, cerea (all in 158 above);

558

Glosses

at Diod. 5.26.2 the same drink is called (in Egypt) ζῦθος.
On the etymology cf. W-H 1.207, 287; E-M ed.2, 230; A.
Mayer KZ 66, 1939, 79 (ceruus) is surely wrong.   The
Oscan caria "bread" in the glossary of Placidus (ID 231)
cannot be connected, unless the meaning runs from "grain"
to "malt" to "beer," which seems unlikely.

Derivative: ceruesarius inscc., Metz, Trier (e.g.
CIL 13.11319, 11360); but in RGKBer. 17, 1927, 41 ceruesarius artis offecturae Rostovtzeff (CRAcInscBL 1933,
250-256) rejects the meaning "brown, dark beer;" probably (et) is to be supplied before artis.   In CIL 13.
597 read ce]ruesario (RA 21, 1931, 476).   And although
it is true that the text h]ospita, repl[e] lag[e]nam
ceru[i]si[a] | copo, h]onori tua[e] bes est repleda
(AcS 1.997,39-41) comes from Paris (CIL 13.10018.7;
Congrès scientifique de France, 35 Session, Montpellier
1868, 2 [1872] 381-83), there is nothing to show where
it was manufactured.   But the word ceruesia is so characteristically Keltic that I have preferred to put it
into Lugdunensis.   Ed. Diocl. 2.11; Jullian Histoire de
la Gaule 5, 183 and 256nn.

cicaro "boy, youth" Petronius 46.3, 71.11

Bertoldi EC 2, 1937, 28-32 identifies this with
the potter's name Cicarus (204), and both of them with
gigarus "draconteum," which is Gallic according to Marc.
Empir. de medic. 10.58.

[cisium PID 2.191; add now ZfCPh 22, 1941, 31]

cladi[b]us (-[m]us?), gladius

Gram. Lat. Suppl. 245.19-20 (gladius quasi cladius,
i.e. cladibos?); see Dottin 246, Marstrander NTS 3, 1929,
255 ("Celt. *kladebo- est emprunté, comme lat. gladius,
d'une source inconnue"), W-H 1.603-604.

Glosses

[? κλοπίας (v.l. κλωπ-) a fish

Caught in the Saône according to Lydus de mens. 8.108, cf. clupea Plin. 9.44, but other localities also are named Anec. Gr. (Boissonade) 1.417, see AcS 1.1046; d'Arcy W. Thompson, Glossary of Greek Fishes, 117.

<u>colisatum</u>   a kind of vehicle, Plin. NH 34.163

Cf. Ir. cul "waggon"

<u>combri</u> "concides" (deriv. combretum?); lib.h.Fr. 25, cf.

Greg. Tur. h.Fr. 3.28 (in Arelauno)

The meaning of combretum (Plin. NH 21.30, 133) is so different that it is hard to bring the words together. But the accepted etymology of combretum (W-H 1.253) involves a root of an unacceptable pattern (*k...dh) as well as a comparison of totally different plants, and Bertoldi Vox Rom. 3, 1938, 229-236 argues for the original meaning as "vegetation in the mass," or the like. Be that as it may, *comb(o)ros (cf. M-L Einf. 241; REW 2075) combros is clearly Keltic, see further J. U. Hubschmied Vox Rom. 3, 1938, 134.

For the formation cf. perhaps cantabrum (cf. Artabri), uergobret-os (?), the etymologies of which are also far from clear. The local names Comberanea and (?)Combretonium are doubtless related; and -etum a well recognized suffix.

κόρνα "argimonia"

Diosc. 2.177 (246.18 W.) gives this as the Gaulish name of the plant.

[?<u>corrigia</u> "shoe-lace"

There are perfect equivalents in Keltic, W-H 1,278,

560

Glosses

but opinion on borrowing from Keltic differs; cf. E-M
ed.2, 223.]

craxantus (-ss-) "toad"

Used by Eucheria (a sixth century poetess in Gaul),
see A. Thomas ALMA 3, 1927, 49-58, and compare the personal names Craxa (-anius), Craxantius, Craxaucus (151
above), Craxxillus (156), Lep. krasanikna (PID 2.321),
Κραυσικνο (61 above). Cf. RC 47, 1930, 463; REW 2304a-b;
SprFK 198. Onomatopoetic?

crocina "mastruca" Schol. ad Prud. Sym. 2.699 (p.89,

Burnam), where mastruca is said to be Gallic, and

crocina rustic usage.

Cf. Ir. crocenn "fell," Bret. kroc'hen "hide,"
Pedersen VKG 1.125, 160; Loth RC 37, 1917-19, 324; discussed in W-H 1.296 (s.v. crux, with which there is no
connexion, cf. rather Penno-crucion 1 above, s.v. pennum); SprFK 198. Hardly to be compared with rachana
(Note xxxiv)?

[?crumilum Paul. Nol. (E-M ed.2, 234)

For curmil(1)um (: κοῦρμι, crama, cremor), either
by a mere scribal error, or a genuine variant? Cf.
ceruesia above, curmi 158.]

crup(p)ellarius "armored combatant" (apud Aeduos) Tac.

an. 3.43

Perhaps borrowed from Germanic (*kruppa REW 4787);
less likely cruppa (ib. 2344; cf. CGL 2.118,16). For
another Germanic word in use in Gaul see framea below;
and on the crupellarii see JRS 32, 1942, 68.

561

Glosses

cucullus (later -a) "hood"

cucullo de birro Gallico scilicet, Schol. ad Iuu. 8.144, see AcS 1.1183-87 for other testimonia; bardo-cucullus 158 above. Deriv. cucullio, cuculliunculus.

Isid. 19.24.17 gives uestis cucullata as an equivalent of casula (cf. capella "chapel," capanna "hut" beside cappa; Aebischer ALMA 5, 1929-30, 5-44). On the Keltic genius Cucullatus see A. B. Cook Zeus 2.1089-90, 3.1182-83, R. Egger in WPZ 19, 1923, 311-323.

Etymology unknown. Holder AcS 1.1186,26-29 gives a variant coc(c)ula, and Toutain BSAF 1919, 257-9 (cf. 1917, 198) would see this in the epithet Cocliensis of Liber Pater in CIL 13.5032 (Germ. Sup.). Despite Latin poets, who make the second syllable of cucullus long, the Romance forms (M-L REW 2356-2359) show that the u was actually short, cf. Fr. coule. No connexion with Cicollus; or with the cutios of Coligny? Svennung (quoted by W-H Addenda s.v.) identifies cucutium with the plant-name cucutia. For the ending cf. carracutium.

cucutium has the meanings (1) "head-dress, hood" (Gallien., quoted AcS 1.346,51) (2) "praeputium," Diosc. Lat. 2.65; its form may have been affected by this very word (for *cucullium?), as representations of the genius cucullatus will readily show.

cumba "locus imus nauis" Isid. 19.2.1

Cf. W. cwmm; cumba is Gallo-Latin for "valley," AcS 1.1189, W-P 1.562; W-H s.v.; Neuph. Mitth. 15, 1913, 75.

dan "iudicem" Endl. Gl., 613.4; on which see Thurneysen

IF 42, 1924, 144

Coins of the Lixouii have arcantodan; otherwise -dan(n)us is better attested in Germania Inf. and Sup. (Notes xlvi, lii below) and Aquitania (cassi- 90, 92, 94, 102), the uncompounded dannus only in Belgica (Note xli below). Cf. Stokes Academy 30, 1886, 43; ZfCPh 8, 1910-12, 373.

Glosses

[?<u>darsus</u> a fish

Dottin 250, M-L REW 2410]

<u>derbitas</u> "impetigines" CGL 3.599,32; deriv. derbiosus?

    For *dérueta cf. W. darwyden, and see SprFK 198,
W-H 1.342-43. The Aquitanian equivalent term was sarna,
serniosus (158 above). But s- : d- (cf. δαρουἰδαι :
δρου - Do. 284 from Diod. 5.31.2; Sirona : Ðirona) is
probably the Keltic affricate. Cf. Darbosa 244?

<u>doga</u> a kind of vase (Vopisc.)

    See E-M ed.2, 279; M-L REW 2714-15 and (better)
Einf. 243; Fr. douve. But the etymology is quite unknown.

<u>dolua</u> (v.l. dulua, dulba) "eruca"

    Euch. Lugd. Instr. 2.12 (158,6 Wotke), quoted AcS
1.367. W-H 1.366 takes this as an ablaut form of *delua
(AcS 1.1263), which in view of the meaning, seems incredible ("form, image" : Lat. dolium?). More likely
(apart from the formal difficulty) connected with -dol-
"leaf" (see πεμπέδουλα below)?

<u>doro</u> "osteo" (i.e. ostium) Endl. gl. 613.15

    Cf. duorico (insc. 142 above), Bret. W., Corn. dor,
Latin fores (W-H 1.529, 866), and -duro- in local names
(SprFK 200) now connected with doro- instead of with
Latin durus. On a possible connexion with -dunum see
Benveniste Origines 1935, 12; but the meanings ("door"
and "fortress") leave some doubts to be resolved (per-
haps "gate, gate-way, courtyard, fortified enclosure,
fortification, hill-top," is the sequence), see dunum
below and isarno-doro (233 below). Cf. Kluge Urg. 6;
Philipon RC 30, 1909, 73-77. For u:o cf. dolua (:du-).

Glosses

*draginos (?) "thorn" (M-L Einf. 42)

?drappus "towel" (vit. Caes. Arelat. etc.)

    Cf. the personal and local names Drappes (182 be-
low), Drappo (237), Drappus (214), cf. AcS 1.1314-15;
Keltic according to W-H 1.373 (cf. M-L Einf. 251; Lane
Language 7, 1931, 279), "Illyrian" Pokorny Urg. 69.
The use of a common noun as a personal name appears also
in sarra, uanga, uimpus; and is common in Liberia and
Nigeria to-day.

druida "druid" Caes. BG 6.13.1-14.6 (in omni Gallia

    13.1) and other testimonia, AcS 1.1321-30; Zwicker

    FHRC, Index, s.v. The first record of the word is

    in Aristotle.

    At present supposed to be for dru-uid- "eichen-
kundig" (Thurneysen ZfCPh 16, 1926, 276-78), which is
virtually the ancient etymology, both expressed (Plin.
NH 16.249) and implied (cf. the variants dryas, etc.);
cf. δρονεμετον (Galatian; v.l. -ναι -); drasidae in
Amm. Marcell. 15.9.4 sqq. must be corrupt; though it
may have been evoked by σαρουιδας Diod. 5.31.2, also
no doubt corrupt and usually emended to δρουιδας. Yet
it is conceivable that σαρουιδας would be a genuine dialectal variant, cf. Dirona, Đirona: Sirona; Diccius:
Điccius; serniosus: derbitae(?).

    I can make nothing of the incantatio ... ex ore
druidum given by Plin. iun. 3.16 (FHRC 100.12) Siculi
uident[ur] iligo uel marino piso adriacicum et iscito
malluli drogoma ex aua mit....unt astandem. The interpretation in gl. Lucan 1.451 (FHRC 53.5) sclaui sunt
appears to be unique.

    *druticare (indruticare is attested in a seventh
cent. text) "grow, prosper" is presumably a derivative
of *druto- "strong," see Jud Arch. Rom. 6, 1922, 313-
339; but this has nothing to do with dru- in druida so
long as the etymology which seeks an intensive particle

Glosses

in dru- (Thurneysen KZ 32, 1872, 563) lies dormant.   In
OE glosses magus "dry" (FHRC 224).

M-L REW 2779a; E-M ed.2, 485.

†δουκωνέ see odocos (158 above)

dunum "montem" Endl. glossary 613.1

Cf. δοῦνον· τόπον ἐξέχοντα (Clitophon ap. ps-Plut.
de fluv. 6), see AcS 1.1375.18-39, and see doro above.
In ASS 1 Nov. 1 p.166A (Passio Benigni), quoted by AcS
1.289,26 we have Augusti dunum id est Augusti montem.
See also lugdunum below; and the discussion by Kaspers
ZfCPh 13, 1920, 164-5; KZ 50, 1922, 155-157; Feist W.u.S.
11, 1928, 47.

dusius "incubus, daemon inmundus"

Aug. c.d., 15.23; Isid. 8.11.103; other testimonia
FHRC Index, s.v.   Cognate with Latin bestia, see W-H
1.102, 386, 861; Loth RC 36, 1915, 63-64; d'Arbois de
Jubainville BSAF 1898, 255; cf. dusmus 233 below, AcS
1.1387,32; Pokorny ZfCPh 14, 1923, 293; Gray Foundations
pp.253-54.

ebulcalium "ungula caballina" CGL 3.582,35, epocalium

id. ib. 589,63

See J. Loth RC 37, 1919, 24-25 (who would read
"inguina caballina" in both places), Bertoldi AGI 22-23,
1929, 498 and 528; cf. calliomarcus 158 above.

[?eglecopala "columbina" Plin. NH 17.46 (Gaulish)]

Glosses

?<u>elea</u>

Holder AcS 1.1413 takes this (from vit. Samsonis
episc. Dolensis, Aremorica) as "buchstab." Cf. perta
(79 above), al (246) and tau (79), runa (222, Proleg.
70 n.140). But both text and interpretation are doubtful.

<u>emarcus</u>: see marcus infr.

[†ennones

The gloss quoted by Holder AcS 1.1440,18 clearly
represents a misunderstanding of some such passage as
Isid. 9.2.106; or (less likely) Mela 3.6.48. But see
also sena below.]

[?<u>farra</u> "bread; spelt"

Ascribed to the Cimbri or Cymbri in Lib. Gloss.
FE 229; cf. Bulletin, Board of Celtic Studies 1, 1923,
309-310. But f- cannot be pure Keltic, and these Cimbri
may not be Cimbri of Gaul (i.e. the Aduatuci). Cf. fara-
buris 207 below, Farraticano CIL 5.7356.

[<u>framea</u> "spear"

Ascribed to the Aremorici by Eucherius Instr. 2.
147,1 W., cf. CGL 5.70,16; 634,43; but the word is Germanic (see 220 below), not Keltic; Greg. Tur. 3.15
(Frankish) and 7.46 (Saxon?). Terracini, Riv. di Filol.
49, 1921, 421-422. On frameafer "hastifer" cf. REA 21,
1919, 228; 22, 1920, 52 (in the worship of Bellona).
There is a garbled gloss in CGL 4.595,37 ganeo....hasta
uel iaculum lingua gallica, which Goetz emends to read
gaesum; but it may be a corruption of framea.]

Glosses

frisgo (-onis) or brisgo (-c-) "holly"

CGL 3.587,41; 608,30; 628,43; cf. Terracini, l.c.
428, SprFK 201. See also 79 above (br-).

[galit "perit," galiuit "periuit"

CGL 5.204,18-19; 600,61; cf. Goetz ib. 6.482 and
Loewe Prodromus 352; Vendryes RC 40, 1923, 435 calls
attention to Paul. ex Fest. 519.3 L., which reads
ualles(s)it: perierit ($\mathfrak{H}^\lambda$-), and it is generally supposed that g- in the Glossary-items represents the OFr
substitution of g- for u- . This substitution, however,
usually rests upon association with a Germanic word,
and such is not here forthcoming. In both branches of
Keltic I.Eu. $\mathfrak{J}^\lambda$ is b, so that g- is anomalous from the
strict Keltic point of view also. Nicholson's account
of valet RLR 5, 1929, 50-58 is of no help.]

?galoxina "two handsful"

In tenth century medical writers, see A. Thomas
ALMA 4, 1928, 94-103, who would claim the word as Keltic,
comparing Ir. glacc "hand," but see the criticisms of
Vendryes RC 47, 1930, 464. In Narbonensis durnus "one
handful" (79 above). For the ending compare aloxinum
(above) and the dubious gallizena (see sena below).

[?gemnades "mulieres"

CGL 5.634,58 (cf. 4.603,31) Lucedemonice [leg.
Lugdunenses?] lingua Gallica. Perhaps cognate with
γυνή, but cf. also galmuda (246 below).]

geusiae "throat, gullet, gums, cheeks" Marcell. Burd.

de medic. 9.37, 12.19, 15.90

Generally accounted Keltic, see W-H 1.596, Dottin
259, Schwyzer KZ 57, 1930, 275. There may be some con-

fusion with guancia (M-L Einf. 243); but more likely,
I think, to be related with Eng. gum (I.Eu. *gheu- W-P
1.565), not with Fr. gueule (Lat. gula, I.Eu. g^uer-),
and hardly with Lat. gingiua (*geu- ?).

[?glebra "arator lingua Gallica" CGL 5.364,8, glebo

    "rusticus" ib. 10

    Evidently corrupt, cf. SprFK 201; but gleba may
have existed independently in Keltic, cf. galba PID 2.
196; and BSAF 1923, 238.]

glenare "glean" (sixth cent.)

    Cf. Ir. glan "clean," and perhaps the local name
Glanum (80 above)? M-L REW 3784; Thurneysen KR 100;
Frings Teuthonista Beih. 4, 1932, 76 n.1; Sofer ZfCPh
22, 1941, 118.

glis[s]omarga "marl, creta fullonia mixta pingui terra"

    Plin. NH 17.46

    Cf. acaunu-marga, marga, *margila (above s.v.
acaunu-); and for the first part of the compound, glastum (as compared with which -ss- is the more normal
Keltic, Pokorny Urg. 43).

    Bertoldi Berl. Beitr. 1, 1929, 279; id. RC 48,
1931, 281; W-H 1.608; Kluge Urgerm. 6.

gnatus "filius...lingua Gallica" CGL 4.598,4 etc.

    See PID 2.184, cf. nate(?) below, gnatha (164),
geneta (Note xxxi g); and many names in -natus, Holder
AcS 1.2029.

Glosses

gulbia and gubia "point or pointed tool, scraper, chisel"

    Cf. Fr. gouge AcS 1.2043-44; W-H 1.625, 868.

gutuater (for -tros)

    A Gaulish priest ap. Carnutes (Hirt. BG 8.38.3, where Cotuatum is merely Frigell's conjecture, though Hirtius may have misunderstood gutuatrum as a proper name, so Klotz l.c.; cf. N. J. De Witt TAPA 69, 1938, 322 n.12); and in inscc. (Aquitania, Lugdunensis, REA 2, 1900, 410; see Notes xxiv, xxix above, CIL 13.1577, 2585, 11225, 11226).

    Repeatedly discussed by J. Loth RC 28, 1907, 119-121; RA 20, 1924, 59 with n.3; 22, 1925, 221; cf. Vendryes MSL 20, 1918, 268-69; Jullian REA 6, 1904, 256 n.3. But the etymology (*ĝhutu-patĕr?) is quite uncertain; the passage in Hirtius suggests that the gutuater had some of the functions of the fetial priests at Rome. In the inscc. he is connected with Mars and Anuallus. Whether he is the same as p. ogen at Mâcon (Note xxix d) we have no means of knowing.

[?heluennaca (uitis)

    Columella 3.2.25, Plin. NH 14.32. Usually counted Latin (: heluus, -ius, -olus) or Etruscan (*Heluenna); but in Columella the context suggests a possible foreign origin. Cf. the ethnica Heluetii, Eluii? There is also a variant in Columella 5.5.16 (quoted AcS 1.733 s.v. candosoccus) viz. eluenaci and Jud in Howald u. Meyer Röm. Schweiz p.371 assumes *heluina (from heluus) as the source of modern arvine (cf. 240). But compare also (H)eluina (Ceres) 82 above. If a local name cf. uitis biturica (Col. 3.2.19 etc.). Thurneysen ZfCPh 14, 1923, 11-12 takes *helu- in Heluetii etc. for *pelu- "much, many."]

ἰουπίκελλουϛ(?) "juniper"

    Diosc. 1.75 (74.20 Wellmann), who makes it Gallic.

Glosses

ἰουπίκελλους ctd.

This is the reading of Wellmann, but Sprengel gives
ἰουπικέλλουσον, of which neither - κελλους nor - λουσον
has been explained; the correct reading is no doubt
Γάλλοι †ἰοῦπι (an ἰοῦπον , ἰουπικόν ?) καλοῦσιν , or the
like (Dioscorides inserts καλοῦσιν about as often as he
omits it).

As for *iup(p)os or ἰουπικόν see W-H 1.731 (s.v.
iuniperus), SprFK 202, with the references given there.
Engadine giop, gioc (*iupco)?

ἰουρβαρούμ "black hellebore" Diosc. 4.16 (183.14 W.)

The resemblance to eusubim, iubron (su-), σουρωρβι,
iorebe, sviorebe (Do.) is superficial.

inter: see ambe above; not necessarily Latin.

iutta, iotta (Rufus, 6th cent.) "soup"

Cf. Ir. ith, OW iot; compare perhaps iottica in
vit. Sancti Eligii (episc. Nouiomagensis i.e. Noyen,
Oise) quoted in Zwicker FHRC 196.19 (from MGH, Ser.
Merov. 4.705): nullus in Kalendas Ianuarii nefanda et
ridiculosa, uetulas aut ceruulos uel iotticas faciat...,
which Du Cange interpreted as ioccicas "jeux." For
iutu- "fat" see Thurneysen ZfCPh 20, 1936, 524; H-M 372
(after W-P 199 and M-L REW s.v.), in a supplement by
Jud, give yet a third word, to be distinguished from
both of these, viz. *iutta "Gerstenkorn." Cf. Svennung
Comp. Lucenses 1941, pp.17, 38, 64, and (iõta) 85; Hofmann Glotta 25, 1936, 118; and note also the personal
names Iutumarus CIL 3.5522, Iutuccus 237 below and (?)
Iutucanus 244.

λάγινον (-ονον), lagine "white hellebore" Diosc. 4.148,

Pliny NH 24.193.

570

Glosses

λάγινον ctd.

Also called exacum and ἀνεψῦ Diosc. ib. (cf. 246
below); see Do. 264, Bertoldi AGI 22-23, 1929, 500-501.
Cf. a-loxinum (above)? Hardly lemigum (158) by metathesis?

lautro "balneo" Endlicher glossary 613.7

Discussed by Stokes Phil. Soc. Trans. 1868-69,
253; cf. Do. 265; W-P 2.441.

?leuaricinus   the name of a fish, Polem. Silu. (MGH scr.

ant. 9) 544.17

Schuchardt's claim, that this word is probably
Keltic, ZfRPh 30, 1906, 722-23 (cf. Terracini Riv. di
Filol. 49, 1921, 428) is generally admitted. But there
is only Romance evidence, nothing from Keltic.

[leda, laia, laya "wood, clearing"

The earliest examples are A.D. 1136, 1307, and
1310, see Du Cange s.vv., and AcS 2.122,33; 213,15
appears to rest only on these. But W. Kaufmann Begriff
"Wald," Diss. Zürich 1913, 65-66 seems to accept Holder
as proof that the word is Keltic. M-L REW 4856 on the
other hand takes Ir. laie back to Frankish laida "way."]

leuga "league"

The Gaulish measure of length, estimated to be
about 2300 metres: leugas Galli uocant...nos milia
dicimus. leuga finitur passibus mille quingentis, CGL
5.217,8-9. Cf. Laterc. Veron., itinn., and inscc., as
well as authors, see AcS 2.197-201, e.g. Hieron. in
Joel 3.18 (A.D. 406; Galli leucas); leuuas Grom. p.373;
Isid. 15.15.3 (cf. Fr. lieue); regularly written leuga
in the very few inscc. which have more than the abbreviated L. From Friolzheim we have a Port(u) [Pforzheim]

571

l(eugas) **v**, cf. Paret Germania 19, 1935, 234-36; Sprater ib. 21, 1937, 28-33 and Nesselhauf 173-75; Bull. Mus. Imp. Rom. 5, 1934, 62.

Local names based upon the number of leagues distant from a given point are said to occur in Belgica and Germania Inferior (see 213 Remark, below). But the word was in use all over Gaul, and is found everywhere in miliaria e.g. CIL 12.5518, 13.9096. Hesychius has λεύγη· μέτρον τι Γ𝛼λ𝛼 -[κ]τικόν or Γ𝛼λ𝛼-τ𝛼ι (γ𝛼λ𝛼κτος cod.); and since there are no Irish or Welsh cognates, it is not certain that it is a Keltic word. The old English borrowing (leowe) probably took place in Britain, for the word does not appear in other Germanic dialects. M. Besnier REA 31, 1929, 336 maintains that the revival of the leuga was not later than the first half of the second century after Christ. See also W-P 2.405; BSAF 1876, 203; Antiquity 10, 1936, 498; REA 39, 1937, 260; Grenier Mnl. 2.1 95; Instinsky Klio 31, 1938, 48.

[**lotta**, **lota** a fish (squilla)

Schol. Iuu. 5.81; cf. Fr. lotte. Keltic?]

lucu[r]parta Polem. Silu. 544.10

Schuchardt ZfRPh 30, 1906, 723. Cf. lucius (207 below), which is possibly the equivalent of lupus (at Forum Iulii Plin. NH 31.94-95, generally supposed to be the Latin lupus, lupa).

λοῦγος "raven"

Ps-Plut. de fluu. 6.4 (AcS 2.307), where the form is cited in explanation of Lugdunum, but it stands entirely alone, and is suspect (Do. 266); other etymologies of the local name itself, both ancient and modern, tend also to discredit this one. Pokorny Urg. 132 has recently come to the defense of lugo- "raven," lit. "black," but not convincingly. Cf. A. H. Krappe Rev. de l'hist. des relig. 114, 1936, 236-246.

Glosses

λοῦγος ctd.

On Lugdunum cf. Loth RC 34, 1914, 384-87. The
Endlicher glossary 613.1 has:

<u>lugdunum</u> "desideratum montem" (dunum enim montem see

dunum above); but "lucidus mons" in Heirici uit.

Germ. 4.298 (AcS 2.308,28)

Cf. Do. 268 and Stokes, Trans. Phil. Soc. 1868-69,
251 (now generally abandoned). Cf. τὴν φίλην Λουκετίαν·
ὀνομάζουσι δ'οὕτως οἱ Κελτοὶ τῶν Παρισίων τὴν πολίχνην ,
Iulianus imp. in Misopog. 340 (CIL 13 pp.464-65). See
also pp.484, 512 above; Schol.Iuu. 1.44 (lucis donum id
est mons FHRC 68.7) and note in ps-Plut. l.c. ὄρος Λούγ-
δουνος, καλούμενον, in which ὄρος is evidently dunum; but
not λιμήν ... δύο κοράκων(Str. 3.1.4, 137C; FHRC 13.4);
M-L Sjoestedt Dieux et héros, Paris 1940, p.60 (cf. xi);
Holwerda REA 25, 1923, 253-54; cf. BSAF 1901, 102-03.

<u>luma</u> "sagum quadratum" CGL 5.602,70

Doubtless an error for linna, cf. Isid. 19.23.3
(158 above s.v. clintinna) with Sofer Lat.u.Rom. 75.

[?<u>maderna</u> "siphon" (and also, sens obs. "penis"?)

Schol. Iuu. 6.310: (longis) siphonibus, quas uulgo

madernas dicimus, teutisce scefolon, Steinmeyer-

Sievers, Die Althochdeutschen Glossen 2, 1882,

348.18-19, cf. ZfdAlt. 15, 1870, 357.1371 (simpho

nadirna dicitur).

maderna may be merely V.L. (: madeo, cf. luceo:
lucerna), whether or not is has both meanings of sipho(n);
yet cf. Gael. maistir "urina," from *mad-tri (Stokes),
μέζεα or μέδεα (Archil., Hesiod; REA 6, 1904, 207), μήδεα

φωτός Hom. "membrum uirile" (W-P 2.231-32; cf. W-H 2.48), Lat. mano from *madsno- (ib.), and, for the general idea, perhaps Petr. madeia perimadeia. It is not likely that there can be any connexion with the local name Maderna (179).

There is no lack of words in -erna (Gradenwitz, Laterc.): e.g. baderna (REW 875), santerna, nasiterna, taberna, lacerna, pincerna; and many adjectives in -ernus.

As for OHG scefolon, cf. perhaps Gr. σκάφαλος· ἀντλητήρ (Hesych.), from *squ̯ep- (-bh-), see W-P 2.562.]

magulus "cinaedus" (?) Schol. Iuu. 2.16

The usual interpretation ("mouth") is wide of the mark. Wessner would take the word as a diminutive of magus "sorcerer." Cf. rather Keltic magu- "youth, slave, vassal" (SprFK 204, Urg. 50), OIr. mug, Goth magus and the large number of derivative personal names AcS 2.373-74, 385-86; Kluge Urg. 7.

[mantellum, mantum (-us) "mantle"

Given as Iberian or Spanish by Isid. 19.24.15; modern authorities claim it for Keltic, see W-H 2.32-33; see 158 above.]

μάρκα "horse"

καὶ ἵππον τὸ ὄνομα ἴστω τις μάρκαν ὄντα ὑπὸ τῶν Κελτῶν Paus. 10.19.11 (279 B.C.), and in local and personal names (AcS 2.417) especially in lower Germany (Marco-durum, -magus 221 below). Cf. τριμαρκισία Paus. l.c. (on - ισία see Hubschmied Vox Rom. 3, 1938, 125 n.1, Kretschmer Glotta 22, 1933, 162).

Only Germanic (*marha-) and Keltic, cf. Marstrander NTS 1, 1928, 122, 142; 7, 1934, 349); -a is masc., as in bagauda, druida, -broga, Belga, Celta, Galba, (?)glebra (above). Welsh march, OIr marc, OHG marh, OE mearh.

Glosses

μάρκα ctd.

The etymology of a word so narrowly distributed is dubious (W-P 2.235), but Loth Mém. de l'Inst. nat. de France 43 (i), 1933, 138-139 identified mar- with Mars, -martis Skt. marúta-s (son of Rudra, cf. Rudiobos 181 below); Dottin Mél. Loth 1927, 92-98, Pokorny Urg. 41; Kluge 6.

marcus (v.l. emarcus) an inferior sort of vine

Gaulish according to Columella 3.2.25, cf. Plin. NH 14.32. Cf. Picard merc, AcS 2.424; Fr. marc; Dottin REA 7, 1905, 43); mar- may be the same as in another plant-name, viz. emerum (220 below).

marga: see acaunumarga above; Kluge Urg. 6

?melinus "color nigrus" CGL 5.371,11

Stokes BB 29, 1905.169 equates this with W. melyn "yellow;" cf. Gr. μέλας (- ανος)? Or better μήλινος "quince yellow"? Perhaps milimindrum (158 above)? But at AcS 2.536,23 remove the asterisk. However, if the gloss in CGL is right, W. melyn etc. are better connected with milimindrum than with μέλας the meaning of which chimes with melinus, not with melyn. Svennung Comp. Luc. 1941, pp.30, 39.

[mentobeto

At one time claimed as Keltic, see Wilhelm Meyer Fragmenta Burana, Berlin 1901, 161-163 (Sonderabdruck aus der Festschr. zur Feier des 150-jährigen Bestehens der Königl. Gesellschaft der Wissenschaften zu Göttingen, 1901), cf. ZfCPh 4, 1902-3, 191 and AcS 3.856, this form is now recognized as Gallo-Latin mente habere Fr. mentevoir, M-L REW 5507, SprFK 155, 204, cf. 194; Terracini Scritti...Trombetti 343 n.1, W-H 2.69, Thurneysen ZfCPh 14, 1923, 11.

575

Glosses

mentobeto ctd.

With it vanishes the supposed Keltic beto "uoce Gallica" notwithstanding.]

mercasius "lacuna"

Vit. Agili Resbacensis (Rebais, dép. Seine-et-Marne), ASS 30 Aug. 6.582 (AcS 2.551), Terracini Scritti ...Trombetti 1938, 339 n.5 (who reads geminam lacunam for geminum lacunar), Do. 272 (cf. REA 7, 1905, 49); M-L REW 5515a (OFr. marchais "marais").

μερισειμόριον· μελισσόφυλλον , Diosc. 3.108

Do. 272 doubtingly compares Ir. semar "trèfle" and AcS 2.573 cites Stokes' view (*semmoro- or *semboro-, cf. Ir. "kleenamen" seamar) and Ernault's (: visumarus).

mesgus "serum (i.e. whey)" CGL 5.623,18

Ir. medg, W. maidd, Fr. mègue. See SprFK 205, W-H 2.79; Jud Arch. Rom. 6, 1922, 201; Do. 272; AcS 2.574.

more "mare;" morinus and moricus "marinus," see Aremorici

above; morimarusa "mare mortuum" (Cimbri, PID 2.188

and 220 below); moritex (207 below)

Cf. Urg. 6, W-H 2.38; in the Endlicher Glossary we evidently have to do mainly with local names (here Aremorici, Morini), cf. Thurneysen IF 42, 1924, 144; 192. On ö:ä Benveniste Origines 81.

?mori "fanum"

Vit. Rigomeri (presb. Subligniacensis, 6th cent., "apud Cenomanos") 6, ASS 24 Aug. 6.787C: in proximo

576

Glosses

loco antiquum fanum esse, quod uocabat populus morifanum
(leg. mori?), quod populus uenerabatur; morifanum may be
a hybrid, like Linguaglossa, ἀμαξάκάρριον and many others.
But mori "fanum" appears to stand alone, apart from the
divine name Moritasgus (181).

?mulicandos (v.l. -dros, mubscandos) ps-Apul.

    See βἐλιοκάνιος (?) above. For b:m see milimin-
drum (158).

nanto "ualle" trinanto "tres ualles" Endlicher Glossary

    613.8

    Cf. the local names Nantuates (or -ae) i.e. "in
Valle (Wallis) habitantes," Nantua; Urg. 166. The meaning "water-course" (cf. W. nant "valley, brook") is also
certain: see J. Jud Bull. dial. Rom. 3, 1911, 74; Aebischer AR 5, 1929, 29-52; Genava 19, 1941, 97; REW 5818;
J. Loth RC 44, 1927, 256. A supposedly different nanto-,
nantu- in divine names (e.g. Nantosuelta) is imaginary.
On Trinanto see Thurneysen IF 42, 1924, 145 n.3 (a local
name, and also "ein singularisches Kompositum").

nate "fili" ib. 613.12

    Also in the uita Symphoriani: nate mi Symphoriane
memorare (v.l. memento dei tui beside nate...to diuo,
see Wilhelm Meyer Fragmenta Burana (mentobeto above) 161-
163; Thurneysen ZfCPh 14, 1923, 11; SprFK 155. But the
correction nato(n) "filum" is highly attractive, see
Language 25, 1949, 390.

[naupreda "lamprey" (Polem. Silu. laterc. 544.10; Anthi-

    mus de obseru. cib. 47; eighth century uit. Hermel-

    andi, see Romania 35, 1906, 185; elsewhere lampreda).

577

Glosses

naupreda ctd.

The form with n- appears to be peculiar to Gaul, and possibly due to popular etymology, see G. M. Messing CP 37, 1942, 155; but W-H 1.756 take it as the original form, and Dottin 274 quotes with approval the dubious etymology which would connect nau- with the numeral "nine" (?naumeto- La Grauf. 104 above). What then is -preda?]

[?netcos "murus" CGL 5.374,13

The emendation of Stokes nectos "merus" BB 29, 1905, 169 is commonly accepted, though violent. Cf. Ir. necht "pure" (older *nictos), Gr. νίπτος, Skt. niktá-s.]

[obsianum a variety of glass-ware

Plin. NH 36.194 (in Gaul), but see also id. ib. 196, where he derives it from an Ethiopian name Obsius.]

[?occabus "bracelet"

In CIL 13.1751 (Lugdunum, A.D. 160), but also 10. 3698 (Baiae, A.D. 289) and in Hesych. (τὰ περὶ τὸν βραχίονα ψέλλια), and Etym. Magn. Presumably not Keltic.]

onno "flumen" Endlicher glossary 613.11

Cf. diuona "fons addite diuis" (AcS 2.875) see 158 above? Or the large number of local names, especially of rivers, in -onna (AcS l.c.)? But Keltic cognates are lacking, and hence Thurneysen IF 42, 1924, 146 proposed to separate the gloss from the lemma and to compare the latter with W. onn "ash-tree;" cf. SprFK 206 (and 199); Terracini Scritti...Trombetti 340.

Glosses

orge "occide" CGL 5.316,70

    Cf. Orgetorix (177, 182); Ir. orgim "murder."
Stokes BB 29, 1905, 170; Do. 277; W-P 2.43.

†oualoida "herba camemelon"

    In an extremely uncertain text, ps-Apul. 23.12
(CML 4.63). Cf. SprFK 206, and ib. 211 (s.v. thauori).

[?parada "awning (of a boat)"

    Auson., Sidon., cart. Senon., see AcS 2.928. I
do not know on what grounds Ernout-Meillet ed.2, 731
write "peutêtre celtique."]

[pelaica (leg. *palaica?) "plaice, sole" Polem. Silu.

    544.18

    Schuchardt ZfRPh 30, 1906, 724 compares Ir. pollan,
Gael. powan; cf. Terracini Riv. di Filol. 49, 1921, 429;
M-L REW 6370. Not Keltic.]

πεμπέδουλα (v.l. πομπε -)· πεντάφυλλον Γάλλοι Diosc. 4.42

    (2.200,15W), cf. pinpedonum (v.l. penpidulum) ps-

    Apul. 2.(CML 4.27,32)

    Marstrander NTS 3, 1929, 254 compares - δουλα (Ir.
duille, W. dail) with Latin folium, but that cannot be
if f- represents bh- (cf. Gr. φύλλον); Weisgerber SprFK
182 (La Grauf. 98 above, pinpetos), 207. The true form
is no doubt *pimpedol(i)- ; cf. dolua above? Bertoldi
AGI 22-23, 1929, 502.

[πεπερίκιουμ Diosc. 1.2 (Γάλλοι), piper apium ps-Apul. 6

(Galli).

Not Keltic; perhaps connected with the names of
the iris discussed in A. Thomas Mélanges ed.2, 1927,
150-152 (pave, paveille, pavot etc., *paveir *paperus)?
Cf. AR 6, 1922, 210.]

?petia "piece"

Thurneysen KR 70-71 on the ground of W. peth, Br.
pez postulates petia (not pettium, -ia) as the source
of Fr. pièce; cf. Ir. cuit "part, portion," i.e. *q%t-
(t)i. But he wrongly connects this with Fr. petit (for
this cf. petisia, piccis 246 and 240 below). Cf. REW
6450; and see tripetia 158 above; pecia Du Cange.

petraria "framea" uita S. Melori (Aremoric.) 5, Anal.

Bol. 5.168

This may be the genuinely local word corresponding
to the Germ. framea (cf. 220 and above; cf. AcS 1.203,4
s.v. Aremorici): quae uulgo uocatur petraria. But is
it Keltic?

Cf. perhaps (ἀκοντισμός) ὁ πέτρινος δὴ ὀνομαζόμενος
τῇ Κελτῶν φωνῇ Arrian. Tact. 37.4. Holder's restoration
of CIL 8.2532B (iaculationem perageretis ⟨petrinam⟩) is
not impossible. But that is usually compared with Latin
peto, and if petraria is from the same root, then, with
its p- , it cannot be Keltic, which has (?) at(h)an
(207 below, cf. AcS 1.251) or *etron (ib. 1.1482, cf.
OHG fēdara). But it is worth calling attention to the
Welsh compound pedryollt (cf. Bull. Board Celt. Stud. 6,
1933, 313-14; Williams Canu Aneirin 1938, 98), the Saxon
angon, i.e. a spear with a four-sided head; petraria (if
not for petuaria, which is also a local name [Note xlv A
below); cf. Petrucorii and perros 158 above] will be
quasi "*quadraria," *pet(u)r- . Cf. 179 Ped- .

Glosses

[† πόνεμ "artemisia" (Diosc. 3.117; 2.125,10 W.)

    This appears to be a ghost-word. It is not con-
firmed by ps-Apul. 10 (CLM 4.43,18) pace AcS 2.1033 and
Bertoldi RC 46, 1929, 17, for ps-Apul. has titumen (cf.
158 above), v.l. nitumen, which may be a corruption of
bricumum (Marcell., see 158 above), and of which πόνεμ
may be a further corruption.]

prenne (renne in cod. V) "arborem grandem" Endl. gl.

    613.16

    Cf. Ir. crann "tree" (o-stem, Thurneysen IF 42,
1924, 146), W. pren "wood." Prenicus (mons) CIL 5.
7749,20 (Tab. Gen.) gives us a satisfactory local name
for comparison, the Endlicher items being almost entirely such. Whether we should compare Coligny (227)
prinni, La Graufesenque (110) prinas is doubtful. The
ogham renni (AcS 2.1042) is now read uorenn(i) by Diack
(The Newton Stone 1922, p.16) and MacAlister (MacNeill
Festschrift 1940, p.193); cf. perhaps ue-rennes(?) below, Prini (193 below), but hardly Pyrene (84) or purpcn
(77 i a) or exprcennio (86). In the Newton stone q]renni
is out of the question.

[prosa pexa tunica: πέξον ἱμάτιον   CGL 2.162,43

    Cf. ars prossaria CIL 13.2023, discussed in Note
xxviii above.]

raia "ray" (the fish) Plin. NH 9.144, CGL 2.168,46

    Cf. M-L REW 7016; for *radia, like leda : laia
(and caia above, with i from gi). Distinguish *rika,
riga (246), whence raie; but cf. perhaps raedo, redo
(207).

Glosses

[ρ̆αιδικᾱνον Ed. Diocl. 19.53 (AcS 2.1072)

    For raeda (PID 2.189) and κανοῦν ?]

-randa

    This important element in local names (cf. Appendix) is entered here only for completeness' sake. It does occur however as a British gloss in a Lugd. setting (*Vindo-randa : Britannica lingua guenran Vit. Alb. ep. Andegau., see AcS 3.350,5) which suggests that in*equoranda the first element equo- is adjectival, not a noun (On this term see ZfFr.Spr.u.Lit. 63, 1940, 166-175; Neophilol. 25, 1939-40, 157).

*rescos M-L Einf. 41 (G. frisch, but Fr. rêche)

rho (v.l. hro) "nimium" Endl. Gl. 614.4

    See roth- below; Thurneysen IF 42, 1924, 144.

rocca "rock"

    A local name, dép. Côte-d-'Or; cf. uita Maximi (Limonicus, ob. 625) 1.8, ASS 2 Jan. 1.91, 2.10 p.92, with whom it may be at least as much an Aquitanian as Lugdunensian word. Perhaps both pre-Keltic and pre-I.Eu. Germanic (m., n-stem) according to M-L Einf. 48.

rottas a fish, Polem. Silu. 544.18

    Perhaps read rocca(s), rucca(s)? Cf. Bened. Crisp. Mediolan. (AcS 2.1239): pisciculos....ruccas nomine dictos. Distinguish OFr. rote (for chrotta) Do. 249; and the fish-names rufus, ra(d)ia.

Glosses

roth "uiolentum" Endl. Gl. 613.4 (....hrodanus "iudex

uiolentus".)

Cf. rho- above, and perhaps the particle ro- (*pro-).
But Thurneysen would reconstruct the gloss so as to make
"uiolentum" apply to danum, which seems improbable. Presumably not a gloss on the river names R[h]odanus AcS
2.1223 cf. 80 above, 212 below; ʽΡοτανός (Corsica), i.e.
read fluuius for iudex?; but note the divine name (Rouen)
Roth(o-) FHRC 278.11,16.

sagum (-s) PID 2.189, cf. 164

„ σάγος Γαλλινὸς, τοῦτ᾽ ἐστὶν Ἀνβιανήσιος(Ambiensis?)
ἤτοι Βιτουρῃικός (-ηγ-?) Ed.Diocl. 19.61.

samauca the name of a fish, Polem. Silu. 544.19

Hubschmied Vox Rom. 3, 1938, 84 (cf. 123) renders
the word "Maifisch," for *samākā from *samos "summer"
(cf. Schuchardt ZfRPh 30, 1906, 728), so that the Romance
forms with -b- (M-L REW 7483, Arabic!) would show lenition. Cf. Jud Arch. Rom. 6, 1922, 210.

Cf. perhaps samera PID 2.205, 3.41 samolum (-s)?
And the large number of items in sab- , sam- , samb-
(AcS 2.1264, 1335; 240 below); FHRC 56.2; W-H s.v. feruo
add.; REW 8081a (after Jud AR 5, 1921, 1) sees *somaron,
*somareton with ŏ due to Germanic influence. Cf. per-
haps μερι- σειμόριον above; SprFK 208. But there can be no
connexion with salmo, salar.

?samolus (-um?) a plant, not certainly identified

Also called selago Plin. NH 34.103-104 (for the
ending cf. similago), used by the druids as a panacea.
Cf. (s)amara (-era) SprFK 208, and samauca above. Holder
AcS 2.1346 would compare also †humalus (1.2058), itself
uncertain and problematical.

Glosses

σαπάνα a variety of anagallis, Diosc. 2.209 (Γάλλοι)

σκοβιήμ "elder" Diosc. 4.171 (Γάλλοι)

Cf. W. y-sgawen, ysgau "alder;" the interpretation of this difficult place in Diosc. is discussed by Sofer Comm. Vindob. 2, 1936, 82-83; Br. scao (see Kerscao, 181 Remark below)?

scobilo, σκούβουλουμ "herba solata"

Ps-Apul. 75.6 (CLM 4.136,17), Diosc. (2.228,2 W), both of whom make it Gaulish; AcS 2.1420 (σκυβ-).

?selago: see samolus above

sena "priestess" (on the isle of Sein)

Mela 3.6.48 (for Gallisenas uocant Rhys reads Galli senas u.); cf. gl. cod. Par. 7648.113,1 zenones (ennones Holder AcS 1.1440; perhaps read henones?): antea dicebantur qui nunc Galli sen[n]ones (Gallis en-nones) uocantur, and the curious item in Serv. A. 8.656 (cf. Isid. 9.2.106) which connects Senones (Lugd.) with ξένος.

The local name Sena (Mela l.c., Sein), as well as the ethnicon Senones and the coin-legend senos (PID 2. 333) may all be related. If so, sena is probably only an ethnicon; but it may be simply "old woman" (Ir. sen, W. hen). Note, however, Sena gallica and the river-name Sena, both in Umbria. There is also a variant Galli-canas...dryades in Scr. Hist. Aug. 2.182 (Hohl), perhaps due to an early misunderstanding of the text of Mela. Cf. senani (?) insc. Paris, 171(c) above, and the per-sonal names Seni(s)seri, Siniser "older of two" SprFK 209 (after Thurneysen).

What are we to make of eccones (-g-) "sacerdotes rustici" CGL 5.633,68 (cf. FHRC 250.1; 260.28; 307.12,18)?

Glosses

sena continued

The similarity of ending (or base) in other words (aloxinum, galoxina above; bazena [bargena] 246; gelasonem
246; personal names in -zena in 244 below) is doubtless
accidental. And the personal names (Illyr.) Enna, Enno
can have no connexion either, despite the v.l. ennones.
V.L. galesegna is of course *gallicinia(AGI 31, 1939,
132-3). See also Weisweiler ZfCPh 21, 1939, 205-279.
Perhaps there is nothing more recondite than Galli Senones.

[?sentius acc. pl., Concil. Autessiodorense (A.D. 578)

        Can. 3: inter sentius aut ad arbores sacriuos uel
ad fontes uota dissoluere, Zwicker FHRC 2.174,12 (AcS 2.
1502). A variant of sentes or sentos? If so, Latin;
see ALMA 17, 1943, 73-77; or is not this rather sent(i)o-
"way"? Cf. Ir. sēt (M-L Einf. 234), Gothic sinþs? Compare the personal names in Sent- , Sint- (214, 237 below).
Hardly sentis "fibula" (207 below).

σιστραμέορ·ἱππομάραθον, Diosc. 3.71 (Γάλλοι)

        SprFK 209; -ορ (and -αρ) Iberian?

socco- : see candosoccus above

σουβίτης (v.l. -ῑτῐς,σουιβίτης) "ivy" Diosc. 2.210 (Γάλλοι)

        Elsewhere called bolusseron q.v. above; AcS 2.1651
sees a diminutive in the personal name Σουβίτιλλος IG 14.
2087 (Torre Nona). Cf. οὐσουβέμ below?

sutis "pig-sty" (Lex Sal.)

        For su-tegis (cf. Eng. sty; OE stig, M.E. stī), cf.
Meyer-Lübke W.u.S. 8, 1923, 185-86, id. REW 8492; compare also *bou-tegon "cow-house," Fr. bo(t), Jud Romania

52, 1926, 347, moritex (?) 207 below, unless that is to be compared with σ-τείχω, like Eng. sty (?). For *t%g- cf. (at)tegia Note lii (k); tugurium 240; ?tigernos (teg-) 207; Tigurini 241; ?στολού -τέγον below.

[?**tamisium** Med. Lat. "sieve"

M-L REW 8551; Th. Frings Teuthonista: Beitr. 4, 1932, 163.]

[?**tancinia** "genus floris" see AcS 2.1717]

taratrum "quasi teratrum" Isid. 19.19.15

Cf. Ir. tarathar, W. taradr (Do. 290; KR 80; Sofer Lat.u.Rom. 105, 175), taradros in the Kassel gl. Greek τέρετρον, Latin terebra. Cf. tarinca (207 below)? AR 6, 1922, 201; REA 7, 1905, 48; 9, 1907, 262.

Ταύρουκ "pond-weed" Diosc. 4.99 (ἄλλοι), cf. taurus (79)

tecco a fish, Polem. Silu. 544.15

Cf. the personal name Tecco (214 below); and, if -cc- is for -ku- (cf. alacco, alaucus PID 2.193, Lepon- tic atekua ib. 302, 319; Raetic tukinua ib. 209); tecu- anbo (?) at La Graufesenque (130 above). Compare also tinca PID 2.186, tuccetum ib. 199 (cf. taxea ib., and 220 below), Tincius 237 below; tucos (?) 158 above. See Loewenthal in W.u.S. 11, 1928, 74.

? θέξιμον a plant-name, Diosc. 3.4 (ἄλλοι)

Zeuss proposed to read δέξιμον (- βον), and an al- leged teuxi[te]mon is cited in AcS 2.1824 from ps-Apul. 19, but there CML 4.57,25 now has feuxiterus.

Glosses

? θῶνα also a plant-name, Diosc. 2.11 (Γάλλοι)

    But if Plin. NH 27.109 means the same plant (othonna?), then in Syria nascitur. Cf. μευτα - σῶνε (79 above) and [Argan]thonius (AcS 1.208)?

tillum "poison" (properly "lime"?)

    uenenum poculo miscuit, tillum quoddam fricans, dedit ei bibere, ASS 28 Iul. 6.577F (uit. Samsonis [abb. Dolensis]). Possibly (like taxus in the death of Catuolcus, see 207 below s.v. eburo- , SprFK 200) a tree-name (πτελέα, tilia; but not Irish teile which is τερέβινθος (RC 44, 1927, 261), unless tillum is "turpentine," not "lime."

†timalus

    AcS 1.2057 q.v. (leg. ⟨h⟩umalus: hoppe, Gl.Ox.); AHDGl. 3.592 anm.; cf. samolus above? Bret. hobilhan, OHG hopfo.

to: a preverb or preposition (Do. 292) or possessive

        adjective (Th.)?

    In the uita S. Symphoriani (ca. 180; Aûtun) Fragm. Burana (Berlin 1901) p.161, in the phrase mementobeto to diuo, paraphrased as "memorare dei;" to diuo is probably Keltic (but [me]mentobeto "mente habeto" see that phrase above); Thurneysen ZfCPh 14, 1923, 11; SprFK 155; Dillon Lg. 19, 1943, 252; no connexion with tau (79).

[toles, tonsillae (tus-) "goitre (?); tonsils"

    Gallic according to Isid. 11.1.57; but this seems unfounded; Sofer Lat.u.Rom. 70. No connexion with tussis, or with the next item.]

587

Glosses

το λούτεγον (**vv.11.** στολ - , τοτούλεγον)

A way of throwing the javelin (not the javelin itself), Keltic according to Arrian Tact. 33. Cf. the
personal name Totulo(n) CIL 3.5485? Another conjecture
Do. 289. For - τέγον (?) see sutis above.

?trade: cabo trade uel caballus AcS 2.1901 (from cod.

Sangall. 238, 29)

This must somehow be connected with treide below
(for *trageto-), cf. uertraha, -gus? See Do. 293 (s.v.
-trago-); but tragula (Caes. BG 1.26.3) pace Holder is
probably Latin (PID 2.190).

treide "pede" Endlicher Glossary 613.17

Cf. W. pl. traed, Ir. traig acc. traigid "foot;"
for *traget-, *traged- (NTS 7, 1934, 346) cf. trade a-
bove; Zimmer KZ 32, 1893, 233 (:τρέχω). Thurneysen IF
42, 1924, 196 acutely combined this gloss with brio
"ponte" (above) as an explanation of the local-name
Briotreide (Greg. Tur. h.Fr. 10.31.4, cf. Meroving. num.
Briotreit). Not for *tripede, cf. petia, tripetia (a-
bove; cf. 158).

tri "tres" ib. 613.8; see nanto above

Cf. tri-garanus (170), Tri-corii (80), Τριμαρκισία
below, trianis (130) and triatalis (La Graufesenque 114),
tri (94) for tris, tidres (Skt. tisras, n. pl. fem.
"three") 130, see SprFK 211; Lig. Tri-contii, Tri-ulli
(PID 2.164); tripetia (158 above), Trepitia (221), Treuidon (80), Tribanti (236), Triputienses (24) are other
examples. It is noteworthy that "three" is so well attested.

Τριμαρκισία see μάρκα , tri above (FHRC 76.13)

588

Glosses

<u>trinanto</u>: See nanto, tri above

<u>trucantus</u> a fish ("trout"?)

    M-L REW 8941, E-M ed.2, 1060 (cf. craxantus above
for the ending), SprFK 212; Terracini Riv. di Filol. 49,
1921, 430; cf. the following item.

<u>tructa</u> "trout"

    Polem. Silu. 544.17, Greg. Tur. in glor. martyr.
75, Isid. 12.6.6; Anthimus, Eucheria, Plin. Val.; Gl.
Cf. trucantus; Kluge Urg. 12.

<u>tunna</u>, <u>tonna</u> "tun, barrel"

    Several times in ASS, see AcS 2.1992, where it is
repeatedly given as the word in current popular use;
CGL 7.374; M-L REW 8986 and Einf. 39; Frings Teuthonista:
Beiheft 4, 1932, 202; KR 87 (the meaning is "skin,"
"hide," then "vessel, tun").

<u>tusillae</u> (<u>tonsilae</u>): see toles above

[?<u>turma</u>

    Not in Latin before Verr. Flaccus (Fest.) or Varro;
if borrowed (E-M ed.2, 1066), cf. perhaps the Spanish
local names Turmogon, Turmodigi?]

<u>ualles(s)it</u>: see galit above

    Whether -ss- is like the -ss- of such Latin verbs
as capesso, or represents the Keltic affricate (as in
Veliocasses) we cannot say. Perhaps cognate with Ir.
atbaill "die" (*bhln- Vendryes RC 39, 1922, 434; W-H 1.
517 s.v. flo).

Glosses

uates "soothsayer" Strabo 4.4.4, 197C (οὐάτεις n. pl.),

Lucan 1.448, al. (AcS 3.126), cf. Ir. faith, OE wōþ

But the Latin uates may be cognate, not borrowed (cf. PID 2.201; E. Bickel Rh. Mus. 87, 1938, 195-6 where, p.198, euhages [i.e. εὐαγής, -εῖς] in Ammianus Marcell. 15.9.8 is defended); Runes' conjecture (Etruscan origin) IF 55, 1937, 122 is most improbable; van Langenhove Studien 2, 1929, 59. The "German" synonym was ueleda (220).

[?**uecturium** "opificem ut pote ferrarium"

Trebell. Pollio trig. tyr. 8.3 (AcS 3.134); if a gloss at all, presumably Latin; cf. uectis.]

uehiegorum "genus fluuialium nauium apud Gallos" CGL 5.

518,13; cf. 4.191,13; 5.613,32

Stokes BB 29, 1905, 170 considered this corrupt: "read perhaps uegorum," i.e. uegoron: ueho, ὄχος , Gaul. couinnus (AcS 3.137). The glossaries have vv.ll. uegei-orum (-et-), uehigelorum; but the form uegeia is actually attested by a mosaic showing a river-boat (Monuments Piot 12, 1905, 137-8), cf. Do. 296 n.2.

Cf. ueheia (PID 2.251; with Svennung Palladius 1935, 612 n.4) "waggon." Probably we have uegeio- : uehei(g)o- , cf. CP 36, 1941, 410.

uela: a plant (ἐρύσιμον)

Plin. NH 22.158: Galli uelam appellant. Cf. Fr. vélar (M-L REW 9178).

uercaria (auerc- cod.) "enclosed field"

First in Polypt. (S. Remy), probably Gaulish, see Jud ZfSchweizGesch. 2, 1922, 420; M-L REW 9223a.

590

Glosses

[?<u>uerennes</u>: instrumentum rusticum; Isid. 20.14.13: a

uehere, id est exportare, nominatae

Read perhaps ueherennes or uehennes (cf. ueheia
above); but what is the ending -ennis? Cf. Ardu-enna?
Or divide at ue-rennes, and cf. prenne, renne above?]

<u>uergobretos</u>: the chief magistrate of the Aedui

Caesar BG 1.16.5, also (-o in dual) on coins of
the Lixouii (177 above); and insc. CIL 13.1048 (Saintes,
Aquitania).

On the etymology see SprFK 212, citing Thurneysen
ZfCPh 16, 1927, 288; Kunze and Voigt in Ph.Woch. 54,
1934, 1440 and 56, 1936, 367-68 (the latter, Ugro-Fin-
nish, is impossible); uergo- W.u.S. 12, 1929, 305. Cf.
perhaps -bretum in combretum; Do. 359.

[are-]<u>uernus</u> "[ante] obs⟨i⟩ta" Endlicher Glossary 613.3

The supposed 2 sg. impv. uernus (AcS 3.228) must
be abandoned, cecos and acrisos (?) notwithstanding.
See areuernus above, with the reference to Thurneysen's
discussion. Nor is uer- to be compared with the prefix
uer-(nemeton etc.).

<u>uertragus</u>, <u>uertraha</u> "greyhound," lit. "swift-footed"

Arrian cyneg. 3.6; Grattius cyneg. 203. This is
the famous canis Gallicus (Mart. 14.200 tit., cf. line
1, and 3.47.11; Ovid. met. 1.533) or Belgicus (Sil. 10.
77); cf. 158 above *perros ("quadruped"); often pic-
tured on vases (e.g. JRS 22, 1942, 143; Rodenwaldt Jahrb.
d. deutsch. Arch. Inst. 48, 1933, 204-225); M. Ginsburg
Hunting Scenes on Roman Glass in the Rhineland (Univ.
of Nebraska Studies 42.1, 1941), cf. CP 37, 1942, 462;
the Corstopitum (Corbridge-on-Tyne) vases are a fine
and well-known example.

The name is good Keltic (uer- intensive, and

trago- , cf. treide above (and trade?), with -ra- from
-re- or -ro- (Kuryłowicz Et. I.-Eu. 1.108); on uertraha
in Grattius see Terracini in Studi...Trombetti 359; and
SprFK 213 (Meillet BSL 22, 1921, 90). Not unnaturally
the word is frequent in the OHG glosses (see AcS 3.247).
AcS 1.1930,6; 1934,17. Cf. segusius PID 2.193.

uidubion: see bidubion above

[uigneta, uigentiana (v.l. uincencia), uigentia "herba

   millefolium"

     Diosc. 3.138 (Γάλλοι οὐίγνητα, note the ending -eta),
ps-Apul. 89.4 (CLM 4.160,13). Latin.]

[uitus: ἴτυς, ἄντυξ, written βίτος in ed. Diocl.

     Also βιτωτός i.e. uitōtus ib.; AcS 3.412, 415. Cf.
uidu- ? If not Latin, then the pure Keltic corresponding to the Aquitanian cantus, q.v. 158 above. Kluge
Urg. 7.]

[?ulucus "owl"

     ululae...quas uulgus ulucos uocant. Serv. E. 8.55
(cf. cauannus above), oluccus and other variants in the
Glossaries (AcS 3.127); not connected with λούγος (Holder
ib.), but onomatopoetic. Not, therefore, peculiar to
Keltic (Ir. ulach, Stokes).]

ura "orchis"

     Ps-Apul. 15.3 (CML 4.50,15), Galli.

Glosses

[?urium (v.l. -num, uranium) Pl. NH 19.52

Not Keltic. But see 158 above; Druidae id sibilis dicunt cet. Detlefsen's reading uranium is accepted and interpreted by Wagenvoort Roman Dynamism, 1947, 178, but is of course Greek, as urium (οὔριον) would be, unless it were the homonym urium (158), which is impossible in this context; Mayhoff's urinum "windy, wind(-egg)" sc. ouum is also Greek.]

οὐσουβέμ· χαμαιδάφνη

Diosc. 4.147 (2.289,20 W.; Γάλλοι), cf. eugubim (leg. [e]usubim?) ps-Apul. 27 (CLM 4.68,7), Galli. Cf. Vssubius, -ium (153, 155 above)?

uxisamo- "top-most"

In local and divine names (e.g. Vxama), cf. uxello- ; the superlative formation, and the usual *uχ-s- from *up-s- make it worth while to quote the form here. Cf. REA 7, 1905, 61; BSL 32, 1931, 164 n.1; W-P 1.193; AcS 3.59-67.

Remark:

To these should be added:

†... ...† πολυάνσριος uel sim.

The name (Gallica lingua...quod ibi fuerint mul-torum hominum cadauera funerata) of a cemetery at Aûtun, is unluckily lost at Greg. Tur. glor. conf. 72.

In Litterae Orientales 55, 1933, 1-6 F. von der Velden expounds his curious view of North African ele-ments in the Keltic vocabulary.

Sources given in AcS are not, as a rule, repeated here, cf. p.174; arabic numerals, without other indication of source, refer to CIL volume 13, viz. part i (1899) 1623-3252 (pp.221-519), with part iv (1916) 11171-11287 (pp.22-39), and part ii.2 (1907) 8951-9025 (pp.667-683). Some few names must either be given twice or assigned arbitrarily to Aquitania or Lugdunensis, the precise location of the frontier being dubious (cf. 148 Remark above). For a corrected text of CIL 13.1663 see REA 23, 1921, 110; on 2580 see the Addendum (the insc. actually belongs to Raetia, CIL 3.5934). Some corrections to CIL 13 by de Ricci REA 4, 1902, 214. On names in -rix (Caesar and Hirtius) see d'Arbois de Jubainville's Noms gaulois (1891; unfinished).

179   Local and Ethnic Names

Aballo TP, -u- Merov. num., Aualensis Pard. dipl. Now Avallon. Cf. gloss 178

?Abrianeco Merov. num. Branges (Saône-et-Loire)

Abrincatui cl., -es Greg. Tur., -cateni ND, Abrenctas Merov. num., Abrincatinus Greg. Tur. Avranches; cf. (221) Abrinca fl. (Rheineck)? REA 20, 1918, 193-8

Achimis, Achmensis (-niencod.) in late authors, now Ach (Finistère), apparently from aximo- , cf. Osismii; RC 5, 1883, 438

?Adalia ND

Adriacus uicaria, now Argy (Indre)

Adrus fl. IA; Arroux

Agedincum cl., uik(ani) Agied(incenses) 2949

Ageius ASS; Ay

Agiedincenses, v. Agedincum

Aedui (H-), Edui, (H)aedues, Αἰδου [σ]οι, Αἰδυες cl.; apparently Eduis n. sg. num., Aeduicus Auson., Aeduensis ASS, Aeduus -a insсc. (e.g. 1676, 1714, 2014-15, 2806, 2828, 2873, 2878, 2877(?), 2924 (on the authenticity of this insc. see addendum and MSAF 1913 [1914] 256-

Local and Ethnic Names

282) 2940 (with add.).
C. p.519; cf. REA 26,
1924, 84; Pro Alesia
1922, 130; Haedui 13.
5110; Aedui 10029.310

Alaona, Aulauna (cf. Al-
anus 80?) Merov. num.,
Alaunensis Pard. Dipl.,
now Allonnes (Sarthe),
cf. AcS 3.548,14; REA
20, 1918, 193

Alauna TP, IA, Aleaume-
les-Vallognes (Manche)

Alba (or -is) fl.; Aube

[Albenses 1954; see 80
above and cf. Albigi
148]

Alesia, Ἀλησία, Alisia,
alisiia (169), alixia
(144), cl.; Alisien-
sis, Alisensis, Alsin-
sis, inscc. 2887,
10029.216a-c; Auxois

Aletum ND

[Algiensis pagus; Auge.
Cf. REA 12, 1910, 196]

Alingauia Merov. num.,
-iensis Greg. Tur.
Langeais

?Aliseio Merov. num.,
Auxey (?)

Alisincum IA, cf. Aquis
Nisincii TP(?); Anizy

Ambatia, Ambacia Sulp.
Sev., -iensis Fortun.,
Greg. Tur., Merov.
num. Amboise

Ambarri (for *ambi-arari?)
cl., Ambarrius inscc.,
12.2575 cf. pers. name
Ambaris? Ambariacus
uicus A.D. 501; Ambé-
rieux

?Ambibarii BG 7.75.4;
Ambrières

?Ambiliati BG 3.9.10

Ambiuareti cl.

?Ἀμνῖται (Σαμ-, Ναμ-)
see 153 above

Andecaui (-g-) -ensis cl.,
-anus and -inus (late);
Anjou, Angers; cf.
Andes below, Andus
(pers. name Aquit.)

Andematunnum TP, IA, and
(abbrev.) on milestones;
now Langres

?Anderetiani ND, cf. REA
13, 1911, 424-28; 24,
1922, 257; Rom. Helv.
14, 1933, 16-21; An-
dresiacus BSAF 1917,
227-33; Andrésy (?)

Andes cl., also Andi (?)
For Andecaui?

Anger, -eris fl. Rav.,
Greg. Tur., Andria(?);
Indre

?Angia ins. AcS 1.153-54

Anisola (-ensis) fl.;
Anile

Ansa, -ensis IA, inscc.,
now Anse (Rhône). Cf.

REA 26, 1924, 68-72;
27, 1925, 333; 28,
1926, 27; 41, 1939,
245

Antrum ins., late authors
(Indre) cf. Anger?
Also Antrensis, Antri-
cinum, -ginum

Apriancum, v. Abrianeco

Arar fl., -icus cl. insc.
(1541, 1688, 1674,
1709, 1918, 2008, 2020
al.; Riese 2451 Arari-
cus; Esp.-de Ruggiero
1141, 1165), -e loc.-
dat. in 1954, 1960,
1966, but -um acc.
2070; once Arecarii
(1709), perhaps an
error, unless this is
actually a different
name (cf. 1688)? Now
the Saône, cf. Saucon-
na or Souconna infr.
Cf. 241 Arar (Aar) in
Switzerland (AcS 3.
654). On Hérault (Ar-
aris 80 above), see
Cuny REA 29, 1927, 49-
51. Confused with Is-
ara, Sulga in Med. ms.
of Livy 21.31 (see 80,
s.v. Sulga)

Arceacensis uilla ASS

Arebrignus pagus Eumen.
pan.6

Arecarii v. Arar

Ἀρηγενούα fl., Ptol., mod.
Argenou, Arguenon; cf.
Ar(a)egenue TP; Orne(?)
but perhaps also Guine
REA 12, 1910, 196?

Arelaunum silua, Arela-
nensis, Arlauno

Aremorici, Armorici, -a,
cl., -icanus ND; Br.
aruorek. Cf. 178
("antemarini"). In
Procopius B.Goth. 1.12
Ἀρβόρυχοι?

Argentoialo, now Argent-
euil (Seine-et-Oise)

Ariolica TP; Avrilly
(Loire)

Artiacus (Arc-), Arcia-
censis; Arcis-sur-
Aube (Aube)

Ἀρούβιοι (v.l. Ἀρούιοι)
Ptol., Aruii Avien.,
perhaps cf. mod. Erue
(a tributary of the
Sarthe)?

Aruii v. the preceding

Asa v. Ansa

?Atesui Pl. 4.107 (or
Es[s]ui?)

Athanacum Greg. Tur.,
-enses, now Ainay
(from Ἀθάνας?) Cf.
pers. names; REA 26,
1924, 235

Aturauus fl., Arroux (REA
39, 1937, 261)

Augustobona TP, IA; Ptol.,
now Troyes

Augustodunum cl., -ensis;
OFr Ostedun, then Os-
teun, now Aûtun; insc.
2678, 2658, Augustiduno

Local and Ethnic Names

13 iv (1916), addendum
to p.402

Augustodurum TP; cf.
8979-81, 8983, 8987
(now Bayeux)

Aulerci (num. -ir-) cl.,
insc. (610, 1390); on
CIL 13 *352-3 see REA
23, 1921, 227-228.
See also Brannouices,
Cenomanni, and Ebur-
ouices

[Aureliani, Orléans]

Autessiodurum 2681b, 2920,
TP; Autissiodurensis
921b, -dorensis late
authors; Auxerre

Autricum TP, NG, Αὔτρικον
Ptol. Cf. Bull. Mon.
64, 1899, 273; CIL 8,
1876 (Dioratus) and
(CIL 13 p.473 add.)
BA 1896, 156, (Lutati-
us); Eure. Cf. pers.
names Autricus (182
below)

Baciuum; Bézu (Eure)

Badi(o)casses, v. Baio-
casses, Bodiocasses

uicani Baiennenses 2450;
Beynost (Ain), cf.
gloss 158; or Bag[
(80)?

Baiocasses, Baiocensis,
v. Bodiocasses

Balatedo Greg. Tur.;

Balesme (Indre-et-
Loire)?

pagus Balbiacinsis Greg.
Tur.; Baugy ?

Balgenti castro Merov.
num.; Baugency
(Loiret)

Bandritum TP; BSAF 1913,
83

Barra(u)o Greg. Tur.
h.F. 10, 31; Barrou
(Indre-et-Loire)

?Barsa ins., not certain-
ly identified. Batz?
Or Île de Sercq?

Baugiacus ASS; Bouhy
(Nièvre)? But see
Boluinnus (181)

uicani Belatu[llenses]
2043; cf. 181 below

Belca TP; Beauche (Loiret)

Belcinaca ins., ASS, Bel-
cionaca(?); Belsignac

Beleno castro Merov. num.;
Beaune (Côte-d'Or);
cf. BSAF 1902, 205;
Belenus (i.e. mons
Beleni), Bull. Phil.
1922-23, 179

Belisium NG; Belley (Ain),
but cf. CIL 13.2500,
read uic(ani) Bel(li-
censium), so Belli-
censis in ASS. Cf.
REA 30, 1928, 68-69

Belsa uilla Fortunat.,

ASS; Beauce. Cf.
belsa gloss (158)

Berraus, Barrao, Berau-
ensis Greg. Tur.;
Barrou (Indre-et-
Loire)

Bibe TP

Bibracte cl.; Mont-Beu-
vray (Nièvre); also
divine name (insc.)

Bidana fl. TP, v. Vidubia

?Blauia, v. Garronenses

Blezis Rav., Blaesenses
Greg. Tur.; Blois
(Loir-et-Cher)

?Boalcha uilla (Cenomanni)
AcS s.v.

Bodiocasses Pl., Οὐαδικάσιοι
Ptol., Bagocassis
Auson., Baiocasses ND,
Baiocassensis Greg.
Tur., Baiocassini Si-
don. Apoll., Baiocen-
sis ASS. The spelling
Badiocasses appears to
be a partial Latiniza-
tion; on Bogiensis see
REA 24, 1922, 128; 25,
1923, 268; Bayeux

Bodonias Rav.

Boii cl., see AcS 1.465,
31; Bouhy, cf. Arzem-
bouy(?) REA 31, 1929,
174 (Nièvre). Cf. REA
14, 1912, 391-94; Boii
CIL 13.11036; Illyrian
according to Krahe IF
57, 1939, 119-20

Aquae Bormonis TP, Bour-
bon-Lancy. Cf. di-
vine names Bormo, Bor-
manus, Boruo; on m:u
see 82 above and note
the reference to ca-
lentes aquae cited in
AcS 1.493,47, but
feruentes ib. 3.913,
40. Cf. the pers.
name Boruonicus (182
below). Some further
modern names AcS 3.
910-11 (*borbo- ,
*bolbro- in Borbro,
Bolbro, Bourberain
etc.); PID 3.10 (Lig.
bormo-)

Bosa or Bosesis fl. (A.D.
1134 and 1005); Bouze,
Bouzoise? OFr bosa,
bouze?

Boxum TP, Buis; cf. Box(s)-
ani (80 above), Bux- infr.

Bradeia uicus Fortun.;
Brie-Comte-Robert
(Seine-et-Marne)

Brannouices (Aulerci) cl.;
Brionnais; branno- is
"raven." Cf. Brando-
brici (80), -nd- from
-nn-?

Breu(i)odurum TP, IA;
Brionne (Eure)

Βριγουλος fl. ps-Plut.
(i.q. Arar, Sauconna);
cf. insc. βριτουλωυ
(165 above)?

Bricca Greg. Tur.; Brèches
(Indre-et-Loire) REA
25, 1923, 151-52; cf.

Local and Ethnic Names

pers. names Briccius,
Brictio?

?Briegio, -ensis AcS 1.77
(s.v. Alta)

Brinnaco; Brenay(?)

Briotreidis uicus Greg.
Tur.; Briodoré (Indre-
et-Loire)? From brio
and treide, see 178
above

Br]ioratenses 2464; Briord

Briouera (Saint-Lô, on
the Vire), Merov. num.
and late documents

Britiniacus (AcS 1.550,
23); Bretigny

Briua Isarae IA, TP
(Pointoise)

Briua Sugnutia 2828;
Brèves (Nièvre)

Βριουάτησ λιμὴν Ptol.,
Brivé (Loire Inf.); cf.
briuatiomu insc. (152
above)?

Briuodurum TP, IA; Briare
(Loiret)

Brixis uicus Greg. Tur.;
Braye-sur-l'Indre

Buxido; Boissy-Maugis
(Orne), AcS 1.1384,33;
cf. Boxum above

Cabillonum cl., Καβυλλίνον
Str., Cabilonnenses

oppidani CRAcInscBL
1912, 677-680, Cabil-
lona Amm. Marcell.,
Caballoduno ND, Cabil-
lonensis and (ASS) Ca-
billonica; Chalon-sur-
Saône. Cf. Armand-
Calliat Le Chalonnais
gallo-romain 1937
(Mém. Soc. hist. et
arch., Chalon-sur-
Saône, 27); REA 15,
1913, 450; 21, 1919,
111-112

?Cadetes, v. Caleti

[Caesarodunum TP, Ptol.,
now Tours]

[Caesarea ins.; Jersey]

Cainon,-ensis Greg. Tur.;
Chinon (Indre-et-
Loire)

Cala Greg. Tur.; Chelle(s)
(Seine-et-Marne)

Calagum TP (for *Caliacum?);
Chailly (Seine-et-
Marne); cf. Calgacus 182?

Calarona fl.; Chalerone
(cf. -ranna, -randa;
*cala 158 above?) AcS
1.689; 3.1043

Calatonno Greg. Tur.;
Chalenton (Indre-et-
Loire)

Caleti (or -es), Κάλετοι,
Caes., Str., but Ga-
leti Pl. 4.107 (Cale-
ti 19.8); Caux cf.
Caudebec. Note also
the divine name Cale-

Local and Ethnic Names

tos (Bitburg), num.
καλετεδου (177), and
gl. 158 above uasso-
galatae (-caleti-?);
personal names Cale-
tiu, Caletius -a; and
possibly Caletanus
(AcS 3.1046,7?), Cale-
tinus (AcS 1.697),
Caltiuus (ASS, ib.)
Cf. FHRC 226.25n.

*Camboritum(?) REA 25,
1923, 385

Cano Fortun.; Chinon
(Indre-et-Loire)

?Cappis gl. Rav.

Caracotinum IA (Harfleur)

?Carifes ND

Carnona castellum Fortun.,
Carnonensis pagus Greg.
Tur.; Chênehutte(?),
see AcS 1.794,31

Carnutes cl., -tus, Car-
nutenus (-inus) inscc.
(1694, 2011, cf. 3150,
3151), cf. add. to CIL
13 p.473; Carnutenus,
-inus, -ensis in eccl.
authors, cf. καρνυξ
(158), carnotina (auis)?
Chartres

?Carronenses ND Occ.
(Aremorici), but v.
Garronenses

Cassiciate insc. (3071),
unless divine; in TP
Tasciaca (pace Holder)
can hardly be the same;
Soyer Bull. Géogr.

1920, 1-16. I do not
believe that cassi-
(caddi- cf. 178) e.g.
in Baio- , Vidu- ,
Velio-casses, Cassi-
gnatus, di Casses can
be connected with
*kassano- "chêne"
(Chasseron); cf. P.
Aebischer ZfSchwGesch
14, 1934, 307

?Catabolon Rav.

?Cauce: see 177 above

[Cauea; Chaâge, v. CIL
13, p.463]

Κελτογαλατια i.e. Gallia
Ptol., Steph. Byz.

Κελτοριοι Plut., AcS 3.
1197,52; cf. REA 8,
1906, 346-47

Cenabon, Genabum, Κηναβον
cl., insc. (Cenabenses
3067), now Orléans;
but Genabum has been
claimed for Gien, see
below; cf. 178

Cenomanni (Aulerci) cl.
Cenomannicus -ensis
in late authors; after-
wards Ceromanni (ND)
and Celemanni (Conc.
Aurel. A.D. 511),
whence Le Mans, cf.
Maine; see Aulerci
above

Cerate Greg. Tur.; Céré

Ceruedo uicus Fortun.;
Cervon (Nièvre)

Chora v. Cora

Cisomagus Greg. Tur.,
Merov. num., now
Ciran-la-Latte (Indre-
et-Loire)?

Clanum IA

?Clitis Sidon. Apollin.

Conbaristum TP

Κουδάτε πόλις , Condate IA;
Cosne (Nièvre); but cf.
CIL 13 ii 2, p.667
(Cóndate, whence Cosne
cannot come directly,
but must be a retro-
formate)

Condate TP, IA; Condé-
sur-Iton (Eure); also
in Seine-et-Marne;
and Candes (Indre-et-
Loire); Condate, Con-
datensis Sulp. Sev.,
Greg. Tur., Fortun.;
in Ille-et-Vilaine
(TP, IA), now Rennes

Condatus pagus, Condaten-
sis insc. e.g. 1670,
1684a (at confluence
of Rhone and Saône,
i.e. Lugdunum), cf.
inter Confluentes
Araris et Rhodani
1668, 1672, 1674, 1676,
1698-1700, 1702, 1710,
1712, 1714, 1719, 2904;
cf. Condeates nautae
1688, 1709; but Con-
fluentes 1541

?Κουδηούικνον (an Condate
uicus?) Ptol., appar-
ently Nantes

Constantia (previously
called Cosedia) ?Con-
stan]tino 8951, cf.
CIL 13 p.497-95; Cou-
tances (Manche), Le
Cotentin

[Conuentus arensis 1671]

C(h)ora Amm., ND, Ion.
uit. Columb., ASS,
both a town and a
river (the latter la
Cure, Yonne), see AcS
1.1114 (cf. 1008),
3.1213 (cf. 1279).
Cf. Meunier cited in
REA 31, 1929, 174

Κορβιλών Polyb. ap. Str.
(near Saint-Nazaire)

Coriallo TP, Merov. num.,
pagus Coriouallensis;
Cherbourg

Coriosolites cl. insccc.
(616,3144); Corseul
(Côtes-du-Nord)

Coriosopites NG, ASS;
Waquet in Mélanges
Loth, 1927, 12-17

Cornutius uicus (i.q.
Carnutenus?) Greg.
Tur.; Cornus (Corps-
Nuds)

Corobilium TP; Corbeil

Cosedia(e) TP, IA

Cotiacus; Cussy, cf. REA
13, 1911, 209

Cracatonnus pagus Greg.
Tur.; Craon (Anjou),
cf. the following item

Κρουκιάτοννον Ptol., Crouciconnum TP; Carentan (Manche)?

Crouio uicus, Crouiensis Greg. Tur.

Cupeda Merov. num.; Queudes (Marne)

Δαριόριτον Ptol., Dartoritum TP (now Vannes)

Decetia (-g-), Deccidae cl., itin.; Decize (Nièvre)

Diablintes cl., Diablinti Plin., Διάβλινται Ptol.; Jublains (Mayenne)

Diodurum v. Iotrus

Dolus (1) Greg. Tur.; Dolus (Indre-et-Loire); (2) ASS, -um, -ensis, Dol-de-Bretagne (Illeet-Vilaine)

Dunum (castellum), Dunensis late authors and Merov. num. Cf. W.u.S. 11, 1928, 47; (1) Châteaudun (Eureet-Loire); (2) Dun-lePoelier (Indre)

Duretie TP

Durocasses TP, IA: Dreux (Eure-et-Loire)

pagus Durocassinus, now Dreugesin

Ebroici v. Eburouices

Eburobriga TP, IA; Avrolles (Yonne)

Eburouices cl., itin., Aulerci [Ebu]r(ouices) insc. 1390; later Ebroici, Ebroicinus; Évreux (Eure). Cf. REA 28, 1926, 24; see also 207, 212 below; W.u.S. 11, 1928, 157; Annales del Ist. de Lit. clasicas 1, 1939, 67-81; 2, 1944, 181-197

?Einode (g)iugo 2446

Esuuii; Esui except in BG (where it is commonly emended to Lexouii but cf. REA 9, 1907, 174; 16, 1914, 346); apparently an ethnicon used in personal names only (and num., see below), AcS 1.1476-78, in particular imp. Esuuius Tetricus 8970, 8977, 9000

[Etifidorum (sic) for Autessiodurum Rav.]

Euina (-ena, -ira); Esvres (Indre-et-Loire)

Exona uicus Fortun.; Essonnes (Seine-etOise); W.u.S. 11, 1928, 61

Fano Martis (Corseul) IA 386 (cf. CIL 13, p.667)

Local and Ethnic Names

Fixtinnum TP, v. Iatinum

[Flauia, Edua CIL 13, p.402]

Forum Segusiauorum Ptol., TP (cf. AcS 2.1454, 21-27); Feurs (Loire)

Γάβαιον ἄκρον Ptol., Κέβαιον in Eratosth. ap. Str. (Finistère)

Gabilona Rav., for Cabillonum

Γαλάται, Γαλατία in Greek authors often for Galli, Gallia cl. inscc. Cf. Proleg. 11 n.9; Galli insc. 1668 ii 38, Gallia Comata ib. 32, Gallia 1817; tres prou. Galliae 1671, 1675, 1679, 1680, 1682, 1685-88, 1690-92, 1695-96, 1700-03, 1706-09, 1712-13, 1715-16, 1720, 3162; Gallicus, Gallicanus cl. inscc.

Gallinaria Sarniensis, v. Sarnia (Guernsey)

Gamapia (-n-) AcS 2.1981; Gamaches

?Garronenses ND, for Carronenses; but if Blauia is a local name (ND Occ. 37.15) either it is (Aremorici) not the Blauia of Aquitania (see 153 above), or Carronenses (G-) is

not a derivative of Garunna

Gegina Fortun., Gien(i)-ensis Greg. Tur.; Gennes (Maine-et-Loire)

Genabum Carnutum, probably a variant of Cenabum (q.v. supr.); but some dispute the identification and claim Genabum for Gien (Loiret), whereas this, according to d'Arbois de Jubainville, is for a Giemagus, older *Di-(ua)emagos; ethn. Genabensis, C-. Cf. Stokes Academy 30, 1886, 210

Gesocribate TP (Brest)

Gienensis uicus Greg. Tur., see Gegina

Gisacum insc. (see AcS 1.2023); Gisay (Eure), cf. 212 below; also divine name. Vicus Gisacus(?) CIL 13.360*, the authenticity of which is accepted by some (cf. REA 31, 1929, 361)

?Gorgobina BG 7.9.6

Grannona ND occ. 37 (Aremorici); cf. REA 23, 1921, 58; 12, 1910, 196; 26, 1924, 345; 29, 1927, 309. Note the divine name Grannus 211, 223, 236 below

Grauinum TP

17

Local and Ethnic Names

Ἥριος fl., Ptol.; Auray
(Morbihan)

Herius ins. (7th cent.)
ASS; at mouth of Loire

Ἰάτινον πόλις Ptol., Fix-
tinnum [leg. Iatinum
(?)] TP, ap. Meldos

Icauna (-g-) fl. ASS, cf.
divine names; Yonne

Ic(c)iodurus (-dunum) Greg.
Tur.; Yzeures-sur-
Creuse (Indre-et-Loire),
cf. CIL 13, p.159

Ictium mare ASS (Ir. muir-
n-Icht, the Channel)

Ἰνγενα πόλις Ptol., also
called Legedia

Intaranum insc. 2681 (cf.
3088?). Is this for
-aunum, -abnum (amnes
178 above, "riuos"
Endl. gl.), or -amum
(cf. divine names In-
tarabos, Entarabos?)
and local names in
Italy such as Inter-
amna, -ium; Entrains
(Nièvre), which looks
like an old plural

Iotrus (-dr-) ASS; Jouarre
(Seine-et-Marne), for
*Diuo-durum?

Isera, Esera, Ysera, Isra,
Ysara, Isara fl. For-
tun., Fredeg., ASS;
miswritten Lura TP
(CIL 13, p.684) cf.

Briua Isarae above;
Oise

Isarnodurus ASS, Merov.
num., cf. gloss 178
above; Izernore (Ain)

Iuliobona Itin., Ptol.;
Lillebonne (Seine-
Inférieure). Cf. Brog-
nard, Bull. Soc. Norm.
24, 1919-21, cited in
REA 28, 1926, 33

Iuliomagos TP, Ptol. (now
Angers); cf. CIL 13,
p.478; REA 17, 1915,
286-87

[Laeti Ammian., ND., cf.
Letaui?]

?Langlo Rav., see AcS 2.
141,38

Latta Greg. Tur., Late
uico Merov. num.

Ledus fl., AcS 2.169,1-
14, cf. 80 above, and
gloss 158, 178?

?Legedia TP; cf. REA 20,
1918, 193

Legia ins. AcS 2.153-54;
but this seems to be
the same as Lesia ins.
(now Lichou?) also in
uit. Sams. (FHRC 241.
25)

Letauia (i.e. Armorica).
See AcS 2.243 and cf.
the personal names
Litauus (? CIL 13.2010),

Litauicus; possibly
also Laeti above.
But see rather W-H
1.815, s.v. litus;
Vendryes EC 3, 1938,
177

Lexouii v. Lix-

Liger, Ligeris fl., cl.;
Loire; Ligerici (naut-
ae) inscc. 1709, 3105,
3114

Ligericus fl., uit. s.
Leobini; Loiret; cf.
Ligericinus (AcS 2.
221)?

Liricantus ASS; Larchant
(Seine-et-Marne), cf.
BSL 32, 1931, 158 n.3,
and Medio- , Canti-
cantus (see REA 24,
1922, 163-64, 260),
Liria 80, Lirensis 221

Lixouii (Lex-), Lixouinus,
Lixoensis, but Lixou-
iatis num., Lixouios,
Lexouius (AcS 2.276);
Lisieux; cf. REA 34,
1932, 159-181 (with 12,
1910, 196; 16, 1914,
346). Lexsouiorum
10022.167. Not to be
connected with lixiuus
(*nips-, νιπτρον)

Loccae Greg. Tur.; Loches
(Indre-et-Loire)

Locoteiacus, Log- (for
Luco-); Ligue (Vienne),
cf. AcS 2.303, CRAc
InscBL 1890, 262-63

?Loium IA, Logio uit. s.
Balthildis

Lucaniacus uilla Fortun.;
Loigny (Eure-et-Loire)

Lucas Greg. Tur. (AcS
1.616, s.v. Brixis)?

Lucdunum ASS; Loudon
(Sarthe), AcS 2.344

Lucotecia (-toc-), Lutecia
(-tic-), -tia, Luco-
ticius cl., itin., ap.
Parisios, see 170, 178
above and p.484; com-
parison with *locu-
"lake" Penne- , Sego-
locus (15) is unlikely

?Ludnomagenses 5923 (an
lud[Nomag[?). On
Lunna, Ludna (Turnel-
les) cf. P. Wuilleu-
mier REA 41, 1939, 245-
251; but see also 241

Lug(u)dunum, -enses (cf.
p.484; items 170, 178
above) cl., inscc.,
viz. Lug[2039, Lug-
udunus 2553, -um 1169,
1428, 1668 ii 29, 1688,
1735, 1751-52, 2008,
2030, 2448 (also Λουγου-
δουνοιο); Lugudunenses
1800, 1806, 1812 (cf.
1813), 1908, 1923,
1931, 2008, 2023;
-iensis 1499, Lugud-
[unensis] 1464, 1807,
1808, 1881, 1942-44,
†Lugdunensis 1855, cf.
1860, 3162(?), -insis
2385. Cf. 11189,
11198, 10029.219, 311-
12; cf. 10006.1; 3.
5832; IG 14.2532; Lug[
7383; Luguduno. lus(?)
CIL 13, p.402 add.; cf.
Λουγδουνον Byvanck 2.827

Local and Ethnic Names

(R. 526; IG ad res
Rom. pert. 3.28,80);
Lugudu | larum insc.
Syria BA 1934-35 [1940]
p.291. For coins of
Lugdunum with Copia
see (e.g.) Congr.
Arch. 1935, 580; Lugi-
dunum BSAF 1928-29,
245-47

Lun(n)a IA; see Ludno-
above

Lutetia, see Lucotecia

Magdunum, -ensis ASS;
Meung-sur-Loire
(Loiret). But this
may be for Maidunum;
and in Schol. Lucan
1.429 (see CIL 13, p.
568) we have Mandunum,
-enses; see also Mog-
dunum

Malliacensis Greg. Tur.;
Maillé (Indre-et-
Loire)

Mandubii cl.

Mandunum; see Magd- ,
Modg-

Masaua TP, -ensis 2895;
Mesues (Nièvre)

Matantes pagus 3148; Le
Mantois (Rennes)? Cf.
RC 18, 1897, 87-88

Materconensis, Matescensis,
v.sq.

Matisco cl., itin., (-asc-),

Matiscensis (-asc- ,
-esc-), Matisconenis
and Materconensis
late; Mâcon. On the
Mâconnais see the
works of Jeanton cited
REA 35, 1933, 171-172;
40, 1938, 300, 411

Matrŏna fl., cl., Auson.,
Greg. Tur.; Materna
ASS, Maderna Rav.;
insc. (Matrona) 5674;
Marne. Cf. maderna
178 above; on the
Middle Welsh mabon uab
modron see VKG 2.45
(cf. ab Mydron EC 4,
1948, 205)

Mauriacensis Greg. Tur.,
MG; Moirey (Aube)

?Meteglo, for Meclo(dunum)

Meclodunum (Mello-?) cl.,
-ensis, Malidunensis
(Mili-) lib. h.Fr.;
Melun, but see Metlo-
sedum

Medalgicum; Les Mauges,
see CIL 13, p.479

Medioconnus Greg. Tur.;
Mougon (Indre-et-
Loire)

Mediolanum (Aulercorum)
Ptol., itin., Ammian.;
Mediolannenses 3202
(cf. 174 above)

Mediolanum (Segusiauorum)
TP; Le Miolan (?)

Meduana fl. ASS, Greg.
Tur.; Mayenne

Local and Ethnic Names

Meduanta TP (now Nohan?)

Meldi (-ae) cl., insc.
2924, Meldensis; Meaux.
Cf. Meldacensis CIL
13, p.479 (Mauges)?

Mellobodii 2801 (or per-
sonal?)

?Meteglo, for Metlo(sedum)

Metlosedum cl., insc.
3012, and -dunum; (or
Metio-); Meudon or
Melun (Meclo-)?

Mogdunum BSAF 1902, 205
(Manche). Cf. Magd-,
Maid-

Moruennum not. Tir., Muru-
innum Greg. Tur.; Moru-
inniccus insc.; Le
Morvan

?Musfa (-ff-) pagus AcS
s.v.

Namnetes cl., Namnis
(6230); Nantes

Nauicellae Greg. Tur.;
Nazelles (Indre-et-
Loire)

Nemetodurus ASS, Greg.
Tur.; Nanterre (Seine),
cf. REA 26, 1924, 343

?Nisincii Aquae, v. Ali-
sincum; but the text
may be sound (cf. niskai
Note xv)

Nortrinsis REA 15, 1913,
442; Norrey

Nostrusa fl., ib. 45,
1943, 252

Nouiliacus uicus Greg.
Tur.; Neuillé-le-
Lierre (Indre-et-
Loire)

Nouigento, Nouiento
Fortun.; Nogent-sur-
Marne

Nouiodunum cl., subse-
quently called Neuir-
num TP, IA, -ensis
Greg. Tur.; Nevers.
(On Gerin's conject-
ures see RA 18, 1918,
180)

Νοιόδουνον Ptol., Nudio-
nnum (?) TP, ap.
Aulercos

Nouiomago IA, Νοιομαγος
Ptol., ap. Lexouios

Odouna insc. 2681b, later
Odona; Ouanne (Yonne)

Olericium ASS; Lirey
(Aube)

Ὄλινα , Olinas fl., Ptol.,
Orne-Saônoise

Orbaniacus Greg. Tur.;
Orbigny (Indre-et-
Loire)

Orna fl., Fortun.; Orne

Os(s)ismi cl., Ossismicus,
Ὠσίσμιοι Pyth. ap. Str.,
Osismiaci Mauri ND, cf.
Vxisama, Vxuma; Vxisama
ins. is the modern

607

Local and Ethnic Names

Eussa, Os(s)ismi
Kerscao (cf. 178), see
RC 38, 1920-21, 259;
CIL 13.2.11 (1907) p.
645. For the work of
G. E. Broche on Pytheas
(Paris 1936) see ZfCPh
23, 1943, 220-223.
Despite the variants
Ostidamni, Ostimii it
is unlikely that the
Oestrymnicae (-ides)
insulae Avien. 130 (96)
should be compared as
some have done

Otlinga (Saxonia) REA 15,
1913, 442; 22, 1920,
52

Oxsello (Vxs-) Merov. num.
AcS 3.6,2

Parisii cl., inscc. 626,
2924, 3034; Parisiacus,
see 171; on Parisius
(adj.) Gray Mélanges
Marouzeau 207

Ped(e)uerius (i.e. Petu-
arius?); Pithiviers
(Loiret); cf. 178 and
REA 39, 1937, 37

Perticus saltus Greg. Tur.,
i.q. Carnutenus pagus;
le Perche. Cf. Note
xlvi below

Petromantalum IA, rendered
Petrum.uiaco in TP, not
far from Paris; cf.
Vendryes BSL 38, 1937,
5 and 113; Loth CRAc
InscBL 1916, 95. In
RA 12, 1938, 332, no.

80 (cf. 13, 1939, 157)
we have a dedication
to the gods Quadruuiae
(cf. 223 below); and
if mantalo- is "ae-
qualitas" it is an
appropriate term for
a boundary (cf. Mantala
80 above), like *equo-
randa (178); see also
REA 19, 1917, 33-34;
BA 1921, ciii; AcS 2.
411 and 977; REA 40,
1938, 62; RA 13, 1939,
p.157 (on identifying
the site); Schwyzer in
ZfCPh 22, 1941, 329
(on -mantalo-); the
early discussion Mém.
Soc. sc. et lettres et
arts, Seine-et-Oise 11,
1878, 343 (Mont. 10)
I have not seen; AE
1922.61

Pocrinium TP; Pringues
(Saône-et-Loire)

Pontachiuggana (?) see
AcS 1.1182 (*Cucana,
Chouanne?)

Ponteleugae; Pontlieu;
see AcS 2.201; perhaps
for -louco, -locu (?)
cf. Sido- , Sede-loco,
-louco below; Penne-
locus 19 Remark (Sege-
locus 1b.)

Portunammetu TP, Portenses
3105-07; Nantes

Ratensis pagus Greg. Tur.;
Retz (CIL 13, p.483)

608

Local and Ethnic Names

Ratumagus, Rot(h)omagus
TP, IA, -enses For-
tun., ASS, num. Ratu-
macus; Rouen. Cf.
Ratum[agenses) uicani,
Pondron(?), see AcS
2.1082, 49-1083,20;
but REA 26, 1924, 123-
24 (Rouen near Beau-
vais, see 212);ʽΡοτό-
μαγοϩ Le Bas-Waddington
3.2036 (cf. CIL 13 iv,
1916, add. p.512)

Redones BG, Riedones Pl.,
insc. 3151; later Rh-
(FHRC 294.33 also
called Rubra); Rennes

Reginca (-ea) TP; Rance

?Renate fonte insc. 2402.3

Resbacis (-baccum) AcS
2.1176

?Riduna ins. TP (near
Sarnia)

Riobe TP

Ritumagus itin.; Rade-
pont (?)

Robrica TP

R(h)odanus fl cl., cf.
inscc. 1541, 1996;
Rhodanicus 1688, 1694,
1716, 1914, 1996, 2002,
2494; Rhône

Rodomagus Greg. Tur.; Ruan
(AcS 2.1083,21)

ʽΡόδουμνα Ptol., Roidomna
TP; Roanne (Loire)

Rotomagenses, see Ratu-

Rumu ins. Pl.

?Saedii insc. 1759 (per-
sonal)

Saii, Sagensis, Sagiensis
ND, ASS, cf. insc.
630; Sées (Orne)

Salioclita, -us IA; Saclas
(Seine-et-Oise), cf.
Jullian REA 32, 1930,
133-38

Σαλιόγκανοϩ λιμήν Ptol.;
Port Sliocan

?Σαμνιται Posid. ap. Str.,
at the mouth of the
Loire (but read Ναμν-?)

Saponaria uicus, Sauonari-
ae portus; now Savon-
nières; MG and ASS

Sarnia ins. (v.l. -mia,
-ma) IA, Sarniensis
insc. CRAcInscBL 1920,
425, cf. REA 23, 1921,
363; now Guernsey

?Sasonien Caroling. num.,
Saosnes (Sarthe)

?Sauara Fortun.; Sèvres
(AcS 2.1385)

Sauconna fl., Sagonna (cf.
divine name Sou-), pre-
viously called Arar;
Saône

Sauiae (near Paris), see
REA 24, 1922, 261

Local and Ethnic Names

Sedelaucum, v. Sidoloucus

aquae Segetae TP, Rav.
also divine name (1641,
1646); perhaps insc.
1630 (?)

Segestrum (-us-) monas-
terium, now Saint-
Seine (Côte-d'Or); cf.
Segessera 237 below

Segusiaui cl.; inscc.
1632, 1640, 1645, 1701,
1711, 1712, 2013; num.

Sena insc. Mela, Sina IA,
off Finistère

?Senona fl.; Sélune (Man-
che), but both Ptol.
and Ammian. have Se-
quana

Senones cl., inscc. 921,
2924, 2942, 2949; Se-
nonius Pol. Silu.,
Sidon. Apoll., inscc.
1676, 1684, 2675, 3067;
Senonicus, Senonensis
in late authors; Senon[
CIL 6.2379b 5.20 accord-
ing to Mommsen Hermes
19,24; for the inter-
pretation of Senones
"pugnaces" (Zeuss) cf.
Galli : senae (?) 178
above and AcS 2.1485-
98 (esp. BG 2.2.3; 5.
24.2); now Sens

Sequäna fl. cl., later
Segone, Sigona, Sigunna,
Sigugna; cf. Sequalina?
Seine; also a divine
name (Siquan[n]a, e.g.
2367, 2864). Cf. Se-
quäni cl., inscc. 1674,

1675, 1991; Sequǎnus
1674, 1675, 1983,
1990, 2023, belonging
to Germ. Sup.

Seudunum, Seo- (Sego-);
Suin (Saône-et-Loire)

Seueriacus Fortun., Greg.
Tur., Civray-sur-Cher
(Indre-et-Loire)

Sextanmanduus pagus 3149
(Rennes); cf. RC 18,
1897, 87-8. Cf. Man-
dubii above; mandu-
"pony" (mannus PID 2.
198) with -nd- from
-nn-? Cf. also Viro-,
Epo-mandui

Siata ins. IA (Bret.
Houat)

Sicdelis ins. IA (509.4)

Sidoloco IA, -louco TP,
Sedelaucum Ammian.;
Saulieu (Côte-d'Or);
cf. Ponte-leugae above

Siduo 2681, IA

Sipia TP; Seiche (Ille-
et-Vilaine), cf. CRAc
InscBL 1944, 421

Sitillia TP; Chizeuil
(Saône-et-Loire). But
distinguish Sicilia
AcS 2.1590 (in Germ.
Sup.)

Solonacensis Greg. Tur.;
Saunay (Indre-et-Loire)

Stampenais pagus Greg.
Tur., Stampas num.
Merov., Étampes

Local and Ethnic Names

Subdinum TP, leg. Syin-
dinum? Or cf. Ὀυίνδινον ?

(Briua) Sugnutia insc.
2828, Brèves (Nièvre).
For loricari (2828)
see 213 Remark below

Sulis TP (Morbihan) AcS
2.1662,47; cf. REA 15,
1913, 449 and the di-
vine name Suleuiae

Sullias see 175 above

Tampium (?) insc. 3162;
cf. Tamfana 223 below

?Tasciaca TP; Thésée
(Loir-et-Cher)

Taurisiacus Greg. Tur.;
Torcy (Indre-et-Loire)

Telonnum TP, Toulon-sur-
Arroux (Saône-et-
Loire); cf. 80

Tincillacensis Fortun.

Tinurtium IA, Spartianus
uit. Seueri 11.1; -c-
TP, -orcensis Greg.
Tur.; Tournus (Saône-
et-Loire); REA 24,
1922, 56-7

Τίτος (?) fl., Ptol., said
to be the Guet (leg.
Γου—?)

Tout[iacus] pagus insc.
2949; Toucy (Yonne)

Tricasses Pl., insc. 1667,
2959; -inus 1691, 2924

and Paneg. Constantio
21; Troyes (Aube). Cf.
Tricastini (80)? See
the glosses caddos and
tri- 178 above; Trica-
[ssius Anb[10003.61

Triconti 2494 (Géligneux),
cf. Vocontii (80),
Petrucorii (153), Tri-
corii (80); REA 13,
1911, 351-52

?Triuortium Trévoux (Ain)

Tudella (near Paris), cf.
86, 154, 181; REA 28,
1926, 252-54

Turnacensis Greg. Tur.;
Ternay (Loir-et-Cher)

Turnomagensis (Tor-) Greg.
Tur.; Tournon-St-Pierre
(Indre-et-Loire); REA
23, 1921, 111-116

Turones, -i cl., inscc.
(1703, 1716, 3076-77),
Turonn[3231 add.;
Turonicus; Tours,
Touraine

Ὀυαδικάσσιοι Str.; Vez
(Oise); or the same
as Baiocasses q.v.?

Ὀυάγοριτον Ptol., cf. Ba-
garidon Rav.?

Vaona uilla AcS 3.101

]ublocnus pagus 1646

Veliocasses cl., insc.
(1998), -caθis num.,

cf. CIL 13, p.512.
Velcassinus, Vil- ,
Vilg- , Vulcasinus
(AcS 3.147,21); le
Vexin. Apparently
πόλις Ούλοκάσσεινος is
ciuitas Veliocassium
(Rouen?) Byvanck 2.
827 (Riese 526, IG ad
res Rom. pert. 3.28,80).
Cf. AcS 3.148,10; Cas-
siciate above and gl.
caddos (178), Vidu-
casses below; RC 38,
1920, 260; Caddarenses
(Illyr.) CIL 13.7268,
7298 (-tth-)

Vellaunodunum BG, perhaps
Château-Landon (Seine-
et-Marne)? Cf. Bull.
Soc. arch. de Sens 40,
1937, 123-28 (APh 15,
1940-41, 355)

Venelli BG, Pl., Ptol.

Veneti cl., inscc. 1709,
2777 (?), 2950; Vannes
(Morbihan); GR 8, 1939,
65-73

Venetonimag(i)enses 2541,
2544, 2564, Viou(n);
in 15th cent. Voinum.
Cf. REA 37, 1935, 211

Vercelliacus Vézelay
(Yonne); see RA 11,
1938, 222

Vernao Greg. Tur.; Vernou-
sur-Brenne (Indre-et-
Loire)

Vertigontes (?) if an
ethnicon; Plin. iun.,
quoted in FHRC 100.3
(with n.)

Vggate IA

Vicinonia (-tin-) fl.
Greg. Tur., Fredeg.;
Vilaine. Cf. Mars
Vicinnus (181 below)?

Ούίδανα λιμήν Ptol.

Vi(n)dilis ins. IA

Vidubia fl. Rav.; La
Vouge

Viducasses Pl., Ptol.,
insc. 3162, 3166;
Veiocae in 14th c.,
now Vieux (Calvados);
cf. MSAF 1910, 225-
335; Note xxiv above.
Vidu- "tree," as in
Sapaudia (15), uidu-
bium (bid-) see 178;
REA 7, 1905, 61

Ούίνδινον Ptol. (Σουί- v.l.)

Vindocinum ASS, Merov.
num., -ensis Greg.
Tur., Vendôme, Ven-
dômois; cf. Seckel,
Preuss. Abh. Ph-H Kl.,
1939.3

*Vindo-randa, now Guér-
ande, see AcS 3, 349-
350; see also the gloss
guenran 178 above
(s. v. -randa)

Vlda fl. Greg. Tur. (H-);
Oust(?)

Vnelli BG; cf. Venelli

Vorganium insc. 9016,
Vorgium cf. CIL 13,
p.409; Ptol.

Modern Local Names

Vrbia fl., Vrbiensis Greg.
   Tur.; Orge; cf. Orbis
   fl. (80); REA 38,
   1936, 345

Οὐξισάμη Ptol., Vxantos
   Pl.(?), -is IA, île

d'Ouessant, Ushant
(Finistère)

Vxuma conc. Aurel. (A.D.
   511), Vxominsis
   Fortun.; Exmes (Orne)

Just as the ancient toponomy (e.g. in terms de-
noting "border" or the like, -margo, -randa, -oiolum,
finis) is of varied origin, so in modern local names,
of which a selection of additional items follows, are
found words that are Keltic, Latin, Keltic again (Breton), Germanic, or French in successive strata in different parts of Lugdunensis.

Aigny-le-Duc, Alançon, Albigny, Alet, Alligny,
Aluze, Ampilly-les-ordes, Anzy, les Areinnes (Paris,
older "ad Arcinas" or "ad Arainas"), Ariengas (Frankish),
Aubigny

Bascerengas (Burg.), Beaumesnil, Bellenod, Ber-
thouville, Biera (REA 13, 1911, 209), Bourge, Bouze,
Branges, Brenne fl., Bresle fl., La Bresse, Les Bries
(Yonne; REA 28, 1925, 327-29), Brignais, St Alban-de-
Bron, Bugey, Bussy-Allieux

Carentan, Chagnon, Chaisieu, Chantenay, Charlieu,
Charrecey, Châtres, Chassenay, Chauffailles, Chavagnes,
Chênoves (Canabae, 9th c.), Chiffrevort, Choulans, St
Laurent-la-Conche, Couville, Clénord, Les Cleons, Crain,
Crot-Volu (Aûtun)

Further modern names

Dennevy, Dol, Salt-en-Donzy, Doué-la-Fontaine

Écuisses (Scotia, Scoteria?), Écully, Eraine, Essey, Eslettes, Étang, St Pierre-l'Étrier

Flavigny, Fourvière

Le Geneste, Gerland, Gilly, Gissey-le-Vieil, Gleizé, Granges (Graniae)

Le Ham, Harfleur

Illeville, St Jouin(-Harfleur)

Laizé, Laye (*Legia REA 13, 1911, 209), Lentilly, Lieusaint, St Lunaire, Luthenay

St Malo, Marclopt, Marmagne, St Maure (Sancta Maura), Mauves, Mellecy, St Méloir, Mérouville, Méspilley (cf. mespilus 158 above?), Meung-sur-Loire, Meusnes, Mienne, Moind (or -ns), Monceaux-le-Comte, Montérollier, Montjou, Moulins, Moutier, Muzin fl.

Néronde, Nemours, Neuvy-en-Sullias, Castel-Noëc, Noyers, Nuits

Orival, Oze fl., Ozerin fl. (Ose, Oserin; cf. REA 41, 1939, 347-348: Alesia Auxois?)

Pommiers, Poncins, Pont-Audemer, Pouilly

Quincey

St Rambert-sur-Loire, Randant, St Révérien, Rive-de-Gier, Rully

Saincaize, Santenay, Sasseney, Savigny, St Seine (Sanctus Sequanus, CIL 13, p.437), Sennecey (Siliciacum, AcS s.v.), Sermizelles, Seua fl. (Guil. Bret.) now Sée (? for *sekua, cf. 19 Remark; cf. pers. name Seua 3228), Serrigny, S(u)èvres

Taluyers, Tard (Taruos, Taruenis BSAF 1902, 205), Tassin

Vaise, Valbonne, Valognes, Valromey, Varennes, Verdun-sur-le-Doubs, Vesiana (Lyons, CIL 13, p.259), Visignot, Vouge fl., Vouvray

Further modern names

The number of specialized studies in modern toponomy is now legion. There follow references to a few of these:

Lyonnais: Devaux, Lyons, 1898 (see REA 39, 1937, 136); REA 36, 1934, 318-322 (Chronique de Toponymie; Lyonnais, Forez).

Mâconnais: Jeanton, Repertoire archéologique, 1926-31 (ib. 35, 1933, 171-72); id., BA 1925, cviii-cix, 91-102 (on names in -acus).

Côte-d'Or: P. Lebel on names of rivers (Mém. Commiss. Ant. Côte-d'Or 1935, 396-240; REA 40, 1938, 155-56).

Burgundy: Chaume, Mém. Commiss. Ant. Côte-d'Or 1927 [1931], Géogr. hist., 3 vols. Dijon, 1927-31 (cf. REA 38, 1936, 341-42; 39, 1937, 364-65); Badet (ib. 39, 1937, 44), Calmette and Drouat, La Bourgogne, Paris 1912 (ib. 15, 1913, 80); A. Dauzat ZNF 5, 1929, 245-251; Chabot, see REA 39, 1937, 261.

Champagne: see the survey by C. Bruneau, Rev. Ling. romane 5, 1929, 87 (cf. pp.128, 143, 169 for neighboring regions). L. Febvre, Hist. de Franche-Comté, Paris 1912 (REA 15, 1913, 72-73).

Bourbonnais: G. Bruel Bull. Soc. Émulation du Bourbonnais, 1922 [Oeil, Aumance], see REA 25, 1923, 384; Fournier, ib. 38, 1936, 346-48.

Nivernais: Meunier ib. 30, 1928, 315.

Picardie: Riez see REA 7, 1905, 249 (cf. Riez in Basses-Alpes 21 above; Reii at Lyons, AE 1935.210).

Île-de-France, Oise, Seine-et-Oise, Seine-et-Marne: Chroniques de Toponymie by Dauzat and Lemoine, REA 40, 1938, 149-51 and 152-54. On Montmartre (Paris and also dép. Yonne), about which there has been much discussion [Mons Martyrum has replaced Mons Mercurii or Martis (?)], see Bull. Phil. 1914, 35-36; REA 36, 1934, 476-78; 35, 1933, 37-40; Bull. Soc. Yonne 1922, 243-266 (REA 26, 1924, 343 and 347); Dauzat, REA 37, 1935, 54; Longnon, Soc. Nat. Ant. Fr.: Centenaire, Recueil des Memoires, 1904, 251-253; CIL 13, p.465 n.5.

Orléannais and Loiret: J. Soyer Bull. géogr. 1912, 56-74 (cf. RC 34, 1913, 486-488); id., numerous articles

18

Further modern names

in Bull. Soc. Orléannais vols. 20, 22, 23, see REA 38,
1936, 40 cf. 53-54; 40, 1938, 53; 41, 1939, 42; 45, 1943,
253-554; Actes Congr. de Toponymie 1938 (cf. APh 15,
1940-41, 207); Ét. Celt. 2, 1937, 361; names in -onnus
(-a), -(o)ialum, -lanum, -randa, -briua, -antia, -entum,
-dunum, -durum, -briga, -magus, -acus, -o(nis), and on
names of "habitations" such as casa, casella, casalis,
casetum (note the suffix -etum); capanna, capanella;
mansio. Id., Bull. géogr. 1920, 1-16 (on Cassiciate);
cf. RC 44, 1927, 406; 46, 1929, 367. Id., Mém. Soc.
Orléannais 37, 1936, 5-108 (ancient roads: Petuarii,
Durocortorum, Metlodunum and others, cf. REA 39, 1937,
37). Id., Ann. Soc...du Gâtinais 40, 1931, 1-16 (on
Gien, older *Giemus; Bull. Soc. Orl. 23, 1936, 43-100
(Latin and Germanic names), 108 (on uassus, arepennis).
See also summaries of papers by Soyer in REA 20, 1918,
126-27; 21, 1919, 224 (Bull. géogr. 1917, on Aquae Seg-
e(s)te, now Sceaux?); 31, 1929, 61 (Vxantia, Ossantia);
35, 1933, 187-194.

Manche: P. Chesnel, Rev. de l'Avranchin 144, 1931,
61-109.

Ille-et-Vilaine: H. Quilgars in Mélanges Loth,
Paris 1927, 386-389.

Maine: Beszard, diss. Nancy (Paris 1910) on local
names (REA 13, 1911, 94).

Vendômois: de Trémault, Cartulaire Marmoutier (REA
24, 1922, 323)

Finistère: Loth and Bernard, on local and personal
names of Cap-Sizurs, Quimper 1926 (ib. 28, 1926, 264).

The whole question of Breton names (cf. Remark below) is closely connected with that of the Breton language itself.

Bretagne: R. Largillière RC 41, 1924, 361-371;
Loth RC 28, 1907, 373-403; A. Oriu in Rev. de Bretagne
49, 1913, 41-52, 309-325. Loth's famous dissertation
(Rennes, 1883: "L'émigration bretonne en Armorique")
is well known (cf. RA 13, 1921, 108-119); a selection
of Breton insc. appears in his Chrestomathie bretonne,
Paris 1890 (cf. C. de Kéranflech, Bull. arch. de l'Assoc.

Further modern names

bretonne 6, 1858, 103; 15, 1897, 1ff.; CIL 13, p.489).
F. Sagot, La Bretagne romaine, Paris 1911; H. Teulié,
Bibl. celt. et neo-celt. (MSS at Rennes), Paris 1916;
Dotton on the dialects of Bas-Maine (see REA 12, 1910,
196); Répertoire...objects anciens (Arch. hist. du Maine
[Le Mans], 11, 1911, cf. REA 14, 1912, 83); Abgrall,
Bull. Soc. arch. Finistère 1919 (on local names of Armorique, Finistère); Jullian, REA 23, 1921, 103-109
(local names of Aremorica in ND). For a Breton history
in Breton see Le Roux and Vallée (reviewed by Dottin
REA 24, 1922, 151-52); and more recently Meven Mordiern,
Notennou diwar-benn ar Gelted Koz (3rd edn., Brest 1944);
A. V. Grand-Marais ("À travers le parler gallo-morbi-
hannais, environs de Malestroit") in Rev. de Bretagne
47, 1912, 181-212; 49, 1913, 123-46; J. de La Passardi-
ère, ib. 47, 1912, 140 sqq.; 48, 1912, 34 sq.; 50, 1913,
94-104 and 185-88; 269-79 (local names of Leon). [Some
older discussions have only a historical interest, e.g.
Gibault in BSAgrSc et Arts (Poitiers) 1, 1828, 294 sqq.].
Abbé France, BSArchBretanne 10, 1891 [1892], 3; du Crest
de Villeneuve, BSArchFinistère 26, 1899 (from Mont. 8).

Chronique de Toponymie (Bretagne, Normandie): REA
34, 1932, 293-300.

On names in -cueille, -plan, -pui cf. Davillé, Bull.
géogr. 1926 (REA 29, 1927, 394).

Caen represents *Catu-magos (cf. Rouen from Ratu-
magus) H. Prentout REA 23, 1921, 229-230; on Arroux
(Atarauus?) cf. 179 above; Adour, Yerre, Yères see Lebel
Mem. Soc. Éduenne 48, 1937, 151-59 (Congrès arch. d'
Autun, 1936), cf. REA 39, 1937, 261.

As to Quimper a large number of suggestions have
been made, cf. REA 25, 1923, 174-5 (none convincing);
presumably it is the Breton kemper i.e. "confluentes."

Remark:

On modern local names in Brittany. The problem is
more complex in Brittany, part of the ancient Lugdunensis.
For here a modern Keltic dialect may still be heard. But
it is a Keltic dialect introduced from Great Britain in

Breton names

the fifth century of the Christian era. Accordingly the
local names of Brittany, so far as they are Keltic, do
not derive necessarily from the ancient Gaulish dialect
of Lugdunensis, though a small minority probably does,
and a few can be proved to come from that source, having
survived not only the Latinization but also the subsequent renewal of Keltic speech. It is important, therefore, to distinguish, wherever possible between the two
strata of Keltic, and to distinguish both from purely
Latin names. Nevertheless, there are many names of the
Gallo-Roman period which have, in addition to the familiar "Keltic" suffix -acus (cf. Loth RC 12, 1891, pp.280;
386-89; 390), a Keltic or partly Keltic base. As evidence of the ancient Keltic speech, then, to be won from
the modern local names of Brittany, we may note the
following, not all of which are claimed as certainly
going back to the Gaulish or Gallo-Roman period. But
all for which any possibility of such origin might
plausibly be advanced have been given the benefit of
the doubt and admitted here.

See, for further details, the careful study published in 1940 by W.B.S. Smith De la toponymie bretonne:
Dictionnaire étymologique (Supplement to Language, 16,
2 [April-June] 1940, Language Monograph 20), to which I
am much indebted.

Ac'h from Os(s)ism- in
Osismi cf. Vxisama,
Vxama (now Eusa), W.
uchaf "highest;" Do.
61. The ancient name
of the tribal centre
was Vorganium (not to
be confused with Vor-
gium, now Carhaix).
See also Corseul,
Vannes, below

Adgat i.e. *Ate-catus

Allineuc i.e. *Alon-acus
AcS 3.574

Arguenon fl., perhaps
*arg- "silver" id. 1.
207, cf. Argellus,
Arganona insce.

Arh Fr. Arz, Art insula
(11th cent.), *arto-
"bear"

Arvor Fr. Armor, cf.
Aremorica

Assérac Gallo-rom. *Acir-
riacus cf. Aiserey
(Côte-d'Or), Azérat
(Haute-Loire), Azérac

618

Breton names

(Dordogne), Aziré
(Vendée; AcS 3.482-3

Aven "river." Cf. id.
1.9; W-P 1.46-7

Avessac Gallo-rom. (Aui-
tiacus from Auitius
-a, according to Hold-
er; Aueriacus accord-
ing to Stokes, cf.
Vassac; see Smith p.13)

Blañvoec'h Van. Blaùéh
(Fr. Blavet) from
*Blauitto- or Blaue-
tium; AcS 3.888, cf.
Loth RC 22, 1901, 88

Bran, Saint-Vran i.e.
Veranus (Bishop of
Cavaillon, Vaucluse)
has replaced the older
bran "crow"

Breiz Van. Breih, Bréh,
Fr. Bretagne, cf.
Brittones, Brittia

Briec: *Brittiacus from
Brittius, see AcS 1.
604, 3.970-1

Brignac (also in Hérault
and Maine-et-Loire):
*Brinniacus from Brin-
nius, -a; AcS 1.546

Brioc from *Brigaco- , cf.
Briavel (Glos.) from
Brigo-maglo- .

Broérec previously Bro-
Warach cf. †Veracius
(inscc.), Loth RC 43,
1926,424

Callac i.e. Callacus
(from Callus), repre-
sented also in Chal-
lex, Chaley (both in
dép. Ain), cf. AcS
3.1049

Campbon from Cambodunum,
found frequently in
Gaul; Do. 87, AcS 1.
714-5, 3.1059-60

Campénéac: Campaniacus
or *Campiniacus, cf.
AcS 1.722, 3.1065

Carentoir contains carant-
"friend"

Carnac from Gaul. Carna-
cus, which, as Smith
has rightly observed
(p.26), does not call
for a personal name
*Carnus (AcS 1.791,
3.1107-8), but rather
contains carn "heap of
stones, cairn." Cf.
καρνιτου (45 above)

Carnoët from *Carnetum,
cf. Carnac. In Latin
-etum normally is used
of areas designated
from flora (cf. uine-
tum, rumpotinetum),
but in Gaulish had a
wider usage (combretum
178)

Catvan, Kaouan Fr. Cavan
cf. Gaul. Catumandos,
AcS 1.858 (catu-
"battle," -mando-
"wise, skillful":
μαν υαν ω W-P 2.270-1)

Kemper, Van. Kimpér Fr.

619

Breton names

Quimper: from *kom-
"with" and bher-
"carry"

Keraez Fr. Carhaise, the
ancient Vorgium (dis-
tinguish Vorganium,
see Ac'h above); the
modern name, according
to Loth (RC 24, 1903,
288-95), stands for
ker- , car- "castrum"
and *agros (cf. Lat.
ager), i.e. "terrain
d'assez grande étendue"

Kerne, Van. Kerneù Fr.
Cornouaille. Cf. Cor-
nouii, Cornubii. As
Smith points out (p.
31), after AcS 1.1130-
1 and others, the name
is extremely ancient

Kerscao (Finistère), from
kéar, ker "castra" and
skaõ "scobies" (V.
Henry Diçt. br.); but
cf. ϲκοβιημ, not ϲκου-
βούλουμ 178 above (cas-
trum alni; castrum
Scotti which has been
proposed is impossible).
For the milliarium dis-
covered there (CIL 13.
9016) cf. CIL 13, p.
490. Cf. Escoublac
below?

Kervignac from Caluiniacus
or Corbiniacus?

Châteaubriant of which
-briant is to be found
in the widespread eth-
nicon Brigantes, Peder-
sen 1.100

Cohiniac earlier Cognuac,
perhaps from the same
form *Conniacus (AcS
3.1274) represented by
the name Cognac that
occurs several times
in France

Comblessac earlier Com-
bliciacus -ca (9th
cent.), which points
to a Gallo-Roman *Cam-
blicius, though the
source might as well
be Calmaciacus or Cal-
misiacus (AcS 1.713,
721; 3.1058 and 1.702-
3; 3.1050)

Condate now Rennes, at
the confluence of the
Ille and Vilaine.
From kom- "with" and
-da-ti i.e. -dha-ti-.
Cf. Condé, common in
modern France; Do.
104; AcS 1.1092-5.
There is a stream Con-
dat not far from Vannes
(Loth RC 28, 1907, 376)

Conmor cf. †Cunomorus,
Conomorus inscc., Greg.
Tur., uit. Gild. From
cuno- "high" (not "dog"?)
and -mor- "large"

Convelin cf. Cunobelinus?

Korle Fr. Corlay, cf. also
Corlay in Indre and
Saône-et-Loire. From
*Corelacum

Corseul the ancient capi-
tal of the Coriosolites,
who with the Osismi

Breton names

(Ac'h) and Veneti
(Vannes) divided wes-
tern Aremorica. AcS
1.1126-7

Crossac Gallo-Rom. Cf.
Crossac (Haute-Loire),
Croussac (Corrèze).
From Crossiacus and
that from *Crossius,
cf. Crossilius. So
Skok, followed by
Smith (p.41). AcS 1.
1203-4 had suggested
Cursiacus or *Curtia-
cus, but that gave
Courcy, Courcais

Darioritum on the site
now occupied by Vannes;
AcS 1.1241

Dinan i.e. din "fortress,"
Gaul. -dunum. See
Loth RC 33, 1912, 302;
Kaspers KZ 50, 1922,
155-7

Dinzak Gallo-Rom., Disin-
sac in 1387, Dinsinsac
1493

Drefféac Gallo-Rom., Smith
(p.45) plausibly sug-
gests that this name
stands, by metathesis,
for *Deruiacus, i.e.
it will contain *deruos
"chestnut tree." Cf.
Deruiacus, Deruetius,
Deruius, Deruonia etc.,
AcS 1.1271; Deruonnae
PID 1.320

Epiniac Gallo-Rom., cf.

Epagny (Aisne, Côte-
d'Or, Haute-Savoie),
Espagnac (Corrèze),
Epaignes (Eure). From
Hispaniacus according
to AcS 1.2055, but
Smith (p.48) has sug-
gested *Spiniacus from
spina (Lat.)

Eréac Gallo-Rom., Ariacus
cf. Héry etc.; AcS 1.
221, better 3.683

Escoublac Gallo-Rom. Sco-
piliacus, Scubiliacus
from Scopilius -a; or
(Smith p.49) *Scoplacus
from Scoplus (AcS 2.
1399, 1418)

Eusa Fr. Ouessant, the
ancient Vxisama. Cf.
Ac'h above, and (BSAF
1932, 163) perhaps
Exmes (Normandy) for
*Oximus; Do. 61, 67,
108, 112, 130, 295;
AcS 3.56-60, 67

Gervér. This modern name
has displaced the for-
mer Guedel, Guezel,
which came from the
ancient *Vidilis (mis-
written Vindilis) in-
sula, according to Loth
"visible," from *uid-
"see." Cf. Vendryes
RC 45, 1928, 387

Glénac Gallo-Rom. *Glan-
nacus, Glannac ca.
1330; cf. Glanna fl.
AcS 1.2024-5 (Glanum
80 above, Br. glann

621

Breton names

"border," Ir. glenn
"valley"). Cf. sq.

Glenan. Cf. Glénac above

Goëlo from *Vellauo- , cf.
Velay (Haute-Loire,
anc. Vellaui), and the
personal name Catuuel-
launus, -i

Gourin in the middle ages
Gururæn i.e. accord-
ing to Loth (cited by
Smith, p.56), for *uor-
Vorganium. But this
appears to confuse Vor-
ganium with Vorgium
(now Carhaix)

Guened Fr. Vannes, capi-
tal of the Veneti, cf.
Darioritum above;
AcS 3.159-67

?Gwiler Fr. Guilers, from
Gallo-Latin uillare
"hamlet" Loth RC 28,
1907, 375

Harnael contains hoiarn-
from isarno- "iron"
(233 below)

Henvic "old town," a hy-
brid (hen "old," and
Lat. uicus, whence
guic)

Herbignac Gallo-Rom.,
*Arbiniacus in Arbigny
(Haute-Marne), Orbinia-
cus (now Orbigny); AcS
3.658. But in the mid-
dle ages, the name was
written Irbiniac (Smith,
p.63)

Hernin older Hoiarnin
from Isarninos, isarno-
"iron" (233 below)

Hervé older Hoiarnovio- ,
cf. Hernin

Hoedic from Gaul. *Atica
(vulg. Arica), accord-
ing to Loth RC 10,
1889, 354; 22, 1901,
86; 42, 1925, 440;
AcS 1.263

Irvilhag Fr. Irvillac,
Gallo-Rom.; older Er-
meliac, which points
to *Armeliacus

Lan-dreger Fr. Tréguier,
probably from Tri-cor-
(i)i (80 above); cf.
Loth RC 44, 1927, 277,
AcS 2.1950

Langon. Since this name
is found also in Gir-
onde, Loir-et-Cher,
and Vendée, Smith (p.
73) conjectures that
it may be Gallo-Roman
in origin

Lantillac Gallo-Rom.,
Lentiliacus from *Len-
tilius, cf. AcS 2.184,
where Lentillac and
Lentilly elsewhere are
cited

Leo-traez Fr. Lieue-de-
Grève, contains leo
"league," leuga (178)

622

Breton names

Lohéac Gallo-Rom., older
Lochiacum (11th cent.),
Lohoiac (in 1101),
Loheauc (ca. 1330)

Loudéac Gallo-Rom., in
the middle ages Lodia-
censis pagus, presum-
ably *Laudiacus from
Laudius

Massérac Gallo-Rom., cf.
Maceracus AcS 2.367

Meillac Gallo-Rom., cf.
*Maeliacus, Miliacus
ib. 2.370-1

Mellac Gallo-Rom., cf.
Mellacus ib. 3.491

Ménéac Gallo-Rom., *Mani-
acus from Magnius.
The name Magny is fre-
quent, AcS 2.407. Cf.
Miniac below

Merdrignac written Med-
regnac c. 1330, Gallo-
Rom. For *Matrinia-
cus, cf. Marnay passim.
AcS 2.468

Mérillac Gallo-Rom., cf.
Marillac (Charente),
*Marilliacus, AcS 2.
428

Milizac Gallo-Rom., from
Miliciacus, also in
other parts of France,
AcS 2.585

Miniac cf. Ménéac above.
Written Méniac in Vit.
S. Machutis (1.84) and

hence from *Magniacus
or *Maniacus, though
*Miniacus has been sug-
gested; in the latter
case cf. Minay (Aube)
from *Minacum and per-
haps Mignault (Hain-
ault)

Missillac Gallo-Rom., as
if *Messilliacus, cf.
Messillus -a, Missil-
lus; AcS 2.575, 601

Missiriac Gallo-Rom.,
from Miceriacus, cf.
Miceriac (1130), AcS
2.582

Molac Gallo-Rom., *Mulla-
cum from Mullus, AcS
2.652, Loth RC 46,
1929, 162. Smith (p.
87) compares Moulac
(St-Jean-Brévelay,
Morbihan)

Morlaix perhaps a hybrid,
for mor- "large" and
-lais from Lat. laxus?

Mordiern according to
Smith (p.88) for *Maw-
diern, i.e. *Magu-
terno-s (-tigernos)
cf. Gaul. Magu-rix

Muzillac Gallo-Rom. according to AcS 2.664, from
Musuliacum

Nantes Br. Naoned, Van.
Nanned from the an-
cient Namnetes (179),
see AcS 2.677-81

623

Breton names

Nanton or Nançon or Nan-
son presumably Gaul-
ish in origin; AcS
2.687

Nivillac Gallo-Rom. *Neu-
illiacus (or Nou-),
cf. Neuilla; AcS 2.
780-2, 739

Noyal in 12th cent. Noial,
then Nuial, Noal,
Noyeal (the last dated
1433), from *Nouio-
ialos, AcS 2.790

Ouat Fr. Houat, formerly
Hoiata, the ancient
Siata (AcS 2.1537);
cf. Loth RC 42, 1925,
440

Ouessant: see Eusa above

Oust formerly U(l)to, Ul-
tum (9th cent.). Cf.
the modern Lot from
Vlta, Oltis (148 a-
bove); AcS 3.26

(Pays-) Gallo from *Gall-
auo-, see Loth RC 6,
1883-85, 115-6

Pennohen "caput boum"
(uit. Pauli Leonensis,
FHRC 234.32-33)

Plessé Smith (p.100) has
suggested a dubious
derivation from Lat.
plebs and *Seo, *Seuo,
cf. Seo below

Pors Liogan the ancient
Portus Saliocanus AcS
2.1309-10, which it-
self may contain the
Ligurian saliu-nca

Priziac Gallo-Rom., cf.
AcS 2.1044-5, Pris-
ciacus (saepe)

Québriac Gallo-Rom.,
*Capriacus from Cap-
rius AcS 1.761, 3.
1087. Cf. Chabrac
(Charente, Corrèze),
cf. W. gafr, OIr.
gabor: Lat. caper.
There is also an even
more frequent Cabiria-
cus from Cabirus AcS
1.665; 3.1025

Quédillac Gallo-Rom.,
from Cadiliaeus, Catil-
iacus, cf. Cadillac

Quistinic, Quistinnic
from older -it, Lat.
castanetum

Radenac, Redené Gallo-
Rom. *Ratinacus, from
Keltic *rati-n- "fern"

Rance Lat. Rencia or
Rentia, fluuius Ren-
cius, Rentius, Rinctus,
Rinctius (AcS 2.1190),
cf. W. rhinc "make a
noise, shout," Do. 89

Redon formerly Roton,
Rodon, modern also

Breton names

Rezon, Réon. Perhaps
not from ritum (AcS
2.1233), cf. Smith
p.111

Réguiny, older Regouiny,
Reguini, Reguyny,
probably Gallo-Rom.
*Ragoniacus (frequent
in Belgium), cf. AcS
2.1071

Réminiac Gallo-Rom. Ro-
maniacus, Rominiacus
ib. 2.1225

Renac Gallo-Rom., cf.
René (Sarthe), from
Ruiniacus, ib. 2.1244

Rennes Br. Roazon, Van.
Rochan, the ancient
Redones or Condate
Redonum see 179 above

Rican, Lanrigan may con-
tain ri "king." Cf.
Rien

Rieux has been compared
with the ancient Du-
retia (for this see
AcS 1.1379), but the
disappearance of du-
is difficult to explain

Rioc for *Rig-aco- (*rig-
"king")

Scorv Fr. Scorff. Loth
explained this as for
*ex-cor-mo "décharge"
(RC 40, 1923, 371-2,
427)

Scrignac Gallo-Rom., cf.

Scauriniacus AcS 2.
1397?

Séné Gallo-Rom., ancient
Senacus AcS 2.1466,
1482

Seo, for *Seųo, cf. sq.

Seoc *Seuocus; see Plessé
above and for *seua-
*sekụa 19 Remark and
180 above (Seua fl.)

Sévérac Gallo-Rom. *Seu-
eracus AcS 2.1531

Sévignac Gallo-Rom. Sa-
biniacus passim, ib.
2.1267-70

Silieg Fr. Silfiac, Gallo-
Rom., but not clearly
for Siluiacus (ib.
2.1564)

Sizun older Seidhun, cf.
Seduni or Sidonius?
Cf. AcS 2.1435-7, 1539-
43

Talensac Gallo-Rom. Cf.
Talentiacum, whence
Talencieux (Ardèche),
Talence (Gironde),
Talencé (Rhône)? Or
Tallentius? (Smith,
p.124)

Tinténiac Gallo-Rom., cf.
Tintiniacus (Tintigny,
Taintignie both in
Belgium) AcS 2.1584;
PID 1.112

tre- (cf. W. tref, Ir.

Breton Names and Divine Names

treb, Osc. triibúm),
saepe

singulative, not for-
mative; however, com-
pare the Io- forms in
personal names (e.g.
182 below)

Yffiniac, Yvigniac Gallo-
Rom. *Iuiniacus, cf.
W. ywen, Br. ivin "if;
yew," but not as yet
known from Gaulish,
and the W. Br. -n is

On St Yves (which
has no relation) see
the paper of Falc'hun
(Les noms bretons de
Saint Yves, Rennes
1943)

If any conclusion is to be drawn from these names, it would be that the Keltic of western Lugdunensis did not differ markedly from other Brythonic Keltic dialects, this when all allowance has been made for Breton influence, over and above the original Keltic (i.e. Gaulish) and Latin strata.

181   Divine Names

See in general Sjoestedt Dieux et Héros des Celtes (reviewed in EC 4, 1948, 155-59) and Vendryes Religion des Celtes (Mana 2, Paris 1948, 239-320). On the numen Augusti of Avallon (2891 sqq.) see S. Ferri cited in REA 35, 1933, 256.

Acionna 3063, 3064, 3065

Aerecura (E-) 2539

Albius 2840 and 11233,
perhaps the same as
Candidus and Loucetius
below?

Alisanus 2843, cf. 161,
178 above

?Amaranus

Amarcolitanus 2600, un-
less personal; but cf.
155 (Cobledu-)

626

Divine Names

?Anexₜlomarus 3190, see
notes ad loc.

Anual(1)os 11225-26 (Anu-
allonor[um?]); AcS 3.
638

[?Arnalia (Minerua) 5639]

[Arus num. i.q. Hercules?]

Ascafotorix fem. (cf. Andebrocirix pers. name 80
above), BA 1932-33
[1936], 35; RA 35,
1932, 145; RC 49, 1933,
306. Other names in
-rix that are feminine
are Aduorix, Bellorix,
Nantiorix, Tancorix,
Visurix. But what is
Ascafo- ? Hardly the
same as Ascapha fl.
(241), itself diffi-
cult. Note, however,
that the insc. was
dredged from the Saône
(ascus 220; Lat.
scapha?)

Atesmerius 3023, see nn.
ad loc.; and RC 38,
1920, 366

[Aufaniae matronae 1766;
cf. 223]

Baco(n) 2603, see nn. ad
loc., AcS 3.787-8, and
Remark below; note also
silua Bacenis 221 be-
low

Belenus num., Auson.;
FHRC 106.4, 225 n.5

?Belisamarus AE 1901.202
and 1913.234; RE 1,
1913, 95; cf. RC 34,
1913, 468; but the
text is identical with
that also read as in
the next item (per-
sonal?)

?Bel[latu]marus 11224

Bemiluciouis 2885, cf.
2886; (-g-?) cf. Lu-
goues, and see p.484
above, lug- (cf. 178);
BSAF 1890, 145

[Berecinthia AcS 1.402]

[?Bereno 2836]

Bergusia 11247; REA 10,
1908, 353, 361; 11,
1909, 255, 358. See
also 169 above; and
cf. local name Ber-
gusia (-ium) 80, Ber-
gusitanus (Narbonne)
from Bergusia in Spain
(Ptol.)? Bergussa 3285,
Berguiahenae 12014

?Bibrax (-acti or -aci
dat.) 2652-53; cf.
REA 4, 1902, 214; the
nom. may be Bibractis,
though not *Bibracis
(2652 add.)

Blanda 2486

Boluinnus 2899, 2900
(modern local name
Bouhy, Nièvre); cf.
also Boulianus (sic)
FHRC 278 n.11?

Bormana 2452, cf. Bormo,
Boruo with local names
(179)

Bormo 2805; cf. Eumen.
calentes aquae quoted
AcS 1.493,47; 3.642,
46-50. Cf. Aquae Bor-
monis 179 above, cf.
RA 21, 1913, 459; RC
er, 1913, 101; BSAF
1912, 401; CRAcInscBL
1912, 341

Boruo 2806, 2807, 2901

Brixantu (dat.? abl.?)
2812

dibus Cabi[or Cael[esti-
bus] 2457, see Remark
below and cf. local
names (179)

Camuloriga (or -i) 3460,
11216 (cf. 4709); un-
less personal; -rix(?)

Candidus 2901 (i.e. Lou-
cetius?); cf. Candiedo
2.2599

Caneton(n)essis, possibly
once Canetus (??),
3183.19-23

[Cassiciatis 3071; or
rather local?]

[?Catharus FHRC 296.27]

Cicollus (-ui dat., o-
stem, see ZfCPh 20,
1936,379), 2887; see
also EC 2, 1937, 28-
32; SprFK 197; to be

compared perhaps with
cicolus "tucus" (158
above); add 5479,
5597-5604 (Dijon or
the vicinity). For
the ending cf. Cocil-
lus (182) and Condol-
lus (237, 244)

Clauariatis m. 3020 (and
4564)

Clutoiθa 2802, 2895 (-da
for -ða), 2946; cf.
Stokes Academy 30,
1886, 210

Condatis AcS 1.1095.8;
REA 20, 1918, 254; in
Britain AcS l.c. and
AE 1938.113

Damona 2805, 2806, 2808,
2840, 11233

Donnia (Minerua) 3100.1

Dunacus(?) 2899, but more
likely -tis

Dunatis 2532, 2899(?);
or nom. Dunas? (Cf.
dunum 178, CIL 13, p.
249; not Dumias 150
above?)

Dunisia 1646

Eburnicae (matrae) 1765;
Yvours

Eolercus (Iuppiter?) CIL
13, p.444 (vit. S.
Peregr. ASS 16 May)

Divine Names

Epona 2902, 2903; AE 1939.
235 (Mt Auxois); REA
35, 1939, 411; FHRC
64.4 (Ἐπονα), 67.26,
69.7, 15 and 20 (ypona),
75.12, 86.5 and 11,
94.3, 115.16, 167.28,
182.25 (irrifa epona
nupsit illegy). See
pp. 541, 564

Erecura 2539

[Esus (H-) Lucan 1.445,
Schol., Lact. div.
inst. 1.21,3; cf. 170
(d) and local name
Esuuii; FHRC 47.24;
50.6 and 12; 51.18;
52.29; 55 n.12; 99.6]

Geniscus FHRC 196.26

Gisacus 3197; Gesacus AcS
1.2015; cf. local name
-um (179), and 212,
223 below

[?Gradiuus Sil. Ital.,
FHRC 60.8; in Spain
insc. RA 18, 1911, p.
211]

Grannus 2600

?Heusta 3023 (unless per-
sonal)

Icauna (or -is?) 2921 with
add. (-i dat.), cf.
βηλησαμι (57) dat. sg.
a-stem; REA 4, 1902,
214 (Yonne)

R]itona 2813 (see below)

Litauis 2887, cf. 5598-
5603. Cf. -litanus
in Amarco-, Bassu-,
Cobledu-, Smerto-
litanus (or -u-)?

Loucetius 3087; Loucius(?)
AcS 2.291

Mairae 2498; cf. 5478,
5622-23

Mabonus (-p-) AcS 2.414,
25-31; cf. W. Mabon
uab Modron

Madius (Maius?) FHRC 196.
28

[Mars AcS 2.442, 10-36]

Matrae (-es) AcS 2.466,
12-23

Mogetius (-c-) 11280

Moltinus 2585, 2878

[?Montiola 2861]

Moritasgus 2028, 2873,
11240-42; AE 1910.
121; REA 12, 1910,
285-86; as pers. name
BG 5.54.2; cf. moritex
(207). See RA 14,
1939, 140-44

Mulius 3096, cf. sq.

Mullo 3101-3, 3148-49,
cf. 3096-97; RC 18,
1897, 87-88

Divine Names

?Nerc[2889

?Nol[3103

Nonissus 2834

[Ratamatus AcS 2.1075; a
misreading of CIL 13.
2583]

Rit[ona] 2892, [R]itona
2813

Rosmerta 2831, 2876. Cf.
Loth RA 24, 1914, 205–
230

Rudiobus 3071; cf. Stokes
Academy 30, 1886, 210;
divine name Rudianus
(82). See also Soyer
Bull. géogr. 35, 1920,
1-16; Loth RA 22, 1925,
210-227; cf. 13, 1939,
241; RC 43, 1926, 471–
72; Sjoestedt Dieux et
Héros, 23 with n.2.
For the ending -bos cf.
Intarabus (Ent-) 213
below

Segeta 1641, 1646; cf.
local names and the
dea Segetia (Wissowa
RK ed.2, 201.9) on
coins of Valerian BA
1932-33 [1936], 96,
cf. 676

Segomo 1675, 2532, 2846;
cf. 5340 and CIL 5.
7868; REA 35, 1933,
411 (a new text from
Lyons)

Sequana 2858-59, 2860-65,
11575; Siquanna 2864;
cf. local and pers.
names; note dia S.
2864, doa S. 2863;
BSAF 1906, 309-311;
Drioux Les Lingons
nos.292, 297

?Serapis 3010 (cf. BSoc.
litt. et hist. de la
Brie, 3, 1903, 43)

Siannus 1669, for Stannus
(?), cf. 950, 953,
1536; cf. 158 above

Silan[3142 with add.;
or personal?

Siluanus 1640, 1779-80

Si..iris (dat. pl.)?

Sirona 3143, once written
Đ- (AcS 1.1286.44),
11243

Sol 2541

Souconna CRAcInscBL 1912,
677-680; REA 21, 1919,
111-112; 20, 1918, 271–
72. Cf. local name
(Sau-)

Suleu(i)ae matres 1787(?);
Sul]eis 2598

Taranis Lucan 1.446,
Schol.; see Heichel-
heim in P-W; FHRC 48.1;
50.7,13; 51.21; 52.30;
260.30

[taurobolium 1751]

630

Divine Names

?Tethios (Thoth?) FHRC
294.33

Temusio dea 11223. Cf.
Toutain, Cultes païens
3.304

Teutates (i.e. the tribal
god) Lucan 1.445; cf.
EC 4, 1948, 156; Rein-
ach RC 18, 1897, 137;
P-W s.v.; cf. Italic
Teutanes at Teuta
(Pisa?) "ipsum oppi-
dum" Serv. auct. A 10.
179 and 2.409 (quoted
FHRC 31.2-4); other
references in FHRC 35
n.8, 47.24, 99.6 (-en),
50.4, 51.16, 52.27-28,
266.32

?Trihianus BA 1913, cxxvi;
cf. REA 15, 1913, 446;
AE 1914.199; but perh.
for Traiano?

Tutela 10024.27, 11227;
AE 1916.123; REA 18,
1916,210; cf. 154 a-
bove and Tudella 179
above

Vcetis 11247, cf. 87
above; REA 10, 1908,
353, 361; 11, 1909,
255, 358; CRAcInscBL
1908, 498-99

[Vesta 1676, 2940]

Vicinnus 3150; cf. REA
28, 1926, 269; Roscher
s.v.

[Victoria 2874 (?); cf.
CIL 13, p.251
(Fuluia?)]

Virotutis 3185

Vm[? 2875, cf. above
157 Remark vii

[Volcanus 1676 (-k-),
3105-07, 3164]

deus patrius Votecuet[
3191; cf. Votepor-(?)
AcS 3.452

[Vssibus 3202, 3207; cf.
usibus 1376, 11151;
see 84, 155 above]

Remark:

In the above list of divine names the following are
worthy of note.

(a)   deae Souconnae ... oppidani Cabilonnenses

Divine Names

from CRAcInscBL 1912, 677-680 (cf. AE 1913.161; REA 15,
1913, 450; RC 34, 1913, 347; REA 21, 1919, 111-112; see
further L. Armand-Calliat "Le Chalonnais gallo-romain"
in Mém. de la Soc. d'hist. et d'arch., Chalon-sur-Saône,
27, 1937 [reviewed in RA 12, 1938, 143-144; REA 40, 1938,
411; Annales de Bourgonne 9, 1937, 323-326; Bull. Mon.
90, 1936, 333]; id. Catalogue des Collections lapidaires
du Musée de Chalon 1936, no.49; cf. J. Roy-Chevrier in
Mém.....Chalon-sur-Saône 15, 1928-29, 87-100, with the
reference to his earlier paper of 1913; Armand-Calliat
"Les Voies romaines du Chalonnais" in 11e Congr. de l'
Assoc. bourguinonne des Soc. Sav., Chalon-sur-Saône,
1934) since it gives us the ancient name both of the
Saône (earlier Arar) and of Chalon; see further P-W s.v.
Sauconna, Souconna, Suconna and compare the modern local
name Sagonne, le Sagonin (Cher); Drioux Cultes des Lingones 1934, 143; AE 1902.205.

(b) CIL 13.2457 (cf. 2462, 2467) has been rediscovered (see Perraut-Dahot "Autel votif de Belley" in
Mém. Soc. d'hist...Chalon-sur-Saône 16, 1930-31, 23-27)
and is said to read

dibus Cabi[| Camulia At | tica aram | posuit

(c) Most interesting of all is the

deus Baco(n)

of CIL 13.2603, giving us a Keltic bacon- "pig," possibly
pre-I.Eu. unlike porcus, sus; cf. the gloss baccones
"stulti, rustici" (AcS 1.323), unless there we should
read buccones (cf. blenni). But the word may be connected with Lat. fagus, so that Bacon- , Baccos (244), Bac-
co (ib.) will refer to the food (beech mast) favored by
swine. In that event -c- for -g- is more difficult to
account for, since we have bagon- also (see Hubschmied
RC 50, 1934, 254, W-H 1.863). Yet note silua Bacenis
(BG 6.10,5), from which it would be evident that Bacon
is the Germanic (not Keltic) form, but with ā not yet
become ō, cf. W-H 1.445, bagon- the true Keltic form (in

Switzerland); Bacon (?) appears also in Aquitania (CIL 13.557, if correctly read).

See further Blanchet "Le dieu Bacon de Cabillonum" in Mélanges Cumont (Annuaire de l'institut de Philologie et d'histoire orientales et slaves vol.4, 1936, 101-106), who quotes also ASS 5 Sept. 2.197 F. (AcS 3.787, 1022) atrium deui Baconis (near the Saône) as well as CIL 13. 557; Bacon as a local name (Lozère, Haute-Savoie, Marne); cf. Jullian HG 6, 1920, 57.4, 429.6, Forêt de Baconais (-es), (?)Bacchonius Onomast., baccones (leg. bucc-?) Du Cange (A.D. 831), French bacon; Jullian REA 4, 1902, 220.4; R. Lantier RGKomm., Ber. 20, 1930, 144-45 (Pl. 15); RA 18, 1941, 281; FHRC 294.3 with n.

(d) CIL 13.3071, a bronze horse, 0.65 m. high, on which is engraved

aug rudiobo sacrum | cur cassiciate d s p d|

seru esumagius sacrouib seriomaglius seuerus |

f c

This name, like Rudianos (divine name, Narb.) and other names connected with horses, has given rise to a good deal of discussion; see Loth RA 22, 1925, 210-227 (cf. RC 43, 1926, 471-472; NTS 1, 1928, 266); id. Mém. Ac. Insc. 43, 1933, 113-148 (cf. REA 28, 1926, 44); J. Soyer Bull. géogr. 1920, 1-16 (cf. RA 16, 1922, 373; RC 44, 1927, 406); RA 13, 1939, 137 cf. 241.

(e) Babelon and Blanchet Catalogue des Bronzes antiques de la Bibl. Nat. 1895, 710-11 no.2306 (after BSAF 1888, 255) report an insc. of unknown provenance

aug[usto sacrum | deo Vxello

in which augusto may be taken as a translation of uxello.

Personal Names

Abba

Abboneso 10024.308
  (Germ.)

Abbula

Abileia

Abillus

Abuccia 2058

Acastos 10008.5

Accauia

Acco BG 6.4.1

Acerranus 10027.4

Aclisianus

Acunus 2379

Acutia 2046

Acutibilus

Adb[

?Aditabb[1816

Adginnius

Admatius

Adnatus (ad-?)

Adonniccus

Aebro (cf. PID 3.2)

Aesarius Fortun.u.Germ.
  10.31

Aetitius 1647-48

Agedouirus

Agisillus

Affra 2237

Aibkixlis

Aiciognu(s)

*Aicus, Aegus AcS 3.526,
  (cf. Egus BC 3.59.1)

?Aido...oi[

Ainni (?)

Airocus

Αἴτετος IG 14.2534

Aiunete..lio

Albillius

Alcus 10017.121

Alexio 2161

?Ali[AE 1910.122

Alibill[us

[Alpinus 1922, 3198; Ale-
  pinni 11234, cf. 2829]

?Aludisas

Ambaci 10024.346

Ambiorix

[Aminorix]

Amitius

Ammatiacus

Personal Names

Ammilla, -us

Amnius

?Ampudius 3173

?Anc[h]iarius 2058

Andangianius 2945 (or local?)

Andi[10027.104

Anθaricus

Andarillu 11263

Andecarus 10025.188

Aneχtlomarus

?Annatus

Annausonius

Antia 2050

Antullus

Aper 1998, 2033, 2979, 3035.30

?Apidius 1815

Apinosus, -ossa

Apinula

?Appa 11226 (apparator?)

Appianus 1727

Appriculus 2709

Apriclius 1978

Apricus

April[2892, -lla 11276

Apronia 2831, 3226; -ius 2500, (Treuer) 1911, 11179; cf. CRAcInscBL 1904, 446

Aproniana 2285, -us 2912, 3226

Apsilla 2702 add.

Apurina 2641

Ἀραγε (νου ?), see Note xxxii(b)

?Ararum (acc.) 2070 (local name?)

Arborius (Auson.)

Arda 1632

Ardonixa

†Arerimus

Aresco REA 16, 1914, 292; Dipl. 133 N.

Areus

Argicius (Auson.)

Argiotalus 6230 (Namnis)

Argutus

[Arimundus 2454]

Ario 10001.48

Ariscula

Arti (Atti?)

Artilia 1937

Personal Names

Artillus

Artius

Aruca

Aruescius

Ἀσχάνδιε πάτεϱ IG 14.2525
(not divine!)

Ascius 1728 (Norbanus)

?Aspetius (Masp-?) 2147

Assule

Assutalus 10006.8

Ateχtus 3017

Ateilius 1834

[Asunna 3051]

Atepomarius 2066a, 3067,
cf. Stokes Acad. 30,
1886, 210; -rus 3242;
cf. ps-Plut. de flu.6

Ateporico 10006.8

Ateruos

Atesmerius (or divine)
3023; Atesmerti 10017.
182; 3080

Atessatia, -ius

Atesmertus

?Atesmerus; cf. RA 12,
1920, 152

Ateurita 11205; AE 1912.
46

?Aθaricus

Ἀθήλεινος, Athelaini (Syrian?) IG 14.2532

Ἀθηνάω

Atilia 1835, -us 10001.
52; 10002.112ff.

?Atoarianus 2833

Atobiles

Atratinus 2452 (for
Atract-?)

Atrianus

Attianus 2536; AE 1946.
101

Attilius

Attillius

?Attin[2500 (divine?)

Attiolus, -a

Attius, -a

Atto 1837

Aucilius 2453

Aucius

?Aucissa 10027.107

†Audoenus 3098

?Auedo 10029.258

Aueseude AcS 1.313

[Aufustius(?) 1649, -ia
1753]

636

Personal Names

?Auirho

Auitus, -a 2510, 2606,
  2828, 2899; 10024.
  354; 10030.12

Auitelu

Auitia 1839

Auitilla 2831

]auorix 3185

?Ausona 2489

Ausus

Autricu[s] p.473 add.
  (cf. 179); but it is
  clearly local here too

†Bacauda 2797, cf. gloss
  178

Baccus 8318

†Baldaridus 2473

Baliario (not Da-) 2598

?Bangn[

Barbiana 2049

Barmasi 10002.126

Bassa 2059, 2518; -us
  1857, 2309

Bastel[(Guernsey) CRAc
  InscBL 1920, 425; REA
  23, 1921, 336

Belatullius

?Becnic[

Belenios, -us, -a, (-in-),
  chiefly on terra sig.
  but cf. gloss (178)
  and IG 14.1801

?Belgis[1687

Bellatu 2697

†Bellausus, Bellosa

Bellicoria 11275

Bellic(c)us

Bellicus 10029.11

Bellinus, -a

Belliolus

Belliosa

Bellius, -ia

Bellosa, v. Bellausus

[Bellouesus]

Bellucana 10002.8

Bemai 10010.2976

Benagius 1854 (Βεναγιος IG
  14.2526)

?Berenus 2836 (or divine?
  Or read Vertanus?)

Bertouinnus 3155

βηρουσ|ηρωμια AcS 1.409,24;
  BSAF 1883,252

[Besius (Viromanduus)
  1688]

Betta 10024.316

Bettonius (V-?) 1913, cf.
  gloss 158

Betuuius 2271

?Bililio 2647

Bill[2908, Billia 1756

Billicca 2555

Billiccatidossus 2541

Billicatus 10003.4

*Billicus 10021.94

Biracus

Bisillus 2848; BA 1932-3
  [1936], 627

Bittia, -ius

Blandina 2687

Blandinia 1983

Blandius

Blandus 1911

†Bodocnous (du Cleuziou
  A.N. 2,92)

Bodua 2853, -os 10027.109

Boiiorix 2656

[Bolanus 3161]

[Bononius 1833]

Borillus 2727

Boruias 2913, cf. Boruoni-

cus 10025.146; AcS 2.
  201,48; BA 1908, 163

Boudia 2699, cf. 174 above

[Bradua 1751]

[Brasius (Treuer) 2012]

Briccius (or -tio) REA
  25, 1923, 151-52;
  ASS; Sulp. Seu.

Βριτόμαρις or -μαρτος

Buolanus (Vol-?) 3183.7

Budacus 10022.47

Burco 10024.178

Burda 10024.362

Caburus(?); cf. 10003.28;
  BG 1.47.4; 7.65.2

Cabutius

Cacilionus

Cacuronius (Treuer)

Calissus 2471

Calter (or -trus) 2463

Caesiccia

Cale[2045

Calenus 2805

Calgacus 10025.161; cf.
  Tac. Agr. 29.4

[Calocaerus 1825]

Personal Names

Caluisia 1904

Caluius 1941

Caluonius

Camaelia AE 1946.101

Camilia 2531

Camilus

Cammius 2700

Camolatia (-u-) 2701

?Campranus 2262

?Camula 2526, 2530

Camulatius 2618

Camulia 2457, 2462, 2467

Camulogenus BG 7.57.3

Camulognata 3183.1

Kaninia 2007

[Κανω θωῖος (Canotha) IG 14.2532]

Cant[3097 g-h

Cantius 2046, 2555, 2557

Cape[

C]apilla 2702

Capillus

Capito 1942

Capril[ius 2652

?Carania 2886

Carantianus 2090. On Ca-
ranto- etc., cf. CRAc
InscBL 1890, 260-263

Carantilla 2936

Carantinus 3183.4, -a
1838

Carantius 1689, 2090,
2525, -a 2089, 2886

Caratuccus 10006.22

Caratus 3081

Carabella

Caricus 2161

Carnutenus 2010; cf.
local names

Carpus

Carugenus (-c-) 2913,
cf. 10027.24

Carussa

†Carusa, -us

Caruti[10008.19

Cassa 10006.20

Cassianus Greg. Tur. gl.
conf. 73

Cassiola, -us

Cassia, -ius

?Castauricia 2039

Castinus AE 1911.25

?Castro 2463

Personal Names

Casuatb[3035.9

Casurinus 1632

Cateri? 2847 add.

?Catia 2467, 2094, -ius
    1985

Catianus 11240, AE 1910.
    121; Greg. Tur. h.Fr.
    1.30

Catidia

Catilla 2245

Catiola 1860

Catonianus 2833 add.

Catta 2455, 2704(?)

Cattea (Catta?) 2704

Cattia 2287

Catu[2576, 10022.79

Catuganis 10017.270

Catulianus 2983

Catulla 2141

Catullinus 1691, 2705

Catullia 2095, -ius 1691

Catullus 2165, 2494

Catulus 3116

Caturcus (-d-) 10027.78

Caturicius 1741

Catussa 1983 (ciuis Se-

quanus), 2983

Cauarillus BG 7.67.7

Cauarinus ib. 5.54.2

Cauda 11254, MSAF 1904-5,
    252

?Caune[2668; Caunus
    10022.61

Caupiola 2292

Caxtos 10010.2930

Celadus 1850

Celadianus 1850

Celianus 3043

?Celtinus 1632

?Cento

Centusmia 2191

Cepula REA 15, 1913, 187;
    AE 1913.124; Byvanck
    2.649

Cerinthus 2969

Cerpus FHRC 167.2,12

Ceruidia 1801

Cerulus 10008.5

?Cettinius (Celt-? Cret-?)
    1632

Ceur[2838

Cextis 10010.2965

Chaudos 10010.2954

Personal Names

Chleuuia 1882 (Clh-
lapis; signo Vinuco,
i.e. Belgic [Sinuca
natione?]?)

Ciarinus 2765

Cicarius 2394; Cicaro
(or -us) on terra sig.,
cf. gloss 178 (Petr.
46.2, 71.11); Cigetou-
tus (Aquit.) on terra
sig.

Cinci 10022.63

Cinto 2525, 2553

Cintonnus

Cinnamus 1996

Cintusmina, -ius (cf.
10021.38)

Cintusmus 2575, -a 2567

Cinu[2707

Cinuralu 10013.6

Cirrus 2968

Cissorina 2641

Ciuttius (Cl-?) 2187

Cl[   ] 2581

?Cleiola

Clheuuia, see Chl-

Clo[10001.366; AcS 3.
1238

Clumarius 2157

Cluttius, see Ciu-

?Cnoditu (sc. conditu[m])

Cnusticus 3199

Cobrūnus 2084

Cocilianus (?) 2840;
Cocillus 11233

Cocillus 1632, 2840 (cf.
11233)

Cocio 11279

Coco[2907

Cocuda 10010.2947

?Codonius RE 1, 1913, 95

Cogitatinius 1797

Coicus 3183.1

Coinnagius 2449

Colona 3017

Comatul[lus, or [la 3083

Combaromarus 3183.7

?Combudouatus (-uc-?)
2583; or divine name?

Co[ ]s[2979

Cominius 2831, Cominos
BA 1932-3 [1936], 627

Comma 10003.28

Commuos 10010.2906

?Comnianus

Personal Names

Conconnetodumnus (-gon-)
   BG 7.3.1

Con.i.rou[2578

Condianus

Connia 1988, 2522, 11218;
   -ius 2113, 11218; cf.
   REA 22, 1920, 215; AcS
   3.1274,45-51

Con(n)imarc[AcS 3.1273;
   Germ. 7, 1923, 16

Connonius 2902

Contedoius 2843

Contestus

Conuictolitauis BG 7.32.
   4; 33.4; 37.1; 39.2

Cor[

Cora (?) AcS 1.1114,26

Corbilla 2001

Cordacio 289

Cordonius AE 1901.202;
   1913.234; RE 1, 1913,
   95

[Corisilla]

?Corsui AcS 1.1138,32

Cospellus (-peitus?) 2539

Cossia 2945

Cossutius 1852

Cosuobnus AE 1922.14; Pro
   Alesia 1922, 130; REA

26, 1914, 84; or di-
   vine name?

*Cotta 10021.72

Cottius 2180; Cotius 11269

Cotuatus

Cotus BG 7.37.4; 33.4;
   39.2

Criciro 2837, -u 2642,
   Crigiru 2711

Crispos

Crixsius, -ia 2117-18

Croca BA 1913, v; cf.
   REA 15, 1913, 446

Cuccei 10022.84

Cucula 2575

Cupari[3104

Curdalus (-o?) 2578

Curuelius 1853

Daccius 10025.34

Dacotoutus 11268

Dagomari 10022.152

Dallario 2598, but Datia-
   rio add.; or divine?

†Dananta 2480

Dan(n)ius 2120-21

Dannus 11268

Personal Names

Danu 2712

?Dap(i)ado 10027.277

Dapssa 2989

Deccius 2122, -ia 2122-23

Decimanus 2008

Decinia 1990 (Sequana)

Decirius 3183.19-20

Decmilla 1990

Decminus 2847, -a AE
   1935.14

Decmius, -ia Decmiola AE
   1946.101

Demincilla (-ilia) 1947

]demuco 2953

Deuia

Dextrius 1758

[Dialis 3163]

Dianta 3091

Didius (Leucus) 2955

Dioratus CIL 8.1876

Diuiciacus 2081; BG 1.3.5;
   num. AcS 1.1262

Diuicus(?) 2095, cf.
   10001.115

Diuiχtus 1991 (Sequanus),
   2531, 3220, 10021.144,
   10025.140; -a 10026.44

Docirix 3183.24

?Donis 2302, Donis[ia
   AcS 1.1306

Δοννίξs RA 1872, p.59;
   10017.76

Donnius 2570

?Douec[2925

Douiccus 2136

?Douiocus 2254

Draccius 2564; 10027.22
   cf. draucus, Draucus,
   Draccus (ter. sig.),
   like alacco : alaucus

Drappes [BG] 8.30.1

Draucus 2564 (dr-?), cf.
   gloss 158

Driburo 1985

?]drienu 2715

Dripenni 10010.2967

Drippi 10010.2917

†Droct[ebodes?] 2389

Dromacius 10024.316

Drusaco 10010.2941

Druta m.

Dubnorix, Dumno- , -reix
   BG 1.3.5; cf. num.177

?Δουλκιῆ(ος) IG 14.2531,
   Dulcitius 2070, 2194.

ctd.
    (On this and similar
    "soubriquets," e.g.
    Viuentius AE 1912.46,
    see H. Wuilleumier REA
    36, 1934, 467-72)

Dumnacus [BG] 8.26.2

Dumnorix, v. Dub-

Dunaus 11262; BSAF 1905,
    358; 1906, 256-57

Dunnius 2129

Duronius, -ia 3092;
    10021.221

Ecaminus 2847 add.

Ecori 10024.191

Ecusi 10010.2975

?Edias 1737

Egnatius dipl. 133 N.

?Einodegiugo 2446 (or
    local name?)

Elafia 2172

Eldruda FHRC 167.2

Elisa(?) 2984

[Elitouius]

(E)latussio? 2802, cf.
    2946

?Eluasso 10020.17

Eluentinus (Fl-?) 2046

[(H)eluius cf. 83 above]

(H)eluetia 2980

(H)eluinius, -ia

?Ennodius

Epaticcus 3183.21; cf.
    212 below

Epedextorix 3064; cf.
    141 above

Epiu 2716

Eporedirix 2728, 2805

Eporedorix BG 7.38.2;
    39.1

Eppius 1678, 1692

Equas(ii?) 10025.53

Esugenus 10027.194

Esuggius

Esumagius 3071; cf.
    Stokes Academy 30,
    1886, 210

Esumopas 3199; Mon. Piot
    31, 1930, 23-38

Esuo[2643

†Eunandus 2481

Euposius 1730

Euoiorix 2530; cf. num.
    239 below

Excingus 2613

Exomnius 1854; IG 14.2526

Personal Names

[Faenius 1776]

?Fenochea

Flacilia

Fl[auius] REA 15, 1913,
    187; Byvanck 2.649

Fredebodus 2816

Gabrilla 2977

[Gaetica]

G(a)esatia

[Γάλατος]

Gallinaria dipl. 16 N.

Gallius 2846

Gallonius

[Gargenus]

Gatisius

Gauius 2148

Gauillius 3042

Geminianus 2975

Gemma 2975

Genetodia 2975

Gentius

Germ[10025.142

Germanilla 2052

Germaninus 2052

Germanissa 3183.17-18

Gessius 1897

Giamillos 3075

Giaucus (Gl-) 2136

?Glgua (Olg-?) 10023.7

Gnata 2915

Gordus (Bononius) 1833

Grania 2151

Grani[ani] 10029.107

Gugua (Ga-?)

Gundis 10024.319

[Habro 2606]

[Hermidius]

?Heusta (-o) 3023

Iaccus 2977; cf. AcS
    2.5,30-40

Iallus 2905

Iarcia 2723

Iarulilus 2631

Iarusci[2950

Iassus 11227; AE 1916.123

Ibetius 10025.188

Ibliomarus 2091, 2839
    (Treuer)

645

Personal Names

Iclius 2911 add.

Icomius 10010.2948

Icotasgus 2902 (or two
  words?)

Idroillus (-gil-) 2844

Ignia 1953, -ius 2070

Ignus 1953; cf. Iginus on
  terra sig.; 10029.120,
  122

B]illicedu 10010.2976

Il(1)iomarus 1988, 2724,
  3063

Inthatius 1954 (Min-?)

Intinca 3179

Ioenalis

Iomaglius 3071

Ioncior 10010.2900

]iopu[2319

Iotacabo 2829, 11234
  (divine?)

?Ippateius (Pat-?) 2978

Isatia 1887 (corrupt?)

Isatt...us 10006.139

†Ismaimalla 3099

?Itacus lib. 1800

Iuati 10024.191

[Iulius Vindex cl.]

Iuimarus (Iuu-?)

Iumileius

Iurincus 2507

Ixisoncitis 2731

?Labella 2459

Laepic[3193

Lanius (or L. Anius or
  Ianius?) RE 1, 1913,
  95

Lannoberga 10024.322

Lantrudes 11281

Lart[1725 (Larttitiola:
  probably two words)

Latinianus

Latius

Latussio 2802 (Elat-?)

Laura 2546

Laurina 2523

Lautius 2603

Lea AE 1946.101

?lectri 3087 (i.e. Cambo-
  lectri, 80 above)

Lentinus

?Letba[2583

Leubacius (-a eius?)
  10024.323

646

Personal Names

Leucus 2955

Leuicus 10001.391

Leuponius 10025.146

Leutachi 3029

Licerius (Luc-) Greg. Tur.

Licinius 1698-1700

Licoidi

Ligurus 3091

Lilli 10028.4

Liomarus 2615

?Liruni 10010.2976

Liscus BG 1.16.5

Lisoui 10010.2965

?Litauat[us 10006.90

Litauiccus BG 7.40.7

Litauus 2010

Litorius (episc. Tur.)

Litugenus 2581, 10001.
   182, 10027.117; -a
   11275

[Litugius]

Litussius 2946, cf. 2802

Liuius

Loiiusus (?Lot-) 2960 add.

Lollon[10022.199

?Lopecenos 2378

Λοῦκις 10002.305

Lucceia 3123

[Lucensis 1961]

Lucilla 1824, 10022.272

Lucinus 2453, 2645 add.

Lucretia IG 14.2533; cf.
   -ius (Campanus) 1959

Lugiola 3043

Luminatus; BA 1932-33
   [1936], 627

?Lupercus 3183.24

Lupula 1830, -us 1846

Lupus 1992, 2006, 2011,
   2037, 2874

?Luselam 2734

Lusenos (-serios?)

[Lutatius CIL 13, p.473
   add.]

Lutea 1872

Luxuris, Λούξουρις 1916,
   IG 14.2528

Macacos

Macciiu[

Maccius 1833, 10017.547

Macena 10010.20; -us CIL
   2.5304

18

Macianus (-g-); BA 1932-33 [1936], 628

Macidula 2010

Macrina 2014, 2015; -us 2186

Magilius 1676, 1687, 2940; cf. Magillius AcS 2.376

Magiusa 3143

Maglius 1701, 1867

Magneius (-er-?) 1650

Magninus 3229

Magus 2698

Magusatia 2278

†Maisrinus 2415

Maiumilus (-el-) 2864

[Maiurus]

Mallo 3123

?Mamaga

Mame[3035.11

Mamma 1827

Mandu[2349

Mansuetus 1868, 2012, 2735, 11269

Maos (Μᾱος ?) 2857

†Marcellus

Marcia 2202

?Marcussus 2528

Mariccus Tac. H. 2.61.2

Mariola 1650, 2864

Maria 1650, 2014, 2015

Mariorum 10029.136

Marlosama

Maro 2567

Martialis 3161

Martinus 2025a

Martna (-in-) 2955

Marullianus 1731

Marullus 1807

Mascel[

Mascellio 2249

Maspetia 2016; cf. Maspeti 2147 (?), if not for M. Asp-

Massa 10010.2929

Massia 2309

Mastonia 1706

Materilla

Materna 3163; on the authenticity of this insc. see REA 12, 1910, 197; 2009; cf. AcS 2. 470,43

Matia 2205

Personal Names

Matinus 2560

Matisoni 2206

Mato 2583

Matronia 2009

Matruso

Matta 2867

Mattius 1761

[Mattonius (Tribocus) 2018, (Germanus) ib.]

Matucia 2207

Maturcus 2846

Maturus 2017, 2153, 2565

Matussius 2555, 2558; cf. 2491

Maurusius BSAF 1909, 179

Mecacus (-eg-) 3232

Meda[tus]

Mediannus 2895

?M]eduillus

Megarus 3233, but cf. Megacus

[Melanio 1729]

Melior 1690

Melissus (-dd-), -a

?Mellobo[di 2801

Mellior

[Memmius 2272; -ia 1811, 1975, 2209]

Mercon[us 2851; BA 1932-33 [1936], 627

Mercullo

Merula 2279

[Messala 1647-48]

Messianus 1992

Messorianus 2075

Messorius 1849, 2742

Metilia 2019, -ius (Treuer) 2029

Mettius 1873, 2214

Metucus

Miccio 2259 (or Micciola?)

Mindo[2743

Mina IG 14.2528

]minius 1992

Minna 1916

Minnuo 2760

Minthatius Cong. Arch. Fr. 1935 [1936], 580; cf. CIL 13.1954

Minucia 2744

Minurio 10006.59

Minuso 1948, 2120-21

Mocetes 11280 (cf. div. names)

Personal Names

Modius 2216

Modso[2746

Mometus 2984

Mominto 2770

Μώμορος ps-Plut. de
  flu. 6

Mon[2829, 11234

?Monna 1893

Montiola 2861 (divine
  name?)

Moricus

Morinus BA 1914, 392

Moritasgus BG 5.54.2; cf.
  REA 16, 1914, 324-28
  (divine name)

Motucus

?Mouerta m. Fortun.

Muccasenia 1874

Mulionis 3097

Mulsus 2738

Murra[2219, Murranus ib.

Murrius 2547

Mutacus 2646

Mutilus 2583

?Naaurmia f. 2093

Nama 2356

Namatius (episc. Aurel.)

Nametus 2987

Nameria 2220

?Nanto, see AcS 2.685

Nau[10027.275

?N]auius AE 1910.122

?Nebrigiac[10006.63

Nennus 2559

[Neratius cos. A.D. 70,
  1675]

Nerrus

?Nertes

Nertinus 2222

Nertius 2223

Nertomarus 2751

?Neru (Nurei?) 3097

Niaos 2857 add.

Nicetius

Nico 1939

Nitiogenus 10006.63

Noil[2783

Nonnicius

†Nonnusi 2420; AcS 2.
  759,52

650

Personal Names

Norbus 2463

Norbaneius 11225

Nosonius 3196

Nouellius 2020, -ia 2748

Nouius 3171

Nunnichius Greg. Tur.

Nunninus

Nunnio

Obellius 1738

Oclatia 1892

Ocusius 10023.12

Oχtai (gen.) 11240; AE
   1910.121; i.e. Oχtaius
   cf. AE 1925.98

Oledo

Olia 2224

?Olibiat[ic]i 10023.13

Olillus 1670

[Omulus 2841 add.]

]onmus 3010

Onixi[3125

Opilio 2359

Oppius 2225; AcS 2.862,42

Orgetorix 3024; AcS 2.875,
   30; cf. W.u.S. 11,
   1928, 47

Orgius 1992, 2608-09

Orum(i)us 10010.2940

Osidius 1702

Otacilia 1643; REA 31,
   1929, 259

?Otrimus 10001.408

]ouano[2850

?Ouondibulus 1970

Paccius 2045

Pama 1701

?Papianus 1913

Patteius (Ip-?) 2978

Pauillus

†Πεκτόριος IG 14.2525

Perrni[1739

Peruia 2853

Pessicinnus 3114

Petanius Gaz. des B-A
   1937, 185-86

Phorci 10002.446; cf.
   CIL 12.5683,276

?Piauonius (imp.)

Pilagus 3092

Piscina 3202

Pistillu 2868, cf. terra

Personal Names

?Resteoris 2754

Restiola 2092

Reticius (episc. Augus-
todun.)

Ricianus

Rictus 10002.427

†Riculphus 2484

]riga 3080

Riotamus Sidon. Apoll.;
Iord. Get. 44.237

Ripc[2753; Ripcicnus
11262, BSAF 1905, 358;
1906, 256-57

Rit[2892

Riunda 2022

?Riχtius 3035.50

Rocco (late authors)

Rottalus 2555

Rottio 2104

Rousonia 2281

Roχt[alus] 2755 with add.
(or Roχta[ni?, Roχtu-
[genus?), cf. Roχtano-
rix 11269 (BA 1904,
cxxxiii; ?Roχtai BSAF
1905, 358; 1906, 256-
57

[Rufus 1776]

?Rullinus 1768

Runatis (gen.) 3183.8-9

Runnui 10001.2952-53

Rusonius 1970, 2251, 2257

Rutio (Rutto?) 2576

Ruttonia 2018

Σαδδου (Sati) IG 14.2532

Sabaricus Fortun.

Sabbatia 2076

Sabellus MSAF 1904-5, 252

Sabiuli 3097 m

Sabius 2761

Sacco 3129, 3183.27

Sacconius (Mediomatricus)
1807

Saccra 2611

Sacer 1924, 1936, 2222,
2516, 2634, 2716,
2761

Saciro 2762-63

Sacirata 2494

Sacrapo 10029.8 (cf. 6;
13a)

Sacrillos cf. Note xxxvi
Remark above

Sacrobena (-nn-) 2533

Sacrouir cl., 3071; cf.

Personal Names

Stokes Acad. 30, 1886, 210

Sacruna 2028

Sacuria 2646

[Saedii 1759]

?Sagila

Salica 1692

Salon(ius); cf. AcS 2. 1328-9

Samilla 2095

Samius 10006.81

Sammia 2257, 2514; -ius 1751

Sammiola 2514

Sammo 1765

Samorix 2615 (Remus)

Sannitillius

Sappiena 1763

Sappossa 3045

†Saraga 2374

Saruscus

Saserus 2912

Sassius 2699; AcS 2.1373, 41

Satia

Satigenus REA 35, 1933, 411; AE 1939.235; AcS (Merov. num.)

Satria 1824, 1888; Satr[BSAF 1933, 198; 10029. 170-172

Sattia 1870, 11175

Sattianus 2035

Sattiolus ib.

Satto 1761, 2035, 2259, 2762; 1984 (Treuer); 10006.19; 10017.763; 10029.169

Sattonius 2259; -ia 2195

Satugenus 10024.271

Satus, Σαύδος 2248

Saχsa 2765; on Decidius Saxa (Hisp.) see JRS 27, 1937, 127-37

Saχsamus 2881; Saχxamus 2766

Scopono 2631

Scorobres

Scottus 2589

Secco 2947; 10022.232

?Secula

Sedatius 2099, 3106; -ia 2264

Sedatianius 11224; RE 1. 1913,95; AE 1901.202; 1913,234

Sedatus 2618, 2706; AcS 2.1429

Sedianus 2151

Sedius 2492; -ia AE 1939. 21

Sedulius 2625; Fortun., Greg. Tur.; -ia 2625

Sedulus 2625

Seg]om[arus] 2803

Segonius Pard. Dipl. 358 (Fleury)

Seia 2265

Selanus (Seia-?) 3204

Selia 1796; -ius 2266

Senaucus 11222

Senecius AE 1939.21; -io 10029.86

Senicio 3229

Senilis 1984; 10003.11

Senillus

Senilos 2770

Sennia 2029; -ius 2029 (Treuer), 3162, 3225, 10021.169

Sennus 2095 (or Sentrus?)

[Seno 3225 (Puteolanus)]

Senodius 3168

Senognatus 3017

?Senouarinus 3086

[Senonius 1676, 1684b, 2675, 3067, 6484; AcS

2.1499,33, 37-38]

Senno 11222

Sentru 10017.789

?Sentrus, see Sennus

Septumanus 2031

[Sequanus Greg. Tur.; Siquana 2367, -nn- 2864]

Seriomaglius 3071

Serotinus 2286

Σεδηρον εύς ps-Plut. de flu. 6.4

Seuio...uiotius 2559

Seua 3228

?Seuinus

Sexauius IG 14.2533

Sico 11203

Siduo 2681b

↑Siggifledis 3099

?Sig(u)dunus

Silanius 2522

Silanus 2021

Silenia AE 1935.17

Silic[2006

Silicia 3147

?Silicnuni

Personal Names

Silius 1852

Sill[ianus?] 2949

]sillin[2852

[Siluius]

Silluuius (v.l. Simil-
    limius)

Similinus

Singu[2615

Sintuciso 10003.72

Siora

Sipurus, -a; cf. 10024.27

Siquan(n)a, see Sequ-

?Smercatus 2741 with add.
    (Merc-)

Smertulitanus (Namnis)
    6230

Smertullus 2876; REA 22,
    1920, 211

?Σοεν|νιλα AcS 2.1597,17

Solicia 2200

Solimarus 3037

Solinus 2274, 2928

Solirix 3095

Solito

Sollicius 3139

Sollemnius REA 35, 1939,
    411; AE 1939.235

Sollius 2560, 2274 -ia
    2560; cf. Sullias be-
    low?

Sonnius 1995

Somonius 2645 add.

Sosandris 1811

Sopatius AE 1935.16

Sosus 1993

Sotullianus 3103

?Spenis 2120

?Steiani 10002.481

Στερκορία [Γαλλιξ] Le Bas-
    Waddington 3.2036
    (Rouen); CIL 13 p.
    543 and add. p.512

Suadugenus 2751

Suadur(i)x BSAF 1912, 401;
    cf. CIL 12.2714, 13.
    5378; Germ. 21, 1937,
    248

?Suaricia 2775

Suarti 10010.2973

Succo 10010.2982

Suillius 3202

Sullias (or local?) cf.
    175 above

Summa 10006.89

Sunilena, -ius 10008.5

†Sunnouira 3159

Personal Names

[Sunucus 2647]

Super Byv. 2.649

Surio 1791

Surtilla 2115

Surilla 2775 add.

Surus [BG] 8.45.2

Suttia 2279

[Suts|sa(?); spurious?]

Syagrius (Su-)

Tallonius 1896

Talusius 2241

Talussius 2570

Tapurus 2552

Taranutius 3083b

Tasgetius BG 5.25.1-5,
   num.

Tasgillus 2581

Tatirius AE 1922.14; Pro
   Alesia 1922,130; REA
   26, 1924, 84

Tatto Greg. Tur.

Tauren(i)us 2429

?Taurentius (L-) 10025.

Tauri[2211

Tauria AE 1935.15

Taurianus 2976

Tauricianus 1709

Tauricius 1709

Tauricus 1698, 1700,
   1709, 2039, 3197,
   3096

Taurino (-us) 2039, 2249;
   AE 1935.15

Taurus 1709, 1988 (Treuer),
   3239

Tautissa 10017.836 (Tout-
   ib. 849)

Tecessi 10006.91

Teθθilla 3161

Teladianus 1850

Teponia 2946

Terpalinus 3244

Tertinius (Treuer) 11200

[Tetricus num., 3035.23;
   cf. Esuuii 179 above]

Theudora 11210

Thallus 11225

[Tiburia 1887]

†Tigridius 2799

Tilande[2600

Tincius 1922

Tipurinius 2028

657

Personal Names

?Tironius 3241

Titiconius 1904

Titiola 2537; AE 1935.15
cf. Lartia 1725?

Titos 10013.22

Tittius 1632

Titulcianus 10025.104

Titulla 2220

Tituri 10027.124

Tossa BA 1932-33 [1936],
35; RA 35, 1932, 145
(cf. CIL 6.26620)

Toutedo 11205; AE 1912.46

Toutia 2285, 2286

Toutilla 3101; -issa v.
Taut-

Toutius 1972, 2286, 2704

Toutona 2014

Toutonius 2287

]trichi[2910

?Trihiano BA 1913, v; REA
15, 1913, 446. Or
divine name?

Trinonus 3095 m.

Tritius 1683

Tritogeno[

]ttusco AcS 3.49,41

Tuoticius 3017

Turbelius (Guernsey) dipl.
16 N.; CRAcInscBL
1920, 425; REA 23,
1921, 336

Turonus 1703, 1716, -nn-
3231 add.

Turranus 2033 (Treuer)

?Tuseius 2673

Tutellus 2572

Tutinatia 2146

Tutus 1691, 3183.15-16

Tyticus

Va.rua 1991

Vagirius 1900

Valetiacus BG 7.32.2;
num.

Valgia 10022.272

Vallo 1925

Vapiladi 10010.2976

Varacius 2778

Varenius 2037

Vario(nis) 10002.524

†Vassio 2363, 3172

Οὐάστα 10017.81

Vasto 2463

[182

658

Personal Names

Ve..pie 2780

Veaio 2779

Vebrullius 11237; Vebrul[
    BA 1932-33 [1936], 628

[Veldumnianus cos.A.D.
    272; N.266]

Velitius, -ia 2300

Vellauus 3240

Velleius 2301

Venantius 2302

[Venetus 1709, 2777]

Vennonia 2057

?Vepia 2780

Veranus 2600

Veratius 1988 (Treuer)

Verce 3017

Vercondaridubnos Liv.
    per. 139; cf. Ven.
    (PID 32a)
    ver·ko·n·zar·na

Vercus 2600

Veretus 2803

Verianus 2837

Verilla 2781

[Verna 1663, 10029.312;
    but cf. REA 23, 1921,
    110, 129 (read Seuer-
    ina)?]

Vernacellus 10002.527

?V(e)rnutas 2883 add.

Vertano 2837

?Vertros[10003.67

Veruco

Vescendus

Vesonticus 2038; Veson[
    10022.279

Ὀυγοπκ[10017.82

?Vianicus 2010

Viattius?

Viccius 10027.186

Victricius (episc. Roto-
    mag.) CIL 13, p.569

Vienna 1956

Viducius 11270

?Vierui 3097o; for ieuru?

†Villancius 11209

?Villaorix 3179; perhaps
    read Vlidorix?

Vindama 5646; cf. PID
    2.196a

Vindex cl.

Vinduro 10006.111

Vinicius 6876

Vinnia 2100

Personal Names

Vinuco 1882

Vintidia 2305

Vinusilla, -us, -ius
2517

Viperius 1856

Vippius 2306

Vireia 1973, 2568

Viri..lo[2758

Viridomarus BG 7.38.2

Viridouix ib. 3.17.2,
Οὐιριδοουιξ Dio Cass.
39.45.1

Viriodu[360*

Virotutus 2010

Viscarius 3183.17

Vithannus, -ia 1858

†Vitigliscus (Vil-) 1657

Vittulinus 2506 (Sumelo-
cennesis)

Vitullus 2506 (Sumel.)

Viuenciolus 2396

Vlati 10027.127

Vlattius 1711, 1926,
1974, 2712; -ia 2518

?Vlidorix, see Villa-

[Vlpius 1826]

]οὐν[10017.90

]υνοὐκιης 10017.91

Voccilus 2634

Voliaetti 2832

Οὐογιτιωυ 10017.83a-b

Volusius 2675

?Vostrus 3180

Οὐρακ[10017.84

Vrinata 2697

Vrittia 2961, -ius 10002.
533; for uritu?

Vrogenius, -ia 1975

Vrogenonertus 1907

Vrsicinus 2428

Vrsina 3033

Vrsio 1901, 2057

Vrsula 1904, 2945

Vrsus 1703, 2365, 2281,
†2370, 3022; -a 1884,
1888, 1896, 2195

?Vruspa 3210

Vsius 3244

?Vspirniol[us AE 1946
[1945].70

Vssedati 2706 (cf.
uχsedia, Ven. Vpsedia)

]ussinus 1999 (C]ussinus?)

?Vteruus 3097

660

Personal Names

Vuistrimundo Greg. Tur.; AcS 2.1753,52	]uxassoni[2309
?Vulidiutus 3097p	[Zotilus REA 14, 1912, 199]

Addenda and Corrigenda

Preface (page 2)   Copies of CIL 13 v (1943) have
                          now begun to reach this country (2
                          May 1950).

In item 79   s.v. brisilis add AcS 3.945; W-H
                          s.v.; cf. brittola 220 below.

ib.   s.v. (para-)ueredos add cf. ZfRPh
                          54, 1934, 197.

Note xxiv   add trigarius (CIL 13.11085), un-
                          less the correct reading is the per-
                          sonal name Arrigarius?

Item 158   s.v. *calmes add cf. M-L Einf. 242
                          s.v. milimindrum add cf. 178 belinuntia?

Page 530   transpose Cabil(l)o and Cabiatus;
                          transpose Cantiori and Cantinorus.

535   place Virlus below Virioru

557   for Vidu-caθis read Velio-caθis
                          and add cf. cassi(s) 177

559   bes is of course "bis" and can
                          have no connexion with the gloss bessus
                          (246)

Belgica

Germania Inferior

1950

The name Belgae was applied at its widest extent
to the people living in the territory stretching from
the Rhine almost to the Seine; and archaeologists find
traces of the same people even as far as the Loire,
but they use the name in a different (cultural) sense,
and are concerned with a different era and with a different problem, all of which may be ignored here.   In
the eastern portion of this territory there were several tribes of "Germani" living among them, the portion, roughly, afterwards set apart by the Roman imperial administration, as Germania inferior.   It was,
in fact, not easy for the ancients themselves to distinguish there between Gauls and Germans in physical
appearance or in customs.   There are some tribes on
the west side of the Rhine that are definitely named
as Germanic (cf. Prolegomena 35), and the eagerness of
the Nervii and Treueri to be reckoned with them, as
reported by Tacitus (G. 28.4), sometimes interpreted
as falsifying the claim, unquestionably had a basis of
fact (see J.G.C. Anderson's note to Tac. ad loc., 1938).

Conjectures as to the etymology of Belga: A. Carnoy Le Muséon NS 14, 1913, 309-321; O'Rahilly Proc.
Brit. Acad. 21, 1935, 328 once more would connect it
with Ir. fir bolg (on which cf. Pokorny ZfCPh 11, 1917,

189-204). As for bulga: μολγός (βολγός ?) see PID 2. 183, 430. For the pers. name Bolgius, Belgius see AcS 1.384; add Belgius and Belgis[ius?] CIL 13.1165, 1687. That the name is Keltic may not be doubted.

On Belgica and the Belgae in general see PW 7. 651, Grenier Mnl 1.134-136; E. Rademacher in Ebert RL 1, 1924, 390-93 (Belgen) and 393-406 (Belgien); Pliny NH 4.105-106. I have not seen J. Breuer La Belgique romaine, Brussels 1944 (CW 38, 1944-45, 111); or these war-time publications of which I learn from APh 18, 1947 [1949], 203-206: Dhondt Frontier linguistique, Ant. Cl. 16, 1947, 261-86; van Kalken Histoire de Belgique, 1946; Tourneur Les Belges, 2 vols. 1944 and Bull. Beaux Arts (Acad. Belgique) 1944, 66-84; R. de Maeyer De overblijfselen der romeinsche villa's en Belgie, Gent 1940 (90 Aflev. Fak. Letteren), cf. RA 23, 1945, 180; three important catalogues of the archaeological collections in the museums of Ghent, Brussels, and Luxembourg are noted in Ant. Cl. 8, 1939, 235-36.

The work of H.G. Moke La Belgique ancienne et ses origines gauloises, germaniques et franques (Gand 1855) is now antiquated.

On the question of the frontier and the Belgic limes see Whatmough Archaeology 2, 1949, 91-94; Faider-Feytmans in Mélanges Marouzeau 1948, 161-172. For the later frontier: L. Roger (and E. Gamillscheg) ZfFrSpr 63, 1939-40, 1-41; L. Bieler RhMus 86, 1937, 285-87 interprets cliens in Ausonius as colonus with reference to the mixed German and Keltic population of the Moselle valley.

But we now reach another crucial case, like that in Aquitania, in which to test the meaning of the ancient tradition. For in language the distinction must have been marked once the first Germanic sound-substitution, which began not later than the fourth century B.C., had produced those most characteristic changes by which

Belgica

Germanic is set off from all the neighboring I.Eu.
tongues. Even the fragmentary evidence of proper
names is enough to suggest a difference of "dialect"
between say the colonia Augusta Treuerorum and the
col. Copia Claudia Augusta Lugdunum, a difference
which is traceable elsewhere in Belgica (even in the
restricted sense), and becomes much more marked in
Germania inferior. Contrariwise certain tribes (e.g.
the Atrebates, Ambiani, Bellouaci) seem to have been
little affected, linguistically or culturally, by the
German influx, which may be supposed barely to have
touched them. We shall have to try to note distinguishing features in dialect; and also to determine,
approximately at least, the ancient linguistic frontier; cf. my paper in Word 5, 1949, 106-115 and further (below) on the relative stability of the frontier.

We have the testimony of Caesar (BG 5.12.1; cf.
Tac. A 11.3) that Belgae had invaded Britain from Gaul,
and the appearance (c. 75 B.C.) of the funerary rite of
incineration, and of "Belgic" urns, in southern and
eastern Britain confirms and dates this migration. Archaeology also reveals a much older movement, in the
third century B.C., and in the same direction, attested

by La Tène remains in Britain, of people who presumably also spoke a Brythonic variety of Keltic.   There
is no linguistic evidence, or no unequivocal linguistic evidence, to sustain the theory, advanced by Rhys
and more recently by Diack, that they had been preceded in Britain by a wave of Goidelic-speaking invaders.   So far as the historically recorded Keltic dialects of Britain may be taken as partial evidence of
the nature of the Keltic dialect spoken by these British Belgae and their Keltic-speaking predecessors,
something may be deduced concerning the dialect spoken
by their kinsmen in Gaul, and in particular, by the
Gaulish Belgae of Gallia Belgica.   It is necessary to
believe that British or Brythonic Keltic (Welsh, Cornish, Breton) represents in part the dialect of the
Belgic invaders, and that any Keltic dialect already
spoken before their arrival in Britain, if not absorbed, was not notably different from it; that is to
say on the assumption that this argument (of comparison of "Belgic" with British) is to be counted valid.
But taken the other way round, the argument would appear to be valid.   For in fact, comparison of the British dialects with the Gaulish at large (for example,
and it is a critical comparison, in the numerals), would

seem to indicate that the latter, the Belgic idiom included, were essentially one and the same with the former. So much is stated by Tacitus (A 11.4: sermo
haud multum diuersus); and our conclusion is borne out
also by the remains of the dialect of the Belgae, a
few brief inscriptions and the usual crop of proper
names and glosses, with the reservation only of Germanic influence, wherever it appears mingled with the
Keltic remains.

Cf. G.C. Dunning and R.F. Jessup Antiquity 10,
1936, 37-53 (with the map at p.40) for another link
between Britain and Belgica, of later date. In no
event do the Belgae appear to have occupied more than
about one-sixth of the area of the British Isles
(Childe), but their Keltic-speaking predecessors spread
far and wide throughout Britain. Comparisons of ethnica such as Atrebates (Brit. and Belg.), Parisii (Brit.
and Lugd.; their capital in Britain is Petuaria, Brough-
on-Humber) are familiar; add now Coritani (Leicestersh.,
Lincs., Notts.) if they came from the Marne (Felix Oswald, Ant. Journ. 21, 1941, 323-332) cf. Καρ(ύ)τανοι
Ptol. 2.11.6 in the agri decumates (if, as is likely,
they had retreated thither, cf. Tac. G 29.4), note Cor-:
Car- (?). In CIL 7.712 C.E. Stevens (Arch. Ael. 4th
Ser. 11, 1934, 138-145; cf. AE 1934.282, and on curia
see REA 36, 1934, 481) now reads curia tex| touerdorum,
but the text is quite uncertain; I conjecture that the
true reading is Texuandruorum or the like. If so, we
may have an ethnicon that derives from Germania inferior (cf. 221 below). The statement reported by Tacitus
(G. 45.2), that the language of Britain and of the
Aestii (on the Baltic) was nearer akin (propior) than
that of the Aestii and Germanic is difficult to interpret, unless it means that British (Keltic) and the
Baltic dialect of the Aestii sounded equally unlike
Germanic to the traveller whose observation Tacitus

recorded (cf. Anderson's note ad loc.); it cannot, in
any event, refer to an Italo-Keltic prototype as Jullian (REA 19, 1917, 133) proposed; after all Bede HE
1.1 brings the Picts from Scythia. A few Keltic items
have somehow made their way into Baltic lands. Thus
Finnish has tarvas and Esthonian tarw from taruo-s
"bull," and the Finnish luode "north-west" may be the
Keltic ledo, liduna with the ō-grade (see 158 above).
A recent summary account of the prehistoric invasions
of Britain may be found in A.H. Williams Introduction
to the History of Wales 1941, 26-27 (cf. 38-39, 45
and for Latin words in modern Welsh pp.61-62).

See, for example, the criticisms of H. Zimmer Auf
welchem Wege kamen die Goidelen vom Kontinent nach
Irland? in Abh K.Preuss Akad, Ph-H Kl, Berlin 1912,
Abh. 3, pp.1-59 (reviewed by Vendryes RC 33, 1912,
384-87). As for Diack's contentions (e.g. Scottish
Gaelic Studies 1, 1926, 12-13), see the negative statements of Fraser (e.g. ib. 2, 1928, pp.172-201 or 5,
1938, 71) or the inconclusive remarks of Childe, Prehistoric Communities of the British Isles 1940, 250-
263.

For a Belgic city recently excavated see R.E.M.
and T.V. Wheeler, Verulamium (Reports of the Research
Committee of the Society of Antiquaries of London 11,
1936), with the criticisms of J.N.L. Myres (Antiquity
12, 1938, 16-25) and Wheeler's reply (ib. 210-17).
The coins (Wheeler 224-27) with uer (uir, uerl, uirl,
uerlamio) | tasc, tascia; dias, deas; cuno(b)elini;
tascio[uanus, tasceouantis, all found in these excavations (as well as elsewhere), like the names to which
they testify (Verulamium, Tasciouanus, Cunobelinus)
and other familiar names (Cassiuellaunus, Commius,
Tincommius, the last perhaps also in Mon. Anc. 6.2,
CIL 3 pp.788 ff.32.2, cf. Sandys Num. Chron. 1918, 97,
together with Dumnouellounus, v.l. -bellaunus) manifestly indicate Belgic settlers or their descendants.

Belgian scholars, notwithstanding the essential
correctness of their assertion that the Belgae spoke
not Germanic, but Keltic, are apt to be uncritical
and to minimize Germanic evidence, out of national
pride; e.g. J. Feller "Quelle langue parlaient les
anciens Belges?" in La Vie wallone 1, 1920-21, 241-47;
289-300.

Belgica

The boundaries of Belgica in the days of Caesar, not to mention free Gaul, were both more and less extensive than those set up by Augustus, or in later centuries; more extensive, since they enclosed the Caleti and Veliocasses, afterwards joined with Lugdunensis; less extensive, since they excluded the peoples south of the Ardennes as far as the Heluetii, all of whom belonged to that part of the "Celtica" of Caesar which we associate with the name of Lugdunensis. But these latter, at first joined with Belgica by Augustus, were most of them afterwards separated once more, to form Germania superior. If we use the later geographical subdivision for its greater convenience (cf. Proleg. p.22), we must not let the geographical label "Germania" lead us to expect necessarily Germanic dialects in those territories. Coligny, with its Keltic calendar, lies within Germania superior as established under the empire. The two Germanies, after all, were military and administrative areas within an older and larger Belgica; and so far as the linguistic evidence goes the influence of Germanic is both more extensive and far more clearly distinguished in Germania Inferior than in Germania Superior.

Belgica

But the linguistic frontier throughout the ages
has been for long periods of time relatively stable
(see above; with 212 bis Remark 2 below, and the Introduction to Germania Inferior); it pushed forward
west of the Rhine, then it was checked or pushed back
once more, and for a time stabilized, but hard to define with precision, in Roman times. In some measure it
agrees, or attempts are made to make it agree, with
political frontiers, especially since the end of the
Roman empire. Actually, and quite apart from the
question of the infiltration of Germanic speech into
Belgica and the two Germanies, the ancient administrative frontier between these three territories is at
several points a matter of dispute and far from being
certain or clearly definable (cf. CIL 13 p.702, and
the more recent arguments of E. Linckenheld REA 34,
1932, 265-87 and 387-410, à propos CIL 13.5989, 5922,
11645-46; id., "Les Limites de la Belgica et de la
Germania en Lorraine," Extrait des Mémoires de la Soc.
d'Arch. lorraine, 1932; cf. Germania 15, 1931, 38;
H. de Weerd Ant. Cl. 4, 1935, 175-189; cf. J.E. Dunlap,
"Tribal Boundaries in Belgic Gaul," CP 26, 1931, 318-
321; on CIL 13.5942 see below, introduction to Germania
Superior). In this admitted confusion, I decided to

stick to the divisions made by the editors of CIL; fortunately it makes little difference for my purpose.

There is a good account of the formation of the
Belgic people and of their migrations to Britain by
C. Hawkes and G.C. Dunning ("The Belgae of Gaul and
Britain") in Archaeological Journal 87, 1930, 150-
335. "It is known" they write (p.154) "that part of
what became the province of Gallia Belgica was occupied in V-II B.C. by the great La Tène culture of the
Marne, while in the north of it a degenerate form of
late Hallstatt culture lingered on among the marches
of the northernmost Celts and the Germans who were
moving down from the north-east. Finally a German or
partly German influx swamped the old Marne culture,
and produced a mixed civilisation, in which cremation
was practiced and the immediate prototypes of the
Aylesford pedestal-urns were made. This characterised
the Belgae whom Caesar found and conquered, whose German blood it was that differentiated them from the
rest of the Gauls." Again (pp.175-76) "the middle
Rhine...was invaded by the Germans in the middle or
later part of III B.C. ...Of course, what happened was
that the two races fused. As there was no further

racial dislocation in this district before I B.C., it
was clearly this fusion that produced the tribe found
there by Caesar and brought by him under Roman rule.
This tribe was the Treueri.... Their racial formation
was thus effected in III B.C., [but] we have to wait
another century or more for that of the true Belgae...
The same half-century is marked by a fresh arrival of
Celts from northern Gaul in Britain." For this reason, as well as on account of the invasion of Britain
by Belgae c.75 B.C., and of late refugees (e.g. Commius, king of the Atrebates), it is often instructive
to compare British items with those of Belgica, and a
few such have been admitted in the lists that follow.

The formation of the Belgic stock thus had been
completed before 113 B.C., when the incursions of the
Cimbri and Teutones begin. The above account of it
agrees with information supplied to Caesar (BG 2.4.1-
2), and the linguistic evidence does not contradict
it. We have material essentially Keltic, with an infusion of Germanic, that tends more and more to be
absorbed unless fortified by new support from more or
purely Germanic regions. But the survival of archaic
types of pottery at Bavai is hardly to be connected
seriously with the possible Keltic inscription recorded

there (183 below), and the large number of settlers from various parts of the Empire inevitably obscures, after the romanization, traces of both Keltic and Germanic speech.

Cf. T.D. Kendrick and C.F.C. Hawkes Archaeology in England and Wales 1914-1931, London 1932, chapter 10 (The Early Iron Age), 153-208. There is a brief summary of the archaeological situation in Belgium proper by de Loë, Catalogue...Musées royaux à Bruxelles: Belgique ancienne, vol. 3, 1937, 4-46. Those whose interests need it, must pursue new discoveries in the journals (often of small local societies, cf. the list in REA 14, 1912, 409-410). For the romanization, see F. Cumont, Comment la Belgique fut romanisée, 1914. Compare also the summary in Hawkes and Dunning, pp.321-324. V. Tourner Les Belges avant César (Acad. royale de Belgique, Bulletin de La Classe des lettres et des Sciences morales et politiques, Sér. 5.30, 1944, 66-84 (a reference, which with the next three I take from Ant. Cl. 13, 1945, 142 and 190-191); on the Belgic limes ib. 28 no.12, 1942; E. Saccasyn della Santa La Belgique préhistorique, 1946; G. Deneck Les origines de la civilisation dans la Nord de La France, 1943.

A movement from Brittany to south-western Britain has been detected (Antiquity 13, 1939, 58-79); it is, of course, independent of the migration from Belgic territory (ib. 7, 1933, 21-35).

Inscriptions of Tortequenne and Bavai

Note xxxviii

CIL 13.3534-37, graffiti on stones ("pierres friables") found at Tortequenne (Pas-de-Calais), each beginning with the word locus or loca, except 3537, which apparently has

loka clesuilitorum

and each showing names, commonly taken as local (e.g. 3534 Caseberesis), with -e(n)sis; but some of the names are certainly personal, and in 3534 Flauiensis is derived from a personal name. Is it possible that locus, -a (loka) is used in the sense of "burial place"? Cf. lokan PID 2.339(a)7.

183

The authorities on terra sigillata have not yet determined the place at which Belgic wares bearing the inscription

uritues cincos

(or simply uritues) were produced. Their distribution is not extensive (Boulogne, Bavai, Andernach CIL 13. 10010, 2097; Weisenau 10017, 839a; Ebernburg, south of

Inscription of Bavai

Kreuznach, Westd. Korrbl. 23, 1940, 135; Titelberg in
Luxemburg, Germania 22, 1938, 238; uncertain origin,
TrZ 8, 1933, 122).   There is a variant uritos recorded
from Colchester (Antiqu. Journal 18, 1938, 270) and
the stamp Euritus f (CIL 13.10010, 871 also read Euretus,
Furitu(s)?) has been compared.   Hence it is held that
we have two names, Vritu(s) and Escingus (Ex-), cf.
Oswald Index 1931, p.346.

But there is something to be said in favor of
reading uritu ("fecit," cf. karnitu, luritu, ieuru)
Escingos, cf. Note xix(b) above, possibly eurises 171b.
For we have a stamp cinge fecit (Bar-le-Duc CIL 13.
10010,564), which Oswald (Index p.77) interprets as
Cinges(s)us of Westerndorf. Cinges(s)us, however, is
not recognized by the editors of CIL, and I suggest
that in cingesus and in euritus we have garbled versions
of escingus and uritu es respectively, f being added
to the latter through sheer misunderstanding, just as
uritu gave place to fecit in the Bar-le-Duc stamp and
es was overlooked and lost. If so, the true reading in
all these would be uritu escingus (-os), preserved completely only in the Bavai specimen.

This specimen unfortunately is now lost. I sought
it in vain at Gussignies (on the Franco-Belgian frontier) in 1929, and attempts to trace even then the collections of former owners of the Château de Gussignies,
said to have moved to Hazebrouck or to Lamballe, were
hopeless. In 1880 Mowat (CRAcInscBL 1880, 250-60) re-

Inscription of Bavai

ported this "assiette" (9 cm. diameter, the stamp in
the centre of the foot) still at Bavai, Bohn in 1901
(CIL l.c.) at Gussignies "ap. de Moras." Mowat's account is, therefore, still important; u in line 1 is
√, in line 2 both n and g are upside down.

Those who interpret uritu as a name may compare
Vrittius (10010,2096), Vritius on an occulist's stamp
RA 26, 1927, 168; Puy-de-Dôme), ουριττακος (33 above),
Vritto and Vrittius at Nîmes, Vienne, Bordeaux and
elsewhere (AcS 3.42), Vritea (Grenoble, ib.), if not
with Eurus (Bavai, AcS 1.1484, probably mis-read);
those who take it as a verb may appeal to ieuru and
eurises, and (for -tu) to luritu(s), karnitu(s).

Loth (cf. Do. 301 n.3) interpreted uritu to mean
"coxit," and more recently Thurneysen (cf. SprFK 214)
is said to have interpreted -urito- in Ate-uritus as
"inuentus," cf. Rituarus (176 above) if to be read
u]ritu ar(uern)us, see JCS 1, 1949, 10; but (es)cinge
fecit seems to be decisive, cf. d'Arbois de Jubainville
ap. AcS 3.42-43, Mowat and Stokes cited in CIL 13.10010,
2097; Do. 56.

Remark:

(a) For the graffito of the La Graufesenque type
found at Bavai, see p.280 above.

(b) CIL 13.3579, on a stone "dont la partie supér-
ieure porte un cartouche"; found at Bavai, and read
inhani or inahni (with Λ a) is possibly Latin; but nh
is noteworthy.

Inscription of Arras; AVOT

(c) For the names of potters who may have worked at or near Bavai, see 194 below.

184

On a bronze octagonal ring discovered at Arras, similar to those of Reims (185-6), Thiaucourt (188), Alzey (Note 1), and Windisch (Note 1v).

ise | car | rua | ≫ xa | ≫ac | sbxxu. | sao

CIL 13.10024,292

Note xxxix

The form auot (on which see Note xi above) appears in Belgica on terra sigillata, e.g.

(i) Vallée Saint Denis (Oise, ager Bellouacorum)

]os au(u)ot

RA 39, 1901, 242 no.54 (AcS 3.781)

Inscriptions with AVOT

(ii) and with the following names, viz.

Acutios auot

Bito auot

Bollo auoti (Trier)

(CIL 13.10010,35,316,335; cf. ib. 337 Bollus fic[it],
Bolli man[u];

Buccos auotis

Casa auo(t)

Citos auo(t)

(ib. 362 Ghent; 468 a Bavai, b Trier, presumably a
potter of "East Gaul" Cas(s)atus, cf. Oswald's Index
pp.63-64; 10010,582 Metz)

Durucu auot

(ib. 834 Trier)

Inticilu au(ot)

(ib. 1035 Trier; also reported, with auot, from Lavoye)

? Orti auo(t)

(AcS 3.880, cf. 3.781,2, Reims)

(iii) alone

auot

(Trier and elsewhere, CIL 13.10010,248; this appears
to have turned up at St. Albans, see Wheeler Verulamium, 1936, 176, where it is given as otau or uato)

Inscriptions with AVOT

(iv) As for the legend asauo on vases of Bavai
(Pro Neruia 2, 1924, 208, cf. RC 46, 1921, 105), and
on a pin found there (Pro Neruia 3, 1927, 357), this
is surely to be read (cf. Oswald 24)

as(iaticus) auo(t)

though Asiaticus (Oswald ib.) is described as being
"of Lezoux;" the reading asauo f (CIL 13.10010,176),
if not an error, implies a confusion between auot and
fecit (cf. 183 above), for in 10010,178 we have Asiaticus fe(cit).

See, in general, CIL 13 iii, 1 p.121 (cf. fasc.
2, p.465); and Notes xi, xxxvi above.

(v) Finally, we have, also from Bavai, a stamp
reading

ateiati|ulioau

(i.e. Ateiat[us?] Iulio[s] au[ot]?); see Pro Neruia 5,
1929, 23; cf. 202 Remark below, uoati, read auoti?)
The item Duru iu (10010,833) if correctly read is especially instructive; for beside Dura (-o) auot, i.e.
Duratus auot 830-31 (Lezoux) it suggests a Duro, -a
(i.e. Duratus) ieuru beside auot (or Duracus auot) and
thus gives ieuru, auot "fecit" like uritu (in uritu
escingos, aruernicus) "fecit." Cf. JCS 1, 1949, 10.

Note xl

(i) It is worth calling attention separately to
CIL 13.3460 (Suessiones) dea|cam|lori|geuo|tum, since
the forms dea and camlorige are presumably dialectal,

Miscellaneous Inscriptions; Reims

the former (with dat. meaning), the latter dat. (e
for i), not miswritings of deae and cam(u)lorigae, as
the editor of CIL l.c. would have it; for -rix fem.
cf. 181 above, and for dea dat. see Word 5, 1949, 112.

(ii) The reading of CIL 13.3467 (also Suessiones)
is far from certain; line 1 appears to be locu [(cf.
Note xxxviii above) or loce[, followed in line 2 by
]nii[or the like, then, in line 3:

locan χuicnin ??

(or, at the beginning, docau-?). Chuic- looks Germanic.

185

On a bronze ring, formerly in the Museum at
Reims, and thought to have been found in the vicinity:

uedzuidiuuognauixuuioni

The third letter was perhaps r; "nomina Celtica

(fortasse uocabulis Celticis inmixtis) uidentur" Bohn,

CIL 13.10024,291; cf. BSAF 1907, 227.

Inscriptions of Reims

186

A similar ring, discovered in 1907 at Reims (in an ancient cemetery, faubourg de Laon), heavily oxidized, so that the reading is uncertain at the places marked:

adepiccade. acnuaumaumuixio

After de possibly f (?); and before the doubtful m, the form of u is given as Y . Probably we should divide de(u)acnua (cf. diuuogna in 185), and uixio (cf. uixuuioni also in 185). Cf. Atepiccus 7.1325.

BSAF 1907, 228

187

Also on a ring, discovered in 1895, at Reims (la Fosse-Pierre-la-Longe).

      ]axu[   ]ax[   ]aldici   ??

in which a is ∧ , u is Y .

BSAF l.c.

Remark:

(i) In the insc. discovered at Reims and published

Inscriptions of Reims

in BSAF 1922, 226 (cf. REA 25, 1923, 383; RA 18, 1923,
388) d m │ Ruson · Nonnae │ Maianus · Primi │ cassidar ·
coniu│gi · etsibi· u · p the editors have seen cassidarius (cf. ND Occ. 9.36 Remensis spatharia); but unless the reading can be verified, it is permissible
to suspect the well-attested cassidan(n)us (see Note
xli below).

(ii) A fragment from Reims given in CIL 13.3335
is said to read]ibroii with which we may compare
brogilus, breialo (79, 178); and in 3418 we have (as
proper names)

Tartos │ Banui

in which Tartos, if a variant of Tritos, Tertius, gives
us the unusual (dialectal?) ar from r̥; comparison with
Osc. trutom "quartum" (cf. Brugmann Grds. ed. 2 vol.
2 ii 54) is not excluded (*tur̥tos).

(iii) For coins of the Remi with ulatos see 206
below.

(iv) Audollent no.107 reports a fragmentary defixio from Durocortorum, said to read doubtfully

illi   ul   otiillca   ?

Inscription of Thiaucourt

188

Dottin's "conservée au musée de Bar-le-Duc," no
doubt echoed from Rhys p.57, and his failure to refer
to CIL 13.10024,164, led me on a wild-goose chase to
Bar-le-Duc in 1929 in search of the octagonal gold
ring discovered c. 1884 at Thiaucourt (Meurthe-et-
Moselle) in a field along the road from Metz to Naix.
All that was ever preserved at Bar-le-Duc is a plaster
cast (which I did see), like the one at St Germain-en-
Laye; the original is reported in 1906 to have passed
into a private collection at Paris. The small size
of the ring (inner diameter 0.625 in.) suggests that
it was intended for a lady's finger. On the eight
sides,

adia | ntun | neni | exue | rtin | inap | piset | u ⟨⟨⟨⟨

in which a is ∧ (except possibly ∧ first letter) and
most letters have slight finials.

Do. 55; Bohn ASA 26, 1924, 86-88

Abecedarium of Lavoye

189

A complete alphabet, described as Gallo-Roman of the fourth century, appears graffito "a pointe seche, après cuisson" on the outside of a shallow dish ("plat") 32 cm. in diameter, 8 cm. deep, base 11 cm. deep (the letters being .8 to 1.00 cm. high), unearthed at Lavoye (Meuse), between Bar-le-Duc and Clermont, and first published by G. Chenet, REA 29, 1927, 201 and Plate 2. The precise date of discovery does not appear, whether accidentally in 1887 or during desultory and incomplete excavations of 1904; Chenet seems to have occupied himself between 1919 and 1923 with remains of terra sigillata obtained at Lavoye, when this object, restored from shattered and scattered fragments, came to his attention. But the restoration seems nearly perfect.

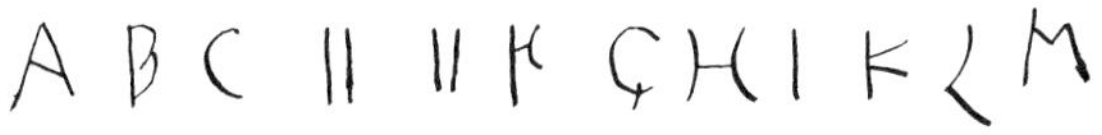

a b c [e] e f g h i k l m

n o p q r s t u x y z

d seems to have been mis-written e, which thus comes twice, unless we regard || as a careless writing of |) .

190

    Another complete alphabet on a vase discovered
at Maar, near Trier; a flagon 17 cm. high, 11 cm. in
diameter. The forms of the letters are similar to
those of Lavoye, e.g. /\ a, || e, ⅄ f, ⊬ k, ∟ l, Ƶ z,
but again q is omitted while r appears twice, unless
the first form ⍴ is intended for q, the second being ⍴,

    Beneath the alphabet are two lines of Latin text,

artus fututor aprilis k l sio

art ligo dercomagni fututor

in which the correct reading is perhaps dercomarcus
(see Note xxv above), and ligo either sens. obsc. or
for the ethnicon Lingo 234 below.

    CIL 13.10008,7

191

    On a marble pawn of circular shape, an incomplete

Latin alphabet, with a space between a and m, the last

letter for which room was available; at Trier in 1906.

This is a regular alphabet of good imperial style (Mm),

but f is ⌐ and k (K)either incomplete or partially

obliterated.

    CIL 13.10035,19

Inscriptions of Trier

Remark:

For the graffito from Montenach (Moselle), of
the type of La Graufesenque, see p.280 above.

Note xli

On the Treueri. Apart from the proper names of
the Treueri (208-211 below), note the following:

(a)   amba[tus

probably as an official title (not a name); cf. for
-aχtus i.e. -actus, Note lvi below (Stockstadt), Ambatus 10010.105 (Ems), and also 206 (coins of the
Mediomatrici).

CIL 13.3686

(b)   per dannum Giamillum

where dannus is clearly a title, cf. 214, Note lii
below, and also 206 arcantodan (coins of the Mediomatrici); CIL 13.4228.

For dannus compare dan "iudicem" Endl. Gl. (178
above), and dannicus (Rauricus) CIL 7.66 (R.1467);
cf. Stokes Phil. Soc. Trans. 1868-9, 251-54; Zimmer
KZ 32, 1893, 230-240; Thurneysen IF 42, 1924, 143-6;
uim danima(?) in the insc. of Poitiers (Note xxvii
above); cassiodanus (La Graufesenque 90, 92, 94, 102);
arcantodan (coins of Lugdenensis 177); platiodannus
at Mainz (CIL 13.6776). Cf. Do. 250; REA 7, 1905,
47; AcS 1.1222; Grenier in Frank 3, 540 cf. 560; Loth
in RC 38, 1920, 380 (cf. REA 21, 1919, 263-70); Blanchet Tr. 1, 85-86; SprFK s.v. (and also s.v. r(h)odanus);
Walde-Hofmann 1.323, 2.319; Ernout-Meillet ed. 2, 253.

Items in Latin Inscriptions

The gloss danus "fenerator uel feneratio" (CGL 4. 327,18) is usually compared with Gr. δᾶνος "loan, gift;" nor does danea "area" (Germ. Inf. 220) seem likely to be related.

(c) AcS 3.696,16 gives after Kraus Insc. Christ. 1.216 (Trier) the form

matir

which, with i for e, would be interesting if the reading were certain; but CIL 13.3909 gives i as ꜣ (e?).

(d) Riese 2491 (from CIL 3.1214, Apulum)

... Ibliomaro domo Augus. Treuer.

quond(am) decur. kanabar.

But the inscription given in Note xlvi below, from Dessau 9450 (R.2368), though found at Trier refers to the kanabis Bonn(ensibus); on canabae in general see 178 above (s.v. cannabis)

(e) For

fara[bur]em

CIL 13.4131 (Bitburg) see 207 below.

(f) CIL 13.10017,94 (AcS 3.1252), graffito found at Soissons:

καμβο | κοιια

In line 2 usually restored κοιια[κος

Items in Latin Inscriptions

(g) leuga, usually abbreviated L (e.g. Igel,
Espérandieu Receuil 6.437; Dragendorf und Krüger Das
Grabmal von Igel; Grenier ap. Frank 3.538 n.97) is
of course a commonplace. The writing febarpias
(†3690) and titiuium (†3909), for Februarias and
titulum respectively, are mere blunders.

Note xlii

A "corrupt" insc., according to CIL 13.4603;

found at Scarponne, first published in MSAF 1839, 207,

seems to read, on the fragment of a column

namandei|dente el a|rmia ... moai|
........i|pppiis ... sc

J. Becker's conjecture (Kuhn and Schleicher's Beiträge
3, 1863, 212-3) "wenn nicht alles trugt, so liegt auch
hier ein uberrest Keltischen idioms vor" has, so far
as I know, generally been forgotten.

Note xliii

Insomuch as the Tungri are included in CIL 13 1

2 (Belgica), I give here the two following items, al-

though there is much to be said for including them in

Names of Potters (Rouen)

Germania inferior, viz.

(i) CIL 13.3595 ("male lecta potius quam ficta")

pertur[

(for petur[, cf. petuar-, petro- "four"?)

(ii) ib. 3622

lubaini

(cf. Goth. lubains ?)

192

Names of potters found at Rouen (see 88 Remark)

In BSAF 1927, 141-45 a list is given of potters' names found at Rouen, of which the following "appear to be unrecorded elsewhere:"

Aii	Dianius?	Iauani?
Ambatus (but cf. 244 below)	Dicaii	Iauaus
	Duicus	Iauui?
Attialus (for -nus?)	Duuius	Icco
Cincissa (cf. Cin-gessus of West-erndorf)	Iasa	Icnus
	Iasatus	Iraχtui

688

Names of Potters (Amiens)

Iuatus	Mum[	Patume?
Lasir(ii) or Lasurii (read C- ?)	Nota?	Potti(ni)
	Oda	Puro
Litumarus	Oncpa (i.e. Nic- ius and Patri- cius of S. Gaul?)	Reso, -i
Lungini		Ri[(i.e. Rialus, as at Amiens?)
Macii (-g-)		
	Onii	Vxiiu?
Manius		Vota

193

In Pro Alesia NS 9, 1923-24, 138-170 a list is given of potters' names found at Amiens, of which the following, said to be "unrecorded elsewhere," may be noted:

Aluitta?	Cenianis?	Diccius?
Amuc(i)us	Ceniobes?	Euhodos
Annicuus?	Cernus	Fantunus?
Anuacus	Ciepus?	Fecinus?
Ateius	Ciuillus	Feufius?
Bussus	Cocinus	Galaliaris?
Caruinus	Comisarus?	Ginatus
Cascus	Cottro?	Illi(a)nus
Cemmius?	Cruppus	Lalianus

Names of Potters (Bavai)

Manianus	Prini lettius	Sextulus
Manurus	Rialus	Sio, Sius?
Mebbianus	Rino?	Statius
Mecan(i)us	Riuicer (no.511); read Diuica-	Titauus?
Mena?	tus?	Vacustinus?
Merecrius?	Rodo	Vassus?
Mildecus	Rontionicus?	Vemius
Nainus	Rub[	Vimor
Neceius?	Sanciro	Viuienus?
Omrius?	Sasin(us)	

194

An unusually large number of names of potters appear on terra sigillata found at or in the vicinity of Bavai, and it is conjectured that they were manufactured not far away. But the site of manufacture has not been discovered, and until it is (with moulds), we must be content to list the following as found at or near Bavai. See further the articles of Darche and Hénault in Pro Nervia 1-6, 1923-30; RC 46, 1921, 89-113; cf. REA 34, 1932, 58-59. It must be observed that some of the readings are very dubious. For the excavations at Bavai conducted in 1934 see BA 1934-35 [1940], 478-84.

Abaciu, -eus	Acidi	Albucius
Abi	Aernui	Aledu
Abno (Adno)	Aiuano?	Asauo (read As[ia-ticus] auo[t]?)
Abudo	Aiui (Aius, Aiuus?)	Atimo (cf. Atimal-is at Mainz)
Acam		

Names of Potters (Bavai)

Atab? (read Atal-?)

Atta(lus?)

Auicos?

Ausios

Aχti

Banillus

Banni (cf. Banuus of Lezoux?)

Beccit

Beliati

Beluxxus

Biruta or Briuat

Botorc

Brariatus (Brabtatus, Brarinius); but cf. 10006.18

Bussieni

Cabiatus (cf. 176)

Cabneius

Calani

Camuco

Canaeti

Canicos (G-?)

Can(n)itus

Carmati

Cauina

Causna

Ceussor

Conicus

Corus

Cossicus (cf. Κοσ|τεγοσ 208)

Cotal

Couii or Couui (read Couni?)

Couoi

Cucanus

Dacouir

Datos

Doms?

Epa

Episi

Eucaris

Fuenis? (or Tuenis? Or read T. Venis[, F. Venis[?)

Galani

Gatisius? (G. Atisius?)

Gialb? (read Giam[?)

?Hamsit (cf. 205; Blanchet Mél. 2, 111)

Iaulla

Iautio? (read Dantio?)

Icurori (cf. Tituro of Lezoux?)

Imia

Inam

Indu, Indutio

Iocos

Iruio

Iumusi

Iunani

Iusio, Iusalis

Lausos

Luas

Maituro

691

Names of Potters (Bavai)

Masalla

Mascuili (cf. 10010.1351)

Masueni

Mettius

?Minacnt (read Mainacni, sc. of Lubié?)

Muscio

Nericcius, Nericcus (Neirx.i.x?)

Ninu, Ninus?

Nocais?

Nonoui

Nuero

Orini

Ouad[

?Outausi

Poria

Priansitit?

?Rinnius (cf. Varinnius)

[Sacciro]

?Saen(i)anesia (read Senani Esia?)

Seueru[

Sossu

?Spori

Subilus

Sumanus (Sunamus)

Tatt[

Tauri

Teurus

Tiuscio

Tricco

Trps(?)

Tueti

Vacasatus

Variatus

Varinnius

Vat·o·x·c

Vateraunus

Vatraunus

Vbera

]ucni

Velignio? (read [Se]ue[rus] and Lic(i)nus of Lezoux?)

Venis (Fuenis, Tuenis; cf. Veniso of Rheinzabern?)

Veruicci

Veruico

Vetera (-us?)

Vinii

Vipac

Virilis

Vit[

Vredus?

Vxpur, Vxpuro

195

Names of potters of Lavoye (see 88 Remark); A.D.120-
200. Cf. G. Chenet REA 40, 1938, 251-286. I have not
been able to procure Chenet's La céramique gallo-romaine
d'Argonne, cf. AJA 49, 1945, 206.

Amenus	Daccius	Mattunus
Aper	Daccus	Matugenus
Auastinus	Diuiχtus	Merco
Belus	Gabrus (not	Messirius
Bodus	*gabros W-H 1.23)	Moscus
Borius	Germanus	Nasso (-us)
Boudil(l)us	Gesatus	Pupus
Boudus	Giamillus	Re(i)dillus
Caper	Iaxus	Sanucius
Carisso (-ius)	Intincilo	Saupi
Catello (-us)	Intinco	Secco
Catucus	Iustus	Susacus
Cicadius (-ael-?)	Latinus	Tocca
Cintugnatus	Libo	Toccius
Cintusmus	Lucupec[	Tribunus
Cocirius	Maccono	Vaccus
Cocus (-cc-)	Macconius	Valdus
Creticus	Maianus	Viducus
Cretto	Marcianus	Vindus
Cucillus (Cucc-)	Martius	

Names of Potters (Avocourt, Les Allieux)

196

Potters' Names of Avocourt (see 88 Remark); A.D. 120-200 and 270-400. Cf. Chenet l.c.; RA 11, 1908, 391-94; 17, 1911, 51-54; AE 1911, 224-5; RA 5, 1917, 154; P-W Suppl. 3, s.v.

Acieillus	Iasso	Pomponianus
Agesillus	Iassus	Serenus
Auonus	Intircius	Sisserus
Boudillus	Iuciussico	Susacus
Carrotalus	Iuciussicus	Tocca, -o
Cominius	Lupus	Veicus
Diseto	Mottius, Motius	Viuentius
Disetus	Mottus	

197

Potters' Names of Les Allieux (A.D. 130-200). Cf. G. Chenet, Germ. 14, 1930, 63-74; REA l.c.; RA 17, 1911, 53; 5, 1917, 157; 15, 1940, 81ff.

Cassutus	Inituicus	Menco
Cas(s)tus	Iunius	Minunus
Cauannus	Leo	Mot(t)ucus
El(l)enius	Manerenus	Pius
Euuodius	Marus	Sab-(inus)
Iasso	Mastrus	Secundus
Iassus		

Names of Potters (Pont-des-Rêmes, La Madeleine)

198

Potters' Names of Pont-des-Rêmes, Florent (A.D. 130-200)

Aenisatus	Mincius	Successus
Anisatus	Minsius	Tarra
Car(r)otalus	Minuso	Tullus
Cos(s)il(l)us	Pugnus (-c-)	Viducillus
Cracuna	Satto	Viducus
Gabrillus		

199

Potters' Names of La Madeleine, Nancy (A.D. 110-130)

Albillus	Cimilus	Oc(c)iso
Amarinus	Gnatius	Orcio (ib.)
?Atei (Oatei, Cnatei?)	Gnatos	Sabellius
	Ianu(s)	Sabellus
Buccius (REA 41, 1939, 334)	Leuca (ib.)	Tritus
Caminus	Misius (ib.)	Virtuus (Vrit-?)
Catusus	Monianus	

695

200

Potters' Names of Eschweilerhof (A.D. 130-160)

Auitus	Cambo	Vimpus
Borius	L·A·L	

201

Potters' Names of Faulquemont-Chémery (Moselle, ca. 15 miles E. of Metz)

See the work of Delort p.280 above (cf. RA 5, 1935, 267; 7, 1936, 126-28; REA 38, 1936, 343-44), and R. Forrer in Germ. 19, 1935, 60-61; Delort in Actes Congrès de Strasbourg [1938], Assoc. Guillaume Budé Paris 1939, 163-168 (on Satto); Les Cahiers Lorrains 17, 1938, 16-20 (AE 1941, p.322); AJA 42, 1938, 580; BSAF 1936, 141-144.

Ateius	Cusio	Peculiar[
Cabila	Graecus	Pecunia
Canaus	Martial[	Sat(t)o
Cassius	Meddicus	Saturni(nus)
Ciamilo (for G-)	Meddu	Siluinus
Crac[	Medicus	Tertus
Cubitus (i.e. Cupidus)	Nopisio (cf. 216)	

202

Potters' Names of Trier (see 88 Remark); A.D. 110-240.

Afer

Amator

Alpinius

Alpinus

Andocaulo

Atilido

Auentinus

Betta

Bollo (-us)

Bollo auoti

Bolsius (V-)

Borlus (Borius)

Botus

Bracio

Braria(tus)

Buccatus (Ba-), -alus

Cassicus Germ 18, 1934, 222ff.

Catus

Censor

Censorinus

Comisillus

Comitillus

Condarillus

Condarus

Conius

Coocus

Corilus

Coris(s)o

Corisus

Couo?

Criciro (-u)

Dessius

Deuus

Dexter

Diutanus

Drappus cf. gl. 178

Dubitatus

Eluissa

Eruimus

Frontunatus (sic)

Ganicos (Can-)

Gatus

Gemillus

Iauenus

Iauurius

Interced[

Irdicos

Lippo

Lossa (cf. -tt- 136)

Maeauus (or Maii-aauus? Or Mai· Iaaua,-us? Maiarus Germ. 18, 1934, 222ff. Perhaps read Matuacus?)

Mainina

Main(i)us, or Maino

Marianus

Matuacus

Masa

(Mediatus?)

Medius

Names of Potters (Trier)

Melus	Obtatus Germ. 18, 1934, 222ff.	Santionus
Meddulus		Sealicus
	Ordilos?	
Mediatus		Serua
	Parentinus	
Metthiatus		Tordilo
	Paterninus	
Melluro		?Vide
	Pituarus (R-)	
Minutius		Virato
	Praeteritus	
Moricus		Vlpicolus
	Pruso	
Morrus		Volontossus
	Ruccatanus	(-unt-)
Nertus		
	?Rxead	Vrsulus
?Noliuiat[(with Interced[ )		

Remark:

    H. Koethe in Festschrift fur August Oxé (Darmstadt, 1938) pp.89-109 gives the following additional potters' names from Trier (cf. RA 14, 1939, 315; TrZ 9, 1934, 171; 12, 1937, 241-247; Germania 18, 1934, 223; 22, 1938, 236-39; Jahresb. des Provinzial-Museums zu Trier 1921-22, 103), viz:

Acalo	Auriso	Capurius (also at Mainz, Rheinzabern)
?Aiuaud[	Benio (Banio)	
Atiassus	Binio	Catonos
?Atisiobus	Bituri	Caura
Atitisus	Boiio	Collosi (cf. Collo of La Graufesenque?)

698

Potters of Belgica

Cottius	Licnio? (Limio?)	Taitra
Couerthi	Lullo	Tappu (I-?)
Couirus	Macianus	Tetarus (cf. Tet-
Cuadrato	Moltus	turo, Lezoux)
Culla	Muic[	Tetio
Datueio (-us)	Namo (cf. Namus,	Troxus
Drucco	La Graufes-	Varo
	enque)	Varos
Durucu	Non[	Vato
Duta	Nonico, -u	Velucnio
?Fillo	Nouidus	Viducuri RA 23,
Furius	Pusso (cf. Pusso-	1945, 163
Fuscinin(u)s	sus, Bavay)	Vitolo, Vitlos
	Rituscia	(Germ. 21,
Iantasio	Senoteno	1937, 194
Induho (-tis)		n.15)
		Voati (or auoti?)

203

Names of Potters found in Belgica (see 88 Remark).
Cf. Journal des Savants 1942, 81-85.

Acanus	Ac(c)o	Aduenac[id. 94
Acero	Acus	Aduentus
Acidus	Adiutex (Tous-	Aeno, Aino (-us)
	saint 94, 107)	

Potters of Belgica

Agilio 10010.60

Aiucaldi Bull.
  Inst. arch.
  Luxembourg 33,
  1937, 9-15

Alesso

Aluitta

Amucus

Andecarus

Andecob 10010.118

Aneacus

Annicuus

Anuacus

Aquenus?

Aranus

Arcad[

Areus

Articianus
  Toussaint p.107

Asus

Atecnudis

Atepus

Attusa (Ati-)

Auendos

Aunodi(?) 10010.
  245; Germ. 22,
  1938, 238

Auritus

Baccinus

Baccos

Banilli 10010.
  269

Becuro

Bisenesus

Bituollus

Bitus

Bolsius

Boutius

Bracisilus

Braria(tus)
  AcS 3.925

Brennos

Britus

Buso

Bussus

Butricus

Cabellio

Cacabus

Caccanus

Caesar

Caeurus

?Caixus

Caledu Germ. l.c.

Camillus

Caninus

?Canoius

Capo Toussaint 94

Cariatus

Carito (-us)

Carnatus

Carpus

Caruinus

Cascus

Cassius

Cauintus

?Ceniobes

Cigetoutus (with
  Asus)

Cinge (fecit)
  Oswald p.77,
  but cf. Cinge
  iouru? (Cintu?
  -toutus?)

Cintuieru,
  Cin(ier)u
  10010.566

?Cispus

Potters of Belgica

Ciuillus

Cocceianus

Cocinus

Cominius Tous-
saint 107

Comisarus

Comnus

Como, -us

Corterus

Cotillus

Crea[

Critobulus

Crubu[Toussaint
101

Cruppus

?Dalisa Bull.
Inst. Lux. l.c.

Decuro

Demioncus

Demo

Democus

Dento

Diauxus

Diuerus

Diuus

Docca

Don(i)us Bull.
Inst. Lux.
l.c.

Dous?

?Ðrapo (V-)
10010.818

Driaso

Duruius

Elius

?Eluinus Bull.
Inst. Lux.
l.c.

Enrius

Errus

Exomn 10010.
874

Fabracus

Futilos

Ginatus

?Gna(s)

Homobonus 10010.
987

Iappus

Icelus

Ictus

Idocius Tous-
saint 142

?Ierius

Illos 10010.
1023

Indutius Bull.
Inst. Lux.
l.c.; 10010.
1031

Ira$_\chi$tus (-ui)
10010.1053

Irmo

Lalus

Lecco

Lintus

Lorius

Lucirus

Maccira (-irilla)
10010.1198

Macrellis

Mado Bull. Inst.
Lux. l.c.

?Maf[

Potters of Belgica

?Magalus 10010.
    1222

Maiudtilus 10010.
    1244

Manianus

Mannus Tous-
    saint 87

Manurus

Marosus

Martianus

Masalla 10010.
    1290

Masclius

Mateius AcS 2.
    459

Matorinus

Matorus

Matugenus

Mecanus

Meddicus

Meddionus

Mercianus

Mercitus

Mercullo

Merecrius

Mildecus

M(a)iudilus

Miuddilo

Monus (-ius)

Moxinus

?Nainus

Namantus, -o
    10010.1403

Namita AcS 2.
    676,35

Nerrus, Nerus

Nisserus

Ociuteso

Olillos

?Orinus

Otocius

Ouilius

Oxeti

Oxittus, -ius
    10010.1482

Pacus

Parus

Peper

Picta

Poppu (Roppus)
    10010.1547

?Purinx (D-)

Pussosus

?Relan[10010.
    1623

Remus

(C)reticus, -ius
    (R-) 10010.
    1631

Rialus

?Riomonus

?Rituarus

Rodo

Romogillus

Runcina Germ. 22,
    1938, 238

Sallidatus

?Samtis

Sa(n)ciro

Sanicus

Sartorius

Saxo

Potters of Belgica

Scotinus

Seclatus

Secorix

Seneca

Siciatus

Siddus

Sucinius

Sosa 10010.
  1836

Sottu 10010.
  1838

Tacitus

Tanconus

Tappu 10010.
  1877

Tassus Bull. Inst.
  Lux. 13, 1937,
  9-15

Tato (Toussaint
  142)

?Tetrecus (Petr-)

Tiotagus

Tintinni 10010.
  1901

Tittilus

Tittullus

Titulus

Torno 10010.
  1929-30

Tritus

Vacustinus

Varicos

Vaso

Vassatius
  10010.1981

Vaonus 10010.
  1970

Vauouus

Vcatus

Veldulus

?Veluonius Bull.
  Inst. Lux.
  l.c.

Vercobius

Veruicus Bull.
  Inst. Lux.
  l.c.

Veus

?Viamus 10010.
  660

Vienus

Vilis

Vimor

Violus

Viriassiu 10010.
  2054

Viriodacus

Virodu

Visero(s)

Visseru(s)

Vocari 10010.
  1930

Volturius

Vossatius 10010.
  2087

Vrittius AcS 3.
  42; 10010.
  2096

Potters of Belgica

Remark:

From Bull. Soc. Académique...Boulogne-sur-Mer 8,
1908-1909, 593 (cf. CIL 13.10010,1623), in a "liste des
Potiers gallo-romains" whose names appear on terra sigillata discovered in Boulogne and the vicinity (pp.555-
609), the work of H.-E. Sauvage, I take the following,
but the reading is doubtful in many cases.

Adacus	Cun	Mancitus
Agate	Daris[	Mopillus (Map-?)
Amillus	Didius	Penti
Arsitiuir	Iluo	?Relanus
Attimani	Iuonus	Rutocius
Cimin m.	Lanianus	Senita
Cinianus	Luinus	Tettaro
Cosmus	Mallianus	?Tica (p.605)

The same criticism is to be applied to names, otherwise unconfirmed, from Le Châtelet (Pro Alesia 7, 1921,
163-169) and from Martelange, Luxembourg (REA 17, 1915,
278-79), viz:

Andeco	Iunillos	Mert[
Arel[	Liun[	Moria
?Bitiruro	Madi	Saius
?Cornuir	Matos	Samotalus
Dacouir	?Mebico	Tuitarri
Dalu(isius)		

Potters of "East Gaul"

Potters' Names of "East Gaul" (see 88 Remark)

A number of potters are said by the authorities on terra sigillata to have worked in "East Gaul," not being assigned to some definite center of production. Although this broader ascription includes the Germanies as well as Belgica, the products of "East Gaulish" potters are in fact, in many cases, found chiefly in Belgica; accordingly, their names are given here, as a matter of convenience, possible as it is that some of them actually worked in Germania Superior or Inferior.

Alibletus

Ambianus

Ambitotus, -toutus 10010. 107

Andecarus

Anducor 10010. 3036

Arantedu(s)

Atiusa

Attiorix

Attissus

Aunedos

Baccatu 10010. 3011

Baccinus

Becuro (-q-)

Bouoririui (iuriu?) 10010.3058

Bracisilus

Bruari 10010. 1033

Cambrus

Cantius

Capi | Mar Germ. 14, 1930, 291 (one name?)

Carus, -o

Cassatus

Catacius

Catus

Catuinus

Caupius

Cauus

Centus, -a

Cicarus, -o; EC 2, 1937, 28-32

Cilenus

Ciltus, Celtus

Cineisso 10010. 2988

Cinninius

Ciruca

Cooarilus 10010. 639

Cobuna

Comio

Commius

Comus (-mm-)

?Coriro (Montsans?)

Potters of "East Gaul"

Corisso, Corisus?	Drillus	Loscius
Cosoi 10010.660	Drilo	Losucus
Cosos	Durotix	Lucco
Cossa 10010.3061		Lued 10010. 3084
Cossous	Gatus	Lugetus
Cossus	Germo 10010. 3040	Lupercus
Cotto	Giamatus	
Cottro	Giamissa	Macnonus
Cuno	Gimissa (C-)	Magnous (-c- 10010.1212)
?Cunopus; Cuno- patus (Col- chester) Germ. 18, 1934, 31	Iarus	Malcio
Cupitus	Ias(s)us	Mardanus
	Imprito (-us)	Marepusius 10010. 3038
Dagobitus	Inticito	Masa
Dagus	Intonius	Maetutus
Dannorix	Inus	Medius
Danuacus	Irdico	Meinus
Deomartus	Issus	Melissus
Dercinus		Melus
Doccalus	Latto	Menda
Doccius	Lauratus	Minuus
Douisico	Lillutius	Mopius 10010. 3027
Douuii 10010. 2985	Lipuca	Morinus

Potters of "East Gaul"

Nas(s)us

Nemes

Nitidus

?Nostili JAOS 58,
  1938, 47

Ortonnus

Papilos

Perimos

Poppillus

Pridianus

Prenio? (Ann.
  Soc. Lorraine,
  1899, 377;
  Blanchet Mél.,
  2.105

Prittius

Prudcus

Prudianus

Ratiatus

Rauitales 10010.
  3024

Remicus

Riginus

Ruittius

Sabinulus

Sanuacus

Sassus

Saluo

Scot(t)o

Senitios

Senoni 10010.
  3011

Siarus

Siddus

Sidus

Smertus

Sucomus

Supputus

Suputo

Taruagus

Tarus

Tassca

Taxnus

Tetricus

Tigomlus (for
  Tigernomaglus?)

Tinus

Tranusa

Tritos, -us

Vaccuro

Valis

Varedo

Vaχtius

Vecorix

Vesnus

Venouus

Viamos

Visiucco 10010.
  2993

Vitro

Viuuus, Viuous

Potters of "East Gaul"

Remark:

(1) For Vaχtius (204) cf. Vaχtus CIL 7.1336, 13. 10010,1986 (Vechten), the personal Vaχtulla (237), but hardly the local name Fectio, Fictio mod. Vechten (221); Oswald records Vaχtius also from South Gaul. Cf. NTS 1, 1928, 112.

(2) Dordu in Bull. Inst. Arch. Luxembourg 15, 1939, 58-59 (cf. Ant. Cl. 8, 1939, 432) I have not seen.

(3) The so-called Belgic ware found in Britain actually was copied from Belgic prototypes (cf. Oxé TrZ 16-17, 1941-42, 92-104 on their forerunners), and some of the names found in Britain should be noted here for comparison; see BA 1932-33 [1936], 683; Wheeler, Verulamium, 176 cf. 182, viz:

Alluci	Magio	Otau (or Vato; auot?)
Gemini	Maialla	
		Tiotag
Inf	Miccioni	
		Vxopilli m.
Iul	Nonico	

205

Of some three hundred "signacula laterculis a priuatis impressa" a large number were made at Trier or at neighboring places in the Mosel valley. A selection of the latter follows, taken from CIL 13 vi (1933), pp.141-176 with TrZ 9, 1934, 163-64; 10, 1935, 63-73;

Names at Trier

cf. Jahresb. des Prov. Museums zu Trier 1921-22; Germania
21, 1937, 107 n.20; Ant. Cl. 8, 1939, 429.

aaf	Armot(riaci)	Cildouiu (G-)
abf	Articianus	Cimagion
adf	Aruernus	Daha
ad Gal	Aruinic	Deaetheri
ad Iou	Assatus	Decidio
ad Pro	Assinno	Drilo
Adiutex (alone, or combined with the following names, viz:	Ateχtos	]enngae
	Attaei	Fecinas Conconikas
	Auitus	Gabinior
Attic Auiti Bel Ben	Balatonaua	Genesis
	Bucus	Gildouiu(s)
Car Crissi	Camar[	Hamsit[(Blan- chet Mél. 2,
Cun Ma Germi	Cano[	111)
Ian Iulissi	Capienacus, -ionacus	?icot
Map Sama	(Kappionnaco)	Irpoix (-s)
Sampu Sen	Capox	Issi
Vass Vassici	Caritosus	(I)uincintius
Vendia)	Casatus (Blan- chet Mél. 2,	Leuc[
Amantiolus	109)	Lupianus
Apianus	Cec[	Lupicinus
Aprio	Ceratius (Blan- chet ib.)	Malico?
Aregius (-ig-)		Mam
	Ceruio	

Names at Trier

Neh[	Sissirius	Tato
Nertomarus	Sontilonnaci	Tigri
Pariator	Streucoi (Sir-?)	Toccius
Placdus	Supetius (for Exs-?)	Vrso
Polla		Vassilo
Remi	Tacato	Viris(i)mi
Sapricius	Tamalicot	Vipsanorum
?Satti (12768)	Tasp	Vincintius (12841)
Secco	Tamne	Vittino

The following item (CIL 13.12844) is not transcribed:

ΓΟ9ΛЯΕΧΙ

For the rare use of the Greek alphabet we have (imported?) in CIL 13.10017,1

ηρακλης

Note xliv

There is very little over and above proper names in the inscribed lead and silver plates (amulets and curses) found in the amphitheatre at Trier in 1908, and published by R. Wuensch BJ 119, 1910, 1-12, cf. Weisgerber SprFK 157; CIL 13 iv, 1916, 11340 1-xiv; Riese 3619, 3629-30. We may note the following:

Inscriptions of Trier; Coin-Legends

(i) 4 dekigo   10 ?d]ekigo

     5 ?Ro]danum   6   eatta

     8 kamapo   10   Bonarius

(iii) 4 in abintiaro uestro (cf. 213 below)

     7 ququma (i.e. Cucuma?)

(v) 1 Racatia (not -nus)   (vi) 2   Acaus?

(vii) 2 Aba?   (viii) 1   Prusia

(xi) 1 Vrsus   2   Vrsula   5   Vrsacia

(xii)   Matrona

206

     Coin-legends of Belgica (from Blanchet Tr., and
AcS with a few items from Blanchet and Dieudonné vol. 1)

aco

αγηδ, agedomapatis,
   cf. esumopas 182
   above

αλαβροδιιοσ (cf. AcS 3.
   545, αβροδιιοσ)

ai

?am(a)

?amandi

ambactu(s), cf. Note
   xli (a) above

andobru(s)

anna | roueci

arcantodan, cf. 177 and
   Note xli (b) above;
   W-H s.v. argentum;
   Loth REA 21, 1919,
   263-70; Tr. 1.85-86;
   Thurneysen IF 42,
   1924, 144 and 192;

Coin-legends of Belgica

SprFK 192, 198. Cf.
αρκαντι Tr. 378

αρδα , arda (Treueri).
Cf. RC 48, 1931, 156

[?atedios]

atesios, atisios

atesos

ateula (cf. AcS 1.261, 3.
402; Tr. 385-86

αθεδιοσ (-η-?) or
aθediac[os

atpilli (cf. 177)

?bao[(but cf. AcS 3.803,
8-14); the coins with
βα οατιγοον , imita-
tions of coins of
Thasos, appear to be
distinct

caic(?) Tr. 107

?caloua, calou, calu
(But l is λ , read
therefore γαλουα etc.
The comparison with
Calua, Galba AcS 1.
706 seems faulty, and
the ascription to
Châlons-sur-Marne Tr.
384 worse, if a refer-
ence to Catuuellauni
is intended). Hardly
caaoua?

Καο (Leuci)

[carausius]

carmanos (g-)

carsicios

κεκν(ι) debased imita-
tion of Augustan coin
Tr. 125; but cf. AcS
3.1177,40

ciu Tr. 110

cnia AcS 3.1242

com(m)i(i)os (also in
Britain; cf. comux
AcS 1.1086?)

coou[Tr. 112. Cf.
Cooarilus 204 above
with CIL 10010.639;
perhaps the same as
couu[Tr. 113, see
245 below

kora[Tr. 486; AcS 1.
1114

coriarcos or corari(li-
ciuci) Tr. 113, cf.
383

cottina Tr. 135 (cf.
pottina)

κρασσυσ (or kraccus?)

cricr, cricru, circiro,
cricuro(-u), criciru
Tr. 114 etc. (v. In-
dex)

cucinacios (cup-)

?κυομ Tr. 385

Coin-legends of Belgica

δειου, δειουιγιια, deiui-
    cac, δειουι ειιαγοσ

epi

epodunac Bl.-D. no.165

?εσθα AcS 1.1406

euornus; cf. Pannonian
    euoiurix (Tr., AcS 1.
    1486)

[galiages(?) ib. 1638,
    but v. Tr. 107 (cal-,
    Bituriges)]

garmanos, cf. car-

germanus Tr. 121 (with
    indutilli, below)
    Treueri?

?ianic AcS 2.8

idoixo (?)

imθniθ AcS 2.31, cf. Tr.
    123

ιμυσ[Tr. 107

indutilli (Treueri?); BA
    1932-33 [1936], 637

inecriturix

iouerc

iouicon[? (Tr. 383; or
    liciuci? With coriar-
    cos q.v.)

lucotios Cf. 179 above

man[(or μαυ- ?)

matucenos (-g-)

[mausaiios (on coins of
    carausios)]

medioma

?mur, mureio Tr. 130

mutinus

nide Cf. Tr. 87n., 97

nirei

nouiiod[

]nr[AcS 2.793

?omaos

ουοαυ AcS 2.892, cf. Tr.
    133

?ουολε ib.; Bl. reads
    θιολε (perhaps λεουο ,
    Leuci?)

[oxokn, oxdkno, okueo,
    see Tr. 133]

πεννοουινδοσ (cf. RN 34,
    1931, 142-43)

pottina, cf. cottina?

Coin-legends of Belgica

remo, remos

rubios

senodon(nos)

sollos, -us

soso

?θex (Treueri or Ebur-
ones) Tr. 147, 356-
57, cf. Bl.-Dieudonné
no. 404. The legend
is given as X∃⊕∃X
and this Forrer Jahrb.
Ges. fur Lothr. Gesch.
u. Altertumsk. 22,
1910, 473 reads as
teθet

?titii (Forrer Kelt.

Num. 293)

uaceco(s)

uartice

uericios, uiricui

uindia, ουινδια   Tr. 394

?uirc[AcS 3.360

uiro(s)

ulatos

uocaran

uocas Tr. 146

uoco (or uoro)

uocu

Remark:

The following British coin-legends (Tr. 479-82;
cf. G.C. Brooke Antiquity 7, 1933, 268-89) are added
for purposes of comparison; see the Introduction to
Belgica above.

a

amminus

andoco(mius?)

antedrigus

aθθedomaros

boduoc

catti

commius, com

British Coin-legends; Glosses

comux	suei? (v. esui)
crab	tasciouanus
cunobelini	tinc(ommius)
dias, deas	ue
dubnouellaunus	uerica (or ui-)
eisu? (or suei?)	uerlamio
epaticcus	uirica (see ue-)
eppillus, eppi | calle	uir(r)i
esupas Tr. 121	uocorio | ad
riconi AcS 2.1183	uose(nos)
seno	]uricon Tr. 141
solidu?	

Glosses

207

(Cf. item 1, Note on Glosses; 79 above; 220 below. Since the migration of Belgic tribes to Britain is well attested, I have put some ancient British glosses into this section.)

ἀγασσαῖος, ἀγασσεύς "dog"

Oppian. cyneg. 1.467–470 (σκυλάκων γένος ... τοὺς τράφεν, ἄγρια, φῦλα, Βρεταννῶν .... | αὐτὰρ ἐπικλείδην σφᾶς ἀγασσαίους ὀνόμηναν). Cf. id. ib. 477 (ἀγασσεύς, hardly a proper name?) Not in L-Sc. Cf. segusius,

Glosses

ἀγασσαῖος ctd.

ἐγούσια PID 2.193; 3.41; REA 7, 1905, 46 (from Arrian
cyneg. 3.4)? Str. 199, Gratt. 174, Nemes. 124, Claud.
Stil. 3.301.

alausa "shad"

Auson. Mos. 127; also in Gargil. Martial. de med.
and Polem. Silv. Etymologists agree that the word is
Keltic; Kluge Urg. 12. Names of birds and of fish, or
of other fauna, are not infrequently associated; cf.
perhaps alauda (d : s?); or, for the ending, bagauda,
bascauda, armilausa, lausiae, baca-lusiae?

amiacum?

Vit. Bandaridi (Suessonis) 2.22, ASS l. Aug. I
67F: in fisca regalia, id est cellam, modum et amiacum.
This does not make the meaning clear: a measure? Or
"chest"? If the latter, perhaps leg. armiacum (cf.
armarium)? But that would be Latin.

areanos (ari-) acc. pl. "uigiles" (in Britain)

Amm. Marcell. 28.3.8. On the etymology see Fick
2 ed.4, 17; W-P 2.29 (*per(i)-).

asseda "sella quadriiugia" CGL 4.476,44

Cf. ἀσσιδάριος Artemid. oneirocrit. 2.32 (AcS l.
1474, 20)? If not for es-, ἐσ-σεδ- (see essedum below),
cf. perhaps the British and Belgic personal names
Aθediacus, Addedomarus (206 Remark) which seem as likely to mean "charioteer" as "spear-man, lancer;" assidarius (i.e. essed-) CIL 13.1997.

716

Glosses

[ἄταν, ἄθαν· πτερωτόν Ptol.

Cf. Ravenn. Pinnatis: only in the local name Athan.
See AcS 1.251; cf. petraria 178 above ?]

ἀτραβατ(τ)ικᾶς (sc. χλαμύδας)

Suidas, Lydus de mag. 1.17 (cf. CIL 13, p.558).
The tapestry of Arras (Atrebates) is famous still in
modern times. Cf. Grenier in Frank 3.587 (Oros. 7.32.
8); and bigerrica (158).

?baniaricia: calmes. Ionae uit. Columbani 18, Sur.

ASS 23 Nov. 471: penes calmem quam baniaricia

uocant

Holder AcS 1.341 makes both lemma and gloss local
names, and certainly baniaricia looks like a local name;
but at 1,704 he seems to think that calmes (sic: not C-)
may not be a local name, even though he records Calmes
as such from Greg. Tur. hist. Fr. 4.29 (Hautes-Alpes).
However we have calmetum "merisc" (i.e. "swamp, marsh")
in CGL 5.354, 46, cf. 31; this is presumably a Keltic
*calmis (cf. W-H 1.249 s.v. columen) cf. Meyer-Lübke
Einf. 241-242 and item 158 above. As for baniaricia
(-tia) cf. Ir. bān "white," banta "waste land," bānach
id., bānaid "lays waste" (Hessen 77-78).

[barbaricarius "goldsmith, jeweler"

Notwithstanding the spelling branbaricarius in
NDOcc. 11,75 (Remenses, Treueri, Arelatenses) and in
one (forged?) insc. CIR p.357 (no.2, Trier) the correct
form is barbar-, v. TLL 2.1731; CIL 13.1945, Ed. Diocl.
20.5-6,8.]

bascauda "conc[h]a aeria"

Ap. Britannos, Mart. 14.99 (tit., and line 1); Iuv.

Glosses

<u>bascauda</u> ctd.

12.46 (v.l. mascaudas), Schol. ad loc., Gloss. (v.l.
vascaudas) and also (AcS 1.322, cf. 3.810, from cod.
Par. 7643, 19^V 1) ba⟨s⟩causa, in which -s- : -d- (-d̄-?)
seems the same as in alausa: alauda, cf. also bagauda
(for the ending); see TGL, Loewe Prodromus 62. English
basket is borrowed from this, Latin fascia cognate.
On b- : m- cf. Jud Arch. Rom. 6, 1922, 203. Presumably
distinct from baccinum "basin" (178 above).

[<u>bastaga</u> "transport"

 Gallicana NDOcc. 11.78. But the word is Greek
(βαστₐγή, βαστάζω), whatever its etymology.]

<u>ben(n)a</u> "canna agrestis" CGL 5.492,51

 Hincmari vita s. Remigii (Remensis) 28 (MG Scr.
Merou. 3.322,13): in uase quod uulgo benna dicitur.
Cf. English bin, OE binn; and perhaps Gaulish benna
PID 2.186. But Cantobennicus (148 above) is clearly
"white-peaked" (candidensis AcS 3.1080,54), not the
equivalent of combenno. It is necessary to distinguish benna "vase," benna "waggon," and benno- "horn,
peak."

βίρρος Νερβικός

 Edict. Diocl. 19.32, cf. 27; 22.21 (CIL 13 p.569).
Cf. also (d.m., Ianuaris nat. Neruius) 13.1056 bur-
(rarii) c(ollegae), and the glosses birrus, burra 158
above; sagum (-s): Ambiensis (178), Atrebaticus above.

<u>bulluca</u> "wild plum" (see 158 above)

 A term common to Aquit. and Belg. (or Brit.); cf.
perhaps bolusseron 178 above?

Glosses

cabuta, cambita, cambut(t)a: see gamba below

[caieu, quayea "quay, sea-wall"

 Cf. the local name Cayeux-sur-Mer (Somme) "hafen"
(AcS 3.1039,31); see 178 above (caio).]

*calmis: see baniaricia above

camba: see gamba below

cam(m)inus "path, way"

 Medieval Latin (Du Cange), from the seventh century, e.g. Not. episc. a Wamba rege confecta; but represented both in Keltic and in Romance according to
KR 52, M-L REW 1552, Do. 240 (not, however, by Ir. céimm
"march," W. cam Br. camm "step"), cf. *caminus, caminare:
Fr. chemin and see the local names below (212 bis Remark
2).

[catthi "Scotti" CGL 5.632,32

 Unless a mere blundering confusion of glosses on
Iuv. 4.147 (Cathis [leg. Chattis] "crudelibus" CGL 5.
520,28, which, pace Holder AcS 3.1151, cf. 1.1408, 41-
43, seems improbable), we may compare either (a) personal names such as Cattus and Scot(t)us, or (b)
-cati, -casses, caddos; but not (c) catta 246 (cf.
cattus) below, which might fit "crudelis" about as well as
Chattus, but hardly Scottus; nor (d) catu- "battle" as
in the Belgic ethnicon Catuslugi (-ogi) Plin. 4.106.]

cennum "acutum" CGL 5.177,8

 See pennum item 1 above (p.37) and compare the
local names Nemeto-cenna (212) Sumelo-cenna (241). The

Glosses

<u>cennum</u> ctd.

latter appears to be a hybrid, like Cuno-pennius (AcS
2.965,27-28), and Cunocenni (ib. 1.982, cf. 1195) to
be patronymic (in personal names there is always the
probability that -cennos should be taken as -genus;
Holder's Saticocenna 1.981, without reference, and his
detached Salicogenne 2.1375,7 must be my Salicogenna
237 below, but cf. Saticenus ib. Pennelocus (15) is
evidently a Keltic equivalent of Summolacu (IA, now
Samolaco, see PID 1.451; cf. SprFK 207) or of Caput
laci (Hubschmied Vox Rom. 3, 1938, 52-58).

We may compare also Penninus (Poen-) 15, Arpeninus
86, personal Pennus (-ius) 83, see AcS 2.966, Penouin-
dus (206), Penobrias 177, local Penno-crucion (Brit.,
cf. Cenn Cruaich; see RC 16, 1895, 36; Antiquity 8,
1934, 350; W-H 1.296); arepennis 158.

[?<u>corroco</u>: a salt-water fish

Auson. Epist. 4.69; perhaps Keltic according to
Thurneysen in TLL; cf. Sofer Comm. Vindob. 2, 1936,
83; but see 158 above]

<u>couinnus</u> "war-chariot" (Belg., Brit.)

Lucan 1.426 al. (AcS 1.1152), glossed as κάρριον
(ib.); couinnarius Tac. Agr. 35-36, cognate with Latin
ueho, quasi *ko-uegh-no-, cf. ueheia (s.v. uehiegorum)
178 above.

<u>cracatius</u>: a fish (Anthimus)

Cf. corroco above?

<u>c[h]rotta</u> "harp" (Brit.)

Fortun. carm. 7.8,64; Ir. crot, W. crwth. On the
Frankish (h)rot(t)a "psalter" see F. Kluge SB Heidelb.

Glosses

c[h]rotta ctd.

Akad. Wiss., Ph-H Kl. 6.12 (1915), 4-5; Do. 249.

[?curucus "coracle, curragh" (insular Keltic only)

   Gildas de excid. Brit. 15; cf. ASS 21 Mar. 3.268B (Scotica lingua curach). Cf. W-H 1.274.]

drusus, drausus "patiens, rigidus, contumax"?

   PID 2.192, with n.1; AcS 1.1317, 1335. Cf. the ethnicon Condrusi (221, Germ. Inf.; AcS 1.1097), and Condrustis ib. 1098. Lindsay's reading durus in the Lib. Gloss. (DR 32, DU 174), if right, would eliminate this item. But DU 174 is more likely to be a corruption of DR 32 than the other way round; drusus (Latin) is for *drut-tos (cf. pagus Condrustis, with -st- : -(s)s- SprFK 186), cf. trutikni PID 2, no.339, Druti f(ilius) ib., Drutalos etc. AcS 1.1354; and also Latin indruticare (Ir. druth, W. drud, W-H 1.694).

[dunocatus?

   dincat "receptaculum pugnae" uit. Paul. Aurel. (Aremor.), 6th century, see AcS 1.1374; RC 5, 1883, 418. British? The gloss is perplexing, but Dunocatus is attested in personal names; Brehant Dincat seems to be a double local name (Breton), and guttur as a rendering of brehant is explained by Loth Chr. 97 by compari- with W. breuant; cf. Smith Topon. Bret. p.21]

eburo- "taxus"

   This is virtually implied by BG 6.31.5; OIr. ibhar gl. "taxus," personal Eburus passim, cf. Eburones (212), Eburouices (179), AcS 1.1400-1403; W.u.S. 11, 1928, 157; Giessener Beitr. z. Rom. Philol. 10, 1922, 67n.1; Do. in Mélanges Loth 1927, 92-98 (note that W. efur is "cow-parsnip," not "yew" which is W. yw, Fr. if); compare also

Glosses

eburo- ctd.

limeum (158), taxus (220), and tillum (178). Eburouices will be "warriors of the yew," Lemouices "of the
lime" (OE wīg "battle"), whether or not the notion of
poisoned arrows (Pl. 27.10,) is explicit. It is barely possible that Texuandri (-ox-, -ax- 221 below) is
rendered Eburones, as it has been conjectured that
Catuuolcus himself is *haþu-walhaz.

Not, of course, connected with OHG ebur "boar,"
nor with Latin ebulus, of which the Gaulish cognate is
odocos (158); nor ἰουμβαρουμ (178) AcS 2.85.

essedum "chariot"

The war chariot of the Belgae and Britanni, as
well as of the Gauls; Belgica...esseda Verg. G. 3.204;
cf. PID 2.196; essedarius insc. Nimes (CIL 12.3323).
Cf. asseda, assedarius above (the latter, insc. Lyon
CIL 13.1997).

φρούδιος ποταμοῦ ἐκβολαί : see 212 below

Ptol. 2.9.1 (the Somme?), AcS 1.1500-1501. Now
commonly compared with Welsh ffrwd "river" (H. Osthoff
ZfCPh 6, 1908, 418-419), and therefore thought to be
a well-attested Keltic f- in an ancient source. See
Heiermeier JCS 1, 1949, 55; and compare perhaps also
Lomb. fruda, fruva, Bret. frot (M-L Einl. 42, cf. 241).
I am not persuaded, however, that sr- had yet become
fr-. Possibly a Germanic *flōd- (with r : l?), and if
so f- is for p-; the Keltic form may appear in liduna
(158).

farra "bread; spelt" (178 above)

Cf. fara(bur)is "granary" (?) in CIL 13.4131
(Bitburg, [Treueri]); Gutenbrunner 6 n.2; Pirson 236
sees Germanic fara "journey" (Mar. Avent. Chron. 2.
238,569); note also pagus Farraticanus PID 3.64. Loth
has a different etymology of Welsh bara Br. barc'h viz
*barga in RC 18, 1897, 99.

722

Glosses

galba "praepinguis" and also "worm, borer"

PID 2.196; the name of a king of the Suessiones, BG 2.4.7, cf. Dio. Cass. 39.1.1. On the etymology see W-H 1.577-78 (distinguish galbus, gaulus 246; cf. Die Sprache 1, 1949, 127); but galbanum, Suet. Galb. 3.1 notwithstanding, is either pre-Indo-European (A. Cuny REA 12, 1910, 162), or Semitic (W-H l.c. and addendum). Its Latin form (g-) was doubtless affected by that of galba.

[gallina "hen"

Caes. BG 5.12.6; but presumably Latin, not "the Gallic bird"?]

gamba "fetlock," adj. gambosus

For the testimonia see AcS 1.710, 3.1055-56. The writing fluctuates between c- and g-, but there is no reason to separate the forms with the different spellings. Either there is a genuine (dialectal?) variation, or else the extremely common confusion of c and g in the writing. The Romance forms point clearly to g-, however, which probably stands for an older c-; cf. perhaps camba "cauis" (CGL 4.29,27); Cambae (scottice) in Adamnan uit. Columb. 1.49; and the large number of local names containing cambo-, or its derivatives, situated in bends of rivers: see Pokorny Urg. 11; L. Davillé REA 31, 1929, 42-50.

That the word is Greek (καμπή, SprFK 201; but see Gamillscheg EWF, s.v. jambe) may be doubted; but many of the modern local names in Belgium and northeast France show Ham-, which points to c-, not Keltic g-. Yet there are several words in camb- meaning "bend, curve," or the like, which are supposed to be Gaulish:

(1) cámbita (camites: modioli CGL 2.607,24 is to be read cambites: radioli, cf. Bret. kammet) "felloe," M-L REW 1542; Einf. 270.

(2) cambut(t)a (v.l. cambota, cabuta) "bishop's staff, crozier," Pardessus Dipl. 1.83 (testam. Remigii,

Glosses

gamba ctd.

episc. Remensis ob. 553); Ion. uit Columb 30; uita S.
Galli (Alemann.) MG Scr. Merov. 4.251,39 (H.E. Loth
Sancti Galli, 1936, 148-10 p.132; cf. CR 51, 1937, 208);
uita Desiderii (Cadurc.) 42.595 (baculum...quod a Gallis
cambutta uocatur); mirac. Winnoci (ab. Wormholtensis)
MG Scr. Merov. 5.781,13. In this form we hardly have
*cambo-butta (cf. andabata, battuo, con-futo: W-H 1.259),
for then we should expect -st- (cf. bastum W-H 1.98).

In Britain Moricambe (now Morcambe); Sicel κάμπος.
The forms with h- show that the word existed at an early
date in Germanic. Surely not all these are borrowed
from one Greek source? We have either a pre-I.Eu., or
a widely spread series of I. Eu. cognates, and I see no
cause for not accepting camb-, gamb- as Keltic. In
Latin it first appears in Flauius Vegetius (ca.388).
Hardly for gamma, i.e. a rectangle (of the leg of a
seated person). However the relation of gambarus "lob-
ster" to cammarus is similar (there can be no connexion
with camurus "curved").

glastum "woad"

Plin. NH 22.2, in Gaul; also in Britain, Caes. BG
5.14.2; Mela 3.6.51, who use the Latin word, uitrum).
Cognate with Germ. glaesum 220 below; glastum is probably the Latin form, for which Keltic would have
*glassum.

gronna "marsh, pool"

Hist. Brit. 76, mirac. Bertini (Belg.) in ASS 15
Sept. 2.602B; also two Irish sources (quoted by AcS 1.
2042). Hardly cf. Grannona (179) or Aque Granni (221),
Grannus (223).

(?) helix: a variety of bear

Venant. Fortun. carm. 7.4,19. Arduenna an Vosa-
gus, cerui caprae helicis uri|caede sagittifera silua
fragrore tonat?

Glosses

(?) <u>helix</u> ctd.

Cf. alces 233 below, OHG elaho.

<u>iottica</u> see 178 above (iutta, iotta)

<u>laeti</u>: see 211 below

<u>lucius</u> "pike"

Auson. Mos. 122, Anthimus 40, cf. Polem. Silv.
544.17, Ruodliep h.v. Seiler 13.39 (lucius et rufus
qui sunt in piscibus hirpus), quoted AcS 2.1243,12;
cf. lucalus Polem. Silv. 544.2 (a reptile or insect).

Apparently the fish called in Narbonensis (and in
Latin) lupus (Foroiulienses piscem...lupum appellant,
Plin. NH 21.95); Polem. Silv. 544.8; cf. id. 544.10
lucuparta, see 79 and 178 above. Keltic according to
W-P 1.411, denied by W-H 1.825!

<u>malagma</u>(?), <u>malina</u> (cf. TLL 8.186,76-79) "spring tide"

Keltic like ledo, liduna "neap-tide," see 178
above; Marcell. de med. 36.49; Isid. ord. creat. 9.4;
4-7; Bede and ASS quoted in AcS 2.395 (uit. Theodulph.
Remensis, as well as Maglorii Dolensis Lugd., Hermen-
landi Antrensis, i.e. Indre-et-Loire); cf. the local
name (ib., no testimonia) malinum: wadum (Ardennes)?
The etymology is unknown. Probably current in Aquit.,
if not Lugd., as well as Belg. and Brit.

[<u>modranicht</u> "matrum noctem" (British)

Bede de temp. rat. 15 (gentili uocabulo); see
Maas Germ. 12, 1928, 59-69 (REA 32, 1930, 253-4).]

725

Glosses

<u>morimarusa</u>: see PID 2.188

<u>moritex</u> "sailor"

    In an insc. of Cologne (CIL 13.8164a; BJ 92, 1892, 261): Apollini C Aurelius Cl Verus negotiator Britannicianus moritex d d etc. (AcS 2.636).

    H. Osthoff ZfCPh 6, 1907-08, 430-432 takes -tex as connected with στείχω , Ir. tiagaim which is more probable than *teg- in *sutegon and other forms listed in 178 s.v. sutis; E. Kleinhaus W.u.S. 9, 1926, 106; Do. 273. For mori- cf. Morirex (CIL 7.409; if correctly read), Moritasgus 181.

<u>nausum</u> "boat"

    Auson. epist. 22.1; 2.37; cf. Adamnan uit. Columban. Praef. 2.9: latine filius nauis, Scottica uero lingua mac naue; Gr. ναῦς , Lat. nauis, Ir. nau, Bret. néau.

<u>olca</u> "campus fecundus"

    Fr. ouche; "champ fertile en Champagne" (so Dottin, REA 7, 1905, 48); for Greg. Tur. in glor. conf. 78 has campus tellure fecundus; tales enim incolae (sc. Remi) olcas uocant. In modern local names, dép. Aisne and Indre (see 152 above).

<u>ordigas</u>: "zaehun" (i.e. Zehen)

    AHDGlossen 2, 1895, 9.35. Cf. OIr. orddu lámae: pollex (gen. sg. ordan); M-L REW 687; SprFK 206. M-L Einf. 240 (after Ascoli AGI 10, 1886-88, 270) compares also Gael. ordag "big toe" and suggests confusion with articulus (Fr. orteil)

Glosses

paximaticus: ?

Vit. s. Geremari (Flauiacensis, dép. Oise), ASS
24 Sept. 6.701D: panis paximaticus cum oleribus paruulis.

Holder AcS 2.960 renders this ἅπαξ λεγόμενον "in-
duratus seu bis coctus." If that is right, we may have
*pₜqʰ-s-, *qᵘₜqʰ-s-, Bryth. *pₛps- i.e. *paχs-. But
Keltic cognates are lacking that would establish this
etymology; W. pobi (Lat. coquo, Skt. pácati) is hardly enough.

pecatus: see picatus

[perca "perch"

Aus. Mosell. 115; not Keltic, but the Latin perca
(from Greek?), Lig. Porco-bera: cf. Bertoldi BSL 32,
1931, 157 with n.2; NTS 4, 1930, 497; Gray AJPh 49,
1929, 343-47. Oribas. 1.127 ἢ ἐν Ῥηνῷ πέρκη .]

[petaso Menapica Ed. Diocl. 4.8

Apparently f. in Ed. Diocl., though the dictionaries make it masc.; Gaulish Varro RR 2.4.10. Cf. W-H
2.296 and distinguish petaso "linteum" ib.]

[picatus (v.l. pecatos, pictas) "skiff"

British (cf. Aquit. acatus 158 above); Veget.,
epit. r. mil. 4.37: scaphae...quae uicenos prope
remiges...habeant, quos Britanni picatos uocant. Perhaps pure Latin, picatus "pitched"? Hardly Lat. pic-
tus. At AcS 2.1004 Holder seems to suggest pincas
"pinace" (i.e.: pinus?).

Butp-, unless for qᵘ-, cannot be Keltic in any
event. Possibly Goth. peika-bagms (whether Lat. ficus
or ON pik "point, tip") i.e. "wood" (in general) or
"mast, tip" may give a clue.]

Glosses

quouenna: see AcS 2.1066 (1.1152,30) and couinnus above

r[h]edo, raedo: the name of a fish

    Auson. Mosell. 89; Polem. Silv. 544.18; cf. raia (if for *radia, *raedia) 178 above, but cf. Thompson Greek Fishes pp.220 and 26 (where they are clearly distinguished).

ronciae: cf. Fr. "ronces;" and also

    runcinellus daemon (at the Somme) ASS 1 Apr. 1. 27A-B cf. Runcina (P-W s.v.), Runcennaeum, Runc(h)o, Runcones AcS 2.1247; J. Zwicker PhW 59, 1939, 431-32.

[Salia (fl.): see 212 below

    de sale Ven. Fort. carm. 7.4.16]

salar "trout"

    Auson. Mosell. 88; Sidon. Apoll. ep. 2.2; Polem. Silv. 544.18; also a local name in Hisp. Baetica. Cf. Gray AJPh 49, 1929, 346; cf. salmo 158 above, and the personal name Salar(i)us 132 above unless this is Latin salarius.

[sciuus "druid" FHRC 147.28 (Latin), for scius]

[sentis "fibula(?)"

    Irish; uit. S. Brigitae ASS 1 Feb. 1.139. But perhaps rather the Latin sentis "thorn," hence "pin, brooch, valuable." But cf. 178 with p.235 above.]

Glosses

[sessum "officina" (at the Salia)

Pard. Dipl. Merov. p.454, quoted by Riese Lit. 15.91.]

spatharii

Ambianensis spatharia et scutaria NDOcc. 9.39 (CIL 13, p.549). But for σπάθη itself cf. OS spado, OE spadu (Boisacq s.v.). Cf. 187 Remark (i) above.

tarinca (-ng-) "iron nail"

Passio ss. Fusciani (Ambianensis) et Victorici (Viromandensis); passio s. Quintini (i.q. Victorici Virom.), ASS 31 Oct. 13.783 A, see AcS 2.1735. Cf. L. Spitzer, Bibl. dell' Arch. Rom. 1, 1921, 128; for -inc- cf. Urg. 86 (Illyr., Lig.). But note *trincare 79 above.

[tauo- "silent, quiet"

AcS 2.1774 takes this as implied in the personal name Tausius...e Tungris (214 below), and in the modern river name Thève. Cf. 79 above.]

tigernius "of royal birth"

Adamn. uit. Columb. 1.43 de duobis tigernis (tit.), duo regii generis uiri (text); cf. W. tigern, teyrn, Bret. tiern, Ir. tigerna, tighearna "overlord," for teg-. Also -tigirno- (in British personal name Catotigirni, AcS 1.845), tigerni, tigirn(i), tigurn(i) in Ogam inscc.; T(h)igernum castrum 148 above, cf. 178 s.v. sutis. But Vendryes REA 42, 1940, 682-85 denies this in favor of an etymology *tig-u-, *tig-r- "point, extremity, top;" cf. ZfCPh 23, 1943, 397.

Glosses

tinca "tench"

Auson. Mosell. 125; Polem. Silv. 544.18; cf. PID 2, 186; M-L REW 8742; cf. tecco 178?

?tufa "crest; standard"

Lydus de mag. Rom. 1.8; Veget. 3.5; Bede: illud genus uexilli quod Romani tufam, Angli uero appellant thuf. Possibly to be compared with Eng. tuft, top (*dəp- W-P 1.765); Romance *ex-tufāre is represented in OHG stŭba (Brüch p.5) but the meaning forbids any relation, and there can be no connexion with Osc.-Umb. tufer, see Ernout Élem. Dial. s.v.; M-L REW 8973 (cf. 8966); AcS 2.1980 cites a local name Tufiacus (Tuffé), dép. Sarthe, with no testimonia.

tossia (Brit[annica): see Note xxxiv (2) above

If Keltic at all, Belgic (British) rather than Lugd. or Aquit.

uabra "silua"

In local names, see AcS 3.71 and 128, cf. M-L REW 9107a; but it is likely that uabra was also a common noun "wood," see W. Kaufmann Gallo-rom. Bezeich. fur den Begriff Wald (Diss. Zurich, 1913), 60; M-L Einf. 271-72; Gamillscheg Rom. Germ. 1, 1934, 271 n.1. Cf. local name Vaberetum (Vouvray, Annecy), cited by Le Roux Boutae p.16. Loth RC 37, 1917-19, 309-11 (*upobhero-) suggests a somewhat different interpretation "ruisseau" (cf. REA 23, 1921, 245); distinguish *uebro- "amber"(?), Loth RC 38, 1920, 283.

?uitrum "woad"

Caes. BG 5.14.2, al.(AcS 3.413-414). It is both asserted (E-M) and denied (W-H) that this is the same as the Latin uitrum "glass"; and another name of woad

Glosses

?uitrum ctd.

(glastum, see above) rather points in that direction.
On the fact of tatooing cf. Isid. 19.23.7 (stigmata
Brittonum); and on woad in antiquity, see J. and Ch.
Cotte REA 21, 1919, 43-57. The word was known also in
Aquitania (158 above).

The Treueri

A complete bibliography would fill a volume.
Note the following: Rau in P-W s.v. (1937); Meister
DLZ 1938, 899 (cf. TrZ 10, 1935, 46); Dragendorff
Gnomon 5, 1929, 219; H. Koethe in Arch. Anz 53, 1938,
752 (cf. Rheinische Vierteljahrs-blätter 9, 1939, 1-
22) ascribes "Illyrian" names to the "urn-field" people, followed by Keltic speakers (see the divine names),
and these by Germanic (from the north and east), who
survived chiefly in border districts. For the newly
discovered divine names, see now S. Loeschcke Die Erforschung des Tempelbezirkes im Altbachtale zu Trier,
Berlin 1928 (reviewed in Gnomon 5, 1929, 214-220; cf.
ib. 278-82); id., Der Tempelbezirk im Altbachtale zu
Trier: Text and Plates vol. 1, Berlin 1938; vol.2,
1942, especially pp.164-179; cf. E. Gose Arch. Anz. 53,
1938, 227-233.

R. Weynand Neue Jahrb. für Antike u. deutsche
Bildung 2, 1939, 229-238 (especially 229-230: Treueri
chiefly Keltic).

J. Steinhausen Archäologische Siedlungskunde des
Trierer Landes, Trier 1936 (reviewed by A. Bach
ZtsfdAltuLit., Anzeiger 58 [Bd. 76], 1939, 80).

J.B. Keune "Religion in den Mosellanden beim
Auftreten des Christentums," Pastor Bonus 45, 1934,
369-398.

G. Baehrens Mainzer Zeitschr. 29, 1934, 44-55 (on
the boundaries of the Treueri and Vangiones.).

W. von Massow Die Grabmäler von Neumagen, Berlin 1932.

E. Linckenheld, ch. iv of Bibliographie Lorraine 14, 1935, published in Annales de l'Est, Nancy 1937; REA 40, 1938, 303.

For a study of the names of the Mediomatrici, see J.B. Keune cited in Rh. Mus. 84, 1935, 311 n.2; and on the survival of Keltic into the early middle ages, L. Weisgerber Zur Sprachenkarte Mitteleuropas im fruhen Mittelalter (in Rh. Vierteljahrsbl. 9, 1939, 23-51).

The introductory notes in CIL 13 cii-cxxviii (Treueri) and cxxix-cl (Mediomatrici) should be supplemented by the additions made in part iv of CIL 13, issued in 1916. M. Toussaint (cf. REA 31, 1929, 174; 32, 1930, 69-70) La Lorraine à l'epoque gallo-romaine 1928; id. Metz à l'epoque gallo-romaine 1948; G. Kentenich Geschichte der stadt Trier 1915, pp.3-50 (now out-of-date, like the same author's Trier, seine Geschichte und Kunstschätze, an illustrated pocket guide, no date; ed.2, Trier, 1933); S. Loeschcke Denkmäler vom Weinbau aus der Zeit der Römerherrschaft an Mosel, Saar, und Ruwer (Trèves, Musée allemand du vin) I have not seen (RA 7, 1936, 152); P. Steiner Römische Brettspiel und Spielgerat aus Trier (Saalburg Jahrbuch 9, 1939, 42-45); J. Bidez on inscriptions of Trèves in Ann. de l'École des hautes études de Gand 2, 1938, 15-28 I have been unable to obtain; H. Koethe Die Erforschung d. Röm. Zeit in Reg. bez. Trier, Nachrichtenblatt f. deutsche Vorzeit 13, 1937, 148-151; P. Steiner in Schumacher Festschrift 1930, 167-170; J.B. Keune ib. 254-259; numerous reports in Trierer Zeitschrift; Forsch. und Fortschr.; Germania 14-18, 1930-34; cf. Die Antike 14, 1938, 252-54 (AE 1938, 142; 1941 p.304).

A. Boinet Le Vieux Metz (see REA 26, 1924, 82); Linckenheld in R.-G.K. Ber. 17 (1927) 108-153, a survey of archaeological research in Lorraine 1915-28, cf. REA 31, 1929, 174; Linckenheld and Herz Sarrebourg depuis les origines (cf. REA 27, 1925, 331); Toussaint Scarponne au temps de la Gaule romaine (in Le Pays Lorrain 30, 1938, 529; cf. Rev. Belge 18, 1939, 714).

The Treueri

Excavation at Trier and in the Moselle valley generally during the second and third decades of this century has directed great interest, archaeological and
linguistic, upon the ancient remains of that important
region. The claim of the Treueri themselves to be Germanic (see Introduction to Belgica) stands in contrast
with archaeological evidence of a pre-Roman "Keltic"
stratum, and with the familiar assertion of Jerome that
the Treueri of his day spoke the same language as the
Galatians, or a similar one (Proleg. 71). But it is
certain that Germanic tribes entered the middle Rhine
in the third century B.C. (cf. Belgica, Introd. above),
to be succeeded by a Keltic revival (see Hawkes and
Dunning l.c., 237-38), the native elements of which are
attested in the proper names of the region. To this
Keltic or Kelticizing period succeeded a Romanizing
period (say c. A.D. 120-360), followed by a new Germanic
infiltration in the third century after Christ, so that
the tribal individuality of the Treueri is strongly
marked within Belgica as a whole. The composition of
the Neruii seems to have been much the same (Linckenheld in P-W, s.v.).

Thus the testimony of archaeology and of history

are not really in conflict. That of nomenclature is
also in agreement (cf. Proleg. 68; and further, below).
But there is evidence of a convincing nature, to suggest strong Germanic influence among the Treueri and
their neighbors the Mediomatrici, as well as in Germania inferior, which, if I mistake not, has been misinterpreted. The fact has often been observed (see,
most recently, Weisgerber in Germania 17, 1933, 97-
104) that the Latin inscriptions of the Moselle valley
show many examples of a-stem names (and occasionally
even common nouns, e.g. dea) with a dative sg. ending
-a. This has been claimed as "Keltic," even though
the Gaulish ending is known to be -i (once, by Greek
influence, - $\alpha\iota$). In 1933 also August Oxé (TrZ 8, 1933,
50-58) called attention to a large number of forms in
-o, dat. sg. fem. of ōn-stems (the corresponding masc.
has -ōni) in inscriptions belonging to the same region.

Attempted explanations of the phenomena are not
adequate. Weisgerber ascribed -a to a Greek influence
(- α or - η); but how could Greek accidence have exer-
cised such a power in the Rhine valley? Oxé ascribed
-ō to the analogy of the nom. sg. (like -ā both n. and
dat. sg.). This is more plausible, since the assimila-

tion of the dat. sg. and nom. sg. in Keltic in the consonant stems is evident in Irish (see Pedersen VKG 2.
98,109; Thurneysen Grammar of Old Irish 1946, 199 and
211-12, cf. Hdb. 192, 201-2; Brugmann Grds. ed. 2,
vol.2 ii.1, 175), and it is right to accept fully this
evidence of agreement with the postulated Keltic datives in -ōn, assuming then the loss of -n in the (suf-
fixless locative?) -ŏn, just as the writing of -u as
the dative sg. of ŏ-stems in Latin inscc. in Gaul may
be compared with the Keltic datives (Ir. fiur, *uiru),
Gaulish -u (once -ουι).

However, Brythonic Keltic lost its declensional
endings at an early date in Britain, so that there is
little or no Welsh evidence. In Welsh y llynnedd (with
ĕ from ĭ as proof of an ending -ā, not -ī) "last year,"
Md. W. er-llynedd, Br. war-lene we seem to have evidence
for an ending -i̯ā from an older -i̯āi (VKG 1.113, 147,
287, 383; 2.87, 89), in contrast with the usual treatment, namely -āi becoming -ai, whence -ī and -i (or -e).
It is right also to take this scrap of evidence into
account, but alone it has little weight. On the other
hand, the syncretism of dat. and instrum. (in part,
also of loc. and abl.) would give a dat. sg. fem. in

-ā in the ā-stems, and this appears also in OHG (e.g.
gebu), like the -ō of ŏ-stems (Goth. wulfa, OHG tagu).
As for on-stems, it is well-known that in Germanic,
the locative -ōni became -ōn, which appears in Gothic
in the feminines as -ōn, OHG -un (tuggon, zungun.) Accordingly, I see Western Germanic forms in the datives
(m. and f.) in -a (of ā-stems), and in the datives
(fem. only) in -o (of on-stems), the latter from -ōn,
with a loss of -n, either in sandhi or by assimilation
to the nom. sg. The latter is also partly a Keltic
phenomenon, just as the dat. sg. masc. -ō (of ŏ-stems),
if instrumental, is both Keltic (-u from -ō) and Germanic, while -a (dat. sg. masc. and fem.) is more definitely West Germanic, and -u (dat. sg. masc.), where
that writing occurs, more definitely Keltic.

In addition to the insc. of Nickenich (Note 11
below), I list here (from Riese Das Rheinische Germanien in den antiken Inschriften, Leipzig 1914, Index
p.468; see also my article in Word 5, 1949, 110-115)
the inscc. showing dat. sg. -a (from Trier, Metz, Arlon,
and a few other places):

R. 427, 2321, 2495, 2499, 3513, 3527, 3652, 3664,
3666, 3675, 3694, 3743, 3753, 3763(?), 3798, 3829,
3893(?), 3894, 3901, 3907, 3952, 3963, 3963a, 3982, 3994,
4027, 4043, 4048, 4057, 4173(?), 4175, 4455; add CIL
13.3460

Dat. sg. fem. -o (cf. Oxé, l.c.):

The Treueri

R. 2662, 3651, 3666, 3703, 3718, 3797, 3850, 3894, 3952, 4004, 4048, 4216; add CIL 13.11453 (and perhaps R. 4003, cf. 4004?)

Both phenomena appear in R. 3666, 3894, 3952, 4048. Thus we have combinations (both names dat. sg. fem.) such as Pruscia Motto "Prusciae Mottoni," Saturninio Sattara "Saturninioni Sattarae," Deuillia Ammillo "Deuilliae Ammilloni," Primia Tauso "Primiae Tausoni;" and dat. sg. fem. -ō, such as Artio, Mat(t)o, Annito, Cridianto, Matuicco, Sacrato(?), Moxsio, Drappo, Nemauso, Varicillo (F.70); and also (m. and f.) in -ā, such as dea, Diana, Seuerina, Nemetona, Modestiniana, Magiona, Eburia (uiua), Iunia, Buccula Titaca(?), Taliounia Lucilla, Bella, Croelonia Sacrilla, Nocturna (auia twice), Secundina, Secundinia, Similia, Saturnina, Attucia Artilla, Acceptia Tasgilla, Mottia Victorina, Ammossa, Bimottia, Amma, Iulinia, Ellia, Euta, Optata, Ategnissa (m.), Aereda (m.). Iumma (m., 13.6460), Ritona, Pritona, Fortuna. (For masc. a-stems in general, of which there are many in Germania Superior and the Agri Decumates, cf. AcS 3.468, 41 to 469,10, cf. Belga, Cracuna, Ciriuna, Lagana, Maina, Pottina, Volca, Allobroga); to these add:

ancil(l)a 12.1412	materna (M-?) 13.4373?
auia 13.4270 (twice)	memoria 13.1258
dea, dia CIL 13.2864, 2892, 3460, 6266, 7624, 7912, 11311, Finke 29	obsequentissima 13.7004
	sua 13.1412?
	uiua 13.4007, 4103
filia 13.7516a, 10023 (cf. 12.4097)	

The only weakness in the above theory is the occasional presence of dat. sg. -ā in Narbonensis; but there it is extremely rare and most likely due to "Italic" influence, since large numbers of Italian settlers lived in Narbonensis, and the dat. sg. -a is not uncommon in the Latin inscc. of Italy.

208

A careful analysis of the names of the Treueri
was made by L. Weisgerber in Rh.Mus. 84, 1935, 289-
359, using CIL 13.3633-4287, 11311-11351, together
with Finke nos. 5-86, 321-27, to which should be added
Nesselhauf nos. 1-57, 264-67 (see Proleg. 7), viz (with
a few from TrZ, and other sources):

Abullius TrZ 6, 1931, 155

Aburius N.4

Aiuinius 1

Alpicus 8, 1933, 116

Ammius 7

Anaillus see Note xxxvi
   Remark above

Annius 1

[Arimaspes (Persian) 1,
   1926, 26-30, 142]

Arte.[7, 1932, 134

Asicius 9

Attillius 47

Ateius Germ. 13, 1929,
   62

Bilius F.26

Brittonius 1

Camaelia AE 1945.101

Capitonius F.238

?Catirius F.30

Cassius 11346, R.3336

†Charalainus R.4417

Κοσ|τεγοσ 8, 1933, 122;
   Germ. 22, 1938, 238;
   cf. gl. 207 above

Cosu[F.30

Cousius 14

Cunomap[7, 1932, 40

Cupria Germ. 18, 1934,
   222

Decmanus 57; cf. Norden
   Altg. 155

Decmilla 16

Demioncus 13 (also div-
   ine name, 84 Vangiones)

The Names of the Treueri

Dentilia 57

Diuiχ[t]us 5, cf. 56

Gallia F.70

Gasculus 8

Gatus 10, 71; cf. Gattus
  77

Gaula (graf.) 11, 1936,
  224

G]iamissa 1

Gnatilla Loeschcke p.51

Iarus 1

Ibliomarus 54

Iedussius (Led-?) 7, 1932,
  134; cf. CIL 13.4137

?Instimenius F.81

†Iunti(?) 5, 1930, 169

Iuti[ni]a[na[7, 1932,
  134

†Lea 34; 13.2577

Leusius 1

Lossa 1

?Lou]citta 8, 1933, 161

†Lubentius R. Lit.p.451

Lucanus R.2456

Lucullus 4

†Ludubertus 23

Mag[7, 1932, 134

Maiianius R.3810

Mascellio 53

Mato 19

Matuinus F.26

Melausus 51

Mesolius 53

]ntisedo(?) F.30

†Nicetius eps.Fort. 3.
  12.6

†Numodoal 31

[Orfita 14]

†Palladius R.4398

†Pancaria 24

†Pascarius 25

Pentius (graff.) 11,
  1936, 226 (cf. ter.
  sig., Westerndorf)

  Porcarius 35

The Names of the Treueri

Pupus 13.7412

?Raddartius (-arpius,
-arius?) 13; cf. AE
1941.170 (Raddarpi)

?Rassura, see p.280
above

Reginus CIL 3.14349,8

†Rotsuintde (graff.) 9,
1934, 77-82, cf. 10,
1935, 17-19

Sabinus 43

Saturnius N.55

Senecianus 14

Senia 11316, Sen[6,
1931, 185

Serotinius F.12, 13

Seuianus 11313, R.2471

Solinus N.55

†Spuria(?) 32

Strambus (graff.) Germ.
14, 1930, 251-4

Suricuia (? -ia) F.62

Taetradius R. Lit.p.331

Ti(gurinus) 12792, cf.
10, 1935, 64; cf. gl.
207 above

Tongonius 1

]tuge (dat.?) N.19, cf.
Germ. 16, 1933, 233

Turpilius 10024.28, cf.
R.3550

Tu]ranius 2033, cf. 7,
1932, 40; cf. 241

Venustus 11346, R.3336

Veranius 11888, R.2489

†Vetranio 34

Virius F.21

Vitorius (for Vict-) F.3

Ουρσικῖνος R.2517

Vrsius 11316

†Vrsola 28, R.4374

Vrsulus 11316 (R.2521),
†Vrsulus R.4299;
Vrsulus grammaticus
Aus. (R. Lit.p.323)

†Vulfilaicus Greg. Tur.
h.Fr. 2.15

†Zoilus R. Lit.p.403

740

The Names of the Treueri

Treueri are named in CIL 13.1795, 1911, 1988, 2012, 2027, 2032, 2577, 2614, 2669, 2956, 7412, (cf. C. pars 1 p.584), 7612, 7613, 7615, 7616, (cf. C. p.478), 11605, 11888; cf. AE 1941.169 (i.q. F.126) and AE 1945.101 (cf. 13.2577)

Weisgerber's study compares favorably with that os J. Scharf "Studien zur Bevölkerungsgeschichte der Rheinlande auf epigraphischer Grundlage" Neue deutsche Forschungen Bd. 185 (Abteilung Alte Geschichte 3, Berlin 1938), reviewed by H. Nesselhauf DLZ 1939, 94 (many inaccuracies), H. van de Weerd L'antiquité classique 7, 1938, 443-44 (adverse), V. Chapot REL 36, 1938, 474-75 (not unfavorable), J.G.C. Anderson CR 52, 1938, 239-240 (uncritical), Gerster PhW 59, 1939, 846-851 (severely critical), W. Schleiermacher Germania 23, 1939, 64-65 (unfavorable); P. Lambrecht Rev. Belge 18, 1939, 762-770; and 19, 1940, 192ff. I have not seen R. Nierhaus in Bad. Fundberichte 15, 1939, 41-104; but compare P. Lambrecht's "Où en est le problème de la nationalité du peuple Trévire?" L'antiquité classique 7, 1938, 359-381 (cf. Rev. Belge 18, 1939, 764); he holds (against Scharf) that the Keltic element was much more conspicuous than the Germanic. Cf. H. Koethe Trevererproblem in Rh. Vierteljahrsbl. 9, 1939, 1-22 (APh 14, 1939 [1941], 323), cf. TrZ 13, 1938, 215; E.B. in JRS 29, 1939, 135 (Arch. Bibl. 1939, 2836); others are listed in APh 15, 1940-41, 322.

Of a total of 1152 names studied, Weisgerber set

aside 729 (i.e. 63.3 per cent) as being of Italic or

Mediterranean origin. Yet observe, even among these,

formations in -inius (e.g. Secundinius, Serotinius) like

the Irish -ne in diminutive forms (Ir. Caittne: Catt as

if *Cattinios: *Cattos, cf. Cattianus 228.iv and Cattaini

228.ix below; catta gl. 246) or the Welsh singulative.

The system of personal nomenclature among the Treueri

The Names of the Treueri

was a compromise between the native and the Roman sys-
tems; but it does not follow that everyone who bore a
Roman name, or a name derived from a Roman, was alien
by birth. Some names of Latin origin were favored because they resembled or recalled native names; others
were virtually translations (e.g. Lat. Vrsus for Keltic
Artos); or again purely personal reasons would induce
the adoption of a Latin name.

208A

But there is a substantial residue (190 names more
or less, say 16.5 per cent) which are manifestly Keltic,
among them in particular the compound single names of
the type represented by Cingetorix, Indutiomarus (Caesar
BG 5.3.2 Treueri). Weisgerber has listed 28 such names,
viz:

Adbugissa 4127

Adia[t]umar(us) 3999

Am[bi]toutus 3991

Andecarus, -ius 3984

Atrectinus 3979

Atrectus 3707

Condollus 11605, R.1488

Dannumara 3979

Dotal[4266

Exsobinno 3970

Ibliomarus -a, -ia 2839,
   3996, 3.1214; F.26

Litugenius 4270

Marouirus 11736

Ollognatus, -ius 4159

Samocna 11888

Samognatius 3.8014

Sintorix 4059

Solimarius 634, 3979,
   4128

Sumaro 4127

The Names of the Treueri

V]ectimarus 4242

Veriugus 4126

Vocaran[tus or [a see 206
  above

208B

We have further (Weisgerber 315) simple (non-compounded) names and their derivatives, to the number of 115:

Artus 4263

Artula 4172

Artillus 4230 (-ius?),
  -a 4106

Artinus 3712

Artisius 4278

Bellica R.2451

Bellicius 3707

Belliciola 6.34676

Betulo 3.4499

Biber 4113

Borinius 11313

Bouus 3987

Bricto 11736

Buccula 4219

Camulinius 3707

Camulissius 3722, F.45

Carantia 4229

Carantinus 4047

Carata 4124

Cappo]nius 11319; REA 18,
  1916, 289; cf. AE
  1913.242

Cattonius 3990

Catus Germ. 21, 1937, 50;
  but G(ratus) or
  G(natus) N.71

Catullius 4247

Cingetius 3707

Cobrouius 4165

Cobruna 4248

Cocus 4059

Cocio F.35

Couirus, -ius 3707, 4200,
  11313; F.7, 26; R.2471

The Names of the Treueri

Dagissius 11313

Dagsillus 4265

Daguus 4265

Dannus, -ius, -issa
4228(?), 3993, 3979
(Ð-)

?Deuas F.20, cf. 6221,
6458

Deuillius, -ia 4159, 4281

Diucia 4244

Donilla 3724, 3994

Donissius 4266

Donicat[ius 3707

Eburia 4103

Ebur[F.321

Gabra, -illa 4011, 4260;
Cabra 4222

Gismillus, -a, -ia 4228,
3996

Gi(a)mmius 3995

Gimmionius, -a 4167

Gnata 3979

Ianetus Ant. Cl. 8, 1939,
232

Iassus, -a, -ius 4146,
4277, F.46

Indutius 4126

Indutillus num.

Ioincissius 4248

Io(u)incatius 3707, 4127;
R.2471

Ioinci[onius 11313
(R.2471)

Iunetius 4116

Iurcinius 4268

Liscius 3707

Lucotios num.

Lugissius 11313

Magius, -io, -iona,
-issius 3731, 4009,
4031, 11313

Mallus 3653

Mammicia F.74

Manduissa 3995

Marul[lus 3715

Masce(llus) 4092

Mascellionius 3733

Masclia 4170

The Names of the Treueri

Mato 4005 (dat. sg. f.)
   F.64, cf. N.19

Matuinius F.26

Mauillo 4003

Melius 3647, 3797

Moxsius, Mogsius 3707,
   4002

Nammauos 3.5901, R.2494

Nant(ius) 3.5901

Nerta 3652

Reticiana 3638

Sacra 3996

Sacrius 4207

Sacratus, -ius 4207

Sacril(l)a 4166, 4227

Sacruna 3641

Sacerianus 4207

Sappulo, -a 3743, 3990

Senecio 3707

Seneconius 4250

Senilius 4028, 4207

Senuria 4162

Sira 4205

Succius 3707

Tasgillus, -a 3695a,
   4106

Tauso 4012 (dt. f.)

Teddiatus 4142

Tessillinius 4047

Totia 4177

Treuerius 3707

Troucetissa 3.14349

Tutia 3725

Vico 4013

Viducus 4007

Vimpuro, -onius 4019

Vinia 4105

Virius F.21

Vriesulius 3649 (Campanus)

208C

   There is also the group of pet names, including
those which were formed by shortening compound single

745

The Names of the Treueri

names, as Eppo, Sammus. A characteristic feature of these is consonant gemination; however, when a formant containing a long consonant (e.g. -issa) also appears, then a preceding "double" consonant is reduced by dissimilation (e.g. Donilla: Donno-). Weisgerber enumerates 20 such names and their derivatives, pointing out that a clear distinction between this and the preceding group cannot always be drawn:

Atepo 4163

Ateponius (or -rus) 4162

Belatulla 4250

Bittius F.11

Cossius 11316, R.2521

Cossus 11313, R.2471

Excingon(ius) 11313

Iattossa 4152

Iblia 4229

Iccius 3717

Iulla 2029, F.67

Luccus 3707

Messionius, -ia 4145, F.45

Jouuius 3707

Secco 3650, 4171, 4202

Senna, -ius, -ia 3707, 4033, 2029

Settus 3980

Sollius, -ia 4013, 4049, 4127

Veccus 11313, R.2471

Vitto REA 38, 1936, 41

Vlittius 3707

On the Germanic origin which has been claimed for some of the above names (e.g. Sinto-, cf. Goth. sinþs "time," lit. "way," OE. siþ) see Weisgerber 320-21.

208D

But there is a remainder of about equivalent bulk (189 names), the source of many of which is not precisely traceable; a few are Germanic, and a few more are probably such:

The Names of the Treueri

Abba 3746, 3985 (Germ.?)

Acaunissa 4009

Adarus 8670 (Germ.?)

Aesiua F.44

Agatillus 4268

†Agroecius eps. R. Lit.
ix 43

Agritius 4203

Aiia 7516a

Aio 3707 (Germ.?)

Alctus 3988

Ambat[us 3686; or
amba[χ]tus?

Amma 4059, 4144, 4176
(Germ.?)

Ammausus F.3

Ammius 4132 (Germ.)

Am(m)illo (f., dat.)
4159, 4281

Am(m)ossa 3995 (Germ.?)

Ammutius 4159

Anauo 4270 (f., dat.)

Ancreianius F.78

Anisatius 4124

Anna 4159, 4200

Annito (dat., fem.) 4168

Apronius R.2451

Aprossus, -ius 4152, 4192

Arbusius F.29

Arda num.

Ar(e)gaippus 4105

Armenius R. Lit. xii 23

Aruesc(ius) 11313

Attauilla 3718

Attedonius 3707

Attioius 4273

Attius R.1437

Atto 3707, 4089, 4162
(Ato), 4177, 4209
(Germ.?)

Attonius F.32, 3.5797

Attucia 4106

Aturiacius 4031, cf. Ateur-
156 above

Atussia 4159

Aunus 3969 (Lig.)

Aχ(s)illius 3641, 3650

†Babbo 3680 (Germ.)

Bataus 3707 (Germ.)

Bimottia 4007

The Names of the Treueri

Bitus 4128 (Thrac.)

Blus(s)in[ius 11313

Boutius 3988

Braetia F.32

Brasius 4261, 2012

Cabilonno 4107

Cacuronius 1984

Calen(a) 4268

Calionius 3721

Capitonius F.238 (AE 1929.
174 Gap-)

Capurillus 11319

Caulnus 4014 (-rn-?)

Caupius F.3

Censonia 4205

Cidionius 3991

Cinianus? 3973

Cletussto 4103

Coblucia 4038

Coiedius 7516a

Coppus 3988

Corobillius 3992

Cossacionius 4166

Cossus, -ius, -ia 3707,
11313, F.33, 11316,
3652

Cossula 4009

Cossillo 7516a

Cosuoni[us 3994

Criccionia 3724

Krilla 4165

Crobus 3778

Cummius F.26

Deccau(us) 7516a

Dedissa 11351

Dimmia 3664 (m.?)

Diseto F.21

Ditias 4084

Doccius 4192

Drappus 4002, 11313

Drindo 4268

Drippia 4247

Ebthocatus 4265

Edullius 4242

Fittio 11605, R.1488
(Germ.?)

Gabso 3681 (Germ.?)

Gamburio 4132 (Germ.?)

The Names of the Treueri

Germanus, -a 3707, 4244,
  F.32, num., see 206
  (Germ.?)

Germania 4060 (Germ.?)

Germaniola 4060 (Germ.?)

Hanhaualdus 3682 (Germ.)

Hariulfus 3682 (Germ.)

H(1)odericus 3683 (Germ.)

Iedussius 4137

Iluatius 11313

Imicius 4146

Indus 3656, 3737, Tac. a.
  3.42 (for ala Indiana
  cf. CIL 13 1, p.584)

Iolsius 4008

Iusia 3637

Iuual[Verh. hist. Vereins
  Oberpfalz 86, 1936,
  439.5

Lagane 4277

Lal(l)us, -a, -ius 3707,
  11313, 4176, 4177,
  4180, 4219, 3998, 4220,
  4269

Lalissus 4176

Lallianus 4002

Ledona F.66

Lellius 3980

Lemafto F.74

Lettius 4168

Losuarca 4008

Loupus 8655 (Germ.?)

Lupercus R.397

Maciatus 11313

Maina, -ius 4095, 11313,
  3707

Mainutius 11313

Maiosa F.65

Mandalonius 4130

Mannius 3652 (Germ.?)

Masgil(us?) 3645 (Germ.?);
  but v. Turmasgade below

Massa 4098

Meccius 3707

Melausus 11351, N.51

?Merital[R.2471, but cf.
  11313

Micco 4089 (Germ.)

Micciona 3984

?Mirio R.2508 (Germ.?)
  but see 11732a

749

The Names of the Treueri

Monnus 3710

Mossa 4042

Mottus 3992

Motto (dat. f.) 3992

Mottio, -a 4257, 4125

Motucius 3735

Nequigo 4007

Nommus 3707

Nouialchus 4123

Ocosuon(i)us F.64

Oledo 3707

Pauto 3992 (Germ.?), cf.
   gl. 220 below

Pennausius 4277

Pessiacus 4003

Piaonius 3679; cf. AcS 2.
   985

Poemenius Amm. 15.6.4

Pop(p)a 4241, 4269

Poppus, -ius 3972, 4217

Popillus 4016

Popillianus 4269

Popira 4248

Pottus (-th-) 4260, F.67

Pottina m., num.

Prisso 4007

Pruscius, -a 4007-09,
   3992

Prusia 11340 (Germ.?)

Puccasius F.47

Quad[11313

Quigilla (Cuigilla, Qui-
   cilla) 3984, 4246,
   4267

Quigo 2669

Reutilo 3682 (Germ.)

Ricenus 4105

Sabinus 3707

Saccius 4206

Sattarus, -a 3745

Satto 3974, 3976, 1984

Sattonius 3650, 4100,
   4106, 4278

Sautus 4123

Seccalus, -ia 4010

The Names of the Treueri

Seisserus 4250

Sementinia 4260

Sen(n)aug(us) 11313
    (Germ.?)

Seranus 4168

Seratia 4180

Sincorius 3707, 4227

Sincorilla 4242

Soiius 4012

Soiianus 4012

Taliounia 4246

Tauena 3701 (cf. 212
    below)

Telionnus 4014

Tetricianus 4211

Teucoriatius F.14 (Germ.?)

Tigidi? (dat. f.) F.44

Titussia 3979

Tonnia 4011

Tornioniius 4016

[?Turmasgade 3645 add:
    (Dac.) i.e. divine
    name]

Vabilis 4179

Varaitio 3707

Varcianus 11313, R.2471

Varedonius 3707

Varicillo (dat. f.) F.70

Varistus 4178 (Germ.?)

Varusius 4177

?Vatichrus 11313, R.2471

Vesecunia 4261

Vildicus 635

Viscareua 4043

Volia 4044

Vollion[ius] 4226

Weisgerber gives a survey (328-29) of the sources
from which the Keltic names derive, as external life
(rix, danno-, cinget-, catu-, ollo-, bitu-, cobro-,
diuic-, touta-, ueni-, -genus, maro-, uiro-, litu-);

Personal Names (Treueri)

personal characteristics (carato-, caranto-, iouinco-,

seno-); the seasons (samo-, giamo-); color or other phy-

sical appearance (adbugio-, bricto-, coc(c)o-, bello-,

uimpo-); place of origin (Deuas, Nantius); animal-names

(arto-, biber, bucco-, epo-) and trees (betulo-, eburo-,

sappulo-).

Those who wish to pursue further the problems presented by the third group of names may take Weisgerber's
remarks (332-359) as a useful starting point. He rightly observes that when a pseudo-gentilicium and a cognomen belonging to one and the same person appear in this
group (e.g. Bimottia Nequigo), it is clear that we have
non-Keltic names. The Germanic names are of late (even
Christian) date; some are due to the enrollment of Germans in the legions, or in a few instances to the beginning of the period of migrations. Some, that are possibly Germanic (marked above: Germ.?), may be in part
even pre-Roman in origin, the rest of the third or fourth
century of our era. It is noteworthy that some of these
last, and a few others, are among those which it is
fashionable to call Illyrian, in defiance of geography;
I am sceptical also of Ligurian identifications (except
the single name Aunus 3969) among the Treueri.

The attempt to discriminate among the rest as being
limited to the Treueri; to the Treueri and their neighbors; as known to the Treueri and found also elsewhere
in Gaul, or in other provinces (notably the Danubian),
or in Cisalpine Gaul, or so widely distributed as not to
merit precise characterization, is only partially conclusive. But some interesting details emerge. Thus beside Sincorius observe Sinccus (Remi) and the divine name
Sinquas (3968-9, Géromont, the most western limit of the
Treueri, accompanied by the Ligurian personal name Aunus;
but note also O.L. seinq i.e. sign[um?] CIL 1, ed. 2,
388, cf. Ihm Rh.Mus. 7, 1902, 316; Muller, Mnemosyne 3rd.
Ser., 2, 1935, 244); beside Nequigo, Quigilla, (Quicilla,
Cuigilla) and Quigo (Germanic? Cf. Goth. qius, OE cwicu?
For qu- cf. also Quad[208D), noteworthy by reason of
qu-, cf. Quiguro at Lyons, to which perhaps he had mi-

The Names of the Treueri

grated from Trier. In general, however, links in nomenclature between the Treueri and the tribes to the west
of them are so good as lacking; and even with the people
of the Cologne region to the north extremely rare. With
the Mediomatrici they are naturally well marked; but
scanty indeed in more remote regions, except in the middle Rhine and upper Danube, and north Italy; even there,
they are not numerous. Finally, attention may be called
to the comparative frequency of diphthongs (e.g. Boutius,
Varaitio); to the peculiar forms in -sto, -fto (Cletussto,
Lemafto); and to the wide extension of Latin -onius,
-anius annexed to older names.

209   Local Names of the Treueri

Trēuerī cl. (Caes., Hirt., Tac.), itinn., inscc.; Treuer

    e.g. N.71, CIL 13.3695a, Treuera 233, Treuir Lucan

    1.441; additional examples 13.11967, Dipl. 23, 84

    Nesselhauf (Treuir); 13.1608 (3.5215, R.395), 13.

    11605, 6.1625a, Dipl. 82, Vollmer 108,236, N.109

    (Treuer, Treueri); 13.7118 (Treuera); 6.1641

    (Treuerica); cf. Cuny Rev. de Philol. 56, 1930,

    24; Τρηούεφι Str., Treuiri late but also Cic.;

    4100; Treuericus Pl., Tac., Τρίβηφοι Ptol., Τίη-

    ούηφοι Dio. Late usage called the Treueri Franci

    or even Sugambri (R. Lit. 13.143-44)

    Thurneysen RhM 84, 1935, 188-92 explains the name
as Keltic: trē- "through," older *trei- (Mid.W. trwy,
OIr. tri, tre, cf. W-P 1.734) and *uer- "water, wet"
attested by local names associated with rivers or

bridgeheads, at least in the form uar- (from *u̯r-) e.g.
Argentouaria, or uōr- (from *uār-) e.g. Vārus. If this
is right, we may count the divine-name Vdrouarinehis (223
below) either as an intensive binomial compound, or
(with Gutenbrunner Götternamen, 1936, 182) as containing
*udro- "otter," and uar- "water;" cf. also the divine
names Vorioni, Voroi (both dat. sg.), i.e. "gods of the
ford" at Trier and Pantenburg (Wittich) respectively
(N.13, F.82). Ir. treoir (ī-stem, or with an old ī fem.)
"water-crossing" also contains uor-, but (like the sg.
Treuir[?], gen. -is, cf. Cuny l.c.) is not an o-stem.
Thurneysen interprets the name Trēueri as active, "die
den Fluss Durchquerenden" i.e. they transported goods
over the Moselle. Vendryes, summarizing Thurneysen,
calls attention (EC 1, 1936, 374-75) to Isid. 20.14.13
uerennes (a uehere, id est exportare nominatae, see 178
above; Sofer 167), in which he sees the same root, and
a suffix -enni or -endi; cf. Dauzat REA 28, 1926, 156
(Merov. Briouera, -o, Briuuiri). To these we may add
uara-, identified by Berthoud in Ambi-uareti, see REA
31, 1929, 60; cf. SprFK 212 (but this is presumably not
the uara of Auson. technop. 4; AcS 3.103; cf. Lat. uarus,
uaratio, uaratus, unless the notion is "curved, winding,"
Vergellus fl. ID 33A; Ernout-Meillet s.vv.; uargus Walde
ed. 2, uarro Do.296).

The remaining names of the district follow, references not being given except to names not included in
212 below; cf. Steinhausen 303-306.

pagus Ac[or Ag[F.238

Ambitaruius (v.l. Ambia-
    tinus?)

Andethanna

?Apollinesses N.53, cf.
    211 below

Arbores Sanctae see 211
    below

[?Aresaces v. P-W Suppl.
    Bd. 6.12, where the

name is treated as
Keltic on the ground
of -āc-. But this
should be -āco-, and
are- is properly pre-
fixed to recognizable
words. Cf. Note
xlviii, 223, 234 below.
Possibly we have Par-
thian troops, cohortes
Arcsacum, cf. Arsaces
(Tac. G.37 ca. 250
B.C.); for Syrians at
Trier cf. IG 14.2559-
60.) See however Beh-

Local Names (Treueri)

rens in MZ 36, 1941,
16-18 (AE 1945.86-87),
and 221 below]

uicus Auetae F.5 (perhaps
divine name)

Ausaua, modern Oos

Beda uicus, uikani
Bedenses

Belginum

pagus Carucum

Contionacum

Crutisiones coloni

[?Deuas 6221, F.20; or
personal?]

Epos(s)ium (Vannérus Bull
Cl. Lettres, Acad. Bel-
gique 21, 1935, 241);
cf. the personal name
Epasius 11298?

Icorigium (v.l. Ego-)

Lusiaco (Steinhausen 577)

Nouiomagus

Oleuia, Oliuia, now Olewig-
Bach, see TrZ 10, 1935,
73

Orolaunum

Ricciacum

Rigodulum

uicus Seniae 11316

Soiaco mod. Schweich
(Steinhausen 577)

?Talliates 13.7777-78,
F.254, Steinhausen 303

pagus Teucorias F.14

pagus Vilcias F.13, said
to be Wiltz fl.

uicus Voclannionum

?Vosugones N.43; see
234, 236 below

Modern Local Names of Trier (Trèves)
and Vicinity

210

Alster, Auweiler (Nieder-Auwen); Beltingen, Berberg,
Bergweiler, Birresborn, Bollendorf, Brecht, Breidweiler,
Bruch; Castel, Consdorf, Conz; Dalheim, Daun, Dreiborn;

Modern Local Names (Treueri)

Echternach; Faha, Ferschweiler, Filsdorf, Fliessem,
Föhren, Franzenheim; Géromont, Gérouville, Greimerath;
Haselbuch, Hemstal, Hermeskeil, Hersberg, Höfchen,
Hollerich, Hondelingen, Hontheim, Hostert; Idenheim,
Igel, Irsch, Irrel; Junglinster, Jünkerath; Kasselt,
Kesslingen; Lampaden, Landscheidburg, Langsur, Limbach,
Longwy, Luxemburg; Majeroux, St-Mard, Merl, Mersch,
Michelbach, Möhn, Mürlenbach; Natterheim, Neidenbach,
Neumagen, Niedaltdorf, Niedersemmel, Niersbach; Olk;
Pachten, Pantenburg, Pelm, Pieckliessen, Poncel; Reins-
porth, Reisweiler, Ruwer; Saarburg, Sassenheim, Schock-
weiler, Schuttringen, Schwarzenbach, Sefferweich, Serrig,
Speicher, Strotzenbusch; Taben, Temmels, Tholey, Thurm
(Weiler-am-), Titelberg, Tossenberg; Udelfangen; Varus-
wald, Veldenz, (Vieux-)-Virton; Wald-, Wasser-, Welsch-
billig, Walderach, Wallerfangen, Weilerbachtal, Wiltingen,
Wittich; Zwalbach

Divine Names of the Treueri

211

(References given in 213 below are not repeated
here)

Abgatiacus F.80   Alauna F.82, 83; Alun[(?)

Divine Names (Treueri)

Linckenheld Annuaire
Soc. d'hist. et. d'Arch.
Lorraine 38, 1929, 143
(cf. RC 46, 1929, 362)

Ancamna F.12, 13, 14(?),
20; cf. 254. Possibly
also in 13.4119(?),
7778(?). On -mna (pre-
I.Eu.?) cf. Kretschmer
Glotta 14, 1925, 319;
28, 1940, 114

Apollinessiu[m] genius
N.53

Arbores sanctae FHRC 299.
36; cf. Fagus and Sex-
arbor 86 above, Robur
155; REA 39, 1937, 44

?Arte...cus 4137 (personal
name?); AcS 1.224,30

Artio 4113, 4203; cf.
Gnomon 5, 1929, 281;
i.e. arto- "bear" (W.
arth), cf. Do. Mélan-
ges Loth 1927, 92-98

Aueta F.5, N.1; for -nta?
Cf. Auentia F.91, and
13.5074 (Avenches)

Bigentius 11346 (cf. mod-
ern local name Pies-
port?); R.3336

Boudina 11975, F.83; cf.
13.8217

Caiua

Camulus

Caprio

Casses, Cassi 4047(?);
F.6-8, N.2; F.33(?).

Cf. 6668; SprFK 196-
197; 80 (Cars-) and
gl. 178 above; 236,
243 below

Cissonius

?[C]reto (T]-?) F.238;
TrZ 2, 1927, 12-21;
AE 1929.174. But it
is remarkable that
an insc. of Dijon (AE
1926.59) also has an
incomplete]rito dat.
sg.m., both insc.
being found in 1925.
Since the writing e
for i is not uncommon,
are the names the
same? Are they cor-
rected for Prito cf.
Ritona: Pritona (F.29)?
Jullian REA 28, 1926,
259 would interpret
T]rito as "Quarto"

Epona N.7; R-GK Ber. 23,
1933 [1934], 126-143;
cf. 7555a, R.2531

[Esus 3656 with ad.]

Gnabetius (for C-) 4258;
ZfCPh 20, 1935, 278-
83

Grannus 3659, 3635, N.71,
Germ. 20, 1936, 60;
FHRC 85.31

Icouellauna

Inciona F.69

Intarabus (Ent-) 4128,
F.11, R.2471, cf.
Germ. 21, 1937, 103

Iouantucarus 4256, cf.
10024.6, F.15-19

Divine Names (Treueri)

[Iunones 3642, N.8; i.q.
matronae, not several
Iuno's. Cf. Mineruae,
Maiae, pl., and Suleua
sg.]

Lenus F.20, 21, cf. 254(?);
N.9; cf.G.21, 1937, 103

Loucetius 7.36; cf. 13.
7412; 11605, R.1488

Matres Treuerae 8634, AcS
2.1935,48

Matronae N.4; cf. RA 10,
1937, 209; Kruger in
Schumacher Festschrift
1930, 239-253; the
matronae are at least
as much Keltic as Ger-
manic (cf. W. Heiligen-
dorf Der Kelt. Matron-
enkultus, Diss. Greif-
swald, Leipzig 1934;
F. Cramer Röm. Matronen-
kultus 1936 [BPhCl. 63.
4414] I have not seen);
for a new interpretation
of their head-dress cf.
Bickel BJ 143-4, 1939,
209-220 (cf. RhM 87,
1938, 193-241, with 88,
1939, 384). But see
also Lambrechts Ant.
Cl. 7, 1938, 378-380;
add the bibliogr. at
223 below (Germ. Inf.);
Sjoestedt Dieux..des
Celtes, 1940, pp.24,
35,75

Meduna 7667

Nemetona 7.36, N.12,
F.324(?)

Pisintus (siue Vertumnus)
F.31

Pritona v.sq.

?deo Regi Cupiti Germ. 18,
1934, 223

Ritona (dat. sg.) F.30;
Ritona Pritona F.29;
cf. 12.2927, 13.2813(?).
What is the relation
of Ritona and Pritona?
Cf. Creto above? Thur-
neysen RhM 84, 1935,
189 interprets rito-
as ritu- "ford"

Rosmerta 4192-95, F.80;
cf. 13.2831

Senia 11316

Sinquas 3968-69; on -qu-
cf. p.752 above, cf.
Gutenbrunner p.72;
Vannérus Bull. Ac.
Belg., Cl. Lett. 21,
1935, 229; note also
Sinati Toutati in CIL
3.5320?

Sirona 4129

Smertrius 4119, 11975

Sucellus F.87

[Toutates (Tut-, Teut-)
see Cocidius 213 below,
Sinquas above]

Treto v. Creto

[?Turmasgadis Dac. or
Syr., 3645; cf. BSAF
1911, 200, 211; 1912,
196]

Vassocaletes 4130; cf.
gl. 158 above; Vasso

Divine Names (Treueri)

kaleti regis CIL 13 iv (1916) p.19 add. to p.194 n.3; Vannérus l.c. p.228

Vegnius 4049

Veraudunus F.69; cf. Virodunum (212 below), REA 29, 1927, 312

Vercana 7667; cf. 4511

Vindoridius 11975

Visucius 3660; cf. 577

Vorio N.13 (for B-?)

Voroi(us?) F.83

?Vosugonum genio N.43; but this (209 above) is probably an ethnicon cf. J. Meyers Ons Hémecht 40, 1934, 120-125. Other references are: Germ. 22, 1938, 190-91 and 239-40; REA 38, 1936, 43; 41, 1939, 261; AE 1939.104; P. Medinger in Cahiers Arch. Hist. Alsace (inaccessible to me) no.99-100, 1934, 219 (from Historia 9, 1935, 680); Linckenheld ib. 216-17. See also below 212 (Vosegus), 213 (?Vogesus), 234 (Vosegus, Vosagus), 236 (Vosegus). R. Forrer in Cahiers... Alsace 28, 1935-38, 155-160 (cf. RA 10, 1937, 352) proposed the reading Mercur(io) Voges(o) Ecate in 13. 4550 (usually read Mercurio Secate or et Hecatae) or, as an alternative Mercur(io) Vassocalete; but the reading is exceedingly difficult and dubious.

Xulsigiae F.21 (a miswriting of Suleuiae??)

Remark:

(a) CIL 13.11319, 11360, F.41 all offer

ceruesarius

at Trier, from which it would appear that both the word and the product ceruesa (see 178 above) were known there. But trade may be responsible for the foreign word (cf. spatharius, cassidarius 207 above; cuparius, saccarius 13.22; uinarius 2033). On F.41 (artis offecturae) see Rostovtzeff CRAcInscBL 1930, 250-256; in view

Names of Belgica

of uinarius et artis cretariae (2033) the explanation
("dealer in beer-colored stuffs") seems mistaken. See
further P.W. s.v. Treueri for other inscriptions of the
district containing ceruesarius.

(b) Germ. 18, 1934, 58 gives a signaculum ocularii
that names a remedy not otherwise recorded and so far
not interpreted, viz.

poscomiuiu

Here pos is perhaps phos (10021.210; cf. fos 211, foos
153), but the rest is unexplained.

Names of Belgica

Sources given in AcS are not, as a rule, repeated
here, cf. p.174; arabic numerals, without other indication of source, refer to CIL 13, viz. i 2 (1904) 3253-
4740 (pp.521-719) with iv (1916) 11288-11467 (pp.40-61),
and ii 2 (1907) 9026-9054 (pp.683-92), together with
Finke 1-4, 87-90, 328-331 (for Finke 5-86, Nesselhauf
1-57 see Proleg. 7). A.W. Byvanck Excerpta Romana (3
volumes) 'S-Gravenhage, 1931-1947, especially 1.534-586;
corrections to CIL 13 by de Ricci REA 4, 1902, 214. The
Bulletin de la Commission des Antiquités départmentales
(Pas-de-Calais 1932-37, St Omer 1892-37, Arras 1883) are
not accessible to me (except 1869-1874 incomplete). V.
Tourneur Recherches sur la Belgique classique in Le
Musée Belge 6, 1902, 423 ff.; 7, 1903, 476 ff. and later
years (9, 1905, cf. ZfCPh 5, 1905, 190 and 587), Latomus
5, 1946, 179-180 are important. On the recent discoveries at Arlon see J. Breuer Bull. Cl. Lettres, Acad. de
Belgique 24, 1938, 136-41 (Jahrb. deutschen Arch. Inst.
53, 1938, 109). On local names in Ravenna see Vincent
Latomus 5, 1946, 373-79.

Local and Ethnic Names

212

[Abrianeco, said to be
Branges (Aisne)?]

Abelica (Ablica, Ebl-
A.D. 712, Albe fl.,
trib. of Saar

[?Abulci ND]

Acciaca uilla mod. Essey

Adsultus A.D. 751, Seux
or Acheux(?), Somme

[Aduatuca v. 221 below]

Aepatiacus v. Itius por-
tus, Epat- below

Agnio fl. A.D. 723, Aa
(Pas-de-Calais, Nord)

[Alamanni CIL 13 p.691]

Alba fl., Aubetin (Seine-
et-Marne)

Alciacus Zudausques (Pas-
de-Calais)

Alisontia fl. Auson., Elz;
cf. ZONF 4, 1928, 269-
71

[Allobriges Ptol., Rav.,
see AcS 1.96,34 and
221 below; Byv. 1.580;
Bull. Soc. Arch. de
Sens 30, 1916, 1-9]

Ambiani cl. inscc. 9032,
14.4468 -ensis, OE
Embéne, Amiens; REA
16, 1914, 97; MSAF
1914, 249-256

Ambitaruius uicus Suet.
(ap. Treueros), Hen-
tern; according to
other accounts, near
Coblenz; cf. 234

Ambiuariti Caes.; cf.
Ambiuareti (Lugd.?).
For Amb(i)-iuara?

Andelaum Fredeg., cf.
CIL 13 p.702, Andelot

Andethanna (-alis) uicus
IA, Sulpic. Seu.,
Fortun.; Anwen (Luxem-
bourg), F. p.23

Andouerpus(-is), Anderpus;
Antwerp. AcS 1.146 and
151 (Merov. num.)

Aperienses coloni F.89

Aquila, -ela fl., Eichel;
Aculinse (A.D. 713)
AcS 1.33; distinguish
Holder's *Aquilensis
(Eflimse A.D. 762)
AcS 3.646, cf. Afliae
223 below

?Arbalo fl. (Erpe) Pl.
11.55

?Arcegeto Merov. num.

Arduenna silua (-in-) cl.,
insc. 3631, also div-
ine name; Ardennes,
cf. W. Kaufmann Bezeichn.
Wald, 63-4, 80; REA 13,
1911, 209; 27, 1925,
330; VKG 1, 50; MLI
prol. xcviii; Glotta 14,

Local and Ethnic Names

1925, 318; RL-Rom. 4,
1928, 246 n.4

Aronna fl., Aronde (trib.
of Oise)

Atrebates cl., insc. 9158,
14.4468 (add REA 16,
1914, 97; MSAF 1914,
249-256), -icus and
-ensis; also in Brit-
ain. Arras

[Atuatuca -i (offspring
of the Cimbri and Teu-
tones, BG 2.29, like
Neruii), Ad- cl., Ἀτ-
ουἀτουκον Ptol.,
insc.(?), cf. 221 be-
low; Vetschau]

Augustomagus itinn., now
Senlis (Oise)

?Autrium (Dict. Top., 17:
Meuse), Autrecourt
(retroformate?)

Axonna fl. cl., later
Assena AcS 3.709,3,
Aisne; cf. sq. For
*ōpsonā(?) W.u.S. 11,
1928, 61

Axuenna itinn. (v.l. Aux-
enna or Muenna cf. C.
p.688), identified
with various sites in
dép. Marne or Aisne

Audaste uillare (near
Malmedy) Pertz Dipl.
2.146 (A.D. 667)

Ausaua uicus and fl.,
itinn., Oos (Trier)?
But v. Aucia 241 below

Baciuum lib. hist. Fr., Bai-
zieux (Somme); cf. 179
above

Baconna, Baconnes (Marne);
cf. 221 below

Baetasii cl. inscc.

Βάγακον, Bag(i)acum
(Baiacum, later Bau-
acum) Ptol., itin.,
Bavay; RC 50, 1933,
245-71; Rom. 61, 1936,
517; Vox Rom. 1, 1936,
186-87

Barisiacum Dipl. A.D. 661,
664; AcS 1.350 (Bari-
zis)

Barrensis (Bar-le-Duc,
Barrois, C. p.705),
see Nasium

?Basilia IA (cf. AcS 3.
812,7; not Basel)

?Bassi Pl. 4.106; cf.
uia Bassoniaca (AcS
1.358) in Germ. Sup.?

Baudobriga(-c-) itin.,
Bodoureca Merov. num.,
Bupprich (near Trier)?
But see 234 below
(Boppard) and distin-
guish also Bodobrio
Budberg (221, 222)

Beda uicus, Bedensis,
Bedenses (uikani)
4131; itinn., late
authors, Bitburg
(near Trier); cf.
Note xlv B (Beda, Rica-
gambeda), AcS 1.364,38-
365,37

762

Local and Ethnic Names

Belgae, -icus cl., inscc. (1042-45, 1687, 1807, cf. 1165) Belge, Belgique

Belginum, -ates(?) itin., inscc. 4085, 7555a

Belgium cl., prouincia Belgica 3.1017, 6.1548; cf. AcS 1.384, Belgius, Belgites. All these names have been again associated of late with Ir. Fir Bolg (e.g. Proc. Brit. Acad., 21, 1935, 328)

Bellouaci cl., -ugui Oros.; -ensis, Beauvais (also called Caesaromagus). Cf. REA 39, 1937, 347-62

Bertunum (V-) Verton (Pas-de-Calais). Cf. 221 and Virodunum below; Dubois Le uicus romaine de Vertunum (Gnomon 15, 1939, 29)

Beuerna uilla, see AcS 2. 281, 28

Bibe TP (near Châlons-sur-Marne); BSAF 1935, 36

Bibrax Remorum Caes.; cf. 179, 181 above

Bitunia Béthune (Pas-de-Calais)

Bleza fl. Rav. 4.26 Blies (trib. of Saar)

Bodatius uicus 4310

Bonomagus Bombogen (Trier)

Bononia (also called Gesoriacus, perhaps the same as Itius portus) OE Bunne, Mid.Ndl. Bönen, now Boulogne-sur-Mer (Pas-de-Calais); itin., Eutrop., MG, ASS, num.; -iensis. See also Mommsen Staatsr. 2.229; Kornemann Klio 9, 1909, 422-449; 10, 1910, 258-260 (REA 12, 1910, 200-201, 417); REA 27, 1925, 334; 28, 1926, 169; Βου-ωνία AE 1910.23, cf. RA 19, 1912, 478, R.7; for the confusion with Bonna-Gesoriacum see 221 below s.vv. and see also Gaesoriacus below

Bratuspantium Caes. (ap. Bellouacos), cf. Glossary s.v. bratu-, and note -sp- Breteuil-sur-Noye (Somme)? REA 39, 1937, 347-362; BSAF 1910, 136

Brinnacus uilla Greg. Tur., Berny-Riviére (Aisne)

Britanni Pl. 4.106; cf. CIL 13 vi (1933), p.135; Britto natine 1981 (cf. natina 2146)

Bri(u)odurum Merov. num., Brières (Ardennes)

Broilus Breuil-sur-Vesle (Marne); AcS 2.546,38; cf. gloss 178

Local and Ethnic Names

[?Buconice, Bou- (Bau-)
-connica, Bruchloch
(Luxembourg) 4085; cf.
221, 234 below]

Buxarias uilla Dipl. Merov.
(Riese Lit. p.410), cf.
gl. 79 and Boxsani 80
above; Bauxeare PID 1.
455 (Bozen). Perhaps
Buxières?

Caero(e)si cl.

Caesaromagos itinn., now
Beauvais (Oise), see
Bellouaci above

Calagum (leg. Caliacum?)
TP, Chailly-en-Brie
(Seine-et-Marne)

Caleti or -es cl. (cf.
Caux, Seine-Inf.),
Belg. and Lugd.(179
above)

Camaracus -ensis itinn.,
ND, Greg. Tur., Cam-
brai, Kameryk (Nord)

[Campania (Remensis) Greg.
Tur., Champagne] cf.
Campanus 3649

Caranusca TP (add AcS 3.
1096), now Garsch
(Kiesel) "stony" (i.e.
*cara- "stone" and Lig.
-usca (Vannérus, see
REA 28, 1926, 364; 31,
1929, 261; 33, 1931,
45-6; 35, 1933, 176);
or Canner pl. (CIL 13,
pp.587-88; cf. Gaunia
below); for *cara- see
85 above

Cardena Rav. 4.26 (Karden)

?Cares fl., Fortun., Chiers(?)
But the reading is prob-
ably corrupt

Caruces, pagus Carucum 4143;
in middle ages Carouuas-
cus, Carascus AcS 3.1113
and 1115; 1128

Casebere(n)sis 3534

Castellum (Menapiorum)
Ptol., TP, IA, cf. AcS
2.546; Cassel (Nord)

Caturiges (-rr-) itinn.
(between Remi and Leuci)

Catusiacum IA (ap. Remos?)

Catuslogi Pl. 4.106; cf.
Do. 244

Catu(u)ellauni, Catalauni
(Cate-) Hieron., Eu-
trop., Ammian., NG.,
Châlons-sur-Marne
(Marne); ethn. -icus
and -ensis

Celbis fl., Auson.; Kyll
(Eifel). But the codd.
have Gelbis, Belgis, or
Gelsis.

Cernone fl., Sanon AcS 1.
993; cf. 153, 179 (Sen-)
above

Ceutrones Caes.; see also
10 above

Chersiacus pagus (ap.
Morinos) Plin. 4.106
(an Gesoriacus?) Cf.
REA 3, 1901, 84n.; cf.
80 (Chars-) above

Local and Ethnic Names

[?Cilicia Ant. Cl. 14,
1946, 177; from Cod.
Theod., see Riese Lit.
p.319 n.1, 320; cf.
Cael- 241. But see
P-W s.v.]

Clauatum v. Lugdunum be-
low; cf. Clauariatis
(213) and REA 26, 1924,
348-49 (clau- "hill,
summit"?)

[Conbulantia Rav. 4.26
and (?) Complatum Cod.
Theod. see Riese Lit.
p.319 n.1 But this
may be Confluentes 234
below]

[Condrusi see 221 below]

Contionacum CTh. and
CIust., now Conz (at
confluence of Saar and
Moselle); or Contern
(Luxembourg)?

Contraginnentes IA, -enses
ND i.e. Condren (Aisne)
cf. AcS 1.58,46; cf.
Byvanck 1.574; 2.465-6
(Condran)

Cortoriacum ND, Courtrai
(Kortrijk) in West-
Flanders

Cotia (-cia) silua Greg.
Tur., ASS, Lib. hist.
Fr., Cuise-lez-Compiègne
(Oise)

Crouiacus (Crouhy, Aisne)
ASS 8 June 2.84

Crutisiones coloni 4228

Curmiliaca IA, Cormeilles
(Oise), cf. pers.
names Curmillus etc.,
gl. curmi (158 above)

Decempagi TP, IA, Ammian.
(Tarquinpol); REA 39,
1937, 259

Deruus v. AcS 1.1272-73

Deruetius pagus 4679

Did(d)ilo fl., tributary
of Recta (Recht-bach),
Pardessus, Dipl. 2.146
(A.D. 667)

Dionantis (Deo-) Rav.,
Merov. num., Dipl.;
Dinant; -um ASS (see
FHRC 244.15)

Diuoduron (now Metz) cl.
itinn.; R.2547 (6.
32623,23)

?Docauχuicnini (??) 3467
(an Catelauni, Catuuell-
-auni? or ...uicini, cf.
sq., and see Note xl a-
bove

Dolucensis uicus 3563

Doso uico Merov. num.,
Dieuze

Drahonus fl. Auson.,
Drohn, Thron

?Dumno TP (east of Trier;
but if this is the
same as Dumnissus in
Auson., it belongs to
Germ. Inf.)

Local and Ethnic Names

Dunum castrum Dun-sur-
Meuse (Meuse)

Durocatelauni IA, cf. CIL
13, p.681; Châlons-sur-
Marne

Duroicoregum TP, perhaps
Donqueur (Somme); or
two words?

Durocortorum cl., inscc.,
Δουρικορτόρα Str.
194 C., Durocorter[
9158, now Reims (Marne)

Duronum TP, IA; south of
Bavai (Nord)

Eboriacus AcS 2.650,17.

Eburones, Ἐβουρωνοί cl.

Egorigium v. Ico-

Epatiaci portus (Aep-)
ND (W. Flanders; or,
cf. CIL 13, p.561, 569,
Le Tréport); see also
Bononia, Gaesoriacus,
Itius portus

Epossium, Epois- itin.,
ND, Greg. Tur., Merov.
num., Yvois, Ipsch
(Ardennes)

Erubris fl., Auson., Ruwer
(trib. of Moselle)

Esera v. Isara

Ex(s)ona Fortun., Merov.
num., now Essones; for
*epsonā(?) W.v.S. 11,
1928, 61 (cf. Axona

above); but cf. Ex(s)-
obnus? And AcS 2.896
reports Oxona(?) for
Uxama (Spain), but with-
out reference

[Fano Martis] Famars,
Byvanck 1.574; cf.
179 above

[Fanum Mineruae IA, Tano-
mia TP, cf. CIL 13,
p.691]

Frudis (-t-) fl., Ptol.
(Φρούδις) Cf. W. ffrwd??

Gaesoriacus portus cl.,
afterwards called Bon-
onia, q.v. But the
town of the same name,
opposite Bonna (v.l.
Borma) ap. Flor. 4.12.
26 is evidently a dif-
ferent place; cf. Aep-
atiacus (Epa-), Itius
portus. However the
Irish monk Dicuil in
Liber de mens. Orb.
terrae (ca. A.D. 825)
treats Gaesoriacus as
identical with ciuitas
Rutupi portus, which
he puts among the Morini.
He seems to have been
following Solinus 22,
but that particular error
his own (Byvanck 1, 584).
Cf. Geso-cribate (Brest),
Lugd.

Gaunia Rav. 234.3 (Schnetz
would read Garania); the
modern Canner (CIL 13 pp.
587-88) implies *Gannia;
see also Caranusca above

Local and Ethnic Names

?Geidumni BG 5.39.1

[Geminiacum -ico itin.]

Germani e.g. BG 2.4, 4.6, 6.32; CIL 13 vi (1933) p.135

[Grannum Merov. num.; now Grand, cf. CIL 13 iv p.77, BA 1941-42, 449]

Grauinum TP C. p.561; or the same as Grannona 179?

Grudii BG 5.39.1

Helenae uicus (5th c.) Hélesmes (Nord), Long-non p.142

Helmini roboretum (in the Ardennes) Pard. Dipl. 2.146 (A.D. 667)

Hermoniacum TP (Bermerain Byvanck 1 p.548)

Hesdinum, Hisdinum Chart. Phil. Aug. a. 1191, Hesdin (ad flumen Quan-tiae), cf. Bull. hist. Soc. Ant. de la Morinie 4, 1867-71, 339

[H]isca fl. Isch (tribu-tary of the Saar)

Hiccosus uicus 4131

Honoris uicus 4301 (Metz)

Hornensis ND occ., cf. Quartensis (Le Crobay, Ant. Cl. 13, 1945, 143)

Ibliodurus IA (ap. Medio-matricos?)

Icorigium (Ego-) itinn., near Trier (Iünkerath)

Ictium mare, muir n-Icht, the English Channel; ASS

Indiana ala (at Trier), cf. AcS 2.40; Tac.h. 3.43; cf. 214 below

Io[pagus 4316 (cf. CIL 13 p.662, Le Sablon)

Isara 9158, Esera fl., also Isra, Isera, and even Sara, Sura(?); now the Oise. No doubt the same name lies behind Yser (Nord)

Isca, Esca: v. Hisca

Itius portus BG 5.2.3, Ἴτιον ἄκρον Ptol. Near Boulogne (v. Bon-onia, Gaesoriacus, Epaticus (Aep-); see REA 46, 1944, 299-317; CRAcInsc BL 1944, 372-86; Ant. Cl. 13, 1945, 143; 14, 1946, 355)

?Itocae[ciuit. insc., see AcS 2.83

[Laeti (e.g. Neruii, Lagen-ses, Teutoniciani) Amm-ian., ND occ., Cod. Th., Eumen. paneg. Const., terra Laetica R. Lit. p.340; cf. AcS 2.120; C. p.574. But this, it would seem, is almost cer-

767

tainly not an ethnicon,
but an appellative, and
Germanic, meaning "free,
liberated," Goth. lētan,
OHG. lāz, cf. P-W 12,
1924, 447; and see also
220 below]

Lege fl., Lys (tributary of
the Scheldt) Rav.

Lesura fl., later Lisera,
Auson., Lieser (tribu-
tary of the Moselle);
cf. 80 above

Leuaci BG 5.39.9

Leuci cl., 4630; cf. CIL
13.2955, 2681, 4338,
10022.225, 10024.255
and 428, 10025.136
(R.2583-84); also as
personal name; BA 1941-
42 [1944], 413-28

Leuca urbs (Tullum) see
CIL 13, p.702 n.3

Lintomagus TP

Listinas MG, ASS; Les-
tines, Estinnes (Hain-
ault, Belgium)

Litanobriga IA

Lomacensis pagus AcS 2.
281; (?)Lamalcensis
BSA Morinie 5, 1872-6,
164; but Camalacensis
ib. 256

Lorica, Lauro, Lauricus
RA 4, 1934, 191; see
further 212 bis Remark
(1) below

Lucofao, Lufao (?) lib.

hist. Fr. 320.10

Lugdunum -ensis, sc. Rem-
orum, commonly called
Clauatum, MG, Greg.
Tur., ASS; Laon (Aisne);
cf. AcS 1.1040, 2.343,
CIL 13, p.523

?Lullia (v.l. ad Iullia)
TP

Marcello (-rs-) uico in
pago Salinense Pard.
Dipl. Merov. 454 (Riese
Lit. p.451)

[Marci or -ae, Marck(?);
-is, now Marquise Ant.
Cl. 13, 1945, 143; Cf.
Byvanck 1.572; Mardick,
Merquise (C. p.561)]

Marosallenses uicani 4565,
-sallo num. Merov.,
Marsal (Lorraine)

Ma[r]tis Fanum ND

Matrŏna fl. cl., later
Maderna (Rav.) or
Materna (ASS), now
Marne

Mauriaci campi (Catalaun-
ici) Iord. Get. 36,
Greg. Tur. h. Fr. 2.7

Mecusa ciuitas Rav. (Metz
according to Schnetz)

Mediol(anum?), Med, Medlu
on leaden tesserae, per-
haps Ru Mélaine (Oise),
10029.220, AcS 2.519;
distinguish (ib. 520,
52) Medelingen(?) Fort.
3.12.10; see also 221
below

Local and Ethnic Names

Mediomatrici cl., inscc.
623, 1807, 2674, 2954,
3656, 4291, 4324, 4327,
8635(?), 11353b (4324b),
11359, 11360; cf. 9053,
9053, Vollmer 259. The
modern Metz cannot rep-
resent this directly
but either a personal
Metti(us), cf. gloss
(246 below) mettica
uitis, hence the late
(5th cent.; ND, For-
tun.) Met(t)is; or (Ven-
dryes MSL 23, 1923-35,
52) is a curtailed fam-
iliar form for Medio-
matrici; cf. Mecusa
above

Meduanto TP, Nohan (Ar-
dennes)? Or Membré
(Desjardins 109)?
Distinguish *Meduenta
(Mantes) 179? AcS 2.
526

[Meldi (-ae) see 179
above]

?Melianum, Meduolanense
castrum, see AcS 2.
520,22, now Moëlan
(Haute-Marne)

Menapii cl., inscc. (e.g.
624); CIL 11.390-91;
13 vi (1933), p.137.
The references to
marshes (Caes., Strabo)
confirm the interpre-
tation of -apio- as
"water"

Mettis (Mediomatrici) see
CIL 13, pp.404, 662;
AcS 2.580; cf. Medio-
matrici above, Fortun.

3.13.9; 7.4.16. For
dat.-abl. pl. of Met-
tius (6235, C. p.583;
Mettus or Metius
10032.17)? Mettensis.
See also Muret Rom. 50,
1924, 451; Bruneau
Bibl...Lorraine 1922-
23 (Rev. Ling. Rom. 1,
1925, 385). Cf. Mecusa
above (Metusa C. p.587)

Minariacum IA

?Minatiticum IA, Ninittaci
TP; Vinictacum and Nina-
tacum (Nizy-le-Comte)
are conjectural. Holder
(AcS 2.586,37, cf. 3.172)
compares pagus Vennecti
(Nennecti), below, cf.
177

Morini cl., inscc. 3560,
8727;11.390-91; ciuitas
Morin[BSAF 1899, 383;
Murrini in an insc. of
Ostia NdSc 1913, 15
(cf. MSAF 3, 1914, 249-
256; REA 16, 1914, 97),
14.4468 (Byvanck 2.102
and 1433; R.729); cas-
trensis Morini (gen. sg.)
C. pp.560, 567

Morta, Murta fl., ASS;
Meurthe

Mosa fl., cl. (OHG Māsa,
OE Masu), Maas or Meuse
In TP Mose (ap. Remos)
may be a different name;
in CIL 13, p.702, iden-
tified with Meuvy; or
i.q. Maceria (ib. p.586)
Mézieres, Ardennes?

Mosella fl., cl., Auson.,

769

Local and Ethnic Names

Mosallici nautae 4335;
Moselle, Mosel

Mosomagus -ensis MG, Mus-
magenses ND, Mouzon
(Ardennes); cf. Musmo
PID 2.165?

Mucra fl. ASS (see AcS 2.
650,16)

Namucum (-g-) MG, Rav.,
Merov. num., now Namur

Nasaga Rav. 4.26; cf.
Nasonacum Cod. Theod.
(R. Lit.p.319 n.1)

Náσιον, Nasium Ptol.,
itinn. Fredeg.; Nasien-
ses 10029.221 (R.2590);
Nasio uico [in Bar-
rense] num. Merov.;
Naix-aux-Forges (Meuse)

[Naua fl. Tac., Auson.,
later Naha, now Nahe;
also Germ. Sup.]

?Nauriacus Ven. Fort. (ap.
Mediomatricos?)

Nemasia Cod.Th., see R.
Lit.p.319 n.1

Nemasa fl., Auson., Nims
(Luxembourg)

Nemetacum -enses (laeti)
itin., ND, at Arras;
insc. (9158), cf. sq.

Nemetocenna Hirt., cf.
insc. 13.806; for
-cenna see 207 above;
Naurpeel (Oise)?

?Nennecti pagus (Vennecti?)
itin.; commonly iden-
tified with Nizy-le-Comte
(Aisne); see Minatiticum
above

?Neonsigo Rav.

Neruicanus tractus Eutrop.,
cf. Neruii

Neruii cl., inscc. 1056,
1702, 3571, 3572(?),
3573, 3606, 7008, 8338-
40, 8725, 8729; EE 3.
103 (R.1863); German
(from Cimbr. and Teut.,
like the Aduatuci BG
2.29) Appian Kelt 1.4;
cf. P-W s.v.; Neruiges
TP

Nida fl. Rav., now Nied
(tributary of the Saar);
distinguish Vida (221
below)

Nouia (for Nouiomagus, cf.
infr.) ap. Treueros,
Rav., Neumagen

Nouiantum A.D. 627, Nouien-
tum (-gentum) Merov.
num., see AcS 2.785

Nouiodunum (ap. Suessiones)
later Augusta Suessonum,
cl., now Soissons (Aisne);
cf. REA 15, 1913, 443,
448

[*Nouiomagos, Νοιόμαγος
Ptol., ap. Meldos]

Nouiomagus TP, Nijon
(Haute-Marne); also
Nouiomago ND, IA, For-
tun. uit. Rad., ASS,

770

Noyon (Oise); Nouio-
magus TP, insc. 9158,
Nouion-Porcien (Arden-
nes); Nouiomago, Noio-
magus IA, Auson., Nobia
Rav., [No]uiomago insc.
4085 Neumagen (see
Nouia above); P-W s.v.
Nouiomagus (Treuerorum);
W. von Massow Grabmäler
von Neumagen 1932

Ὀββρίγκας , -ος (Ἀβρ-) fl.,
Ptol., according to
some the Vinxtbach
(Fines)

Odornensis pagus 9th cent.,
BA 1941-42, 413

Ὀριγίανον (Ριγιακόν)
Ptol., Orchies? (cf.
CIL 13, p.558)

[?Orna fl., Fortun., Or-
nain]

Orolaunum IA, cf. AE 1939.
46; insc. Orol[Arlon
(Belg.), cf. RA 12,
1938, 108, Ant. Cl. 7,
1938, 350; Bull. Acad.
Belg. Cl. Lett. 1938,
136-37; P-W s.v.

?Oromarsaci Pl. 4.106, pays
de Marks (?); but the
correct reading must be
ora Marsacis (C. p.560
n.3) see 221 below

[Osimi TP, Byvanck 1.542
seems to be a blunder]

Pacis uicus 4303 (Metz)

Paemani (Poe-) cl., Famène
according to Riese

Pernaco, Perniciacum itin.,
Perwez (?), but see 221
below; Branchon, Braives
according to Byvanck 1.
540 and 547

Perta, Pertensis, Petra on
lead tesserae 10029.
222, Merov. num., Per-
thes-en-Perthois (Haute-
Marne); cf. 79, 82
above

Pleumoxii BG 5.39.1 cf.
Moxhe (in the valley
of the Mehaigne, a
tributary of the Meuse?)
PID 2.63

Pontibus IA, Ponches (Somme)

Vic in Pontio Merov. num.,
Ponthieu (Pas-de-Calais),
cf. Quentavic below

Prin castellum Rav., Bern-
castel (Trier)

Promea fl., Auson., later
Prumia, now Prum

Quantia fl., Quanta, Quen-
ta, Quentauic(us): see
AcS 2.1060, 1062, with
Pokorny Urg. 153 (mod.
Canche, Cance in Pas-
de-Calais, and [Lugd.]
Manche, Crne), 3.281-
282; Alcuin ep. 12;
93; and other sources
(A.D. 858, 1191) cited
in Bull. Hist. Soc.
Antiquaires de la Mor-
inie 4, 1867-71 [1872],

Local and Ethnic Names

339; 5, 1872-76, 163-177
cf. 255-56 and 317-320;
Journal de Verdun 83,
1758, 35-39. Cf. Pontio
above

?Quartensis locus ND occ.
(siue Hornensis) see
AcS 1.2056,25; or Quan-
tensis, ib. 2.1336,5;
Hornensis is identified
with Cap Hornez, Quar-
tensis with Le Crotay
(-oy) CIL 13, p.561;
cf. Ant. Cl. 13, 1945,
143

Ratum[agensis?] 3475; cf.
REA 26, 1924, 123-24;
C.p.543 and 179 above;
Rouen (near Beauvais),
the Ῥατόμαγος of Ptol.
2.9.6 being Pondron
(Pont-de-Ront, Rodomun
9th cent., Longnon)

Raurobaccio fl. (A.D. 664),
cf. CIL 13, p.703,
Robache

[R(h)ēnus fl. cl.]

Recta (not Refta or Resta),
A.D. 667 (Pardessus),
now Recht, see AcS 2.
1093

Remi cl., inscc. CIL 6.46;
12.1855, 1869-70; 13.
628; 1055, 1091, 1796,
1844, 2008, 2615, 3255,
8701, 10012.5; Remus
Sagarius 2008; Reims,
Rémois (R[h]emensis
ASS). Cf. CIL 13 p.521

Ricciacum 10029.223; -o
TP (Holder identifies
this with Ritzingen
Lorraine; Dalheim ac-
cording to Vannérus
Publ. de la Sect. hist.
de la Gd-Duché de Lux-
embourg 62, 1926 and
65, 1929 (see the ref-
erences to REA at Cara-
nusca above)

Rigodulum (ap. Treueros)
Tac. h. 4.71, now Riol
(near Trier)

R[h]odanus fl., Ven. For-
tun. 3.12.7 (cf. AcS
2.1223,10)

Roudium TP (Nod-), insc.
9158; cf. AcS 2.1235,
28 (Roiglisse, Roye;
Somme?)

Rufiacum (Rof-) AcS 2.
1240; cf. CR. Com.
arch. de Noyon 1872,
173-177

Sabis fl. BG 2.16.1 (tributary of Meuse?). Cf.
Sambra below; REA 46,
1944, 155

Salia fl. Fortun., Seille
(tributary of the Mos-
elle), Salinensis pagus
Dipl., Salins, or Saul-
nois?

Salmon(n)a fl. Auson.,
Salm (tributary of the
Moselle)

*Samara, *Sambra, Sambri-
cus (ND occ.), Samari-
cus (BSAF 1897, 342),
cf. Samaro-bruia below;
variants in Fortun.,
ASS, MG are Somena,
Sumina, Sumena, Somena,
whence Somme; but *Sam-
ara is compared also
with Sabis, Sambra
(Sambre) and with Sim-
mer (tributary of the
Nahe) i.e. *Simara

Samarobriua cl. (Cic.,
Caes.), Ptol., itin.,
inscc. 3490 (div.
name?), 9032, 9158; now
Amiens (Somme)

Sambra fl. ASS, Sambre;
classis Sambrica Ant.
Cl. 13, 1945, 143, cf.
CIL 13 p.561 Sam[(or
*Samara above?), and
vi (1933) p.135

Sana fl. (Sal-?), Selle
(tributary of the
Scheldt)

?Sara fl., Ven. Fort.,
Saar. But the read-
ings are disputed,
and Sarauus seems to
be the true ancient
name of the Saar, cf.
sq.

Sarauus uicus 4549 (Loer-
chingen), cf. Ponte
Saraui itinn. (not
Saarebruck), Saraburg-
gum Merov. num. Saar-
burg (CIL 13 pp.688,
690)

Sarauus fl. Auson. Mos.
367, Saar; Saruba Rav.
4.26

[Sarmasia, see AcS 2.1368;
Sarmatae, -arum uia,
tractus cf. P-W s.v.;
Sairmaize, Ser-]

[Sate fl., lect. dub. at
Fortun. 7.4.15; per-
haps read Salia]

Sauromates Aus. Mos. 9;
Sohren (P-W s.v. Saur-
omates)

Scaldis fl., cl., itinn.
ASS., Scheldt (Fr.
Escault); Scaldea Rav.
Cf. Rev. Belge 14, 1938,
894-96

Scarpon(n)a itinn., Ammian.,
pagus Scarponinsis A.D.
745, Merov. num.; Scar-
ponne (Serpone), Scar-
ponais (Serpanais, Char-
peigne) in Meurthe-et-
Moselle

Sefulae insc. 9158 (also
read Seeuiae), cf. Set-
ucis TP? See AcS 2.
1437

Segni BG 6.32.1, Oesseninc
(Oesling; but cf. REA
22, 1920, 128)

?Senon[CIL 6.2379b 5.
20; Senonensis A.D.
1127; cf. 153 above
and perhaps Cernone
(AcS 1.993), Senones
179? BA 1922, 127-144
(REA 26, 1924, 348)

Local and Ethnic Names

[Senones 4304]

?Sensuna fl., tributary
of Sana (AcS 2.1348, 2)

[Sequanus 3492]

Siluanectes Pl., Ptol.,
itinn., Siluanectensis,
Selnectis (post Merov.)
Senlectis; Senlis (Oise)

Sinduno uico; now Senuc
(Longnon, NLF 32)

Soliciae uicus 4679, Sou-
losse (Vosges)? cf. sq.

Solimariaca IA, 2681c;
-ensis 4681, 4683; AE
1926.65 Sol[icia or
[imariaca, cf. R.2591
(CIL 13.10029,221 and
224) which reads R.
Sol[. Whether Solicia
and Solimariaca are the
same, and whether Belg.
or Germ. Sup. is dis-
puted; CIL 13 clvi
(pp.702, 711); REA 20,
1918, 255; BSAF 1902,
194; 1937, 140-43; on
the names see Bruneau
in Mélanges A. Thomas
1927, 61-70 (cf. REA
33, 1931, 45; RC 44,
1927, 45). See 237
below

*Somena v. *Samara

Suaeuconi Pl.4.106

Suessiones,-ssones cl.,
inscc. 3538, 11299,
Suessio 3261, N.10,
cf. 1609, 3204, 9028,
9031, 9158, AE 1910.19,

1934.218; -icus and
-ensis, Soissons (Aisne).
The vv. ll. without
s-, here and in Siluan-
ectes (cf. CIL 13 p.543)
can hardly imply a var-
iant with the loss of
s-, in view of the mod-
ern forms which show it

Suggentensis pagus 9th
cent., BA 1941-42, 413;
cf. CIL 13.7048?

Sura fl. Auson., Sure
(Sauer, tributary of
the Moselle)

Τκβούλος fl. Ptol., thought
to be the Scheldt

Taionnacus Sidon. Apoll.
(near Soissons?)

Tantalinum AcS 2.1723; cf.
148 above

Tardunensis pagus, Tarde-
nois

Ταρουάννα Ptol., Taruenna
IA, Teruanna TP, Tar-
uanensis NG., Thérouanne
(Pas-de-Calais), Ter-
waen

?Tauena, Tabena 3701,
Taben (Saar); or per-
sonal name?

Teucera TP (leg. Teuara?)
fl., Thièvres (Pas-
de-Calais); cf. 209
above

[Thara, Thérain AcS 2.
1821]

774

Tingus -ensis, Tignus
AcS 2.1853; Thin-le-
Moutier

?T]regouicou[ium AcS 2.
1909; but v. CIL 13.
4481

Τρηούα, Treueri see 209
above; Treoris Rav. 4.
26

Trunciniae ASS, Tronchien-
nes (East Flanders)

Τούλλιον Ptol., Tulla Rav.;
Tullium, Tullum itinn.,
NG, Tullensis, Tollen-
sis, Toul (Meurthe-et-
Moselle); see also
Leuca urbs; Tullum Leu-
co]rum 2681?

Tungri (see also Germ.
Inf.) cl., 3599, 3606,
later Tongri (itin.);
Τούνγροι Ptol., -icanus
(-ec-). (Note: CIL 13.
3591-3632 [Tungri] have
been included in Belgic
names, even though this
is inconsistent with
Kiepert's maps) Tongern;
cf. Ant. Cl. 12, 1943,
37-46; see further C.
p.506; Weerd in Ant. Cl.
4, 1935, 175-89; Scher-
ling in P-W, s.v. (Ant.
Cl. 14, 1946, 174); 3.
12030,5 (R.2600), 13.
7036

Turnacus itinn., Hieron.,
Turnace(n)sis 3565,
(Tor-) Greg. Tur.,
ASS, Tournai (Doornik,
Dornick)

Vabra silua, Vabrensis
Greg. Tur., Woevre or
Voivre (Meuse); cf.
REA 23, 1921, 245;
gloss 207 above

Οὐαδικάσιοι Ptol. 2.8.11,
but cf. 179 above

?Valcedorum ASS; Waulsort,
see AcS 3.86

Vangius fl. Vignore (Haute
Marne); cf. 234 below

[Vellau(u)us pagus 7.1072;
Veluwe, Byvanck 2.1236,
R.1878a]

Vennectis pagus 3450; cf.
TP Nimittaci (leg. Vini-
ctaci?). Cf. num.
ueneχtos 177 above

Verbinum IA, Vironum (Vir-
uinum?) TP, Vervins
(Aisne)

Verris fl., Vair 13 p.702

Vicus[... ...] 4481
(Herapel)

Vicus portus Wic en Pon-
thieu AcS 3.281-82,
see Quentauic(us)
above

Vicus Aus. Mos. 2; perhaps
read Vingus or Vinco,
i.q. Vungus

Vidum fl., A.D. 627 (AcS
2.785,18), now Void
(Meuse)

Local and Ethnic Names

Villiacum (B-), later
Billicke, now Wasser-
billig; AcS 3.318,41
and cf. Belgica uicus
221 below

Virodunum (Ver-) -ensis
itinn., NG, ND, Verdun
(Meuse)

Viromandui cl., inscc.
1465, 1688, 3528, 8341,
10010.1882; itinn.,
Vero-; Vermandois

Virouiacus IA, Virouino
TP Werwick, Vervicq
(West Flanders)

Vlmanectes v.l. Silu- AcS
2.1554, 3.25

Voclannionum uicus 3648-
50

Vod(o)goriacus (v.l. Vogod-)
itinn., now Waudrez
(Hainault)

[?Vosegus mons (Luxem-
bourg), see 211 above]

[Vrsarienses 3492, R.1803;
ND Occ. Dalmatia]

Vungus, pagus Vongensis
IA, MG, ASS; Voncq (Ar-
dennes)

212 bis   Further Modern Names

Aa fl., Aire, St Amande, Ambleterre, Arleux, Armen-

tières, Ars-Laquenexy, Assche (Brabant), St Avold;

Ballée, Bittersdorf, Blieskastel, Boussières, Bréquereque;

Capron mt., Carvin, Chanville, Le Châtelet; Deneuvre

(*Donnobriga?), St Dié (i.e. Deodatus), Diedendorf, Die-

denhofen, Dieulouard, Differten, Dizier, Dombasle, Donon

mt., Donneley, Douai, Durstel, Dyle fl.; Ernstweiler;

Filsdorf; Gerpinnes, Gerhardsbrunnen, [Grand, CIL iv p.77

on 5942]; Haarberg, Halingem, Haudiomont, Haumont, Havingen,

Modern Local Names

Herbitzheim, Hermes (Oise), Hinges (on this variant of
Fins see J. Orr, Proc. Manchester Philological Club, 1924,
2-3; Rev. Ling. Rom. 12, 1936, 10-35), Holving, Hond (at
mouth of Scheldt), Hüttigweiler; Jouy-devant-Dombasle;
Kirchnaumen, Kreuzwald; Lohr, Lorenzen, Louvroil, Lys;
Manheulles, Merlebach, Merville, St Momelin, Moderbach
(Cf. Matrona REA 30, 1932, 401), Monthureux; Nancy, Nie-
derwürzbach, Norroy; Oberhomburg, Obernheim, St Omer;
Plombières; Raillencourt, Rebouville, Remiremont, Riedel-
berg, Rieschweiler; Le Sablon, Saareguemines (Saar-
gemünd; in 8th cent. Gaimundia "confluence," cf. Condate),
(Wald-Neu-) Scheuer, La Sensée fl., La Scarpe fl.; Tar-
quinpol, Thienes, Tintilleries, Torquetenne; St Venant,
Vezouse fl. (REA 40, 1938, 418); Vitry; Wallers, Watten,
Wahlscheidt, Waldfischbach, Waresswald (cf. CIL 13.4257),
Wieres, Wissant, Wüstweiler; Xertigny

Remark:

(1) In those areas of Gaul, such as Belgica, in
which no clearly Keltic insc. has yet been discovered,
we depend for some notion of their pre-Latin speech upon
glosses and proper names, and in some measure on the

Modern Local Names

history of the modern languages. Ancient divine and
personal names are as useful as local names; among modern names it is chiefly, if not solely, local names that
are significant. But it must be admitted that the study
of names (see the works NLF, NLB, FrON listed in Proleg.
7-8; cf. A. Dauzat Les noms de lieu, origine et évolution
ed. 4, Paris 1937, and La Toponymie française 1939; A.
Carnoy "De Plaatsnamen van de Brusselsche Omgening," in
Verslagen en Mededeelingen d.k. Vlaam. Acad. voor Taal
en Letterk. (Gent), 1925, 364-392; and some other items
to be cited below) does not and cannot give results of
the precision that continuous ancient texts would give,
but only a general indication of the former presence of
speakers of this or that language, and tells us virtually
nothing of differences of dialect within such languages,
Keltic or Germanic. At the most we can distinguish the
distribution (a) of different types of names (see, for
example the instructive maps in Dauzat, Top. fr., pp.21,
23), Keltic more thickly in the central and north central
regions of France, less densely in regions corresponding
to the ancient Narbonensis and Aquitania, and also along
the Rhine, and, rather strangely in the north-western
peninsula of France (west of a line drawn from Calvados)
to the Vendée.) This last peculiarity probably means
only that the population of that region in pre-Roman

778

Modern Local Names

times was meagre. And (b) we can also distinguish Ligurian, Iberian (i.e. Aquitanian), and Germanic names in
precisely those areas where the Keltic names are thinly
sown. It is important, however, to distinguish the later
stratum of Germanic names from the older, the latter with
few exceptions (e.g. Scaldis) being names not of places,
but of divinities and of persons.

Cf. A. Carnoy Dictionnaire étymologique du nom des
communes de Belgique, 2 volumes Louvain 1938-40, ed. 2
1949; cf. BSL 45, 1949, 117-20; id. Les éléments latins
dans la toponymie de La Flandre, Ant. Cl., 11, 1942,
199-212; note especially the periodical founded in 1947
as Onomastica, continued in 1948 as Revue internationale
d'Onomastique; Beiträge zur Namenforschung (since 1949),
e.g. Kaspers (105-104, 209-247) Untersuchungen zu den
politischen Ortsnamen des Frankenreiches; K. de Flou Woor-
denboek de toponymie van West-Vlaanderen, 1914-38; G.
Bernaerts Études étymologiques et linguistiques sur les
noms de lieux...de la Belgique, 2 vols., ca. 1890; Sou-
beiran Archéologie du département de l'Oise, vol. 2
Toponymie ancienne 1937; A. de Smet Une carte très rare;
la Gallia Belgica de Gilles Boileau de Bouillon, see
Rev. Belge 18, 1939, 100-107; Ch. Bruneau Les parlers
lorrains anciens et modernes (Bibl. critique, 1908-24)
Rev. Ling. Rom. 1, 1925, 348-413; W. Blochwitz Germ.
Ortsnamen im Dép. Ardennes (Volkstum u. Kultur d. Romanen
12, Hamburg 1939; see REA 44, 1942, 250)

Something, not very much, may be gleaned from the
history of French and of the several dialects of France
and Belgium and of the adjoining lands to the east (see
the works of Brunot and Nyrop, and others, listed in
Proleg. 68, n.138). Thus it is noteworthy that an iso-
gloss which runs for some two hundred miles between
Picard and Wallon, separating them from the French

Modern Local Names

of the Île de France (Latin en becoming nasal e and
nasal a respectively) coincides with the ancient boundaries of the Nouiomagenses and Camaraci and of the
Bellouaci, as well as with those of the old dioceses of
Noyon and Cambrai and of Beauvais (see Iorgu Iordan
Intro. to Romance Linguistics, London 1937, 220) and
also recalls a Keltic dialectal distinction between en
and an from n̥ or ₂n (cf. SprFK 185-6).

The fullest account of French local names, but
still incomplete (begun in 1863, no parts issued since
1912) is the Dictionnaire topographique de la France,
comprenant les noms de lieux anciens et modernes (publié
par l'ordre du Ministère de l'Instruction Publique); cf.
Paul Joanne Dictionnaire géographique et administratif
de la France, 7 volumes, Paris 1905. The Dictionnaire
des Postes (since 1859; the 1913 edition does not include Alsace and Lorraine) is sometimes useful in identifying small places. The work of Léon Maury Les noms
de lieux des montagnes françaises, Paris 1929, is of
small value. As for personal names (not important except the ancient names), see A. Dauzat Les noms de personnes, origine et évolution, Paris 1925; P. Aebischer
L'anthroponymie wallone in Bull. du Dict. wallon 13,
1924, (Liège); and on divine names, Hans Maver Einfluss
der vorchristlichen Kulte auf die Toponomastik Frankreichs in Sitzungsberichte der Kais. Akad. der Wissenschaften in Wien, Ph. Hist. Kl., 175.2 (1914), 155 pp.
For older works (1872-1908), see Rev. de Ling. Rom. 5,
1929 (e.g. pp.87, 111, 143, 169); and for recent studies,
the critical survey by J. Vannérus, Rev. Belge 12, 1933,
1244-73; 14, 1935, 527-554 and 1451-1481; the Chroniques
de toponymie in REA (34, 1932, 192-95: Alsace, Belgique
Wallone, Luxembourg; ib. 293-94: Nord; 35, 1933, 303-
308: Lorraine; 37, 1935, 461-66: Champagne; 41, 1939,
147-154: La Flandre Belge; and later years), cf. the
annual summaries that appear in Bulletin de la Commission
royale de Toponymie et Dialectologie [Handelingen van de
koninklijke Commissie voor T. en D.], Brussels since 1927,

780

Modern Local Names

which also contains many important studies, among them:
J.-M. Remouchamps Carte systématique de la Wallonie (with
a discussion of the modern linguistic frontier, and a
list of names: "double nomenclature des communes belges
de langue romane," cf. REA 38, 1936, 421) viz. 9, 1935,
211-271 (also in Enquêtes du Musée de la vie wallone 3,
1935, 11ᵉ année, nos.34-36 [April-Dec.], 323-384); J.
Feller, Toponymie de la Commune de Jalhay 1936 (454 pp.)

The number of special studies in this field is now
very great. I mention only a few (cf. Bibliographie
Lorraine, see REA 38, 1936, 51 and 41, 1939, 139):

F. Vercauteren Étude sur les Ciuitates de la Belgique seconde (contribution à l'histoire urbaine du Nord
de la France de la fin du IIIᵉ à la fin du XIᵉ siècle)
in Académie royale de Belgique, Mémoires: Collection en
8°, no.1445; Classe des lettres et des sciences morales
et politiques 2ᵉ Série, 33, 1934, 488 pp. (reviewed in
Rev. Belge 14, 1935, 939-950)

W. Kaspers, three studies on names in -acum, -anum,
-ascum, -uscum in northern France and in the Rhineland,
Haller 1918-24 (see ZfCPh 14, 1923, 291-92; REA 31, 1929,
63; Rev. de ling. rom. 2, 1926, 130; cf. Carnoy De plaatsnamen met — acum in het vlaamische Land, Kon. vl. Akad.
voor Taal-en-Letterkende, Versl. en Mededell. 1933, 17-
27), supplemented by the same writer's paper on similar
names in Alsace-Lorraine ZNF 12, 1936, 193-228 (id., ib.
3, 1927, 82-106; 8, 1932, 26-39; 10, 1934, 293-308; 11,
1935, 28-43, on names in -ingen in the Rhine valley, on
which see also Vannérus [-ing, -ingen in Luxembourg] Bull.
de La Comm. d'études linguistiques et dial. vol. 2, Liège
1928, 225-63, cf. REA 33, 1931, 46)

J. Vannérus (on Thoul, Tol), Jahrb. d. Gesellschaft
für Sprach- u. Dialektforschung 1928, 12-38 (cf. Aebischer
RC 47, 1930, 427-32 and 437-440; note Paul. ex Fest.
tullius "spring, source" Gloss. Lat. 4.443; but tul-
"mountain" Vannérus Ann. [Jahrb.] Soc. Lux. d'Études ling.
et dialect. 1928, 12-38, cf. Ir. tul and Tuledo, Tulelasca
PID 1.362, Tolo-durum [Nièvre], Tullum 212 above); (on
Nennig; cf. Nennectis 212, -us 213, 214) Cahiers Luxemb.
1931, 93-103 and 1932, 3-16; (on Les Chaumont germaniques)
Rev. Belge 1, 1922, 283-292; (on Binche, Pintsch) Jahrb.

Modern Local Names

1931-2, 32-60 (cf. REA 34, 1932, 418); (toponymie de Larochette) Cahiers Luxemb. 15, 1938, 7-20; (ancient local names of Luxembourg-Chiny) Bull. Acad. royale de Belgique, Cl. des Lettres etc., 5e Série 21, 1935, 150-175 and 226-256; (Lorch, Luerken, Lorrite, from Lat. lorica "rampart" not from Lauro-), Congrès arch. de Belgique, Liège: 1932, 113-123 (cf. RA 4, 1934, 198; ib. p.191 Steinhausen; but cf. Lauriacus, Lauro AcS 2.160, 163; another possibility is loricarii eg. CIL 13.2828 at Briua Sugnutia 179 above; note that the Congrès arch. de Belgique, formerly in Annales Acad. royale de Belgique, since 1930 was united with its Bulletin to form the Revue Belge d'archéologie et d'histoire d'art)

Davillé (on Bar) Bull. Phil. et hist. 1924, 85-95, cf. RC 44, 1927, 220-22; Lebel Appellatifs forestiers dans le Nord de France REA 46, 1944, 134-153; Lalance (on names in -ac, -curtis, -ham) Bull. Soc. Industr. de l'Est no.147 Nancy 1919 ("Origines gauloises sur le Rhin et en Lorraine," see REA 22, 1920, 56)

P. Marchot Noms de lieux belgo-romains dans la fôret d'Ardenne, Musée Belge 26, 1922, 121-126

F. Lot (on names in -ville, -court): Romania 59, 1933, 199-246

de Loisne Les anciens localités disparues du Pas de Calais, MSAF 6, 1906, 57-133

R. Müller on the names given in Tab. Peut. for Belgica, in Geogr. Anz. 1926, nos.9-10, 1-8 (Gotha, 1926), and separately; cf. his paper in Festschrift für Geheimrat Prof. Dr. Peter Meyer, 1933. But see the criticisms of X (i.e. S. Reinach?) RA 24, 1926, 296-7 on the former.

J. Steinhausen Die Flurnamen im Dienste der Bodenforschung, Rheinische Vierteljahrsblätter 3, 1933, 192-204.

A. Vincent (on river-names) Rev. Belge 7, 1928, 21-47

For Trion ("la 30e lieue"?) and Bar cf. REA 29, 1927, 300; Kohn (i.e. *caunus "mountain" cf. the gloss acaunus 178 above, ad montem Chaunum Liv. 40.50.2 in

Modern Local Names

Spain, Acaunum 15 above, Acaunissa 214 below) ib. 30,
1928, 310 with n.3, cf. Vannérus Annuaire Soc. Lux.
d'Études ling. et dialect. 1927, 77-99; Taison, cf.
tais(s)on (Lat. taxus, -o) ib. 37, 1935, 214-15 and 38,
1936, 50; Senon (near Verdun), cf. Senon[212 above,
Matres Senonum (at Metz AcS 2.1498,8) ibid.; Bilhem
(Bilo, Billus and -heim, -haim?) BSAF 1917, 156; Canda
(Flanders), see Bertoldi BSL 32, 1931, 112 n.1 (pre-
I.Eu.); Jaillon (Gauillo) and Xon (older Sixons cf.
213 below Saxanus?), see Davillé BA 1926, 27-37 (with
map at p.29); on the names of the Eupen-Malmédy region,
J. Bochmer in ZNF 12, 1936, 67-82; on names of the
Frankish type *setr-ûth in northern Gaul, A. Bayot,
Bull. Comm. royale de Topon. et Dialectologie 13, 1939,
141-49 (cf. Neophilologus 15, 1939-40, 236)

(2) The evidence of local names is important
chiefly for its bearing on the question of the linguistic frontier, i.e. between Romance and Germanic, and,
in pre-Roman times, between Keltic and Germanic. Despite some deviations the former does not appear to be
radically different in modern times from what we believe the latter to have been in ancient times; see,
for example, Map 1 in W. von Wartburg Die Entstehung
der Romanischen Völker, Halle 1939, which shows the
modern boundary of Romance following a line that would
comprise most of Belgica (the northern pocket excepted),
the southern part only of Germania Inferior, but a substantial part of that portion of Germania Superior
which lay west of the Rhine. In other words, the
slight extension of the Latin area to the boundaries

Modern Local Names

of the Empire (von Wartburg, Map 2) subsequently failed;
and likewise the temporary expansions of Germanic into
Romance territory afterwards shrank back once more.
That is to say, notwithstanding those fluctuations
which have occurred from time to time, since the end
of the Roman Empire, as the tide of invasion and occupation has flowed and ebbed, the linguistic frontiers
have not diverged significantly from the lines at which
they were established when the entire region first
became settled and reasonably well populated in the second half of the last millenium B.C. True, French has
been substituted for Keltic; but Latin was not substituted, or not for very long, for Germanic; and wherever
Germanic obtained a hold inside the truly and permanently Romance area, it has nearly always and everywhere
lost ground again. The endurance, or even re-emergence,
of an old linguistic frontier presumably is determined
by the degree to which a region has once and for all,
short of the forcible removal or extermination of its
inhabitants, become and remained densely enough inhabited to have a more or less settled population, repro-
ducing itself generation after generation, so that the
linguistic boundary also remains relatively stable even
over many centuries, later disturbances and intrusions

Modern Local Names

notwithstanding. That is what seems to have happened
to the western limit of Germanic speech, on the continent of Europe, shortly before the Roman conquest of
Gaul. Thus the descendents of the Menapii have become
entirely Germanized; on the other hand, the great bulge
along the river valleys of the Sambre and Maas has been
in considerable measure Latinized, that is to say, has
taken over a Romance dialect, since ancient times. In
other words the old boundary between Keltic and Germanic, as established by Caesar and his successors,
though it has dragged here and there, has remained, on
the whole, well anchored. Later Germanic incursions,
down to our own day, have proved evanescent.

Cf. F. Petri Die frankische Landnahme und das
Rheinland 1936 (reviewed unfavorably by Gamillscheg
DLZ 59, 1938, 370); id. Germanisches Volkserbe, 2 vols.
Bonn 1937 (but see the criticisms in Rev. Belge 17,
1938, 319 ff.; cf. REA 44, 1942, 250; Tackenberg Oxé
Festschrift 1938, 265); J. Vannérus Le limes et les
fortifications gallo-romaines de Belgique in Mém. de
l'Acad. royale de Belgique, collection en 4°, vol. 11
(2) 1943 (cf. REA 46, 1944, 333); Whatmough Archaeology
2, 1949, 91-94 and Word 5, 1949, 110-115; Dhondt in
Ant. Cl. 16, 1947, 261-86 (cf. BSL 45, 1949, 124-25).
On Gamillscheg's work (cf. Remark 3 below also) see R.
von Kienle in Abh. zur Saarpfälzischen Landes- u. Volks-
forsch.1, 1937, 234-240; REA 44, 1942, 246 ff.; F. Lot
in CRAcInscBL 1945, 289-98; see also Gamillscheg's
article Zur Frage der fränkische Siedlung in Belgien
und Nordfrankreich in Welt als Geschichte 4, 1938, 78-
94 (with map of the linguistic frontier); Petri's map
(Volkserbe 2, 990) clearly puts the boundary too far to
the west and the south, making the Condrusi, Paemani,

Modern Local Names

and Coerosi (as well as the Vangiones, Nemetes, and
Triboci) all pure German; R. Much SB Akad. Wiss. Wien
Ph-H Kl 195.2, 1920, 26-33

 See also H. van de W(eerd) Ant. Cl. 7, 1938, 356-
57; G. Gilissen Rev. Belge 17, 1938, 71-102; A. Dauzat
(on the Germanic "substratum" in French) in Mélanges
van Ginneken 1937, 267-272; J. de Vries Tijdschrift
voor Nederlandsche Taal en Letterkunde 50, 1931, 181-
221; Godefroid Kurth La Frontière linguistique en Belgique et dans le Nord de la France, in Mémoires cour-
onnés et autres mémoires publiés par l'Acad. royale
de Belgique 48, in two parts (1895 and 1898), Brussels;
the works of Gamillscheg and Frings cited in Proleg.
69 n.139; A. Lesmaries in REA 27, 1925, 318-326; G.
des Marez Le problème de la Colonisation franque, Acad.
Royale de Belgique, Classe des Lettres, Mémoires, collection en 8°, 2e Série 9.4, 1926; W. Rolle The Franco-
German Frontier, in Greece and Rome 8, 1938, 36-49; F.
Lot Les invasions germaniques, Paris 1935; L. Roger La
frontière linguistique in Z. f. franz. Spr. u. Lit. 63,
1939, 1-19 (cf. ZNF 15, 1939, 277); J.J. Manley Germanic
Invasions (A.D. 234-284), 1934; Léon Vanderkindere Recherches sur l'ethnologie de la Belgique, Brussels 1872;
id., L'ethnologie de la Belgique in Patria Belgica 2,
1874, 1-26; id., Nouvelles recherches sur l'ethnologie
de la Belgique, 1879; id., Les origines de la population flamande in Choix d'études historiques, Brussels
1909, 65-92; id., Introduction à l'histoire des Institutions de la Belgique, Brussels 1890, 5-90.

 The attempt has been made by A. Carnoy (De Taal

der Plaatsnamen in Nomina Geographica Flandrica Studiën

2.1, Inleiding tot de studie van de vlaamische Plaats-

namen 1, Brussels 1929, 69-100) to identify Keltic

names (e.g. Mosa, Nervii, Menapii, Aduatuci, Morini,

*isaros in Yser) as distinguished from Germanic (e.g.

Texuandri, Scaldis, and doubtfully Tungri); cf. the

analysis of Flemish local names made by J. Mansion

Modern Local Names

(Studiën 3, 1935), and also of personal names by the
same author, Oud-Gentsche Naamkunde: bijdrage tot de
kennis van het Oud-Nederlandsch (1924), pp.120-131,
where it is pointed out that a number of names recorded
at late dates (e.g. Mummolenus, A.D. 677) are Keltic.
Recently attempts have been made to claim as Illyrian
certain elements which hitherto had been counted Keltic or Germanic, notably -apa in names of rivers; Carnoy still claims it for Keltic (Rev. Belge 18, 1939,
269-70; for some other Keltic names, according to Carnoy, cf. Ant. Cl. 6, 1937, 27-34). But since forms
with -p- are attested outside the Germanic area (Skt.,
Gr., Baltic, as well as Illyr.), beside forms in -b-
(Ital. and Keltic), see Walde-Pokorny 1.46-47, the
association of the names in -apa specifically with the
late bronze age urn-field people (ZNF 2, 1926, 72-83;
3, 1927, 1-65) seems unjustifiable; if -apa is not
common I.Eu., it is either Germanic for an older -aba
(which may be Keltic), or a Keltic equivalent of Latin
aqua, but not specifically Illyrian.

   Cf. Marchot ZfRPh 44, 1924, 206-214; Schnetz ZNF
15, 1939, 49-51 (on Wallon names in -effe); Pokorny
Mélanges Pedersen 541-549; id. Urg. 110-112

Keltic elements are easily traced in areas which
became more or less Germanic-speaking in the course of

Modern Local Names

the last half millenium B.C. (cf. Introduction to Belgica; Proleg. 41), and these appear in modern, as well
as in ancient names, e.g.:

brogilo- (178 above): Groot-, Klein-brogel (hybrid
forms)

nouioialo- (neu-): Nijvel, Nevele (on -oialo- cf. A.
Thomas RC 39, 1922, 334-37)

-acum: -aken (in contrast with Germanic -ingen)

-magalos (cf. Magalona, Maglone AcS s.vv.): Wijg-maal,
Mechelen (cf. Carnoy Contaminates tusschen Germaansch,
Keltisch, en Romaansch in de Vlaamische Toponymie in
Bull. Comm. roy. de Toponymie et Dialectologie 10,
1936, 65-66)

There are also to be noted a few items of vocabulary in these western Germanic dialects e.g. glinnen
(Fr. glaner) from a Keltic glenare (Steinhausen 571
after Frings, who adds benna, carruca, tamisium, cumba
cf. 178, 207, 240, 178, 158 respectively; Steinhausen
p.573), as well as several local names that are entirely Keltic, viz.:

Kemm (Trier), Kiém (Luxembourg), Tchin (Liège),
see Vannérus Bull. Comm. roy. Topon. et Dialectol. 9,
1935, 277-332 (cf. Rev. Belge 17, 1938, 619); 11, 1937,
31-57; REA 39, 1937, 261; Steinhausen 100 n.49: from
an assumed *camminos (but not Ir. céimm "walk," W. cam,
Br. camm "step," Do. 240, which has another etymology
*kng- cf. *cinge- VKG, W-P Wtb. 1.588) beside *caminus
(Fr. chemin etc., M-L Wtb. 1552, citing Thurneysen KR
52); this last rests upon the doubtful caminare "walk"
of Fort. carm. app. 16.6 (see TLL 3.205,55)

Modern Local Names

Karel (Karelweg, Aachen): carraria (Kelt, carrus
240 below), see Gamillscheg 1.5; and a series of names
believed (Steinhausen 573; Oxé BJ 130, 1925, 71-3; cf.
J. Hagen Römerstrassen der Rheinprovinz, Bonn 1931) to
contain Keltic numerals, viz. Finthen (near Mainz cf.
MZ 35, 1940, 21-30), Schweich, Sedtem (older Sechteme,
Sethenie, Segtene according to Steinhausen; 7 leagues
from Cologne), Detzem, cf. Keltic (90 ff.) pinpetos,
suexos: W. chwech, sextametos: Ir. sechtmad, W. seith-
fad; decametos cf. decumates), all of them Germanized
(V.L. -ts- or -tz- not before the fifth century), leugas being understood in each case, see Gamillscheg 1.5
(denied by Frings, Zfdeutsch Altert. 73, 1936-37, Anzeiger 55, p.8). It might be argued that Latin sources
are possible for some of these names (but not for Finthen, nor for Schweich), and certainly the palataliza-
tion -ts- for -c- is V.L.; and that -cht- (from -kt-)
is a "Niederfränkische" pronunciation, and so Frings
does argue. But the change -pt- to -xt- is Keltic,
not Germanic, and is attested as Gaulish (as well as
Irish, and in the older shape of the Welsh form it
must be assumed). Similarly in Uchaud (Gard) "(ad)
octauum (lapidem)," and Delmes (Lorraine) i.e. (ad)
duodecimum (lapidem), whether miles or leagues are involved, numerals are believed to have given rise to
local names, the former either Keltic (Gaul. oxtumetos)
or Latin, the latter probably Latin, but all dependent
upon the Roman system of roads. The numerals themselves,
however, may well antedate the Roman occupation, and at
least in Finthen, Schweich (if correctly interpreted),
Sechtem they must. Whether Cochem and Treis (southwest
of Koblenz) also disguise numerals, as has been suggested, seems more doubtful.

Further evidence for Keltic is to be had from

names in -magos (Neumagen, Narmagen, Remagen) or treb-

or -bonna (again Frings is sceptical), and such names

must have been formed when these elements were still

in use on the linguistic frontier. But names in -acus

attest Keltic speech less clearly, for the type was

freely copied by the Romans and their subjects, so

789

Modern Local Names

that contrasted with such a name as Ebernach (near
Koblenz), of which the first element also is Keltic,
viz. *Auernus (cf. Averney, Loire), are many others in
which a Latin personal name has taken on the familiar
-(i)acus ending. Nevertheless, there can be no good
reason against assuming that there were some Keltic
fragments in the Rhine-district as late as the first
century of our era, when neither Latin nor German could
have succeeded in uprooting Keltic speech completely.
The famous assertion of Jerome (see Proleg. p.71) would,
on the face of it, imply a much later date. But these
are all survivals of Keltic in a region overrun by Germanic speech even in pre-Roman times.

The names in -iacum in Rhine-districts are collected by Gamillscheg vol. 1, pp.58-63. It appears
from his researches that this suffix was still produc-
tive in Gallo-Roman at the time of the Frankish occupation; and parallel with it there often was used the corresponding Germanic suffix -ing(en). Thus we have not
only Donnelay (dép. Moselle), for *Duninacum, but also
(1178) Dunningen; similarly Hutingas, Hutinges (1263),
Hittingen (15th cent.), but also mod. Hattigny from
*Hutiniacum, in 1359 Haitegny. The reverse process ap-

Modern Local Names

pears in Metzingen as compared with Mellecey (1594)

from Militiacum, i.e. -ey was replaced by -ingen.

I have not seen P. Aebischer on names in -ing-
published in Mélanges Ch. Gilliard, 1944, 103-13, or
Lebel on names in -ensis and -ingen, and on frontier-
names (Onomastica 1, 1947, 35-40 and 127-136), which
are known to me only from APh 17, 1945-46 [1948], 214
and 18, 1947 [1949], 128 respectively.

(3) In Belgica itself, on the ancient linguistic

frontier, there still survives, even into modern times,

abundant evidence from local names to testify to an-

cient Keltic speech. Note, for example, the following

items (cf. Ernst Gamillscheg, Germanische Siedlung in

Belgien und Nordfrankreich in Abhandlungen der Preuss-

ischen Akademie der Wissenschaften Jahrgang 1937, Phil.-

Hist. Klasse nr. 12, Berlin 1938. References to Gamill-

scheg in this paragraph are to that work)

Betz (Oise), from Gaulish *bettium "alder" (126 n.1.).

Brabant: *brakobantum (p.5) i.e. *bracum "morass,"
    (Gaulish? See M-L ed. 3, 1258a) and *bant, which
    (cf. Bantia) some would now claim as Illyrian.

Darnau (Namur), cf. Keltic *darnauo- Do. p.250 (Gamill-
    scheg 107 n.1)

Duncq (Abbeville, Somme) older Dun i.e. dunum "fortress"
    (id. 78 n.5)

Veset, Fr. Visé; Visato in 983 (Dalhem, Luttich), cf.
    Kelt. Visurix, Visucio, OIr. fiach "raven," SprFK
    213 (id. 101 n.5)

791

Modern Local Names

Landenne; Landinas in 1091 (Héron, Luttich), according
to Gamillscheg (98 n.2) from Gaulish *landa "moor"
(Charleroi); cf. Do. 264

Machault (dép. Ardennes); probably Keltic, cf. Maccaus
AcS 2.364, Gamillscheg 119 with n.1 (ad fin.)

Rèves, formerly Rodava (980) represents the Keltic
*rótauo- (Gamillscheg 90 n.2); AcS 2.1232

Théaurne (Béthune) from Taiorna, Keltic *tag- (AcS 2.
1700), id. 69 n.1; but cf. 207 above

?Thennes, Tanes in 1128 (Amiens); Gallo-Rom. *tana,
tanna "hollow" M-L 8554; id. 80 n.3

Thorin, Thorenc 1164 (Château-Porcien, dép. Ardennes)
from Keltic *taurincus, id. 119 n.1? Cf. 207 above

Heure, Oire in 1181 (Lüttich), cf. L'Heure (Abbeville),
both from Illyr. Vrium, Vriacum (AcS 3.41), mod.
Oria (Calabria, PID 2.344), see Gamillscheg 78 n.1,
96 n.1. If this is correct, then pre-Roman, even
if not Keltic

Vanne fl. (near Sens), Vennes (Brabant) cf. Lüttich
dial. vène "dyke," all three from Gaulish *uenna 96
n.2 (on p.97), 151 n.3; M-L 9201

Less significant for us are the later borrowings:

OHG channeta, now Kante, from Gallo-Rom. *canna,
*cannata, *cannada, Gamillscheg Rom. Germ. 1, 9, 28

OHG sehtari, from sextarius, which was taken over by
Keltic (Pedersen VKG 1.216, 218, 491). But see
Frings' criticism (p.9) of Gamillscheg (1, 10)

Pfette, borrowed in the fifth century (id. 13), from
*padina, Fr. panne "roof-beam;" but if this is Kel-
tic its p- is important

bannasta, bennesta, Reichenau bansta "basket," Gallo-
Rom., and probably pre-Roman, even if not Gallic
(cf. Messapic benna PID 3.9); see M-L 935.

Modern Local Names

galleta, a liquid measure (Fr. jaloie), perh. Gaulish;
    M-L 3565, Gamillscheg 1, 22. Cited by CGL 5.364,48
    (see 158 above)

paraueredus is represented by OHG pfarfrit, German
    Pferd

*uaura "meadow" (web Ardennes, waver Schleswig, Wavre-
    ville dép. Meuse), Gaulish according to Gamillscheg
    1.271n. See 207 above; Woëvre, dép. Meuse and Marne;
    Voivre dép. Troyes (cf. nemus Wevre 1152, Woevre 1269
    dép. Aube); Wavre (Switzerland REA 29, 1927, 396),
    mod. Limous. vavre "Brachacker" (Gamillscheg 1, 271n.)

Even Burgundian personal names show a few Keltic ele-

ments; e.g. catu- "battle," as in Catbertus (Chabers),

Kaþubrands (Chabrant) both in the Calais region; or

-nerto "strength," Gailanerþs (Nerta 208 B above, cf.

Germanic Nerthus fem., Tac. G. 40, ON Njørðr) see

Gamillscheg 3, 1936, 134 and 166 (cf. 141). A valu-

able clue to the extent of the Germanic frontier in

Roman times is the appearance of -baccus (German -bach)

beside the Latin riuus, e.g. (in the Malmédy region)

Stagno-baccus, Rarobaccus, but Didioloni riuus (see

Bastin Ant. Cl. 3, 1934, 381 n.1).

It is obviously no easy matter to disentangle

conclusively evidence of such disparate quality and

varied dates. But the scanty records of the Roman

period, combined with the historical tradition and the

archaeological indications (see Belgica, Introduction),

Modern Local Names

suggest that the frontier of Keltic had receded well
to the west of the Rhine, not very far from the boundaries of Belgica (except the northern pocket of Belgica, the Atrebates, Morini, and Menapii) and of the
two Germanies, to become more or less stabilized there,
leaving isolated patches of Keltic further east, and
itself passed more than once by a westerly Germanic
tide that never stayed long or deep enough, however,
to form permanent Germanic dialects west of the old
frontier, beyond which Latin itself never became permanently established in the opposite, easterly direction.

The Germani of the tradition appear to have been
armed warriors who pushed west of the Rhine and south
along it as pioneers and settlers into territory that,
in the areas corresponding to the northern part of Belgica and the whole of the later Germania inferior was
but sparsely populated, perhaps not so sparsely along
the middle and lower Rhine. On both sides of the Rhine
remains of Keltic speech are to be observed. But these
Germani were not destroyed or absorbed; instead they
formed a frontier which Germanic has often overflowed,
but which in general has remained fairly stable, re-

Modern Local Names

inforced by subsequent Germanic immigrations and settlements during the period of the barbarian invasions.
The Anglo-Frisian and Franconian dialects represent
the outcome of that expansion and superimposition, in
successive waves, of West Germanic speech upon fragmentary Keltic dialects, that began perhaps as far
back as 400-300 B.C. Further south the modifications
introduced into High German dialects along the Rhine
complicate the situation, but essentially it is not a
different picture in Roman times, save for the Germanic
expansion of a few centuries later in date. Thus we
account for the ancient Keltic influence on the formation of the German vocabulary (-rix, ambactus), the
presence of Keltic local names (Rhein, Main, Neckar,
Lech, Inn, Eisack) in what is now Germanic territory,
as well as for Germanic influence, of various dates,
in Keltic and later in Romance areas, on which see J.
Brüch Der Einfluss der Germanischen Sprachen auf das
Vulgarlatein, Heidelberg 1913.

795

213

Adcenec[us 4476; an epi-
thet of the divine
name (a local god?)
Nennic(us?) ib., cf.
Nemnic[div. name 3.
4805, and the *Nen-
necti(s) pagus 212
above? PID 3.81 (Ad-
cen-, Adgan-, Aggan-)

Ammaca 3615, R.2626; see
Gamaleda below

?Ancamna 4119; and cf.
Pomana below, 211
above s.v.

Arduinna CIL 6.46 (a dedication by Sabinus Re-
mus); cf. RA 13, 1939,
246-7

[Arcecius? 3600]

Aruernus Pl. 34, 45; By-
vanck 2, p.563

[Atesmerius (-t-?) 3023]

Atesmerte (dat.) AE 1925.
98; REA 22, 1924, 327-
330

Bugios 4555

Caiua 4149 (not Calua)

Camloriga (or -rix, cf.
AcS 2.1197, and Asca-
fotorix 181 above, for
-rix f.) dea 3460

Campestres R.3008-9

Camulorix 4709

Camulus 3980, 6.46 (cf.
Arduinna), BSAF 1934,
167-68, 173-74; AE
1935.64; Musée Belge
8, 1904, 26-28; AE
1910, p.456 (cf. no.
65)

Cantrusteihiabus matron-
is 3585

Caprio 4142

Cassibodua 4525

Cautopatis 4540

Cissonius 3659, 4500

[Clauariatis 4564 (by
neg. uest. ex [Germ.]
Sup.)]

Cnabetius 4258, (G-)
4507, 4508

[Coaetiae matronae (?)
Riese Geog. Min. p.33
(with apparatus, as
if Matrona for Marne?
But cf. p.78, Eiotiae);
AcS 1.1053]

Cocidius 7.642; Cocidius
Tutatis EE 3, 1877,
128 (i.q. CIL 7.335)

Cosumis 4304 (epithet of
Mercurius). But the
reading is doubtful
(Cossuonius?); cf.

Divine Names

R.3316, P-W 4.1675.
Perhaps corrupt for a
personal name?

Degouexi (dat. sg.) 4506

[Diana (ap. Treueros)
Greg. Tur. h.F. 8.15]

Đirona 4498, R.2719; Sir-
ona 4661, 4129, AE
1941.89

Entarabus deus, 3632, In-
tarabus 3653, 4128,
11313

Epona 4630, 4649, 4320
(R.2431a), R.3008-9;
cf. AcS 1.1450; on the
worship of Epona see
further Grenier REA
38, 1936, 200; Keune
TrZ 6, 1931, 152-54
(REA 35, 1933, 411)

Gamaleda 3615 (see R.2626;
cf. Gutenbrunner 109-
10; and Ricagambeda
below)

[Genio Leucorum 4630]

Gesacus 3488; cf. Gisacus
(181), Gesahenis (223)

Icouellauna 4294-98; and
at Trier 3644. Linck-
enheld Études de myth-
ologie celtique (on

Alouna, Icouellauna
and others), Ann. de
La Soc. d'hist. et
d'arch. Lorraine 1928
(see REA 31, 1929,
260; 33, 1931, 44)

Intarabus v. Entarabus

Iunones 4704

Lenus 3654, 3970, 4030,
4122, 4137, cf. Λῆνος
7661

]leni (dat. sg.?), epi-
thet, incomplete, of
Mercurius (or personal
name?) 4552; not for
Lenus

Loucetius 7.36

Magusanus 7.1090; cf. 13.
10027,212

Maiiabus (for Magiabus?)
4303; read Matribus
REA 16, 1914, 233

[*Matra? Jullian would see
this divine name in the
local name Mediomatrici,
see REA 9, 1907, 370-
71]

[matres] Neruinae 3569
(ap. Neruios); cf.
Genius Neruorum AE 1931.
29, N.185

Menapus (deus) Mirac. S
Bertini (Bertincourt,
ob. ca. 700), see FHRC

Divine Names

242.24 (MG Scr. rer.
Merov. 5.779)

Minurae 4475 (for Miner-
uae?); cf. 12.2974

Mogontia 4313

[?Mogounus AcS 2.616,40;
but this, CIL 13.4668,
is more like a person-
al name, Magounus]

?Nam daemon, Nammutum ASS
14 Sept. 4, 388D (FHRC
244.25-8) at Namur

Nantosuelta 4542. On Nan-
tosuelta and Sucellus
see, among many others,
Linckenheld RA 24,
1926, 212 (REA 34,
1932, 56); Rev. hist.
rel. 99, 1929, 40-92
(REA 35, 1933, 183; RC
47, 1930, 461); Drioux
RA 30, 1929, 14-19;
Hubert in Mélanges Cag-
nat 281-296 and RA 5,
1915, 26-39; Reinach
RC 17, 1896, 45-59 and
66; Stokes Academy 49,
1896, 263 and 307
(ZfCPh 8, 1910-12, 386);
Lantier in Mon. Piot 34,
1934, 58; Keune in P-W
s.v. Sucellus (cf.
Drioux Cultes indigènes
104 n.); Lambrechts Ant.
Cl. 7, 1938, 376 n.5;
Behn MZ 24-25, 1929-30,
68-99

[N(emesis) 3661, 4052]

Nemetona 7.36

Nennic(us 4476, cf.
Nemnic[3.4805 and
pagus Nennectis 212
above (?)

[Neruinae deae] v. matres
above

?Olim[(for Olympio?)
4573; but note names
in Ollo-

Oglius 11295 (or Oglaius?
Cf. BSAF 1909, 255,
384 where it is sugges-
ted that in Lucan Herak.
1, for Ὀγμιον the cor-
rect reading is Ὀγλαῖον
RC 30, 1909, 268; RA
10, 1919, 369); AE 1910.
57

Ouniorix 4651; cf. 10010.
1464 Onniorix?

?Po]mana 4119, cf. Arnob.
adv. nat. 3.30 (AcS 2.
1030), but the reading
Ancamna is now sugges-
ted (see P.W. 2te R.,
6.2314)

Recmo[4722

?Ratum[3475; or local
name?

[Ricagambeda 7.1072]

deo Rio[3529

Rosmerta 4192-95, 4237,

Divine Names

4208, 4311, 4683-85,
4705, 4732; cf. Cahiers
...Alsace 5, 1927, 68-
74; P-W s.v.; REA 16,
1914, 233

Runcinellus (daemon) see
207 above

Samarobriua (dea?) 3490

Saxanus 4623-25, 3475 (?);
cf. REA 26, 1924, 123-
4

Saxsetanus F.90

Secate(?) 4550

?Senomatris R.3316, CIL
13.4304; but (P-W 4.
1675 and 2te Reihe 2.
1540) Senuonum tris
(i.e. tribus). Cf.
AcS 2.1498,8; Guten-
brunner 155. However
we have Senomatro 243
below

Siluanus 3968, cf. R.3008-
09

Sinquas or Sinquatis (-tes)
3968, 3969 (dedicated
by Aunus)

Sirona, v. Đirona

Smertrius 4119 (previous-
ly read Smertatius or
-utius, but see P-W,
2te Reihe 6.2314); cf.
236 below

Sucellus 4542, F.87,
Toussaint 147

Suleu(i)ae Iunones 3561

Suleu(i)a 3664, cf. R.3008-
09

[Sul or Sulis, Belgic ac-
cording to REA 15, 1913,
449]

[Surburus (-o) Forrer
L'Alsace rom. 171; but
it is better (4554, cf.
AcS 2.1673) taken as
personal]

Tutatis v. Cocidius

Vassocaletis 4130; 4550(?)
also read Vogeso Sec-
ate, see 211 above
(Vosugonum)

Vegnius 4049

Vercana[4511

Veriugodumnus 3487

Vihansa 3592 (cf. Ven.
ahsus, Goth. anses;
Aꭓsi- 223 below)

Viradectis (-sthis, -cdis)
dea 7.1073, 13.8815,
but Belgic, in so far
as the Tungri are; cf.
223, 236, 243 below

V[irotuti or V[indonno
AE 1939.46

Visucius 3660, 4257, 4478;
-ia 3665

Divine Names; Personal Names

213 ctd.

Visuna 11714 (R.2570)   Volkanus 3528, 3593

214   Personal Names

A[ ]oteg[AcS 3.469

Abadr[10010.2998a

Abba 3985

Abbo (episc. Mettensis)
    ASS

]abresu[10017.939

?Abro AcS 1.10

Acaunissa 4004; cf. 212
    bis Remark (1) above
    (Cauno-)

Accedo 4347

Acern[10010.3042

Acharius (episc. Viro-
    manduensis) v. CIL 13
    p.556 n.2

Ayrotalus 10010.3095v;
    cf. Do. 223; W-P 1.28,
    W-H 1.7

?Acirgus 10002.5-6

?Aci]carus (poeta?) 3710,
    R.4485

Acisillia 11362

Acomn[10010.3042b

Acuitus 10010.29

Adac[10010.3020a

Adaris(?) C. p.583

Adaucius 10006.2

Adbugissa 4127

†Adelhaidis BSAF 1922,
    227

†Adeisfia 3851

?Adiatumarus 3999 (corr.
    for Adiaumar)

Adinc[10010.2986c

Adiutex (Adiutece, Adiu-
    ticeben[ ) AcS 3.508

Adnatus 1807

Adrucius 10010.3008a

]aduci 4446

Aduital[10010.2988a

Aedai[10010. 2986c

Personal Names

Aedius 3.15163 (R.2594)

Agatillus 4268

Age 3778 saepe (or mason's mark, at Trier)

Agisilius (-c-) AcS 3. 522,32; Agisilla R.4132

Agorix 10027.3

Agritius 4203

Agsatus AcS 1.62

Aiausa 3580

?Aiccardi (Aicadrus AcS 3.526)

?Ailicotdi 10006.170

Aio 3703.2,12

Aiullus 3778

Aiunus 3280

Alb[3705

Albi[, Albian[Ant. Cl. 1, 1932, 349 (Liberchies i.e. Geminiacum?), Albinus 4158, Albinius 4158

Alctus 3988

†Aldahildis 3507

Alfenus R.403; AE 1911. 491

Alona 10010.3016b

Alpicus 3644, 3655, AE 1934.219, cf. 10027.10

Alpinius Montanus Tac. h 3.15

?Amadis 10010.3095n

?]amarce[4491

Amarius 10010.101

Amasa 10010.3016

Amb[10017.139

Amba[ctus?] 3686; not necessarily a name, cf. gloss 178 above

[Ambatus 10010.105]

Ambitoutus 3991(?), cf. 10010.107

Amianus 4583, cf. 10010. 108a

Amilius 4310

Aminnus 10010.3020b

Amma 3620, 4059, 4176 (-a dat.)

?Ammaca 3615, but see 213 above

Amme 4144

Ammausus F.3

Am(m)illus 4159, 4281, 4579; -a 4590-91

Ammius, -a 3624, 4132, 11453

Ammo.mus 4136

Ammonius 4516

Personal Names

Ammossa (dat.) 3995

Ammus 3261

Ammutius 4159

Amo 10010.3044b, 3051h

Amretoutus (an Ambi-?)
3991, cf. Amrat[
7859

Anaillus 4714

Anauo 4270

?Andebrogius v.l. BG 2.3.
1 (but see Andecombo-
gius)

?Andecanus AcS 1.140

Andecarius 3984

Andecarus 3268 (-rr-),
3474, 3984, 4346,
10025.188

Andecombogius BG 2.3.1;
num.

Anducor 10010.3036e

Andus 10027.24

Anectius Liv. per. 139
(Neruius)

?Anion 10010.129

Anisatius 4124

Anitius 10001.38

Anna 4159, 4200

Annaius 7088 (Neruius),
R.2163a

Annitus 4168

†Ansebertus 3508

Antia 10010.3020c

Antigus 4301

?Antoccini 10010.3006

Anulinus 11311, R.427

?]anuni AcS 3.638

Anusiccus 3717

?Anxus 10010.2985b

[?Aoχ (Atioχtus?) AcS 1.
164; also read Attio-
rix]

?Apecius (-lius?) 10027.
241

Apiciola 3799

Apinossa 3271, cf. -us
10025.132

Apiu 10017.159

Appianus 3585

Appinosa 11298; BSAF 1912,
282

Appus 4734, cf. F.90 (-ius)

Aprionius 3591

†Aprilia 3693

Aprill(us) 4004

Apronius 3696, 4202, 4421

Personal Names

Aprossus 4152, 4192; Germ.
   10, 1926, 139-44; REA
   29, 1927, 315

†Aquilinus N.22

Aquilo 4152

Aquinius 6687

Aqustrani 10010.3016c

†Arablia 3800

†]aralaicus 11440

Arantia 4419

Arantillus 600* (now said
   to be genuine)

Arauatius episc. Tung.
   (C. p.574)

Arbo[g]astis (Treuir) v.
   TLL; R. Lit. pp.355-
   56; cf. 237 below

Arcus 10010.164,166;
   10015.91

†Aregius 3802

†A]relocus 3785

Armot[AcS 3.687

Arrimr[10010, 3038b

Arsitiuus 10010, 3020d

['Ἀρτας (Syr.) 10025.1]

Arthemius Greg. Tur. h.
   F. 1.46

Artilla 4106

]artima 4161

Artisius 4278

Artula 3909, 4737; cf.
   AcS 3.696,15

Artus 4090

Aruescius AcS 3.703,14

Asania 3274

Asariuus R. Lit.12.23

Asicius 3707

?Asso (or Neuo?) 11459

Assutalus 10006.8; 10010.
   182

Astimo[3275

Astuor, Asturius Saalb.
   Jb. 9, 1939, 44

Asurio 3500

Atab[10010.3040

Atacos 4136

Atbil[10015.59

Atecnudis 10010.185a

Ategnia 4681, cf. C. p.702

Atepa 3276, 4388

Atepo 4163

Ateponius 4162

Ate]uritus 11295; BSAF
   1909, 255, 384

Personal Names

Atiassus 10010.193

Atillia 3985, -us N.47

Atisius 10006.9

Atitisus 10010.199

Atitta 10002.114

Atot[3778

Atrectinus 3979

Atreχtus 4301, Atrectus
3707

Attaedio (nom.) 3452

Attauilla 3718

Attedonius 3707

Atteius 4081

Attianus 4264

Attilius 3986 (mis-
printed 3896)

Attillius 4670, cf. 3985
(Ati-)

Attioius 4273

Attiolus 3622; cf. 10010.
125, 10027.72; -a BA
1922, 138

Attiorix 10010.206

Attius 4248, 3.4391; C.
p.584

Attli (gen.?) 4002

Attonia 4330, -ius 3.5797

Atuindi Saalb. Jb. 9,
1939, 42

Aturena 4043, cf. Ateur-?

Aturiacius 4031-32

Atussia 4159

Aucalus 3529

Aucissa 10027.107

Auco 3529

[?Aucous 10010.3007b]

[?Aucus 10010.215; 10017.
200]

Auectius Liv. per. 141

[Auentina 3696, 7.55],
-us 4206

Auerra 4338

]auiatuc[3480

Auidus 3606

?Auirho AcS 1.314

Auitus 4172, 4628, 11366,
Ant. Cl. 6, 1937, 304;
11396, -a AE 1932.23;
BSAF 1931, 100; cf.
1938, 162; 3641 (Aui-
tus siue Sacruna)

Auius 3987

Aulio (nom.) 3280; -ius
N.71

Aullus (ciuis Treuerus)
Germ. 20, 1936, 60

Personal Names

Aunatus 3281

Aunillus 11288; BSAF 1907,
225

Aunodi 10010.245

Aunus 3258

Aupius 4348

Aurorianus 4218

Aurusius 4273

Ausicus 10010.3016g

[Iulius Auspex Tac. h 4.
69]

Ausus Ant. Cl. 6, 1937,
304

Auua 3375

?Axida[10006.117

Axilius 3641

?Axus 10010.261

Azinas 3.8762, R.1902

Bacca BSAF 1922, 227

Bae[10010.2999e

Baius 6.31870; R.399

Balatonus 3283

†Bancio 3805

Banio AcS 1.341

Banna (-nua?) 10027.190

Banuos 3418

Bassa 10001.66

[Bassilia R.4562; 10026.
41]

Bat[10010.2139-40

Battis[3878

Bau[10010.2139-40

†Baudiricus 3472

[Beladius (Pannonius)
3451]

Belatonus 3284

Belatulla 4250, 4560,
Toussaint 147; cf. div.
name (Brit.) Belatuca-
drus (AcS 1.367, 3.823;
AE 1933, 130-131)

Belatulus 4547

Beliniccus 4349

Bellator 4547

Bellausus 4542

Bellianus Toussaint 150;
AE 1941.152

Bellicca 3407, -us 4554;
cf. AcS 2.1673,35; Anz.
Schw. Alt. 26, 1924,
89-91; RE 4, 1902,
1479; modern local name
Belley (Ain)

Bellicianus 10027.244

Bellosa 3510

Personal Names

†Belsoaldus 3511; cf.
   Belsa 136, 158 above

Beni[10001.68,240
   (Ben[)

Bergussa 3285

Betulo (Treuerus) 3.4499

Biatuccus 3286

Billicedo 10027.205

Bimottia 4007

Bio[3287

?Birius 4071

Bittius 3288

Bitucar[10010.318

Biturix 4661

Bloturix 4350

Blussinius AcS 3.890

Boancus(?) 4722 (Boia-
   cus?)

Bocca 3289

Boduognatus BG 2.23.4

Bodus 10010.33 (i.q.
   Boudus, see 195 above)

Boipus(?) 10010.3040

Bononia 3290

†Bonosa 3786, -us 3807

Boram[10010.3044g

Borias 3259

Borinius AcS 3.912

Borissa 3289

Bouda 3291-93

Boudillus 3294, Toussaint
   150; AE 1941.152

Boutius 3988

Boru[10010.3094r

?Brariatus (cf. Braria
   202.203 above) 10005.
   6; 25 (cf. 10006.18;
   95)

Brasilus(?) 10010.351
   (but cf. Bracisilus
   204 above)

Brasius 4261

Βρέννος Ioh. Lyd. de mag.
   1.50 (or βρέννος PID
   2.184?)

Bricia 3295

Briga 3296 (or read
   Brigan[?)

Brigin[4691

Brilla R.3905

Britto episc. Treuer.
   R. Lit. 15, 76

Brixa 4401

Broccius 3578, or (better)
   Brocchus

Personal Names

Bruarus 10010.3033d

Bucculia AcS 3.995

Buccula 4219

Busi 10027.273

Butu 10010.373

?Buus AcS 1.646

Ca[ ]nsunea 4389

Kaba 3909

Cabrilla 11461

Cacetius (v.l. Cass-)
   600* (possibly genuine)

Cacuo 4482

Cacuronius 4100

Cacussius 4482

Caeticcus 3260

Caein[10010.2986e

Cag[4703

?Caina 10010.3044c; cf.
   AcS 3.1039,50

Cainus 4514

?Caletanus AcS 3.1046
   (Scaeu. dig. 36.1.80);
   cf. Caleti 212 above?

Caletinus AcS 1.697

Calionius 3721

Callid[4691

Cam[4550

Camama 4352, cf. AcS 1.
   721,15 (read Κάμαμα ?)

Καμβο|Κοιια (?) 10017.94
   (Soissons)

Cambo 4627

Cambrus 10010.4131, cf.
   AcS 3.1061,33

Camillus 3580

Camulinius 3707

Camulissius 3722

Camulus 3297, 3529, 4353

Camus 3385

Can[ ]unus 10010.3049a

Canetus 4551

Caninia R.415, -ius 7.706

Cano 10010.431; Canus 4229,
   4237

Cantaber 7033

Cantaius 4582

Cantebosis 4663

Cantedo 11367

Canto 10006.118

Cantognatus 4547

Caontius Saalb. Jb. 9,
   1939, 43

Personal Names

Capienaci (-on-) AcS 3.
1085

Capito F.90

Capria Saalb. Jb. 9, 1939,
42

Caprasius 4354

Caprissus(?) 4445

Capurlus 4445, Capurus 7.
691

Capurillus ceruesarius
(Trier) R.2467a (Add.)

Carad[d]ouna 3298, 4355-
57; -us BA 1922, 137

Caraddounus 4499, cf.
Caraddounius 6468;
written Carathounus
4325, 4362, Carassouni-
(os) 11454, cf. AcS 3.
1096, Carassoun[11393;
R.4051

[Caranius, Caraniusa(?)
AcS 1.766]

Carantia 3300, 4229, 4363

Carantil(l)a 4358, 11368

Carantillus 4485, 11454

Carantinus 4047

Carantinius 4239

Carantius 4602 (Carantus?),
cf. 7369 and 10025.136
(Leucus)

Carantodius 4359, 4483
add., 4583, 10025.136,

AE 1941.151; -ia 4359,
4583. Cf. Toussaint
150, AE 1941.25,27

Carantus 3299, 3301, 4363,
·4602, 4732

Carantusa 3449

Carantusarus(?) 4363

Caras(s)ounius, v. Caradd-

Carathounus, v. Caradd-

Caratila 3302

]caratius 4358, cf. 590*
(Caratius)?

Carata 4124

Caratulla 4385, 4584; -us
600* (genuine?)

Caratuccus 10001.83

Caratus 3081

[Carausius AcS 1.775;
Menapius Mausi(ai)us
Dessau 8928, Byv. 2.
1428; cf. 10010.498b
and CIL 13 iii p.121;
for coins, see Mat-
tingly Ant. 19, 1945,
122; CW 1946 no.11,
p.88; for Maus- cf.
Ceamausa 10027.79, or
perhaps Mosa 212 above?]

Carianus AE 1941.152;
Toussaint 150

Cariatus 4545

Caril[10027.110

Personal Names

Cariolus, -a (G-) 4167

Carmulus (or Carmillus?) 4582 (hardly for Curm-?)

Cernarus 10010.3038f

Carnus 10027.206

Caro 4360

Carosa 4672

Carrarius 3344

Cartulla 11369

[Caruilius BG 5.22.1]

Carulirus 10010.3038g

Carussa 4652

Caruus F.304(?)

Casa[? 10010.468 (followed by auo[t?)

Casatua(?) 590* (if genuine); cf. 6283, 10027. 15

Cassibodua(?) 4525

Cassillus 4572

Cassius 3707

Caseli AcS 1.834

Casseus 10010.477; cf. 4572 (Cassius?)

Casurius 4615; cf. 10010. 479

Catacius 10010.482

Cathirig[ius (or Cathirix?) 4291

Caticcus 3304

Catillus 3303

Catilus 4570

Catonius 4517

Catonos 10010.490

Catonius 3990

Cattus 3305, 3592; cf. AcS 1.846,42; gl. 207, 246

Catuimus (Cr-?) 10010. 2470

Catullia REA 38, 1936, 41

Catullianus 4362

Catullinus 3723, 4362, 4517, 4669, 10035.23

Catullius 4247, 4669

Catuos 10010.3094w

Catus 4486, N.71 (Treuer); or Gattus?

Catusius AE 1926.65

Caudo 4273

?Caulnus (read Cauanus?) 4014

Caupa 10017.273

Caupius F.3; Mus. Belge 25, 1921, 51

Caupo 3650

Caura 10010.506

Cauua (G-? Or C. Auua?) 3306, cf. 3409

?Ccilui 10010.3044k (cf. 3159b)

Ccoiedius 7516a (Cocied- ius?)

?Cdius 10010.3017h

[?Ce.ostasii 10010.3078b]

?Ceamausa (or read Cem- musa?) 10027.79

?Cebeus 10025.33

Cecus 10010.3044cc

?Cellius 3285 (or read Vernacellius, AcS 3. 1181,35)

?Cemmusa, v. Ceamausa

?Cenia 4018

Cenopi[llus] 10027.80ab

Censonia 4205, -ius 4288

Centilis 10006.109

?Cercit[3493

?Ceruca 10017.1088

Cesianus 10010.547d

Cesua 4628

Cetronia (for Cae-) 4363

Charietto (Francus) A.D. 358, C. p.584

Chartius R.2593

Childeriks 10024.307

?Chonus AcS 1.1008

Chumstinctus Liv. per. 141; cf. 228 iv below?

?Cianico AcS 1.1009,44

Ciat[10010.3038i

?Ciceuns[10006.122 (for Cicenus?)

Cidionius 3991

Cientius (Scottus) 3310, cf. 10010.2868

Cilta 11413, cf. -us 10010.561

Cilu, v. Ccilui

Cinaes[10010.2986g

Cimuo[10010.3042d

Cinges 4422 (-entis, gen. sg.), cf. 10010.564, 12014.199

Cingetius 3707

Cingetorix (Treuer) BG 5. 3.2 sq.; also in Bri- tain (5.22.1)

Cincisso[10010.2988b (or read Cingessus, cf. 238 below)

Personal Names

Cinia, -ius v. AcS 1.1020

Cinianus 10010.3020f

Cinno 10006.123

Cinto 3284

Cintusma 4397

C]intu[s]minus 3311

Cintusmus 4301, 11373;
Ci[n]tusmus 4685; cf.
R.3932

Cintussus 4364

]cionius 3650

?Cipio 4042, Cipi 10027.
17-19

Cirata 7088

?Cisc[AcS 1.1029

[? ciudendu(s) 4489, per-
haps not a name, but
for claudendus?]

Ciurna 3281

Clamosa (ciuis Treuera)
233, cf. Clamos(s)us
10006.26, 10011.181

Clarebenu[3334

Clceaua (?) 10010.3009d

[?Clebibullici AcS 1.1041]

?Clesuilitus 3537

Cletusstus 4103

?Clicici[10010.3094i

?Cliucil[3354

Cloa[4585

[Cluaniducus AcS 1.1047]

Cober[4382

[Coberatius AcS 1.1053,
Coberillus ib.; cf.
11660]

Coblucia 4038

Cobruna 4248

[Cobuitua AcS 1.1055]

Cobrouius 4165

Cocio TrZ 3, 1928, 190

?Codaria 10010.3015b

Codora 3904

?Coecoe[10010.3020g

Coenilia R.415

Cofilus 3904

Coinnagus 4468

?Co[ll]inus 4532

Comi[3312

Comilu[10010.2986h

Comisarus 4587

Comitilla (Mediomatrica)
7007

?Comitu[AcS 1.1074

Commius BG 4.21.6-8, cf.
C. p.558; AcS 1.1074-5

Personal Names

[Communis AcS 1.1079,23]

Comus 3312, cf. Commus 10010.620ab

Comn(i)us 10010.621b

Conattus 10017.517

Condarillus 10016.630

[Condrusus dipl. 125]

]conia 10010.2496

Connius 3314 (?); or read Connisuca?

Contua 3315

Cooarilus AcS 1.1113

Copiensis 3.2049

Coppus 3988, cf. 10010. 2851m

Corio 3548

Corobus 4301c, cf. 10006. 27

Correus BG 8.6.2 etc.; also in Britain (num.), AcS 1.1135

Corterus

Cossacionius 4166

Cossilus 4588, cf. 10010. 653 (also Cossillus)

Cossus F.33

?Cosumus; but v. 213

Cosuonnia 4715

Cot[3316

Cotilius 4706

Cotina 11461, -us 11461, R.3905

Cotira 4499

Cottalus 4366

Cotto 10016.24

[Cottus 4366; 574*, possibly genuine]

Couirius F.7, 26

Couirus 3707 ii 8, 4200; cf. 11313

†Couol[3811 (for Quoduoltdeus?)

Courunus 4519

Cricconia 3724

Cridiantus 4367

Crispus 10029.32

Crixus 4647, cf. AcS 1. 1171-72

Crobus AE 1941, 152; Toussaint 150

Croelonia 4239

Cuienpnn 10035.23

?Cuna 4383 (or]cuna)

Curmilla 4393

Cusa 4141

Personal Names

?Dabesu[F.115

Da[g]illus 4520 (read
   Daxillus?)

Dagsillus 4265

Daguus 4265

Dannumara 3979

Dannus 3993, 4228 (but
   in this, more likely
   a common noun dannus,
   cf. 6676; Note xli b
   above)

Danomarus 3349

Danus 3317

Darra AcS 1.1242

Dassi 10024.188

Datinis(?) 3813

Datius 3262; cf. AcS 1.
   1243,53; 10027.73

Dauius AcS 1.1245

Deccosus 11374

Decemi(us) 6687

Decma 4590-91

Decmanus R.2575

Decmina 4190; cf. Norden
   Altgerm. 155 n.2

Decuma 3318

Dedissa R.4231

Degouexus 4506

?Depardosa (or Pardosa,
   Pardosus?) 4604

Dercoiedus 4301, 4576

Deru[us 4679 (or Deruensis?)

?Dessillus 3313

Desticius R.402

Deuillia (dat.) 4159

Dicaeue(?) AcS 1.1281,475

Diceratus (Remus) 1055

?Dimis AcS 1.1283

Dimmia[3664

Diucia 4244

Diuciana 4306

Diucius 11377

Diuicia 4371, -ius 11376

Diuiciacus BG 2.4.7 (Dei-),
   cf. C. p.544

Diuiciana 4306

Diuiχta 4592, -us 6.32623,
   23; N.5

Diuiχtilla 3454

Diuos AcS 1.1296,28-31

Diuuogna 10024.291

Doccius 4192

Dogir[ix? AcS 1.1301

Donicat[ius?] 3707

Personal Names

Donicus 3.14214

Donilla 3724, 3994

Donissius 4266

Donna 4301

Donnetius (or -tus?) 4521

Donnus 4355

Dotalus 4266

Dotilla 3400

Dou[11293; BSAF 1907, 225

†Doxates 3817

Drappo 4516

Drappus 4002

~~Drauso~~ 3618

Drinus AcS 1.1319

Drippia 4247

Dru.a.i 11290; BSAF 1912, 281

Druca 4356

Dubitatus 3707, 4227

Dubna 4468

Dubnotalus 4711

Duccenus 4692 (Doc-?)

Dunamiola 3889

Durianios(?) AcS 1.1380

Durio 3493

Durnacus 3253

Durra 10027.113; 10028.2

Duteria 3321 (Δω-?)

Duian[10001.370

†Duuiadius(?) 3512, or read Dun- with ∨∨ un(?), cf. 3600

Ecitumus 4693

Ecritunius 10006.31

Edullius 4242 (cf. 6058, AcS 1.1407-08)

?Efutius 4080

Egidius Lib. h. Fr. 8

†Egrebaldus 3513

Eica R.3905

Elantia 3320 (cf. 241 below)

Elicus 10027.82

Eloppo 3321

Elox 4101 (Ve-?), Elogs AE 1941.88

Eluo[4407

Eluorix 4301

Emin[us?] AcS 1.1434

Epasius 11298; BSAF 1912, 282

Personal Names

?Epaχta 4371, Eppaχta
(-xia?) 4372

Ericco AcS 1.1463; or
Fricco 10006.35

[??Ertixus AcS 1.1466]

[Esciepeda (?) ib. 1467]

Escitatus 4614

Estius 10029.16

Esuc(cius) 3322

Esuggus 3487 (-ccus, cf.
Esuccus 5366a, Vesan-
tio)

Esui 10024.194

Etenianus 3323

Etiainanus 3358

Etullilia R.4082

Eucc[4490 (for Esucc-?)

Euentius Saalb. Jb. 9,
1939, 43

?Eull[(AcS 1.1483)

?Eurinus ib. 1484

?Euta 4373

Excingillus 4239

Exobnus 6460 (Mediomatr.)

Exomnius 4470

Fandus (?) 4562

Fanu, Fanus AcS 1.1492

[?Fecinus AcS 1.1493]

Fedula (P-?) 3726

Flauius 3.4391; 3.7415

Focatus R.4181

†Francola 3880

Freio 3614; cf. Freiouerus
7036 (Tunger)

Friatto 3614

Fricco 10006.35

Fronto F.33

Frontonius F.88

Fullofandes Amm. 27.8.1

Gabra 4911 (C- 4222)

Gabrilla 3325-26, 4260,
cf. 3327

?Gaitus 4545

Gai.iuus(?) AcS 1.1513

Gaiolus AE 1941.151;
Toussaint 150

Galba cl., BG 2.4.7, cf.
C. p.544

†Galla 3832

Gallionio 4099

?Galoua AcS 1.1980, cf.
706.21 and num. caloua
(γαλουα?) 206 above

Personal Names

[Gamaleda 3615; but see
213 above]

Gamburio 4132

Gangusso (C-?) 3596

Garmullus 10002.242

[Garrus(?) AcS 1.1985,
for Galrus]

Gauinius 10001.146

Gauio 3676

Gauua 3409 (cf. 3306)

Gelos 3707

Genoesugenus 4674 (two
words?)

†Geronius 3838

Germanio 3899

Gesacus 3488

Giama 3328

Giamillius 3456, -ia
3996 (C-)

Giamil(l)o 10017.432

Giamillus 4228, Giamil[
3329

Giamius 4301, cf. Gi(a)-
mmius 3995

?Giamos AcS 1.2019,45

]giannus(?) 4523 ( ]cl-?)

Gimmionius (and -ia) 4167

Gimmius 3995

Gionis 4087

Gogo Fort. 7.4.3

Gnasi[AcS 1.2029

?Gnatilla N.7a

Grannica 4704

Graptus 3725

†Hagdulfus 3840

Haldacco 3622

Haldauuo[nis] 8340
(Neruius)

?Haricura 10024.311

[Healissus REA 27, 1925,
28; but Espérandieu,
in Mém. Soc. acad.
Arch., Sc., et Arts...
Oise, 19, 1904-06, 411-
412 (cf. CIL 13.378*)
suggested Thallusus as
the correct reading]

Heluius 3707

Heluetius 4521

Heptois R.4181

[Hermidius AcS 1.2053]

Hibern(ius?) 6687

†Hildulfus 3513

†Hillidius Greg. Tur.
h.Fr. 1.45

Personal Names

Hirniosus 10027.252

Homullia R.415

†Hubold[BSAF 1922, 228

Hurmius 7.692

Iacioni[3331

?Iaecca 3420-21

Iaisius 3741

Iancus 11376

Ianotissa 3332

]iapicinc[3799

Iaretius 6202

Iasetus 3334

Iassia 4695, R.4190, -ius
    F.46

Iassus 4146, 4277; -a
    4382

I(i)auius(?) 3548

Ibetius 3474

]ibroii 3335

?Iberari[di] 11383

Iblia 4229

Ibliomarus C. p.584; cf.
    above 208B; N.54

Iccius cl., BG 2.3.1

Icran[3717 (-g-)

Icum[4406; Icurm[or
    Icurn[10006.129

Iedurcius

Iedussius 4137 (Led-?)

Ientius 3310

Iiauius (Iau-?) 3548

]ildoniui (F-?) F.329;
    cf. 224 below

†Iledius 3844

Illanuissa 4301 (Lan-?)

Imbrius 3586

Imbetansius episc. (Remi)
    Duchesne 3.81

Impaut[10027.274

Ina 3901

Indus Tac. a. 3.42; cf.
    CIL 13.3656 (ad.); RC
    28, 1907, 41-2, ala
    Indiana R.1461, 1467

Indutiomarus cl., BG 5.
    3.2; cf. C. p.568

Indutissa 10029.321

[Indutus AcS 2.45]

Inecius (Imi-) 4146

Inedo 4488

Ingenus 4260

Inginossus 3337

?Inhani 3579

Inoincius 11313; cf. AcS
2.47

Intincius 4281 (cf. 3.
12031,19 Intincu f.)

?Intuminus 3311

Inturix R.4601

Inuiricus 3743

Io, Ius 4098

Iocus (Iu-) 11390

Ioimarus 3464

Ioincatius 3707

Ioinchus 3339-40

Ioincissius 4248

Ioppillo, Ioppios AcS 2.64

Io[...]cusell[4338

Iou|coniu 4098

?Iosion[ius(M-) 4136

Iouina 3846

Iouinca 4127

Iouincillus 4427

Irmidius (Herm-) 8709;
AcS 1.2053; cf. 224
below

Isanis[10027.63

†Iseontius 3851

Istatillius 4659

Isuiius·4406 (E-)

Itaiccus 10027.115

?Ithacius C. p.584

Iuccosa 4394

Iucundinius AE 1935.64

Iuent[4711

Iulius (Auspex, Classicus,
Florus, Indus, Tutor,
Valentius) Treuer (ex-
cept Auspex Remus)
Ritterling Fasti 140-
42; R. Lit. Index

Iumma m. 6460 (Mediomatricus)

?Iurici 3743

Lalissus 4176

Lalla 4177

ᴸallius 4269 (Halkin Serta
Leodiensia 1930, 180)

Lallus 3290, 3349, 3707
p.10; Lal- v. Massow,
482

Lalus 4176

Latinianus AcS 2.152

Laucus (Menapius) 5.885;
cf. PID 196a (laχes̃)

Lauena 4596 (Tau-? Tab-?)

Lausic[Pro Neruia 2,

Personal Names

1925, 94; cf. Note xv above, PID 158, Lascus 132 above

Lenius AcS 2.120,13

Lettius 4168

Leubasna 3601, -us 7. 691; cf. Lobasinus (Tunger 3.3400)

†Leuboricus 3485

†Lecontia 3871

†Lea, †Leo 3848, 3850, 3852; Saalburg Jb. 9, 1939, 43

Leodenus 11024.324

Leuus 3351

Liamiarus(?) 2615

Liaoius 4472, 4477

Libentio 3634

Libo 3592

Liccatulia 11386 (two words?)

Liccus 3350

Licinus 3459, -ius N.58, 60

Licnius AcS 2.211,44

Lillius 4288

Lillutius 4311

Liscius 3707

Litauiccus 4711

†Litorius 3848, AcS 2. 246,48

Lituccus 3452

Litugeni 10027.117

Litumara 4711

Lollianus 4412

Longinus AE 1945.58

Lopolus 3854

Lorius AcS 2.288,42

Lossius 3547

Losunio 6202

Lottius 3547, 11354

Lotto AcS 2.290,41

Louessus ib. 294, 22

Loupus C. p.583 (AcS 2. 292); cf. 8655

?Lsulpo 4550 (L.S. Vlp-?)

Lubaini 3622 (dat. sg. f.)

Lucana F.69

Luccus 3707 a.2,4

†Lucec[3915

Lucillius 4548

Lucretius R.1946

Luculentus Saalb. Jb. 9, 1939, 42

Personal Names

†Ludula 3787

]lulna 4546

Lup[4598, Lupio 6687,
    Lupius Toussaint 149;
    Lupus 3730

†Lupantia 3855

Luperca 3905

Lupicinus 3856

Lusia 4229

?Luxus AcS 2.359

†Lycontia R.4328

[Macaritinus AcS 2.363;
    367 (Macerati-)]

[Maccius 3501]

Macco 4670

Macio (-g-) 4397

Macribalata(?) 3381 (two
    words?)

Macrinus 3454

Macumus AcS 2.369

Madicua 3624

Magiatius 11453

Magiatus 4498

Magiaxu REA 24, 1926,
    328; AE 1925.98
    (-gi-?); cf. Caixu Do.
    34; or -χu?

Magillius AcS 2.376, Mag
    ...uilla 4137

Magio 4397, 4420

?Magiona AcS 2.378

Magiorix 4534

Magnianus 4398, R.4211

Magunus 10025.151

Magurio AcS 2.386

Maiana 4007, -us BSAF
    1922, 226; REA 25,
    1923, 383; AE 1923.20

Maiinternus 4147

?Mainnatus F.330 (cf. 83
    above)

Mainnonia R.4213

Mainus 11391, cf. AcS 2.
    391

[?Maiurilus AcS 2.392]

Maiusus 4560

Maliut[4098

Mallius (Seneca) Dig. 36.
    1.48

Mallus 3653

Manaua 4343

Mandalonius 4130

[Mandubracius BG 5.20.1]

Manedu AcS 2.406

Personal Names

Mania 4266

Mansuetus, -inus TrZ 3, 1928, 189

Mantidia 4653

Mapa 3445

[?Mapnusus AcS 2.414]

Marcu[s 4355

Marsus 4445

Marontius 3895

Martialis N.45

Martisano[AcS 2.448

Martus 4023, Martia 4266

Marullus R.3845

Marus 3862

[Masalla AcS 2.449]

Mascellio 4532, N.53

Masclo 3365

Massa 4542; cf. 3.12361 (Tuncer), 12.166

Massius 4325, -ia AcS 2.455

Masueta 3360, -us 3361

Masurus 10027.27

Matona 3367

Matta 3621

Matto 11385, 11395

Mattos 4325

Matuiccus 4405

[Matutinius CIL 5.5929]

Matus AcS 2.483

[Mausaeus(?) v. Carausius]

Meccius 3707 a.2,6

Meddugnatus 4681

Medeticca 3503

Medilus AcS 2.497

[Mediuiχta ib. 524; or Diu-?]

[Melanasia 4273; cf. gl. 178]

Melausus R.4231

Melindus 4672

Melio 4510

Melius 3707a 2,3

Mellis(?) 4640

Melonius 11396

Melus 3449

Memmiolus 4264, Memmius 4274

Merculo 10006.56

Meroclia[4408

Mesol[N.53

Messia 4001

Personal Names

Messicus 3453

Messo 3371

Messonius AcS 2.576

Mettus 10032.17

Miaenus AcS 2.581

Micco 4089, Mico[4283

?Micrus AcS 2.584

†Mictianus 3693

Middei (gen.) 6395 (Med-
    iomatricus)

Milidea (Me-) AcS 2.585

?Miliduo 10006.58

[Miner[AcS 2.588]

Minna 3426

[?Miori AcS 2.599]

Mirani 10035.15

[Mircio AcS 2.599]

Miscuro BSAF 1931, 100;
    1938, 162; AE 1932.23

?Mogounus 4668 (or div-
    ine name)

Mogsius 3707 p.1.5

?Mommo 4135

Monianus 4555

?Monimene 4602

Morius AcS 2.636

Mottio 4257

Mottus 3992

Motuacus 4171

Motucus -ius 3735

[?Motuso AcS 2.647]

Mouesius R.3860

Moxius 4406

Moχsius 4002

Musa AcS 2.661; cf.
    Mausaius?

Mussidius 10002.351-52

?Naca AcS 2.671

[Nacusso ib. 672]

]naiionus R.4051

Nais(?) 4640

Nammia 4388

Nammota 4353

Nanninus C.p.584

?Nasola 3521

Nant[3.5901

Natto 11454

Nasso 10025.99

Nauos(?) 3570

Nectaridus Amm. 27.8.1

Personal Names

Nedo 11398

]nebnicca 4673

?Nebrius 4705

[Nemausus 11453]

Nennicus 4476

Nequigo 4007; cf. Quigo,
   Quigonius 2669

Nera[10027.100

Nered[4147

Nericcus AcS 2.719;
   10006.62

?Neuo (or Asso?) 11459

†Nesisu (Germanio) 3899

Neutto 3628

Niem[4161

Ninnius 3618

[Nistus(a) AcS 2.750]

?Nitieeuirico (Ne-) 3743

Nomarus 3349

Nommus 3707

Nonianus 3729

Nonna 3376, 4331; BSAF
   1922, 226; REA 25,
   1923, 383; AE 1923.20

Nonnillus 3729

†Nonnita 3517, cf. AcS 2.
   758

Nonnius (Germanus) 3707

Nonnita 3859, 3867

Nonusa 3868

Noseta 11454

Notta 3377

Nouialchus 4123

Nouianus 4163

Nunechius 3869

Oassos (Vassos?) AcS 2.
   821

[?Occo AcS 2.825,50; prob-
   ably misreading for
   Oc(c)iso or (cf. Fort.)
   Coco; Gogo above]

Oclatius (Tunger) F.304

?Oconius 4258

Ocratia 3573

Ocusonius F.64

Odua 4525

[?Oico AcS 2.839-40]

[?Oinencilo ib. 840]

[?Oitoccius ib. 841]

[?Olco[ib. 843]

Oledo 3707

]ollius 3650 (read Axill-
   ius?)

Personal Names

Ollodagus 3632

Ollognatus, -ius 4159

Omullius 3507

?Opetius AcS 2.861

Orbissa 10006.64

Oricla 4293

Osidius 1702

Ossuac[3915

Otalus 10002.589

Ouina 4409

Ounicco 11399

Oχtaioius AE 1925.98, cf.
  Oχtaius 11240 (Lugd.);
  RÉA 26, 1924, 327-30;
  cf. 5408

?Ouint[3742 (Q-?)

[Ousanna AcS 2.892]

Pacuuianus 3.2049

Padula 4704

Pagadunus R.3593

Papinia 4165

Parcilius AE 1941.74

Pardius 3650, Pardus
  4006

Partus C. p.583

Paricus AcS 2.932

Passuio 11401

Pauto 3992; cf. gl. 220

Penci 4147

Pennausius 4277

Perra 3379

Perssicila 4674

Pertur[3595

Petturo 4704

Pexius Ant. Cl. 6, 1937,
  304

[Pia(u)onius 3679, R.285;
  Pauunius Num. Chr. 78,
  1940, 85]

Piccienus 10017.681; cf.
  gl. 240

[?Pieris 3706]

[Pinarius (Sabinus) 3531]

Pisc[BSAF 1912, 281

[Plaianus (Dalm.) 3458]

Pluncus AE 1941.74

Pomentina 11323 (for Pomp-
  tina?)

Popillius 3503

Popira 4248

Poppus 3972, -ius 4217
  (Oppius?)

Personal Names

Poppusa 11403

Pottus 4260

Priectus 3875-76

Primanus C. p.583; cf.
   3635, 4139-40 (perh.
   "of Belgica Prima,"
   cf. TrZ 6, 1931, 56)?
   Primanius 4004-5, 4260

Primilla F.331

Primnia 7007 (Medio-
   matrica)

Primulius 4006

Prisso 4007

Priti 3878

Prittio 4692

Prudca 4418

Pruscia 4007, -ius 4009,
   3992; -s- 4008

Prusonius 4579

[?Pucatus AcS 2.1051]

Puetus 4440

Pupus 7412 (C. p.584)

Pusena 3858

Quicilla 4246

Quigilla 4276; cf. Quigo
   2669; Nequigo above

Radogi(sil)us 3486

Ratisc[4338

Rebricus 4700; R.3886

Recmo[4722

Regina BA 1922, 138

Regulus 4700

Renatus 4531

?Reputia 4606

Resta Ant. Cl. 6, 1937,
   304

Restutus N.19

†Retecius 11333a, R.4328

Reticianus 3638

Ridiantus R.3888

Riguiru 4722

?Rimentus 4606

Rio[ ]a 3389

[Riomonus AcS 2.1191]

]risua 3890

Rocca 10002.429

Rodana, -us (Rh-): for
   these as personal names
   see AcS 2.1221-23

?Romaim[3327

Romogillus 4170

Personal Names

[?Ruesarius AcS 2.1240]

Rusonia 7.55 (Medio-
matrica), Ruson[REA
25, 1923, 383; AE 1923.
20; BSAF 1922, 226

Sabinus (Remus) 6.46;
R.2661; -eius R.3721

Saccetius 4547

Saccomainus 4547 (two
words?)

Sacconius 1807

Sacc(i)us AE 1945.58

Sacgedo (i.e. -cc-) 3367

Sacerius F.3; -ianus 4207

Sacio 3391

Sacirobena 4712, -cr- 4425

[Sacrapus AcS 2.1280]

Sacratius 4207; -tus
4538, 4559

Sacricia(?) 4166

Sacrilla 4166

[Sacrillius 7555a]

Sacrius 4207

[Sacrouir cl.]

Sacruna 3641

Sacuna 4405

Sailo 4584

Sallidatus 10010.1705

Saluius 11714

Sambatius 3861

Samocna (Treuer) AE 1913.
130

Samogenus 4720

Samognatius 3.8014

?Samoialus 10006.82

Samorix (Remus) 2615

Samotalus 4685, cf.
10006.82; num.

Samrs 10001.420

Sanctinius CIL 5.5929

Santinus 4426

Sanuacus 4663, cf. 10010.
1721ab; BA 1922, 137

Sapo 10017.760; cf. gl.
220

Sappula 3990

Sappulo 3743 (or Sappul-
us?)

Sarracina 3885

Sassius 5.5033

Satia 4007

Sator 10001.424

Satta 3395

Personal Names

Sattara m. 3745, cf. 7754
a.2

Sattarus 3745

Satto 3401, 3974, 3976;
10017.763

Sattonius 4100, 4106,
4278

Sattus AcS 2.1378

Satullinus

?]saudes 3854

Sautus 4123

Scaripus 11.1356

?Scomius 4586

?Scorobres 10002.54-55

Scottius 4706

Scotto 3887

Scottus 3310, -a 3887,
10002.459

Secate 4550 (or divine
name?)

Seccius 3463, 3488

Sec[c]ula AcS 2.1425,13

Secco 3650, 4171, 4204;
10027.122

Sedatus 4609

Sedulius AcS 2.1434,36

[Segouax BG 5.22.1, Bri-
tain]

Seisserus AcS 2.1459

Seius 3707; cf. 8.19333;
Dig. 36.1.48

Sementinia 4260

Semmi 10022.233

Senecianus N.14

Senecio 3453, 6687; cf.
7.269; F.238

Seneconius 4250

Senectius Liv. per. 139

Senicatius 3503

Senilius 4207, 7369 (Med-
iomatricus)

Senitios 10010.1783

Senna 4522

Sennaugus 11313.2,19

Senniola 3407

Sennius 3394, 3558; 10021.
73, 10025.193

Sennus 4428

Senorix 4403

Senouir 4711

Sentiauis(?) REA 38, 1936,
41

Senurius 6687

?Seppa 3408

Personal Names

Sernatius episc. Tung.
  C. p.574

Serms[10002.469

Seronnus AcS 2.1523

Serotinus 4211

?Sertus 3980; better
  Settus?

Sesuggus 3487 (or Esu-?)

Setubogius 3487

Sicco AcS 2.1539,20

Sicnobenus 4613

Sicogninus 4432

Siluanus 8655

Siluius (Britto) Auson.
  (AcS 2.1565)

Similia 4007, -ius AE
  1941.88

Similinia 3983

]simnus dipl. 125 (S-?)

Sinccu(s) 3411

[S]incorilla 4242

Sincorius 3707 a.8

Sioi (?) 3866

Siora 4613, 11461

Sittia 4200

[?Smertucus AcS 2.1593,
  51]

?Snata 10006.140

Soianus 3293, Soiianus
  4592 (cf. 4012)

Soiionia R.4049

Soiius 4012

Solidia 4561

Solimarius 3979

Solinus 3426

Solitum(arus?) 11454

Solitus 10010.1829

Sollanus (-ii-) 4012

Sollauius 3632

Sollius 4013

Sollus 3445

Solu[AcS 2.1612.50

Somo[ib. 1614

?Sottillius F.330

Sottu 10010.1838

Strambus 10015.110a

Sualiccia 3562

Suarigillus 4433; cf.
  Suagrius 182 above

Suc[3413

Suca 3314 (or Connisuca?)

Sucarus 10010.2408

Personal Names

Succius 3707 a.10

†Sucio 3891

Sueonila 3414

[Suessio 3261]

Suiccius 3528

Sumaro 10017.821

[Sumelio AcS 2.1666]

Sun...ninus 3892

Suniducus 4627

?Suommoiius AcS 2.1671

Surbur[us 4554

[Taccitus 7667?]

Tagausius 3628

Tagia 3456, -ius ib.

[Talanus 3541 (Pann.)]

Taliounus 4293, -nia
   Hettner 198

Talissa 4715

Talia 3416

Tallus 3664

Talpidius 4625

Tamne AcS 2.1716

Tanehi (gen. sg.m.)
   3607; AcS 2.1719

Tappu 10010.1877c

?Targilia 4615 (read Tas-)

Tarsica[3417

Tartos 3418

Taruco 10010.1882

Tasgilia(?) 4615

Tasgillus 4380, 4506, 4507

Tatira 10010.1889

Tauricus 4225

Tauso f. 4012

Tausius (Tunger) AcS 2.
   1773 (Capit. Pert. 9.
   9), cf. C. p.574;
   10015.87

[Taximagulus BG 5.22.1,
   Britain]

Tecco 10002.497

Teddiatius 4142

?Temony 4035

?Teriono 4014

Tertinius 4114, -nn- (?)
   RE 1229

Tertus 4062; -ius 4114,
   F.328

Tetius 4108

[Tetricus REA 13, 1911,
   350; Rev. Num. 4, 1940,
   83; RA 26, 1946, 109;

cf. 83 and 182 above;
C. p.584; inscc. saepe
e.g. 1292, 2271, 2921,
2993, 3035, 3308, 4434,
5010; Rh. Mus. 84,
1935, 349 n.5]

Tet(ti) 10027.45

Teuto 4273

Thalia 4079

Tica[10002.602

Ticherno AcS 2.1834

Tigernomaglus ib. 1841

[T]igorilla, [T]incorilla
see [S]incorilla

Timincius 3568

Tinntus (or Tinntirus)
10001.439; 10010.1910a

Tiola 4686

]tionius (Remus) 7439

Tippa F.330

Tippausus 4435

Titiola BSAF 1912, 282

Tittalius 4468

Tittausus 11402

Titullina 11412

Tiua 10006.164

?Tlob[10010.1920

Toccia AcS 2.1865

Tocnaius F.63

Togenetus 3321

Tonnia 4011

?Topiuri 4427

[Tornacus (if genuine)
10001.318, cf. local
names]

Totia 4177

Tounus 4436

Toutissia 4713

Toutos 11413

Treuerius (apparently as
personal name) 3707b
2.8; 3855

[Tribocius 4046]

Tricus 3499; cf. Tricc(i)
10027.45

Tris[4304 (perhaps div-
ine?)

Tritus 4578, cf. 10010.
194

Troucetissa m. C. p.584;
3.14349,8

]ttini 3584

Tutia 3725

[?Tuinisu 10006.144]

]tulla 4400

Tu]ranius (?) 2033; TrZ
7, 1932, 57; Turrani
10027.201

Personal Names

Vaa[10010.1952, cf.
   10017.1085; 83 above

?Vabilis 4179

Vacasatus 10006.94

Vaccia 3456; -io 11.1356

Vaduna 3603

Vaiani[10010.1958

Valatonius 3283

Vanaenia 3624

Vanero AcS 3.99

?Vaonus 10010.1970

Varacatus 4348

Varaitio 3707

Varedonius 3707

Varicillus 4301

Varinnius 10006.99

?Varistus 4178

Varrotalus AcS 3.111

Varusius 4177; Varrusius
   Pro Neruia 2, 1925, 94

Vasaenus 3626, cf. Vannen-
   us 10003.64

Vasnus 10027.184

Vassatius 10010.1981

Vassillus 4433, 11382

Vasso (or -us) F.330 (fem.)

Vassorix 3532

Vateraunus 10006.101

Vatus(?) AcS 3.127,7

Vc[4553

Vceou[10027.276

Vci[10015.64

Ve[3456

V]ectimarus 4242

Vectissus 7555b

Vedastus episc. R. Lit.
   12.99

Ve]getus F.1

Vegisonius 4317, 4318

Vegiso 10017.877

Veldulus 10010.1993

Velidoreti 10022.274

Vellango 8340 (Neruius)

Vellau[AcS 3.149

[Vellocatus Tac. h. 3.45,
   in Britain]

Velmada 3596

Vellorius 7555a

Velugnius 3632, cf. 10010.
   1995

Vendus AcS 3.158.33

Venulinus F.88

Personal Names

Venulus 4411

[Venutius Tac. a. 12.40,
    in Britain]

Ver[4103

[Veransatus (Tunger)
    7036]

Veratius 3586

Vercobius 10010.2008

Verinus 6687

Veriugodumnus 3487

Vertico BG 5.45.2

Vertiscus BG 8.12.4

Veruecco (-us?) 3612;
    cf. Veruicius C. p.584

Verzu 10024.291

Ves[10017.892; 10029.
    100

Vesecunia 4261

Vest[10010.1023

Vestina 4713, -us 10027.
    48

Vesuca[AcS 3.260

?Veteranus 10006.104

Vettius 10001.330

Vetulenus 3.793

]ueus[3288

?Vgustus 4497

Vibiasena 4441

[Vibius 4624]

Vico 4013

?Vicsus (or Vrsus?) 10028.
    23

Victurus 5.8762

Viducus 4007

Viducillus 10027.98

Viducius 10010.2039a

Viduco 10017.912

Vienus 10010.2041

Viena 4024

†Vigur 3903

Vildix C. p.584

Vilieus episc. Mettensis
    (Fort.)

Vimpata 4616

Vimpuril(l)a 3294

Vimpuro, -onius 4019

Vimpus 4707, cf. 10010.
    2044, 10019.20 (Vimpus
    of Blickweiler and Esch-
    weilerhof, perhaps ear-
    lier at Lezoux)

Vinardu 3905

Vindillus 3313

Vindoinissa 4665

Personal Names

Vin.ia 4105

Viniccius

Vipi 10027.155

[Virdomarus Prop. 5.10.
   41; cf. AcS 3.381,48]

Viredo 4468

Virialcus 4514

Viriassiu 10010.2054

Virodu 10010.2058, cf.
   Virodd[(divine name)
   6486, Virodu num. 78
   above

Viromarus 4659

Virotus 7033

Viscareua 4043

Visuiius 4406, cf. sq.
   (also at Metz)

Visutlus 10017.919

Vitalia 4281

Vittata (B-?) 3504

Vittatius 4445

[Vittio 6484.11, cf.
   8339]

Vitto REA 38, 1936, 41

Vitubena 3428

Viuous 10010.2069

Vixuuio 10024.291

Vlittius 3707

[?Vlloir[10006.167]

Vlpius R.2599; AE 1945.
   58

Vo..mi AcS 3.422

Vocarus 10010.1930, 2075

[Vocula Tac. h. 4.33]

?Vodadasus 10034.1

Volia 4044

Vollio 4226

Vongidia 3555

Vosecunnus 10010.2085

Votla 10010.2088

Vraθarus 4407

Vrbicius 3426

Vrbicus 3426, 4439, 4732,
   cf. 10010.2092

Vrdo 3404

Vris[10023.19

Vrissulius 3649

Vrnacus 10027.131 (Durn-;
   or Vrsinus?)

Vrsa (dat.) 3718; 3906-07

↑Vrsacius 3690, -t- 3789
   ↑Ουρσάκιος R. Lit.
   p.246

Personal Names

Vrsicinus 3522, 3908, cf.
  Ουρσικῖνος IG 14.2561

Vrsicius 4152

Vrsina, -ianus 3033

Vrsinus 3650

Vrsio 3908a, 4108

Vrsola R.4374

Vrsolus 3907, -ulus 4114,
  4121

†Vrsuius 3801, -a 3909

†Vrsula 3693

Vrsus 3624, 3861

?Vsca[3666 (or
  u.s.l.m.?)

Vsilla 3426

]usmarus AcS 3.54

Vtilius 4261

Vttubena 3428

?Uufre[AcS 3.58

†Vuidargildus 3902

Xinai 3429

Yllici 10025.33a; cf. num.
  177 above and 239 below?

?Zurdigi 3495 (cf. 3493
  Durio?)

Note xlv   British Names

    Many proper names recorded in Britain reflect an
indirect light upon Belgica and Germania inferior (cf.
Belgica Introduction). But besides Keltic items, there
are Germanic, due to Germanic-speaking recruits stationed in Britain. These also are part of the record.
Most of the evidence useful for this purpose is given
by Holder from CIL volume 7 (1873), and from supplements
of later date down to about 1894 (EE volumes 3, 4, 7;
Arch. Journal volumes 47, 49, 50), and from non-epigraphic
sources. These items are not repeated below. Subsequent
additions, or corrections of texts previously published,
we owe to Haverfield, Macdonald and others (EE vol. 9
and annual reports in Proc.Br.Acad., JRS); a selection
follows (arabic numerals are references to EE 9, 1913;
references by volume, year, and item-number are to JRS);
note also C. Hawkes RGKBer. 21, 1931, 87ff.; Antiquity
7, 1933, 493; Kendrick and Hawkes Archaeology in England
and Wales 1914-31, London 1932; Haverfield Roman Occupa-

British Names

tion of Britain 1924, p.246; V.E. Nash-Williams, Early
Christian Monuments of Wales, 1950.

(A) Local Names

Aballaua ND, cf. JRS 28,
    1938, 203

Albion Scottish Gael.
    Stud. 5, 1938, 72-75

Atrebates 988a

Brigantes p.623

Caledo 1005

Calleua 986

Cornouii 14, 1924, 244.5

Deua 1274

Deceangl(i) p.642; 12,
    1922, 284.15

Dobuni p.636

Durobriuae 30, 1940, 190

Gleuum 1283-84

Londinium 1372

Lutudarenses 1265-66;
    31, 1941, 146

locus Maboni (Clochmaben-
    stane) see 33, 1943,
    37.20 (cf. p.77); fons
    Mabonus (Savigny) RC
    14, 1893, 152; see also
    divine names

Maridunum p.634

Petuaria uicus 28, 1938,
    199.1

Silures 1012

[?Textouerdi p.593; but
    cf. p.666 above]

Vindolandesses uicani Rn.
    Brit. in 1914 31.5;
    AE 1917-18.131

(B) Divine Names

Alaisiagae 11, 1921, 237.
    6; cf. Gutenbrunner
    Gotternamen, 202;
    Krappe MLR 21, 1926,
    56

Anociticus, Antenociticus
    1164; AE 1924. 4

Arecurius 27, 1937, 246

835

British Names

Aruolecia 27, 1927, 217. 29

?Autocidius RA 33, 1931, 183

Baudihillia 11, 1921, 237.6

Beda R.2440

Belatucadrus (-cairus, -caurus) p.567; 17, 1937, 212, cf. 217; 22, 1932, 223

Boudig[a] see 155 above

Brigantia 1138, 1141, 1120; cf. CIL 7.1062, 13.7945; Caelestis B. 7.1345; cf. 27, 1937, 208-09; 33, 1943, 78

Callirio (dat.) 37, 1947, 178

deo genio Chocunc[32, 1942, 42; cf. 13.7923-24, 12008-09

Cocidius 1177, 1227; 12, 1922, 277; 15, 1925, 247.9; 28, 1938, 15a-b; cf. RA 33, 1931, 183; AE 1924.3; 1927. 91; JRS 27, 1937, 246; 31, 1941, 140; AE 1938. 113

Condatis 27, 1937, 246

Fersomaris 1124 (unless a personal name)

Fimmilena Dessau 4760, R.2440

Friagabis 11, 1921, 237.6

Garmangabis 1135

Germ[(if divine name) R.1986; 7.796

Harimella 7.1065

Lenus 1009; 39, 1949, 114

Maponus p.579; 15, 1925, 248; cf. local names (Mab-)

Medocius Campesium 1005

Nodens, Nu- (Ir. Núadu), deuo N. in 7.140, cf. Lith. naudà "profit, money," Umb. nu̯rpener "nudi-pondiis," nudi-pineum Gloss. Lat. 4. 1930, N 10; cf. Soc. Ant. London, Reports 9, 1932, 132-37; AJPh 59, 1938, 252; RC 49, 1932, 91-95

Ocelus Vellaunus 1009, Oce-lus 1010, 1219; cf. AE 1912.6, Byvanck 1416; and 82 (above), 223 (below)

Ocianus (i.e. Oceanus?) 1162

Ollototae matres 1133; 22, 1932, 224; AE 1933.134

Rata, Ratis 1213

Ricagambeda 7.1072-73

Riga (m.) 1119

Saiiada p.593; but cf. 15, 1925, 249.11

Sul 994-95; AE 1924.92

British Names

Suleuae, -iae 998-99; EE 7.844

Thingsus (Tincsus) R.1854, 2440; Gutenbrunner pp. 6 n.2, 25

Tra(ns)marinae matres 7. 303; R.1858

deo Trida[16, 1926, 242. 10

Tutela see 155 above

?Vagdauarcustus 1124

Vellaunus v. Ocelus

Vernostonus 7.9*, genuine according to 31, 1941, 140

Veteres, Viteres, Vitiris, Hueteres, Vhiteres 1122, 1134, 1181-83; 31, 1941, 141; 27, 1937, 247

Vitonus 36, 1946, 146; 37, 1947, 179

Viradecthis p.614; -esthis R.1878

Vnseni 1124

(C) Personal Names

Aaiotio(?) 17, 1927, 217. 29

Abascantus 1266

Abellius (Tab-?) 1191

Acontius(?) 1103

Ahtehe 38, 1938, 202.11

Albanus 1077

Albillus 1359.2

Albucianus 1358.2-3

Anauillus 32, 1942, 118

Andria 1281 (or local name?)

Anicius 17, 1927, 217.15

Annius 1073-74

Antestius 1075

Apronius 1076

Arcauius 1124.5

Ariouistus CIL 13.10021, 195

Arponatus 27, 1937, 246

Ari[983

Arrius 1234-35

Artius 1028

Asurius 1103

Ateancti dat. f. (Atencti?) p.587, ad EE 3.201

837

British Names

Atgiuuios 33, 1943, 81
  (cf. CIL 13.10027,105
  Mainz, brooch of Au-
  cissa type)

Attius 1045, 1348

Auar[(?) 17, 1927, 218.
  35

Aueus 14, 1924, 246.13

A]ucissa Rn. Brit. in
  1913, 32.9; 1313

Au(e)sina(?) 30, 1940,
  188

Auita m. 1058; 12, 1922,
  280.6; -us 1058

Auntinus 38, 1938, 204.
  15b

Babudius p.556 ad 7.184

Bacura 30, 1940, 189

Barita 11, 1921, 236

Barrius 1327

Bebius 1375

Belen[Wheeler Verulamium,
  176

Belsa 1358.6

Bitudaccus(?) 27, 1937,
  250 (but cf. Dago-
  bitus 204 above)

Bodicca CIL 8.2877; cf.
  JRS 2, 1912, 21-24

Brice 1117

Bruceti (gen.) 998

Burcanius 1124

Cabriabanus (-ntus?) 1289

Cadarus 1063

Caiatius 1059

Calenus p.556, ad CIL 7.
  182

Caletus 1358.7

Caluentus 1047, 1186

Camulogenus 1310

Camulus 1077

Capienius 1078

Capitonius 1108

Carantus Proc. Ant. Scot.
  70, 1936, 33-39

Caratilus 1358.9

Carina m. 983; 12, 1922,
  280.6; Karino 984

Car(isius?) 1216a

Caristanius 1242

Catianus 1358.10

Catu(s) 1300

Caul[(f.) 1119

British Names

†Cauudus Rn. Brit. in 1913, p.41

Cesti 1074

Cicereius 18, 1928, 213; cf. gloss 158

Cintusmus 1358.12; 37, 1947, 178

Cipius 1312bc; p.660 ad 7.1293ab

Cocceia 1065, -us 16, 1926, 243.17

Cogitatus 1007

Congenniccus 1138

Congess[29, 1939, 228 (cf. Congeistlus)

Coninia (Ertiria?) Proc. Ant. Scot. 70, 1936, 33-39

Corsm[1284a

Cracina (-u-) 1358.15-16

Cunobarrus 21, 1931, 249

Cunopectus Germ. 18, 1934, 31

Curatia 1102

Dagualda p.592, ad 7.692

Decimin(us) 1338

Decmus 1358.16

Desidienius p.589, ad CIL 7.769

Dobunnus dipl. 49

Donicus 3.14214

Doninas 11, 1921, 234.1

Eberesto(?) 15, 1925, 250. 17

Ebutius (for Ae-) 1329

Ecum[35, 1945, 92.8

[Eptacentus 1354 (Thracian); cf. F.293]

Ertole nomine 29, 1939, 226

Etacontius (Acontius?) 1103

[Faenius p.614 ad 7.1066]

Fersomaris EE 9.1124

Galerus 1090

Gamidiahus p.614, ad 7. 1065; -nus Byvanck 2. 1246

Gecus 21, 1931, 248

Ger(manus) 1186

Gessius 1320

Gipp(ius) 1358.18

Glabrio 1009

British Names

Hnaudifridus 11, 1921,
237.6; cf. Nodens (B)
above

Iau[olenus] 11, 1921, 234.
1; i.e. the jurist, cf.
P-W s.v.?

Ingenuina 1002, -us 1019

Ingenus p.594, ad 7.724;
1094

Isatis (gen.) 1257

Itosius 17, 1927, 216.22

Iullinus 1358.19

Lanuccus 1198

Ledicca 1019

Libo p.588, ad 7.688

Licinianus 1339

Lollia v. Bodicca above

Lossio(?) 1005

Louesia 17, 1927, 213.8,
-us 1063

Lucco dipl. 49

Luonercus dipl. 110

Maccalus 1358.21

Macillio 32, 1942, 118

Macrianus 1358.22

Macrinus 1007

Magunna 1229

Mainacnus(?) 1358.23

Mantia 11, 1921, 236.5

Marcus 1359.6

Marinus 1212

Martia 1104

Martina 1117

Marullinus 1085

Marullus 27, 1937, 250

Mascellio 1358.27

Matunus 15, 1925, 250.20

Maurusi Verulamium 138

Mettius 1056

Minthonius p.620, ad 7.
1038

Molacus dipl. 110

Mucianus 1122

Muχtullus 1358.30

Namilianus 1358.31

Nemnogenus p.564, ad 7.
276

Nonico (Belgic potter's

British Names

name) Wheeler Verulam-
ium (Soc. Ant. Lond.
Reports) 11, 1936, 175-
6

Nonius 1009

Nouellius 1198

Ocel(lio) 30, 1940, 189

o]phoi[an]kn 30, 1940,
189; probably for Op-
pianicnos, cf. 83
above; AE 1912.6; Cic.
pro Clu. 4.9

Olbius or Olennius 30,
1940, 118

Oriuendus 32, 1942, 42

Ouineus(?) 14, 1924, 247.
15

Papittedo 37, 1947, 181

Patto 1358.32

Pedioui(?) 16, 1926, 243.
16

Peisius 17, 1927, 217.30

Peltrasius 1227

Pertacus 1293

[Platorius R.1836]

Primanus 1358.34

Pou...iarus 1124

Purcio 14, 1924, 245.8

?Quilis (Quirillus) 34,
1945, 90.5 Limerick

]qquittu[30, 1940, 188;
]uccuit 34, 1944, 85;
a bronze patera (Llan-
beris, from Gaul?)

Sabinus 1075

Sacrillus 1358.36

Sadius (or Sauius) 17,
1927, 213.10

Salica p.558, ad 7.186

Sallienus p.527, ad 7.
100-01

Sarimarcus (?) Rn. Brit.
in 1914, p.36

Scirus 1119

Sebdius 1087

Seccius 1205

Seneca 1053; 15, 1925,
249.16; Senilis 249.
12

Senecio 18, 1928, 212.2;
1322

Sennianus 30, 1940, 190

Senopianus 1120

Sextinus 1059

British Names

Sigilius 1128

Sita 38, 1942, 43

Socellinus 1190

[†Spesindeo ("Espéran-
  dieu") 1263b]

Sulinus 998

[Syagrius 1263ac]

Sudrenus 28, 1938, 203.11

Tabellius (Ab-) 1191

Tanicus p.627, ad 7.1124

Taurinus 1358.45

Tertullus 1337

Tiotag[Verulamium 176

Toutius 995

Trenus dipl. 49

Vassedo 34, 1944, 91

Veda 1005

Vellibia 29, 1939, 226

Velua 11, 1921, 235-4

Venuleius 17, 1927, 216.
  23

Vepogenus 1005

Verinus p.536, ad 7.165

Vesuius 1208

Vibennius 1363

Vibius 1047, 1066

Vindaticius 1354

Vlpro 1060

Voeiic (Doueccus?) 15,
  1925, 250.18

Volcacius 16, 1926, 240.1

Voteporix 1030

Remark:

An incomplete alphabet (a-g, i) from Lydney Park
is given in Reports of the Research Committee, Soc. of
Antiquaries of London 9, 1932, p.101; and a graffito
from Ospringe (Kent) on a Belgic flagon, ib. 8, 1931,
p.44 no. 389, Pl. 52, which reads

diuiⅩti metti iacona

British Names

Another alphabet (abc only) from Chichester is given in
JRS 30, 1940, 188. No native potters signed their names
(see Collingwood in Frank 3, 1937, 66) in Britain.

The famous insc. of Colchester (CIL 7.1005) is
given in the Appendix (*247 vi.b). For personal names
in British Coins see C. V. Sutherland Coinage and Currency in Roman Britain, pp.62, 162 ff.; and Romano-
British Imitations of coins of Claudius in Numismatic
Notes and Monographs 65 (see JRS 26, 1936, 109).

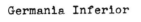Germania Inferior

It is manifest that the dialects of the Belgic
tribes of the Rhineland were subjected to strong Germanic influence by the beginning of the Empire. So
soon as written records, that is Latin inscriptions,
are available, Germanic names, conspicuously local and
divine names but also some personal names of Germanic
origin, are noteworthy. Proper names and glosses are
in fact, the only evidence to hand, apart from a few
isolated words that appear in the Latin inscriptions
of the area. Germania inferior extended from the sea,
on both sides of the Rhine as far as the junction of
the Lupia (Lippe), and then west of the Rhine along
that river as far as the Abrinca (now the Vinxtbach,
from Latin Fines). At first a military administrative
district, immediately adjoining the Rhine (cf. Proleg.
22 n.26), where the population, originally Keltic-
speaking, may be described as Germanized Kelts rather
than Germans, Germania inferior (or secunda), seems to
have extended westwards as far as the boundary (about
4.20° east of Greenwich) between the Neruii and the
Tungri; and as far south as the Ardennes.

    See Plin. NH 4.98-101; Ernst Stein Kaiserliche Beam-
ten ... im Römischen Deutschland, Vienna 1932, 1-22;
Grenier Mnl. 1.136-38; CAH 10, 1934, 784-789, 940-45,
987-991; P-W Suppl. Bd. 3 s.v. Germani (R. Much), 546-
585. Some further references: H.E. Stier "Zur Varussch-

lacht" in Hist. Zeitschr. 147, 1932-33, 489-506; Vendryès Ét. Germ. 3, 1948, 131-137 (on early borrowings
into Latin); popular accounts of the frontier by O.
Brogan and W. Rollo in Greece and Rome 3, 1933, 23-30
and 8, 1938, 36-49 (cf. ib. 5, 1936, 73-89 D.P. Dobson
on Roman influence in the north). Note especially that
Caligula is said to have studied German (Suet. Cal. 47)
and, much later, Syagrius (ca. A.D. 475, Sidon. Apoll.
Ep. 5.5), see Sofer ZfCPh 22, 1941, 108-09); H.J. and
G.A.J. Beckers Voorgeschiedenis van Zuid-Limburg, Maastricht 1940 and A.W. Byvanck De Voorgeschiedenis van
Nederland, Leiden 1941, and Nederland in den Romischen
Tijd, Leiden 1943, and H. Hardenberg Lugdunum Batauorum
(1943?) I have not seen (Kl. Bibl. 15, 1943 [1944]
pp.ii,v); Much "Ulixes in Germanien" in WuS 12, 1929,
342-361 (especially 347 and 355, cf. Jullian REA 14,
1912, 283); cf. Norden Die germ. Urg. in Tacitus Germania, ed. 3 1923, and id. Altgermanien, 1934; Norden's
suggestion was that Vxello- underlies the story of
Ulysses in Germany, and Jullian's that an imaginary
insc. ...ϭμϵρτ... (Tac. G. 3.3) should be read
᾿Οδυϭϭϵυ]ϭ Λϰϵρτ[, whereas Much interprets it better as
Ro]smert[a. Perhaps Germani is but a Latin version of
Suebi (su̯e%- and bho-).

The presence in the two Germanies of large numbers

of Roman troops, eight legions and their auxiliaries,

contributed to a Romanization, superficial perhaps,

but outwardly at least as obvious as that of the three

Gauls, and surpassed in the west only by that of Nar-

bonensis. It is to this that we owe, through the Latin

inscriptions of Germania Inferior (CIL 13 ii.2 7776-8860,

and iv 11981-12086a) much of our information, scanty and

fragmentary as it is, about the linguistic situation.

The contrast with the comparatively unorganized communi-

ties that dwelt on the right bank of the Rhine is clear

from the use of the term saltus (as also in some parts
of Aquitania) instead of ciuitas (cf. Grenier in Frank
Economic Survey of Ancient Rome 3, 502). Had any of
the revolts, such as that led by Florus and Sacrouir
in A.D. 21, succeeded, this Romanization would have
failed, or at best been greatly weakened, but the linguistic situation along the Rhine hardly much changed;
our knowledge of it, however, given a better acquaintance with the art of writing, might have been corres-
pondingly greater.

Of these peoples of Gaul, then, whose forbears had
come from a "Keltic cradle" east of the middle Rhine,
those who lived along that river had a varied fate. The
Treueri, as we have already seen (208 above), remained
largely Keltic, but had been partly Germanized in language; but there were also Germani cisrhenani, the Germani par excellence, (Tac. G 2.5; for a recent attempt
to cope with the troublesome a uictore: a uicto re⟨or⟩
Hirschfeld, viz. read a uiciniore, see R. Meissner
Rh.Mus. 88, 1939, 379-84, E. B[ickel] ib. 384), not only
the Eburones (eburo- "yew" cf. BG 6.31.5 taxus, whence
V. Tourneur Mélanges Paul Thomas 1930, 663-64 ingeniously
explains Texuandri, Toxiandria, phonetic difficulties

notwithstanding, as a translation, like Bleyberg beside
Plombières), Condrusi, Caerosi, Paemani, and Segni (cf.
Proleg. 35), who by Caesar's time had become partly
Kelticized in nomenclature and political sympathies,
but also the Belgic Nervii, who show some Germanic evidence in their proper names, the Tungri, who are perhaps
the most conspicuous of them all after the Eburones had
been all but exterminated by Caesar, the Texuandri, the
Baetasii, and others.

The infusion of Germanic speaking tribes increased
again in the territory that is now southern Holland and
eastern Belgium c. 125-100 B.C., at the time, that is,
of the disturbances caused by the migrations of the Cimbri and Teutones and Ambrones, so that the displaced
population was forced back upon the Aisne and Marne, a
movement that completed (cf. Belgica Introduction) the
fusion of German and Keltic tribes that produced the
Belgic people as described in Caesar and Strabo.

The Keltic element among them was far from being
completely submerged, just as a Keltic fragment still
remained, from much earlier times, even in central Germany, namely the Volcae in the Hercynian forest (BG 6.

4.2). But along the Rhine, where new Germanic tribes
had come in, the situation was different. Whatever the
origin of the name Germani (Keltic according to Schnetz
ZfNF 13, 1937, 33-60, in a reply to Pokorny ZfCPh 20,
1936, 461-475, who would make it Illyrian; other discussions Feist Teuthonista 4, 1927, 1-13; G. Stümpel
Klio: Beiheft 25 [NF 12], 1932; Bickel BJ 139, 1934,
14-20; W. Krogmann Der Name der Germanen, Wismar 1933),
the most ancient use of it known to us makes it a col-
lective designation of those tribes from the east of
the Rhine, presumably Germanic speaking, who had settled
(c. 250 B.C.) between the Menapii and the Treueri (cf.
BG 2.3-4; 6.2; 6.32); the text of Tacitus (l.c.) seems
to imply that this use originated among the Gauls from
what had been previously a tribal name. If this is
correct, the name is presumably Germanic in origin, just
as Grai (Greek) is Hellenic, and Germani no more to be
subjected to etymological speculation than Graeci.

More explicit evidence is wanting, simply because
knowledge of writing was not yet common, and the use
of it severely restricted. Mentz (Rh.Mus. 87, 1937,
193-205), in the course of a discussion of the use of
Germani by Tacitus in general, argues that notae (G. 10)

means "runes;" but writing remained a peculiar accom-
plishment in the days of Theodoric (ob. 526) and even
of Charlemagne (ob. 814). Actually, however, no Runic
inscription has yet been found in the area with which
this book deals of a date early enough to be pertinent
to our problem.

Nevertheless, there can be no question that there
is much that is Germanic of much earlier date is on
record, conspicuously among the proper names of the
Vbii and neighboring tribes (see, e.g. S. Gutenbrunner
"Neue Zeugnisse zur Sprache der Ubier," in Teuthonista
[Ztschr. für Mundartforschung] NF 13, 1937, 65-77; cf.
A. Oxé in Die Heimat [Krefeld] 14, 1935, 175-182; Rudolf
Much in Stzb. d. Akad. d. W. in Wien, Ph.-H. Kl., 195.2,
1920, 26-33), not merely such distinctive items as
Freiatto, Friatto, Friattius (with Germanic -tt-), but
also Germanic phonematic substitutions as o from u by
a-umlaut (Flossia, note also fl-, which is not Keltic:
*flus(s)a(n)-; Stirr(i)us: *sterna- with W. Germanic
-rr-?). On the other hand the distant Metuonis at the
mouth of the Elbe is Keltic (W.J. Beckers Rh.Mus. 88,
1939, 56-57), no less than Boiorix (king of the Cimbri),
or Moenus fl. or Hercynia silua or Taunus mons, not to

mention the numerous names of rivers in -apa, if indeed that suffix is Keltic (Kluge Urg., ed. 3, p.7).
Presumably these Keltic names, on the right bank of the
Rhine, are relics of the pre-German Keltic occupation
(cf. Gutenbrunner in Hirt Festschr. 2, 1936, 454-5),
and far less likely due to occasional later Keltic penetration of Germanic territory. Some names to the west
of the Rhine, once all too ardently claimed by Much as
Germanic (ibid.495), viz. Eburones, Condrusi, Caerosi,
are generally recognized as Keltic. As for the Cimbri,
who are said to have used the Keltic term morimarusa
(Pl. 4.94), our informant may be in error, and Streitberg actually contended that this word is German (cf.
PID 3.31), it is far from clear to what extent the Cimbri and Teutones, if they originally spoke Germanic at
all (cf. S. Feist in Zeits. f. schweiz. Gesch. 9, 1929,
129-160), had been affected by the Keltic-speaking
tribes whose land they invaded and occupied. That the
agri decumates have a title Keltic in form has been
proved by E. Norden (Altgermanien 1934, q.v. passim), and
it is to be observed that, in general, discussion of the
problem prior to 1914 (e.g. F. Kaufmann Deutsche Altertumskunde 1, 1913, 209-254) is much more sober than some
of the work of the second, third, and fourth decades of
this century.

Germania Inferior

Weight is not to be denied to Germanic items other
than proper names, provided that they are well-attested
and of early date, and that the history of their etymology is clear, e.g. bar(r)itus, burgus (cf. Asci-
burgium "ash-to[w]n"), framea, ganta, glaesum, laeti,
melca, sapo, uibones (220 below).

It is noteworthy, whatever the correct explanation
in each case, that certain Germanic tribal names bear
a striking resemblance to those of other i.e. non-German
tribes. Thus beside Lemouii (Tac. G. 43.6) one sets
Lemouices, Lem-urinus, Lem-anus; Lugii (43.3) recalls
Lugudunum, Quadi the Ligurian Quadiates (and the name
of their prince Vannius the Lepontic Venia), Naharuali
the Illyrian Naharkum, Ναρήσιοι, Peucini (cf. Dessau
1722 Nereus nat[ione] German[us] Peucennus, and for
-ennus cf. Clarenna, Sumolocenna) the south Italic
Peucetii. But some of these are doubtless fortuitous,
mere accidental similarity of the outward shape of
words. In any event, the argument (e.g. in Neckel's
Germanen und Kelten, Heidelberg 1929) has been vitiated
by a reaction against "Keltomania" that can only be
described as "Germanomania;" actually only a purely linguistic test can guarantee valid conclusions.

It is frequently remarked that names which are
claimed as purely Germanic in origin nevertheless are
recorded in a Keltic writing (e.g. Teutoboduus, Claodicus), or even in a hyper-Keltic form, as when c
(occasionally ch) is written instead of h (e.g. Cantru-
beside Chandru-, Andru- and Belgic Condru-), or ollo-
for alla- (cf. Ollogabiae, Germ. Sup.). But such
variations from the Germanic can only mean that Germanic
words had fallen into a Keltic mouth, so to speak; and
to claim them as evidence for pure or stable Germanic
settlements can only be regarded as special pleading.
Evidently Germanic-speaking tribes had occupied the
territory of an early Keltic-speaking people, whose
utterance in some cases persisted strictly enough to
modify the Germanic forms, perhaps here and there accomplished a sort of temporary revival. On the other
hand, the unequivocally Germanic Freiouerus, Haldacco,
Laubasnius, Lubaina (or -is), Vihansa must be taken at
their face value. Evidence of such a kind is extensive
enough and weighty enough to prove that Germanic tribes
had pushed as far west as 4.20° E. Greenwich (the Tungri)
by or before the last century B.C. Some Germanic names
are of Christian date, it is true; but their proportion
is fewer than, for example, in Belgica itself. In fact

the total number of early Christian inscriptions included in CIL 13 ii 2 (Germ. Inf.) strikes me as, by
comparison, small. Pagan inscriptions containing Germanic names, unless there is clear internal evidence,
are not easily assigned an accurate date; and since a
Frankish grave at Gellep has been dated as early as
ca. A.D. 450 (see A. Steeger, Germania 21, 1937, 182-
188), it is well to be cautious about the date of some
of our Germanic evidence. Nevertheless, it is clear
from many of the inscriptions containing Germanic names
that the bearers of them had lived west of the Rhine
long enough, they or their families for some generations,
to have made themselves thoroughly at home. This fact,
taken with the evidence of history and archaeology,
agrees with the conservative estimate already given of
the western limit, and of the chronology, of the Germanic
pre-Roman westward expansion.

See, in general: E. Babelon Le Rhin dans l'histoire
vol. 1, L'Antiquité: Gaulois et Germains, 1916; W. J.
Beckers "Die Völkerschaften der Teutonen und Kimbern in
der neueren Forschung," RhM NF 88, 1939, 52-92 and 101-
122; H. Brunsting Het Grafveld onder Hees bij Nijmegen,
Amsterdam 1937 (reviewed by H. Comfort AJA 43, 1939, 179;
Vollgraff REA 40, 1938, 92-93, but Brunsting's contention that the Bataui were Kelticized before their arrival
in the Low Countries is to me improbable); A.W. Byvanck
Excerpta Romana vol. (ancient texts) 1931, vol. 2 (inscriptions of Holland) 1935, vol. 3 (Roman remains) 1947,

see 221 below; id. in Mnemosyne 9, 1940-41, 87-96 (on
the northern frontier of Gaul and Not. Dig.); W. Capelle
Das alte Germanien (ancient sources), Jena 1929 (reprinted 1937); H. Dragendorff Westdeutschland zur Römerzeit, Leipzig 1912; S. Feist, in PBB 36, 1912, 307 ff.
and 562 ff., 37, 1913, 112 ff.; id. "Das Volkstum der
Kimbern u. Teutonen," in Zeitschr. f. schweizerische
Geschichte 9, 1929, 129-160; H. Friedrich "Die Anfänge
des Christentums ... im Gebiet des Nieder- u. Mittel-
rheins...," BJ 131, 1926, 10-113, cf. Proleg. 73 n.153
(Neuss); A. Grenier Études d'archéologie rhénane: quatre
villes romaines de la Rhénanie: Trèves, Mayence, Bonn,
Cologne (Paris, 1925); S. Gutenbrunner Germanische
Frühzeit in den Berichten der Antike, Halle 1939; J.H.
Holwerda "Die Tungrischen Stämme am Niederrhein," Oud-
heidkundige Mededeelingen (Leiden), NR 16, 1935 (vol.
34, 1937), 18-24; T.E. Karsten Die Germanen, Berlin and
Leipzig 1928 (Paul's Grundriss, vol. 9); G. Kossina
Ursprung u. Verbreitung der Germanen, ed. 1 1911 (reviewed, together with his Deutsche Vorgeschichte 1912,
in REA 15, 1913, 107-109), ed. 2 Wurzburg 1934 (Mannus
Bibliothek 6); G.S. Lane "The Germano-Keltic Vocabulary,"
Language 9, 1933, 244-264; R. Much Deutsche Stammsitze
1893 (with maps; also in PBB 17, 1893, 1-224); id. Die
Germania des Tacitus, Heidelberg 1937; A. Norlind Die
geographische Entwicklung des Rheindeltas bis um das Jahr
1500, Lund and Amsterdam 1912; H. v. Petrovits BJ 142,
1937, 365 (review of Brunsting as above; makes the Bataui
mainly German-speaking); id. in Festschrift für A. Oxé
Darmstadt 1938 (pp.220 ff., on boundaries in the lower
Rhine valley in the 3rd and 4th cent. after Christ); G.
Röttger Altgermanien, Leipzig and Berlin 1937 (on the
Germania; reviewed by G. Trathnigg Prähist. Zeitschr. 27,
1937, 309; cf. PhW 58, 1938, 840-41); Ludwig Schmidt
Geschichte der deutschen Stämme bis zum Ausgang der Vol-
kerwanderungen: vol. 2 Die Westgermanen (in four parts,
Berlin 1911-1918; Part 1, ed. 2, Beck Munchen 1938; re-
viewed by U. Kahrstedt GGA 1938, 416-420; A. Klotz PhW
59, 1939, 575-78; cf., on Die Ostgermanen, ZfDAlt., Anz.
54, 1935, 4-9); id. Geschichte der germanischen Frühzeit,
Bonn 1924; Hermann Schneider Germ. Altertumskunde, Mün-
chen 1938 (articles by Gutenbrunner, Mohr, Kuhn, Sch-
neider, de Boor, Reichhardt, von Jenny; reviewed by Hans
Philipp PhW 59, 1939, 1091-1111); Gudmund Schütte (vol. 1,
Eng. Tr. by Jean Young) Our Forefathers: the Gothonic
Nations, 2 vols. Cambridge (England), vol. 1 1929 [Vor
Folkegruppe Gottjod], vol. 2 [apparently English text

Germania Inferior

only] 1933; K. Schumacher Gallische u. Germanische
Stämme und Kulturen im Ober- u. Mittel-Rheingebiet zur
späteren La Tenezeit (in Prähist. Zeitschr. 6, 1914,
230-292); id. Siedelungs- u. Kulturgeschichte der
Rheinlande von der Urzeit bis in das Mittelalter, Mainz
1921-25 (cf. RA 18, 1923, 179-180); Karl Simon, "Früh-
geschichtliche Siedlungsstudien," in Zeitschr. f. d.
Alterthum 74, 1937, 165-210 and 229-268; J. Steinhausen,
Arachaeologische Karte der Rheinprovinz vol. 1, Bonn
1932 (reviewed in Antiquity 7, 1933, 108); Streitberg,
Michels, Jellinek in Streitberg's Gesch. d. indogermanischen Sprachwissenschaft vol. 2 ii 1927-36 (e.g. pp.61-
63, 78-81, 109-123, 316-318); R. Weynand l.c. 208 above.
E. Schwartz Deutsche Namenforschung, Gottingen 1950; A.
Bach Deutsche Namenkunde, Berlin since 1943 (in Paul's
Grundriss); E. Schröder Deutsche Namenkunde (ed. 2
by L. Wolff) 1944; L. Weisberger Der Sinn des Wortes
"Deutsch," Gottingen 1949 (cf. id. Theudisk, der deutsche Volksname unde die Westliche Sprachgrenze, Mar-
burger Universitätsreden 5, Marburg 1940; reviewed in
Geistige Arbeit 8, 1941, 2); W. Levinson Aus rheinischer
und fränkischer Frühzeit, Dusseldorf 1948; Reche in
Ebert's Reallexikon 4, 1926, s.v. Germanen (273-390);
G. Lüdtke u. L. Mackensen Deutsche Kulturatlas (Vorzeit
und Frühzeit; Germanische Sprachen) Berlin 1931; W.
Karsten and R. von Uslar Germanen u. Kelten in Monatschr.
für Höheren Schülen 36, 1937, 1-27; O. Brogan "Romans
and trade with the Free Germans," JRS 26, 1936, 195-222;
R. Stampfuss Rheinische Vorzeit (Volk u. Kunst 1, Köln
1934, 77 pp., see Gnomon 10, 1935, 5); id. Die ersten
Germanen am Rhein (Germanen-Erbe 2, 1937, 130-136); L.
Schmidt "Zur Kimbern- u. Teutonenfrage," Klio 21, 1929,
95-104; R. von Uslar Westgermanische Bodenfunde, Berlin
1938; H. van der Weerd Inleidung tot de Gallo-Romeinsch
archeologie der Nederlander, 1944.

Note xlvi

A few forms in the Latin inscriptions of Germania
Inferior are worthy of note. References in parentheses

Words in Latin Inscriptions

are to CIL 13.

i. (7778, Ripsdorf), if correctly read

ancam

appears to denote some object of sacrifice or dedication;
cf. perhaps Umb. ançif ("pateras"?), Gr. ἄγγος , less
likely Gaul. anax (178 above); possibly the object is the
same as that described as καντενα in Gaulish inscc. A
Germanic cognate may be found in OHG ancha "testa," cf.
angom *247(iv) below; but (F.254) we may actually have
the divine name (Trier) Ancamna.

ii. (7816, Rigomagus)

pertica uiatoria

is evidently the Latin "measuring rod"; but it stands
for an older per(c)tica, and in perc- (cf. Umb. perkaf,
perstu, Osc. perek, Pael. pracom, v. ID 642-43) we have
the most likely source of V.L. parricus (cf. Dutch perk,
Germ. Pferch) of the Lex Ripuaria; Brüch Einfl, 8-9.

iii. (7833, Heilstein)

]lailon

wears a Germanic look ("lamentum"??), with its final -n;
but most likely it is a proper name, incomplete.

iv. (7861a, Hasselweiler, a dedication Vatuims)

atucum

possibly a local or personal name; conceivably a common
noun (quasi "monstrum, ostentum, portentum"?).

Words in Latin Inscriptions

v. (7867, Bonsdorf): this reads clearly

deae idbans gabiae sacru(m) ex

(i)mp P Albanius Primu(s) s l l

in which idbans (acc. pl.?) may be the object of gabiae.

vi. (8164a, Cologne)

[negotiator Britannicianus] moritex

See 207 above.

vii. (8184, Cologne). Cf. 12.1814 (Vienne), 13.
7281, 7313 (Kastel; but not 7250, Mainz). Taken at its
face value, 8184 has

hastiferi

However, an insc. of Madaura, alleged to have this word,
actually has cisthiferi (see CRAcInscBL 1913, 256-260;
1918, 312-323), and the nature of the hastiferi is in
doubt, for framefer (Rudston, Yorks; JRS 24, 1934, 220)
is the epithet of a lion. In view of the frequent alternation h-: ch- for c- in proper names, is it conceivable that L. cistiferi was, on being borrowed, mis-
pronounced chistiferi (?), cf. cisthiferi, and this afterwards reshaped as hastiferi, which seemed more intelligible? Cf. h]ast[Byvanck Exc. Rom. 2.1335? A
curious variant appears in BSAF 1908, 305, viz cistiber
(unless that is "cis Tiberim," cistiber CIL 6.32316, TLL
3.1194, which also is at least once written -fer ib. 22)
accompanied by the personal name Gaionas (cf. 237 below),
like Porcobera (Polcevra), with -b- for -f-. The two
words would be readily confused in spoken Latin: on
framea see further REA 21, 1919, 228; 22, 1940, 50; 178
and 220 above.

viii. (8218, Cologne)

gantunis

Words in Latin Inscriptions

For a discussion of this word (cf. ad gantunas nouas)
see Note xlix (b) below.

ix. (8244, Cologne)

ob honorem sacri matratus

This tu-stem, comparable to Goth. -ōdus, -ōþus, is attested only here

x. (8251, Cologne)

pl[ateae

and 7261 (Castellum Mattiacorum), 7335-37 (Heddernheim)

platiodannus

Compare Note lii below. Grenier Les Gaulois (1945) 307
appears to think the word Keltic, which is impossible.
The resemblance between 7263-64 (cf. 6776, 7335-36) and
the Oscan eítuns-inscc. is striking. On the meaning of
platea (uicus, angiportus) see Harsh CP 32, 1937, 44-58.

x bis (8331, Cologne)

c(e)nt[enarius?

The neuter centenarium is interpreted as genus aedificii,
fortasse castri uel burgi (cf. ND Occ 33.62 ad burgum
centarium in Pannonia Inf., πύργον κεντινάριον CIG 8664,
Nicaea; for the general meaning cf. perhaps Osc. dekkviarím); see now Oxé RhM 89, 1940, 127-151 and Leschi
CRAcInscBL 1941, 163-176. If burgum is to be supplied
or understood, then see (for other occurences) 220,
Notes lii (g?) and (p), lvi below.

Words in Latin Inscriptions

xi. (8348, Cologne)

mango

Not Greek (W-H s.v., Kleberg Eranos Lofstedtianus 1945,
276-284; cf. CP 42, 1947, 203); but Germanic (Hempl
AJPh 22, 1901, 429) or more likely Alpine (see item 15
above), note especially Dessau 4851 (NdSc 1892, 68) a
dedication to Iuppiter Poeninus from the Gt St Bernhard,
the definition gallodromus in CGL 5.620,8; μαγγάνα "wine
cask" Ital. (Hesych.), mango in CIL 5.4600 (Brixia) and
4879 (Benacenses), the personal name Mangius (12.4218,
see 83 above) and Mangandius 237 below. Perhaps originally a pedlar, huckster, trader in cheap trinkets for
personal adornment *mon(i)k- or *mong-, cf. W-H s.v.
monile, PID 2.198? The word spread throughout the Mediterranean area. OE mangere "merchant," mangian "to
sell."

xii. (8492, Deutz)

uered(arius)

See 79 above, and for the ending -arius Note lvii below.

xiii. (8718, Nouiomagus)

brato

If not a personal name, cf. βράτου(δε) , less likely
brado 220 below.

xiv. (8775, Domburg)

deae Burorine quod uodum fecit etc.

in which uodum apparently stands for uotum, cf. uodiuus
in Lex Sal. But note that in

Words in Latin Inscriptions

xv. (8788, Domburg), we have th for t, viz.

ambacthius

xvi. (8860, inc. or.)

]fpromis

I can make nothing of this; f(ilius) promissis seems
improbable.

xvii. (R.2368, Dessau 9450, cf. Germ. 10, 1926,
27). Found at Trier.

Atticus fecit kanabis Bon[nensibus

Cf. 178 above.

xviii. (REA 18, 1916, 289; cf. RG KBl 8, 1915, 12.
Cachet d'oculiste, Bonn)

Tiberii Iulii Asonis aliso etc.

in which aliso is interpreted as al[bum iso[chrysum (?).
But cf. 178 above, 221, 241 below; ala 158 above, al
246 below.

Note xlvii

To the above may be added, from IG 14

1. (2573.10, a bronze statuette, Haag-Westreen)

ΤΕΚΟΥϛ(ον?) | dugiti(um?)

Cf. dugiiontiio 169 above, dugiaua PID 3.18.

860

Words in Greek Inscriptions

ii. (2578.1, on a vase at Dimesser, Mainz)

] λ ε υ χ υ ε ι μ ν α ν α . . . υ α ι λ ω ν [??

iii. (2576.1 b, Cologne)

λ υ ν γ ε υ σ

This may be Greek.

iv. (2577.8, Bonn)

λ υ σ ε τ ο υ (?)

v. (2575.2, Saalburg) illegible; apparently Greek alphabet, but not deciphered, and therefore it is not clear whether the language is Greek or not.

Cf. on Greek inscc. at Cologne, Wilhelm Reusch Germania 22, 1938, 172-17; a gnostic amulet from Gellep is given in R.3617.

Note xlviii   On an Inscription of Utrecht

The modern name Utrecht is explained as containing ut "out" by Förstemann 2, 1157-58; but the vernacular was formerly Oude i.e. "old" and Trecht, Latinized as Vltraiectum[!]; W. traeth "strand," Ir. tracht are borrowed from L. tractus, and traiectum is Latin, not Keltic pace Bede h.e. 5.11 accepted by Holder AcS s.v.;

Utrecht

the true Keltic for "ford" is *tre-ueri-, Ir. treoir,
cf. Treueri 208 above.

From excavations conducted in 1929 near the Cathedral in the centre of Utrecht (Traiectum ad Rhenum,
i.e. "bridge-head," apparently Vada colonia in this
insc., cf. Tac. h. 5.20-21, opposite the Albiobola of
the insc.[?] but cf. P-W s.v. Vada; distinguish Traiectus [superior] portus, now Maastricht (Greg. Tur.,
Troia Rav.) and Traiectus [between Caerleon and Silchester, IA])come two long inscriptions and three brief
fragments of a similar one, discovered on 17 December
of that year. They record certain dedications to the
gods of the Bataui; they give further, if accurately
deciphered, a number of names, local, personal, and
divine, hitherto unknown. They have been assigned on
epigraphical grounds, notably the abbreviations and
suspensions, to the third century of the Christian era.
There is, in my opinion, no question of their authenticity; but they were defaced in ancient times, and Vollgraff's readings and interpretation, given below, are
open to grave suspicion. But the texts are problematical enough to merit reproduction in full. The military organization supposed by Vollgraff in his interpretation is also extraordinary, if not both unique and
impossible in itself from all that we know on that head.
It is not for a moment suggested that the text is a
forgery; but that it is now out of the question to restore the original readings. I learn (brieflich) that
the Netherlands authorities have now covered up the
stones and "forgotten" about them.

On Roman Utrecht see van Giffen, Vollgraff, and
van Hoorn Opgravingen op het Domplein te Utrecht, Haar-
lem 1934 (Provinciaal Utrechtsch Genootschap van Kunsten
en Wetenschappen), cf. H. Comfort AJA 43, 1939, 178-179;
Vannérus RA 4, 1934, 55-60; Byvanck Mnemosyne 2, 1935,
309-320; G. van Hoorn Hermeneus 1, 1929, 153-160. The
discovery of the inscc. was made known by Radet (after
Vollgraff) in REA 32, 1930, 416; cf. 35, 1933, 177-78
(Grenier); 36, 1934, 70-71 (A. Roes) and 497. The text
was published, with notes on linguistic matters by A.G.
van Hamel, who points out the mixed Germanic and Keltic
character of the proper names, as read by C.W. Vollgraff,
in Mededeelingen der Koninklijke Akademie van Wetten-

Utrecht

schappen (Amsterdam), Afd. Letterkunde, Deel 70, Ser.
B, no. 5, 1930 (pp.127-148); and also by Vollgraff, much
the same account, in Mnemosyne 59, 1931, 249-265. Doubts
were quickly raised by S. de Ricci RA 34, 1931, 209-210
(cf. AE 1931, pp.357-58), as well as by A.W. Byvanck in
Mnemosyne 60, 1932-33, 193-98, whose suspicions were
aroused by the naming of four different sites as colonia,
and who also found the names of the cohorts and of deities
mentioned all astonishing. He was sceptical of the date
assigned to the texts, and concluded (p.198) that the inscriptions were mutilated after the time of Geta, and
are, as we now have them, unintelligible. This throws
considerable doubt on the names claimed to be read by
Vollgraff; who, however, defended their authenticity in
Mededeel. d. K. Akad. d. Wetensch., Afd. Letterk., Dl.
80, B 1, 1935, pp.1-25; cf. RA 2, 1933, 405 (AE 1933);
8, 1936, 279; REA 38, 1936, 198-99; PhW 57, 1937, 62;
Glotta 23, 1935, 121-22.

The text is not given by Nesselhauf (p.119, no.257);
in Gutenbrunner Götternamen, it is no.75 (p.218). See
also the discussion by I. Lindquist in K. Hum. Veten-
skapssamfundet i Lund, Aarsterättelse 1932-33 VI 165-
175; P. Goessler in P-W 2te R., 7, 1948, 2045-46.

The alleged local names are:

Albaniana colonia (also TP, IA n.pl., now Alfen);

Albiobola col. (albio- Kelt., -bola Germ.) ethn.

Alb[i]o[bolanus]; Batabi; Borbetolego abl. (Kelt.; for

-lego cf. W. lle "place;" or Osc. slaagid, Ir. slicht

"track"); Brabones; Sudobeb[a] col. (i.e. -u-eua [?],

cf. $\Sigma o\acute{u}\delta\epsilon\tau\alpha$ $\ddot{o}\rho\eta$, $\Sigma o\upsilon$ [$\sigma o\upsilon$]$\delta\alpha\prime\nu\alpha$ Ptol.), Vada col.

Divine names (?):

Alabuandus Baldruus (Germ.[?]; but he shows

certain Semitic features, and perhaps first reached

the Rhine through Roman troops, in this text possibly

Utrecht

of Phoenician extraction, viz. from Barcino i.e. Barcelona; on Baldur cf. G. Neckel Der Gott Balder, 1920);
Boruoboendoa and -boedoa (Kelt.), Cobba (Kelt.); Aeques
(i.e. Eques?); Erecou[leus] and Ercouleus Alabuandus
(Germ.) or Macusanus (Kelt., Magu-), g(enius) s(anctus)
Lobbon[n]us (Germ.), Lunus masc. (i.e. $M\acute{\eta}v$, deus lunaris
orientalis, Vollgraff); Vabusoa.

Personal name (?): Bodaro (Kelt.?)

Vollgraff's text (mere fragments being omitted) is
as follows:
(A) 1. hs coor ii albo uict ae deo bb g sa lobbon col
col albiobolae batabor coor vi alb

2. colo albiobo ba genio s lobbonno deo bb albiobolae babo col uada bb

3. g s lobbo bb albiobolae ba luno albiobo ba sena
p q albiobo batabor col

4. deo lobbo col albiobo ba optio bals coor x
albo sag bba aresa brabo deodḍḍu

5. borbetolego uol tribun coho v bob x sa geio
albiobo ba

864

Utrecht

6. seuir aug col albiobolae ba genio lobbon d bb
coloniae albiobolae

7. albiobo ba barcinone albiobolae ba coliae

8. libb col albo ba f r p d bb e decreto decurio
albiobo ba d bb lobbono pos colo albio

(B) 1. es lobbo colo uada gno lobbon bai cool deo
babo albiobol.. babo   genio lobbo albiobolae batabo
colo

2. lbb aa genio colon lobbo albiobo bba bodaro ab
aerar albiobo ba genio sa lobbo batabo albiobol

3. aedd deo ercouleo alabuando albiobo ba u s deo
lobbo ba   bb colon albiobolae ba

4. tss l ppos colon sudobeb brab lobbo albiobo
g s lbe a u solu deab boruoboedoae cobbae albiobo ba
pos

5. oul macusao baldruo lobbo sol ddecur uabusoae
deo lobbo boruoboendoae uo ss a lbb

6. deo bb deo aeq genio sa albiobolae bra colon
b o batabor d decur colo alba po deo lobbo colon
albaniana batabor

865

Doubtful Inscription of Utrecht

7. colo albiobolae ba monum d bba lobbo f cnt et
erecoul macusano uoot lbb sol

8. colon uot lbb a sol colo albiobolae bbtor deo
ercou lobbo deo albiobo ba col p uuot ssol lbb a

This Vollgraff expands as follows:

(A) 1. Hispanorum cohors II Albiobolana uictrix aeterna
deo Bataborum, genio sancto Lobbonno coloniae Albiobolae.
Bataborum cohors VI Albiobolana

2. coloniae Albiobolae Bataborum genio sancto
Lobbonno, deo Bataborum, Albiobolae Bataborum. Colonia
Vada Bataborum

3. genio sancto Lobbonno Bataborum, Albiobolae
Bataborum, Luno Albiobolae Bataborum. Senatus populus-
que Albiobolae Bataborum coloniae

4. deo Lobbonno coloniae Albiobolae Bataborum.
Optio ballistariorum cohortis X Albiobolanae sagittariorum Bataborum Aresacum Brabonum deo DDDV

5. Borbetolego Voltinia, tribunus cohortis uolun-
tariorum Bob. X sagittariorum genio Albiobolae Bataborum,

6. seuir Augustalis coloniae Albiobolae Bataborum
genio Lobbonno, deo Bataborum, coloniae Albiobolae

7. Albiobolae Bataborum, Barcinone Albiobolae
Bataborum coloniae;

8. liberti coloniae Albiobolae Bataborum fecerunt
rei publicae deo Bataborum. E decreto decurionum Albiobolae Bataborum deo Bataborum Lobbono posuit colonia Albio

Doubtful Inscription of Utrecht

(B) 1. [g]e[nio] sancto Lobbono. Colonia Vada genio
Lobbonno Bataborum cooloniae, deo Bataborum, Albiobolae
Bataborum. .... genio Lobbonno Albiobolae Bataborum
coloniae.

2. libentes animis genio coloniae Lobbonno Albiobolae Bataborum. Bodaro, ab aerario Albiobolae Bataborum, genio sancto Lobbonno Bataborum Albiobolae.

3. aediles deo Ercouleo Alabuando Albiobolae Bataborum uotum soluerunt deo Lobbonno Bataborum. - - - - -
bb coloniae Albiobolae Bataborum.

4. [u]otis susceptis libentes posuerunt. Colonia
Sudobeba Brabonum Lobbono, Albiobolae Bataborum genio
sancto, libens animo uotum soluit, deabus Boruoboedoae
Cobbae Albiobolae Bataborum posuit.

5. [uota Erc]ouleo Macusa(n)o, Baldruo, Lobbono,
soluerunt decuriones, Vabusoae, deo Lobbono, Boruoboendoae uota soluerunt animo libentes.

6. deo Bataborum, deo aequiti, genio sancto Albiobolae Bataborum coloniae. B[on]o Bataborum decreto
decurionum coloniae Albanianae posuit deo Lobbono colonia Albaniana Bataborum.

7. coloniae Albiobolae Bataborum monumentum deo
Bataborum Lobbono faciundum curauerunt et Erecouleo
Macusano uoota libentes soluerunt.

8. coloniae uotum libentes animo soluerunt.
Colo[ni] Albiobolae Bataborum deo Ercouleo, Lobbonno,
deo Albiobolae Bataborum coloniae, pia uota soluerunt
libentes animis.

215

Potters' Names of Germania Inferior (Remagen A.D. 180-220, Sinzig A.D. 180-200), or found in Germania Inferior (Xanten, Vechten). Cf. 88 Remark above.

Abilus	Caesus	Homobonus
Abud(os	Cainu(s)	Iappus
Aciani	Cariatus	Iauenus (Tau?)
Agilio	Carisso	Iocara (Voc-?)
Amarius	Ceccus	Ionio
Anisiedo	Celinus	Iraχtui
Aruernus	Communis	Laco
Axus	Commus	Locco
Bellius	Condarillus	Luscus
Benio	Cosedo	Macellus
Beritonus	Costutia	Marillus
Biracautus	Crax[	Mianus
Bituus	Dadas	Musa
Bituollus	Darionus(?)	Nerrucus
Bolsius	Diuerus	Ordilos
Bracdilus	Diuiχtui	Ouidius
Buccas	Diuiχtullus	Rituscia
Cabiatus	Driedocius	Rituarus
Cabillus	Drucus	Sadiodtus (-thus)
Cabuctus	Ebarus (-ur-)	Samus
Cacunius	?Futrat[(for Tartus)	Sentio

868

Names of Potters

Serra	Taruillus	Varus
Seruti	Tinntus	Vauus
Sio	Tituius, Titullus	Viruico
Socco	Tocco, Tocca	Vocara
Sosa	Tosa	Votla
Talussius	Vadus	Vreu
Tantalus	Vail[	

To these may be added from BJ 140-141, 1936, 452:

Oponius

(commonly read ?Otonius, Rheinzabern);

ib. 122, 1912, 417 (graffito, Vetera)

Dami

p.374

Vapusu

(cf. Vapus, Vapuso of La Graufesenque, see 132 above) and, graffiti, from Ockenburgh bij den Haag, see Oud-heidkundige Mededeelingen (Internat. Archiv fur Ethnographie, Leiden) 37, 1939, pp.47-48:

Icto

Vene[?

Beson

all on terra sigillata with known stamps.

Names on Terra Sigillata

216

From many names on Terra Sigillata found at Nijmegen (Nouiomagus Batauorum) or in the vicinity (see the works of F.J. de Waele Romeinsch Nijmegen, Amsterdam 1931; reviewed in BJ 140-141, 1936, 514-516 by H. v. Petrikovits, cf. RA 35, 1932, 172 and de Waele in P-W s.v. Nouiomagus; cf. W. Vermeulen Een Romeinsch gravfeld op den Hunnerberg te Nijmegen uit den tijd van Tiberius-Nero, reviewed in BJ l.c., 517-522 by the same reviewer; and of H. Brunsting, cited above Introd., add the reviews of Koethe Germania 22, 1938, 61; Schleiermacher DLZ 59, 1938, 242; v. Petrikovits BJ 142, 1937, 363-65, cf. RA 12, 1938, 141-42; O. Brogan CR 52, 1938, 78; E. Gerster PhW 58, 1938, 829-831) the following appear not to be recorded elsewhere:

Aicorus (but cf. 83)	Iogeni	Perecarni?
Carunai	Iriuna	Senonius
Cetius	Locco (-us)	Tabus?
Crasonius	Mauaonii?	Tauenus
Egenus (-in-)	Mucatra	Tisinus
Exsomni	Muc(i)us?	Trelus
Iluci?	Ninuso?	Vercissius
Inalius?	Nisiusa	Viu(o)us
	Oiefa?	

Remark:

O.E. Meyer Germania 18, 1934, 106-107 gives a graffito from Schönforst (Aachen) which appears to read

ruthya

i.e. Rut[ilius] Hya[los] (cf. AJA 42, 1938, 580)? Or cf. Note xx above? Or is it a local designation?

Names on Terra Sigillata

As for the Meoilli (Nijmegen) reported in Schumacher Festschrift 309-314 (Knorr), is it not a mis-writing of Meθillus? But the

Cicelauius

(Cologne), if correctly read, R-G Forsch. 6, 1933, 83 (cf. Cigetoutos, Lezoux?) is to be compared not only with the divine name Cicollus (236 below; SprFK 197), but also with the personal name Cicelauus 156 above and gl. 158; the name

Viradius

on a Belgic flagon (ib. 84) with Virodu(s) (Soissons, terra sigillata, see 203 above), and the divine name Viradectis (213).

On moritex (8164a) see 207 above.

At Oberaden (in Germ. Magna), which is commonly identified with Aliso (cf. O. Prein Aliso bei Oberaden, Munster 1930; Werner, Wo lag Aliso? Leipzig n.d.) a few names have come to light not hitherto recorded on terra sigillata (see Albrecht, Regling, Oxé Das Römerlager in Oberaden 2 vols., Dortmund 1938-1942), of which only these need be noted here, viz.

Ac(c)o

Crito (for Cristo?)

Epidius

Memmius

Vmbricius

Of names of centurions on pila (pp.78ff.), note the following: Cald(i), Munni(i), Paq(uuii), Poniui(?).

On the name Aliso (formerly identified with Haltern, cf. REA 15, 1913, 441; Germania 10, 1926, 113-114; Albrecht p.10), with which Alesia is perhaps to be compared,

Names on Terra Sigillata; AVOT

see 178 above. From Haltern itself comes a lead lid
with an insc. ex radice Britanica (Plin. 25.20) on
which cf. REA 32, 1930, 260; Germania 12, 1928, 76-77;
cf. 220 below (uibones)

Finally, at Cologne we have also (CIL 13.10008,47)

uilbru (?)

perhaps to be read uabru (cf. 207 above) or uebru (cf.
237, 244; *uebro- "amber" Loth RC 38, 1920, 283; but
uabra "wood" 37, 1917-19, 309-11); hardly uibbru- (cf.
Wipper?).

Note xlix

(a) The word auot, auoti(s), cf. Notes xi, xix,
xxxvi, xxxix, liv, lx; 136 Rem. 1, 175, appears on
terra sigillata found in Germania Inferior, thus:

i.   Nijmegen (CIL 13.10010,217)

Aucirix auoti(s)

ii.   Cologne (834)

Durucu auot

iii.   Dalheim, Tongern, Cologne (1177)

Lullo(I-?) a(uot)

Also on a fibula (Dalheim, 10027.116)

Iulius auo(t)

AVOT, CANTVNAE

Cf. CIL 13 iii.1 p.121, 2 p.465; AcS 3.780. I do
not think that the cruciform arrangement in 10010.248
(East Gaulish) is a disguised monogram such as $\overline{\alpha f \omega}$ (on
monograms see Gardthausen Das Alte Monogram, 1924; Gr.
Pal. ed. 2, 1913; id. P-W s.v. Monogram; Dornseiff Alphabet in Magie u. Mystic ed. 2, 1925; for uita is so
arranged in 2062, and Melissus in 1333, Roppus in 1653.

(b) Of peculiar interest are the terracotta "statunculae" manufactured at Cologne (CIL 13 iii 2, p.465,
and 10015.99b, 105, 115a-d, 118; cf. Pirson 237, Riese
2308-2311, Dessau 9448, 9449a; Blanchet Mélanges
d'archéologie gallo-Romaine 2, 1902, p.92; id. MSAF 10,
1901, 214-230), containing the phrase

ad cantunas nouas (fecit)

(in 115a written gantunas), believed to designate pars
urbis Coloniae (CCAA A[grippinensium]), like the modern Hahnentor. But the word cantuna or gantuna (TLL)
is not completely explained; Keltic (?) W-H s.v.; cf.
Bertoldi BSL 32, 1931, 155 and see above 158, Note
xlvi, 220 below; the Gaulish καντευα may contain a
clue, and in 10015.108a we have a parallel, but not
equivalent, phrase ad forum hordia(rium). But in 8218
(Cologne) gantunis is commonly taken as a divine name
(Gutenbrunner pp.168, 250). Cf. Fremersdorf Saalburgjb.
9, 1939, 6-11; cf. Mnemosyne 5, 1937, 79.

It is, I think, clear that we must distinguish between Gantunae and cantunae, no less than between ganta
(220 below) and canta- in cantalon (160) and perhaps in
καντευα. But the meaning of cantunae ("market"?) remains obscure. There is, unfortunately, nothing in the
character of the "statunculae" themselves that is decisive.

(c) Note, among other names as well as Vindex (b)
on the terracottas, the following (R.2311 Anm., CIL 13.
10015)

Names on Terracottas and Tiles

(c) ctd.

Alfius	Ianetus
Amoco(?)	Lucius
]atto	Seruandus
Fabricius	Vrsio

217

Names on tile-stamps (Germania Inferior), cf. 205 above.
The following are taken from CIL l.c., and from BJ 118,
1909, 246-256; 122, 1912, 388-393; 135, 1930, 194; 136-
37, 1932, 185, 305-306; 140-141, 1936, 453; cf. R.697a
(p.454); Byvanck Exc. Rom. 2, 115; Germ. 10, 1926, 364;
AE 1927, p.364; RGKBer. 26, 1938, 97.

a (i.e. Aquae, Aachen?)	Laetus
Andris	?Linaius
Auitus	Luse[nus]
Blaes(i)us	Metius
Candilonius	Musanus
Crispus	Pupli
Cupitus	Ricom
Euntius	Rin
Exgerin[	Rio
Flenatis (cf. local names)	Sabl[
Idroc[ ]ticus	Sapricius
?Ieius	Seui

Sorini   Tra   Tritus

Coin-legend; Abecedarium of Holdoorn

218 Coin Legend of the Tungri

From Blanchet Tr. 1.103,375; cf. Forrer Les monnaies
gauloises ou celtiques trouvées ... en Alsace, Mulhouse
1926, p.24, I take what seems to be the sole coin-legend
of Republican date that may be assigned to Germania Inferior, viz.

auaucia

Cf. MSAF 5, 1904, 84; at least the legend given in AcS
3.252 ueruio ⊕ k seems to lack confirmation.

The coins found at Bochum (Germania Magna) in 1907
(Blätter für Münzfreunde, Dresden 1908, 3935-36; R. Forrer,
"Die Keltogermanische Triquetrumgepräge der Marser, Sugam-
brer, Tenkterer und Ubier," Jahrb. der Gesellschaft für
lothringische Geschichte und Altertumskunde 22, 1910, 442-
486) are, if a true Germanic coinage, inarticulate imitations of the Keltic coins of the Danube-region (see 239
below). The Bochum hoard is now at Dortmund, cf. Albrecht,
Frühgeschichtliche Funde aus Westfalen 1936, p.11. Forrer
dated the coins 50-20 B.C.

219

That the art of writing was not diffused in the Germanies before the spread of Latin is certain. An abecedarium found at Holdoorn near Nijmegen in 1840 was published by L[eonhardt] J[ohannes] F[riedrich] Janssen,
Beschreibung eines römischen Ziegels mit zweifachem lat-
einischen Alphabet, Leyden (S.u.J. Luchtmans) 1841; cf.
J.W.C. Steiner, Codex Insc. Rom. Danubii et Rheni, Seligenstadt 1851, vol. 2 p.254 no.1391; Walters History of
Ancient Pottery 2, 1905, 395. A square tile, 5.5 cm. each
side,

(1) ABCDIIF CHIKLMN OPQRSTVVX

(11) ABODIITCHI KLMN

Abecedarium of Holdoorn; Glosses

In (i) either u is repeated, or the order t u x y disturbed; in (ii) evidently (Ɗ is intended. Cf. R.4506, 3.

For the potter's tally of Holdoorn see La Graufesenque (90 above).

Glosses

(Cf. l above, Note on
Glosses; 79 above)

It is far from an easy matter to classify the Glosses. I believe that most of those in IV (Lugdunensis) may be broadly assigned to Gaul; but some of those put into III (Aquitania) may well have had a wider currency, and some of those in V (Belgica) evidently have what may be called "British" associations also. As for the Germanies, it is clear, on other grounds, that Germania Inferior was more affected by Germanic than Germania Superior ever was during the early Empire, so that it is at least arguable that many Germanic words of early date entered Gaul, if not Latin, through that channel. Hence, unless there is clear evidence to the contrary, I have put most Germanic items into this section, not into VII (Germania

Glosses

Superior). A certain number of glosses, however, for
which I could find no reason, not even a probability, that
they might be, though doubtfully, considered as belonging
to one of my eight geographical sections, have been put
together into one and the same section (IX) as alien and
doubtful inscc., and these may be called "glosses of uncertain provenance" (246).

Chronology is as doubtful as geography. Words
cited from authors (Pliny's ganta, or the saio of Cas-
siodorus) may be given a terminus ante quem; but items
in the glossaries, unless independently attested (e.g.
brutis) may be, but cannot be proved to be, actually
much older borrowings than the date of the compilation
of the glossary (e.g. the Liber Glossarum) itself, many
of them doubtless taken over by soldiers of the Imperial
armies. Whenever the Romance languages agree in the use
of a word borrowed from Germanic, and if the form may
be shown to have undergone early Romance changes, it is
safe to assume early borrowing (cf. Kluge Urg. 17-18);
on the contrary, specific and late Germanic dialect
changes exclude such an assumption. Similarly words
known only from later literary texts (e.g. strontus, or
proper names like Flocenna, Ludibrut in Salomon et Mar-

colfus), though they may represent a much older tradition
that may have been formed on the old linguistic frontier
in Flanders (cf. Bennary's edition, pp. ix-x), are excluded.

See, in general, Ernout-Meillet p.1104; Josef Brüch
Der Einfluss der germanischen Sprachen auf das Vulgärlatein, Heidelberg 1913; id. "Die bisherige Forschung
über die germ. Einflussen auf die rom. Sprachen," Rev.
de Linguistique rom. 2, 1926, 25-112; cf. W. Meyer-Lübke
Einführung ed. 3, 1920, pp.45-53, 227-228, 272-3; F.
Kluge in Grober's Grundriss vol. 1 ed. 2, 1904-06, pp.498-
501; id. in Paul's Grundriss ed. 3, 1.2 (Urgermanisch)
1913, pp.16-18; T.E. Karsten ibid. 9 (Die Germanen) 1928,
pp.153-154; Johann Sofer Lat. u. Rom. aus den Etymologiae
des Isidorus von Sevilla 1930, 166-168 (cf. 186); G.
Devoto Storia della Lingua di Roma 1940, 294-95; H. Hirt
Geschichte der deutschen Sprache ed. 2, 1925, 91 (on the
spread of Germanic over Keltic-speaking territory), 137
(on the Germanic frontier, but Hirt wrongly makes the
Rhine the frontier, even in the north, in ancient times),
277 (notes to pp.76,77), 279 (notes to p.82), 280 (notes
to pp.91 and 92).

Brüch (87-88) found that some 102 words had passed
into Latin before ca. A.D. 400. Cf. my article in Word
5, 1949, 106-115. According to Waitz (Das Alte Recht
der Salischen Franken, 1846) the Lex Salica reflects
"German institutions as they were after the disappearance of free ancient institutions, as described by Tacitus, but before the foundation of German kingdoms on
Roman territory" and originated in Toxandria; Krusch
dated it from A.D. 507 and ascribed it to Clovis (Hist.
Vierteljahresschrift 31, 1937-39, 427). These views are
attacked by Stein (Speculum 22, 1947, 113-134 and 395-
418) who maintains that it is a ninth-century forgery.
But laws notoriously are archaic in vocabulary and expression, and I have thought some of their terms admiss-
ible. As for the Salic law see Franz Schramm Sprachliches
zur Lex Salica, Marburg 1911; there is a handy text of
the Leges Barbarorum by H.F.W.D. Fischer (1948 ff.) in
Brill's Textus Minores.

Glosses

On Roman trade with the "Free Germans," which must
have contributed to linguistic borrowing, see Brogan JRS
26, 1936, 195-222. The influence of military encampments
(e.g. the legio V Alauda at Vetera CIL 13 vi 1933, 14)
has long been recognized.

On Germanic items in Latin glossaries see the four
articles of F. Kluge in SB Akad. Wiss. Heidelberg Ph-H
Kl. 6, 1915, Abh. 12; ZfRPh 41, 1921, 678-685; AR 6, 1922,
231-240 and 299-312. Kretschmer KZ 69, 1948, 1-25 deals
with the earliest linguistic evidence of a Germanic character.

abantonia "ancilla" (Lex Sal. 6.5; cf. E-M ed. 2, 41)

See ambacthius below

ablinda "blind-worm"

Polem. Silv. 544.1 (cf. 18 abelindeas). For the
meaning cf. Latin caecilia, with W-H 1.4,129 and 842.
What is a-? Prov. blendo (M-L 7525) is "salamander;"
perhaps conflation with ab oculis (ib. 33)?

?abonnis "a sort of cap, bonnet"

Lex Sal. 1.11.1 (Ernout-Meillet, ed. 2, 6).

?achasius

A payment made, on re-marriage, by a widow to her
first husband's parents; ib. 1.7; E-M ed. 2, p.10.

[?aeranis: see guaranis below]

879

Glosses

aesis

Apparently a Germanic (?) term, of unknown meaning, Anth. Lat. Riese, 204.10-12.

aggripare "to finger"

anagrip agrippare carnem feminae cum manu CGL 5. 491, cf. MG Leg. 4.652 (aggripare), OE ætgrǣpe (Beowulf 1269); Kluge AR 6, 1922, 299.

ala "awl" Comp. Luc. L 20

The operation described is that of dividing gold leaf, apparently by pricking. Cf. OHG āla, OE ǣl. French alêne from *alisna, Svennung 61 (with n.73).

alabarda "burr, burdock"

gigarone alabardan CGL 3.587; Med. Lat. bardana "lappa" Matth. Silv. c. 387 (AR 6, 1922, 300).

*alisna "awl"

See ala above, and OHG alansa, alunsa (W-P 1, 156); M-L 346. In Ahd. Gl. 3.678b alesna; Kluge ZfRPh 41, 1921, 678; Svennung Comp. Luc. 61 and n.73.

?amactum "coined gold"

Quoted from Cart. Senon by AcS 1.111 (which gives this definition); the text would seem to have been inspired by the coins of the Mediomatrici (206 above, cf. Note xli) which read arc | ambacti (misread arg and ascribed to Strasbourg Rev. Num. 1, 1883, 110).

Glosses

[?amalchium "septentrionalis Oceanus"

Plin. NH 4.94, who says the word means "congelatum" in "Scythian," like morimarusa in Keltic (see below); Sol. 19.2]

ambacthius

See Note xlvi above; perhaps for -cht-, cf. ambaχtus (Stockstadt-am-Main, Dessau 9254), Goth andbahts (διάκονος). Hence the two items abantonia (above) and ambascia (below).

ambascia "mission"

Lex Burg. and Lex Sal. Cf. AcS 3.582; M-L 408, Kluge Urg. 6.

amistrum "mistletoe" (v.l. -ost-; anstrum)

Known only from the glossaries CGL 3.596,22 al. uiscus et anstrus in arbore; but amostro..de uisco 3. 552,47, anstrum (-a), amstrum, and amistrum "mistil" in Ahd. Gl., see Kluge AR 6, 1922, 301.

anc[h]orago (-rauus) a fish, caught in the Rhine (male

salmon?)

Cassiod. var. 12.4; Polem. Silv. 544.17; a Keltic etymology (*anco- "gekrümmt" and raco- "vorne" for *prōk-) ap. W-H 1, 45; cf. Howald and Meyer Röm. Schweiz, 369; d'Arcy W. Thompson p.14; ZfCPh 22, 1941, 216

ango "spear"

uncinus (-ce-) CGL 5.340, see Kluge AR 6, 1922, 301. Cf. petraria 178 above.

Glosses

[?**ansa** "handle" (Plaut.)

"Mot du vocabulaire du Nord-Ouest, comme barba etc." E-M ed. 2, 55. Cf. Ven. ahsun acc. sg., -uš acc. pl.]

aringus (**ha**-) "herring"

Ps.-Garg. Mart. app. 62.209 (TLL 2.577,27-30). OHG hāring, OE hǣring. Given in CGL 5.390,15 as the definition of sardina.

armilausa "sleeve-less garment"

Isid. 19.22.28; Sofer Lat. u. Rom. 74; armi- is an i-stem, cf. the local name Armi-lausi (Kluge Urg. 35), but Arma- TP, cf. TLL s.vv.; Ar(a)mici 241 below.

arpa v. harpa below

ascus "boat (sc. of ash)"

Lex Sal.; Germanic (OHG ask), cf. the local names in Asci- 221, 234, 241; divine name 181.

aspellis "extra sermonem regis positus (?)"

Lex Sal. 70.1, cf. Goth spill "sermo," W-H 1.73.

?**austerauia** i.q. glaesaria Pl. 4.97, 37.42; cf. 221 below

?**baiulos** Germanicos, also attested ap. Celtas, v. Riese
  Lit. 15.69 with n.; but cf. 158

Glosses

baltha "audax" CGL 4.210,38; 5.492,31

As an ethnicon in Iord. 42 and (with this definition) 146, see TLL s.v.

bandum (-s), bannum (-s). There are two words, indif-

ferently spelled, which must be distinguished,

probably both Germanic, though the second has been

considered Keltic, viz.

(i) bandus (-m) "standard, sign"

CGL 5.505,7 labarum: bandus uel sceptrum, 2.
28,40 bandum: σίγνον (for λίγνον, Scaliger); cf. ban:
segn (OE), Goth bandwa (-wo), see M-L REW 929, Brüch
Einfl. 58; Du Cange s.v. bandum 1, bannum 4; Procop.
Vand. 2.2 (σημεῖον), Veget. 3.9; sinnum (Brüch 15,
from CIL 9.2893); Welt als Gesch. 1, 1935, 87 n.28;
Kluge Urg. 12.

(ii) bannus (-m) "ban, banns; edict; penalty"

(Du Cange: bandum 2, bannum 1-3), cf. Ir. for-
-banda, -bonnim (AcS 1.340). It is more likely that the
Keltic words are borrowed from the Germanic (W-P 2.124,
-nn- for -nu-) than the other way round (as d'Arbois de
Jubainville ap. AcS 1.340).

Greg. Tur. h.Fr. 5.26; Chilpericus ... bannos
iussit exigi; Cart. Senon. 19.193 ut de ... omnibus
bannis seu et arribannus (sic) sit conseruatus.

Du Cange takes arribannum as standing for here-
bannum, and here- he connects with Germ. Heer "army."
If this is so, we have a hybrid. But (reading arri-
bannis in Cart. Sen. above), we may have a true Keltic
compound *are-banno-. Presumably not connected, unless by popular etymology, with arr(h)abo.

Cognate with fas, fari, fabula (W-H 1.438). Distinguish *banno- *benno- "horn" (see 78 above) from both
of these words.

Glosses

<u>barditus</u> (so Norden Germ. Urgesch. in Tac. Germania ed.

3, 1923, 115 ff. and 180 ff.; v.l. baritus, both

readings with ms. authority) "carminum (de uiris

fortibus) relatus"

       Tac. Germ. 3.1, cf. Amm. Marcell. 16.12.43
(barritus or u-). Perhaps not connected with bardus
(see Anderson ad loc.; Kluge Urg. 12) at all. Grimm's
explanation (cf. ON bardi "shield") is still accepted
by some, though the ON word is both late and ἅπ. λέγ.

       The connexion with băro "fortis in bello" (see
below) seems to me possible, denials notwithstanding:
*bar-os, *bar(i)d-os, whence *barditus (not băro "stul-
tus," though that has a derivative bar(r)idus: CGL 4.
600,17); but bar(r)itus, if right, is probably onomatopoetic (cf. Festus s.v. barrire; Isid. 12.2.14) and not
specifically Germanic. Brüch Einfl. 16, 18; H. Klenck
in Schumacher Festschrift 1930, 210-212; W. Brückner
Festschr., 49 Versammlung deutscher Philol. und Schulm.,
Basel 1907, 65-77.

<u>bargus</u> "gallows" Lex Sal. 41 al.

       Distinguish barga (158); cf. TLL, s.v.; cognate
with Latin furca (Kluge SB Heidelb. Akad. Ph-H.Kl. 6,
1915, 3).

<u>băro</u> (-ōnis) "fortis in bello," lit. "free-born"

       CGL 5.592,13, cf. Isid. 9.4.31; ingenuus (Lex Sal.)
See TLL 2.1756, Lindsay ALMA 4, 1928, 39-42.

<u>battuo</u> (-<u>ere</u>) "beat, strike"

       See the testimonia (from Plautus onwards) in PID
2, 191; AcS 3.815-16. Pure Latin f- (in confuto, futuo);
but if the Keltic form is Boduo- (Ir. bodb), then battu-

Glosses

(OHG Batu-) will be Germanic (so also in andabata, cambutta?), and one of the earliest Germanic words, perhaps of characteristic significance, to enter either Keltic or Latin. Ir. bath, W. bathu are borrowed from Latin (Loth RC 18, 1897, 99). Deriv. battualia, battitura, battuator.

[beber, biber "beaver"

Wartburg FEW 1.304; Terracini Riv. di Fil. class. 49, 1921, 425-46; and Brüch Einfl. 68, prefer to regard Germanic not Keltic (see 178 above) as the source of VL beber, cf. M-L REW 1012, W-H 1, 490. The Keltic proper names seem to favour a Keltic origin.]

becarius (v.l. bac-) "orceoli genus" CGL 4.591; "uas uinarium" 599, 2

In the OHG glosses bechar, pec(h)ar; perhaps from bacarium (Loewe Prodr. 55, 292; cf. Thes. Gloss. Emend. 1.124), i.e. "wine-vessel." From ba(c)car, bacca? Cf. TLL s.vv. Or from beccus (158 above), like German Schnabelkanne?

bigardo-   v. caia 178 above

[bison "bison"

Plin. NH 8.38 (Germania); Isid. 14.4.4 (Hercynia silua); OHG wisant; cf. Vesontio, Bisontii? Brüch Einfl. 18 (Vesontio, bison the Keltic forms); Kluge Urg. 6,13].

bitus "pole, stick"

bitus: lignum quo uincti flagellantur CGL 2.579, 3; Kluge AR 6, 1922, 301

Glosses

<u>blada</u> "leaf, flower"

illa blada quem ibidem deos dederit..., Formulae
Andecauenses 12.11, 32Z (AcS 1.449); cf. Ir. blath
"flower;" and perhaps blata "corn" (Godefroy), Jud.
Rom. 49, 1923, 409; M-L REW 1160 (OE blæd). Cf. 151
above.

[<u>blanco-</u> "white" Kluge Urg. 13, Devoto Storia d. Lingua
di Roma 295]

<u>blauus</u> "blue" from older *blēu̯-

CGL 2.570,12 blat(t)a: pigmentum hawiblauum (OE
hawi "caeruleus"); OHG blāo "blue," OE blāw; Ir. bla
borrowed from Germanic; cf. Lat. flāuus; OL flōrus is
the OIr. blār, W. blawr (W-H 1.513). Cf. Sofer Lat. u.
Rom. 108 (Isid. 19.28.8); Kluge Urg. 13, M-L Einf. 52;
Ital. biava etc. (beside biado), which goes with blada
above, would appear to rest upon a bookish confusion of
blata, blada "flower" with blatta "purple."

<u>blundus</u> "blond;" see Kluge ZfRPh 41, 1921, 679; ML Einf. 52

<u>borda</u> "border" CGL 5.596,9 (see AR 6, 1922, 302)

<u>bordum</u> "board" CGL 3.586,10

Kluge AR 6, 1922, 302 compares OE, OS bord, Goth.
baúrd

<u>brado</u> "ham" Anthim. 14

Brüch Einfl. 32-33 (Germanic); cf. OHG brato "calf
(of the leg)" and Note xlvi above?

886

Glosses

branca "paw," hence "branch"

Aug. serm. 161.4, Grom. Lat. 309.2, cf. 4; AcS 3.
924. We are now told that this is not Germanic, but
Keltic (for *urānca, Lith. rankà "hand"), see J.U.
Hubschmied Vox Rom. 2.1937, 24-33, W-H 1.114, M-L REW
1271; Pokorny Urg. 67. But where are the Keltic cognates? However Vendryes Rev. de Phil. 72, 1946, 94
has a new etymology. In modern Germ. Pranke; hardly
cf. Brancus (king of the Allobroges) Liv. 21.31.6?

bridum "frying-pan" Anthim. 43

Cf. OHG bratan, OE. brǣdan "assare"

brio graece latine bullio

E. Merchie Musée Belge 26, 1922, 263.15. Evidently Germanic (cf. OHG briuwan "brew"); read germanice?

?brit(t)ia: cressa, CGL 5.404,1

Cf. divine names (matres Brittae) and personal
(Britta, -us, Brittula, Britto); brittola "cepa
minuta" CGL 3.587,49 al. (TLL, s.v.) is of uncertain
origin. Not to be connected with brisilis, brisare
(79)? Cf. crisson(us) below.

britischae "zetae (domus) hiemales" CGL 5.586

The description given by the gloss suggests a
house heated by a hypocaust, and the word itself is
apparently British (Breton?), see Kluge AR 6, 1922,
302.

*bros(s)a "brush"

See Note xxviii above, ars prossaria (CIL 13.
2023) or (Rostovtzeff) brossaria; the usual recon-

Glosses

*bros(s)a ctd.

struction (REW 1417, cf. 1340a) has -st-, compared with
which -ss- may be Keltic; prosa 178 above.

brunicus: see buricus (158 above)

E-M ed. 2, 122 suggest that the writing brunicus
arose "d'après le germ. brun?" (Sofer Lat.u.Rom. 68).
Cf. TLL s.vv.; Kluge ZfRPh 41, 1921, 679; Devoto 295;
AcS 3.988.

[**brun(n)ia** "breast; cuirass"

Kluge Urg. 17; cf. Meyer-Lübke WuS 12, 1929, 4
who takes the word as originally Keltic. In Lex Sal.
bructis (read perhaps brustis) TLL, may contain the
same root.]

[**brunus** "furuus" Reichenau Gl.

Germanic, but late; see Brüch Einfl. 87, Sofer
Lat.u.Rom. 68; E-M ed. 1, 1104; Kluge Urg. 13, M-L
Einf. 46, 52]

brutis "bride, daughter-in-law," cf. CGL 5.314,32:

bruta "nurus"; βρύτα Lydus mag. 1.33

In inscc. of Noricum (CIL 3.4746) and (ib. 12377,
12666) Moesia (not "Moselle" E-M ed. 2, 119); Goth.
brūþes "bride" (on the etym. of which see van Langenhove Ling. Stud. 2, 1939, 48-50 and 62; but see HSCP
54, 1943, 21), Ir. bru; Ven. vhrutana·i· (PID 136b),
Vegl. bertain (M-L 1345), but not Latin Frutis "Venus"
(van Langenhove 60); W-H 1, 117, cf. 853; Gamillscheg
Rom. Germ. 2, 1935, 236. Note also the personal names
Brutis CIL 9.1974 and Bruto 3.5697; cf. TLL 2.2212.
Older references: Pirson p.236, AE 1893.34, cf. Pauli
Altital. Forsch. 2 ii 1894, 181.

Glosses

bultio "pike"

Only in the Glossaries, see AR 6, 1922, 302-03;
OE bolt, OHG bolz; Ital. bolzone, OFr. bousson, OProv.
boson?

burcana "fabaria" Pl. 4.97; 37.42 (Riese Lit. 4.61);

see 221 below Burcana (v.l. Baunonia)

burdatio "tribute, tax; corvée?"

Greg. M. reg. ind. 9 May 1.42, quoted AcS 1.632-
33; Germanic (OE. byrden)? Or cf. burdo, -us -unculus
etc. TLL s.vv., 158 above; E-M ed. 2, 121.

burgus "watch-tower, fortification"

Isid. 9.2.99 (per limites habitaculum) cf. 4.28,
15.1.64. Germanic (borrowed into Greek through an
Illyrian channel), Kretschmer Glotta 22, 1934, 100-122
(Gr. πύργος Zos. 2.34, R. Lit. 4.26; castra Fredeg.
Chr. 2.46, R. Lit. 11.34), cf. Sofer Lat.u.Rom. 85-87;
E-M ed. 2, 122. Other theories are cited by W-H 1,
124, cf. 853. It is improbable, however, that burgus
is borrowed from πύργος , cf. rather Goth. baúrgs, OHG
burg. Cf. burge (BSAF 1920, 182), burgarii ib. 1911,
128, Asci-burgium (G. Esche "ash") 221 below, cf. 241;
Burginatio (-acum?) TP, IA (Monterberg) also 221, cf.
Burgenae (Pannon. inf.), and other local and personal
names AcS 1.639-640, 3.1005; mod. Bourg, Jullian REA 3,
1901, 341; Brüch Einfl. 15 (burgus CIL 3.3653); AE 1940,
p.238: Mélanges de l'École fr. de Rome 56, 1939, pp.151-
167 on burgi, burgarii; for burgarii "cultivators" see
also G. Behrens Germ. 15, 1931, 81-3 (REA 34, 1932, 52).
M-L Einf. 45, Pirson 230 (Kbl. 1884, col. 85); Veget. re
mil. 2.10; E. Penninck L'origine hellénique de burgus,
Latomus 4, 1940-45, 5-21. The relevant inscc. are noted
in Notes xlvi above, lii and lvi below.

Glosses

caliga, caligula "soldier's boot"

On the Rhine, Sen. dial. 2.18.4, cf. Suet. Cal.
47, Tac. Ann. 1.41, and probably a Germanized equivalent (*caliza) of the Gaulish gallica, gallicula, cf.
Oxé Germ. 15, 1931, 17, which pace Walde-Hofmann, is
essentially right; possibly influenced by cālo "boot"
(itself from calo "booted (soldier)"? See gallica 79
above; kalones: gallicae (v.l. Galliae) militum CGL
4.103 (AcS 1.704,12-13); καλικα (-ῶν), καλικαρικός,
but hardly καλτίον Ed. Diocl. 9.1 cf. 7-9; for the distinction (in price) between gallica and caliga ib. 9.5,
cf. 9.12. W-H would connect caliga with calx, calceus
(s.v. 1. calx) and explain καλτίον as Tarentine or
Oscan (s.v. calcar); for herba caligularis see FHRC
135.26; and for the meaning calo "boat" (TLL 3.179,33)
cf. barca 158 above.

cammarus "cray-fish"

From Varro onwards; gambarus Oribasius, cambarus
Caper GL 7.108,13; gammariunculus Gl. (for the formation cf. burdunculus).

Cf. κάμμαρος . Both early borrowings from the
north (Kretschmer Glotta 22, 1934, 103-104), cf. the
early Germanic borrowings burgus, battuo?

cambortus "hedge-pole" Lex Sal. 34.1, quoted AcS 1.716

Declared to be Germanic by W-H and E-M; but possibly a corruption of cambutta (207), or if only related to that, then not Germanic but Keltic. Note Cam-
bortese pago AcS 3.1064,44-48; cambotre 157 above.

camisia Lex Sal.: see cama (158 above)

cana(?), canna "can"

Vit. Austregisili (ep. Biturig.) ASS 20 May 6.230*
D canana (leg. cana, or better canna); Ven. Fort. vit.

Glosses

cana(?), canna ctd.

Radegund. (reginae Franc.) 1.19,44 canna insc. 88
above (Montans), and at La Graufesenque 94 above (cf.
REA 5, 1903, 69); since La Graufesenque has also panna
(90 ff.; cf. 237), we have apparently two series of
words of parallel semantic development (probably not
related as p : q^u), and here may be the clue to the
obscure gloss benna (leg. panna?) "id est tufera" (CGL
3.608,63; unless we read banna: tufa, cf. Thes. Gl.
s.vv. tubera, trulla, canna; and for tufa see 207 above),
bena "canna agrestis" (ib. 5.492,51) cf. Hincmari vita
s. Remigii MG scr. Merov., 3.322,13 (in uase quod uulgo
benna [leg. panna?] dicitur) quoted s.v. benna 207
above. Beside panna at La grauf., which is not for
patina (W-H., SprFK), we have panaca 240 below and perhaps canecosedlon (162) quasi ὑποκρατήριον (?), but
canipa "basket" Frat. Arv., Marini 323.15 appears to
be a ghost-word (read Tus]canicas with Henzen); canistrum (later canister); derived from canna "can" or from
canna "reed" (Greek κάνιστρον , κάναστρον), appears "to
be borrowed into Latin" W-H 1.154, s.v. canna, "from Latin" E-M.

The whole is probably pre-I.Eu., cf. Sicel κανθός
"pot, vessel" PID 2.465, and just as "vessel" has both
meanings in English (cf. barca 158), so canna "skiff"
may be the same as canna "pot," (whether or not canna
"reed" is connected, cf. canistrum "basket made of
rushes, or of willow twigs"?); from can-to- (-tho-)
"pot," may come "round object, circle, tire" (cf. 158
above). The range of these words (Greece, Sicily,
Italy, Spain, i.e. the Mediterranean generally; Gaul
and Germany) points to a word of Mediterranean origin
widely distributed in the course of trade, as names of
objects, themselves in trade, commonly are. So Cuny
REA 12, 1910, 162.

Add canua gl. 4.29,36; Note xxvii Remark above.
Cf. κανοῦν , cana (-orum)Paul. ex Fest. 40.5 L., cani-
fera 57.8, canastri La Grauf. (-i for -a, n. pl., cf.
Terracini in Scritti Trombetti 1938, 356); καντενα
Narb.; cantuna (g-) "canteen"(?) Note xlix below (cf.
above xlvi). But -cannae in divine names (AcS 3.1076,
1) and in local names is not likely to be connected unless -cann "stadt" (Holder) in the sense of "enclosure"
(cf. cantuna) and canna "reed" or "willow" passed
through the intermediate stage "hut" (mapalia), cf. S.
Gutenbrunner Germ. Götternamen 167-68. [For canna

Glosses

<u>cana</u>(?), <u>canna</u> ctd.

"zelus" Isid. 7.9.18 which is Hebr., and Can(n)aneus
"Zelotes," see K. Meyer SB.K.Pr.Akad., Ph-H Kl. 1912,
2.1144)].

    Walde-Hofmann 1.154; Brüch Einfl. 15.

<u>carenum</u> "sweet-wine, nectar"

    caroenum in CGL 5.11,1, specified as Maeonian Ed.
Diocl. 2.13; κάρηνον 3.218,5; cf. Thes. Gloss. s.v.
nectar; Isid. 20.3.15; OE ceren.

    This is commonly supposed to be Greek κάροινον
(- ρυν-), but the Greek word is late (Ed. Diocl.) and
of uncertain origin (L.-Sc. suggest καρύτνος "nut
brown," or a geographical name). It is remarkable that
there is an OE form (with umlaut at that), but no Romance derivatives. Hardly compare cerea, ceruesia.

[<u>cateia</u>: see PID 2, 187 (lingua Theotisca)

    Add now Weisgerber RhM 86, 1937, 118; W. Kaspers
KZ 67, 1940-41, 218-19 (APh 15, 1940-41, 201) "boomerang," from a Germanic *kat- "curve."]

<u>c[h]attica</u> <u>spuma</u> "soap" Mart. 14.26 (v.l. caustica)

    Cf. Chatti 221 below, and sapo (infr. 220); not
catthus or Cattus 207, 214 above (unless Cattus is an
older form of Chat[h]us i.e. Chattus, Hattus), though
catt[h]us "crudelis" may be the ethnicon, or the animal
name.

[*<u>caua</u> "owl"

    Cf. cauannus 178 above; but M-L Einf. 52 would
see a Frankish form with a from ē (?), cf. REW 1785.]

Glosses

caupulus (-ll-) "a boat; cable"

Gell. 10.25.5, Isid. 19.1.25, Leg. Burg. (see AcS 1.869), gl. (ib. 3.1168), caupuli Germanorum Hegesipp. The etymology and the source are entirely unknown. Span. and Prov. have representatives, but no other Romance language. Pre-I.Eu.?

cinnibar "coiffure" (Gotorum)

Isid. 19.23.7; cf. Sofer Lat.u.Rom. 19, 170, who postulates *kinnu-bar(d)s, which is possible.

coacula, quaccola "quail"

Onomatopoetic (cf. cerceris W-H 1.202). Only in glosses (cf. E-M ed. 2, 833); quaquara Schol. Isid. Valicell. 12.161, cf. Fest. 32.8; Netherlandish kwakkel is hardly enough to prove a Germanic source (E-M ed. 2, 200). Cf. Lat. coaxo? Van Langenhove Ling. Stud. 2, 1939, 82 ff. discusses this whole series of words meaning "cry, call." Cf. ciculus 158 above, W-H 2.404.

cofea, cufia "coiffure"

Ven. Fort., Reichenau Gl. Germanic (*kupfja) according to Brüch RLR 2, 1926, 80; W-H 1, 857; Kluge Urg. 18.

[crisson(us) "cress, nasturtium"

Gl. (9th cent.); W-H 1.293. Cf. brittia above.]

[croccus "uncinus" CGL 5.624,42

Cf. E-M ed. 2, 234 "germanique;" ON krōkr, M-L REW 4780.]

Glosses

danea "area, threshing-floor" Reichenau Gl.

    See Kluge Urg. 17-18 and 148, who observes the absence of W. Germ. consonant gemination. For the etymology W-P 1.853.

deraubare "rob" Not. Tir. 128.53

    From Germanic roubon; E-M ed. 2, 262.

dosinus "cinereus" (of a horse)

    Isid. 12.1.54, cf. CGL 5.597,33 (178, 18); OHG dosan, dusin, tosan (Ahd. Gl. 2.716,19; 702,44; 4.229, 3): Lat. fuscus, Kelt. donnus. Cf. Sofer Lat.u.Rom. 20-21, M-L REW 2755a; Fick Wtb. ed. 4, 2.152.

drensare, drensitare "cry" (of a swan)

    Suet. fr. 161 (p.251 R.); Anth. Lat. 762.23 R.; Gl. Probably Keltic (AcS 1.1317), cf. M.Ir. dresacht "cry;" cognate with θρῆνος. But the word is much better represented in Germanic than in the Keltic languages (W-P 1, 861; cf. W-H 1, 861).

drosca: a bird (throstle?)

    Also in Anth. Lat. 762.11 R.; cf. OE þrostle, OHG droscala (*þrusko), Lat. turdus; d is probably đ. Cf. also Eng. thrush.

drungus "troop, military detachment"

    Vopisc. Prob. 19.2, Veget. epit. r. mil. 3.16 al., Gl Basil. (AcS 1.1331) δρουγγάριος · χιλίαρχος (also in a Christian insc. of Kiev, Holder l.c.). It is now held that this is Germanic, and borrowed into Keltic (SprFK 199, after Terracini Riv. di Filol. 49, 1921, 426), cf. OE þrang "throng."

Glosses

drungus ctd.

Distinguish drungo- "nose," which is Keltic, and which appears in Galatian δροῦγγος, Τασκοδρουγῖται· ἀδσαλορυγχῖται Epiphan. 2.14, see Weisgerber Natalicium Geffcken 1931, 162-64; Sofer Comm. Vindob. 2, 1936, 88 n.44; it has cognates in Ir. and Welsh, as well as representatives in the Romance area; but the forms with initial t- point to a *trugno- in Gaul (not dr-), beside str-, sr-, Welsh ffr-, viz. Ir. trogne, Prov. drougno- and trougno-, W. trwyn and ffroen. As for tasco- cf. *tascone, Prov. tascoun, Cat. tasconar, Jud Rom. 49, 1923, 411-16; *taska- "pocket" (Brüch 6), and tasconium (158 above) are distinct.

dulgo (-ere) "give (in reprisal)"

Lex Sal. 78.5; cf. Thurneysen in TLL 5 (i) 2199.35.

emerum "spelt"

Gl. Prud. c. Sym. 2.23, Ahd.Gl. 2.469 (ZfdAlt. 16, 1872, 73.23) far: amar, quod Galli emerum dicunt. On the etymology cf. W-P 1.53; Kluge Et.Wtb. s.v. emmer "sommerdinkel."

esox "salmon (?) or pike (?)"

Pl. 9.44 (in Rheno); but also in the Loire (Sulp. Serv. dial. 2[3]10.4), and see the other testimonia in AcS 1.1470, d'Arcy W. Thompson Glossary of Greek Fishes 1947, 95; spelled also isox; cf. the personal name Esucius (Reims) 214 above. Gray AJPh 49, 1928, 343: Ir. eó (iach), W. eich; W-H 1, 421; perhaps connected somehow with piscis, fisks (cf. Marstrander NTS 1, 1928, 237); for Basque izokin see Aquitania Introd.

faluus "fallow, pale" CGL 4.341 al.

See Kluge AR 6, 1922, 304; OE fealo, OHG falo (Germ. stem falwa-).

Glosses

fario "salmon-trout"

Thompson Glossary of Greek Fishes 1947, 73 rightly accepts this word from Aus. Mos. 128. It is justified by OHG vorhe, forhana, Swiss fore and Fr. forelle; omitted by TLL, and rejected in favor of sario by W-H; Loewenthal WuS 10, 1927, 194 sees lenition in f: s.

filtrum "lana coactilis"

Cf. filtra "centones," filtrus (filistrus cod.) "fimbria," CGL 5.295,4 and 584,5; felte "garment" vit. Radegund (see Thes. Ling. 6.1, 456.56). Hence Eng. felt, filter, about which the dictionaries are vague; cf. M-L Einf. 47; W-H 1, 497. Suebian according to Brüch RLR 2, 1926, 32.

flado "cake"

Ven. Fort. vit. Radegund., 15.35; see W-H 1, 508.

flasca, -ō "flask"

Isid. 20.6.2; Ennod. Carm. 2.147,1. Cf. Sofer, Lat.u.Rom. 132-133, W-H 1.513.

framea "spear" (AcS 1.203,4; 3.675,15)

Of the Germans (Tac. G 6.1) as well as of the Aremorici (178 above), SprFK 201; on the etymology see W. Krause in Festschrift für Hirt 2, 1936, 585-589 (*pro-mo-; cf. Promea 212,]fpromis Note xlvi above), so Müllenhof fram "onward" (W-H 1, 866); leo framefer (Rudston, Yorks.) AE 1935, 116; JRS 24, 1934, 220.

fredianus "subject to fredum (?)"

Cod. Theod. 16.10,20,2; from Germ. fredum "aes collatum, amende(?);" the latter appears as fritus in Greg. Tur. Mart. 4.26 and in Lex Sal. 13.6 al. (TLL).

Glosses

friscos: see rescos

fristitus, fristatitus "postponed(?)"

Lex Sal. 61 rubr.; cf. Germ. fristan (TLL).

[?**galbinus** "yellow" (Petron. and later writers); Germ.

or Kelt.?]

ganta "ganot" (in Germania) Pl. 10.53

Clearly a Germanic, rather than a Keltic, form; cf. Latin anser (W-H 1, 52; cf. 583); and presumably distinct from gantunae, cantunae above (Note xlvi) unless that means "goose-market" or simply "market, canteen" (cf. P-W s.v.; Grenier in Frank 3.446; Pirson 237). Not gant "glabretum" in a late gloss BSL 32, 1931, 96 (cf. 108; 163 glaretum).

garba "sheaf (of grain)"

CGL 5.363 (Épinal) garbas: sceabas, in which one Germanic word is defined by another. Kluge AR 6, 1922, 305.

[**gardingus** "palace official"

Lex Visig.; Brüch RLR 2, 1926, 40.]

[**gargala** "uvula" (Orib. eup. 2.1 G 6)

Cf. Germ. Gurgel, gurgula "throat" (so TLL s.v.), but W-H 1, 583 accept Mørland's hypothesis of gurgulio conflated with γαργαρεών.]

Glosses

gasacio "aduersarius" Lex Sal. 50.2 (*ga-sakja)

gauranəm: see guaranem below

[?gibatus

Unless connected with Latin gibber, this word,
which occurs only in Anth. Lat. 204.12 R., beside a
number of other alien words, may be Germanic. But the
meaning is unknown. Cf. perhaps Fr. gibet, Eng.
gibbet?]

glaesum, glesum "amber" (Aestii)

Plin. 37.42, Tac. Germ. 45; cf. Glesaria insula
(Cimbri, 221 below), OE glǣr and glǣs; cf. glastum
207 above. According to Tac. l.c. the Aestii spoke a
language Britannicae propior (cf. Bede HE 1.1 on the
Picts and Scythians). W-H 1.604 (cf. 868); Krappe CP
37, 1942, 353-70.

glen(n)are "glean"

Lex Sal. 87.48 (AcS 1.2027); cf. M-L REW 3784
(Gaulish); Ir. glan "clean," W. glan. For the alternation en: an cf. granus below and ambannus (79 above).

[?globa "inctura" CGL 3.495,75; 513, 26

Germanic M-L 3790; but TLL gives also Slavonic
cognates.]

[?glōcio (-ire) "cluck" Columella 8.5.4 (and later

writers)

Onomatopoetic (cf. glattio), rather than borrowed
from Germanic; OE cloccian.]

Glosses

granus and grana "moustache"

Apparently a Germanic word (OE gronu, ON grǫn) borrowed into Latin; Isid. 19.23.7 assigns it to the Goths (Sofer Lat.u.Rom. 136); but cf. Apollo Grannus in Germ. Inf. and Sup. (223, 236 below), and, on a possible wider distribution of the word, Pokorny Urg. 50. Ir. grenn "beard," Prov. gren "moustache;" cf. Jud Arch. Rom. 6, 1922, 208 who called attention to the alternation en: an (see glennare above); Brüch RLR 2, 1926, 54.

grunda: see suggrunda below

guaranis (v.l. gaur-) "ceruinus" (of a horse)

Isid. 12.1.53, who continues: aeranem idem uulgus uocat (aeramen, see CGL 6.35). Cf. guaranio, waranio "stallion" in Lex Sal. 38.2, M-L 9573, perhaps conflated with warantia "brown madder" (Sofer Lat.u.Rom. 21-25, 170), cf. W-H 1.624,868. But aeranem (-m-) is presumably Latin (E-M ed. 2, 19).

hairo "heron"

ASS Aug. 3.619b uolucres quas hairones nuncupat locutio uolgaris; CGL 5.615b ardea id est auis id est hairo. Cf. OFr. hairon M-L 3991; Kluge AR 6, 1922, 305-06.

hanappus "cup"

CGL 5.583,8 al., uas uinarium; OS hnap Germ. Napf., cf. Gesta abb. Fontanell., ASS July 5.94; Cornish gl. hanapus, hanaf; nappus in OHG Gl. The glossaries have also a corrupt, would-be learned spelling, anaphus. In Comp. Luc. 16-17, 45 at F 27 (Svennung) [h]anfus. Cf. Kluge AR 6, 1922, 233-34, and see 178 above (s.v. annapum).

Glosses

harpa (v.l. arpa) "harp" Ven. Fort. Praef. 5 (2.14 Leo)

haring: see aringus above

hosa (osa) "hose"

Isid. 19.34.9; an early borrowing from Germanic;
Brüch Einfl. 91, Sofer Lat.u.Rom. 138; cf. OHG hosa.

ἴσοξ , issicius

See esox above; less likely hysex (240), ὕσος
(ib.), or hυσουι[in Note xx above.

laetus (v.l. letus, litus) "serf"

Paneg. 5.21.1, adj. laeticus cod. Theod. See the
discussion in W-H 1.750; Anderson on Tac. G 25.1;
Schoenfeld in P-W 2, 1924, 447; Laeti 212 (above).

latta "lath" Lib. Gloss. AS 8 (CGL 5.169,7)

Cf. OE læt, OHG latza; Kluge AR 6, 1922, 306

laubia "bower" CGL 2.558 n.2

Properly "made of leaves;" on Ital. loggia, Finn.
laupio see Kluge AR 6, 1922, 306-07.

lec(c)ator "gulosus" CGL 5.602,51

Cf. lectuosus Virg. Gram. 28.2. Evidently the
Germanic lick, OE liccian; cf. W-H 1.777, W-P 2.400.

Glosses

lellus: a pet appellative (VL), MHG Rer. Merov. Scr.

4.547, vita S. Desiderii 33

leudis "blood-price"

Greg. Tur. h.Fr. 2.42 al.; Lex Sal. 16.1 al. Cf.
Latin liber (W-H 1.787; E-M ed. 2, 541)? Note also
the divine names Leudinae, Leud[223 below; P-W s.v.
Leud[cites a personal name (7th cent.) Leudesius.

leudus "song"

Fortunatus e.g. carm. Praef. 5 (2.14 Leo): bar-
baros leudos arpa relidens; cf. 7.6.89.

liciscus "a kind of dog"

Also spelled ly- and defined (e.g. Isid. 12.2.28)
as a cross between a wolf and a dog. OFr. leisse;
CGL 5.370,2. Also called braccus, pracho. Kluge AR 6,
1922, 307 explains it as "Hund aus dem Lechgebiet,"
like Pinscher from Pinzgau(?).

lixare "polish"

Comp. Luc. K 15, Svennung 58; not to be confused
with Lat. lixare, but from Germ. lisi "smooth," lisc(h)a-
Du Cange. Svennung take -x- in Comp. Luc. as standing
for -s-; but note lipsa in Mappa Clavicula; lissare,
Ital. lisciare, M-L 5081; Pirson Berl. Beitr. zur Rom.
Philol. 1, 1939, 372 compares lix "lye," but cf. 240.

[?lōdix "coverlet"

Pollio ap. Quint. 1.6.42; Iuv. 7.66; Martial (14.
152,1) puts it in Cisalpine Gaul; it has been suggested,

Glosses

[?lodix ctd.

not very enthusiastically, that we have a Germanic
word borrowed into Keltic and thence into Latin (OHG
lodo, OE loþa), see W-H 1.819.]

machalum, mahalum (v.l. ma[u]f-) "open barn, shed"

  Lex Sal. 16.3; etym. uncertain. Cf. magalia

mac(h)io (-onis) "mason"

  Isid. 19.8.2; perhaps Germanic (cognate with make,
machen?); Sofer Lat. u. Rom. 142-144; M-L 5208. Cf.
comacinus "maurer" AcS 3.1264,31 (ed. Roth.).

mahunus (-onus) "poppy, opium" CGL 3.589,22 al.

  See Thes. Gl. s. vv. mahunus, papauer. The variant mich- appears to be due to confusion with μήκων,
W-H 2.12. Cf. OS māho; Kluge AR 6, 1922, 236; M-L
5232.

[?maladrinixia: fauus mellus CGL 3.569,27; cf. TLL

  8.615,10]

[malahereda: see TLL 8.162,66]

mallus "court of law," gamallus "qui suscipit causam...

  in uicem alterius," mallobergus "court of law" (lit.

  iudicii mons), admallare(?) Lex Sal. 1.1; 46; 48.4;

  54.4; 50.2 al.

Glosses

[mallus etc.ctd.

See TLL s.vv., W-H 2.16 (Germ. *maðlá-), OHG
mahal (W-P 2.304). P. Rolland sees mallo- in Rue des
Maux at Tournai, see Ann. de l'Acad. roy. d'archaéol-
ogie de Belgique 75, 1929, 103-09. mannio (-ire) "in
ius uocare" Lex Sal. 1.1; 1.2; 50.2 belongs here also
(W-H 2.29). For -mallus perhaps compare Canto-mallus
AcS 1.754; 136 above?]

marc(h)a "boundary" CGL 1.298; cf. M-L 5364

?maria "adnuntatio" Lex Sal. 5.8; marha(?) Amm. 19,11,10

Cf. TLL s.vv.; for marha Reinesius proposed warra.

marisca "caenum" CGL 5.621,20

Germ., cf. OE mer(i)sk, E. marsh. Does mariscus
"sedge" Plin. 21.112 not belong here rather than with
mariscus (-a) "fig"? Cf. (more-)marusa ("stagnant"?)
below; dea Marica Wissowa RK 49 n.6.

mariscalcus "agaso" Gl. 5.583,7; Lex Sal. 10.4.1

Cf. OHG marah-scalc "marshall". Cognate with
Latin merx according to Schrader and Niedermann; but
marah "horse" is as far back as we need to go in tracing the meaning; as for scalco- see W-P 2, 594. Cf.
μάρκα 178 above, marcosior Note xxxi (e). To the references given at 178 add Krogmann (*markos) ZfCPh 20,
1933-35, 284-92.

*marsuppa, marisopa: a fish

Vit. Filiberti (Lugd.) ASS 20 Aug. 4.80C; Polem.
Silv. 544.5; lit. "Meer-saufer" (W-H 2.40). Distin-

Glosses

*marsuppa, marisopa ctd.

guish maforte (-ium): marsuppius, bazena CGL 5.220,10
(see s.v. bazena 246 below), which is presumably marsuppius "purse" (Semitic?). But cf. the next item.

[marsopicus "fina" (OE) i.e. "woodpecker," Gl. 5.372,

   22; Corp. M 35.

      M-L 6484a; Rev. dial. Rom. 2, 1910, 192; from
marso- and picus, but it is the Italic Marso- (Martio-),
not the Germanic Marsi.]

[martola(?) "felis" Gl. 3.259,27

   Germanic, M-L REW 5384; cf. Fr. martre]

marusa(?) "dead" (perhaps "stagnant")

   See morimarusa below, marisca above.

[mastruca (-g-) "sheep-skin, sheep-skin coat"

      In the glosses it is said to be "uestis Germanica,"
or the word itself to be Gaulish, see AcS 2.456; but
Quintilian 1.5.8 reckoned it Sardinian; perhaps actually
Ligurian, PID 2.165; see also 178 above, s.v. crocina]

μέδος (for medu-?) "mead" Anthim., Isid.

      Priscus hist. Goth. fr. 8, p.300 Dindorf; see AcS
2.524-525, where the word is actually assigned (with
κέγχρος i.e. σῖτος , and κάμος apparently "beer," see
240 below) to Pannonian. Cf. W. medd, OE meodo, E.
mead; Germanic (cf. Sofer Lat.u.Rom. 145-146), but Keltic has independent cognates (W-H 2.59).

Glosses

melca: a spiced dish, made from curdled milk

CE 862 (first century), Anthim. 78; Apicius 7.300 tit.; in Greek μέλκα. Evidently one of the oldest borrowings from Germanic into Latin; OE meoluk, cf. Brüch Einfl. 17; W-H 2.62-63.

morimarusa "mare congelatum" Pl. NH 4.95

See 207 above (PID 2.188); but it is difficult to be certain what Cimbri Pliny meant (North Italy, Narbonensis, Belgica, or Germania magna?); but the context (cronium concretum Plin. 4.104, mare Cronium, see AcS 1.1175) does indicate the last named (or Denmark) as the locality of the Cimbri Pliny had in mind. Hence Streitberg IF 14, 1903, 490 (cf. Much quoted in AcS 2. 449) maintained that morimarusa is Germanic, not Keltic (despite more, and maru-, which are well established; for the latter see now also W. von Wartburg "La Marve" ZfRPh. 56, 1936, 760; RLR 13, 1937, 44). Called Amalchium by the Scythians Plin. 4.94.

pauta "paw" (Germ. Pfote; Eng. dial. pote)

On the geographical distribution of this word see Frings Germ. Rom. (Beiheft 4, Teuthonista) 1932, 179-80, where it is considered pre-Roman, but not Germanic; the etymology proposed by Brüch Wiener Studien 54, 1936, 173-180 (*plauta from plautus) is too hypothetical (cf. PhW 58, 1938, 505); see now Die Sprache 1, 1949, 126; Word 5, 1949, 195.

[perna Marsica Ed. Diocl. 4.9 (Marsi in Italy, not Germany, which would be -acus]

rac(h)ana "huitil saxonice" CGL 5.327,45; raganus: coopertorium uel panniculus 5.623,17; dimin. rachan-

Glosses

rac(h)ana ctd.

ella Leontii vita s. Ioannis eleemosyn. 20 (Migne

P.L. 73.356.)

Holder AcS 2.1069 cites the following sources: Ed. D.
7.60; 22.4 (rachana, ῥακάνη); CTh. 14.10.3 (nemo uel
ragis uel tzangis [sagis??] utatur); Ennod. ep., Greg.
M., vit. S. Radegund., as well as the insc. of Vieux
(Note xxxiv above). M-L 6983; the Romance derivatives
suggest rather an Illyrian than a Germanic source. Cf.
Lat. rica (-ium) "veil" ricinus? Distinguish rica Note
xxv Remark above (cf. SprFK 208). And there are other
possible explanations: (1) cf. Eng. rag, ME ragge which
must then be separated from ON rǫggr; (2) cf. λάχαινος,
lacchena Ed. Diocl. 8.4 (with r: l), whatever its etymology (Svennung Comp. Luc. 42); (3) cf. crocina (178
above), i.e. Germanic *(h)rach-, or with loss of c- in
cr- (Illyrian), as of g- in gr- (Rae-ti: Grae-ci, rauistellus: gr-), i.e. κροκίνη (Athenaeus, cf. HSCP 56-7,
1947, 142 n.53). Cf. 246 below.

rasta "two leuuae" or "three miliarii" Grom. 373

Cf. AcS 2.198,44; Hieron. Ioel 3.18; Riese Lit.
14.42; Grenier Mnl. 2.95. On the value of the leuga
(2300 m.) see Sprater Germ. 21, 1937, 28-33. Goth.
rasta "mile, lit. rest" W-P 1.144 (not, as sometimes
said, Russ. versta).

reno "garment of skins"

Germanic (Sallust) or Keltic (Varro)? Cf. PID 2.
199. For the testimonia in full see AcS 2.1129-1130.
The etymology proposed by Walde (*urenō) would, if
right, make the otherwise satisfactory Keltic cognates
(Dottin REA 7, 1905, 39) loanwords. This, then, is
one of a number of terms, whose attribution, to Germanic or to Keltic, must remain undecided. Cf. sq.

Glosses

reptus "reno" Isid. 19.23.4

    Germanic, cf. OE ript, rift "cloak;" reipus, repus "rope" Lex Sal. 44? Sofer Lat.u.Rom. 43-44.

*rescos Fr. rêche

    Cf. Germ. frisch; the form without p- will be a Keltic borrowing from Germanic, Meyer-Lübke Einf. p.41.

runa "secret, mystery"

    Ven. Fort. carm. 7.18.19; cf. Goth. runa, OIcl. rún rúnar, OE run. The Keltic forms (AcS 2.1246, cf. Do. 283) are probably borrowed; and runa "genus teli" in Ennius (pace E-M ed. 2, 877) unconnected. Proleg. 169, n.140.

sadol "saddle"

    CGL 5.390,40 (s.v. sella), v.l. satul, i.e. we have a low as well as a high German form. According to Gutenbrunner Frühzeit 29, Keltic *sodulo-.

saio "judge" (poenator, tortor: see CGL 7, 224)

    Cassiodorus e.g. Var. 1.24.2, 2.4; Isid. 10.262 (cf. Lib. Gloss. SA 162); OE secgan i.e. *sagjan, OHG sagen; Sofer Lat.u.Rom. 153-154.

[sapa "must, syrup"

    The relationship of this word (e.g. graffiti Genava 18, 1940, 46) to OE sæp etc., has never been made clear; and the Romance derivatives have the meaning of sæp rather than of sapa; has not the latter been borrowed from a Germanic or Keltic source?]

Glosses

<u>sāpo</u> "a bleach for the hair; soap"

Gallic according to Pliny 28.191 (presumably Germanic borrowed into Gallic), cf. Martial 14.27 (Mattiaci, cf. 26 Chatti), 8.33.19 (Bataui) and other testimonia, AcS 2.1360-1362; saponem Gallicum (Marcell. de med. 19.41); σάπων Ed. Diocl. Troiz. 3 (p.2211).

Borrowed from Germanic (Walde ed. 2, 677), probably through Keltic, but not itself Keltic in form (both ā and p conflict with that assumption); cognate with Latin sēbum (cf. e.g. sebaciaria Dessau 2174-77; Sebosus AcS 2.1421, Sebosiana [ala] ib.?); E-M ed. 2, 894; Grenier ap. Frank 3.587. Called chattica spuma (q.v. above); sapo mitis insc. (an amphora, Westphalia) Germ. 17, 1933, 239. On sapo see also Kretschmer Einl. 24 with n.2; Pisani Die Sprache 1, 1949, 141. Jullian's Iuno Saponaria (REA 19, 1917, 199-205) is imaginary. No connexion with σαπάνα 178 above. On the Romance development (Fr. suif) see Ascoli AGI 10, 1886-88, 260-69.

Deriv.: Saponius, -onianus (personal names); ars saponaria in CIL 13.2030 (Trion), Saponaria uicus (Maine-et-Loire), see AcS 2.1362.

<u>scadd-</u>, <u>sceadd-</u> "shad"

Cf. OE sceadd, W. ysgadan, MIr. scatán (W-P 2. 538), the Keltic forms perhaps by borrowing. The OE form appears first in Monasticon Anglicanum (Dugdale) 1.266, 45-6 in the will of Wulfric earl of Mercia, founder of Burton Abbey temp. Eadred (dated A.D. 1004).

<u>scala</u> "cup, goblet"

Isid. 20.5.5, cf. Lib. Gloss SC 13, CGL 5.564,48; Germanic, see Sofer Lat.u.Rom. 154-155. Does Scalensia (fictilia) e.g. 10002.48 (R.4544) belong here? But cf. P-W s.v.

Glosses

scaptus "sagitta" Isid. 18.8.2

Probably Germanic (OE sceaft "shaft," OS and ON skapt), see Sofer Lat.u.Rom. 44-45.

scarfia "egg shell" CGL 3.553,15

As Kluge points out (AR 6, 1922, 308) f (:b) represents p (OChSl. črěpъ "Scherbe"). Cognate with L. corbis, Gaulish carpentum, cf. W-P 2.582.

scarpa "wrapping" (for the feet) vit. S. Honorii (M. 19, 10)

Honorius was bishop of Arles 426-429. On the Germanic origin of this word see Blatt in Eranos Löfstedtianus 73-4 (1945). Cf. perhaps English scarf?

scramasaxus "culter" Greg. Tur. h.Fr. 4.51

[?silurus: a fish (sturgeon)

Although the name was known to Lucilius (ap. Varro), Pliny puts the fish in Moeno Germaniae .. et in Danuuio (9.45), Ausonius Mos. 135 in the Moselle; but the identification both of the fish and of the origin of its name is far from certain; Thompson Greek Fishes 235.]

[siser (at Gellep, Pl. NH 19.90): see 79 above]

sodinga "steaming pan" Anthimus de obs. cib. 3

spelta "spelt" Ed. Diocl. 1.8

Cf. OE spelt, OHG spelza; E-M ed. 2, 963; M-L 8139; Brüch Einfl. 12.

909

Glosses

spitu "ueru" CGL 5.518,32, cf. Kluge Urg. 17

straua (-b-) "tumulus, sepulcrum" CGL 5.516,9; 578, 43

Cf. Mommsen on Iord. 198 (Walde ed. 2, 743);
Goth straujan "streuen."

strundius, struntus: σπέλεθος ("ordure") CGL 2.189,38

E-M ed. 2, 989; Brüch 13.

[?sucinum "amber" Plin. 37.30; Iuv. 6.573; Mart. 3.

65.5; sucineus Pl. 22.99

"Wohl Umbildung eine nordeurop. Wortes," quasi
*socinum (conflated with sūcus), Walde ed. 2, 752.]

[?su(g)grunda (for sub-) "eaves" Varro RR 3.3.5,

sucrunda CIL 1 ed. 2, 687

Cf. suggrundium (-atio, -arium) "burial place
(of an infant) under the eaves" Vitruv. 2.9.16; sub-
runda CGL 3.365.14. Cf. grunda: στέγη καὶ τὸ ὑπὲρ
τὸν πυλεῶνα ἔξοχον [ὑποστέγιον] CGL 2.36,42; G.L. 2.
163; Engad. gronda, M-L 8438a; E-M ed. 2, 436. TLL 6.
2. s.v. grunda compares Baltic words, and OHG gruntis
"tignum," Walde ed. 2, 354 OE grindel "bar, bolt," cf.
W-P 1.657. But conflation with the root of OE grund
"ground" is not impossible (Lat. frendo); W-H 1.625.
From "grind" to "saw," and thence to "beam, post" is a
conceivable shift of meaning.]

sulzica (v.l. -t-), salzica (v.l. -t-) "uas aptum

salibus" Isid. 20.4.12.

Cf. OS sultia, OHG sulza "Salzwasser, Salzwurst"
Sofer Lat.u.Rom. 167.

Glosses

supa "sop"

Only in late sources (see Kluge AR 6, 1922, 309-10); cf. Ptg. sopa, but A. Thomas in Mél. Louis Havet cites an earlier suppa from an Oribasius text of 5th-6th cent. A Germanic *supa (cf. Goth. supōn?) is postulated, I.Eu. *s(e)ub- W-P 2.469.

?**tanda**: the name of a tree(?)

Anth. Lat. 204.11 R; cf. nabras tanos (one word?) ib. 10; and perhaps sq. if a punishment (some kind of torture) is meant in this context (-nd- is perhaps a Keltic pronunciation of -nn-). In pop. Eng. "to tan" is "to thrash, beat." Possibly therefore the name of a tree associated with the underworld (Tartareo carcere v.2) like the reputedly poisonous taxus (Pl. 16. 51; cf. Ovid m. 4.432) which is fatal in another setting (cf. 207 above, s.v. eburo-).

tan(n)are "tan" CGL 2.565,44; 566,14:

aluta locus ubi pelles in calce pilantur uel **tan(n)-antur**; alumen locus ubi **tannantur** coria.

Cf. OHG tanne ("abies, quercus"), Fr. tan (M-L 8555a), Bret. tann. But the meaning of the Keltic cognates is disputed (see SprFK 210, Do. 290); AcS 2. 1719-20. Kluge's objections (ZfRPh 41, 1921, 683) to this explanation by Thurneysen are not, I think, valid. The evidence for an earlier dating of W. Germ. shifts than is commonly believed is such as to leave the question open. Connexion with tonna, tunna (178 above, cf. 240) seems unlikely, though not impossible.

The use of oak-galls, or bark, for tanning makes it at least likely that the name of the tree and of the process of tanning are connected, though M-L l.c. does not even consider such a possibility. So far as a notion of color (brown, dark yellow) is found in some of the Romance cognates, cf. perhaps Lat. tamnus, taminia (uua).

911

Glosses

?targa "shield, target"

    AcS 2.1734, M-L REW 8579 (Frankish). Cf. OE targe,
originally of hide; cf. therefore Lat. tergus.

taxea: see PID 2.199

    If actually Germanic, again an early borrowing.
But Isid. 20.2.24, like his source Afranius, makes the
word Keltic. The related (?) taxo, taxus "badger,"
taxoninus, on the other hand, seem to be Germanic
(Walde 765); they occur only in the glossaries and Marcellus Empiricius. Sofer 88, Brüch 16, M-L Einf. 45,
Kluge 13.

    The names of trees taxa (Pl. 15.130 "laurel, bay,"
Keltic?), taxus "yew" (cl., Caes., Verg., Pl., al.) can
hardly be connected in any way; but tucca, tuccetum,
tuccetosus, Umb. toco, the root-meaning of which is
again "fat," ultimately are probably related, notwithstanding the vocalism. The ethnicon Texuandri (221
below), if connected with taxus, translates Eburones
(cf. eburo- 207 above) as pointed out by Tourneur (see
Introduction to Germania Inferior).

[?traiectum "bridge-head"

    Bede h.e. 5.11 would make this Keltic, see AcS 2.
1903, 3.319; and it is possible that some native word
is concealed in the Latinized Vltraiectum (quasi Vltra-
traiectum.) But see Note xlviii above, and Vilti 221
below.]

tubruci, tibraci "trousers"

    Isid. 19.22.30; Gl.; Bede (see AcS 2.1974-75).
Whatever -braci (braces, -ae), -bruci may be, Germ.
or Kelt. (see 178 above), tu- is evidently Germanic
(OE Þeóh "thigh"), see Sofer Lat.u.Rom. 160-161.

Glosses

[uadum "ford"

The influence of Germanic (OHG wat, watan, OIc.
vada, cf. Vada 221 and Note xlviii) is manifest in the
Romance forms in g-, gu- (Fr. gué, Ital. guado, Prov.
ga).]

uuaisdus "woad" CGL 3.583,48

Capit. de uillis (ca. 800) 43, see Kluge AR 6,
1922, 311; OFr. guesde, Fr. guède, OE wād with loss of
-s- as in mēd (meord, Goth mizdo); in Comp. Luc. 16-17,
71 (Svennung) Q 33 uuatum; and in Oribasius uuisdil
(Kluge, Svennung l.c.); cf. uitrum (207 above)

uanga "hoe, spade" CGL 5.399,43; 423,25; 625,1

Greg. M. vit. Deodati (Nivernersis), al.; see AcS
3.99-100; G. Behrens Mainzer Zts 29, 1934, 44-55.
"Wohl aus dem Grm." Walde (so Ernout). Cf. Vangiones;
and scotta "ferrum anceps" (beside Scotti; so Saxones,
Dorieus). Cf. uangas: spadan (n. acc. pl.) Corpus
Glossary (ed. Lindsay, 1921); but in Musée Belge 26,
1922, 282 we have a different word uanga: est mensile
fosfarium (sic), ib. p.263 mensis Iunius Bosporius (p.
275). Cf. uangroni Note xxi, Vangio 237, 244; Vangiones
234.

uuantus "glove"

Ion. vit. Columb. 1.15 (tegumenta mannuum quos
Galli uuantos uocant), vit. Bertharii, vit. Filiberti,
see AcS 3.100-101; Fr. gant (M-L 9500); Buck Synonyms
435.

uargus "vagabond" Eum. pan. Const. 9.3, Sid. ep. 6.4

Cf. ON vargr? Germanic (Walde, Ernout).

Glosses

uuarantia "Färbkraut, sandyx"

This I take from Kluge AR 6, 1922, 311-12, citing
Thes. Gloss. Emend. s.vv. rubis, sandyx, uarantia; OFr.
guarance. Kluge compares OHG rezza "für Germ. wratja"
which he sees in the OChSl. (borrowed) broštь "purple."

uassus "cliens" (cf. BG 6.15.2; 19.4) Schol. Hor. ars

p. 32 "imus: pro uassu[s];" then in Lex Sal., Alamann.,

Baiuvar. and in Marculfi form.; **uassalus** (AcS 3.119)

Apparently a name at Soluthurn (CIL 13.5173), and
perhaps in vit. Segolenae (Troclarensis) ASS 24 Iul. 5.
635E: puer nomine uassus (?). Cf. uasso-caletis CIL
13.4130, see 158 above; and the numerous names containing uasso- AcS 3.122-3; W. guas "seruus," Ir. foss
"servant." Cf. Grenier in Frank 3.529. From *upo-dhē-
Osthoff (cf. Marstrander NTS 1, 1928, 107) quasi "sub-
ditus"; *upo-sto- ("oder zu gr. ἄστος ?"), Pokorny Urg.
43, Gutenbrunner 179; better *upo-st(h)ə-.

uuatum "woad" see uuaisdus

ueleda "prophetess" Tac. G 8; h. 4.61 (apud Bructeros);

Stat. S. 1.4.9

Though ancient historians make this a proper name,
it is more probably a common noun, Ir. fili "seer," W.
gweled "see," Chadwick Growth of Literature 1, 1932,
606; cf. id. Nationalities of Europe (1945), 157. A
recently discovered insc. from Ardea (Rend. d. Pont.
Acad. Rom. d'Arch. 21, 1945-46, 163-67; REA 49, 1947,
377-78) is addressed to Βελήσα by Ῥηνοπότκι, on which
see further Anz.f.Alt. 1, 1948, 63. Cf. ganna, Ganna
240-1.

Glosses

<u>uibones</u> "flower of the plant Britannica" Plin. 25.21

    Germanic (Frisian) according to Gutenbrunner Germ. 23, 1939, 122-123 (*wiban: OE wifel, OHG wibil, MHG uibelen); insc. radix britanica (Haltern) Germ. 12, 1928, 70 (cf. 75, 172).

<u>uuisdil</u> "woad" see uuaisdus above; cf. uitrum (207)

<u>urus</u> "aurochs" BG 6.28.1 (in Hercynia silua)

    Cf. PID 2.201. Borrowed into Latin (Verg. G. 2. 374, cf. Serv. ad loc.); Plin 8.38 (Germania), cf. Isid. 12.1.34; CGL 2.211,55 (βοῦς Γερμανός); AcS 3.44-46.

Names of Germania Inferior

Sources given in AcS are not, as a rule, repeated
here, cf. p.174; arabic numerals, without other indication of source, refer to CIL 13, viz. ii 2 (1907) 7776-
8860 (pp.505-644) with iv (1916) 11981-12086a (pp.133-
145) and ii 2 (1907) 9133-9165 (pp.707-713) and iv
(1916) 12087-12090, together with Finke 254-317, 359-372
and Nesselhauf 142-275 (on F.333 and N.144, 241 see AE
1937, p.332, Siebourg BJ 160-161, 1936, 422-28); A. Riese
Das rheinische Germanien in der antiken Literatur 1892
(abbreviated R. Lit.); id., Das rh. Germ. in den ant.
Inschriften 1914 (abbrev. R.) with RGKBer. 7, 1913-15,
pp.7-29 (additions to R. Lit.) 9, 1916, pp.115-147 (additions to R.); for the diplomata see CIL 16, 1916; Hans
Lehner Die antiken Steindenkmäler des Provinzialmuseums
in Bonn, 1918; reference is made occasionally to Förstemann's Altdeutsches Namenbuch: Ortsnamen ed. 3 (1911-
1916) and to A.W. Byvanck Excerpta Romana (De Bronnen
der romeinsche Geschiedenis van Nederland; 1. Teksten
1931, 2. Inscripties 1935), in Rijks Geschiedkundige
Publikatien, 'S-Gravenhage, Nijhoff, vols. 73 and 81).

A few names admitted from adjacent parts of Germania Magna are marked thus⟨ ⟩. Byvanck 1.534-586
gives some new identifications of ancient and modern
local names in Belgica and Germania Inferior.

On local names in TP see J. Schoo Die Wegen door
het land der Bataven op de Kaart van Peutinger, Tijdschrift van het Koninklijk Ned. Aardrijkskundig Genootschap 54, 1937, 649-700 (with maps); B.H. Stolte De
romeinsche Wegen in het land der Bataven en de Tab.
Peut. (with notes by H. Hettema Jr. and F. Kroon) ibid.
55, 1938, 700-722; in Mnemosyne 8, 1939, 67-71 Byvanck
has discussed the date and importance of Not. Dig. for
this area; see also P.J. Blok en A.W. Byvanck De romeinsche Tijd en de frankische Tijd (in the Geschiedkundige Atlas van Nederland, 'S-Gravenhage 1929); Franz
Cramer Rheinische Ortsnamen aus vorrömischer und römischer Zeit, 1901; A. Berthelot La Germanie d'après
Ptolémée, REA 37, 1935, 34-44; Th. Steche Altgermanien
im Erdkundebuch des Claudius Ptolemaeus, 1937 (reviewed
in CW 31, 1937-38, 176-78); Langewiesche Germ. Siedel-
ungen im nordwestlichen Deutschland zwischen Rhein und
Weser nach dem Berichte des Ptolemaeus, 1909 (reviewed
in REA 15, 1913, 469); R. Müller Die geographie der
Peutingerschen Tafel in der Rheinprovinz, in Holland
und Belgie, Geogr. Anzeiger Heft 9-10, 1926 (cf. RA 24,

Local Names

1926, 296; REA 35, 1933, 178); J. Hagen Römerstrassen
der Rheinprovinz ed. 2, Bonn 1931 (cf. REA 35, 1933,
45-46); Jan de Groot (on Utrecht, Fectio, Fleuus, Albis,
and other local names) in Oxé Festschrift, Darmstadt
1938, pp.210 ff.; S. Gutenbrunner (on river names in
the lower Rhine area) ZfCPh 20, 1933-36, 448-460;
E. Kranzmayer Zur Ortsnamenforschung im Grenzland,
ZNF 10, 1934, 105-148; J. Schnetz ZfCPh 15, 1924-25,
212-222 on the names Weser and Wipper (for the latter
cf. uebru 10008.47, see 216 Remark above).

Other references: M. Schönfeld Wörterbuch der
altgermanischen Personen- u. Völkernamen, Heidelberg
1911; G. Schütte Ptolemy's Maps of Northern Europe,
København 1917 (cf. Acta Philol. Scand. 18, 1948, 308-
314); U. Kahrstedt Claudius Ptolemaeus u.d. Gesch.d.
Südgermanen, Mitth. d. praehist. Komm. d. Akad. d. Wiss.
Wien 3.4, 1938; Riesmann-Grone Ptolemaeus...Niederrhein
u. Westfalen, Beitr. zur Gesch. von Stadt u. Stift
Essen. 57, 1938, 5-38 (known to me from Idg. Jahrb. 25.
149); J. Beckers Des Claudius Ptolemaeus Germania Karte
in der frühgeschichtliche Forschung Geogr. Zeitschr. 44,
1938, 220-229; Kaspers (on names in -rich) Beitrage zur
Namenforschung 1, 1949-50, 106-148; Bach (on Latin mons
in Germanic local names) ib., 170-180; Stempel Klio 23,
1930, 346-7; R. Much SB Akad. Wiss. Wien, Ph-H. Kl.
195.2, 1920; id. in P-W Suppl. 3, 1918 s.v. Germani (545-
585); W. Krause Herkunft der Germani Jahrb. d. Akad.
Wiss. Göttingen 1940-41, 18-36; Jost Trier Welt als
Gesch. 9, 1943, 83-86

E. Förstemann Altdeutsches Namenbuch ed. 2, vol. 1
(1900-01) Personennamen; ed. 3, vol. 2 (1911-16) Ortsnamen.

The name Germanus (Gar-) is endlessly discussed;
I give a few references merely: Pokorny ZfCPh 20, 1933-
36, 461-475; W.J. Beckers Rh.Mus. 88, 1939, 122; Walde-
Hofmann s.v. (with Addendum); Norden Altgermanien 1934,
pp.259ff.; Schnetz ZONF 12, 1936, 91-96; 13, 1937-38,
33-42; E. Hesselmeyer in Der Schwabenspiegel 33, 1936,
233-34, 243; E. Bickel BJ 139, 1934, 14-20; Gustav
Stümpel Klio Beiheft 26 (NF 12), 1932, Name und Nation-
alität der Germanen; Fr. Pfister Tacitus und die Germanen in Studien zu Tacitus (pp.59-93, of Würzburger
Stud. zur Altertumswissenschaft 9, 1936); R. Much Mannus
24, 1932, 465-478 (untrustworthy); W. Kaspers Ph.Woch.
56, 1936, 1022-1024; during the middle thirties a flood

Local Names

of monographs about the Germani appeared in Germany,
to refer to the reviews of some of which, by Hans
Philipp, will suffice viz. Ph.Woch. 55, 1935, 275-79,
651-53, 1123-24, 1203-04; 56, 1936, 162-64, 270-71, 579-
580; 757-59; 1385-1390; 57, 1937, 610-614. These are
of unequal value, some of them quite worthless.

In my opinion the testimony of Caesar and Tacitus
makes it clear that Germani was originally the name of
a German tribe, subsequently applied by the Gauls and
the Romans to all Germanic-speaking tribes. It is not
clear that the word itself was German (cf. Teutones,
which is certainly a Keltic form), though that is the
more likely assumption.

Local and Ethnic Names

Remark:

Many divine epithets (see 223 below) are strictly
local, e.g. Abirenes (matronae), i.e. "ambi-rhenae,
am Rhein," cf. the personal name (Germ. Sup.) Ambirenus
Rauricus, which is (strictly construed) also local.
But I give divine epithets with the divine names, and
personal with the personal, lest misunderstanding and
confusion arise to set any reader hunting for a place
that never existed, if I should give here Abirenes or
the like as a local name.

A[8053.16

[Aballauenses (Frisiones)
at Aballaua (Brit.),
Byv. 2.1284-85; R.1853,
cf. sq. (or AR 6, 1922,
199?)]

[?Abalus ins. i.q. Basil-
ia Pl. 37.35; Germ. 25,
1941, 90-97]

Abrinca v. Ob-

?Actania ins. Pl. 4.97

Local and Ethnic Names

⟨Adrana fl.⟩

Aduatuca (At-) BG 2.29;
ᾈΤΟΥᾼΤΟΥΚΟΥ Ptol.,
Aduaca Tongrorum IA
(At- TP); Aduatuci
(At-), sprung, like
the Neruii (212), from
Cimbri and Teutones,
BG Oros.; ᾈΤ - Dio;
auaucia(?) num.; cf.
CIL 13 i pp.506, 573-
74. Vetschau. Bull.
Comm. Topon. 5, 1931,
115-16; R. Müller
Aduatuca Eburonum
(Jülich 1943)

⟨Aestii Tac. G. 45.2⟩

[?Agenappio uicus; cf.
NLB p.101 (Genappe?)]

Albaniana (-in- IA) TP
Alfen, cf. Note xlviii
(Utrecht)

?Albiobola (-anus) Note
xlviii above

Albios Dio Cass. R. Lit.
3.59

Albis Tac. G. 41; Elbe.
Cf. REL 11, 1933, 203-
11; C. p.297. Identi-
fied with Eridanos
Germ. 25, 1941, 90-97

Allobriges (-it-) Appian,
Procop., Rav. But cf.
212 above.

⟨Aliso; Ἄλεισος R. Lit.
13.80; Metz Iter soli-
tum und Aliso, Wetzlar
1935 (PhW 56, 1936, 8-
9; Gnomon 12, 1936,
285-286); also on the

Aliso question Werner
Wo lag Aliso? Sadée
in BJ 130, 1935, 302-
309; Lonke in Giessener
Beitrage z. d. Philol.
86, 1946, 5-22; 88,
1946, 5-12; cf. Metz
Die röm. Fernstrasse by
Wetzlar, 1937⟩

[Alutum flumen 8213; but
cf. Ptol. 5.8.6 Ἀλόντα ,
which flows into the
Caspian; gl. 158]

⟨Amalchium Byv. 1.584; cf.
220⟩

[Ambiuariti v. 212]

[Ambrones cl.; cf. Om-]

⟨Amisia f. Emms⟩

Ampsiuarii Tac. a 13.55-
56; Byv. 2.495

Angriuarii cl., eg. Tac.
a 2.19

⟨Angleuarii Byv. 2.496⟩

Aquae Granni AcS 1.2039,
8-15; but is not this
medieval form for
*aqui(g)ranni, cf. *ewi-
(egui-)randa ib. 1485
and Appendix; Iculisna
(Aqui-, Equo-) ib. 2.
24. Not ancient (CIL
13 ii p.517); ad Achas
795, Ahha 972 (Förste-
mann 1.38), now Aachen.
P-W 2.300 n.44; 7.1824.
Other possibilities
Grannus (div. name 211,
236); gl. gron(n)a 207;
Granona 179; but not
granus 220?

919

Local and Ethnic Names

Arenacum Tac h 5.20, Har-
enatium TP, cf. CIL
13 ii p.616; Rindern
(or Arnheim?)

Arbalo fl. Pl. 11.55;
Erpe

[Aresaces Note xlviii,
209, 223, 234, 237?]

Arnefala fl. (older -apa)
Rav. 4.24; Erft(?)

[Ascarii Klio 31, 1938.
51-59; cf. 234; Am.
27.2.8]

Asciburgium Tac. g. 3
(cf. Anderson ad loc.),
h. 4.33; itinn.Ἀσκι-
βούργιον Ptol., CIL 13
ii pp.507, 600; Asberg.
On aski- (an i-stem)
Kluge Urg. 35

Austerauia ins., v. Glae-
saria and gl. 220

Bacenis silua BG 6.10.5
(cf. 181 Remark above),
OHG Buohhunna (-ch-);
Kluge Urg. 33

Badu[h]enna v. div. names

Baetasii (Bet-) cl., inscc.
Betasius 7025, Bait- 3.
3079. Cf. CIL 13 ii
p.598; R.2380; R.1838-
43; Dipl. 48, 69, 70,
82

[Baia AcS 1.332-3; ZNF
14, 1938, 90; gl. 158]

Balcia Rav.

[Basilia ins., v. Abalus]

Bătāui (-āui Lucan 1.431)
cl., inscc. e.g. 1847,
8771, Vollmer 511,
Dessau 8852; IG 14.
2433. Cf. CIL 13 ii
pp.618-19; Robert Mne-
mosyne 5, 1937, 302
(Βατάοveς in Greek
insc.); Βαταβία Zos.;
B]ataeus R.2396; Bad-
auus R.2409; Batai R.
864; Badaus (Rome) 6.
31140, cf. Gutenbrunner
p.7.4; Batabi Note
xlviii; Bataui 6.31162;
Bataus 7833, 3.11936,
11.1070; V.275; Bataua
8339, Dipl. 105; Batauus
6.4341; cf. 10001.69;
R. Lit. 13.139; Kluge
Urg. 32; Βατάβοι Plut.;
-άουοι Diod. Bataui 3.
3681; Betau[us] 3.10513;
Βατάο[υ]οι R. 1778; Bata-
orum 8.21668; Betauos
R.2414; oppidum Batauorum
REA 19, 1917, 209; 20,
1918, 116; 22, 1920, 299.
    In TP Patabus fl.
(Batauus) is the mouth
of the Vaal or Mass; and
in Rav. 4.28, 5.3 Pat-
auum appears to be an
error for Matauo. Cf.
Patauio Iul. Hon. Occ. 22
(Geogr. Lat. Min. p.37).
    Cf. Betewe (between
Vaal and Lek); and see in
general J.W. Muller Nomina
geogr. Neerlandica 8, 1932,
112-158. Patauia (B-) TP.

Batauodurum cl., -δουρον
Ptol., C. 618

Baunonia v. Burcana, cf.
220 above; Pl. 4.97

?Beeosus (tribus) F.372;
see further Byv. 2.
224; AE 1919 p.420;
REA 21, 1919, 91-96

Belgica uicus IA, appar-
ently Billig. (But
this is hardly a clue
to the etymology of
billig.) Cf. Villia-
cum 212; AcS 1.383

Bertunum, -ensis Greg.
Tur., Beurtina(?) Rav.
Cf. above 212 Bertunum
(Verton, Virton). For
*Virodunum? Now Birten
with which, however,
Vetera also is identi-
fied, cf. CIL 73 ii
p.507, 602; AcS 1.408

Blariacum TP, mod. Blerik

Bodobrio(?) AcS 3.917,36;
Hohen-Budberg

⟨Βογάδιον   Ptol. 2.11.13⟩

Bonna, Βόννα , -ensis cl.,
inscc. (AcS 1.480,19;
3.904, but not CIL 13.
8648 Bon[, which is
Bononia in Italy); mis-
written Borma in Florus
4.12.26 (cf. CIL 13 ii
p.560, and v. 212 above);
now Bonn

?Borbetolego (loc. sg.)
Note xlviii above

?Bordonchar Rav., Byv. 1.
579

Βούδορις   Ptol. 2.11.14,
Büderich

?Brabo(nes) Note xlviii

[(Britan)nicianus 8793]

Βριττία, -ωνες , -ιοι
Procop. h.G. 4.20, AcS
1.603-605

Bructĕri Vell. 2.105, cf.
Str. 7.1.3, 290C; Bur-
cturi TP, Brucherum 5.
8768 (R.1929); Byv. 2.
496

?Buconia silua Greg. Tur.
h.F. 2.40; but v. Buc-
onica (Bau-, Bou-) 212
above, and cf. Bucco,
Bucconius etc. (pers.
names) e.g. 83

Burcana ins. Pl. 4.97,
i.q. "Fabaria" cf. gl.
220; Str. 7.1.3, 291C,
Steph. Byz. Borkum?

Burginatium itinn., cf. C
ii pp.602, 611; Kluge
Urg. 9; Bornsche veld?

Burungum itinn. (for -nc-)
ib. pp.507, 590; Wor-
ringen (Burgel Byv.)

[Caemani falsa lect. BG 2.
4.10, whence Oros. 6.7.
14]

Caerosi cl., CIL 13 i
p.573

Caesia silua Hesiwald, or
Forêt d'Hesse? Cf. RhM
87, 1938, 177-88; SB
Akad Wien, Ph-H Kl. 1934,
143-4. Cf. 223 below

Local and Ethnic Names

?Calidona Amm. 27.1.2 (an
Caletus?)

?Calcaria R.2374; 2375;
Kalkofen, Calkar

Calone IA

?Camppil[8558

ᵛΚαμψ(ι)ανοί Str., v. R.
Lit. 4.68, 13.29

Cannanefates cl., inscc.
(C ii p.619) e.g.
7227, 7628, 8316,
R.46; Canafates R.1434,
Canonefas R.2427. On
9165 cf. H. Hettema Jr.
De Gids 99, 1935, iv
108-117. Described as
lingua par Batauis Tac.
h. 4.15; cf. possibly
Hannanefates (v.l. K-),
Annaneptiae 223 below.
Regularly -an- inscc.,
-in- Tac., -en- Pl. 4.
101, cf. Vell. 2.105(?);
Kennemerland.

[?Carambucis fl. Pl. 6.34
(mouth of Elbe; or of
Thames?)]

Caruium (ad molem) REA 42,
1940, 688, Herwen; but
cf. AE 1939.107, cf.
130; Germ. 23, 1939,
32; Vollgraff Med. k.
Akad. Afd. Letterk.,
1.12, 1938, 560-564
(cf. Rev. Belge 18,
1939, 807-08); caruo-
"stag" cf. 224 below

Caruo(ne) itinn., hardly
cf. Carbonaria (silua)

Greg. Tur. h.Fr. 2.9;
Harawa? (Förstemann 1.
1234); or Herwen?

Caspingium TP

[Castra Herculis Amm.,
itinn.; Kesteren?]

⟨Casuarii cf. Ch-⟩

Κάθ[ου]λκοι Str. 7.1.4,
291C; cf. pers. name
Catuolcus (224)

Catual[iensis or -inus?]
pagus AE 1926.129;
F.306 Cf. Catualium TP
(wrongly identified in
AcS 3.1155 with Kessel
near Blerik, on the
Maas). Note also the
pers. name Catuolcus
(224); Ant. Cl. 4, 1935,
175-189; C p.619; Heel
according to REA 44,
1942, 125; Catualium
Vannérus Bull. Acad roy.
Belgique, Cl. Lettres
1939, 141-69

Celbis fl. (Belgis mss.)
v. 212 above

Celtae on r. bank of Rhine,
Dio 39.49.1; [Celtae
8007]

Ceuclum (not Ceuelum) TP,
Kui(j)k

⟨Chemaui (cf. Bat-aui)⟩

⟨Charini (H-?) Pl. 4.99⟩

⟨Chasuarii, Cas-⟩

Local and Ethnic Names

⟨Chatti Tac. G. 29.1
   Hessen⟩

Chattuarii, see Riese
   Lit. 3.93 (v.l. Att-),
   4.68, 13.98

⟨Chauci C p.618; R. Lit.
   13.44; insc.⟩

⟨Χдοῦλκοι Str. (R. Lit.
   13.29) v. Κдθ[ο]υλκοι⟩

⟨Cherusci cl. TLL Onom.
   s.v. C p.297 n.9⟩

[Cimbri cl. (e.g. Pl. 4.
   98) R.7; cf. RhMus 88,
   1939, 52-92, 101-122;
   Die Sprache 1, 1949,
   140; REA 10, 1908, 71-
   75]

[Cliua A.D. 1134, Cleve;
   cf. Förstemann 1.1692;
   van Hamel compares
   Caleua, Note xlviii]

Coadulfaueris lect. cor-
   rupta Rav.; corres-
   ponds to Caruone (q.v.
   supr.) in itinn.; cf.
   AcS 3.1244,29. Coad-
   fulueris ZONF 15,
   1939, 86-96. But cf.
   ulf- (i.e. wulf?):
   Vlpia?

[Colonia Agrippinensis
   (oppidum, ara Vbiorum)
   cl. inscc. C ii p.505,
   Köln, Cologne, Keulen]

[colonia Traiana IA, 6.
   31140; ciues Traianen-
   ses 8185; now Xanten
   (Lat. sanctus?)]

Condrusi, -ustis pagus,
   v. 212, 213 above, 223
   below; C i pp.573-74;
   7.1234 (-usi), 1073
   (-stis); cf. Byv. 2.
   1250; -us Vollmer 514;
   ZfRPh 54, 1934, 218-20;
   Condroz

Coriouall(i)um itinn.,
   Heerlen. But the v.l.
   -rt- has suggested
   Kerten to Riese (see
   his Index); C ii p.506

⟨Cronium prom., Byv. 1.
   584; cf. morimarusa 220⟩

(Cuberni Pl. iv 106); Χου-
   βερ[νωροι] R.1906, Cuberni R.1848, Cugerni R.
   1849

Cugerni (G-) Tac. h 4.26;
   C ii.598; v. Cub-

Deuso v. Diuitia

?Dispargum Greg. Tur.
   h.Fr. 2.9

Diuitia, -tensis Amm.,
   Greg. Tur., inscc.,
   8274, R.1765-1774, 3.
   728, R.1774 (Diuitesim
   gen. pl. 8274); cf.
   CIL 13 ii p.587;
   Deuso(?) Hieronym., cf.
   D(i)eusoniensis num.
   Postumus; Deuso and -us
   also pers. name (AcS 1.
   1273), but in origin
   probably distinct;
   Diuitienses insc. 11828,
   11979; Deutz. Cf.C.pp.499,

Local and Ethnic Names

549, 574; exploratores
Germ. Diuitiensium on
r. bank of Rhine 7750-
51, 7761, cf. 6814,
7054; 8.9059

⟨Dulgubnii Tac. G. 34;
cf. REA 24, 1922, 329⟩

Dumnissus Aus., v. 212
supr.; Denzen?

[ad Duodecim]

Durnomagus itinn., Dor-
magen; cf. AcS 2.
1451,10; Loth REA 23,
1921, 116

Durostates (Do-) Rav. 1.
10, 4.24; cf. Philo-
logus 89, 1934, 88;
Duurstede (Byv.)

Eburones, Ἐβούρονες cl.;
CIL 13 1 p.573; cf.
Intro. above

⟨Eridanos v. Albis above⟩

(H)ermiones Tac. G. 2.3

Eustrachia Rav. (i.q.
Austerauia?)

Fabaria ins., v. Burcana;
Φαβιράνον Ptol. 2, 11,
12

Falchouarii ND; cf. P-W
s.v.

Fectio 8815 (on which see
H. Wagenvoort Mnemosyne

8, 1939, 58-64), itinn.
TP (Fletio, Fictio),
CIL 13 ii pp.619, 638;
Vechten

Feresne TP, Vucht? (Read
Teresne Dilsen, REA 44,
1942, 125); Vannérus
l.c., s.v. Catualium
above; R. Lit. 13, 114

Flenio TP; cf. Mnem. 3,
1935-36, 289-304 (on
9165); not the same
place as sq.; Brunsting
Grafveld 1937 p.1 would
read (H)elenium, q.v.
below

Fleuum ins. et lacus; os-
tium Rheni; castellum:
Mela 3.24, cf. Geogr.
Lat. min. p.128; Pl. 4.
101; Tac. h. 4.72;
Φληούμ Ptol.; Latomus
3, 1939, 107-110

Franci, Φράγγοι confused
with Sugambri and Treu-
eri Lyd. de mag. 1.50;
with Germani Procop.
Goth. 1.12; described
as Keltic (!) Libanius
Constant. 3.316R., and
their name written Φρά-
κτοι as if from φρασ-
σω (!) ibid.; used to
include the Salii Amm.
17.8.3; Francia prac-
tically "Gallia" but
with reference to Ger-
mania Superior Paneg.
Const. [Pan. Lat. 7]
6 and Hieron. vit. Hil.
22 (Riese, Lit. 9.102);
Francus insc. 8274 (cf.
pers. names), Franci
8502 at Deutz (temp.

Local and Ethnic Names

Const.); Francia Rinensis (i.q. Gallia Belgia †Alobrites) Rav. 4. 24, cf. 26; Celtici et Francici Trebell. Pollio vit. Gallieni 8.1; see also Riese Lit., Index s.v.; Amm. Marc. quoted in CIL 13 ii p.603

Frigones (-xon-) Rav. 1. 10, 4.24 (cf. Durostate); but v. also sq.

Frisiauones Pl. 4.101, 106; ND Occ.40; Kluge Urg. 34

Frisiaui Geog. Lat. Min. p.128; Frisii Tac h. 4.72; Frisius Vollmer 510, R.1854, 2438; 6. 4342; Frisauones R. 1835, Dipl. 51, 69, 70; Frisiauus R.2436; Frisiaus 7.68; Frisaus 8040, R.2437, cf. Tac. G.34; Pl. 4.101; Frisio R.1853, 1856; Frisiaeus 6.4343; Frisius 3 p.879; Dipl. 105; 6.3321a; Frisaeus 6.3260; Friseus 6.3230, cf. R.2430-38; Frisaeuo R.2434, -aeuus R.2435; cf. P-W s.vv., CIL 13 ii p.618; and divine names (222 below)

[?Gaesati v. CIL 13 i p.574]

?Gaesoriacum, opposite Bonna (q.v. supr.), Florus 4.12.26, cf. Pl. 4.106, and see 212 above

[Γαμβρίουι Str. 7.1.3, 291C; Gambriuii Tac. G 2.4]

Gelduba cl., itin.; Tac. h 4.26, Pl. 19.90; Gellep; C p.597

?Geminiacum itinn., -ensis ND, now Liberchies? (But cf. CIL 13 i p.574, where Gembloux, Gimnée, Gemmenich are all considered)

?Gensouiacum (Florus) AcS 1.2003, mod. Gensem? (or Gaesoriacus 212 above?)

Germania inferior 1807, -ae duae 1807; Germani, -ia cl., inscc., see Intro.; Germanus 2018

Glaesaria ins. Pl. 4.97, 37.42; i.q. Austerauia. Cf. gloss 220.

⟨Granni(?) Aquae, v. Aquae⟩

Grinnes cl., TP

⟨Guiones Pl. 37.35⟩

Guberni (or Cug-?) Pl. 4. 94

[Hadrani forum TP; cf. CIL 13 ii p.637; Arentsburg]

Hanaua (Ch-?) Honnef (AcS 3.606,9)

Harenatium itinn., v. Arenacum

Helinium (v.l. Helium) ostium Pl. 4.101; cf. Mnem. 3, 1935-36, 289-304; Hettema De Gids 99, 1935, iv 108-117

⟨Heruli nom. prov.; Byv. 1.550⟩

⟨Hiustia fl. Rav.; Byv. 1.584⟩

Hoium (-gi-) Pertz Dipl. 97 (A.D.743-47), ASS; Cho(a)e Merov. num. (cf. AcS 1.1077; 2005), Oim(?) Rav. (ib. 2.841), modern Huy

⟨Idistauiso campus Tac. A. 2.16⟩

Inda fl. Rav. 4.24; cf. ala Indiana, and Indus pers. name 214 above; Inde

⟨Inguaeo, -ones Pl. 4.99; Tac. G. 2; cf. Kluge 34; Klio 31, 1938, 57⟩

⟨Ipada Pader? Byv. 2.579⟩

⟨Istaeuones Tac. G. 2.3⟩

Iuliacum itinn., Amm.; CIL 13 ii p.521; Iülich, older Gulik, Gulich

laeti (L-), -icus, e.g. Laeti Bataui ND, Franci; cf. 212 above; Lagenses ND Occ. 42. 43; now not Lowaige (L'haut weg) REA 44, 1942, 112; 46, 1944, 157, but Luik Byv. 1. p.574; see, however, P-W s.v.

⟨Lamizon Emms Rav.⟩

⟨Λανδοί Str. (R. Lit. 4.68)⟩

⟨Langobardi⟩

[Latab[ici 8316, prob. for Latou[ici, see 234, 241; cf. Grenier Mélanges Paul Thomas 1930, p.385; cf. Byv. 2.511]

⟨Lauri⟩

Laurum TP

Leuaci cl., cf. divine name Liuicus 223 and Leuefano below (?), Lèves?

Leuefano TP (Euitano Rav.), Λευφανο Ptol., commonly taken as Leuae (div. name) fanum; AcS 2.202 gives also Leua fl., an error for Lege(?), 212 above; cf. Tamfana 223

⟨Lina Leine⟩

Lirensis portus N.161 (Bonn); Rostovtzeff CR

Local and Ethnic Names

AcInscBL 1930, 250-
260; portus is "dépôt;"
Germ. 16, 1932, 104-
108; BJ 138, 1933,
112-13; Stein Beamten
46 n.31; cf. 80 above;
Walters Pottery 2.363

[Lopetei uil(l)a (or PN?)
F.372]

Lucretius uicus 8254; cf.
80 above

⟨Lup(p)ia, Λουπίας fl.,
cl., Lippa Rav., Lippe;
Kluge Urg. 32⟩

Lug(u)dunum (Batauorum)
itinn., num. Merov.;
Λουγόδουνον Ptol.;
Leyden

Mannaritium IA

? Μαραμανις λιμήν Ptol.
2.11.1 (R. Lit. 13.
87) cf. AcS 2.417,12
(Marc. Heracl.), v.l.
μαρναμανός . Cf. Mar-
comanni 241? Hardly
read μοριμαρουδα ?

Marcodurum Tac. h. 4.28;
Duren

Marcomagus itinn., Mar-
magen; C. p.560 n.3

Marsaci Tac. h. 4.56;
-us ciuis 8303; -ii
Pl. 4.101, Marsaquius
6.3263; Dessau 2508;
cf. Marsacae 223

⟨Marsi⟩

Matilo TP, Matellio Rav.,
now Roomburg (Stein
Beamten 227)

⟨Mattium Tac. a 1.56; cf.
Mattiana (mala) Ed.
Diocl. 6.65⟩

Μεδιολάνιον Ptol. 2.11.13,
Metelen or Mylen (near
Gellep)? Bethoud Pro
Alesia 10, 1924, 234-
247

Mederiacum IA, Melick?
But in TP we have M...
nerica, variously iden-
tified (cf. Desjardins
Geogr. p.109)

⟨Melibocus⟩

Metuonis oceanus Pl. 37.
35

Μουνδιακόν (τῆς ἑτέρας Γερ-
μανίας) Olympiodorus
fr. 17 (FHG 4.61).
Cf. Montiacum Hist.
Aug. vet. Aurel. 7.1
(v.l.), Montiacesenam
Leterc. Veron. 15,
mod. Montzen(?). This
name, usually identi-
fied with Moguntiacum
(Mainz) 234 below, and
emended accordingly,
has been much discussed
of late. See Nessel-
hauf Abh. Pr. Ak. Ph-H
Kl 1938, no.2, 74 with
n.1; Ant. Cl. 8, 1939,
233; Byvanck Mnem. 6,
1938, 380-81; 7, 1939,
76-79; Rev. Belge 14,
1935, 1577-8; Vannérus
15, 1936, 5-22 and Gré-
goire 815-16; id. Byzan-

tion 5, 1930, 767; 10,
1935, 236-37; Stein RGK
Ber. 18, 1928, 98-100;
L. Schmidt Germ. 21,
1937, 264-66; cf. div-
ine names 213, Note xlv
B, 236

Mosa fl., Pons Mosae, cl.;
Maas

Mouit fl. (evidently cor-
rupt; read Mosa? or
Mosella?) Rav. 4.24

[Nabalia fl. Tac., Ναυαλία
Ptol., Naualia Isala
fl., now the Leck]

Namucum (-g-) Fredegarius,
Merov. num.; uit. Bert.
Namon Rav., Namur. Cf.
Rev. Belge 10, 1931,
531-39

Nasaga Rav.

Nersa (A.D. 856), mod.
Niers; cf. div. names
223; Gutenbrunner 164,
194

⟨Nictrenses nom. prov.
(Byv. 1.550); or Tenc-
teri?⟩

Nida fl., v. Vida

[Nigropullo TP]

[?Nistricus Rav., Byv. 1.
581]

[?Nocdac Rav., Byv. 1.
579]

Noita Rav. 4.24 (read
Nouia?)

[Nordostracha ins., i.q.
Actania above?]

[Northomanni Rav.]

Nouaesium insc.(?) 8569;
cl., Ptol.; -es-
itinn., Amm.; Niuisium
Greg. Tur.; Neuss

Nouiomagus CIL 3.11936,
cf. 5918b, 6.3237,
3284; CIL 13 11 p.620;
TP; Nymwegen. Cf. AE
1945.97; P-W s.v.; and
on the question of
chronology REA 30,
1928, 219

Ὀβρίγκας fl. (v.l. Ἀ-)
Ptol., now the Vinxt-
bach (from fines); cf.
Abrincatui 179 above,
Abrianeco 212, Obrege
148

[Oeocenae ins. Rav. (Byv.
1.584)]

Oi(u)m v. Hoium

⟨Ombrones, Ὀμβρωνες
Ptol.⟩

Paemani (-oe-) cl., cf.
212; C i p.573

Parisii TP (between Rhine
and Maas), Byv. 1.542;
this ethnicon occurs also
in Lugd. and in Britain

?Peruiciacum (vv. ll.
-nic-, -uc-) IA, Per-
naco TP (:pernae?),
Perwez (Taviers?), cf.
CIL 13 1 p.574 (Hannut)
Byv. 1.540 (Branchon,
Braives)

[Praetorium Agrippinae
TP; Byv. 3.139; van
Giffen (and others)
Opgravingen ... Val-
kenburg Z.-H., 1948

[?Pullus (Niger), v.
Nigropullo]

?Purdenses v. Voredenses
below

?Quadriburgium Amm. Marc.
18.2.4 (or Asci-?);
Qualberg

Quadruuiae AE 1922.61; cf.
179 above

Rausaconfinitio Rav. 4.24

Renus fl., ʿΡῆνος cl.,
inscc., Rhenicus 3045;
R.3,7; N.186; OHG Rîn,
Rhîn; divine name in
5255; Rhine, Rhein.
Among the large num-
ber of discussions of
Renus note REA 7,
1905, 61; AGI 22-3,
1929, 419; SprFK 207,
KZ 59, 1931-2, 15; RC
44, 1927, 256; ZfcPh
23, 1943, 401; Geist.
Arb. 8, 1941, 1; Mél-
anges Pedersen 1937,

77; Pokorny Urg. 75;
RC 45, 1928, 312-317;
Glotta 26, 1938, 193;
M-L Einf. 241; Zwicker
(see index s.v. R[h]enus)
together with AcS col-
lects the relevant
notices

Retom[agus?] 8614 (or divine or personal?)

⟨Reudigni⟩

Rigomagus Amm., Rav., TP;
Remagen

[Ripari Jordan. Get.36]

⟨Rusbeas prom. Pl. 4.95,
Rav.; Byv. 1.p.584⟩

⟨Rugi nom. prov.⟩

]rum (gen. pl.) R.1854

?Rungon (or Burungo q.v.
supr.?)

Rura fl. (for *Rau-?)
Rav., Roer (cf. Ruhr,
Rauricus)

⟨Rura fl. Ruhr⟩

Sabis, Sambra fl., cl.;
Sambre. See 212 above

Sablones IA

⟨Σάλας Str. Saale, trib.
of Elbe⟩

Salii (i.e. Franci) ap.
Texuandros Amm. 17.8.3;
CIL 13 ii p.630; Byv.

Local and Ethnic Names

2.1290 (Zalii Byv. 2,
p.496)

[Sarmatae v. AcS 2.1368.
Cf. 212 above.]

⟨Saxones Eutrop. 9.21;
cf. litus Saxonicus
ND Occ. 38⟩

Scaldis fl., cf. 212
above

[Scubuli R.36; cf. P-W
1.1259]

Segni, v. 212 above; cf.
CIL 13 i p.573

Segorigienses 8518; Holder
gives a possible Segor-
igium after the Serima
of Rav.; cf. Segora
(Aquit.)?

⟨Σημανὰ ὕλη Ptol.⟩

⟨Semnŏnes cl., e.g. Tac.
G 39⟩

Serima, v. Segorigium and
CIL 13 ii p.507

⟨Σετουία (v.l. -γ-) both
in Germ. Magna and in
Dalmatia; cf. AcS 2.
1453 s.v. Segouia (3)
and (4)⟩

⟨Σιατουτανδα(?) Ptol. 2.
11.12; perhaps merely
sua tutanda Tac. A 4.
73! R. Lit. 13.88⟩

?Stablesiani R.1800, cf.
RA 26, 1927, 386-87;
REA 28, 1926, 256;
the Stablesiani are

commonly put in Phry-
gia (cf. P-W s.v.),
but note the local
names Stabulae etc.
both Germ. Inf. and
Germ. Sup. (AcS 2.
1630)

⟨Στερεόντιον Ptol. 2.11.12⟩

Sturii Pl. 4.101

[Sudobeb(a) Note xlviii
(Utrecht)]

[Suebi e.g. EE ix 1135;
Stein Beamten p.240;
Sueui Semnones R.1864;
cf. Anderson on Tac.
G. 181-2]

⟨Sugambri Caes. BG 4.16;
Mon. Anc. 5.54; Sicam-
bri Prop. 5.6.77; Sid.
Apoll. 23.246; Σούγαμ-
βροι Strabo 7.1.4, 291C,
Sygambri Hor.4.2.34,
14.52. Cf. Supeni,
Cugerni; ap. Treueros
Ioh. Lyd. de mag. 1.50.
On the Sugambri west
of the Rhine (8 B.C.)
cf. Tac. G 2.4 and And-
erson ad loc.⟩

Sunuci inscc., -ici cl.,
(?)Sunix 7904, dipl.
70; v. CIL 13 i p.567,
ii p.598. But -ici
insc. EE 3.103, R.1863;
cf. divine names (-ux-)

Supeni(?) IA; or Cugerni?
(R. Lit., Index)

Tablae TP, perhaps same

Local and Ethnic Names

as sq. (Brunsting Graf-
veld p.11, cf. Flenio
above)

?Tαβούλα fl., Ptol.; cf.
212; CIL 13 i p.573

Talliates 7777-78; cf.
Germ. 15, 1931, 191

Τεκελία Ptol. 2.11.12,
Texel

⟨Tencteri BG 4.1, Tenc-
terus 3.728, cf.
7387, R.1774⟩

Texuandri Pl. 4.106, Tox-
iandria Amm. Marc. 7.
8.1, Texandri EE 3.
103, Texu[CIL 3.
14214, cf. 13.i p.567,
ii p.630. Cf. Bel-
gica Introd. (CIL 7.
712, a dedication to
dea Saiiada, Note xlv
A), Tex[uander(?), 13.
6239 (R.2602), cf.
R.1863; Texandrio in
8th cent. (Tourner in
Mélanges P. Thomas
664, who sees taxo-
as "yew" cf. Eburones).
Variously identified
as Tessenderloo (R.),
Testerup (Med. uitgeven
door Vlaam. Top. Ver-
eeniging te Leuven 21,
1945, 1-9), Zundert(C)

Τευδέριον (v.l. -τ-) Ptol.,
Theudurum IA, Tüddern

⟨Teutoburgiensis saltus
Tac. A 1.60; cf. P-W
s.v.; Welt als Gesch.
2, 1936, 368-375⟩

Teutones or -i cl. See
P-W s.v. On teutoni-
cus "deutsch" see Rh
Mus 86, 1937, 97-126

Tiberiacum IA, Ziverich

Tolbiacum cl., itinn.;
Tulbiacensis Greg. Tur.,
Tholbiaco Fredeg., Tul-
biecum lib. h.Fr.; Tul-
biaco num. Merov.; per-
haps uica[ni T]o[l
7920? Zülpich

[Traiana colonia; Traia-
nensis 6955, Byv. 2.
1380, CIL 13 ii p.602;
v. Colonia above, now
Xanten; Cf. Ara Traiana
(Vetera) BSAF 1928-29,
245-47; Troianensis 2034
(Byv. 2.1381), Troianus(?)
Byv. 2.1379; Troiae(?)
i.e. Traienes (Köln)
R. Lit. 13.151 (or is
this for Treueri 209
cf. 212 above?)]

Traiectum "bridge-head"
IA; Latin, not Latinized
for a Keltic name (as
Bede declares, cf. AcS
2.1903, 3.319, v. Vilti
infr.); cf. Treiecten-
sium urbs (Maastricht)
Greg. Tur. h.Fr. 2.5;
Troia Rav 4.24, Trega
Rav. 4.26 (but v. 212
above, insc. T]regoui-
cou[ium), Tro[g]ia
Fredeg. Chron 3.3 (not
Treueri?); cf. CIL 13
ii p.638, Utrecht. Per-
haps Τρηούα Ptol. 2.11.
12 (though this also
has been claimed for

Local and Ethnic Names

Treueri.) See above
Note xlviii.

Traiectus Maastricht,
see Note xlviii and
the preceding item

[Tricensimae Amm. 18.2.
4]

⟨Τουβάττιοι Str. 6.1.4,
291 C; Tubantes Lat.
Veron.; v. P-W s.v.;
cf. gloss battuo 220⟩

[Tuihanti R.1855, 2440;
Dessau 4760; Guten-
brunner pp.8, 202]

Tungri cl., insc. 8815,
3.12030,5; Tuncri
Sid. Apoll. 23.244,
Tongrecani ND Occ. 5.
28; Amm. Marc. 26.6.
12; Tungrecani 13.
5190, cf. CIL 13 1
pp.573-74; Ant. Cl.
4, 1935, 175-189; Ton-
gern. Tunger 3.12361;
-ri R.1869, 1874; on
13.8815 cf. Mnem. 8,
1939-40, 58-64 (cf.
244-49, 250-54). On
the Tungri see P. Mar-
chot ZfRPh 48, 1928,
651-56; 50, 1930, 346-
48; 54, 1934, 218-220

Vacalus fl. Caes. BG 4.
10.1 (-ulus v.l.), Vach-
alis Sidon. Apoll.,
Vahalis Tac.; CIL 13
1 p.574, cf. 11 pp.618,
629; Kretschmer Einl.
112; now Vaal. See
also 223 below

Vada (-m acc.) castra Tac.
h. 5.20-21, now Gouda-
ter-Gouw; cf. Vada Note
xlviii above (Utrecht)

Vahalis v. Vacalus

Varii TP (Byv. 1 p.542)

⟨Varini Tac. G 40.1; cf.
Varinnae Pl. 4.99?⟩

Varnenum(?) F.260, cf.
223 below

Vbii, Οὔβιοι cl., inscc.;
Albanus Excingi f.
Vbius 13.2613; mis-
written Veiorum (Vbior-
um) insc. BSAF 1928-29,
245-47

*Vebro- Wipper (RC 38,
1930, 283; distinguish
*uabra- ib. 37, 1917-
19, 309-11)

Veius (not Vbius?), Vein[
6.4337, 4339; but cf.
Vinouia AcS 3.354

Vella(u)us pagus 7.1072,
see 212 above; CIL 13
1 p.574; Veluwe

[Versulatii insc. (dis-
covered 1939), see Germ.
25, 1941, 98-104 (APh
15, 1940-41, 290); cf.
Bersula (Versala) fl.?]

Vetera (Beurtina? or Ber-
tina?) cl., inscc.,
itinn.; cf. C p.602,
and 223 below; not nec-
essarily Latin (REA 29,
1927, 311-12)

Local and Ethnic Names

Vida fl. (for N-) Rav. 4.
  24 (not the same as
  Nida 4.26), Wied

⟨Οὐίδρος fl. Ptol. 2.11.
  1⟩

Vilti, Viltaburg Bede
  h.e. 5.11 (lingua
  autem Gallica traiec-
  tum), now Wiltenburg
  (near Utrecht); cf.
  gloss 220 above

Vineta cf. R. Hennig Wo
  lag Vineta? 1935

Vinouie[nses] R.1856;
  Vein

⟨Visurgis fl. Weser; C
  p.297 n.9⟩

?Vlmanectes Pl. 4.106
  (leg. Silua-)

Οὐλπίας R.1778 col. Vlpia

Traiana (Xanten, for
  Sanct-?)

Vodgoriacum itinn., CIL
  13 i p.574, Waudrez;
  v.l. Vodo- (cf. 212)
  AcS 3.434

?Vordenses R.1858 (Pur-
  denses)

⟨Vsipetes BG 4.1, Οὐσί -
  πέται Diod., Vsipi(i)
  Byv. 2.473, 521; cf.
  Οὐίσπιοι 241

?Vsistrati fanum 8660
  (at Vetera)

uici[(V-?) fines 8695
  (at Cleve)

uici ... [8838 (inc.)

uican[ ]oii[.. 7920
  (Zülpich) uicani 11983

Addendum: Trepitia Rav., cf. gloss 158; Drůpt or Trůpt.
  But in Germ. Sup. we have also Triputienses, see
  241 infr.

222   Further Modern Names

  Alt-dorf, -enburg, -essen, -kerk, Antweiler

  Bandorf, Bedberg, Beetgum, Berg, Berkum, Bettenhoven,
Blatzheim, Bocklemündt, Bonsdorf, Born, Braives, Budberg,
Büderich, Bürgel

  Calcar, Commern

  Dernau, Dodewaard, Dollendorf, Domburg, Düsseldorf,
Dyck

Modern Local Names

Egmond, Elsdorf, Elten, (Ober-)Elvenich, Embresin (Am-), Endenich, Enzen, Erkelenz, Erp, Eschweiler, Euskirchen

Flémelle, Floisdorf, Friesdorf

Geich, Gey, Gielsdorf, (München-)Gladbach, Gleuel, Godesberg, Gripswald, Gresserich, Grünthal, Gürzenich, Güslen

Haseltsweiler, Heilstein, Hemmen, Hersel, Hochkirchen, Hoven

Iversheim

Kaiserstein, Katwijk aan Zee, Kirchheim

Lechenich, Lessenich, Lipp, Loevenich, Lommersen

Meckenheim, Merkenich, Meschenich, Merten, Merzenich, Millingen, Monterberg, Morken, Müddersheim, Munstereifel, Müntz

Netterheim, Niederdollendorf, Nierendorf, Nieukerk, Neu-Luisendorf

Oberwinter, Odendorf, Odenhausen

Pattern, Pont, Pützdorf; (Poortugaal Byv. 2.218)

Quaalburg

Ravensbosch, Rheinkessel, Ripsdorf, Roedingen, Roermund, Roevenich, Rohr, Roomburg, Ruimel

Sechtem (see 212 bis, Remark 2; but what is to be made of the insc. 8155 Xehndea at Sechtem? Cf. Xantia 8355 [Sanctia, Xanten?]), Sinzenich, Soller, Spellen, Stockum, Stommeln

Tetz, Thorr, Toterdonk, Tzum (Tolsum F.372)

Urhbach

Vellekoven, Voorburg

Wallseifen, Weissweiler, Weingarten Rheder, Wesseling, Wenau, Weltweis, Wollersheim

Zingsheim

Modern Local Names, Divine Names

See, in general, Nomina Geographica Neerlandica
(since 1885), Nomina Geographica Flandrica (since 1928);
J. Vannérus "Chronique de Toponymie: Rhénanie," in REA
35, 1933, 419-428; H. Maryan Keltische u. Lateinische
Ortsnamen in der Rheinprovinz (inaccessible to me; cf.
Bull. de la Commission de Toponymie et Dialectologie 5,
1931, 117 n.1); geographical names are discussed among
others by E. Schröder Deutsche Namenkunde 1938. There
is a very large number of discussions of proper names
in Bull. Dict. Wallon (e.g. the river name Thièle, by
E. Muret, 17, 1922, 261-68). See also the items enumerated (221 Introduction) above, and add: R. Kleinpaul
Ortsnamen im Deutschen (Göschen Sammlung, 1912) cf. REA
15, 1913, 109-110.

223   Divine Names

Remark:

    In this item m. stands for matronae, matres and
the like. On the cult of the matronae see Ernst Bickel
BJ 143-144, 1938-39, 209-220; id. Festschrift für Oxé,
Darmstadt 1938, 164-169; J. de Vries in Tijdsr. voor
nederlandsche Taal- en Letterkunde 50, 1931, 85-125;
id., Altgermanische Religionsgeschichte 1, 1935, 188-
210; H. Güntert Altgerm. Glaube 1937 (reviewed in GGA
200, 1938, 81 ff., DLZ 59, 1938, 1567 ff.); Hahl in
Arch. Inst. 6th Internat. Congress 1939, 564-565 ("to
appear in full in BJ"); Heichelheim in P-W s.v. Matronae; W. Heiligendorf Der Keltische Matronenkultus
und seine Fortentwicklung im deutschen Mythos, Form
und Geist 33, Diss. Greifswald 1934; M. Ihm in BJ 83,
1887, pp.1 ff.; Johansson in Skr. utg. av Hum. Veten-
skaps Samfundet i Uppsala 20, 1917 (see the summary by
A. Cuny REA 22, 1920, 310-311; cf. Meillet MSL 21, 249);
Koethe RA 10, 1937, 208-09 (sees the extent of the matronae as the boundary line between the Vbii and Treueri);
Lambrechts Ant. Cl. 7, 1938, 380 (the cult of three
mother goddesses in a group peculiar to Germ. Inf.);
H. Lehner BJ 135, 1930, 1-48; id., ib. 125, 1919, 75-162

Divine Names

(on Gebrinius, Vacallinehae, cf. CIL 13.7951-7964, 8003a,
12035, 12037, 12039 etc.); id., with W. Bader, 136-137,
1932, 136-154; F.N. Robinson in ERE 4, 1911, 406-411,
and in Oxford Class. Dict. 1949, s.v. Deae Matres; M.
Siebourg de Suleuis Campestribus Fatis diss. Bonn 1886;
id., BJ 138, 1933, 103-129 (also 113 on Gabrinius);
J. Weisweiler ZfCPh 21, 1939, 205-279 (especially 217
ff.), cf. PhW 61, 1941, 334; but the evidence, to any
unprejudiced observer, is entirely against the Germanic
origin of the cult of the Matronae (pace Altheim-Mattingly
453-4), cf. REA 22, 1920, 56.

It is well to call attention to the forms that h
frequently takes in these matronae-inscc., e.g. ⟨ (Aser-
icinehae 7978-79, 7981); ⟨(he) 7854; ⟨(h) 7851. On
the interpretation of the various endings -nehae,
-henae and on the value of -h- (in some places certainly χ) cf. Gutenbrunner Götternamen pp.132-145, 188.

For early Germanic religion in general, cf. AJA
42, 1938, 579 (Nixibus sanctis; cf. dis genibus and 243
below); Drexel in RGKBer. 14, 1922 [1923], 1-68 (reviewed by Wissowa PhW 44, 1924, 712; cf. Gutenbrunner
22 n.2); G. Dumézil Mythes et dieux des Germains (Mythes
et Religions 1, Leroux Paris 1939; reviewed in EC 4,
1948, 143-146); S. Gutenbrunner Die Germanische Götternamen der antiken Inschriften, Niemeyer Halle 1936
(Rheinische Beiträge und Hülfsbücher zur germ. Philologie
u. Volkskunde, Bd. 24) reviewed by H. Arntz Germania 21,
1937, 54-55; Heichelheim in P-W s.v. Tierdämonen; Karl
Helm Altgermanische Religionsgeschichte vol. 1, Heidelberg 1913; vol. 2, 1937; F. Jostes Sonnenwende (vol. 1
Die Religion der Keltogermanen, Munich 1926; reviewed
unfavorably by Heusler DLZ 1927, 298); Koethe in RGKBer.
23, 1933 [1934], 10-108; von Leers in Nordische Welt
May 1935 (on pagan deities in Frisia), cf. PhW 55, 1935,
946; von der Leyen Götter der Germanen 1938, 72-122;
G. Neckel Der Gott Balder, Dortmund 1920; A.N. Newell
in Greece and Rome 3, 1934, 74-84; W. Schleiermacher
in RGKBer. 23, 1933 [1934], 109-143; H. Schneider Die
Götter der Germanen, Tübingen 1938 (cf. Geistige Arbeit
1939, no.14); F.R. Schröder Quellenbuch zur Germ. Religionsgeschichte Berlin 1933 (cf. NTS 7, 1934, 424);
M. Siebourg BJ 140-141, 1936, 422-428 (cf. RA 10, 1937,
332). Byvanck Exc. Rom. 2, 1935, pp.535-571 gives many
valuable references.

Divine Names

E.A. Philippson MLN 65, 1950, 462-65; Prähistorische
Rassenkunde und Germanische Religionsgeschichte (Monat-
shefte für deutschen Unterricht 32, 1940, 241-265); id.
the three Matres or Matronae (Michigan Alumnus Quarterly
Review 53, 1946, 73-79); id. Der germanische Mütter- und
Matronenkulten am Niederrhein (Germanic Review 19, 1944,
81-142); Usener RhM 58, 1903, 1-47 and 161-208 and 321-
362; the review of Dumézil by Heiermeier IF 59, 1944,
115-116 (Tiwaz: Thingsus: Mars); for the variants matribus, matris, matrabus see TLL s.v. 443.61 - 444.27 (not
divine names only, but also the common noun), cf. matro-
nis 483.66 (but contrast -ona in Epŏna, Diuŏna; -ōna in
Local names e.g. Verona); Bickel RhM 87, 1938, 193-241;
id. ib. 88, 1939, 384; E. Maas Heilige Nacht Germ. 12,
1928, 59-69 (cf. REA 32, 1930, 253-4; Bede de temp. rat.
15 de mensibus Anglorum has gentili uocabulo modranicht);
Rostovtzeff BSAF 1925, 205-211; cf. Schumacher Festschrift
1930, 249-253 on Matronae (: Parcae), see REA 34, 1932,
47 (cf. Bibliogr. Lorraine 1930, 97); Siebourg BJ 140-
141, 1936, 425 discusses ollo- (as Keltic) in 13.6751,
7280; H. Hommel Die Hauptgottheiten der Germanen bei
Tacitus in Archiv für Religionswissenschaft 37, 1941,
144-173. I know of E. Peterich Kl. Mythologie: Götter
und Helden der Germanen, 1938; E. Jung Germ. Götter,
1939; W. Baetke Religion der Germanen in Quellenzeug-
nissen, 1937, only from APh 14, 1939 [1941], 352-361.

Abiamarcae m. 7898, cf.
Ambiomarci (-ae?) 7789;
abi is for ambi-

Abirēnes m. 8492; see 221
above

Aduernus (i.e. Aru-) 8164;
v. also Ar-; AcS 3.
700,3

Aeques Note xlviii above
(Utrecht)

Aflims 8157, Afliabus m.
8211, both dat. pl.
Cf. Eifel-gau, i.e.

pagus Eiflensis (Guten-
brunner 162; AcS 3.646,
53), cf. Aquil-; or
equo- iguo-, see Appen-
dix (?); cf. Iflibus
8520; to be compared
with Ἀπόλλων Glotta
13, 1924, 242 n.1

Ahinehiae m. 8845

Ahueccanae (or -iae) 8161
cf. Octocannae, Secca-
nehae

?Aianoua R.509 (8728)

Divine Names

Alabuandus see Note
xlviii above

Alaferhuiae 7862 (-ph-
for -f-?) with Suppl.
12012, F.303, R.3082

Alagabiae m. 8529; Ollo-
236 below

[Alaisiagae duae R.1855,
-ae- 2440; JRS 11,
1921, 237.6]

Albruna Tac. G. 8 (v.l.
Aurinia) Germ. 12,
1940, 270-71

Alateiuia 8606; cf. teiua
(Negau) PID vol. 2,
2*, and possibly
Elitiuae m. (82), but
hardly Alateruiae m.
Note xlv A? Cf. also
Finnish Runkoteivas
(I.Eu. *deiuo-), see
Gr. d. idg. Spr. u.
Altertumsk., Germanish
1.370 (IF 55, 1937,
147)

Albiahenae m. 7933-36,
cf. Albis (Elbe)?
Hardly to be read
Alh- (cf. 243; Gutten-
brunner 189)

Almauiahenae m. 12065

?Alus v. AcS 3.579

Ambi- v. also Abi-

Ambiomarc(i)ae (or
-marci?) 7789

Amnesahenae m. 12066

Ana[ ].bane (or -bante?)
dae (dat. sg.) 8004;
cf. FHRC 246.21, 32:
Ir. ana, buanann

Andrusteihiae m. 7995,
8212; N.145; BJ 135,
1930, 38. Perhaps for
Handru-, Chandru- (i.e.
Condru-, cf. Cantrus-
teihiae 3858, 7880,
and local name Condrus-
tis (220); so Annan-
eptae below (-f-?) in
8629 (cf. Cannanefates
220), Hannanef[(?) in
8219

Anesaminehae m. 7926

Annaneptiae m. (cf. 220
Cannanefates?) 8629,
cf. Andru-, Chandru-,
Condru-, Cantru-?

Ardbinna dea 7848

Arsacis paternis siue
maternis 8630, cf. 221
above, 237 below. Are-
saces 7252. Not Par-
thian? Or read M]arsa-
cis?

Aruernus 7845, 8235, 8579,
8709; see also Ad-, and
cf. 150 and 158 (s.v.
uassogalate) above

Aruagastiae m. 7855; for
Hari(a)-, cf. harixasti
at Negau (PID vol.2, 2*)

Asericinaehae m. 7981,
-ec- 7978-79; hi in
7981 is Ꞔ . Cf. the
personal name Aseriecix
224 below

Divine Names

Atufrafinehae 7984-89

Audrinehae m. F.280 (d),
282-84, 286; 285 (-th-);
Autriahenae 281; REA
32, 1930, 253

Aueha 8161

Aufaniae m. 7897, 7920-22,
8021-22, 8213-14, 8530,
8724, 11983-996, N.146-
182; AE 1939.235, F.256;
Lehner Steindenkm. 299;
BJ 135, 1930, 1-37;
136-7, 1932, 73-74; in
Spain CIL 2.5413, Lugd.
13.1766, Germ. Sup.
6665; in all nearly
seventy items.
Compared with Latin
uber by d'Arbois de
Jubainville RC 2,
1873-75, 111 (cf. Walde
ed. 2, s.v.)

?Auiaitinehae m. 8531
(item Rum[a]nehae)

?Auiua[m. 7866

Aumenahenae m. 8215,
12054

?Aurinia v. Albruna

Autr- v. Audr-

Aχsinginehae m. 8216.
Cf. Vihansa 213, Ven.
·a· hsu·s·? Or Asci-
(Acsi-)? Or Excing-?

Bacurdus 8166-67

Baduhenna Tac. A 4.73; cf.
Ir. Badhbh (a goddess
of war, Cormac's gloss-
ary ed. Stokes p.25
and n. ad loc., FHRC 3.
247,21); for bodu-

[?Baldruus see Note
xlviii]

[Baudihillia JRS 11, 1921,
237.6]

[Beda R.2440]

Be]rguiahenae 12014,
Ber]guinehae(?) m.
7878 (or Guinehae,
Cu-?), cf. sq. (and
note also Bergusia 181)

Berhuiahenae m. 12013

??Biausius (Mercurius)
8726 (so AcS 1.415) is
a misreading; but the
correct text is uncer-
tain (Eriausius R.3353;
or Friausius?)

[Boruoboendoa(?) Note
xlviii]

Boudunn[eae or -ehae]
m. 8217

Brittae m. 8631-32; in
8632 the epithet (part-
ly illegible) may have
been Marsacae

]bus 8532, 8539;]iabu[
8708, presumably all
dat. pl. f. (i.e. dedi-
cations to m., but see
Lugoues below)

Buronina 8775

Divine Names

C[m. 7950

Caimineae m. 7969; cf.
gloss *caminus 207
above

Campestres N.183; R.1869;
Byv. 2.1471, 1473-74;
CIL 6.31140, 31158

[Camulus 8701 (dedication
by Remi)]

Kannanefates m. (v.l. H-
or Hi-) 8219, cf. An-
nan- above?

Cantrusteihiae m. 7880
(cf. 3585, Belgica),
i.e. Condru-? (C- for
Ch-) cf. Chandru-
below, and Andrustei-
hiae (i.e. Handru-)
7995; and local name
Condrust- (221)

[Cartouallenses m. Byv.
2.1575]

]cdonib[8026 (sc. matron-
is)

Chandrumanehae (v.l. Gh-)
7968; cf. Andru-, Cantru-
(7880, 7995; 3585 [Belg.]
and local name (221) Con-
drustis; possibly Ha[ṇ(?)
... m. 7847?

Channinae m. AE 1945.5

Channinus 7781

Chuchinehae m., v. Cu-

Cissonius 8237

Cobba v. Note xlviii
above, 236 below

Cocidius R.1862, 1872

[Couentina R.1857, 1845,
1848, 1985, 1987; see
Note xlv B]

Cuchenehae m. 7923-24,
written Chuch- 12008-
90; cf. C[7950 (if
to be restores C[u-
or C[huchinehae]) and
7878 Guinehae (Cu-?),
but v. Berguinehae.
Cf. mod. Chuchenheim
(TLL)

Deana 12048; cf. 243 be-
low

[D(i)eusoniensis, Dieu-
senensis as epithet
of Hercules, num.
Postumus, cf. 221]

Diginibus (dat. pl.)
8176; cf. Digenibus
82, and perhaps Nixi-
bus 243

[Domesticus IOM 8718]
-ae (matres) N.182

Duspro (-y-?) dat. sg.
(Apollini) 8607

]ehis m. 7983

]enis m. 8030

Divine Names

Epona 6.31141, 3.788

[Ercouleus, Erec- Note
  xlviii (Utrecht)]

?Eriausius v. Biausius

[?Esus v. Mars below]

Etrahenae m. 7890, Ettra-
  7895 (for Ettra- or
  Ethra-(?), Gutenbrunner
  191

]euthungae m. 8225 (or
  Eu-?)

Fachinehae m. 7830, -eihae
  7829, Fahineihae 7970

Fernouineae 7980

[Fersomaris v. Note xlv B]

[Fimmilena R.2440]

[Formanus R.2858, cf.
  R.2704?]

[Fortuna Gubernatrix 7792]

[Friagabis JRS 11, 1921,
  237.6]

?Friausius see Biausius

Frisauae m. 8633, cf.
  local names

Fr. liaup[(Mercurius)
  8859, cf. Friausius(?)
  above; but more likely
  Fr. Liaup (both per-
  sonal?)

Gabiae m. 7856,]iabus
  7780; 7937-40, 8192,
  8612, F.273, Cab-
  7950; Gabia dea 7867?

Gantunae 8218, if a div-
  ine name; R.2308,
  2310, 2311. But see
  Notes xlvi, xlix

[Garmangabis R.1864, EE
  9.1135]

Gauadiae m. 7885-88, 7984,
  8536; -s- 12067, R.3149

Gebrin(n)ius N.186-195;
  cf. Germ. 16, 1932,
  104-8; BJ 135, 1930,
  19 ff. (no.45-52), 136-
  37, 1932, 145 (no.80);
  138, 1933, 113; cf. AE
  1930.19; 1931.11; 1939,
  p.306; ZfCPh 20, 1936,
  391

?Ger]manae m. 8224, cf.
  7.5

Gesahenae m. 7889, 7895,
  7957(?), 8491, 8496;
  Cesahenae 7890. Cf.
  Gesacus 213 above; v.l.
  at 7889 is Gesaienae,
  but i is probably a
  misreading of ꝉ h (cf.
  7890)

Ghandrumanehae v. Chandru-

Grannus 7975, 8007, 8712,
  10036.60; cf. 224?

Gratich[iae] m. 7971; cf.
  Ratheih(i)ae 7972;
  ?Gratius *1326 (Byv.
  2.198)

Guinehae (Cu-?) 7878, but
v. Cuchenehae, Berguin-
ehae

dea H. Lucena 8661, cf.
6761; read perhaps
Hluðena?

Haeua 8705 (hardly for
Hebe?); Heaua (de
Vries), Haiua (Helm 1,
301), cf. Caiua 213
above

Halamard[us] (Mars) 8707

Hamauehiae m. 7864, 12072;
cf. 7847? R.3155

?Han[m. 7847, see Hamaue-
hae and Chandrumanehae,
Channinus, or any of
the names beginning with
An-

Hariasa 8185

[Harimella 7.1065; cf. ZfD
Alt 63, 1926, 19-22;
KZ 64, 1937, 269]

Helliuesa 8161

Herclinti (dat. sg.) 8188,
cf. 7693 and 6.31158
(-en-)

Hiannanef(ates) or Hann-
m., v. Kannanefates
(C-)

Hiheraiae(?) m. (v.l.
-apae) 7900

Hludana 8611, 8830,
8723(?), Hluðena 7944;

hence in 8661 possibly
read Hlu- for H.Lucena(?)

[Huiteres, Vh-, Huet- see
Note xlv B above, Ros-
cher Lex. s.v.]

Ianehiae m. (v.l. Lan-)
7976

Idban[ae] Gabiae(?) 7867
(v.l. Idbangabis, deae
Idbans Gabiae dat. sg.
lapis; Idian- Guten-
brunner 62)

Ifles (n. pl.) 8520, cf.
Afliae

Ineae m. 8147; cf. Inui
Isid. 8.11.103 (FHRC
194.12), i.q. Gaulish
dusii?

Ise]nbucaega REA 34, 1932,
417; AE 1933.157; cf.
Mnem. 5, 1937, 318-20;
N.256 reads -euc-;
Gutenbrunner 110 (-aega
Iber.), de Vries 1,
1935, 207 (with plate 8)

Iulineihiae m. 7882 (cf.
221)

[Iuno Regina 8623, 8625;
dea Regina 8518]

[Iuno Virtutis 8193; for
Virtus i.q. Vagdauer-
custis see Germ. 22,
1938, p.102, rejected
ib. p.253]

[Iunones: 7860, 7920,
8158, 8192, 8612, 8622]

Divine Names

[Iuppiter: saepe, v.
R.2852-3009]

Lanehiae v. Ian-; Or]lan-
Gutenbrunner 171

Λῆνος IG 14.2562,3 (Kob-
lenz); cf. F.254 (13.
7778); Lenus EE 9.1009

?Leua cf. 221 above Leue-
fano

Leud[(Mercurius?) 7859,
(Hlud-, Hleud-?) but
cf. sq.

Leudinae m. 12020, Lehner
Steindenkm. 365; cf.
RA 12, 1920, 352

Liuicus (Apollo) 8006, cf.
local name Leuaci?

[Lobbon(n)us(?) Note
xlviii; cf. Lubicae?
Gutenbrunner 65-66]

Lubicae m. 8220 (hardly
for Lyb-)

?Lucena v. H. dea (and
also Hluθena) 8661

Lucretiae deae 8171, F.362,
cf. REA 32, 1930, 252-
53

Lugoues(?), vix.]uibus
8026; but the dedica-
tion may be to m. do-
mesticae rather (cf.
8023-25); however
Jullian REA 18, 1916,
63 (following Loth, see

Lugdunensis Introduc-
tion above) would see
(Iunones) Lucinae in
Lougiae (2.5797, 13.
2849), Lugoues

[Luna 8812; deus Luna
F.164]

[Lunus (masc.) see Note
xlviii (Utrecht)]

Macniacus (Mercurius) see
Note xlv B, Byv. 1.
1416, 147; cf. 12.
2373

Magusanus 8010, 8610, 8492,
8705, 8771, 8777; 6.
31162, cf. 7.1090 (Tun-
gri); 13.10027,212
(Tongern, Bonn, Köln,
Grimlinghausen); also
at Utrecht (Mac-), see
Note xlviii above; and
on coins of Postumus,
Cohen 6.29, 129-30.
Germanic according to
Lambrechts Ant. cl. 7,
1938, 373 n.1

Mahalinehae (m.) 8492; cf.
sq.

Mahlinehae m. 8221; Germ.
19, 1935, 132; 21, 1937,
55 n.4; N.241 cf. AJA
42, 1938, 579

Maluisae 8208, 8598

]manis (m.) Suebis 8224,
v. also Suebae, Ger-
manae

Mannus Tac. G 2.3

?Mars Esus. The insc. CIL 13.1328* is now accepted as genuine (Finke in Oxé Festschrift, Darmstadt 1938, pp.122-24; R.723). The first line appears to read Mar Esui (or et Sui?), for which Oxé (Germ. 11, 1937, 31-33, cf. REA 32, 1930, 250) would read Matribus et Suleuiis, Finke Mar(ti) e(t) Sul(sigiis), but for the latter we have as yet only the writing Xulsigiae (F.21); AE 1939, p.316. A u-stem? Cf. 170 above

[Maponus R.1984 (Brit.)]

?Marsacae m. 8630, 8632 (v. Brittae above); but in 8630 M- is lacking, and in 8632 -rs- quite uncertain (-x-? -xi-?)

Masanae m. 8223

matres, matrae, matronae; on the distribution of dedications to these goddesses, and on their general character, see the Introd. to 223 above and the references given there; add R.1858 (tramarinae); N.221; R. p.324 (3069 sq.), Gutenbrunner 120

??Mauiaitinehae m. 8531; cf. Aviait- and v. Gutenbrunner 178

?Maxacae v. Marsacae

Medicinis (d.pl.) 832

Mediotautehae m. 8222

[Menmanhia 6.31178, Dessau 4747]

[Mopates m. suae 8725 (dedicated by ciuis Neruius), cf. Agedemopas, Gatpas, Esumopas for the ending]

Nait(i)enae m. 12068, R.3163, G.194

Nahalennia 8498-99 (-aenn- and -n- for -enn-), 8776, 8779-80, 8782-97, 8799-8803; interpreted (e.g. by Cumont, Comment la Belgique fut romanisée, p.28) as a "Keltic"(!) "goddess of navigation"(!), Germanic according to Grenier in Frank 3.556; Jullian's notion (Basque Néhe!) REA 3, 1901, 211-12 is impossible

Nersihenae m. 7883

Nerthus f. Tac. G 40.2; cf. Kluge Urg. 31, 35; Bickel BJ 139, 1934, 8-10

[Neruiorum genius N.185]

[Noricae m. 8813; perhaps the same as Nixae, cf. Germ. 18, 1938, 216-17 and 243 below]

Divine Names

[Numidae m. N.196; but cf.
Nimid- insc. 86 above]

Ocelus EE 9.1009

[Olist[m. Byv. 2.1575]

Octocannae m. 8571-77; cf.
Sec-, A]huec-

[Quadruuiae 7928, 8240-
43, 8638, 8637; though
this word is Latin it
is cited here (a) for
comparison with Petro-
mantalum 179 above;
(b) because it is pos-
sible that the divine
name Huitires, Hueteres,
Vheteri Note xlv B a-
bove, may conceal a
related Germanic form;
cf. Ettrahenae (Vet-?)
above, and perhaps the
local name Vetera i.e.
"cross-roads"? Local
names containing the
numeral "four" are not
rare. In 8638 an old
but poor reading has
matribus Quadriburg[
(for Quadrubiis)]

Ratheih(i)ae m. 7972, but
cf. Gratichiae, and for
g-: gr- see PID 2.473

Regina (i.e. Iuno) 8518,
formerly mis-read Rega
dea

Renahae (or]renaeae) m.
F.315

Requaliuahanus 8512; Boi-
sacq 273, G. p.69
(Brugmann Grds. 2 i 83)

Rhenus 7790-91; on the
magical powers attrib-
uted to the Rhine see
FHRC 1, 7.24 (and other
passages in Zwicker's
Index)

Ricagambeda 7.1072

?Roin[ ]iae (matronae?)
8702, AcS 2.1224; but
the reading is doubtful

?Ro]smert[a see Introd.
above; not to be read
'Οδυσσεύς (cf. Tac. G 3)
or Vlyxes (REA 14,
1912, 283-4)!

Rumanehae m. 7869, 7927(?),
7973, 8027-28, 8148-49,
8531, F.264; written
-mn- in 8531, Rumon-(?)
in 8148 (cf. Goth Rum-
oneis?), Roman[in
7973

Saitchamimis (d.pl.) m.
7916 (v.l. -ms), writ-
ten Saitham (-ia[bus)
7915

[Salutares fortunae 7994]

Sandraudiga 8774

??Saxanus (Hercules) 7820;
cf. 236 below

?Se[(or Sii[?) 7794

Seccanehae m. 8846 (cf.
A]hueccaniae 8161?)

Divine Names

[Semele et Sorores eius
8244]

Setuaianus AE 1941.22

Sii[v. Se[

Suebae m. (strictly eth-
nic, see 241 below)
8224, 8225, 8497; cf.
Gutenbrunner 145, 158.
So in 8224]manis Sue-
bis is most likely
Ger], though other
names contain -man- or
the like (-an-), e.g.
Chandrumanehae, Men-
manhia, Masanae, Aufan-
iae. In no event is
manissuebis one word.
Again, in 8225 Euthun-
gabus (or T]euth-?) is
an ethnicon (Guten-
brunner ll.cc.)

Suleuiae m. 7725, 8247,
12055-56; R.3516; cf.
6.767-68, 31140-41,
31145-46, 31148-49,
31161, Byv. 2.1465-68,
1470-74; 6.31171,
31174-75; on 13.1328* v.
Mars Esus above; Peder-
sen 2.15; G. 195-198;
AE 1928.89; REA 32,
1930, 250; Germ. 11,
1927, 31-33

?S]un[i]cia AcS 2.1668,
but the insc. 13.7870
has Vncia; yet cf. sq.

Sunuχsalis (cf. 221 above
Sunuci?) 7858, 8248,
12004, Byv. 2.1548,
F.261, BJ 135, 1930,
56; N.199; written -cs-

7912, -x- 7917, 7795,
8546, and (unless
-x[s- i.e. -χ[s-) also
in 12011; -sallis 7912.
Cf. Sunix[7904; add.
to 7917; Behn Kat. R-G
Central-Museums no.2,
1910, p.113.788. In
13.8546 we have dae Sun-
xalis, where dae is dat.
sg. fem. (cf. 3664). Cf.
Gutenbrunner 87, Lehner
23, P-W s.v.

[(Mercurius) Susurrio
12005, cf. Ἑρμῆς ψιθ-
υριστής, but perhaps
identified with Wuotan
Omi, see notes ad loc.]

[Talliatium genius 7777-
78]

[Tamfana (in Germ. Magna)
Tac. A 1.51; but cf.
the difficult local
name Leuefano 221 a-
bove?]

Teniauehae m. 8847

T[....] Batau[o]r[um 7.
350, usually read
T[errae]

T]euthungae m., see Euth-
ungae and Suebae

Teχtumeihae 7849, 7899

[Thingsus R.2440, Dessau
4760; cf. Note xlv B
above; cf. Kluge Urg.
34; Tincsus 224 below]

Titica dea 8853 (Titaca?);
cf. 7624, R.2299, 3535

Divine Names

[Treuerae m. 8634, see
211 above]

[Triuiae uiae semitae
8243]

Tuisto (father of Mannus)
Tac. G 2.3; cf. HThR
35, 1942, 83 on Skt.
tvaṣṭr

?Tummaestiae m. 7902 (read
Teχ]tum-?)

Tutela 8251, -lla N.184

Vabusoa see Note xlviii
above (Utrecht)

Vaccal- and Vacallinehae
m. 7952, 8003a, 12018,
12020, 12023-28, 12030-
32, 12033 (or -1-?),
12034-35, 12037-39;
F.257, 264(?), 266-67,
270-72; Lehner, Stein-
denkemäler...Bonn 361,
363, 376, 379, 380,
383-84, 388-92, 394-
403, 405-07, 417, 1434-
48; written -l- (not
-ll-) 7951, 7953, 12021,
Lehner 387, 404; R.3178,
3181-82
    See also Voc-, and
cf. the local name
Vacalus, Vahalis 221
above; BJ 125, 1919,
75-162 (REA 25, 1923,
63)

Vaeau[m. 8665

Vagdauercustis 8662, 8702-
3, 8805, 12057, AE
1935.163 (-dae-); cf.

EE 9.1124 (Note xlv B
above), see Germ. 22,
1938, 100-104, 252-253;
24, 1940, 255-266; and
cf. Iuno Virtutis, Vir-
tus; R.450; Mnem. 5,
1937, 318-30; Germ. 24,
1940, 255-66 (AE 1941
p.327); Pannonia 1935.
184

Vallabneihiae m. 8226,
Valabneiae 8227; cf. sq.

Vallamaeneihiae 8228; if
ae (i.e. e) is anapty-
ctic, we have mn: bn
(un), cf. Gram.

?Vanamian(i)ae 12069

Vapthiae m. 8841

Varneno F.262, cf. Varnenus
260; i.e. -ōn- : -o-stem

Vataranehae m. 7903-05;
cf. Veter-; but 7904
has Va]- (i.e. Taran-
ehae?) and 7903 has
V]a-

Vatuiae m. (-uims d.pl.,
as well as -uiabus)
7861a, 7883-4, 7893,
7891-93, 8510

Vdrauarinehae m. 8229,
12069, R.3197; 8147
doubtful

[Veleda see 220, 224; G.
182]

[Vellaunus EE 9.1009, Byv.
2.1416, 1417; cf. also
Macniacus above, with
Velauni PID 1, 364;

Divine Names

Οὐελαῦνοι 80 above,
Vellauus pagus 221; and
Note xlv B]

[Vesta 8642, 8729]

Vesuniahenae m. 7850-54
(but 7053 doubtful),
7925; Pedersen 1, 74;
G.192

Veterahenae m. 7823, 7911;
but Veteranehae 7821-
22, 7906-7910. Cf. the
local name Vetera (221),
divine name Vataranehae
(above); REA 29, 1927,
311-12; and the divine
name Veteres, Huiteres
Note xlv B above

]uibus 8026, v. Lugoues(?)

[Victoria 8252, 8492; V.
Francica Byv. 2.465]

Vihansa (Tungri, see 213
above)

Viradecdis 8815; cf. 213
above, CIL 13 i p.574;
Viradectis in 213, cf.
ZfRPh 54, 1934, 218-
220; Hermeneus 12, 1940,
96-98 (Kl. Bibl. 12,
1940 [1941], 22); Keune
in Roscher s.v.; REA 15,
1913, 78 and 455; G.108;
RG Korrbl. 1913, 9-35;

R.2253; Mnem. 8, 1939-
-40, 58-64, 244-254 (AE
1940 p.240); see also
236, 243 below. The
distribution of the
cult ranges from Birrens
through Vechten and
Mainz to Trebur

Virtus 8514, F.363; cf.
R.2227, 2319, 2846,
3437, 3561, 3562; see
also Iuno Virtutis,
Vagdauercustis above

Vlauhinehae m. 7932 (v.l.
Vlatu-)

?Vncia 7870, according to
some to be read Sunucia
(or -icia); cf. AcS 2.
1668, 3.30; cf. perhaps
Vruncis 235?

[Vnseni EE 9.1124, see
Note xlv B above, cf.
Vagdauercustis]

Vocalline(i)hae 12022,
12029; Lehner Stein-
denkm. 367, 369-371,
1433; note Voc- beside
Vacallinehae q.v. above

[Volkanus 3593]

?Xehndea 8155 (Sechtem)

?Xulsigiae v. Mars Esus
above

Personal Names

For sources see 211 above; something may be gleaned from Martin Bang Die Germanen im römischen Dienst, Berlin 1906; S. Gutenbrunner in Zts f. Mundartsforschung 13, 1937, 76; E. Ritterling Fasti des röm. Deutschland, Vienna 1932; E. Stein Die Kaiserlichen Beamten...im röm. Deutschland, Vienna 1932; G. Werle Die ältesten germ. Personennamen, 1910; A. Wienicke Keltisches Söldnertum im Mittelmeerwelt, Diss. Breslau, 1927; Nesselhauf Diplomata (CIL 16, 1936).

224

Aba|cluuii 10010.1814

?Abilicedo 10010.11 (for Bill-?)

Abud(o)s 10010.15

Abruna R.1927 (cf. Albruna Wackernagel's reading at Tac. G 8.3?)

Abuta 7964

Acacua 8834

Acconius 8226

Acirgi Byv. 2.361

Acis 7932

Aclonius 13 vi p.18, no.42

Actius R.1990, cf. 6. 20216 (Byv. 2.1318)

⟨Actumerus (v.l. Cat-) Tac. A 11, 16-17⟩

?Acus 8691

Acutius 6.3348

[Adarus 8670]

Adaucius (-g-) 10006.2

?Admetus F.372

Adnamatia 8819; -ius N.187, -ius Gal(l)icanus 8357

Adraxius 10027.2

Aebutia 8358

Aerio (-onis) 8656

Aesarius Fort. v. Germ. 31

Aeto 7923, [8097]

Aex[10017.112

Agausus 10001.29

Agisiaca 8820

Agisilia 8545

Agorix 10027.3 (R.4600)

Personal Names

Agra[R.2433

Agu[10010.65

Ai[8691

Aiacius (mango) 8348

??Ailicotdius 10006.170

Aiua F.270, N.247

Aius F.372

?Aixixi 10010.3301a

Aladius 10017.124; -tus 10010.74

[Albanius (ala Indiana) Treuerus 8519, cf. N.160]

Albanus (Vbius) 2613, Albanus 8337

Albinus 2611, F.265, N.266

Alcidicus, Vollgraff Dijk van Drusus (in Med. Kon. Ned. Akad., Afd. Letterk., NR 1, 12, 1938) p.2, cf. REA 42, 1940, 686, but see AE 1939.106, cf. 129 (C[h]alcidicus), Germ. 23, 1939, 31

Alcimachus R.2399

Aleb[o 7806

Alfius 10015.100

Allectius 12051

Allius 8739, N.237; cf. Alio 10001.347

Allua 8229

Almer[10010.3073b

Alpius see Vlpius

?Altaulus 10010.3068

Alus[8441

Alutiraius 10017.137; Holder compares Pliny 3.130 Alutrenses (Liburnian)

†Aluuefa Byv. 2.3 cf. Arnefa (local name 234)

Amacis 10010.3292c

Amaio 8822

Amandinius N.189

Amarius 10001.36; 10010.101

Ambacthius 8788 (unless a common noun)

Ambiorix (Eburones) cl., BG 5.24.4; C p.573

Amilo N.249, 250

Amma 8152, cf. 3620

Ammaca 7929; -cius 8779

Ammaeus 8108

Ammaua 8705

Ammausius 7831, 8639

[Ammillius 10036.60]

Ammilusima Byv. 2.1379

Personal Names

Ammius 8803, 10017.143,
-ia N.255; cf. Sammius?

??Amnomieiius 7951; but
the reading is uncer-
tain (Am. Norui eiius
lapis)

Amrat[7859; cf. Amret-
outus 3991

Amusanus Byv. 2.1331

Amuro R.1854

An[10010.2120, Ana[
10017.146

Anaillius N.190

?Anailus Germ. 13, 1929,
132

Anaridus Rav. (Byv. 1,
p.579)

[Ancitatus R.4491]

?Andd[10006.115

?A]nnaeluci AcS 3.628

Annauso (-us) 7025 cf.
Annausonius 12.2206

Anneus 8813

Annius 3.14214

Annua 7905; cf. 10003.23,
10010.2122

Annusonius R.1768

Ansehis Rav. 5.31 (Henget?
Cf. ansis 240 below;
or ansa- 220 above)

Ansius 10027.5 (R.4599)

Antulla 8231, -us R.4601

Anu[10001.43; 10010.
2816b

Apa[10010.2123

[Aper 8035, 8607]

Apigianus Byv. 2.1195

Apius 10017.159, 10027.
216

Aponius, -ia Byv. 2.1204

Apra N.199

Aprianus 8512, -a 8525

Aprilio 8324, -ius R.1774

Aprilius 3.728, 13.738?

Apronius 7984, 8153, 8378,
10017.163; cf. -onianus
Byv. 2.1158

Aprus R.3583

]apurisscu[Byv. 2.363

Aquileia 7872

Aquilinus F.314

Aquilo AE 1941.87

Aquina F.295, -nius N.166

Aramo Byv. 2.178

[†Arauatius (Tunger) CIL
13 i p.574; Greg. Tur.
h.Fr. 2.5, cf. Arua-
tius 7577]

Personal Names

[Arcauius EE 9.1124]

?Arcus 10010.164

?Areli[10003.3

?Areui[AcS 3.678

Aribo 10010.3292

⟨Arminius Vell. 2.105;
  Tac. A. 2.9-10; 11.16;
  RhM 84, 1935, 17-18;
  Niedersachs. Jahrb.
  13, 1936, 235-37⟩

Aroastes Ven. Fort., Aro-
  gastus Lib. h.F.; see
  TLL s.v., Arbo- 214,
  237

Arrad[(Baetasius, Ripan-
  us) 6.31140, R.2380

Arragenus 8317

Arrius R.4598

[Arruntius 8833]

Arsulana 8268

Artesi[10010.3061d

Artis 8119

Aruania 8065

Aruo AE 1928.20 (for Auuo,
  i.e. Sammo?)

Arusenus 8066

Aryacus RGKBer 27, 1937,
  p.40

?Asauo 10010.176

Ascattinius 8780; cf.
  local names in Asci-

?Aseriecix 7904; cf. 223
  above

Aso Note xlvi above, REA
  18, 1916, 289

[Aspadius 8654; †Asp[(?)
  F.277]

Asprius N.167

?Assinno 10010.180

Assonius 8781

Atectius AcS 1.254,35;
  Att- 12538.1

Ateuus F.372, Ateius R.2417

Athama (m.) 8342

Atidenus 8627

[Atil(l)us (Vocontius)
  8761]

[Atissa 8096]

Atrectus 8342

Attalus Byv. 2.1470

Attarachus 8423

Attectius 12538.1

Attiganus 8845

?Attimua 10017.192

Attius R.1839, 1897 (cf.
  1840, 1842), Byv. 2.
  1467

Personal Names

Atto 7880, N.190

Attonius N.190; AE 1945.
13

]atuga[8119

Atusso 8238 (cf. Atussia
4159)

Aual[7897

?Audeo[10010.3283e

?Auentinus R.2286

Auia (Bataua) 8339

Auillia, -ius 8368

Auiscus 10010.3052

Auitianus 8066, 8658

Auitus 7860, 8050; -a
8066, 8368, 11982;
R.2379, 2381, 865; CIL
13 vi (1933) p.14,
no.32

Auonius Byv. 2.208

[Aulupor R.1818]

?Aurinia Tac. G 8.3

Auritus 10010.253

?]auruin[8163a

Auua N.245

?Auuo BJ 132, 1927, 188;
cf. AE 1928.20 (F.285),
also read Sammo

[Baccus (Thrax) 8318]

Baebius R.865, 2401

Baen[8008

?Baliens R.2390

⟨Βαιτόριξ Str. 7.1.4,
2910⟩

?Baluus R.2414

Banna 10027.190

Barbus Byv. 2.1.124

Basea 8415

Bassiana 7890, 8419, N.172,
-us N.168, 155

[Bassilas R.596]

Bassus 7795, 6.4337-38,
4342; 3, p.879; 1980;
R.4598

?Β[άτα]λος IG 14.2566,2

Bato 8824

Baudio R.1930

Beh[10010.3058

Belec[or Beli Icc[i
10027.97

Bella 7995

Bellanco 7819

Bellina 8559

Personal Names

Bellicus N.176, -cc-
  R.4601

]berenio Byv. 2.363

Bers[Byv. 2.1124

?Bertus AcS 3.854

Besius R.866

Bessula 8307, Bessus
  8312; cf. Byv. 2.1360

Betto R.524

Betu 10017.223

Betuinianus R.866

[Biarta 8312, v.l. Blarta]

Bienus 8341 (Viromanduus)
  8342, 8409; cf. num.
  157 above

Bilanu AcS 3.863

Bio 12086a

Bir[8470

?Birinico 10010.3064
  (Bell-?)

Bisa 8312

Bisicco 10017.224

Bisius (domo Brixsae)
  8733

[Bissula Auson. Biss. e.g.
  2.1; 4.2 (Suebian or
  German) cf. Vistlus
  AcS s.v.]

[Bititralus (Thrax) 8818]

Bitucarus 10010.318-19

Bituios 10010.321, -uos
  10010.320

Bituollus 10010.323

[Biturix 8092, 10017.226
  apparently a name]

Bitus (i.e. Vitus RGKBer.
  27, 1937 [1939], p.40)

Blandus Mnem. 6, 1938, 222
  cf. 8.2769(?), R.2278

Blarta 8312, v.l. Bia-

Blesio 1326* (Oud. Med.
  NS 8, 1928, 103)

]bltata 8737

⟨Boccus, Bochus 10036.19⟩

Bodaro (Utrecht, Note xlv
  above)

⟨Bodua[cus 10027.108⟩

⟨Boicalus (Ampsiuarius)
  Tac. A 13.55⟩

Boiorix (Cimber) Liv. per.
  67, Plut. Mar. 5.3,
  Florus 1.3 (3.3) 18;
  Oros. 5.16.20

Bonius Byv. 2.1209

Bonosa Byv. 2.1217

Bori 8188 (or Pirobori?)

[Borissus (Vindel.) 8320]

?Bouoririui 10010.3058a

Personal Names

[Bradua Byv. 2, p.258]

Brariatus 10006.95

Brato 8718 (or divine name?)

Brim[10010.353

Briganticus (Batauus) Tac. H 2.22, 4.70, 5.21; cf. num.

Brinno Tac. H 4.15

Britannicianus 8793, 8164a

[Brucetus Byv. 2.1465-66]

Bruttius 12058

Bubalus 8378

Bubens R.1818

Buc[8523

Bucca 10001.70

[?Bucrelim[AcS 1.627,40]

Bupu 10025.108-9

[Burcanius EE 9.1124]

Burdo Tac. h 1.58

Burgio 1326* (Oud. Med. NS 8, 1928, 103)

Burrius R.1844

[Burrus (Aniensis) 8284]

Burspra 8362, 8392

?Busenus 7920, hardly a divine name (cf. Buxenus 82 above)

Caballus Byv. 2.1343

Cabirus 8342, cf. Καβιριο 10027.255

?Cadndi 10010.3312c

Cadulinus 10010.3305

Cadunus R.2382

Caecina (Germ.) Tac. h 2.20-22

[Caelius 8648]

[Caesius (Sauaria) 8772]

Caesarix (G-?) Oros. 5. 16.20 (Cimber); cf. 174, 212 above

?Caicu 10010.3301

Calbanius 7882

Caldinius 8215, N.169

Caldius 7894

Callienius R.535

?Kaliunis AcS 1.700,43

Κάλωνος IG 14.2574,4

Callus 8607

Caluio R.570

Cam[8741, 12041

Personal Names

Camaidus 10017.393

Camilla 12048

Campa.t[R.3182 n.

[Campanius 7939, 8147]

Campanius Byv. 2.1136,
 -us 1209

Campester R.1848

Campilius 10001.79

[?Camppilus 8558, unless
 a local name]

Campusius R.710

Camula 7783

[Camurius Byv. 2.725]

Candida N.156a, -us N.166,
 241

Candidinius 7834, 8042,
 8373-4, 8719, 12080,
 F.296, N.163, R.2409,
 3076, 3931

Candidus 7.215, Byv. 2.
 1279

Candilonius 13 vi (1933)
 p.14, no.35

?Canicc(i)us AcS 1.717;
 10036.36a

Cann[Byv. 2.1468

Cannicus (g-) Frontin.
 strat. 2.4.7, Κυννίκ –
 ιος Plut. Crass. 11;
 cf. gloss 220?

Cannutius 8607

Cant[8442

Cantarus R.2379

Cantinus R.4598

[Cantius Byv. 2.1467]

Canto 10006.118

Capito 8238

Capitonia 7827

?Capnus 10010.445

Capurus R.1874

Caracco AcS 3.1090

[Carantius 8649, 8669]

[Caretis (gen.) 8593
 (domo Turo)]

?Careuus 10010.3280a

Caricus 10004.1

?Carilic[ib. 3279a

Carisius 8055

Carminius R.544

Carnunt[10017.258

Carpilius R.1921

Cart[10017.260, cf.
 Carto AcS 1.818

Carugenus 10027.14

Caruus F.304 (cf. 221)

Personal Names

Cascellius 8656

Cassius 8039, 8176, 8215,
8320, 8321, 8375,
8734, 11982, **F**.268

Casua (Vlpia) 8601

Catho[10001.86

?Catica AcS 1.841

Catonius 8588

Catranus AcS 3.1150

Cattara 10010.3282a

Catullinius 8216, -nus
10003.1

Catullus 8244, -a R.544

Catulus 8170

Catusso 8238

Catuuolcus cl., e.g. BG
5.24.4 (usually ex-
plained as *Haþu-wulfaz)

Cauonius 12038, R.3178

?Cebeus 10025.33

Ceionius Vell. 2.119.4

Cellius BJ 142, 1937, 267

Cellissus F.290

Celorius 7937

Celsinus F.268

Cen[8661

Cenicus 10010.2903d

Cennu[7780, cf. 10010.
532

[Cergaepur (Afr.) 8304]

Cersucus 10017.1045

Certilianus N.234

Certus N.168, 169

[Ceruuli 10026.73 (Ital.)]

Cesdius? F.372

?Cess[ib. 284

Cessorinius 8639

?Cexal[v. AcS 3.1211

Chalcidicus v. Alcidicus

Chalehenius 7976, appar-
ently written also
Cchallinius ib.; or
Hal-, Chal-?

Charioualda (Batauus) Tac.
A 2.11

Chartius R.2593

?Chirisophos F.317

Chiu[R.2433

Chleuuia 13.1882 (R.1278)

Chloreus R.2400

Cigemma 10010.557

Cilo N.175

Cimber F.366 (cf. REA 32,
1930, 255; Germ. 13,
1929, 132-8)

Personal Names

?Cimni 10010.3061g

]cinius 7836

Cinno[10006.123

?Cintusmus N.242 (or Cin-
    tus?)

Cipius 10027.17, R.4599

Cisso Byv. 2.1548

Cisson(1)us F.261, cf.
    R.711

?Citecianot[10001.365

Cittius Byv. 2.1206

[Ciuilis (Batauus) Tac. H
    1.59]

?Cixsun[7904 (or read
    Sunix, cf. 221, 223)

Claodicus (Cimber) Oros.
    5.16.20 (Hludihho AcS
    1.1045)

Claudius F.271, 297

[Claudius Labeo CIL 13 i
    p.573]

?Cm.enios 10001.451

Coail.a(?) 8321

Cocceius N.153, 3.806,
    Byv. 2.1207 (Noric.),
    8243

Cocceianus R.2417

Codunus 10001.97

?Coeiius 10010.3278e

Coeo[10011.314

[?Coil[10036.59]

Colonius F.287

?Colsi 10002.3

Cominius 8057, -ia N.199

Cominus (or -ius) AE 1938.
    77, i.q. 13.10027,219;
    see Germ. 21, 1937,
    275-6

?Comius AE 1928.21, but
    Cottius F.287

Comminius 8176

?Comurin[10010.3011a

Cons(i)us 10004.1

Copiritus 10027.193

[Coponius N.170 (Noricus)]

?Corilis AcS 1.1125

Corumbus 8337

?Coruus BJ 142, 1937, 196

Cosconianus R.1845; EE
    3185

Cotinus R.2364?

Cottius F.287 (but cf. AE
    1928.21)

Counertus see AcS 1.1055,1

?Couuiliu[AcS 1.1153

Cracinus 8511

Personal Names

Creperi 10027.224

Crotilo R.1983

Crotus R.1987

Cruptorix Tac. A 4.73

Cuasus(?) AcS 1.1180

Cullonius R.1434

Cumius 8521

Cu[ ]onius N.191

Cupitus 13 vi (1933) p.15, no.40

Curmillus 8352

?Curnus AcS 1.1203

Curtauius 7818

Cururio 8833

Cuspius R.1379

Daccius 8124, F.272, R.3182

Dacinus 8783

?Daciscus 2322

?Dacomot[AcS 1.1213

?Dacorius ib.

[Dacraio N.242 (Tribocus)]

Dagania 8279, 8414

Dagionius 7934

Dagonus 7934

[Dansala (al. Noric.) strictly a local name, 8308]

Dartoed[(?) AcS 1.1242

Dasaticenus Byv. 2.1124

[Dasius (Nor.) 8243]

[Dasmenus (Breuc.) 7801-2]

Dassiu(s) 8050, cf. R.1949.8a (p.455)

[Dasus 7801-2]

[?Dax[AcS 1.1245; cf. Daxna (i.e. Daχna?) 10010.761]

Deccius, -ia N.234; Deccius (Ticin.) 8287

Decminia 8072

Decol[7816

Decumidis RGKBer. 27, 1937, p.42

Degala 7227

[Dellius Byv. 2.p.329; cf. Germ. 21, 1937, 274-6, AE 1938.76]

Demionca 8342

Dento 10027.247

Deomarti 10010.771

Deoratus 10027.21

959

Personal Names

Deospor 8607

⟨Δευδόριξ (Sugamber) Str. 7.1.4, 292C⟩

?Diasenius AcS 1.1280

[?Điccius ib. 1281]

[Didil[(Thrax) 8524]

[Didius 12058; cf. R.1510]

Dignius 8378

?Dinia 7847 (or read Ate]-dinia?)

[Di[ui]χtus (Vocontius) 8671]

Dirmesus 8492 (or Dri-?)

Diuos 8606

Diχti 10017.365

?Dregenius (Vbius) F.352, MZ 23, 1928, p.85; ZfCPh 20, 1933-35, 391

Dribus 10010.3292

Drind[8109

Drousa 8171

]dubi[8581

Dubitatus N.187

[Dubius (Mediolan.) 8071]

Duco 8095

Ductus R.1991

?Duerretus F.372

Dugiti[IG 14.2573,9

Duhus R.1985

Duiau[10001.370

Dullius 10027.223

Dupal[8185

Durio R.1984, 10006.30

Durises 8311

[Duuius v. TLL Onom. 3. 263]

Ebon 10025.54

?Ebusius R.1434

]ecosco[8365

Ecua RGKBer. 27, 1937 [1939], p.38; cf. (-qu-) 10025.35b-g; Equasius R.4580-81 (Ecua-); 10025.36,54

Edistrus 8011

[Egrilius 8159]

Eldebaldus Rav. (Byv. 1. p.579)

Elicus AcS 1.1414

Elollcinna 8737

Eluadius R.2394

Eluissus 10017.340

?Emaicu(s) AcS 1.1433

Personal Names

†Emeterius 8331

]enepo 8295

Enteius R.4600; 10027.83

Epiens[7991

?Epon(ius) see AcS 1.1450

[Epta(centus) F.293]

?Erce 7967

Erdico AcS 1.1463

?Erepus F.372

?Ermuipia ib. 1464 (from
    CIR 194)

Erualio 8641

Erucius 8512 (or Fructus?)

Erucua (Vlpia) AcS 1.1466

Euali (gen.) 8422

Euesea AcS 1.1485

[Eupulus 8499]

Excingius (Vbius) 2613;
    Exscingius 10010.875

Exomna 8409

Exomnianius 8784

Exomnius 7932, 3.4465,
    F.266

[Exsochus i.e. -χs- F.366]

[?Fabius Valens C p.584]

[Faedus (Biturix) 8092]

Fahena 8572

Falco N.238

Fannia 8405, -ius Byv. 2.
    1182, cf. R.1860-61

Farsuleius 12035; cf.
    Fersomarus 223?

Farus(?) 7950

Fasta m. R.1922

Feldunius F.293

Feruesa N.241; cf. Z. f.
    Mundartsforsch. 13,
    1937, 73

Firmanus 7909 (cf. 8590,
    v.l. -marus?)

Firmus 11982

Filinus (Ph-?) N.256

Flaccinia 12024, -ius
    R.1846, 3.14214

Flaccinius 7.617, cf. Byv.
    2.1400

Flauius 7577, F.316, N.157,
    252, 256, -ia 149;
    R.1922-25, 1928

Flauus 8771, N.156, Flaus
    Mnem. 6, 1938, 222

Flaunus 7.541 (Byv. 2.
    1280)

Flettius 8786

Flossia 8218

Personal Names

Fledimella 8821

[Francus 8274, cf. R.1951]

Frapia 8525

†Fregadius CIL 13 1 p.574
(Tunger)

Freiatto 7916

Freiania 8396

Freiouerus see 214 above
(13.7036)

Friannius 8536

Friattius 8324, 8498
(Erilapis)

Friausio 8726, cf. 221

Frisus AcS 2.1237,5 (TS)
for Rrisus

Fritus AcS 1.1500

Fronto (Vbius) F.352,
N.175

Fruendus N.234?

Fua (lib.) 8338

Fucissius F.262

†Fugilo f. 8479-80

Fufius F.289

Fuscus N.237

Gabrillus 10001.76

Gabrius 8084

?Gadunus (T. |gad-?) N.255;
cf. 7.323

Gaesorix see Caesorix

Gailla N.172

[Gaisio (Afr.) 8806]

?Galeneti (dat.sg.f.)
8364

Galeta 8070

Gallianus 8810

[Gallicanus 8357)

Gallus 10.4862

[Gamidiahus R.2796]

[?Gamicus RGKBer. 27,
1937 (39), 49; γαμικός ?]

Gangusso 3596

Ganna (-icus) AcS 1.1982

Gannascus (Canninefas)
Tac. A 11.18; cf. Γάννα
"fatidica" Dio Cass.
67.5.3; Gannoduron 241

Gargilius F.372

?Garisianus 7833, but see
Madd-

Gastinasius 8565

[Gatus 8409, Viromanduus
8341-43]

Gauallianius N.171

Gauillius 3.14214

Personal Names

Gauius 7947, 8268; Byv. 2.
1044; cf. gloss 158

Gellius 6894

Gemellinus 8406

Gemellus 12022

Genalnius 6.3240 (Byv. 2.
1358)

Genetius 8228

Ge]nn[a(?) see AcS 3.2002.
1-2

Gennalo 8786

⟨Gennoboudes Mamertinus
Paneg. Max. 10; Geno-
baudes Greg. Tur. h.
Fr. 2.9⟩

Genucius 12006

Ger[8470

Germanio 8359; Germanilla
8268, Germanus 7577,
8281; 6.4337-4341,
4344; Germa[ni 10017.
430

Geron[8334

Gesatius 8346, -tus 8320

?Gescus AcS 1.2016 (for
Gesac-?)

Giamillus 10025.82

Gimmo 7819

⟨Girisonius (Obernburg)
Germ. 13, 1929, p.63⟩

[Glitius (Gallus) Byv.
2.684, cf. p.329]

Gracileius 3599

Gradonus 7950

Graecinius N.226

Granianus Byv. 2.490

Granius 8615; cf. 136,
211, 220

Gru[8586

[Gumattius 8806 (Afr?)]
Read as Traianus Iuc-
gumattius (Keltic,
Iugum-) by J.C. van
Slee Bijdr. voor vaderl.
Geschiedenis en Oud-
heidkunde 9, 1930, p.131

Hal- v. Chal-

[Haldacco see 211]

Haldauuo[nis] gen. 8340

Haldauonius 8068

Halenius F.303 (cf. 221
Hel-?)

[?Halotus see AcS 1.2049]

Haparonius 8354

Hari 10024.320

†Helacius F.259

[?Hellius 7693, cf. AcS
1.2051]

Personal Names

Helluesa 8161; cf. 223

?Hemata Byv. 2.363

Herculianus F.300

Hiannane f. 8219

Hinge[(or Ih-[(?)] for
    Ch-, C-?) 8683; not
    for Ingen-

Hitarinius 8791

Hostilius Byv. 2.1407

Hristo F.303, cf. R.4613.
    3, and see Germ. 9,
    1925, 119

Hucdionis (gen.) 8779

Hunicius (Vlpius) 7858

Hurmius R.1874

Iabe[10017.454

Iabitiana 7837

Ialdania 8387 (read Hald-?)

Ialehenius 7976

?Iamnia AcS 2.8 (Iamuua?)

Ianda (L-?) 8632

Ianetus Ant. Cl. 8, 1939,
    232; cf. 10015.104;
    Iunetius 4116

Ianuarinius 8788

Iassa 8833, -us

Ibuiodif(?) 8746 (I.
    f[ilius]?)

?Icoppi AcS 2.23

?Iesanno 8595

]igausia 8443

Illanuo 8409

?Illusus AcS 2.35

Iluro 10001.387

?Imbetius AcS 2.36

Inanna 7965

Incenus (for Ingenuus?)
    8251

Indiana (ala)8519; cf.
    221 above; R.1461,
    1467

Ingenuinius Byv. 2.1331

Ingonius 8820

Insius R.1948,17

?Iocara AcS 2.62

Ioctaunus 7965

Ioincatius R.1773

Ioiua m. Byv. 2.1206

?Iothur AcS 2.65

Irmidius 8709

Istaca N.174

?Iucgumattius see Gumattius

Personal Names

Iucundinius 7817, F.280

Iulius F.306, N.198 al.;
and note the histori-
cal figures who bore
this name Arminius
(Cheruscus), Brigan-
tinus, and Ciuilis,
(Bataui). Cf. Ritter-
ling Fasti 140-142

Iullinus 12538.1

Iunnius F.372

Iuo Byv. 2.1548

Iurius 7966

Iusiutina (sic) 12004;
R.3535

Lada 8727

[Laertes(!) Tac. Germ. 3;
On Jullian's conjec-
tured]s Λαερτ[for an
imagined]σμερτ[(REA
14, 1912, 283-4) see
the Introduction]

Laetus 8513

Laetillus Byv. 2.1219

]lailon 7833

?Landa see Ianda

Lanicus Byv. 2.363

Lari...us 8237

Latronius Byv. 2.208

?Latuo AcS 2.156, Byv. 2.
195

Laubasnius 8744; cf. Leub-
3601, with Byv. 2, p.395

Lauinus 7789

Launius R.1923; 5.8752

Lectu[R.2412

Lefa 7872, 12024; cf. 221,
223 above

?Legiminn[8809

Lella m.f. 7899, 8228; cf.
M-L Einf. 251, G.10

Lellauus -auuus 7789

Lella 8411, N.241; Serta
Leodiensia 1930, 180
n.3

Lem[8648 (sc. tribus?)

Lentinus R.1900

Leontius N.227

Lepontia RGKBer. 27, 1937,
p.43

?Leubasnus R.1874; 12019;
-ius F.266; cf. Laub-
above

Leu[7839; but cf. 223

Liaup[8859

Liberalinius 8267b

Libo N.175

[Liccaius 8313]

⟨Λίβης (Chattorum sacer-
dos) Str. 7.1.4, 291C⟩

Personal Names

Licco 12062

Licinius 8716

Liffio 8783

?Lilus F.372

[?Limocinctus 8334; cf.
  AcS 2.180,20 and 227,
  38; but this is hardly
  likely to be a name,
  cf. BJ 140-141, 1936,
  426]

Linus R.2397

Lipi[8595

Liss[8238

?Lixucus AcS 2.276

?Loceaneolus R.2428; but
  see Byv. 2.1369

Lollius 8403, 10024.430;
  3.14214; cf. Lollianus
  3.14428

Longinus Byv. 2.1133

?Lopoteius F.372

Louba (Vbia) 8565

[Loupus (Treuerus) 8655]

Loxus RGKBer. 27, 1937, p.50

[Lubaina (or -us) see 214;
  cf. Λούβαινοι Ptol. 2.
  6.47 (in Spain)? Byv.
  2.p.395]

Lucanus R.2414; -ius
  13.2719

Lucceius 8201

Luccius 10021.126; cf.
  10029.109

Lucretia 8568, -ius 11986;
  cf. 221, 223

Lucullus 7798

Lucius 8061

Lug[7816 (or divine
  name?)

Lugius (Cimber) Oros. 5.
  16.20

?Lullo(s) AcS 2.346

Lupassius 8404

[Lupercus CIL 13 ii p.505]

Lupio 8105, (Vlpius) 8705;
  10025.36

Lupua 7860

Lupula 8240, 8356

Lupulinus 7825

Lupulus 8296, 8499 (Eup-
  ulus i.e. Εὔπλους Byv.
  2.1584), N.201 cf. 230

Lupus 8430

Lurius 8008, Lurio R.1984,
  Luria R.1991

Lusen[AcS 2.350; 13 vi
  p.15, no.69

Λυρέτου IG 14.2576,8

Lusius 10.4862

Personal Names

⟨Lussius Schumacher Fest-
schr. 316-8; REA 34,
1932, 49⟩

[Lutatia (Suebia) 8745]

Lutocis AcS 2.354

Macellus 8556

Macena (-g-?) AcS 2.366;
10001.20; cf. Macenus
2.5304 but -g- (Aquit.)
10016.2

Macer 6.4340

Macerius 7844

?Macnous, for -gnous (see
204 above)? Cf. also
AcS 2.368,34

Macrinius 7936, N.164

Macrinus 8198, F.307,
F.374, N.165, 225

Macro 8709, 6.4339

?Macuatus AcS 2.368

Maddgarisianus (Bataus)
7833; perhaps two words?

[Madicua see 214]

Maduio 10006.47

Maecius 8647

Magalus 10010.1220

[Magilo (Segontilieses)
8093]

Magius 8071

Μαικίου IG 14.2574,7

?Maieris 8307

Maiorius 8819

⟨Μαίλων, Maelo (Sugamber)
Mon. Anc. 5.54,32; cf.
Μέλων⟩

Mainonius 8351

Maiora 8819

Maiorena 8819

[?Mallius Germ. 23, 1939,
32, but cf. AE 1939.
107 and 130]

Mal(l)orix Tac. A 13.54
(king of Frisii,
A.D. 59)

Mallouendus Tac. A 2.64

]maloger[R.1458

Mandia 7893

Manerta 8055

Maniu(s) 8710

Manicius 8744

Manionius Byv. 2.1289

Mannius 7970, Manius N.192

Mansuetus 8213, [8317];
F.307

Marc[8801

Personal Names

Marcia 8283, 8706, N.174;
-ius 7923

Marcus 7998, 8520; †F.302

⟨Marcomeres Greg. Tur. h.
Fr. 2.9⟩

Mar[N.143

?Marenia Byv. 2.1369

Mari (dat. sg.?) 7872

[Marinus 7786], 6895,
F.278

Marius 7994

Maro 7879

[Maroboduus cl.; Kluge
Urg. 33]

?Marsus R.2364

Masauo (n.sg.m.) Byv. 2.
1274; cf. Förstemann 1.
1107

Mascellio N.201

Masclinia F.295

Masclus Germ. 13, 1939,
136

Massa (Tunger) 3.12361

Massula 7983, 8423

Masucua N.251

⟨Μάσυος Dio Cass. 67.5.3⟩

Masueta 8301

Masuri 10027.27

Masuua N.248

Matacus(?) AcS 2.457

Matidia R.634

Matio N.247, 248; cf.
gloss 220 above, Kluge
Urg. 18

Matr (or Matb[?] 10024.16-
17; perhaps divine?

Matrinius 7907

[Matta v. 214]

Maturinius N.184

Matutio 10027.28

?Mauus AcS 2.488

Medamus 10026.23 (Illyr.,
or Iberian?)

Mediana Byv. 2.361

Mefitus R.1850

Meletene N.198

[?Melisusus AcS 2.538]

Mel(l)onia 8114; -ius
8405, 8.2769; cf.
R.1963, R.2278

⟨Μέλων (Sugamber) Str. 7.
1.4, 291C., cf. Μαίλων
above⟩

Memmia 7985, cf. R.2337,
Memmius R.866

?Men.us N.243

Meruelfa(?) 10025.189

Personal Names

Messeanus R.2437

Messius N.207

Messor 7922, R.2437

Messulenus 8407

[†Meteriola 7813]

Metius 8556

Mettius 1328* (REA 32,
 1930, 250; Oxé Fest-
 schrift 1938, 122-24)

Miccius AcS 2.582; Miccio
 10017.601

Micco ib.

Milenius Byv. 2.1132

[Miniata (ala) Dipl. 69]

Minus 7881

?Mirido AcS 2.599

Mirius R.2428

Mogontinius 8850; cf. 221,
 223

?Moi[7991

Montius R.1849

Monrepus 13 vi (1933),
 p.18 no.52

Monus AcS 2.627

?Moritex 8164a; or a
 common noun, see 207
 above

?Mos[10033 (cf. REA 20,
 1918, 250)

[Mucala 8308; cf. Muccala
 AcS 2.648]

[Mucatra 8607; cf. Byv.
 2.1216, and 1211-12]

Mucianus N.184

Mucro 6.3263

Mucronia 8706

Mum[10003.47

Munatia R.3163

Muranus AE 1941.87

Murranius F.269

Musa N.246

Musanus AcS 2.661

Musicus 8055

Mutio AcS 2.665

Mutus F.372

Nacca AcS 2.671

Namanto 10010.1403

?Nanna see Inanna

Nardus RGKBer. 27, 1937,
 p.43

[?Nasennius R.2348]

Personal Names

Natalinia F.300

Natio(?) 8092

]ncernus Byv. 2.1124

Neg[8513

?Nelli(us) Germ. 13, 1929,
  136

Nema[8649

Nemesia 8410

?Nem[onius] cf. AcS 2.
  714, 23-24; Nemis(?)
  Byv. 2.925,1208; Nemoni
  10027.1208

Ncoides (?) 8352

[Nepele 12059]

Nepot[ianus F.292, R.3108

Nepotinius R.3108

Nerius 10001.228

Nerrus 10010.1420

Nertomarius 8792

Nertonus 8792

]nertus AcS 2.723,43

[Neutto see 214]

[Nicasius 8384]

Nigrinius 8217, cf. 6.
  3360; -nus 7.1090;
  R.1865

?Nistus, -usa AcS 2.750;
  10010.3313

Noihus, Noiius F.274 (or
  Nothus? Notius?)

?Nomi.eiius 7951

Nonius EE 9.1009; R.2105

[Nonnus 8094; cf. num.
  239]

Noreiianus 8163

Nouellius N.179

]nou[...]urius Germ. 11,
  1927, 43

?Nouius AcS 2.793,32

?]nux[ib. 809

Ocellio 8409; (Viroman-
  duus) 8341

Occo AcS 2.825

Ocel[ib. 826

Oclatius (Tunger) F.304

?Oecmus AcS 2.835

?Oecus ib.

Olennius Tac. A 4.72

Ollius|cus(?) 8008

Olugnia 8406 (Teol-,
  Etol-?)

[Oluper (Cergaepur) 8304]

]oluta 8450

Omui (if pers.; cf. Omiuii
  12.3911?) 8644

Personal Names

?Oninit[RGKBer. 27, 1937, 40

?Onoiic[AcS 2.860, prob. for Onniorix (terra sig., Rheinzabern)

?Opara[ib. 861

?Opiso ib. 862

Oppi 10027.32

Opponius 8002, 8082 (or Copp-?)

?Orcos AcS 2.869

Orgius ib. 877

Ottidius CIR 4; CIL 13 vi p.18, no.45

]ouetinio[8667

?Ouetus (Qu-?) R.1782

[Ouf[, no doubt trib. 8644]

Ouiorix 10006.65

[Pabecus (Alexandr.) 8322]

Paccius N.193

Paetinus R.2398

Pagadunus R.2593

?Paiurin[AcS 2.922

Panno 7789

Paranus AcS 2.929

Pardin(ius) N.185

Paris N.193

Pa[t]erna 7890, -us F.309, N.185

Patirnius 7868

Patroilus R.2413

Pattua N.252

[Paulus (Batauus) Tac. H 4.13]

[Pedilicus 8098]

Pegu[10001.412 (an Pecu[liaris?)

Pentis f. 8277

Perrus 10027.34; cf. 158 above

Pertic[ia] 7816

†Peruincus F.302, -ius N.224

Perula N.186

Peticius AcS 2.972

Petrusus(?) BJ 143-44, 1938-39, 435

Pettronius 11989

[Pintaius 8098]

Pintio 7825

[Piperacius 8080]

Piro 8188

Personal Names

Pisinius 7784

Pla[N.216

Polla R.634

Pom[7932

Pontius 8657

Potentinus F.263, -ius
  N.197

Porparcu[10002.28

[Pou...iarus EE 9.1124]

[Prepis 8427]

?Prid[ ]ucanus Byv. 2.
  363

[Prifernius Byv. 2.743]

Priga 12020

Primanus 8795

?Primeuis 8777

Primio F.290

Priminia 7883, F.299, -ius
  F.276, 299, N.184

Pritonius AE 1938.77; cf.
  Germ. 21, 1937, 275-76;
  10027.219

Prosius N.150

Proximenia 12004

Pulmilenus 7973

Pupinaia 8594

Pusinnio 7912

Pusua 8529

Quettius 8175

?Rabutus R.2491; cf. 2395

Rac[AcS 2.1069, for
  Crac[una, Crac[issa?

Ramio R.1984

⟨Ῥαμίς Str. 7.1.4, 291C⟩

[Rasuco 8780]

Reburrinus 6305

Reburrus 7045, 8367; cf.
  158 above; 13 vi p.18,
  no.40

]rdapi[8764-5

Rebui 10017.731

Reginia 8244

Reginus 8650, -a N.147,
  148

[?Regiso 1324*, cf. Byv.
  2.198]

[Regtugnus i.e. Rectuge-
  nus (Segontiliensis)
  8093]

Regula N.227

Reitugenus R.2414

?Reperius F.372

Retom[arus] 8614

Personal Names

⟨Richomeres Amm. 31.7.4⟩

[Rigasis R.1818]

?Ri]gedus F.289

†Rignetrudis F.279

Ripanus R.2380

]rispint[8853

?Rituscia 10010.459a

Robin(i)us Germ. 13, 1929,
   137; cf. 10028.26

Romanius 7875, -us R.2014

Roestu[12063

?Rotama AcS 2.1232

Roχtanus RGKBer. 27, 1937,
   44 (cf. AcS 2.1237)

Rubbius 8349

Rubri[8415

Rucletianius (Apru-?)
   8242

?Ruil(i) 10027.224

[Ruimus (Thrax) 7803]

Ru...nilia 12029

?Ruppus AcS 2.1248, prob-
   ably for Roppus 136
   above

Ruso Germ. 23, 1939, 32;
   AE 1939.130; REA 42,
   1940, 607; cf. 13.7031

[Rutaenus 12060]

?Ruterius 8083

Sabaricus Fort. v. Germ.
   31

Sa]bidius R.702

Sabina 7906, -us 7905,
   R.866

Sabinius N.158

[Sacrilus or Sacrius
   (Remus) 8309]

Sacsena(?) 8683

Sadiod[10010.1702 (Saci-)

Sagurus R.1342, cf. Byv.
   2, p.379

?Saibe[AcS 2.1296

Sallion 10017.755

Samai 10017.758

Samdus N.245; Sambius G.
   p.12

Saminia 7871

S]ammius 8723 (or Ammius?)

?Sammo G. p.210 (F.285),
   also read Auuo(?)

Samm(i)us 8607, 10010.
   1714 (Samus)

Sarra 10010.1728; cf. 132
   above

†Saroaldus F.250

Personal Names

Personal Names

Seuro (-us?) 12044

?Sexinsius 12053 (Insius?)

Sextantius R.2384, Byv. 2.1380

Saiei f. gen. 8384

Sidonius 8355

Sidua m.(?) 8084

Sige Byv. 2.1208

[Silauciensis 8593]

Silena BJ 142, 1937, 196

Silius F.317

?Silla 8852

[Silo 10010.1811-12, mis- reading of Silu(anus)]

Siluanus 8655, F.271

Siluinius N.184

Similinius 8492

Similis 7899, N.189

Simmo 7910, 8522

†Simplex F.302

?Si[nt]us 8019

Sirius 10010.45

⟨Sirus Greg. Tur. h.Fr. 2.9⟩

Sitas[10001.434

Siuitus R.1854

[Slanius (cos. A.D.190) 8809]

?Smat[8441

Smertuccus 8822

[Sollauius cf. 214]

Soiio f. 8352

]sonius 8838

Speratus 8357

Statilius N.151

?Stelus F.372

Stertinius 7776

Stirr(i)us 7940

]stis 8492

[Stu[R.4491]

Su[10010.1561

?Suaduanus ib. 1845

Suandacca R.1927

?Subilus 10010.1848

Successinia N.157

Suhetius 7911

?Suilius (D-?) 10001.437

[Sulinus Byv. 2.1465-66]

[Sulla (Remus argentar- ius) 8104]

Sulpicius N.236

Personal Names

Sumaronius 8795

Sumatrius F.281

Summius 11990

?Suni[10006.151

Sunicius 8036

?Sunix (or Clysun-?) 7904
  (but cf. 223 above)

⟨Sunno Greg. Tur. h.Fr.
  2.9⟩

Sunnuuesa 7846

Super N.160

Superinia, -ius F.263,
  284

Superimus R.2410

Suppo R.3182n.

[Surco (Breucus) 8693]

Surilla 8351

Surius AcS 2.1677,14;
  Surio 10027.270

?Surninus 10010.3293b

Surus 7876

Sutoria N.151

Tabi 10010.1867

[Tabusus (Thrax?) 7803]

Tacitia R.2348, -tus
  R.3931; 13.7834

Tacitnius 8173

Taelius 8353

?T.gadunus N.255 (or Gad-
  unus?)

[Tagausus see 214]

?Taiuba (Tal-?) 10010.1871

]talu[10010.2727

?Tam[AcS 2.1712

[Tanehi see 214]

[Tantalus 10010.1876]

Tap[10009.248

?Tarasius R.1783

[Tarquitius 8170, 12048;
  AE 1910.61, R.3549]

Taruillus 10010.1833

Tasgo 10010.1887

Taticenus 8221

Tatta 8390

Tatucus 8173

Tauius 7929

Tauricius 8841, N.159

[Taurinus 8080]

Taurus 8734, R.1354

Tausius (Tunger) CIL 13 i
  p.574; Cap. v. Pert.
  11.8

Personal Names

Tecchallinus 7976

? Τεκουσι (ος ?) IG 14.2573, 17

Tertinius 7899, F.300, 306-8

Tertius N.170 al.

Tettius R.1037

Teutoboduus (Teutonum rex) Flor. 1.38 (3.3). 10; Eutrop. 5.1.4; Oros. 5.16.11; written Teutomodus in Hieron. chr. 1915; not Teutoboc(c)hus 12.1231

[Teutomatus see 156 above]

Tex[quisi]us 8778 (for Tex[uand]rus? (221)

[Tharsa R.1818]

Themaes, Thementianus Byv. 2.1201

[Theronis filius 8794]

[Thiaminus 8648]

⟨Θουμέλικος Str. 7.1.4, 291C⟩

Θουσνέλλα ib.; cf. RhM 92, 1944, 285-86, and Schmidt l.c. Arminius above

Tiar[8691

[Timauius 8371]

Thincso (PN?) R.1854, EE 8.85; cf. 223

? Tinnti, Tintinni[10001. 439, cf. 1901; now believed to be a misreading for Ainibinus (139 above)

Tita N.157, R.1840-43

Titianus N.164, 173

Togius 7054, R.1770

Tontianus R.1037

Totus AcS 2.1896,7

Tra[10017.851

Trauc[(-g-) AcS 2.1905

Treboc[8671

? Treiu R.1857

Tritos, -us 10010.1941

Troxus (Roxus?) 10027.125

Trupo R.1984

[ ]ttios (Neruius) 8339]

? Tulicris 10017.856

Tullius 8611

Turano 10025.196; Ant. Cl. 7, 1938, 208

? Τουνέδος IG 14.2570

Turesius 8066, cf. Turesus Oros. 5.8.1

Turillo 10017.858

Turius 8426

Personal Names

Turranio 12045

Turr(an)ixx 10017.859;
but read perhaps
tudd(os) ixx?

Turtuinus (Frankish) Germ.
11, 1927, 40

Turullius (Germ.) Tac. H.
2.20-22

Tusci[10017.860

[Tuttius (Virunum) 8289]

Vacasatus 10005.26

]uacimius Byv. 2.1074

Vadinus 12005

]uadrin[10017.949

[Vaduna see 214]

Vage 8662

Valc[10017.867

Vale v. Vol[below

Valgas(?) 8307

?Val(1)o[nius R.1800, cf.
REA 28, 1926, 256; RA
26, 1927, 386-87

Vanan[(or Vainan?) 7932

(Vanaenia see 214)

Vannius N.223; cf. Tac. A
2.63, 12.29

Varenius F.295

Variatus 10006.98 (Br-?)

Varisa 10006.100

Varissa 8238

Varus N.220

Vassionius R.1927

Vassius BJ 136-137, 1932,
p.345

†Vassus F.303

Vatnan(?) 7932, v. Vanan[
above

?Vatta Germ. 13, 1929, 136

Vaua[10010.1984

Vauettius N.1788

]ucci 7953

⟨Ὀὐκρόμηρος Str. 7.1.4,
291C; v.l. Ἀκρο-, v.
Actumerus?⟩

Vesperianus 7877; cf. Vx-
below

Ve[N.234

Vecconius N.179

Vegetinius 8541

Vegetus 7893; BJ 142, 1937,
p.193; F.359

Veldaf (or Velda f?) 8663

Veldes (Texuander) 3.14214

[Veldumnianus (imp.) N.266]

Personal Names

⟨Veleda (perhaps a common
    noun) Tac. H 4.61; 5.22;
    24; G 8; Stat. Silv. 1.
    4.90 (v.l. Velda); Dio
    Cass. 67.5.3 (Οὐελήδα);
    see 220 above⟩

Vellango (Neruius) 8340

[Vellaunus (Biturix)
    8094]

[?Velmada 214 above]

Venconius 8015

[Venidius Rufus 8825,
    8828; Prosop. Imp. Rom.
    3, 395 no.245]

Vennenus 12020

Venni 10001.440

Vennonius F.270

Veranius 7803, N.201

Veransatus see 214 (13.
    7036)

Veratius 10003.1

Vercu 8662, cf. Werle 15-
    6; and perhaps 211,
    236

Vereius Byv. 2.1183

Vergilius 10.4862

Verina Byv. 2.1338

Verinus 7777, 6.3260,
    R.3118, F.280, 296;
    N.201

Vernaclo 8375

Veronius 8630

Verritus Tac. A 13.54

Versulatius AE 1941, 87

Verucua (Vlpia) 8374,
    F.296

Verus N.159, 163

Vestinus 10027.48

Vetera[10006.104

[Vettius (Verona) 8590;
    N.165, 182, 237, Byv.
    2.1468; Vetius R.2013;
    Vettius 8650 (Reginus),
    8652, F.275]

Vettulenus R.1912

Vex[10017.894

Vgginius (Vcc-?) 7921

Viator N.249, 250

?Viatoria 7816

Viatorinus 8274

†Vibius(?) F.259, 274

Vibrius R.1002

Vicdiccius 10036.36; 10006.
    106 (Vicd-)

Vicsus (Vrsus?) 10028.23

?Victeati 10017.903

Victimarius 8292

?Vidaco AcS 3.288

Personal Names

Viddic[10010.2038

Viducius 10010.2039a

Vien...deius 10013.34;
R.4617

Vihirmatis (gen. sg.)
8771

Villana N.229

Vimpa N.144; cf. on Kel-
tic uimpo RhMus 84,
1935, 329; BJ 136-137,
1932, 343; 140-141,
1936, 427; Language
25, 1949, 388-391

Vinda (Vlpia) 3.4110, cf.
AcS 3.342-43

Vindex 10015.115, 6.3237,
R.1933, 2409

Vipac[10010.2049

Viperinus 8353

Viponius N.241

Vircus 10002.606

Viriodacus 10010.2057

?Virus R.2398

Viscus F.274

Visellio 7905

Vithannus, -ia 1858 (cf.
Vithones Tac. G 40)

Vitalinius F.306

Vitolo 10010.2065

[?Vittio (Neruius) 8339]

Viuatianus 8584

Vlfenus N.250

Vlp[7789, 8696; Vlpius
(Tribocus) 6.31139,
R.2288, R.4527, N.194
al.; cf. C p.505;
Vlpius (Noreianus)
8163; Vlpia F.296;
Vlpius, -ia Byv. 2.
1137, 1141, 1613; cf.
Latomus 3, 1939, 79-
83; Vlpius (Filinus)
Mnem. 5, 1937, 319;
AE 1933.157; in N.194
read as Alpius BJ 135,
1935, 21

Vmrianus 12034

Vocara 10010.1042: V.
fecit and auoti(?)
10010.2075-76; Vocn[
10010.2077

[Vocula C p.505; Tac. H
4.25-27]

Vol[Lucus 8059, 8060;
but Vale[Luci 8061

Volcinius R.1940

Volerius 7912

Volsonius N.144; cf. BJ
140-141, 1936, 428

Voltedius R.721

Vonatorix 8095

Vossatilli 10029.324

Vrb[10017.101,928; Vrbb[
ib. 930

Personal Names

Vrbicus 10017.931

Vrsa 7897, 8406, 8414, N.249

Vrsacius R.1926

Vrsarius 8639

†Vrsicinus N.217

Vrsinia F.276

Vrsinus Patr. Lat. 13. 583 (Riese, Lit. p.327; ciuis Agripp. 13.6968)

Vrsio 8418, N.229; 10001. 342

Vrsula 8422, (†)8485, 8885, 12072

Vrsulus 7868, 8053.12; R.2276

Vs[N.216

Vsara 10010.2105

Vsia R.4245

Vxper[10017.937, Vxs-perus N.247, cf. Gam-uxperus 13.7086; cf. Vcs- above and on *uks-sep- (from *seku̯-) see Pedersen 1.77; 2. 620 (Gutenbrunner 12 n.4)

Xantia 8355

?Xaue AcS 3.462

Addenda and Corrigenda

Item 78   add Κχστικο[σ], -γ- Tr. 240; AcS 1. 836; cf. 237 below

82   add Maia REA 15, 1913, 74

83   add Litumarus CIL 12.5749

88 Remark   on terra sigillata see now P-W Suppl. 7, 1950, s.v.

Addenda and Corrigenda

Note xx   for ὕσσος (158 below, s.v. coccolobis)
                         read ὕσσος (240 below; and ὕσγη· κόκκος 246,
                         cf. 158 above s.v. coccolobis)

Note xxv Remark   for bregan cf. brigantes 158 below

Item 154 Remark   add Dauzat RLR 14, 1928, 1-20

157   add uandailos Gallia 6, 1949, 61
                         (with some new readings of other dubious
                         coins)

158   gammus "stag." Iberian E-M ed.2;
                         Keltic Loewenthal WuS 10, 1927, 185; 11,
                         1928, 73; W-H suggests conflation of camox
                         and dammus

                         draucus: Germanic according to Ven-
                         dryes Ét. Germ. 2, 1948, 135-36

                         tripetia: on Pictish Pit- (older
                         Pett- cf. W. peth "piece, portion [of land]")
                         see now H.M. Chadwick Early Scotland 1949,
                         pp.53-60 and 63

                         uassogalate (not -ete): cf. 214 below

Note xxviii   add assidarius (i.e. essed-) CIL 13.
                   1997

Note xxxiv   on CIL 13.3162 see now H.G. Pflaum Le
                   Marbre de Thorigny, Paris 1948, reviewed
                   in CP 45, 1950, 254-55

Addenda and Corrigenda

Item 177   read κοιιακα   read ulluci

on "punning" types, especially κοιιακα
(onomatopoetic?), eburo "yew," ullucci and
ulacos "raven" (cf. 178 λοῦγος , to which
add λῦκος "crow" Arist. HA 9.24, cf.
uluc[c]us), see now Blanchet EC 5, 1949,
82-86

178   dunum cf. dunum castrum 212 below

add, from AJPh 21, 1900, 189-192 q.v.:

?cloes: pluuia CGL 4.45,17 al.

gergenna "cross-bar, bolt" (vit. Adamn.
2.16)?

ludari(u)s: steor CGL 5.369,30

?triueta: thriu uuintri steor CGL 5.381,8

Keltic etymologies are possible for all of
these

Item 179   read *Meduanta (now Mantes, Seine-et-
Oise; AcS 2.526)?

207   corroco: cf. κορακῖνος Thompson Greek
Fishes p.123, and see 246 below at calicarca;
hardly curucus (207)

helix: for fragrore read fragore

tossia: cf. 246 below s.v. toscia

212   on p.762 transpose Audaste, Ausaua to
correct alphabetical order

983

Addenda and Corrigenda

Item 214   on p.823 transpose Nonnita above Nonnius

p.845   line 12 from above for Romischen read Romeinschen

p.849   on an early Runic insc. of relevant date from Arguel (near Besançon) see Ét. Germ. 3, 1948, 1-12

p.854   line 21 from below for Petrovits read Petrikovits

p.962   transpose Fledimella to 961 after Flaunus

RA 15, 1940, Jan.-March is not to be had in this country; it appears to have contained (pp.108-113) relevant articles for Aquitania (Un village gaulois près de La Mouthe, Corréze); Belgica (Incinérations au début du Ier Siècle à Xivry-Circourt, Meurthe-et-Moselle; Au musée de Trèves); and Germania Superior (Les fouilles du Temple des Sources de La Seine en 1939); and a note by Chenet (pp.81-83) on terra sigillata in the Argonne (Belgica).

Germania Superior

The Agri Decumates with the
Upper Rhine and Danube

Appendices

1951

VII GERMANIA SVPERIOR
(West of the Rhine)

The Roman province of Germania Superior extended
from the Raetic frontier and the western end of Lake
Constance to the Vinxtbach, just north of Andernach
on the west bank of the Rhine (cf. Pliny NH 4.79, 98-
101; Grenier Mnl. 1, 136-138). Its western boundary
ran, according to accepted opinion, along the crest
of the Vosges in Alsace; and north of that the territory of the old Germanic, but, like the Triboci, thoroughly Kelticized tribes, the Nemetes and Vangiones perhaps
coincided, more or less, it is suggested, with those of
the old dioceses of Speyer (Nouiomagus Nemetum), Worms
(Borbetomagus) and Mainz (Moguntiacum). South and west
the problem of fixing a dividing line, even for my purpose, is unduly complicated by the fact that the editors
of CIL 13 decided to include the Sequani, Heluetii, and
Lingones in Germania Superior. This decision was afterwards retracted (see CIL 13 iv, 1916, p.72, note to ii
fasc. 1, 1905, p.83), as well as the erroneous attribution of Grand to the Lingones instead of to the Leuci
(p.77, note to 5942; cf. 13 i p.702 n.9). The Augustan
attribution of the three tribes just named to Belgica,
would, however, be equally misleading. The Heluetii I
have included in my next subdivision (VIII) "Upper Rhine
and Middle Danube," which also comprehends the territory

between the Rhine and the Limes Germanicus and Raeticus
as far as Ratisbon on the Danube, thus including the
"agri decumates" and the basins of the Neckar and Main.
Presumably, with the Sequani and the Lingones, they
belonged to the great Celtica of Caesar. At all events,
it is clear from the evidence collected here, notably
the local and divine names, but also from the coin-
legends and the personal names, that nothing like the
Germanic influence we have found in Germania inferior
is to be traced in this restricted upper Germany, nor
even in the Germania Superior of CIL at its widest.
Even among the admittedly erstwhile Germanic Vangiones,
Nemetes, and Triboci, traces of their older Germanic
tongue are not to be read; it had yielded, if not to
Keltic, then to Latin, or first to the one and then to
the other (cf. U. Karhstedt "Die germanische Sprachgrenze im antiken Elsass," in Nachr. v. d. Gesellsch.
der Wissensch. zu Göttingen, Ph-H Kl, 1930, 381-395).
The Germanic evidence is all late and, so to speak
"alien;" and even the oldest of it is in the Christian
inscriptions of the area. Since the Germanies were established as military commands, political organization
was loose or non-existent.

Germania Superior

See, in general, in addition to the works cited above (Germania Inferior, Introduction): Bibliographie Alsacienne (Publications de la Faculté des Lettres de l'Université de Strasbourg), the most recent available to me being Vol. 6, 1934-36 (REA 41, 1939, 139); J.A. Brein Saarpfälzische Bibliographie 1936 (Beiheft 2, Abhandlungen zur Saarpfälzischen Landes- und Volksforschung, 1939); G. Drioux Bibliographie, lingone (in Bull. de la Société historique et archéologique de Langres, April 1931); R. Forrer L'Alsace romaine, Paris 1935; A. Fuchs Die Kultur der Keltischen Vogesensiedelungen 1914 (cf. REA 21, 1919, 147-148; 24, 1922, 57); Grenier Notes d'archéologie rhénane in REA, e.g. 25, 1923, 61-67; 26, 1924, 133-143; 27, 1925, 140-148 (cf. Proleg. p.8); R. Henning Denkmäler der elsässischen Altertumssammlung zu Strassburg 1, 1912; C. Jullian in REA 16, 1914, 317-323 ("De l'origine des Francs saliens"), 20, 1918, 169-180 ("Dans l'Alsace gallo-romaine"); Pauly-Wissowa s.vv. Nemetes, Triboci; F. Sprater "Die Pfalz unter den Römern" (Speier-am-Rhein 1929-30, Veröffentlichungen der Pfalzischen Gesellschaft zur Förderung der Wissenschaften 7-8); G. Stümpel "Das Germanenproblem" (cf. 221 above) in Zeitschrift für die Geschichte des Oberrheins 84 (NF 45), 1932, 536-565; A. Weirich Histoire d'une vieille demeure à l'époque gallo-romaine, Strasbourg 1936, cf. Koethe Gnomon 14, 1938, 222.

O. Tschumi (ed.) Urgeschichte der Schweiz vol. 1, 1949; F. Staehelin Die Schweiz im römischen Zeit ed. 3, 1948; R. Laur-Belart Führer durch Augusta Raurica, Basel 1937 (reviewed in ASA 40, 1938, 158; ZfSchwGesch 18, 1938, 223). On the text of Ammianus Marcellinus 14.7-11 see P. de Jonge Spr. u. Hist. Kommentar, Groningen 1939.

Note 1

On a ring, found at Alzey; diameter 9 cm., width 1.5 cm. The insc. is described as "an der Lötstelle geplatzt," and leaf-designs (here represented by ∴)

Miscellaneous Inscriptions

are interspersed, thus

ue∴rinus∴con∴nou∴ca∴su∴ua∴sal

This is probably to be read as Verinus Connoucasu uasal.

Finke 178

Note 11

Of greater interest is an inscription discovered in 1931 at Nickenich (near Mayen), now published in Nesselhauf (no.136), which reads

contuinda esucconis f | siluano

ategnissa f | h(eres) ex tes(tamento) f(ecit)

Cf. Germania 16, 1932, 22-28 and 286-288; 17, 1933, 14-22 and 95-105; BJ 138, 1933, 99-102 cf. 155, 158; RA 10, 1937, 206-08; MZ 32, 1937, 97-98; REA 41, 1939, 33.

Note 111

Here is collected such occasional evidence of dialect as the Latin inscriptions of Germania Superior afford (CIL 13 ii 1, 1905).

(a) 5502 (Dijon)

moni | minto | cacud | ia | sua | dugeni | ceni

In moniminto we have i for e before nt, and it is possible that the final syllable was -on (cf. 5628 at

988

Items in Latin Inscriptions

Til-Châtel, monimenton Do. pp.70-71); but in 5495
(which also may have had Cacudia) we have monimet[,
and in 2646 (Beaune, Note xxxi Remark above) monimentu,
5635 (Til-Châtel) monem, and at Chagnon (Note xxv
above) monimont; cf. mon[im]entu 5557.

Cacudia (-o) turns up as Cacusso in 6125 (cf.
Contedio, v.l. Contesoio 161 above). The final ceni
is commonly taken as a blunder (geni repeated); it is
worth asking whether we have not a noun ("tumulus") or
verb ("posuit") cf. W-P 1, 390-399.

(b)   5525 (Dijon)

This is known only from a late sixteenth century
copy and an early seventeenth. The former has monumentum Iuniani in lines 1-2; the latter, though the
author is not in general so trustworthy, is in this instance perhaps the better copy, since in the meantime
the stone (a small pyramid) may have dried out to reveal the letters more clearly; it reads

momniius │ iaxiu │ ouxxrii │ aiscs⌇⌐

(the older copy in line 3 has oxpibhi), which, whatever it may be, is not Latin; ieuru may be the true
reading (line 3).

(c)   5623 (Til-Châtel), in a dedication "deabus Mairis"
line 6

c]absarius

On capsa and its derivatives see TLL, and W-H s.v.
The word may well have come into Latin from Gaul or the
Germanies.

Items in Latin Inscriptions

(d) On monimenton (note the ending -on) see above (a).

(e) 5664 (Vertault). Again the readings are confused;
beside d.m. [?M]aiuri (doubtful) we have a variant that
differs widely, viz.

? tudos m. satur..i

in which u is $\wedge$ (?). Cf. 224 (Turr-).

(f) 5924 (Bourbonne-les-Bains)

maponus | histriorocaba | tus decessit ann xxx

Since Maponus as a proper name is a divine epithet,
here we may have simply the adj. or common noun maponus,
Rocabatus (or -lus) being the personal name; if Maponus
is taken as a name, rocabatus (-lus?) needs explanation.
Cf. AcS 2.414 (Rouen); Maponus (Apollo) AE 1927.90
(Corbridge); Fons Maboni (Lugdunensis) AcS 2.414,30 (cf.
RC 14, 1893, 152); Locus Maponi Rav. 5.31 p.436.20 (now
Clochmabenstane), cf. W. mabon "youth," mid. W. Mabon
uab Modron "Mabon, son of Matrona (Modron)," Pedersen
VKG 2.45; Note xlv A above.

(g) 5653 (Essarois)

? ientenniqupt

"titulus num Latinus sit dubito" ed. CIL. Perhaps centenarium?

(h) 5967 (Koenigshoffen, Strassburg)

genio uici canabar et uicanor canabensium

Items in Latin Inscriptions

(h) ctd.

Cf. Bohn Germania 10, 1926, 25-36. We have also at
Mainz canabarius (6730, cf. 11806) and canabenses
(6780). See 178 above (s.v. cannabis).

(i) Finke 163a, 165, 166 (Speyer) offer the forms

inuihtus (i.e. inuictus) and carax, carx, cf. F.366

corx (i.e. corax); but the puzzling girece F.122 (Vin-

donissa) is clearly a different word.

(j) 6017 (Hagenau, Brumath)

   d(eo) Medru Matutina Cobnert(i filia)

Here Medru can hardly be the equivalent of Mithrae, see
R. von Kienle AR 35, 1938, 254; -u is apparently a dat.
ending.

(k) 6054 (Wasenburg)

   deo Mercurio attegiam teguliciam cet.

Cf. TLL s.v. (in Iuv. 14.196 for Maurorum read perhaps
Raetorum or Rauracum?); W-H 78; cf. tugurium, *tegis,
mori-tex and the other items cited at 178 above s.v.
sutis; to the references given there add WuS 9, 1926,
106; Do. 273; SprFK 240. The word is said to survive
in the modern Tyrol and Graubünden, and in no event is
to be accounted Moorish (Iuv. l.c.) even though the
name Maurus occurs in CIL 13 (see Index: Cognomina).

Items in Latin Inscriptions

(1)   6691 (Mainz)

genio p[lateae?]

The restoration is based on the far-better attested
platiodanni uici Noui (6776, Mainz; for uicus Nouus
there cf. 6722); on dannus see Note xli(b) above, and
for platio compare Gothic plaÞjo (or platjo), erroneously written plapjo (τῶν πλατειῶν Mark 6.5), genium
pla(teae) in 7261 (Castellum Mattiacorum), genium
plateae noui uici (7335-36, Heddernheim), plat(eae)
praetor(iae) in 7337 (Heddernheim), plat(eae) dext(rae)
euntibus Nidam 7263-64 (Cast. Matt.), platiae d[   ]
Sumelocenes... uici Grinar(ionis) 11727 (Kongen), plat-
earum M M L 8251 (Köln), pla]tea noua cet. 8.304 (Suppl.
11529); and the modern Romance and German derivatives
(place, Platz; but not W. plas). On platiodannus cf.
Weisgerber Germ. 17, 1933, 21 n.23; dannicus (D-?)
CIL 7.66 (Rauricus), H-M 478. In addition to the references given in Note xli(b), see also Note xlvi above;
and note the remarkable similarity of the Oscan eítuns-
inscriptions (ID 60-63).

(m)   7066 (Mainz)

baiulus

Cf. 158 above; and 7754 (Niederbieber) baioli.

(m bis) On hastiferi (7250 Mainz) see Note xlvi above,
Note lvi below.

(n)   The personal name (7256 Klein-Winternheim) Summula
may be a translation of Vpsedia (CP 29, 1934, 290), i.e.
uχsedia, as at La Graufesenque (90 ff. above) see ZfCPh
20, 1936, 369.

Items in Latin Inscriptions

(n bis)   7501 (Ober-Ingelheim)

uittue

Commonly taken as a personal name (cf. Vittio 6484.11, Vittuo 6401, ?Vituo 6118. The two last citations are dedications to Mercury, and in 6118 at least a divine epithet seems to be intended).

(o)   †7660 (Carden) has fimini (gen.) and ricinae (-g-?) with the pers. name Rasnehildi; the close pronunciation of long e as i is noteworthy.

(p)   11976 (Zell), cf. R.286, 3467, with 220, Note xlvi above and Note lvi below

qui burgum (a)edificauerunt

Cf. 11537, 11538, both with burgum: NDOcc. 33.62 ad burgum centenarium (Pannonia Inf.), CIG 8664 (Nicaea) πύργον κεντεν άρι [ον] and CIL 13.8331 cent[enarium]; P-W 3.1926. On burgarii (and ueredarii) cf. Stein Beamten pp.235 n.12, 272 n.214.

(q)   The potter's name

uenicarus

(Heiligenberg and Rheinzabern, cf. 13.11806) may well be a hybrid compound, Keltic or Germanic *ueni- "friend" (AcS 3.168) and Latin carus; or, less likely, we may have (cf. Weisgerber s.v.) ueni- "woman," with u-: b- (-bena cf. AcS 3.845). OE wine, OHG wini "friend" (W-P 1, 259).

Inscriptions of Moirans

Remark:

  1. ocecit (6668) is interpreted by the ed. as
"q(uorum) c(ura) egit."

  2. On ambatus (10010.105) see Note xli above.

  3. For the potter's tally of Hummetroth see La
Graufesenque (90 ff.) above.

225

  Engraved in punched letters ("au pointillé") on
a bronze cauldron or kettle, dredged from the Rhine in
1892; Dottin reported it as in the Museum at Mainz.

    nettas | mucurue

CIL 13.10027,90; Do. 57

226

  A bronze fragment, similar (peg-hole and all) to

those of the calendar of Coligny, dredged in 1802 from

the Lac d'Antre (Jura), about 2 km. from Moirans. Now

lost; enquiries made about 1898 or 1899 of the widow

of M. Fornier of Rennes, to whom it had been sold about

fifteen years earlier, and who was the last known owner

of it, failed to discover its whereabouts, and nothing

has since been learnt of it. The text is based upon a

Inscription of Moirans

comparison of the copies of Bruand (in CIL) and of that
made by Héron de Villefosse from an imprint secured by
R. Mowat.

First published by A.J. Bruand Annuaire de la Pré-
fecture du Jura pour l'année 1814 (Lons-le-Saulnier,
1814), p.209; cf. CIL 13.5345.

Clearly we have parts of two adjoining columns of
letters:

(i)			(ii)
	]mb		
	]do		
	]mb		x[
	]d		xi[
5	]mu		xy[
	]ro		n
	]d		[
			i[
			i[

of which the first has been compared appropriately with
the end of the second fortnight of the fourth month at
Coligny and the beginning of the first fortnight of the
fifth month (ogron); thus -mu (line 5) will end the word
diuirtomu, and -ro (line 6) the word ogro(n).

H. de Villefosse CRAcInscBL 26, 1898, 264-272;
Seymour de Ricci RC 21, 1900, 14-15; Do. 54. There is
nothing to suggest that 226 could possibly have been
part of 227.

The Calendar of Coligny

227

The first announcement of the discovery of the Calendar of Coligny, as it has come to be known, was made by Héron de Villefosse at a meeting of the Académie des Inscriptions et Belles-Lettres on 17 December 1897 (CR 4e Série vol. 25, 1897, 703-04). The actual site is "sur le territoire de la commune de Coligny" (arrondissement de Bourg-en-Bresse, the capital of the département de l'Ain). Coligny stands about 15 miles north-east of Bourg. The discovery was made in Nov. 1897, on the land of a M. Victor Roux. The precise circumstances are described by P. Dissard, then conservateur des Musées de Lyon (ap. de Villefosse l.c., cf. Rev. épigr. du Midi de la France vol. 3 no.87, Oct.-Dec. 1897, pp.493f.) in the following words: "Un cultivateur du hameau de Charmoux, en minant une terre nommée Verpois, située à peu de distance de la route nationale de Lyon à Strasbourg, près des confins des départements, de l'Ain et du Jura, et non loins des restes d'une voie romaine, a trouvé enfouis à environ trente centimètres du sol le debris d'une magnifique statue de bronze remontant à l'époque gallo-romaine. Cette statue, grande comme nature, est très probablement une image d'Apollon....

The Calendar of Coligny

"En même temps que les restes de la statue et
mêlés avec eux, on recueillait les fragments de deux
grandes tables de bronze; ces fragments sont au nombre
de près de cent cinquante, dont plus de cent vingt
sont couverts d'inscriptions gauloises." The nature of
the document as a calendar was recognized at once by de
Villefosse, who called attention to the division of the
months into two periods of fourteen or fifteen days
each; to the holes drilled beside each day's number for
the purpose of marking, by means of a peg inserted in
the appropriate place, successive dates, viz. day,
month, and year; and to the entries describing the different days, festivals and the like, of the calendar
through an entire lustrum.

The identification of the statue, we may note in
passing, has been disputed, the first report claiming
it, as we have seen, as an Apollo, later ones identifying it as Mars (CRAcInscBL 1898, 9-10).

Dissard's first account of the precise circumstances of discovery he also amplified (ibid., p.163) as
follows: "Nous rappellerons sommairement qu'avec les
débris de l'inscription, et mêlés avec eux, se trouvaient

The Calendar of Coligny

ceux d'une magnifique statue, également en bronze repré-
sentant une figure virile entièrement nue et debout;
le tout était enfoui à 0.30m. du sol, dans une excavation dont la forme spéciale a suggéré l'idée que tous
les fragments avaient été au préalable réunis dans une
espèce de panier en forme de hotte." From this information the conclusion was drawn by Héron de Villefosse
(ibid. p.265, with n.3) that the calendar had been
broken deliberately into small pieces and hidden "in-
tentionnellement pour être soustraits à une profanation
ou à un péril qu'il est impossible de définir." On
epigraphical grounds, the calendar has been dated
c. A.D.50-80; it would appear, therefore, that the
troubles connected with the uprising of Sabinus in
A.D.69 may have caused its destruction.

The same fate overtook another calendar, a single
fragment of which was recovered from lake d'Antre in
1802 (see 226). To judge from that one fragment the
calendar d'Antre was, as de Villefosse remarked, contemporary with that of Coligny, and its very twin.
Certainly it is hard to imagine that a bronze plate
would have been shattered into so many tiny fragments
as the Calendar of Coligny, save by some extraordinary
accident. There is little or nothing in the accounts

The Calendar of Coligny

of its discovery to suggest that it was broken by the operations of the viticulturist who first chanced upon it; observe, however, that the term used in Dissard's account as quoted above is miner; and défoncer in Rev. épigr. 3, 1897, p.493. But it is probable enough that had the discovery been made in the course of systematic excavations we might have had the whole of the calendar before us, even if in pieces. For there were persistent rumors in 1898 that some pieces were lost: "Je sais de la façon la plus positive que quelques-unes des fragments ont été soustraits" (de Villefosse p.270, n.3 ad fin [p.271]).

Preserved in the Musée de Lyon (case no.32), the 149 fragments have been arranged so as to reconstruct, with reasonable likelihood, an original that measured 1.48m. (58 in.) by 80cm. (35.25 in.); the text is engraved within a border 2 in. wide.

The following transcription follows this arrangement, beginning with column 1 on the left, which, like all the other columns, contains space for the entry of four months, then column 2 and so on to the end, column 16. This would make a total entry of 64 months, namely a cycle of five years, each of twelve months (total sixty months); and, in addition two intercalary months, the first before the first month of the first year of the cycle, the second before the seventh month of the third year, i.e. halfway through the cycle, each of the intercalary months having its entries so widely spaced as to occupy twice the amount of space as the rest. Thus we have actually sixty-two months set forth, two of them intercalary.

The Calendar of Coligny

Abbreviations are numerous, and it is not always easy to determine what words they represent. After the date, day by day, there often follows the symbol †||, |†| , or ||†, the meaning of which is unknown.

The chief peculiarities of the writing are Λ for A, and the failure to distinguish (and G; i is often taller, so as to pass above the top line; and the cross-bars of e and t slant upwards (cf. Dissard CRAcInscBL 1898, 163-167). The alphabet is in the style of fine late republican or early imperial Latin, with finials and long-tailed Q. There are two sizes of letters, a larger (in headings of the months) .375 in. high or a little more, and a smaller (in the daily enumerations), about .19 or .20 in.; coinjoint letters appear (e.g. atenoux).

Fragments the proper place of which has not been yet discovered are placed together at the end. The following text is based upon a collation of Dottin's text with the original in the Musées de la ville de Lyon (Palais des Arts), where the Director, M. L. Rosenthal, to whom I am grateful, afforded me all possible facilities for its study (25 and 26 July, 1929).

Facsimile, after drawings of Dissard, CRAcInscBL 1897, p.730 (transcription 1898, 299-336); reproduced in RC 19, 1898 at p.213; in color, by E. Espérandieu, supplement to RE 3, 1898, p.557 (cf. pp.493, 541); RC 21, 1900, at p.413.

Bibliography (cf. CRAcInscBL 1898, pp.9, 161-2, 163-7, 167-70, 175, 264, 273, 299-336, 611, 612-14,

The Calendar of Coligny

718, 724, 725; RA 34, 1899, 145 ff.; RE 4, 1899, pp.1,
13, 22. Most of the early notices are repetitious;
and of the early discussions antiquated): to 1899 by
Seymour de Ricci RC 21, 1900, 10-27 (cf. Espérandieu
RC 21, 1900,100) and in Montandan Bibl. Générale 1,
1917 (items 171, 177, 209, 210, 212, 377, 1903), Suppl.
1, 1921 (items 8712, 8715-16, 8732-33, 8735), including, among others Seymour de Ricci RC 19, 1898, 213-
223 (cf. p.357, d'Arbois de Jubainville); J. Loth
CRAcInscBL 1898, 175-76; E.W.B. Nicholson Sequanian,
London 1898 (cf. RC 19, 1898, 346); R. Thurneysen in
ZfCPh 2, 1898-99, 523-544 (cf. RC 20, 1899, 108).

Since 1899: Nicholson ZfCPh 3, 1901, 329-331;
S. de Ricci RC 24, 1903, 313-316; J. Loth CRAcInscBL
1904, 25; id. RC 25, 1904, 113-162; Nicholson Keltic
Researches, London 1904; Rhys Celtae and Galli, London
1906 (cf. Thurneysen ZfCPh 6, 1907-08, 244-45, cf. 557-
58); Loth CRAcInscBL 1909, 16-28; Rhys Notes on the
Coligny Calendar, London 1910 (cf. RC 32, 1911, 205-209);
id. Celtic Inscriptions: additions and corrections, London 1911, 77-100; Dottin Langue Gauloise, Paris 1918,
172-207; Eóin MacNeill Ériu 10, 1926-28, 1-67; Seymour
de Ricci Journal des Savants 1926, 448-449 (with facsimile); W. Kubitscheck Grundriss der antiken Zeit-
rechnung (Müllers Hdb 1.7) 1928, 6, 36 n.3, 136-140;
J. Cuillandre RC 47, 1930, 10-29; Weisgerber SprFK,
pp.184, 220; T. O'Rahilly Proc. Br. Acad. 21, 1935, 322-
372; so far as I can discover, a paper presented by J.
Phelps to LSA in 1939 has not been published; E. Linckenheld RC 48, 1931, 137-44; C. Lainé-Kerjean ZfCPh 23,
1943, 249-84; O. Haas ib. 297-301 (on cantlos *kuntó-
"dog").

In many of the months the indication in(n)is ap-

pears, most frequently to mark the sixth to the twelfth

days, occasionally the fourth and fifth. That the

Coligny calendar is a lunar calendar is certain from

internal evidence, and is also what we should expect

from Caesar's statement (BG 6.18) about Keltic time-

The Calendar of Coligny

reckoning; thus the day is reckoned from sunset to sunset, each period of twenty-four hours corresponding to
successive phases of the moon. On the sixth such phase
(sexta luna) a Keltic month was held to begin (Pliny
NH 16.250) as well as the New Year (in the first month
of the year). Thus the days marked in(n)is correspond
roughly to the second quarter of the moon, and this
seems to give a clue to the meaning (cf. Gr. μηνὸς
ἱσταμένου?). It is a period that corresponds roughly
also to the Roman nonae; the preceding dark nights are,
so to speak, a preparation for the new month and the
several feriae begin with the nones (Varro LL 6.28, cf.
Macr. 1.15.12). There is also marked in each month of
twenty-nine days, after the 29th day, a sort of retro-
spect to the departing month (diuertomu), like the
Greek ἕνη καὶ νέα (rather than μηνὸς φθίνοντος), and
perhaps other fixed or variable points (exo near the
beginning; and petiux and prinni), the meanings of
which are not clear. The fourteen-month Keltic year
alleged in Dio Cass. 54.21.3 is perhaps not entirely
fictitious (cf. Jullian HG 4.83, n.7; Grenier ap. Frank
3.499); apparently a fraudulent tax-collector contrived
to count an intercalary month twice in one year.

The Calendar of Coligny

CIL 13.5955 is a fragment of a Latin "menologium aeneum" discovered at Grand, but of much later date; however it uses the Roman divisions of the month, not the system of seven-day weeks, and marks the aequinoct[ium. Cf. Do. p.44 on intercalary days. On some of the problems of adjusting non-Roman to Roman calendars in Augustan times cf. AJPh 66, 1945, 191. For later evidence on time-reckoning in Gaul see FHRC 165.4-15 (Concilium Arelatense), ib. 20-25 (Palchus astrologus) with Zwicker's notes. Although the druids are said by Caesar (BG 6.13) to have come from Britain to Gaul, just as Jullian maintains (REA 30, 1928, 309) that the name Scottus was introduced from Ireland, the suggestion that they constructed our calendar is usually rejected (e.g. T.D. Kendrick The Druids, 1927, 115-120); even if it were valid, it might hardly be invoked as a solution of linguistic difficulties. Svennung Palladius, 1935, 254-259 (cf. 256 n.1) has some interesting comments. The Gaulish new-year was perhaps Halloween (31 Oct.-1 Nov.) see EC 4, 1948, 157 (Samain). In REA 10, 1908, 174 cf. 196, it is maintained that the seven-day week was indigenous in Gaul. On peti ux (perhaps "relatively small, brief"?) see Die Sprache 1, 1949, 128; W-H 1, 850 ad fin. on ogro-no-. For a map showing the temple of Mars Augustus near the lac d'Antre see Mém. Soc. d'Emul. Jura 3, 1910, 257-264. Cf. JCS 1, 1950, 144-47.

In the original, when the entry for a certain day, extends over more than one line, the second and following lines are sometimes indented, but by no means invariably. This is shown as accurately as possible in the Commentary, but no attempt has been made to reproduce it in the transcription which follows. In the transcription of the Calendar only the extant lines are reproduced, with some estimate of the possible number of missing lines. This estimate is based, where possible, upon the number of days not indicated in the existing fragments. In the Commentary, however, where a restoration of the calendar is offered, the lacunae are largely filled from the entries of one year or another. The exception to this statement is, of course, the intercalary months.

Unless explicitly stated, a point beneath a letter means merely that the bronze is broken through it, but that the letter is otherwise extant and certain. How-

The Calendar of Coligny I

ever, I have omitted broken peg-holes (since to write
° would be confusing) and marked only the unbroken ones
(thus °).

The numbering is by columns and lines of each column.

Column I   Notes

   ḍ[3. Ṃ i.e. mẹ? 4. a
          has the form Ʌ The
   meịdx̣[fourth letter could not
          have been anything other
   matu[than x 5. s broken
          but certain 6. g is
5 ° i mat s ṣ[‖ gia[⊂, but in 51 ᴳ 8. ˙ a
          is Ʌ, and so often
  ° ii mat d[| sonna[

  ° iii ma[

10 iiiị[

11, 12 desunt

          13. m seemed more prob-
15 ° vii ṃ[| tinad[| ne[‖   able to me than n, i.e.
          Ṃ broken (for Ʌ) than N
    ui[

  ° viiị[| ma[20. Possibly the last
          extant letter was not o
20 ° viiii ma[| edutiọ[‖   but q; only the left up-
    me[per portion of the letter
          remains

  ° x[

  ° xị[

24-29 desunt

30]rini   30. rini is certain

]ṃb riur

]ni

v d dumanni amb riu r

° vi iiɫ md ᵗb iuri

35　° vii nsds sam.ni anagan ‖

inni si[　]tit

viii nsds[　]ṭọ ‖ inn[

40　°viiii ṇ[│ eḍ[│ su[

° x[

43-45 desunt

° x[iiii

xv[│].ḅ ṛịχtio │ cob[

] cariedit

50　　oχ.antia ‖

pogdedortonin │ quimon

mid samm

i d dumanni iuoṣ

55　ii m d iuos

iii ɫii d exingidum iuos

iiii m d iuos

v d amb·rix·ri

vi　m d

60　°vii n dumann iniṣ.r

°viii m d .mo

33.　The final r of riur
was added so as to avoid
the punch-hole, i.e. it
comes in between lines 33
and 34 of Column II
But though thus separated
from riu it makes one word
with it　34.　The en-
graver wrote β (not ℝ) by
mistake.　ɫ is ⱦ.
36.　There is a space af-
ter inni, then s followed
by the upper half of i
(not t)　　Nothing is
lacking after tit

47.　Before ḅ nothing cer-
tain

52.　q, as usual, Q

58.　a is not ∧ but ⋀
The interpuncts are both
certain, between b and r,
and after x

60.　Space after dumann
61.　I doubt s before m
as being original; or, at

The Calendar of Coligny I

° viiii d dumanni

° x m d

° xi d amb

65 x]ii d m

x]iii d m

x]iiii d m

xv d m

atenoux

70 i d dumanni

ii m d trinosam·sindiu

iii d amb

iiii m d

v d amb

75 vi iii m d

vii d dumanni amb

vi]ii iii dumanni

]n dumanni·in·r

79 deest

80]amb

81-91 desunt

]m·et amb

93 deest

]riuri

95]riuri

best, as intended. It is Ϟ, not the usual S The o is open at the top (ʊ)

71. The interpunct between m and s is very doubtful

78. n is read from comparison with line 60; not enough remains of the letter to make the reading anything but doubtful

90. The bottom of the two final strokes of m is visible before the interpunct; then et 94. r corroded but certain

The Calendar of Coligny I, II

]ḍ riuri

]ḍ

]ịnis r

]d

100]ịuos

101-105 desunt

  v iꝉ[[

  vi iiꝉ[

  ° viiꞔ

  ° viiiꞔ

110 viiiiꞔ

  ° x̣ iiꞔ

  ° xiꞔ

  ° xii nꞔ

  ° xiii . amb iuoꞔ

115 ° xiiii nẹḍs iuoꞔ

  díuertiọmu

106. The bottom portions of the letters indicated are faintly to be observed immediately above those of line 107

116. i longa

Column II

1-4 desunt

  5]ọmuriuo

  ]nịs

  vi]ị iꝉi d anagantio

  viii iiꝉ d anagantio

5. No spacing between words 8. ꝉ is Ŧ (sic) 8-10. g: or c?

The Calendar of Coligny II

10	viiii d	anagantio
	x m d	
	xi n	inis·r
	xii m d |	deouuori·uo
	piu:[	
15	xiiii m d	
	xv m d	
	ate]noux	
	]d	
19 deest		
20	]amb	
21-34 desunt		
35	ii[	
	iii[	
	iiii m[	
	v n[	
	vi p.[	
40	vii m d og[	
	viii m d ogron[	
	viiii m d ogroni	
	x d	
	xi d amb	
45	xii ɫii d	
	°xiii iɫi d	

14. In this line, after e, we have apparently ℣ superimposed upon o, as if the engraver had hesitated between VV and o, or between ᵒV and V   There is no space before ri·, but a clear punct after i, then uo followed by a space, and next p, not r; after u comes what might be the top of b or p or r, followed by a letter now lost at the break   On deou uori.uo see the Glossary   17. A small corner of e may perhaps be detected by the confident before the broken n.

40-42. g is ⅁ , not ᴄ

45. ɫ is ⊤, in 46 it is †

1008

The Calendar of Coligny II

```
  °xiiii ·  iil d

     ]d

  at]enoux

50   ]d

     ]d

     ]amb

53 deest

     ]amb

55   ]inis  r

     ]ogro  amb

     ]m d cutio                58. ogron is corroded,
                               n broken; and above ogr
     viiii  d ogron[           a line is drawn, thus
                               OGR      There is no
     x †i   iil d              trace of a following amb
                               59.  1 of xi in rasura
60   xi  iil  d                61.  Formerly xiii, the
                               final i having been era-
     xii.[                     sed; a following d (if
                               any) has been erased
     xiii.  d  am[             62.  Formerly xiiii, the
                               final i having been
     xiiii  d                  erased      64.  The up-
                               per portions of diuer
     diuertomu                 still are faintly dis-
                               cernible      65.  The
65   ]mat[                     lower portions of mat
                               still are faintly dis-
66-68 desunt                   cernible

     iiii  m[

70   v  d[

     vi  m d[

     vii  m d[

     viii  m d cu[
```

The Calendar of Coligny II

```
       viiii  n  cut[
75     xmd
       xi  d a[
       xii  m d
       xiii  m d
       xiiii  m d
80     xv  m d
       atenoux                      81.  a is A
       i  m d cuti[
       ii  m d cut[
       iii  d cu[
85     iiii  m[
86-96  desunt
       m[
       i  m d iuos
       ii  m d iuos
100    iii  m d iuos
       iiii  prini loud            101.  p is ⌐, little dif-
                                    ferent from ⌐ (i)
       v  n inis·r
       vi  m d
       vii  giam pri lag           104.  The second g is G
105    viii  d giamoni
       viiii†  n giamo inir r      106.  It is viii, not
                                    viiii, evidently a cut-
       x  m d                       ter's error
```

The Calendar of Coligny II

```
      xi   d amb
      xii  m d
110   xiii  m d
      xiiii  m d
      xv  m d
      atenoux
      i  m d ogron[
115   ii  m d ogron[
      iii  d ogro[
      iiii  n in[
      v   d amb[
      vi  n inis[
120   vii  n giam[
      viii  n gia[
      viiii  d amb[
      x   m d
      xi   d
125   xiim  d
      ]d  [  ]b
127 deest
      ]amb
```

The Calendar of Coligny III

Column III

1-18 desunt

]n[ ]s[

20	iii d amb	
	iiii łii d	
	v iłi d amb	
	vi iił d	
	vii d simiuiamb	24-26. i longa in sim-, and also (24) in -ui
25	viii m d si*miuiso	25. m is ǀ ǀ (for M)
	viiii d simiuis amb	26. b is in column IV, the line being filled as far as the peg-hole in col. III
	x łii d	
	xi n inis r	
	xii iił d	
30	xiii d amb	
	xiiii d	
	diuertomu	
	m simiuimąt	33. t in column IV
	i giamo prin lag	
35	ii m d	
	°iii d equi	
	iiii m d	
	v n inis r	
	vi d equi	
40	vii d equi	

The Calendar of Coligny III

viii equ pri la

viiii d equi

x m d

xi d amb

45 xii m d

xiii d equi

]iiii neds

]s equi

49-53 desunt

v d [

55 vi ili d equi

vii ili d equi amb

viii d equi

viiii d amb equi

x m d

60 xi d amb equi

xii m d iuos

xiii d amb iuos

xiiii m d iuos

xv d amb iuos

65 m equos anm

i d iuos

ii prini lag iuos

iii m d simi iuos

iiii d iuos

41. l hardly to be dis-
tinguished from i; but
cf. 34 above

48. Before s, probably
n (or i), not u
54. All of d except the
top right corner is plain-
ly discernible

65. a is A not ∧
66. d is perfect (pace
Rhys, Dottin)

The Calendar of Coligny III

70   v d amb

      vi m d simiuiso

      vii d elembi

      viii d elembi

      viiii d elembi

75   x d

      xi d amb

      ]ii d

      xiii m d semiuis

      xiiii m d semiuis

80   xv m d semicano

      atenoux

      °i m d semiuis

      °ii m d semiuis   84. The letters is at

                                          the end of this line are

      °iii d amb simiuis   placed beyond the peg-

                                          hole in Column IV

85   °iiii d

      °v Ɨii d amb   85-89. The Ɨ-group sym-

                                          bols are as I report them

      vi iiɨ d simiso   from the original

      vii iɨi d elem amb

      viii iiɨ d elemb

90   viiii d amb elemb

      x d

      xi Ɨii d amb

      xii iɨi d

      xiii iiɨ d amb

The Calendar of Coligny III, IV

```
95     xiiii  d

       xv  d  amb                    96.  sic       99.  Top
                                      of d survives
       m elemb  an[

             ]d[

                ]i  d [

100    ]s[                           100.  The sole surviving
                                     letter is in Column IV
101-118 desunt

       ]d

120    ]d  edri amb

       ]m d edrini

       ]iiii   d amb edrini

       x   d  sind iuos

      °xi   d  amb

125   °xii  lii  d               125.  lii, not łii

      °xiii  iłi  d amb

      °xiiii  ilł  d

       diuertomu
```

Column IV

```
       m edrini mat

       ]cantli

3-5 desunt

       ]amb
```

The Calendar of Coligny IV

7 deest

    ]nt

9-25 desunt   17.   The x which Rhys
                                            reports I did not see

    viiii d

    x m d

    xi d a[

    xii m d

30   xiii d amb iuos

    xiiii m d iuos

    xv d amb iuos

    m cantlos anm

    i d aedrin

35   ii d

    iii d

    iiii prinni lag

    v d amb

    vi d

40   v[ii] d cantli

      ]d cantli

      ]ii d cantli

      ]d

    xi d amb

45   xii d

    xiii d

    xiiii d

The Calendar of Coligny IV

xv	d	tiocobr.χt

49-55 desunt

°vii[

°·viii[

°viiii iɫi[   ]r

°x ḍ[

60   °xi ḍ[

°xii d[

°xiii iiɫ d amb iụ[

°xiiii iɫi diuodibcant

diuertomu

65   m samon mat

i n dumaniuos

ii iɫi m d iuos

iii iɫi ḍ dum iuos

iiii m d

70   v d amb

vi m d

vii prin loudin

viii d dum

viiii iiɫ m d

75   x m d

xi d amd

xii m d

48. Probably i not e is
the missing letter
Of the rest only the
merest top remains in
each   The reading is
based on other years

58. iii aes   r is in
column V

68. ḍ: here the en-
graver first wrote l
and then superimposed
d, but the reading is
certain

72. sic; not prini

74. iil aes

76. sic; but amd is
presumably an error for
amb

```
         xiii  Iii m d
         xiiii iIi m d
80       xv  iiI  m d
         atenoux
         i  d̤ duman
         ii  iiI  trinuxsamo            83.  or -Xs-?
         iii  d amb
85       iiii  Iii  d
         v  iIi  d amb
         vi  iiI  m d
         vii  d amb
         viii  n inis r
90       viiii  n inis r
         x  Iii  m d
         xi  iIi  m d amb íuos
         xii Iii  m d íuos
         xiii  d amb iuos
95       xiiii  m d iuos
         xv  d amb iuos
         m  duman anm
         i  samon prioudixiuọn        98.  oṇ corroded; but the
         ii  n íuos                         last letter at end is n,
100      iii  d íuos                        not s
         iiii  d íuos
```

The Calendar of Coligny IV

v .rinni iaget		102. iaget aes, not
		lagit (as Rhys, Dottin)

103 deest

]n inis r

105   ]iⱦ m d samoni

viiii d

x d

xi n inis r

xii d

110   xiii d

xiiii d

xv d

atenoux

i m d samoni

115   ii m d samoni

iii iⱦi d amb

iiii iiⱦ d

v d amb

vi iiⱦ m d

120   vii d amb

viii ⱦii d

viiii n inis r

x d

xi d amb

125   xii n inis r

124. amb presumably
belongs to day xi but it
is placed between this
line and the line above

The Calendar of Coligny IV, V

xiii　d amb

xiiii　ns ds

diuertomu

Column V

　　　]os mat

　　　]nagant　　　　　　　2.　g is (

　　　]loud

4 deest

5　　]g riuros　　　　　　5.　g: or c?

　　　]nis r

7-8 desunt

　　　]nni loud

10 deest

　　　]m　　　　　　　　　11.　No letters ever
　　　　　　　　　　　　　　　　followed m
　　　]inis r

13 deest

　　　]m　iug riu

15　　]iuo　　　　　　　　15.　or inc?

16-21 desunt

　　　]s

23 deest

　　　]mb

25　　]etiux anag

The Calendar of Coligny V

```
      ]d amb

   x   iiƚ m d petiuxriuri

   xi  ƚii  d amb íuos

   xii  iƚi m d íuos
```

30   xiii iiƚ d amb íuos

```
      xiiii  m d íuos

      xv  d amb íuos

      m   anagan anm

      i   m d riuri iui[
```

35-42 desunt

```
      ]d

      °xi  d
```

45   °xii d

```
      °xiii  d

      °xiiii  d

      xv  d

      atenoux
```

50   i d

```
      ii  d

      iii  ƚii d   amb

      iiii  iƚƚ  d
```

```
      v  iiƚ  d ạmb
```

55   vi n inis r

```
      vii  n inis r

      viii  d
```

34. Every letter in
this line is broken
through the middle;
but at the end I saw
iui, not iuo[

53. For iƚi; but the
original clearly has iƚƚ

The Calendar of Coligny V, VI

```
      viiii  n inis r
      x  iłi d
60    xi  iił  d amb
      xii  d
      xiii  d amb
      xiiii  d
      diuortomu
65    m ogron mat
66-128 desunt
```

59. iłi appears to have been overlooked by previous editors

Column VI

```
      ]on[
2-7 desunt
      v[
      viii[
10    viiii  m[
      x [
      xi  d[
     °xii  d[
      ]iii  d
15    ]ii  d
      xv  d
      atenoux
```

The Calendar of Coligny VI

```
        i   d
        ii  nsds
20      iii  amb              20.  am corroded, but
                              visible    21.  For iii
       °iiii  iii d           22.  For iti
       °v iii  d amb
       °vi  iit  d
       °vii  n ini r
25     °viii  n ini r
       °viiii  d amb
       °x  tii d
       °xi  n ini r
       °xii  iit  d
30     °xiii  d amb           30.  amb between lines
                              29 and 30
       °xiiii  d
       †x  diuortomu          32.  x in rasura
        m  semiu[
34-45 desunt
       °xii[
       °xiii[
       °xv  d equi
        atenoux
50      i  d  equi
        ii  d  equi
        iii  d amb equi
```

```
        iiii   iiɫ m d

        °v   d   amb                          54.  amb between lines
                                              53 and 54
55      °vi  iiɫ  d equi

        °vii  d   amb

        °[ ] ɪii  m d

        °[ ] iii  d amb r

        °[ ] m d

60      °[ ] d amb

        °[ ] d

        °[ ] amb

        °[ ] s amb                            63, 64.  The reading s
                                              amb is certain in both
        °[ ] s amb                            lines

65      ]uos[

        i[

        ii  pri[

        iii  m d[

        iiii [

70      v  [

        vi  iɫi  n[

        vii  d[

        viii  d[

        viiii  d[

75      x  d[

76-96 desunt
```

The Calendar of Coligny VI

```
      m    elembiu anm
      i    d   iuo                       98-102.  No trace of
                                         final s
      ii   d  iuo
100   iii  prinni     lag iuo            100, 106.  l is ⌐, g is ⊂
      iiii  d   iuo
      v   d   iuo
      vi   d   amb                       103.  After amb the en-
                                         graver began to write i
      vii  d                             in iuo again, and then
                                         thought better of it
105   viii  d
      viiii  prinni   lag
      x   n   ini   r
      xi   d   amb
      xii  d
110   xiii  d
      xiiii  d
      xv   n                             112.  n, not d
      atenoux
      i   m  d   edrini
115   ii   m  d edrini
      iii  ɫii   d amb edrin
      iiii   d
        ]d   amb
        ]d
120      ]amb
121-128 desunt
```

The Calendar of Coligny VII

Column VII

     ]s mat

     ]iuo   2. iuo, not iuos

     ]iuos

     ]uos

5-12 desunt

     xii iii [

     xiii iɫi m[

15   xiiii iiɫ m[15-16. Between these

     xv d m[two lines stands $\overset{\times}{\times}$ in

     ateno.x   rasura and, apart from

                       these symbols space for

     i d elemb   about two lines Evi-

                       dently the engraver cut

     ii d elemb   a series of numerals

                       first, and in this case

20   iii d elembi amb   had cut × twice too of-

                       ten before realising his

     iiii iɫi m d   error and correcting it

     v iiɫ d amb   21. Not ii

     vi iiɫ m d   22. Not i i

     vii d amb

25   viii d

     viiii ɫii d amb

     x iɫi d sínd íuos

     xi iiɫ d amb

     xii m d

30   xiii ᵗm d amb   30. m in rasura

The Calendar of Coligny VII

xiiii m d

.v n

m   cantlos anm

i m d edrini

35   ii d

iii d

iiii prinni lage   37. Or lace?

v d amb

vi d

40   vii d

viii d

viiii d

x d

]amb

45-47 desunt

]iocobrextio   48. e is [, scarcely
                             distinguishable from i
]oux

50-51 desunt

iii d amb   52. A small part of d
                             remains on left
iiii n inis r

v d amb   54. The engraver put in
                             ˜ of β and left it at
55   vi iii d   that

vii d amb

viii d

The Calendar of Coligny VII

	viiii	d	am[		60. The first stroke of
	x	d			m is barely visible
60	xi	d	am[		
	xii	d			
	xiii	iii	amb		62. iii not ii
	xiiii	iii	d[		

64–65 desunt

]iuo[

]iuos

]mele iuo

69–71 desunt

]d

]mani

74–96 desunt

m dum[

i samon prin lodex[

ii n iuos

100 iii d iuos

iiii d iuos

v prinni lage

vi d

vii n inis r

105 viii iii m d samoni

viiii d

72. From its position
d is the final letter of
loud, not the common ab-
breviation d   73.
mani is all clear and certain

98. ex certain, even
though only a portion on
left survives of x; e is
very clear

102. Or lace?

The Calendar of Coligny VII

```
       x    d
       xi   n   inis r
       xii  d
110    xiii  d
       xiiii  n
       xv   d
       atenoux
       i[
115    ii   m[
       iii [
       iiii [
       v   [
       vi  iii d
120    vii  d
       viii  d
       viiii  n   inis r
       x    d
       xi   n   amb
125    xii  n  inis r
       xiii  d amb
       xiiii  nsds
       diuortom
```

128. -u was omitted by
the engraver himself

The Calendar of Coligny VIII

Column VIII

      m riuros mat

     °i d anag

     °ii prinni loud

     °iii n

  5   °iiii m d brig riu

     °v n ínis r

     °vi m d

     °vii m d

     °viii prini lo[

 10   viiii ɫii m d

     x iiɫ m d

12-13 desunt

     °x[

 15   °xiiii[

     °xv m[

     ateno[

     °i m d

     °ii m d [ ]o

 20   °iii d am[ ]uo

     °iiii m d

     °v ɫii d am. iuo

     °vi iɫi m d   23. iiɫ aes

     °vii iiɫ d amb

The Calendar of Coligny VIII

25 °viii d peti riuri anag

°viiii n

]riuri †d riuri iii m d

]iuos

]uos

30]iuos

]iuos

]iuos

m ..agtio anm

°i m[ ] riuri exo iuo

35 °ii [ ]iuos

.[ ]iuos

]ociom riuri

]n inis r

]prinni lag

40]ns ds

]d

]ii d

]d

]d amb

45]d

46-48 desunt

]oux

50-51 desunt

27. A good piece of r is visible; d is merely Ɔ and probably is to be omitted, being an erroneous anticipation of d at the end of the line, where it has been put into Column IX

34. A peg-hole has been drilled through the lower left part of o, in anticipation of the next column

The Calendar of Coligny VIII

]amb

53 deest

]amb

55   ]ínis r

]inis r

57 deest

]inis r

59 deest

60   ]mb

61-72 desunt

viii m ḍ

viiii ɫii m d

75   x iɫi m d

xi   iiɫ d amb

xii m d

]d

79-80 desunt

]ṇoux

]m d cutio

]n cutio

]iiɫ d cutio amb

85   iiii m d

v   d amb

vi ɫii m d

57-58. In the fragment
that is left it is hard
to say whether inis r
belongs to 57 or to 58;
comparison with other
years favors the latter

The Calendar of Coligny VIII

```
        vii   iꟷi   d amb
        viii  iꟷi   m d cutio
90      viiii   d amb
        x   m d
        xi   d amb
        xii   n ínis r
        x̣iii  iꟷi   d amb
95      ]iiii  iiꟷ m d
        ]ṿ   d amb
        ]c̣ụṭ[
98-117 desunt
        v   [
        ·vi   [
120     ·vii   ꟷi[
        ·viii   iꟷ[
        ·viiii  iiꟷ[
        ·x   m ḍ [
        ·xi   d[
125     ·xii   m d
        ·xiii   ꟷii ḍ
        ·xiii[
        ·xv[
```

122. iiꟷ (not iꟷi) aes

<table>
<tr><td></td><td>ciallosb.is | sonnocingos</td><td>1. No trace whatever of the letter that stood between b and i   2. The sixth and the ninth letters are identical in the original</td></tr>
</table>

ciallosb.is | sonnocingos

amman·m·m·xiii |]lat·

5   ccclxxxv |]b antaran·m ‖

]d simiuis

]manni iuos

]man iuos

]ri iuo

10   ]iuriurian

]anag |]roc

]n[

13ª-15 desunt

viii d[

° viiii no[inis[

20   °x n el[

°xi ... d edri[

°xii iii d cantl[

°xiii iii md samoni

°xiiii d duman[

25   °xv ds ma · ns riur

atenoux

° i d anagan

° ii iii md quti in ogr

° iii d ogroni qu[

30   iiii d giamoni

1. No trace whatever of the letter that stood between b and i   2. The sixth and the ninth letters are identical in the original

11. The t reported by Rhys before anag is not to be seen; g: or c? 12. r is broken, but c is perfect

16. n very doubtful 17. d broken   This entire fragment of bronze is buckled and difficult to read   19. After inis a mere fragment of an upright at bottom (b, d, e, h, i, k, l, m or what? r is possible, but by no means certain) 20. Corroded   21. Either edrini or idrini, quite uncertain which 23. ni corroded 24. After dum the rest is cracked and broken; probably an, but no trace of ni to follow

25. Ꮇ

28. ogr and then the bronze is buckled over 29. I saw no t to follow qu

The Calendar of Coligny IX

°v d simis amb

vi ііɬ d simiuisonn

qutio

35 °vii n giamoni | elembi ‖

°viii n giamoni

aedrini

°viiii d giamo cant

amb riur

40 °x ɬіi m d samon

°xi d dumn amb

°xii iii md riuri

°xiii d anag. amb

°xiiii iiɬ d ogronu

45 °xv iiɬ d amb qut

m giamon an[

i m d simiuison gia

°ii d

°iii d

50 iiii ḍ

v d amb

vi d

°vii iiɬ m d simiuitiocbr

°viii m d simiuis

55 °viiii m d simi sind íuos

35-36. I do not agree
with Rhys that a line
of writing may have
stood between these two
lines, or between 22
and 23   The bronze is
blank in both places,
without traces of writ-
ing   39. There is no
space for Rhys' ant be-
tween amb and riur

47. Or c?

48-50. Corroded

53. Corroded c: or g?

The Calendar of Coligny IX

```
        °x    d
        °xi   d amb
        °xii  d
        °xiii d
60      °xiiii  d
        °xv   d
        atenoux
        i   d
        ii  ns ds
65      iii  d amb
        iiii  d
        v   d  amb
        vi  iil  d
        ]d  simi amb
70      ]simiui
        ]miuis amb              71.  m very doubtful
72 deest
        ]r
74-77 desunt
        m  simiui[
        ]giamon p[              79.  Or c?
80      ii  m d
        iii  d  eq[
        iiii  m d
```

The Calendar of Coligny IX, X

```
        v   n[
        vi    d  equi
85      vii   d  equi
        viii   equi   prinni la
        viiii   d   equi
        x   m  d
        xi   iii   amb
90      xii   iii   m  d
        xiii   d   equí
        xiiii   d  equí
        xv    d equí
        atenoux
95      i    d   equi
        ii    d   equi
        iii    d   equi   amb
98-109  desunt
```

Column X

```
        m    equos anm
        °i   d   iuos              2.   d easily visible
        °ii   prin   lag   iuos
        i[ii]   m d iuos
    5    ]iuos
```

The Calendar of Coligny X

6-40 desunt

    viii [ ]uis tiocob   41. The lower part of
                                uis is all that remains;
    viiii m d edrini   but the reading is cer-
                                  tain, cf. IX 53 sq.

    x   n inis r

    xi   d amb

45   xii d

    xiii d

    xiiii d

    xv d

    atenou.

50   i[

    ii[

52-72 desunt

    ] cantl

    ] canti

75 deest

    xi   d anb

    xii ǂii m d

    xiii iǂi m d

    xiiii iil m d   79. iil sic

80   xv m d

    atenoux

    i d elemb

    ii d elemb

The Calendar of Coligny X

```
        iii   d   elem amb
85      iiii  iíi  m  d
        v   iił  d  amb
        vi  iił  m  d
        vii   d   cantl   amb
        viii  d   cantl
90      viiii   d   cantl amb
        x   iłi  m  d
        xi  iił  d  amb
        xii  m  d
        xiii  d  amb  iuo
95      xiiii  m  d  iuo
        xv   n   iuo
        m   cantlos an.
        i   m  d aedbini íuos
        ii   d   íuos
100     iii   d   íuos
        iiii   prinni  lag
        v   d  amb
        vi   d
        vii   samon prini loud
105     viii   d   dumani
        viiii  m  d  samoni
        x   d
```

90. amb at the end, and likewise iuo 94-96, seem to have been overlooked hitherto

98. For aedrini

1039

xi d amb   108. amb is placed be-
                             tween x d and xi d rather
xii d   than with the latter

110   xiii d

xiiii ḍ

xv d tiocobreχ[

atenoux

i d

115   ii d

iii d aṃ[

iiii n iṇi[

v ḍ [

vi [

120-128 desunt

Column XI

ṃ[

2-6 desunt

vi m d

vii d

viii m d

10   viiii d duman[

x m d

xi d amb

The Calendar of Coligny XI

```
      xii  m d

      xiii  Iii m d

15    xiiii  iiI m d

      xv  iiI  m d

      atenoux

      i  d  dumani

      ii  d  prini sam sindí

20    iii  d  amb

      iiii  Iii m d          21.  Iii corrected from
                             iii
      v iii  d  amb

      vi  iii  m d

      vii  d  dum amb

25    viii  d  dum

      viiii  n  dum  ínis r

      x  Iii  m d

      xi  iIii  d amb        28.  iIi and 29 iiI m d
                             corroded
      xii  iiIi  m d

30    xiii  d amb

      xiiii  m d

      xv  d amb              33.  ann    The last let-
                             ter is badly corroded; but
      m duman ann            I too think it was n rather
                             than m, though it is a wide
      i  samon prini loud    n if it was n

35    ii  d

      iii  d
```

iiii   d

v prin[38.   prin corroded

vi[

40-67 desunt

]iuos

]ig riuri

70   ]nis r

71 deest

]anagtios

]anag

]nag

75 deest

]s r

77 deest

]iu· g· riuri   78.   g or c?

]mat

80   ]at ns

]oux

82-96 desunt

]nn

]m d riuri   98.   riuri not -o

ii d

100   iii d

iiii m d ociomu riuri

The Calendar of Coligny XI

```
        v   n  inis r
        vi prinni  anag
        vii  m d ogroni
105     viii  m d ogroni
        viiii  m d ogroni
        x   d
        [  ] mb
```

109-111 desunt

```
        xv[
        ateno[
        i   d
115     ii   d
        iii  d  am[
        iiii  d  amb
        v   d  amb
        vi  n  inis·r
120     vii  iti d amb   ogron
        viii  iti m d quti ogron
        viiii  d ogron am
        x   ns ds
        xi   d amb
125     xii   d
        xiii  d amb
        xiiii  d
        x  diuirtomu
```

102. r is clear
103. vi is preceded by a small o, which, if not accidental, ought to have belonged to the preceding column; prinni is now clear (the verdigris having been removed); then I saw, according to my notes, anag not the expected lag   106. ogroni now all distinct

117. amb deleted by the engraver   b incomplete

119. iiiis aes (‖ for N)

The Calendar of Coligny XII

Column XII

    ]rom m[

2-12 desunt

    ° [

    ° x[

15 ° xii[

    ° xv

    atenou[

    i   Ꞽii m d qutio

    ii iꞼi m d qutio

20   iii   iiꞼ   d amb qutio

    °iiii   m d

    v   d amb

    vi   d   Ꞽii

    vii iꞼi amb qutio

25   viii iiꞼ md ogro quti   25. g is ⟨

    viiii iiꞼ d amb q[

    x   m d

    xi [   ] amb

    xii[

30 xiii[

    xii[

    x[

33-87 desunt

The Calendar of Coligny XII

```
        ]r
        ]s  r
90      ]mb
91 deest
        ]ini  r
93 deest
        ]d amb
95      ]iii  d
        diuertomu
        m  simiuis mat
        i  giamo prini lago       98.  g is ᐸ (twice)
        ii  n
100     iii  iɫi  d equi
        iiii  m d
        v  n  inis r
        vi  d  equi
        vii  m d tiocobreχtio
105     viii  m d
        viiii  m d sindiu iuos
        x  m d
        xi  n
        ]  m d
110     ]d  equi
111-126 desunt
```

°xii[

°xv[

Column XIII

    m   equos a[

    i d

    ii prini lag[

    iii n semiu[

5   iiii iiƗ d

    v d amb

    vi m d sim

    vii d

    ]prini lag

10   ]i iiƗ d

    ]iƗi d

    ]d amb

    ]d

    ]m d simi

15   ]m d simi

    ]m d simi

    ]noux

    ]semiu

    ]semiu

20   ]emiu

12. amb is clear, but
(though it must belong
to 12) is placed between
lines 11 and 12

The Calendar of Coligny XIII

21 deest

]b

]bu

24-64 desunt

65   ]mat

]s íuo

67-80 desunt

]ux

]elembi

]elembi

]d   ami elemb

85   ]lii m d

v   iiƚ d amb

vi iiƚ m d

°vii   d amb

°viii   m d

90   °viiii ƚii   ᵗin d amb

°x   iƚi   m d sindiu íuo

°xi iiƚ d amb

°xii   m d

°xiii   d .mb

95   °xiiii   m d

°xv   n

m   cantlos anm

90.   What looks like in
is presumably an incom-
plete ∧ partly erased

```
        °i   m d aedrini

        °ii  d

100     °iii  d

        °iiii  prinni lag

        v  iłi  d amb

        vi  n

        vii  ḍ

105     viii  d

        viiii  ḍ

        x   łii[

        xi  iłi[

        °xii[

110     °x[

111-128 desunt
```

Column XIV

1-16 desunt

```
        ạ[  ]ux

        °i  ḍ  ḍumani

        °ii  m d .rino samon          19.  p is very doubtful;
                                      perhaps read trinosamon?
20      °iii  d amb                   Not ed-

        °iiii  łii m d

        °v  iłi  d amb

        °vi  iił m d
```

The Calendar of Coligny XIV

```
       °vi[

 25    °vi[

       °v[

27-57 desunt

       ] n  in[

       ] d[

 60    ] d amb[

       ]i  n ini r[

       xiii  d amb[

       xiiii  ns ds [

       diuirtomu

 65    m  riuros mat

       °i  d anagantio

       °ii  prinni loud

       ]m  d

       ]tio riuro

70-87 desunt

       ]b

       ]iuri anag

 90    ]b

       ]uri

92-98 desunt

       ]d  go riuri

100    ]d iuo
```

At 33 Rhys reported a
fragment m[duman anm],
and at 55-57 another
fragment vi[vii[
viii[which I did not see

62. d certain

64. corroded

The Calendar of Coligny XIV

    iiii m d ociomu riuri

    ]n ini·r

    ]prin lag

    ]d

105   ]d

    ]d

107 deest

    ]amb

109-112 desunt

    ]ux

114 deest

115   ]d

    iii ɫii d a[

    ˙iiii iɫi d

    v iiɫ d amb   118. v entered twice
    v   by error
    vi n in.r

120   vii n ini·r

    viii d

    viiii n ini r

    x ɫii d

    xi iiɫ d a[

125   ]ii d

    ]ii d [

127-128 desunt

The Calendar of Coligny XV

Column XV

    ]mat

2 deest

    ]loud

4 deest

5   ]d̤[

    ]r

7-12 desunt

    ]ii̤ m d̤

    xi̤ii m d

15   xiiii m d

    xv m d

    atenoux̤

    i m d qutio

    ii m d qutio

20   iii d amb qutio

    iiii m d

    v d am̤b

    vi iil m d

    vii d am̤b   24. amb is placed be-

25   viii m d qutio   tween lines 23 and 24

    viiii d am̤b

    x m d

    xi d am̤b

```
       xii  n inis r
30     xiii  iii  d amb
       xiiii  ii  m d
       xv  d amb
       m  cutios mat
       i  m d
35     ii  m d
       iii  m d
       iiii  prinno loud
       v  n ini  r
       vi  n d
40     vii  m d
       viii  m d
       viiii  n ini  r
       x  m d
       xi  d amb
45     xii  n
       xiii  m d
       xiiii  m d
       xv  m d
       atenoux
50     i  m d ogroni
       ii  m d ogro
       iii  d amb ogr
```

44. amb stands between
lines 44 and 43

The Calendar of Coligny XV

```
      ]n  ini  r
      ]d  amb
55    ]n  ini  r
      ]ḍ   amb
      ]d  ogroni
      ]amb
      ]ḍ
60    ]ḍ   amb
      ]ḍ
      ]ḍ  amb   íuo
      ]ṃ  d   íuo
      ]   amb  íuo
65    ]mom   anm
      ]mius  exoiu
      ]iuo
68-84 desunt
85    iiii   iii[
      v   iii[
      vi   iii[
      °vii  [
      °viii[
90    °viiii[
      x
      xi
      xii
```

65. m in anm falls in
column XVI

In 81 Rhys reports a
fragment at[, and in
83-84 a fragment ii[
iii[which I did not
see

The Calendar of Coligny XV, XVI

94-96 desunt

    ]at   97. In column XVI

98-99 desunt

100   °iii

      °iiii

      ˑv[

      ˑvi[

      °vii[104-105. There are traces of d between the two lines

105   ˑv[

106-128 desunt

Column XVI

    m equos anm

    i d

    ii prin la[

    iii n simiui

5   iiii iiꝉ d

    v d amb   6. d is incomplete Ɔ (sic)

    vi m d sem[

    vii d

    viii prino la[

10   viiii iꝉi d

    ]iiꝉ[

The Calendar of Coligny XVI

12-18 desunt

 ii m [19-26. This fragment
             may not be correctly
20 iii d amb s   placed here 20. sic

 iiii d

 v iii d amb

 vi iii d amb

 vii iii d amb

25 viii d

 ]d amb

27 deest

 ]mb iuo

 ]iuo

30]amb iuo

 ]iuo

 ]mb iuo

 ]biu anm

 ]iuo

35]iuo

 ]l[36. l part of lag? No
            trace of iuo in this
37-42 desunt   line

 ]n[

 ]iii d[

45 xii d

 xiii d

 xiiii d

```
         xv   n
         atenoux
  50     i    n   edrin[            50.  e scarcely distin-
                                         guished from i
         ii   d   edri[
         iii  d   amb  e[
         iiii d
         v    d amb
  55     vi   iii  d
         vii  iii  d amb
         viii iii  d
         viiii d amb
         x    d
  60     xi   d amb
         xii  iii  d
         xiii iii  d amb
         xiiii iii d
         diuertomu
  65     m    edrini mat
         i    d   si[
         ii   m[
         iii  [
69-76 desunt
         xii  m d
         xiii m d
```

The Calendar of Coligny XVI

```
        xiiii  m d
 80     xv  m d
        atenoux
        i   d elemb
        ii   n
        iii  d amb elemb
 85     iiii  m d
        v   d amb              86.  amb is placed be-
        vi  iii m d            tween lines 86 and 87
        vii  d amb             88.  amb is placed be-
        viii  m d              tween lines 88 and 89
 90     viiii  d amb
        x  m d sindiu iuo
        xi   d amb
        xii  m d
        xiii  d amb
 95     xiiii  m d
        xv   n
        m   cantlos anm
        i   m d edrini
        ii   d
100     iii   d
        iiii  prinn·n·lag
        v   iii  d amb
        vi   n
```

The Calendar of Coligny XVI

vii d

105   viii d

viiii d

]d[

]amb

109-121 desunt

]amb

]d

xi   d amb

125   xii d

xiii iii d amb íuo

xiiii   d íuo

diuertomu

Unplaced Fragments

(a)   ]x

]ui

]ui

]i amb

(b) Two pieces, now fitted together:

vi   d m

vii   prinni la[

The Calendar of Coligny: Fragments

```
            viii  iιi  d

            viiii  n ini r

5           x  d

            xi  d amb

            ]ii  d

            ]ii  [

            ]ii  [
```

Here, with the removal in time of small pieces of verdigris, it has been possible to correct earlier readings (lines 1, 3, 4)

```
(c)         ]semiuiso

            ]d  semiuiso    1-3.  se-, not
                                  si-
            ]d  semi

            ]noux

            ]miu

            ]u


(d)         vi[

            vii[

            viii[


(e)         ]m d t

            ]m d ti

            ]m d

            ]d
```

Calendar of Coligny: Fragments; Names
of Potters (Luxeuil, Heiligenberg)

]d

]d

(f)   ]umman (AcS 3.29)

228   Names of Potters

On potteries in Germania Superior (including Windisch and other manufacturies given below) see in general
Grenier in Frank 3, 1937, 550; and 88 Remark above.

(i)   Luxeuil (A.D. 80-120)

Agedillus	Ioenalis	Pritmanus
Anteros	Maro	Ranto
Birrantus	Maronus	?Satto
Britann[	Musicus	?Saturninus

(ii)   Heiligenberg (A.D. 100-130)

Aenisatus	Belsus	Censorinus
Aimiadus		Cerialis
Alpinus	Carisius	Cintugnatus
Anisatus	Cassius	Ciriuna
Apirilis	Cassus	Coixoinus
Auernia	Cauirinus	Consta(n)s
Auinius	Celsus	Cracus

Names of Potters (Heiligenberg)

Cristo, Crissto

Curinnus

Domitianus

Drombus (-n-)

Firmus

Gemellus

Geminius

Ianus

Ibilirius

Iuliccus

Iulius

Iuriunn[

Lucanus

Lut(a)eus or
   Luteu(o)s

Magnus

Mammillianus

Marcellinus

Marcinus

Marinus

Maritanus

Maro

Maso

Maxaxius

Melausus

Miccio

Minus

Niualis

Oc(c)iso
   (-ioso)

Patruitus

Paullinus

Repanus (Ri-)

Respectus (Medi-
   [omatricus?)

Ripanus

Rufinus

Sacco

Saciantrus

Saciiantro

Saciratus

Sacratus

Sedatus

Seuerinus

Sollemnis

Sollenbenis

Successus

Suinus

Tartus

Toccinus

Tribocus

Tullio

Turtunnus

Vaccul(us)

Valentinus

Vannius

Veniantus

Venicarus (-ne-)

Verecundus

Viccius

Viducus

Virauus

Names of Potters (Ittenweiler,
Rheinzabern)

(iii) Ittenweiler (A.D. 110-130)

Agressus	Cintus	Gesatus
Auitus	Cintugnatus	Suadeuillus
Austalis	Cintusmus	Suadullius
Carantus	Ganniceius	Toccinus
C(i)elsinus	Gannicus (C-)	Verecundus

(iv) Rheinzabern (A.D. 130-200 or 250). Cf. W. Ludowici
Stempelnamen....in Rheinzabern 1901-1914 (RA 29, 1929,
202)

Abbo	Amunus	Attianus
Acceptus	Aper	Attillus
Acussa	Aprianus	Attiolus
Aesto, Aisto, Aistus	Apris (-us)	Attisio
	Arala	Atto
Aeuinius	Arminus	Attoni
Aibre	Aroitus	Atulrus
Albinus	Arrus	Auena
Alc	Aruernicus	Auetedo
Alca	Ascilli	Augustalis
Alloni	Atreius	Augustinus
Amabilis	Atrestus	Auitus
Amandus	Atrextus (-χs-), Atreχtus	Aunus
Amator		Austinus
Ammo	Atretus, -ius	

1062

Names of Potters (Rheinzabern)

Austrus	Catus	Crassiacus
Autillus	Cefalio	Crissi, Crissio
Auus	Cenno	for Cris(s)to
	Censorinus	see (ii) above (Germ. 11, 1925, 119)
Belatullus	Cerialis	Crummus
Bellator	Cibisus (-ius)	Cucio, Cucus
Belsus	Cillutius	Cullatius
Birius	Cintugnatus	Cunissa
Bisso	Cintusmus	Cusius
Borlus	Cinus	Cuxus
Buccius	Clemens	Cuᵪsus
	Cobnertus	
Capitolinus	Comitialis	Datius
?Capurio	Conatius	Decminus
Caranus	?Constaeni	Dignus
Carisius	Constans	Diuiᵪtus
Caromarus	Constantinus	Docilis
Carus	Coradus	Domitius
Casatos	Costillius	Donatus
Casiatis	Costio	Dubitatus
Castor	Co(n)stinuti (cf.	
Castus	214 Chumstinc- tus?)	Eluentinus
Cattianus	Cottalus	[Errumocito?]
Catullus	Couentio	Euritus

Names of Potters (Rheinzabern)

Eustadius	Iatta 10010.3166	Lillus
	Iassus	Lillutius, -io
Fato	Icouicus	Liltani
Fauo, Fauuo	Impetrati	Luceanus
Ferminus	Ioincorix	Lucinus
Firmanus	Iouanti	Lupercus
Firminus	Iouentus	Lupus
Firmi, -us	Ippus	Luscero
Flauianus	Iscatus	Lutaeus, -aius,
Florentinus	Iuanius	-eus, -euos
Fortio, -onis	Iuaus	
		Maginus
	Iulianus	Magio
Gemellus	Iulius	Maianus
Genialis	Iuratus	Mammilianus
Gimillus	Iustio	Marcellini
Gorio	Iuuenis	Marcellus
		Marcianus
Haisto (cf. Aisto)	Laitilo	Marinus
	Latinianus	
Helenius	Latinnus, Latinus	Meritus
Honoratus		Marthus
	Launio, Lannio Cf. Germ. 9, 1925, 119	Martinus
Ianinus		Martius
	Leo	
Ianuco		Marus
	Liberalis	
Ianus		Mascellio

Names of Potters (Rheinzabern)

Mas(s)imus	Niuires 10010.3166	Pattusa
Maternianus	(for Nequres, Necures?)	?Pepius
Materninus	Nouanus	Peppo
Maternus	Nundinus, Nudinus	Peregrinus
Matianus		Perimitius
Matinus, -a	Oc(c)iso	Perpetus
Mattato, -us	Oenias	Peruincus
Matto	Onar	Petilianus
Matugenus	Oneratus	Pippius
Maturus	Onniorix	Placidus
Mecco	(cf. Ouniorix 213 above; Onnio AcS 2.857; 13.	Polianus
Melausus	10010,1464)	Polio
Mettus	Orninus	Potitusio
Mica	Otonius	Pottalus
Miccio		Potulus
Minna	Pacatus	Primantius
Minus	Paidus	Primanus
Mixius (-o-?)	Pastenaius	Primitiuos, -us
Modestus	Paternianus	Primitius
Motus	Paternus	Probus
	Patricianus	Proclienus
Naris	Patruinus	Properatus
Natus	Patruitus	Proppius
Nenarius	Pattosus	Prouincialis

Names of Potters (Rheinzabern)

Pupus	Secundanus	Vacator
	?Secundinaui (i.e. Secundinus Auitus)	Vaccura
Regalis		Vasianus
Reginus	Sedulus	Vcumus
Regulinus	Sendatus, Sedatus	Vector
Rep	Seuerianus	Venicarus (-ne-)
Reppo	Seuuo	Veniso
Respectinus	Sextus	Venus
Respectus	Sintanius	Venustus
Restio	Sinto	Veratius
Restitutus	Sollius	Verecundus
Restutus	Sollo	Verinus
Resulinus	Sollus	Verus
Ritus	Statutus	Victor
Rufiani	Suadeuillus or Suadullius	Victorinus
Rullinus		Viducus
		Vindemialis
	Tasellus	Vinxus
Sabienus	Tatratius	Viratilus
Sabinianus	Taurus	Vitus
Sabinus	Temporinus	Viuinus
Satinus	Toccinus, Tocci 10010.3166	Vrsianus
Sattara	Torf[	Vrsico
Saturio	Trescantus	Vrsinus
Saturrus		Vrsus

Names of Potters (Vindonissa, Mandeure,
Vertault)

(v) Vindonissa (A.D. 100-120)

Apirilis	Paullinus	Siluinus
Cintugnatus	Reginus	?Vdes
Mercator	Rufinus	Verecundus
Montanus	Secundinus	Virilis
Patricius		

(vi) Mandeure (A.D. 110-130)

Atimus	Marcellinus

(vii) Vertault (cf. Germ. 6, 1922, 123-25; Drioux Les
Lingons, 695)

Aetussa	Cienso	Eluinus
Andeco	Ciruca	Ganicos (C-)
Arilus	Comacus (-g-)	Iaunus (F-?)
Biant[	Cotthios (auoti)	Inauus
Boiius	Crixus, -ius	Ἰολλο (cf. FHRC 32.2)
Buoric	Darrantus	
Βυℸιολυ	Dassos	Iotobito (?Dari-)
Candillus	Disio	Laguaudus
Cariatus	Eilo	Messinius

Names of Potters (Vertault, Blickweiler)

Nem[es?]	Rudus	Tinntus
Noiobito?	Sacatta? (-ttha)	Viriodaci
Noue	Secoios (auote)	Vlatos (cf. AcS 8.
Orcos	Silciatus	421,26)
Ronsus	Suncius	Voranus
		Vta

(viii) Blickweiler (A.D. 105-140)

Albillus	Caprasius	Paternus
Albinus	Cocus	Petrullus
Aper	Doeccus	Pottus
Austrus	Eburus	Saciro, -us
Bitunus (not the Arretine -hus?)	Gemellinus	Sacro
	Mattio	Satto
Borillus	Mattius	Saturninus
Borius	Marro	Secco
Cambo	Miccio	Tocca
Campinus	Moscus	Vimpus
Candidus		

Names of Potters

(ix) Names of Potters found in Germania Superior (items marked [1] are taken from R. Forrer Strasbourg-Argentorate, 1927; a few other items come from BA 1934-35 [1940] pp.531-535; Behn Röm. Keramik, Mainz 1910; Mylius R-G Forsch. 12, 1936, 130. As to Forrer's readings I feel the gravest doubts.)

Abudo[1]	Atitisus 10010.199	Caddiro
Acca	Atta[10010.201	Caddiron 10010.392
Acinnus[1]	Attro	Cadilon 10010.392
Acilnus	Attusa, -os 10010.211	Cainus
Aciani		Camillianus
Acinnus	Axanticus	Camorinus
Adius	Axinus	Canduionus[1]
Adiutor	Auctus	Canicae (Behn 1387)
Ager	Audatus	
Agillito	Audilus	Can(n)icos (G-) 10010.430
Alinnus 10010.90	Auetus	Cananus 10010.426
Alpinus		Cantomallus
Alrus[1]	Bippa	Capinus
Ambatus	Bitucaro	Capurio 10010.447
Amoco (R.2311 n.)	Borius 10010. 3089	Carantolo[1]
Aspr[	Bracciatus	Cariatus
Astaurus	Bubalus; cf. Germ. 14, 1930, 255	Cattaini (Behn 1771)
Atecnudis (-tis)		
Atias(s)us 10010. 193	Buturi 10010.375	Caura 10010.506
		Celatus
Atitio 10010.198	Cacabus	Celtianus

Names of Potters

Cenna, -us

Cicanus (-m-?)

Cocceianus

Coruinus

Credus

Crixus, -χsus

Dappui 10010.3247

Datueius 10010.
758

Dauica 10010.759

Diuerus

Dinatus?

Docca

Dolccus (not -e-)
10010.802

Doria

Dubintius

Ducius

Ebredus

?Emaus

Espucus (or Eup-)

Etrulios[1]

Excingius 10010.
875

Forianus[1]

Fou[[1]

Fritus[1]

Ganicos (C-)

Genatis[1]

Germani 10010.375

Gessius

Giamilus

Grassia[1]

Homobon[

Iaoafo[1]

Ialussa[1]

Ianetus (R.2311
n.)

Iantui[1]

Icurnus

Iducinus[1]

Intus

Ioicato[1]

Irmo

Iuccus 10010.3089

Iueratius[1]

Iumesa

Iusico

Laco

Laguaudus

Lassenius 10010.
1115

Lauratus

Lexius

Magitanus[1]

Mantius

Mappa

Meuillus

Miacinus[1]

Moilo (?)[1]

Monus

Musa

Namantus

Nemausus[1]

Nerrus[1]

Nertus

Nilus

Names of Potters

Noiobito (-uio-) 10010.1438

Nonus[1]

Nudinus[1]

Nutis?

Octorinus[1]

Ollecnos 10010. 3214

Ollilos

Onirini[1]

]onoχs.[1

?Opurimus 10010. 1471

Origesus

?Oxmiro (Behn 533; Mirus?)

Pera

Procalius(?)

Prueini 10010. 3214

Rascio

Ratinus

Renus[1]

Ritu(arus)

Rubali[1

Rutac[1

Sacadisus

Sakkn[1]

Sapito[1]

Sattiθ[1

Sauuo[1]

Seccali[1]

Sedatus

Senilis

Sequanus

Simirinus[1]

Sintillus 10010. 1891

Soilos[1]

Sollenbeni[1]

Sosa

Strambus (R.2311 n.)

Tabus 10010.1867

Tagonus

Taiuba (Tal-?) 10010.1871

Tanconius

Tascouanus[1]

Tata, -us

Tatira

Tiotagus

Tocirnus (-g-)[1]

Tornus

Torosu(s) 10010. 1931

Toroxo, Troχso 10010.1943

Treuir

Tribocus 10010. 1938

Tritus

Varicos

Vcatus

Vegiso

Velugni 10010. 1995

Vepu[1 (R.2311 n.)

Vesi[

Vestrus[1]

?Vicoius

Vid(o)ucus

Violus

Names of Potters

Vipac[10010.   Vonus   Vossatius
   2049

Virto

Remark:

    Loring BA 1926, 116-136 and Drioux (Les Lingons
no.695, 696) give a few additional names from Langres
and the vicinity, viz:

Aiulli	Comagus	Pucatus (Canru-?)
Ates	Dassos	Ronsius
Bauri	Ducius	Rouinus
Buadusi	Egualarus	Rudus
Buturo	?Feluius	Viainos (?)
Cananus	Germanus	Volusenus
Candillus	Nonico	?Zacada
?Cenratius		

    At Coblenz (BJ 142, 1937, 44-46) we have (chiefly
on Belgic ware or lamps):

Acoieuso?	Aru	Daponi
Acundius	Attillus	Drapon
Acutus	Capr	Exscincius

1072

Names of Potters; Graffito of Blickweiler

Iiuotuii (Euo-?)	Otii (Ote[?)	Strobili
Iuima	Osir	Torno
Mario	?Oxmiro	Varo
Maros	]ruid	Veio
Naritus	Rumius	Vocaris (-a)
Nauo		

229   Graffito of Blickweiler

The Blickweiler graffito which follows, and which
so clearly resembles those of La Graufesenque, was discovered in 1912-13 (AE 1924, p.398) and published by
O. Bohn in Pfälzische Museum, Pfälzische Heimat 1923,
pp.39-40, whence it was repeated verbatim by R. Knorr
and Fr. Sprater in their work Die westpfälzischen Sigillata: Töpfereien von Blickweiler und Eschweiler Hof,
Speier-am-Rhein 1927 (Histor. Museum der Pfalz, Histor.
Verein der Pfalz, Veröffentlichungen, 3 Band), pp.115-
118, on which, together with Hermet's notices of it, the
following account is based. Hermet gives it as no.44 in
his plates, merely for comparison; there is no reason to
suppose that it came from La Graufesenque.

The fragment came to light "in den letzten Jahren
vor dem Kriege." Bohn published his copy, which he
describes as "zwar flüchtig," from inspection of the
original; the writing was done after firing, as in the
La Graufesenque graffiti (90-131 above). In fact, once
the nature of these graffiti is realized, obviously it
could not have been done at any other time, or, indeed,
before a vase had been broken or at least discarded as
imperfect.

Graffito of Blickweiler

Bohn at once saw the general nature of the contents
of the text, and compared the specimens published by
Hermet in RA 1904, as well as the Montans fragment (CIL
13.10017,46). He further pointed out that in contrast
with the Montans-La Graufesenque lists (nom.), this
gives the names of potters in the gen. -i, e.g. -rulli
(cf. Petrullus 228 viii above, better than Verullus,
CIL 3.5220, or Vocrullus 13.5295), and similarly Lituui,
Carletisoni, Saq(u)anoli, all of which are otherwise unrecorded, "ihre Elemente aber gut keltisch."

Under names of vases, Bohn places uas and uass cf.
CIL 13.6086: uassa decem; -nnias he identifies with an
imaginary cauannis at CIL 13.10017,46; catilli and
paruspi (παροψίδες) we have at La Graufesenque; gollati
he explains as colati cf. lucernae colatae CIL 13.10001,
19; 8.10478,1 and Suppl. 22643, 2-9, TLL s.v. colare;
at is interpreted as "up to," before numerals, and it
as "item" (cf. CIL 13.10017,47).

I.]i |].lxx   uass at ccxxxx |

]rulli |].nnias at dccc uass at ᴎ dc

Graffiti of Blickweiler

II.] licuui | parusp aequat at[

5 carletisoni[| catilli golla[| saqanoli ‖

cantilli carnuata | paruspi gollat si init

I 2. uas Bohn 4. pa]nnias At La Graufesenque we have both panna and pannia, pania (cf. Oxé BJ
130, 1925, 52-55); cf. panna 10017.663 and ORL 8 (Zugmantel, 1909) p.156

II 1. lituui Bohn; perhaps licuias? 7. gollat
at it Bohn; perhaps li at it? 2. q differs from the
q of line 5, but no other reading seems possible (Bohn)

See further O. Bohn Germania 7, 1923, 64-67
(REA 28, 1926, 37); J. Loth RC 42, 1924, 221-22; id.,
CRAcInscBL 1924, 67-74; Oxé l.c.; Knorr Töpfer u. Fabri-
ken Verzierter Terra-Sigillata des ersten Jahrhanderts,
Stuttgart 1919.

But uass is "about, more or less" (*upo-sta-),
while gollat corresponds to bol at La Graufesenque;
hence aequat[(Lat.) at Blickweiler translates us at La
Graufesenque. Thus uass corresponds to uχsedia (?) and
carnuat to luχtos (?).

230

A similar graffito of Rheinzabern is given by Oxé
BJ 130, 1925, 52 after Ludowici Rheinzab. Töpfer 2,
1901-1905, p.138; Sprater Pfalz unter den Römern 2, 1930,
141.

Graffiti of Rheinzabern; Miscellaneous
Graffiti

(a) Ia]nuarius

(b) | aci]tabla(?) |]xxx |]ria(?)

5   lxxv |]xxv ‖

(c)]tata

230 bis

And yet another, Ludowici ib. p.x.

]xl |]ccc | | | cer]uesa[ri(?)

5   ]cl ‖]cccc

In line 5 Ludowici reads uesti

Note 1iii

A number of graffiti found at Vertault, some in
Greek alphabet, were reported in BA 1926 [1927] 138-39,
viz.

(a) eburii[

(b)]atu[?

(c)]ουε[

(d) καμουλα

(e) λουο

(f) mat

Miscellaneous Graffiti

(g) ?atped

(h) ?atpor (miswriting for Gaipor?)

(i) sen

(k) dam

(l) rutilo curmilo auitia de[

Cf. Drioux Les Lingons pp.171-73.

F.A. Schaeffer Un Dépot...à Seltz 1927, gives a graffito, p.32

uribus

Similarly R. Forrer Strasbourg-Argentorate 1927 vol. 1, 304-06 reports the following graffiti from Strassburg, viz.

Attilsi	Germi[
Cassognati	Renicos
Dabiro	Moriconis
Finillae	Vertos

The same author reports the following names on lamps and amphorae (pp.607-608) from the same place:

Apocc[	Mocta[
Beruca (V-?)	Sequan[
Ites	Talutius

Miscellaneous Graffiti; AVOT

Finally he gives (p.730) a fragment of Runic or quasi-Runic writing (not in Arntz); this last is of much later date than the records collected in this book.

Note liv

Potter's marks with auot(i) appear in Germania Superior as follows (CIL 13 iii 1, p.121; cf. fasc. 2 p.465); see Note xi above.

(a) auot

10010.248 (Bingen, Weisenau, Andernach)

(b) Iullo auot

10010.1084 (Rheintürkheim)

(c) Trous auot

10010.1944 (Bingen)

(d) Vasen[auot

10010.2911

(e) uocar | auoti

BJ 142, 1937, 44 (Coblenz, Belgic ware), not uoati. In CIL 13.10010,2075 uocari (sc. auoti?), but 10010.2076 uocara fecit. Other names accompanied by auot are Bollo (10010.335) and Ericu (10010.859). Cf. Note xlix above, 228 (vii).

Tile-stamps and Coin-legends

231

 Names on Tile-Stamps (Germania Superior), cf. 205 above. The following are taken from CIL l.c. (cf. CIL 13 ii 1, p.302, Castell), Riese 1094 (cf. 4611-22).

Amasonius	Didius	Sedule
Arbo(g)astis (episc.)	Dun[	Sedularcoi
	Heluius	Sentius
Arcas	Latti	Sucio
Auitius	Lupi	Ti(gurinus?)
Bellicus	Mestr(i)us	cf. TrZ 10, 1935, 64; 13.
Bricic		12792; and
	Mogontia	gloss 207 above
Camulus	Montanus	Toude (13.12864)
Celaic[	Ricom[	Vatus
Cinturi AE 1934. 131	Sabalius	Vinds[(C p.302)
Consius	Sarda	Vrsi
Decuma		

232

 Coin-legends of Germania Superior (from Blanchet Traité des monnaies gauloises 1905; R. Forrer Monnaies gauloises ou celtiques trouvées en Alsace, Mulhouse 1926; cf. BA 1932-33 [1936], 636-37; R. Forrer Strasbourg-Argentorate, vol. 1, 1927, 34* 35* [for the items marked*]; however, some of these are proper to Lugdunensis.)

Coin-legends

auχustus

biteotei*

kal, kaledou, kaletedou;
   but cf. 177 above.
   A reading kaletaedui
   (Vogt l.c. 239 below),
   if correct, is gar-
   bled or corrupt

caniccos (Forrer MG 71)

cantorix (cf. 177)

cel

? ΚѠΚΟΓΙΟΓ

doci (docius, docirix?)

ekrito

?imioci

?iminocirix

ιολου

?iotuos v. sequano-

sam (samotalos?)

sequa, sequano, sequa-
   niotuos (sequano
   iotuos i.e. two words?)

solima

ΤΟΥLΚϪΙΟΙΤΟΓ (?), ΚλΙΟΙΤΟΓ
   (-ϪΥΤ-?) AcS 2.1867

togirix

turonos (or Lugd.?)

Remark:

   CIL 13.10016,12 (Mainz) testifies to the spread
of the Latin alphabet, especially as used by potters.
This one has ‖ e, Γ f, Κ k, Ⱶ l, and at the end ΧΥΖ(sic).

   Besides several of the graffiti given above (Note
1111), CIL 13.10017,217 (R.4531) shows a few letters
of the Greek alphabet in a text not obviously articulate:

   ααγκσ   κκο   ατμρ   σδακ

Coin-legends; Glosses

IG 14.2573,9 (Benfeld, Alsace) reads

$$\kappa \alpha \nu \zeta \alpha \,|\, \pi \iota o \upsilon$$

But the Greek inscription noted at CIL 13 iv, 1916, p.75
(πλωτικα etc.) is possibly false.

233

Glosses

(Cf. Note on Glosses 1 above; 79; and 220 above)

[abaso "infirmatorium; seoccra manna hus" Gl. Aelfric

185.21

The other gloss infirma (v.l. infima, infama)
quasi sine base (CGL 5.591,32) obviously is etymologiz-
ing; and Hesych. ἀβάς· εὐήθης καί ἱερά νόσος, cited in
TLL not obviously related (a garbled variant of ἀβάνας
178?). Etymology? Perhaps not Germanic at all.]

alces, ἄλκη "elk, moose-deer," see PID 2.194

In Hercynia silua BG 6.27. Cf. Alce local name
(Celtiberia), helix 207 above, Alcouindus 151 above,
Lep. alkouinos PID 2.274. On the etymology W-H 1, 28,
cf. 845.; pers. name Alciacus 212 above; adj. alcinus
13.5708. The form alcis Tac. G 43.3 is a Germanic nom-
pl. i-stem. Cf. Dottin Mélanges Loth 1927, 92; other
discussions RhM 89, 1940, 1-6, 6-7, 12-16, 151-152 (PhW
60, 1940, 398-9, 614-15), TrZ 15, 1940, 8-27 and 16-17,
1941-2, 1-66 (RA 23, 1945, 160; 26, 1946, 105); GRM 28,
1940, 245-58; AR 6, 1922, 300; REA 46, 1944, 328-29;
Kluge Urg. ed. 3, 13 cf. 35.

Glosses

altitona (i.e. *alto-dunum) "hohenburc"

    Presumably Hohenburg (Alsace) MGSS 23.434,25 (AcS 1.110); cf. Ir. alt "cliff," O.W. allt "collis" ib. 3. 578.

[besant (O.Fr.) "pièce d'or, auri solidum"

    Properly "(nummus) byzantinus," but apparently associated by popular etymology with the local names Vesontio, Besantio, Bisontii and Crusinia (quasi Chryso-polis), cf. the modern Orchamp(s); perhaps names such as Argentorate, -uaria contributed to the confusion. Cf. C. fasc. ii p.70; and for gold-workings at Ehl (Ill) see REA 15, 1913, 311.]

?brittola "cepa minuta" CGL 3.608,40

    Other testimonia and forms (britton[i]?) in AcS 3. 971. Cf. OChSl. briti "cut;" Vosges bratte, brotte, Lothr. brat, brot (M-L REW 1315), Sp. breton?

caesia silua "Hesiwald" (OLG., in the Ruhr) Tac. A 1.50

    W-H 1, 133 (s.v. caesaries) cites MLG heister, hester "young oak or beech;" cf. Much Anz. Akad. Wiss. Wien Ph-H Kl. 71, 1934, 143-144; Gomoll RhM 87, 1938, 177-188; Kluge Urg. ed. 3, pp.9, 31, 34.

dusmus gl. Luxem. "diabolus"

    AcS 1.1387,32; on which see W-H 1, 386 and 861 (dusius 178 above), comparing Westph. dūs "devil" (ac-cording to Holthausen Anglia Beibl. 43, 1932, 270 borrowed from OF. dieus "God," cf. Pokorny ZfCPh 14, 1923, 293; SprFK 200).

1082

Glosses

?ἐμπονή "heroine"

So Do 255, from Plut. amat. 25, p.770E: ἦν δὲ
(Σαβῖνος,) γυναῖκα πασῶν ἀρίστην ἡγμένος, ἣν, ἐκεῖ μὲν ἐμπονὴν
('E-?) ἐκάλουν, Ἑλληνιστὶ δ'ἄν τις ἡρωίδα ('Η-?) προσ-
αγορεύσειεν , but the conjecture Σεμόνην, as a proper
name, has been advanced; Dio Cass. 66.16.1 gives Πεπο-
νίλλα and Tac. h 4.67 Epponina. Etym.? Perhaps cf.
epona?

fara "journey"?

Mar. Avent. Chron. 2.238, 569, cf. TLL s.v. (OHG
faran).

?gleton, glis "bur, burdock"

See the glosses quoted in AcS 1.2027 (Stuttg.):
glis etiam uocatur herba, quam uulgus gleton uocatur,
and (Évreux) cleton "lappa;" cf. OHG chletto, OE clide.

The gloss glis: humus tenax CGL 5.601.7 must be
related, and presumably glittus in Cato de agr. cult.
45.1, cf. Paul. ex Fest. 87 (: Lat. gluten, glus).

Cf. also OFr. cleton (Frank. kletto), Fr. gletton,
Norm. kyatrō, M-L REW 4709. If gleton, glis "burdock"
is actually Germanic, it must be older than the first
Germanic sound-shift, which seems improbable, unless,
in view of OFr. cleton, the spelling gleton is for
*cleton (under the influence of glutto).

*hora "locus palustris" CIL 13 ii p.58

This is believed to appear in Chorost (234 below),
modern Hor-burg; the accepted etymologies of OHG koro
(W-P 1.409, cf. 325) make it Germanic (h- for k-), but
cf. Chora fl. (AcS 1.1008), hardly Horo-latis divine
name 86 above?

Glosses

isarno- "iron"

Vit. Eugendi (abb. Iurensis), ASS 1 Jan. 1.50:
Gallica lingua Isarnodori (gen. sg.), id est ferrei
ostii.

For doro- "ostium" see 178 above; isarno- in proper
names is well-established (AcS 2.75-76), OIr. iarn, OW.
hearn. The question is to what language isarno- properly belongs. Holder roundly asserted that in ASS above
"Gallica lingua" is "falsch," "wohl burgundisch oder
gotisch oder frankisch," "got. daur und eisarn," and
there has been much discussion of this point. Pokorny
in particular, Urg. 75 (cf. KZ 44, 1914, 290-292; 49,
1920, 126-128; Ipsen IF 39, 1921, 232-236; cf. BSL 37,
1936, 10; Loth RC 36, 1915-16, 230) maintains that the
word is Illyrian (with ĭ for ei, cf. Rīnus, but Keltic
ē as in Rēnus from ei); Kluge Urg. 6.

On the etymology see W-P 1.4, W-H 1.19-20 (: Isara,
ἱερός, Skt. isirá-s, which is doubtful, for these all
seem to be more connected with water and rivers than
with metals, cf. HSCP 48, 1937, 188-89).

Mod. Izernore (Ain); compare also local names such
as Eisenberg, Eisenach.

nimida "woodland shrine"

For this O. Saxon or Frankish form of the Gaulish
nemeto- see 79 above and BSL 32, 1931, 81-2

?rufus a fish ("Rufolk"?)

Ruodlieb 13.39 (ed. Seiler). Perhaps related to
rucca (178 above) as lupus (79) to lucius "luce" (207).

stludio χαμού'λκιον, sclodia καμουλκίς CGL 2.188,53;

180,16

Hubschmied Vox Rom. 3, 1938, 111-112 (:lubricus?);
cf. Eng. sled, slide? On s(t)l- see Phelps in Language
13, 1937, 278-84. See also (?) γλευδία 246 below.

Glosses

uuantus "gant; glove" see AcS 3.100-101

Names of Germania Superior

From CIL 13 ii 1 (1905), viz. 5001-5024, 5258-5332, 5339-6282a, 6661-7260, 7502-7563c, 7623-7732; iv (1916) 11468-11470, 11539-11709a, 11799-11937, 11962-11964a, 11975-11978a; Finke 132-179, 202-220, 225-237[238], 241-252, 332-336, 350-352; 356-358; Nesselhauf 64-65, 67-89, 111-120, 123-141; with the two works of Riese cited at 221 above; cf. G. Drioux Les Lingons, Strasbourg 1934.

See also (in part on modern local names): P. Aebischer in Zts. f. schweizerische Geschichte 14, 1934, 284-309 (on Chasseron); H. Carrez "Une voie antique dans le Haut-Jura" (Mémoires de la Société d'Emulation du Jura 3, 1909, 257-264); Chaume "Les anciens domaines gallo-romaines de la région bourguignonne" (Mémoires de la Commission des antiquités de la Côte d'Or 20.2, 1934, 201-310) and other studies by the same author (cf. REA 38, 1936, 341-42); id., "La question des limites des nations gauloises: Dijon, bourgade des Sequanes" (Annales de Bourgogne 21.1, 1939, pp.7ff.); A. Dauzat Bibliographie toponymique de la Bourgogne in ZONF 5, 1929, 245-251; J.E. Gerock on Faucilles in REA 12, 1910, 390-398; A. Goux "La voie romaine de Langres au Rhin supérieur," ib. 32, 1930, 355-360; Grenier REA 27, 1925, 146-147; P. Lebel (on Cure, Cousain, Arce) in Annales de Bourgogne 10.4, 1938, pp.290 ff.; id., Chronique de Toponymie in REA 37, 1935, 341-42 (Haute Saône, Côte d'Or); F. Mossé ib. 34, 1932, 189-191 (Alsace); F. Mentz "Der name Elsass" Zts. f. Gesch. des Oberrheins NF 48, 1935, 109-125; Th. Perrenot "La répartition des établissements Burgondes: noms de lieux en -ange, -ans (Franche-Comté) in Mémoires de la Société d'Emulation du Jura 8e Sér. 3, 1909, 227-243; id. "Études de toponymie franc-comtoise" in Mém. Soc. Emulation du Doubs 8e Sér. 6, 1911 (301-307, Bibliographie; 308-323 "Noms de lieu en -ans, -ange") and 9, 1914-1918 [1919], 135-195 (the same, continued);

id. "Études des noms de lieu les plus anciens (!)
[actually Alemannic] du territoire de Belfort" in Bulletin de la Société Belfortaise d'Émulation no.27, 1908,
37-42; id. "Des difficultés que presente l'interpretation des noms de lieu d'origine germanique dans le
territoire de Belfort" ib. no.28, 1909, 85-101; id.,
"Les Alamans et les Burgondes dans la trouée de Belfort
vers la fin du Ve siècle" ib. no.27, 1908, 31-42; M.
Piroutet "Voies principales du Jura...sous la domination
romaine" REA 21, 1919, 115-137; cf. ib. 24, 1922, 57
("Routes romaines de Franche-Comté"); REA 37, 1935, 341
(on Anjeux from *Andiocasses); A. Philippe on Vosges in
REA 12, 1910, 168-69; A. Schwaederle Vorgerm. Fluss-
u. Bachnamen in Elsass, Colmar 1912 (this I have not
seen; condemned in Jahresb. Germ. Philol. 34, 1912
[1914], p.145, no.60); J. Schnetz on the battle-site
BG 1.31.12 (Admagetobriga) in ZONF 10, 1934, 25-28;
F. Sprater "Von den ältesten Strassen der Pfalz" (Abh.
zur Saarpf. Landes-u. Volksforschung 1, 1937, 18-22);
Violot (on names in -ey and -é in Burgundy) REA 26,
1934, 401-02. E. Christmann on names in -heim, -ingen
ZONF 12, 1936, 96-107; Bibliogr. (Palatinate) ib. 153-
163 (REA 39, 1937, 42); id. "Von Stallbühl, Langmacher
u. Römerstrasse bei Godramstein-Siebeldingen" Westmark
4 ii, 1936-37, 186-89. E. Schwartz Deutsche Namen-
Forschung, 2 vols. Göttingen 1949-50.

234

Abiolica

Abucini portus NG 9.9
(v.l. Bucini), cf. ASS
22 Oct. 9.533B

[pagus Ac[(Belg?) F.238]

[Acerrani muro Vic[....
Amantes 7546 (Kreuz-
nach)]

Admagetobriga BG 1.31.12,
now La Moigte Broye

(or Broye-les Pesmes,
Pontailler-sur-Saône;
but see also REA 18,
1916, 206 and 24, 1922,
57 on the question of
identification: Dôle,
Mt Ardou); the insc.
Magetob[(C p.66) is
not authentic; cf. RA
20, 1924, 271-72

[Aeotreenses 7544 (Mace-
donia; Pl. 3.19.16;
4.35.111)]

Local and Ethnic Names

Alaia Rav. 4.26, 232.3
  (Ehl C p.142)

Alamanni ("Germani" Fl.
  Vopiscus uit. Proculi
  13.3), -a plebs (in
  Belgica, Amm. 16.2.9);
  at Mainz Amm. 29.4.7;
  at Argentouaria Oros.
  7.33.8, Cassiod. Chr.
  a.377, both after
  Hieron.; crossed the
  Rhine A.D. 275. Ala-
  mannia v. C p.67, 139;
  cf. 241 below. Cf.
  Lohmann in F.u.F.13,
  1937, 159-60 (RA 10,
  1937, 354); Oberdeutsch
  Z. f. Volkskunde 10,
  1936, 65-75. Alamanna
  R.2610 (CIL 11.1731),
  -icus R.313, 317. Cf.
  CIL 5.6395.

[Alba, Albis fl., now
  Aube; cf. C p.59 and item
  221 above; perhaps Alb]-
  anenses 11538]

Albisi Rav. 4.26, 232.10

*Alciacus pagus (Hauxiaco
  A.D. 696) Auxey; cf.
  divine name Alhiahenae
  243 below

?Alduasdubis corrupt (see
  Dubis below and C p.70
  n.3). The personal
  names in Aldua- (237,
  cf. C p.66 n.1) may be
  in part responsible
  for the error

Alsacia, Alsatia MG; Alisa-
  cinsa (Fred. 4.37.43),
  cf. Alesaciones, -cius,
  -tius; C p.139 (Dipl.

A.D. 695); at first be-
  tween Selz and Eckenbach;
  mod. Alsace, Elsass. Cf.
  REA 31, 1929, 54

Altaripa NDOcc., CTh, Sym-
  machi Laud. 2 ad Val.,
  Altripe Rav., mod.
  Altripp

Alteium CTh, uicani Altiai-
  enses 6265; Alzey

Altitona AcS 1.110,8, cf.
  gl. 233 above

[Amantes (Maced., Afr.?)
  v. Acerrani]

Ambitaruius uicus (near
  Coblenz? Trier?), see
  212 above

Andematunnum itinn. (-ant-
  TP), ᾽Ανδο - Ptol., now
  Langres; cf. sequ., and
  Automadenses?

?Anderetiani milites NDOcc.
  41.17 (uico Iulio), sub
  disp. ducis Mogunt.
  (Endertbach?); v.l.
  -rec-; also at Paris
  (42.22). But see 148
  above

?Andesina v. Lindesina

Andomo pag[o] consistentes
  135475 (cf. 5474,
  p[agani] A[ndomenses?])

?Anipi[ciu[5629

Antro uico Merov. num.,
  Antre; cf. Antros ins.
  (148)

Local and Ethnic Names

Antunnacum insc., itinn.,
Merov. num; Antennacum
Fort.; Andernach (so
Andernachum Pard. Dipl.
A.D. 745, Anternacha
Rav.)

Aon Rav. 4.26, 232.7

Apolline(n)sis uicus 6688

Arar (-is) fl., cl. itinn.
inscc. (cf. 179); nauta
Araricus 5489, cf. Ara-
ricus (pers.) 5711

?Aresaces 7552 with add.
11825; cf. divine
name (223) Arsacae;
but 7252 has been read
silua Resacesis instead
of uican[Aresaces; cf.
Resbacis AcS 2.1176,
8-26? R.2131-31a;
Stein Beamten 162-163;
cf. Behrens MZ 36,
1941, 8-21 (AE 1945.
86-7); REA 32, 1930,
252; Note xlviii, 209,
221 above, 223 s.v.
Brittae. Or is there
some confusion with
Arusaces (Persian) Pl.
6.93?

Argentaria (-ea), Argen-
touaria itinn., Ptol.,
Amm., Oros., Casiod.,
Hieron.; Argentariensis
NG

Argentilla fl. ASS 19
June 3.873E, Arentelle

Argentorate itinn., Ptol.
(- τον), Amm.; -ensis
5966; now Strassburg;
Argentinus ASS

Argentouaria v. Argentaria

Arialbinnum itinn., now
Binning(en)

?Ariolica (Ab- TP, -rica
IA) itinn., Pontarlier

Ascis Rav. 4.26, 232.23

?Atrenses F.351 (if local)

Auderienses 7063, cf.
7353

??Automadenses (inc.) 5679;
cf. Andematunnum?

[Basilia, -ienses Amm.,
NG., Basel; cf. 221]

Bassoniaca v. 212 above

Baudobriga (Boud-, Bod-)
itinn., ND, Bodorecas
Rav. 4.24, now Boppard
(St Goar); it is im-
probable that IA 374.2
names a different place
(Bupprich, Belgica)
from 254.2 (Holder); as
for his Hohenbudberg
(Düsseldorf) AcS 3.917,
36 (Bodobrio), it also
is doubtful;]udobriga
(Ba- or Bo-?) 9158 i 5;
but see also CIL 13 ii
1 p.467 and 2. p.645 (cf.
241?) K. Miller It. Rom.
49, 79

[Belg(ini) uicani 7555a;
cf. 4085; but this is
the Belginum of 212
above]

Local and Ethnic Names

Belicenses NG 9.7 (pre-
viously Argentaria)

Bingium Tac. h 4.70; 6211,
9158 i 7; itinn. (Vin-
gium IA); B[r]ingentes
NDOcc.; Binc[enses
F.232

Bisontii Amm., cf. gl.
bison (220) and Veson-
tio below; gl. 233?

Borbetomagus itinn., Ptol.,
NG., Warmacenses Comm.
Luc. 1.431; insc.
9158 i 11, cf. 10010.
588g; Warmatia NG;
Gormetia Rav. 4.26, 231.
1; the forms with W-
and G- prove the etym.
(:L. formus, not
ferueo); Worms

Borbona Merov. num., cf.
divine names Bormo,
Boruo; Eumen. paneg.
Const. 22 (calentes
aquae), and finis Bur-
burensis (A.D. 815),
now Bourberain (Côte
d'Or); Bourbonne-les
Bains. Cf. above items
80, 82, 179, 181-2;
AcS 3.914

Boudobriga v. Bau-

Brara Rav. 4.26, 232.9

Βρευκόμαγος Ptol., v.
Broco-magus; cf. Breuci
6213?

Βρίγουλος Ps.-Plut., de
fluu. 6, the old name
of the Arar, Souconna
(Saône)

Brisiacus mons, -um itinn.;
cf. 11538]iaco (?);
Cod. Th. Rav., Breisach

Britinacha A.D. 1179,
Brettnach; Breteniachum
1198, Bretenat; see AcS
3.945-46

Brocomagus itinn., Amm.
(Brot-), Ptol. (Βρευκο-),
Vroc- insc. 9097; Bru-
math

Bucinobantes (at Mainz)
Amm. 29.4.7; ND; cf.
Buconia silua (221)
and sq.

Bucinus (Abucinus) portus
NG, ASS, now Port-sur-
Saône

Buconica itinn.; inscc.
4085, 9158; Bau- IA;
cf. Buconia silua (but
not Bacenis?), offi-
cina Buconiana 15.1556;
CIL 13 ii, pp.194, 301

[Burgundia C pp.66, 269n.;
-ii, -iones; cf. Riese
Lit. Index s.v. Bur-
godiones Pl. 4.99;
Burgundiones R.1830]

Buxuillare v. AcS 2.1056,
1, Buchsweiler; cf. gl.
79, Buxarias uilla 212
above

Caeracates Tac. h 4.70

Cambate (-et-) itinn.,
Kembs

Local and Ethnic Names

Local and Ethnic Names

Ptol. 2.9.9 (Ἕλκηβος leg. -βητ- ?), v. C pp.57, 59, 149; mod. Ell (Ehl), Ill fl. The Helellum of TP, distinguished by Kiepert, appears to be the same place. Cf. REA 15, 1913, 51 and n.1; BA 1928-29, 507-512; cf. Alaia above (?)

Epamanduodurum (-mantudur-um) itinn., ASS (Man-datumdurum, Mandorum), now Mandeure; cf. BA 1934-35 [1940], 581-86

[Filomusiaco TP]

Fines, now Vinxtbach; cf. Fines 7732

Foro Aug[(or Vag[) 6958

Franci -icus R.308, 312, 317, 2367; Paneg. Const. 6; Francia Rinensis Rav. 4.24; 26.

Frincina(e) Rav. 4.26; for Virinc-, Vrinc- (?) see Vruncae below, cf. C p.149

[Gallia (unless pers.) 7234?]

[Germania 6823; G. superior 5090, 6749, 6754, 6762, 6806; cl.; Germaniae duae 1807; Germani cl., e.g. BG 6.24; Tac. G

37; Κελτῶν τινες, οὓς δὴ Γερμανοὺς καλοῦμεν Dio 53.12.6; -us 2018]

Gormetia Rav. (Worms), v. Borbetomagus

?Gramatum IA 349.2, cf. C p.66 (for Epamantu-duro?)

Gunzinus fl. Zingel (Alsace) AcS 2.2044

[Haliqu[6763, cf. 7495, R.3042(?), 8.21814a, 21053; Stein Beamten 266]

[?Hammii R.1784; Hemis[R.199; but cf. P-W s.v. Hammi(s)]

Heluetos, v. El-

Isarnodurum ASS 1 Jan. 1.50; cf. gloss 233; Merov. num.; Izernore (Ain)

Iulio uico v. Anderetiani

Iura mons, pl. Iures, Ἰουράσιος (-κσσος), Iurenses Alpes, Ἴορα(ς), Iorensis cl. (BG, Str. Pl.), itinn., Ptol., ASS; cf. C p.6, 65-66 (at 6027); *iorum M-L Einf. 242

Laeti Amm. 16.11, 1 (cf.
20.8.2, 21.13.16)
NDOcc. 42 (Lingonenses),
cf. Zos. 2.54, Cod.Th.
7.20.12 (cf. 13.11.10
terrae Laeticae); as
pers. name 6271, 7754;
properly laeti see 221
above. Further Grenier
Mnl 1.537 (fig. 202)
and in Frank 3.596;
W-H s.v.

Laguirion Rav. 4.26

Langiones gens Iul. Honor.
Occ. 26 (Lingones?
Vangiones?)

Larga opp. and fl., itinn.;
Largitzen

Latauienses NDOcc. 36.5,
Lavans. But Grenier
(Mélanges Paul Thomas
1930, p.385) would
read Latouici Veson-
tione at NDOcc. 36.5
for Latabienses Olinone
(v.l. Olitione), cf.
Latab[13.8316 (Germ.
Inf.). Cf. REA 25,
1923, 57-60; 27, 1925,
135-36; AcS 2.150; for
Latouici see 241 below,
Latobius divine name
(243)

Latiscensis pagus 7th cent.,
v. AcS 2.154

[Laugona Fort. 7.7.58, cf.
Rav. 4.24 (Logna), now
Lahn]

[Leuci v. Belg.]

Lindesina TP; cf. regio
Lindinsis F.98; BSAF

1937, 140-43 (Andesina?)

Lingauster 7038 (cf. 5917,
7030, 3.10514), prob-
ably the same as Lingo-
(nes)

Lingŏnes cl. (Polyb., BG,
Liv., Str., Lucan,
Tac.), -as (acc. pl.)
2873; itinn., insec.
2681, 3606, 4654(?),
5681, 5488, 5661, 5682,
5685, 5693, 5694, 5708,
5883; Lingonus 5911,
Ling[5917 (or pers.
name?), Lingo[5920;
Lingo 7034, 5942 (-nus),
cf. AE 1941 p.333 (8.
21669) Lingoni 10012.4;
-es 10029.218; Lingonum
R.318 (H-M 341; 13.
11543) -is dat. pl.
10012.4 (cf. C 13 iv
p.72); cf. Cuny Rev.
de Philol. 56, 1936, 24;
cf. REA 42, 1940, 622;
Lingonum 5942 (C p.84),
formerly held to prove
that Grand belonged to
the Lingones instead of
the Leuci (cf. Suppl.,
xliii), for]nni[(local
or divine) is insuffi-
cient; Lingonas NDOcc.
69 (Sarmatorum gentilium);
uomer Lingonicus Frontin.
4.3.14, bardocucullus
Mart. 1.53.4; Langres

?Liomena Lehmen v. AcS 2.
227,25

?Litauicrari (local name,
loc. sg., hardly pers.
gen.) 5708 ii 11; cf.
Crarus 82?

Local and Ethnic Names

Liticiani (Laet-) Iord.
  Get.36

Loposagium TP, now Luxiol
  (Baume-les-Dames)?

[Ludna IA, v. Gallia 1,
  1943, 227; Ludnomagen-
  ses 5923?]

Lugnesses 7640 (Gondorf)

Lut(t)ra fl. v. AcS 2.
  354; Lauter

Luxouium, -iensis ASS,
  Lib. h.Fr., cf.Διττ-
  αούιον above (Lix-?);
  C pp.66, 149; cf. the
  divine names Lussoius,
  Luxouius; aquae cali-
  dae AcS 2.356,54; Lux-
  euil

murum Magid[unensem (Augst)
  11543 (H-M 341, R.318);
  cf. REA 28, 1926, 365
  and 33, 1931, 45; RC
  44, 1927, 222-23; now
  Moëdon (Rheinfelder)

Magione AcS 2.378,5, cf.
  C p.194, 301 (uetere
  Magione)

?Mansuerisca uia and
  Marleiensis strata v.
  Riese Lit. p.410

Matra fl. AcS 2.463,25;
  Moder

Maresacensis uicus (Gren-
  ier Quatre villes p.84)

Melenuenses 3.7387, 8.
  9060 (AcS 2.535), cf.

uicus nouus Meloniorum
  13.7270? Stein Beamten
  271

Moenus see 241 below

Moguntiacum (-ont-),
  -enses 6705, 6722,
  6727, 6733, 11810,
  11827; cl. (Tac.), ND,
  itinn., inscc.; Mainz,
  cf. C pp.194, 296-99,
  301; (for Mundiacum v.
  221 above); cf. R.724
  (Moguntiacus as pers.
  name); 293. Grenier
  Mnl. 1.537, fig. 202.

[Mosella fl., v. Belg.]

Mosa IA 585.8, cf. C p.85

?Nantes ciuitas Rav. 4.26,
  p.230.17; cf. Nantiorix
  (f.) 5485, Namnes -is
  6230

Naua fl. Tac., Auson; Nahe
  (Bingen)

Nemesia R. Lit. 319 n.1

Nemetes, -ensis cl. BG,
  Lucan, Pl., Tac., Amm.
  16.2.12 (-as acc.),
  itinn., inscc. (6404,
  6106, 11690) Nemis (sg.)
  3.9735, -es (sg.) 13.
  6659, 3.5902 (cf. BJ
  135, 1930, 71), AcS 2.
  708-710; C p.161; ND
  (Nemetis castellum,
  praef. militum uindi-
  cum); Nemetus 3.5902
  (Vollmer 247); Nemes
  204 above; Nemens R.
  2105 (6.31171); -ae n.

Local and Ethnic Names

pl. in Amm.; Nemetenses
in late documents

[Noialenses (-y-) 7544;
cf. Pl. 3.116; 4.111]

Nouiodunum cl., inscc.,
itinn. (C p.1) Nyon

Nouiomagus (Nemetum)
itinn., Ptol., now
Speyer; cf. P-W s.v.

?Nouiomagus (C p.132;
Notre Dame-les-Piliers?)

?Olibriones Iord. Get.36

Olino fl. NDOcc. 36.3,
ib. 5 (cf. Olinas
[Lugd.], Olonna
[Isère]); REA 23, 1921,
57; 27, 1925, 135-37

Oscara fl., Greg. Tur. h.
Fr. 2.23 (32), 3.19;
Ouche? Cf. 158 above

?Oxsello num. Merov. AcS
2.62

[Pacenses milites (at
Saletio, sub disp. duc.
Mogunt. NDOcc. 41; Byv.
1.573 refers to Pax
Iulia, but see also
Pacis uicus 212 above]

[pallas, palus see C p.255
(cf. p.149) Pfahl,
Pfalzburg, Fahlburg;
cf. pers. name Palanta
7039, divine name Pallas
6746, and Capellatium
above]

[Portin Rav. 4.27, p.242.
2, Port-sur-Saône (cf.
Bucinus)]

Portis[ienses] R.1793; cf.
Porza?

[?Pranci (Fr-?) TP]

[Raetinium 7023]

Rauraci, -ici cl. (BG,
Pl.), itinn. inscc.
(7325, cf. 6503, 6509,
6604, 6609), Rau[
5264, Augusta Rauricum
(5273?), Raurica 10.
6807 (R.1, H-M 334),
now Basel-Augst, cas-
trum Rauracense (now
Kaiser-Augst), cf. 7.
66 (EE 7.834); Stein
Beamten 142; C pp.67,
63, 238, 281

R(h)enus cl., inscc.
5255, 6211; cf. R.293,
1796

?silua Resa[censis (?)
7522 (or uicani Are-
saces? or cf. Resbacis,
-ccum 179?)

[Ripa v. Alta ripa; cf.
Ripari Iord. Get.36]

Robur (Basilia) Amm. 30.
3.1; interpreted by
Niedermann as "for-
tress" i.q. Magidunum
(Festschr. Oeri, see
APh 18, 5)

Rubiacum AcS 2.1237,35-36;
the same as Rufiniana
(Ptol. Ῥουφινιάνα 2.9.9)

[Salutares uicani 6723]

Saletio Amm., itinn., ND;
now Seltz

Salisio IA, now Salzig

Saluxsia fl. 8th cent.
AcS 2.1332, Selzbach;
explained as *sal-
ups- W.u.S. 11, 1928,
60; cf. Saloissa 241
below

Sarmatae ND, cf. Sauromates
Aus. Mos. 9, Strata Sar-
matorum (see Riese Lit.
p.410), cf. AcS 2.1368,
21

Sauconna (Arar, Brigulus)
Saône, cf. 179, 181
above

Scotingorum pagus, Scud-
ingius see P-W s.vv.

[Scubuli 6212, 6821, 7032;
R.46, 737, 1497; dipl.
20, 28, 36, 62-3; P-W
1.1259; cf. gloss scu-
bulum 178?]

Sedusii BG 1.51 (for Eud-
usi?) cf. Oros. 6.7.8
(Euduses Ed-, cf. Tac.
G 40, Eudoses); hardly
for Seduni?

[Sefiniacum, num. Merov.,
Savigna (Jura)]

Segessera TP (now Bar-sur-
Aube), cf. C p.85;
Segest- 179

Segobodium TP; Seveux

Sequani cl., inscc. (e.g.
5353, 5367, 5592 [-a],
6503, 6509, 6604,
6609, 7325, 3.5782),
Secuanus CIR 1525; cf.
Sēquăna fl. (Lucan 1.
425), now Seine; Se-
quanica tutrix Mart.
4.9.1; Σηκοανοί (-κο-
for qu?) Str. and Ptol.
(2.9.10) usually -κου-
(Plut., Dio Cass.); cf.
C pp.65-66, 238; Verg.
E 1.62 assigns the
Sequani to the Germani
as interpreted in C
p.156(!), and the late
prov. Maxima Sequanorum
includes part of the old
Germania Superior; Eutrop.
6.17 extends the name to
the Heluetii; Sequanus
Vollmer 92, 510; Athen-
aeum 25, 1947, 80-82

?Sicilia Lampr. Alex. Sev.
59.6, cf. C p.178 (AcS
2.1540); cf. (??) Sit-
illia TP, probably not
the same place (179
above); an error for
Cilic- (212)?

[Solicia 4679; Soulosse
212]

Solimariaca, -enses see
212

Spira, -ensis NG, Merov.
num., and late docu-
ments, Sph- Rav.; the
older Nouiomagus (Nem-
etum), Speyer

Stabulis (-a or -ae?) IA,
Stafulon Rav. 4.26,

232.14; Étaules? Cf.
Stablesiani R.1800; 5.
4376. Cf. 221 above

Stratisburgum Rav. 4.26,
-te- Greg. Tur., ND
(cf. C p.161), the
older Argentorate,
Strassburg

[Sueui see 221, 241]

Sura fl., Sauer (AcS 2.
1673, 11-17); cf. P-W
s.v.

[(Tres) Tabernae Amm.,
later Ziaberna (?).
Cf. C p.149 n.1; Za-
bern (Fr. Saverne),
cf. Bergzabern (C
p.162)]

[Tabernae itinn., ND,
Rheinzabern (ib. p.
164)]

Te[ciuis 6239 (if Tex-
uander, then see 221)

Ternodorensis (-der-)
pagus, -e castrum
Fort., Greg. Tur., ASS;
mod. Tonnerre

[Teutoniciani laeti NDOcc.
42; cf. Τευτονοάροι
Ptol. 2.11.9%]

Tilena(?), written Filema
TP; Tala Castro num.
Merov., Thil-Châtel,
cf. Tille

Triboci cl. (Caes., Str.,
Tac.), inscc. (e.g. 3.

3164, 9816, 6.22981,
3.9760 [Tre-], 13.
2018, 6054, 6448-49,
6553, N.242). In
Strabo Τρίβοκχοι ; as-
signed BG 1.51, with
Vangiones and Nemetes,
to the Germani; cf.
REA 15, 1913, 52; Tri-
bunci Amm. 16.12.58 is
probably a variant form;
cf. C p.139

[Οὐαδικάσιοι, if correct
reading at Str. 4.1.11,
see 179]

Vangiŏnes Lucan 1.430
(Sarmata), cl. (Caes.,
Tac.), Vangio as pers.
name (cf. uanga 220)
6.31149 c 5; inscc.
6225, 6244, 6249. Cf.
Vannius (pers. name)
Tac. A 2.63; 12.29;
and Vangius fl. (per-
haps Vignory, Haute-
Marne); cf. C pp.178-
79; N.75; AE 1940.110;
Stein Beamten 240 (CIL
7.987,1002); Arch. Anz.
1909, 290

Varcia TP, IA; for Var-
cianus see 241; mod.
Vars?

Velatudurum IA, cf. Velle-
rot-les-Bains?

Vertillenses uikani 5661,
Vertello (12th c.),
i.e. *Vertillum, Ver-
tault

Vesontio cl. (Caes., Diod.),

itinn., inscc., e.g. 9078, 9081 (Vesant-), Vesonticus 2038, Vesontiensis; later Vesontine, Visontione (cf. C pp.7, 66), Besanciaeum (ib.), Βεσοντιωνα (acc.) and Ουεσοντιωνι (dat.) Dio; now Besançon; cf. gloss 233; Vi[6156 (Stein Beamten 273), unless this is Vindelici; Besuncin num. BSAF 1915, 213; perhaps bison (220), wisund-Kluge Urg. 6

?uetere Mogontiaci C pp. 194, 301 (but uetere may go with Magione)

[Vettones 7544 (Sp.); cf. gloss 158]

]ni uicani R.2136

Vicus Iulius v. Iulius

?u[i]c[ani R.2704

uici......6676 (cf. C p.303)

uicus Nouus (at Mainz) 6722, 6776, cf. F.204-05 and 7335 (at Heddernheim)

muro Vic[7546

Vidubia fl. TP, Vouge; cf. gloss 158

qui uix...Vincen[(?) R.318

?Vindices milites v. Nemetes; cf. R.1804

Vingio (IA) v. Bingium

Vobergensis iuuentus 6689 (Mainz), cf. Verbigenus pagus BG 1.27. 4 (241 below)?

Vocara AcS 3.423

Vocrullus mons 5295 (Basel-Augst)

Vosĕgus mons cl. (Caes., Lucan, Pl.), Vogesus v.l. mss and schol. Lucan; Vosegus as pers. name Sil. Ital. 4.213; Vosagus TP, Fort., Greg., Fredeg. Vosegus in 9c.; see C pp.66, 139, 156; Vogesen, Wasgau, Vosges. Cf. REA 12, 1910, 165-66; for Vosugones see 209; cf. 9023 ii 2 and items 209, 211-13 above, 234, 236-37 below

Vosoluia, Vosouia TP, Rav.; cf. 4085, 9158 ii 6; Wasaliacinse vit. St Goar (AcS 3.451.42), Wesel; the name of modern Vesoul (235) is given as Vesulium castrum in 9th cent., later Visolium, see FrON 1, 56

Vrba fl. IA, NG, cf. Orba uilla Fredeg.; Orbe

Vrocomagus, v. Broco-; cf. R.270, 13.9097

Vruncis IA, Frincina Rav.; ?Orincis IA, N.242(?); cf. AcS 3.455

Local and Ethnic Names; Further
Modern Names

Vxellus uicus Merov. num.;
Oselle; cf. AcS 3.63,3
(Oxsello see above)

235   Further Modern Names

Ain, Alsheim, Altdorf, Altenkirchen, Altenstadt,
Alzey, Andelot, Lac d'Antre, Arbois, Arc-en-Barrois,
Arinthod, Aube, Aubonne fl., Les Auges, Auxon, Avolsheim

Balesmes, Banzenheim, Barjon, Barrois, Battenheim,
Beaulmes, Becherbach, Beire-le-Châtel, Benfeld, Bermel,
Bertrich, Nieder-Betschdorf, Bière, Biesheim, Binger-
brück, Birkenfeld, Blieskastel, Bregeille, Bretzenheim
(uilla Britannorum, near Mainz; perhaps Sicilia v. AcS
2.1540, Sitillia TP?), Büdesheim, Burckheim

Stein-Callenfels, Carden, Céligny, Les Chaprais,
Chorst (Chorust, Hor-burg), Fort-les-Cluses, Cobern,
Cochem, Colmar, Coppet, Corre, Cuarnens

Dagsburg, Dampierre, Dannstadt, Daun (Dhaun i.e.
Dunum?), Dienheim, Dôle, Donnersberg (Thonar?), Drais,
Dudenhofen, Dunhusen, Dürkheim

Ebersheim, Eckenbach, Edenburg, Edenkoben, Eisen-
burg, Erpolzheim, Essarois, Esthal

St Ferjeux, Fleury-sur-Ouche

Geitershof, Gerstheim, Gimbsheim, Gissey-sur-Ouche,
Glan fl., Godramstein, Godrons, Görsdorf, Gondorf, Gon-
senheim, Grancey, Grand, Grassendorf, Greifenstein,
Griselles, Gross-Limersberg, Grozon, Grussenheim

Hagenau, Harterkopf, Hatten, Hechtsheim, Heidesberg,
Heiligenstein, Heiteren, Herrgott, Hinzerath, Hohenburg,
Hohengeroldseck, Horburg (nr. Colmar, cf. gloss horo
"swamp," Chorust Rav., Chorst; Chora fluuius AcS 1.1008),
Hottenbach

Modern Local Names

Idar, Iebsheim, Iggelheim, Imflingen, Ingweiler

Jeure, Jodils, St Julian

Kärlich, Katzeneck, Keferstein, Hirchheim an der
Eck, Kirn, Kleinwinterheim, Kreimbach, Kretz, Kreutznach
(Caroling, Cruciniacum, *Crut- see Kaspers ZfCPh 15,
1924-25, 206-211), Kritzhof, Kusel

Landau, Landstuhl, Langensulzbach, Lautenheim,
Lauter fl. (Lutera?), Lautzkirchen (cf. Lauter-burg),
Lehwen, Lernbach, Lons-les-Sau(1)nier, Les Loyes

Mâlain, Mariaborn, Maudach, St Maur, Mayen, Mémont,
Mertzweiler, Mettenheim, Mietesheim, Millières, Mire-
beau, Moirans, Mombach, Montéclair, Mülhausen, Mumpf,
Mundenheim

Nähweiler, Nette fl., Nettehammer, Neustadt an der
Hardt, Niederbronn, Niedermodern, Nierstein, Nonfous

Oberholm, Oberstaufenbach, Ochtendung, Öden, Oggers-
heim, Openheim, Orchamp (cf. 234 Chrys-, Crusina), Ott-
marsheim

Pfaffenhofen, Pfalzburg (pallas), Pfeffingen, Plaidt,
Polch, Pommern, Pomy, Pothières, Pouilley-sur-Vingeanne,
Prangins

Reichshofen, Reinhardsmünster, Rehweiler, Ringel-
dorf, Rockenhausen, Romainmoutier, Ruchheim, Ruffey

Säckingen, Salins, Sauer fl., Saulx-le-Duc, Schoenau,
Schwarzenden, Selongey, Selz fl., Sierenz, Stambach,
Starckenburg, Stephansfelder, Suzon

Tavaux, Treis (south of Coblenz)

Valeyres-sous-Ursins, Vanvey, Varois, Versoix,
Vesoul (see 234), Vincy, Viry, St Vit, Vitrey, Vix, Voll-
mersbach

Waldfischbach, Wasenburg, Wasselnheim, Weissenburg

Zell, Zinsel, Zinsweiler, Zurzach

Divine Names

Remark:

CIL 13 ii 1 (1905) p.298 n.1 calls attention to a gloss on Orosius giving the local name (10th cent.)

Trúsileh

interpreted as *Drusi-(lage)[?]; ib. p.302 Zahlbach, in A.D. 1190 Zagel-bach (tegulae?); cf. (ib. p.302, n.7) *Drusilacus modern Drusenloch (cf. Förstemann ON 1.754); see 19 Remark above and 241 below on -locus "lake, pool."

For Treis, Finthen, Sechtem ("three, five, seven" sc. leagues?), Sweich ("six"?) and Cochem (with the same ending?) see 212 bis Remark (2) above; but Finthen has been connected with fontes MZ 1, 1849, 359 (CIL 13 ii 1 p.399 cf. p.312; the reference is to the Zeitschrift des Vereins zur Erforschung der rheinischen Geschichte und Alterthümer in Mainz 1, 1845-51, not to the later Mainzer Zeitschrift 1, 1906); cf. also Forstemann 1.969.

236   Divine Names

See, in general, Beck MZ 31, 1936, 23-32 (matronae not purely Keltic in origin); E. Christmann "Wotans- u. Donarsbergen in der Pfalz" (Abh. zur Saarpfälzischen Landes- u. Volksforschung 1, 1937, 5-17); G. Drioux Cultes indigènes des Lingons, Paris 1934 (but cf. the reviews of Grenier REA 36, 1934, 478-480; and Rev. critique 68, 1934, 113-115; H. van de Weerd, Ant. cl. 3, 1934, 543; Lenschau PhW 55, 1935, 41; Vannérus Rev. Belge 14, 1935, 485; and, above all, Vendryes EC 3, 1938, 175-77); Dumézil Mythes et dieux des Germains, Paris 1939 (reviewed in RA 17, 1941, 309; EC 4, 1948, 143-146); R. Forrer 25, 1927, 97-103 (on Epona at Strassburg); id., Jahrb. des Hagenauer Geschichtes- u. Altertumsverein 14-18, 1933-37, 9-46 (on Sirona in Alsace); R. von Kienle "Das Auftreten Keltischer u. germanischer Gottheiten

Divine Names

zwischen Oberrhein und Limes" (actually includes Germania Superior as a whole), Archiv für Religionswissenschaft 35, 1938, 252-287; id. in Abh. zur Saarpf. Landes- u. Volksforschung 1, 1937, 23-36 (native deities under Latin names); W. Schleiermacher in RGKBer. 23, 1933 [1934], 109-143.

The Mercurius of 7213-7225 (cf. 7326) is supposed to be Wodan (cf. Donnersberg, CIL 13 ii pp.180, 399); so in Godesberg Wodan has been displaced. Similarly Taranis and Taranucnus are set beside OE Þunar, OHG donar (i.e. Odin), with metathesis of -r- : -n-. On divine names at Mainz see Behrens MZ 39-40, 1944-45, 1-10. According to BG 6.21 the Germans worshipped only the sun, the moon, and fire; but the situation as revealed in inscc. is as complex as in non-Roman Italy (cf. Foundations 381-388).

??Add[(if div. name) 6128

Alcis Tac. G 43.3; see 233 above

g(enius) c(astrorum) Argent(oratensium) 5966

Arm[ogius 6738 (or [iger?)

??Arnalia (not genuine?) 5639

Attini deo (i.e. Attis?) 6664, Atti (dat.) 11606

Aufaniae 6665

Bell[(if div. name) 5670, cf. 5408 but probably Latin, cf. Bellon[5351, Bellona

N.78; cf. RA 43, 1882, 271 (Pl.8)

Biuiae 5621, 6096; miswritten Bidiae (Ð for B) 6667; cf. 6060 (RE 1, 1913, 408; AE 1914. 205)

Boruo 5911-20, cf. 5922; modern local name, Bourbonne (les-Bains)

Boud[e]na 11975 (R.3467)

Bricia 5425; Brixia (or -χtia?) 5426; Briχta AE 1939.48; cf. Pro Alesia 3, 1908-09, 389 n.1

B]rito (dat.) Drioux p. 158; but see 211 above

Camulus 11818, R.3034; cf.

213 above

Campestres e.g. R.2092, 2105, 3008-9

Can[a 6021, 6022; cf. CGL 2.97,2

Casses 6116, 6153; bonis Cassubus 6668; cf. bonum euentum 6669 [dedic. by ciues Sumeloc.], bono euentu 6670, Casebono 3.8256 add., Κασιβόνων (local name, Thrace); cf. gloss caddos 178 above; Casibanus num. Commodus (AcS 1.822)

Caturix 5046, 5054; cf. AcS 3.1163,10

Cicollus (-ui dat., o-stem, Thurneysen) 5479, 5597-5604, 5600 add.; cf. 181 above

?Cimbrianus 6742 (C.mab-rianus lapis); Guten-brunner 52-54

Cisonius 6119; Cissonius 5373, 6085, 11607 (R. 3346)

?Cobeia 5412; AcS 1.1053, 25; or personal? Cf. Note xlviii above and OE Cobbo (Searle Onom. 138)

[Concordia 6127, probably not local, but Latin divine name]

?Crepellius 5666

C]reto F.238 (or Tr-?)

C.sp[nymphae 7210 (local?)

Damona 5911, 5914, 5921

Demioncus N.84; cf. 8342 (-a)

de(a) Dia(na?) 5936

?]dobi[F.358

Epona 5622, 7555a, 7555b, 7680, 11539, 11801; R.1116, 2734, 3008-9

Excingorigias BJ 139, 1934, 225; REA 38, 1936, 44 (cf. pers. name Excingius); N.137

[Fortuna Supera (i.e. Ger-maniae Sup?) 6679]

Garmangabae see Note xlv (B), 223 above

Grannus 5315, cf. R.2647; N.71, 88; RA 8, 1936, 273-4; 10, 1937, 341; Germ. 20, 1936, 60; REA 29, 1927, 55-56; BSAF 1936, 182-187, AE 1937.55. Cf. 5942; modern local name Grand

Divine Names

Herclenti 7693

[honor Aquilae leg. 22.
6679]

Ianuaria 5619

[IOM Sabasio Germanus 6708]

inuihtus deus F.165, 166

[Iouantucarus 10024.6;
but see 211 above]

La[ ]natunili R.3024

[Laurentes nymphae (from
local name? Cf. Lau-
rentia personal name
7108?) 7212]

Λῆνος 7661

Leucetius (Louc-) 6131,
6221, 7241, 7242,
7249a, 7252, 7253(?),
MZ 36, 1941, 16-18
(AE 1945 p.164); cf.
R.1488 (11605); 7.36;
see also 243 below

Litauis 5599-5602, 5603(?),
5600 add.

Loucetius v. Leuc-

Lucena 6761 (not neces-
sarily for Lucina), cf.
Hluc- 223 above?

Luna 6733; deus Luna F.164
(cf. Note xlviii)

Lussoius 5425, cf. local
names; so Luxouius
5426

Mairae 5478, 5622, 5623

Matrae 5344, 5369-73,
5959; Matres 6729,
11577

Matrona 5674

?Medru (dat. sg.) 6017
RC 25, 1904, 47; REA
20, 1918, 118; note
also Toutati Medurini
6.31182

Meduna 7667; cf. Guten-
brunner 108; Germania
2, 1918, 8-10; AE 1921
p.463; Glotta 11, 1921,
115 cf. 267; NTS 1,
1938, 160

?Moccus 5676 (or Mocco
pers.?); cf. modern
local names Moque, Le
Moche; see also Blan-
chet Mélanges Cumont
(Ann. Inst. Orient.-
Slave 4, Brussels 1936)
p.105 n.4; but hardly
exmuccauit (CIL 4.1391)
with AcS 2.603,17; W.
moch (Do. Mélanges Loth,
1927, 92-8)

Mogounus 5315, cf. C p.
296-97; Mogonti (dat.)
AcS 2.611, dea Mogontia,
Mogontiacum (234); 5650?

Nemesis dea (apud Lingones)
see FHRC 213.11; 15; 21

Nemetona 6131, 7253

numen G(erm) S(up) 7417

Divine Names

Noadat(?) deo Mar[ti]
6740; cf. Nodens Note
xlv B above

Ollogabiae 6751; cf. 7280
and Al(l)a- 8529

]ore (dat. sg.) 6673

]ouno (if div. name) 5650,
cf. Mogounus (213
above)

[Pallas 6746; cf. 234]

[Parcae 6223]

Quadriuiae (-ru-) 5621,
5671, 6091, 6667,
6731 (Compitales)
7623, R.813; 11647,
F.244

?Rauini (dat.?) v.l. 6094

Rosmerta 5677, 5939, 6222,
6263, 7683, 11696; REA
38, 1936, 44; BJ 139,
1933, 225; N.137; cf.
BSAF 1900, 168-69

[Sabasius 6708]

Sam[6077, Samm[6083

Saxanus 7697-7712, 7716-
7719, 7719 add., 7720;

F.242, 251 (-xs-); BJ
140-41, 1936, 449;
R.352-55; 7715?

Sequana 11575, Dr.292;
10024.23

Sil[uanus?] F.134

Sirona 5424, 6272, 6753,
N.85; 86; AJA 47,
1943, 239; ZfSchw.
Arch.u.Kunstg. 3,
1941, 241

Smertrius 11975 sq.

Sucellus 6224, 6730
(-cael-), F.134 (cf.
REA 26, 1924, 344);
H-M 352

Sul dea 6266; Sol 5992

Suleu(i)ae 7504, 7725,
R.723, 2105, 3008-9;
11740

?Ti[taca] 7624 (cf. 8853)

Taranucnus 6094; cf. Taranis 181 above

genio tectorum 11803

Temusio f.11223; Dessau
9314, AcS 2.1793

[Toutates see Medru above]

Toutenus 6122, F.225; MZ
37-38, 1942-3, 38; RC
44, 1927, 427; Guten-
brunner 53-54; AE 1940
p.238

Divine Names

?T]reto v. Creto; cf. 211 above

?Tribanti (dat. sg.) 6061

?T]rito (dat.) v. Brito, cf. de Ricci CRAcInscBL 1925, 249 (Britouius 12.3082-83); Jullian REA 28, 1926, 259 would interpret Trito as "dea Quartana." Note however the Lugd. pers.-name Brictio (Goelzer REA 25, 1923, 151-52); AE 1926.59, cf. RA 26, 1927, 387. A restoration F]rito is unlikely; cf. 211 above

Triuiae 5621, 6096, 6667 (-b-)

?Vatin[eae] matres 5673

]uco (genuine?) 5638

Vercana 7667, cf. 4311; see also Meduna above

Vesontius 5368

uicanorum genio 7655

uiciniae (?) Genius 6115

Vindonnus 5644-46; in 5646 the pers. name Vindama has been read (v. AcS 3.329 but cf. 5646)

Vindoridi (dat. sg.) 11975, R.3467

Virodactis 6761

uirtus Bellonae N.78

Visucius 5991; cf. 213 above; AcS 3.406-7

?Vituus 6118 (or Visucuus?); cf. pers. names Vittuo 6401, Vittua 7501

Volpinae nimpae 7691 (cf. Vulpis fl., 2 above)

Vosegus 6027, 6059, 6080; R.3563-65; also as personal name 237; N.73; cf. Germ. 22, 1938, 239; Forrer Cahiers d'Arch. et d'hist. d'Alsace 28, 1937, 155-160, and see above 209, 211, 212, 213, 234

237   Personal Names

Abilius 7551

Abbo 10017.27

Abre×tubogius 5665

Abrius 5709

Personal Names

[Abronius 7055]

Acceptus 7667, -io 11976

Acconius 6101

?Aciro, ?Acirgi[Dr.692.
  1-2

Aco 6196

?Acocaulo 10010.20

Acuitus ib. 29

Acum[i]na CRAcInscBL 1925,
  247; Dr.233, AE 1926.
  59; cf. RA 26, 1927,
  p.387

Acutius, -ia 6688, ?715-
  16

†Adalharius 7200

[Adbogius 7031]

Adbugius 11877; 10010.
  3080(?); Adebugius
  5491 with add.

Addo[(unless divine)
  6128

?Ad]gentius 11589, cf.
  AcS 3.506,17

Adginnius (Sequanus)
  1674, 1675 (insc. Lyon);
  Adgini[5710

Adiantanus 5278

Adic[6940 (for Ande-
  cauus?)

Aditiedtotian[5452 (or
  -tostiaai?); perhaps
  two names

Adledus 5278

Adn[amatius] AcS 1.43,44;
  Adn[amatus or -amius
  3.509,30; 6765; Adna-
  matius F.137, -tus BJ
  142, 1937, 322

Adnametus 5278

Adnamius v. -namatius
  (6765)

Adnamus 6027

?Adnas[10010.3259a

Aduenas f. AcS 1.48,29

?Aeaindus 10010.3248a

Aeauius ib. 3177

?Aebauus AcS 3.514

Aebutius 6885

Aecissa 5738

Aeginus 10010.3169a

Aenionus AcS 1.51,46

Aemasu[5762 add.

]aetoma[5949

Aetn[10016.16

Aetrius R.1597

?Afegii 5512

[Afer, Afra 7256; Afro
  (case?) 7098

Agedinius 5929, cf. AcS
  1.56,20 (-nus)

Personal Names

Agenarichus Amm. 16.12.25;
  cf. [Serapion] below

Agero 11555

[Agileius....Luco 6882]

Agilo Amm. 14.10.8

Agis(i)llus (-stilus) AcS
  1.59,4; 11579, Agisilus
  (or -stlus?) 5787; cf.
  (for -stl-) Congeistlus
  239 below

Agriccos (gen. sg.?) 5640

Agrilies 5480

Aiassasius F.176

†Aiberga 7525

Aigioninus 10010.3132b

Aiia (dat.) 7516a (filia
  dat. ib.)

?Ainia (Ae-) AcS 1.71,19

Aiiuua[7280

Airo (Atro?) 6122

Aitillus 10011.35

Aiussa 7097

Aiuus 5732

?Alanux 5402 (or ann. V
  ux[or]?)

Albanus 5374, 6892

Albisia 6237

†Aldualuhi 6256

Alefius 7643

Alendiola R.3988

Alesso 10010.87

Allinus AcS 1.95, cf. 3.
  6227; 7594

Allontius, -ia 7103

Alpina 7504, -ius R.781;
  10028.25

Altianius R.2136

Am[N.124

Amancius 7238

Amb[5550

Ambe[6195 (or -ii[?)

[Ambirenus (Rauricus) 3
  p.865 (D. xxii), H-M
  477, R.2077-78]

?Ambiti 7551

Aminorix 5595

?Aminus 5429

Amm[5410, 7116

Amma 7120

]amma 6766,]ammius 6767

Ammeius 10010.3246b

Ammianus 6801

Ammillus 6283, -ius R.2647

Amminus 11976, -ius BJ
  142, 1937, 322

Personal Names

Ammius 4470; 10017.142

Ammo(n) 7551, 7553; terra
  sig. (Rheinzabern)

Ammonius 11823

Ammosa (or Ammosatari)
  dat. 7075

Ammosius N.129

Ammula 6184

Ananus 10010.3246a

Anarus 10017.149

Andangi 7086

Andedunis D ii (Varcianus)

[Andes 7023]

ᵗAndic[cus 6940

Andossa F.171

Androurus 7579

Anexia (or -χta?) 5781

Aneχtlomarus 11583; BSAF
  1902, 217

Aniancant[5464

Aniatus 10010.3232

Anicius 7506

Anienus 5981

Aniex- (i.e. Aneχ[tlo-?)
  6004

Aninius 7553

Annaius 7088, 7507

ᵗAnnasus 10010.3259n

[Annauso (Betasius) 7025]

Annauus 10035.25

Annicensa 5548

Annionius N.80,7

ᵗAnnius 6723 (cf. 10004.
  13)

Anonanus 5469

†Anserico 7671

Ansi 10027.6

Antesta 10001.350; C
  p.307

Antestius 6936, Antistius
  -ia N.118

Antullus R.3752 (cf. 1552);
  11874

Anua 10010.2122

Anullus F.162

Aper N.118; AE 1933.250

Aperinus 5491 with add.

Aperonius F.356

Apinosa 5466, -ossus 10025.
  132, cf. Appinius R.692

Apius 10025.132

Aponinus 7718

Personal Names

]aporigi (dat.) R.3926

Apra N.118

Aprilis 7038

Aprilla 5718, N.82

April(l)ius, -is 5716,
  5717; -ianus 5716

Apro 6826

Apronius 6794, R.2163a;
  -ia N.118; -ianus
  5279, cf. R.1286, Dr.
  693.1

Aprosus 6133

Apulio(?) 6005

Aquila 5708

?Aquilinus 5942

Aragante 6013

Araricus (cf. local
  names?) 5711

Arator Amm. 28.2.1

Araurica 5312

?Arbina 5714

Arbirius (? for Are-)
  11690, R.2106

Arbo[g]astis Greg. Tur.
  h.Fr. 2.9; cf. R. Lit.
  pp.355-56 (Treuir);
  TLL s.v.; and 214
  above

Arcosus Dr.528

Arcus 10010.164

Arem[5594

Areobindus (-u-) 10032.3

†Arerimus (episc. Ling.)
  2628

Argelius 10006.7

Argiotalus 6230

Aribo AcS 3.684,5

Ariouistus cl. (e.g. BG
  1.31)

†Armentarius 7558 (arm-?)

Armonius RE 1, 1913, p.383

Arp[AcS 3.689,30

Arrecinius dipl.36

Arric[5550

Arrius 6095, -ia 7551

?Arrotia 5647 (or Arrotala;
  cf. AcS 1.221,33-7; 3.
  690,31)

?Arrteius 6212

Arruntius 6884, F.176 (cf.
  Arruns and the Etr. Lartius, Lartidius infr.)

]arsi 10010.2456

Artacus 6084

?Artissius 7626, F.174

Arto 11876

Personal Names

Artu 10017.174

Arua 10002.7

?Artossius 5706

Ascaricus Paneg. Const.
11

Ascyla Greg. Tur. h.Fr.
2.9

[?Aspadiacus R.1201; cf.
Aspadius 224 above]

[Assenio 7511]

Assonius N.82

Ategniomarus 7101

Ategnissa (dat.) N.136

Atepo 5706

?Ate]porix 11675

Atessas 6013, 6711, cf.
7263

Atessatius 6740

Atgiuios 10027.105

Atiacus MZ 35, 1940, 80

Atilia 7629, -ius 6750,
Atilianus 6681

Atius 6676, 6854

Atitio 10010.1981

Atlus 10027.189

Atpor (for Ateporix?)
10017.1089

Atrectius 6681

Atrectus 6994; 13 vi p.56,
no.299

Atre$_\chi$stus 6140

Atri$_\chi$tos 10027.106b

Atro 6122 (or Airo?)

Atta 5611, 7551, 7678

Attalus Aur. Vict. Caes.
33

Attia 5614, 5720; -ius
5258, 5259, 5685, 5720,
6853-54, 6994, 7047,
7678, 11606, 11848

Attianus 6803, -a 7076

Atticia 5484, -ius 5484

Atticianus 5608

Atticina 7655a, -us 7551,
7553

Atticus 7659, F.356

Attillia 7077, 7627

Attillus 11678c, Attilus
N.80,10

Attio 10027.242

Atto 6130, 6175, 6277,
7678, 7713, 10027.242

Attonius 5279, 6266,
11688, -ia 6175, R.2136

Attiso 7551

A]ttisonius AcS 3.736,44;
R.2136

Personal Names

Attisso 7553

Attucius 7555b

Atturus 6114

Attusa 7072, 10010.211,
   10011.24c

At]tusilla 7072

Atu[llius] 6085

Atuqua R.3896

Atusa 10001.57

Atusirus 7067; cf. Grenier
   in Frank 3.505 and
   n.171

Attuusas 7149

Auais[10017.196

Aucissa 10027.107

†Audolendis 7201

Auentinius, -ia 6208

?Augtus AcS 1.285,47

Augustio (n. sg.) F.137

Auiana 7678

Auidus 6954

Auii[7115

?Auisa 10010.3262a

Auita 7656-58

Auitia 7656-58

Auitianomara 5495

Auitianus 5560, cf. 5494;
   11647; F.168, R.813

Auitus 6102, 6105, 6803,
   11575, 11603, N.123
   (-ius); cf. Pl. Ep. 8.
   23.5

Aulus 6176, -ius N.71

?Auno 11682

[Aur[(Germanus nat.
   Dacus) 6824]

Aura 5384

Aurelius N.111a

Ausonius 6858

[Autronius (Spain) 5975]

Axsinia 6184

?Auuufus (Anulf-?) 10010.
   3240c

Baburius 6212

[Babuleius Brocchus and
   B. Garrulus (both
   Milan) 5976]

Bainobaudes e.g. Amm. 16.
   11.8

Baiulus 7066

Balatulla 5496-7

Balchobaudes Amm. 27.2.6

Baldomarus Aur. Vict. Caes.
   42.17

Personal Names

Balinis 5498

Bandulia 5644 with add.

Banogalis Dr.501

Banuo 5323

Barbatius R.2106

Barin[Dr.692,8

Barnaeus 7011, cf. 10002.
127

Banna 10027.190

Basilida 5954

Bassianus 5007, -a N.78

Bassus 5007, cf. R.1008,
1288

[Bato (Dalm.) 7508]

†Bauderisima (?) 5463

†Baudo(a)ldus 5308 with
add.

?Bauri 10010.3154b

Begulus 5727

?Beip[(or Bienus?) 7166

Belatulus 5993, cf. 5864;
-tullus 11649, -a
5694; ?5742 (Latuna?);
R.3759

Belina 11564, -us 5498

?Beli]samus R.33

Bella 5995, cf. Dr.319
(m.)

Bellator 5722

Bellatorix 6019

Bellicia 5499, -ius
11650, R.3761

Bellico 5723

Bellicus (-a) 5499, 6214,
11650; R.3761

Bellinus 5281; 10017.3

Bellius 6159; cf. AE
1920.125

Bello (n. sg. m.) F.208

Bellognatus 5724

Bellorix 5665 (fem.)

Bellucus (?) Dr.692,9

Bellustius R.3409

Benusa 5341

Beritonus 10017.113

†Bertichildis (not Ber-
thus) 7526; Germ. 21,
1937, 114; MZ 1938,
45-46

†Bertisindis 7202

[Bessus 7213]

Betulonius(?) 3.9760

Beusas 7509 (Dalm.),
11962

Biccus 5366a

Biddu[7512

Personal Names

Bienus 5977, cf. 7166(?) and 157 above

Bilcaisio 5018

Billicedni (dat.) 6154

Bina, -us R.4008

Biracatus 5522-23, 5529

Biraci[5630, -cus 1b.

Biracillus 5522

Biracius 6776

Biracus (-g-?) 5630

[?Biribam 7328; cf. 5328 add.]

Birrius 5318

Bissus 5726; cf. Bissula Aus. 326-330

Bitia AE 1941.85

[Bit(h)us (Thr.) 6955; cf. Bessus; Bitus Hor. S. 1.7.20]

Bitheridus Amm. 29.4.7

Bittius 7249

Bitumus AcS 3.875,11

[Biturix 5725, 5831, 11565]

?Biuilo (or B[e]lullo) 5726

[Blaedarius (Breucus) 7510]

Blandinus 5568

Blandula 5676

Blandus 5282, 5500, 5543, 5536; R.643; -a 5500

[Blattius R.656]

Blullo (?) v. Biuilo

Blussus 7067; cf. Grenier Mnl 2.2.550

†Boddus 6528

Bocc(h)us

Bodicca 7519

Bodico 6740a

Bodi[l]icus 5596

Boduacus 10027.108

?Boiussila 5727 (or Bonu-?)

Bonicia 11876

Bonitus Amm. 15.5.33

Bononia (pers.) 7062, 11628, [11865 (Italy)]

Bonosus 11917; R.4281

Bonussa 5501

Bonussil(l)a 5727

Bora 5728

Boritus 10010.343

Boruonicus 10025.146

Personal Names

?Bot[5422

Bou[5797

Boudillus 5316, 5332

Βουδομάριος v. Vado-

Boudus 5729

Braetius 6887

Brequa[(or Bre[Qua[)
    Lat. xxii primigen.;
    Bre[Brige[13 vi
    p.56, nos.241, 273

[Breucus 7510]

†Bricius AcS 3.933,44

Brigi[5576

?Brigic[AcS 3.940,52

Brigio 7067

Brigiu 5662

Brigius 5576

Brigo 6.31141, R.3008-9;
    cf. 241 below

Britomartus 7068

Britta m. 5020

Britto 11954a

[Briu (Breucorum?) 6213
    add.]

Broc[10002.13

Brocchus 5007 (cf. 5976
    Milan); gl. 158

?Bruso AcS 1.624,14

[Bruttius domo Tucci
    (Spain; v. Itucci,
    Tucci P-W) 6856]

?Buodasi[10010.3156a

Bucco 6907; cf. gl. 79

Buccus 5730

Buculus 6837

Burdo 5866; cf. gloss 158

Burrius 3.9760 (Trebocus)

]bussia 5737

[Bytytralis (Thr.) cf.
    Mucutralis 7213]

Ca[6675

Cabirus 10017.241

Cacirus (-g-) 6154, 6185

Cacudia 5502, cf. 5495

Cacusso 6125

Caerellius 6806

Caesernius 5609

Caesia 5001

Caesonius 6223

[Caeus (Itur.) 7040]

Cagius 7680, cf. 10010.
    3292d; gl. 178

Personal Names

Caia R.3774; 11653

Caiunus 5279

[Caledius -id- (Pisaur.)
    214]

Calenus 7719

[Calipunis 7551]

[Caliphontis 7551]

Callaeus (Sequanus) 5.907

[Caluaster Dio Cass. 67.
    11.4; cf. Ritterling
    p.141]

Caluisia 7531

Cam[5977, cf. 10010.
    476

Cambad[5550 (cf. 234
    above)

Cambo 6091

Camellius 5358

Camelus 11583 (Cameius?)

Camerinus 5556, 7210

Camill[ius 5046, -us
    5063-4

Camilus 10002.161

Campilius 10001.79

Camula 7551; -us (Cam[)
    13 vi p.56, nos.237,
    241

Camulatus 5411, cf. N.124

?Can[   ]unus 10027.173-4

?Candeco AcS 1.732,38

Candidianius 6197

Candidius 6243, R.2140

Candidus AE 1940.110

Canisius R.4008

?Canlos AcS 1.735,29

[Cantaber 5013, 7033]

Cantianus RE 2, 1914,
    p.163

Cantilius N.88a

Cantin[11606

Cantistius 5005

Cantius 5677, cf. AcS 1.
    752,35

Cantognatus 11652

?Cantrus (leg. Scantrus?)
    5408

Canuleius 7082

Capalus 11559

Capell[11606

Capenus Liv. per. 120

Caper 5766

Capito 5816

[Capitonius F.238]

Personal Names

Capratinus 5730, Capr[
R.4202

Capurillus 11659, 11666

Capusoi 7626

Caracus 11652a

Carado[11652b

Caradouni, Caraddouni (for
-dd-) 11653; Carathouni
(for -d-) 11656; cf.
Carassounus, -onus

Caraisioun[11653, R.
3774

Caran[6176a

Caranitanus 7551

Caranta 11652c

Carantia 5782

Carantianus 5503

Carantilla 5996, R.4156;
-us 5476, 5570, F.148,
150

Carantius 7659, 11666;
10025.136

Caranto 11652d; Caranto
a( )u( )10025.32

Carantodius 11654, 11657;
10025.136; -ia 11654;
R.3971

Carantus -ius 5508, 6013,
6059, 6175, 7665,
11664, 11655, 11686;
R.3862, 3882, 4157

Carasius 6003, 6005,
11653, R.3774

Carasus 11653, R.3774

Carassonus 11566

Carassounus 11653; -ius
5279

Carata 5983, F.144

Caratacus 11669, R.3706

Carathounus R.3778; 11656

Caratilla 5740

Caratius 5997

Caratodius 11656

Caratullus 5731-32, 11657;
F.143; -a 5740

Caratun[R.4160

Caratus 5313, 11657;
R.4157

?Caraus[10010.498

Careius 6958

?Carenta R.4484 add.

†C(h)ariatto (H-) and
-ttho Conc. Araus.,
Genau., Matisc. (A.D.
529, 585) see TLL Onom.
3.191

Carietto Greg. Tur. h.Fr.
2.9; cf. Char-

Carinius 2138, 11827, -ia
2138

Personal Names

Carinus 5732-33, 6681

?C(h)ariogaesus (H-) see
Ario- 244

[Carisius (Aruernus?)
11658]

Carisso 10010.549a

Carmanius N.87

[Carminius (Sp.) 6233]

Karonius 7682

Carpullus 5430

?Carpus (or]carpus) 5944

Carrotalus 5436, -a 5390

Casa 5997

Casia N.129

Casialus 10017.263 (or
Casiatis?)

Cassauus 7.69

Cassitalus 5789

Cassius 6265, N.87, F.357

Casticus BG 1.3.4; cf.
num. Narb. καστικο[σ
(-γ-) Tr. 240, see 78
add. above; κοσττεγος
208

Castius 5284

Castonius 6265

[Casua 8601]

Catalus (Sequanus) 5.907

Catamantoloedis BG 1.3.4

Catianus 5470

Catilia 5346, 5506; -ius
5346; Catilus 5970

Catiola 5737-38

Catius 5368 (?), 5388,
5504 with add., 5739;
-ia 6756

[Cattonius (Virunum)
6860]

Catulianus 11658a (-ll-)

Catullinius 5703, 6198
(-nus?)

Catullinus 5703, 6002 -l-,
6198, 11659, AE 1923.
27, R.780 (6.3350), cf.
R.1979 (6.3315); 10030.
5

Catullius 5368, 6085, 6.
3350 (R.780)

Catullus 5416-18, 11659,
10001.87

?Catulo 10010.497

Catulus 5706, 6801, Catul[
6085

?Catunius 5729

?Catuellaunus 10003.5

Catus N.71(?)

?Caudesus AcS 1.867,30

?Cauinilu(s) 10010.3167b

Personal Names

Caupillius 6121

Ceintusa 10017.275

Celianus 6075

]celima 6773

Cellerus 5740

Cellius 6246, 7685

Celsinius 11608, R.831

Celtillus v. Cilt-

?Cemenus 5756 (leg.
   Gemin-?)

?Cendrinus 10010.3220a

?Ceniratus AcS 3.1200

?Cerasio 10010.542

Κερκίων Eunap. fr. 11

Cetturo 5317

Cetus 5945 (cf. G-)

Cexa 5222 (or Cexauicti?)
   cf. sq.

Cexuari 10026.25a

Charietto Amm. 17.10.5;
   cf. 27.1.2; and Cari-
   above; Χαριέττων Eunap.
   fr. 11; cf. R.1998

Chlodouechus Greg. Tur.
   h.Fr. 2.27

Chlogio ib. 2.9

Chnodomarius (rex Alem.)
   Amm. 16.12.18, cf. C

pp.152, 162; v.l.
   Chonod-

C[h]rocus Greg. Tur. 1.
   32, Aur. Vict. Epit.
   41.3; cf. REA 13,
   1911, 99

†Chrodebertus 7559

?Ciauid[10001.449

Cidius 6001

Cileio 6196

]cillina 5825

Ciltius (G-) 5269, H-M
   344

Ciltillus (Celt-?) ib.

?Cincor[10005.27

Cinnamus 5456, 5929

Cinnena 6201

Cino 6146

Cintri (gen.) R.3882

Cin]tugena AcS 1.1022,
   37

Cintullius R.748 add.

?Cintuma[rus (or Cintu[s]ma?)
   AcS 1.1023,41

?Cintus (or Cintusmus)
   N.242

Cintusma 5533; -us 5641,
   5741, 5939, 6002,
   11585; N.242; cf. 4685

Personal Names

Cintussa 6002

Cipi 10027.19

Cippa v. Gippa

[Cirata (Neruia) 7088]

Cirim[10035.1

Cirniu 10010.3237b
  (Cirinus?)

Cirir 7181

Cirratus R.2000,3

Cir(r)ius 7534

?Cirus AcS 1.1029,35

Cisa[5303

?Cisinebi 10010.3255k

Cissalus ad 6018

Ciuerumn[AcS 3.1231,
  R.1492; 11869

Cladaeus AcS 1.1035,55

]clantrus (Saci-?) 5742

Claupus (missicius) 11709

Clod[ius F.132

Clossus 6234

Clu[5744

Clusiodus 11868

Cnatillus 11667

Cnatius ib.

Coactilus 5444

Coberatius 11660

Cob...til[5412 add.

Coblunius N.124

Cobnertus 6017, 6681
  (-ius); R.4631a

Cocceia 6962, cf. Cocce[
  5017

Cocilla 5756, 5916; -us
  5722, 5929; -ia 5745

Cocum[bus] Dr.700,2

Cocus 5675, 5843

Cocusia 5285

?Coddis 5826

Coddacatus 5368

Codol...na(?) 5998 (Sen-
  urus or Senu..rus, or
  Codosenus?)

Codom[5319

Codo[nius?] AcS 1.1060,
  41

Coetius (not -i-?) 7698,
  cf. Coetus 10010.3259c,
  Coitus ib. 3167c
  matronae Coaetiae(?)
  AcS 1.1053

[Coiedius (Treuer) 7516]

[Coinagus (Petrucorius)
  7031]

[Colinus (Eporedia) 11854]

Personal Names

Comi[5848

Cominius 7517, -ia 7094

?Cominiat(a) 7517

[Comitilla (Mediomatrica)
    7007]

Como[5874

Condollius 11605

?Conesini 10010.3241

Coniletus 10010.3249

Connoucasuua(?) F.178

Consiuius AE 1937.55;
    BSAF 1936, 180-186

Conteddius 6013

Contuinda (dat.) N.136

Con[ ]nis 7505

[Coranus R.1560]

Corcianus (or Gorgias?)
    6085

Cordinus R.47

Cordus 6954, 7255, R.1066

Corisilla 5917

Corobilius R.2136

[Corotures (Sp.) 7045]

Cosminus 5809

Cossa Dr.358; Kossa AcS
    1.1139

Cossattio 6013

Cossetio 11703

Cossianus R.3795

Cossillus 7516a

Cossus 5260, 7551, 7553;
    -ius 5292, 5747,
    R.3795

Cossutus 7715-16

Coteus 5312 (Coteius)

[Cotallus (Africanus)
    5466]

Cottius 6194; 6860(?), or
    contirones?

Couentius 6028

?Couiuicii AcS 1.1153,5

Courunus ib. 1.1151,4

Coxxe[ib. 1.1153,35

Cra..aχ(t?)alius 5686

Crasarcinus 5851

Craxallus 11584 (5748)

Craxanus 5748

Crecus 10029.314

Cricirus 5750

Crippo 7665

Crispinius 7623, Crispus
    10029.32

Cri..talus 5686

Personal Names

Criticus 5783

Crobus 11653, R.3774

Crodius R.3024

Cuasus AcS 1.1180

Cuatasius 5510 (v.l.
  Culn-)

Cucumilla 5454; cf.
  cucuma TLL

Cudelo(?) 6951b

?Culnasius 5510 (or Cuat-?);
  Curisius R.1080

Curio F.176

Curtilia 7241

Curtius Germ. 7, 1923,
  15; 8, 1924, 81

[Cuses (Raet.) 7048]

Custadge 11574 (Germ.?)

Cybira 6819, Cyria F.143

Dacraio N.242

Dagalaifus Amm. 26.4.5

?Dagillus AcS 1.1214

Dagoberctus MGH Dipl. 1
  p.41

Dagomarus 5995, 11892

Dagouassus AcS 1.1216

Dagus 5340

Damus 5751, 7535

Daminius 5911

Dammula 5720

Damo AcS 1.1220,48; div-
  ine?

Damuio 5762

Dan[7626

Dann[5734, cf. Dannius
  AcS 1.1223,17

Dannicus (Rauricus) 7.66;
  H-M 478; perh. adj.
  (Note lii above)

[Dasus (Dalm.) 7508]

?Dasillinisoia 5465

Datiba 5697

[Datiuius 6705, 11810
  (Taunensis)]

Dauina 5762

Dauus[5732

[Dauerzus (Dalm., local)
  7507]

Decantilla 5412 with add.

Decauus 7516a

Decemius 6687

D(ecimus) N.129

Decentio 5627

Decia[5648

Personal Names

Decmanius 5511

[Decmanus neg. Mog(unt.)
  ciuis Taun. 7222]

Decmia 5466

Decmilla 5462, -us 5511

Decmin[5873, -us 5755

Decmo 5753, -us 5755

Decorata N.75

Decumilla 6100

Decumina (-us) 5045

[?Degala (Cannenaf.) or
  -ula; or read Desala?
  7227]

[Degus (Bithyn.) 6851]

Δηιοταριανος R.1122

Deipses 5512

Demia 5466

Dentilia Sprater 2.34

Deomartus 6734, cf. 10010.
  771, 10026.75

?Deruius AcS 1.1271

?Deua[lis 13 vi p.56,
  no.284

Deuillius 6710

Di[ ]busia(?) 5737

Diccia 5754

Diddignatus 11701

Didius 5756, 7253

Diginianus F.137

Dignilla 6243

Dillius R.41

?Dimisin[7643

[†Diopella(?) 5448]

[Disacentus (Thr.?) 7051]

Diuiciacus F.216

Diuicianus 11663

Diuicus 5434

Diuixta 5759, 6000, 6001,
  6022, 11664

Diuixtius 5425

Diuixtus 5281, 5321;
  Diuixtus (Sequanus)
  insc. Lyon C p.66, n.3

Diuilla 11678c

Diuitiosa BA 1925, p.lx

[Dizzaca (Parth.) 6231]

Domatus, -a 7627

Domitus 5761

Donicatus 5433

Donius 6723, 6892

Donnius 7717

Dorepus 5761

Doss[5020

Dosso 7732

Dossus N.80,1

Dousonna 5561, -us 5532
    (for L-?)

Drappo AcS 1.1315,21,
    Draponi 10010.818; cf.
    gl. 178

Dr.c.ca 5519

[Dregenius (Belg.) F.352]

Dribionos (or Dib-?) 5494

Drimmius 11559

Drombinus 6108

Druciedo (-tedo?) 10027.
    112

†Dructacharius 7203

[Drudelinus 6219, a late
    (15th c.?) addition;
    see 6219 ad loc.]

[Dubitatia (Syria) 5373]

Dubitatus 6131, cf. R.805;
    10017.332

†Ducia Dr.676

?Dugenicani (or Suadugeni?)
    5502

†Duda (f.) 6257

?Dullius (Auentinus)
    11658; but see Sua-
    below

Dumnedo[rix 5708.2,20

Dumnotalus R.1459

[?Durasmeas AcS s.v.]

D]uroti[x 10027.130

Durotus 11664

Durra F.145

Duspala 5513; cf. Dieu-
    pala PID 2.59

Eari[nus R.4533

Ebregisil[us Germ. 21,
    1927, 114; MZ 33,
    1938, 46

[Eburo (ethn.) 6216]

[Ecco (Raet.) 7684]

]ecissa 5872

]edioni F.174

?Edobeccus Greg. Tur.
    h.Fr. 2.9

Edullius 6058

?Ef...ias AcS 1.1408

?Egnicax ib. 1409

?Eiodi 5512

]eiouus 5669

Eirmio (or F-?) 5320

Elia 5711, -ius 7640

?El(l)ima 6773

Personal Names

Elurus Dr.412

Enius 6919, Ennius 7238,
?Ennias 7660

Epidius(?) 7089

Epilla AcS 1.1445

Eppo 6125

Epponina Tac. h. 4.67;
ἐμπονή Plut. am. 25
(770E), Πετονίλλα Dio
Cass. 66.16.2; but cf.
gloss 233

†Epta[(uidua?) 7526;
but cf. Eptacentus
(Thr., e.g. 6821, 3.
2328,69; cf. Disa-
centus)

Equonius 6034

[?Erga.onius 10033.7]

Erpa Fred. chr. 4.42 (C
p.15, at Vrba)

[Eronis (Itur.) 7042]

[?Erumo (spur.?) 6014]

?Escupius 5435

]essus 11692

Esucco N.136

Esuccus (-gg-) 5366a

Esunertus 11644

Etima(?) v. Elima

Etipe 7183

E]trius 5613

†Euharia 7558

Eunus 7168, 7520

?Euotalis AcS 1.1486 (or
Eustadius?)

Exascas 5451a

[Eximnus (Vindel.) N.114]

Exomnius 11632; cf. R.3988

Exsomnus 6939; cf. 11669

Facundanus 6072, -ina
6348 (cf. 2.3326;
Facineihae 223 above;
pagi Facanis NdSc 1892,
336)

[Faltonius 6950, cf. 6960
(Dertona)]

?Fanula 5713

Fauio 6118

Fecu[5290

?Felius 6120

Fers[7060; cf. 223

Festius F.145

Fett[7161

Fiertius AcS 1.1495

F]irmanus AE 1939.48

Firminius F.137

Personal Names

Firmio 6122

Fittio 11605

[Flaccilla 7066]

[Flauoleius (Mutina) 7253]

Florius N.71; MZ 35, 1940, 80

Flu[11976

Focuronia 7519 (cf. Runa f. 7604? Or Focunates?)

†Forandus R.4410

†Francio 7558

Fraomarius Amm. 29.4.7 (king of Bucinobantes)

†Frederico N.140

Freorin[(?) 6124

Fronto F.209; 11818; [F. 352, Vbius]

Frot[5915

Fuscus F.236

G[ ]tus N.71

Gabrie[5516

Gabrila AcS 1.1510

Gabro 5961 cf. Gabrila, -llus, Gabreta, Gabro-magus, -se(n)tum etc., cited ad loc.

†Gaereholdus R.4418

Gaio(n) N.80,17

Gaipor BJ 160-161, 1936, 450

Galbus 7253

Gall[5860

Galla 5954, Gallia (if pers.) 7234

Gallicanus 5743

Gallus R.1053, cf. 10017. 420

Gamatus 7551

Gamuxpero (dat.) 7086; cf. -poris, -por? Or two names? Gutenbrunner 12

Gapr[5325

Gario AE 1941.108; MZ 35, 1940, 79

Gattus N.77, cf. 71

Gauius 7085; cf. 6893 (Histonium); Gauius RE 1, 1913, p.383

Gauisa (?) 7551

Gedus 5391

Geddius 6154

?Geius AcS 1.1993

Gellio 5957

Gellius (...Celerianus Nemes) 6659

Gemellus 5700, 5771,
6281(?), F.205; cf.
10017.424

Gemellonius 6682

?Gemenus 5756

[Geminia Titulla Arau-
siensis 5384]

Gemino 5700, -inus v.
Gemenus

Germanus N.111a, -icus
N.129, [Germanus (sic)
natione Dacus, AE 1940.
117; cf. 6824]

Germanilla 6806

†Gennarius R.4308

?Gentius 11589 (or Satta
...gen[?)

Gettonius N.80,1

Giamillus 5946, cf. Gia-
millius (Virunum) AcS
1.2018,30

Giamonius 6145

?Giappa 5774

Giltius (C-?) 5260, cf.
H-M 344

Gimio 6133, cf. 224

Gippa (C-?) 5754, cf.
11585(?), AcS 3.1226,
40

Gippo(n) 5518, 11585

Gittonius 11607; REA 20,

1918, 180 (divine name
Ciss- 236)

[?Glucu[R.841]

Gnatillus R.3837

Gnatius 6262, Gnatus
11610, -a 6025

[Goar Greg. Tur. h.Fr. 2.
9, cf. Olympiod. fr.
17]

[Gorgias 6085]

Granianus R.1728

Grannicus 5515a, -a AcS 1.
2037,3; cf. Grannus
223, 237

Gratinus N.75

Gratius F.226

[Grumensis R.4533-34]

†Grutilo 6259

†Gundoaldus N.141

Gundomadus Amm. 14.10.1,
16.12.17

Gundicarius (-ch-) Cassiod.
Chr. p.653 M.; Prosper.
Chr.

Gunduicus Pass. Sig. (ap.
Fredegar. p.333 Krusch)

Guntiarius Olympiod. fr.
17

?Haeb[7555

Personal Names

Haledona F.215 (cf. Hal-
  dania 224)

[Haneli (Itur.) 7040]

Hariobaudus Amm. 18.2.15
  (cf. -des ib. 2)

[Hastaius 7515]

Hedius R.1461, cf. 1109

[Hegontis? 7083]

Helluis 7694

Helues[(or Heluetius?)
  R.2136

Heluius 6723, 6907, 6928,
  -ia R.41; -us R.4598

[Hendinos Amm. 28.5.14;
  but see 240]

H]ere[o]llus AcS 1.2052

Hibern[7083, Hibern(ius)
  6687, R.3988; Hiber-
  nalis 7083(?)

Hilariclus 11575

†Hisagogus 5449

Hispel(1)o 6943, 7016; but
  cf. Hispali(?) R.4535,
  4541 (Spain)

[Hordeonius e.g. Tac. h.
  4.25]

Hortarius Amm. 16.12.1

(H)ostilius N.80,3

Ia[ ]inius 5916

Iader 6827

Iadestinus 6827

?Iadromus 10026.25c

]iaino 6176a

Iamailiora(?) 11470 (or
  two words Iamai Liora?)

[Iamlicus (Itur.) 7040]

Iamma 7120

?Iamnia AcS 2.8

Iantumarus (Varcianus)
  Dipl. ii

Ianuconius 5983

Ianussa 11615c

Ianussius, Ianussus 5391

Iappus 10010.1004; Behn
  526

Iaretius 6202

Iassus 5968

Iasus 6190, -a; 11647;
  R.813

Iatinius (Romanus) 5916

Iauius (Varcianus) 6.3257

[Iauolenus Priscus 6821,
  cf. Iaolenus 3 Suppl.
  9960 al.]

Iaχtia (or Iaχtila; hardly Laχtia) 5793

Ibliomar(i)us 6018 with
  add.

Personal Names

Iblissa 11978

Idmus 5694

]ieammo[6199

Iedurcius 7666 (cf.
   Iedussius 4137)

Iegidi 10001.161

Iemietl[us] 5666

[Ierombalus (Itur.) 7041]

†Ieuninus (L-?) 7636

Iladecda 11573

Iliomarus 5392

Inderci[11584 (5748)

Indercilea (-ia, -la?)
   5748; better Indercilli
   filia; Indercinia BSAF
   1910, 237; but see
   11584

[Indiana ala 6230, 7027,
   7257, Gallorum 6495;
   R.1461 cf. Indus (Tre-
   uerus) Tac. a 3.42;
   dipl. 80]

Indu[AcS 2.40,50

]indus 5802

Indutius 5317, 7243;
   [Lusitania 5311]

Indutus 6776

Ingeldus 10027.207

Intamelus (Eburus) 6216;
   cf. Lig. Intimilium?

AcS 3.633 suggests
   Antamelus (-te-)

?Inuetius 5393

Io..c..a 6021

Iodauin[5762 add.

Ioenilis 5794

Ioincatia 5287

Ioincorix 11689

Ionillus 5663

Iouinus Oros. 7.42.6

Irdutus 6156

?Irenillus 5440

Isuria 5778

Itamon R.2004 (3.7387,
   cf. 8.9060)

Ituuerus R.2004

[Ituraeus 6278]

Iuisus (?) F.236

Iulichus 5698

Iulinius N.129

Iulliacus AcS 2.88

Iullonius 7219

Iuenis 6061 (RE 1, 1913,
   p.408)

Iulu(s) 5843, 5628(?)

?Iumileius AcS 2.88

Personal Names

Iunianus 5524, 5786a

Iunilla 5787

Iunni[5545

Iurus 5628(?)

Iutuccus 5788; cf. EC 2, 1937, 30, n.1

Iuuencus R.2077-78; Dipl. 50

La[N.128

Labeo 5789 (Lib-?)

Laetilius F.215

Laetus 6271, cf. R.1998

?Laficis 5943

Lagussa 5437

Lallius AcS 2.127

?Lambre[us] ib. 129

?Lamma (or Iamma; Amma?) 7120

†Landulfus R.4418

Laniogaisus Amm. 15.5.16

[Lanus (Raet.) AcS 2.143]

Lapius ib.; 5467, cf. Lappius Dr.168

[Lappa 7513; Stein Beamten 210.357 interprets as a Syrian local name]

Lappianuc AcS 2.143

Largennius 5978

Lartius 5792; cf. TS Lezoux

Lartidius 6942 (cf. Etr. Arruntius above)

Lasionius 6349

Lassonius AcS 2.149

Latinius 5353 (Aeduus), 5916

?Latuna 5742 (v. Bela-tulla)

Laxtia 5793(?), v. Ia-

?Lauta F.351

[Lemonia 11628; cf. AcS 2.176-77]

Leon[F.241

†Leoncia R.4324

Lepontius 5980

?Lesto(u)n[5693

Leubius 11709

[†Leuninius (Ieun-?) 7636]

†Leupa[7636

Leuponus 10025.146

Liaeniuus(?) 6150

†Libefridus 7560

Personal Names

[Licaius (Pann.) AcS 2.
  206]

Licina N.116

Licinius N.116, 11591

Licontius 6250

?Lictauius AcS 2.213

Liguris 5795, -ius 5987

Lillutius AE 1914, 286

Lin[7034

Lindo 6679, †Lindis 7260;
  cf. local name Lin-
  desina 234 above,
  †Thudelindi(?) 7260

Ling[5917 (ethn.?)

Linicinius AcS 2.237

Lippo 5528

Litauiccus 5797

Litauicrarus 5708 2.11,
  cf. 234 above

Litugenus 5529, 5950

Liuia N.116; AcS 2.266,39

Liuilla N.116

Locu[ ]ulla R.3926

Lollio 5700

?Lonis (or local name, or
  Apol]loni?) 5316

Loro[7235

]lorta 6753

Losunius 6202

Lubitiata (Du-?) 6005

Lucania 6279, R.1205a
  (add.)

Lucanus 6266

Lucceius 5639

Lucconius 5010 (Lucco?)

Luceua R.4254

Lucinius 6010

Lucretianus R.35; 11.
  1331

Lucrio 5697

Lucudeca 5926

Luculla 7536

Lucunessus N.87

Lucus 7013

†Ludinus 6257

[?Ludnomagens[5923,
  prob. local, cf. Ludna,
  Lunna TP (between
  Lugudunum and Matisco,
  in Lugdunensis); 179,
  234 above]

Lug[6941

]lugena 6783 (or Ve]lugena,
  cf. Vela- 9 above)

?Lullo(s) AcS 2.346,19-20

Personal Names

Luna 6107

Lupercus 6247

Lupio 6687

Luppus 11976

Lupula 5437, 6163, 6728a

?Lupulinus 11976

Lupulius 6247, -ia R.2011

Lupulus 6250, 6252

Lupus 11810, cf. R.1124,
  1205a (add.)

?Lurius 7191a

Luso 6947, Luse Dr.681.11

[Lustrostaius (Viennensis)
  5011]

Luteuus 6025

Luto 5323

Lutoria 7519

Luttonius 6252

Lutullus 6031

Lutumarus (Li- or La-?)
  7553

[Lycnis 7089]

?Macato 5806

Maccio 5321

[Macco (Eporedia) AcS 2.
  365,28]

Macer F.236

Macnilla (-g-) 5802

Macrianus Amm. 18.2.15,
  28.5.8

Macrina 5718, -us -ius
  6669, cf. C p.114

Mactichildis Germ. 21,
  1937, 114; MZ 33,
  1938, 46

Maddacatus 11587

Maelo 5258 cf. Mon. Anc.;
  Μέλων Str. 7.1.4,
  2910; cf. gloss 246
  below

?Maeiu[5643 (AcS 2.362)

Maesi 7551, Maesius R.657

?Mafius 7267 (v. BJ 142,
  1937, 54 n.1) or ?Mafu
  (Oxé Festschr. 128-
  134)

Magalius AcS 2.373

Magal[us 5593

?Magetob[(if genuine)
  Dr.692.36

Magian[5531

Magillius 6723

Magiorix 5992

Magissa m. 6078, 6154

Magissius (Hibernus) 6078

Magius R.802, 807

Personal Names

Magnianus 5801

Mago 5375

Magunia 5803

Maianus 6214

Maie[F.241

Mainetius 10028.5

Mainus 11652, cf. 11667
(-nn-), 11670a (-nn-),
11672 (-nn-); 10010.
1240; 10010.1234c-d;
R.3874

?Maiuro 5739; -us 5642,
5664

Maius 5646

Malarichus Amm. 15.5.11

Malia R.3706

Mallius 6217

Mallobaudes Amm. 30.3.7

Mallus 5804

Mamma 5783

Mammaius 5372

Mammilianius 6771

Mammisso 5871

Manatia 6151

Mandatus AcS 2.402,9

Mandubilus (-bius?) 5532
(-blius?) ethn? (179)

Manertus 5850

?Mangandius AcS 2.406.36;
cf. gloss mango 15;
Note xlvi (xi) above

[?Manno[(?) 6128]

Mansuanius R.1053

Mansuetus 5988, 6084,
6092, 6685, 7553, 7555;
-a R.4104

Maponus 5924 (but cf. 181)

Marcatus 5806

Marciainus 5438, -nus
11647, R.813

Marcio R.4510a

Maridus 10004.4

Marinianus Sprater 2, p.34

Marinus 5291

Mariscus 5801

Maronianus 5431

Maroboduus cl. (Vell.,
Tac.)

Marsius 5809

Martasus 10005.16

Martilla 5810

Martialis N.87

Martio (n. sg. m.) F.162

Martius 5318, 6071, N.88;
-ia 6693a, 11587

Personal Names

Marullus F.236

Marulus, -ina 5278

Masc[5455

Mascel(1)io 5538-39, 6097, 6262

Masclius 7532

Masculus 5676

Masonius AcS 2.454,10

[Massa (Heluet.?) 7024]

Massianus 7732

Masucia 5285

Masuaeta F.244

Masuco 5292; Gutenbrunner 12

Massuinnus 6156

Masuonia AcS 2.457

Masurius 11952

Mata (or Sattomata?) 5834

Mataris 10028.6

[Maternius (Nemausus) 7007]

Matidonnus 5793

Mato 6140

Matrainno 11658, R.3972

Matta 6003 (or -aius?)

Mattaius ib., -aus(?)

[Matteius (Bononia) AcS 2.474]

Mattius 5601, 6114

Matto 7072, 11610; cf. Mattonius (Tribocus) 2018; R.3412; C p.139

Matucus 5496-97

Matugen[a or -us 5853

Matuinus 6153, 7553

Matura 5950, -us F.236

Maturia 5918, -ius 6151

Maturix F.148

Matutina(?) 6017, -nus 6204, R.831, F.146

†Mauricia F.229, -ius 7645

Maurus N.80,8

Maurusius 11561

Maxima 5984, F.139

Maxseminus 6080

Maxsumus F.236

Me[5824

Mederichus Amm. 16.12.25

[Med(iomatrica?) 5919]

Meddillius 11689, Meddil[F.142

Melausus F.170

Personal Names

Meliddius 5439 (cf. 10002. 296-97)

?Melisattius 5553

Mellonius 6682, R.782, 785, Dr.699.4

Melonius AcS 2.541,26-7; R.2009 (cf. local names?); 7.632

Melosattus AcS 2.541,45

Memusus 5280

Menimanius 7067, cf. div. name Menmanhia 6.31178 (Dessau 4747); cf. Men[R.3260-1; 223 above

Mepilla 5427

Mercurina 5778

Merdi 10027.243

Mergenialis(?) 5812

]meritanius(?) 6834

Meritus AE 1923.27

Merobaudes Amm. 30.10.3

Merogaisus Paneg. Const. 11

[Messius AcS 2.576,26]

Messo[7280

Messor 5258-59, F.202

Messorius 5370; -ia AcS 2.576,50

Messue(?) 6182

Meteellus R.2143

[Metillius (Taurini) AcS 2.579,1]

Metonius 6935

Mettius 5367, 7700

Mettus 10032.15, R.4630

Mezzentius F.235; AE 1945.1; BJ 146, 1941, 218

?Midicsine 7627; BJ 142, 1937, 54 n.1

Mimir[AcS 2.586,15

Mineru[(divine name?) 5366a

Minedo 10026.26

Minet[5397

Minicius 6679

Minius 5780

Minno 10002.272

Minusilla 5958

Minusonius 11828

Minutus 5543

?Miono 5617

Misionius N.87

Miucenus 5341

?Miuinua 11670a

Personal Names

Moenia(?) F.138

Mogetia 7092

?Mogo 5315

†Mommolenus AcS 2.620 (13. 905?)

[Monimus (Itur.) 7041]

?M]onnus 6013

Montanus R.2108

Mopesu[N.80,16

Moriena R.4058

Mossianus 5694

Mossimo[5546

Mossia 5921

Motti 10017.607

Motuacus AcS 2.646

Motuca 6247

Moxsius 6140

[Mucapor (Thr., cf. Gaipor) 5269; 6821, cf. 3.10411]

Mucuru(s) R.4600; 10027. 90

[Mucutralis 6716, 6740]

Mullius 5912

[Munnis N.114a (Vindel.)]

Muranus 7579

Murrasius 6930a, cf. Murra (m.) R.655

Murr(i)nius R.2146

Muscidius 5782

Musentius 6935

Musicus 5817

Musina 5440

[Musius (Veleias) AcS 2. 662]

Mutace 5818, -us 5413, 5859; 631, cf. AcS 2. 664,42

[Mutius (Treuerus) 6235]

?Nalmanoti 7146

?Nammius 6711 (Mem-R.1227)

[Namnis 6230 (Lugd.?)]

Nanius 5563

Nanniensis Amm. 31.10.6

Nannus (-o?) 6704

Nantia Dr.501, -ius F.147

Nantil(us) 5514

Nantiorix f. 5485

Natironius 11707

Nantuas AcS 2.687 (ethn.?), v.l. Nantuasius

Personal Names

]nareg[f. 5488

Natalis N.80,4; F.147, 220

Natuspardo Amm. 27.10.16

Naunius 11801a; R.2774

Nauius 5563

]nctinu.do[5880

[Nemausus (cos.) 7007]

Nemonius 6676

Nen[10001.227

Nerius 10001.228

Nertus 5965; R.1459, 3. 10514

Nertomarus 6027, cf. Nertomarus Irducissae f. Boius (3. p.1975); AcS 2.725,42; Nertomer[10027.118

Ne]ruinus? F.236

Nestica Amm. 17.10.5

?Nettas 10027.90; R.4600

?Nibo AcS 2.742,3

?Nicarinus 1041*

Nicer R.3752

Niccus 6175

Nicinia 6099

Nicronius 11707

Nigellio 6109

Nigidia 5478, -ius 6680

Nigidianus 5383

Nigrina 7093

Nigrius 6.22981 (Tribocus)

Nimeius AcS 2.748,21

Nis[6118

Niualius 5929c; AcS 2. 752,27

Niugenus 5504 with add.

]nnio 10004.13

Noctedius 7127

Noluntiossus AcS 2.757,17

Nominator(!) N.70; 80,14

Noniso 11579

†Nonnus 7561

[Norbania 7055; Norbanus 5366, 5773, 7055]

Nothi[R.2000,5

]noturin[5841

Nouanus R.1205a (add.)

Nouellius 7062; 2020 (Vangio)

Nouellus 5694, 5821; N.88

Nouionia 6247

Nouia 6159, 6218

Personal Names

Nouim[arus F.236

Nouirius 7210

]nucco 6125

[Nunadus (Vindel.) N.114a]

Nundina 5287

]nussata F.174

?Nux AcS 2.809,47

O[ ]us 6018 with add.

Occo 7655

Occonia (-mia?) 7655

Ocellio 5003, 6723

Oclatia 6084, 6177

Oclauia 6349

Octa 5827

[Octiumei 7060]

Octonius 6265

Octutis(?) 7646

Ogrigenus (Sp.?) 7037

Olaatius 5429 (or Ocla-?)

Olisaius 6150

Olitius BJ 140-41, 1936, 450

Ollecnus AcS 2.846,17

Ollus 6037

[Omfalenis 5515c]

Omullus 5295

]onacianus R.1726

?Oppet[AcS 2.862,35

†Optoualda R.4410

?Opurim[AcS 2.863,15

]oredo 7655a

]organ[5949

[Orgilus AcS 2.876,37]

Ostilis N.80,3 (Ho-?)

Otacilius 6809

Ouiorix 10006.65

Oxia 5370 (for Oχta?)

Oχta 5408 (or Oχtaia)

Oχtaia 5441; RA 43, 1882, 271 Pl.8

?Oχtaius 5525 (?Oχtirius, ?Ouχt[lapis)

P[ ]ruti 6005

?Pabenn[5965

Paccius 7725

?Panna 10017.663 (panna?)

[Pannonius (ethn.) 6211]

[Pamius Dr.687; cf. RA 26, 1927, p.164 no.247]

Personal Names

Panturo 5279

Pappius 7714

Parameius 5824; cf. gloss
   paramus 158 above

Pardus 6999

[Parra (Baeterr.) 6857]

[Partus (Treuerus) 6235]

Paterio 6013

Patta 7519

Paturius 11869

Patruitus 6095

Paulla N.113

†Pauta 6258, cf. gloss 220

[Pelidianus r.1727]

?Pellius 5666 (but v.
   also divine names, s.v.
   Cre-)

Pelto (or Peito) 6149

Pennausius AcS 2.965

Peppo 6683

Perclla (sic) 5673

Perrius AcS 2.969

Petianus ib. 972

Peticio, -ius ib.

Petra R.3874

Petrullus 5557

Petturo AcS 2.981

Pinossus ib. 1005

Pintilus 7037

Pipa (or Pipara) Aurel.
   Vict. Caes. 33 (cf.
   Epit. 33, and Trebell.
   vit. Gallien. 21.3)

Pippausus 11607

†Pipuuan?? (Rip-?) 7525

Piraucobruna AcS 2.1007
   (two words?)

Pistillus 6214

?Pisulus AcS 2.1010

Piχtacus 5788

Pla[F.351

[Plassus (Dalm.) AcS 2.
   1013]

?Plinius ib. 1019.11

Πωλλῖνα R.1975

Pollionia 7072

[Pomptina m. (Aeduus)
   5353]

Popa AcS 2.1035

Popillianus ib.

Popp[6200

Poppausius 11703

Poppillus N.84

Personal Names

Poppio 7098

Poppua 6132

Pora[5781

Pradus AE 1945.78 (ex
  coh. Breuc.); MZ 37-
  38, 1942-43, 28

Praua m. 7507

[Prauaus (Dalm.) 7507]

Pressus BA 1920, p.307

Pre[ ]nus R.3988

Primanus 5983; (Ibernus)
  6130

Primius N.84

[Primnia 7007]

?Prionia 7060a

Priunus F.236

?Pritmanus AcS 2.1046,48

Prittillius 5323

Prittusa 5280

?Prognus AcS 2.1047

Prop[(genuine?) C p.164

Prunicus (Phryn-) 5699,
  Phrunicus (-y-) 5966

]p[ti]mo[n]ius? 6675

†Puasi 6258

Pugnus R.3882

Pullius 6821

Pupa f. 5976

Pus[6207

Pusa m. and f. 7101

Pusio F.236

Pusinna 5002, -us 7516a,
  -io 6849

Puster (or -rus) AcS 2.
  1054-55

Puttius 5473

]quannensis 6779

Quartus(?) 6061 (v. [Q.]
  Varius)

Quintianus R.3676, cf.
  N.74

Quinto 6175

Quintus N.81

†Quito 6258

?Quir[6679

Ra[10002.424

†Radelindis 7204

Radoara 5309

†Ragnoaldus N.139

Ramus 5457

Personal Names

Rando (Alamannus regalis)
  at Mainz, Amm. 27.10.1

†Randoaldus 7202

†Rasnehilda 7660

Ratu[5732

Ratulla 6025

Rauinus (or Tr-?) 6094

Rautionis (ex Germ. Sup.)
  7.693

Rebleni 10017.48

Rebrica 5551; -us 5487,
  5534 (Rib-), 5838

[Reburrus (Sp.) 7045]

?Recalem AcS 2.1092

Refidius R.1008

Regalis 5552-54; 11548,
  R.3887

Regallia 7627

Reginius 6129, 7301; -us
  cf. C p.114 (5708 ii
  19, 5840)

[Regus 7048]

Remigius Amm. 30.2.10

?Resius 5555

Restia BJ 142, 1937, 323

Restutus N.80

]retiso 10008.42

Rhenic(i)us 11548; REA
  28, 1926, 365

Rhenus F.176

Ric.ina 7660

Ribricus 5534

Richimeres Greg. Tur.
  h.Fr. 2.9

?Rinnus AcS 2.1191

]riossi 5706

Ripanus 5007-08, 7655

[Rittius (Vienna) 6969]

Ritu(m)arus 10006.73

Rituscia 10010.459a

]rix 5367

]rmini|nuari[? 7654

Riuens[10002.35

?Riuouatus 5868

?Rocabalus 5924

Rocus AcS 2.1201 (-χ-)

?Ronsius ib. 1228

?Roscus ib. 1229

Roχtanus 5557

Rubrius 7554

?Rucui 11959

?Rugus AcS 2.1243

Rulius R.4110

Runa 7077

Runi[5481

[Runicas (ethn.?) N.114a]

Rundo 6177

Ruscus 10006.74-75

Ruticus AcS 2.1256,44

Sabinianus F.137

Sabinus (Lingo) Tac. h.
  4.55

[Sabini 7060; cf. R.802,
  1080]

[Sabionius R.782]

Saccius AcS 2.1274.5;
  10021.166

[Sacco (Mediolan.) R.996]

Sacerilla 7536

Saceronia 7536

Saci[5323a

Sacer N.114a

Sacini[5845

Saciro 5660

Sacra 5743

Sacrillius 7555a

Sacrillus 5838

?Sacrobarus 5856

Sacroben(n)a 5516, 5821
  with add., 5846 (?)

?Sacrodiuus 5830

Sacromaini (dat.) 5561

Sacrouir cl. C p.65,
  Sacrouiru[5619,
  Sacrouirus 5838

Sacruna 5562, 5840 (m.);
  10028.10

Sacurilla F.148

Sacurius, -ia 5563

Saecular N.125

Saedius 5022

Saenianensis 10002.36

Sagarius 11597 (sag-?)

Sagil[lus] 5564

Sagius AcS 2.1288

Saiot[5927

Sair[AcS 2.1297

[Sal[(Lusitania) 5311]

Salicilla 5442

Salicogenna 5784

Sallio 5566

Salutus 6953

Sam[6077 (or divine
  name, cf. 6083?)

Personal Names

Sambatiola 5458

Samel[5836

Samicius 5847

Samilla 5434

Samio (-ius?) 6189

Samis 10002.71

Samm[6083 (v. Sam[above)

Sammo 7120, cf. 7348; F.148

Sammonius 6970, 7120, 10017.3

Samocinus 5848

Samocus 5849

Samoricos (gen.) 5788

Samus 11806; perhaps Beli]samus? R.33; cf. 10027.129, RGKBer. 3, 1906-7, p.94 no.171

Samus....essus 11692; R.3266

San[6030

Santius (also div. name?) 7552; cf. 6607

Sanu[ ]ni 11582

Sanuaca 5618 with add.

Sanuc(i)us 5258, 5818

Sappo m. N.82; cf. RhM 84, 1935, 325

Sarasus 5833

Sarenus AcS 2.1367,5

†Sarmanna BJ 140-141, 1936, 456-57

[Sarnus (Raet.) AcS 2. 1369,50; cf. MZ 37-38, 1942-3, 28]

Sasmi 10001.423

Sasso 5565

Sassula 5913

Saticenus 11580, -g- Dr.693.7

Satrio ad 5566; -ius 7242, cf. 6945; Satri 10034.2

Satt[5553

Satta 11589 (or Sattagen[?)

?Satta]ro R.2781; R.4036; 11877

Satti 10017.764

Sattiolus and Attiola (Ling.) 2035

Sattianus 2035

Satto 5277, 5834, 7532

Sattonius 5622, F.217

Sattulinius ad 6054

Saturio 6684

Satur[n]inius REA 38, 1936, 44; N.137

Personal Names

?Saturus 5638

Sau[(or San[?) 6038

?Sauaria (local?) 11847

Saurius, -ia 7659

S]amax[a Dr.358

Saxxamus 5641 (i.e. -χs-)

[?Scalensis 10002.48
   (Spain)]

Scantrus 5408; RA 43,
   1882, 271

?Scaper 5851

Scatnilla 5567 cf. Scato
   R.644

[Scenus (Pann.) 7511; cf.
   P-W s.vv. Sceno-barbus,
   -bardus]

Scitus AcS 2.1398,52

Scottus 5372, 5759

[Scruttarius 11857]

Scudilo Amm. 14.10.8

Seblasius 11891

[Sebosiana ala R.1834,
   cf. (Sp.) 6236; dipl.
   48, 69; Sebosus (Kel-
   tic) Stein Beamten
   151-152]

Seccalus 5178, 11604

Seccius 6275, 7105-06

Secco 6024, cf. 10003.77;
   AcS 2.1425,9

Secius 7104

Sedan[t]ianus 5642

Sedatius 7083, -ia 5676,
   5009, 5551

Sedatus 5988, 6709, 6929,
   11587

Sedauo 7025; Gutenbrunner
   13

Sedulius 5688

Sigileius 6013

Segillius 6019

Seginius F.236

Seglatius 6740a

Segomarus 5568, AcS 2.
   1448,10 (Dr.278)

Seius 6175

Seionius 6841

?Seiuolius 5854

Seluanus N.113

S.uola (Scae-?) 5855

Selma 6175

[Σέμνων Zosimus 1.67]

Semus· |· Abt 7631

Sena AcS 2.1465,54

Senai(us) ib. 1466,50

Seneca 6907, 7700, cf.
   10010.1772, 10017.787

Personal Names

Senecio 6676, 6693, 6740b, 6776, 6881, R.807; cf. F.238 (Belg.)

Senecionius 6687

Senetius R.3738

Senicianus 5871

Senil[7537, cf. 6765 (-ia?); Senilius 7222

Senilis 5567, 5930; 7. 632

Senio 6243

Senim[5600 with add.

Senimar[5600

Senius R.4513

Senn[5569

Sennaeus 6130

Sennaius AcS 2.1478,44

Sennaucia 7072, -ius (Damasc.) 6270; cf. Seniauchus Amm. 15.4. 10, 25.10.6-7

Sennaus 6025

Sennicia AcS 2.1479

Sennonis (gen.?) 10017. 788

Senobena 5363

?Senocenna AcS 2.1483

Senocondus 7301

?Senoisu 10010.1788

Senopatius 7553(?), -ius N.88

Senotaeunus 7553

Senouir 5569

Sentianus 6794

Sentinus 10001.226

Sentius 5053, 6933, 7108; cf. Sint-; 13 vi p.56, no.284

Sentrus 5570

Senurius 6687

Senurus 5998; but v. Codol-

†Seoira 7637

Sepetumienus 7109

Seppianus 6730

[Sequana C p.66 n.3]

Sequentia 7037

Seranus F.149

[Serapio v. Agenarichus]

?Ser[ ]olus 5611

Serdus 10002.468

Sergius 6971

Sero 6150

Serotina 6282

Personal Names

Serro 6151

?Serus (Tettoserus?) 6087;
   cf. AcS 2.1525,34

?Set[5683

Seuerinus (or -ius) 6054

Seunuri(?) 7073

Seuuo 11604

Se𝜒stinus 5766

[Sextio(?) 7516a]

Sextocus 6001 (Sextus?)

Sextus N.70

Siano (St-?) 5571

[Sibbaeus (Itur.) 7042]

Sicanus 10001.427

†Sicco 6258

Si𝑑[7073

Sido Tac. A 12.29

†Sidonius (episc. Mogunt.)
   Ven. Fort. 11.7

Silius 6842; 6277 (Picent.)

Silo 7551, 7553; 5975 (Sp.);
   cf. 10010.1812; AcS 2.
   1151,30-42

Solonia 7550

Siluanius N.81

Siluester F.135

Siluis O. p.584

Siluius 11690; H-M 352,
   F.134; -o R.2106

Similio 7681

Similis AcS 2.1566,33

Sincorilla 11876, cf.
   4242 (Trier); AE 1941.
   108 (-ila); MZ 35,
   1940, 79

Sinisserus 5366

[Sinistus Amm. 28.5.14;
   i.e. sinistas
   "eldest"?]

Sinorus 10001.432

Sintillius 6707

Sintillus 10010.1819

]sinto 7519 (Sintus?)

Sinto 7553-54, cf. Sent-

Siron(i)us 10001.433

Sisgus 6204

Sisses 5012

Sitta 5988

Siui[AcS 2.1591

]slamo[5721

Smertuca F.216

Smertulitanus (Namnis)
   6230

1145

Personal Names

S]mer[tullus AcS 2.1594,
  28

[Socmus (Damasc.) ib.
  1597]

[Soenus (Pann.) ib.]

Sofio 6217

Soi[7038

Soigelasius 5752

Soius 5752, 7038; cf. AcS
  2.1599,1 (Soia?)

Solenus 5459

Solimarius 7034

Solimarus 6200

Solimutus 5572, 6773

Solitus 7095

Solius 6972

Solle AcS 2.1608 (Soia?)

Sollius 5573, 6739 (Gal-
  licanus), 11539

Sollus 5573

?Soman[5355

Somniciosus 11650

?Sono[ ]dus 10010.2406

Sounus 11644

So.uus 10027.129

Spart[F.134

Sparucus 3.9816 (cf.
  3163)

Spatalus 6013

Spautus H-M 352, F.134

[Spendusa N.116]

Speratus F.155, 216; -ius,
  -ia F.171; cf. 6539

Spinia 5736

[Staberius R.738, cf. 47]

Statilius 7701, -ia AE
  1941, 109; MZ 35, 1940,
  80

[Sterna (Flor.) N.111c]

[Sterio (Vindel.) N.114]

[Stlaccius R.1560]

Su[7192, 5574

Sua[ ]do 5276

Suadugenus 5502 (-genicenus
  lapis; sua Dugenicanus?)

Suadulla 7117

Suadullius 11658

Suadurx (for -rix?) 5378;
  cf. Germ. 21, 1937,
  248

Suarica 5532

Suauilla ad 5633

Suausia 7673

Succ[11543

Personal Names

Successus 5674

]sucius 6794

?Sucroraripi 5856

Suecconius 5171

Suemoni[5512

(Sugent[(Raet.) 7048)

[Suggiricus BJ 140-141,
    1936, 460]

Sul[11579

Sulpo AcS 2.1665-66

Sunlila (for Sunilla?)
    5633

?Sun]ucco 6125 (not div-
    ine?)

Suolc[5857

Suomarius Amm. 16.12.1

?Super 6.31141

[Sura (leg.) F.251]

?Suramill[5539

Surdonedonus 5048

Surillius 10001.311

Surius 7673, 6737; -ia
    5342

Surus 7550, cf. 3.9816
    (Tribocus)

Sutta N.88a

[Sutti (Dalm.) 7509, cf.
    11962]

?Tacitianius R.2713

Tacitus 6087, 6197, -a
    N.78

Tallom[6189

Taluppa 6028, 6116

Tannogenus 5785

Tanusius N.111b

Tarronius 11815

Tascilla 5443, -us 10027.
    43

Tasgillus 6194, 11976;
    -a R.3671 (?)

Tata 6013

Tatico 11978

Tatto AE 1941.109; MZ 35,
    1940, 80

Tatucanius 6201, cf. Tatu-
    cus CIR 339

?Taudaci 10017.21

Tauricus 5312

Taurinus 5766, F.137

Taurus 5424, 6721, 6887,
    6899 (for Taurinus?),
    [6817 (Itur.)]; cf.
    R.1999, 2000.1

Tecco 10003.77(?), cf.
    10002.497 and gloss
    178

Teddiatius F.206

Teddilos 6013

Personal Names

Tegeddos 6154

Ten[6844

Temporinus F.206

Ternicus 5720

Tertinus F.203, 227, -ius
    CIR 650

Tertius 5321

Tessiatus 11978

Tetto 5295; 6087 (or
    Tetto Serus? But cf.
    Sinisserus 5366, Sis-
    serus TS Avocourt,
    Seisserus CIR 1773)

Teutomeres, Theudo-
    (Franc.) Amm. 15.3.10,
    Greg. Tur. h.Fr. 2.9

†Thudelindi 7260; cf.
    Lindis, Radelindis
    above and local name
    Lindesina 234 above

?Tilia 5785

Tilicius 5696

Tillicus (cf. local names)
    5575

Tillius 6762

Tincius (Alpinus)...Lingo
    [C p.84, cf. 5686 (?)]
    13.1922; gloss 207
    above

Titianius R.2136

Titilia 11978

Titinia 7116

Titiola 11647, R.813

Tituconius 11826

[Tituleius 5382 (Raet.)]

[Titulla (Araus.) 5384]

Titurus 6114

[Tiultus (Bithyn.) domo
    Tiu 6851]

Toccia 7665

Tocco 10010.1924

Tocissa m. 5969, 6018

Togirix num. (Sequani),
    cf. 5055

Togitio 7034

Togius, -ia 7054

Toi[5584

Tonianus 7146

Tor[N.68

Torniss[5710, cf. Tor-
    nius (TS Belg.)

Tornos 10010.1929

Torogilla 5859

Toutio 5278

Tr[7033

[Trautio R.2008]

Trio (cogn.) 5315

Personal Names

?Trauinus (or Rau-) 6094; but cf. 236 (R-)

Trita 5855

Troni(?) 11818

Trougillus 7101

?Troxo 10010.1943a (or Toroxo, i.e. Torosus 228 ix) cf. Truxus

Truxus 10015.50

Tucius 11695

Tuil[(Tull[?) 6135

Tullinus (if pers. not local) 6115

Tullius 6135

?Tummo (N-?) 6237

Tunia 10027.263

Turicus F.236

Turrania 7117

Turullius Tac. h. 2.22

]tussi[5949

⌐Turpericus 5593

Tuticanus 5684

?Tutinus 5845

Va[|]indus 5802, 11590

Vaaro 7521

?Vabnuai[us 10002.603

Vacus (or Valdus?) 10010. 1953a

Vadamalis AcS 3.81

Vadomarius Amm. 14.10.1, Βαδομάριος (Βουδο-) Zos. 3.3

Vaeutinus 5845, cf. Valeutinus R.2006a

[Vafrius R.1298]

Vag[6958

Vallus(?) F.236

Vanatastus 5392

Vanataχta 11689

[Vangio (pers.) Tac. A 12.29; 6.31141, R.3008-9]

Vannius Tac. A 2.63; 12. 29 (king of the Quadi), for -ng-?; cf. Vannius N.110

Vap[6167

Vapinus 6232

Va[rius?] 6113, Varius 6061 (not Quartus) v. RE 1, 1913, p.408

Varucius 6468

Vassatus 10028.17

Vassitu(s) AE 1941.84; MZ 24, 1940, 127

Personal Names

Vassorix 6071

Vat[10010.1983, N.124

Vatasius 5510

?Vatin[5673

Vato[AcS 3.127

Vatto 5058

Vaχ[5769

Vaχtulla 5864

Vbius 6241

Vbtio 6102

Vccux(?) [sagarius] AcS 3.13

?Vciecus Dr.637,2

Vebro 5576 (cf. R.1002, Vibrius); 216 Remark

Veccinius 6100

Vecilius R.1053

Vectissus 7555b

[Vedennius R.1030]

Vegeius 7627 (Vec- BJ 142, 1937, p.54 n.1, cf. Oxé Festschr. p.128-134); Vegetus? -ius?

Vegeta 5001

Vegetius 5910, cf. N.77

[Veiagenus (Vel-?) Raetus 6240]

†Velandu 7260

[Veldumnianus (imp.) H-M 384, 13.9056]

[Velenius R.1121]

]uellicus R.1784

Velorius 7555a

Velsius 6934

Velu[6169

[Velugnus (Deuas) 6221; cf. 10010.1995]

Ven[Dr.692.12

Venatius 6794

Venedi 10034.4

Venicarus R.33; 11806; RGKBer. 3, 1906-7, no.171; AE 1919, p.433

Venixamus F.142

Veranius 5344, cf. R.3397

Veransatus 7036

†Veratdar(?) 7527

?Vergatur[(if pers.) 5735

Verillia 5920

Verinus F.178

?Verius R.2704

Verocilla 5739

Personal Names

Verpatus H·M 321

Verrea 5920

Versenius R.1728

Verus 5366a, -a 7118

Verula 5866

Vescius 7521

Vestralpus Amm. 16.12.1

Vetia 7087, 7118

Veticus 5540

Vettius 6845

?Via[10017.897

Viana (or divine name?) 11859; cf. F.210 but see notes ad loc. (for Vienna local name, Viennensis?); or Viama (82)?

[Vibullius 1121]

[Vibennius 7255]

Vicerina (Victor-?) 6151

Victurus 6010, cf. 10026. 69?

Vidoucus 10010.2040v

Viduca 5389, -us 5950, -ius 11976; -a or -ia Dr.640

[Veiento cos. 7253]

[Viennensis 5922]

Vim[10017.913

Vimpurilla 5634

(Vi)mpu[? (or murum pedes V, m. pass. V?) 5828

Vin[6273

Vincent[ASA 15, 1913, p.38

Vinda 7101

Vindaluco 5282

Vindamai 5646 (Raet.?)

Vindedo 5059 (but divine at 5078 Momms.; why not local like Tuledo, Tenedo?)

[Vindelicius F.203]

Vindex C p.64; 7717 (perh. Latinized for Vindos)

Vindicila 5869

Vin[dillus?] 6059

Vindillius 6215

Vinicarus 7043; cf. Ven-

Vinicius 7014

Vinilla 5431; cf. BSL 32, 1931, 158 n.2

Vinnonia 7072; BSL l.c.; Germ. 15, 1931, 166- 169

Vintedo 11577

Personal Names

Vintilius 5870

?Vipuro 10010.2050

?Viralira (Viraria?)
  R.4254

Vire[6025 (not Vire...
  ratulla)

Vireius 5411, 6778, 6998

Viriaucus BJ 139, 1933,
  225 (REA 38, 1936, 44),
  N.137

Viril(l)io 6241, 6975

Virius (v.l. Vlpius) 6105,
  6914; cf. 10017.752

Virotalus 5990

Virotius 7033

Visellio 5871

Visionius 6190

?Visollu AcS 3.403

Visurio 6058

Visurix (f.) 5295

Vitalia 5913, Vitalis
  11591

Vithecabius Amm. 27.10.3

Vittue 7501; cf. Vittuo
  (-onis) 6401

[Vittullinus (Sumeloc.)
  2506]

[Vitullus ib.]

Vitunis (m.) N.73

Vituus 6118

Vituso 10003.70

?Viuato AcS 3.418

Viuilenus 5504

Vlagius 5247

?Vletus 10027.127

Vlmio 7756

Vlpius 6105, cf. R.2092
  (Tribocus), 2105
  (Nemes); 6.31139; cf.
  Latomus 3, 1939, 79-83

Vmidion(i)us 10027.90

?]uncelf[6134

†Vnfalchus 6260

?Vocara 10010.1042

Vocula (m.) R.41

Vogl[N.80,6

Voltodaga 5816

Voltius 7123

Voluntossus 10010.2082

Volusius 6801

Volusus 6686

Vonu 10017.928

Vo[piscus] N.111b; AE
  1940.113

?Vorgio (Ongio lapis) 6723
  (or local, Lugd? Cf.
  Desjardins 197)

Personal Names

Vosegus (also local and divine names) Sil. Ital. 4.213

?Vosonicus 10010.2086

?Vot(l)a 10010.2088

†Votrilo 7603

Vppilius 6198

Vpulalus 7501

Vrbicius 5644

Vrbicus 5693

?Vrcunus 10027.131

Vriata 11592

Vrius Amm. 16.12.1

Vrsa 6688, 7076, 7057, F.155; 10017.933?

?Vrsaius 10017.933

[ursarius, not Vr-, 5703]

[Vrsatius Amm. 16.4.7]

Vrsia 7083

Vrsicinus Amm. 16.12.1, cf. 15.5.2

Vrsic[us 6123

Vrsio 7083, 11638; R.4058

Vrsinus (emeritus) 6735; 6803; cf. R. Lit. p.327

Vrsula 6774, 7072, 7083

Vrsulia 11821

Vrsulus 5482, 6050, 6707, 11976

Vrsus 6794, 6801, 7083, 11810, R.2136, R.4377 (†); N.80,1

Vruinus (Vrb-?) 11629, 11817; R.1964a, 3013

Vscus AcS 3.49

Vssus 5988

[Zetus F.214]

The Agri Decumates with the
Upper Rhine and Danube

1.   The agri decumates

In Tacitus G 29, the only place in which the expression decumates agri occurs, the extent of territory
implied seems to be that enclosed by the Main, the
Rhine, and the Danube. This is not very different from
what Ptolemy seems to imply by ἡ τῶν Ἐλουητίων ἔρημος
(2.11.6, 256.2). The meaning of decumates, as Norden
has shown, is most likely "ten fold" rather than "tenth"
(OIr dechmad), and the term comparable with Decempagi,
Nouempopuli, Quinquegentani and the like. Apparently
the area had at one time been occupied by the Heluetii,
who abandoned it, perhaps about the end of the second
century B.C., under pressure of invading Germans, and
crossed the Rhine into Switzerland. No doubt some few
of the Keltic population remained in occupation of their
old homes; but a new influx of Keltic-speaking groups,
economically or politically ruined by the events of the
last century B.C., made their way thither as refugees
to territory which, except along the valley of the Rhine,
was sparsely inhabited.

Colonization of the area, the settlements of Arae
Flauiae (Rottweil, earth-fort, A.D. 50-83, then a civil

settlement), Sumelocenna (Rottenburg, earth-fort, A.D.
90-102, then a uicus), Condate (Cannstatt, earth-fort
A.D. 90, stone-fort 98-154; uicus to 250), belongs to
a later date, from which most of our evidence also comes.
Nevertheless it is easy to see traces of Keltic nomenclature, commingled with Germanic and occasionally other
elements.   These, however, are by no means so impressive
as in Germania inferior, and we may conclude that prior
to the imposition of Latin, the language of the area
was Keltic, not Germanic.

See, in general, Anderson's edition of the Germania
1938, pp.148-49; Grenier Mnl. 2 ii p.902, and in Frank
vol. 3, 547; CIL 13 ii, 1905, pp.5,215; and above all
Norden's Altgermanien (1934), pp.137-190 (with the references to RC 41, 1924, 38, Keltic dekametos, see 108
above; and to Pedersen VKG 2.35 on collectives in Keltic), with the reviews by Syme JRS 26, 1936, 75-80; by
Schnetz ZONF 10, 1934, 310-314 (and 11, 1935, 44-61, cf.
id. Klio 28, 1935, 133-179); by Kornemann in Gnomon 11,
1935, 289-300; and by H.J. Rose CR 49, 1935, 34.   Other
discussions of decumates agri: Hertlein Germ. 13, 1929,
51-52; Hesselmeyer, a series of articles in Klio, viz
19, 1925, 253-276; 20, 1926, 344-353; 24, 1930, 1-37;
28, 1935, 133-179; and 31, 1938, 92-103; id. Welt als
Geschichte 2, 1936, 203-258; U. Kahrstedt "Die Kelten in
den decumates agri" Nachr. von d. Gesellschaft der Wissenschaften zu Göttingen Ph-H Kl. 1933, 261-305; Mommsen
Provinces of the Roman Empire 1, 1909, 152 n.1; R. Much
Die Germania des Tacitus (Heidelberg 1937), 276-284 (unconvincing); Grenier in Frank 3 p.535 ("settlers who paid
tithes," cf. REA 32, 1930, 248); K. Schiffmann PhW 59,
1939, 622-24 reads decumatos (-thes codd.), in which he
agrees with Schnetz (ZONF 11, 1935, 209-218, cf. 14, 1938,
227-233, rejecting Norden's interpretation, see also
Pokorny ZONF 11, 1935, 184-185); the discussion in Bericht
über dem achten Verbandstag der west- u. sud-deutschen

Agri Decumates

Verein für römisch-germanische Altertumsforschung (at
Heidelberg and Mannheim 14-17 Sept. 1907), cf. REA 10,
1908, 196, is inaccessible to me. Add: Schnetz ZNF 16,
1940, 121-153 and 238; 18, 1942, 14-22; WuS 3, 1940,
172-185; Sontheimer P-W Suppl. 7, 1940, 3-15; Gutenbrunner
Klio 34, 1941, 357-63; Kaspers Hermes 76, 1941, 315-16.
The fact is that the only pre-Roman linguistic material
in the agri decumates is Keltic, not Germanic.

2.   The Vindelici, with the

Upper Rhine and the Danube

No ancient authority makes the Vindelici Keltic in
language or extraction. In fact Servius (Aen. 1.243)
would reckon them Liburnian, and Porphyrion (on Hor. Od
4.4.18) Thracian. But their own name, and that of many
places within their boundaries, as well as of persons
living there, reveals their Keltic affiliation clearly
enough. Similar evidence points to Keltic tribes or
individuals in the upper valley of the Rhine, and along
the upper and middle Danube, or even further east. But
German, Thracian, and Dacian names also make an appearance, and even Greek, as well as Illyrian. In Tacitus
G 43.1 the Cotini are described as speaking "Gaulish"
(lingua Gallica), which perhaps does not mean more than
Keltic. This tribe is commonly regarded as a remnant of

Keltic stock, more or less submerged by their German
neighbors (see Anderson's note on Tac. l.c.); Schmid,
therefore, can hardly be right (RGKBer. 15, 1926, 189-
202, cited by H-S p.1) in making the eastern boundary
of Noricum (16 B.C.) also the eastern boundary of Keltic
speech, though it may be doubted whether the presence
of Gallic cavalry in the Danubian provinces in Imperial
times (JRS 32, 1942, 138-39) necessarily implies even
the occasional use of Gaulish or Keltic there at that
date. The interpres Germanorum named in an inscription
of Alt-Ofen (CIL 3.10505) seems to be good testimony to
the use of a German dialect, presumably among troops of
German origin (cf. 3.14349 interpres Sarmatarum; AE 1947.
35 Dacorum). So too Amm. Marc. 18.2.1 alludes to the
sermo barbaricus (sc. of the Alamanni) spoken, or at
least known, by Hariobaudes, and in Iulianus Misopogon
(Riese Lit. p.448; 434 H.) there is explicit mention of
the language of τοὺς ὑπὲρ Ῥῆνον βαρβάρους as being λέξει
παραπλησίᾳ τοῖς κρωγμοῖς τῶν τραχὺ βοώντων ὀργίθων
this last detail being a misapprehension that may well
be ignored. Ariouistus himself, however, spoke Gaulish
(BG 1.47). Interpretes diuersarum gentium at NDOr. 11.
52 is too general to be helpful, though Illyrian and
Thracian, and (NDOcc. 9.46) also the Gaulish of Lugdun-

ensis (and Germanic in Belgica?), might be understood
to be implied.

Gutenbrunner (Frühzeit, 1939, p.44) and Arntz (Hdb.
d. Runenkunde 1944, 61-64) happily interpret the name
of the Tulingi (BG 1.25; cf. 28 and 29), after Noreen
and others, as "highlanders" (Germanic), and similarly
Daliterni (also Germanic) as "lowlanders, valley-dwellers,"
so that the latter would be an equivalent of Keltic Nantuates and Latin Vallenses (on these see 19 Remark above),
a substitution characteristic of a linguistic frontier
(cf. Eburones: Texuandri). Again it is possible to see
in Mattiaci a Germanic name with -tt- (Matti, cf. Chatti)
and the Keltic suffix -aco-, so that this tribe might
conceivably be regarded as Kelticized Germans.

Weisgerber (l.c. infr.) has recently sought to
question the view that Keltic survived not only in the
Rhineland, but also (Goidelic?) in southern Germany,
and in Switzerland as late as the early middle ages.
Such survivals, however, are clearly of isolated items,
possibly even of a small isolated community of speakers
here and there in remote districts, not of a consistent
system of speech-habits that could be called a "dialect."

On the archaeological side mention may be made of
the pre-Roman settlements (e.g. the Helvetian cemetery
near Baden, of the 4th to 2nd centuries B.C., Germania
14, 1930, 77-82, cf. REA 34, 1932, 41), the occupants
of which presumably were Keltic-speaking. Bittel (Die
Kelten in Württemberg) has surveyed a typical area.
He finds a Keltic movement, in an easterly direction,
c. 400 B.C., succeeded by Germanic invasions which in
the second and first centuries overwhelmed and more or
less completely absorbed or expelled, or even exterminated, all but mere remnants of the older Keltic-speaking
stock. The linguistic evidence, such as it is, agrees
in the main with this conclusion.

See, in general: F. Altheim (with E. Trautmann)
WuS NF 1, 1938, 12-45, where it is argued (on the basis
of rock-engravings) that early Scandinavian wanderers
reached as far as the south side of the Alps (the Camunni) at a very early date (disputed by Jacobsthal JRS
28, 1938, 65-69), and that evidence for Cernunnus (cf.
243 below) is to be found in the same rock-engravings,
which seems more plausible; A. Alföldi "Zur Geschichte
des Karpathenbeckens im ersten Jahrhundert vor Christus,"
Östmittel-europäische Bibliothek (Lukinich) no. 37
(Budapest and Leipzig) 1942 (known to me only from RA 25,
1946, 254); A. Alföldi Jr. "Zur Entstehung der colonia
Claudia Sauaria," Arch. Ertes. 56, 1943, 71-79 (German
text 80-86), v. AE 1945 p.171; A. Betz (on Carnuntum)
Wiener Stud. 54, 1936, 188-192 (cf. PhW 58, 1938, 505);
Kurt Bittel Die Kelten in Württemberg RGK Forschungen 8,
1934), reviewed by Grenier REA 38, 1935, 496-98; among
other publications of the RGK note (Germ. Denkmäler der
Frühzeit vols. 1-3) G. Behrens (Denkmäler des Wangionen-

gebietes 1923; H. Hofmeister Die Chatten 1930; R. von
Uslar Westgerm. Bodenfunde 1938; and also (Germ. Denkmäler der Völkerwanderungszeit vols. 1 and 3) W. Veeck
Die Alamannen in Württemberg 1931; J. Werner Münzdatierte
austrasische Grabfund 1935 (reviewed in Antiquity 10,
1936, 253); O. Brogan "Trade between the Roman Empire
and the Free Germans," JRS 26, 1936, 195-222; CAH 11,
1939 (chapters 2, 12 iv, 13 ii-iii) and 12, 1939 ch. 5;
E. Fabricius Die Besitzname Badens durch die Römer (Neu-
jahrsbl. der Badischen Hist. Kommission, NF 8, Heidelberg
1905); S. Förster "Süddeutschland zur Keltenzeit," Kultur
u. Leben 3, 1926, 65-71 (from Idg. Jahrb. 12, 1928, 67);
L. Franz "Die Germanen in Niederösterreich" RGKBer. 18,
1928 [1929], 115-148; the article by J. Gruaz "Les Hel-
vètes et la question gallo-romaine" (Bibliothèque Uni-
verselle 1920), cf. REA 23, 1921, 62, I have not seen;
on Heluetii, Heluii, see the articles by Haug in P-W
(other articles in P-W Hercules im West: agri decumates
[with references there], Alpes [with references], Octo-
durus, Seduni, Noricum); Fr. Hertlein, P. Goessler, O.
Paret Die Römer in Württemberg vols. 1-3, Stuttgart 1928-
32; R. Heuberger in Klio 31, 1938, 60-80 ("Die Gaesaten");
30, 1937, 78-79 ("Das Ostgotische Raetien"); 24, 1931,
348-366 (on Raetia prima and secunda); for new discoveries
and interpretations see the summaries in Jahresbericht
der schweiz. Gesellschaft für Urgeschichte; H.U. Instinsky in Klio 31, 1938, 33-50, "Septimius Severus u. der
Aufbau des raetischen Strassennetzes" (discusses the
Raetic limes, tres Galliae and Germania, and the leuga),
cf. P-W 32, p.34; J. Klose "Roms Klientel-Randstaaten am
Rhein und an der Donau" (Breslau 1934, Hist. Untersuch.
14), reviewed in Gnomon 12, 1936, 171; in Germania 22,
1939, 133-136, and in JRS 25, 1935, 95-99; H. Krahe IF
57, 1939, 119-122 makes the ethnic name Boii "Illyrian"
(!), after Pokorny Urg. p.9; for an ancient linguistic
stratum in the Danube area see P. Kretschmer "Die donau-
ländische Schicht" Glotta 28, 1940, 255-278 (especially
p.258 on names in -ss-, with which cf. Pokorny Urg. 42-
47); id. "Die frühesten sprachliche Spuren von Germanen"
KZ 69, 1948, 1-25; R. Laur-Belart Vindonissa: Lager und
Vicus (RGK Forsch. 10, 1935), reviewed in REA 37, 1935,
498-503 by Grenier, in RA 7, 1936, 150-152 by Lantier;
for excavations on the "limes" see Der Röm. Limes in
Oesterreich of the Vienna Akad. d. Wissenschaft. since
1900 Wien and Leipzig (cf. DLZ 59, 1938, 1335) with indices of proper names, part 17 (1933) 1-72 on Carnuntum
(AE, 1934, 297-299, nos.263-273), and Der Obergerm.-
Raetisch Limes, begun in 1894 (cf. YW 1938, p.54); note

also the map at p.4 of Germania Romana (Bilder-Atlas RGK, Bamberg 1922), reproduced in REA 12, 1910, Pl. xi; G. Neumann "Kelten in Thüringen," Die Thüringer Erzieher 3, 1935, 143-154; Norden Die germ. Urgeschichte in Tacitus Germania ed. 3, Berlin 1923, with an excursus by Hans Philipp on Switzerland in ancient authors, pp.472-484; see also the review of the first edition by F. Stahelin "Zur Gesch. der Helvetier," ZtsfSchwGesch. 1, 1921, 129-157 (cf. REA 24, 1922, 55-56); V. Pârvan Dacia (Eng. tr.), Cambridge 1928 (reviewed by Besnier REA 31, 1929, 201-202, cf. 54-55); id. Getica (Roumanian, French résumé) published in Acad. Rômâna: Mem. Sect. ist., ser. 3, vol. 3, 1926; id. "Les Celtes en Dacie," CRAcInscBL 1926 (REA 29, 1927, 57); id. Durostorum in Riv. di Filol. 2, 1924, 307-340 (REA 27, 1925, 331; Idg. Iahrb. 12, 1928, 67); F. Reinecke "Die Kaiserzeitliche Germanenfunde aus dem bayerischen Anteil an der Germania Magna," RGKBer. 23, 1933, 144-206; the work of Ludwig Reinhardt Heluetien unter den Roemern, Berlin and Vienna 1924, is condemned in REA 26, 1924, 344; P.E. Scherer "Vorgesch. u. Frühgesch. Altertümer der Ur-Schweiz," Mitth. d. Ant. Gesellsch. in Zurich 27 no.4, 1916, 195-269; L. Schmidt on the Hermunduri, Germania 23, 1939, 262-269; C. Schuchhardt Alteuropa 1919 ("Urkelten" in the Danube valley); W. Schulz Das Fürstengrab von Hassleben (in RGK Forschungen 7, 1933, with contributions by Weidenreich and R. Zahn), see the review in JRS 24, 1934, 239; K. Schumacher Siedelungs- u. Kulturgesch. d. Rheinlande vols. 1-3, Mainz 1921-1925; E. Šimek "Keltové a Germáni v. nãsich zemích," (Kelts and Germans in Bohemia), publications of the Ph. Faculty of the Masaryk Univ. at Brno (Brünn) 1934, v. PhW 56, 1936, 330; F. Stähelin "Die vorrömische Schweiz," ZtsfSchwGesch. 15, 1935, 337-368; id. Schweiz in d. rom. Zeit ed. 3, 1948, (especially pp.3-65); A. Stein Die Legaten von Moesien Diss. Pann. 1 xi 1940 (AE 1941 p.356; reviewed in JRS 1945, 108-115) and Die Reichsbeamten von Dazien Diss. Pann. 1 xii 1944 (AE 1945, pp.159 and 182, and at AE 1945.57); A. Stuhlfauth "Keltische Ringwall am Schlossberg zur Burggailenreuth," Jahresb. Hist. Vereins von Oberfranken, Beilage 1938 (see DLZ 59, 1938, 1767; 60, 1939, 647); E. Täubler Tyche (Berlin 1926) ch. 6 "Orgetorix" (pp.137-166) and 7 "Die letzte Erhebung der Helvetier" (pp.167-179); D. Viollier Carte archéologique du canton de Vaud, Lausanne 1927; J. Vogt "Rassenmischung im röm. Reich," Vergangenheit und Gegenwart 26, 1936, 1-11; von Duhn (on Alpine trade-routes) Neue Heidelberger Jahrbucher 2, 1892, 55-92; N. Vulič "Les Celtes dans le

Nord de la peninsule Balkanique," Musée Belge 30, 1926,
231-243; E. Wahle Vorzeit am Oberrhein 1 (Neujahrsblätter der badischen Historischen Kommission, Heft 19,
Heidelberg 1937), cf. DLZ 60, 1939, 1172-4; F. Wagner
in Schumacher Festschrift 1930, pp.53-55 (on the pre-
Roman Bavarian Alps); K.H. Wagner, Germ. 22, 1938, 159-
169 on the pre-Roman oppidum at Manching-Ingolstadt;
L. Weisgerber "Zur Sprachenkarte Mitteleuropas im früheren
Mittelalter," Rheinische Vierteljahrsblätter 11, 1939,
23-51. The Bulletin of the Association pro Auentico
(since 1887) contains a number of preliminary reports
of new discoveries; and so do many other, often inaccessible, local publications, e.g. Bericht über die 13te
Hauptversammlung des Südwestdeutschen Verbandes fur Al-
terthumforschung in Würzburg 10-12 Sept. 1912 (see REA
15, 1913, 309); a "popular" account of the limes in O.
Brogan Greece and Rome 3, 1933, 23-30. Cf. E. Stein
"Die Organisation der weströmische Grenzverteidgung in
5te Jahrhundert und das Burgunderreich am Rhein,"
RGKBer. 18, 1928 [1929], 92-114; R. Giessler "Untersuchungen zur früheren u. alteren Latènezeit am Oberrhein
und in der Schweiz" RGKBer. 32, 1942 [1945], 20-116;
E. Meyer Die Schweiz im Altertum, Bern 1946; P.E. Martin
on the Germanic occupation of Switzerland in Bull. Soc.
d'hist. et d'arch. Genève 6, 1935, 1-30 (cf. ZfSchwGesch.
16, 1936, 216-218); L. Schmidt (on the Alamanni in Switzerland) ZfSchwGesch. 18, 1938, 369-379; A. Alföldi's
book (with that of Daicoviciù, both inaccessible to me)
Zu den Schicksalen Siebenburgens im Altertum (and Sie-
benburg in Altertum) is reviewed in AJA 52, 1948, 410;
a summary of Weisgerber (against Hubschmied) appeared in
ZfCPh 22, 1941, 368-369; Gutenbrunner Germanische Frühzeit 1939; H. Arntz Hdb. der Runenkunde, Halle 1944,
makes the Seduni, Veragri, Nantuates Germanic or half-
Germanic (pp.61-64; also on Mercurius Cimbrianus and on
the Toutoni-stones); E. Meyer Römisches und Keltisches
in der romischen Schweiz ZfSchwGesch. 22, 1942, 405-419
(ZfCPh 23, 1943, 391); G. Kraft Der Oberrhein als Kel-
tenheimat, Oberrh. Heimat (Freiburg in Breisgau) 27, 1940,
141-156 (ib. 405); N. Reissard Carte archéologique du
Canton de Fribourg, 1941.

Words in Latin Inscriptions

Note lv

On a silver ring (1.7 cm. diameter), octagonal in shape (compare the ring from Thiaucourt, 184 above), discovered inside the Roman camp at Vindonissa, first published by O. Bohn ASA 26, 1924, 86-88.

auo |mio| toc |nai| ixu| tio| udr |uto

("Auomio Tocnai [filio] Ixutioudruto" is one of Bohn's suggestions); a is ∧ , not A , otherwise normal Latin alphabet. Could not auo stand for auot? If so, it should be the last, not the first word.

Cf. AE 1925.3; REA 28, 1926, 266; H-M 427; F.110

Note lvi

There are, as usual, a number of items, other than mere proper names in the Latin inscc. of this area, to which it is worth while calling attention. From CIL 13

5166 (Pierre Pertuis)

uia ... per m dunium paternum

Cf. Dunum, Dunensis (Thun), mod. Donon. H-M 244 construe as a personal name, and read duouirum in the following line, where CIL has duouiri.

Words in Latin Inscriptions

5222 (Windisch)

cexa uicti

"prius uocabulum quid significet, non liquet" ed. CIL ad loc.; cf. cexuari(?) 10026.25a, perhaps personal names. Hardly for cesa (i.e. gaesa?), still less ceyx "kingfisher" Pl. 32.86 (κῆϋξ).

5234 (Baden) on a patera (read perhaps boletaria; or cf. ieuru?)

rinionibolittiuri (?)

5246 (Kempraten, on Lake Zurich)

.... |]ro · hesus | u s l l m

Unless a personal name, hesus may designate the votive object. Note also the divine name Esus?

5338 (a defixio, in Greek alphabet, from Baden-weiler)

Besides the formula quem peperit Leib[, we have the (Semitic, or quasi-Semitic?) ablathanalba, semisilam, sesengem. The item Ein unbekanntes Fluchtäfelchen aus Frankfurt-am-Main-Prauheim (Mus. für heimische Vor- u. Frühgesch., Frankfurt 2, 1938) noted in APh 15, 1940-41, 319 is inaccessible to me; and also Laur-Belart on an insc. of Augst published in Urschweiz 1942, 20-23 (see Jahrb. Schw. Gesellsch. Urgesch. 33, 1942, 168).

6287 (Offenburg)

ΣΣΣΛ

This recalls only the Massiliote coins with μασσα (PID 2.130)

Words in Latin Inscriptions

6391 (Lobenfield). This begins

deo inuicto lu itur

(or luitur?). Riese (3432) has L. Vitur[, which may
well be right.

6455 (Benningen), a dedication to Mars Cnabetius;
at the end

car | tsrcon · u·s·l·l·m

C Ar[Tsr(?)con i.e. a proper name; or possibly an official title (Becker, BJ 50, 1871, 162); but the word
cartsrcon may apply to simulacrum immediately preceding.

6463 (Bürg) in line 3

ambaxius (fort. leg. -χtus?)

Cf. 11774 (Dessau 9254, R.2760, Stockstadt) ambaχtus;
and 206 above (num. Belg., Mediomatrici).

6484 (Wimpfen) begins

reae gortiai | ogl sunt aquibus

percollectae

followed by a list of personal names. Read perhaps deae
Fortunae (?) ogl sunt Aquibus (i.e. Aquis) etc., in which
ogl may conceal some term of local usage.

Words in Latin Inscriptions

6509 (Schlossau) in line 8

ob burg(um) explic(itum)

Cf. Note lii above; CIL 13 ii 1, p.263; R.150d (CIL 3.
3385, cf. AE 1910.145); 3.13796 (R.130) burgarii; and
the local name Quadriburg[ium AE 1947.28; 13.11537
(R.320, H-M 339) from Koblenz (Aargau) line 5

in summa rapida [burgum...

(in which rapida is the forerunner of rávia of the Canton
Ticino, see H-M p.310, quoting Jud); 11538 (R.319, also
from Koblenz) burgum ...iaco confine ( ]iaco being a
local name), cf. C p.59 col. 2; perhaps read Bris]iaco
confine..... | Alb]anensium, cf. Alba fl. In 11537 Riese
takes Summa as the proper name, instead of Rapida. In
11538 other restorations (CIL 13 iv p.69) August] or
Grati[anensium are possible. Ravennas has not only
Brezecha (Breisach, Brisiacum and -us mons 231 above), but
also Wrzacha (said to be Zurzach, C p.59) and the ancient
form of this may be concealed in]iaco. Another text
containing burgus is 3.12376 (Fiebiger-Schmidt 140). In
CIL 8.20816 (R.150e) instead of burgus we find turris.
Is Summa Rapida similar to Sumelocenna in meaning?

6569 (Osterburken) has

t(urma)

a word not known in Latin before Caesar's BG. If it is
related to turba (v. Ernout-Meillet), then perhaps we
have lenition (m:b). Or turba may stand for *tubra,
*tumra (cf. turma): tumeo?

6590-91 (Osterburken, Rinschhein), branding irons
with the marks

AS   and   M

Words in Latin Inscriptions

The former appears also at Büchig (6340) and at Heidelberg (6408a); yet another (Mitt.Zür.Ges. 15, 1864, p.158) has

$$S \cdot I \cdot S$$

Cf. C p.265.

EE 6, 1885, p.xxx (cf. C p.259), a sling-shot with insc. in Greek alphabet, appears to be recorded only in Christian Kehrer's Beschreibung meiner Sammlung antiker Waffen 1810, pl.24, no.10 (inaccessible to me).

7261, 7263-64 (all three from Kastel), 7335-37 (Heddernheim), 11726-27 (Köngen) give respectively

    pla[tea]   p[ost]   p[ortam]   pr[a]et[oriam]

    plat[ea]   dex[tra]   eunt[ibus]   Nid[am]

    platea   noui   uici

    platea praetoria

    platia Sumeloce[nsis]

    platia d[extra] Sumelocenes[is]

(or, in the last, cf. R.2170-71, less likely, platiae-danni [Zangemeister], cf. 6776). The resemblance of some of these to the Oscan eítuns-inscc. is striking. It is not likely that danea (220 above) is combined with platea in a hybrid binominal intensive compound.

7281 (Kastel)

        hastiferi ciuitatis Mattiacorum

Words in Latin Inscriptions

see Note xlvi(above); 7250? (Mainz); 12.1814 (astiferi; Vienne) and 7317 (hastiferii). We should, however, have expected rather frame-feri in Germania.

7274 (Kastel) gives the days of the week (Saturnus, Sol etc.). In 7749 (Neuwied) we have ogto for "Octobres;" H-S 232 (AE 1934.73) has idibus octosribus (sic).

7439 (Kapersburg), and perhaps 7610a (see R.2791, Zugmantel), cf. 3.13796, R.130

ueredarii

7425 (Mithraeum at Oberflorstadt)

uirtut(i) uisdl(?) Leccus l d d

Can uisdl (so R.3561) designate the object of d d? Or cf. perhaps uaisdus, uisdil 220 above?

7754 (Niederbieber)

baioli

(cf. 7066 Mainz, baiulus; with gloss 158 above)

and

Dago uassus

(sic; not one word?)

R.4476 (Heddernheim)

nassas faciunt piscatores

Words in Latin Inscriptions

Cf. Gothic nati, natja "net(s)"? But it may be the
Latin nassa "fish-basket," and Nasso is the name of a
potter at Heddernheim (see 238 i below). Cf. 225 above.

F.122 (H-M 320), from Windisch

in girece Vindoinsa

girece has been (1) taken as a local designation, (2)
read as gynece[io?], (3) identified with grege (see
F. p.2*), or (4) compared even with corax, carax, carx
(F. 163, 165-6; Note lii above; REA 28, 1926, 259; RA
26, 1927, 390).

R.2053 (H-M 82, Dessau 4851), cf. Kleberg in Loef-
stedt Eranos (1945), p.277

mango

But see also Note xlvi above.

R.2181 (Bietigheim an der Metter)

odissei d d

Not dative, for the insc. begins collegio Matisonensium;
if not part of the name, perhaps the object of d d, corrupt; in CIL 13.11749 read as (optio) co[llegii] s(upra)
s(cripta) ei.

Vollmer 361 (3.14370,10) has

k(anabae) R(egenses)

if correctly supplemented; cf. R.2337 (3.10548 canab-
[ensis). See above 178 (s.v. cannabis), Notes xli, xlvi,
and lii.

Words in Latin Inscriptions

R.4504 (Zugmantel), on dice

uirisloiiuana

F.100 (Windisch)

pullum u s l l m

"eine Voltivegabe aus ton" (Bohn); either "chicken" or "nigrum"?

3.14373,13 (p.2325 53-54)

VDⲖEBKⲪXBDo⋏Φ†

I can make nothing of this. The same remark applies to the markings on a glass amulet (see Note xxxvii above) from Münsingen (Switzerland), reproduced by Déchelette Mnl 2.1321 (REA 17, 1915, p.68), which are certainly not alphabetic or, so far as I can see, articulate at all. They may be magical, but hardly gnostic.

H-S 412 (Poetouio), in mixed Greek and Latin alphabet

t]auta

Note for P]auta? Cf. 3.4075; and on tauta 12.874; FHRC 31.4

To which may be added:

cinnaminum (Berne) Vorg. Jahrb. 1, 1926, p.56 (RA 24, 1926, 349)

Words in Latin Inscriptions

diapsoricum (Berne) RA 24, 1927, 159 (cf. p.168); cf.
    H-M 441 (-bs-); Gr. ψώρα "itch" (sc. on the edges
    of the eyelids)

nardinum (Augst) H-M 444; cf. gloss PID 2.160; Pl. NH
    12.46, cf. 13.15

bardus (not B-?) H-M 471 (Traunstein), Vollmer 509, CIL
    3 p.846; cf. gloss 178 above

lembus CIL 3 p.721 (on Danube) Amm. 21.9.2; cf. gloss
    PID 2.64

uatis "priest" (rather than "poet") H-S †16.3 (RGKBer.
    15, 1923-24, 207); cf. gloss 178 above, PID 2.201

cod[(a kind of drink?) ASA 28, 1926, 203 no.7

defrutum H-M 432

garum H-M 433-34; cf. gloss 79 (and 158)

muria H-M 435-36; cf. ASA 28, 1926, 203 nos.5, 6   Cf.
    gloss 79

πυ∠ ASA 28, 1926, 202 no.1 (on an amphora)

sapa AE 1946.164

scomber 3.12010,48; garum scombri H-M 434

thamnum H-M 437; cf. Columella 12.7.1; Tert. An. 32.2
    (cf. Waszink p.386); a plant preserved to be eaten
    as a vegetable. Schneider (Col. l.c.) gives a v.l.
    tann-, cf. perhaps θάμνος (: OHG tanna "fir"
    Boisacq)

Words in Latin Inscriptions

Remark:

Attention may be called to the model axes, inscribed with divine names CIL 13.5158, 5172 (cf. 5164;
and Jahrb. Schw. Ges. für Urgeschichte 37, 1946, 120),
for the bearing which they have, I think, on the formula sub ascia. As to it, see most recently H. Wuilleumier Rev. de l'hist. des religions 128, 1944, 40-63.

Note lvii

Observe the following derivatives in -ario- (cf.
Gothic bokarja-):

barcarii (Ebrudunum) Zts.f.Schw.Gesch. 17, 1937, 86; cf.
    P-W s.v.

canaliclarius (from canalicula "quill pen") H-S 314
    (p.147)

flaturaria sigillaria (ars) CIL 3.5833

lintiaria (ars) CIL 3.5800

molin(arii) ib. 5866, i.e. molae aquariae (cf. Cod. Theod.
    14.15.4), molina (-arius)

ratiarii (Geneva) Zts.f.Schw.Gesch. 17, 1937, 94

salariarius AE 1947.35

In contrast with canabarius (178, Note xli) we have
the more normal canabensis (Note lvi; cf. Note lii).

Germanic Words in Latin Inscriptions

Note lviii

The following Germanic items in Latin inscriptions should be noted (cf. Brüch Einfluss p.15)

brutis and bruta "nurus" (CGL 5.314,32); Dessau 8558 (3.12377 cf. p.2316.[45]), 8558 add. (viz. 3.4746; Pais Suppl. CIL 5.255),

guitanos (cf. witan) 6.1208

moder 5.4151

suecerio (cf. *swēʒrū W-P 2.522) 3.5974

sinnum (cf. OHG sin, Germ. Sinn) 9.2893

uindi leuis umbra 5.6714,3

Remark:

In R.3580 ("am obern Hauenstein") observe liberttus with gemination of t. But the spellings nomene, siuis (F.188), xancto (F.184) are merely vulgar. Note, however, cuntra and cauntra in H-S 557 (a defixio; cf. AE 1921.95; RGKBer. 16, 1927, 111). The spelling Daccisca occurs in H-S 45 (3.11691), and Gutica (i.e. Gotico) hoste in H-S 10 (3.11700).

In the ancient local name Aramici (13.5096) Jud (ap. H-M p.374-75; cf. ZfCPh 23, 1943, 217) sees *aram-on- (cf. 12.2971), i.e. arm- "bracchium" (cf. Armi-lausi 220 above); and in the modern Zihl, Fr. Thièle a Gaulish *tela "bullock" (Hubschmied Actes prem. Congr. internat. de Toponymie 1938, p.149) cf. REA 40, 1938, 292; ZfCPh 22,

Inscription from the Danube

1941, 370. But this *tela is a figment; and as for
Aramici, something is to be said for comparison with W.
araf "peaceful" (W-P 1.144). Or may we not compare Arar
(r : m) see 179, 234, 241 and Arauris, Aruranci, Arurensis
(with a:au:u) see 80, 241? Note also arimo 157 Remark?

Not much should be made of the dat. sg. Transitu
(H-S 291, 292; cf. Cumont Textes et Monuments Mithra 1,
1899, 171).

The new "Fluchttäfelchen" found at Praunheim, noted
in APh 15, 1940-41, 319 (Exner) remains unknown in Cis-
atlantic libraries.

Note lix

The insc. that follows, if χσ stands for an older

-p(o)s-, may be Keltic (with -st- as in Brythonic),

rather than Thracian or Illyrian; cf. La Grauf. uχsedia:

Ven. upsedia.

It is apparently complete, though not certainly

read. On a silver beaker, 18 cm. high, 15.5 cm. in

diameter. Recently in the Brummer Gallery in New York

(the contents of which are said to have been dispersed),

it was discovered in the River Danube, downstream from

the Iron Gates.

Inscription from the Danube

The decorative patterns are believed to have come
"overland from S. Russia"; there are also drawings of
"horses" (not stags?).

After

a private (owner's?) mark, probably not alphabetic,
comes, right to left in line 1, left to right in line 2

$$ |||\cdot\cdot\ \pi\upsilon\digamma\upsilon o\ |\ \chi\sigma\tau\alpha\,\delta\epsilon\epsilon $$

(with $]\digamma$, $\times\,\chi$), which may be interpreted as "for
whom (i.e. the person identified by the private mark)
it was set up, established, built (i.e. the stable, or
racing establishment)," $\pi\upsilon\digamma\upsilon$ (or $\pi\upsilon\digamma$?) being dat. (loc.?)
sg., from qǔu (W-P 1.522), cf. Skt. kúva, and $o\chi\sigma\tau\alpha\delta\epsilon\epsilon$
(or $\upsilon o\chi\sigma\tau\alpha\delta\epsilon\epsilon$), standing for *upo-sta-d-e-i(t), cf. W.
gwastad, Ir. foss (Pedersen-Lewis pp.20-21) OChSl. stado,
OLith. stodas "Pferdeherd," L. stabulum (*stadhlo-) but
Gr. $\sigma\tau\acute{\alpha}\delta\iota o\nu$ "champ de course" (for $\sigma\pi$-?) may not belong
here, though the adjective $\sigma\tau\acute{\alpha}\delta\iota o\varsigma$ does; p- for qǔ, and
-χst- for -p(o)st- would point to Brythonic Keltic.

See Griessmaier Wiener Beiträge zur Kunst- u. Kulturgeschichte Asiens 9, 1935, 49 (fig. 9); "The Dark
Ages," Loan Exhibition of Pagan and Christian Art, Wor-
cester Art Museum, 1937, no.66; Nestor RGKBer. 22, 1933,
150; Rostovtzeff Skythien und der Bosporos 534; Jacobsthal

Names of Potters

Early Celtic Art 1944, vol. 1 p.36 n.3, cf. p.58; vol. 2 Plates 226-27; Whatmough Die Sprache 1, 1949, 128-29.

238   Names of Potters

Cf. 88 Remark above; besides Oswald see also Bibliographia Aquincensis (vol. 5 including instrumentum domesticum; inaccessible to me, but see RA 16, 1940, 88-89, and Blanchet's article on terra sigillata of the Danube valley, ibid. pp.29-45); von Bonis Keramik von Pannonien (other than terra sig.?), also inaccessible to me (Dissertationes Pannonicae II 20) cf. RA 25, 1946, 253; E. Vogt Zts. f. Schw. Arch. u. Kunst 3, 1941, 95-109, cf. 164-166; Chr. Simonett ib. 2, 1940, 1-9; R. von Uslar, K. Bettermann, H. Ricken in Saalburger Jahrbuch 8, 1934, 61-182; R. Knorr Die Verzierten Terra-Sigillata-Gefässe von Rottenburg-Sumelocenna, Stuttgart 1910; C. Englert ASA 26, 1924, 263-266; 27, 1925, 59-63; Georgine Juhász Die Sigillaten von Brigetio (Diss. Pann. II 3, 1935), cf. A. Hild in Jahresh. d. öst.-arch. Inst. in Wien 26, 1930, Beibl. 115-176 and F. Eichler in Diss. Pann. II 10, 1938, 151-160. A few new "Keltic and Illyrian" names are given in AJA 52, 1948, 239; Behn Mainz Katalog (part 2: Keramik).

(i) Heddernheim (A.D. 120-130)

Ammius	Augustio	Meddulus, Meddu
Aponianus	Coocus	Melluro
Atrestus (-gtus, -χtus)	Dessus	Nasso
	Gatus	Ouidius
Atrextus (?)	Graca	

Names of Potters

(ii)   Bregonz (A.D. 100-120)

Apirilis   Cerialis

(iii)   Kräherwald (A.D. 140-200)

Camulatus   Edui[ ]s   Marinus

Carataculus   Firmus   Reginus

Domitianus

(iv)   Westerndorf (A.D. 160-200)

Agisillus   Erotus   Maianus

Albinus   Fidanus   Mancius

Amio   Gallo   Matto

Anno   Garmanus   Muscella

Belatullus   ?I]assus and   Nocturacus
                         Iassus
Caccuro   Peintius
                       Intusmus (Ci-)
Callo   Pentius
                       Lall(i)us
Catullinus   Repanus
                       Lillus
Cinges, Cingessus   Sacero, -iro
                       Lima
Comitialis   Taruagus (-c-)
                       Liuius
CSS (a mark of   Venerus
   capacity?)   Lucceius
                                             Vologesus
El(l)enius (He-)   Luppo

Er[

Names of Potters

(v) Middle Rhine and Upper Danube

Aio

Alexianus

Aricantus

Atuortes

Aucasus

Auec[Oxé
    Festschr. 71

Axinus

Bai[

Banasius

Cabiatus

Camillus

Cananidonius

Cea REA 38, 1936,
    427-38

?Ceniamus (-n-)

Cocina

Communis

Copillus Germ. 21,
    1937, 129

Cospius

Eburio RA 16, 1940,
    32

Eluinus

Exsobnus

Gennus

Iopu | diu

Lintus AcS 2.
    237

Miccinus

Oica

Pacatus

Plaus

Pussocus

?Putrimus (i.e.
    Butrio m?)

Rauinius

Rauracus

Reginus (Boden)

Rimunatus

Rina[

Rodu[

Romacillus

Sarda REA l.c.

Senonius

Sequanus

Siluinus

Sintillius (Diss.
    Pann. 2.10,
    158)

Sottilus (for
    Scotnus?)

Tacitus ASA 36,
    1934, 97

Taluba

Tanco

Vaccuui

Varucus

Vasco ASA l.c.

Vekuso (for -gi-?)
    cf. 176

Vipuro

Vritti[cf. 176

Vssomarius cf. 176

Vxoniso

Abecedaria

Remark:

1. A few abecedaria may be noted here:

(a) Stein-am-Anger, a complete alphabet from a to z, CIL 3, p.962 (cap. xxvii, no.1, on a tegula); Walters Ancient Pottery 2, 359.

(b) CIL 13.10017,69 (Saalburg), R.4506.6, only a-e.

(c) From Palézieux (canton Wallis), Mommsen Insc. Heluet. (Mitth. antiqu. Gesellsch. in Zürich 10, 1854) 347.4, R.4506,1. After excudite, apparently we have a garbled alphabet a-z, but with some peculiar forms (unless mis-copied).

ii. The bronze letters CIL 3.11941 (Pfünz) are not relevant here; on the cursive writing of Gaulish potters cf. Oswald JRS 17, 1927, 162-64. As for Tac. G. 10.1, the notae there mentioned were perhaps not alphabetic (litterae 3.3); but see now Mentz Rh.Mus. 86, 1937, 193-205.

iii. There is one brief text in Greek alphabet IG 14.2575,2 from Saalburg, described by the editor as "uix Graeca," viz.

]γισλαρετου

in which -ετου (cf. karnitu) may be a verbal ending.

Coin-Legends

Note lx

The only example here of

auot

appears to be CIL 3.6010,34 (Vienna).

239   Coin-Legends

From Blanchet Tr., and AcS; see further: PID 2,
pp.129, 616-617; von Koblitz WPZ 17, 1931, 5; Karl Pink
WPZ 24, 1937, 57-75; R. Paulsen Die Münzprägungen der
Boier 2 vols., Text and Plates, Leipzig and Vienna, 1933
(part of Pink's Die Ostkeltischen Münzprägungen); E.
Polaschek in P-W 17, 1936, 975; Pink Die Münzprägung der
Ostkelten und ihren Nachbarn (Diss. Pann. II 15, Budapest 1939), reviewed in CW 35, 1941-42, p.100; cf. Pink
in WPZ 23, 1936, 8-76; FuF 13, 1937, 99-100; Num. Ztschr.
25, 1932, 9-15; 29, 1936, 10-28; AJA 47, 1943, 363; R.
Forrer Triquetrumgepräger l.c. 218 above (esp. p.474,
nos.13-29); Déchelette Mnl. 2, 1914, p.1569 n.2 (bibliogr.;
ed. 2, vol. 4, 1927, p.1075); Blanchet Rev. Num. 6, 1902,
36-51, 157; id. Mém. et Notes, 1909, 406-24; L. Piotrowicz
Eos 34, 1932-3, 413-426; Forrer Reallexikon (1908), s.v.
Münzen (Kelt.); E. Vogt in Jahresb. d. Schweizerisches
Landesmuseums 41, 1932 [1933], 91-101; R. Forrer ASA 37,
1935, 90-92; M. Miller Die Münzen des Altertums 1933, 20-
23; Blanchet RC 48, 1931, 158; G. Wüthrich Celtic Numis-
matics in Switzerland, Num. Chron. 5, 1945, 1-33.

The problem of text at BG 5.12.3 has little rele-
vance here, though it does bear on the question of currency among the Kelts in Britain. Read perhaps ut
taleis ferreis (for aut) cf. Kalinka in Bursian Jahresber.
264, 1939, 176; Wiman Eranos 27, 1929, 151-52; the identification of supposed currency bars in England is disputed
(see Antiquity 7, 1933, 61, 210; 8, 1934, 210 and 336).

Coin-Legends

adnamati[

ainorix

ansali Tr. 463

?ap[, ar[AcS 1.169, 30; Tr. 462

ɑπολ

atta

[atullos Tr. 103, 468; cf. ʋλ below?]

au[Tr. 462

aunulcos (cauln, cauanos?)

[βαλλαιου (Illyr.) Tr. 103-104]

belinos or bienos Tr. 81, 104, 169, 423; unless to be assigned to Aquit.

βιαλεσ (Pannonia), or biatec(?), biat, bia

boio

busu, bussumar[, also read lu-, and perh. also written uu-

br, brig

cambodunnon, cambiduno

casibanus AcS 1.822; num. imp. Commodus, cf. 236 above

[κυαρου (Thr.) AcS 3. 1173]

κδ|ιεικϙ (?) PID 2.616

[κερσι βαυλοσ (Thr.) AcS 3.1206]

ciecim(?), ciecimui; but Paulsen p.29 has ceg-naze or ϝεγναϳε , be-side ciecin, cegna|ze, gena|za(?), and the text and interpretation are highly dubious

cobrouomar(us)

cocestlus i.e. Congeist-lus, conges[(Styria); AcS 1.1099 and 1057; 3.1271

coisa; cf. koiša PID 3.14

copo, coppo(u) Tr. 112

connos, counos (-ou)

couio[marus]

?kouises Forrer p.474 no.29, but v. PID 331

kritasiros (Paulsen p.4), for ekritus-?

cur (i.e. Curia?), cf. Paulsen p.37

deua (?), δηυα Tr. 447; deuila; cf. dem[AcS 1.1263?

domisa Tr. 463

(?)earairix AcS 1.1393

eccaio, eiccaio

?εχο οθος (Forrer p.478
  no.17)

·e·kr (Ven. alphabet,
  Paulsen p.26)

ecritusiri v. gesatorix;
  Pink WPZ 24, 1937, 74
  has ecritusiri regi h;
  P-W 17.975 ecritasiros;
  cf. ekrit[AcS 1.1405;
  Ecritomarus ib. 1406
  (from Cic. Verr. 2.ii
  47.118 Aegrit-), but
  the correct reading is
  -u-; for e- see AcS 1.
  1393,11

? ερονσμτρ Tr. 458

etu | iul; Kremer Publ.
  sect. hist. de l'In-
  stitut grand-ducal de
  Luxembourg 67, 1938,
  531-533; cf. υλ below

euoiurix (Udine) AcS 1.
  1486

·e·n·no (Ven. alphabet),
  Paulsen p.26

?euno Tr. 458; οχ χeuno
  Forrer p.478, no.14

??fapiarius (u-?) Tr. 450,
  fariarix (Paulsen)
  which Much (ap. Paul-
  sen, p.90) interprets
  as Germanic

gesatorix | ecritusiri;
  Jahresh. Öst. Arch.
  Inst. 9, 1906, 70-74
  (REA 8, 1926, 266)

iantumar

lauumarus (-om-), for
  iantu-?

?liki Forrer p.474 no.26,
  but cf. PID 331

mau, maus, mausaiios

?minu Tr. 462

mu[or um[AcS 3.27

nemet, nemetos (Udine),
  cf. P-W s.v. Noricum;
  AcS 2.713

ninno[s Tr. 470

nonnos (Pannonia)

ote

rauis, rauisci, rauit,
  irauisci, irausci Tr.
  462-63, i.e. Rausci,
  Arauisci?

?roueca (uerica??)

romano (Paulsen)

samillus

sauumarus

sissau Tr. 462

suicca

?θk·i·tr euθ Forrer p.474,
  no.14

ti[, tinco[(Noricum),
  tincommius

titto (Paulsen)

Coin-Legends; Glosses

ĭucca (Kremer l.c.; mis-
reading of suicca?)

υλ (Pannonia); cf. 177

ues (Ven. alphabet, Paul-
sen p.26; cf. PID 2.
616b)

uolc Tr. 472 n.1, cf.
Bittel pp.29-30

·u·on·n: (Ven. alphabet,
Paulsen p.26)

240   Glosses

    Cf. 1 above (Note on Glosses), 79 and 220 above.
That early Germanic peoples penetrated as far as the
Alps at a much more remote date than is commonly sup-
posed is now held to be shown by the rock-engravings of
the Val Camonica as interpreted by F. Altheim and E.
Trautmann, see WuS NF 1, 1938, 12-45; cf. Jacobsthal l.c.
170 above. An index of words in Ed. Diocl. appears in
CIL 3, pp.1188-1194, 2608-2622; the text is given in
Frank 5, 1940, 305-421.

alpes (Suebian)

    Strabo's καὶ δὴ καὶ ἀπεφήναντό τινες οὕτως, διά τε
τὴν λεχθεῖσαν θέσιν καὶ διὰ τὸ τὴν αὐτὴν ὕλην ἐκφέρειν
(7.1.3, 290C; R. Lit. 367) is not illuminating.

amblatium "strap for a plough"

    According to M-L REW 408b, attested from the 9th
century; the modern distribution of the word (Graubünden,
Tyrol, Carinthia) suggests an eastern Keltic origin.
Meyer-Lübke rejects *slatta (Jud; cf. W-H 1, 741; Loth
RC 40, 1923, 156); amb- is for ambi- 178 above. Cf.
Raeto—rom. umblaz, Graub. amblaz, OFr. amblais.

Glosses

[aminnaea (uitis) is the source of modern amigne (see
   H-M p.371); but the ancient name (Pl. 14.21) belongs
   to Picenum.]

anses "semidei" Iord. 13.78 (ap. Gothos)

βάνατα : an article of clothing?

   Diocl. Ed., fr. Megalop. 19.43,45 βάνατα Νωρική
διπλῆ ἤτοι καταβίων ... βάνατα Γαλλική , see AcS 1.340, cf.
TLL s.v. Perhaps a travelling-cloak; cf. βαννάται PID
2.429, ID 49? Keltic (b from gᵘ̯?).

basium (-iare, -iabor, -iatio, -iolum) "kiss"

   PID 2.206. The word undoubtedly had, or acquired,
an obscene meaning (M-L REW 971, 976); cf. possibly
bessus 246 below?

βέδοξ "covering"?

   Ed. Diocl., fr. Megalop. 19.44,46 βέδοξ Νωρικὸς
κάλλιστος ἤτοι βῆλον (uelum)... βέδοξ Γαλλικός . For the
ending cf. camox 1 above.

βίτος "felly," βίτωτος "with fellies"

   Ed. Diocl. 15.31a,34. Cf. Gr. ἴτυσ, fίτυς , and 220
above; Brüch p.10.

blattearius, blattosemus Ed. Diocl. 29.10, 29.12; cf.

   βλάττη "purple," - όσημος ib. 24.2, 29.38

   Germanic (cf. W-H), μεταξβλάττη ib. 24.1a, 24.13
(for μεταξα see below); ὑπο-βλάττη ib. 19.9, 29.33. Cf.
blauus, blada 220 above?

1184

Glosses

βρίʒα "rye" Ed. Diocl. 1, 3 (232858), secale cereale

    Thracian or Macedonian(?) L.-Sc. Distinguish brisa (βρύτεα) 79 above. Cf. Lith. rugiaĩ "rye" and Eng. rye.

?βρύʒα "refined (gold)"

    χρουσοῦ βρύʒης ἐν ῥηγλίοις ἢ ἐν ὁλοκοττίνοις (gold coin, solidi), Ed. Diocl. 30.1a.

bulga, μολγός

    This word, usually counted Keltic (cf. PID 2.183 and 430), is maintained by Vendryes BSL 41, 1940, 134-139 to have been "North European" (whence it entered Thracian and Greek), or Thracian (whence it passed to Germanic and Keltic.)

βύρνη "myrrh" Ed. Diocl. Troez. 30 (p.2211)

    Perhaps lenition (b : m), cf. μουν- : βουν-ιαδικόν below? But μύρρα is usually counted Semitic (Boisacq), notwithstanding σμύρνα like (σ)μυρο- (e.g. μυρο-βάλανος Ed. Diocl. 19) "unguent" cf. Smertullus, Smerius? Distinguish muria 79 above.

camum "beer"

    In Pannonia; see the testimonia in AcS 1.728-729, 3.1069-1070; cf. CIL 3 p.827 (Ed. Diocl., but at 2.11 p.2328.58 it is μάκαμον. W-H 1.149 compares Med. Lat. camba "Braustube," and counts the word probably Keltic in origin. For ca(r)mo-, cramo- (cf. 158)?

carpa "carp"

    In the Danube, Cassiod. var. 12.4. But probably Germanic rather than Keltic; cf. OHG karpo, whence the

Glosses

Romance (and English) forms, M-L 1708, W-H 1.171, Brüch Einfl. 8.

carrago "saepes carrorum"

Amm. Marc. 31.7.7; from carrus (see below) and -hagô, the Germanic equivalent of Keltic caio (see 178 above). Cf. Kluge Urg. ed. 3, pp.12, 35, 66, 102; Brüch, Einfluss p.16; Holthausen OE haga. Gothic according to Amm. l.c.; W-H would make it Keltic.

cartallus (-ell-) and -um "basket" (in LXX)

CGL 5.349.41, but the word appears to survive in Sic. karteḍḍu M-L 1722; W-H 1.286; cf. κυρτία , caetra 158 above. Usually supposed to be Greek, but the ending suggests the same source as caballus (178). Cf. cartalamon 79 above.

carrus "carriage, wagon," with a large number of derivatives: carralis, carrare, carrarius, carreus, carricare, carricatio (-g-), καρρικός , κάρριον , car(r)uca, καρροῦχα (-ον), carrulus, carrucarius; carracutium, carrada, carroballista, carrocarpentarius, carropera, [?carrocapsum], carradeci(?), καρραρικός , and also of hybrids καρρόπηγος , ἁμαξοκάρριον (- κάρινον) carrucotechnites; but carra f. (AcS 1.808) appears to be a by-form

Cf. PID 2.195, 3.12; AcS 1.810-815, 3.1119-1123; W. Enslin Klio 32, 1939, 89-105; Sofer 165; SprFK 196. carratum "fôdir" AHDGl 3.646,27 is probably the same word (i.e. "fodder," namely a waggon-load, i.q. carra, carrada AcS 1.808,48). As a personal name Carrarius

Glosses

214 above. carruca is also a wheeled-plough (on such inventions see Plin. NH 18.172 and 296, cf. Serv. G 1. 174 and Plin. NH 17.42; Jud Rom. 52, 1926, 347), cf. mod. carîga H-M 373. See Chr. Hawkes in Antiquity 9, 1935, 341 (citing J.B.P. Karslake Antiqu. Journal 13, 1933, 455-463 on British ploughshares). Hawkes connects the heavy plough with the development of the villa, perhaps "as far back as the Belgic invasions."

Cf. W-H 1.173 (on carrago, carracutium), 174 (on carrus); OIr, MW carr (but these may have been borrowed from Latin). The ending -(c)utium as in cucutium (178 above).

The word was adopted into Latin early and, clearly enough, carried all over the Empire; its immediate source seems to have been Alpine or Transalpine regions (cf. the local name Καρρόδουνον, Carrodunum) which appears in Germania Magna, ap. Vindelici, in Pannonia Superior, and ap. Sarmatae). To be distinguished from Bertoldi's pre-Roman *kar(r)a "stone, rock, crag" (BSL 32, 1931, 161). The pure Latin may be currus (so W-H 1.315); sarracum, serracum seems to have been borrowed into Latin from some satem-dialect (Thracian?), not from Illyrian (which preserves k), see below; cf. Σαράγαρον

In Sisenna (fr. 61, p.287 P.) carrus and sarracum are joined together; in Varro (sat. Men. 111.9 R.): Gallica petorrita, carros Tadcura, Tusca pilenta, it is obvious that Tadcura is an error for some ethnicon (leg. Alpinos, or some derivative of Adula or Curia?); in Caesar BG 1.3.1 it is the Heluetii (cf. 6.1, between the Jura and the Rhône), in 51.2 and 4.14.4 the Germani who use the carrus.

? κατα βίων an article of apparel; see βάνατα above

? κέρκερ "pimpernel"

Diosc. 2.209 has a v.1. Γάλλοι κέρκερ, Δακοὶ τούρα (for Σάπανα , Δακοὶ κέρκερ). If actually Dacian, κ may stand for qʰ; cf. also the local name Quarqueni Pl. 3.130 (Histria)? W-H s.v. cerceris.

Glosses

[dalmatica (laodicia) CIL 13.3162 ii 10; cf. Ed. Diocl.,

e.g. 26.37

    See Note xxxiv above; the same term is applied to sethaus (or sethrus) dalmaticum on a lead pig from Chesterton-on-Fosse, Warwicks; JRS 11, 1921, 239 no.16.]

δόρκιος Ed. Diocl. 8.21; 4.45

    Evidently the same word as iurca (1 above), Boisacq s.v. δορκάς, i.e. δ is presumably ḍ, from i-. But durgo in IA Plac. A 39 (TLL s.v.).

drappus "cloth, fabric, drape," cf. 178 above

    Oribas. (W-H, no reference), uit. Caes. Arel. 2.42, not. Tir., Marculfi formulae, Pactus Alam. fr. (cf. AcS 1.1315); cf. personal names Drappes, Drappo, Drappus, mod. local name Drap (Alp. Marit.). Claimed as Illyrian by Pokorny Urg. 69 (Lith. drãpana "clothing") with (?) a for o; but see Lane in Language 7, 1931, 279.

δύβρις· θάλασσα (Illyr.?), Schol. Theocrit.

    Cf. OIr dobor, OW dufr (W. dwfr) "water," Dubris (TP, IA, NDOcc., Rav.) now Dover; Dubra fl. (Tauber, trib. of Main) Rav., AcS 1.1362-63; Tubri- 241 below, cf. 242. Apparently both Keltic and Illyrian; see Kretschmer Glotta 22, 1934, 216; Pokorny Urg. pp.63, 98-99.

[duracina Ed. Diocl. 6.80

    (-ae siue bumastae) uuae; duracina CIL 13.10004,13; persica 10008.50; R.4548; duracenum at Isid. 17.7.7 (hence no need to write *duracenum Vox Rom. 2, 1937, 367); cf. durize 240 Remark below, and duratia 246]

Glosses

enoc(h)ilis "piscis stagneus, id est anguilla"

CGL 6.389 (Gloss. Lat. 3.34, 18) Illyrian? See
Krahe IF 54, 1936, 118 (Illyr. Enoclia in CIL 5.2221).

gadalis "whore" MG 1, p.298.25-27

Hludovici Pii capit. de discip. palatii Aquis-
granensis (on this see AcS 1.2039,8-17), quoted AcS
1.1511-12. Frankish? Cf. OF r jael, Prov. gazal; M-L
3631.

Holder cites (as the source of the medieval Latin
gadalis) MBret. gadales "meretrix," mod. Br. gadalez,
gadal "libidinosus," but there is no reason to suppose
that the borrowing was not in the opposite direction.
Eng. gad, OE gædeling, Goth. gadiliggs "companion"?
Bruch ZfRPh 38, 1914, 688 (Goth. gadaila).

gaesatae "armed with the gaesum"

Heuberger Klio NF 13, 1938, quotes (p.68) from
EM the absurd παρὰ τὸ τὴν γῆν ζητεῖν (!); but what are we
to make of Polyb. 2.22.1 διὰ τὸ μισθοῦ στρατεύειν ...
ἡ γὰρ λέξις ... σημαίνει κυρίως (a suggestion of gain, cf.
Goth. ga-geigan, Lith. giežiu?), which perhaps finds an
echo in Orosius (4.13.8) nomen non gentis sed mercennariorum Gallorum est. Cf. Feist Wtb. ed.3, 181. But
the original meaning must have been "spearmen."

? γάννα · θεάζουσα Dio Cass. 67.5.3; cf. 241 below

gausape (or -a) "coarse woollen cloth"

See PID 2.204-205; probably a Balkan or Illyrian
word (Alb. gezóf), cf. W-H 1.585, 867; Pokorny Urg. 125;
Glotta 27, 1939, 89 gaunape, galnape, gaunaca, and gunna
(below); gaunape(s) or -um (galnapes Isid. 19.26.2, v.l.
gannapes; testam. Caes. Arelet., Pardessus Dipl. 1.105,
cf. galnabis Du Cange) is perhaps merely a conflation of

gaunaca (Persian according to the etymologists; Varro
L.L. 5.167 is corrupt, and he may have thought it Gallic)
with gausape; or perhaps ultimately cognate with gausape,
gunna (Mid.Ir. guaire "hair," W-P 1.557, cf. W-H l.c.).
Cf. Ganapo personal name (Nimes), Espérandieu ILG 482.
See also TLL s.vv.

gunna "robe," gunnarii "artepell⟨i⟩ones"

For the latter (CGL 5.441,32) see AJPh 21, 1900,
191; the former (OFr gonne, Engl. gown, whence W. gwn)
occurs in Anth. Lat. 209.4 R, then in MG epist. Cin-
hardus Lullo and Gutbertus Lullo, and (dim. gunnela) in
the vita Savini, quoted in AcS 1.2044. Probably an Illyrian or Ligurian loanword, see Pokorny ZslPh 4, 1927,
103-4, Jokl quoted by W-H 1.626; M-L 3319. Ultimately
related to gaunape, gausape.

heluina (Ceres)

See Schol. Juv. 3.320 (quoted in FHRC 68.13-15),
clearly from Heluus; and observe the name of a vine
arvine (quasi *heluina) H-M 371; heluennaca 178, ethnicon Heluetii?

hendinos (leg. kindinas) "rex" Amm. 18.5.14

Cf. Goth. kindins; H.M. Chadwick Nationalities of
Europe 1945, 55n. suggests theudinos.

hysex: an unidentified animal (Pl. Val.), adj. (h)ysicinus

For esox 220 above? Cf. for the ending laurex 158,
ibex 1, helix 207.

ύσσος "javelin, pilum"

Polyb. 6.23.8, Plut. **Pyrrh.** 21, Dion. Hal. 5.64; in
Appian Kelt. 1.1 the context is Keltic (Boii), though the

ascription in Roman: τὸ δὲ δόρατα ἦν οὐκ ἀπ εοικότα ἀκοντίοις· ἃ Ῥωμαῖοι καλοῦσιν ὕσσους. Cf. ὕσταξ (ὕσσαξ ?) and ὕστακος (ὕσσ-) in Et. Mag. (785.7) and Hesych. The pronunciation with -ss- for older -st- is no doubt Keltic, whatever the ultimate origin of the word may be. Cf. ηυσσουι[Note xx above, ὕσγη 246 below. The suggestion of Bezzenberger BB 27, 1903, 178 *udzdho- (OE ord, OHG ort "pike, stake, point") is at least as likely as Bechtel's guess ib. 30, 1906, 271 of a Carian loan-word.

labarum "national standard, flag"

Keltic according to Pisani Rend. Lincei, Sc. Mor. 6.8, 1932, 338 (not important), cf. OS lappo, OHG lappa "cloth, rag." In Sil. Ital. Pun. 4.232 the personal name Labarus is in a Keltic (or Raetic) context; and labarum at Tertull. Apol. 16 (ed. Beati Rhenani, which represents a lost ms; the v.l. cantabrorum is probably a gloss, and candelabrorum a corruption of it) is also in a Keltic context (Epona). Cf. the divine name Laburus at Kaltenbrunn CIL 3.3840; local *Labara AcS 2.113

If Holder's conjecture (ib. 114) is correct, the literal meaning is probably "effigy, speaking emblem," hence "standard."

lama "loam, marshy ground"

First in Ennius (Paul. ex Fest. 117), cf. also (?)lamatus "lutatus" CGL 5.469,37; 508,1; Hor. epist. 1.13.10.

Illyrian according to C. Hernando Balmori Emerita 4, 1936, 74-85; cf. *247 iv below. For conjectures as to the etymology see W-H 1.753, 870-871; here is another, viz. cf. Eng. loam, OE lām "clay," with OE (and OHG, ON) līm "lime" (cf. Lat. līmus), i.e. ā from ai, older oi? The change from ǒ to ǎ is Illyrian, if not from ai to a. Not OIr lām, W. llaw (: palma).

Glosses

[**lixiuus** and **-um** "lye" (for nips- cf. νίπτρον ?) Pl. NH

28.244

Cf. Lixa (pers. name, 244 below); hardly lixa,
lixio "sutler, aquarum portitor" Gl.), but cf. lix
"ashes, lye" for which W-H 1.816 has a different etymology; ligo 246 below; distinguish lixare 220 above.]

λούγεον "marsh"

This I deduce from Str. 7.5.2, 213C. Not Illyrian
(IF 47, 1929, 323 no.1) but Keltic, see Lugdunensis
Introduction above, with 170 and 178.

?[μάκαμον]: see camum above

mannus: see PID 2.198, 3.30 (Illyrian)

Dimin. mannulus (Plin. epist. 4.2.3); in Keltic
-nd- (Epomanduodurum; Manduessedum), cf. Basque mando
"mule."

W-H 2.29-30 (but I still think both man(n)isnauius
and udisna PID 2.49 to be I.Eu., the former rather in
the sense of "hand-washing" cf. ὑδατώλενος PID 2.499,
malluuiae); SprFK 204, FHRC 29.22, q.v. (Serv. G 1.12).

[? μαραμανίς (v.l. -ός)· λίμήν (R. Lit. 13.87)

Perhaps a local name (AcS 2.417,12) cf. Ptol. 2.
11.1, but it may be a corruption of morimarusa 220 above?
Less likely of marco-mann-o, marca "boundary," since
water is often a boundary line.]

[μάρκα: see 178 above

But τριμαρκισία is Galatian, not Gaulish (Do 25)]

Glosses

mataris (-er-), madaris: see PID 2.192, 3.30

Used by the Heluetii, Boii, and Tulingi, R. Lit.
2.24; 15.19; deriv. mat(t)iarius (Ammianus, cf. AcS
2.476,12; mattzari insc. Cilli CIL 3.5234), and mattio-
barbulus; pers. name Mataris 237.

From a Keltic *mattia (cf. mateola?) TLL s.v.? Cf.
Mattiaci 241 below? See also W-H 2, pp.48, and 51-53
(but the combination with Medio-matrici W-P 2.230 is
not to be hastily dismissed, at least so far as concerns
mataris).

North Italian dial. (cf. OFr. matras Do 271, REA
7, 1905, 48) M-L 5402. Cf. MSL 23, 1930-35, 64; and
the following item?

μάταξα, μέταξα "thread" and "raw silk" in μέταξα βλάττα

Ed. Diocl. 24.1a, 24.13; metaxa in Lucil.; cf.

blattearius above

Etymology unknown (Schrader-Nehring 2.383; W-H 2.
49); P-W s.v. serica (1923) 2.1727. But observe matta
"threads" in Note xxxi (d) above, on which see my paper
in Language 25, 1949, 391 and add Ital. matasse (-ato,
-ino, -ina) "skein," Fr. mateau. Conjectures of Persian, or some Semitic, source are facile but idle.

mazuuia "club"

Gloss. cod Brux. quoted AcS 2.489; claua: genus
teli qua Hercules utebatur, quod rustici mazuuiam uocant.

For *mattuia, *mattea, *mattua? (cf. mataris); the
curious distribution of modern forms (M-L 5426) points
to a Danubian source.

mēlēs, mel(l)ina "marten" (Plaut., Plin., Ed. Diocl.)

An Alpine word? Cf. W-H 1.474 (feles: W. bele

Glosses

from *bhelegs- VKG 1.98, 2.24); for b : m cf. milimindrum, melinus 158 above.

μουνιαδικόν "turnip" Ed. Diocl., 6.16, with μ- for β-?

Cf. μουνίας (- δος): napus CGL 2.132,24; βουνίας L-Sc.

[mustela Pl. NH 9.63, a fish in lacus Brigantinus; cf.

H-M p.368; Thompson Greek Fishes, 1937, 168-69]

nauda "marsh-land" (9th cent., see Du Cange)

For *snauda (Ir. snuad "brook"). Hubschmied Vox
Rom. 3, 1938, 115 sees a survival in the local name
Nöschikon (Zürich), for *naudisk-inga.

panaca "cup, goblet"

Mart. 14.100 tit., cf. 1-2 si non ignota est docti
tibi terra Catulli | potasti testa Raetica uina mea.
Cf. can(n)a 220 above, pannas at La Graufesenque (according to some for Latin patina, e.g. E-M ed. 2, 741; SprFK
206). But probably a dialect form (*c- in Germanic or
pure Latin?), like W. pann, La Grauf. panna: canna. The
chief difficulty here arises from the existence of anax
"pitcher" 178 above, which, if related at all, and if
it has lost p- (cf. ibid. anam "paludem": Pannonia?),
puts canna out of court. If canna and panna go together,
then anax is not related, unless panna(: canna) is hyper-
Keltic.

The skill of the Gauls at tinning (cf. stannum 158;
the Volcae are "smiths" or "tinkers") suggests that words,
referring both to metal-ware and to earthenware, may
well be native, even though the etymology is not clear.
Distinguish panacum 79.

1194

Glosses

[parma: see PID 2.199

If actually Thracian, it may be included in these
Danubian glosses, though it probably reached Latin
through Greek.]

[piccis "peak," Fr. pic

This long standing riddle (REW abandons it) appears to be solved at last; Jordanes G 42.219 assigns
the word to the Veneti (mons Piccis); cf. perhaps Piccienus (terr. sig., Scarpone) and Picusus Ceunus 3.2859?
Cf. 10th cent. pizzius W-H 2.313, and perhaps pitulus
(pisinnus) ib. 311; Fr. petit, see Die Sprache 1, 1949,
127-8.]

[ploum "plough": see PID 2.63

Cf. ploxenum ib. 204, for *ploʒ-s-enom? H-M p.373-
74 see in Surselv. fléua, Engad. fleja and fliana the
same word; SprFK 207; Kluge Urg. 46]

[pontō (-ōnis) "boat; pontoon; bridge of boats," pontonium

"punt"

Caes. BC 3.29.3: pontones, quod est genus nauium
Gallicarum, Lissi (in Dalmatia) reliquit (cf. AcS 2.
1035); pontonium: Isid. XIX 1.24. No doubt from Latin
pons.]

[pulluga (-ca): cf. bulluca, pulluga 158 above]

[sabaia, -um "beer" (Illyr. and Pannonia)

Amm. 26.8.2, Hieron. in Isae. 19 (see AcS 2.1262-
1263).]

Glosses

sal- "salt"

See Salas fl., 241 below (with Tac. A 13.57), and
cf. salinae (ap. Burgundios) CIL 13 p.269 n.1 (marshes
at Hall, cf. Halle, Salzburg, Saal-burg; Riese Lit.,
Index p.487).

[sambucus "elder-tree" Plin. 16, 74 al.

Written sabucus Ser. Samm. 7.100, gl. 3.358,71 al.
Cf. Dacian σέβα (MSL 16, 1910-11, 329); E-M ed. 2, 892.
Cf. σκοβιημ, scobilo 178 above.]

σαράγαρον see serracum below, carrus above

[secale, sicale Plin. NH 18.140 (rye?)

Some kind of grain (centenum) Ed. Diocl. 1.3. A
word of Balkan origin?]

σέγεστρον "blanket" Ed. Diocl. 8.42a

Cf. ib. 8.43 pulicare tenerrimum et maximum:
σεγεστρου καθαρείου πουλικαρίου.

selio (-onis) "strip of ground for sowing"

Medieval Latin (Ducange); perhaps Keltic, Jud in
Jaberg Festschrift, Zurich 1937, 131-192, summarized in
EC 4, 1948, 181-182.

senoca, seneca (-en), sinocus "inveterate, chronic"

From CGL 5.586,3; 654,40. Cf. 5.393,1 (OE gundaes-
uelgiae). Abbruz. saniče "scar, wound," cf. OItal. senici
"swollen glands," see M-L 7819; Jud AR 6, 1922, 210. Presumably Keltic or Latin.

Glosses

?serracum, sarracum "waggon"

    See the testimonia AcS 2.1524-25, and cf. carrus
above, with which it is frequently joined, σαράγγρον
in Ed. Diocl. 15.31a (AcS 2.1364). Persian according
to Heraeus Kl. Schriften 1937, 8-10; but cf. Pirie CR
53, 1939, 82. With s- from k- not Illyrian but some
satem-language, perhaps Thracian?

silurus: see 220 above (in Danuuio)

[silvr- "silver"(?)

    An Alpine word, modern local name Silvretta; OChSl.
sьrebro, Basque cillara; see Feist Got. Wtb. s.v. silubr;
Schrader-Nehring 2.395. But the correct origin was identified by Hubert RC 44, 1927, 82.]

sinistus (leg. -as) "sacerdos (natu) maximus"

    Amm. 28.5.14; cf. Goth. sinista; if this conjecture
(cf. hendinos above) is correct, Germanic.

[?singilio "a garment;" cf. mod. Eng. "singlet"?

    Dalmatensis according to Trebell. Pollio Claud. 17.
6; Ed. Diocl. frag. Megalop. 19.47-50 (JHS 11, 1890, 299)
Νωρικός and Γαλλικός (as well as Νουμεδικός , φρυγιακος
and Βέσσος !), cf. AcS 2.1573. Presumably from Lat. sin-
gulus, hardly the local name Singilia (Spain).]

sinocus: see senoca above

sparus, dim. sparulus "spear"

    See PID 2.193, AcS 2.1624-1625 also "nomen piscis"

Glosses

sparus ctd.

CGL 5.393,41; on this cf. Thompson Greek Fishes, 1947, 100, 255). But I now consider the word to have been either Germanic (OHG spër), or Thracian (Sparadokos: i.e. Spartacus, see Kretschmer Spr. 18); cf. PID 2.430 σπαρα βάραι (i.e. -φόροι), hardly Spariani 84 above. But the fish name and bird name (sparrow) may be connected.

-stro- in capistrum Ed. Diocl. 10.4, cf. σέγεστρον

(tegestre) 8.42a (?); this suffix has several possible sources

sturnus "starling" Pl. 10.72 al.; Ed. Diocl. 4.42

Of Germanic origin; cf. st- in OE storc, Sicel τόργος PID 2.464.

sulaga "uolutabrum; slough" (C 13 ii 1, p.215) cf. 241

below Sülchen (Sumelocenna?)

sybina "telum uenabuli simile"

Illyrian according to Paul. ex Fest. 453 L., citing Ennius; Lib. Gl. ZI 1-2, CGL 4.198,6a; CR 36, 1922, 92. Cf. σιβύνη, σιγύνης (Cypriote, Macedonian, Thracian, or Scythian according to various authorities), see Jacobsohn Hermes 45, 1910, 214 (PID 2.629, cf. 159); BSA 37, 1936-37 [1940], 187-191.

[terriberum, terracuberum Ed. Diocl. 6.94, p.232860

Apparently a form of truffle]

Glosses

tina "wine-butt" Varro Non. 544.6

Perhaps the same word as tunna, tonna (178 above); chiefly in the lives of the saints. Possibly an Alpine word Walde ed. 2, cf. Gröber ALL 6, 1889, 125; E-M ed. 2, 1040; Brüch Einfl. 5-6. Cortsen Glotta 23, 1935, 157 compared Etr. tun.

trahonas (acc. pl.): a kind of goose, Pl. NH 10.56

Usually corrected to tetraonas; but v. H-M p.369, where the modern traoss (Unterengadin) is cited.

tugurium (teg-, tig-), **tuguriunculum** "hut" (inscc.,

Fest.)

Cf. attegia Note lii above, sutis and *bou-tego-n 178 above, but perhaps not mori-tex 207 (:στείχω); cognate with Lat. tego. Probably Keltic, see Haberl ZfCPh 8, 1910-12, 92-3; SprFK 212; ALL 9, 1894-5, 436; Walde ed. 2, s.v., Sofer 124; cf. tigerno- 207 above, κοσ|τεγος 208, Tigurini 241 (cf. 244), and στολούτεγον 178?

? τύρχη "furca" Gl.; Ed. Diocl. 15.47

But Ed. Diocl. 15.9 has φοῦρκα . See bargus 207 above (I.Eu. dh...ĝh... in τύρχη , but furca either dh- or bh-?)

uatusicus v.l. uathusiccus (caseus)

Pl. NH 11.240 (apud Ceutronas) Compare the personal name Vaturus (12.2349) H-M p.77 n.?

ueleda "prophetess"

See 200 above (add REG 62, 1949, 88 and 160); the

Glosses

ueleda ctd.

Germanic term was perhaps ganna (Dio Cass. 67.5.3, R.
Lit. p.156), q.v. above.

uennu(n)cula (uitis or uua)

Hor. Sat. 2.4.71; Colum. 3.2.2; Plin. NH 14.34.
Walde accepts Schulze's account (ZGLE 410), connecting
the word with a personal name Venno; but cf. rather
Vennones, Vennonetes (Raetic PID 1.446, 2.56), and compare such names of vines or grapes as biturica, mettica,
heluennaca.

? οὐολκαῖα · ἕλη

Cf. Ir. folc "wasserflut," Krahe RhM 89, 1940, 192
(Dio Cass. 55.32.3); not Alb. ułk "wolf." But why not
Volcaea (:Volcae)? Cf. olca 178? Or Volsci?

Remark:

In Mélanges Duraffour (Vol. 14 of Romanica Helvetica
1939) H. Brossard has studied "parole prelatine (soprat-
tutto celtiche)" in Alpine regions, among others, in the
Trentino (p.170), and the Grisons (p.175), of which the
following may be listed here as reflecting partially the
vocabulary current before the spread of Latin, viz.

Glosses

bladum, blaua "frumentum, segale, auena;" benna
"cesta su carretta;" clocca "campana;" sarrus "virgulto;"
ambilatium "chiorolo;" assum, asculum "pascolo;" balma
"riparo sotto una roccia sporgente;" poina, puina
"ricotta," i.e. *popina; briva, brevia "ponte."

More ambitious is the "Contributo al Lessico Pre-
romanzo" of R.A. Stampa Rom. Helv. 2, 1937. Of the
words which he lists (pp.201-203) the following may be
noted here, viz.:

albulana "pernice bianca;" barga "recinto;" benna
"slitta;" broccu "legna minuta;" dérbita "erpete;"
galleta "recipiente..;" ganda "scoscendimento di sassi
in montagna;" glastu "mirtillo;" macco "bambino;"
mappetto "bambino;" marg- "sornacchio;" mascarpa "ricol-
to;" (s)leudia "slitta;" talopenno "impalcato."

Jud (Romania 52, 1926, 347, cf. 47, 1921, 493) sees
in Prov. treva (: Lat. trabs, W. tref) an Alpine *trebo
of Keltic origin; cf. Hubschmied Vox Rom. 1, 1936, 89-
105 (Allem. senn, ziger Lomb. mascarpa); id. Schw.
Lehrerzeitung 27 Jan. 1933 (v. REA 29, 1937, 36) on
Keltic rit-, briga, taruos, tinn-, *iūlo; H-M p.242 (cf.
370-371) mod. arvine (uitis, uua heluina), rèze (raetica),
amigne (aminea [Paelign.]), durize (duratia, duracina);
J. Hubschmid Praeromanica, 1949 (Rom. Helv. 30). Many
of these are discussed above, see the Glossary.

Germanic glosses of late date, where proper names
are concerned, are usually wide of the mark as when,
à propos of the saints Vincent and Valentine (Luthers
Werke, Weimar edn., 1, 1883, 412) we have vinden
"inuenire" and vallen "cadere." There is an interesting
place in Walafridus Strabo (Libellus de exordiis. cet.,

1201

Glosses; Proper Names

Mon. Germ. Hist., Leges, II 2 Capitularia regum Franc.
ed Boretus and Krause, 1897), cap. 7 (p.481) on the
knowledge of Greek and Latin words by the Goths, and on
the passage of Gothic words into Greek and Latin.

241 - 244 Names of the Agri Decumates
with Upper Rhine and Danube

From CIL 13 ii, 1905, viz. 5025-5257, 5333-5338,
6283-6660, 7261-7501, 7564-7622, 7733-7775; iv, 1916,
11471-11538, 11710-11798, 11938-11961, 11965-11974,
11979-11980; Finke 91-131, 180-201, 221-224, 239-240,
253, 337-349, 353-355; Nesselhauf 58-63, 66, 90-110,
121-122; with the two works of Riese cited above (221),
and also Ernst Howald and Ernst Meyer Die Römische
Schweiz: Texte und Inschriften, Zürich 1940; CIL 3 ii,
1873, 5768-6021, 6529-6540, 6570-6573, with the Supplement i, fasc. 3, 1893, and ii, 1902, 11879-12034, 13542-
13562, 14370-14376, 15209-15220, and occasionally other
inscc. which illustrate the matter in hand, including
the Edict of Diocletian (CIL 3 pp.801-841, 1909-1953,
2208-2211, 2328 57-63 and [Index] pp.1188-1194, 2608-

Proper Names

2622; Frank 5, 1940, 305-421) and the Diplomata Mili-
taria. These last are now best published in CIL 16,
1936; and, so far as possible I have followed that text,
though references to the numeration in CIL 3 are also
used. Something has been gleaned also from Vollmer's
Inscriptiones Baiuariae Romanae (Abh. d. Kgl. Bay. Akad.
d. Wissenschaften, Philol.-philos. u. Hist. Kl., Supplement-
Band) 1915, here abbreviated V.; and from the work of
Viktor Hoffiller and Baldwin Saria Antiken Inschriften
aus Jugoslavien, Heft I (Noricum und Pannonia Superior)
1938 (Internat. Verband der Akademien), Zagreb (in Kommission b. den Buchhandlungen F. Pelikan, Beograd; St
Kugli, Zagreb); finally the Dacian waxtablets (CIL 3
pp.921-966, 1058, 2215) yield a few forms of peculiar
interest (notably [Iuppiter] Cernenus).

Cf. F. Haug and G. Sixt Die römischen Inschriften
und Bildwerke Württembergs ed. 2 (by Haug and P. Gössler),
Stuttgart 1912-1914 [1915].

A. Kerényi (personal names of Dacia) Diss. Pann. I
9 (1941) is still inaccessible to me; but, like I.
Gronovsky (personal names of Pannonia) Diss. Pann, I 2
(1933) it doubtless contains much that is Keltic; the
Harvard dissertation of J.T. Barrs (cf. HSCP 47, 1936,
211-14) deals with Moesia and Dacia; see also Martin
Bang Die Germanen im römischen Dienst, Berlin 1906. See
also the Indices to CIL 3.

P. Aebischer Noms de cours d'eau vaudois (in Mélanges
Duraffour, Rom. Helvet. 14, 1939) 80-92 (modern local
names of Keltic origin); J.U. Hubschmied ib. 211-270

Proper Names

(-inco, -anco; Germanic names; cf. on personal names
in -ingos id. Mélanges Gilliard, Lausanne 1944, 103-
113); R. von Planta and A. Schorta Rätisches Namenbuch,
since 1939, Rom. Helv. 8, see Vox Rom. 5, 1940, 248 and
323; E. Muret Romania 50, 1924, 439-452 (on Keltic names
in Switzerland); Förster in Streitberg Festgabe, 1924,
pp.59-85 (river names); U. Kahrstedt "Claudius Ptolemaeus
und die Geschichte der Südgermanen," Mitteilungen der
prähistorische Kommission der Akad. der Wissenschaften
Wien, 3 part 4 (Vienna, 1938); Aebisher RC 42, 1925, 97-
118 (local names of Gaulish origin in Switzerland); id.
RC 50, 1933, 254 (*bagako-, *bagon[o]), 263 (*deruo-),
cf. Gauchat Festschrift (Aarau, 1926), 435; and Z. f.
deutsche Mundarten 19, 1924, 169; P. Reinecke "Örtliche
Bestimmung geogr. Namen" (in Der Bayerische Vorgeschichts-
freund 5, 1925, p.19); W. Deonna Genava 4, 1926, 317-18;
P. Aebischer "Témoinage hydronomique du culte de la
déesse Vroica en Suisse romande," RC 48, 1938, 312-324
(cf. Jud Romania 58, 1933, 599-601); id. "Un Auenticum
fribourgeois," RC 47, 1930, 63-71; id. "Le nom de
Lausanne" Zts. f. Schw. Gesch. 11, 1931, 265-296 (*lousa-
"flat stone," -on(n)a a goddess; but A. quotes Kuryłowicz,
as suggesting *ple/ousa- "flow," and this seems to me
better, though it is possible that we have the Germanic
laus- "less," of which *lous- would be a hyper-Keltic
form); cf. RC 49, 1932, 307, and P.S. Pasquali "Lausanne
nell' onomastica medievale valdostana" Aosta, 1934, 8
pp. [Bolletino dell' Academia di S. Anselmo 23], a reference which I take from Z. f. Rom. Phil. Suppl. 47-55,
1927-35, item 3179; Konrad Schifmann Das Land ob der Enns,
1922; id. Hist. O-N Lexikon Oberöstereichs 2 vols., Linz
1935; J. Schnetz "Süddeutsche Orts- u. Flussnamen aus
keltischer Zeit," ZfCPh 13, 1919-21, 92-100 (Sumelocenna),
365-69 (Businca, Sumelocenna; and mod. Albig); 14, 1923,
35-42 (Rednitz), 274-288 (Rednitz again, Kissingen, names
in -acum); 15, 1925, 212-219 (Wipper; Weser, Visurgis);
R. von Kienle, "Der Alamannen-Name," in Oberdeutsche
Zeitschrift für Volkskunde 10, 1935, 65-75; J. Schnetz
ZONF 6, 1930, 141 (cf. Verhandlungen des historischen
Vereins von Oberpfalz u. Regensburg 86, 1936, 155-58);
on Ratisbona, Regensburg, Castra Regina; E. Muret "L'En-
quête sur les noms de lieu de la Suisse romande dans le
canton de Valais," and R. von Planta "Über Ortsnamen,
Sprach- u. Landes-geschichte von Graubünden," both in
Rev. Ling. rom. 7, 1931, 52-70 and 80-100 respectively;
a fair illustration of the theory and method of recon-
structing ancient from modern local names may be seen in

Proper Names

the contributions of Jud to H-M, e.g. p.363 Swiss Lugnez
from *Leponetia, Prättigau i.e. *Pritanni, cf. regio
Britannia (Chur 11th cent.); Engadin: uallis Eniatina
(A.D. 930), *Eniates; p.374 Zihl (Fr. Thièle): Gaulish
*tela; p.375 Broye: -brogia, -broga; Orbe: *urba (fl.);
Aramici (see 241 below): Gaulish *aramon (I.Eu. ar(ə)mo-,
Germ. arm-, aram- "bracchium," used as a term of toponymy);
p.376 n.1 Safneren: *Sabinaria.

Berthelot RA 8, 1936, 199-200 (on some of the local
names of the Heluetii in Ptolemy).

O. Fiebiger and L. Schmidt Inschriftensammlung zur
Gesch. d. Ostgermanen (Denkschriften Akad. d. Wissenschaften in Wien, Ph-H Kl. 60 iii, 1917) and NF (Fiebiger
alone) 70 iii 1939, and 72 ii 1944 (cf. AE 1949, p.244).

For maps, in addition to those in CIL 3 and 13, and
in Mommsen's Insc. conf. Helu. Lat. (Mitt. Antiqu.
Gesellsch. Zürich 10, 1856) and Kiepert's Formae Orbis
antiquae 23 and 24, see the excellent ones in H-M,
Vollmer, Norden, and Staehelin. For a map of the Limes
see RGKBer. 6, 1910-11 [1913].

P. Aebischer "Sur l'origine et la formation des
noms de famille dans le Canton de Fribourg," Bibl. Arch.
Rom. 2 vi (1924) hardly falls within our subject.

Terra Sigillata Diss. Pann. II 20 (by Bónes), cf.
Laureae Aquinc. ib. II 11; Dacian personal names ib. I
12 (cf. CR 61, 1947, 35-36).

241   Local and Ethnic Names

A G ciuitas 6462; cf. C
p.245 (Cochina fl.
11th cent., Gochsen),
or Oehringen, v.
Aurel[

[Ab(e)rins(-berg) medi-
aeval C p.224]

Ἀβίλουον (v.l. -λουον)
Ptol.

Local and Ethnic Names

Abnoba mons Tac. (-oua
Pl.), Ἀβνόβαια ὄρη
Ptol.; Avien., Mart.
Cap.; also as a div-
ine name; uallis
*Abnobensis in Oos fl.,
and Aquae Abnobenses(?)
C p.62 and 197; cf.
perhaps Ab-ona(?) AcS
1.9

[Abrettenus dipl. 44,
q.v.]

Ἀβουδίακον Epfach, PID 1.
443

Abusina fl. (v.l. Aru-
sena) IA, TP, ND;
Abens

Aceruo (-bo) Rav., TP

Acronus lacus Mela 3.2.24,
cf. P-W s.v. Rhenus
734; note also Accio
(lacus Lemannus), see
80 above and 243 below

Acincenses milites CIL
13 ii 1, 1905, cxxx;
vi, 1933, p.137; ND
Occ. 41, and see
Aquincum (Alt-Ofen)

Ἀδούλας (mons and fl.)
Str. 4.3.3, 192C

Ἀδραβαικάμποι Ptol.

Adrana fl. Tac., Eder(?);
Cf. Adriana and (Dalm.)
Atiranus?

[?Aeg(issus) dipl. 22]

Aelia Augusta (Vindel.)
6741

[Agrippinenses Transal-
pine AE 1933.111]

[Aguontum, now Lienz;
CIL 3 p.707. Aguntum,
-iensis AcS 1.62, 3.
524; dipl. 98]

Αἶνος , Aenus fl. Ptol.,
Tac., itinn.; ad Ae-
num; v. statio Enensis,
Pons Aeni

Αἰτουία Ptol. 267.3

Alamanni -icus chron.
Fred., C pp.62, 66,
421; NDOcc.; cf. 234
above (-ia) R.2610 and
CIL 3 p.721 (-ia)

⟨Alani (Hal-) Iord.⟩

[Alauni (Noricum), cf.
6425, and 243 below]

Alba (Vopisc.) v. Ἄλπεια
and cf. 6324, C p.251,
(Swabian) Alps; cf.
Albis (C pp.280, 301;
and 234, 240 above),
Albisi Rav.; Albia,
Alpes, Σάλπια , Ὄλβια ,
Ἄλβιον ὄρος Str. 7.5.
2, 314C; mod. Albis

Albianum IA

[Alburnus (Dacia) 3 p.925;
as divine name P-W s.v.]

Ἀλκιμόεννις Ptol. 2.11.
15

Alisinensis ciuitas 6462,
6482 (cf. C pp.231,
238; Aliso p.406), El-
senz fl.; Alisinenses

Local and Ethnic Names

Gordiani R.2183, cf.
Ἀλεισόν Ptol. (R. Lit.
p.384); 221 above

⟨Alma mons Vopisc. uit.
Prob. 18.8⟩

Ἄλπεια ὄρη Ptol. 2.11.5,
Str. 7.1.3, 290C; Alba
Vopisc. uit. Prob. 13.
7, cf. P-W 1.1299;
(Swabian) Alps

Alpini v. Nesselhauf Dipl.
p.179

[Altoburgium (mediaev.)
C 3 p.724, Altenburg]

Ἀμασίας fl. Str. 7.1.3,
290C, cf. Amissis Mela,
Amisis Pl., R. Lit.
p.52 n.1

[Ambi-lici (Noricum)
Ptol.]

Amb-isontes v. Isonta

Ambra mansio, *Amber fl.,
Ammer; PID 1.448

A[mbrones?] 6610, cf.
Oros. 5.16.13 where
they are mentioned
with the Tigurini

Anartes BG 6.25.2, cf.
Dessau 8965

Ἄναυον Ptol. 272.5

Andautonia (Daut- IA);
cf. 3.4008

Ἀνδουαίτιον Ptol. 275.9

Apollinesis uicus 6688
(Mainz)

[Aprensis dipl. 10]

Aquae v. Abnobenses, Hel-
ueticae (10027.204),
Mattiaci; cf. sqq.

Aquenses uikani 5233
(Baden, Switz.)

Aquenses 6339, cf. ciuitas
(Aurelia) Aquensis,
Aquae Aureliae C p.297;
now Baden-Baden; ciu-
itas Aquens[, ab Aquis
9116; note also prae-
fectus Aquae (or Aque-
[nsium) 7279, presum-
ably a different place;
cf. AE 1941.90

[Aquesiani (Dalm.) V.10]

Aquileia TP, cf. CIL 3
p.739; AcS 1.168,39
and 168,47; Aal, Aalen

Aquincum dipl. 61, Aquinc-
(ences) 3.13396, v.
Acinc- above

[Arae Flauiae, now Hoch-
mauern near Rottweil]

Aramici v. Arurensis

Arar (-is) fl., Switzer-
land; v. AcS 3.654,
cf. C p.5, add. p.59;
Araris Rheni Conflu-
entes (-ia) Coblenz;
Arares, -um C pp.211-
212; Aar (two rivers,
cf. Arola)

[Arauissca Diss. Pann. ii
10, 1938, p.3; cf. 3.
3325, 13389; Tac. G 28.
3 (cf. Anderson ad loc.),
Arauisci Pl. 3.148 (Er-)]

Local and Ethnic Names

[Arbenses AE 1948.242]

Arbor Felix, Arbore (Brigantium); Arbona, Arbon PID 1.450, cf. C p.5, 47.

Arcunia, Ἀρκυνία cf. Ercunion, Hercynia silua; AcS 1.1458 sqq.

Ἀρελετία Ptol. 270.2 (v.l. -γ-)

Armilausi TP, cf. gl. 220; P-W, TLL s.v.

Armisses, -isia fl. 6378-79, Erms fl.

Arola fl. Fredegar., ASS, AcS 1.219, 3.689, now Aar; Arula Eucher. (ib. 3.696,35, cf. 1. 230,7); cf. Arurensis

Ar(r)abo itinn., ND, Ptol.; Raab

Ἀροίκουα Ptol. 273.15

Ἀρσόνιον Ptol. 271.3

Ἄρταυνον Ptol. 2.11.12, cf. Taunus

Artobriga TP, Ptol.

Aruranci v. Arurensis

Arurensis regio 5161 (C p.7); nautae Aruranci Aramici 5096 (cf. Aramo divine name 12. 2971), Aar(-gau), *Arura (-ae uallis) Aare, Aarau; cf. C

p.31; REA 29, 1927, 49. Cf. Arar above and Arauris 80; distinguish yet another Aar fl. (cf. C p.478), Bingen, from the Swiss Aar (Arar, Arola, Aruris)

Ascafa (uilla) A.D. 980, Ascapha Rav. (Main-) aschaff (Moenus), Aschaffenburg; C p.289

Ἀσκαλίνγιον Ptol. 269.5

Ἀσκαῦλις ib. 268.1

⟨Asciburgius mons in Germ. Magn., cf. -ium 221⟩

Ascis Rav. (R. Lit. 409)

Atiliensis colonia 3.5887

?Atergum 3.5793, cf. Opitergium (-inus)

[Atilia (mediaev.) C 3 p.724]

Atrans H-S p.94; itinn., insc. (-dr-)

Aucia, Auciacensis Ossgau (Baden-Baden) AcS 1. 282, R. Lit. p.174. Distinguish Ausaua 212 above

Aude[riensis] ciuitas 7353, but cf. 7063 (see 234 above), F.183; C p.426

Auenticum Tac., itinn., NG, -a Greg. Tur., Ἀουεντικόν Ptol., insc.

Local and Ethnic Names

(9065, 9062, 9067, 9071, 9072, 9076); coloni Auenticenses 5102, cf. 5042, 5072, 5091, 5518, cf. 4085; divine name Auentia; Auennica A.D. 517, Auenticulum IA, Lausanus quae prius Auenticus NG (cf. AcS 3. 770,50), mod. Avenches; distinguish Auantici (80)

Augusta (mansio) IA

Augusta Vindelicum v. Vindelici

Augustana ND Occ.

uicani August[R.2253

c(iuitas) Aur[G[S[, N.106, cf. A G above

uicani Aurel[ianenses] 6541, 6542, cf. 11. 3104, i.e. Aurelius (-ianus) uicus (cf. Aureliana Orléans), now Oehringen, C pp.5, 197, 281, 269; cf. Ohrn fl., Orin-gawe (later Oehringen), like Orinwalt, Oren-huc. Possibly]aur, Auer[on tiles (C p.270) belong here

[Azalus dipl. 96-7, 99, 104; -a 49]

Bac fl. Rav. 4.229,18

Bacensis cf. AcS 3.787, 20

Βαγινοχαῖμαι Ptol. 262.7

Βαῖμοι Ptol. 265.10, cf. Boiohaemum?

Ba(i)uuarii Rav., also written Bag- Bauuarii AcS 3.819, cf. 896.54; Bavaria

Balissae (Aquae) H-S p. 269

Βαλύσεινος Ed. Diocl. 19. 52

?Balr[(tegulae, Oehringen), C p.270

⟨Βάνδιλοι v. Vand-⟩

[Bassianus dipl. 132; cf. 212]

Bastarnae (-er-) cl.; -aei Pl. 4.81; cf. Tac. G 46.1; REA 8, 1906, 263-4

Batauum (-a) castra v. C 3 p.734, ND Occ. 25; Stein Beamten 168-69, now Passau

Βατίνοι Ptol. 262.7

Bedaium (Bid-) itinn., cf. Βέδακον Ptol.

⟨Berga (Thrace)RA 24, 1945, 38⟩

Βέργιον Ptol. 273.3

[Bergomum 5210]

[Bessi dipl. 46, 50, 75 cet.]

Local and Ethnic Names

Βίβακον   Ptol. 274.12

uicani Bibienses (i.e.
  probably from "biuium,"
  but cf. AcS 1.415)
  6315; or Vib-?

⟨Βικούργιον   Ptol. 273.5;
  Vic-?⟩

Biricianae (-a) TP

[Bituriges F.342 (Viuisci)]

Bodamicus lacus (mediaev.)
  C p.297, Boden See

Bodungo Rav. 4.26

Boiodurum Ptol., itinn.,
  ND Occ.; 3.5121, 5755
  (Boho-?), cf. C 3 p.734.
  Beiderbach (or Innstadt?)

Boiohaemum Vell., Tac.;
  Βουίαιμον Str., Βοι-
  χαῖμαι Ptol.; C p.262,
  AcS 1.473

Boii 6448, 6553, cf. C
  p.238; Boius V. 510,
  Βοίων ἐρημία Ptol.; cf.
  dipl. 55, 61; 3.14359,
  23; 9.5363-64. BG 1.5;
  Str. 7.2.2, p.292

Βραγόδουνον Ptol., cf. C
  p.211 (-δουρον), Vin-
  del.; cf. Brigobanne,
  Brocodu[num?] R.4531a,
  AcS 1.618

Bratananium TP

[Brega fl. C p.211, cf.
  Brigach]

[Breuci 3.5918, 5918a,
  11933; dipl. 26, 31,
  55 cet.]

Brigantium, -ia, -inus
  lacus, Brigantienses,
  Βριγάντιοι   v. PID 1.
  477, 452 (?Brixenetes);
  Bregenz. Cf. Venetus
  lacus ibid.; cf. Bri-
  gantia (pers. name) 3.
  5468; Bracantia Rav.
  4.26, Brec- N.D.

[Brigetio (Pannonia) AcS
  1.540]

Brigobanne (now Hüfingen)
  TP; cf. C p.211 (Bra-
  godurum)

Brisiacum, -us; Brezecha
  (mons) cod. Th. Rav.,
  Brezach (Rav.), cf.
  Breisach (234)

Brisigaui ND Occ., Bris-
  icau MG; AcS 1.549,
  cf. C p.62

Βριτολάγαι (v.l. -γολατ-)
  v. Latobrigi

[Britones 6622, 7752 add.,
  Brit[6592 add., Bri-
  ttones 7749, 7762; cf.
  Brit(tones) Mu(rrenses),
  Elant(ienses), Triputien-
  ses, C p.238; Cal[
  12498, Stein Beamten 250,
  AcS 3.1041; see also
  Grinario and Guruedenses
  Lunenses, Vro[below]

Briu 6231 add., but cf.
  Briuines ciues 3.5878
  (for Breu- cf. Breuci[?]
  or Brix-[?]; Brimienses
  AcS 3.943,4

[Brix⟨i⟩a 5241, Brixsa 8733;
  cf. AcS 1.612, 615; cf.
  PID 1.452]

Local and Ethnic Names

Βροδεντία Ptol.

Bromagus v. Viro-

?Brucherus Sid. Apoll.,
cf. R.1929; but see
221 above

Bucinobantes Amm. 29.4.7

Βουδόριγον Ptol. 271.1,
Brieg

Βουδορίς Ptol. 2.11.14,
cf. C p.225; Büderich

Βουνίτιον (M-) Ptol. 2.11.
12-3, AcS 3.1000; cf.
Bounis ib. 981; gloss
240 (μουνίας)

[Βουργονόβορε Procop. de
aedif. 4.6, 289D]

[Buri Tac. G 43.1, cf.
Byrrus fl. Ven. Fort.
uit. Mart. 4.168, and
ab expeditione Burica
3.5937, V. 353 (for
Burae v. Zeuss p.458);
"prope fontes Vistulae"
Tac. l.c. But note
also Biraci 224)]

Businca fl. (cf. Quintana)
v. C 3 p.734

Caelius mons IA, ND, now
Kellmünz; cf. Coel-
aletae Tac. A 3.38,
Cel- Pl. 4.41, Cololet-
icus (?) dipl. 33

[Caesarisburgium (mediaev.),
C 3 p.724, Kaysersburg]

Caistena Rav., cf. C p.59,
now Kaisten; ZONF 15,
1939, 86-96

ciues (sg.) Kal[(or
Ial[?] 3.5932, V. 207,
Cal[13 vi, 1933,
p.122, cf. Chalitani
below? Cal[(Brittones)
12498 (Stein Beamten
p.250, C pp.265, 270)

Καλαιγία Ptol. 270.3

Καλαμαντία (v.l. Κελ -)
Ptol. 275.10; cf.
Caelius mons

Calatinum, Callatia (med-
iaev.) C 3 p.724 (ad
5898)

Καλισία Ptol. 271.4

[Calsum 3.14207,15]

Καλούκωνες Ptol. 2.11.10,
cf. Καλοῦλκοι Str. 7.1.
3, 291C

Cambodunum Str., Ptol.,
ND, Merov. num., itinn.;
3.5987, cf. PID 1.446;
Kempten

⟨?Campus fl., v. Adrabae-
campi⟩

Camunni H-M 364; v. Duhn
Gräberk. 2, 1939, 16
n.21

Κάνδουνον Ptol. 269.8

[Canobiaca ND]

Canini campi Amm. 15.4.1

Local and Ethnic Names

Καντιοιβίς Ptol. 274.11

[Καπέδουνον Str.]

Capellati(i) Amm. 18.2.
15, see also Palas
below; cf. mod. Cappel?
And possibly the gloss
capellus (178). See
also C pp.225 n.4, 269
n.1

Καρίταμοι (v.1. - νοι) Ptol.
2.11.6, cf. C p.197

[Carnariis 3.3893]

⟨Carnuntum cl.⟩

Carrodunum (v.1. -no-)
Ptol. 274.3

Κάρπις Ptol. 252.3, Cirpi
IA

Καρουάγκας Ptol. 2.13.1,
Caruancas

?Cartusa C p.144 n.1

Cassangita Rav., cf. C
p.59, Gansingen; ZONF
15, 1939, 86-96

Cassiliacum ND, Kisslegg

Κασουάροι Ptol., Casuarii
Nom. Prov.

Κασουργίς Ptol. 273.10

Catenates Pl. 3.137, CIL
5.7817,3; Cattenates
Germ. 19, 1935, 226-
28; cf. AJA 42, 1938,
584

Cattharenses (numeri)

7298, written Caddar-
enses 7268, cf. 13 vi,
1933, p.123, Catthar-
or Catther-(enses) on
tile-stamps, cf. AcS
1.844, 3.1151, C p.4;
Catarienses Pl., ND
Occ., cf. Catta-(renses)
Mauri 7545; Cater-
(ienses?) 13.3493 (or
Catafr-?); cf. Catthi
(v. infra Chatti) and
note C...th... :
Ch...t(t). Not Catari
(Pannonia), or mod.
Cattaro (Dalm.), v. adn.
ad 7268

[Kauieretium (Dacia) 3
p.937]

Κελκμαντία Ptol.; cf.
Caelius mons?

[Celeia now Cilli, 7029;
H-S 8, 22, 370]

Celeusum TP Kellsbach,
Kells

Celius mons IA, Kellmünz

Κέλτρος λίμνη Schol.
Lycophr. Alex. 189;
for Istros?

Κένεννον Ptol. 267.2 (cf.
for the ending Παριέννα
below)

?Cenni Florus, Dio Cass.

[Cepasiae IA]

Cetium, Cetienses v. AcS
1.1001 (itinn., inscc.)

Chaibones Mamert. Paneg.
Maxim. 5

Local and Ethnic Names

Χαιτούωρος Ptol. 265.3

Chalitani 6763.12; cf.
  Halicenses below, and
  P-W s.vv. Chali, Chal-
  usus (Cimbri)

Chatti C pp.297, 468,
  Χάττοι p.406, Catthi
  pp.212, 243, 262 n.7
  (Tac. A 1.56, Vell. 2.
  109); Catthi Meliboci
  p.243; cf. Cattharen-
  ses?

[Χαῦβοι Str. 7.1.3, 290C]

[Chunni Lib. h.Fr., i.q.
  Hunni]

C[imbri?] 6610; Cimbri
  (ap. Boios, in Pan-
  nonia, Str. 7.2, cf.
  Schulz Germ. 13, 1929,
  139-143)

⟨Cirpi itin., Κάρπις Ptol.⟩

Κλάνις fl. Str. 4.6.9,
  207C

Clarenna TP, cf. C pp.216,
  238; for the form cf.
  Clauenna (PID 1.451),
  Sumelocenna, Κέvεννον ,
  Παρίεννα

Κλαυτονάτιοι(-την-) Str.

Clemidium Rav.

Clunia TP

[Cochengowe A.D. 788, see
  C p.245 n.1, Chochina
  fl. 9th cent.; cf.
  ciuitas A G above?]

Κολάγκωρον (-oρ-) Ptol.
  270.6

Κόλαπις fl., Str. 7.5.2,
  314C

[Colatio TP]

Comacia, -ienses 3.5650,
  cf. Comagena, -enses
  IA, TP, ND Occ.

Condate (Seyssel?) C
  p.693

Condistat (in 8th cent.)
  now Cannstatt (cf.
  Canbach) C p.238

Κονδοργίς Ptol. 275.5

Κόγνοι Ptol. 263.3

[*Confluentes (Koblenz,
  Switz.), v. Arar above]

Constantia Konstanz Rav.

Contiensis Eumen.; C 3
  p.721

⟨Coralli: cf. REA 8,
  1906, 263-4⟩

Κόρκοντοι Ptol. 263.1

Κορκόρας Str. 7.5.2, 314C
  (Chadwick Nationalities
  of Europe 1945, 154 n.1
  (cf. 166) compares mod-
  ern Krkonoške and de-
  rives the name from the
  same root as Hercynia
  :Lat. quercus)

[Coritani (Lincs.) from
  Bavaria via Marne, Os-

Local and Ethnic Names

wald Ant. J. 21, 1941,
323-332]

[Cormones v. AcS 1.1129]

Cornac[R.1764, cf. AcS
1.1129, Cornacates
dipl. 2; CIL 13 vi,
1933, p.137; Jacobsthal
Celtic Art 1944, 10
(Cornacenses)

Cosuanetes Pl. 3.137, CIL
5.7817,10; cf. Ptol.
2.12.3 (Κωντουάνται)
and perhaps Κωτουάντιοι
Str. 4.6.8,206C

⟨Cotini 6.2831; Klio 30,
1937, 215; Tac. G 43.
1; cf. BG 6.24; orig.
Volcae Tectosages
(lingua Gallica Tac.);
Dio Cass 71.12.3; CIL
6.32544g, 32557, Dessau
8965⟩

Κωτουάντιοι v. Cosuanetes

?Coueliacae TP

?Crhepstini TP (corrupt)

Cr[v. Gr[below; C
p.265 suggests Rems
(i.e. Ch-?), Ramesdal
in A.D. 1080, cf.
Hramisitha in 11th
cent., Förstemann p.
834

Cubii Frontin. strat. 1.
3.10; C p.263 n.4;
and see deus Santius
below (243); cf. also
Cuballum (local name,
Galatia)

[Cuculla TP, Kuchl]

Curia itinn., Paul Diac.,
Curiensis cf. PID 1.
450, AcS 1.1200, C
p.49; probably not
Latin, but cf. REA 36,
1934, 481; perhaps
Κουριώνες Ptol. 2.11.
11. Modern Chur,
Coire, Coira

Κούρτα Ptol. 252.3

Curuedenses v. G-

[Daesitiates 9.2546,
Desidias dipl. 11]

Δαρμάσια Str.

Δανδοῦται Ptol. 2.11.11

?Da.sag[enses] N.102

Dānuuius (-b-) cl. inscc.
(also as divine and
personal name, cf. AcS
1.1238-39), cf. C pp.63,
197; possibly to be
compared with Rhodanus
(80 above) cf. Glossary;
but Kretschmer Glotta
24, 1935, 1-11 makes
Danuuius (cf. Skt. dānu-
Avest. dānu-, Osset. Don
"river") a Scythian
word; cf. Förster ZfSlPh
1,1924, 1-25, 418; Ven-
dryes MSL 20, 1918, 265-
85 (RA 8, 1918, 347);
cf. less probably Eri-
danus, Pokorny in Mélan-
ges Boisacq (Ann. Inst.
Orient. et Slav. 5, 1937),
193-197

Local and Ethnic Names

[Dalmata V.265]

[Dardani 8.9990; IG 14 2433; dipl. 45, 50, 78]

[?Darnithithi AE 1945.57]

[Dauersus dipl. 38]

decumates (agri) v. p.1154 above; cf. C p.238

Δηούονα Ptol. 273.2, cf. Diuona 148

[Didines-Haim 770 A.D. Förstemann 1.705; Didissen C p.252; Diedes-heim]

?Dinax AE 1929.194, cf. BSAF 1928-29, p.247

[?Dipscurtus dipl. 1]

[exploratores Germ. Diuitiensium 7750-51, 7761; cf. 6814, 7054; 8.9059; Diuitienses 11828, 11979. Cf. C p.499. Diuitia (Deutz) is of course Germ. Inf., but the large number of troops thence, stationed on the r. bank of the Rhine in Germ. Sup., should be noted]

[Δορτικόν Procop. de aedif. 4.6, 289D; ND Or. 42.3]

Δρακούινα Ptol. 2.12.3

[Drauus, Drave H-S 361; cf. AcS 2.1905]

⟨Drobeta (Dacia) ND Drub[AE 1945.61, D[robeten- ses?] AE 1949.197⟩

Dubra fl. Rav., cf. Dubra- goe and Tubrigowe 8th cent., Tubera fl. 11th cent., now Tauber; C p.279 n.1; but some read Bubra (the Wipper) C p.279 n.3; cf. gl. 240 and see on this and other terms for "water" or "river" (*abona, frudis, onno, uara cf. uerno-) ZfCPh 23, 1943, 397

Duebon Rav. 4.26

Dunensis lacus Fredeg. chron., AcS 1.1376,28; Thuner see; hence *Dunum, now Thun, is assumed; cf. possibly dunium(?) 5166 (si uera lectio)

Duria fl. Pl. 4.81; Δοῦρας Str. 4.6.9,207C

castra E...id[(?) 6658

Eburodunum TP, ND Occ., Eburodunenses 5063- 64 Yverdun cf. RC 44, 1927, 320-335; ZfSchw- Gesch 17, 1937, 83- 95; REA 40, 1938, 62; distinguish the next item

[Eburodunum in Germ. Magn., Ptol. 2.11.15, now Brünn, C p.16]

Local and Ethnic Names

Local and Ethnic Names

Gallisueba salus Fort. 5.
2.22

Γαν(v)όδουρον Ptol. 2.9.
10, often read Σαλ-
q.v.; or cf. Γάννα 244,
but perhaps Kandern-
in-Baden, see ZfSchw.
Gesch. 17, 1937, 418-
26

?Gantisci Aurel. Vict.
uir. il. 72.7, cf.
AcS 2.1769,24; cf.
Gannascus 224? Hardly
for Taurisci?

⟨Γαζωρία, -ιος Thr., RA
24, 1945, 46⟩

Gen(n)aua see 80 above

Germani 6405, -us 6485,
7341a; Cermani (sic)
6552; 6.4344; Pl. 4.
81; Germanicum TP
(Kösching)

[Geta dipl. 96 cet.]

Γελιδύα Ptol. 271.5

[Gipedes R. Lit. p.346;
cf. C p.299]

[Gothi R. Lit. p.226]

uicus Grinario, uicani
Grinarionenses 11726-
27, cf. TP, Ptol. 2.
11.12 (Γραυιοναριον),
said to be Köngen;
Gr[inarionenses?]
B[tiyyones] 12499. Cf.
C p.264 (Cr-?); Stein
Beamten 251

Guntia itin., ND, Eumen.;

Guntiensis Paneg. Const.
2; cf. C p.144; Günzberg

[Gutones Str., Pl.]

[Gurbita(?) TP]

Guruedenses (Brittones)
7343 (C-), R.1750,
CIR 1455

Haci TP

Halani i.q. Alani

Halicenses 7495, cf.
Haliq[et Chalit[
6763,12; and probably
]q(u)annensis (-canna?)
6776. The latter ap-
pear to be on the limes
Germ.; C p.297 puts
Halicanum ap. Boios (in
Pannonia), P-W near Hom-
burg. Alicano, Hali-
cano (Salle) itinn.,
H-S p.195; cf. Chali,
Chalusus (Cimbri);
Chalitani (if for Hali-
tani), v. above, and
under Ch-

[Harii Tac. G 43.3; cf.
Zdeutsch.Alt.77, 1940,
27-8]

H(arudes??) 6610. Harudes
BG 1.37, 1.51; cf. Mon.
Anc. (Charydes and
Χάλυβες)

Helmanabinde uilla A.D.
796, now Helmbund (C
p.245)

Heluetii, -icus cl.,

inscc., cf. C pp.5-7;
5089, 5093, 5085,
5090, 5092, 5098,
5099, 5079, 5110,
5166, 6472, 12.2597;
etc.; V.536 (gaesati,
q.v.) R.1775; F.96;
Heluetia 2980, 6369,
6372, cf. H-M 471;
-ius 6372, 6234, H-M
471; dipl. 5, 76;
Helueti H-M 190; con-
uentus Hel[ueticus]
11478; Eluetius 7024,
7026; ἡ τῶν ἘλουηΤίων
ἔρημος , deserti Helue-
tiorum v. C l.c.;
ἘλουήΤΡιοι ibid.; Aquae
Helueticae (or Helue-
tiorum) ibid., AcS 1.
1429, now Baden, cf.
uikani Aquenses (but
not 7566a, Wiesbaden?),
and CIL 3.6017,2, 13.
10027,204 (R.2074, H-M
448); colonia Heluetio-
rum (i.e. Auenticum)
5079; He(luetius) V.
260B (an Heduus?), 509;
Insc. Hel. 241

[Helisii Tac. G 43.3]

?Hem[iseni] R.199; cf.
Hemesa prou. (Moesia);
not Syrian? 3.3844,
13398 cf. p.1734; H-S
172

[ἘόρΤα (Scordisci) Str.]

Hercynia silua cl., AcS
1.1458-63 (cf. C p.5).
On Hercynia (cf. ἀρκυ-
νία ὄρη) see Do. 228,
Walde ed. 2, 632; hard-
ly arcomus (gloss 246,

AcS 3.662, cf. rather
are-comici?) Kluge Urg.
6; now Bakorny (Chad-
wick Nationalities of
Europe 166 n.1)

[Hermunduri Tac. G 41, 42;
cf. C p.262, Hermiones
Tac. G 2.3; Germ. 23,
1939, 262-69]

⟨Heruli C p.299⟩

[Hunni (Ch-) Ambros. Ep.
24; according to Pris-
cus 59 the Hunni had
adopted German]

[Iadestinus dipl. 11]

[Iapodes (Illyr.) see
Serta Hoffill. 189-
199; APh 15, 1940-41,
355 and 463]

[Iasulones (Pannonia) IA]

Iasus (Pannonia) dipl. 31;
Iasi 3.4000, H-S 586,
587; Aquae Iasae 3.
4121

[Iazyges Dio Cass.; R.501]

Iciniacum TP, now Itzing

ἸλιγμαΤία Ptol. 273.12

Ἰνκρίονες (?) v. Nicretes

Ἰντούεργοι Ptol. 2.11.6;
cf. P-W s.v., and C
p.197 n.1; cf. perhaps
Itiui[below

Local and Ethnic Names

Ἰνούτριον see PID 1.453

Iouisura IA; cf. 3 p.1051,
    hardly Isar?

Ἰσάρας fl., Str.; Isar

[Ἴσκος Procop.]

?Isonta fl. (v.l. -g-),
    Bisontia Pinz-gau,
    PID 1.447; cf. Amb-
    isontes Pl. 3.137

Istaeuones Tac., Pl.

Ἴστρος , Hister cl., cf.
    Danuuius; C p.212;
    R.3, 6.1207

Isunisca (v.l. -in-)
    itinn., Izny or Isny(?)

ciu. Itiiu[7321; cf.
    perhaps Ituuerus, (ex
    Germ. Sup.) 8.9060, or
    Ἰντούεργοι above?
    ..]ii[.. 7394; C p.426

Iuarus fl. TP, Ivar; PID
    1.447

Iuliomagus TP (now Schleit-
    heim)

[Iuthungi Ambros. Ep. 24]

[Iuuauum Pl., Ptol., itinn.,
    inscc. (3.5536 al.),
    AcS 2.96-97; Iuuauenses.
    Salzburg; V.6, 31]

[Λακκοβοῦργο Procop.,
    Λακιβούργιον Ptol. 267.
    5]

Laciacum IA

laeti 6378, see 212, 221,
    234 above; cf. laetus
    (L-?) 7754, but hardly
    ]letus 6603; in the
    formula u s l l m, com-
    mon on the Rhine and
    Danube, is laetus Latin
    or Germanic?

[Laianci 5.1838]

[Lamatini 3.9864a, cf.
    (TP, Rav.) Lamatis?]

?Lamizonipada fl. Rav. 4.
    17; but Müllenhof read
    Amisa, Visara

Langobardi Vell. 2.106,
    Str.

Larga fl. itin.

Latauienses ND Occ. 36.4;
    AcS 2.150

[Latobici, -uici Pl.,
    Ptol., itinn., cf. 3.
    3925, 10804; AE 1945
    p.181; cf. 221, 234,
    243; Dessau 9132]

Latobrigi BG; -bogii Oros.;
    cf. Λατόβριξ (v.l. Ἀλιό-)
    gl. Ptol. 3.10, where
    apparently we have
    Βριτολάγαι for Βριγο-
    λάται?

Laugona fl. Fortun., Lahn

Laurissa 8th cent., C
    p.234; Lorsch; Laur-
    eacus 1136, Lorcha
    1102 C p.265 Lorch (cf.

Local and Ethnic Names

lorica p.212 bis Remark
1 above)

Lausonna v. Leus-

Lemannus lacus cl., v.
also 80; H-M 152; on
nautae lacus Lemanni
Toutain BSAF 1925,
271; S.R. in RA 21-22,
1925, 311; ZONF 4,
1928, 269-71

Lentienses Amm. Marc.,
who calls them Ala-
manni; Linz

Leubaccii (Germani) 7613a
add.; unless a personal
name?

Λευκάριστος Ptol. 271.2

Λεῦνοι Ptol. 2.12.13

Leusonna, Leusonnenses
H-M 152-54, cf. p.243,
where the etymology
*lausa "Felsblock" is
offered; but au appears
to be a later writing
than eu: ou; uikani
Lousonnenses 5026, cf.
]oeusona(?) 12.2040;
lacus Losonne, Lausonna,
Lausonius itinn., C
p.7 (Lausonicensis eps.
ib.), cf. AcS 2.202 and
292. Cf. REA 19, 1917,
274-6; Lousonna Esp.-
de Rugg. 84; on nautae
qui Leusonnae consis-
tunt Rev. Hist. Vau-
doise 47, 1939, 127-45;
49, 1941, 60-65; cf.
Rev. Suisse d'Art et
d'Arch. 2, 1940, 157-9;
3, 1941, 1-24 (inscc.

of Avenches and Bas-
Valais, see APh 14,
1939 [1941], 285; 15,
1940-41, 318); nautae
Leuson[nenses AE 1946,
256; Jahrb. Schw. Ges.
Urg. 31, 1936, 86.
In 12.2040 read perhaps
Leusona. As to the ety-
mology, other possibili-
ties are *pleu- "sail"
and Germ. laus- "less"
(though not with *onno
"water")

Λικίας fl., Licca; Licates,
Λικάτ(τ)ιοι, Lech (Fred-
egar.), cf. PID 1.443;
in Zos. 1.68 (R. Lit.
p.219) Ἄιγυος has been
read Λίγυος (Lech) or
Νίγρος (Neckar)

Licus fl. C 3 p.740; cf.
Ambi-lici, Vinde-lici?

Ligano (H-S p.195) itin.

Λίμιος ἄλσος Ptol. 270.9

uicani capite limitis 6764
(cf. for caput limitis
CIL 5.2546), limitis
Germaniae 6763. See C
p.234

Linac(?) Rav.

Lind(ensis) regio H-M 234,
F.98, AE 1927.6; 1929.
12

L(inenses) [Brittones] C
p.264, 265 but now
taken as l(unenses) q.v.
infr. (Stein Beamten
p.252); Leyn (1251)

Local and Ethnic Names

Λιριμηρίς Ptol. 265.9

Littamo IA

Λοκόριτον Ptol. 2.11.14,
   Lohr

Logana, Logna i.q. Lau-
   gona

Loncio IA

⟨?Λογγίωνες R. Lit. 219
   n., i.q. Lugii?⟩

Lopodunum, -ensis inscc.,
   6421, cf. C pp.225,
   229-31; Lupodunum
   Auson.; Lobodone in
   8th cent., then Lobo-
   den-gau, now Lodenburg,
   the ciuitas Vlpia
   S(ueborum) N(icretum),
   v. Nicretes below

Losodica TP

Los-, Lousonna v. Leus-

[Lotodos itin.]

Λουγίδουνον Ptol. 270.7;
   AcS 2.306

[Lugii Tac. G 43.3]

L[(Brittones) 12500
   (L[unenses Stein Beam-
   ten p.252)

ad Lunam TP (R. Lit. p.394);
   Dina fl. Rav. 4.17, 4.
   13 is perhaps for Lina
   (Byvanck 1, p.578-9),
   Leine, Lone(?), C p.215;
   Λοῦνα ὕλη Ptol. 2.11.3
   (and 11); C p.265 ad
   Lunam TP, not Leyn, Lein,
   but Lone fl.

Lunares[6422 (cf. C p.216?)

Lunenses CIL 13 vi, 1933,
   p.123

Λούπφουρδον Ptol. 270.4

Λουπίας , Lupia fl. Str.
   Vell., Mela, Tac.,
   now Lippe; Lippa Rav.,
   cf. C p.406

Magia TP, cf. Maiensis 5.
   5090? Now Maienfeld

[Maezii 9.2546, Maesaeus
   Fiebiger-Schmidt 13,
   Maezeius dipl. 14]

[mons Mal(s)cus(?) C
   p.234; Malchen, Mal-
   schen]

[Maluensis col. dipl.
   144; cf. Maluesates
   AE 1948.242; P-W 14.
   927]

[Manimi Tac. G 43.3]

Μαραμανός see 240 above;
   R. Lit. 13.87

silua Marciana itin.,
   Ammian. (-ae); Murg.
   Cf. C p.63; from marca
   "boundary" (gloss 220)
   so Marco-manni, Thur-
   nina marca (C p.279)

Marcomanni BG 1.51; Mon.
   Anc.; cf. Zdeutsch.
   Alt. 77, 1940, 27-8;
   C pp.65

Μαριανίς Ptol. 266.10

Local and Ethnic Names

Μαρόβουδον Ptol. 273.6

Marsi Tac. G 2; Μαρσικός Ed. Diocl. 4.9

Marsigni Tac. G 43

Μαρουίγγοι Ptol. 2.11.11

Martenses (milites) CIL 13 vi, 1933, p.137

Masciacum IA, Matzen

Matisonenses 11749, R.2181; cf. Metter fl.

Mattiaci 11803, 11804; Plin., Tac., ND. Cf. C p.469; Mattiaci Gallicani ND, cf. 5.8737, 8739, 8744, 8751. ciuitas Mattiacorum 7061-62, 7266, 7271, 7281, 7587; Aquae Mattiacorum (Wiesbaden) 9124, inscc. C pp.197, 407, 469, fontes calidi Pl. 31.20 (cf. Mart., Amm.), uicani Aquenses 7566a; Mattiaci Seniores or Senii 11032 (cf. gallisenae gloss 178; Senii divine name); Mattiaci (Gordiani) 7205; the Mattiac[or]um castellum (cf. C pp.298, 406, 407 n.3) num., 6740a, 7317 (k-), 7250, 7271, 7281 is now Castél, Kassél (distinguish other places of the same name, e.g. in Belgica), the birthplace of the emperor Vlpianus; Mattium Tac. A 1.56; ?Mattiatici Cod. Th. 10.19.6; cf. R. Lit. 319 n.1; Matiaci

R.1788, Matiorum 7250, Nattiaci 11032, R.1937; Mattius, Matius terr. sig., AcS 2.477; Anderson's Tac. G pp.146-47; Riese p.246; Ματτιακόν Ptol., uicus uetus Castellum Mattiac[or]um R.2220; AE 1910.59, REA 12, 1910, 68; cf. AcS 1.1376, 29-32

[Mattzara (-i) Scyth. or Armen., H-S 49; 3. 5234]

[Mauri Cattarenses, v. Cattharenses]

?Mediae itin.

Mediana TP, said to be Gnotzheim

Μεδιολάνιον (Germ.) Ptol. 275.6

Μέδουλλον Ptol. 2.12.4, now Muln (?), cf. PID 1.451

Melenuensium numeri see 7321, cf. 8.9060 (Melenuenses); see 234, and cf. personal name Melonius 244, gloss 178 and Melonii below; Maluensis above

Μηλίβοκον ὄρος Ptol. 2.11. 5, cf. Catthi Melibodi C p.243

Μηλόκαβος Ptol. 2.11.14; cf. C pp.407, 426; AcS 2.541

Μελιόδουνον Ptol. 273.9

Local and Ethnic Names

Melitomoge(n)sis (v.l.
Vedito-) Ed. Diocl.
19.37

uicus nouus Meloniorum
7270; cf. pers. names
and Melenuenses above;
uicus nouus 234

[Menneiana IA]

Μηνόσγαδα Ptol. 273.4
i.q. Μοινοσταδα fl.
AcS 2.548

[?Meromenni App. Illyr.
16]

Μερ[ρ]ούσιον Ptol. 270.1

[Metlenses AE 1948.242;
cf. Metlosedum 179
above]

Metubarbis insula (in
Sauo) Plin. 3.148

[Micienses(?) AE 1944.74;
-censes 3.7852]

uicani Min(n)odunenses
5042-43, Min(n)odunum
itinn., Moudon; C
pp.7, 15; cf. PhW 59,
1939, 1190; ZtSchw.
Arch. u. Kunstgesch.
1, 1939, 15-20

Moenus fl. Pl., Tac., -is
Mela; 7070(?), cf. C
pp.5, 212, 234, 262,
421; Main; Pokorny
Urg. 73

Mogetiana (Pann.) 3.10993,
11043, 10900, IA; cf.
C p.297 (5.5747)

Moguntiacum see 234 above

[Montani dipl., Nessel-
hauf Index p.183]

?Μουγίλωναι Str. 7.1.3,
290C

Μουνίτιον Ptol. 267.6

Murga v. Marciana; cf.
H-M p.240 Murg (C
p.162)

uikani Murrenses 6454,
Murrenses (Brittones)
6471; cf. C p.238
(item xcviii, cf.
lxxxix), *Murra fl.
(ib. p.242) now Murr
(cf. Murrhardt) being
inferred; Murrenses
CIL 13 vi, 1933, p.123;
cf. C p.270 (tegulae)
Brit[M[; or Marbach-
Benningen? See Britt-
tones above

[Mursa (Pannonia) R. Lit.
9.85; Aelia Mursa
(Pann. Inf.) dipl. 151]

numeri N[7439, 7441

Nablis fl. Ven. Fort.,
perhaps Naab (cf. AcS
2.671)

Nagalta Nagold AcS 2.672

Naharuali Tac. G 43 (-os
n. pl., cf. ARW 36,
1939, 398-405; cf. APh
14, 1939 [1941], 359;
Idg. Jahrb. 26.132
Naruali AcS 2.689

Local and Ethnic Names

[Nantuates see 15 above;
   semi-German, Arntz
   Hdb. Runenkunde 1944,
   61-64]

Ναραβών fl. Ptol. 252.1

[Nardina ZfCPh 20, 1933-35,
   396]

[Naristi Tac. G 42.1]

Nattiaci v. Mattiaci

Naua fl. Tac., Auson.,
   now Nahe (near Bingen)

[Nauata (Pannonia) ND
   Occ.]

Nauoa TP

[Nauportus Pann. Sup.]

[Neditanus dipl. 11]

Nedienses (-ss-) 6388,
   6389; Niedenstein, but
   cf. Nid- below

Nemanin[genses] 6629, 6642;
   on exploratores Neman-
   ingenses AE 1910 p.339

Νερτερεονοί Ptol. 2.11.11

Nemauia IA

Neuiodunum (Latobicorum)
   3.3919, 3921, 11322

Nicer (-g-) fl. Auson.,
   Sid. Apoll., Symm.,
   paneg., Neckar (-au,
   -burken); as pers.
   name 3.11582, 12.5008;
   cf. C pp.197, 231, 234,

237; hence Nicer: cf.
   fluuius...Nigra dea
   FHRC 205.25(?) sc. dubh
   bandea; cf. Nigropullo
   221

Nicretes (Suebi) 6404;
   ciuitas Vlpia Suebor-
   um Nicretum 6417, cf.
   6420, 6420a, 9099;
   Holder would add here
   also the Ἰνκριονες
   (leg. Νικ -) of Ptol.
   2.11.6

Nictrienses Nom. Prov.,
   cf. Nictrenses AcS 2.
   746

Nida fl., 7263-64, cf.
   9123, Rav. (both Nied
   and Nidda, cf. also
   Nidder); hence

Nidenses, viz. (uic)us
   Nidensis 11944, R.2253;
   cf. 7441 add., at Tre-
   bur, REA 15, 1913, 78,
   455, cf. Nedienses
   above

Νομιστήριον Ptol. 273.8

⟨Noreia BG 1.5⟩

[Norici, -um cl., so far
   as Keltic? Νωρικὸν
   πόλις Procop. Goth. 3.
   33.10; ciuitas Noricum
   Geogr. Lat. Min. ed.
   Riese p.121]

[Νο(ϝ)κρος fl. Str. 7.5.
   2, 314C]

?Noua (-ia?) 11.6053 (R.
   141, cf. R. Lit. p.178

Local and Ethnic Names

with n.l); TP, IA;
Nouenses (see P-W, s.v.
Nouae)

Nouae C 3 p.735

Nouarienses Nom. Prov. 14

Nouiodunum -ensis Nyon;
AE 1945.68

Nouus Vicus 7335-36, cf.
C p.426 (Heddernheim;
cf. p.303 Mainz, 407
Cassel), see Melonii
above

[Nurritani dipl. 56]

Ocra mons Str., Ptol.,
cf. Ocra Pl. 3.131(?);
see P-W s.v.

[Οἴσκος Ptol. (Dacia), 3.
14416 Oescenses; cf.
Viuisci below]

Ὄλβια (Alps) Poseidonius
ap. Athen. 6.23, 233D-
E

Opia TP, perhaps Bopfin-
gen?

Orcynia BG 6.24.2, v.
Herc-

Ὀσανία Ptol. 274.4 (v.l.
Ἄσανκα)

[Osi Tac. G 28.3; 43.1]

⟨Osiniates Sinj AE 1941.
52⟩

Ottonis siluae, iugum C
p.215

⟨Ouilaua itinn., Wels⟩

Palas Amm. 18.2.15, cf.
Pfahl-bach A.D. 796
(C p.269-270); and
perhaps pers. name
Palanto 7039, if not
dea Pallas 6746; Amm.
l.c. gives Capellatii
as another name for the
same place; cf. Pfalz

[Pannonius 7046, 7247;
dipl. 17, 20, 69; C
p.299]

Παριέννα Ptol. 274.1;
for the ending cf.
Clarenna

Πάρισος fl. Str. 7.5.2,
314C?

⟨Parmaecampi Ptol. 265.4⟩

?Parrodunum ND (for Car-
rodunum?)

Partanum TP, IA, now Par-
tenkirchen; v.l. Tar-
teno

Patrensibus V. p.219

[Pautalia cf. AE 1940.165]

[Pelso lacus Pl., Aurel.
Vict., Iordan., Rav.]

Petinesca (-enisc-) itinn.,
cf. C pp.7, 31

Local and Ethnic Names

⟨Peuce ins., at mouth of
Danube, v. AcS s.v.,
Anderson on Tac. G
p.218; Peucennus CIL
6.4344, Peucini Tac.
G 46.1, Pl. 4.98-101⟩

Φαινιάνα Ptol. 2.12.3,
Pin(i)ana C 3 p.721
(ND)

Piri (Pirus?) mons Amm.
28.2.5, cf. C pp.224-
25, Pirum itin. Burd.
560.4

[Pirustae (Dacia) e.g. C
3 p.937]

[Poeninus, -a]

[Poetouio dipl. 142, 155,
now Pettau; -ionensis;
Παταβίων (or cf.
Bataui, Pa-?) Priscus
FHG 4 p.84; R.558; cf.
Pult-?]

Ποίναι Ptol. 2.12.1, cf.
3.1.1

Pomona TP

[?Pone (Pannonia) ND Occ.]

?Ponione TP

Pons Aeni itinn., ND; cf.
V. p.219 (not Innsbruck
but Rosenheim)

[Porolissium dipl. 132,
cf. AE 1945.50,54]

?Portic[6457, cf.
Por[t]za Rav. 4.26,
Portis[R.1793, CIL

13 vi, 1933, p.137, a
Port[N.263, Pforz-
heim; cf. C p.161. On
N.263 v. also Goessler
in Jacobi Festschrift
(Saalburg Jahrb. 9,
1939, 23-33; AE 1939.
293) port[a Hercynia(?)

Προδεντία Ptol. 274.13

[Pultouia itinn. (an
Poet-?)]

[Ποσηνοί Appian Illyr. 21]

⟨Quadi Tac. G 42.1; inscc.⟩

Quintanesis 7749; Quint(i)-
ana itinn., ND, Eugipp.;
Künzing

Ῥακάτριαι Ptol. 265.12,
i.q. Ῥακάται Ptol.
ib.(?)

Radasponensis (-is-) 9th
and 10th cent., Ratis-
bon (or Regensburg, v.
Castra Regina); -bona
AcS 2.1070

Raetinium 7023

Raitia CIL 5.3936; Raeti
dipl. (Nesselhauf pp.
183-84); Serv. A 1.243
makes both Raeti and
Vindelici "Liburnians."
Raetus (-i, -ia) cl.,
inscc. (6240; 5382,
6806, 6821, 7048),
Raiti 7027; Raetica

Local and Ethnic Names

tellus 5251; cf. 7444-
45, 7452, 7457, 7460,
7462, 7465-68, 7470,
7584; Raeticus 3.5924
(11911, cf. 12011.13),
Raet[3.11997;
p(rouincia) R(aetia)
3.5785, 5862; cf. C
pp.469 (tegulae) 261,
265; 7.1002 (R.1880),
6.2806 (R.186, Acta
Fr. Aru.), 3.1017
(R.252); Cuny REA 20,
1918, 164-68

Raetobarii NDOr. 5.10

[Ragundone -and-, -ind-(?)
itinn.; cf. p.2328.47]

Ῥαιδίκανος Ed. Diocl. 19.
53?

[Ramista It. Burg.]

Rapae TP

Ratiaria (Rait-) Ptol.,
itinn., 3.6294, 6295,
7429, dipl. 120

Rausa confinitio ZONF 15,
1939, 86-96

Ῥεδινγουίνον Ptol. 273.7;
i.q. Ῥεδιντούινον ? Cf.
AcS 2.1102,4

Reginum, Castra Regina TP,
IA, ND, now Regensburg
(cf. Radasponensis);
in V. 361, 3.14370,10
(cf. REA 18, 1916, 287)
k R is better inter-
preted as k(anabarum)
R(eginensium) than as
k(astrorum) R(eginorum);
C p.197. On the etym.

(Germ. *regn) Beitr.
z. Namenforschung 1,
1949, 55

Reg(a)nus fl. Rav., ASS,
now Regen(s-burg)

Regus 7048

R(h)enus fl. cl., inscc.;
Kretschmer Glotta 24,
1935, 2 on Rēnos
"stream" (Keltic?),
cf. Lat. riuos? Rhein,
Rheineck

?Rensibus TP (Per-, Pr-,
Pons R-?), but see
Patrensibus

Retico mons Mela 3.3.30

[Ῥιουσιαουά Ptol. 2.11.
15; cf. Bittel p.112]

Rizinis Rav. 4.26

R[h]odanus cl.

[Ῥιγινοκάστελλον Procop.]

[Risinitanus dipl. 14]

Robur (Basilia) see 234

Rota (Hr-, Chr-) fl., 9th
cent., cf. Förstemann
2.613

Rotunuilla A.D. 792 (cf.
C p.213), Rottweil

Ῥουκάντιοι Str., Rucin-
ates 5.1817,11; Runi-
cates PID 1.441; Runi-
cas N.114a

Rugium Rav. 4.26, p.231.
16; cf. Ptol. 267.9

Local and Ethnic Names

Rugusci (-ig-) Ptol., cf. 5.7817,15

Runicas see Ruc-

Rut[3.5936 (V. 350)

?Rut[ciuis V. 350

ciuitas S T 6482, R.2607-08; variously interpreted, v. C p.251; but the correct reading may be St[, cf. Stu[6592

?S[ ]llatinian[i] (riui) 6405

[Saeuates 5.1838]

Σάλᾰς fl., Str. 6.1.3, 291C; cf. Tac. A 13. 57 (flumen gignendo sali fecundum; but this is "inter Hermunudros Chattosque") Sale fl., or Saale, Saalburg? C p.297

Saldis TP, Rav., Ptol.; cf. perhaps domo Saldas 6620 (unless this is in Africa)

[ad Salices 1 Aug. (Moesia Inf.), cf. Saligniana (mala) Ed. Diocl.?]

[Salle H-S p.195, itin.]

Saloatum 3.11846, V.485

Salodurum IA, TP, Ptol., Eucherius; uicus Salod[5170, Salodur[

3.6331, R.2067; Solothurn or Soleure; ZONF 16, 1940, 58-73; Vox Rom. 5, 1940, 310

Saloissa Fredeg. (R. Lit. p.410), Sette (?)

[Salonitanus dipl. 11]

[Salsouia IA]

Samulocenis v. Sumelocenna

Sanctio (for Cassangita?)

[Sappaeus dipl. 12; cf. Pl. 4.11.40]

[Sapuates 3.9864a, cf. Sapua itinn.]

[Σερδική, Serdica v. R. Lit. p.244]

[Sarmaticus, Sarmatae C p.299, cf. Sarmasia 212]

[Sarmizegetusa C 3 p.711]

Sarunetes Pl. 3.135, PID 1.450; cf. Σαρούηνα (Cappadocia) Ptol.(?)

[Sauaria (-b-) in Pannonia, cl., itinn., inscc., AcS 1.1385-86; Sauariensis dipl. 18]

[Saua, Sauaria 6825, 6829, 6832, 6850]

[Sauia, -iensis (Pannonia) Laterc. Polem. Silv. 5. 12]

[Sauos, -us, Saus fl. Str.,

Local and Ethnic Names

Plin., inscc.; also as
divine name]

uicani Sc[3.5898 p.723
(Nassenfels) cf. Scar-
bia?

⟨Saxones C p.299; Ptol.⟩

Scarbia TP, cf. Scarbantia
[H-S 450] (Pannonia)
Pl., Ptol., itinn.?

[Scirto dipl. 100]

[Scordisci cl., inscc.,
Γαλάται according to
Strabo 7.2.2,293C;
scordiscus Ed. Diocl.
10.2 "saddle" REA 8,
1906, 263-4]

?Scubuli see 234

[Scupinia (Moes. Sup.)
6823]

Σκοῦργον Ptol. 267.10

Scutt[arenses] uikani 3.
5898, Schutter fl.,
Scu[3 p.1050

Sebatum IA

?Σεγαστική Str. 7.5.2,
p.314C (i.q. Σισκία ?)

Σεγοδοῦνον Ptol. 2.11.14
(Burg-Sinn)

Seiopenses 6600, 6605, 11.
3104; C p.280-81; P-W
s.v. Seiopa; R. Lit. 8.
4,28 ff.

[?castra Selgi, an old
reading in 6658 (cf.

C p.294 n.1) is dub-
ious (v. castra E...
id[above), despite
modern local names
(Zell-hausen, -kirche;
Seligenstadt) or the
Σελγοούαι of Ptol.
(Britain)]

⟨Σήμανος ὕλη Ptol. 2.11.
5⟩

Semnones Mon. Anc. 26.17;
Tac. G 39.1; Vell.
Paterc.

[Senonius 6484]

Senot[enses] uicani 6329,
cf. Seno[243 below

Septemiacum C 3 p.739,
V. p.223, Sechtenhausen

[Serretes Pl. 3.147]

Seruitium itin., H-S p.275

Σετουία Ptol. 274.2

Σετουάκωτον Ptol. 275.1

[Seuaces, Σεούακες Ptol.
2.13.2]

?Σιβινοί Str. 7.1.3,209C

[?Sicilia Lampr. Alex.
Sev. 59.6]

Σίδονες Ptol. 263.3

Σινγόνη Ptol. 275.11

[Silacenae IA cf. Silau-
cienses 8593, R.1672]

?Sinic[6243, C p.231 n.1

Local and Ethnic Names

[Sintia Liv. 26.25.3]

[Sirmion Pann. Inf., -um
itin.; dipl. 18, 156]

[Siscia Str., Plin.,
itinn., inscc., num.,
dipl. 18, Dessau 9132;
cf. Siscii Procop., v.
AcS 2.1584-87, Sis-
ciani 3.3977 (*sesquos
"dry"?), now Sisak]

Solicinium (v.l. Solicom-
num) Amm. 27.10.8, 30.
7.7; cf. Sulihgeiuua,
now Sülichgau; gloss
suliga "uolutabrum"
240 (C p.215); Oxé
Festschrift 1938, 175;
C p.230; cf. insc.
Sol[AE 1926.25 unless
that belongs in 212
above

Solist[Rav. 4.26

[Sopianae Pann. Inf.]

?Sonsi (i.e. Osi?) Byv.
2.592

Soruiodurum TP; Straubing

[?Spiurus dipl. 3]

[Splonistae AE 1948.242]

Stanacum IA

?Starb[3.5956

Στράγόνα Ptol. 270.8 (-τ-)

exploratores Stu[(or S[
Tu[?) 6592, cf. C p.279
n.5

Στρεουιντία Ptol. 273.11

Suanetes PID 1.450; cf.
Cosuanetes above?

Sublauio itinn.

Submunturium ND, cf. Summ-

Σούδετα (-η-) ὄρη Ptol.
2.11.5; Sudeten. Cf.
Σουσούδανα Ptol. 270.5?

Suebi BG 1.51, Mon. Anc.;
Suebicus e.g. R.55,
?Suefia 5.374, R.2610;
-us R.1311, Sueua 12.
480, Suaui Iord. (R.
Lit. 12.70), Suebi Pl.
4.81; Sueui (Sua-) Rav.
4.24, 4.26 cf. 221
above

Suebi Nicretes 6404; ciu-
itas Vlpia Sueborum
Nicretorum 6417, cf.
6420-20a, C pp.197,
229-231 (Suebus [Per-
inthus]); in 6243 the
reading is doubtful
(Sinic[or S[ueb]
Nic[?); S N 6399,
9099, 12.2604

?Suebi T[C p.251, 264,
à propos of 6482; how-
ever, for its S T,
there have been proposed
saltus translimitanus
i.e. χώρα ὑπερλιμιτάνη ,
Seiopenses, Suebi, Tou-
toni, to which might be
added Tubantes, Turninu
(cf. C p.279 n.5),Τουρ-
ωνοί (ibid.), Tu[6592,
Tu[ ]tensis 7750

Local and Ethnic Names

?Suesia (palus) Mela 3.3.
29

Sumelocenna, -ensis, Σομελο-
κεννήσια (R.409) inscc.,
itinn., cf. C pp.208-
215; 2506, 6358, 6365,
6384, 6669, 9084,
11726-27; cf. AcS 2.
1666-67, and (for Nemeto-
Nitio- Satio-, Seno-
cenna) ib. 1.981; TP
has Samul- for Sumel-;
cf. perhaps modern Sül-
chen, Sulicha in 11th
cent., Germ. sulaga
(sol-)? See also Nor-
den Altgermanien p.305;
WuS 11, 1928, 136; cf.
Oxé Festschrift 1938,
175; P-W s.v.; ZfCPh
13, 1919, 93-100, 368;
PID 1.451; W-H 1.865
(s.v. feruo). For the
formation of Penne-,
Sege-locus, and Κενεννον
Clarenna above; perhaps
translated in the next
item; 19 Remark above

Summa Rapida 11537

Summuntorium IA, ND Occ.
(now Schrobenhausen),
see Sub- above

T[6482, v. Suebi

Ta[7301

Talar (Hyrcania), Ταλαβρόκη
Str. 11.508C, v. Ber-
toldi RLR 4, 1928,
236 n.2

Ταρόδουνον Ptol. 2.11.15,

Zarduna, Zarten (C
pp.63, 211)

Tarnaiae itinn.

Taruessedum TP, IA

[murum] Tasg[aetium 5256,
uik[ani] Tasg[aetini
5254-56, Ταξγαίτιον
Ptol. 2.12.2 cf. Tas-
gaetius (pers. name)
BG 5.26,29; Exientia
in the middle ages,
Eschenz; Jahrb. d.
Schw. Ges. fur Urgesch.
31, 1939, 157-160

Taunus mons Mela, Tac.;
Taunenses 6705, 6770,
6985, 7064, 722
7265, 7301, 7335-36,
7352, 7360, 7370,
7386, 7394; cf. Ἀρταυ-
νον above; ZONF 4,
1928, 269-271; 17,
1941, 115; ZfCPh 23,
1943, 399 ("gross")

[Taurisci cl., inscc.,
4401 al., AcS 2.1770;
P-W s.v.]

Taurodunum Greg. Tur.;
chron.

Ταξγαίτιον v. Tasg-

Τένκεροι Ptol., cf. Tenc-
teri (Inf.)

Tenedo TP; cf. gl. AcS 2.
1794,30 (cf. 2)

uicus Tera[7734

Terioli (-a) ND Occ., now
Zirl, PID 1.448

Local and Ethnic Names

[Tertiaci equites Amm. 25. 1.7]

Tessenii (-inos) IA, Diessen?

Τευριοχαῖμαι Ptol. 2.11, 11 cf. Teurius 5. 7850(?)

[Teurisci (Dacia), Ptol., insc.; cf. Τευρίσται Str.]

[Teurnia (Noricum) V.8, 9]

Teutoburgiensis saltus Tac. A 1.60 (for the name cf. Teutoburgion Ptol., itinn., ND)

Τευτονοάρροι (-ουάριοι ?) Ptol. 2.11.9

Tiaus 6985, if for Taunensis (?)

[Thedoricopolis Rav. 4. 26]

[?Tiguntia Eugipp. vit. Seuerini 3.4]

Tigurini BG 1.12.4-7 (-us pagus), pag(i) Tigor(ini) genio 5076; cf. modern local names Tegernau, Tegernsee, Tegernbach, and the gloss tigernos 207. Oros. 5.16.13, (FHRC 125.33), Τιγοῦ-ρινοι (-ην-) Str. 7.2. 2, 293C; Τιγούριοι Appian (R. Lit. 1.20); Catutigernus (Brit. pers. name); cf. ASA 21, 1919, 15-68; AE

1922.6; if *teg- cf. attegia, moritex(?)

[Tilurion itinn.]

[Τιμένα Procop. de aedif. 4.6]

Tinnetio IA, Tinzen

[Toleses 3.10982]

Toringia Ven. Fort. 6.1. 75, Th- Greg. Tur., Turringia Rav.

Τωυγένοι Str. 4.1.8, 183C, 7.2.2, 293C; but H-M pp.356-7 identify them with the Toutoni (taking γ as a miswriting of τ)

Toutoni 6610; this inscription, variously interpreted (see most recently Norden Alt-Germanien 191 ff.), reads inter Toutonos C A H F(inis?); cf. C p.279; and see T[above, and Tu[, Τουρωνοί below; for Teutoni (-es) v. AcS 2.1808-1820, 1899. On Norden see Kahrstedt BJ 139, 1934, 46-49. Cf. Gutenbrunner Hdb. Runenkunde 1944, 61-64; Kretschmer KZ 69, 1948, 12; on 6610 see further F. Quilling Mannus 6, 1914, 334 (RC 42, 1925, 266); Gutenbrunner Frühzeit 1939, 116 (i[ussu]... at the end); Syme's review of Norden, JRS 26, 1936, 75; cf. RA 8, 1936, 302; F. Miltner Klio 33, 1940-41, 229 n.1

Local and Ethnic Names

(cf. AE 1945, p.162)
who takes Toutoni as
a Keltic ethnicon, but
Cimbrius, Cimbrianus
as Germanic divine
names. R. Egger (Ger-
manenstein) in Mélanges
Kuszinski (APh 14, 1939
[1941], 322); W. Fin-
sterwalder is reported
to have published a
new insc. inter Teu-
tonos F.u.F. 1942, 324-
5 (ib. 1942-44, 329).
I conjecture inter
Toutonos Cimbros Ab-
nobam Heluetios fines

[Tragisa fl. Orelli 1331
(if genuine), in the
10th cent. Treisima,
now Traisen; for the
name compare also mod.
Dreisam (C p.63), re-
corded as Dreisima (9th
cent.), and Tragisamo
TP (Zeuss) now Trais-
mauer, gloss tragula
PID 2.199(?), uertra-
gos 178 above; but not
Traiectum 221]

?Trernahensis 3.2715

[Tricornium dipl. 67]

[Trimontium dipl. 139]

Triputienses (Brittones)
6502, 6511, 6514,
6517-19, 6599, 6606,
cf. C pp.238, 280-1,
258 n.1. Many sugges-
tions are offered:
(1) cf. Tripetia, Tre-
pitia 221, and gloss
tripetia 158, cf. 178

petia; (2) Tripontium
IA (in Britain); (3)
is -put- for -qu(e)t-
cf. Triquetra, trique-
trus, -r- being lost
by dissimilation(?);
(4) the locality is
identified with Amor-
bach, quasi "Dreiborn"
(cf. W. pydaw); (5) the
older form of Trennfort
(6599), which is Tribun-
furt, Tribenford; (6)
but Trebur stands for
Tubri-, Dubri (q.v.,
above), and Trienz is
still further off; cf.
modern Drüpt?

[Troi[smi, -smenses?]
V.516 (Moesia)]

Tu[6592 v. Suebi (above);
cf. Stu[and T[(6482,
above; add also Tu...
tensis 7750. Again the
possibilities are num-
erous: (1) Tubantes
see 221; Tac. A 1.51,
Ptol.; (2) Tulingi see
infr., or Turicum, sta-
tio Turicensis below, or
Toutoni above; (3)Τουρω-
νοί see below with Tur-
ninu; (4) Tungri 221,
Tungrecani below; (5)
Tulbiacum, Tolb- 221

Tu[ ]tensis 7750

⟨Tubantes Tac. see 221⟩

Tubri v. Dubri

[Τουλκοβουργο(ς), - ιον
Procop., de aedif. 4.4;
Τουλισουργιον AcS]

Tulingi BG 1.5.4, cf. R.
Lit. pp.11, 12; and
Τουλισούργιον Ptol. 2.
11.13 (vv. 11. -βούργιον
-φούρδιον , cf. Kluge
Urg. ed. 3, pp.32-33)
and the next item

[Τοῦλλον Str. 4.6.9,207C,
with which compare
Tullum (212), Tullia-
sses PID 1.448, Tuledo
ib. 263]

[Tungrecani 5190, cf. 3.
12030,5; Amm. 26.6.12,
ND Occ.]

Turego, Turicum implied
by (statio) Turicen(sis)
5244, cf. C p.7, now
Zürich; Tyrici Cod.
Theod. 1.29.2 (A.D.
365), Durgaugensis Par-
dessus Dipl. 2.391
(A.D. 744) Ziurichi
Rav., Turico (castro)
MGSS Merov. 3 p.629.1,
Turigoberga Rav. 4.26

Τουρωνοί Ptol. 2.11.11,
see C p.279 n.5 (on
6610), commonly changed
to Τουτονοί but if gen-
uine cf. Turninu (A.D.
795), which may mean
that the Turones of
Aquit. had originally
lived here, like the
Bituriges Viuisci.
Yet we have Turnin(a)
marca (C ibid.), com-
pared with mod. Wall-
dürn; and domo Turonus
13.8593, R.1672 is Tyre
(Sdebdas)

Turninu (Wall-dürn) see
the preceding item

Turum C 3 p.724 (IA)

Οὐαγρίωνες Ptol. 2.16.6

Valdensis pagus Pard.
Dipl. 1.70 (A.D. 523)

Vallatum ND Occ., at Cas-
tra Regina

Vallenses 6361, see 15
above

[Vandali, -ilii, -uli
Tac., Oros., Vopisc.]

Vannianum regnum Pl. 4.
81, see Vannius 244
below

Varciani (F.365) cl.,
inscc. 7707, 7804,
8188, 6.3257, 3.9796;
Varcianus dipl. 4, cf.
Pl. 3.148; P-W 4.347;
Stein, Beamten p.222;
Varciani Dessau 9132,
Varcia 234 above

Varistae Capit. vit. Ant.
20.1

†Vapii (corrupt) TP

[Vaticanus 7281]

Vburzis Rav. 4.26

[Vcenni Pl. 3.137]

Οὐέβιον Ptol. 275.2

Veditomagensis Ed. Diocl. 19.37 (p.2209); an Melitomagensis?

Veldidena Wilten, PID 1. 443

Vemania itinn., ND, PID 1.450

Venaxamodurum ND Occ., cf. Venixama, -sama 3.3797, 3820, 3825 and Venixxamus pers. name 156 above

Οὐένδων Str. 7.5.4,315C (Auendo?)

Venetus lacus see Brigantinus and PID 1.447

[Venethi Tac. G 46.1]

Οὐέννωνες Str. 4.6.6, 204C; 8,206C

Vennonetes Pl. 3.135; CIL 5.7817,4; Ptol. 2.12.2 (Οὐέννοντες), cf. PID 1.446-47

Venostes 5253, cf. Pl. 3. 137, CIL 5.7817,3, Vintschgau

pagus Verbigenus (in Belgica, but of Helvetian origin) BG 1.27.4; in view of Vobergensis 6689 (cf. C n. to 5171) some would emend BG to agree; but see REA 38, 1936, 345

Vermegaton Rav. 4.26 (Bremgarten?)

Vet[ciues 3.5889, cf. p.1050

Vetoniana TP

Viaca TP

Οὐιαδούας Ptol. 2.11.2; Ipada; see ZONF 13, 1938, 141-50

Οὐιάνα Ptol. 2.12.3; cf. Vienna

Wibili chron. Fred., cf. C p.18, Wiflis

Οὔικος Ptol. 2.12.2, Igis (?); but see Viuiscus, and PID 1.453

Victohali Amm. 17.12.19, Victoali Eutrop., Victouali V. Capit. M. Ant. 14.1

[Vien(n)a, Vian(n)a, 5011, 5214, 5239, 6969, 6871-73, 6909, 6912, 6944, 6969, 6972; 11859 (unless personal name); Vienne, 80 above]

Wimpina 9th cent., now Wimpfen; cf. uimpa, Vimpuro; or Vindobona?

Vindelici, -ia cl., inscc. (6821, 7048, 7331), Vindol[6242. Vindolici 9.3044, -al- R.407. Add 6495, 7410-11, 7418-19, 11947, 3.5780, 5969. Vendelici N.114, Vindelici dipl. 20, 36,

46, 62-3, 80, 90, 107;
Vindelici N.114a. In
3.5905 perhaps c(o)h
R(aet) V(i)nd, but
the text Chrun is cap-
able of other inter-
pretations, cf. Run-
icas 237 above(?);
for tegulae cf. C
p.469; Augusta Vindel-
icum (or -orum), now
Augsburg; Augusta Vin-
delicenss C 3 p.711;
Vindelicia Ptol., cf.
inscc. 5.3936, 9.4964
al.; Vindelici CIL 13
vi, 1933, p.115

[Vindenae itinn., cf.
Vindinates Pl. 3.114
(Umbria)]

Vindobona inscc., itinn.
Vienna

Vindonii Campi Paneg.
Constant. 4; R. Lit.
229

Vindonissa Tac., num.
Merov., itinn.; uicani
Vindonissenses 5194-
95, -ense NG, cf. C
pp.7, 211; now Windisch
H-M p.332, no.398e (but
cf. p.378) interpret
12306 as s(ub) c(ura)
[or c(astris)] Vi[ndon-
issensibus], Vindoin-
issa (pers. name) 4665,
Vindoinsa F.122 (H-M
320), Vindonissenses
13 vi, 1933, p.50

[Vipitenum itinn. Wipp-
thal]

Virdo fl. Ven. Fort. now
Wertach

?Virolouicium 11970a, R.
3532 (Virolo pers.
name, n. sg., uictum).
But cf. R.2373, (13.
7845) uici V[(at
Wenau)

Viromagus, Vromagus (Br-)
itinn. C pp.7, 15;
Oron(?) or Broye fl.;
for Oron see de Saus-
ure Anz. f. Schw.
Gesch. 51, 1920, 1-11

Οὐιρίτιον   Ptol. 267.8

[Virunon (Noricum) 7287]

Οὐισβούργιοι   Ptol. 263.4

Οὐίσποι Ptol. 2.11.6, cf.
C p.197; R. Lit. 13.87

[Visurgis fl. cl. Weser;
cf. C p.406]

Vitudurum IA, murus Vitu-
durensis 5249, now
Winterthur; cf. C p.6,
3 p.707; REA 19, 1917,
293

Viuisci (originally Hel-
vetians) Str. 42.1,
190C; cf. Viuiscus
itinn., Ptol.(?); now
Vevey

⟨Vlmo It. Burd. 566.5, C
3 p.720⟩

uicus V(lpius) V[6433
(cf. 7845; ciuitas
Vlpia Sueborum Nicre-
tum above; Vispi; or
Volouicus pers. name
3.5552); cf. C p.422;
Vlpia (Heddernheim) C
p.426

Local and Ethnic Names

Vndius 3.3224

Vnione (i.q. Musaro) Rav.
4.16

Vobergensis 6689, cf.
Verbigenus

Vocetius mons Tac. H 1.
68; REA 15, 1939, 281;
cf. Vogesus?

Volcae (Tectosages) in
the Danube valley,
earlier on the Rhine,
cf. BG 6.24.1-2; cf.
OHG Walha

[Voturi Pl. 5.146]

Vrba fl. IA, NG, Fredeg.,
Orbe; REA 28, 1936,
345

ciues Vro[(Brittones)
Haug-Sixt 44, R.2610a

Vromagus (Bro-) v. Viro-

Vrpanus fl. Pl. 3.148

Vrusa TP

[Vrsarienses milites ND
Occ. (Gantia), cf. 13
vi, 1933, p.124; from
Vrsaria ins. (Dalmatia);
Stein Beamten p.273;
CIL 13 i (1), p.512
and 13.3492]

?Οὔσινοι Ptol., R. Lit.
4.68

[Vsipi, -etes C p.469 BG
4.1.1; Tac. A 1.51]

Wrzacha Rav. 4.26, now
Zurzach(?)

?Ζοῦμοι Str. 7.1.3, 290C

See also J. Striedinger "Wie alt is der Baiern-
Name?" Z. f. bayer. Landesgesch. 10, 1937, 1-11; A.
Duraffour "Notes linguistiques," Rev. de geogr. Alpine
17, 1929, 793-98; Wilhelm Hübner "Die Bedeutung der
Ortsnamen fur die Erkenntnis alter Sprach- u. Siedelungs-
grenzen in den Westschweiz," Vox Rom. 1, 1936, 235-63;
J.U. Hubschmied (on Ogo, Oex, Uechtland) in Zts. f.
deutsche Mundarten 19, 1924, pp.169-198 (cf. REA 26,
1924, 348; 39, 1937, 133-38); id. (on Gaulish names in
-pi, -pā: -kui, -kua) in Gauchat Festschrift 1926, 435-
38 (cf. Idg. Jahrb. 12, 1928, 40-41 [Slotty], Litt.
Zentralbl. 1926, p.1947 [Karg-Gasterstädt], RC 43, 1926,
216 Vendryes]); id. Über Ortsnamen des Amtes Frutigen
1940 (see Jahrb. d. Schw. Gesellsch. für Urgesch. 31,
1939, 162); P. Aebischer in REA 31, 1929, 237-252
("matres" in local names in Latin Switzerland); Charles
de Roche "Les noms de lieu de la Vallée Moutier-Grandval
(Jura Bernois)" ZfRPh Beiheft 4, 1906; there has been

Local and Ethnic Names

much discussion of Vevey: C. Jullian REA 22, 1920, 47
would substitute Viuiscum for biuium in a medieval text,
but thinks uiuiscum means "carrefour," like biuium (cf.
the divine names Biuiae etc.), which is absurd (uiuiscum
"gui," Aebischer Zf.Schw.Gesch. 14, 1934, 307 cf. EC 1,
1936, 178), cf. Jullian REA 15, 1913, 47-50 and D.
Viollier, ib. p.186 (he would bring the Viuisci from the
Garonne to Switzerland, not vice versa); Aebischer l.c.
284-309 (on Chasseron, di Casses)

Chronique de Toponymie (Suisse Romande) REA 38,
1936, 201-215 (by J. Jeanjaquet)

G. Binz Festschrift...Tappolet (Schwabe, Basel
1935), against Hubschmied's theory of late date (and
translation) of Keltic local names (summary in REA 38,
1936, 139 by Cuny)

As for Trebur (trub-, Turb-), this apparently is
for Dubris; yet cf. the gloss (79) trebo cf. Prov.
treva: Latin trabs, Jud Romania 52, 1926, 347; 47, 1929,
493; and Contubrici, Contrubii item 2, Turbellius Note ii
above

On local names of Friulian cf. A. Prati Rev. Ling.
rom. 12, 1936, 43-143

J.U. Hubschmied, "Über Ortsnamen des Silvretta und
Samnaun-gebietes," in Clubführer durch die Bündner Alpen
Bd. 8, Chur 1934, 421-460 (cf. ZfRPh Suppl. 47-55, 1927-
35, item 2239a; Idg. Iahrb. 20, 1934 [1936], 195); "Über
Ortsnamen des Bernina-gebietes," ib. Bd. 5 (Berninagruppe),
Chur 1932, 349-363 (cf. ZfRPh. l.c., item 2239; RC 50,
1933, 245-271), but both these articles are inaccessible
to me; "Über schweizerische Flussnamen," Der kleine Bund
Bern, 29 Nov. 1931, 380-382 (ZfRPh. l.c., item 1865); cf.
Vox Rom. 1, 1936, 88-105; 2, 1937, 24-33 (cf. Idg. Jahrb.
22, 1936 [1938], 112)

K. Bittel Die Kelten in Württemberg, 1934

On Emme (*Ambia), Önz (*Abonetia cf. *abona), Ach-
seten (*asko-: pascua), Tietscheten (*tegia), Gürmschi
(*kormisio- "sorbus," or cf. curmi, ceruesia?), all
highly conjectural, see ZfCPh 22, 1941, 370-71; on Silvretta (Piz) : silver Hubert RC 44, 1927, 78-89 especially
p.81 (cf. Arganthonios SprFK 157, 193); on names in -ingos

Further Modern Names

P. Aebischer Mélanges Gilliard 103-113 (APh 17, 214);
id. Mélanges Duraffour 80-92 (on cambo-, craxantos,
*senouia, uinouia in river-names of the Vaudois); id.
on mediaeval names and ancient routes in Switzerland
Zeitsch. Schw. Gesch. 19, 1939, 155-164 (APh 14, 1939
[1941], 328); M. Galotti Elementi prelatini (viz. Keltic)
nella toponomastica della Val Camonica in Universo 18,
1937, 593-602 (APh 15, 1940-41, 189).

    Aalen, Abbach, Achern, Aising, Aislingen, Aitingen,
Aitrach fl., Altenhofen, Allmendingen, Alpirsbach, Alt-
dorf, Altenbaindt, Altenburg, Amoeneburg, Ammer fl.,
Amorbach, Amsoldingen, Anhausen, Ansbach, Argen fl.,
Arnheiten, Arnsburg, Arzbach, Auerberg

    Baar (P-), Babenwohl, Baccon (cf. REA 18, 1916,
146), Baden (i.e. Aquae, nr. Zürich), Badenweiler,
Bahnbrücken, Baierbrunn, Balg, Baumburg, Baumgarten, Bélon,
Bendorf, Benningen, Bergen, Bergheim, Berkach, ad Bernam
in 11th cent. (Berne), Bernau, Beutelsbach, Biberbach,
Bierstein, Biesenhard, Birkenbuckel, Bischofsheim, Blau
fl., Bleiche, Blochingen, Böckingen, Böhming, Bonfeld,
(Gross-)bottwar, Brachstadt, Brenz fl., Brettach, Bröbin-
gen, Buch, Büchig, Bühl, Bühler fl., Bürg, Bullau, Burg,
Burg-hausen (-heim, -höfe, -mannshofen, -weinting),
Burkwang, Burladingen

    Cannstatt, Carouge (*Quadriuium Genava 18, 1940,
54), Castelfeder, Chieming, Chiemsee, Ciernaz, Craichgau,
Cressier

    Dambach, Daxlanden, Demling, Derching, Dieburg,
Dienbach, Dietfurt, Dietingen, Dillingen, Donaueschingen,
Donnstetten, Dornheim, Dotzheim, Dreisam fl., Druisheim,
Dünhausen, Dünz(e)lau, Dürrmenz, Durlach, Dux

Further Modern Names

Ebnisee, Ebranzhausen (-nts-), Echatz fl., Egau fl.,
Eger fl., Egerndach, Eggenthal, Eggstatt, Egweil, Ehingen,
Eholfing, Eigeltingen, Eining, Eisenbach, Ellmendingen,
Ellmosen, Emerkingen, Em(m)etzheim, Ems, Endorf, Engel-
hartszell, Ennetach, Enz, Erbach, Erding, Erling, Erl-
statt, Erms fl., Erbstetten, Etting, Ettling, Ettlingen,
Eutingen, Eyrs

Faimingen, Falting, Feldkirchen, Fils fl., Finnengen,
Flörsheim, Forchheim, Forsthof, Frauenchiemsee, Frauen-
stein, Freinfeld, Freundpolz, Freutsmoos, Freymühle,
Friedberg, Fridolfing

Gaimersheim (Gei-), Gammelsdorf, Gansheim, Gauting,
Gehaborn, Geiselbrechting, Geisslingen, Gemmingen, Gemür,
(Gross-)Gerau, Gersthofen, Gersprenz fl. (Caspenze in
8th cent., -sa 11th cent.), Gex, St Gilla, Gingen, Glems
fl., Glött, Gmünd, Gnotzheim, Gochsen, Göggingen, Göhren,
Gomadingen, Graben, Grabenstädt, Greinberg (Gran-, Krain-),
Grüningen, Grossaitingen, Grosskrotzenburg, Gundelfingen
(Gr-), Güglingen, Günzelhofen, Gunzenhausen

Halheim, Hammerschmiede, Hammerstein, Hanau, Happing,
Hardt (part of Vosegus), Harlach, Haselbach, Hasse, Hassel-
burg, Haunsheim, Hausen, Heddernheim, Heddesdorf, Heft-
rich, Heidelberg, Heidekringen, Heidenheim, Heidenstock,
Heilbronn, Heiligenberg, Heldenbergen, Hemmingen, Hennen-
weidach, Henningen, Herrenwörth, Hesselbach, Heune-berg
(-säulen, Hain-säulen), Hockenheim, Höchst, Höchstädt,
Höllenbach, Högelwörth, Hofen, Hofheim, Hofolding, Hohe-
wald, Hohengebraching, Holzhausen, Homburg, Huefingen,
Hunzel

Ickstetten, Iffezheim, Unter-iflingen, Igstetterhof,
Ilbenstadt, Illingen, Ingelheim, Inheiden, Inningen,
Innstadt (-Passau), Iona, Irgetsheim, Irnsing, Irrsee

Iägerweise, Iagsthausen (Iagst fl. in 11th cent.,
Iagas on which see Blind Würt. Vierteljahresheft 1889,
182)

Kaiserstuhl, Kanzach fl., Kappellenberg, Karlsruhe,
Kaufbeuren, Kelheim, Kemel, Kempraten, Kerslach, Kessel-
stadt, Kinzig, Kirnach (or Kirnau) fl., Bad Kissingen
(on this see W. Kaspers ZfCPh 15, 1924-28, 206-211),
Kleindeinbach, Klein-Gemund, Kochendorf, Kocher, Kösching,
Köngen, Köppern, Kornberg, Kriegshaber, Kumpfmühl, Kun-
tersweg, Künzing (or Künzen, Quintana), Kusterdingen

Further Modern Names

Lahn fl., Laimerstadt (Lei-), Laimbach, Laiz,
Langenau, Langenerringen, Lauchringen, Laufen, Lauingen,
Lauber fl., Laupersdorf, Lechsgmünd, Lein fl., Lengfeld,
St Leon, Linde fl., Lindenberg, Lingenthalerhof, Loben-
feld, Loch (Lueg), Lone fl., Lonthal, Lorch, Lorsch,
Ludenhausen, Lueg, Lützelbach, Lug, Lugberg

Machtfling, Mainhardt, Maisel, Mals, Manching,
Mannheim, Marbach, Marienhausen, Marköbel, Massohl,
Mäurich, Maurkirchen, Mauls, Meerweisen, Meimsheim,
Meisterstall, Mengen, Metter fl., Merching, Messkirch,
Metzingen, Miltenburg, Mitte(n)wald, Mochenwangen,
Moosdorf, Morrens, Mudbach, Mühlberg, Mühlenbach, Müm-
ling fl. (Mimelinga in 9th cent.), Mümlingen, Münster,
Munningen, Münsingen, Murg (explained as *morga "boun-
dary" by Hubschmied Vox Rom. 3, 1938, 139; H-M p.244),
Murr

Nagold fl., Nals, Nassenfels, Nau fl., Nauis fl.,
Neu-burg, -wied, Neuen-haus, -heim, -stadt, Niederstot-
zingen, Nidder fl., Niederbieber, Niederberg, Noetingen

Ober-dorf, -günzberg, -hausen, -kirchen, -stimm,
Obernburg, Obing, Odenwald, Oedheim, Offenburg, Okarben,
Olten, Oos (-Scheuern), Oos, Osterburken, Osterdorf,
Otterswang

Pappenheim, Parr (B-), Passau, Paudex, Pfaffenhofen,
Pfarrhofen, Pfelling, Pfersee, Pfin, Pfinz fl., Pfon-
dorf, Pföring, Pforzheim, Pfünz, Pierre-Pertuis (cf. 13.
5166 and C p.7), Pietenfeld, Pittenhart, Platling, Pohl,
Praunheim, St Prex, Prim fl., Promasens, Prutting

Quettich

Rabenden, Rabland, Rastatt, Reichenhall, Reith,
Remchingen, Rems fl., Rettich (-g), Riaz, Ries, Riess,
Riez, Riss fl., Risstissen, Riegel, Rinschheim, Robern,
Roth fl., Rott, Rotthof, Roetelsee, Rottum, Rottweil,
Röthenbach, Röthenberg, Rotenburg, Ruffenhofen

Saalburg (near Frankfurt; cf. CIL 13 p.455; exploratores Halicenses 7495, Haliq et Chalit[?] 6763, on
the limes Germ.; but CIL 13 p.297 puts Halicanum among
the Boii [Pannonia]; cf. Saluia 13.6538, at Halle,
Saluiatos 3.9860, Ptol., IA), Saaldorf, Saale fl.
(Σάλας Str. 7.1.3,291C; cf. P-W, related to Sale fl.,

Further Modern Names

between Chatti and Hermunduri, Tac. A 13.57; and perhaps
Halle : sal-, a dialect variation like Keltic s-: h-,
either Goid.: Bryth., or both Brythonic, cf. Sabrina,
Severn: Hafren, Sæfern, see Pedersen VKG 1 p.71); cf.
Salz-burg?), Salisburg, [Salzach fl., Salz-burg, Salz-
burghofen], Sandweier, Sattelbach, Sayn fl. (for
*Sequana?), Scharnitz, Schaan, Schalchen, (Ober-)Scheid-
enthal, Schieren-dorf, -hof, Schierstein, Schlanders,
Schlossau, Schmiechen, Schussen fl., Schönberg, Schön-
geising, Schretzheim, Sechta fl., Seebruck, Seligenstadt
(not "castra Selgi," but "martyrs-town"), Siebeneich-hofe
(cf. Sex Arbor 86 above), Sennbuch, Sillersdorf, Sind-
ringen, Sinkingen, Söchentau, Sollern, Spechbach, Stamm-
heim, Starkenburg, Steinbach, Steinheim, Steinleinsfurth,
Stetten, Stappach, Stepping, Stettfeld, Sterzing, Stockstadt, Stoddenstadt, Stöttham, Strasslach, Straubing,
Strassenheim, Studenberg, Stuttgart, Surheim, Surrberg,
Sulm fl., Sulz-bach, -brunn

Taimering, Tann (silua, C p.265), Tarsdorf, Tegernsee, Teisendorf, Tettelham, Theilenhofen, Tittlmoos,
Titmoning, Tolnaishof, Traubing, Trauchtlingen, Trennfurt (older Tribunfurt, Tribinford, Triebenfurt, Dreien-
furt; cf. Trebur and Tubri- [Dub-?] but hardly Triputienses, though insc. 6599 comes from Trennfurt), Treucht-
lingen, Trienz (Triputienses?), Trostberg, Trostburg,
Tübingen, Türkheim

Uffkirche, Ummerdorf, Untertöbingen, Unterfinningen,
Unterhausen, Unter-saal, Urspring, Utzmemmingen

Vaihingen, Valley (C 3 p.738), Vidy, Vielbrunn,
Vilbel, Vilbelerwald, Vils fl., Vilshofen, Vuippens

Wagenschwerd, Wahlheim (-haim), Waldmössingen,
Waldmühlbach, Walldürn, Weihmorting, Weilheim, Weissenburg, -dorf, Welzheim, Wengen (in Allgäu), Wernstein,
Westheim, Wetter fl., Wetterhausen, Wezikon, Wieslauf
fl., Wiesbaden, Wiflisburg, Wilferdingen (Senot[ienses),
Wilten, Wimpfen, Wörth, Wössingen, Wolkertshofen, Würm
fl., Württemberg, Würzburg

Zaber fl., Zaehringen (Zaringen), Zainingen, Zell-
hausen, Zellkircke, Zugmantel, Zurzach, Zwiefalten.

Divine Names

243

See further Stähelin (on divine names in Roman
Heluetia) in ASA 23, 1921, 17-30; AE 1922, p.366; P.
Aebischer "Témoinages du culte de l'Apollon gaulois
dans l'Helvétie romaine" (Grannus and Belenus in local
names, e.g. p.40 Belna 1142, modern Bienne, Biel) RC 51,
1934, 34-45; id., ZfSchw.Gesch. 14, 1934, 284-309 (di
Casses in Chasseron); on divine names of Baden-Baden
(6296, 6296a) see Germ. 2, 1918, 77-83; 3, 1919, 15-17
(cf. RA 14, 1921, 463; REA 20, 1918, 256); W. Cart ASA
NF 21, 1919, 7-19; A. Closs "Die Religion des Semnonen-
stammes," Wiener Beiträge zur Kulturgeschichte und
Linguistik (vol. 4 Die Indogermanen- und Germanenfrage,
Salzburg-Leipzig, 1936, ed. by W. Koppers), pp.549-673,
cf. id "Das Heiligtum der Semnone," Congr. Hist. Religions 1935, 18; L.W. Jones "Cults of Dacia," Publ. in
Class Philol. of Univ. of California vol. 9, part 8,
1929, 245-305 (reviewed by Besnier REA 32, 1930, 90);
D. van Berchem "Le Culte de Jupiter en Suisse," Rev.
historique vaudoise 1944 (Lausanne) sees Lucan's Taranis
in Tarnaiae (Rav., canton Wallis, see 241 above), AE
1945, p.177; G. Steinmetz "Vom Merkurtempel auf dem
Ziegetsdorfer Berg," Verhandlungen des historischen
Vereins von Oberpfalz und Regensburg 86, 1936, 434-440

"Restoration" plagues divine as well as local names.
Thus Weisweiler ZfCPh 21, 1939, 218-19 cites as "divine
names" f., Druantia and Onniona, appealing to Aebischer
RC 48, 1931, 312-14, and he to Hubschmied. But I find
no ancient source; presumably the former rests on the
modern local name Drance fl., the latter being a postulated *Onniona pure and simple.

On the divine(?) name

Nix[

on a ring from Rembracht (Tettnang, Boden See) in Wür-
temberg; and on the certain divine name

Nixibus sanctis (v.l. Nixabus)

on a vase from Amstetten, Niederösterreich, with which cf.
Nixibus Lucinis (Aquileia) see Paret Germ. 18, 1934, 193-

Divine Names

197, Strade ib. 216-217, Gutenbrunner pp.198-199, Grenier REA 37, 1935, 343 (cf. 101). The question is whether we have merely the Roman Nixi and Nixae or the Germanic (OHG nicchussa, Mod Low Ger. nixe) Nixen.

As for the former cf. Ovid met. 9.294, cf. Paul. ex Fest. 182-183 L., cal. Philocal. CIL vol. 1 (ed. 2) i p.332, Notitia ap. Richter Topogr. d. Stadt Rom 1901, pp.224, 373 (cf. Wissowa RK ed. 2, 249 n.1; and in Roscher Lex. s.v. Nixi).

The texts themselves are reported in Jahresh. öst. Arch. Inst. Beiblatt 23, 1933, 135-138 cf. 29, 1935, 217-220; Germania ll. cc.; Brusin Scavi di Aquileia 1934, p.86 no.10 (cf. AE 1933.127, 1934-238; 1935 p.242 and 1936 p.267; Rassegna Epigr. rom. 1129, 1197, 1262), summary in AJA 42, 1938, 579.

Note also Fatis]ixibus in PID 1 p.322, from Pais 739; and, if pre-Roman, the ending in

uibebos

Villach, Kärnten (Glotta 23, 1935, 202). For the meaning cf. perhaps di(s) genibus(?) see 82 and 223 above. Compare on mother-goddesses in general Siebourg BJ 137, 1933, 103-123.

The plant-name nixa Isid. 17.7.10 (Sofer p.100) can hardly be connected.

Abnoba 5334, 6283, 6326, 6332, 6342, 6356, 6357, 11746-47, cf. 11721; and local names; R.2611, 2613; BA 1920, clvi-vii, 95-100

Accio (Iuppiter) 3.3428 (cf. Accio, Lake Geneva PhW 59, 1939, 1100; 80 above)

Adsalluta 3.5134-36, 5138; 11684-85, H-S 26, 27, 255 (Atsaluta); also fl.

Aericur[a] 6322, cf. Er-, Her-; Aecur[na 3.3831, Aecorna H-S 149, Aec[150; cf. Glasnik MDS 13, 1931, 6; Pannonia 1, 1935, 171f.; H-S p.68 cite also Aequorna

Agaunus 3.14359,27

Alaunus (unless local) 6425

Alcis Tac. G 43.4; Gutenbrunner 189

Divine Names

Divine Names

Divine Names

Ei.obeia(?) 6296a (cf.
   6296, R.2730), read
   also as Einobera Germ.
   2.1918,77-83, cf. 3,
   1919, 15-17; REA 20,
   1918, 256

[Εἰτιόσαρος AE 1945.1]

Epona 5170, 7438, 7610a,
   R.3008, EC 3, 1938,
   198; CIL 3.5910
   (11909); Epona Augusta
   3.5312 (H-M 304); E-
   ponae (pl.) 3.7904,
   ?Epona Germ. 16, 1932,
   62 (Eponfaum?), i.e.
   -(a)e Aum[? or fanum(?),
   Epona V.261; RA 25,
   1927, 101; 6.31149

Eraecura 6631a (cf. Aer-,
   Her-), Ercura H-S 29,
   Erecura N.100

[Fortuna balinearis redux
   6552, cf. 5066]

Garmangabis Gutenbrunner
   55

[genius optionum 6567]

Gerionis 6441 (apparently
   divine name, dat. pl.;
   or for Cerfonius per-
   sonal (?); or cf. Ger-
   ontia, i.e. Ageruchia
   C p.303 n.5?)

Gontia Germ. 14, 1930, 39-
   40, AE 1930.74 cf.
   local names; REA 32,
   1930, 255

?Gortia 6484

Grannus 6462; 3.5861,
   5870-71, 5873-74, 5876,
   5881; cf. R.2651, V.
   201, 213, 219, 224; 13.
   10036,60

Hal[icanus] R.3042

Harcecius, see A-

Harmogius 3.4014, 5320,
   5672 (M-)

Herecura 6359, 6438, 6439;
   Cf. Er-, Aer-

Herequra(?) 6360

Heroni (dat.) 3.8147

Hesui(?) dat. sg. 5246

Idennicae v. Suleuiae

Indercus 5042 (Mélanges
   Gilliard 71; APh 17,
   319)

[?Intarabus AcS 2.56,30]

[Laburus 3.3840; cf.
   laburnum, -rusca PID
   2.203, W-H 740]

Latobius 3.5097-98, 5320-
   21; cf. local name
   Latabienses 221, 234
   above; Latauio (PID 1.
   390); AE 1929 p.375;
   Anz. Akad. Wiss. Wien
   Ph-H Kl. 64, 1927, 9

Divine Names

L]enus (?) 11775

Leucetius 7608, 7412

Liber, Libera H-S 288,
289; cf. 3.10834-5;
PID 1.159,163-4

?Lopo]du[nenses (matres)]
AcS 2.286

Lugoues 5078

Magla 3.3963

deo Malag[RA 20, 1912,
494 (Sarmizegetusa)

[maliator (Hercules) 6619,
sc. Thunar see C p.265]

Marmogius v. Har-, Ar-

[Mars (et) Aquila H-M
304]

[? *Martis fons see 6593,
Morsbach, Mors- (or
Mars-) -brunnen (?),
C p.279]

Matres 3.5972 ad. (p.2201);
M. Pannoniorum et Del-
matarum 13.1766

[matri castrorum ob uic-
toriam Germanicam 6459]

Matronae Germ. 24, 1940,
128-40

Mattiaca (Diana) 7565

[Mercurius domesticus 7757]

[militaris (Mars) 6574]

[Mithra 7397]

[Naissatis 3.8260, cf.
local names AcS 2.673]

Naria 5161; Naria Nousan-
tia 5151, cf. H-M
p.252

?Nemesis 3.4241, 11153,
13423; cf. AcS 3.138,
250, 733

[?Nemnic[3.4805]

?Nerta v. Auert-

[genio ciuitatis Vlpiae
S(ueb.) N(icr.) 6417,
cf. 6420, 6420a]

Nixibus Brusin Aquileia
p.86; REA 37, 1935,
342; see p.1243 above

⟨Noreia AcS 2.761, V.434⟩

Nousantia v. Naria

Numfhae 7460, R.145; Nym-
phae 6606, 7278-79,
11507; N. Perennes
11759-11760, Apollin-
ares 6649; R.341,
3475; AcS 3.643,16

Nundinarius (Iuppiter) H-S
500

Nutrices Augustae H-S
324-335

Nymphae (salutares, Augustae) H-S 460-65; cf.
Numfhae

Divine Names

Ollogabiae 7280

?Obila 3.6263, cf. Obil-
edus 3.11794

?Ogl[6484

Oraee H-S 162 (i.e. ᾽Ορ-
εία ?)

Pallas 6746

Petra Genetrix H-S 294,
Dessau 4244

Poeninus H-M 82, cf.
Poin- 3.6143

Quadriuiae (-uu-, -ii,
-ubus) 5069-70, 5198,
6315, 6343, 6429a,
6437, 7398, 7430-31;
cf. AE 1938.80 and 1947.
24; F.345; ZfSchw. Arch.
u. Kunstgesch. 2, 1940,
8

Rhenus 5255, V.178; cf.
FHRC Index s.v. (p.
329)

Rosmerta 6388, R.2607

diuabus S[7331 (cf.
Suleuis?)

Santius 6607 (cf. San-
tones [Aquit.] who,
with the Turones, were
earlier located in

Germ. Sup., C p.215
col.2, p.279 n.5; cf.
Cubii p.263 n.4, Cubus
6626; so the Viuisci,
cf. Hirschfeld SB Akad
Berl. 1896, p.453); cf.
Sentius pers. (and div?)
name, Santius (personal
name), sentis gloss (79);
cf. 208 (2); Sentona
below

[Σαρνευδηνός 3.7762, AE
1945.22]

Sauus 3.3896, 4009, 5138,
11680, 11684, H-S 27,
S. Augustus 3.4009

dea Scarbantia (dat., cf.
local names) AE 1912.8

?Secat[4450, R.3371

Sedatus 3.11929 (5918),
cf. H-M 62, V.273

his sedibus (i.e. genio
loci) 6558

Segomo 5340

[Senam[us(?) Iuppiter 3.
10833; cf. P-W 2te
R. 2.1545]

[Sentona 3.3026]

Seno[6335, Senomatro(?)
6475 (read as genio
Martis by some); cf.
Galli-zenae 178 above;
cf. dis M[atris] Sen-
onum 4304(?) or Senuon-
um see 213 above; and
possibly S]enus (or
L]enus?) 11775(?)

Divine Names

[Silumius 3.1306; for
  Siluanus?]

Siluani Augusti H-S 467,
  468

Sinatis 3.5320

Sirona 6327, 6458, 7570,
  V.33, 222; Jahresb.
  Schw. Ges. Urg. 32,
  1940-41, 112

[Σιττακωμικος AE 1945.26]

Su[3.7748

Sucellus 5057, F.134,
  H-M 352; cf. P-W s.v.,
  pp.515-516

Suleuiae, Suleuae, Suleae
  11477, (suae) 11499;
  Idennicae 5027 (also
  suae; at Rome meae C
  p.7), S. sorores 11740;
  H-M 162, 242; R.3008,
  6.31149, 3.5900; cf. 3.
  7331 (?), 3.1156, 1601
  (montanae); AE 1937.212;
  V.245; Gutenbrunner 95;
  Sul[eis] suis Jahresb.
  Schw. Ges. Urg. 31,
  1939, 85-6

[Summanus 3.4443, 11156]

[?Surburus 4554, cf.
  10010.1859 (pers. name);
  see 213 above]

Tamitenus (I.O.M.) AE
  1912.54 (Riben, Bul-
  garia)

[T(anarus?) 3.10418]

[Tadenus (Apollo) RA 18,
  1911, 213]

Taranucnos 6478, cf.
  6094

Termunes 3.5036; AE 1948.
  238

Tesera (dat.) 11970a, R.
  3532

Thana H-S 516-518; 3.
  3941, 10819

[Tifatina (Diana) AE 1910.
  140]

dea Titaca (dat.) 7624
  q.v., cf. 8853

T(i)outatis 3.5320, cf.
  6.31182 (Medurini T.)
  On Teutates cf. Rein-
  ach RC 18, 1897, 137

Tor[(if divine) 3.10829

Toutiorix 7564

Triuiae 5069-70, 6429a,
  6437

Tutela 3.3345

V[5164

[Vagdaeuercustis Guten-
  brunner p.233, item
  104.7; cf. Mnem. 5,
  1937, 320 de Vries
  Altgerm. Rel. 208-9]

Vidasus H-S 516-18, 3.
  3941, 10819

Divine Names

Vindedo 5059 (unless pers.),
but cf. 5078

?Viradec]dis Haug-Sixt
433, 13.6543

Viroddis 6486, cf. Guten-
brunner 111 n.1

Virodacθi 11944, R.2253,
at Trebur; cf. 7441
add., REA 15, 1913,
78, 455; Gutenbrunner
104; cf. 6761 (V. siue
Lucena); see 223, 237
above

Virttut(i) 7425 (inter-
preted as Virtus Mith-
rae cf. 7399, 7400;
but see 223 above on
Virtus i.q. Viradectis,
Vagdauercustis

Virtus Bellonae 6481; dea
Virtus Bellona 7281;
Virtus inuicti Imp.
7400; Virtus dea 6385

Visucia 6384; -ius 6347,
6384, 6404; cf. 155,
213 above

[Visuna 11714, see notes
ad loc.; dedicated by
Mediomatr.; Gutenbrun-
ner 194]

Volkanus 6454

Volpinae nymphae 6649

Vxellimus 3.5154

[Vxlemitanus (Brunn, Steier-
mark) RA 13, 1938, 335;
cf. Jahresb. d. Österr.
Arch. Inst. 31, 1938,
Beiblatt 95]

[Ζυλμυ]δριηνός AE 1945.
77, cf. 80; cf. Thr. Ζαλ-
μοξις (?) Hdt. 4.94-6;
Thr. ζαλμός : Skt. šarman
Hirt Idg. 2.592]

Personal Names

Abalu[13 vi, 1933, p.
129, no.14

Abascantus dipl.42,
-ianus N.66

?Abbo 3.12010,15 (F abb;
but of abb Rheinzabern)

Abcar Lex. Burg., TLL 1.
74,36

[Abdedat[(Semitic) Germ.
15, 1931, 6-10; Abde-
tathus N.103]

['Αβεζελμίs AE 1945.1]

Abissetus 10003.18

Abonius 10022.14

Abrosus 7281

Absucus AcS 3.510,34

Aca[10027.60

Aka[10017.1093

Acauconi (dat.) 3.11732

Acconius 6425

Acesonius (-g-) 3.4871,
10509

Acirgus 10002.5-6

]acmaχtus 3.11441

Acoci[10010.3209

Aconius dipl.18, -ia 3.
10866

Acresa 3.15216,21

Acrilla Germ. 22, 1938,
54

Acrinius 10036.68

Adatilia 3.10865

Ἀδκοῦλφος Olymiod. fr.17

Adbugiouna 3.10883

Adcobrouatis AE 1945.57,
see pp.182, 159; Diss.
Pann. 1.11; 12 (cf. AE
1941, p.349)

Adelgerius Fiebiger 3.23h

Adginna 3.11586

Adiaturix AE 1939.260

Adietumarus 3.10867

⟨Adigillus RA 24, 1945,
54; AE 1946.230⟩

Adioui...ius 5333

Adiutorius R.2607-08

Adiutus 3.11711

Admata 3.14101

Adnamatius 6539, 11775,
3.11699; -ia 6539, 3.
11816; -tus 7281, V.9,
Adnamatus AE 1920.59;
cf. 8357, 8819

Adnamo AE 1945.133, Ad-
namo (-u) AcS 3.510,34;
on names of the type
Adnamu see Frühgesch. u.
Sprachwiss. 1, 1948, 38-
53

Personal Names

Adnamus, -a, An(n)- cf.
   AcS 3.509-510; 1.44

Adnomatus, 3.10740

]adua m. 6.32623 (Suebus)

Aduentius R.2654

Aeauius 10010.3177, 3238e

[Aebutius R.558]

A]edilus Germ. 16, 1932,
   62

Aegus 10017.114; cf. 83
   above

†Aelloldus (v.l. Aegiol-
   dus) Genava 5, 1927,
   126

?Aex[10010.3102

Agecius Fred. Chr. 2.53

Agilis 11504 (not Aquili-
   [nus, F. p.35)

Agisillus JÖAI 26, 1930,
   Beibl. 189-200

Agisius H-M 450

Agisl[7367-8

Agisus 3.5542, 10883

Agramianus R.3568

[Agraptus 6586; R.1947.4]

Aiacius 7417, 7441

?Aiatu[3.11427, cf.
   12012.106

Aico (n. sg. m.) 3.3853

Aido 10010.310

Aiiuca 3.14359,21, Aiuca
   3.4991

?Aiiuua m. 7280 (Atiuuar-
   rius?)

?Aipinus 10010.3180 (Alp-?)

Aisius 3.14373,57

Aisogius 3.14359.24 (i.e.
   Esu-)

Alba 5105

Albanus 6304

Albess[3.12014,108(1)

Albio 3.6010,10

Albucinus 3.14370,9; Al-
   bucius Verh. hist.
   Vereins Oberpfalz 86,
   1936, 437

Alc[5123

Alci[3.6014,3

Alcimus dipl.33

Aldanus Diss. Pann. 2.14,
   713

?Aliania 7450

Alil[10010.3102h

Aliquandus 6324, cf. CIR
   1668

[Allius (dom. Dert.) 5206]

Personal Names

Allo 3.11568

Allounus (not Ali-) 3.
5242 (pp.1830, 2285)

?Almexllius 3.10355; cf.
Thr. Ζάλμοξις ? Or Al[
Mex-? Ἀβεξελμίς above

Alpinia 5233, -ius 7741,
cf. R.2688

Alpinula 5233, Alpinulus
3.12014 (p.1900)

Alpinus 5130, 3.11938, -a
3.5815

Alpnius 3.6010,11

Alpus 3.5835

Alueiu[10010.3115b

Alumin[10010.3111o

Amalricus Fiebiger-Schmidt
281

Amantia H-S 70, 84

Amasonius 12634, H-M 406

Ambatus (-χt-?) 10010.105

Ambaxius 6463

Ambiorix R.4611

Ambisauus (ethn.) Gron.
75

Ambiurus AE 1945.64

Amelius Fiebiger-Schmidt
130

?Amepis 11525a, but see
H-M 312 (C. Valerius)

Amma R.3788, V.304

Amemu 3.6010,292 (An-)

Ammisia F.224 (cf. local
names)

Ammius R.2630

Ammo 10017.615 (Ma-?)

Ammon[ius] 7264

Ampio (Mattiacus) 5.8739,
cf. Ampius dipl.46

Ana AE 1939.260, Diss.
Pann. 2.10, 1938, p.7

Anarius 10010.3202

Anartios J. Öst. Arch.
Inst. 28, 1933, 140

Anatelo 10001.37

?Anatissa 3.6570 (p.1063)

Anaus 10022.303, H-M 308

Anbo Arch. Ert. 44, 1930,
242-243, 316

Anbusulus 3.4858

Ancarius (Etr.?) 7307

Ancharis Zts. f. Schw.
Arch. u. Kunstgesch.
3, 1941, 68

?Ancirius 3.14355,9

Andeca (Sueuus) Isid. reg.
Goth. 92

[Andedu dipl.4]

Personal Names

[Andes Raetinius (Dalm.)
7023]

Androuri 7579 (cf. 12.
2876, 2891, 4577)

[Andueia, Anduenna 3 p.
960]

[Andunocnes 3 p.960]

Aneχtlati 10010.124

?Aneroestos or -es(?)
i.e. Ariouistos(?)
Polyb. 2.22.2 (Gaesata)

Angulatus H-S 100

Anici[6305

Anilina Fiebiger-Schmidt
127

Animo (-em-) 3.12014, 113-
114

Annaeus dipl.100, cf. 3
p.960

Annama Gron. 1 al.

Annamatus Gron. 2

Annamus 3 p.962 (14)

Annauus 10035.25; R.4504

Anneius dipl.155

Annesis 3 p.960

Annilio 3.14368,30

Annius R.4076, ASA 31,
1929, 184

Annusius 5233

Ano AE 1945.133, Anno V.54

?Anotius 5168

Ansia H-S 576

Anta[H-S 256

Antabagius Val. Max. 5.5
3 (for Adnamatobogius??)

Anteius H-M 309, R.1947.2,
F.109

Antonius 6484

Antullus R.1552, 3752

Anuea 10010.3184c

Anuxi (-χti?) 10002.648

Apalaustus 3 p.960

Aper 7301; dipl.4, 107;
3.3851, H-S 313, cf.
3.15156

Apeus 10022.303; H-M 308

Apidius dipl. 55, cf. 61,
65; V.510

Apis 6484

Aplo 3.4344; cf. Guten-
brunner Frühzeit 22

Aponius 3.14354,31

Appius 10003.24

Appuleiu(s) H-S 9, 121

Apra 6351, F.353

Ἀπρήων (i.e. Aprio?) H-S
526

Personal Names

Aprianus 6484

Aprilius N.101, -is JÖAI
26, 1930, Beibl. 189-
90

Aprio 10001.45

Aprionius 6484 ad.

Aprius 3.5835, V.417,
Diss. Pann. 2.14, 712

[Apronianus cos. A.D. 191,
6604]

[Apronius (luco Aug.) 5185,
5207, cf. R.392]

Apronius 3 p.963 (15),
H-S 501

Aprunculeius 7290

Aprus 10036.65

?Apsorius ASA 28, 1926,
6

Aptus H-M 208

Apulus dipl.10, Apul[3
p.960

Aquensis N.92

Aquessi[10017.165

Aquila dipl.10, 30

Aquinus 6468

?Aran[3.11430a

Arator Amm. 28.2.5 (at
Mons Pirus)

[Arbetius Amm. 15.4.1]

Arcino(s) 3.6010,246

Arellius 11525a, H-M 312,
cf. F. p.35

Areobindus (A.D. 506)
5245, 10032.3, Fiebiger-
Schmidt 299 (i.e. Ario-
uindus?); Fiebiger 62-
64

Argata 11786

Ariaua 10010.3102

Arimanus (i.e. -io-) 3.
11502, 11661

[?Arintheus Amm. 15.4.10]

Ἀριόγαισος (king of Quadi)
Dio Cass. 71.13.3

Ariomanus 3.4594, AE 1939.
261, AJA 52, 1948, 237

Ariouistus see Aneroestes;
cf. 237 above

Ariuaria 3.12014,129

?Ἀρφγέ(νου) 10026.24

Arpus Tac. A 2.7

Arriae C p.208 (with add.)

Arricus (eps. Lauson.) C
p.7

Arrius 7247

Art[H-S 7

Artaunus AcS 1.224,18-25,
cf. Ἀρταυνον 241 above

Artissius 3.14370,10; V.
361

Personal Names

?Artlaus 3.11240

Artorius 6.32929, V.50

Artu[AcS 3.696,10

Aruatius 7577

[Aruernus 3.12014,130]

Arusi[us 3.12014,131

Ἀρξάκειος AE 1945.23

Ascaricus (rex Franc.)
  Paneg. Const. 11, cf.
  16

Asinio (eps. Curia) C
  p.49

Asson[ius 6533

Assupa H-S 176 (cf. Assu-
  paris)

Asucius 3.13552

[Asuodana m. dipl.118;
  V.518]

Asurius 3.12014,133 (or
  Casurius, Lubié La
  Palisse)

Atalis 10010.3100a

Atalo AE 1941.16

Atebla (i.e. -eu-?) 3.
  10946

[Ateboduus 3.4732]

[Atecina 3.11650; cf.
  Emerita 3, 1935, 212-
  224]

Atecurus AE 1948.234

Atedunus AcS 3.715,
  Gron. 2

[Ategnate 3.4732]

Ateius 3.6010,19; N.109

?Ateixanti AcS 1.256,28

Atemerus V.48

Atera 3.11514

Aterissa 3.5784, V.93

Aterius 3.12014,134

Ἀτερόνιος RA 15, 1940,
  209

Atesiatis H-M 325, F.112

Atesso AcS 3.719,42

Atestatis (-iat-?) 3.4724

Ateu[3.6010,247

?Atiextus 3.12014,140;
  for Atr-?

Atilis 3.5889

Atilius 7342, 10002.112
  sq., 3.5115

Atimetus 3.6475, CE 1310

Atinius V.122

Atioucius 3.5242

Atiougo (-onis) 3.4724

Atitto 3.5523

Personal Names

Atiu- see Ailu-

Atnamatus Gron. 2

Ato H-S 75

?Atortus 3.1111,17

Atrec[6466

[Atreccesianus 3.12896]

Atrect[6317

Atrectus 11947, cf. 6994

Atregtius 7281

Atressus Gron. 57

Atriχto(s) 10027.106a

Atropus 10002.544

Atta dipl. 96, -(i)us F.
 108

[?Attaps 3.13423]

Atte.i...7450

Attectius (Atr-?) CIL 13
 vi, 1933, p.129 no.17

Attes[anius] 6740a

Attessas 7263

Attialus 10010.3097a

Attianus 6283, 7753

At(t)ianus 6569

Attienus 11525b

Attillus 5222, 7291,
 7570b

Attisionius 11940

Attius 7047, 11726

Atto 10017.193

Attonius 6480, 6575, 7281,
 11940, V.9, 108, H-S
 154, 274

[?Atuacis (gen.) 3.11761]

Atulus 3.11556

At[ ]umara 11477

Atuns (-nis?) 6460

Aturo 7754

Atusonius 6554

Atuus AE 1920.59

Au[5190

[Auamacimaria 3.10576]

Aucissa 3.12031,18

Aucus (lib.) 3.5932,
 R.4084

?Aucusus 3.12014,146;
 Aucus V.207

Auentina 5192

[Aueta (for Auentia) 5074]

Auetontia V.11

?Aufatr 3.6010,30

Augisa Fiebiger-Schmidt
 129

?Augustanius 6484

Personal Names

Augustus 6484

Auiana AE 1945.124

Auilima ASA 38, 1936, 169
(Auili ma?)

?Auiola 7353

Auita 6486, -us 5179,
6646, 6648a, cf. 5112
(cos. A.D. 209), 5142,
10001.62; 3.3853, 3892,
10780, 13403; H-S 241,
243; N.91; Auitus
10036.90, Auitus, -a
V.31; 3.13562, 14106;
H-S 159, 163; F.181
-1a F.353; -ius N.106

Auitianus H-S 37

Aulenus dipl.90

[Aulupor, Aulusanus (or
]nusanus) Thrac., see
nn. ad loc. (ex ciu.
Anchealo) 7292, cf.
dipl.136, R.1818]

Aulutra m. 6955

Aurotra m. 6955

Aunus H-M 218, F.94

?Auomius F.110

??Aupain[10010.3184a

Aurac[10022.39

Aurelius N.111a

Aureolus Aur. Vict. 33.
17; 3.11999

Aurgais Fiebiger 33; cf.

Germ. 22, 1938, 54;
ZfdAlt. 75, 1938, 115-
117

Auscus 3.5265, -a 3.11715;
Ausscus H-S 107

?Auteta 3.4929

Autus 6337

[Axius R.424]

Azala dipl.49 (ethn.)

[Azinas R.1902]

Baai.iu. 10010.3190c

Bacadus 3.5922, V.328

Baccara (Raetus) Martial
11.74.1

Bacco(s) 10010.264a; 3.
12014,157

Baebius 6285

Baiauso 3.6010,36

Baienius 3.5870, V.201;
cf. Bien(n)us AcS s.v.

?Baiolus 7754, cf. baiulus
7006, and gloss 158
above

Baius see V. p.221

Baldomarius (king of Mar-
comanni) Dio Cass.;
v.l. Bad-, Ball-

Baldricus Fiebiger-Schmidt
315

Personal Names

Balio Pac. Drep., Pan.
Theod. 28

[Banira 5027]

Banona 3.4724

Banna 3.6017,8

Bappo Amm. 15.4.10; cf.
AcS 1.343

Barbius 3.11682, H-S 165,
175

Barbus H-S 392

Bardo f. 3.11657, m. H-S
13

Bardus H-M 471; V.509, C
p.6, C 3 p.846); hard-
ly bardus gloss 178
above; dipl.5

Baricio 7336

Barmasi 10002.126a

Barus 3.5265

Basia Gron. 2 al.

Basilla Gron. 4

Bassianus H-S 275

Bassidius 3.10738

Bassina 7347

Bassinius 3.5794

Bastarnus Fiebiger-Schmidt
13

Basterna dipl.42

Bathana AE 1945.109

[Bato..ex Saluia 6538; 3.
p.960; cf. RA 20.
1912, 464 a sobriquet]

Baturio (or But-?) 3.
12014,157 (1)

Bauila 3.14348

?Bausig[3.12014,158

Bauto Ambr. Ep. 24.7

Beginus Val. Max. 7.8.4

?Behanc[Fiebiger-Schmidt
285a

Belatullus 5026, 7281,
10017.219, 11473

Belatumarus AJA 52, 1948,
237

Belatus(s)a 3.11552,
14359.23

Beleizis Hdt. 4.94 (Thr.
or Getae), for Mel-
("honey-eater"?); not
Gebel-

Belica H-M 326

[Bella dipl.61]

Bellatumara V.34

Bellianus F.349

Bellicianus H-S 491

Bellicinia H-S 491

Bellicus 3 p.960

Personal Names

[Bellius dipl.108]

Bello n. sg. f. H-S 217

Bellonius 6488

[Bennus 3.2785; Ben(n)o Fiebiger 3.23c-d]

Berta m. 7574

Berullus 3.10775

Beruus 11737, Berus R. 2205

Besius R.866

Bessa 3.5796, V.7, 107

Betubius V.63

[Betuedius dipl.12]

Betuinianus R.866

Betuscius H-S 370

Betuuius 11508, R.893

[Beusas 6538, 7509, 11962; C 3 p.960]

Biatec Gron. 6, 72 (num.); better Βιατεσ

Biausco dipl.112

Bibulla (Vib-?) 6626

Bicarus 3.12014,160

Bienus N.97; cf. num. (Aquit. or Upp. Danube, Tr. 104, 202, 423)

Bilicius 7438

Bilisa 3.6010,248

?Bilix 3.12010,9

]bini[10010.2477

Bippa 10010.303

Birrus AcS 3.870,14

Bison AE 1945.24

Bissula Auson. de Biss.

[Bithus (Bessus) dipl.35, V.143]

Biticnus 10010.3201d

Bito 3.12014,163

Bittius 3.12014,680 (p. 1900)

Bitua 3.14359,21

Bitugenitus Gron. 7 al.

Bitunus 3.12014,164

[Biturix 3.5831; F.343]

Bitus 6955

[Bituuant[3.917]

Biuallo 3.12014

Bla[7586

Blandus R.4068, 3.10782

Blastus AE 1945.102

Blatto 3.12014

Blendo 3.11647

Personal Names

Bodica F.224

Bodico 6740a

Boccus 10036.19

?Bo... τoσ 10010,3198b

Boius see V. p.222
  (Vopisc. Aurel. 13.1)

Bolerianus 3.3816

Bolittiurus 5234

Bolsius 10010.338

Boltus 5234(?)

Boniatus H-S 13

Bonosus see V. p.222

Boraides 10032.9

Borili 3.12017

Borus (-ius) dipl.101,
  V.515

Boudillu(s) 10027.77

Bounia 3.11481

Bra[6317, cf. 10010.
  2146

[Bradua cos. A.D. 185,
  6581, cf. 3 p.960]

Brem[H-S 75

Breucus Byv. 2.1090,
  dipl.49, 69; 3 p.960;
  13 vi, 1933, p.129
  no.14

Briamius 10010.3232b

Bricco 3.4724

Bricomarus AcS 2.1177

[Bricto (Treuer?) 11736]

Brilo Gron. 4

Brinnia H-S 179

?Br. tut[10010.3255a

Britto 11954a

Βρίζενις Diss. Pann. 2.
  14, 182 al.

Broccus 3.3970, -cchus
  3.4360

[Brogimarus 3.15151; cf.
  AcS 1.620]

Broi[10002.131a

Broxu[5086

Brutta 3.11882, V.76,
  Bruttius V.312, 515

Bubens R.1818

Bucatioi 3.12014

Bucca Gron. 22

Buccinius 3.5838, V.150

Bucia 3.5265

Bucio 3.3790

Buco 3.10728

Buctor 3.3823

Bugia 3.3862

Personal Names

Buia 3.10745, cf. 10739, 3970

Buio 3.3790, cf. AcS 3. 997,30-34; 3.3866 (cf. p.1731), 3826 (and pp.1731, 2328.188), H-S 140; Buiio 3.3860, 13397 (pp.2328.26,189)

Bul(i)us Gron. 5, 65

Bunna 6460 add.

Buomi 3.2753, 9803

Buquorsa 3.10740, H-S 133

Burco Sidon. Apoll. 5.378

Burga Fiebiger 3.23k

Burrus 11508

Bussugnata Gron. 56

Bussurigius AE 1945.32

Bussuro 3.14359,17

Busturo dipl.104

Butto Gron. 2, 44

But(t)us Gron. 78

[Butus dipl.13]

Cab[3.12014, 170

[Cabalio 3.5487, 11740]

Caballarius Procop. Goth 3.2

[Cabdnus 3.11111,6]

Caccuso 3.6010,45

?Cacirspinae 3.12010,2

Cacurio AcS 1.668,44

Cacus H-M 407

Cadaric[ius] 3.14214,3; 12

Caesernius H-S 176, 177, 209, 450, 493 (-ia)

[Caetenius dipl.14]

Caiuca 3.12014,175

[Calaetus AcS 3.1042,30]

Calamus 3.6014,2

Calandina 3.5106, H-S 87, 394; Kalandina 3.11711, -us 3.11718, Calandinus 3.11715

Calaua m. 3.13552,53

Calemerus 3.10852

Calla 3.6549

[Callidius dipl.42]

Callo 10010.407; 3.6010, 46

Callus 11500

Calo 3.6010,249; 11586

Caluo 3.10729; Caluus F. 109

Cambioui AcS 3.1058,24

[Camidienus dipl.42]

Camil(l)us, -ius 5075,
5083, 5093, 5094,
5097, 5110, 5154,
6654, R.1947.1; Ritter-
ling Fasti p.142

[Camirnus 3.11059]

Camona (Can-?) H-S 75

Campilius 3.6008,9

Camu[10019.1

Camulianus 3.4893

Camurius R.1652; 3.12014,
178; 13552,119

Canauillus 3.5802, Can-
auilus V.113

Canda 6626

Can[didianae f(iglinae)
3.12527; cf. AE 1945.
8; P-W 12.1700-01

Candidius 6399, H-S 232

Candidus 6305, N.91, cf.
R.2205, 4068 (: Blan-
dus)

Caniccius 10036.36, R.
3005 (Oldenburg)

Canina 5129

Canius (Cainus), -ia AcS
3.1074,40-50

Cannicus Front. strat. 2.
4.7, Καννίκιος Plut.
Crass. 11; AcS 1.735,
3.1074; cf. Gannicus
1.1982 and perhaps
Ganna 224, 240 above

Cannutius 3.6020,4; dipl.
20

Cantabriacus 3.4471

Cantarro 3.12014,180

Canteχta H-M 242

Cantius 3.3857, N.90; -us
13.10010,438

Cantomiti 3.12014, 436

Canuatr[10010.3184d

[Kanus (Romanus) 7573]

?Capado AcS 1.757,23

Capito (Raet.) 7246, 7247,
3.3952

Cappo 5027

[Capponius 3.13397 p.2328.
26]

Caprasius 5166

Cara[6484

?Caradeann[(leg. Caraddoun-
[ius) 6484

[Caragonius AE 1940.100]

Caramallus TLL Onom. s.v.;
AcS 1.766

Carantia 6534, -ius 6410,
7302

Carantiniu(s) 7279

[Carantinus (Mediomatricus)
7369]

Personal Names

Carantus 6410, 6534, 7270

?Carasaou 10010.3203

Carassounus (Heluetius)
　R.2053, H-M 82; cf.
　Caraddounius 6484

?Caratacul[10010.3199a

Caratilia 5034

Caratinus 6600

Caratullus 6369, cf. C
　p.6; H-M 468

[Cardacanus 11601]

Cereius H-M 300, F.101

Cares (-entis) 3 p.960

Careus 7655a

Cariccus 3 p.960

Karita 3.4087, AcS 1.790

Carmeus, -ae- H-S 583 (or
　Garm-?)

Karodius AE 1945.123; 3.
　4296

Carpinius 3.10721

Carpus 10021.121, cf. AE
　1934.99; 3 p.960

Carrunius 6320

Cartoria H-S 394

Cartus 10010.646, 3.14373,
　15

Carueicionius Gron. 2

[Carullius dipl.10]

Caruonia 3.5115

Caruus Germ. 21, 1937,
　129

Casatus 6283; dipl.55,
　V.510 (Sequanus)

Casius 6310

?Casioouninius 7330

Cassianus 6283

Cassius 6343, 6471, F.113

Cassus 3.5451

Castilla AE 1945.124

[Castinus cf. AcS 3.1141,
　22]

Castori (d. sg. f.) H-S
　256

Κάστος Plut. Crass. 11;
　AcS 3.1076,13

Castricius R.1303

Caterto 10036.2

[Catielus 3.10721]

Catius 6484, V.26

Catomocus Gron. 32

Cattanus 3.11969, V.387

Cattaus (Heluetius) H-M
　471, V.509; cf. C p.6,
　C 3 iii p.846; dipl.5

Cattia 3.11884, V.77

Personal Names

Personal Names

[Χαριόμηρος Dio.]

?Chisen 10010.3201a

Χracciatus 3.14373,65

[Chrocus Fred. Chr. 2.60]

Cials 3.6007,7

?Ciaso AcS 1.1010; V.180

Ciatus AcS 3.1215,4

Ciba (G-) H-S 557

?Cicafus 3.5878 (leg Tet-
   rici Ca. f.?)

Cilnius V.166

Cilo 3.4120, cf. P-W
   Suppl. 6.1763; H-S
   608

Ciltus 5257, cf. Giltius
   237 above

Cilaustianus AE 1945.38

Cimberius (Suebus) BG 1.
   37

Cingen[6484

Cingetius 7349

Cinnamus dipl.38

Cinnenius 5191

Cinto 10006.25

Cintusmus 6533, 10017.
   286, 3.15215

Cintussia 3.12014.201

Cipi[3.6017,9

Cirraba Gron. 57

Cirrata 3.3857

Cirrus H-M 452; 10014.3

Ciruna JÖAI 26, 1930, 189

Cisiacus V. p.221

Cisoni[us] 3.6013

Cissus dipl.31, cf. 3
   p.960

Cladaeus (for Claudius?)
   5129; R.1886

[Clagissa (Bessus) dipl.83]

Clamosus 10011.181

Claturnius 3.3858 (Sabinus)

Claudius (Heluetius)
   dipl.76

Cletus 3.10852

?Clirionis 3 p.962 (12)

Clito 3.4552

Closius C p.6 (Mainz)

Clossius (Heluetius) 6234

Clusiodus R.1653

Cluuius 5098, 5100

Cnodauus Gron. 32, 63

Cns 10006.124

1267

Personal Names

Coaeddus (or Coneddus?)
7348

Cobnertus 10011.57b, H-M
460; cf. Counertus 3.
5108, 6491, 11644,
14373.26, 15205f; AcS
1.1054, 3.1245; -a 3.
5430; Laur-Belart Vin-
donissa p.10

Cobromarus Gron. 23,
R.4611

Cobromara 3.3598

Cobrunius N.108

Cobua m. AJA 52, 1948,
237

Cocaius 3.14565

Cocate f. AJA 52, 1948,
237

Cocc[3.5903, cf. 4382

Cocca R.1688a

Cocceius 6343, AE 1945.
115, V.252, 3.10888

Cocillus 10036.39

Cocliensis 5032

Cocusio 3.13519a

Codopit 3.12034.8

[Coelenus dipl.55; V.510]

Cogit[H-S 347

Cogitatus AJA 52, 1948,
238

Coius Gron. 2

Coluedu Gron. 12 al.

Comacia 3.5650, cf. gloss
79?

Comalus 3.14359,24

Comatius -a 3.1002, 1095,
1096, 1154

Comato AE 1941.15, 1910.
139; Comatus 3.11711

Comatuia AE 1941.15

Comatullus (Boius) dipl.
55, V.510

Comatumarus 3.3377

Combrissa 3.14359.21

Cominius 5214, H-S 74

Como[7301

[Cona 3.5311, cf. AcS 3.
1278,23]

Conatus 3.12031,2; cf.
177 above

Concolitanus (Gaisata)
Polyb. 2.22.2

Condatie 3.5905, 11906

Condatius H-M 310

Condollius 7460a

Condollus 6453, 6464

?Coneddus v. Coae-

Personal Names

Conginna 3.7523

Congonetus 3.11578

[Cono 3.8065,14]

Conridatus 3.5905

Cons[7424

?Consiueteni 3.6010,70

Consius dipl.33

Consta.e.ni 3.1010,70

Contlius V.30

Conus -a AcS 1.1111, 3.
    1278

[Copiesilla 3.13903]

Copponia V.438

Corb[10002.11

[Corbulo 5178]

Corcolonius Ann. Inst. de
    St. Cl. 2, 1933-35,
    219-222

Cordius ASA 28, 1926, 210.
    19

[Corellius dipl. p.1960]

Coresus(?) 7753

Corippus H-S 78-9

Corobilius 11940

Corrodu f. 3.5801, V.112

Cosa 3.120,11

Cosillus 6603

Cossinius 3.5795

Cossius 6740a, -us F.354

Cosso 3.5542

Costinus 3.12010,12

Costio V.311A

?Cosuactia CIL 1, ed. 2
    1196

Cottal(i) 3.15217

Cottio 3.12014

Cottius 5195

Cotto 10017.299; Cotto
    (Bastarna) Livy 40.57.
    3

Cottus 6438

Κοτύος (gen. sg.) RA 15,
    1940, 202

Coudomarus 3.5131

Counertus v. Cob-

Couria 3.5262

Courunus, Gouruna (i.e.
    Cob-?) 3.12014,216;
    cf. AcS 1.1151, 2033

Couso 3.14106

Coutusuatius (Heluetius)
    7026; or Coutus Vati?

Craanianus (ter. sig.) i.e.
    Gran- (of Lezoux), at
    Riegel, AcS 1.1153,47

Personal Names

Cracissiu (dat.?) 7369; or for Coracesium (Cilicia)?

Crassicius 11499, 3.5842

Credanus H-M 315, F.114

Cred(i)us AcS 1.1158

Creiscns H-M 315

Crinuo 3.4982

Crispianus AE 1945.127, Crispinus H-S 443; 3. 4098,1; 3.10844

Crispus 7362, 7574, 7589; 3.5789, 5835

[Κειτάσιρος Str. 7.3.11, 304C]

Crixsius 7281

Crobiso 3.14373,47

?Crocus Aur. Vict. ep. 41.3

?Crollus 3.12014,613

Crougen[3.14373,7

Crouta m. 3.4959, 5028

C.run 3.5905, 11906

Cubus 6626

Cucius 3.12014,231; cf. 4936

Cudius 3.12014,235

Culuas 3.12014,237

Cumius 10010.721

?Cundius 3.5858

Cupitus, -ius AcS 1.1197, 33; 1198, 8-10

[Curadro dipl.72]

?Curio R.2969

Curmisagius Diss. Pann. 2.10, 1938, 3; AE 1939.260 cf. κοθρμι Curmillus (-issus) and (for the ending) Depro-sagilos ("eater, glutton" Loth)

Cusala Gron. 84

Cusides Gron. 7

Cusentis (gen.) 3.12014 (p.1900)

Cuses 7048

Cusseius 3.11895, V.187, R.4601

[Custa dipl.61]

Cutio 3.4083

Dab[AJA 52, 1948, 236

Δάβεις Diss. Pann. 2.14, 384

Dabesu[H-M 325, F.115

Daccus 6389

Dacumena H-S 457; 3.4116

†Dadilo F.188; Germ. 3, 1919, 48-51

Personal Names

[Daetor (coh. Delm.) 7581]

Dagal(aifus) 5245 (A.D.
506) 10032.3; Fiebiger-
Schmidt 299, Fiebiger
62-64

Dago uassus (sic) 7754

Dagodnadus V.30

Dagorix 3.10951

Dagualdus Fiebiger 3.21

Daiberi Gron. 52, 66

[Dallo 3.3594]

Dam]matius 6740a

Dando Val. Max. 8.13.7;
cf. Gutenbrunner
Frühzeit 22

[Dannius 6891]

[Dansala (Thr., ethn., cf.
Denseletae Pl.?) 7049,
7050, R.1688a]

Danus AcS 1.1225,15, cf.
Amm. 14.8.3

Danuuius 3.3581, 4544

Darbosa H-S 75

Δάρδανος Olympiod. fr.17

Dari(ka?) 3.12014,246

†Darstus F.188; cf. Germ.
3, 1919, 48

[Dasas (-antis, -entis)
6538 (Dalm., ex Magno),
dipl.2, 30; 3 p.960]

Dasius 11952, R.149; dipl.
30, 100; AE 1947.134;
Das(s)ius 3 p.960,
Fiebiger-Schmidt 13

Dasmenus dipl.2, 97

Dasodunus 3.14373,45

Dassiolus (Mattiacus) 5.
8744

[Dassius (coh. Delm.)
7581]

[Dasumius R.330]

Datuus (Bessus) dipl.10

Ddron H-M 454

Deccius 3.5923; cf. Germ.
21, 1937, 52, N.96

[Decebalus (Dac.) R.66,
cf. R.382]

Dec[, Decim[, Decima
5180, -us 3.13551,14

Decimanus 5172

Decmanus 7222

Decuminius 11946, R.2986

Deisan Gron. 56

Delmatia 3.4013 (cf. p.
1746)

Demecenus 5171

Demittius 3.11926

Dento 3.12014

[Dentubrise (Thr.) 7051]

1271

Personal Names

?Deotitano 3.5965, V.407

Depo 3.12014

[Deramista (local name)
  dipl.38]

†Derstus F.188

[Derzizenus dipl.83]

Dessius 3.6008,18

[Desticius dipl.121,
  V.517]

[†Detibaldus late insc.,
  TLL Onom. s.v.]

Deua 6458

Deuonia 3.3863

Deuontia 3.10759

Deuso 3.10883, -a 3.5303

Deusus 3.5303, 5370, 5425

Deuua 3.4724

Dextrianus R.145

Dianu[3.11555

Di...anus (Dioni-, Digni-?)
  6571

Diassumarus Gron. 23

[Diatr[(Thr.) 7292]

Dibugius 3.4595

Dicae 3.15212,3

Diceus 3.14374,1

Didius AE 1948.56

Diindihildi Fiebiger-
  Schmidt 239

Diligius Gron. 31

Dindius H-S 158, 3.10782

Diocaitus 3.14107

[Disacentus (Thr.) 7051]

Disaucus 10036.51

[Ditus dipl.38]

Diueca 3.5956, V.396

Diuico BG 1.13.2

Diuiχtus 6484, 7302, N.108,
  Diuiχtus 10021.19,
  ?Diuiχti 3.12014
  (p.1900), Diuiχtullus(?)
  10010.790

[Diuzenus dipl.1]

Δυ̒α̒λας AE 1945.78

Δί̒χς RA 15, 1940, 204

[Docleas (Dalm.) 7039]

Docnimarus AE 1948.234;
  Docnim[3.11733

[Dolanus (Thr., Bessus)
  7585]

Dolccus (for Doeccus?)
  10010.802

Doles dipl.12

Dome[(or Domeius?) 6460

1272

Personal Names

Dometius H-S 557

Domisus 3.4597

Domi[itius?] 7367-68

Donco 3.11653

Donico 3.5085, Doncius 3.
14044; -icus 3.14214
ii 9

[Donius (Virunum) 6892]

Doninda 5027

Donnetus AcS 1.1305,49

Donnoc[atius?] 7756

Doroturma dipl.67

[Δορπανἃς AE 1945.1]

Dos(?) 7326-27

Dotocha dipl.67

Doueccus(?) Genava 13,
1935, 209-10

Doui[, Doue[10027.248

[Draco 3.13551,15, F.104]

Drigisa Gron. 84

Dromb[3.15216,24

Drusus 7490

Druto F.110

Drutus 3.11304

Dubintius 10010.3245

Dubitatus 7267, 7409;

10017.332; 3.5936,
V.350

Dubna 3.12031,19

Dubnia AE 1948.237

Dubp[10036.45

†Duccio F.188; Germ. 3,
1919, 48

Dudis Gron. 83, 84

[Dulazenus dipl.12]

Dules (Bessus) dipl.10

Dullauus EC 3, 1938, 198

Dullius (Gallus) 9.3044;
cf. Dullius Auentinus
13.11658

[Dumnotalus 3.10514]

[Dumragmithres (gen.) 3.
6020,5]

Dun[12765, H-M 409

Dunius 5166 add., cf. Dur-

[Duppius (pp written Ϥ)
3.12014.260]

?Dupu[AcS 1.1378

Durinius 6484

Durissa Gron. 7

Durius(?) 6456, cf. Dun-;
Durrius 3.3892; Duria
v. TLL

Durpacisa Gron. 61

Personal Names

Duttius 6544

Ebius AE 1945.124

Ebonicus 3.10732, 10741

Ebonius 3.10774

Ἐββύξενις Diss. Pann. 2.
  14,323

Eburus Gron. 3

Eccaio Gron. 31

Ecco 7684 (coh. Raet.,
  nat. Montanus) cf. 3.
  3796,]ecconis 10003.
  77

Ecdici 3.12014,253 (or
  Ec | Dici?)

Eceius 3.12014,261

?Ecetius H-S 347

?Eciosu[6515

Ecouta 3.11711

Eftecenthus Diss. Pann.
  2.14, 325 (but Ἐπτήκ-
  ενθος ib. 1010); cf.
  Epta- below

Egotalus 3.12014

Egnatuleius 3.10860

Eleius dipl.31

(H)elico Pl. 12.5

Eliomarus, -a 3.4838,
  4959; cf. Eliamarus
  (Aquit.)

Eluima 3.5446

Eluisianus 3.5486

Eluisso 3.5523

Emanneanus 3.11642

[Emerita, -us dipl.2]

Emon AcS 1.1434

Enena Gron. 60

Engenaldo (-co lapis)
  Fiebiger 3.23f

Enico (n. sg. m.) H-S
  140

Enignus 3.3871

Eninna 3.3823, 3860 (En-
  nina)

Ennius (Placentia) H-M
  278

Enobux (-bug[i]us?) 3.
  4725

Entionius 6484

Epicadius 3 p.960

Epidius 10036.8, -ia 10036.
  70

Epilius 10036.86

Eppius 3.3925

Epo 3.10740

†Eppo (hardly Eppocu[?],
  rather cu i.e. qui
  [...uixit]) 7599; cf.
  Eppo 3.3598, 3790, 3816,
  3872, 10735

Personal Names

Eptacentis dipl.36, -us
   83

Eptaperis dipl.83

Epuria H-S 459

[Equester 6.31145, 31149]

Erauiscus (ethn.) Gron.
   30, 83

Erepta F.353

?Eronu AE 1939,105

Erredius dipl.78, V.511

[Esbenus (Thr.) 7585]

Esrinus Gron. 49

Essibnus V.7

Essidi[3.6008,81

Essimnus Germ. 19, 1935,
   236

Ettiunia Gron. 69

Eudam[F.93

Eu]melus H-S 166; 3.
   10767

Eunus Gron. 36

Excingomarus 3.11711

Eximnus N.114

Exobna R.3788

Exobnus 6460, Exomnius
   12.2604

Exouna 3.13403

Exsoratus (Gallius), -a
   H-S 188

Exxuperatus H-S 324

Fabius Fabullus H-S 463

?Fabrac[us] AcS 1.1491

Fanius dipl.14, Fannius
   H-S 446

[Fato 3.6010,84]

Fauentianus Germ. 14,
   1930, 39

[Feletheus Eugipp. vit.
   Sev.]

Ferrasius 6646

Feua[3.10725

Feucontis gen. sg. 3.
   10722-24; cf. Ven.
   vhouχont-

Fidspk(?) 12782, H-M 410

Finitius 7268, Finitus 3.
   5316

Firmus, -ina 3.13402

Flama 11525a, H-M 312,
   cf. F. p.34

Flainus REA 12, 1910, 68;
   R.1937

Flanallus 3.4228, R.2259

[Flauius Gallicus 7565a;
   Flauius H-S 313; 11508,
   R.893; N.102

Personal Names

Flauos R.2078a

Foca (?) 3.12030

Focoronia 7519

Foebadius AE 1912.39

Fortionius 7753

Fraomarius Amm. 29.4.7

Fracca Fiebiger 3.23k (ON
  frakkr?)

Fresius (Hisp.) V.203

Frigiridus Greg. Tur. h.Fr.
  2.9; P-W 7.102; Frigeri-
  dus Fiebiger-Schmidt 296

Fronto F.102; H-M 301, 433,
  dipl.31, 3.5108; Fron-
  tinus AE 1946.262

[Fufidius 7300]

Fuluius (Boius) Vopisc.
  vit. Aurel. 13.1

[Funisulanus (Aniensis) 3.
  4013]

Gabinius 6421

Gabril(l)a 6309, 7299

Γκεινός H-S 525

Gaianus dipl.143, H-S 269

?Galiatia CIR 1723

Galla H-S 220

Gallicus V.220

Gallio (-eo) Gron. 11

Gallionius 11740

Gallonius AE 1945.127

Gallitta Gron. 11

Galunus 3.3815

Gam[10003.35, 10017.422

Gammus H-M 471; V.509,
  dipl.5 (Heluetius); cf.
  W.u.S. 11, 1928, 73

Gamus 3 p.1053

Γάννα Dio. 67.5.3, Ganna
  3.12012,109

Gannica (lib.) 5137; cf.
  terra sig. Gan(n)ic(c)us,
  -ius (Oswald Index; It-
  tenweiler)

Gargilius H-S 375

Garmo 3.5644 (C-?)

Garomarus 3.6010,94

?Garuon AE 1939.260; Garuo
  Diss. Pann. 2.10, 1938,
  p.3

Gasce AcS 1.1989

Gatlus (or Gallus?) AE
  1948.56

Gauidius 3.12031,3; V.75A,
  1

?Gauitus (or C Auitus?)
  6586a

Gauius 10001.145, 3.5813,
  V.121

Personal Names

Personal Names

Personal Names

Iammo (or Simmo?) 7348,
cf. Iamo (or Iallo?)
AcS 2.8

Ianisius AcS 2.8

Iantu[3.12014 (p.1900)

Iantullus, -a 3.4988,
5045, 11622, 5143,
5191, 5274a

Iantumalius Gron. 28

Iantumarus AcS 2.9; dipl.
4, V.48, -a V.28

Iantuna Gron. 28

Ianu f. 3.5963

Ianuconius F.353

[Iaolenus 3 Suppl. 9960
al., R.312 cf. 6821(?);
Tidius Tossianus Iauo-
lenus, born at Nedinum
(Dalm.)]

Iasdius 3.797-98, cf. 6.
1428

[Iasus dipl.96 al.; cf.
local names]

Iauennius CIR 1381

Iausus AcS 2.14,28

Iauius Gron. 61

[Iauus 3.2781, cf.
Iauuo(s) 3.6010,101;
12014.301, 13552]

Ibernalis 6436

Iblia 6740a

Ibliendus 3.4151, 5144a

Ibliomarius 7749; Verh.
hist. Vereins Ober-
pfalz 86, 1936, 439;
-ia F.324

Icarus 5027

Iccius 10036.52

[Icus 3.2951]

Iegidi C p.248, 10001.161;
cf. add. 3.6008,30

Ientumarus 3.4731

]iessillus 3.4604

[Iestinus 3.1221]

Iezena Gron. 57, AE 1910.
131

Ἰγίλλος Zos. 1.68

Iliatus 3.4594, 11302

Ilius, -ia 3.5071

Illus V.30

Iluin[3.12014,303

Im...alus 3 p.960

Imber(us) AE 1946.274

I]mmo 7348

Inc[3.4549

?Incopio CIR 1621

Indercus 5042 (Mélanges
Gilliard 71), but see
243 above

Personal Names

Induti(llus) 3.5777, V.87
  (or Indutus?)

Ingenius (Eluetius) 7024

†Ingildo 7600

Inguiomerus Tac. A 1.68

]inincanus 5163

Intimius 3.4098,1

Inoreiχs 3.12014,752

[Insteius dipl.55, V.510]

Intincu f. 3.12031,19

Ioincius 6484; read as
  Ioinooius add.

Ioncutus AE 1945.62

Iono AE 1945.62

?Iora see Lora

Iouentina 3.5665

Iouincus 10027.253, AcS
  2.60,20

[Iouinus dipl.20, 3.3844]

Iouitus 3.5131

Iounius 3.13561,13

Iradco 5057

Irducissa dipl.61

?Iru[3.12010,25, cf.
  Irus 3.6010,270

Isaisimus 3.6010,257

Isaurus 3.11740

Isin[3.12014,309

Isnir[cius] AE 1910.146

Issus 10017.475

Isus (Bessus) dipl.108

Itta 3.5041

Ittu 3.4784, 5242 (-o)
  al.

Itulus 4.4934, 5425 al.

Iuaccius 3.6540,13

Iucus, Iucc(?) 11718;
  R.3818; cf. Iuncus cos.
  dipl.72?

Iuenilis C p.16

Iuitorinus 3.14373,42

[Iumma (dat.) Mediomatr.
  6460]

Iuncatus V.417

Iuncinus 3.5202

Iungatus 3.5968

[Iunia (Deua) 6458]

Iunilla 3.5078

Iunna v. Bunna

Iutucanus 5029

Ixutiou[cius?] F.110

Personal Names

Λάβερις H-S 526

Laco 10010.1105, 3.6010, 115; cf. dipl.83

[Lacomo 3.10558]

Laeca R.750

Laepius H-S 134

Laetus (1-?) 7754

[Laidus dipl.11]

Laletus H-S 159

Lallo 3.6010,116; -us ib. 117

Lalus 3.11144a, AE 1920. 59

Lamia AE 1948.56

Landinus 3.5292

Lappius dipl.37

Lappus 3.5361

Larcius H-S 557

Lartia 3.3846

Lasciua 3.5824

[Lascontia 3.3855, 3895]

Laso 3.3790

Lassaiu Gron. 44

Lassonia 3.10723

?Latinianus 3.4365

Latinnus 3.6010,119

[Latinus 3.5822]

?Latumarus 3.4724 see Lutu-

Lauiania 3.5840

Lauieu[3.15216,13

Launio 3.4222

[Laurus dipl.72]

Lautinus R.4512

Leburna m. 3.3980

Leccus 7425

Ledia 3.4743

Leib[5338

Lensus dipl.17

[Lenula (Thrac.) 7049]

[?Leporus 8.6473; AcS 2. 187]

Lesus AcS 2.191

Leubaccus (-ius) 7613 with add. 7613a; for names in Laubasn- (13.8744), Leubasn- (7.691; 13. 3601), Lobasin- (Byv. 2.927; 3.3400), Lubain- (13.3622) see Oxé BJ 135, 1930, 68-69; cf. Leubius 11709, Leubinus 3.14420

[Leubinus 3.14420]

Leucena 3.10793

Leucimara 3.5265

Personal Names

[Leuganus 3.1158]

Leuinnus 7281

Lianus 7047 (cf. 3 pp.952, 960)

Libino Amm. 21.3.2

?Libo 6602

Licaius (coh. Pann.) 7582, 3.3224

[Licca 3.11051, dipl.99]

Liccaeus 3 p.960

Liccaius 3.3665, 11227; 3.14216,8; dipl.99

Liccana Gron. 30

Liccauus 3.3224

Licco Gron. 32, 63

Lichus 3.12012,112

Licinus (Heluetius) 6234, cf. C p.6 (insc., Mainz), -ius F.183, N.58, 60; AcS 2.211,15

Licouia, -ius 3.5265

Liga 3 p.960

Lillus 3.5907, V.242, 259

Lillu(tius?) 10027.99

Limenius Zos. 5.32.4

Limmo AcS 2.262

†Linculfus Kraus 1.10 (C p.37)

Linda 3.14216,8

[Lipor 3.3393]

Lirus 3.4376

Lisinius 3.5167

Liso 3.6426

Lissinia (Galla) 3.10321

Litogena 3.6008,35a, -e 3.12012,8; 13551,1

Litu 3.5501

Litugena 3.5066, 5099, 5269, 5430, V.19; -es 10001.181

Litullina (Tullina?) 5135

Liuia AJA 52, 1948, 238

[Liuima 3.5698]

Lixa 3.11259; cf. gloss 240 above

Lobasinus 3.3400

Loce[3.12014,328

Loceaneolus (Luc-?) 3. 5194

Locita H-S 239

Loco 3.11578, Locco AcS 3.510,34; Gron. 2, 49

Logus (Ermundurus) 3.14350a

[Lollius 6275, 7362; 3. 4746, 3.11882; dipl.22, 23 al.; V.35, 76]

Personal Names

Longinius Germ. 10, 1926,
  67

?Lonio 5199 (or Pomponius?)

Lonus 3 p.960

(?Loponius 3.13397)

Lora (Iora?) dipl.2

Loriqus Gron. 31, 34

[Loscus 3.3059]

Lossa 3 p.960

Loto AJA 52, 1948, 236

Loturus 3.5487

Lscscr H-M 414; 13.12863

Luca Gron. 3

Lucana H-M 184, F.92

Lucc[3.5111, cf. 12014.
  333b

Lucca dipl.49

[Luccius (cos) F.111]

Lucco 3.4599 al.

Luccus 3.12014

Lucerinis (gen. sg. fem.)
  3.3991

Lucernio 3.3987

Lucianus F.122

Lucic.c 3.12010,21, cf.
  12011,8

Luciolus 5338

Λούκις AE 1945.2

Lucretius 3.5844, cf.
  10029,36; H-M 428, 3.
  12014, cf. 14106

onis|ucri (for Lucri?)
  3.12014,337

Lugidamus 3.12027f.

[Luinus (Biturix) 6434]

Luo 3.4908a

Lupatius 10001.189

Lupatus 3.6008,37a

Lupercus dipl.128

Lupianus H-S 399

Lupio 6484

Lupionius (Suebus) C p.231;
  3.14207,7; R.1311

Lupius 3.6010,123

Luppo 3.6010,124, cf.
  11479

Λούππος AE 1945.81

Lupulus 7570a-c; -a H-S
  10; 3.11700

Lupus 3.6008,38, cf. dipl.
  3; 3 p.960 Lu(pus)
  Vlp(ius) 3.15184,12

[Lurius dipl.14; 3.12011,
  9]

Lusius 6400, dipl.5

Lusseorianus H-M 323

Personal Names

[Luχsonius (Ateste) H-M
281, F.108]

Lustus 3.5664

[Lutatius (Corfinium; or
Corinium Dalm.) 6869;
cf. AE 1948.56]

Luteia 6410

Lutetua 3.11589

Luteuius 7359, -euos 3.
14373,18

Lutriuos 3.12014,340 (or
-taeuos?)

Lutropi Jahrb. Schw. Urg.
31, 1939, 85

Lutumarus 3.4724 (for
Latu-?)

Lytra m. 3.5835

Ma[5170

Mac[3.4373

Macarius 3 p.960

[Maccaus (Verona) 5211]

[Maccius (Sabinus) H-M
243; F.99]

Macedo H-S 451

Macelus 6430

[Macer 5098-5100]

Macerina H-S 34

Macimarus 3.3377

Macrinus 7754

Macrius 5098-5100

Macuri (-g-) 3.6010,128

[Madena dipl.38]

[Maecius dipl.61; cf. AE
1946.255]

[Maenius R.392]

Maeseius (Delm.) 7581;
i.e. Moesius?

[Maeticus dipl.139]

Magaia 6296

Ma[ga]pilius H-M 245
(Ma[...0]pilius 5170)

Magetiu f. 3.11498

Magianus 5233

Magiatus N.108

Magil(i)us H-M 315, F.114

Magio (-c-) 3.4555, 4600,
Gron. 12

Magiomarus 3.11579

Magissa Gron. 60

Magius 5211, 11499, dipl.
3, F.349

Magnensis 3.3183a (unless
local name)

Magniancus Gron. 69

Personal Names

[Magnus dipl.61]

Magurius 3.4962, N.96

Maianus 7733; cf. terra
  sig. (Westerndorf)

?Maiaχia AcS 2.389

Maiorinus 5182, Maiiorinius
  N.106

Maiorius F.189

Maius F.116

Malchus 6606

Maleius 3.5498

Malia H-S 329

?Malo[AcS 2.398

Malusia 3.11565

Mam[3.12014,353

Mamma 10017.560

Mammius H-S 219; cf. JÖAI
  26, 1931, Beibl. 189-
  200

Μάμμος H-S 526; Mammus
  7301

Managnius -ia 3.5817, V.
  128

Mancius (-g-) terr. sig.
  (Westerndorf), cf.
  Mangius 12.4218, and
  Mango 5.4600, 4879;
  gloss mango 15 above

Manertus 10002.579

Manius 7050

Mann[3.12014

Manno 3.4908a

Ma[n]suetinca 11737

Mansuetinius 6604

Mansuetus 6304; id. (Viana)
  6871

Manu f. 3.3871

??Manurxi AcS 2.413 (a
  misreading for Vranarus,
  Vrbanus?)

Map[3.12014,700

Mar[3.10786

Mar[ ]us AcS 2.417,9

Marcellinus H-S 31, F.92

Marcinesius 3 p.960

Marcio dipl.128

[Marcius dipl.14]

?Marclus 6515

Marcomarus Aurel. Vict.
  de caes. 16.13; -mirus
  Rav. 4.17-18,23; Byv.
  1.578-9

Marcrinius 7281

Marcrotta 3.4945

Marcunus 11479

Marcus dipl.44

Personal Names

Marica 3.11647

Mariccus Tac. H 2.61, cf.
3.5257, 6850

Marina H-S 23

Marinius, -ia 7564

Mariorius (sic) Germ. 9,
1925, 2-3, but Maior-
ius F.189

Marnius 3.12014,362

Maro Gron. 40, 60

Maroboduus cl., Vell. 2.
108; C p.262 n.7

Maronius 3.5127

Marsus 10036.20

Martialius F.224

Martianus 3.15220

?Martiaqs ASA 28, 1926,
1-7; H-M 304, ??Mar-
tiaquos AE 1926.7

Martionius 6740a

Marus 7640a; cf. AcS 2.
417,9 (?), †Μαροῦ(s)
Arch.-Epigr. Mitth.
1896, p.103.57; 1897,
p.60-116

Masc[7263

Mascellio 7302

[Mascillius 3.4781]

Mascius 3.5637

Mascutius AcS 2.452,34

Masiac[ius 7344

Massa m. 6347, 7024

Massarus 3.11499

Masso 3.5623

Massurius 3 p.960

?Mastao 3.11299

Masterna R.896

Mastius H-M 415; 12888

?Mastus AcS 2.456,37

Masue R.4022 (Mansuetinca?)

Masuet- v. Mansuet-

Masunnus 3.4927

Masurius 11952, R.149

Masuus Dio. Cass. 67.5.3

Mataura Gron. 66

?Matera 3.4146

Materia 3.12014,704

Materiona H-M 471, V.509,
C 3 p.846 (dipl.5)

Materiu f. 3.5435

Mati Gron. 40, 80

Matia Gron. 33, 40, 80

Maticius, -ia 5156, cf. 3.
6010,137, dipl.37

Personal Names

Matiera 3.4083

Mato 3.11860, cf. 12013.6, 12014.369

Matomarus Gron. 23 al.

Matrona 3.5905, 6209

Matrulla dipl.55, V.510

[Matsiu 3.3602]

Matta 3.5836, 11574

Matti[o] 3.12014

Mattius 5234, 11737; terra sig. (Westerndorf]

Matto 5195, 3.5868, V.211 (f)

Mattosa AcS 2.479, R.4451

Mattua Gron. 41

Matuco 3.5624; -us 6010. 139

Matugenia 5185, -us terra sig. (Westerndorf)

Matui[3.11581

Matuia AE 1910.139

Matumarus 3.3409, 3546

Matuna 3.5905

Matur 5034

Maturus 3.6010,140; 6498; F.120; 10036.53

?Mauai (or Maiai?) 3. 12014,348(i)

?Maximinus (Thrax) cf. Rh. Mus. 90, 1941, 1- 17

Mecco 10017.592; 3.14373, 23

Me | Cre 3.12014,376

Medalus 3.12014,381

Μεδχ(μου) 10026.24

Medianus R.4537-8

Meddignatius 7281

Meddila 6393

Meddillius 6543, cf. Meddu ter. sig. (Heddernheim)

Meduliuia Arch. Ert. 44, 1930, 242-3, 316

Medullia 3.4083

Meita 3.10794

Melesme 3.13403

Meliddatius 6451

Melisa 3.5635

Melissus 5165

Melito 3.12014,382

Melonius 7270, 11938; cf. 6682, 7328, 6.632 (Melonius Senilis ex prou. Germ. Sup.); -ia AcS 2. 541,40; cf. 241 above

Meluro ter. sig. (Heddernheim)

Melus 5195

Personal Names

Memandus 3.11884, V.77

Memausus 3.12014,60

Memmusus 3.6010,144

Menaudonius H-S 9

Mengausus AcS 2.547

Meranius AE 1946, 262

Merator F.109 (for Merc-?)

?Mercasius 3.3625

Mercusenus AcS 2.572

Mercus(s)a 5338, cf. ter.
  sig. (Lezoux)

Mereccusa 10299

Mesia 3.11578

Mesinus 3.11299

Messicus 3.11502

Messinus 3.4537b

Messius 6366, 3.11552,
  H-S 265, 3 p.960

Me.sso 10005.17

Messorina R.3064, 3278

Messorius 6400, H-S 265,
  F.183

Mestuid[(?) 6574

[Meticus (Bessus) dipl.45]

Metilius H-S 258

Metius 7288, Metia m. 5055

Mettius 5216 (cf. 6900)

?Meussius (Sumeloc.) Blanchet, Mélanges d'arch.
  gallo-rom. 2, 1902, 109

?Mexllius see Almex-

?Michu[3.5409

Miccio F.224, 3.14373,50

Miccionia F.224

†Micco f. F.188

Mico 3 p.960

Micu 3.4459

[Middilus (not Middeus)
  6394 (Mediomatr.)]

Miletumarus 3.3404-5

Minicius 7414

Mirio (dat.) V.266

?Mirpa V.213

Misaucus 3.5891, V.235
  Misso..us AcS 2.601,11

Mixalus (-il-) AcS 2.601

?Mocilo(te) 3.12020

Mociuncius 3.1194

Mocius 3.11083, 13523 (-c-
  for -g-?)

Mocus Gron. 32

Moderat[6484

Mogetio Gron. 13 al.

Personal Names

Mogetissa m. dipl.55,
   V.510

Mogetius 6740a (Mattiacus),
   6394 (Mediomatr.), AE
   1929.194 (Carnuntum)

Mogia H-S 13

Mogienius 3.5320

Mogii[3.12014,706

Mogil(l)onius 7444

Mogio AE 1948.237

Mogitmarus Gron. 5 al.

Moienus Gron. 80

Moiota 3.3785, 3804, H-S
   134, 140

Molinus 3.5866

Momma AE 1920.59

Mommeius 3.11626

Mommius 3.5523

[Μώμω f. RA 24, 1945, 46]

Momus 3.15211

Monimus Gron. 56

Monnus 3.15211,4

Montaio 3.11595

Montanus 3.5820, cf.
   dipl.22, 33

Mo/ota AcS 2.627

Mosicu 3.5373

Mosso 3.3820

?Motrus 3.11493

Mottius H-M 472; 3 p.1978,
   R.1886, dipl.76

Mottu f. 3.5624

[Μουκάκενθος AE 1940.33]

Mucapius 3.809

[Mucapor, Muca-tralis (Thr.)
   7292, v. nn. ad loc.;
   cf. AE 1945.15; RA 15,
   1940, pp.202, 206; 3.
   799; dipl.36]

Mucarus Gron. 5, 55

Mucatri 3.787

Mufo 3.5485

Mulinus Verh. hist. Vereins
   von Oberpfalz 86, 1936,
   438

Munatius R.2634

†Municerna 7601

Munn[3.12014 (s.v. Cu-
   sentis p.1900)

Munnis N.114a

Muraesus 11947

Muranus 7579

Murranianus AcS 2.658

Murius 7370

Musaeus dipl.11

Personal Names

[Muscellus dipl.26; 3.
13552]

Muscio 3.5265

Musculeius, -a 3.13414

Muso 3.5365

Musonius 7307

Mussa 3.5344

Mussatis 3.4369

Nabra 6317; cf. 246 below

Nacinos 3.12012,114

Naeuio dipl.123

[Namiorix AcS 2.676]

Namm[7587

Namma 3.5487

Nammauos (lib.) 3.5901,
V.236

Nammeius BG 1.7.3

Nam(m)o 3.3871, H-S 133

[Namuso 3.3377]

Nan[3.12014,400

Nannenus Amm. 28.5.1; cf.
Greg. Tur. h.Fr. 2.9

†Nansa Fiebiger-Schmidt
125

[Nant(ius) 3.5901 (Treuir),
V.236]

Nanus 11947

Nasellius 6469, 6472,
6477 (cf. Nis-)

Nasoni(us) 10036.16

[Nassius dipl.11]

Nasua m. (Suebus) BG 1.37

†Nasualdus Fiebiger-
Schmidt 125

Natalius 6468

Natotus 3.6010,150 (or
-mus ter. sig. S.
Gaul?)

Νεβιογάστης Eunap. fr.12;
cf. R. Lit. 291

Nebtus Gron. 57

[Nebus dipl.151]

[Necca[(Tunger) 3.6485]

Nemausus 5214

Nemeto 3.4945, AE 1945.
133

Nemetus 5209, -a H-S 4

Nene Gron. 7

Nennius 11947

Neratius Gron. 59, 80

Nereus 6.4344

Nerianus dipl.11

Neritanus Gron. 5, 55

Personal Names

Nerius 6008.42

Nert[10008.30

Nertes 3.13552,93

Nertinius 6740a

Nertomarius 3.10794, -1a
  3.5109

Nertomarus dipl.61 (Boius),
  cf. 3.4552, 5131, 5196
  al.; Nerto[mar.. 13.
  6496, Nertomar[10027.
  118; AcS 3.510,34

[Nertus (Lingauster) 3.
  10514]

Neuia 7766

Neuiriola 3.14370,8; V.226

Neuntius 3.10776

Niarius 6484

Nicennius 5198

Nicer 3.11587, cf. C p.231;
  6.31141, 31143

Nico 3 p.960

Nido 10017.1031; R.4620

Nigellio H-S 4

Niger 3.11882

Nigilla 3.14354,17

Nipius dipl.30

?Nisellius 7756 (cf. Nas-)

Niualis 5099

Niugi AcS 2.752

Niuio dipl.96

Niuus V.4

Noebia (lib.) 3.4990a,
  cf. Noeibio 3.11558;
  Noiibio[3.11733

Nomes 3.13552,94

Nonius H-M 162 (-ios),
  440; cf. 3.4725; dipl.
  69; Jahrb. Schw. Urg.
  31, 1939, 85-6

Nonnosa H-S 69

Nonnula R.2969

Nonnus 11738, -a 3.5955,
  H-S 76; num., cf. AcS
  2.759

Nontr[ius] H-M 160; Jahrb.
  Schw. Urg. 31, 1939,
  85-6

Noreius V.223

Notria 3.3858

[Nouantico AE 1945.57]

Nouanus (Heluetius) dipl.
  76, R.1886, H-M 472;
  cf. ter. sig. (Rhein-
  zabern)

[Nouellius dipl.10]

[Nouellus 3.5471, 5567 al.
  Nouella AcS 2.783,38]

[Nouena v. AcS 2.783]

Nouetius 3.3902

Personal Names

[Nouius N.61]

[Numa ASA 31, 1939, 182]

[Numisius AE 1945.14; 3. 3935]

Nunadus (Runicas) RGKBer. 27, 1937, 86; N.114a

]nupica(?) H-S 506

[Nutrius dipl.1]

Obilia 3.4979, 6503

Obilus 3.5664

?Obucior 3.3790

?Occo[3.5529

Occus 3.4987

Ocellio H-M 449, 3.11895, V.187; cf. AcS 2.828; R.4601

[Ocilius dipl.96, 97 al.]

Ocilotes V.231

Oclatio, -ius 7307; 3. 10780; AE 1946.274

Octo AcS 2.830

[Odouacre Fiebiger- Schmidt 2]

Oeccia 3.4833

Offas 3 p.960

Oitil[10001.405

Ollia 3.3893

]ollode[3.6501

]olni 5214

Olus V. p.221

†Omharus Fiebiger-Schmidt 285

Omulus H-M 440

]onissa R.3788

?Onotnius 3.4748

Ontio H-M 319, F.121 (D]o-?)

On vi AcS 2.860,37

Oppalo, Opalo 3.3866, 10726

Oppalus 3.5422a

Oppius 3.12014

?Opniθ 3.6010,263

Opras (i.e. Of. Prasini?) 3.6010,264

?Optu f. V.46

Op.....us 7749

Orcetius (-g-) 3.11803

Or[cu]arrus (?) 3.4947, cf. 87 above

Orfatus H-S 18

?Orficius dipl.37, Orfius 38-9

Personal Names

Orgetius -ia 3.5630, 11803

Orgetorix BG 1.2.1; cf.
  W.u.S. 11, 1928, 47

Ories[R.4494

Ostilia 3.3853

Ostius 3.10732

Ostus 3.10726, cf. 3806

Otacilius, -ia 5106, 5107,
  5155, 6359, 11471,
  11480-83; add. 5106;
  R.2048, 2640; F.93

[...otgarius 3.6449]

??Oticeioccus AcS 2.889

Otto 3.3817

Oueranus V.183

]oupuna 3.5422a

?Ouuenis 3.5976, V.414

?Ouinius 7330, cf. R.927

Oxetius (-χs-?) dipl.123
  (Erauiscus)

Oxidubna (-χs-?) 3.3546

Pacata dipl.49; AJA 52,
  1948, 237

Pacci[us] 3.6014,3

Paconius 6.32933

Pacus R.4022

Paetinius H-S 220

Paettusius see Patt-

?Paii[AcS 2.922; but
  cf. ter. sig. Pallio
  (Lezoux), or Paidus
  (Rheinzabern)?

Pairk[3.6010,265

[Palanto Plassi f. (Dalm.)
  7039]

Pallo 3.5109

Pama 3.2065, cf. 182
  above

Pameta 3.5426, 5576, V.21

Pamius H-M 317, F.117

Pansiana AE 1912, p.469
  (at no.59)

[Panto f. 3.2773, 2786]

Panun[H-S 476; 3 p.2328,
  28; 14354.24

Papus (-r-?) AcS 2.928

[Paquar[3.1757; or div-
  ine name?]

Parasenus 3.4550

Pardu[lianus? 5177

?Paricus, Parus AcS 2.932
  (cf. ter. sig. Patricius)

Partus 3.11578

Passia 3 p.960

Personal Names

?Pata AcS 2.951

?Paterio 6572

Patiaanta 3.4945

Patiratus 6.6010,160

Pattusius 5169, 11499
  (Paet-)

Pau[3.6019,2

?Pauti 3.12014,711

Peccia 3.4775, 5081, 5625

Pedania 3.5947

Pellic[ius 3.12010,24

Pempte (Dalm.) 3.5913,
  V.265; not Pemptena
  Dalmata (i.e. natione)?
  Germ. 17, 1933, 127

Pentius ter. sig. (Westerndorf)

[?Perasis dipl.82]

?Pere[3.12014,425

Perpetuus 6484, F.186,
  187 (-tus), 182 (-tuius)

Perrius 7281

Perrus 7590; cf. ter. sig.
  (Banassac) and gloss
  158 above

]pessa 3.4769

Peticio f. AcS 2.972

Petissena Gron. 36

Peto 3.3820

Petronis F.103

[Petronius (Viana) 6871,
  cf. R.252]

[Petrucilus 3.12031,8]

Pettu 3.5370

Pettunatius(?) 6636

Petus 6393

Peucinia 3.4991

Piaius 3.5131

Picus 10036.55

Pileto 3.4765

[Pinarius 7566a, R.46]

Piperas 3.5837, V.149

Piru[6574 (cf. local
  names)

Pisani 3.12014 (?Rasini)

Pistaucus (or -e) f.
  (Isaurica) 3.5844, V.
  160

Pitius 3.4602, 4518

Pladomenus 3.6410

Planius 3 p.960, H-S 123,
  124

Plares (-entis) 3 p.960

[Plarentis (gen.) dipl.
  38]

Personal Names

Plassarus 3.4376

[Plassius (Delm.) 7039]

[Plator dipl.14; 3 p.960]

Plauio[3.5966 (?Fl-)

Pletor 3.10723, 10724,
H-S 134

Plinius (domo Trumplia)
3.7452

Plotia AJA 52, 1948, 237

Plunco 3.3793, 3825; -us
3.5474

Pocca V.54

Pofititus(?) 3.5965 (Pot-?
or Potit[i]us?)

[Pola dipl.8]

Polinus 3.6010,175; 12014,
67; Pollinus R.2048

Pollia 5240, Pollianus
R.252; Pollius 3.14354

Politta 3.3858, Gron. 44

Pom[H-M 470; 6.32789,
P]ompe[? 3.11703

Pontius 3.15183

Popp[3.5865

Poppo 3.12014 (or Roppus?
[Lezoux])

Porcpr[10002.32

Porcus 7565

Pormur[10002.31

Posenna 10026.66 (for
Pusinna?)

Posimarus 3.10589

Potamilia H-S 591

Poteius 3.10723

Potens 6484

Potitius(?) 3.5965, 13526;
cf. Potitus dipl.23

Pradus AE 1945.78

Pre[cio?] 3.11227, cf.
3400

Prentius 3.5878

Priarius Amm. 31.10.10

Pricus 3.6010,169

Primanius 6484

Priscinius F.184, 185

Proballa Gron. 30, 69

Procri AcS 2.1047

Prosius Gron. 15 al.

Prososius dipl.2

Prota JÖAI 26, 1930, Beibl.
189-200

Proximonia 6436

Prou[7301

?Prouino[m 3.6010,75; 3.

Personal Names

12014,448; or Prouin-
cialis?

Prouius 3.3797

Pr...uus 3 p.960

[Pruca 3.3311]

Pruso 6294, 6310

†Puleualdus F.253

Pullinius 7293

[Pullius dipl.37, et
saepe]

Pullus AE 1945.102 (cf.
57, 58); or pullus?

Pureius 6584, R.1947.5

Pusinna 5155-56, V.158,
3.5846; Fiebiger 3.21;
-us 3.5944, -io V.364
(ii 16)

Pusintus 3.5846, cf. 3335;
V.158

?Quai[3.3858

†Qalqit[? 7602

Queranus 3.11894

Quintio Gron. 11 al.

Quita 3.3621; cf. †Quito
(Sup.)

Quordaio 3.7523

Rabilus Gron. 57

Raecus 3.5789, V.100

Raeticianus V.62, Raeticus
V.312, Reticus V.377,
-ius V.151

†Rainoualdus 7748

[Rando Amm. 27.10.1]

?R]anismor[a 3.13550,3

Rantillus 3.5513

Ranucius 10036.67

[Rasinius R.1631; 3.12014
(or Pr-?)]

Rauricia 3.11613, cf. 83
above

Rauius H-S 402

Raus 3.3249

Reburrinius 6305

Reburrus 3.5087

Recinus H-M 455; 10010,
1618

Recolfi Fiebiger-Schmidt
131

Redsatus 3.4753, 4962a

Redsomarus 3.4727

Refius Gron. 37

Rega 3.3787, 3793, 3866,
3871; cf. Sup.

Regilius 3.3598

Reginius 7302

Personal Names

[Regrethus Germ. 15, 1931,
6-15 (Semitic); N.103;
F.u.F. 7, 1931, 109]

Reidomarus AE 1945.105

?Reientus 3.12014,466

[Reitugenus (Itur.) 3.
4368

†Remico F.188; cf. Germ.
3, 1919, 48-51

Renatus Greg. Tur. h.Fr.
2.9; Gron. 64

Rennius 3.5550, dipl.5,
V.509; AE 1947.33

Repenia 6571

?Resatus 3.6010,181;
12014, 467; H-S 75

[Rescentus dipl.3]

Resculus 3 p.960

Rescupor Gron. 30

?]resiaesi[7766

R(h)esius 3.4727, cf.
2883, 9973

Respendial Greg. Tur.
h.Fr. 2.9

[Ressatu f. 3.3358; -us
3.4962a, 5643 al.;
H-S 256, Gron. 1 al.
cf. Reds-]

Ressil(l)a 3.3358, 5496;
Gron. 44, 62

Ressimarus 3.5469, 5496;

H-S 217; cf. Reds-

Ressius AcS 2.1177

Ressona 3.3377

Restio 5170

Restumarus 3.5289

?Retia 3.5788, 5789

Reticintis Gron. 33

Reticius 3.5839

Reticus 3.11968

Retonius AE 1945.116

Reuso 3.11304

Richelda Fiebiger 3.23g

Ricmara Gron. 1

Ridaus 3.5905 (11906),
for -atus? (V.255)

Rifus V.30

Rigasis R.1818

Rinio 5234

Rin.ius 11947 (for Grin-
ius? Hardly G. Ran-
tius)

??Rinx AcS 2.1191

Ripanus 6476; cf. 6010.
183 and ter. sig. Rep-
anus (Rip-) of West-
erndorf; Ripanus 3.
12014,72

Riparius 5177

Personal Names

Ritogenus 3.14373,70

Rittius 6969

[Ritulla 3.11739]

[Ritumara 3.11654]

Ro[ ]scus AcS 2.1199

Robilius 10036.72 (cf. 85), 3.6017,12

[Roburus 3.12018]

†Rodoberto (gen.) 7320; cf. Le Blant nouv. rec. 1892, 426

Ro]gatinus 5192

[ʹῬοῖμος AE 1945.77]

[Romaesta m. dipl.3]

Romogilli 3.12014

Ropli AcS 2.1228

†Roteldis 7320

Ruca 3.10292

Ructicnus 3.4849

Ruega Germ. 16, 1932, 62

Rufe[R.908

Rufonius Verh. hist. Vereins Oberpfalz 86, 1936, 438

Rufrinia R.2969

Ru[f]uis (-t-?) 3.5936, but cf. p.1050

Rugus 3.12014

?Ruma 3.5350

Rumo (n. sg. m.) H-S 75

†Runa 7604

Ruscus 3.5107; cf. 13. 10006,74-75; Rudscus 3.11650

Russ[AcS 2.1249

?Ruus 3.3821

S...me[6356

S[ ]anus 6504

Sabi[3.4969

Sabianius AcS 3.528,7

Sabidianus 6.32929

Sabina H-M 471; dipl.5, V.509, -us F.99, 125

[Sabinilla 5160]

Sabinus 5106, H-M 243

Sabucinus 5102-04 (for Samb-?)

[Saccarius 3.2512]

Saccauus 3.4604

Sacciarius 3.3874

Sacconius R.2760

Sacero (ter. sig. Western-

Personal Names

dorf) cf. 10010.
1684e (3)

Saciro (-u) 6585

?Saciun (Sacrun[a?) 6376

Saco AE 1940.5

Sacra 3.5351; -atius AcS
2.1280,25

Sacretius 3.5512, 11630

Sacro 3.11579, 11630; cf.
Sacronius 3.5106

?Sac[r]una 6376

?Sacta 3.4603

[Saenienses (Span.) 10002.
36]

Saetibolus Gron. 60

Safinius AE 1912.42

Saggo 3.5465

Sagillia 3.11788

Saidel(1)us AcS 2.1296

Sait[AcS 2.1297

?Saiu(s) 3.12014,492

?Salamallianus R.392

[Sallienus dipl.33]

[Saloninus F.109; R.1947.
2]

Salon(ius) 10022.231

Saltuinus 3.5820, V.131

Saluda (dat.) Germ. 15,
1931, 10 (Semitic,
like Regrethus?), N.103

Saluonius 11751

?Salusa 10001.419

Sam[3.6506; cf. 13.
10002,97

Samaconius Diss. Pann. 2.
10, 1938, p.6

[(?)Samaria 6646; but cf.
nat. Isaurica 6656]

Sambarra 3.5565, V.5

Samianta 3.5550

Samicantu 3.5480

Samis 7306

Sammio 3.5319

Sammo H-M 311, F.107; cf.
7348; 3.4282, 11732

Sammo[V.355

Sammola 3.5939

Sammus, -a 3.5052, 5372,
F.107

Samogeni 10017.757

[Samognatius (Treuir) 3.
8014]

[Samuco 3.4971]

[Samuconius 3.10937]

Samuda 3.5365

Personal Names

Sanc[3.11813

Sancteius 5236; 12.2597;
  Urg. Jahrb. 31, 1939,
  96

Sanctinus 7277, 7335

[Sangibanus (Sambida?)
  Iord. Get. 37.194-5;
  cf. P-W s.v.]

[Sangurius(?) Tac. A 6.7;
  v.l. -nquin-]

Sanillus 3.12014,494

Sanusso 3.13552,103

Sepidius 5108

[Saplius, -ia 3.5606,
  5589]

Sappaus 7580

[Sapurda 3.3358]

?[Saraba dipl.103]

Sarda 12983; H-M 416

Sarinus Gron. 12

?Sarius 3.12014,493

†Sarmanne 3.5972, †Sar-
  mannina V.419

Sarnus 3.4501

[Sarturonius 3.4972]

?Sasirus dipl.101, Sasipus
  V.515

Sassa Gron. 31, 64

Sassaius Gron. 31

Sassus 3.5139, 6101.188;
  cf. ter. sig. (East
  Gaul)

Sasulus Gron. 31, 64

Sattara 7754

Satto 7276, H-M 317,
  F.117; 10017.763

Sattonius 6437 (with add.),
  7337, 7448; cf. 7373

Satricanius ASA 31, 1928,
  181

[Satrienus H-M 288; F.
  106]

Satucio 3.11595

Satula 3.5680

Satullus 7754, 3.3865

Saturio 7494-7494b; cf.
  3.11571

Saturius 7442

Satus 3.5465

?Saudu|ca (or Sanduca?)
  3.12010,41

Σαύφιος AE 1912.83

Sauricus dipl.2

Sauro 3.5351

Sauilo[ ]rialis 6370

Sautes Gron. 7

Personal Names

Sauus (PN?) H-S 456, 557

Saxamus 3.4909, 4960;
  -χs- 3.4864; cf. ter.
  sig. (Lezoux?); Saxan-
  us(?) H-S 100

Saχsio 3.5552

Saχxu 3.11656

?Sc:l.o. 3.12014,504

Scaenu[10002.49

Scalla 6371

Scalus 3.4582

[Scarbantilla 3.10946;
  -ina 3.4201 ethn.]

Scatonis 10036.21

Scenus dipl.31

Sceolinus Gron. 44

Scerulo Gron. 69

Scilus Gron. 5

Sclaies 3 p.960

[Scorilo (Dacus) AcS 2.
  1405]

Scu[3.5898

[Sebacauso 3.5027]

Seca 3.4555

Secca 5111

Seccalus 5178

Seccia dipl.52

Seccianus 6516

Seccio 3.4756, 5057, 5589,
  V.34; -ius V.4, JÖAI
  26, 1930, Beibl. 189-
  200

Seccionius 3 p.962 (19)

Secco 3.5786, cf. 3810,
  3861; dipl.121, V.517,
  3.3871 (p.1734)

Seccu 10010.2399

Seccus 3.5057

Secionius 6638

Sectatus 3.10937

Secuanus 7579

Secues (signifer) 6611,
  perhaps for Sequens?

Secundin[6484

Sedatus 3.6010,194 (ter.
  sig., Westerndorf);
  -ius 7352

Sedida Gron. 33

Sedulius 6440, F.184, 185

?Segillus 3.11302

Seglatius 6740a

Segunion 3.13548 (p.2202)

[Seidunate 3.10576]

Seiedius V.301

Seius 3.12014

Personal Names

Sementiuus dipl.26

？Semius AcS 2.1464

Sena 3.12014,721

Seneca 3.5411

？Senatius 5192

Seneca 5095, 7609; cf. 3.
5067, 5598, V.43

Senecianii 6338

Senecianus 6480, 6544,
6740a, N.102

Senecio 6544, 7363, V.5,
cf. V. p.222; N.60;
10017.11, AE 1912.8

Senecionius 6484

Senecius, -ia 3.4988,
5469 al.

Seniauchus Amm. 15.4.10

Seniccus 3.12014,513

Senilic[7499

Senilis 6638, cf. 6.632,
3.5097

Senilius, -ia 7369; 3.
5818, 5821, 5824

？Senillus 3.5121; -a 6435

Senio AE 1941.15, AE 1910.
139 (Erauiscus)

Sennantis (gen.) 7403

Sen(n)on[6484; Senno 3.

5792 cf. 5668; V.103

Senonius 10010.1787

Sennius 3.3860

Sennonius 6484

Sennus 3.3860, 5311

？Seno[(unless divine
name) 6335

Senocondus 7301

Senope (gen. sg. m.?)
6502

Sentilius dipl.96-98 al.

Sentius 3.12014, 13552.
Cf. R.4631; dipl.120
al. [Sentius (Beryto)
6658; cf. C p.262 n.7]

Sensuta Gron. 52

Senucus 3.4893, 5034

Senu[r]us 7281

Senus 3.5426

Seppienus dipl.22

Seppius (Creon) 7262,
7275, -ia V.8

Sequana dipl.55

Sequna Pauli no.36* (p.77;
cf. PID 1.459 Sqnna)

Sera (m.) Gron. 31

Serdi 10002.468

Personal Names

Serenus 7312

Sergius H-S 563

?Sero 7.1337,23

Serotinus 7272, 10028.12;
   Verh. hist. Vereins
   Oberpfalz 86, 1936,
   439

Serranus 11525b

Seruandio 6484; Seruandius
   Verh. hist. Vereins
   Oberpfalz 86, 1936, 439

Seruatius 6484

Serus 7582; cf. 3.6016.269

Setonius 3.5572

?Setundius 6484

[?Seubrinubi 3.5153]

Seuerra 3.4867

Seuerus 6484

Seuolus 3.12006

[Seuthus dipl.35; -es m
   dipl.33; (?)Seuthius
   3.3854]

Seχstilia, -ius H-S 123

Sextilla 3.4962

Sextus 6442

?Sibiaenus 3.3285

?Sibulla 3.5877

Sicco (Secco) dipl.73,
   V.96

Sioconia 3.11896, V.188

Sido Tac. A 12.30

Sigismundus Genava 18,
   1940, 54

Signius 6559

Sile Gron. 7

Silici (dat.) AE 1946.262

Silinus F.187

Silius (Heluetius) 6372;
   cf. 237 above; dipl.
   33

Silla 3.4460

Silo 6357, cf. 3.5165,
   dipl.14, 11508, R.893;
   but the Silu of AcS 2.
   1551,57 is probably
   Silu(anus) or Sil(uinus,
   -uius)

Silo | Tic[3.12014

Siluimarus Fiebiger 69

Siluinius F.187

Siluius H-M 352

Similis dipl.49

Simirasi Gron. 15

Simmo 7348 (or Iammo?)

Simnus dipl.125 (Condru-
   sus?)

[Sincoria 3.4769; cf.
   Singoria 3.11568]

Personal Names

?Sinic[6243 (or Suebo
Nicreti?)

[Sinomarus 3.11650]

Sintacus 3.4545

Sipa 3.12014

Sipurus AcS 2.1576; 10017.
808

Sira 3.5625, 11647, 13526
(m.)

Sirius (or Sirus) AJA 52,
1948, 238

Sirmia H-S 591 (cf. local
names)

Siro 3.5441, 11699; H-S
325; -us 3.5096, cf.
AcS 2.1583,35-6

Siscia Gron. 70; Sisgus
6240, cf. local name
Siscia

Sisia 3.4983a, 4998, 5630;
(-ss-) 5075, Sissa
Gron. 84

Sisiunus H-S 112

Sitalcis 10036.85, cf.
72

?Sitid[12014.530

Siuppus AE 1945.102

[Slauius dipl.9 (Putio-
lanus Caralitanus)]

Sledius 3.15209,1

[Soio (Bessus) dipl.26]

Sola (m.) 3.787; dipl.45

Solimari 3.12014

Solitus ASA 28, 1926, 201

Solius 6972, -ia 3.5487

Sollius 11946; R.2986

Sollonius 3.4868

Solua 3.5331, R.1897

Somario 3.11597

[Sonius AE 1940.46]

Sopron AE 1912.8

Sorina AE 1913.132

Sorn[3.14358

Σόῦις H-S 526

Sosius 7404, 7448, -ss-
R.1303

Sossianus dipl.2

[Sparticus (Bessus) dipl.1]

Spartus H-M 352

Spendo 3.13549,7

Speratus 3.5441, 13.6458;
Germ. 10, 1926, 67-71;
AE 1927.364

Spicius 3.5835

Spittulus 3.5315

[Spor dipl.83]

Sporilla Gron. 18 al.

Personal Names

Spumarus dipl.112

Sta[ ]nincanus 5163

Statianus dipl.104 al.

Statorius dipl.18

Statutus 7054, 3.5554 al.

Staus V.411

Sterius 6328, -io N.114

[Stiontia 3.3792]

Stipo Gron. 35

Stlaccius dipl.22, 24, 26

Stledius 3.15209,1; R.2747

?Stolo (-onis) 11504

Strambus AcS 2.1639,42

Strito H-S 75

Strobili 3.13551,3

Strubiloscalleo Fiebiger-
Schmidt 334

Stu[(or S. Tu[) 6592

Su[3.12014,540

Suadinus 10006.88

Suadra 3.5025, 5031, 5371
al.

Suadru f. 3.4922, cf.
14359.18

Suaducco 3.14115,76

Suaducia 3.5418, 5421

Suadulla Gron. 66

[Suaemedus 3.1120]

[Suanus 3.1185]

Suationia N.99

S]u..atius 7281

Subloanus 3.3855

Succus 10010.3186

Sucomus 10010.1850

Suecconi(us) 5171

Suerus (-b-) 6978

Suetrius V. p.221

Suetus R.2688

Suges(?), -entis 7048

Suitinus 3.6010,214

Sul[3.5643

Sule[11477

[Sullius (Viana) 6872]

Sumarius 3.4985

Sumeliu 3.11783, cf. CIR
1783

Sumelo 3.5638

Summinus 3.5424

Sumotus 3.4595

Suputa 3.5262

Sura (m.) Gron. 31; AJA
52, 1948, 237

Personal Names

[Suratus 3.5153]

Surburu (-o) 10010.1859

Surco Gron. 38

Surianus H-S 156

Surica 3.4197

Surillio 3.5319,7

Suril(l)us, -a 3.4834,
    4856 al., Surillus 3.
    13552

Surinus 3.5969, 12008

Surio 3.11805 al., 14108
    cf. 14368.21

Surius, -ia 3.4590; 12014.
    726

Suro 3.5095, cf. 6103

Surus 3.3815, 3821, 4205,
    4883 al., cf. R.1688a,
    H-S 257, 451

Susacus -g- (cf. ter. sig.,
    Avocourt) Pl. Ep. 10.
    74.1

[Sutti (Dalm.) 7509,
    11962]

Suttihus 3.4831, Suttius
    AE 1945.21

Sutuedus 3.4898

Tacilus (sic) 7365

Tacitus 6544, 3.5450, 5838
    al., 11971 (torquatus)

Tal[10002.600

Talasse 3.6018,1

Talism.s 3.12014,547

Tallarius 3.11235

Talsius 3.3811

Tam[3.12012,19

Tamacus 3.5080

Tampiana (ala) Byv. 2.
    1090; dipl.48, 69, 93

Tanconi 3.12014

]tantius N.121

Taparu f. 3.5469

Tapetius 3.6260-61, cf.
    999

Tappo 3.11302, cf. Cat.
    104.4

Tapponius 3.4773, 4866;
    cf. ter. sig.

Tara Gron. 39

Tarasi (gen.) AE 1910.152

?Tarfna 3.4995

Tari[3.12010,30

Tartonius 3.4184

Taruacus (-g-) 10010.1881,
    3.6010,217

Tas[3.12014,549

Tasgo 10010.1887

Personal Names

Tato 5027, H-S 590

Tatu Arch. Ert. 44, 1930, 242-3, 316

Tatsoria 3.10722

Tattaia Gron. 44

Tatto 3.11600

Tattus 3.11522, cf. 5310, 13523

Tatucus, -a 3.4555, 5350; -ius H-S 76

Tatue 3.4983a

[Tatulus R.1678; H-S 34]

?Taulus 3.4847

Taurinus 5820

Taurus 3.14049

Tauurus 3.6010,218

Tauus (or Tauu...s) 3. 12014,553

Te[5338

Tedd[6544, cf. 3.14368, 29 (Tess-)

Tedsicnatus (-c- for -g-) H-S 74

Telauia Gron. 64

Telesinus (cos.) F.111

?Temaio 3.11603

Teni[3.12014,728

Teraniscio AE 1941.16

Terit[3.6517

Terso 3.3400

Tertic[3.5019

Tertinius 3.4867 al.

?Tertinus 3.5300

Tertius 3.13552,108

Tessia (Heluetia) 6372, cf. C p.6 (H-M 469); -ius V.18

Tessillus 3.14368,28

Tetiunia 3.10734

Teθθ[6544

Tetra[N.92

Tetricus 3.5944, V.364 iii 1, -a F.183

Tettius 5212, F.182, dipl.72; 3.4038

Tetto 3.5929, 11912, V. 204; R.4243

Tettus, -a 3.10736, cf. ter. sig.

Teuegetus Gron. 64

Teuganiius Fiebiger 3.23e

Teurigo 10010.3186

Teuriscus Gron. 78

Teuta Gron. 81

Personal Names

?Teutana Gutenbrunner
  Frühzeit 22

Teutius Gron. 73 al.

Teutomus dipl.20; R.46

Tharsa m. R.1818

?Tharton 3.2065

Tidius 3 S. 9960 (cf. 13.
  6821), R.326

Tigurinus 5076 (Tigurinus
  pagus), cf. C pp.5,7
  (local name Caes BG 1.
  12, Str., Liv.); cf.
  gloss 207 above

Tilea AcS 2.1846

Tilurinus 3.4503

?Timi (gen. sg.) dipl.67

Timonia 6401

Tin[10017.844

Tincius, -ia 3.5849, cf.
  Tincus V.35, 161; -a
  11737, R.4022; gloss
  178

Tinco 3.4753; cf. AcS 2.
  1853

Tincus 5.5590; V.35, 161

Titennius 5213

Titianus 3.3846

Titiu f. 3.11513, cf. -o
  m. 5316

Tittionius 3.5054

Tittius 3.6010,223

Tituca 3.5080

Titulenia V.428, -ius
  see V. p.221

Titullinus 11505

Tituro 3.12014,560

Tit(t)us 3.6366, 13406

Tiu[6550, Tiuri(?) 5234

Tloantius Gron. 63

Tlo...cona 3.15216,15

Tocca m. 5028, 11472;
  R.2654

Toccinus 10010.1922; 3.
  6010,224; 12048.85

Toccus 10010.3245

Tocies 3.13552,110

Tocinus 3.15216,16

Tod[ia 3.14370,15, V.385

]todius H-M 299, F.100;
  for Carantodius?

Togio 3.4898, 5355, 5506
  al.

Togionius 3.5533

Togirix 5055; cf. num.
  232 above

Togius, -ia 7054; 3.5986,
  cf. 14101 (-c-),
  15205 1, V.412

Personal Names

Personal Names

Tu[(see Stu) 6592

Tuccius 3.4868; -ia AE
1948.236

Tuccus 6377

Tudrus Tac. G 42; Diss.
Pann. 2.10, 1939, 148;
AE 1939.261; AJA 52,
1948, 236

Tuio Arch. Ert. 44, 1930,
242-3, 316

Tugnatius 7265

Tulia 3.5968

?Tullina (Litullina?) 5135

Tunn[3.14359.4a

Turalba 3.12014,731

Turbo AE 1939.260; Diss.
Pann. 2.10, 1938, 3;
dipl.60

Turelius Gron. 77

?Turetedius 3.12031,4;
V.75A

Turicus F.236

Turius 3.12014,563

?Turma 3.1195

Turoius 3.17024-25

Turonis 3.12014 (or Ti-
Lezoux?)

Turran[6365, Turranius
dipl.23, cf. 3.12031,
15

Turana dipl.2

Tut[3.13552,63

Tuticanius V.510

Tutio Gron. 35 al.

Tutius 7050, cf. 3.11650,
dipl.13

Tutula dipl.49

Va.ullius 3.12014,568

Vabrilo 3.4600

Vacarus H-S 557

Vaeerius 3.5506, cf. 1860

?Vafo[3.11590

Valagenta 3.4184

Valeia 3.12014

Valerius F.121, cf. 11525
(-is) F. p.35

Valgius (or Vlag-) 5247

Vallaunus 3.10951

Vallesia 3.5915

Valmarus 6400

Vanamiu 3.4244

Vanatactus H-M 160; Urg.
Jahrb. 31, 1939, 85-6

?Vangio C p.231 n.1

Vannius 3.4149, N.110;

Personal Names

cf. 223, and Tac. A 12.
29; 2.63 (king of
Quadi); cf. Sido (his
nephew) above

?Vanonb[3.3665

Vantit[3.11671

[Varanes 3.6150]

Ούάριος AE 1945.81

Varisaticus F.122

Varisidius 3.10740

Varonius 7570a-c

Vartia H-S 18

Varucius 6468

[Varuso 3.12014,567; prob.
for Vapuso, ter. sig.
La Grauf.]

Vassen[10003.64

Vasidius 3 p.960

Vasilius 3.12014,315 (cf.
ter. sig., S. Gaul)

Vassius 5173

Vassus 5173, cf. AcS 3.
123

Vaterculius 6548

[Vates 3.1967]

Vati(?), see Coutusuatius;
cf. AcS 2.1243

Vatto 5035

]ubitni 10017.1060

Vcborue Gron. 24

??Vcciomarus H-S 133

[Vcc(o) 3.3362, cf. 5048,
5463]

Vccus 3.5451

Ve[10006.102

Vecco Gron. 39, 69

Vecisus 3.5464

Veco 3.10795

Vecto 10017.1031; R.4620

↑Vector V.71

Vederna AE 1948.236

Vedius V.436, 3.13526

[?Vedisouna 3.10062]

[Vegelus (Cremona) 5216]

Vegeto 3.4763; -us 13.
5209, F.126

Vegiso 3.6010,277; uegisom
3.6539 (p.1052), cf.
134 Remark iv above,
Vegiso 10010.1992

Vegisonius 7328

Vegnatius 5215

Vehe[3.5778; cf. gloss
178 above

Veiagenus (Vel-?) 6240

Personal Names

Veico m. AJA 52, 1948,
237

?Veieas (-i-) 3.4241

Veitro Gron. 2

Vela-, Velei- see Vei-

Velat[3.10774

Velidaen[7589

Velideatus AE 1941.16

Vellecia 3.5347, cf. 1247

Vello 10017.880

[Venetus dipl.14, 38; cf.
3 p.960]

Veni[3.11644

[Veniann[3.13552,115]

Veniantus 3.15216,21

Venicarus 3.12014

Venidius 11747a

Venimarus 3.4753, cf.
13975

Venisa 3.14359,19

Venisama 3.3825

Venixama (-ema, -iema) 3.
3797, 3820, 3825

Vennian[3.13552,115

Vennonius 6356, 6421

Ventinus (Au-?) V.260B
(He[luetius? or
He[duus?)

Venulanta 3.5965, V.407

Venulus 3.14354,31

Venussimus 11749

Vepintania AE 1933.111

Vepitta 3.11234

Vepo 3.5232, cf. 10795

Vepotalus H-M 457; cf. 3.
5350, num. 157 above

Veponius, -ia 3.4857,
5148, 5225, 11275,
11565

Vera[3.5319

Veranes 3 p.960

Veranius R.3397

Veracapit[AcS 3.180

Veratius 6325, 6478

Veraunius 3.11894

Verbigenus (-t-?) C p.7;
BG 1.27.4)

[Verbugia 3.10544]

Vercaius (-g-) 3.5698,
cf. 6010.271

Verciouus 3.14359,24;
AJA 52, 1948, 237

[Vercombogius 3.4732,
15205.1; Vercombogio
Gron. 73, 81; -bogus
ib.]

Vercondarius AE 1939.260

Personal Names

Verecunda dipl.55

Verecundus 6848, dipl.24
al.

Vereius 6397

[?Verio 3.11826]

Verinus 3.5106

Verissimus 3.10800

Veriugus 3.14101

Vernasius H-S 312

[Verpatus (Vasio) H-M 321
F.123]

?Vertigenus see Verbi-

Veru[3.6178,3 and 30

Veruccius 3.11153

Veruclo Gron. 32, 63

Verucloetius BG 1.7.3,
R. Lit. 2.18; v.l.
-clou-

Veruicia 11741, Veruicus
Gron. 3 al.

Verzo 3 p.960

?Ves[3.13519a

Veseca 3.5922, V.328

[Vesnius 9.6053]

[Vestalis m. Ovid ex P.
4.7.1; cf. 6, 29, 54;
Donnus "rex," ib.
Alpine]

?Veta 3.4474

[Vetidius dipl.10]

[Vettienus dipl.46 al.;
Vettenius V.510]

Vetra AE 1948.237

Vetu[3.4443

Vetulenus 3.5937, Vett-
dipl.22, 28 (cf. 3 p.
1960)

Veturius 5195, R.46, dipl.
20, 22

Veuarius F.124; H-M 325

]ugiacus 5240

Viacus 3.12014,581a

Viatica H-S 451

Vibennius 3.4991

Vibennus 3.5104-05

Vibenus 3.4149

Vibilius Tac. A 2.63; 12.
29

Vib[ius?] 7425, dipl.2,
H-S 4; 3.5131, 5142
(also -a)

Vibuleius 3.14372,7

Vibunius H-S 163

Vibunna 3.10759

Vicarius 3.5450, 5467, 5678

Personal Names

Vicasius 6.32929

?Viccus f. 3.15196,2

Vicdiccius 10036.36a;
R.3605

Victor 6484

?Victum[arius 11970a;
R.3532

Vidius 3.5861, 12014,
V.176

Vidos 3.6008,84 (for
Vind-?)

Viducius 6445, -cus 10017.
912

[Vietaucus 3.7870]

Vigellius 11738

Vigius 3.11779

Vimaic 5176

Vimpia 3.4251

Vin[7425a

Vinco F.353

Vinconia F.353

Vind[3.11429

Vind[ ]umiaii AcS 3.328

Vinda m. 3.11661

Vindaina (-ania) AJA 52,
1948, 237

Vindedo 5059

Vindelicus -a C p.6; cf.
H-M 471; V.509; C 3
p.846), cf. the next
item

Vindel[icius?] 3.5969,
F.203; V]indelec[
10001.163

Vindemi[3.6008,64

[Vindex see 237 above]

Vindicilla 3.11297

Vindilius 3.11494, 11152

Vindil[l]ius 5333

Vindillus, -a 3.11494,
11658

Vindio 3.5505

Vindius 7294; cf. dipl.84
(cos. A.D. 138); 3.
5414, 5503, 5575 al.;
3 p.960, V.15

Vindo Gron. 45

Vindobius 3.6017,10

Vindonius 6487

Vindorisus H-M 322, F.125
(-d-)

Vindus 3.12008, cf. AcS
3.342-43 (Vindo, Vindu)

Vinens 3.14216,8

??Ving[3.5916 (local?)

Vinicia 3.14370

Virate 3.12014,757

Personal Names

Vircaio 3.4911

[Viredo 3.11576]

Vireus 10002.606

Viriatus 3.15192a, cf. 3.
11650? Cf. gloss 158
above?

Virillio 3.12011,18

Viritus 3.13552,108

Virius 3.5938, -ia 3.
11650

Virolo 11970a; R.3532,
cf. Virula R.1944.1;
gloss 158 above

Vironianus AE 1941.16

Vironic.ui 3.15212,4

Virotouta H-S 168

Virrus 10017.918

Viselius 11507

Visulanius R.412

Vitalinius 7281

Vithus see Bithus

?Vitimik[AcS 3.411

Vittio 6484

Vittue 7501

Vittuo 6401

Vitullinus C p.214

Vitullus C p.214

Vitulus 7608

Viuenus 3.5550

Viuia Gron. 33

[Viuibius 3.4224]

Vix[3.12014,739

?Vlagius (Valg-) 5247

Vlbius 3.4802

Vlen[7378

?Vlmio (-ionis) 7756, not
Vlmius, perh. Vlmionius(?)

Vlpius (Helu.) 6.3302, AE
1945.102, Vlp(ius)
Lu(pus) 3.15184,12; -ius,
-ia AJA 52, 1948, 237

?Vl[tinia?] 3.11258

Vm....(us?) 7749

Vmp[10017.924 (Vimp-?)

Vne[3.12014,591

Vngario 11737, R.4022; AcS
3.31; but cf. 212 above

Vnna (B-, I-unna?) 6460

Vnno[3.12031,16

Vntilis Gron. 69

[Voccio (B-) BG 1.53.4;
cf. Voccius AcS 3.424]

Vocco 6362

Voconius 7608

Personal Names

Vocontius H-M 325, F.126

Vogitoutus 3.4724, 4908

Volcenius 3.10834, 13408;
 -ia H-S 521; cf.
 Volcae?

Volcius 6410

Volouicus 3.5552; cf.
 uicus VV C p.234 and
 6433; local name (241
 above?)

[Volsenus dipl.3]

Volterex 3.3823 cf. p.
 1731, Voltrex Gron. 22
 cet.

Volta 3.10723

Voltani 3.3790

Voltaro (n. sg. f.) 3.3860

Voltaront- Gron. 67

Voltia 3.10729

[Voltielus 3.10748]

Voltilius 3.13402

Voltio Gron. 44

Voltognas 3.13402

Voltrex 3.3797, 3825,
 3860; Gron. 22 al.

Voltuparis 3.10729

Volusius H-M 465; 3.5312,
 6020.9, H-S 168; 3.
 14354,17

[?Vomera 3.13378]

?Vomun[(-an[?) 3.12014,
 592

Vossatius 10010.2098; cf.
 3.12014,593

Vot..i(us) 3.10725

†Votrilo 7603

Vppia 3.11571

Vppo (-u) 3.5061, 10895

[Vptarus Socr. h. eccl. 7.
 30]

Vpulalus 7501

Vragiso 3.14368,28

[?Vranariu 3.14115,70]

Vrbanius 5195, R.2990

Vrbicus 5244, 6450, F.189;
 ASA 31, 1929, 183

Vrbo 3.12014,595

Vreticus 3.15220

[?Vriacius 3.10531]

Vrsa 3.5947, 5955; V.154,
 379, 391, 394; H-S 73

Vrsacius 3.5830, 5834,
 5852; V.141, 145

Vrsarius 5243

Vrsicinus H-S 69

Vrsinia 6343, -ius 6484,
 V.32

Personal Names

Vrsinus 6343, 6484, 6522,
  7302; 3.3826

Vrsio 3.11968, 12009; V.
  377, Vrsio 3.6008,65;
  dipl.104; 3.12012,96;
  H-S 591

Vrsius 7281

?Vrsuius 3.12012,14

Vrsulus 6484, 3.5944, V.
  364 iii 8, H-S 100

Vrsus V.437; 6419, 6464,
  6484, 7301; dipl.120;
  cf. †Vrsus Euch. Agaun.
  martyr.6; Vrsus 10003.
  71, 10017.934; 3.13551,
  2; H-S 69, 232

Vrue 3.15212,5

Vsou[3.14116,36

Vss[3.10759

Vsseorianius F.127

?Vteuos 3.12014,596 (for
  Luteus, ter. sig. Heil-
  igenberg, Rheinzabern?)

Vtta 3.10552

Vttedianius see V. p.221

Vttu f. 3.5523, cf. Vtto
  m. 3.11304

Vuillimeres Fiebiger-
  Schmidt 126

Vxauillus Gron. 75

Vxela 3.13406

Vxopillus Gron. 75

Zaca Gron. 15 al.

Zenas H-S 242, Zeno ZE
  1910.152

[Zerula dipl.146]

[Zina dipl.83]

Zinama 3.8147

[Ziraeus (Dalm.) 7039]

Appendices

IX   APPENDICES

245   Coins of unknown or uncertain ascription

From AcS, Blanchet Tr.; see also Forrer in Ebert's Reallexikon 6, 1926, 301-326; Blanchet and Dieudonné Mnl. de Numismatique française 1, 1912; Blanchet "Chronique de numismatique celtique," RC 28, 1907, 73-78; 29, 1908, 72-79; 30, 1909, 189-197; 31, 1910, 49-59; 32, 1911, 396-406; 34, 1913, 397-405; 39, 1922, 338-347; 48, 1931, 149-162; id., REA 12, 1910, 21-46 (against Forrer's theory of the invasion of the Cimbri); 13, 1911, 350 (on Tetricus); id., Rev. Num. 11, 1907, 461-470; 25, 1922, 124; 29, 1932, 175-184. Gleanings from collections published in recent years (Lloyd, de Luynes, Fitzwilliam) are insignificant.

annoc AcS 1.157

ασινογη (?) Tr. 95; or ηγουισα(?), cf. (μ)ησ- below

ateura (for -la, see 177 above?)

[calminoxou Tr. 107, 602]

?καιητοσ Tr. 124, also read hαιριτοσ(?), Carnutes(?)

calitix | cosii

.ccu Tr. 109

cel

kenueia Tr. 125

ki (ib., cf. 515)

cou(u)[

counertomotul Bl.-D. 124

coura ib.

cupinacios Bl.-D. 130

δι·αγα RN 29, 1932, 175

donnus | esianni (ib. 141)

?eburouix ib. 185

]eduninni[ib. 155

eiqitiako (-co) possibly to be assigned to Aquitania

επηα ib. 171

?επθσ Bl.-D. 170

εχy ib. 175

?γονοσ AcS 3.1275, cf. RN 11, 1907, 470

ie.isa. AcS, vv. ll. σελισυ (or σεγ-?), aliisia(??)

imioci Bl.-D. 189

ιυκοχ ib. 194

Coins of Unknown or Uncertain Ascription

lantos ib. 100

?matundus

(μ)ησουαγογι Bl.-D. 182

?mor[

oiiuko AcS 2.840

olutetio(s), son of Tetricus

οππιλι RN 11, 1907, 461

ouu[, ou[, oud[(?)

?πντρο (μ) retrograde RN 29, 1932, 180

πρι |σελ.ο οα ib. 183

rn AcS 2.1199

segusiaus Bl.-D. 322   But σεσισου ib. 331 is probably for σεγισου RN 29, 1932, 184; and likewise cesisu, σεσισου (?) 177 above

sobius Bl.-D. 338

?]ssatusioi

υη|&δ RN 29, 1932, 176

uepotal Bl.-D. 375

?ueruio ⊕ k AcS 3.253

uiu[

?ugoex Tr. 147 (or uegorix?)

]uot AcS 3.452

246   Glosses: Unassigned or Alien

(Cf. 1 above, Note on Glosses; 79, 178, 220 above)

F. Lot "Index scriptorum operumque latino-gallicorum medii aevi" (i.e. 500-1000 A.D.), ALMA (Bulletin du Cange) 14, 1939, 113-230; id. "Liste des cartulaires et recueils contenant des pièces antérieures à l'an 1000," 15, 1940 pp.5-24, are useful clues to medieval sources which occasionally preserve older words.

Glosses

absus "poor, inadequate"

I learn of this word from Svennung Compositiones
Lucenses (1941) pp.17, 36; I do not understand why he
considers it "veilleicht keltisch."

acina: the name of an insect, Polem. Silv. M.G. auct.

ant. 11.544,3

Given by Holder AcS 3.482, cf. Ernout-Meillet ed.
2, 11; but Plin. NH 11.120 (cf. Cic. Tusc. Disp. 1.94),
which seems generally to be overlooked, would locate
the word on the Hypanis if it has the meaning alleged
by Polem. Silv., and is not merely a misunderstanding,
through successive glossaries, of Pliny, where, of
course, it is the same as acinus "grape seed" (cf.
duracinus, whatever the origin of that may be, cf. 240
and duratia below). "Mediterranean" W-H, E-M, s.v.;
not Keltic. Perhaps connected with uaccinium (below)?

[?actaca "duck" Greg. Magn. Ep. 5.46

Doubtless nothing more than an error for anaticus,
so TLL s.v.; only an etymological dictionary appears to
be capable of taking it more seriously.]

al: see PID 2.186

ἀνεψᾶ "hellebore" Diosc. 4.145

The equivalent of λάγινον Γάλλοι (see 178 above).
It is odd to find a personal name Anepsia (Ammian. 28.
1.49), cf. Anextia AcS 1.153, Anexia (i.e. -χs-) ib.
AcS 3.662, Anissen[1.156?

Glosses

?arcomus: the name of an animal, Polem. Silv. 543.10

    In TLL the suggestion is made that this item, following arcolion (ἀρκο - λέων) is for ἀρκο - μῦς, or that it is corrupt (for artomus?); perhaps it is for arcomus as in are-comici (cf. aruernus beside are-uernus)?

[? ἀρούσιον "woad" Diosc. 1.253.16

    Cf. Ps.-Apul. 70.1, CML 4.127,6 adn.; cf. παρεία, Lesb. παραύα "cheek"?

attanus "sacred vessel"

    Nigid. ap. Non.40 (in Saliaribus); dim. atalla (Act. lud. saec. Aug., 107.132); atanulus: ἅγιον ἱερέως σκεῦος, κειμήλιον CGL 2.22,47; "genus uasis" CGL 4.406, 33 al.; cf. athannuium, atena (TLL), ἄττανα, ἀττανίτης (Hesych.).

    Usually counted Etruscan (aθene), but (Leumann, Glotta 27, 1939, 88) perhaps ultimately Keltic (cf. -t(t)- : -th-), and so for patina; cf. anax:panaca 178, 240 above.

auedo "uerbascum" CGL 3.596,28

    See Bertoldi RC 50, 1933, 332-335: lëvon Côte-d'Or, Beaune; Saône-et-Loire; cf. the personal name Auedonis (gen. sg.) CIL 5.4304 (Brescia); M-L REW 816a.

bancus: a fish (Cael. Aurel.), see W-H 1.96

βαράκακαι· ἅγιοι διάφεραι Hesych. (Zwicker FHRC 138.21)

Glosses

bardala, bardea "crested lark" CGL 3.90,9-10; 361,14

Cf. bardus (178 above, cf. 240) i.e. "the song bird" (so Do. 231) par excellence? But cf. rather (W-H 2.53) barbulus a fish, the bearded pike?

bardana "herba personacia"

Ps.-Apul. 36.7 (CML 4.82,22); i.q. betilolen (178 above), whence Fr. bardane, see SprFK 194. Cf. alabarda 240 above?

bauina: a sea-bird

Martyr. s. Porcarii (abb. Lerinensis ca. A.D. 500) ASS 12 Aug. 2.738 F: bauinarum, id est auium maritimarum innumerabilis multitudo. Only conjecture can be offered, gauia 158 above (g : b)? bouinari "screech"? Or cf. Fr. bevée, Eng. bevy?

?bazena "mafortia, marsuppius" CGL 5.220,10; 221,31

Perhaps read *bargena (cf. barga 158 above) "hut, cabin," hence "head-dress, cap," cf. capella, capanna caracalla (cf. 178); this *bargena is to be distinguished from the bargena of the glossaries, the true meaning of which it may have ousted. But Meyer-Lübke's *besena (OFr. bazeina "bee hive") Einf. 241 may find its origin here.

bessus (-ūs, m.) "mos feritatis" Virg. Gram. 14, 85.18

"Mot gaulois?" E-M ed. 2, 108. Perhaps actually, as Virg. Gram. conjectured, the Keltic form of Lat. bestia, with -ss- from -st-; hardly cf. basium 240 above. If bessus is Aquitanian, then this item belongs in 158 above.

Glosses

bessus ctd.

Ir. dāsacht "fury" (of a wild beast), dāsaim "in-
furiate" (I.Eu. *dhuōs-ta-) Vendryes RC 43, 1926, 210-
11, Loth ib. 399 (see W-H 1.102).

blandonia, bladon(n)a "mullein"

CGL 3.590,55; 612,14; 624,20; Bertoldi W.u.S. 11,
1929, 9 suggests a Keltic (Gallic) origin; and sees
also a meaning "candle-wick."

[?**bolona** "cetarius" Arnob., Donat.

Cf. bolona redemptor cetariarum, tabernarum....
quas tabernas uolgo cetarias uocant CGL 5.50,11; see
Thes. Gloss. Emend., s.v.

Thurneysen TLL explains bolona as * βολώνη (cf. E-M
ed. 2, 113, from βόλος and ὠνεῖσθαι). If so, Greek.
But note also: bolonicum "ubi liquamen fit," bullonium
"luto quod lacerarii salsamenta dixerunt" and "lutum"
Gl.]

bria "uas uinarium" Arnob.

E-M ed. 2, 117; cf. briensis ib. 118? Hardly a
mis-writing of b⟨ac⟩ria?

βρία "city" Str. 7.6.1; 319C; "village" Hesych.

Thracian; Cuny REA 11, 1909, 213 n.3 (cf. 15, 1913,
402) explains βρία as extracted from local names in
- μβρία and standing for an older -mria (Lydian).

But there is always the possibility, in names
otherwise Keltic, of seeing the familiar -briga (-bria),
see Dottin REA 9, 1907, 179-178, Jullian ib. 8, 1906,
48-51, cf. 2 above and passim; AcS 1.529. Distinguish

1323

Glosses

βρίχ ctd.

brio "bridge" (178 above), for which bria appears at
AcS 1.529,23 (from Pardessus Dipl. 2.143): in bria
quae est super fluuium Flirante; and also brio "brew"
(220 above). REA 39, 1937, 36 cites Hubschmied in
Schw. Lehrerzeitung 27 Jan. 1933 (inaccessible to me).

?cabarus: the name of an insect or reptile, Polem.

   Silv. 544.1

   Holder suggests carabus (i.e. κάραβος "crawfish")
AcS 3.1020; but a crawfish is neither insect nor reptile. If the word has got into the wrong list, Holder
may be right; or (on the same assumption) cf. *cabros,
*gabros "goat;" and the *cabrostos postulated by Ber-
toldi RC 47, 1930, 184-196 (cf. Rev. de Philol. 4,
1930, 134; REA 33, 1931, 201; Pokorny Urg. 9), from the
same source, is a plant-name

?caburtarius

   Pelagius I, quoted AcS 1.667: Iohanni patricio
caburtario inter cetera. Cf. cambutta (207), or cambortus (220 above)?

?cacabasia: the name of a plant CGL 3.628,61 al.

   If an error for caccabos, also used as a plant-
name, then not Keltic; AcS 3.1027.

cada "aruina," cadula "frusta ex adipe" CGL 5.14,34

   Thought to be "germ. Wort zur Sippe von botulus"
(W-H 1.127).

Glosses

?caesar "dimitte"

Serv. A 11.743: namque Gaius Iulius Caesar

cum dimicaret in Gallia et ab hoste raptus equo

eius portaretur armatus, occurrit quidam ex hos-

tibus, qui eum nosset, et insultans ait "caesar

caesar" (v.l. cecos ac caesar), quod Gallorum

lingua "dimitte" significat. Hoc autem ipse

Caesar in ephemeride sua dicit.

But Bern. 165 (s. ix) has : hoc de de historia
romana sumptum est. Iulius siquidem Caesar scripsit
historiam de bello germanico ubi aliquid tale de se
ipso commemorat. dicit enim quod cum esset in bello a
quodam milite raptus est de equo. et cum ab eo portaretur, obuia[uia]uit alius miles recognoscens caesarem
cumque crepit eum appellare et dicere caesar caesar,
putauit ille quia dixisset "dimitte dimitte;" caesar
enim lingua germanica est dimitte, sicque contigit ut
dimitteretur. hoc enim praecipuum esse commemorat
inter alia omnia suae fortunae miracula.

The source is probably the same as that which explains uarro as Illyrian, and other proper names as
Punic or the like. Weisgerber RhMus 86, 1937, 97-126
has discussed Serv. A 7.741 in the same MSS; cf. Savage
TAPA 73, 1942, 411. Plutarch spoke of the commentarii
as ἐφημερίδες (Schanz-Hosius Gesch. 1, 1927, 437), and
presumably "de bello germanico" is the sixth book of
the BG, possibly the events described in BG 1.31-54.

Etymologies of caesar are many; besides the well
known account in Suetonius (aesar "deus" Aug. 97) we
have (Manitius Neues Archiv 36, 1910-11, 48, from cod.
Rotomag. 1470 on Phocas GL 5.415,10 K.: Cesar uel a
cesarie, id est capillis, uel a ceso, id est secto
utero matris, a quo extractus est, uel ab elefante,
quem fertur pater eius occidisse in die natiuitatis
eius, que cesa lingua Etrusca uocatur. However Serv.
A 1.286 has caesa "elephas" lingua Poenorum, cf. (Elder
HSCP 56, 1946-47, 149), caesa "elephas" lingua Afrorum.

Glosses

?caesar "dimitte" ctd.

If caesar "dimitte" is a corruption of gaesa cf.
also Gaesatae; and note too Caesarea, the island of
Jersey.

If the expression cecos ac caesar is to be interpreted as Germanic (it being assumed that "lingua
germanica" is not absurd, in view of the fact that
Ariouistus was a German, though Keltic-speaking, and
bearing a Keltic name), then read perhaps gagus ak,
Caesar (or ge-gus?) "Unhorse (him) now, (it is) Caesar"?
Or gagus, ak gais-ar (or ge-gus?) "Unhorse (him), but
let (him) go, i.e. dimitte." (i) If ge- we have re-
duplication, if ga- the prefix ga- (cf. Gothic galūkan
aor.); as for ac cf. OE ac "but" (:L. age W-P 1.35);
(ii) gus "pour out, throw, unhorse" (ib. 1.564) cf.
O.Icelandic gióta "unhorse, throw;" (iii) -ar (ur-)
"out" (ib. 1.190 *ūd-s, ūs); (iv) gais cf. Lith. gaĩšti
"nachlassen" (ib. 1.528).

A "Germanic" interpretation of sorts is more fea-
sible than a Keltic. At AcS 3.1036,19 (on 1.677,48)
Holder compares OIr. cuire "throw" (cuirim) in Bede
Carlsr. 32ᶜ 11 (though doubtfully); Latin caesar "mur-
derer" glosses OBr. orgiat (cf. O.Ir. orgim, Orgetorix
AcS 2.875), but this is no help. The item really is
not to be taken seriously at all.

?calicarca "hyoscyamus" CGL 3.195,38

Read caligularis (-c-), cf. ps-Apul. 4.7 (CLM 4.
33.26) i.e. calcy-? But note also calocatanus and
milimindrum 158 above; not caligula (220)? However
calox, also the name of a plant, ps-Apul. 25 cf. AcS
1.705, emending alii to read Galli, may go with calocatanus, W-H 1.142; for the ending cf. camox 1 and
βέδοξ 240 above. As for coracinum (AcS 1.2063,5) that
is perhaps the same as κοράκιον (ib. 1.1114,49), cf.
corroco (207 addendum), not that ὑόγη , ὕς has anything
to do with ὑοσκύαμος.

Glosses

κανθήλη "tuft, candle-wick" Ed. Diocl. 18.6

 Commonly supposed to stand for καλαμανθήλη i.e. ανθήλη "tuft" (cf. ἄνθος); or compare candela?

 caracalla, καράκαλλα "tunic" Ed. Diocl. 26.120

caris(s)a: see PID 2.195, 3.12; W-H 1.169

casamo: see PID 2.195, 3.12; W-H 1.176; BSL 30, 1930, 110

 Keltic or Illyrian? But Quintilian 1.5.8 has a v.l. casnar (which would be Oscan, with a different meaning); and there is also some doubt about his interpretation of casamo itself, viz. "assectator" or "affectator." Cf. Illyr. pers. name Casamo CIL 3.10348? And what, if any, is the relation of the gloss cassamo (-u): id est semen balsami CGL 3.527,50 (AcS 1.821, 3.1130)?

catta: a bird

 Pannonian according to Martial 13.69.1; cf. Heraeus RhMus 74, 1925, 325 n.3; Phelps Lg. 7, 1931, 254 (Greek, cf. κόττος· ὄρνις). Cf. gattula below. But cattu(s) "cat" must be the same word (so TLL; cf. Vulg. Bar. 6.21); cf. 207 and (cateia) 220 above; Brüch p.7.

cecos: see caesar above

? κινάρα "artichoke" Ed. Diocl. 6.1

claures "porci domestici"

 E. Merchie Musée Belge 26, 1922, 263; Merchie

(p.268) compares χλούνης "sanglier, porc sauvage,"
which is not the meaning. Read perhaps ciaures (-les)
cf. Lith. kiaũlė "swine" W-P 1.467?

κοαδάμα· ποταμογείτων Diosc. 4.100 (Dacian)

It has been supposed by Pokorny (Urg. 3) that we
have to do with an I. Eu. *qᵘa- (Dacian *kua) "water;"
but ποταμός means "river," and κοα-, if that analysis
is correct, would mean "river, boundary" also, rather
than "water."

Hence cf. Lydian Καδαυας, Καδοας Lycian Kada-wãti
(see Cuny REA 15, 1913, 401), a frontier-name; -dama
may appear in the Thracian local name Vscu-dama, and
*qᵘa- "water" is thought to appear in Skt. ka- "water"
(cf. now on this W-H 1.60, 848, 863).

?* Κορορ....ορι (perhaps a woman's tunic?) Ed. Diocl. 7.
54

κόστα : the wooden parts of a cart, Ed. Diocl. 15.19

crientae "quisquiliae, paleae" CGL 4.559,55

Possibly Keltic, see Jud Arch. Rom. 6, 1922, 207;
Rom. 49, 1923, 403-404; M-L 2324a. Cognate with criblum?
(W-H 1.291); derivative: *crientare (or -iare) "winnow,
bolt"

κρώσσος "globular jug, pitcher"

Apparently "Sicel" in Aesch. but cf. Vendryes
REGr 32, 1921, 495-496 and W.B. Stanford, Proc. Roy.
Ir. Acad. 44, 1937-38, C p.234 (cf. CR 52, 1938, 240);
probably this word passed into Sicel from Keltic (for

Glosses

the Gauls in Sicily, see PID 2.168 n.2, Diod. 15.70.1
al.), cf. SprFK 162, 221; the Keltic word (cf. Ir.
cruach, W. crug "mound, heap") plays only a restricted
rôle in Romance, M-L 2340, cf. Jud AR 6, 1922, 199.
Cf. Penno-crucium item 1 (s.v. pennum) above; Idg.
Jahrb. 11, 1924, 41; Geffcken Festschrift 152; Kluge
Urg. ed. 3, 46; W.u.S. 12, 1929, 243.

krukia "crozier" Brüch p.9; Lat. or Germ.?

δηλάβρα "mattock(?)" Ed. Diocl. 15.44

Cf. Latin dolabra W-H 1.364, perhaps, conflated
with δηλ- as in ἰάδηλος "full of holes," δηλέομαι "damage."
In TLL 5.415,74 Thurneysen would regard the word as
modified for uelabrum, but CGL 2.425,47 and 522,25 has
delabra (-um): πτύον ("winnowing fan") with which dolabra
is more easily reconciled. Not delab(o)ro.

diodela "millefolium"

Dacian ps-Apul. 89.4 (CML 4.160,13), presumably
-dela "leaf," cf. πεμπέ - δουλα 178 above, W-P 1.826,
δουωδηλα in Diosc. (W-H 1.352). But what is dio- or
δουω-?

dolsa "root of garlic" (8th cent.)

Misc. Tir. p.65, 17. The etymology is unknown;
and the word survives chiefly in southern France. M-L
REW 2726.

drauoca "personacia, lappa" CGL 3.592,30 al.

Cf. Sicel δρακιά· φύλλα PID 2.467. This is, then,
another Keltic word that found its way into Sicel. Cf.
W. drewg, Bret. draok, dreok "darnel," which need not

be borrowed from vulgar Latin; Eng. tare; W-H 1.374. Also called bardana q.v. above, alabardan 220; cf. SprFK 199, Kluge AR 6, 1922, 304.

δρυνάιμετον (-νεμ-) "place of assembly" (Galatian)

Str. 12.5.1,567C.

Cf. uernenetis, nimida see 158 (and 79) above; Weisgerber Natalicium Geffcken, 1931, 159-160.

duratia "mespola" (-il-) CGL 3.585,4

According to Aebischer Vox Rom. 2, 1937, 365 merely a vulgar form of duracinus (Pl. 14.14 [Narb.], 15.39 cf. 103 [Belg.], 113, see also 240 above), usually taken as a Latin cpd. (durus, acinus, for the latter see above); but cf. the Gallic personal name Duratius, Duratis (Aquit.), BG 8.26.1-2, 27.1, and silver coins of the Pictones, AcS 1.1379. Now durize (Aebischer); for mespilus see 158 above, and distinguish dureta ibid.

[eccones "sacerdotes rustici" CGL 3.520,13 al., 5.597,

56 (-g-)

Cf. FHRC 209.2; 250.1; 260.28; 307.12,18; but Lindsay CR 31, 1917, 127 would read agones Etrusci(?), cf. W-H 1.391; yet see ennones 178 above?]

ἔρινον· χαμαίδρυς (germander)

Diosc. 3.98 (Gallic); cf. Plin. 23.131, 24.130 (erineus, ἐρινεός ?), SprFK 200; v.l. ἐχῖνος Diosc. 4. 141.

Glosses

exacum "centaurium" Pl. NH 25.68

For exago-? (W-H 1.424); Gray AJPh 50, 1929, 370 rejects Holder's and Dottin's account of this word, viz. *ex-aug- in favor of a compound of ag-. Also called aloxinum, see 178 above, gontaurion at Poitiers (Note xxvii); bricumus elsewhere in Aquitania 158; on c : g cf. Terracini in Studi...Trombetti 359, n.2.

exedum the name of a plant, Plin. NH 24.175

For -etum (cf. nimida 79 above, and many other examples of intervocalic voicing?).

[ex(s)ufflans

Stigmatized as "parum Latinum uerbum," Sulp. uit. Mart. 7.2; the word was used by Tertullian, and it was borrowed into Keltic, W. eissyfflat "backbiter." But it is Latin.]

?fesmerion "herba ibiscum"

Ps-Apul. 38 (codd.-β, Gallic), CLM 4.85,17 adn.; see SprFK 201. Cf. θέξιμον 178 above.

gaesatae "spear-men" (gaesum, PID 2.184)

Etym. Magn. offers παρὰ τὸ τὴν γῆν ζητεῖν (!), cf. Polyb. 2.22.1 διὰ τὸ μισθοῦ στρατεύειν ... ἡ γὰρ λέξις .... σημαίνει κυρίως , Amm. Marc. 4.13.5 nomen non gentis sed mercennariorum Gallorum est. Cf. Klio 13, 1938, 65-66. These can have no connexion of course with caesar "dimitte," unless that is a corruption of gaesa, which is unlikely. For gaesum cf. 1, 240, 241 above.

Glosses

gaganus: a princely and royal appelation (Greg. Tur. h.Fr. 4.29)

Said to be a title of the king of the Huns or Avars, cf. χαγᾶνος (W-H 1.576), see TLL s.v.; cf. Coripp. Iust. 3.271, Ioh. 8.418 Cagan as a proper name (rex Auarum), Caggun (Maurus); and Cagius 13.7680, cf. 10010.3292d?

galmuda "menstruous woman" (Akiba)

Galatian? (Th. Reinach RA 7, 1886, 59-60), SprFK 201; Natalicium Geffcken 160. Said to occur in O.T. in the sense "abandoned." Akiba was a Jew of the time of Hadrian. Note, however, gemnades 178 above.

gattula "blackcock" Oribas., syn. 4.3

Diminutive of catta above; but there is a v.l. gantula, apparently for cantula Plin. Val.; hardly cf. ganta 220 above, TLL? W-H 1.183 s.v. catta.

γελασονέμ· γναφάλλιον, i.e. "cotton-weed" Diosc. 3.122, Gallic

See Bertoldi AGI 22-23, 1929, 499; RC 48, 1931, 282 (Ir. gel- "white")? But cf. gilarum 158 above.

? γελανδρόν· ψυχρόν Hesych.

Hitherto counted Sicel (see PID 2.452, 482), but Hubschmied Vox Rom 3, 1938, 130 (Grenoble jalandro "cold winter") has made out a case for reckoning it Galatian and Gallo-Latin. But are there any Keltic cognates?

Glosses

γερδία   "weaver" Ed. Diocl. 20.12,13

γλεύδια   see παύγλα   below

(g)rauistellus "grey-head"

   In Plaut. Epid. 620 A (grauastellus P, and Paul.
ex Fest. 96, 272). I believe that r- is the Illyrian
form (cf. rauicellus Taurini : granum PID 2.160; Raeti,
Raii, Ῥαικός (Epicharmus) : [Alpes] Graiae, Messap.
graias, graivaihi, grahis, see PID 3.22; 2.261, 429,
473; note Grai Ocelli in the Cottian Alps), gr- the
Latin. Cf. W-H 1.620.

[haematites "heliotropa"

   AcS 1.2047, from ps-Apul. 49.2 (CLM 4.99,8-100,1);
but the text is corrupt: alii ema Titanu, v.l. Galli
ematites, profetae ematites, αἷμα Τιτᾶνου Diosc. 2.194,
13; and either we have Greek forms, or, less likely,
some equivalent, not necessarily Gallic, now hopelessly
lost.]

[ὕσγη i.q. κόκκος , i.e. kermes-oak, quercus coccifera

   Galatian, Paus. 10.36.1 (for ὗς of the codd., see
LSc ed. 9 s.v.), ὕσγινον the dye extracted from ὕσγη,
spelled ἱσ- in Edict. Diocl. AcS 1.2064-2062 accepts
ὗς. But is the word connected with ὗς ? Acorns and
berries are good food for pigs, like beech-mast. Cf.
baco- ("beech") and deus Bacon 181 Remark above. Ed.
Diocl. 19.8,31; 24.9-12; 29.20 al. (ἱσ-), 29.30; cf.
Suidas s.v. On coccum (oak-gall) REA 7, 1905, 47; Do.
247; but coccolobis (158) is a vine; no connexion with
hysex (240), ὕσσος (ib.), or ὑοσκύαμος (calicarca above);
h ὑσουι Note xx above is unexplained.]

Glosses

λάκχαινος "dyed indigo" Ed. Diocl. 8.4-5

 Cf. lacca, pellis lacchēna (Dacian?) W-H 1.742.
Perhaps rachana (220) belongs here? If so, not crocina
178.

lacrimusa "green lizard" Polem. Silv. 543.2

 Modern forms suggest a Lyonese source, M-L 4826,
but that fact throws little light on the ultimate origin.

ligo "tinctura uel fosorium" CGL 5.572,1 (AJPh 21,

 1900, 192)

linum "flax"

 "Wohl...aus einer unbekannten nichtidg. Quelle
stammend," W-H 1.810. Polyb. 3.114.4 no more justifies
an Iberian than a Keltic ascription. The Keltic words
(Ir. lin, W. llin) are borrowed. Distinguish linna (an
early Cisalpine loan into Latin), PID 2.198, cf. 158
above; Ed. Diocl. 26.1a al.

[maforte, -ium (v.l. mau-): a woman's head-dress,

 Serv. A 1.282

 Formerly claimed as Keltic (Sofer, Wilamowitz),
now traced to Semitic, W-H 2.9 q.v.]

[?manutantum (if the correct reading)

 AcS 3.413, from Caes. Arel., Pardessus Dipl. 1.
107; perhaps read manutergium "mappa," Thes. Ling. Lat.
8.369,23, gl. OE "lin." Or compare mantum (-us) 158
above?]

Glosses

<u>masca</u> "hag, witch"

Edict. Rothari 197: strigam quod est mascam, 376 quem dicunt mascam; masca "mask" is supposed to be Arabic; but is this the same word? Cf. Du Cange (Gervasius Tilb., lamias quas uulgo mascas, aut in Gallica lingua strigas); cf. M-L REW 5394, Kluge Wtb. s.v. and AR 6, 1922, 307-8; W-H 2.47. But note uascus : inanis, -m : nugatorium gl.; Aquit. divine name Bascei(?) CIL 13.26; Vascones (84, 86 above), Mascator Ennod. epist. 3.24, 9.20; Mascarpio CIL 13.5876, Greg. Tur. uit. patr. 14.4, i.q. masturbator(?) Petr. 134.5; not Masclus etc. (ter. sg.); bacuceus 79 above; talamasca (d-) 158 above.

? μαστίχη (-τύχη) "mastich" Ed. Diocl. Tr. 11 (p.2211)

<u>mēles</u> (<u>mēlo</u>, <u>mēlus</u>) "marten, badger" (Varro, Plin.);

cf. 240 above

Evidently the same as bele "marten" (I.Eu. *bh-, Latin feles), and perhaps, therefore, showing lenition (m : b), cf. W-H 1.474, Pedersen VKG 1.98, 2.24.

[<u>melinus</u> "color nigrus" CGL 5.371,11

Stokes BB 19, 1905, 169, W. melyn; cf. AcS 2.536, Terracini Riv. di Filol. 49, 1921, 428. But "black" is not "yellow" any more than it is white, pace Weisgerber SprFK 204, and this gloss must be a corruption of μέλας, -ανος , while *melinus "yellow" is surely the Greek μήλινος (cf. TLL 8.617.35); cf. milimindrum 158 above. Not adj. of meles.]

μέταξα "raw silk" Ed. Diocl. 24.1a, 24.13

At least as old as Lucilius (mat-); cf. 240 above, and matta Lang. 25, 1949, 391.

Glosses

mettica (uitis): Col. 3.2.27, Pl. 14.35

Possibly derived from a personal name or a local
name (cf. Mettius, Metiosedum; Mettus or Mettiacus,
see d'Arbois de Jubainville Propr. Fonc. 423, Metz),
like biturica (balisca), uennuncula, heluennaca and
other names of vines. Less likely Mattiaci (241) or
Matisco. For Mettis see 212 (mettis 207); Gröhler
FrON 269.

?nabras: an instrument of torture

Anth. Lat. 204.10 R. Cf. napurae "ropes of straw"
(in 204.6 paleae are mentioned); -pr- becoming -br- as
in *cabros : caper, Pokorny Urg. 9), Umb. kabru. Cf.
OHG snuaba "uitta"? Less likely Nabrissa (Span. local
name AcS 2.671); or naupreda 178 above; not Nebres,
Nebrigiac(us) AcS 2.695-696. Usually joined to the following word of the text (tanos) for which see 220 above
(tanda in line 11).

?nagarba "hard earth"

AcS 2.672, from ps-Augustine 3.1269 Migne (garba
Mart.), where OHG garba is cited. Irish? Cf. Lyd.
mag. 1.2? E-M ed. 2, 411.

[natrix "water snake"

Dottin Mélanges Loth 1927, 98 suggests borrowing
from Keltic, OIr. nathir. W-H 2.147.]

ogma, ogmius: FHRC 78.1; 182.28; 272.34; 216.4

Cf. Oglaius 213 above.

Glosses

ondax "genus marmoris" CGL 5.377,3 (ontax codd.)

    Cf. Ir. ond "stone" Stokes BB 19, 1905, 170; and perhaps Ontio 244 above? If so ontax (see 158), not ondax.

ἰωθόνη a kind of linen, Ed. Diocl. 26.64

    ωθονία "holoserica" Cf. P-W s.v. serica col. 1727.

?parada "curtain or awning on a ship"

    Auson. ep. 5.29, Sidon. ep. 8.12.5; parata in Marculfi form. "Peut-être celtique" E-M seems pure conjecture.

?patus "master" (Querolus ed. Peiper 16-17)

    Goth -faÞs, Latin potis, see van Langenhove 2.52. Not Keltic, but perhaps to be recognized in the names Agademopas, Gatpos, Esumopas? But again p- should be from qᵘ.

παῦγλα ἤτοι γλευδία parts of κάρρος , Ed. Diocl. 15.43?

    But στλευδία or σλ- may be the correct reading, cf. 233 above; hardly cf. gladius? Yet γλευδία is also rendered "tamp" or "lump-breaker."

pelax: see pilax below

pelora "thrush"?

    Anth. Lat. 762.11 R (dulce pelora sonat quam dicunt nomine drostam (drosca see 220), but the text is uncer-

tain: per ora BV, pelora M, accepted by Niedermann,
*palara E-M ed. 2, 723; cf. M-L 6156) Germ. pirol
"thrush"?

petisia "small apple"

Plin. NH 15.50; cf. perhaps petīlus Non. 149, CGL
7.81 (Fest. 244 P-Th), Isid. 12.1.52? If OW edil is
cognate, then petisia with p- is not, but -s- suggests
that it is not pure Latin either; Do. 278 Cf. Fr.
petit, on which see M-L 6544a pit [Lallform] "klein,"
6548 *pittula "kleiner Kuchen," KR 71-72? More recently Die Sprache 1, 1949, 127-8 (with 158, 178, 240 above).

?pilax "cattus murilegus"

AcS 2.1002 quotes from the vita Samsonis (Dolensis)
ASS 20 Iul. 6.518 A, and from Irish sources; Stokes considered the word borrowed from Latin, an improbable
assumption, since it does not appear in Latin. Stokes
appealed to pilare and (ex)pilare. The ending -ax suggests a non-I.Eu. (Iberian?) source.

[poipia Med. Lat. "conical mound of earth"

In eastern France; C. Jullian REA 23, 1921, 37-42.]

rattus, -a, raturus "rat" (Med. Lat.)

"Schallwort" M-L 7089a; perhaps it came in with
cattus (above)? But cf. Brüch p.6, and rotta 178 above.

rauistellus: see gr- above

Glosses

rica, ricinus, ricinium (re-) "head-dress, coiffure"

Varro LL 5.130, Paul. ex Fest. 369.1, Fest. 342. 20; Isid. 19.25.4; CGL 4.278,30; 5.525,41 and 623,13; Serv. A 1.282 and 4.137. Etymology unknown; if the conjectures in Walde ed. 2 are correct, not Keltic (ur-, W. gw-). Not rac(h)ana, crocina 178, 220.

riga Med. Lat. "furrow," for an older *rica?

See Thurneysen KR 74-75, AcS 2.1182; for *prkā, Lat. porca, Germ. furche, Eng. furrow. Cf. rica (Marcellus 8.191), SprFK 208.

?sabina (herba) "juniper"

From Cato onwards; perhaps connected with sapo 220 above? Or with the numerous names in sab- cf. Alessio L'Italia antichissima 11, 1937, 53-59, AcS 2.1264-1273? Or with sambucus (i.q. ebulus) cf. 240 above (Walde ed. 2, 675; cf. E-M ed. 2, 982); the supposed connexion with the Italic Sabini is probably no more than popular etymology.

santerna "borax" Plin. 30.93, 34.116

Used for soldering gold; perhaps Iberian (cf. -erna in maderna 178 above; Santones?), rather than Etruscan (E-M ed. 2, 893); Runes Etr. Mum. 72.

? σαύνιον "iron-shod javelin"

, Cf. perhaps the Iberian local-name Saunium or Σαυνῖτον 2 above; for the testimonia see AcS 2.1382-1383 (inter alia Diod. 5.34.5). On the ὁλοσίδηρον cf. Julian HG 2,194.1; Cuny RC 28, 1907, 413-15; Déchelette REA 13, 1911, 453-56; Breuil RA 6, 1917, 68-74 (on Iberian arms in Gaul) Is ξύνημκ (AcS 3.462) a Greek corruption of σαύνιον ?

Glosses

scordiscus "saddle" (Ed. Diocl.), **-um** "raw hide"

    scordiscarii "cavalry"

    Presumably the ethnicon Scordiscus (Illyr.). For the scordiscus itself see REA 14, 1912, 256 n.2 (cf. p.250 fig.9); AcS 2.1403-1404

selago Plin. 24.103 (a plant like sabina above)

?seruitia (uina)

    Pl. 14.69 (ab Ausonio mari); but cf. the local name Seruitti IA 268.7 (cf. 241; Pannonia). English "service-tree" is totally different (Latin sorbus "mountain-ash").

sisimbriorum Ed. Diocl. 6.24, i.e. σισύμβριον "bergomot-

    mint" or "hedge-mustard" (L.Sc. s.v. ἐρύσιμον i.q.

    uela below)

    But what is its source? The formant -brio- suggests a local name, cf. Mesembria, and βρία above.

?simila "flour"

    See Lewy KZ 58, 1930, 16-35; PID 2.473; REA 36, 1934, 32-46; E-M ed. 2, 941 Cf. σιμιδάλια , σεμ - Ed. Diocl. 15.57 ("flour"). Sicel or Illyrian?

[**sipōneis** "disciples"

    Goth., from Keltic? Cuny REA 12, 1910, 15; Weisgerber Natalicium Geffcken 165-166 (cf. Vendryes RC 49, 1932, 300); Proleg. 19; AcS 2.1576. But cf. Osc. sīpus?]

Glosses

? σιπποκλαστων Ed. Diocl. 28.67, σιππο – "tow"

    See L-Sc., s.v.; or read στυππο- i.e. stuppa?

?sirus "silo"

    Varro r.r. 1.63: in iis quos uocant sirus, quod cum periculo introitur recenti apertione; AcS 2.1583.

[σισυρα "a cloak" Polyaen. strat. 8.16.2

    Galatian according to Polyaenus; Thraco-Phrygian Boisacq; Greek AcS 2.1589.]

σπαραβέραι· οἱ γερροφόροι Hesych.

    See PID 2.430, cf. p.193 (sparus), Germanic or Illyrian? Cf. 240 above.

?spionia (spinea?) uitis

    Plin. 14.34 (at Ravenna); but cf. Columella 3.2. 27, 3.7.1, 3.21.3 Possibly Keltic SprFK 209 (after Terracini Riv. di Filol. 49, 1921, 429), cf. Pedersen VKG 1.68, 2.533 (Mid.Ir. sion, OW. fionou "rosarum," W. ffion "digitalis").

striga: see masca above

tamisium "sieve" (178 above)

    Add Brüch 13; Thurneysen KR 80; cf. possibly the divine name Temusio Dessau 9314, AcS 2.1793, see 180 above; apparently a hair-sieve, and too well attested in Romance to be a mis-writing of *camisium (linen being often used as a sieve), cf. 158, 220 above?

Glosses

[Τάρανδος , tarandrus "reindeer"

See the testimonia in AcS 2.1726-1728; Scythian.]

[titta: see Brüch p.13; but it is mere baby-language]

[θυρεός "the Keltic (Galatian) shield"

Polyb. 2.30.3, Pausan. 1.13.2, cf. 8.50.1, and the other testimonia AcS 2.1831-1832. But presumably Greek (θύρα), from its oblong shape; strictly the scutum.]

?toscia CGL 5.413,61

lena toscia; Goetz reads toga, but laena: tossia (207) is no doubt correct.

telo "well-sweep"

quo hauriant aquas Isid. 20.15.3; cf. Festus Gl. Lat. 4.447 tolenno, tolleno (gl.) qua trahitur aqua; Walde ed. 2, 767; Aebischer RC 47, 1930, 440; cf. 80, 179 above; 212 with Remark (1) ad finem, sub Vannérus: tullius Festus 482 (Gl. Lat. 4.443) Τούλλον 241, and perhaps Tullianum?

uaccīnium "blueberry" or (?) "hyacinth" (Verg.)

uaccīnus M-L 9111; whatever the origin of this word (Mediterranean? Cf. REA 36, 1934, 32-46), it evidently became confused with uacca, uaccinus; Cuny REA 12, 1910, 154-5; but cf. Vaco-magi, Vacalus (itself, according to Pokorny ZfCPh 18, 1930, 437, connected with uaccilare).

Glosses

<u>uara</u>: Auson. Technopaeg. 4; see 158 above, s.v. urium;

uargus 220?

<u>uela</u> i.q. ἐρύσιμον "hedge-mustard" (cf. sisymbrium

above)

Gallic Pl. 22.158.

<u>uerpa</u> "membrum uirile;" <u>uerpus</u> "circumcised"

Catull., Mart., Iuv. (AcS 3.241). Cf. PID 2.201-
202. Lith. varpstis "spindle," uerpiù "spin." Alessio
Stud. Etr. 13, 1939, 317-330 would connect uerbascum
(Lig.?) cf. RC 50, 1933, 330-335 (see item 1 above).
W-P 1.276; cf. δρῖλος sens. obsc.; Verpa(n)tus 83 above,
Ando-uerpus 212?

?<u>uallus</u> "reaper" (in Gaul)

Plin. 18.296 (AcS 3.96), but presumably the same
as Latin uallus "pole." Cf. Goth walus "staff," Ir.
fal "hedge," W. gwawl?

<u>uo-</u> (in Voretus and other names); see W-P 1.193 (s.v.

upo-)

[ζῦθος, <u>zuthum</u> "barley brew" (Egyptian)

Athen. 4.151 (from Poseidonius), cf. Diod. 5.25.6;
Ed. Diocl. 2.12; cf. 158 above, s.v. celia, cili(ci)a;
ζῦτος in papyri (L.Sc.) But possibly I.Eu., cf. ζύμη,
Latin ius, and iutta 178 above. Cf. Truscelli l.c.
Proleg. 9.8, p.618 n.1.]

Glosses; Spurious Inscriptions

Remark:

AcS 2.1588 offers *sisqᵘos "dry." If Latin siccus
and Sicel ϭάῠκος belong here, this would apparently be
the fifth word now observed to have reached Sicily from
Gaulish, or at least to be common to Sicel and Gaulish.
On siccus, secu-, si-sqᵘ- cf. Walde ed. 2.709; Meyer
[-Lübke] KZ 28, 1887, 172; Pokorny Urg. 155; Proleg. 51
with n.94. The same formation in *sisqᵘ- (-ku-?) as in
tescua, -qua.

Runic inscriptions are discovered within the territorial limits covered in this book, but all are outside its chronological limits except a possibly genuine
text from Arguel (4 km. s.w. of Besançon), for which
see Études Germaniques 3, 1948, 1-12. For runa see 200
above.

Tovar has recently shown that Keltic or Keltic in-
fluence is not altogether to be discounted in Iberian
(Boletín de la Real Acad. Española 25, 1946, 7-42;
Eranos 45, 1947, 81-87; Emerita 16, 1948, 75-91. Cf.
Publ. de la Real Sociedad Vascongada de Amigos del País,
San Sebastián 1945; Bol. del Seminario de Estudios de
Arte e Arqueología, Consejo Superior de Investigaciones
Científicas 43-45, 1946-47, 21-35; Univisidad de Buenos
Aires, Facultad de Filosofía y Letras, Inst. de Filol.,
Sección Classica 4, 1949, 353-356); Zephyrus (Seminario
de Arqueología, Salamanca) 1, 1950, 33-37.

There follow three texts nos. *v (Lugdunensis),
*vii (Germ. Inf.), and *viii (Germ. Sup.) that are

spurious. The rest are genuine, but alien to the ter-

ritory covered in this book, and not easily accessible

elsewhere (cf. PID 2 nos.337-341).

Alien Inscriptions

*247

Of known Keltic inscriptions of Italy, and of other
lands outside the boundaries of Gaul, the following additional texts may be included here.

(i) On strigils found at Filottrano (see JRAI 67,
1937, pl.26 no.6) and in the Gaulish necropolis at
Bologna (Montelius Civ. prim. plate 111 no.1, cf. Mon.
Ant. 9, 1899, 742; Brizio Atti e Memorie della R.
Deputazione di Storia patria per la provincia di Romag-
na 1886-87, 457 ff., references which I take from
Jacobsthal Early Celtic Art 1, 1944, p.145), retrograde,
in Greek alphabet, the stamped signature

$$o\lambda\lambda o\,\omega\rho\omega$$

(Ollo- being a well-known Keltic element in proper names,
Do. 110, 276, 292). This is claimed by Jacobsthal as
being, if correct, the oldest Keltic insc. known; but
that claim may be questioned. Cf. PID 2 nos.337-339,
especially 338.

(ii) From Arroyo del Puerco, see Hübner MLI p.181
no.46, CIL 2.738):

```
         ambatus  |  scripsi  |  carlaepraisom   |
5        secias · erba· muitie|as · arimo · praeson ‖ do ·
         singeie[t]o | ini · aua · indi · uea  |  un ·
         indi · uedaga|rom · teucaecom  |  indi · nurim ·
10       i[t]e ‖ ude[a]ec · rurseeco  |  ampilua  |  indi
```

Alien Inscriptions

(iii) From Muro de Agreda, CIL 2.2848:

umtrubos | ....roni.... |

...ero | urouii | u·s·l·m

in which Holder (3.29) takes umtrubos as "matribus,"
but that is Latin as much as Keltic (ματρεβο).

(iv) CIL 2.416 (p.695), MLI p.184 no.57. See C.
Hernando Balmori in Emerita 3, 1935, 77-119, cf. EC 1,
1936, 379-81. From Lamas de Meledo (Portugal). Balmori
gives a facsimile (pp.86, 88 Plates 1 and 2), and on
p.89 the text:

rufinus et | tiro scrip|serunt | ueamini

5   cori doenti ‖ angom lamaticom | croucea

10   maga | reaigoi petranioir|adom porgomioueas ‖

caeilobrigoi

in which lama- and croucea (cf. crougin, Hübner 48) may
be compared with lama (240) and κρωσσός (246). But
Balmori (Emerita 4, 1936, 74-85) compares also lama
(Hor. Epist. 1.13.10), which he thinks is "Illyrian"
(cf. the local names Lamatis, Ναμητος) and passed thence
into Ligurian (both as a common noun and in toponymy)
and into Corsica and Spain; ioueas and -brigoi may well
be Keltic.

To judge from Balmori's facsimile c and g are not
well distinguished; a occurs once (line 10) in the form
Λ. He holds that the insc. begins in Latin, the rest
being in a Keltic dialect, with Ligurian proper names.

*(v) Spurious? Reported about 1660 by a certain
Buat to Ménestrier (L'Art du blason justifié Lyon, 1661,

Alien Inscriptions

93); since this Buat was stationed at Meyriat (Ain), perhaps the "insc." was discovered in the vicinity (cf. REA 20, 1918, 246-47). Said to have been engraved on a gold circlet placed on the head of a gigantic figure the tomb of which Buat claimed to have discovered.

μεγασδρυ[

(vi)

A. Said to contain names of "Pictish" kings (cf. Antiquity 11, 1937, 471), the well-known cross-shaft from St Vigeans, near Arbroth, Angus, ornamented with vine and tendril-scrolls (ibid. Pl.4); the inscription "has never been examined by a palaeographer" (sic; sc. "epigraphist") according to Crawford, who gives the text as follows:

drosten ipe | uoret ett | forcus

B. The insc. of Colchester (CIL 7.1005):

deo Marti Medocio camp|esium et uictorie

Alexan|dri Pii felicis Augusti nosi|donum

Lossio Veda de suo | posuit nepos Vepogeni

Caledo

(v.l. sos[s]io in line 4?) has been discussed by J. Loth RC 47, 1930, 2-4, and by G.C. Diack Scottish Gaelic Studies 1, 1926, 195-202; id., The Newton Stone and other Pictish Insc., Paisley 1922 (cf. YW in Mod. Lang. Studies 3, 1933, p.148). Cf. now Diack's Inscriptions of Pictland, 1944, 54 and 75; Chadwick Early Scotland, 1949, 8.

Alien Inscriptions

*(vii) Spurious. An alleged Keltic insc. which
turned up at Bonn during the winter of 1917-18:

Κασιαν | σαγκα | τνιυπ | ωυολη

was owned and published by F. Marx "Über eine Marmor-
statuette der grossen Mütter mit der ältesten Inschrift
der Rheinländer in Keltischen Sprache," Bonn 1922
(Verein vom Altertums Freunden im Rheinlande). The
monument itself, as well as the insc., has been condemned as a fabrication. See Vossische Zeitung 6 March
1918; Th. Reinach REA 25, 1923, 399 (cf. 20, 1918, 196);
J. Vendryes RC 41, 1924, 287 (cf. 44, 1927, 431). See
also ZfCPh 14, 1923, 424; Germ. 8, 1924, 44f.

*(viii) Spurious. From Philol. Woch. 46, 1926,
923-28 (Ch. Mehlis "Eine griechisch-gallische[?]
Inschrift aus der Nemetergau"); found at Lachen (Neustadt a.d. Hardt, Speyerbach), and read by Mehlis as

Mehlis treated this seriously, and read it as ch·n·ph·ch·i
i.e. konpokios "Combogius;" but Sprater PhW 46, 1926,
1293, exposed thoroughly the true nature of the alleged
"insc." as childish scribbles of modern date.

(ix) On the Negau insc. considered to be Keltic
see PID 2 pp.611-12 no.1* bis; to the references given
there add RC 44, 1927, 403 and 470-471; AcS 3.845 s.v.
*bena; SprFK 155 (on *bena-; but note also banuo- "porc"
Do. 231); RGKBer. 32, 1942, 117-198.

Alien Inscriptions

(x) Names of Keltic mercenaries (Greek alphabet)
on stelae from an Alexandrian tomb, and on a Lydian
from Hadra, see Mon. Piot. 18, 1910, 37-62; REA 13,
1911, 50 (note also Ἀκάννων ib. 55 n.1; Gauisidius 67
n.3, cf. 73 n.1; Matiscus, -sco 73-74); Jacobsthal
Early Celtic Art vol. 1, 1944, 212 (addendum to 145
n.6):

Αἰδεπράτης

Λιδοσότιος

Ἄτυιος (Κελτός)

Βίτος (Γαλάτης)

Βούδορις (Γαλάτη)

Κετόσιτος (Γαλάτης)

Δοννωναταιεύς
(Γαλάτης)

Λοστοίεκο (ς?)

Σισόνων

(xi) I have not been able to see, or to obtain any
notion of the contents of Bruno Schweizer Zimbrische
Sprachreste part 1 Texte aus Giazza (in the Tredici
Communi), Deutsches Ahnenerbe: Reihe B (Abt.: Arb. z.
Germanenkunde) no.5 (Halle, Niemeyer 1939), nor am I
at all certain of what is meant by "Zimbrische" (sc.
Cimbrian? But Keltic or Germanic or what? And of what
date are the texts?).

Alien Local Names

248 Local names of alien or uncertain provenance (from
AcS)

Abalcia (v.l. Balc-,
Balt-) AcS 3.470

?Alites

Ἀλοκίαι νῆσοι Ptol.

Ἀμψιανοί Str. (for Amp-
siuarii?)

Ἀπειλοκάριον

Balcia (-t-) v. Abal-

Caletanus

?Casaecongidunus AcS 3.
1130, cf. 1271

Catalienses?

Χάλουας fl., Ptol.

Κιτουία Ptol.

Κοβανδοί

?Cursarienses (but cf.
Vrsaria ins.)

Cylipenus Pl. 4.97

Dacringi (L-?) AcS 1.1213

Δριλώνιος Steph. Byz.

Αἰβουρο βισυγγησία (i.e.
Eb-)

Fanesii Pl. 4.95; ZfdA 77,
1940, 25

Gayra fl.

Γέρμαρα Steph. Byz.

Lagnus Pl. 4.97

Latris ins. ib.

Lenna uicus Merov. num.

Lygdus fl.

Melfigia, Malfigienses

Melsyagum palus Mela 3.3.
29

Memficus silua

Μηρίων

Metia palus Mela l.c.

?Mulcha fl.

Oeonae insula Mela 3.6.56,
Pl. 4.95

?Pauum silua, Pauvain?

Πραῦσος Str.

?Rauelae AcS 2.1087

Salautensis

Σάντις Steph. Byz.

?Sarute (for Sapua see 241
above?)

?Σέρραι

Σισύγιλις

Alien Local Names; Divine Names

Soneffia

Suesia palus Mela 3.3.29

Summias (Padani?)

Ταρκυναῖοι (Draganum?)

Tastris prom. Pl. 4.97

?Tauronia

Trisfagium

?Ούιαδούα fl. AcS 3.273

?Visi

?Vist(u)la Weichsel AcS
   3.404-06

?Ούρίτιον Ptol. 2.11.12

249   Divine Names

Zwicker FHRC (see Proleg. p.7); M-L Sjoestedt Dieux et héros des Celtes, 1940 (reviewed in EC 4, 1948, 155-159, q.v.); G. Dumézil Mythes et Dieux des Germains, 1939; P. Lambrechts, Contributions à l'étude des divinités celtiques (Gent, Fac. van de Wijsbegeerte en Letteren, 93 Aflevering, Bruges, 1942; reviewed in RA 26, 1946, 126-27; cf. PhW 63, 1943, 96); and (now somewhat antiquated) J. Toutain Les Cultes de la Gaule romaine (Vol. 3 of his Cultes païens de l'empire romaine) 1920.

A few special discussions may be noted here: Artio (Bitburg BJ 55-56, 1875, 245; Bern CIL 13.5160, cf. 211 above), linked with Ἄρτεμις by Pisani REA 37, 1935, 145-150, no doubt contains artos "bear" (with ar from $_z$r or r̥, cf. NTS 1, 1928, 235); cf. RC 10, 1889, 160-66 and 174-75. Aquit. Artahe REA 10, 1908, 96 (cf. 86 above) is presumably not cognate, nor Messap. arta-, or W. arddwr, though Arthur may be.

Candidus (DN, Nièvre) may be Keltic (cf. Candetum, Cando-soccus, W. cann: see BSL 32, 1931, 111 n.2, AcS 3.1072; there are, apparently, variants with -nt- : -nd- as well as -nn-; SprFK 196). In the Nièvre Candidus is joined with Boruo, but most likely he corresponds rather to Loucetius or Leucetius, cf. AcS 1.494,5.

1351

Divine Names

di Casses: on cassi- cf. REA 3, 1901, 87 n.3, 212; 4, 1902, 276n.; caddos (-ss-) see 178 above

Cernunnos (not connected with κάρνον , κάρνυξ , SprFK 197); note †Cernuus in the eighth century (Bull. Mon. 1935, 143), and Cernenus 243 above.

Cicolus Gutenbrunner ZfCPh 20, 1933-35, 379

Cnabetius ib. 278-83

Gebrin(n)ius ib. 391

Lobbonus Pokorny ib. 399

Loucetius (Leuc-) see Candidus above

matronae Bickel Rh.Mus. 88, 1938, 193-241

Nantosuelta: etym., see BSAF 1896, 95

Nodens (Nu-), Ir. Nuada Krappe RC 44, 1927, 374; cf. Note xlv (B) above

Ogmios Arntz Hdb. d. Arch. 3, 1939, 353-356 (Müller's Hdb. d. Kl. Altertumswiss., Abteilung 6); cf. gloss 246 above; AcS vol. 2 s.v.; FHRC 216.4; Hermathena 62, 1943, 96-105; SprFK 205; in inscc. Arntz would read Oglios. Cf. Index in FHRC s.v. Ἡρακλῆς Ὄγμιος . Other references: Koepp BJ 125, 1919, 38-73; REA 25, 1923, 61; NTS 1, 1928, 184; REA 1, 1899, 112; 6, 1904, 61n., 140; Macalister Proc. Roy. Irish Ac. 44, 1937-38, C 246.

Ollo-gabiae, -totae REA 5, 1903, 387; but at least the former has not Keltic ollo-, but a hyper-Kelticism of Germ. ala-, as Gutenbrunner rightly contends.

Ritona Gutenbrunner ZfCPh 20, 1933-35, 397-99; NTS 1, 1928, 158-59

Sucellus: etym. BSAF 1896, 95

Vgium (local and divine) at Lavalduc, see H. Rolland REA 42, 1940, 653-59.

Alien Personal Names

250

    These genuine personal names of alien or uncertain
provenance are given here either for their intrinsic interest or for purposes of comparison. They are taken
from AcS in all except a few cases.

Ἀκιχώριος (or
   Κιχώριος ?)

Ἀδαῖος (gl. ἀλεκ-
   τρυών)

Adduus

Adiatorix

Agusius

Alauda (cf. 178
   above; also the
   legion; and OHG
   gloss laudula:
   lericha AcS 3.
   547,41)

Alarnus

Aliso

Ἀλούκκιος

Ἄμβατος

Ambenus

Ammilius

Andouarto

Anepsia (cf. 246
   above)

Apaudulus

Araus

Arcontia

Argutis

Ἄρτικνος

Asuuius

Ἀτεπόριξ

?Attaeus

Attusius

Aucissa

Aurius

Autaritos

Auil(l)ius, cf.
   Auili ma ASA
   1936, 169

Auitus 10024.
   354

Baeculonius

Bagauda

Balanos

Balsamo 10024.
   354

Bappo

Βαθανάτιος (-αττος)

Baudus

Becca, Becco

Bellouaedius

Βέλγιος (Βόλγ-)

Benaia

Beralcha

Biumus AE 1914.
   255

Boculus, -a

Βόλγιος, cf. Βελγ-

Bonus

Breccanus

Brennos cf. Brinno
   (224 above)

Bricomarus

Brigomarus

Brinca

Brinnius

Brittomarus

Buomi

Alien Personal Names

Bursacus AE 1914. 255

Bussenius

Caballina

Caballus

?Calacissus

?Calupio

Calocissus

?Calussa

Καμβαύλης

Canterius

Carissus

Caromarus

Carominius

Carsidius

Catmelus

Cattabus (-uus)

Cattura

Catucius, -ia

Catullus

?Ceccius

?Κινᾶτος

Cincibilus

Cingonius

Cipi 10026.45

?Comdaius

Κουᾶτος

Corbis

Cotilus

Cotyla

Crato

?Crepereius

Cretonius

Curandius

Damio

Datius

*Deces

Dignidi 10024. 354

Δοκ(κ)ούριος

Docila

Δομνόκλειος

Δομνόριξ

Drinnacius

Drusillianus

Duronius 10021. 221

Ecritomarus (Aegrit-)

Edasius

Epos(s)ognatus

Erminuscius

Etitica 10025. 162

Euronius

Fadius (Gallus)

Γάλλατις

Γαλλείνας

Gallienus

Gallio

Gargilius

Gargonius

Gargorix

Garricus

Garutos

Gaulotus

?Gicegatus (Cig-?)

Glitius

Gorgonius

?Iagumus

Alien Personal Names

?Iaules

?Iectofian

Intro 10027.114

Iogenan(us)

?Iouincilli 10027.
138

Itotagus

Labarus

?Labrases

Laenilla

Laniogaesus (or
lanio:
gaes⟨at⟩us?)

Lasemo

Laudio (Breucus
Laudionis f.)

?Leucanus

Leucis (-as?)
10024.428

Leuconicus

Libino

Lic(c)aius (-ae-)

Licco

Ligusti 10024.429

Lucconia 10024.
432

Lucontius

Luppa AE 1914.255

Lupus 10024.434

Luxorius

Maccarus

Magulla

Maiu

Malisianus

Μαναδός

Mancia

Martoualus (Me-)

Mascator (cf. gl.
246)

Mastucis

Matho

Mat(t)ius

Melimoni

Menulla

Meterius

?Methuinus

Miuddilo

Μολίστομος

Mui(elius) AE
1914.256

?Mustacus

Mutto

Nanneiuo

Nenni[

Netacagnos

Nirellius

Nurdi 10024.
532

Ocuni 10027.
178

Oenianus, cf.
Aenus (Inn)

Ὀλτίσκος

Opianicus

Oppius

Oresius

Ὀρεστόριος

Orsua (see Cor-
bis)

Ὀρτιάγων

Padus

Paterius

Patiscos

Pennus

Pestika

Peticio

Petrucius

Alien Personal Names

?Petrosidius

Pistaucus AE 1914.
255

Pisus

Pitulo 10026.47

Πλέννιος

Pordaca (see Sal-
sula)

Porius

Qusonia (i.e. Cus-)

Radagasos (Ro-)

Ranuicus

Riccim[

Riciouarus

]ricus

Rufinus

Sabaiarius (cf. gl.
sabaia 240
above)

Salanius

Salluuius

Salsula

Sammulla

Sannio

Sannius

Saocondarus

?Sapala (cf. gl.
220 above)

Sarmens

?Sarnacus

Σάρος

Scotticus

Sebennos

Sedecinnis

Sedulat[us

Segauianus

Segius

Sindilla

Sipio 10024.501

Smertomaro

Σμερτόρειξ

Solatius

Sormatius

Stratonabios

Suedius

Sueius

Talisius

Tanusius

Τάρβος , Taruus

?Ταρβούλα

Tarcondarius, cf. Ταρκω-
δήμαντος, Ταρκονδημος,
Ταρκονδιμοτος

Tarculius

Targuro

?Tasuit[

Taurou 10024.561
(Ταύρου ?)

Tautanus

Tebassus

Temisus

Tessignius (Tedd-)

Teutagonus

Teutalus

Teutamatos

??Tharasia

Thyrmis

Tiamo

Τιλλόβορος

Togonius

Tongillianus

Tongillius

Torasius

Alien Personal Names

Torisa	Varitinna	Vesulus
Tosio	Vatanaus	Vindullus
Touto[	Vatiuesca	Virdius
Troginus	Venedius 10027. 185	?Vmorci
Tucca		Viriola
Tugio	Venutius	?Vissi BSAF 1881, 247
Turnus	Veoclautus	
Turullius	?Veqoanai	Vituriga (quae et Samso)
Turus AE 1914.255	Veraniolus (Cat. 47.3)	Volaginius (Ve-)
	Vertacus	Vrsicinus 10030.11
?Vahalus	Versius	Vurga

H. Dragendorff BJ 96, 1895, 18-155 (Gaulish names on terra sigillata, e.g. Seuuo, Vallo, Buddarus "mit dem keltischen aspirierten dental" etc., see especially pp.93, 106-07; ou in Boudus, Boutius; n. sg. -os for -us; peculiarities of script, e.g. Ð đ, ʘ o, Λ or Λ a, ‖ e, ʌ i, ⌐ f); P-W s.v. Namenwesen; on Signa see Hélène Wuilleumier Mém. Ac. Inscc. BL 13.2, 1933, 559-696 (cf. REA 35, 1933, 310); on Keltic names, Thédenat RC 8, 1887, 378 ff.; 12, 1891, 131, 254, 354; 13, 1892, 301; 14, 1893, 163; Creuly RC 3, 1876-78, 153-67 and 297-312; Thomas RC 14, 1893, 303 (Comprinnus); d'Arbois de Jubainville "Les noms hypocoristiques d'hommes et de lieux en celtique" MSL 9, 189-91; id. with Ernault and Dottin Les noms gaulois chez César et Hirtius Paris, 1891; C. Marstrander RC 36, 1915-16, 335-390 (on Lugenicus : Ir. Luignech; Corobilium : Corrbil; Conguinna : Congend; Inaepius; Babrinius : Bauber); Zimmer KZ 32, 1893, 158-197; Vendryes MSL 23, 1930-35, 52 (Mettis, Bottus, Eppius; matara).

Many names are discussed by Kuno Meyer Zur keltischen Wortkunde in SB d. Königlich preussischen Akademie der Wissenschaften 1912 vol. 2, no.23 p.800: -bios : Ir. -be; -bion in uidubion; ib. Betuuius, Latobius [-m-] Etarbae; no.24, p.801: Gaulish personal names in Virg. Gram., viz., besides Latomius, pp.802-03:

Alien Personal Names

Andrianus	Gallienus	Plaetus
Arca	Gelbidius	Regilus
Asporius	Gergesus	Rigas
Bientius	Glengus	Rithea
Bregandus	Lapidius	Sagillius
Don	Lassius	Samminius
Fassica	Lucenicus	Sarbon
Gabritius	Martulis	Sarricius
Galbarius	Mitterius	Senenus
Galbungus (-ugnos)	Ninus	Sulpita
Gallirius	Perrichius	

id. ib., p.1144 no.25 (on suapte); no.26 (on Asmerius, Assianus, Gurgilius, Iuuanus, Ossius, Prassius, Saurinus, Sedulus, Vrsinus); p.1153 no.39 (Ir. Cruthen, W. Pryden "Pict"; cf. now H.M. Chadwick Early Scotland 1949; Diack Inscriptions of Pictland 1944; p.1156, 40 (on Artur; cf. p.1351 above).

Id. ib. 1913 vol. 1 pp.445-455 no.41, on Ἐπίδιον ἄκρον : Epidius, Ebude; 1913 vol. 2, 950-59 no.62 Gaulish Corobilium, no.72 Conginna f.; no.73 Viro-cantus; 1914 vol. 1, 630-42, no.91 Gallic and early British personal names, viz.

Affinus	Camulaeus	Concessa
Alfinus	Cancen	Falertus
Bernicius	Catneus, -ea	Hernicius
Caetiacus	Caturus	Inaepius
Calpornus	Chataceus	Maceleus

Alien Personal Names; Notes on Proper Names

Mathona	Odissus	Segetius
Melus	Ordius	Sencaticus
Mosamoc	Potitus	Siluister
Nitria	Rufin[us	Solonius
Ocmus		

1914 vol. 2, 952-54 (addenda) and 955-58 (index; note no.33 -icnī). On Bregandus, Gelbidius, Lugenicus (Luc-) v. also (K.M.) ZfCPh 9, 1913, 182.

REA Tables vol. 1-15, NTS Index vols. 1 and 7 (Sequana); for names on terra sigillata, Oswald's Index, 1931; and Oswald and Pryce Introduction to the study of Terra Sigillata, London 1920 are useful; for Dauzat Les Noms de personne, Paris 1925, see REA 28, 1926, 43; Jullian ibid. 14, 1921, 282-3 (on Camulixus and other such names, "Ulysse en Germanie" [!]); id. (with Prinet) ib. 21, 1919, 35-42 (anthroponomie gallo-romaine). Discussions of particular names are legion: REA 24, 1922, 260 (Liricantus Larchant cf. Cati-cantus ib. 163-4, and 25, 1923, 379); BSAF 1896, 95 (etym. of Iouantucarus); 1902, 139-144; 1904, 149-50 (on Ansenses); 1906, 252-53, 403; 1910, 237 (Craxallus or Craxanus, Indercinia or -ilia, but v. CIL 13.5748); 238 (crax-, derc-); 243 (Catius); 1926, 265-67 (Auei, Aulli[?], Crucuro). Cf. also:

Briccius (-ctius?): Goelzer REA 25, 1923, 151-2

Diuiχtus, Corcolonius: Bologa Anuarul Inst. Stud. Cl. 2, 1933-35, 219-222

Vopiscus "qui a deux âmes" (Keltic or Ligurian): Vendryes Miscelânea scientifica e literária.... J. Leite de Vasconcellos, Coimbra 1934, 428-33 (cf. EC 1, 1936, 366-7)

Agrippa ibid.

Notes on Proper Names

Pauto, Pottus (Gaulish): Frings ZfRPh 56, 1936,
    371-74 (on Weisgerber's views); but cf. Die
    Sprache 1, 1949, 126-27

Crixos: Devoto Storia 31

Andelius (Gaulish): Gray AJPh 50, 1929, 370-72

Senica (terra sig.): Bull. Arch. 1932-33 [1936],
    220; ib. 231 num. TΡΡοΤΧΧ (?), leg. Tutorix(?);
    ib. 266 num. Vercingetorix

Bull. Arch. 1905, 164 (on non-Latin proper names);
K. Simon (early Germanic names) ZfdA 74, 1937, 165-210
and 229-268; J.C. van Slee Bijdragen voor vaderl. gesch.
en oudheidk. 9, 1929, 129-140.

Cauar- in personal names, see SprFK 197

Cingo-: W-H s.v. cingo, cf. Κοyyo -, congius,
    cingeto- (NTS 1, 1928, 248)

Crapp(a)l-: Do. 248; Pokorny Urg. 69

Gobannitio: AcS 1.2030.27-2031.36; REA 7, 1905, 60

iantu-: NTS 3, 1929, p.253 s.v. "inuidia"

(Virido-)marus : ἐγχεσί - μωρος, Goth. waila-mers,
    Slav. Vladi-merz, Kuryłowicz Études p.99. But
    cf. Brito-mar[t]us PID 2.183

(Mori-)tex (if a name): cf. glosses su-tegis,
    *bouteg-, Meyer-Lübke WuS 8, 1923, 185-6, sutis
    Lex Sal. (REW 8492); and (s.v.) 207 above

uindo-: Bertoldi Berl. Beitr. 1, 1929, 278; ZfRPh
    57, 1937, 139

Bibliographical Notes on Proper Names

    It may be useful to bring together here references
to a number of discussions of proper names (local, divine, and personal), viz.:

Notes on Proper Names

Dauzat in ZONF (e.g. 2, 1927, 216; 4, 1928, 257;
6, 1930, 234; 8, 1932, 206; 9, 1933, 210; 10, 1934,
340); Gutenbrunner ZfCPh 20, 1936, 391-99 and 448-460
(names of rivers), cf. Idg. Jahrb. 22, 1938, 287-88; id.
ib. [1935] 278-83 (on Cnabetius); on Gutenbrunner's
Götternamen cf. Arntz in Germania 21, 1937, 54-55; E.
Polaschek on Not. Dign. in P-W; Ch. W. Glück Die bei C.J.
Caesar vorkommenden keltischen Namen Munich 1859; H.
d'Arbois de Jubainville Noms gaulois chez César et Hirtius Ser. 1, 1899 (names in -rix; no more published);
id. Recherches sur l'origine de la propriété foncière
et des noms de lieux habités en France Paris 1890 (reviewed by Thurneysen ZfRPh 15, 1891, 266-268); R. Pichon
Les Sources de Lucain (p.26 on Cinga), cf. Samse in RhM
88, 1939, 164-179 (on Lucan 1.396-465); Mendell Yale Cl.
Stud. 8, 1942, 1-22; Marstrander NTS 7, 1934, 344-46
(river names); H. Mayer Einfluss der vorchr. Kulte auf
die Toponomastik Frankreichs, SB Akad. Wiss. Wien, Ph-H
Kl. 175.2, 1914 (cf. RC 4, 1879-80, 6 on Bormana in CIL
12.1561); Medinger TrZ 9, 1934, 122-167; A. Mayer KZ 66,
1939, 79 (on Aballo, Eposognatus); E.O. Mayer Germania
13, 1929, 47-49 (on terra sigillata names: Bassus, Firmo,
Melus, Murranus, Namus); Meillet Introd. ed. 5 (p.130
Litauia, 218 Dumno-rix, 236 Ritu-magus); P. Aebischer La
divinité aquatique Telo et l'hydronomie de la Gaule RC
47, 1930, 427-441 (also on Stanna as a divine name CIL
13.950-54), deals with Le Toulon; Tullum (BG), Telonnum
(IA), Mistral touroum "fontaine, source" (Var); J.
Hopfner ZfCP 12, 1918, 185-194 (cf. Jahresb. d. off.-
privatgym. a.d. Stella Matutina zu Feldkirch 24, 1915,
3-34 [Idg. Jahrb. 5.174, no.2]) on diminutives in river-
names, and -ara (also in river-names); id., on nemorensis
PhW 56, 1936, 479 (Lig. *Rem- cf. 55, 1935, 1024); Hubschmied Vox Rom. 2, 1937, 24-33 (-etum); id. Festschr.
Gauchat, Aarau 1926, 435-438 (-pi, Vimpi); C. Vaillat Le
Culte des Sources dans la Gaule antique, Paris 1932 (cf.
R. Cagnat Journal des Savants 1934, 41-42).

The names restored as

*Aequo-randa (Equo-, Egui-, Igui-, Eui-) cf. AcS
1.1485, 2.24, 2.45 have given rise to endless discussion,
see SprFK 202. The name Iculisna (Aquit.) is often
brought into consideration; and it is possible that Aquis-
granni (Germ. Inf.) is a late re-shaping of the same name,
despite appearances to the contrary.

Notes on Proper Names

On -randa (-nn-) cf. Loth RC 41, 1924, 400 (372 ff.) and see 178 above; as for the alleged ico- "water" see Vendryes RC 46, 1929, 362; and any connexion with equos -i (REA 7, 1905, 36) is surely out of the question.

Among the numerous discussions I may cite Drioux REA 31, 1929, 358; P. Lebel Romania 63, 1937, 145-203; Hubschmied Vox Rom. 3, 1938, 142 n. (I.Eu. *eu̯g̑ᵘʰ- : εὔχομαι); Jud Arch. Rom. 6, 1922, 192 (on -randa 210); F. Lot Romania 45, 1919, 492-96 (cf. REA 18, 1920, 130; 22, 1920, 300); Grenier REA 20, 1918, 231-36; 38, 1936, 199.

The possibility that this local name, if not the month-name equos at Coligny, is related to Umb. eikve-, eitipens, Lat. aequus (not equos), with -ku̯- (like equos) not qᵘ seems not to have been considered. It would give the meaning of "common" border, which is what is required. Cf. W-H s.vv. equus, aequus (with addenda); and (on the Umbrian forms) von Planta vol. 1, 347; von Blumenthal Ig. Taf. 1931, 41; Devoto Tab. Ig. 1937, 386; Norden Priesterbüchern pp.79-80, 284 (on aestimo, cortumio). Cf. perhaps -mantalo- for the meaning.

Other discussions: Longnon Noms de Lieu pp.72-74; Dauzat Toponyme française 1939, 122-25 (on -apa "water" cf. p.106); Vannérus Bull. de la Commission de Toponymie et Dialectologie 11, 1935, 129-163 (cf. ZfRPh Suppl. 47-55 Bibliogr. 1927-35, p.145); 12, 1938, 321-344; Vox Rom. 2, 1937, 16; Lot REA 26, 1924, 125-129; Dauzat ib. 28, 1926, 159-163; other references ap. A. Brun RLR 12, 1936, 217-219 (p.218 n.1); Durand in BSAF 1893, 116; but is Holder's *Aquilanda (AcS 3.646), the modern Églandes, also for -randa?

Bertoldi RLR 4, 1928, 236 n.2; P. Lebel Bull. Soc. histor. et arch. Langres 1936, 107-122 (REA 39, 1937, 131); P-F Fournier Bull. geogr. 1931, 135-138; Lebel Romania 61, 1935, 483-488; -randa is identified also in Chamerande (cama- cf. *camina, chemin?) in REA 22, 1920, 130 (cf. 300), but see also 23, 1921, 52-4.

Dauzat ZONF 11, 1935, 240-255; G. Gagnon REA 30, 1928, 313; Carnoy Rev. Belge 15, 1936, 752 (cf. Ant. Cl. 6, 1937, 27); Besnier REL 7, 1929, 92; Grenier Mnl. 1. 173. Cf. Rev. Belge 17, 1938, 618-19.

Grenier Rev. des Cours et Conf. 32.1, 1931, 577-94 (on the penetration of Gaul by Roman roads), and 705-20 (La toponymie des voies romaines), where, inter alia Grenier discusses Petro-mantalum (Keltic combined with Keltic) : Petro-uiaco (TP, Keltic combined with Latin) : Quadriuium (Latin combined with Latin), accepting Jullian's (and Vendryes') account of mantalum (as also Jullian's account of Viuiscus "biuium"!); cambo- beside Ham- in the north and east; briua- (distinguish Germ. briga, brica); ritum (Keltic) : uadum (Latin); Belenus (divine) in local names.

On the Mediterranean substratum in Gaulish names see Bertoldi ZfRPh 57, 1937, 169; in Sardinia id., RLR 4, 1928, 222-250; on *alisa ib. 3, 1927, 263-282; combretum id. Vox Rom. 3, 1938, 229-236.

There are numerous contributions, of varying quality, on ancient local names in Gaul, in BSAF e.g. at 1897, 275; 1898, 262; 1917, 227-33; 1920, 135, 265; 1937, 140-43 (Favret: on Lindesina or Andesina of TP).

So in ZNF (formerly ZONF) e.g. Loewenthal 4, 1929, 269-271; Schnetz 10, 1934, 25-32; 215 and 311-314 (Germani), 275-279, 293 (-ingen), 314 ff. (reviews and bibliography); 11, 1935, especially 209-218 (decumates, cf. 14, 1938, 227); 240-255 (Dauzat on Gallo-Rom., an important contribution); 14, 1938, 82-5 (Lebel), 129-141 (Kaspers), 221-27 (Schnetz; also on garma), with the bibliogr. 303-07 (Derivière, Haust, Lebel, Vincent) and 15, 1939, 277-280 (Gaillard, Lebel, Payot and Chaume, Rostaing, Soyer, Aebischer, Hubschmied, Vannérus); Index, vols. 1-13 (1939).

Similarly ZfCPh, e.g. E.W.B. Nicholson 3, 1901, 324-326 (Aquitania); J. Schnetz "Suddeutsche Orts- u. Flussnamen aus Keltische Zeit," ZfCPh 13, 1919-21, 365-69 and 14, 1923, 35-42 and 274-288; J. Hopfner "Verkleinerungsformen altkeltischer Flussnamen" 12, 1918, 185-194.

Similarly REA e.g. A. Dauzat Chronique de toponymie (since 34, 1932, 63-71) no.29: travaux de l'année 1938, REA 41, 1939, 41-48; P. Lebel Les noms de rivière de la

Gaule chez l'Anonyme de Ravenne, ib. pp.121-137, cf.
Schnetz in Philologus 87, 1932 p.107 and (on Ligeris)
Ganshof in Tait Festschrift 1933, 111-120; A. Dauzat
Toponymie gauloise de l'Auvergne et du Velay, 32, 1930,
139-48 (-oialum -ialo-), 33, 1931, 357-88 (-acu-, -asc-,
-osc-, -usc-, -isc-; -inc-, -anc-; -ate-; -aru-; -etu-;
-enna etc.; Gallic compounds 373-79; isolated words 380-
387; Belisama 380; map at p.388); C. Jullian La Gaule
dans les "Notae Tironianae" 15, 1913, 181-184; and the
other chroniques de toponymie, e.g. 34, 1932, 65-71
(includes Bourgogne and the Franche-Comté); 35, 1933,
49-50; 36, 1934, 77-80; 14, 1912 has La Gaule dans la
Table de Peutinger (p.60) with eight plates (after
p.116); 13, 1911, p.96 on names in -aua, -aach, -aqua
(C. Taeubler, Globus 98.21, 1910, 333-337); 23, 1921,
212-218 (Jullian: de Pontchartrain à *Icoranda); 17,
1915, 271-74 (id. de l'exactitude topographique dans
la legende carolingienne); 38, 1936, 201-15 (Jeanjaquet,
on "Suisse romande"); 45, 1943, 253-264.

Of historical interest only is F. Pratbernon in
Mém. Commis. Arch. Haute-Saône 1, 1839, 5 (cf. Bibl. 2
p.638 item 37761; Mont. 1, 1917, 259 item 4721); reprinted in 1854.

Similarly RC e.g. F. Lot RC 45, 1928, 312-317; J.
Loth 44, 1927, 76-77 (on Malènes); A. Longnon Les noms
de lieu celtiques en France 13, 1892, 361-367; A. Thomas
38, 1920, 88-89; A. Thomas Quelques noms de lieux français d'origine gauloise 20, 1899, 1-6, 438-44; 22, 1901,
216-26.

On E. Muret Les noms de lieu dans les langues
romanes, Paris 1930, see Meillet BSL 31, 1931, 114-116;
Kübler Litteraturbl. f. germ. u. rom. Philol. 52, 1931,
191-193; Zauner ZONF 7, 1931, 103-04. On C.A. Williams
Die französischen Ortsnamen keltischer Abkunft (diss.
Strasbourg, 1891) see RC 12, 1891, 479 and Vollmöllers
Jahresbericht 2.175.

P. Marchot (on -inos, -a, -on in local names) in
Z.f.fr.Spr.u.Lit. 47, 1925, 455-61.

d'Arbois de Jubainville Les noms de lieu dans le
cartulaire de Gellone, CRAcInscBL 1899, 229-236 (cf.

ZfCPh 3, 1901, 434); Hubschmied Verkehrswege in den Alpen zur Gallierzeit nach den Zeugnissen der Ortsnamen, Schweiz. Lehrerztg. 27 Jan. 1933 (from ZfRPh Suppl. 47-55, 1927-35, no.1068); W. Bofinger Lat. Personenamen in d. rom. Ortsnamen auf -anum, -acum u. -anicum, Diss. Tübingen 1938 (Gnomon 15, 1939, Bibl. Beil. p.3); Pokorny ZfCPh 19, 1931-33, p.368 (on Mindel fl.); A. Vincent (on -icinus in local names) Mélanges Thomas, Paris 1932, 728-37; ZfRPh Suppl. 47-55, 1927-35, items 3132-3197, 3425-3434; P. Skok (south French local names in -anum, -ascum, -uscum) Diss. Halle 1906 (cf. RC 29, 1908, 87-88); F. Lot (on names containing uxellos, oxellos) in Mélanges d'Arbois de Jubainville, Paris 1906, 169ff.; W. Kaspers (north French local names in -acum, -anum, -ascum, -uscum) Diss. Halle, 1914 (with two other relevant monographs 1918 and 1921, cf. REA 31, 1929, 63 and ZfCPh 14, 1923, 291-2); J. Loth RC 41, 1924, 372sqq.; 43, 1926, 132-167 (Notes étymologiques); Dauzat Quelques noms prélatins de l'eau dans la toponomie de nos rivières REA 28, 1926, 152-168; id. Les noms de lieu La Nature 9 mai 1925 (cf. REA 28, 1926, 30); id. ZONF 2, 1927, 216-221 (cf. REA 29, 1927, 310); id. La toponomie française, ses méthodes, ses resultats Revue des Cours et Conferences 37, 1935-36, 593-605; J. Loth Le Gaulois turno- dans les noms de lieux REA 23, 1921, 111-116; Lebel REA 39, 1937, 44 (Arroux fl. for Aturauus, in which -auus corresponds to -ensis); Aebischer RC 47, 1930, 427-441 (on telo- in names of rivers); J. Feller Rev. belge 1, 1922, 41-49 (on Astanetum now Staneux see REA 22, 1924, 255); Jullian REA 25, 1923, 169 (on Triarnum); F. Lot RC 45, 1928, 312-317 (on Rhine, Rhône, Dordogne, Garonne, Cévennes, Belisama) see REA 31, 1929, 258; Bertoldi Stud. Etr. 3, 1929, 293-320 (*gaua in river-names, cf. NTS 4, 1930, 496); for other works of Bertoldi, Aebischer, Jud see REA 39, 1937, 135-136; Berthelot REA 36, 1934, 51-69 attempts to reconstruct the Gaul of Ptolemy; for Hubschmied's discussion of names in -pi, -pa (Gauchat Festschrift, Aarau 1926, 435-438) see Idg. Jahrb. 12, 1926, 40 and NTS 1, 1928, 266; Marstrander NTS 7, 1934, 344-46 (on river-names); Aebischer Le thème garg- et ses derivés dans la toponomie de la Gaule, in Archivum Romanicum 14, 1930, 436-39; id. Toponymie et épigraphie: l'origine du nom de Perpignan et le gentilice "Perperna," Barcelona 1931 (and also in Butlletí de dialectología catalana 19, 1931, 1-18); H. Strobel Diss. Tübingen 1936 deals with French local names derived from names of plants (see below).

Notes on Proper Names

Etymological studies of individual names or parts of names are numerous, and vary greatly in merit, e.g., among the meritorious: d'Arbois de Jubainville BSAF 1890, 266 (petru-corii, bodio-casses, teuto-bōdiaci; cf. Fr. butin from ON bytin); Dunbabin CR 56, 1942, 69 (litana "broad"): Gutenbrunner ZfDA 72, 1935, 173 (on the names in -βουρο - in Procopius); Carnoy L'élément sentimental dans la toponymie gallo-rom. Ant. Cl. 6, 1937, 27-34 (cf. Rev. Belge 15, 1936, 752), not to be taken very seriously; H. Jacobsohn, see Idg. Iahrb. 1, 1914, 236 (on the gender of Keltic river-names in Germanic territory); Vendryes BSL 38, 1937, 113-116 mantalon "chemin" (cf. Mantala ap. Allobroges), Petromantalon : Petrum-uiaco "carrefour, les Quatre-chemins," not connected with W. mantawl "balance" (Do.) but W. mathru, Br. mantra (Pedersen VKG 1.139, cf. Jullian REA 19, 1917, 39), Catamantaloedis gen. sg. (BG 1.3.4) "qui marche au combat" (for another explanation "of equal weight," cata-, cant- W. gan- "with," see Schwyzer ZfCPh 22, 1941, 325-329); Vendryes EC 3, 1938, 201-2 denies that mare Cronium Pl. 4.30 can be Keltic; Dottin Manuel pour servir à l'etude de l'antiquité celtique ed. 2, Paris 1915, passim; Loth BSL 31 fasc. 1, 1931, xxv and 8-19 (cf. NTS 5, 1932, 376); H. Strobel Die von pflanzennamen abgeleiteten Ortsnamen einiger südfranzösischen Departments," Diss. Tübingen 1936 (not important); note especially Thurneysen KZ 59, 1931-32, 14 (cf. IF 42, 1924, 144) on Rhodanus (cf. gl. Endl. 178 above, s. vv. dan, rho):

*dānu- "heftige Strömung, stark fliessendes Wasser," OIr. dane "kühn, drauf-gängerisch," Danuuius (on which cf. Pokorny Mél. Boisacq 2.193) and (Yorks., the Don) Danum

ib. p.15: Condate (acc. -em, Auson.), Fr. Condé, Condes beside Confluens, -ntes (Ger. Koblenz); on the latter cf. Meyer-Lübke in Mélanges Chabaneau Rom. Forsch. 23, 1907, 591-96 (see REA 9, 1907, 371)

ib. pp.15-16: on R(h)ēnus, *Reinos cf. O.Ir. rían "Meer, Strömung," but note Dīuiciacus (ī from ē), Dīuona (Auson., near Bordeaux, Divonne dép. Ain), Dīuogenus (-a) beside Dēuognata, Dēuignata, from which it is evident that the development of ē from ei is not universal in

Gaulish (cf. RC 51, 1934, 179). So eu, ou
have also a varied treatment: Leuci but Teutates, Toutius, Totius, Tutius.

Hopfner PhW 57, 1937, 847-48 (on Ricomagus, Rigo-);
on Gaulish and Ligurian names in Sil. Ital. 8.588 ff.,
cf. CR 50, 1936, p.56. On the text of Strabo 4.1.1-12
cf. A. Jacob Curae Strabonianae in Rev. de Philol. 36,
1912, pp.151-158 (4.1.1 read τὸ Κέμμενον not Κέμμενον,
Γαρούννα not - ούνα or - μνα; 4.1.3 Σάλλυες not -λ-, so
also 4.1.11; 4.1.5 restore Ῥοδανουσίαν καὶ τὴν Ἀγάθην
[for Ῥόην καὶ Ἀγάθην], Σούλγας fl., Οὐνδαλον i.e. Vindalium; ib. Ἀκουσίων (?); 4.1.12 read Ἀρηκομικούς not
- ίσκους. At p.167 a long discussion of the Ἀτάγις - problem.

Chaume Mém. Commission Côte d'Or 20, 1933, 17-19,
29-34 (on etymology of Dijon), 58-59 (Étang), Bèze
(134-36), Bourguignonne (201-310).

Note also the Congr. Internat. de toponymie et
d'Anthroponymie (Actes, Premier Congr. 88-91, P.F.
Fournier on names of Puy-de-Dôme, see ZONF 15, 1939,
277; cf. REA 39, 1937, 41-44; 40, 1938, 287-294).

The papers of Longnon have been deposited in the
Bibl. nationale at Paris (see Besnier REA 34, 1932, 26-
36).

T. Sävborg Étude sur le rôle de la préposition
dans les expressions de lieu relatives en latin vulgaire et en ancien gallo-romain, Diss. Uppsala (APh 15,
1940-41, 207).

But in all these discussions there is too much
that is speculative and hypothetical. The criticisms
of Weisgerber SprFK 182 (e.g. on taro- "swift," a mere
figment) are well taken.

A. Dauzat Les noms de lieux, origine et evolution,
Paris 1926; id. Noms des personnes, origine et evolution, 1925; M. Besnier Lexique de géographie ancienne
Paris, 1914; id. Les routes de la Gaule romaine: questions de méthode REA 26, 1924, 331-340 (cf. 25, 1923,
153-64; 27, 1925, 209; 28, 1926, 335-351); Bull. arch.
1923, 75-96; id. REL 7, 1929, 85-95 (Estrée : strate,
Septèmes : septimas, Maizan : mansio etc.).

Notes on Proper Names

In addition to the great, but incomplete, Dictionnaire topographique of the French Ministère de l'Instruction publique (for several recent volumes, down to 1912, see, for example REA 15, 1913, 308; cf. 22, 1920, 125, Isère), the useful Joanne (see p.780 above) and the works named in my Prolegomena pp.7-8 (to which add now A. Carnoy Dictionnaire étymologique du nom des communes de Belgique, y compris...noms de hameaux et de rivières vol. 1, A-K 1939; 2, L-Z 1940), there are several other departmental repertories, of varying merit, e.g. de Saint-Vénant Dictionnaire topographique etc. de Vendômais, 4 volumes, Paris 1912-17, see REA 24, 1922, 323).

The work of Auguste Vincent Toponymie de la France 4° (Brussels 1937) is, in my opinion, the best treatment of this complicated subject. Since the work is not to be found in some even of the larger libraries of the United States, it may be useful to give here a summary of its contents: pp.23ff. §§ 40-49 on bilingual names or (modern) translations; p.25 -iaco- (-ay, -ey) : -ingen or -heim (e.g. Bannay : Bizingen, Cernay : Sennenheim cf. ZONF 12, 1936, 96-107); Ligurian names (§§ 160-167) -asco- etc., -inco-, -elo- (Κεμενέλεον); Iberian (§§ 168-169) e.g. Eliberris, Βου(ρ)δίγαλα, with (§170) Phoenician: e.g. Barcelonne, Carcassone, Narbonne; Greek (§§ 171-172): Μασσαλία, Ἀντίπολις, Ἐμπόριον, Ἀθαθῆ (τύχη).

§§ 173-277 on the Gaulish element -acus but Latin -anus in local names, inscc. with father's name of Keltic type but son's Romanized, local names derived from personal names (-acus, -as [-atis], -ausus, -auus, -iacus and other suffixes). Keltic elements of vocabulary in local names (§§ 203-229): e.g. apa, apia "water," arganto- (-c-) "silver," benno- "point," bona "base," -briga "height," briua "bridge," doro "door," dunum "fortress," durum "fortification," -ialo "district," nantu- "valley;" names of plants and trees: auallo-, brug-, *cassano-, *eburos, lemo-, limo-, tanno-, *uerna (-us); adjectival elements, e.g. canto-, deuo-, maros, nouio-, seno-, uindo-. §§ 278-311 Roman period; §§ 312-435 early middle ages (§§ 313-369 Germanic influence, including -apa?); §§ 383-384 Basque elements; §§ 385-393 Breton elements, e.g. banadloc "genêtraie," coat, coet "wood," guern, wern "aune," guic "bourg," kemper "confluent," ker or caer "camp," lann "parish," lenic

"saline," les and lis "cour," loc "oratory," mané and
mené(z) "mountain," pen "summit," plou "parish," poul
"mare," ran "region," run "colline," tré and tref
"village." Cf. above 180 Remark.

On names in -court, -ville see F. Lot Romania 69,
1933, 199-246 (cf. RA 12, 1938, 75-78, 275-276 on the
incursions of the Franks and Alamanni, and the destruction of old established sites).

A not dissimilar source of knowledge, namely the
history of Gallo-Roman, is as meagre in its results.
Apart from lexical elements (see, for example, von
Wartburg's etymological dictionary, with Pedersen's
review of fasc. 17-28 in EC 1, 1936, pp.169-173), certain phonetic changes, when known also to be Keltic,
are attributed to the influence of the substratum. This
explanation is valid when the change can be shown to
belong to Gallo-Roman; thus too, certain archaisms
(e.g. the survival of -s, see Vendryes EC 1, 1936, 367)
are explained.

Dauzat Rev. des Cours et Conf. 37 1, 1935-36, 593-
605 seeks to distinguish various strata: pre.-I.Eu.,
Iberian, Ligurian, Greek, Italo-Keltic, Keltic, and Latin
(but this is partly a geographical matter); cf. id. in
Où en sont les Études de Français? Paris 1935, 210-26.
Cf. Survivances celtiques, Revue du Vivarais 1927 (REA
30, 1928, 313); Boisonnade REA 14, 1912, 194-196 (pas-
tellum : waisda, waisdium, guède etc.); Vendryes MSL 21,
1920, 43 (bief from Keltic *bedo or Germanic bed?);
Mennier RLR 3, 1927, 313-317 (etym. of assiette).

Note lxi: On the Alphabets

The forms of alphabet, Greek and Latin, present no

problem. Nor need we consider here the more difficult

On the Alphabets

question of the ogam script (cf. Proleg. 30, with n.39;
Arntz considers briefly the Gaulish alphabet in PBB 59,
1935, 321-413, cf. 61, 1937, 188-208; Keller Beiblatt
zur Anglia 47, 1936, 33-37; cf. the gloss ogmios 246
and see also the references given 249 above, s.v. Ogmios;
on Gaulish cursive cf. Oswald JRS 17, 1927, 162-64).
The Latin alphabet of Germania Inferior is distinguished
by the lavish use of ligatures, as well as by ├ (or ┤)
for h.

Outside Narbonensis the Greek alphabet appears
sporadically; and, as a rule, on portable objects save
for a few inscc. of Alesia. On coins, however, it is
not uncommon. Presumably the Greek alphabet of Narbonensis came from Greek settlements at Massilia and
other sites, even though early Greek products in Gaul
passed over the Alps and not through Narbonensis, see
Jacobsthal Early Celtic Art vol. 1, 1944, p.142 n.4,
where Schuchhardt in Ebert's Reallexikon 3, 1925, 162
is cited, whose view was that the use of Greek writing,
e.g. by the Heluetii BG 1.29, and at Mt. Beuvray (Bibracte see Note xxxi Remark vi above), had come to the
Kelts of Gaul from the East. But the Greek alphabet
in use, not only in Narbonensis, but also at Alesia

On the Alphabets

and at Bibracte, does not differ notably from the Attic-
Ionic, is not ancient, and cannot be shown genuinely to
have penetrated Celtica at all. There illiteracy prevailed before the spread of Latin and of the Latin alphabet. Accordingly the Greek alphabet of Narbonensis
may be taken as the standard Hellenistic Greek alphabet
adapted to the writing of Gaulish. Schuchhardt's view
is extreme, and not accepted even by Jacobsthal. The
use of Γ with the value η (before γ) is clear evidence
of the comparatively late type of Greek alphabet in
use in Narbonensis, not to mention the vocalic value
of H, or the letter forms C (σ), $\in$, A (α), ω
(ω) and Y (υ), or the use of ω as well as of ου to
designate ou and u. Cf. Robert's Gr. Epigr. 1.311;
Schwyzer Gr. Gr. 1.158-159. Greek influence appears
in the Latin alphabet of Gaul in $Ð$ or $\oplus$(ð), and in X
i.e. χ (before s and t).

The few, complete or partial, abecedaria, chiefly
of cursive type, found in Aquitania (Martres-de-Veyre,
Moulins, Vichy, Vouroux); Belgica (Lavoye, Maar, Trier);
Germania Inferior (Holdoorn); Germania Superior (Mainz),
and in the Upper Rhine and Danube (Palézieux [Wallis],
Saalburg, Stein-am-Anger) are given in the body of the

On the Alphabets

work (CIL 13.10016,2; 12; 67-69; 10008.7; cf. 134
Remark). The last named is dated by Loeschcke in the
first half of the second century. See also Déchlette
Vases ornées 1.133-35; Dieterich RhM 56, 1901, 77-105;
Dornseiff Alphabete in Mystik u. Magie, Leipzig 1922).
They are manifestly associated with pottery-manufacture;
cf. REA 29, 1927, 199-204; ib. p.203 n.; and Hermet's
and Oxé's discussion of the several hands at La Graufesenque; Grenier in Frank 3.557; perhaps four different hands, but only one style and one epoch. At La
Graufesenque I have, in general, ignored slight variations in letter-forms, despite Oxé's classification,
based chiefly on the style of writing a, viz:

(i) ⊢ ⋔ ⊢ Γ

(ii) ⋔

(iii) ᴧ λ λ ᴧ

(iv) ⊢

except when a question of transcription arises. But
I have sought to distinguish there between Đ or ᴆ (ᴅ),
and θ (θ), granted even that the distinction is merely
graphic, as it appears to be. In numerals d is usual;
elsewhere θ and θ, and perhaps also Đ are used indif-
ferently. The interpuncts of the La Graufesenque sherds
are reproduced faithfully, and also the symbols ⌅ (=)
and ⌅ ⌅ (= =).

On the Alphabets

Throughout the book I have noted forms such as ‖ for e, |ᴵ for f, ⊖ (θ) and Ð (đ); but c and g are often not clearly distinguished in the originals, nor χ (before t and s) and x, u and v (y̨) hardly ever. In graffiti (La Graufesenque) ∿ and m (ᛙ), ⏀ and m (ᛙ) are also confused, and variant forms of i (𝑙, 𝑖), including í (ᶥ, ⌡), hardly worth noting. But in 89 lines 15-16 for example we have conjoint -us (not -os). The phonetic value of o, ου, ŭ̥ and the like is noted in the Glossary for each word, so far as it can be determined.

As to chronology, see the notes to the inscc., especially at Cavaillon, St-Remy-de-Provence, and Montagnac. The last named (ca. 250-225 B.C.) is the oldest insc. of Gaul (cf. 247 i above for older texts in Italy, where a few other brief texts, both on stone and on bronze, are known); at Glanum the best estimate of date is ca. 100 B.C. (SprFK 155, after Jacobsthal Schumacher Festschrift 189-194, esp. p.191 n.4; cf. AA 44, 1930, 236 and n.1). The Glozel "symbols" (and the Sancerre terracotta, Blanchet REA 29, 1927, 187-89) are of course ignored. The use of θ, đ and of χ presupposes the later (spirant) value of the Greek symbols, not the older (aspirate) use.

1373

Corrigenda and Addenda

Contents, p.10   At 245 for inscription read ascription

Item 6   Bodi[AE 1948.123

    10   Ceutrones ib. 163

    39   Ippo[nae (for Eponae) AE 1946.151

    80   On Mastrabala RA 36, 1950, 77-83

Page 241   andere: cf. JCS 1, 1950, 131-33

Item 84   ?Gomferani AE 1949.126; cf. RA 31,
    1949, 511; Géry according to Lizop.
    But I am suspicious of the new inscc.
    reported in AE 1949.113-129. Here
    the improbable Gomferani (Comberani,
    Conforani, Consorani?) and Eriape
    etc. (Priapus?), Tauricus Taurinus
    (124, 128) and Amandus Amaradus (113,
    129) are difficult to accept.

    86   deo Er(r)iap(p)e or Er(r)ap(p)e and -o,
    viz. Eriape, Erapius (114), Erriappus,
    Eriapus, Erriapus, Erriape AE 1949.
    113-127. Cf. RA 31, 1949, 499-515
    (arri- "rock;" or perhaps ari-, are-,
    and -ap(p)o- "water"??).

    Sutugius RA 31, 1949, 501

    87   Amandus AE 1949.113   Borsus 117

        Amaradus ib. 129   Nuc[119

        Bambiolus 123   Sennetarus 116

        Bedo 127   Sintus 130

Corrigenda and Addenda

87 ctd.   Tauricus 124, 128   Taurinus 124, 128

           Cf. RA 31, 1949, 499–521

84–87   Cf. de Ricci RC 24, 1903, 71–83; BSA
           Midi 29–31, 1901–03, 362–74

141   Cf. [Esmonnot Néris, Moulins 1885]
           plate 3, no.6

158   uergobreto (13.1047–48) AE 1948.166

Page 672   On the evolution of Belgic ware cf.
           Oxé TrZ 16–17, 1941–42, 92–104

Item 179   Vid[ucasses (13.3162 Thorigny) AE 1949.
           136; cf. REA 46, 1944, 136 and JCS
           1, 1950, 135

182   Namantobogius AE 1949.75

           Nertomarius ib.

Note xlv C   Smert[ri]us JRS 40, 1950, 116.10; cf.
           236 above

Page 854   Add Hans Philipp Germania: die Ent-
           deckungsgeschichte der Germanen-
           länder nach Tacitus und anderen
           Quellen ed. 2, Leipzig, 1936

Item 220   s(apa) Euboiedis uini **AE** 1946.164

236   Transpose numen G S and Noadat

Corrigenda and Addenda

Item 241   s.v. Elant[for Atlantia read Alantia

246   Transpose uallus (p.1343) to correct
           alphabetical order (p.1342)

249   AJA 55, 1951, 13-51 (Cernunnos)

Books on ~~reg~~ ... ~~~~ out for two we~~~~
must be presented at the Circulation Desk in order to be renewed.

A fine of **five cents** a day is charged after date due.

Special books are subject to special regulations at the discretion
of library staff.